Kitchen & Bath Source Book 1996/97

Sweet's Group

A Division of The **McGraw·Hill** Companies

1221 Avenue of the Americas
New York, New York 10020-1095

Great Homes Demand Broan Products.

When selecting built-in products for your residential construction projects, chances are you'll make your decision on the basis of style, convenience and – undoubtedly – quality.

For decades, builders of America's most beautiful homes have turned to Broan for these very reasons. As the leader in home ventilation, Broan products can make any home a healthier and more comfortable place to be. All fifteen product lines provide the added convenience that new home buyers demand.

Remember, it's your reputation on the line, so be sure to ask for more information about our quality product lines. Just check the appropriate boxes and send your request to Broan, along with your name and address.

❑ Range Hoods
❑ Medicine Cabinets & Lights
❑ Bath Fans & Fan Lights
❑ Indoor Air Quality Systems
❑ Door Chimes
❑ Central Vacuum Systems
❑ Music/Intercom Systems
❑ Ceiling Fans

❑ Trash Compactors
❑ Whole House Ventilators
❑ Powered Attic Ventilators
❑ Wall Mounted Hair Dryers
❑ Ironing Centers
❑ Vanities
❑ Heaters

BROAN ®
A NORTEK COMPANY

There really is a difference with Broan.
It's in the details.

To hear more, call 1-800-548-0790.

P.O. Box 140, Hartford, WI 53027. In Canada: Broan Limited 905-670-2500.

1221 Avenue of the Americas
New York, NY 10020-1095
Tel 212 512 6566
Fax 212 512 4460
russellb@mcgraw-hill.com

Robert M. Russell, Jr.
President
Construction Information Group

The **McGraw·Hill** Companies

May 1996

Welcome to the *Kitchen & Bath Source Book!*

Would it make your life easier if you could go to one source to develop your ideas for designing a new kitchen or bath?

McGraw-Hill's *Kitchen & Bath Source Book* shows you literally thousands of products, colors and design ideas **using the manufacturers' own catalogs,** in an easy-to-use book format. No need to hunt down dozens of brochures, only to misplace the one you really wanted at the moment you're ready to move ahead. Everything is right where you left it — between the covers of the *Kitchen & Bath Source Book.*

At Sweet's we are serious about our commitment to customer satisfaction. I personally welcome your ideas, thoughts and questions concerning Sweet's products and services. Please don't hesitate to contact me by phone or fax.

In the meantime, I hope the *Kitchen & Bath Source Book* provides the products and ideas you need to successfully plan and build a kitchen or bath perfectly designed to suit your needs, or those of your customers.

Sincerely,

Bob Russell

Sweet's Group

A Division of The McGraw·Hill Companies

1221 Avenue of the Americas
New York, NY 10020-1095

Our Customer Service Hotline is available to answer your inquiries regarding Sweet's products and services:
1-800-442-2258
fax 212-512-2348

Officers of The McGraw-Hill Companies

Chairman & Chief Executive Officer
Joseph L. Dionne
President & Chief Operating Officer
Harold W. McGraw III
Senior Vice President - General Counsel
Kenneth M. Vittor
Executive Vice President - Chief Financial Officer
Robert J. Bahash
Senior Vice President - Treasury Operations
Frank D. Penglase
President - Information Services Group
Michael K. Hehir

President - Construction Information Group
Robert M. Russell, Jr.
Senior Vice President - Marketing, CIG
Eric J. Cantor
Senior Vice President - Finance, CIG
Stephen L. Kessler
Vice President - Sales
Nancy M. Porter
Vice President - Finance & Planning
Scott J. August
Vice President - Publishing
Adam R. Lefton
Vice President - New Business Ventures
Daniel L. Peak
Vice President - Sales Programs
Craig B. Soderstrom
Director - Advertising & Promotion
Daryl D. Brach
Director - Federal Government Affairs
Mary E. Fenelon
Director - Client Services
Brenda Griffin
Director - Sales Planning & Training
Elizabeth F. Hazlett
Director - Consulting Services
Gary B. Keclik, AIA, IFMA
Director - Systems Development
William E. Keller
Director - Publishing Operations
Thomas H. Koster
Director - Product Services
Jane Alex Mendelson
Product Manager, Kitchen & Bath Source Book
Jane T. Morrison
Director - Technical Services
Stanley Shapiro
Director - Distribution/Customer Service
Linda Shapray
Director - Direct Response Programs
M. Louise Slater
Director - Market Research
Alma L. Weinstein

Sweet's Consultants

Cynthia Belisle, AIA, CSI
Robert C. Boettcher, AIA, CSI
Joseph V. Bower, AIA, CSI
Donna Burns, AIA, CSI
Robert C. Chandler, AIA
Daniel C. Colella, AIA
Dorothy H. Cox, CSI
John W. Embler, AIA, CSI
Raymond M. Hennig, AIA, CSI
E. Michael Hollander, AIA
Richard J. Mazzuca, AIA, CSI
Wayne W. Puchkors, AIA, CSI
Barbara Ruppel, AIA, CSI
Peter G. Schramm, AIA
G. Robert Steiner, S.E., ASCE, CSI
Albert J. Thomas, AIA, CSI
John S. Vaci, AIA
William E. White, AIA, CSI

Regional Offices

Chicago, IL 60601
Two Prudential Plaza
180 North Stetson Avenue, Suite 700
312-565-1818 • 312-616-3236 – fax
Regional Director of Sales –
Joseph J. Pepitone

Cleveland, OH 44115
1255 Euclid Avenue, 3rd Floor
216-621-6460 • 216-771-2857 – fax
Regional Director of Sales – Gary E. Darbey

Dallas, TX 75240
14850 Quorum Drive, Suite 380
214-991-9155 • 214-991-8630 – fax
Regional Director of Sales –
Katherine Louis Foster

Miami, FL 33174
8700 West Flagler Street, Suite 100
305-223-4470 • 305-220-7444 – fax
Regional Director of Sales – John A. Fox

New York, NY 10019
1633 Broadway, 13th Floor
212-512-3181 • 212-512-6831 – fax
Regional Director of Sales – Douglas Runner

San Francisco, CA 94105
221 Main Street, Suite 800
415-882-2885 • 415-882-2824 – fax
Regional Director of Sales – Nancy E. Harmon

Sweet's Electronic Publishing
99 Monroe Avenue N.W., Suite 400
Grand Rapids, MI 49503
616-454-0000 • 616-454-4140 – fax
National Sales Manager – Michael Fowler

International Offices

Chicago, IL 60601 USA
Two Prudential Plaza
180 North Stetson Avenue, Suite 700
312-616-3230 • 312-616-3236 – fax
International Marketing Specialist,
Steven Gilberg

Montreal, PQ H3G 2A5 Canada
3495 de la Montagne, Suite 11
514-842-9573 • 514-843-3166 – fax
Regional Manager – Pierre Savoie

North York, ON M2J 1R8 Canada
270 Yorkland Boulevard
416-496-3118 • 416-496-3104 – fax
Director of Manufacturing – Bruce Irish

Philadelphia, PA 19107 USA
1700 Market Street, Suite 1500
215-496-4964 • 215-569-8078 – fax
International Marketing Specialist,
Anthony Mancini

Cover Photos:

Top left: Courtesy of Gerard Valentini.
Top right and bottom: Images © 1996 PhotoDisc, Inc.

Kitchen & Bath Source Book

Table of Contents

To Find Information Quickly

The *Kitchen & Bath Source Book* is organized in an easy-to-use format. Catalogs are grouped by similar product type to help you quickly locate information on manufacturers and products for your kitchen and bath projects.

Coding System

Catalogs are assigned a four-character code indicating their position in the *Kitchen & Bath Source Book.*

As an example: C123

In addition, each catalog displays a unique BuyLine® number for use when calling Sweet's BuyLine® service (see page 5). You will find a two-tiered code on Kitchen & Bath catalog covers:

C123
BuyLine 1234

Refer to the Indexes

The *Kitchen & Bath Source Book* contains complete Firms, Products and Trade Name indexes:

The **Firms** index is an alphabetical list of manufacturers and their catalog codes.

The **Products** index is an alphabetical list of all products within the Book. Manufacturers and their catalog codes appear for each product heading.

The **Trade Names** index contains an alphabetical list of trade names accompanied by a brief product description and the catalog code.

Sweet's BuyLine is a service for kitchen & bath professionals. It does NOT provide information of use to consumers.

Attention Kitchen & Bath Professionals:
Need to contact the local sales representative for any manufacturer in Sweet's *Kitchen & Bath Source Book*? **Call Sweet's BuyLine®.**

Here's how to use BuyLine®

1. When you want to locate a manufacturer's local sales representative, just dial 1-800-892-1165. When using a touch-tone line, you will be greeted by a voice response from the Sweet's computer. If you are using a rotary dial telephone, or if your touch-tone telephone uses a rotary line, an operator will answer the call (between 8 AM and 9 PM EST).

2. You will be asked to communicate with the computer using the numerical buttons on your telephone keyboard. The system will instruct you to enter the four-digit BuyLine® code assigned to the manufacturer's catalog, as well as your telephone number (including area code).

3. After you've entered the four-digit BuyLine® code and telephone number, the system will answer with the requested information (i.e., the name and telephone number of the manufacturer's sales representative serving your area).

4. When you call the rep, please say "Sweet's BuyLine® sent me." Telling the representative that BuyLine® made your contact possible indicates to manufacturers that BuyLine® is working for you and for them. It's the best way to be sure Sweet's can continue to provide and improve the valuable BuyLine® service in the future.

Toll-free throughout the U.S., including Alaska and Hawaii.

Call 1-800-442-2258

Sweet's wants to provide you with the quickest and easiest access to the wealth of information within the *Kitchen & Bath Source Book*. This guide outlines several of the special services we offer.

To answer any questions you may have regarding the *Kitchen & Bath Source Book*, our Customer Service representatives are available Monday through Friday from 8:30 AM to 4:30 PM (EST). Use our toll-free number for any of the following.

Shipping Inquiries

Please call us if your book arrives damaged or if you have received a duplicate copy.

Qualification or Additional Orders

If you have any questions concerning your qualification for the *Kitchen & Bath Source Book*, or any of Sweet's Catalog Files, please call. You will be immediately directed to the proper individual for assistance.

Change of Address

Please let us know if you have moved recently or plan to move in the near future. We need to keep our address records current to make sure you continue to receive the *Kitchen & Bath Source Book*.

If you wish to contact Sweet's Group in writing, please send correspondence to:

Sweet's Group
A Division of The McGraw-Hill Companies
1221 Avenue of the Americas
Room 2040
New York, New York 10020
USA

Do You Know Someone Else Who Needs a Kitchen & Bath Source Book?

Let them know about the Kitchen & Bath Source Book by passing along the handy order card below.
Or better yet, give them the Kitchen & Bath Source Book as a gift.
Professionals may wish to order additional copies for their businesses.

❑ **YES!** Please send me my copies of the 1996/1997 Kitchen & Bath Source Book, ONLY $29.95 each.

No. of copies _____ × $29.95 for a total of $_____
❑ Check enclosed (Do not send cash)
❑ Please charge my: ❑ Amex   ❑ Visa   ❑ MC

Acct. #_____ Exp. Date_____

Name: _____

Signature: _____

Telephone (   )_____

City:_____State:_____Zip: _____

Mail to:

Sweet's Group/A Division of The McGraw-Hill Companies
Distribution Department, Room 2040
1221 Avenue of the Americas, 20th Floor • New York, NY 10020

If you're building or remodeling your home, the bathroom is one space you can't afford to overlook. When you consider how much time you spend in this room, you realize that this is one space you definitely want to be comfortable and functional, as well as good looking.

The bathroom is more than a space for three necessary fixtures; it's the place where you can relax after a long day, change your clothes, mend your wounds, apply your make up, comb your hair and take care of a multitude of other grooming and hygiene needs. It's probably the first room you visit in the morning, and the last room you visit at night.

But, how do you begin to make it the luxury room of your dreams? The National Kitchen & Bath Association (NKBA) recommends beginning by assessing your needs for the space.

"First, you must determine who will use the bathroom," says NKBA Director of Societies John Spitz, CBD, CKD. "This will affect the mood of the space as well as the features included in it."

According to Spitz, bathrooms should be designed around the users - a family bathroom, a children's bathroom, an adult's or master suite bathroom, a powder room or guest bathroom.

Each of these types of spaces has its own specific needs and concerns.

The Family Bathroom

"Traditionally, all of the fixtures in the bathroom are placed in one open space," adds Spitz. "But, for a family of four or more who is sharing one bathroom, zoning the fixtures would work much better."

By separating the fixtures into individualized compartments, several family members can use the space together while retaining some privacy. For example, the tub/shower and toilet could be placed in one space and a single- or double-bowl vanity in a second area. This would allow one person to use the vanity area while someone else was using the tub/shower area. Dividing the space into three separate areas may be the best approach for a larger family - one long vanity with the toilet and tub/shower in their own nooks allows three people to use the space concurrently.

The Children's Bathroom

"Small children always pose unique concerns in the home," Spitz says. "They require more safety features and lower heights, but also adaptability as they grow."

According to Spitz, some features which should be included for children are safety latches on drawers and cabinets; door locks which can be opened from outside the space; above-floor storage for cleaning supplies; shower valves which balance water pressure and temperature; pull-out step under the vanity; and adjustable pole-mounted showerheads or hand-held shower-heads.

"Many of the safety features listed for a child's bath can and should be included in all bathrooms," notes Spitz.

The Adult's Bathroom or Master Bath Suite

When planning a bathroom for adults only, or a master bath suite, it is important to note the reasons for the space - privacy, relaxation, efficiency. Again, the reason will affect the fixtures, the lighting, etc.

"When space is limited, but you want a large private bathroom, the master bath suite is the answer," Spitz adds. "By 'stealing' space from the bedroom, the master bathroom can be enlarged creating a private retreat."

According to Spitz, adult baths may also incorporate added amenities such as whirlpool tubs, saunas and bidets, which increase the level of relaxation and luxury for the user. And for those who dream of a more efficient place to dress and groom, Spitz suggests improving the storage and closet area.

"Adequate cabinets with interior storage are a must in the adult bath," says Spitz. "Built-in drawers, racks, and hooks should be added for clothing storage, and divided, shallow drawers as well as deeper drawers and adjustable shelves should be added for grooming supplies in the bathroom area."

The Powder Room or Guest Bath

This specialized space is also known as the "half bath" because it does not include the tub/shower fixture. This is the bathroom that is typically used by guests.

"Obviously this type of bathroom requires less space than a full bath; however, comfort is still important and should not be overlooked," Spitz adds.

According to Spitz, the powder room should incorporate enough space for the fixtures as well as for storage, and enough room for the user to comfortably enter and exit the space.

It is also important that the room include proper soundproofing and ventilation.

As you can see, a bathroom remodel, no matter what style, is a major undertaking. Beyond planning the type of bathroom it will be and the users it will serve, there are electrical, plumbing and clearance considerations which must also be carefully planned. With all these things to consider, it's easy to see that this is not a do-it-yourself project. Spitz recommends working with a bathroom specialist, or a Certified Bathroom Designer (CBD). These are professionals who know the ins and outs of bathroom planning and can make your dreams become reality.

The National Kitchen & Bath Association offers a complete planning kit to help you get started. This kit includes a list of specialists in your area. To order your kit call 1-800-401-NKBA, ext. 700.

The decision has been made! You've decided that the time has come to turn your dream kitchen or bathroom into a reality. Great! Now what?

The Beginning

Your first step should be locating and hiring a professional kitchen/bathroom designer. What can a professional do for you? Plenty!

A kitchen/bathroom specialist can guide you through every phase of your project — decorating, design, construction and plumbing and electrical systems.

Specifically, kitchen/bathroom specialists are able to:

- work with contractors, electricians and plumbers
- answer any questions you have about design, products and colors, as well as anticipate and prevent problems that you may not have considered.
- create designs that reflect your individual personality through color, style and pattern selection

"To ensure a successful project, it is important to find a kitchen or bathroom professional who is right for you," explains Gail Olsen, CKD, Ducci Kitchens, Torrington, Conn. "Similar to finding a doctor or dentist, you need to locate someone who is capable of completing the job, but who also meshes with your personality."

The National Kitchen & Bath Association (NKBA) provides a list of its retail members, including Certified Kitchen and Bathroom Designers (CKDs and CBDs), in your area who can help you with your project.

The Middle

"Once you have found the kitchen/bathroom planners near you, it is a good idea to visit them in person," says Olsen. "This gives you the opportunity to see kitchens and bathrooms on display and to talk with designers about products, materials and colors. This will help you discover which designer is right for you."

Olsen also suggests that you prepare for your visit. Here's how:

- Collect and clip photographs of kitchens or bathrooms that appeal to you. Examining these with the designers during your visits will give them a good idea of the styles to which you are attracted.
- Evaluate your current kitchen or bathroom to find out what works and what doesn't.

For example, is there enough cabinet shelf space? Is there enough counter space? Is there adequate task lighting above the countertop? In the bathroom, is the bathtub big enough? Is the showerhead at a comfortable height for all users? Is the bathroom safe — does it include grab bars and non-slip flooring?

- ◆ Write down the answers to these questions and bring them with you when you visit the kitchen/bathroom planners. They will play an important role in the design of your new space.

The Completion

After you choose a firm, a designer will visit your home to take precise measurements. He or she will also spend a great deal of time interviewing you to discover the exact type and style of kitchen or bathroom you desire. Then, a plan, which includes material costs, specifications and design details, will be prepared. When the design is approved and the budget is set, a payment schedule will be arranged. Typically, a schedule is set up where 50% of the total is paid at the signing of the contract, 40% upon start of installation and the remaining 10% when the job is completed. NKBA member firms will usually offer a contract that outlines project responsibilities and a payment schedule.

The time frame for completion of projects will vary. Generally, kitchen and bathroom projects take two weeks to several months to complete. Although living with construction is not easy, it will all seem worth it once your new kitchen or bathroom is complete.

To obtain a list of NKBA member firms in your area, and a remodeling organizer kit call (800) 401-NKBA, ext. 700.

Universal Design: Planning Kitchens That Last a Lifetime

People come in all sizes, shapes and varieties. So do their kitchens. But this space should do more than just reflect personal tastes in regard to color and style. The kitchen must be functional, and it must be designed to suit the needs of all users throughout their lifecycles. This is the basis of universal design.

"When planning a new kitchen, it is just as important to consider who will use the space and how they will use it as it is to choose colors, appliances and styles," explains Mary Jo Peterson, CKD, CBD, Mary Jo Peterson Design Consultants, Brookfield, Conn.

For example, the kitchen is no longer the sole domain of the female of the household. According to the National Kitchen & Bath Association (NKBA), men, women and children are sharing in kitchen activities such as cooking, doing homework, paying the bills, entertaining, etc., and this has an effect on how the space is designed.

Another aspect to consider when conducting a kitchen project is aging. According to the American Association of Retired Persons (AARP), by the year 2020, over 20 percent of the population will be over 65 years old. A survey completed by the AARP shows that a majority of these people wish to stay in their homes and age in place.

"In order to achieve this, it is essential to plan kitchens that allow for independent living," Peterson says. "Although you may not currently need special features, it is a strong possibility that you will someday. So why not plan for it now?"

Planning a universally designed kitchen requires special consideration of every aspect of the space: countertops, cabinets, appliances, etc.

Countertops and Cabinets

Countertops, for example, must be designed within easy reach of the user. Therefore, countertop height must be carefully considered.

A standard countertop is 36″ high, but this height is often uncomfortable for children or adults who are shorter or taller than average or for those who prefer to work while seated. For a universally designed kitchen, NKBA recommends including some countertops that are 28″ - 32″ high. This height is appropriate for seated or shorter users and for use as a chopping or baking center. For taller users, countertops that are 42″ - 45″ high are suitable. This height will work well as a snack bar also. The space should also include some countertops at 36″ high for general use by standing users. In addition, adjustable countertops can be incorporated into the space. By doing so, the kitchen becomes functional for all who will use it, both now and in the future.

NKBA also offers the following suggestions for cabinets:

- Lowering wall cabinets via motorized or mechanical system

- Interior storage systems such as divider drawers, roll-out shelves and tray dividers to provide clear accessibility and easy retrieval of items

- Open shelves for quick detection of items and to eliminate the hazard of open doors

- Drawers instead of doors to eliminate the need to get around the open door

- Lever handles as opposed to knobs to allow easier opening of doors

Appliances

As more and more manufacturers become aware of universal design, more appliance options become available. This allows universally designed appliances to be incorporated into the space without sacrificing aesthetics.

Consider the following items when planning a universal kitchen:

- Side-by-side refrigerators or bottom freezer models provide ideal access for all users — young and old

- Separate cooktop and oven accommodate height differences

- Appliance controls placed at the front allow easy access

- Easy-to-read numbers and touch-pad controls rather than knobs are easier to see and use

- Microwave placement within reach and sight of the individuals who will use it

By including these items in the kitchen and considering carefully their placement in the design, you ensure that the space can be used by everyone, regardless of their abilities or stage of life.

Hiring a Professional

Peterson cautions that the above suggestions are just that — suggestions. And they only scratch the surface.

"Each kitchen is unique — a reflection of the person who uses it," she says.

To be certain that your kitchen suits your needs, it is a good idea to consult with a professional. NKBA provides a list of its retail members, including Certified Kitchen and Bathroom Designers (CKDs and CBDs), in your area who can help you with your project. These professionals will work with you to plan a space that is right for you.

"Your new kitchen should last a lifetime," Peterson says. "A professional kitchen designer will help see that it does."

For a list of designers in your area, contact NKBA at (800) 401-NKBA, ext. 700.

Remodeling can be an overwhelming process, whether you're remodeling your kitchen, bathroom or any room in your home. It's easy to build an idea file that is overflowing with products and styles that you like. But, how do you turn your idea file into your dream kitchen or bath?

The National Kitchen & Bath Association (NKBA) recommends making two lists to narrow your options:

1. what you need for your new space to be functional

2. things you want, if budget permits

Some things you'll need to consider for the kitchen include:

	Need	Want
◆ cabinets	_____	_____
◆ countertops	_____	_____
◆ flooring	_____	_____
◆ oven/range/cooktop	_____	_____
◆ refrigerator/freezer	_____	_____
◆ dishwasher	_____	_____
◆ sink	_____	_____
◆ lighting	_____	_____
◆ waste disposal	_____	_____
◆ recycling bins	_____	_____
◆ desk area	_____	_____

For the bathroom, the following should be considered:

◆ vanity	_____	_____
◆ separate tub/shower	_____	_____
◆ whirlpool tub	_____	_____
◆ toilet	_____	_____
◆ sink	_____	_____
◆ faucets	_____	_____
◆ storage	_____	_____
◆ flooring	_____	_____
◆ countertops	_____	_____

Keep in mind that the way you use the space(s) should also be a determining factor in the amenities that you choose for you new kitchen or bath. For example, is there one primary cook in the household, or do all family members share in the cooking process? Do you normally make heat-and-serve meals, or full-course "from scratch" meals? Is the kitchen a socializing place? Who will use the bathroom - children, guests? How many people will use the bathroom at one time? What activities will take place in the bathroom - make up application, dressing, laundry?

Since the kitchen and bath pose their own unique remodeling challenges, the NKBA recommends working with a kitchen and bathroom specialist to help you plan your new space. He/she will look at your idea file and talk with you in depth about your needs and wants. A kitchen or bathroom specialist can make recommendations for your new space based on the way you live that will save you time and money before, during and after the remodeling process. And, he/she can help you choose products and colors to fit your individual style.

To receive a list of NKBA members in your area, and a kitchen and bathroom planning kit call 1-800-401-NKBA, ext. 700.

Creating Your Dream Kitchen or Bathroom

More than four million kitchens will be built or remodeled in 1996. Some of the projects will be dreams come true. The rest can be nightmares.

When you stop and think about the effects that every alteration has on a room, you realize just how complicated remodeling or building can be. Besides the logistical questions, many decisions must be made in terms of color, hardware, appliances, lighting, plumbing fixtures, countertops, and the overall style of your new room.

"With so many decisions to make and so much to think about, the average consumer needs a professional to organize this project — someone who understands all of the complexities involved," said Donna M. Luzzo, Director of Communications for the *National Kitchen & Bath Association* (NKBA). "Kitchen and bathroom design is a specialized trade. It requires a good deal of experience and know-how to accomplish successful projects."

The first step in creating a successful new room is a simple one — find an NKBA member to design and coordinate the construction of your room.

"Someone remodeling a kitchen or bathroom wants the project to get off to a good start, and a kitchen and bath professional is definitely the way to go," said Luzzo. "An NKBA member will coordinate every aspect of the design and installation. They are experienced at working with contractors, electricians, plumbers, etc., and can efficiently schedule the jobs involved. And, most important, they are experts at working with the client. They listen to client needs and translate them into the kind of rooms they want."

To help consumers get ready for a remodeling and help them work with a kitchen or bathroom designer, the NKBA offers consumers a complete planning kit, including a listing of kitchen and bathroom designers. **Contact NKBA at 1-800-401-NKBA, Ext. 700.**

IN KITCHENS AND BATHS, IT'S THE THOUGHT THAT COUNTS.

Getting your kitchen or bath project under way takes good ideas. Then a plan to put those ideas into action. That's what you'll find in *The what, where and the who to start your dream kitchen or bath*, from the National Kitchen & Bath Association. We're the professional association that represents the entire industry. And our complete kit of strategies and checklists—along with resources for product information and a list of our member professionals in your area—can help make your dream a reality.

NATIONAL KITCHEN
NKBA
& BATH ASSOCIATION

FROM INSPIRATION TO SENSATION

**Creating Your
Dream Kitchen
Or Bathroom**

OFF TO A GOOD START

So, you've decided to create your dream kitchen or bathroom. Great idea. You'll finally be able to apply all of those wishes you've collected on your list over the years, like that kitchen island with a cooktop (and more of that invaluable countertop and cabinet space), or maybe you've always wanted a bathtub-for-two. Whether it's the kitchen or bathroom (or both), you can look forward to an exciting transformation into the room you've always wanted.

But when you stop and think about the effects that every alteration has on a room, you realize just how complicated remodeling or building can be. Take, for instance, the kitchen island with a cooktop. Where there's a cooktop, there's smoke and steam. And where there's smoke and steam, there has to be ventilation. So an overhead hood must be added, unless you have a downventing cooktop. Also, any time you have work space like the added countertop, you need electrical outlets. So wiring will be necessary for the outlets, as well as the cooktop and vent hood. And that's just the beginning.

Besides the logistical questions, many decisions must be made in terms of color, hardware, appliances, lighting, plumbing fixtures, countertops, and the overall style of your new room.

With so many decisions to make and so much to think about, you need a professional to organize this project — someone who understands all of the complexities involved. That's where the National Kitchen and Bath Association (NKBA) comes in.

FINDING THE NKBA MEMBER FOR THE JOB

The first step in creating your new room is a simple one — find an NKBA member to design and coordinate the construction of your room. You want your project to get off to a good start, and a kitchen and bath professional is definitely the way to go.

WHY?

The National Kitchen & Bath Association is an organization of professionals who focus specifically on kitchens and bathrooms. When you deal with an NKBA member, you'll benefit from specialized expertise, years of experience, a commitment to quality, and a high degree of professionalism. They maintain showrooms with products and complete designs on display so you can get a feel for the type and quality of work they can do.

A kitchen and bath professional can offer sound advice and suggest solutions to any problems that may arise, or, better yet, prevent problems from occurring. They also understand the ways families and individuals relate to their surroundings, and therefore may be able to troubleshoot and meet needs in ways that may not occur to those who don't specialize in kitchens and bathrooms.

An NKBA member will coordinate every aspect of the design and installation. They are experienced at working with contractors — electricians, plumbers, etc. — and can efficiently schedule the jobs involved. And, most important, they are expert at working with you, the client. They listen to your needs and translate them into the kind of room you want.

Don't take chances with your investment. When you make the decision for a new kitchen or bathroom, make the decision to find an NKBA member.

HOW?

NATIONAL KITCHEN
NKBA
& BATH ASSOCIATION

It's easy to find an NKBA member, if you know what to look for. And easy identification begins with the NKBA logo, a symbol of quality, dedication and expertise in kitchens and bathrooms.

When visiting kitchen and bath showrooms, look for the logo in windows or on the counter.

If you know anyone who has recently remodeled, talk with them. Ask them who they used and if he or she is associated with the NKBA. Referrals are an excellent source for finding an industry professional, but be sure you're dealing with someone qualified in kitchens and bathrooms specifically — an NKBA member.

You can find all of the NKBA members in your area by contacting the National Kitchen and Bath Association at 687 Willow Grove Street, Hackettstown, New Jersey 07840, **1-800-401-NKBA, Ext. 700.** They will provide you with a directory of NKBA firms who design, supply and install residential kitchens and bathrooms.

HAVE YOU FINISHED YOUR HOMEWORK?

Now that you have a name in mind (or possibly more than one — you may want to talk with several NKBA professionals to find the one with whom you feel most comfortable), you can go ahead and set up an appointment to discuss your project. But before you actually sit down with the designer, there are several things you should do in preparation. (This is the fun part.)

Chances are you've been thinking about this for a while, but if not, start reading magazines geared toward the home, remodeling, architecture, and especially those that focus on kitchens and bathrooms. Clip out pictures of kitchens or bathrooms that interest you — this will help the designer get a feel for the styles you like. You may even find features that would work in your new room.

Visit kitchen and bath showrooms to see the many options for new countertops and other surfaces, and to collect brochures on fixtures, cabinets, appliances and any other items or materials that interest you.

As you visit different showrooms in your search for ideas and NKBA designers, you should make notes on each one. The best way to find the NKBA member with whom you're most comfortable is to evaluate the designers and their showrooms. Use the following checklist to help you in your decision:

Evaluating the kitchen and bath dealership

	Showrooms				Showrooms		
	#1	#2	#3		#1	#2	#3
Showroom Clean and Neat	___	___	___	Designers Ask Questions About Your Project	___	___	___
Displays Highlight Interesting Design	___	___	___	NKBA Membership Identified	___	___	___
Displays Well-Constructed and Presented	___	___	___	Firm Has Been In Business for at Least Two Years	___	___	___
Broad Range of Styles Offered	___	___	___	Firm Provides Complete Design and Installation Services	___	___	___
Staff Friendly and Helpful	___	___	___	Referrals Provided	___	___	___
Staff Knowledgeable About Products and Design	___	___	___				

As you visit showrooms and gather notes, clippings, photographs, brochures and samples, you may want to organize them into an "idea file." As your file grows, you'll see a definite style emerge from the decorating trends you've chosen — *your* style.

KITCHEN PLANNING WITH YOUR NKBA SPECIALIST

You can save a lot of time and money, and greatly reduce guesswork by first evaluating your needs. Before even your initial consultation, write down some basic lifestyle facts.

Simple facts, like how many hours a week you work, will affect how often you cook and what appliances you use. If you work a lot of hours out of the home, you may cook less often, opting instead for microwave meals, in which case you'd need your microwave in a convenient location and a lot of freezer space.

Who uses your kitchen? Is it a setting for family gatherings, or the private domain of a gourmet chef? Will it function well with two or more cooks? Do you entertain often? All of these answers will affect the size, layout and type of equipment you need for your kitchen.

When preparing your evaluation, first consider your normal cooking habits. For instance, if your family shares in the meal preparation, you may need two sinks and built-in cutting and chopping boards strategically placed throughout the kitchen to maximize food preparation areas.

Will children be active in the kitchen? If so, easy-to-clean surfaces are a must. You may also want to consider a desk or counter setup for homework and after-school snacks.

If you like to entertain, often cooking for large groups of guests, you may need two ovens and a wide-shelved refrigerator.

Do you recycle? You'll need the separating and storage space, depending on your involvement and the requirements in your area.

All of the variables mentioned here (and others your designer will pose) will affect the layout of your kitchen. Each shape — U-shaped, L-shaped, Corridor, Island, One-Wall, or Peninsula — has its own functionality and advantages. Once the NKBA kitchen specialist has laid out your kitchen, he or she will guide you in selecting components. With all of the advances in materials, appliances and designs, this selection process would be overwhelming without the help of a professional.

Your decision-making becomes much easier once you have related your needs to your lifestyle. By providing your NKBA professional with a clear picture of what works best for your family, you'll be off to a head start.

BATHROOM PLANNING WITH YOUR NKBA SPECIALIST

Do you look forward to spending time in your bathroom? Sounds like a strange question to most people. Most bathrooms are cold and claustrophobic, places where comfort is either kept to a bare minimum, or simply not an option. But with the shift in society back toward the home also come changes in the bathroom.

Bathrooms have become more than a necessity. Their role has now expanded to that of "bodyroom," incorporating such amenities as whirlpool tubs, exercise equipment, dual-head showers, heat lamps and entertainment systems.

Before you talk to an NKBA professional about your new bathroom, evaluate your needs by first looking at who will use it, and how. The best way to do that is to examine present bathroom usage. Some NKBA members suggest taking notes as you use the room on a typical weekday and weekend. By mapping out your routine, you and your bath designer will be better-equipped to create a floorplan that is efficient and incorporates the features you need.

For example, you may think the first thing you do when you step out of the shower is to reach for your towel. Keeping a diary, however, might reveal that oftentimes the first move after exiting the shower is to drip, drip, drip across the hall to the linen closet. So, by simply focusing on details and making note of them, you've discovered the need for bathroom towel storage.

If several girls or women use the bathroom, adequate circuits and outlets are necessary for hair dryers and curling irons, as well as appropriate lighting for makeup application.

Special safety and convenience features should be considered for elderly, very young and handicapped family members. High water closet seats, grab bars and locking cabinets are practical options, and your designer will likely have other suggestions.

For family bathrooms which are shared by several people, privacy zones isolating the shower, tub, lavatory and water closet will allow simultaneous use.

Your NKBA bathroom specialist will take into consideration all of these factors and more. They have the experience to anticipate potential problems and point out options that may help you with your choices.

SETTING
PRIORITIES

When your idea file is overflowing with clippings and photographs, you've thought about style and color, and evaluated your needs, there is one final step that will really help your NKBA professional: your "must-have" and "want" lists. You simply make two lists which include:

1) features you consider essential for your new room, and
2) features you'd like to have, if possible and if budget permits.

It sounds easy, right? Well, this one may force you to make some tough decisions and possibly even some sacrifices, but it is a very valuable step. Just listing and distinguishing the "must-haves" from the "wants" will help you focus on the features most important to you and your family. In fact, you may want to let each member of the family make their own lists. When you can actually see them on paper, it puts your needs into better perspective.

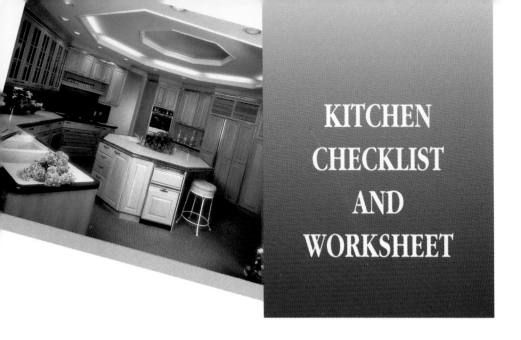

KITCHEN CHECKLIST AND WORKSHEET

Needs and Wants

Check the items you feel your kitchen must have in the "need" column, and the items you would like, if the budget and design allow, in the "want" column. (This should be used as a preliminary guideline; they may change along the way.)

	Need	Want		Need	Want
New cabinets	___	___	Recycling bins	___	___
New countertop	___	___	More workspace	___	___
New floor	___	___	More storage	___	___
New oven(s)	___	___	Pantry	___	___
New refrigerator/freezer	___	___	Wet bar	___	___
New cooktop	___	___	New window(s)	___	___
New microwave	___	___	Desk area	___	___
New dishwasher	___	___	Eating area	___	___
New sink(s)	___	___	Media/TV center	___	___
New light fixtures	___	___	Others _____	___	___
Cutting/chopping surfaces	___	___	_____	___	___
Waste disposal	___	___	_____	___	___
Trash compactor	___	___	_____	___	___

Lifestyle/Room Use

This worksheet will give you some things to think about in your initial planning, but it's only the beginning. Your NKBA kitchen specialist will conduct an in-depth interview with you in order to create a design that suits your lifestyle and satisfies your needs and wants.

Who is the primary cook? _____

How many other household members cook? _____

Do any of these members have physical limitations? _____

What type of cooking do you normally do?
    ____ Heat and serve meals
    ____ Full-course, "from scratch" meals
    ____ Bulk cooking for freezing/leftovers
    ____ Other _____

Do you entertain frequently? ____ Formally ____ Informally

Is the kitchen a socializing place? _____

Where do you plan to sort recyclables?
    ___ Kitchen   ___ Laundry   ___ Garage   ___ Other

What type of feeling would you like your new kitchen space to have?
    ___ Sleek/Contemporary   ___ Warm & Cozy Country
    ___ Traditional   ___ Open & Airy
    ___ Strictly Functional   ___ Formal
    ___ Family Retreat   ___ Personal Design Statement

BATHROOM CHECKLIST AND WORKSHEET

Needs and Wants

Check the items you feel your bathroom must have in the "need" column, and the items you would like, if the budget and design allow, in the "want" column. (This should be used as a preliminary guideline; they may change along the way.)

	Need	Want		Need	Want
New vanity	____	____	Heat lamp	____	____
Separate shower	____	____	Bidet	____	____
New lavatory (sink)	____	____	New floor/wall surfaces	____	____
Tub for two	____	____	New countertops	____	____
Whirlpool tub	____	____	Customized storage	____	____
New water closet (toilet)	____	____	Others _____	____	____
Exercise area	____	____	_____	____	____
Entertainment center	____	____	_____	____	____
Linen storage	____	____	_____	____	____
Lighting fixtures	____	____	_____	____	____

Lifestyle/Room Use

This worksheet will give you some things to think about in your initial planning, but it's only the beginning. Your NKBA bathroom specialist will conduct an in-depth interview with you in order to create a design that suits your lifestyle and satisfies your needs and wants.

Who will use this bathroom (i.e., client, spouse, child, guests)?
_____

Type of bathroom?
__ Powder   __ Children's   __ Mastersuite   __ Hall

How many will use it at one time? _____

What activities will take place in the bathroom?
__ Makeup application   __ Bathing
__ Hair care   __ Dressing
__ Exercising   __ Lounging
__ Laundering   __ Other _____

Would you like his and hers facilities? _____

Do you prefer the water closet and/or bidet to be isolated from the other fixtures? _____

Would you like a closet planned as part of your new bathroom?
          ___ Yes   ___ No

What type of feeling would you like your new bathroom to have?
___ Sleek/Contemporary   ___ Warm/Country
___ Traditional   ___ Open & Airy
___ Personal Design Statement

THE DESIGN CONFERENCE

O.K., you've done your homework — you stand ready with your ideas, lists, samples, photographs, maybe even rough plans. And now it's time to meet with your designer.

You may first meet with the NKBA member at the showroom to look over samples and displays, but then he or she will come out to your house and really get to work. Here's where you'll begin to see what sets NKBA specialists apart from other designers. The NKBA member will take careful and thorough measurements, right down to locating the pipes in the walls (something often overlooked by those who do not specialize in kitchen and bathroom planning).

He or she will look at your idea file and talk with you in depth about your needs. This is an opportunity for both of you to discuss thoughts and opinions, ask questions and determine a direction for your room design. Think of it as an exchange of ideas, a "design conference." This is another advantage of working with an NKBA member. He or she will work *with you* to achieve the best results, instead of simply dictating a design.

One very important determinant for your new room design is your budget. You should have a figure established as you go into this — one that's realistic for your situation. And the initial design conference is the time to talk budgets. Your NKBA specialist will let you know what can be achieved — in the way of materials, construction, appliances, etc. — for what you want to spend. And together, you can set priorities for your design that will allow your new dream room to stay within your budget.

When you both agree on a general direction and a budget, you can make arrangements for payment.

With many firms, payment begins with 50% at the signing of the contract, then 40% when installation begins, and the remaining 10% upon completion of the job. Financing can be arranged through a home improvement loan, or you may be able to negotiate the price into the mortgage when purchasing a home. Remember, your new room is an investment in your home's equity. It increases with the value of your home, and may be recovered when the home is sold.

LET THE TRANS-FORMATION BEGIN

From the first meeting, you'll begin to see how working with an NKBA member will make the project easier, and the results, better. When you've got the knowledge and experience of an NKBA professional on your side, you can rest assured that your new room will be everything you dreamed it would be, and more.

First, your NKBA specialist will design the complete layout, choose the final materials, and begin coordinating the contractors — all with your approval, of course. Then, the construction begins.

Living under construction is never easy, but your NKBA professional will do everything possible to minimize the inconvenience for you. Ask him or her for tips on living under construction. For example, setting up temporary facilities for cooking and cleanup. Your NKBA designer has experience in these matters and will undoubtedly have ideas to make you more comfortable during this phase.

And now it's only a matter of time before you see your dream room become a reality. Exactly how long depends on many variables (whether or not you are having cabinets custom-designed, for example), but in somewhere between two weeks and several months, you'll see the results.

You'll soon see your room taking shape. The ideas you've envisioned, the style you've developed, the colors you've decided upon, you'll see it all materialize at the hands of the craftsmen.

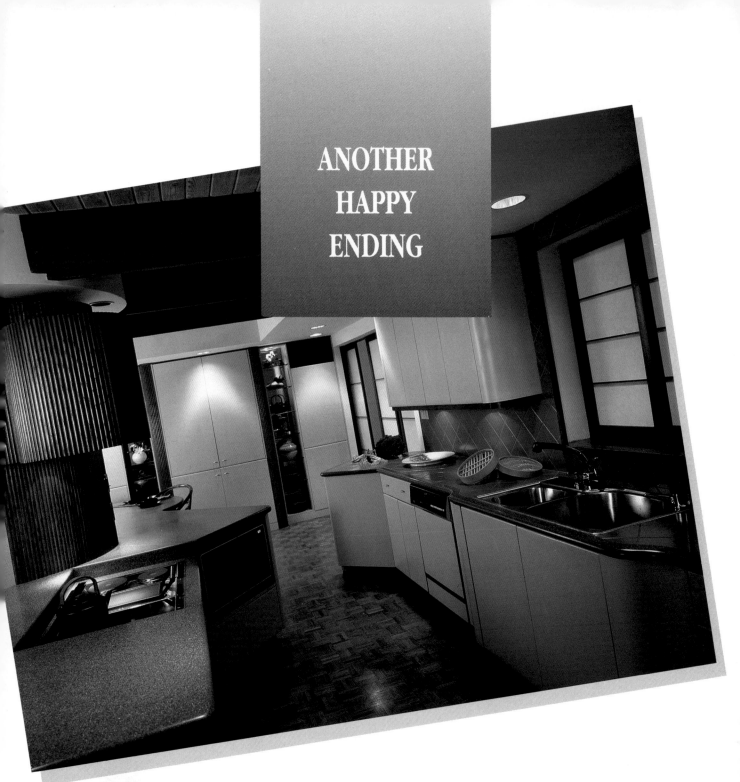

ANOTHER HAPPY ENDING

It's evening, you're dining in your new kitchen, or soaking in your new whirlpool tub. You proudly gaze around the room. For the next few weeks you'll have to open an extra drawer or two looking for the silverware. Or you may catch yourself walking across the room to where the towels *used to* be. But you'll enjoy getting to know your new room and growing with it. After all, you created it (with a little help from NKBA).

National Kitchen & Bath Association
687 Willow Grove St.
Hackettstown, New Jersey 07840
1-800-401-NKBA, Ext. 700.

Firms

Catalogs are coded by position within the volume in numerical sequence, e.g., C345.

Products

Catalogs are coded by position within the volume in numerical sequence, e.g., C345.

Index headings listed below are based on the manufacturers' descriptions of their products as those descriptions appear in the catalogs distributed by Sweet's. SWEET'S MAKES NO REPRESENTATIONS OR WARRANTIES OF ANY KIND, EXPRESS OR IMPLIED, INCLUDING BUT NOT LIMITED TO IMPLIED WARRANTIES OF MERCHANTABILITY OR FITNESS FOR ANY PARTICULAR PURPOSE AS TO THESE INDEX HEADINGS OR AS TO THE PRODUCTS DESCRIBED BY THESE INDEX HEADINGS. Users of Sweet's Files should not rely on these index headings in connection with selecting products. Users of Sweet's Files should refer to the manufacturers' catalogs for further information regarding characteristics of products indexed below.

a

Accelerators
see
admixtures: —accelerators

Access doors
see
doors—application: —access—specific type

Access floors
see
flooring—access, raised

Accessible products for the disabled
see
bathroom accessories: —grab bars—specific material
elevators—passenger
faucets—application: —disabled persons' use
faucets—types: —sensor-actuated
flooring—clay or ceramic tile: —detectable, tactile warning strips
hardware—window
lavatories and accessories: —disabled persons' use
mirrors: —tilting
plumbing fittings and trim
railings—types: —handrail—safety: —handrail—wall-mounted
showers: —disabled persons' use
showers: —seats—wall-mounted
surfacing—detectable, tactile—disabled persons' use
toilets: —units—disabled persons' use
washroom accessories —grab bars

Acoustic isolation and control
see
partitions—properties: —sound-insulating or retarding—specific type
windows—properties: —insulating—sound—specific type

Acrylic products
see
grout—materials: —acrylic
skylights—materials: —acrylic

Address systems—public
see
intercommunicating systems—specific type

Adhesives for
ceramic or clay tiles
Summitville Tiles, Inc. C190

Adhesives for cont.
flooring—brick, pavers
Summitville Tiles, Inc. C190
flooring—clay or ceramic tile
Summitville Tiles, Inc. C190
flooring—marble
Summitville Tiles, Inc. C190

Admixtures
see also
cement
accelerators
Summitville Tiles, Inc. C190
acid-resistant
Summitville Tiles, Inc. C190
anti-freeze
Summitville Tiles, Inc. C190
bonding agents
Summitville Tiles, Inc. C190
curing
Summitville Tiles, Inc. C190
hardeners and densifiers
Summitville Tiles, Inc. C190
plasticizers
see
sealers
water-reducing or water-repellent
see also
dampproofing
Summitville Tiles, Inc. C190

Aerators
see
liquid waste disposal or treatment equipment: —filters, strainers, aerators, interceptors
water conditioning equipment: —filters, aerators, deodorizers, hydrators, strainers

Air conditioners
packaged—unitary
see
heaters—unit
packaged—window or thru-wall
Frigidaire Co. C493

Air-conditioning equipment
see
air conditioners
dehumidifiers

Air distribution equipment
see
fans
ventilators

Air handlers
see
air conditioners

Air/liquid treatment equipment
see
air conditioners
dehumidifiers
liquid waste disposal or treatment equipment
waste handling equipment and systems
water conditioning equipment

Air pollution, quality control equipment
see
dehumidifiers
vacuum cleaning systems

Alarms and alarm systems
horns, bells, chimes, sirens
see
bells, buzzers, chimes (entrance and alarm)

Aluminum products
see
railings—materials: —aluminum or aluminum alloy
skylights—framing: —aluminum or aluminum alloy
veneers: —aluminum
windows—replacement: —wood-aluminum—specific type
windows—wood-aluminum/operation

Appliances—residential—kitchen
see
ice making machines: —residential
kitchen appliances—residential
kitchen or kitchenette units

Architectural artwork
cornices
see
moldings and cornices
surfacing and paneling—interior—materials: —moldings and trim for—specific material
ironwork—ornamental
see
specific products
moldings and cornices
see
moldings and cornices
murals
see
murals

Architectural artwork *cont.*

plaques, insignia and tablets
see
  plaques, insignia and tablets

Architectural woodwork
see
  woodwork

Art and decorative objects
see
  murals
  plaques, insignia and tablets

Ash handling equipment
see
  vacuum cleaning systems

Ash trays
see
  washroom accessories: —ash trays, urns

Association catalogs
see
  specific products

Athletic equipment and facilities
see
  bathtubs: —hydro-massage combination
  consultants and services
  health club equipment
  saunas and equipment
  steam bath rooms and equipment

Audio and visual equipment
see
  intercommunicating systems

b

Balusters, balustrades
see
  railings

Barbecue grills
see
  grills—barbecue

Bar furniture and equipment
see also
  ice making machines

elbow rests, tops
  Nevamar Corp. .C467
  Wilsonart International, Inc. C478

sinks
  Elkay Mfg. Co. C550; C551
  Franke, Inc., Kitchen
    Systems Div. C555
  Nevamar Corp. C467
  Swan Corp. (The) C562

Barrier-free design products
see
  bathroom accessories: —grab bars—specific
    material
  elevators—passenger
  faucets—application: —disabled persons' use
  faucets—types: —sensor-actuated
  flooring—clay or ceramic tile: —detectable,
    tactile warning strips
  hardware—window
  lavatories and accessories: —disabled persons'
    use
  mirrors: —tilting
  plumbing fittings and trim

Barrier-free design products *cont.*
see cont.
  railings—types: —handrail—safety:
    —handrail—wall-mounted
  showers: —disabled persons' use: —seats—
    wall-mounted
  surfacing—detectable, tactile—disabled persons'
    use
  toilets: —units—disabled persons' use
  washroom accessories —grab bars

Bars
see
  bathroom accessories: —grab bars—specific
    material
  washroom accessories: —grab bars

Bases
see
  flooring—specific materials
  showers: —stalls and receptors—specific
    material

Bathroom accessories
see also
  washroom accessories

cabinets and mirrors
see also
  cabinets: —medicine
  mirrors
  Broan Mfg. Co., Inc. C587
  Dornbracht, Santile
    International Corp. C568
  NuTone C590

cabinets and mirrors—with lighting fixtures
see also
  lighting—application: —accent and display
    —cabinets and mirrors
  Broan Mfg. Co., Inc. C587
  Dornbracht, Santile
    International Corp. C568
  NuTone C590

dispensers—facial tissue
  AQUASTYL, M-K-F, S.a.r.l.,
    Menager International
    Corp. C584A
  JADO C588

dryers—hand or hair
see
  washroom accessories: —dryers—specific
    type—hand or hair

fans for
see
  fans: —kitchen or bathroom

fittings for
see
  plumbing fittings and trim

grab bars, safety toilet seats, safety towel bars—metal
see also
  plumbing fittings and trim: —toilet seats
  AQUASTYL, M-K-F, S.a.r.l.,
    Menager International
    Corp. C584A

holders—toilet brush
  AQUASTYL, M-K-F, S.a.r.l.,
    Menager International
    Corp. C584A
  Baldwin Hardware Corp. C584B

holders—toothbrush and/or tumbler—ceramic
  Dornbracht, Santile
    International Corp. C568
  Hastings Pavement Co., Inc. C572

holders—toothbrush and/or tumbler—metal
  AQUASTYL, M-K-F, S.a.r.l.,
    Menager International
    Corp. C584A

Bathroom accessories *cont.*

holders—toothbrush and/or tumbler—metal *cont.*
  Hastings Pavement Co., Inc. C572
  JADO C588
  NuTone C590
  Opella, Inc. C561; C575

holders—toothbrush and/or tumbler—plastic
  Hastings Pavement Co., Inc. C572

hooks—coat or robe
  AQUASTYL, M-K-F, S.a.r.l.,
    Menager International
    Corp. C584A
  Hastings Pavement Co., Inc. C572
  JADO C588
  NuTone C590
  Opella, Inc. C561; C575

lighting—accent
see
  lighting—application: —accent and display

mirrors
see
  mirrors

partitions for
see
  partitions—shower, toilet, urinal

shelves
see
  shelving: —bathroom or washroom—specific
    material

sinks
see
  sinks—residential

toilet paper holders, soap dishes—ceramic
  Hastings Pavement Co., Inc. C572

toilet paper holders, soap dishes—metal
  AQUASTYL, M-K-F, S.a.r.l.,
    Menager International
    Corp. C584A
  Baldwin Hardware Corp. C584B
  Hastings Pavement Co., Inc. C572
  JADO C588
  NuTone C590
  Opella, Inc. C561; C575

toilet paper holders, soap dishes—plastic
  Hastings Pavement Co., Inc. C572

towel holders
  AQUASTYL, M-K-F, S.a.r.l.,
    Menager International
    Corp. C584A
  Baldwin Hardware Corp. C584B
  Dornbracht, Santile
    International Corp. C568
  Hastings Pavement Co., Inc. C572
  JADO C588
  NuTone C590
  Opella, Inc. C561; C575
  Strom Plumbing, Sign of the
    Crab C584

vanity cabinets
see
  cabinets: —bathroom vanity

waste receptacles
  AQUASTYL, M-K-F, S.a.r.l.,
    Menager International
    Corp. C584A

water closets
see
  toilets

Bathroom planning and design
see
  consultants and services: —kitchen and bath
    planning and design

Baths—recirculating

see

bathtubs: —hydro-massage combination

Baths—steam

see

saunas and equipment
steam bath rooms and equipment

Bathtubs

accessories for

Absolute by American
Standard, Inc. C565
American Standard, Inc. C566
Clarion Bathware C566B
DuPont Co. C474
Jason International, Inc. C573A
Strom Plumbing, Sign of the
Crab C584
TradeWind Industries, Inc. C665

enclosures for

American Shower Door C591
DuPont Co. C474
Formica Corp., Nuvel C476
Formica Corp., Surell C477
Jason International, Inc. C573A
Nevamar Corp. C467
Strom Plumbing, Sign of the
Crab C584
Swan Corp. (The) C562
Wilsonart International, Inc. C478

enclosures for—folding door

American Shower Door C591

enclosures for—sliding door

American Shower Door C591
Jason International, Inc. C573A

enclosures for—swinging door

American Shower Door C591
Crane Plumbing/Fiat
Products, Fiat Products C567

fiberglass, fiberglass-reinforced, plastic

Clarion Bathware C566B
Formica Corp., Nuvel C476
Formica Corp., Surell C477
Jason International, Inc. C573A

fittings for

see

faucets—application: —bathtub
plumbing fittings and trim

hydro-massage combination

Absolute by American
Standard, Inc. C565
American Standard, Inc. C566
Clarion Bathware C566B
Crane Plumbing/Fiat
Products, Fiat Products C567
Jason International, Inc. C573A
Kohler Co., Plumbing Div. C574
TradeWind Industries, Inc. C665

porcelain enamel, vitreous china

American Standard, Inc. C566

wall liners for, surrounds

see

bathtubs: —enclosures for

whirlpools

see

bathtubs: —hydro-massage combination

Bathtub/shower—prefabricated unit

Clarion Bathware C566B
Crane Plumbing/Fiat
Products, Fiat Products C567
Jason International, Inc. C573A

Beads

see

flooring—specific material

Bells, buzzers, chimes (entrance and alarm)

Broan Mfg. Co., Inc. ii
NuTone C590

Bidets

see also

faucets—application: —bidet
Absolute by American
Standard, Inc. C565
American Standard, Inc. C566
Dornbracht, Santile
International Corp. C568
Gerber Plumbing Fixtures
Corp. C571

Blenders

see

kitchen appliances—residential: —blenders

Blinds—venetian

door—built-in

see

doors—swinging—by materials/construction:
—specific material—frame and glass—built-in
venetian blind

window—built-in

see

windows—replacement: —specific material—
double-glazed—built-in blind, shade
windows—specific material/operation

Blinds—vertical

window—built-in

see

windows—replacement —specific material—
double-glazed—built-in heat-reflective blind,
shade

Blocks—concrete

cement, mortar for

see

cement

Blocks—glass

see also

glass—form: —block
panels—building—materials: —glass, glass block
partitions—materials: —glass block
windows—replacement: —glass blocks for
Weck, Glashaus Div. B687

Blocks—glass—anchors, caulking, joints for

see

sealants: —caulking compound for—specific
material

Blocks—wood

see

flooring—wood: —blocks—specific type

Blowers—centrifugal or axial

see

fans
ventilators

Bluestone

see

specific products—flagstone

Bond

see

cement: —bond: —masonry or mortar—high
strength

Bookcases

residential

Wellborn Cabinet, Inc. C536

Bookstacks

see

bookcases

Brass products

see

piping and tubing—accessories for: —fittings—
brass

Brick

acid and chemical-resistant

Summitville Tiles, Inc. C190

unglazed

Summitville Tiles, Inc. C190

Brick face—simulated/manufactured

see

fireplaces: —facings for—simulated/
manufactured—stone or brick

Brick products

see

fireplaces: —facings for—simulated/
manufactured stone or brick
flooring—brick
surfacing and paneling—interior—materials:
—brick
veneers: —brick

Brick—simulated/manufactured products

see

fireplaces: —facings for—simulated/
manufactured stone or brick

Bridges

railings for

see

railings—types

Broilers

residential

see also

ranges and ovens—residential: —cooktops/
smoker/broiler combination: —ranges—
griddle/broiler/oven combination
Dynasty C491
Jenn-Air Corp. C502

Building panels

see

panels—building

Bulletin boards

see

directories/message boards

Bumpers

door

see

guards: —door
hardware—door: —holders and stops—specific
type

wall

see

guards: —wall

Ceramic or clay tile *cont.*

unglazed

American Olean Tile Co.
Sub., Armstrong World
Industries, Inc., Dal-Tile
International Corp. C171
Daltile, Dal-Tile International
Corp. C173
Summitville Tiles, Inc. C190

Ceramic products

see
*bathroom accessories: —holders—toothbrush
and/or tumbler—ceramic: —toilet paper
holders, soap dishes—ceramic
ceramic or clay tile
fireplaces: —facings for—ceramic
flooring—clay or ceramic tile
moldings and cornices: —ceramic
mosaic tile: —ceramic
panels—building—materials: —ceramic—specific
type
paving: —ceramic or clay tile
plaques, insignia and tablets: —ceramic
sinks—residential: —ceramic, composite
stair treads, risers: —clay or ceramic tile
surfacing and paneling—interior—materials:
—ceramic—specific type
veneers: —ceramic
washroom accessories: —holders—toothbrush
and/or tumbler—ceramic*

Chimes

see
bells, buzzers, chimes (entrance and alarm)

Church equipment

directories
see
directories/message boards

signs
see
signs

windows—inserts for
see
*glass
plastic*

Chutes

rubbish and waste
see
waste handling equipment and systems

Clay products

see
*ceramic or clay tile
flooring—clay or ceramic tile
paving: —ceramic or clay tile
stair treads, risers: —clay or ceramic tile
surfacing and paneling—interior—materials:
—ceramic or clay tile—specific type: —clay
tile—quarry*

Cleaners—masonry, stone

see
masonry cleaners

Cleaning systems

see
vacuum cleaning systems

Closers—door

see
*hardware—door —holders and stops—specific
type*

Closets

accessories for
see
shelving

water
see
toilets

Clothes racks, hooks, hook panels

see
washroom accessories: —hooks—coat or robe

Clothes washers

see
laundry equipment—specific use

Coatings and toppings— concrete or masonry

see
sealers

primers
see
primers: —masonry or concrete

sealers
see
sealers —masonry—specific type

transparent
see
sealers —masonry—specific type

waterproof, water-repellent—brush, roller or sprayed-on
see
*dampproofing
waterproofing membranes*

waterproof, water-repellent—troweled
see
*dampproofing
waterproofing membranes*

Coatings—roof

see
*dampproofing
sealants
sealers
waterproofing membranes*

Coatings—slip-resistant

see
flooring—specific material

Coffee area equipment

see
dispensers

Communicating systems

see
*directories/message boards
intercommunicating systems—specific type
wiring devices—electrical*

Compact kitchens

see
kitchen or kitchenette units

Compactors—waste

see
*waste handling equipment and systems:
—compactors—specific type*

Concrete

admixtures for
see
admixtures

Concrete *cont.*

caulking
see
*sealants: —caulking compounds for concrete or
masonry*

cleaners, surface preparation for
Summitville Tiles, Inc. C190

expansion, contraction control for
see
sealants

primer
see
primers: —masonry or concrete

sealers
see
*sealants: —caulking compounds for concrete or
masonry*

Conduits—electrical

covers for—fire-resistant, fire-stop penetration
Arden Architectural
Specialties, Inc. C357

underfloor
see also
*floorings—access, raised: —accessories (caster
pads, grilles, pedestals, ramps, wiring
modules)*
Arden Architectural
Specialties, Inc. C357

Construction joints

see
sealants

Consultants and services

construction loans, project financial information
Green Tree Financial Corp. . . . inside front cover

financial information
see
*consultants and services: —construction loans,
project financial information*

kitchen and bath planning and design
Maytag Co. .C507

Contractors

see
*flooring—clay or ceramic tile: —ceramic
mosaic—contractors for*

Control joints

see
sealants

Controls

electric, electronic—centralized
Broan Mfg. Co., Inc. C486

pest
see
specific products: —fungus, vermin, rot-resistant

rodent
see
specific products: —fungus, vermin, rot-resistant

system—interface—air, audio/video, lighting, security
Broan Mfg. Co., Inc. C486

Controls—lighting

see also
*transformers
wiring devices—electrical*

dimmers—manual
Task Lighting Corp. C950

Controls—lighting *cont.*

sensors—occupancy—infrared, ultrasonic
Task Lighting Corp. C950

Conveyors or conveying systems

elevators
see
elevators—specific type

pneumatic—tubing or fittings for
see
piping and tubing—accessories for

Cooktops

see
ranges and ovens—residential: —cooktops: —cooktops/grills—convertible: —cooktops/ smoker/broiler combination

Copper products

see
veneers: —copper or copper alloy

Cornices

see
moldings and cornices
surfacing and paneling—interior

Counters

lighting for—accent
see
lighting—application: —accent and display

tops for
American Olean Tile Co.
 Sub., Armstrong World
 Industries, Inc., Dal-Tile
 International Corp. C171
Daltile, Dal-Tile International
 Corp. C173
DuPont Co. C474
Florida Tile Industries, Inc. C176
Formica Corp. C379
Formica Corp., Nuvel C476
Formica Corp., Surell C477
Nevamar Corp. C467
Summitville Tiles, Inc. C190
Wilsonart International, Inc. C478

Couplings

piping and tubing
see
piping and tubing—accessories for

Covers and frames

catchbasin, manhole, pit, sump, trench, trough
Arden Architectural
 Specialties, Inc. C357

floor cleanouts
Arden Architectural
 Specialties, Inc. C357

Covers—with fire-resistant properties

see
conduits—electrical: —covers for—fire-resistant, fire-stop penetration

Coves

see
flooring—specific material
luminaires—types: —cove

Crash guards

see
guards: —crash—wall, door

Curbing

roof—skylight, smokestack, ventilator
see
skylights—general: —curb combination

Curtain walls

see
panels—building
storefronts

Curtain walls—window framing systems

adhesives, caulking and sealing compounds for
see
sealants: —caulking compound for—specific type

panels for
see
panels—building

d

Dampers

air pollution control
Broan Mfg. Co., Inc. C486

air volume control or duct
Broan Mfg. Co., Inc. C486

moderate pressure and temperature
Broan Mfg. Co., Inc. C486

regulators for
Broan Mfg. Co., Inc. C486

Dampproofing

see also
admixtures: —water-reducing or water-repellent
waterproofing membranes
Summitville Tiles, Inc. C190

Dehumidifiers

Frigidaire Co. C493

Densifiers

see
admixtures: —hardeners and densifiers

Dentils

see
moldings and cornices

Desks

tops, pads for
Formica Corp. C379

Diffusers—air distribution

see
ventilators

Dimmers—light

see
controls—lighting: —dimmers—specific type

Directories/message boards

see also
signs

extrusions for
Nevamar Corp. C467

wall or ceiling-mounted
Nevamar Corp. C467

Disabled persons' products

see
bathroom accessories: —grab bars—specific material
elevators—passenger
faucets—application: —disabled persons' use
faucets—types: —sensor-actuated
flooring—clay or ceramic tile: —detectable, tactile warning strips
hardware—window
lavatories and accessories: —disabled persons' use
mirrors: —tilting
plumbing fittings and trim
railings—types: —handrail—safety: —handrail—wall-mounted
showers: —disabled persons' use: —seats— wall-mounted
surfacing—detectable, tactile—disabled persons' use
toilets: —units—disabled persons' use
washroom accessories —grab bars

Dishes

see
bathroom accessories: —toilet paper holders, soap dishes—specific material

Dishwashers—residential

built-in
Frigidaire Co. C493
Jenn-Air Corp. C502
KitchenAid, Whirlpool Corp. C503
Maytag Co. C507

energy-saving
Jenn-Air Corp. C502
KitchenAid, Whirlpool Corp. C503

free-standing or mobile
Frigidaire Co. C493
Jenn-Air Corp. C502
KitchenAid, Whirlpool Corp. C503
Maytag Co. C507

kitchenette combination
Maytag Co. C507

under-sink
Jenn-Air Corp. C502
KitchenAid, Whirlpool Corp. C503
Maytag Co. C507

Dispensers

chilled water
In-Sink-Erator Div., Emerson
 Electric Co. C501; C501A

facial tissue, lotion, paper cup, soap
see
washroom accessories: —dispensers—specific type

hot water
Franke, Inc., Kitchen
 Systems Div. C555
In-Sink-Erator Div., Emerson
 Electric Co. C501; C501A
Jenn-Air Corp. C502
KitchenAid, Whirlpool Corp. C503

Display equipment

see
shelving

cabinets and cases
see
cabinets

Faucets—types cont.

wall-mounted
Grohe C564
JADO C588

water-saving
Elkay Mfg. Co. C550
Franke, Inc., Kitchen
  Systems Div. C555
Gerber Plumbing Fixtures
  Corp. C580; C563; C578; C579
JADO C588
Kohler Co., Plumbing Div. C581

Fiberglass products

see
  *bathtubs: —fiberglass, fiberglass-reinforced,
    plastic*
  *showers: —stalls and receptors—fiberglass,
    plastic*

Fillers

see
  *plastic—form: —corrugated or flat sheet—filler
    strips for
  sealants*

Filters

air, dust, fume, gas or grease
Broan Mfg. Co., Inc. C486

water
see
  *water conditioning equipment: —filters, aerators,
    deodorizers, hydrators, strainers*

Filters—industrial processing

liquid
see
  *liquid waste disposal or treatment equipment:
    —filters—specific type*
  *water conditioning equipment: —filters—specific
    type*

Financial loan services

see
  *consultants and services: —construction loans,
    project financial information*

Fireplaces

accessories for
Heat-N-Glo Fireplace
  Products, Inc. C824

facings for—ceramic
American Olean Tile Co.
  Sub., Armstrong World
  Industries, Inc., Dal-Tile
  International Corp. C171
Summitville Tiles, Inc. C190

facings for—metal
Heat-N-Glo Fireplace
  Products, Inc. C824

**facings for—simulated/manufactured
stone or brick**
American Olean Tile Co.
  Sub., Armstrong World
  Industries, Inc., Dal-Tile
  International Corp. C171
Heat-N-Glo Fireplace
  Products, Inc. C824

fireplaces—packaged unit
Heat-N-Glo Fireplace
  Products, Inc. C824

gas/electric heat
Heat-N-Glo Fireplace
  Products, Inc. C824

**hearths—simulated/manufactured—
stone**
American Olean Tile Co.
  Sub., Armstrong World
  Industries, Inc., Dal-Tile
  International Corp. C171

Fireplaces cont.

logs—synthetic—for gas/electric heat
Heat-N-Glo Fireplace
  Products, Inc. C824

Fireproofing

see
  *conduits—electrical: —covers for—fire-resistant,
    fire-stop penetration*

Fire protection equipment and systems

partitions
see
  *partitions—properties: —fire-rated: —fire-
    resistant—specific type*

Fire-stops, firestopping

see
  *conduits—electrical: —covers for—fire-resistant,
    fire-stop penetration*

Fitness equipment

see
  *health club equipment
  saunas and equipment
  steam bath rooms and equipment*

Fittings

see
  plumbing fittings and trim

Flitches

see
  woodwork

Floor cleaning and maintenance equipment

see
  covers and frames: —floor cleanouts

vacuum cleaning systems
see
  vacuum cleaning systems

Flooring

see
  *flooring—access, raised
  flooring—brick
  flooring—clay or ceramic tile
  flooring—granite
  flooring—marble
  flooring—properties
  flooring—slate
  flooring—underlayments for
  flooring—underlayments—general
  flooring—underlayments—materials
  flooring—underlayments—properties
  flooring—wood*

Flooring—access, raised

access doors for
see
  *doors—application: —access—ceiling, duct, floor
    or wall*

**accessories (caster pads, grilles,
pedestals, ramps, wiring modules)**
Arden Architectural
  Specialties, Inc. C357

**metal—carpet, clay, rubber, terrazzo or
vinyl tile-covered**
Arden Architectural
  Specialties, Inc. C357

Flooring—brick

adhesives for
see also
  adhesives for: —flooring—brick, pavers
Summitville Tiles, Inc. C190

glazed or unglazed
Summitville Tiles, Inc. C190

Flooring—clay or ceramic tile

adhesives for
see also
  adhesives for: —flooring—clay or ceramic tile
Summitville Tiles, Inc. C190

bases, dividers, edgings and inserts for
American Olean Tile Co.
  Sub., Armstrong World
  Industries, Inc., Dal-Tile
  International Corp. C171
Daltile, Dal-Tile International
  Corp. C173
Florida Tile Industries, Inc. C176

ceramic mosaic
American Olean Tile Co.
  Sub., Armstrong World
  Industries, Inc., Dal-Tile
  International Corp. C171
Daltile, Dal-Tile International
  Corp. C173
Florida Tile Industries, Inc. C176
Summitville Tiles, Inc. C190

ceramic mosaic—contractors for
Summitville Tiles, Inc. C190

custom-designed
American Olean Tile Co.
  Sub., Armstrong World
  Industries, Inc., Dal-Tile
  International Corp. C171
Daltile, Dal-Tile International
  Corp. C173
Florida Tile Industries, Inc. C176
Summitville Tiles, Inc. C190

detectable, tactile warning strips
Daltile, Dal-Tile International
  Corp. C173

glazed
American Olean Tile Co.
  Sub., Armstrong World
  Industries, Inc., Dal-Tile
  International Corp. C171
Daltile, Dal-Tile International
  Corp. C173
Florida Tile Industries, Inc. C176
Summitville Tiles, Inc. C190

grouting or mortar for
Summitville Tiles, Inc. C190

patterned, decorative or textured
American Olean Tile Co.
  Sub., Armstrong World
  Industries, Inc., Dal-Tile
  International Corp. C171
Daltile, Dal-Tile International
  Corp. C173
Florida Tile Industries, Inc. C176
Summitville Tiles, Inc. C190

premounted sheets
American Olean Tile Co.
  Sub., Armstrong World
  Industries, Inc., Dal-Tile
  International Corp. C171
Summitville Tiles, Inc. C190

quarry
American Olean Tile Co.
  Sub., Armstrong World
  Industries, Inc., Dal-Tile
  International Corp. C171
Daltile, Dal-Tile International
  Corp. C173
Summitville Tiles, Inc. C190

Flooring—clay or ceramic tile *cont.*

unglazed
American Olean Tile Co.
Sub., Armstrong World
Industries, Inc., Dal-Tile
International Corp. C171
Daltile, Dal-Tile International
Corp. C173
Summitville Tiles, Inc. C190

Flooring—computer installation
see
flooring—access, raised

Flooring—granite
Daltile, Dal-Tile International
Corp. C173
Summitville Tiles, Inc. C190

Flooring—marble

adhesives for
see also
adhesives for: —flooring—marble
Summitville Tiles, Inc. C190

panel or tile
Daltile, Dal-Tile International
Corp. C173
Summitville Tiles, Inc. C190

Flooring—metal—grid
see
gratings

Flooring—plastic

grid
see
gratings

Flooring—properties

acid or alkali-resistant—commercial or institutional use
Florida Tile Industries, Inc. C176
Summitville Tiles, Inc. C190

acid or alkali-resistant—industrial use
Summitville Tiles, Inc. C190

acid or alkali-resistant—residential use
American Olean Tile Co.
Sub., Armstrong World
Industries, Inc., Dal-Tile
International Corp. C171
Florida Tile Industries, Inc. C176
Summitville Tiles, Inc. C190

antimicrobial
see
flooring—properties: —fungus, decay, insect, rot, vermin-resistant

corrosion-resistant
Florida Tile Industries, Inc. C176

detectable, tactile
see
surfacing—detectable, tactile—disabled persons' use

fire-resistant
Bruce Hardwood Floors,
Triangle Pacific Co. C246
Florida Tile Industries, Inc. C176
Summitville Tiles, Inc. C190

frostproof
American Olean Tile Co.
Sub., Armstrong World
Industries, Inc., Dal-Tile
International Corp. C171
Florida Tile Industries, Inc. C176
Summitville Tiles, Inc. C190

fungus, decay, insect, rot, vermin-resistant
Summitville Tiles, Inc. C190

Flooring—properties *cont.*

grease-resistant—commercial or institutional use
Daltile, Dal-Tile International
Corp. C173
Summitville Tiles, Inc. C190

grease-resistant—industrial use
Summitville Tiles, Inc. C190

grease-resistant—residential use
Daltile, Dal-Tile International
Corp. C173
Summitville Tiles, Inc. C190

slip-resistant—commercial or institutional use
Bruce Hardwood Floors,
Triangle Pacific Co. C246
Daltile, Dal-Tile International
Corp. C173
Summitville Tiles, Inc. C190

slip-resistant—industrial use
Summitville Tiles, Inc. C190

slip-resistant—residential use
American Olean Tile Co.
Sub., Armstrong World
Industries, Inc., Dal-Tile
International Corp. C171
Bruce Hardwood Floors,
Triangle Pacific Co. C246
Daltile, Dal-Tile International
Corp. C173
Summitville Tiles, Inc. C190

Flooring—raised
see
flooring—access, raised

Flooring—slate
Daltile, Dal-Tile International
Corp. C173

Flooring—treatments, maintenance and resurfacing
see
sealers
wax—floor or wall

Flooring—underlayments for

tile flooring
Summitville Tiles, Inc. C190

Flooring—underlayments—general

adhesives
Summitville Tiles, Inc. C190

joint compounds
Summitville Tiles, Inc. C190

Flooring—underlayments—materials

cement-based
Summitville Tiles, Inc. C190

Flooring—underlayments—properties

fire-resistant
Summitville Tiles, Inc. C190

Flooring—wood

adhesives for
Bruce Hardwood Floors,
Triangle Pacific Co. C246

blocks—residential (parquet)
Bruce Hardwood Floors,
Triangle Pacific Co. C246

Flooring—wood *cont.*

borders, inlays, inserts—ornamental design
Bruce Hardwood Floors,
Triangle Pacific Co. C246

coatings for—slip-resistant
Bruce Hardwood Floors,
Triangle Pacific Co. C246

hickory
Bruce Hardwood Floors,
Triangle Pacific Co. C246

maple or elm
Bruce Hardwood Floors,
Triangle Pacific Co. C246

oak
Bruce Hardwood Floors,
Triangle Pacific Co. C246

planks
Bruce Hardwood Floors,
Triangle Pacific Co. C246

plastic-impregnated
Bruce Hardwood Floors,
Triangle Pacific Co. C246

prefinished
Bruce Hardwood Floors,
Triangle Pacific Co. C246

strips
Bruce Hardwood Floors,
Triangle Pacific Co. C246

unfinished
Bruce Hardwood Floors,
Triangle Pacific Co. C246

Floor plates
see
gratings

Floor proximity egress path-marking system
see
lighting—application: —stair, aisle, path

Floors—floating
see
flooring—access, raised

Food service equipment—commercial or institutional

compactors—waste
see
waste handling equipment and systems: —compactors—specific type

dispensers
see
dispensers
washroom accessories

food waste disposers
see
food waste disposers: —commercial or institutional

ice making machines
see
ice making machines

menu boards
see
directories/message boards
signs

ventilators
see
ventilators

waste handling equipment
see
waste handling equipment and systems

water conditioning equipment
see
water conditioning equipment

Food waste disposers

see also
*waste handling equipment and systems:
—compactors—specific type*

commercial or institutional
In-Sink-Erator Div., Emerson
Electric Co. .C501

residential
Franke, Inc., Kitchen
Systems Div. C555
Frigidaire Co. C493
In-Sink-Erator Div., Emerson
Electric Co. C501
Jenn-Air Corp. C502
KitchenAid, Whirlpool Corp. C503

Fountains—decorative

lighting for
see
lighting—application: —underwater

Fountains—soda

beverage dispensers
see
dispensers

Frames

see
*doors—frames for
windows—specific material/operation*

Freezers—residential

see also
*refrigerator-freezer combination: —residential—
specific type*

built-in
Jenn-Air Corp. C502
Sub-Zero Freezer Co., Inc. C514; C515

energy-saving
Jenn-Air Corp. C502
Sub-Zero Freezer Co., Inc. C514; C515

free-standing
Frigidaire Co. C493
Jenn-Air Corp. C502
Sub-Zero Freezer Co., Inc. C514; C515

undercounter
Sub-Zero Freezer Co., Inc. C514; C515

Fume hoods

see
ventilators

Furnaces

see
heaters—unit

Furniture

see
*bar furniture and equipment
bookcases
cabinets
desks
hardware—cabinet
hardware—drawer
laboratory equipment
shelving
tables*

g

Garbage disposal equipment

see
*food waste disposers
waste handling equipment and systems*

Garden equipment

see
*lighting—application: —landscape—deck,
garden, patio/terrace, walk*

Gas equipment and products

see
*piping and tubing—application: —gas, water,
electrical or sewer system*

Generators

steam
see also
steam bath rooms and equipment
Helo Saunas, Saunatec, Inc. C647

Generic information

see
specific products/materials

Glass block products

see
*blocks—glass
glass—form: —block
panels—building—materials: —glass, glass block
partitions—materials: —glass block
skylights—materials: —glass—corrugated, plain,
wired or block
windows—replacement: —glass blocks for*

Glass—film finish for

see
glass—properties

Glass—form

bent, curved
Weck, Glashaus Div. B687

block
see also
blocks—glass
Weck, Glashaus Div. B687

**patterned, carved, decorative, etched,
sandblasted or textured**
Weck, Glashaus Div. B687

structural
see
panels—building—materials: —glass, glass block

Glass products

see
*doors—operation: —sliding—frame and glass—
specific type
doors—swinging—by materials/construction:
—glass—specific type
mirrors: —glass
panels—building—materials: —glass—specific
type
shelving: —bathroom or washroom—glass
skylights—materials: —glass—corrugated, plain,
wired or block*

Glass—properties

anti-glare/shading
Weck, Glashaus Div. B687

bullet, blast-resistant
Weck, Glashaus Div. B687

burglar-resistant
Weck, Glashaus Div. B687

diffusing
see
*glass—form: —patterned, carved, decorative,
etched, sandblasted or textured*

fire-rated
Weck, Glashaus Div. B687

fire-resistant
Weck, Glashaus Div. B687

Glass—properties *cont.*

heat-absorbing
Weck, Glashaus Div. B687

insulating panel
Weck, Glashaus Div. B687

security and detention
see
glass—properties

sound-resistant
Weck, Glashaus Div. B687

Glazing

see
*glass—form
glass—properties
plastic—form
plastic—properties*

Glazing compounds or accessories

see
sealants

Glazing film

see
*glass—properties
plastic—properties*

Grab bars

see
*bathroom accessories: —grab bars—specific
material
washroom accessories: —grab bars*

Granite products

see
*flooring—granite
panels—building—materials: —granite
paving: —granite, limestone, marble, slate—
paving blocks and stones
surfacing and paneling—interior—materials:
—granite*

Graphics

see
*murals
plaques, insignia and tablets
signs*

Grates

fireplace
see
fireplaces: —accessories for

trench
see
*covers and frames: —catchbasin, manhole, pit,
sump, trench, trough*

Gratings

frames for
Arden Architectural
Specialties, Inc. C357

trench covers
see
*covers and frames: —catchbasin, manhole, pit,
sump, trench, trough*

Griddles

see
*ranges and ovens—residential: —ranges—
griddle/broiler/oven combination*

Grids—flooring—for armoring

see
gratings

Hose

connectors for
see
> *piping and tubing—accessories for*

shower
see
> *plumbing fittings and trim: —shower or spray—
>   hoses for*

Hospital equipment

air conditioning units
see
> *air conditioners*

corridor railings
see
> *railings—types: —handrail—specific type*

desks—registration, reservation
see
> *intercommunicating systems—specific type*

**grab bars, safety toilet seats, safety
towel bars**
see
> *bathroom accessories: —grab bars—specific
>   material*
> *plumbing fittings and trim: —toilet seats*

plumbing fittings
see
> *plumbing fittings and trim*

wall guards
see
> *guards: —wall*

Hotel, motel equipment

appliances—compact
see
> *kitchen or kitchenette units—specific type*

bathroom
see
> *bathroom accessories*

lighting for
see
> *lighting—application*

Hvac terminal units

see
> *heaters—unit*

i

Ice making machines

residential
Jenn-Air Corp. C502
KitchenAid, Whirlpool Corp. C503

Identifying devices

see
> *directories/message boards*
> *nameplates or number plates*
> *plaques, insignia and tablets*
> *signs*

Impact absorption devices—
vehicles

see
> *guards: —crash—wall, door*

Indicators

see
> *directories/message boards*
> *nameplates or number plates*
> *plaques, insignia and tablets*
> *signs*

Insignia

see
> *plaques, insignia and tablets*

Intercommunicating systems

NuTone C590

Ironing boards

see also
> *laundry equipment—specific type: —ironing
>   board—built-in*
NuTone C590

J

Jail equipment

see
> *specific products*

Janitors' stations

mop sinks, receptors
see
> *faucets—application: —sinks—service, laundry*

k

Kick plates

see
> *hardware—door: —kick and push plates*

Kitchen appliances—residential

blenders
NuTone C590

can openers
NuTone C590

combination food preparation center
NuTone C590

mixers
NuTone C590

Kitchen equipment—residential

see
> *cabinets: —kitchen—residential—specific type*
> *consultants and services: —kitchen and bath
>   planning and design*
> *dishwashers—residential*
> *fans: —kitchen or bathroom*
> *faucets—application: —sink—kitchen*
> *food waste disposers: —residential*
> *freezers—residential*
> *grills—barbecue*
> *kitchen appliances—residential*
> *kitchen or kitchenette units*
> *kitchen planning*
> *ranges and ovens—residential*
> *refrigerator-freezer combination: --residential—
>   specific type*
> *refrigerators: —residential—specific type*
> *sinks—residential*
> *ventilators: —hoods—residential kitchen—
>   specific type*
> *waste handling equipment and systems:
>   —compactors—residential or institutional*

Kitchen or kitchenette units

Frigidaire Co. C493
Maytag Co. .C507

Kitchen planning

see also
> *consultants and services: —kitchen and bath
>   planning and design*
Maytag Co. .C507

Knobs

see
> *hardware—cabinet: knobs, pulls and slides*
> *hardware—door: —knobs*
> *hardware—drawer: —knobs, pulls and slides*

L

Laboratory equipment

plumbing fittings
see
> *plumbing fittings and trim*

sinks, drainboards, troughs
Nevamar Corp. C467

work surfaces for
Formica Corp. C379
Nevamar Corp. C467
Wilsonart International, Inc. C478

Laminates

see
> *metal laminate sheets*
> *plastic laminate sheets*
> *veneers*

Landscape accessories

lighting
see
> *lighting—application: —landscape—deck,
>   garden, patio/terrace, walk*

Latches

see
> *hardware—door: —latches*

Lath and plasterwork
accessories and trim

casings and corner guards
see
> *guards: —corner—specific material*
> *guards: —wall*

Laundry equipment—commercial
or institutional use

faucets for
see
> *faucets—application: —sink—service, laundry*

ironing board—built-in
see
> *ironing boards*

Laundry equipment—residential
use

dryers
Frigidaire Co. C493
Jenn-Air Corp. C502
KitchenAid, Whirlpool Corp. C503
Maytag Co. .C507

dryers—energy-saving
Jenn-Air Corp. C502
KitchenAid, Whirlpool Corp. C503

faucets
see
> *faucets—application: —sink—service, laundry*

ironing board—built-in
see also
> *ironing boards*
Broan Mfg. Co., Inc. ii
Maytag Co. .C507
NuTone C590

washer/dryer combination
Frigidaire Co. C493
Jenn-Air Corp. C502
KitchenAid, Whirlpool Corp. C503
Maytag Co. .C507

Laundry equipment—residential use *cont.*

washers

Frigidaire Co.	C493
Jenn-Air Corp.	C502
KitchenAid, Whirlpool Corp.	C503
Maytag Co.	C507

washers—energy-saving

Jenn-Air Corp.	C502
KitchenAid, Whirlpool Corp.	C503

Lavatories and accessories

cabinets for

Absolute by American Standard, Inc.	C565
Dornbracht, Santile International Corp.	C568
Gerber Plumbing Fixtures Corp.	C571
Wellborn Cabinet, Inc.	C536

disabled persons' use

American Standard, Inc.	C566

fittings and trim for
see
> *faucets—application: —lavatory*
> *plumbing fittings and trim*

lavatories

Absolute by American Standard, Inc.	C565
American Standard, Inc.	C566
Dornbracht, Santile International Corp.	C568
DuPont Co.	C474
Formica Corp., Nuvel	C476
Formica Corp., Surell	C477
Gerber Plumbing Fixtures Corp.	C571
Kohler Co., Plumbing Div.	C574
Nevamar Corp.	C467
Strom Plumbing, Sign of the Crab	C584

modular

Dornbracht, Santile International Corp.	C568

tops for

Absolute by American Standard, Inc.	C565
American Standard, Inc.	C566
DuPont Co.	C474
Formica Corp.	C379
Formica Corp., Nuvel	C476
Formica Corp., Surell	C477
Gerber Plumbing Fixtures Corp.	C571
Kohler Co., Plumbing Div.	C574
Nevamar Corp.	C467
Swan Corp. (The)	C562
Wilsonart International, Inc.	C478

vanity top and bowl—molded—one-piece

Absolute by American Standard, Inc.	C565
American Standard, Inc.	C566
DuPont Co.	C474
Formica Corp., Nuvel	C476
Formica Corp., Surell	C477
Gerber Plumbing Fixtures Corp.	C571
Kohler Co., Plumbing Div.	C574
Nevamar Corp.	C467
Swan Corp. (The)	C562

wash centers
see
> *washroom accessories: —wash centers (lavatory with accessories)—specific type*

Learning systems
see
> *intercommunicating systems—specific type*

Letters—architectural
see
> *signs*

Lifts
see
> *elevators—specific type*

Lift stations
see
> *pumps: —grinder—sewage*

Lighting
see
> *controls—lighting*
> *fans: —fan-light combination—specific type*
> *heaters—unit: —electric—with lighting*
> *lighting—application*
> *luminaires—components for*
> *luminaires—types*
> *signs*
> *wiring devices—electrical*

Lighting—application
see also
> *luminaires—types*

accent and display

AQUASTYL, M-K-F, S.a.r.l., Menager International Corp.	C584A
Task Lighting Corp.	C950

cabinets and mirrors
see also
> *bathroom accessories: —cabinets and mirrors— with lighting fixtures*

Broan Mfg. Co., Inc.	ii; C587
NuTone	C590
Task Lighting Corp.	C950

display
see
> *lighting—application: —accent and display*

floor proximity egress path-marking system
see
> *lighting—application: —stair, aisle, path*

fountain
see
> *lighting—application: —underwater*

landscape—deck, garden, patio/terrace, walk

Task Lighting Corp.	C950

railings
see
> *luminaires—types: —railings*

showcase
see
> *lighting—application: —accent and display*

stair, aisle, path

Task Lighting Corp.	C950

street
see
> *lighting—application: —landscape—deck, garden, patio/terrace, walk*

underwater

Jason International, Inc.	C573A

walkway
see
> *lighting—application: —landscape—deck, garden, patio/terrace, walk: —stair, aisle, path*

Lights

dome
see
> *skylights—form: —dome—specific type*

window
see
> *glass*

Lights *cont.*

window *cont.*
see cont.
> *plastic*

Limestone

mortar
see
> *cement: —mortar—specific type*

Limestone products
see
> *paving: —granite, limestone, marble, slate— paving blocks and stones*

Linings or liners

coatings and waterproofing
see
> *dampproofing*
> *waterproofing membranes*

Liquid waste disposal or treatment equipment
see also
> *waste handling equipment and systems*
> *water conditioning equipment*

filters, strainers, aerators, interceptors

In-Sink-Erator Div., Emerson Electric Co.	C501

piping for
see
> *piping and tubing—application: —gas, water, electrical or sewer system*

Loan services—construction
see
> *consultants and services: —construction loans, project financial information*

Locks

door
see
> *hardware—door*

Locksets
see
> *hardware—door: —locks, locksets*

Louvers
see
> *ventilators*

Luminaires—components for

controls
see
> *controls—lighting*

housings—reflector

Task Lighting Corp.	C950

Luminaires—types
see also
> *lighting—application*

cove

Task Lighting Corp.	C950

fan
see
> *fans: —fan-light combination—specific type*

heater combination
see
> *heaters—unit: —electric—with lighting*

incandescent

NuTone	C590
Task Lighting Corp.	C950

Luminaires—types cont.

low voltage
Task Lighting Corp. C950

motion detector combination
Task Lighting Corp. C950

railings
Task Lighting Corp. C950

signs
see
signs

task
Task Lighting Corp. C950

tube lighting
Task Lighting Corp. C950

m

Manholes

covers and frames for
see
covers and frames: —catchbasin, manhole, pit,
sump, trench, trough

Marble

counter tops
see
counters: —tops for

mortar for
see
cement: —mortar—specific type

Marble products
see
flooring—marble
panels—building—materials: —marble
paving: —granite, limestone, marble, slate—
paving blocks and stones
surfacing and paneling—interior—materials:
—marble—specific type

Masonry
see
grout
sealants: —caulking compounds for concrete or
masonry
sealers: —masonry—specific type

Masonry cleaners
Summitville Tiles, Inc. C190

Masonry toppings
see
admixtures
cement
primers: —masonry or concrete

Materials handling equipment/
systems
see
storage equipment

Medical equipment
see
laboratory equipment

Menu boards
see
directories/message boards
signs

Merchandising equipment
see
dispensers
storage equipment

Message, announcement boards
see
directories/message boards
signs

Metal laminate sheets
Formica Corp. C379

Metalwork—ornamental
see
murals
plaques, insignia and tablets

Microphones and accessories
see
intercommunicating systems—specific type

Microwave ovens
see
ranges and ovens—residential: —ovens-
microwave—specific type
ranges and ovens—residential: —ranges—
microwave/conventional oven combination

Millwork

wood
see
woodwork

Mirrors
see also
bathroom accessories: —cabinets and mirrors—
specific type

frames for—metal
AQUASTYL, M-K-F, S.a.r.l.,
Menager International
Corp. C584A
Hastings Pavement Co., Inc. C572

glass
AQUASTYL, M-K-F, S.a.r.l.,
Menager International
Corp. C584A
Broan Mfg. Co., Inc. C587
Dornbracht, Santile
International Corp. C568
Hastings Pavement Co., Inc. C572
JADO C588

tilting
Hastings Pavement Co., Inc. C572

Mixers—food

residential
see
kitchen appliances—residential: —mixers

Moistureproofing
see
admixtures: —water-reducing or water-repellent
dampproofing
sealants
sealers
waterproofing membranes

Moldings and cornices

ceramic
see also
surfacing and paneling—interior—materials:
—moldings and trim for—ceramic
Florida Tile Industries, Inc. C176

lighting for
see
luminaires—types: —cove

plastic, composite
see also
surfacing and paneling—interior—materials:
—moldings and trim for—plastic, composite
DuPont Co. C474

Moldings and cornices cont.

simulated/manufactured stone
DuPont Co. C474

tile
see
surfacing and paneling—interior—materials:
—moldings and trim for—tile

Mortar
see
admixtures
cement: —masonry or mortar—high strength
cement: —mortar—specific type
concrete
flooring—clay or ceramic tile: —grouting or
mortar for
grout
surfacing and paneling—interior: —ceramic or
clay tile—adhesives, grouting or mortar for

Mosaic tile

ceramic
American Olean Tile Co.
Sub., Armstrong World
Industries, Inc., Dal-Tile
International Corp. C171
Florida Tile Industries, Inc. C176

Murals
Summitville Tiles, Inc. C190

n

Nameplates or number plates

door, ceiling or wall
Summitville Tiles, Inc. C190

Number plates
see
nameplates or number plates

o

Office equipment
see
storage equipment

appliances—compact
see
kitchen appliances—residential
kitchen or kitchenette units—specific type

shelving
see
shelving

Operators—powered/door type
see
hardware—door

Ovens
see
kitchen or kitchenette units
ranges and ovens—specific type

p

Paging or signaling systems
see
intercommunicating systems—specific type

Paint
water-repellent or waterproof
see
dampproofing

Paneling—prefinished
see
surfacing and paneling—interior

Panels—building
see
panels—building—general
panels—building—materials
panels—building—properties

Panels—building—general
curved
Weck, Glashaus Div. B687

Panels—building—materials
ceramic tile or veneer
Daltile, Dal-Tile International
Corp. C173
glass, glass block
Weck, Glashaus Div. B687
granite
Daltile, Dal-Tile International
Corp. C173
granite—simulated/manufactured
see
panels—building—materials: —stone—
simulated/manufactured
limestone—simulated/manufactured
see
panels—building—materials: —stone—
simulated/manufactured
marble
Daltile, Dal-Tile International
Corp. C173
marble—simulated/manufactured
see
panels—building—materials: —stone—
simulated/manufactured
slate
Daltile, Dal-Tile International
Corp. C173
slate—simulated/manufactured
see
panels—building—materials: —stone—
simulated/manufactured
stone—simulated/manufactured
American Olean Tile Co.
Sub., Armstrong World
Industries, Inc., Dal-Tile
International Corp. C171

Panels—building—properties
bullet or burglar-resistant
Weck, Glashaus Div. B687
fire-resistant
Weck, Glashaus Div. B687
insulating
Weck, Glashaus Div. B687

Pans—shower
see
showers: —pans

Park equipment
see
consultants and services

Partitions
see
partitions—materials

Partitions *cont.*
see cont.
partitions—properties
partitions—shower, toilet, urinal

Partitions—application
shower
see
partitions—shower, toilet, urinal
toilet, urinal
see
partitions—shower, toilet, urinal

Partitions—general
blocks for
see
blocks—specific material
partitions—materials: —glass block
wall, corner guards for
see
guards: —corner—specific material
guards: —wall

Partitions—materials
glass block
see also
blocks—glass
Weck, Glashaus Div. B687
plastic laminate-faced
Formica Corp. C379
shoji
see
plastic—form: —patterned or textured

Partitions—properties
bullet or burglar-resistant
Weck, Glashaus Div. B687
fire-rated
Weck, Glashaus Div. B687
Wilsonart International, Inc. C478
fire-resistant
Formica Corp. C379
Weck, Glashaus Div. B687
sound-insulating or retarding—floor-to-ceiling partitions
Weck, Glashaus Div. B687

Partitions—shower, toilet, urinal
shower—plastic
Swan Corp. (The) C562
Wilsonart International, Inc. C478
toilet, urinal—plastic
Wilsonart International, Inc. C478
toilet, urinal—plastic laminate-faced
Aristech Chemical Corp. A026
Formica Corp. C379

Patio equipment
see
doors—application: —patio/terrace—specific
operation
lighting—application: —landscape—deck,
garden, patio/terrace, walk

Pavers
see
paving

Paving
see also
surfacing—detectable, tactile—disabled persons'
use

Paving *cont.*
ceramic or clay tile
American Olean Tile Co.
Sub., Armstrong World
Industries, Inc., Dal-Tile
International Corp. C171
Daltile, Dal-Tile International
Corp. C173
Florida Tile Industries, Inc. C176
Summitville Tiles, Inc. C190
colors for
Summitville Tiles, Inc. C190
granite, limestone, marble, slate—paving blocks and stones
Daltile, Dal-Tile International
Corp. C173
Summitville Tiles, Inc. C190
sealers for
see
sealers
slate
Daltile, Dal-Tile International
Corp. C173

Photographic artwork—prints, transparencies
see
murals

Physical fitness equipment
see
health club equipment

Pigments
see
specific products—colors/pigments for

Piping and tubing
see
piping and tubing—accessories for
piping and tubing—application

Piping and tubing—accessories for
see also
plumbing fittings and trim
fittings—brass
Absolute by American
Standard, Inc. C565
Gerber Plumbing Fixtures
Corp. C580; C563; C578; C579
Interbath C572A
Jason International, Inc. C573A
Kohler Co., Plumbing Div. C581
traps
see
plumbing fittings and trim: —drainage, drains

Piping and tubing—application
gas, water, electrical or sewer system
Zoeller Co. .C576

Pit covers and frames
see
covers and frames: —catchbasin, manhole, pit,
sump, trench, trough

Planning services—manufacturers
see
kitchen planning

Planning services—professional consultants
see
consultants and services

Plaques, insignia and tablets
ceramic
  Summittville Tiles, Inc. C190

Plastic
see
  plastic—form
  plastic laminate sheets
  plastic materials—custom-molded
  plastic—properties

Plastic—form
colored
  Aristech Chemical Corp. A026
  DuPont Co. C474
  Formica Corp. C379
  Formica Corp., Nuvel C476
  Formica Corp., Surell C477
  Nevamar Corp. C467
  Wilsonart International, Inc. C478

corrugated or flat sheet
  Aristech Chemical Corp. A026
  DuPont Co. C474
  Formica Corp. C379
  Formica Corp., Nuvel C476
  Formica Corp., Surell C477
  Nevamar Corp. C467
  Wilsonart International, Inc. C478

corrugated or flat sheet—filler strips for
  Wilsonart International, Inc. C478

engraved, etched
  Aristech Chemical Corp. A026
  Formica Corp. C379
  Nevamar Corp. C467

patterned or textured
  Aristech Chemical Corp. A026
  DuPont Co. C474
  Formica Corp. C379
  Nevamar Corp. C467

sheet, coil
  Aristech Chemical Corp. A026
  DuPont Co. C474
  Formica Corp. C379
  Formica Corp., Nuvel C476
  Formica Corp., Surell C477
  Nevamar Corp. C467

Plastic laminate products
see
  partitions—materials: —plastic laminate-faced
  partitions—shower, toilet, urinal —toilet, urinal—
    plastic laminate-faced
  plastic laminate sheets
  surfacing and paneling—interior—materials:
    —plastic laminate-faced

Plastic laminate sheets
  Aristech Chemical Corp. A026
  Formica Corp. C379
  Formica Corp., Nuvel C476
  Formica Corp., Surell C477
  Nevamar Corp. C467

Plastic materials—custom-molded
  DuPont Co. C474

Plastic products
see
  bathroom accessories: —plastic—specific type
  elevators—passenger: —cars—interior—plastic
    or vinyl
  fascias: —plastic—specific type
  flooring—wood: —plastic-impregnated
  moldings and cornices—plastic, composite
  partitions—shower, toilet, urinal: —shower—
    plastic: —toilet, urinal—plastic
  plastic materials—custom-molded

Plastic products *cont.*
see cont.
  showers: —stalls and receptors—fiberglass,
    plastic
  surfacing and paneling—interior—materials:
    —moldings and trim for—plastic, composite:
    —plastic—specific type
  wall coverings—flexible
  washroom accessories: —holders—toothbrush
    and/or tumbler—plastic

Plastic—properties
abrasion-resistant
see
  plastic—properties: —shock-resistant

anti-glare
  Nevamar Corp. C467

chemical-resistant
  DuPont Co. C474
  Formica Corp. C379
  Formica Corp., Nuvel C476
  Formica Corp., Surell C477
  Nevamar Corp. C467

fire-resistant
  Formica Corp. C379
  Formica Corp., Surell C477
  Nevamar Corp. C467
  Wilsonart International, Inc. C478

moldable
  Nevamar Corp. C467

safety
  Formica Corp., Nuvel C476
  Formica Corp., Surell C477
  Nevamar Corp. C467
  Wilsonart International, Inc. C478

shock-resistant
  Formica Corp. C379
  Formica Corp., Surell C477
  Nevamar Corp. C467

Plates
floor
see
  gratings

wall
see
  wiring devices—electrical: —wall plates

Plumbing fittings and trim
see also
  piping and tubing—accessories for

carrier fittings—lavatory or sink
  Absolute by American
    Standard, Inc. C565

carrier fittings—water closet
  Absolute by American
    Standard, Inc. C565

drainage, drains
  Elkay Mfg. Co. C550

faucets/fixture trim
see
  faucets

shower or spray
  Absolute by American
    Standard, Inc. C565
  Grohe C564
  Hastings Pavement Co., Inc. C572
  Interbath C572A
  JADO C588
  Jason International, Inc. C573A
  Kohler Co., Plumbing Div. C581
  Opella, Inc. C561; C575
  Strom Plumbing, Sign of the
    Crab C584

shower or spray—group—column, wall-mounted
  Grohe C564
  Hastings Pavement Co., Inc. C572
  Interbath C572A

Plumbing fittings and trim *cont.*
shower or spray—group—column, wall-mounted *cont.*
  Jason International, Inc. C573A

shower or spray—hoses for
  Hastings Pavement Co., Inc. C572
  JADO C588
  Opella, Inc. C561; C575

shower or spray—water-saving
  Interbath C572A
  JADO C588
  Kohler Co., Plumbing Div. C581

thermostatic
see
  plumbing fittings and trim: —valves—mixing—
    pressure-balancing, thermostatic

toilet seats
  American Standard, Inc. C566

valves—diverter
  JADO C588

valves—flush—manually-operated—toilet, urinal, sink
  Opella, Inc. C561; C575

valves—mixing—pressure-balancing, thermostatic
  Grohe C564
  Interbath C572A
  JADO C588
  Jason International, Inc. C573A

Plumbing fixtures
see
  bar furniture and equipment: —sinks
  bathtubs
  bidets
  faucets
  laboratory equipment: —sinks, drainboards,
    troughs
  lavatories and accessories
  plumbing fittings and trim
  showers
  sinks—commercial or institutional
  sinks—residential
  toilets

Plywood products
see
  doors—facings for: —plywood, wood
  doors—frames for: —wood or plywood
  shelving: —wood, wood fiber, plywood

Pollution control equipment and systems
see
  air conditioners
  fans
  liquid waste disposal or treatment equipment
  pumps: —grinder—sewage
  vacuum cleaning systems
  ventilators
  waste handling equipment and systems
  water conditioning equipment

Porcelain or baked enamel products
see
  bathtubs: —porcelain enamel, vitreous china

Power supplies, protection/conditioning equipment
see
  transformers
  wiring devices—electrical

Prefinished paneling
see
  surfacing and paneling—interior

Refacings or facings
see
> fascias
> panels—building
> surfacing and paneling—interior
> veneers
> wall coverings—flexible

Reflectors—electrical
see
> luminaires—components for: —housings—
> reflector—specific type

Refrigerator-freezer combination
residential
> Frigidaire Co. .C493
> Jenn-Air Corp. C502
> KitchenAid, Whirlpool Corp. C503
> Maytag Co. .C507
> Sub-Zero Freezer Co., Inc. C514; C515; C515A

residential—built-in
> Jenn-Air Corp. C502
> KitchenAid, Whirlpool Corp. C503
> Maytag Co. .C507
> Sub-Zero Freezer Co., Inc. C514; C515; C515A

residential—energy-saving
> Jenn-Air Corp. C502
> KitchenAid, Whirlpool Corp. C503
> Sub-Zero Freezer Co., Inc. C514; C515; C515A

Refrigerators
see also
> refrigerator-freezer combination

commercial or institutional
see
> kitchen or kitchenette units

residential
> Frigidaire Co. .C493
> Jenn-Air Corp. C502
> KitchenAid, Whirlpool Corp. C503
> Maytag Co. .C507
> Sub-Zero Freezer Co., Inc. C514; C515; C515A

residential—built-in
> Jenn-Air Corp. C502
> KitchenAid, Whirlpool Corp. C503
> Maytag Co. .C507
> Sub-Zero Freezer Co., Inc. C514; C515; C515A

residential—energy-saving
> Jenn-Air Corp. C502
> KitchenAid, Whirlpool Corp. C503
> Sub-Zero Freezer Co., Inc. C514; C515; C515A

residential—ice, chilled water dispensers
> Frigidaire Co. .C493
> Jenn-Air Corp. C502
> KitchenAid, Whirlpool Corp. C503
> Sub-Zero Freezer Co., Inc. C514; C515

residential—kitchenette combination
see also
> kitchen or kitchenette units
> Maytag Co. .C507

residential—undercounter
> Sub-Zero Freezer Co., Inc. C514; C515; C515A

water cooler combination
see
> refrigerators: —residential—ice, chilled water
> dispensers

Registers and grilles
see
> ventilators

Rehabilitation equipment
see
> bathtubs: —hydro-massage combination

Renovation—building
see
> consultants and services

56

Restaurant equipment and furniture
see
> dispensers
> refrigerator-freezer combination

Risers
see
> stair treads, risers

Roadway construction
see
> paving

Rods and bars
see
> bathroom accessories: —grab bars—specific
> material
> showers: —rods, hardware and tracks
> washroom accessories: —grab bars

Roof assemblies
see
> skylights

Roofing specialties and construction products
see
> waterproofing membranes

coatings
see
> dampproofing
> sealants
> sealers
> waterproofing membranes

fascias
see
> fascias

ventilators
see
> ventilators: —roof—specific type

windows
see
> windows—roof

Roof windows
see
> windows—roof

Room assemblies
dressing
see
> showers: —dressing rooms, compartments

partitions for
see
> partitions

saunas
see
> saunas and equipment

showers
see
> showers: —dressing rooms, compartments

steam
see
> steam bath rooms and equipment

Room dividers
see
> partitions

Rotisseries
see
> ranges and ovens—residential: —ranges—
> rotisserie combination

S

Saddles
see
> sills and stools
> thresholds

Safety equipment
plastic
see
> plastic—properties: —safety

Sandwich panels or walls
see
> panels—building

Saunas and equipment
see also
> doors—application: —sauna
> Helo Saunas, Saunatec, Inc. C647

Scale control—water treatment
see
> water conditioning equipment

School equipment
intercommunicators
see
> intercommunicating systems—specific type

laboratories
see
> laboratory equipment

partitions
see
> partitions

storage
see
> storage equipment

Screens
fireplace
see
> fireplaces: —accessories for

partitions
see
> partitions

space dividers
see
> partitions

Sealants
see also
> adhesives for

caulking compounds for concrete or masonry
> Summitville Tiles, Inc. C190

Sealers
masonry—liquid
> Summitville Tiles, Inc. C190

Seals
sill, door, window
see
> sealants

Seats—shower, toilet
see
> bathroom accessories: —grab bars—specific
> material
> plumbing fittings and trim: —toilet seats
> showers: —seats—specific type

Security and bullet-resistant equipment
see
> consultants and services
> glass—properties: —bullet, blast-resistant:
> —burglar-resistant
> guards: —doorway
> hardware—door
> luminaires—types: —motion detector—specific
> type
> panels—building—properties: —bullet or
> burglar-resistant
> partitions—properties: —bullet or burglar-
> resistant

Sensors—light
see
> controls—lighting: —sensors—occupancy—
> infrared, ultrasonic
> luminaires—types: —motion detector
> combination

Septic tanks and accessories
see
> liquid waste disposal or treatment equipment
> waste handling equipment and systems

Service basins
see
> sinks—commercial or institutional

Sewage treatment equipment and systems
see
> liquid waste disposal or treatment equipment
> piping and tubing—application: —gas, water,
> electrical or sewer system
> pumps: —grinder—sewage
> waste handling equipment and systems
> water conditioning equipment

Sheet metal for fabrications
see
> metal laminate sheets

Sheets, strips, plates, coils
glass
see
> glass—form

metal laminate
see
> metal laminate sheets

plastic
see
> plastic—form

Shelving
see also
> storage equipment

bathroom or washroom—glass
Baldwin Hardware Corp. C584B
Hastings Pavement Co., Inc. C572
JADO C588
NuTone C590
Opella, Inc. C561; C575

bathroom or washroom—metal
AQUASTYL, M-K-F, S.a.r.l.,
Menager International
Corp. C584A
Baldwin Hardware Corp. C584B
Hastings Pavement Co., Inc. C572
Opella, Inc. C561; C575

bathroom or washroom—wood
Hastings Pavement Co., Inc. C572

filing and storage—high density
see
> specific equipment: —filing and storage—high
> density

Shelving *cont.*
wood, wood fiber, plywood
Wellborn Cabinet, Inc. C536

Shower heads
see
> plumbing fittings and trim: —shower or spray

Showers
see also
> bathtub/shower—prefabricated unit

cabinets and enclosures
Aristech Chemical Corp. A026
Clarion Bathware C566B
DuPont Co. C474
Formica Corp. C379
Formica Corp., Nuvel C476
Formica Corp., Surell C477
Jason International, Inc. C573A
Nevamar Corp. C467
Strom Plumbing, Sign of the
Crab C584

disabled persons' use
American Shower Door C591

doors
see
> doors—application: —shower, tub

dressing rooms, compartments
Wilsonart International, Inc. C478

enclosures—folding
American Shower Door C591

fittings, levers, valves for
see
> plumbing fittings and trim

group
see
> plumbing fittings and trim: —shower or spray—
> group—column, wall-mounted

hydro-massage combination
Clarion Bathware C566B
Crane Plumbing/Fiat
Products, Fiat Products C567
Jason International, Inc. C573A
TradeWind Industries, Inc. C665

pans
American Olean Tile Co.
Sub., Armstrong World
Industries, Inc., Dal-Tile
International Corp. C171

partitions for
see
> partitions—shower, toilet, urinal

rods, hardware and tracks
Hiawatha, Inc., Activar
Companies, Inc. B420
Strom Plumbing, Sign of the
Crab C584

seats—wall-mounted
Crane Plumbing/Fiat
Products, Fiat Products C567

stalls and receptors—fiberglass, plastic
Aristech Chemical Corp. A026
Formica Corp. C379
Formica Corp., Nuvel C476
Formica Corp., Surell C477
Jason International, Inc. C573A

systems
Crane Plumbing/Fiat
Products, Fiat Products C567
Jason International, Inc. C573A
TradeWind Industries, Inc. C665

Shutters and louvers—ventilating
see
> ventilators

Siding—materials
stone
see
> specific type

Signage
see
> directories/message boards
> nameplates or number plates
> plaques, insignia and tablets
> signs

Signaling systems
see
> bells, buzzers, chimes (entrance and alarm)

Signs
see also
> directories/message boards
> nameplates or number plates
> plaques, insignia and tablets

exterior—non-illuminated
Summitville Tiles, Inc. C190

extrusions for
Nevamar Corp. C467

interior—non-illuminated
Summitville Tiles, Inc. C190

Sills and stools
see also
> thresholds

slate
American Olean Tile Co.
Sub., Armstrong World
Industries, Inc., Dal-Tile
International Corp. C171

stone—simulated/manufactured
American Olean Tile Co.
Sub., Armstrong World
Industries, Inc., Dal-Tile
International Corp. C171
Wilsonart International, Inc. C478

Sinks—commercial or institutional
fittings and trim for
see
> plumbing fittings and trim

laboratory
see
> laboratory equipment: —sinks, drainboards,
> troughs

tops for
Swan Corp. (The) C562

Sinks—residential
bar
see
> bar furniture and equipment: —sinks

ceramic, composite
Hastings Pavement Co., Inc. C572
Nevamar Corp. C467

faucets
see
> faucets—application: —sink—specific type

fittings for
see
> plumbing fittings and trim

food waste disposers for
see
> food waste disposers

stainless steel
Elkay Mfg. Co. C550; C551
Franke, Inc., Kitchen
Systems Div. C555
Kohler Co., Plumbing Div. C574

Sinks—residential *cont.*

tops for
DuPont Co. C474
Elkay Mfg. Co. C550; C551; C552
Formica Corp., Nuvel C476
Formica Corp., Surell C477
Franke, Inc., Kitchen
  Systems Div. C555
Hastings Pavement Co., Inc. C572
Kohler Co., Plumbing Div. C574
Nevamar Corp. C467
Swan Corp. (The) C562

Skirting
see
  fascias

Skylights
see
  skylights—form
  skylights—framing
  skylights—general
  skylights—materials
  skylights—operation
  skylights—properties

Skylights—form
cone or polygon
Sunglo Skylight Products,
  Plastic Sales & Mfg. Co.,
  Inc. B367

dome
Sunglo Skylight Products,
  Plastic Sales & Mfg. Co.,
  Inc. B367
Tubular Skylight, Inc. B368A

flat panel
Andersen Corp. B357
Sunglo Skylight Products,
  Plastic Sales & Mfg. Co.,
  Inc. B367

pyramid
Sunglo Skylight Products,
  Plastic Sales & Mfg. Co.,
  Inc. B367

tubular
Tubular Skylight, Inc. B368A

Skylights—framing
aluminum or aluminum alloy
Sunglo Skylight Products,
  Plastic Sales & Mfg. Co.,
  Inc. B367
Tubular Skylight, Inc. B368A

steel or stainless steel
Sunglo Skylight Products,
  Plastic Sales & Mfg. Co.,
  Inc. B367

wood
Andersen Corp. B357

Skylights—general
curb combination
Sunglo Skylight Products,
  Plastic Sales & Mfg. Co.,
  Inc. B367

custom-designed
Andersen Corp. B357
Tubular Skylight, Inc. B368A

double-glazed
Sunglo Skylight Products,
  Plastic Sales & Mfg. Co.,
  Inc. B367

Skylights—materials
acrylic
Sunglo Skylight Products,
  Plastic Sales & Mfg. Co.,
  Inc. B367
Tubular Skylight, Inc. B368A

glass—corrugated, plain, wired or block
Sunglo Skylight Products,
  Plastic Sales & Mfg. Co.,
  Inc. B367

Skylights—operation
ventilating
Sunglo Skylight Products,
  Plastic Sales & Mfg. Co.,
  Inc. B367

ventilators—power-driven
see
  ventilators: —adjustable—manual or power-
  operated

Skylights—properties
heat and glare-retarding
Sunglo Skylight Products,
  Plastic Sales & Mfg. Co.,
  Inc. B367
Tubular Skylight, Inc. B368A

insulating
Tubular Skylight, Inc. B368A

Slate products
see
  flooring—slate
  panels—building—materials: —slate
  paving: —slate
  sills and stools: —slate
  surfacing and paneling—interior—materials:
  —slate

Slides
cabinet
see
  hardware—cabinet: —knobs, pulls and slides
drawer
see
  hardware—drawer: —knobs, pulls and slides

Smokers—cooking
see
  ranges and ovens—residential: —cooktops/
  smoker/broiler combination

Soap, soap dispensers and holders
see
  bathroom accessories: —toilet paper holders,
  soap dishes—specific materials
  washroom accessories: —dispensers—soap:
  —soap—cake, lather, leaf, liquid, powder

Solar energy conversion— components for—passive
glazing—insulating
see
  glass—properties: —insulating—specific type
  windows—properties: —insulating—thermal—
  specific type

panels—building
see
  panels—building—properties: —insulating

Sound control products
see
  partitions—properties: —sound-insulating or
  retarding—specific type
  windows—properties: —insulating—sound—
  specific type

Space dividers—interior
see
  partitions

Spandrel panels
see
  panels—building—materials

Speak holes
see
  hardware—window

Sports training equipment
see
  bathtubs: —hydro-massage combination
  health club equipment
  steam bath rooms and equipment

Stained or faceted glass
see
  windows—specific material/operation

Stainless steel products
see
  sinks—residential: —stainless steel
  skylights—framing: —steel or stainless steel

Stain removers
see
  masonry cleaners

Stairs—metal
treads and risers
see
  stair treads, risers

Stair treads, risers
clay or ceramic tile
American Olean Tile Co.
  Sub., Armstrong World
  Industries, Inc., Dal-Tile
  International Corp. C171
Summitville Tiles, Inc. C190

grating
see
  gratings

lighting for
see
  lighting—application: —stair, path, aisle

stone—simulated/manufactured
American Olean Tile Co.
  Sub., Armstrong World
  Industries, Inc., Dal-Tile
  International Corp. C171

Stalls—shower
see
  showers

Steam bath rooms and equipment
see also
  generators: —steam
  health club equipment
American Shower Door C591
Helo Saunas, Saunatec, Inc. C647

Steam products
see
  generators: —steam

Steel products
see
  skylights—framing: —steel or stainless steel

Surveillance equipment and systems
see
> luminaires—types: —motion detector combination

Swimming pool equipment
chlorination
see
> water conditioning equipment

filters
see
> water conditioning equipment: —filters, aerators, deodorizers, hydrators, strainers

lighting
see
> lighting—application: —underwater

pumps
see
> pumps

underwater lighting
see
> lighting—application: —underwater

waterproofing and coatings
see
> waterproofing membranes

water treatment apparatus
see
> water conditioning equipment

Switches
dimmer
see
> controls—lighting

t

Tables
tops for
Formica Corp. C379
Formica Corp., Nuvel C476
Formica Corp., Surell C477
Nevamar Corp. C467
Wilsonart International, Inc. C478

Tablets
see
> plaques, insignia and tablets

Telephone equipment
see
> intercommunicating systems

Testing equipment
water
see
> water conditioning equipment

Theatrical equipment
see
> directories/message boards

Theft detection/protection equipment and systems
see
> consultants and services
> glass—properties: —bullet, blast-resistant: —burglar-resistant
> guards: —doorway
> hardware—door
> luminaires—types: —motion detector combination
> panels—building—properties: —bullet or burglar-resistant

Theft detection/protection equipment and systems *cont.*
see cont.
> partitions—properties: —bullet or burglar-resistant

Therapeutic equipment
see
> bathtubs: —hydro-massage combination
> showers: —hydro-massage combination

Thresholds
see also
> sills and stools

stone—simulated/manufactured
American Olean Tile Co.
Sub., Armstrong World
Industries, Inc., Dal-Tile
International Corp. C171

Toilets
compartments
see
> partitions—shower, toilet, urinal

paper, dispensers
see
> washroom accessories —holders—toilet paper

partitions
see
> partitions—shower, toilet, urinal

plumbing for
see
> plumbing fittings and trim

seats
see
> plumbing fittings and trim: —toilet seats

sewage removal pump compartments
Zoeller Co. C576

units
Absolute by American
Standard, Inc. C565
American Standard, Inc. C566
Dornbracht, Santile
International Corp. C568
Gerber Plumbing Fixtures
Corp. C571
Kohler Co., Plumbing Div. C574

units—disabled persons' use
American Standard, Inc. C566

Toilet seats
see
> plumbing fittings and trim: —toilet seats

Tops
see
> cabinets: —tops for
> counters: —tops for
> desks: —tops, pads for
> laboratory equipment: —work surfaces for
> lavatories and accessories: —tops for
> sinks—commercial or institutional: —tops for
> sinks—residential: —tops for
> tables: —tops for

Towel bars—safety
see
> bathroom accessories: —grab bars—specific material
> washroom accessories: —grab bars

Towels
see
> bathroom accessories: —towel holders

Tracks
shower cubicles
see
> showers: —rods, hardware and tracks

Transformers
power and distribution
Task Lighting Corp. C950

Traps
see
> plumbing fittings and trim: —drainage, drains

Trash cans
see
> bathroom accessories: —waste receptacles

Treads—stair
see
> stair treads, risers

Treatments
see
> primers

Trenches
see
> covers and frames: —catchbasin, manhole, pit, sump, trench, trough

Trim
see
> hardware—door: —lock trim
> moldings and cornices

Troughs
see
> covers and frames: —catchbasin, manhole, pit, sump, trench, trough
> laboratory equipment: —sinks, drainboards, troughs

Tubing
see
> piping and tubing

Tubs
see
> bathtubs
> bathtub/shower—prefabricated unit
> doors—application: —shower, tub

u

Underlayments
see
> flooring—underlayments for

Universal design products
see
> bathroom accessories: —grab bars—specific material
> elevators—passenger
> faucets—application: —disabled persons' use
> faucets—types: —sensor-actuated
> flooring—clay or ceramic tile: —detectable, tactile warning strips
> hardware—window
> lavatories and accessories: —disabled persons' use
> mirrors: —tilting
> plumbing fittings and trim
> railings—types: —handrail—safety: —handrail—wall-mounted
> showers: —disabled persons' use: —seats— wall-mounted

Wood products *cont.*
see cont.
  windows—roof: —wood—specific type
  windows—wood-aluminum/operation
  windows—wood/operation
  windows—wood-vinyl/operation

Wood—simulated/
manufactured—products
see
  surfacing and paneling—interior—materials:
    —wood—simulated/manufactured—specific
    type
  veneers: —wood or simulated/manufactured
    wood

Woodwork
custom-built
  Eurodesign Cabinets, Inc. C524
  KraftMaid Cabinetry, Inc. A017
  Wellborn Cabinet, Inc. C536

Woodwork—simulated/
manufactured
moldings, cornices, door and window
trim
see
  moldings and cornices: —plastic, composite

Woven wire mesh products
see
  specific products

Trade Names

Catalogs are coded by positions within the volume in numerical sequence, e.g., C345

Sweet's has been requested by manufacturers to include the following trade names and trademarks in this index. Sweet's makes no representations or warranties as to the rights of any manufacturer to any trade name or trademark listed in this index.

---

a

ABSOLUTE (plumbing fixtures) C565
ACTIVAR (architectural hardware) B420
AKTIS (glass blocks) B687
ALLBEND (glass blocks) B687
AMERICAN (shower doors & tub enclosures) C591
AMERICAN OLEAN (ceramic floor & wall tile) C171
AMERICAN STANDARD (plumbing fixtures) C566
ANTELL PLANK (oak planks) C246
ANTIQUITY (glazed floor tile—matte stone look with cut accents & borders) C171
AQUASTYL (bath accessories) C584A
ARDEN (floor access panels) C357
ARDEN (handrail & corner guards) B479
ARISTECH (acrylic sheet) A026
ARTURA (ceramic wall tile) C176
ATRIUM (wood windows) B269

b

BALDWIN (bath & cabinet hardware) C584B
BAY (3-sided fireplace) C824
BAY GDV (3-sided AFUE-rated direct vent fireplace) C824
BAY INSERT (3-sided masonry or prefab insert) C824
BAY SUPREME (3-sided heat circulating fireplace) C824
BAY 30 (3-sided direct vent fireplace w/h/v technology) C824
BLOKUP (mortarless glass block installations) B687
BLUE CREEK (cooking system) C502
BORGO ANTICO (natural stone look tex. porcelain paver w/color variation) C171
BRANDON (oak flooring) C246
BRIGHT (high gloss glazed wall tile in basic & contemporary colors) C171
BRIGHT GLAZE (ceramic tile) C176
BROAN (residential appliances) .... ii; C484
BROAN (toilet & bath accessories) C587
BROAN (ventilating fans) C486
BROOKHOLLOW (oak flooring) C246
BROOKSIDE (oak flooring) C246
BRUCE (hardwood flooring products) C246
BUILDER SELECTION CENTER (ceramic tile display) C171

c

CAMBRIDGE (oak planks) C246
CAROUSEL (convection/microwave ovens) C512
CARUTH PLANK (oak planks) C246
CATHEDRAL (oak planks) C246
CERAMIC MOSAICS (unglazed floor tile for slip-resistence/shower floors) C171
CERAMIC TILE DESIGN PACKAGES (coordinate floors walls; w/accents/strips) C171
CH (nylon architectural door pulls) B420
CHARLEMONT PLANK (oak planks) C246
CHRYSTAL GLAZE (ceramic tile) C176
CLAIRMONT ELEGANCE (custom-crafted wood tile) C246

CLARION (whirlpools) C566B
CLARITY (glass blocks) B687
CLASSIC (oak planks) C246
CLASSIC (two-handle faucets, valves-tub/ shower/diverters) C564
CLEAN BURN SYSTEM 41-CB41 (clean burning wood fireplace) C824
CLEAN 'N' STRIP (cleaner for wood flooring) ... C246
COFFEE TABLE (power vent fireplace w/ceramic fiber logs) C824
COLD-STIK MASTIC (adhesive) C246
COLORADO (glazed floor tile—stone look with wall tile & accent strip) C171
COLORADO PEAKS (glazed wall tile in stone look w/floor tile & accents) C171
COLORCORE (surfacing material) C379
COLORJET INFUSION (color process) C246
COMPRI (glazed marble look wall tile w/accent strips & accent tiles) C171
COMPUCOOK (convection/microwave ovens) C512
CORIAN (plastic material) C474
CORNER-DV (2-sided gas fireplace) C824
CORNER TV (2-sided top vent fireplace) C824
COUNTRY CLASSICS (decorative glazed quarry tile) C190
COUNTRY OAK (oak planks) C246
CRANE (showerbathing) C567
CREEKSTONES (glazed floor tile fume glaze with pillowed edges) C171
CREEKSTONES (glazed wall tile has texture, fume & matching floor tile) C171
CROSSFYRE GAS STOVE (dvt-stove) C824
CRYSTALLINE (glazed textured wall & floor tile) C171

d

DACOR (cook tops & oven) C489
DAL-TILE (ceramic tile) C173
DALTILE (ceramic tile) C173
DAMASK (has look of satin stripe in glazed wall tile with accent strip) C171
DAPPLE GLAZE (ceramic tile) C176
DARK 'N' RICH (wax for wood flooring) C246
DEBUT (custom-crafted wood tile) C246
DECORATIVE INSERTS (decorative glazed tile) C190
DELANCY (gloss glaze wall tile with floral accent strip; marble look) C171
DESIGNER ACCENTS (high gloss glazed wall tile for accent w/sizzle strips) C171
DESIGNER LINE (cooking system) C502
DESIGNER STEPS (glazed floor tile fume & solid smooth glaze) C171
DEVON PLANK (oak planks) C246
DIAMOND ACCENTS (maple flooring) C246
DORNBRACHT (plumbing fixtures) C568
DOUBLEND (glass blocks) B687
DURA-LUSTER (cleaner, fresh finish) C246
DURA-SATIN (wax finish for wood flooring) C246
DYNASTY (range tops) C491

e

EARTHSTONE (ceramic tile) C176

8000 DVT FL (42"(1.067m) direct vent top vent fireplace w/fiber logs) C824
8000 GDV (42"(1.067m) direct vent fireplace) C824
8000 GDVFL (42"(1.067m) direct vent fireplace w/ceramic fiber logs) C824
8000 TV (42"(1.067m) top vent fireplace) C824
ELEGRIL (stainless steel grates) C357
ELKAY (sinks) C550; C551; C552
EMERSON (food waste disposer) C501
ENERGY MASTER 41 (1-sided high-efficiency fireplace) C824
ENERGY MASTER 42 (1-sided high-efficiency fireplace) C824
ENERGY MASTER 48 (1-sided high-efficiency fireplace) C824
EURODESIGN (kitchen cabinets) C524
EUROPA (Hiawatha shower door hinge) B420
EUROPLUS (single-handle kitchen faucets, ceramic disc) C564
EVERBOND LP ADHESIVE (adhesive) C246
EXPRESSIONS COLLECTION (cooking system) C502
EXQUISIT (two-handle faucets, valves-tub/ shower, ceramic disc) C564
EXTERIOR CLADDING (glazed porcelain paver) C190

f

FIRESIDE (oak planks) C246
FITZ & FLOYD (sculptured decorative tiles) C190
5000 GDV (32"(81.3cm) direct vent fireplace) C824
5000 TV (32"(81.3cm) top vent fireplace) C824
FLOOR BRICK (extruded/indust./plain or abrasive chem.-resist. floor brick) C190
FLORIDA (ceramic tile) C176
FLS24 (ceramic fiber logs) C824
FLS24LO (ceramic fiber logs) C824
FORMICA (plastic laminates) C379
FORTRESS (glass blocks) B687
4000 INS (masonry insert-supreme) C824
FRANKE (plumbing fixtures) C555
FRESCO (glazed floor tile—semigloss marble look) C171
FRESH FINISH (urethane finish for wood flooring) C246
FRIGIDAIRE (appliances) C493

g

GAS STOVE - GS 4000 (freestanding gas stove) C824
GERBER (fittings, trim & accessories) C563; C578; C579; C580
GERBER (plumbing fixtures) C571
GLEN COVE (wood flooring) C246
GLS18 (gas log sets) C824
GLS24 (gas log sets) C824
GLS30 (gas log sets) C824
GOLDEN FLAME GAS SERIES (direct vent & top vent gas fireplaces) C824
GRATEDESIGN (entrance grates) C357
GREEN TREE (financial services) .... inside front cover
GROHMIX (thermostat & thermostat pressure balance valves) C564

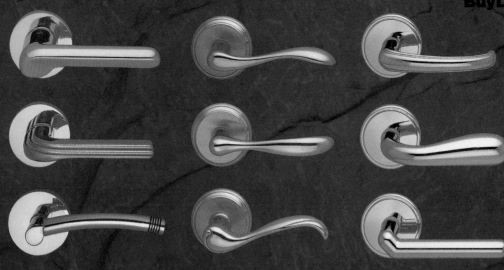

A T R I U M

Aluminum Clad & Wood
Windows & Doors

THE ATRIUM
DOOR® & WINDOW
COMPANY

TABLE OF CONTENTS

WINDOWS AND DOORS BY ATRIUM.

SINCE 1976, THE ATRIUM DOOR® & WINDOW COMPANY HAS BUILT A REPUTATION FOR OFFERING THE FINEST, MOST BEAUTIFULLY BUILT PRODUCTS ON THE MARKET TODAY. OUR ATTENTION TO QUALITY AND DETAIL IS SECOND TO NONE. AND OUR SELECTION AND DESIGN OPTIONS ARE SO EXTENSIVE, WE HAVE WINDOWS AND DOORS TO FIT VIRTUALLY ANY OPENING OR BUDGET THAT EXISTS. BUT WE DON'T STOP THERE.

WE ALSO PROVIDE THE MOST COMPREHENSIVE, ONE-SOURCE SERVICE AVAILABLE. EVERYTHING FROM PRODUCTION AND SHIPPING TO WARRANTIES AND CUSTOMER SERVICE IS COORDINATED ALL UNDER ONE ROOF. AND WE'RE ALWAYS THERE TO HELP, THROUGH OUR CONVENIENT TOLL-FREE NUMBER, FOR CUSTOMER QUESTIONS AND TECHNICAL SUPPORT.

SO WHEN YOU CHOOSE THE ATRIUM DOOR® AND WINDOW COMPANY, YOU'LL NOT ONLY GET THE HIGHEST QUALITY WINDOWS AND DOORS, YOU'LL GET A COMPANY THAT STANDS BEHIND ITS PRODUCTS.

1

Construction

- Kiln-dried Ponderosa Pine
- Optional low maintenance aluminum clad exterior in WHITE (WH), EARTHTONE (ET) or SANDSTONE (ST)

Swing Door Sill

- Multi-chambered weep system extruded in aluminum
- Celluka® PVC inside threshold
- Bronze aluminum extrusion

Glazing Options

- Atrium Door, Atrium French Classic and Atrium Glider units feature 3/4" High Performance insulated glass, double sealed and bedded; Professional series doors and casements utilize 3/4" clear insulated glass, double hungs and horizontal sliders utilize 5/8"
- Single glazed or insulated clear
- Gray, bronze or obscure
- All door glazings use safety tempered glass

Grilles

- Doors supplied with full wood surround frame. Clear wood interior grilles 7/8" muntins. Atrium Door series doors also available with 1 3/16" muntins
- Windows offer KD wood grilles with 7/8" muntins or 5/8" internal muntins bars

Weatherstrip

- Wood units feature engineered extruded dual durometer thermoplastic weatherstripping system
- Clad units feature high efficiency foam filled weatherstripping

Hardware

- Windows feature white hardware standard, brown and polished brass optional
- Atrium Series doors feature polished brass hardware
- Multipoint and singlepoint hardware available on Atrium Series
- Professional Series doors are pre-bored for hardware, allowing personal choice of handle and lock

Atrium Classic Lites

- 1 1/8" or 7/8" bars simulate a true divided lite unit with interior and exterior bars

Insect Screen

- Windows offer aluminum frame, fiberglass screen cloth, vinyl corners and tension springs and lift tab. Available in WHITE (WH), EARTHTONE (ET), OR SANDSTONE (ST)
- Doors come with heavy duty tubular extruded steel frame in WHITE(WH), EARTHTONE (ET), OR SANDSTONE (ST) and adjustable ball bearing wheels

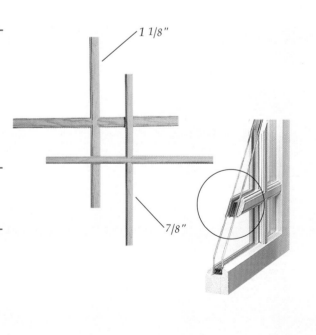

1 1/8"

7/8"

THE ATRIUM DOOR®

*T*he Atrium Door® is one of the most solidly-constructed doors on the market today, and one of the most beautiful. Each door offers 3/4" high performance insulated glass, double sealed and bedded. The Low E glass offers energy efficiency and reduced fading. Our attention to detail is a reflection of the quality in every Atrium Door, from the sills to the grilles.

STANDARD SIZES

Fixed Coordinates

Dimensions shown are for unfinished units only. For CLAD UNITS add 3/16" to all RO and UD dimensions. The Atrium Door is also available in 8-0' heights. The RO height per 8-0' is 96".

○ NARROW STILE   ● WIDE STILE

6-8' UNIT HEIGHT RO 80" UD 79 1/2"							
RO 24 13/16" UD 24 5/16" AU2168UN	RO 47 9/16" UD 47 1/16" AU4068UN	RO 70 5/16" UD 69 13/16" AU6068/3UN	RO 141 1/16" UD 140 9/16" AU12068UN	RO 14 11/16" UD 14 3/16" AU1268UN ○	RO 16 9/16" UD 16 1/16" AU1468UN ○	RO 28 9/16" UD 28 1/16" AU2468UN ○
RO 30 13/16" UD 30 5/16" AU2768UN *	RO 59 9/16" UD 59 1/16" AU5068UN *	RO 88 5/16" UD 87 13/16" AU7668UN *		RO 16 15/16" UD 16 7/16" AU1568UN ●	RO 18 13/16" UD 18 5/16" AU1768UN ●	RO 30 13/16" UD 30 5/16" AU2768UN ●
RO 33 1/4" UD 32 3/4" AU2968UN *	RO 64 9/16" UD 63 15/16" AU5468UN *	RO 95 5/8" UD 95 1/8" AU8068UN *			RO 22 9/16" UD 22 1/16" AU11068UN ○	
RO 36 13/16" UD 36 5/16" AU3168UN *	RO 71 9/16" UD 71 1/16" AU6068/2UN *	RO 106 5/16" UD 105 13/16" AU9068UN *			RO 24 13/16" UD 24 5/16" AU2168UN ●	

* Lite Pattern is 3 wide and 5 high per panel

Notes:
1. *Muntin bars illustrated represent the patterns of optional grilles or Atrium Classic Lite bars. 8-0 height doors are 6 lites high.*
2. *For ARCHITECTURAL DETAILS & SPECIFICATIONS refer to Atrium Door & Window Company's **SweetSource** program or call: **1-800-935-2000**.*

THE FRENCH CLASSIC® DOOR

A new interpretation of the Traditional French Door, the French Classic® Door features a polished brass multipoint locking system with a dead bolt for added security, stability and weather-tightness. Four heavy-duty hinges made of commercial grade steel, triple plated and hand polished to bright brass, matching the lockset, provide added strength and beauty. These doors are turning a tradition into a classic.

STANDARD SIZES

Fixed Coordinates

Dimensions shown are for unfinished units only. For CLAD UNITS add 3/16" to all RO and UD dimensions. The French Classic Door is also available in 8-0' heights. The RO height per 8-0' is 96".

○ NARROW STILE ● WIDE STILE

6-8' UNIT HEIGHT RO 80" UD 79 1/2"							
RO 35 9/16" UD 35 1/16" FC3068UN	RO 59 9/16" UD 59 1/16" FC5068UN	RO 69 1/8" UD 68 5/8" FC6068/4UN	RO 141 1/16" UD 140 9/16" FC12068UN	RO 14 11/16" UD 14 3/16" FC1268UN ○	RO 16 9/16" UD 16 1/16" FC1468UN ○	RO 28 9/16" UD 28 1/16" FC2468UN ○
RO 47 9/16" UD 47 1/16" FC4068UN	RO 64 7/16" UD 63 15/16" FC5468UN	RO 93 1/16" UD 92 9/16" FC8068UN		RO 16 15/16" UD 16 7/16" FC1568UN ●	RO 18 13/16" UD 18 5/16" FC1768UN ●	RO 30 13/16" UD 30 5/16" FC2768UN ●
	RO 71 9/16" UD 71 1/16" FC6068UN				RO 22 9/16" UD 22 1/16" FC11068UN ○	RO 33 1/4" UD 32 3/4" FC2968UN ●
					RO 24 13/16" UD 24 5/16" FC2168UN ●	RO 36 13/16" UD 36 5/16" FC3168UN ●

Notes:
1. *Muntin bars illustrated represent the patterns of optional grilles or Atrium Classic Lite bars. 8-0 height doors are 6 lites high.*
2. *For ARCHITECTURAL DETAILS & SPECIFICATIONS refer to Atrium Door & Window Company's* **SweetSource** *program or call:* **1-800-935-2000**.

THE ATRIUM ENTRY SYSTEM

*C*lad units from the Professional Series™ Swing Door and French Door can be used in combinations to create unique entry systems, whether it's your front door or back door, patio or backyard entrance. Mix and match standard single or double panels along with *fixed or venting sidelites to fill most openings.*

STANDARD SIZES

Coordinates

Dimensions shown are for Clad Units only.

6-8' UNIT HEIGHT RO 80" UD 79 1/2"	RO 32 3/4" UD 32 1/4" PF2968UN	RO 63 7/8" UD 63 3/8" PF5468UN	RO 15 7/8" UD 15 3/8" PF1368UN
	RO 36 3/4" UD 36 1/4" PF3168UN	RO 71 7/8" UD 71 3/8" PF6068UN	RO 17 3/8" UD 16 7/8" PF1568UN

Other sizes and options available

Entry System Combinations

Notes:
1. *Muntin bars illustrated represent the patterns of optional grilles or Atrium Classic Lite bars.*
2. *For ARCHITECTURAL DETAILS & SPECIFICATIONS refer to Atrium Door & Window Company's* **SweetSource** *program or call:* **1-800-935-2000.**

PROFESSIONAL SERIES™ SWING DOOR

*T*he Atrium Swing Door is available in The Professional Series™ as an affordable swinging unit. Units can be left or right-hand swing, in both clad and unfinished, with 3/4" safety tempered insulated glazing, and optional high performance or tinted glass. Multi-chambered sill with PVC threshold channels water away from the interior of the home. Units are complete with weatherstripping and optional screens.

STANDARD SIZES

Fixed Coordinates

Dimensions shown are for unfinished units only. For CLAD UNITS add 3/16" to all RO and UD dimensions.

6-8' UNIT HEIGHT
RO 80"
UD 79 1/2"

○ NARROW STILE ● WIDE STILE

RO 49 1/8" UD 48 5/8" PD4068UN	RO 86 1/4" UD 85 3/4" PD7668UN	RO 14 3/8" UD 13 7/8" PD1268UN ○	RO 16 1/4" UD 15 3/4" PD1468UN ○	RO 25 3/4" UD 25 1/4" PD2268UN ○
RO 59 7/8" UD 59 3/8" PD5068UN *	RO 92 1/4" UD 91 3/4" PD8068UN	RO 19 3/8" UD 18 7/8" PD1768UN ●	RO 21 1/4" UD 20 3/4" PD1968UN ●	RO 30 3/4" UD 30 1/4" PD2768UN ●
RO 63 7/8" UD 63 3/8" PD5468UN *	RO 104 1/4" UD 103 3/4" PD9068UN		RO 20 3/8" UD 19 7/8" PD1868UN ○	RO 27 3/4" UD 27 1/4" PD2468UN ○
RO 71 7/8" UD 71 3/8" PD6068UN *			RO 25 3/8" UD 24 7/8" PD2168UN ●	RO 32 3/4" UD 32 1/4" PD2968UN ●
				RO 31 3/4" UD 31 1/4" PD2868UN ○
				RO 36 3/4" UD 36 1/4" PD3168UN ●

* Lite Pattern is 3 wide and 5 high per panel

Notes:
1. *Muntin bars illustrated represent the patterns of optional grilles or Atrium Classic Lite bars.*
2. *For ARCHITECTURAL DETAILS & SPECIFICATIONS refer to Atrium Door & Window Company's **SweetSource** program or call: **1-800-935-2000.***

PROFESSIONAL SERIES™ FRENCH DOOR

*O*ur Professional Series™ French Doors recreate traditional elegance at a very affordable price. Standard units utilize 3/4" safety tempered insulated glass, one lite or optional Atrium Classic Lite for that divided lite look. Units are available in clad or unfinished wood and are fully weather-stripped for energy efficiency. Choose from many glazing options.

STANDARD SIZES

Fixed Coordinates

Dimensions shown are for unfinished units only. For CLAD UNITS add 3/16" to all RO and UD dimensions.

6-8' UNIT HEIGHT
RO 80"
UD 79 1/2"

○ NARROW STILE ● WIDE STILE

RO 59 7/8" UD 59 3/8" PF5068UN	RO 14 3/8" UD 13 7/8" PF1268UN ○	RO 16 1/4" UD 15 3/4" PF1468UN ○	RO 25 3/4" UD 25 1/4" PF2268UN ○
RO 63 7/8" UD 63 3/8" PF5468UN	RO 19 3/8" UD 18 7/8" PF1768UN ●	RO 21 1/4" UD 20 3/4" PF1968UN ●	RO 30 3/4" UD 30 1/4" PF2768UN ●
RO 71 7/8" UD 71 3/8" PF6068UN		RO 20 3/8" UD 19 7/8" PF1868UN ○	RO 27 3/4" UD 27 1/4" PF2468UN ○
		RO 25 3/8" UD 24 7/8" PF2168UN ●	RO 32 3/4" UD 32 1/4" PF2968UN ●
			RO 31 3/4" UD 31 1/4" PF2868UN ○
			RO 36 3/4" UD 36 1/4" PF3168UN ●

Notes:
1. Muntin bars illustrated represent the patterns of optional grilles or Atrium Classic Lite bars.
2. For ARCHITECTURAL DETAILS & SPECIFICATIONS refer to Atrium Door & Window Company's *SweetSource* program or call: **1-800-935-2000.**

THE ATRIUM GLIDER ®

The Atrium Glider® is a simple way to upgrade from an old-fashioned aluminum sliding glass door. Available in left or right-hand units in standard 3/4" clear insulated glass with optional high performance or tinted glass. Atrium Classic Lite and snap-in wood grille options are available. Attractive polished brass handleset included, optional white or brown. Units utilize a heavy-duty extruded aluminum sill with intergral screen track.

STANDARD SIZES

The Atrium Glider is also available in 8-0' heights. The RO height per 8-0' is 96".

6-8' UNIT HEIGHT RO 80" UD 79 9/16"	RO 32 1/4" UD 31 3/4" AG2868UN	RO 34 1/4" UD 33 3/4" AG21068UN	RO 50 1/4" UD 49 3/4" AG4268UN	RO 60" UD 59 1/2" AG5068UN	RO 72" UD 71 1/2" AG6068UN	RO 96" UD 95 1/2" AG8068UN	
		RO 38 1/4" UD 37 3/4" AG3268UN					

Notes:
1. *Muntin bars illustrated represent the patterns of optional grilles or Atrium Classic Lite bars. 8-0 height doors are 6 lites high.*
2. *For ARCHITECTURAL DETAILS & SPECIFICATIONS refer to Atrium Door & Window Company's SweetSource program or call: 1-800-935-2000.*

PROFESSIONAL SERIES™ SLIDING DOOR

The Professional Series Sliding™ Door provides years of energy efficiency as its frame is fitted with weatherstripping and panels interlock with heavy duty extruded vinyl. This maximum door to frame seal is extremely effective in keeping out air and water. Choose from white or earthtone clad color. Standard glass is 3/4" clear insulated, safety tempered with high performance and tinted options. Atrium Classic Lite and snap-in full surround wood grilles also available.

STANDARD SIZES

6-8' UNIT HEIGHT RO 80" UD 79 1/2"	RO 32 3/16" UD 31 11/16" PS2868UN	RO 34 3/16" UD 33 11/16" PS21068UN	RO 37 3/16" UD 36 11/16" PS3268UN	RO 50 3/16" UD 49 11/16" PS4268UN	RO 59 13/16" UD 59 5/16" PS5068UN	RO 71 13/16" UD 71 5/16" PS6068UN	RO 95 13/16" UD 95 5/16" PS8068UN

Notes:
1. *Muntin bars illustrated represent the patterns of optional grilles or Atrium Classic Lite bars.*
2. *For ARCHITECTURAL DETAILS & SPECIFICATIONS refer to Atrium Door & Window Company's SweetSource program or call: 1-800-935-2000.*

9

THE ATRIUM DOUBLE HUNG WINDOW

*T*he Atrium Double Hung Windows are crafted with traditional styling and are available in the Atrium Classic Lite, colonial grilles, internal grids or one lite. Units are manufactured in either extruded aluminum clad or exterior primed wood units and are available in white, earthtone or sandstone. High security surface mounted cam locks and aluminum frame screens are supplied. Units are weatherstripped for energy efficiency.

STANDARD SIZES

UNIT WIDTH ▶ / UNIT HEIGHT ▼	RO 21 13/16" UD 21 5/16"	RO 23 13/16" UD 23 5/16"	RO 25 13/16" UD 25 5/16"	RO 29 13/16" UD 29 5/16"	RO 31 13/16" UD 31 5/16"	RO 33 13/16" UD 33 5/16"	RO 35 13/16" UD 35 5/16"	RO 37 13/16" UD 37 5/16"	RO 41 13/16" UD 41 5/16"	RO 45 13/16" UD 45 5/16"	RO 47 13/16" UD 47 5/16"
RO 36" UD 35 5/8"	DH18210	DH110210	DH20210	DH24210	DH26210	DH28210	DH210210	DH30210	DH34210	DH38210	DH310210
RO 40" UD 39 5/8"	DH1832	DH11032	DH2032	DH2432	DH2632	DH2832	DH21032	DH3032	DH3432	DH3832	
RO 48" UD 47 5/8"	DH18310	DH110310	DH20310	DH24310	DH26310	DH28310	DH210310	DH30310	DH34310	DH38310	DH310310
RO 52" UD 51 5/8"	DH1842	DH11042	DH2042	DH2442	DH2642	DH2842	DH21042	DH3042	DH3442	DH3842	
RO 56" UD 55 5/8"	DH1846	DH11046	DH2046	DH2446	DH2646	DH2846	DH21046	DH3046	DH3446	DH3846	

Dimensions shown are for CLAD UNITS only. For PRIMED UNITS add 1/16" to RO width and 2" to RO height.

*Standard unit as Cottage Style, Reverse Cottage or equal lite also available.
** These units single hung, only bottom sash operates, tilts and removes.

Notes:
1. *Muntin bars illustrated represent the patterns of optional grilles or Atrium Classic Lite bars.*
2. *For ARCHITECTURAL DETAILS & SPECIFICATIONS refer to Atrium Door & Window Company's **SweetSource** program or call: **1-800-935-2000**.*

STANDARD SIZES

UNIT WIDTH ▶ / UNIT HEIGHT ▼	RO 21 13/16" UD 21 5/16"	RO 23 13/16" UD 23 5/16"	RO 25 13/16" UD 25 5/16"	RO 29 13/16" UD 29 5/16"	RO 31 13/16" UD 31 5/16"	RO 33 13/16" UD 33 5/16"	RO 35 13/16" UD 35 5/16"	RO 37 13/16" UD 37 5/16"	RO 41 13/16" UD 41 5/16"	RO 45 13/16" UD 45 5/16"	RO 47 13/16" UD 47 5/16"
RO 60" UD 59 5/8"	DH18410	DH110410	DH20410	DH24410	DH26410	DH28410	DH210410	DH30410	DH34410	DH38410	DH310410
RO 64" UD 63 5/8"	DH1852	DH11052	DH2052	DH2452	DH2652	DH2852	DH21052	DH3052	DH3452	DH3852	
RO 68" UD 67 5/8"	DH1856C *	DH11056C *	DH2056C *	DH2456C *	DH2656C *	DH2856C *	DH21056C *	DH3056C *	DH3456C *	DH3856C *	
RO 72" UD 71 5/8"	DH18510	DH110510	DH20510	DH24510	DH26510	DH28510	DH210510	DH30510	DH34510	DH38510	DH310510
RO 76" UD 75 5/8"	DH1862	DH11062	DH2062	DH2462	DH2662	DH2862	DH21062	DH3062	DH3462	DH3862	
RO 80" UD 79 5/8"	DH1866	DH11066	DH2066	DH2466	DH2666	DH2866	DH21066	DH3066			
RO 84" UD 83 5/8"	DH18610 **	DH110610 **	DH20610 **	DH24610 **	DH26610 **	DH28610 **	DH210610 **	DH30610 **			
RO 96" UD 95 5/8"	DH18710 **	DH110710 **	DH20710 **	DH24710 **	DH26710 **	DH28710 **	DH210710 **	DH30710 **			

Fixed Picture Units

UNIT WIDTH ▶ / UNIT HEIGHT ▼	RO 49 13/16" UD 49 5/16"	RO 61 13/16" UD 61 5/16"	RO 73 13/16" UD 73 5/16"
RO 48" UD 47 5/8"	DH40310	DH50310	DH60310
RO 56" UD 55 5/8"	DH4046	DH5046	DH6046
RO 60" UD 59 5/8"	DH40410	DH50410	DH60410
RO 64" UD 63 5/8"	DH4052	DH5052	
RO 68" UD 67 5/8"	DH4056	DH5056	
RO 72" UD 71 5/8"	DH40510		

Dimensions shown are for CLAD UNITS only. For PRIMED UNITS add 1/16" to RO width and 2" to RO height.

*Standard unit as Cottage Style, Reverse Cottage or equal lite also available.
** These units single hung, only bottom sash operates, tilts and removes.

Notes:
1. *Muntin bars illustrated represent the patterns of optional grilles or Atrium Classic Lite bars.*
2. *For ARCHITECTURAL DETAILS & SPECIFICATIONS refer to Atrium Door & Window Company's **SweetSource** program or call: **1-800-935-2000**.*

THE ATRIUM CASEMENT WINDOW

*O*ur Casement Window brings all the outdoors in. With a vast assortment of sizes, our window fits the same openings as worn-out wood or aluminum windows. That makes them ideal for either replacement, remodeling or new construction projects.

STANDARD SIZES

Fixed Picture Units

UNIT HEIGHT ▼ / UNIT WIDTH ►	RO 18" UD 17 1/2"	RO 20" UD 19 1/2"	RO 24" UD 23 1/2"	RO 28" UD 27 1/2"	RO 30" UD 29 1/2"	RO 32" UD 31 1/2"	RO 36" UD 35 1/2"	RO 48" UD 47 1/2"	RO 60" UD 59 1/2"	RO 72" UD 71 1/2"
RO 24" UD 23 1/2"	CS1620	CS1820	CS2020	CS2420	CS2620	CS2820				
RO 36" UD 35 1/2"	CS1630	CS1830	CS2030	CS2430	CS2630	CS2830	CS3030	CS4030		
RO 42" UD 41 1/2"	CS1636	CS1836	CS2036	CS2436	CS2636	CS2836	CS3036	CS4036	CS5036	
RO 48" UD 47 1/2"	CS1640	CS1840	CS2040	CS2440	CS2640	CS2840	CS3040	CS4040	CS5040	CS6040
RO 52" UD 51 1/2"	CS1644	CS1844	CS2044	CS2444	CS2644	CS2844	CS3044	CS4044	CS5044	CS6044
RO 57" UD 56 1/2"	CS1649	CS1849	CS2049	CS2449	CS2649	CS2849	CS3049	CS4049	CS5049	CS6049
RO 60" UD 59 1/2"	CS1650	CS1850	CS2050	CS2450	CS2650	CS2850	CS3050	CS4050	CS5050	
RO 66" UD 65 1/2"	CS1656	CS1856	CS2056	CS2456	CS2656	CS2856	CS3056	CS4056	CS5056	
RO 72" UD 71 1/2"	CS1660	CS1860	CS2060	CS2460	CS2660	CS2860	CS3060	CS4060		

Dimensions shown are for CLAD UNITS only. For PRIMED UNITS add 1/2" to UD & RO height.

Notes:
1. Muntin bars illustrated represent the patterns of optional grilles or Atrium Classic Lite bars.
*2. For ARCHITECTURAL DETAILS & SPECIFICATIONS refer to Atrium Door & Window Company's **SweetSource** program or call: **1-800-935-2000**.*

THE ATRIUM HORIZONTAL SLIDING WINDOW

*C*lear wood interior sash can be finished to match any decor, providing the natural insulating properties of wood. Frame is a 4 9/16" extruded aluminum and wood with vinyl head and sill track. Frame and sash are available in white, earthtone or sandstone.

STANDARD SIZES

UNIT WIDTH ▶	RO 36 1/2" UD 36"	RO 48 1/2" UD 48"	RO 60 1/2" UD 60"	RO 72 1/2" UD 72"	RO 72 1/2" UD 72" 15" x 35 1/2" x 15"	RO 96 1/2" UD 96" 21" x 47 1/2" x 21"
UNIT HEIGHT ▼						
RO 23 3/4" UD 23 1/4"	HS3020	HS4020				
RO 29 3/4" UD 29 1/4"	HS3026	HS4026	HS5026			
RO 35 3/4" UD 35 1/4"	HS3030	HS4030	HS5030	HS6030	HS6030P	HS8030P
RO 41 3/4" UD 41 1/4"	HS3036	HS4036	HS5036	HS6036	HS6036P	HS8036P
RO 43 3/4" UD 43 1/4"	HS3038	HS4038	HS5038	HS6038		
RO 47 3/4" UD 47 1/4"	HS3040	HS4040	HS5040	HS6040	HS6040P	HS8040P
RO 53 3/4" UD 53 1/4"	HS3046	HS4046	HS5046	HS6046	HS6046P	HS8046P
RO 59 3/4" UD 59 1/4"	HS3050	HS4050	HS5050	HS6050	HS6050P	HS8050P

Dimensions shown are for CLAD UNITS only.

Notes:
1. Muntin bars illustrated represent the patterns of optional grilles or Atrium Classic Lite bars.
2. For ARCHITECTURAL DETAILS & SPECIFICATIONS refer to Atrium Door & Window Company's *SweetSource* program or call: 1-800-935-2000.

ARCHITECTURAL MILLWORK

*A*trium offers a wide selection of unique architectural millwork in a vast array of configurations. In just about any shape and size imaginable, you will find solidly-constructed, finely finished accent windows.

RADIUS & POLYGONAL SHAPES

Standard Door Sizes		Standard Windows Sizes		Other Shapes Available	Polygonal Direct Set Units—Unfinished & Clad		
2-9/3-0/3-3	HALF ROUND	2-0	4-8	FULL ROUND	RECTANGLE	SQUARE	TRIANGLE
4-0		2-4	5-0				
5-0		2-6	5-4				
5-4	QUARTER ROUND*	2-8	6-0	HALF ROUND WITH EXTENDED LEGS	PENTAGON	RIGHT TRIANGLE	
6-0		3-0	6-8				
7-6		3-4	7-0				
8-0	ELLIPSE	3-6	7-4	GOTHIC	OCTAGON	TRAPEZOID	
9-0		3-8	8-0				
12-0 (Ellipse Only)		4-0		EYEBROW			

Quarter Round units available through 6-0 widths.

Specifications

Frame— **Unfinished units** constructed of fingerjoint Ponderosa Pine exterior. Interior units are clear, unfinished. Frame and brickmould are unprimed. **Clad Units—** 4 9/16" extruded aluminum and wood frame with nailing fin. Units have a prefinished exterior in WHITE (WH), EARTHTONE (ET) and SANDSTONE (ST). Interior is unfinished.

Glazing— Clear insulated glass. Other glazing options:

3/4" HDG Insulating Glass Bronze, Gray or Obscure Safety Tempered	ACL 3/4" Insulating Glass rectangular lites only ACL single glazed-rectangular lites only

Grilles— Unfinished wood grilles, 7/8" and 1 3/16" muntins available.

Atrium Classic Lite Units— Supplied with white exterior paintable and interior wood stainable bars. All designed to simulate a true divided lite. Clad units have exterior prefinished bars available in WHITE (WH), EARTHTONE (ET) and SANDSTONE (ST).

Note:
1. *All Polygonal shapes are viewed from the exterior. Please note measurements accordingly at the appropriate jamb legs.*
2. *Half Round Unit dimensions heights are equal to 1/2 of the width.*
3. *Frame unit type must be specified.*

THE ATRIUM
DOOR® & WINDOW
COMPANY

Distributed by

P.O. Box 226957 Dallas, Texas 75222-6957 214/634-9663 WATS 800/935-2000 FAX 214/637-6724

SEVEN FOOT WIDE
OPERATING SASH.

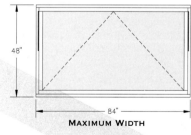

TO AN ARCHITECT THIS IS A HUGE WINDOW OF O

SIX OPERATING
WINDOWS IN A
SINGLE FRAME.

H WINDOW SYSTEMS. THE CHOICE FOR ARCHITECTS WITH BIG IDEAS.

You don't just design houses – you design living, breathing space. You know that bringing space alive means opening up your design, painting with broad strokes of light and air.

When you want the largest possible operating windows, H Window Systems offer the elegant solution, custom crafted to your exact design specifications.

DESIGN FREEDOM HINGES ON THIS.

H Window Systems are so amazingly strong, so perfectly balanced, they let you think in completely new dimensions. Dimensions like seven feet wide for a single operating sash. Dimensions like ten feet high or ten feet wide with virtually any combination of vertically or horizontally operable sash and stationary windows in a single massive frame.

Choose huge expanses of *glass, true divided lite* (TDL) or *simulated TDL* with a removable wood interior or extruded aluminum exterior grille, all available in a virtually infinite number of configurations and combinations.

THINK BIG.

FULLY REVERSIBLE
PROJECTED STYLE
H WINDOW (FRP)

48"

84"

MAXIMUM WIDTH

64"

48"

MAXIMUM HEIGHT

FULLY REVERSIBLE
CASEMENT STYLE
H WINDOW (FRC)

68"

36"

MAXIMUM WIDTH

76"

32"

MAXIMUM HEIGHT

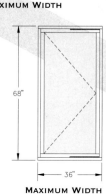

AT H WINDOW
COMPANY, WE'RE
CREATING A
REVOLUTION...

WITH WINDOWS THAT
SIMPLY WORK BETTER
FOR...

- ARCHITECTS
- BUILDERS
- HOMEOWNERS

...FOR GENERATIONS.

A REVOLUTIONARY TRADITION COMES TO AMERICA.

All over the world, the sun pours through more than 10 million very special windows. Revolutionary windows. H Windows.

So sensible, so surprisingly simple, H Window Systems revolve a full 180° for easy cleaning and maintenance without intruding into the room. But that's just one part of the H Window story…as you'll see in the pages ahead.

A remarkable hinge system is the H Window secret. Crafted in Norway by Spilka Industries, the H hinge has been the Scandinavian market leader for decades. The superior performance and design of the Spilka hinge has been proven millions of times by the 44 companies in 10 countries using H Window Hinge Systems around the world.

Today, H Window Systems are available in America, custom built in Minnesota for architects, builders and homeowners who refuse to compromise on style, function and quality.

The possibilities, we think you'll agree, are revolutionary.

WHAT MAKES THE H WINDOW THE FINEST WINDOW SYSTEM IN THE WORLD?

PROVEN PERFORMANCE
AROUND THE WORLD
SINCE 1959.

- THE ONLY FULLY REVERSIBLE WINDOW SYSTEM IN THE MARKET.

- THE HIGHEST PERFORMANCE RATINGS IN THE INDUSTRY.

- THE LARGEST OPERATING WINDOWS IN THE U.S.

- THE MOST ADVANCED ENGINEERING AND TECHNOLOGICAL DESIGN CURRENTLY AVAILABLE.

- MORE COLORS, FINE WOODS AND GLASS CHOICES THAN ANY OTHER MANUFACTURER.

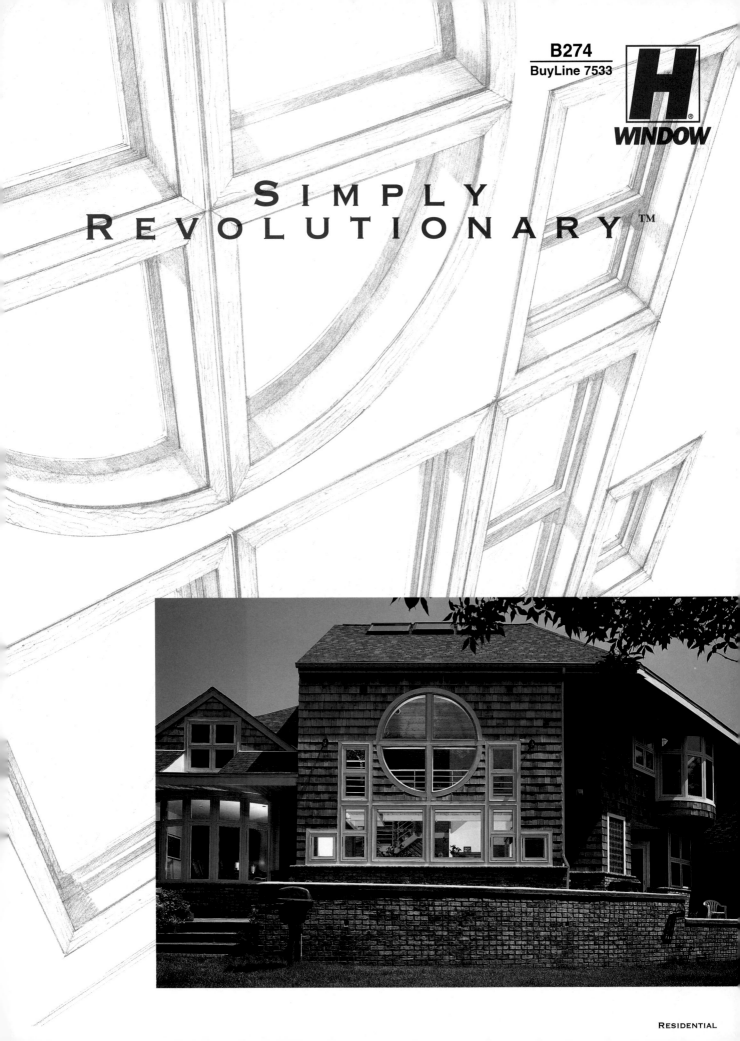

B274
BuyLine 7533

H
WINDOW

SIMPLY REVOLUTIONARY™

RESIDENTIAL

THE H HINGE SYSTEM LETS
YOU CONCENTRATE ON THE
BIG PICTURE.

Whether you choose the traditional
Fully Reversible Projected Style
H Window or the new Fully
Reversible Casement Style H Window,
the revolutionary H hinge design
provides superior weight distribution.

ORTUNITY.

H Window Systems' superior engineering makes it possible to operate
even huge picture windows with one
hand. In fact, even a large H Window
requires less than 5 pounds of force
to operate.

The unequaled ruggedness and
superior weight distribution of
H Window Systems let you explore
new vistas in architectural excellence.

Combine towering vertical casements up to 76" high or panoramic
views with a 7' wide sash. Reveal a
glorious sunrise across the lake or
afternoon warmth splashing across
a room.

Feel free to think big, because
H Window Systems can bring your
biggest ideas to light… beautifully.

MAXIMUM FRAME SIZE WITH MULTIPLE
OPERATING SASH, FIXED SASH OR
STATIONARY UNITS.

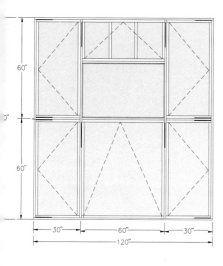

14' X 17' INTEGRATED UNIT COMBINING LARGE OPERATING SASH, FIXED
GEOMETRIC SASH AND A SPECIAL HEAT ABSORPTION GREEN TINTED GLASS.

4

HOMEOWNERS COULD EASILY FLIP OVER AN H WINDOW.

REVOLUTIONARY SIMPLICITY. A CLEAR ADVANTAGE.

THE INS AND OUTS OF H WINDOWS.

Open the window, release the handle mechanism, and the entire sash revolves 180°, without intruding into interior space or disturbing window treatments. Now you know why H Windows are revolutionary in design and operation.

From the first floor to the fourth, you can wash every window – inside and out – in just moments. No window stays cleaner than an H Window, because no window is easier to clean.

With H Windows, there's no perching precariously on a ladder to clean second or third story windows. We bring the outside inside.

That's an important story all by itself, but H Windows are also a great choice for first floors or below ground applications. That's because an H Window offers easy exit in case of fire or emergency. In fact, H Windows meet egress requirements in sizes as small as 38 by 43 inches. It's a small feature that could make a big difference.

FULLY REVERSIBLE OPERATION FOR

THE H WINDOW PUSH BAR LOCKS TO AN UNLIMITED
NUMBER OF VENTING POSITIONS. HARDWARE
OPTIONS FOR H WINDOWS INCLUDE EUROPEAN
PUSH BARS, EURO, CRANK AND CUSTODIAL HANDLES
IN VARIOUS COLORS TO COMPLEMENT YOUR DESIGN
SCHEME.

TRADITIONAL DOUBLE HUNG CONFIGURATION.

SIMPLE ONE HAND
OPERATION FOR
ADA APPROVAL.

EASILY
REMOVABLE,
EXTRUDED
ALUMINUM
INTERIOR
SCREEN.

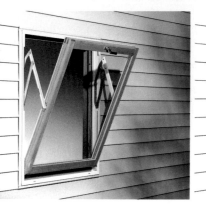

ING AND MAINTENANCE. WINDOW DOES NOT INTRUDE INTO INTERIOR OR INTERFERE WITH WINDOW TREATMENTS.

INTRO
THE FIRST
ENOUGH

**CASEMENT WINDOWS TAKE A
TURN FOR THE BETTER.**

Architects know H Windows for our
revolutionary hinge design and superior performance. They know we
won't compromise. That's why we
haven't built a casement
window...until now.

Our Fully Reversible Casement
Style H Window System sets a new
standard for function and performance in casement windows.

H WINDOW

COMPETITOR

68"
64"
32"
36"
MAXIMUM WIDTH

H WINDOW

H WINDOW
CASEMENTS
CAN BE MADE
WIDER AND
TALLER THAN
ANY OTHER
CASEMENT IN
THE INDUSTRY.

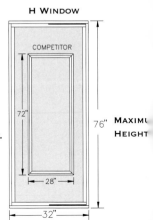

COMPETITOR

72"
76" MAXIMUM
HEIGHT
28"
32"

UCING
ASEMENT REVOLUTIONARY
O BE AN H WINDOW.

UNIQUE TROLLEY CAR
TRACK SYSTEM HANGS
THE WEIGHT OF THE
WINDOW FROM THE TOP.

Like the Fully Reversible Projected Style H Window, our casement is built with a sturdy extruded aluminum exterior and an all wood interior.

Like the Fully Reversible Projected Style H Window, our casement provides superior thermal, structural, air, water and sound attenuation performance.

The difference is it opens sideways, and it just might turn the casement window market inside out.

**THE GRAVITY
OF THE SITUATION.**

Typical casement windows are inherently weak. The lower corner hinge and handle mechanism supports all

the weight when the window is open, leading to sagging and poor fit over time.

The unique, patented hinge design of the Fully Reversible Casement Style H Window dramatically outperforms the competition. The weight of the window is displaced by hanging the majority of the weight from the top hinge guide.

Tests have proven that the H Window Hinge System holds up to 2000 lbs. That's why we can build the H Window casement taller and wider than the competition.

Our casement is one casement window that's built to last, or H Window would never have built it at all.

UNLIKE TRADITIONAL CASEMENTS, OUR CASEMENT WINDOW REVOLVES A FULL 180° WITHOUT DISTURBING WINDOW TREATMENTS.

FULLY RETRACTABLE
INTERIOR SCREEN,
OUT OF SIGHT WHEN
NOT IN USE.

THE NORDIC OUT-SWING PATIO DOOR. OUTWARD DIFFERENCES MAKE IT BETTER.

EVERYTHING YOU'D EXPECT IN A PATIO DOOR...AND MORE.

No typical in-swing french door can protect precious floorspace like the Nordic Out-Swing Patio Door from H Window. Our wood interior and extruded aluminum exterior patio doors combine superior functional design with exceptional durability.

Notice that our Patio Door opens outward, not inward like most others. It's a smarter way to build a patio door.

- You save interior floorspace.
- The weather seal is inside, protected from harsh conditions.
- Both sides of a double-wide door are fully operable.

FOR EXTRA SECURITY, WE'VE TRIPLED THE LOCKS.

Patio doors shouldn't be a standing invitation to burglars. Our 3-point locking mechanism combined with a composite frame of extruded aluminum and wood make an H Patio Door nearly impossible to force, providing more peace of mind than typical patio door systems. To force our Patio Door, you'd have to break through the entire frame, not just the locking points.

We also let you secure your door in an open position. Our unique locking system lets you open the door as much or as little as you like and secure it firmly in place with just a twist of the handle.

YOU WOULDN'T EXPECT THE SAME OLD HINGE SYSTEM FROM H WINDOW.

Our Patio Doors feature an extra fourth hinge, at the top where the weight load is greatest. That means an H Patio Door will fit perfectly with less sagging than competitive doors.

ZINC-PLATED, YELLOW
CHROMATED STEEL HINGES
WITH PROTECTIVE LIQUIDON
80 SEALER AND PAINTED TO
MATCH EXTERIOR COLOR.
MEETS COASTAL PERFOR-
MANCE REQUIREMENTS.

NOBODY
SUPPORTS THEIR WINDOWS
BECAUSE NOBODY GIVES

**H WINDOWS.
HARDWARE THAT'S GUARANTEED
FOR LIFE.**

We believe that windows, like homes, should be built to last for generations. That's how we build H Windows.

We support that commitment with this extraordinary guarantee of quality and craftsmanship.

IF THE HINGE SYSTEM OF ANY
H WINDOW SYSTEM FAILS, WE'LL
REPLACE IT...FREE...
FOR AS LONG AS YOU OWN
YOUR HOME.

The durability of the H hinge, the heart of every H Window, has been proven more than 20 million times for more than three decades.

**OUR ALUMINUM/WOOD COMBINA-
TION GIVES HOMEOWNERS
EXACTLY WHAT THEY WANT MOST,
INSIDE AND OUT.**

We only build H Windows one way. The right way. Every H Window combines the beauty and warmth of interior wood with the unparalleled strength, weather resistance and durability of a custom-finished extruded aluminum exterior.

**FOR THE OUTSIDE...
A RUGGED BARRIER,
BUILT TO LAST.**

Just look at an H Window System side by side with other standard "premium" windows, and you'll see the difference.

H Window extruded aluminum joints are screwed together by hand,

not quick-crimped. They are sealed with a special closed-cell gasket, not just a squirt of silicone. The H Window sill is sloped to allow better drainage. A special venting space is designed beneath the glass to help reduce potential seal failure. Moving parts have special protective coatings and sealed ball bearings to resist wear.

You'll feel the quality of an H Window every time you open and close it.

**FOR THE INSIDE...
THE ENDURING BEAUTY
OF FINE WOOD.**

At H Window, we may be tough on the outside, but we've always appreciated a cozy inside. We build our wood interiors like heirloom furniture. True mortised and tenoned joints strengthen each corner, doubly reinforced with glue and hidden heavy-gauge staples.

We constantly search out the world's finest lumber for highlighting America's finest homes. Choose our standard top grade pine or specify, oak, maple, walnut, cherry or perhaps something even more exotic. H Windows can find it, build it, and ship it unfinished or prefinished to your specifications.

For stained samples of your choice of wood, call H Window toll-free at 1-800-THE-H-WAY (800-843-4929).

AIA AWARD WINNING DESIGN.

AIR INFILTRATION
Amount of Air Leakage in a 25 mph wind.

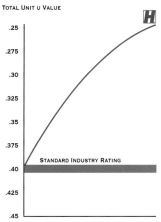

CFM/FT

Bar chart values:
- TYPICAL DOUBLE HUNG: .15
- TYPICAL SLIDER: .18
- TYPICAL CASEMENT: .03
- H WINDOW: .008

TEST STANDARDS REFERENCED:
NWWDA I.S. 2-88 AND 2-93,
AAMA 101-93, AND NFRC 100-91.

THERMAL
Choice of high performance glazing options
can greatly improve u values.

TOTAL UNIT U VALUE

STANDARD INDUSTRY RATING

WITH H WINDOW, THERMAL
PERFORMANCE IS A CHOICE,
NOT A LIMITATION.

WATER PENETRATION
Wind/Rain velocity that window is able to
withstand without leakage.

POUNDS PER SQUARE
FOOT (PSF)

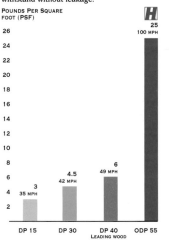

Bar chart values:
- DP 15: 3 (35 MPH)
- DP 30: 4.5 (42 MPH)
- DP 40 LEADING WOOD WINDOW MFGS.: 6 (49 MPH)
- ODP 55: 25 (100 MPH)

TEST SIMULATES AN 8"
RAINFALL IN ONE HOUR
AT VARYING WIND SPEEDS.

STRUCTURAL
Ability to withstand physical force
of high wind velocity.

POUNDS PER
SQUARE FOOT (PSF)

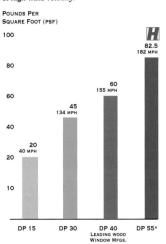

Bar chart values:
- DP 15: 20 (40 MPH)
- DP 30: 45 (134 MPH)
- DP 40 LEADING WOOD WINDOW MFGS.: 60 (155 MPH)
- DP 55*: 82.5 (182 MPH)

*H WINDOW RUNS AN OPTIONAL
TEST TO A LEVEL THAT SURPASSES
STANDARD TESTING.

THERMAL TESTING COMPLIES WITH NEW NFRC STANDARDS.

WEATHER OR NOT, TURN TO H WINDOW SYSTEMS FOR SUPERIOR ENVIRONMENTAL CONTROL.

OPTIONAL SPILVENT VENTILATOR FOR CONTROLLED VENTILATION WHEN WINDOW IS LOCKED AND SECURED.

H WINDOW SYSTEMS. INDUSTRY-LEADING PERFORMANCE.

As you might expect from Scandinavian window technology, outstanding performance comes standard in every H Window we build here in America.

In fact, no operable window seals tighter than an H Window. H Window Systems score better on 50 mph air infiltration tests than most windows can at 25 mph, and not just in the lab. We set our benchmarks in real-world tests on installed windows.

It's in the design. The harder the wind blows, the tighter an H Window seals. The continuous weatherstripping system around the window and the unique hinge design seals the sash firmly against the entire frame.

We also pass water infiltration tests in excess of 100 mph winds and 8 inches of rainfall per hour. Most competitors can't pass similar tests at 60 mph.

In addition to being the tightest window in the industry, we also offer one of the widest selections of glazing options available, making thermal performance a choice, not a limitation.

SPILVENT—ONE OF THE FINEST IDEAS IN CIRCULATION.

H Windows seal tight. That's why we offer the Spilvent, a unique air circulation device built right into the frame. During the winter or while you're away, the Spilvent allows a breath of fresh air to circulate while the window is closed and secured.

It's like having a tiny extra window built into your regular window. Once you've used it, you'll wonder why no other window has a Spilvent.

QUIET LEADERS IN SOUND ATTENUATION.

H Windows stand up to trains, planes and automobiles as well as wind and rain. Solid construction and superior materials help keep out noise as well as weather, making H Windows the obvious choice for your most challenging noise abatement applications. We'd like you to hear our lab and field test results for yourself, but you'll have to listen closely. Not much sound got through.

- Maintenance-free extruded aluminum exterior

- All wood interior with optional custom woods or prefinishing available

- Custom sizes up to 78″ wide and up to eight feet high

- Both doors operate without a center obstruction

- Tightest air and water infiltration performance in the industry

- Custom exterior colors, including anodized, powder coating, and Kynar™

- Decorative interior wood or exterior extruded aluminum grilles

- Superior thermal performance with a variety of glazing options (dual pane, triple pane, Heat Mirror™, etc.)

- Triple point locks and composite frame design for added security

- Brass or chrome handle hardware

- Retractable interior screen

- Fully operable miniblinds protected by glass

BETTER,
THEIR WINDOWS BETTER SUPPORT.

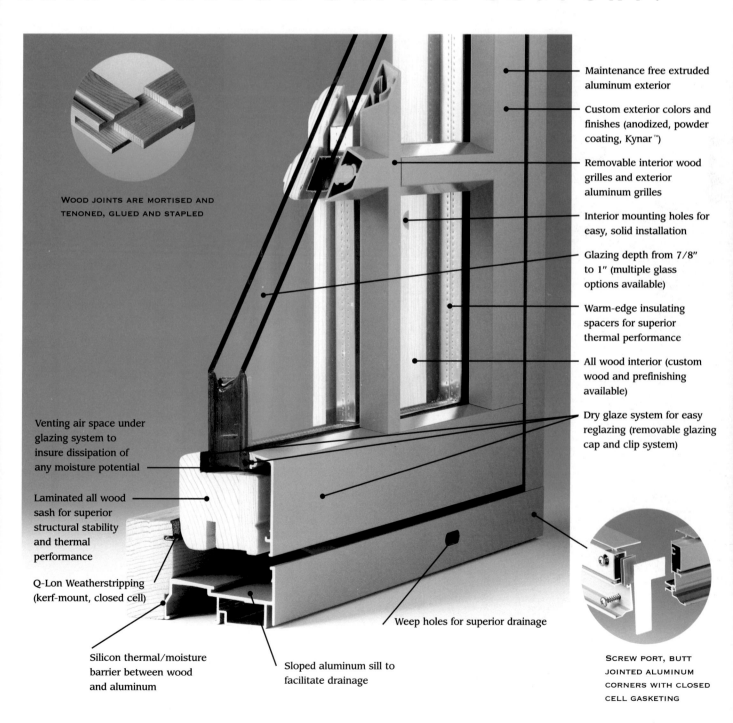

WOOD JOINTS ARE MORTISED AND TENONED, GLUED AND STAPLED

Maintenance free extruded aluminum exterior

Custom exterior colors and finishes (anodized, powder coating, Kynar ™)

Removable interior wood grilles and exterior aluminum grilles

Interior mounting holes for easy, solid installation

Glazing depth from 7/8" to 1" (multiple glass options available)

Warm-edge insulating spacers for superior thermal performance

All wood interior (custom wood and prefinishing available)

Dry glaze system for easy reglazing (removable glazing cap and clip system)

Venting air space under glazing system to insure dissipation of any moisture potential

Laminated all wood sash for superior structural stability and thermal performance

Q-Lon Weatherstripping (kerf-mount, closed cell)

Silicon thermal/moisture barrier between wood and aluminum

Sloped aluminum sill to facilitate drainage

Weep holes for superior drainage

SCREW PORT, BUTT JOINTED ALUMINUM CORNERS WITH CLOSED CELL GASKETING

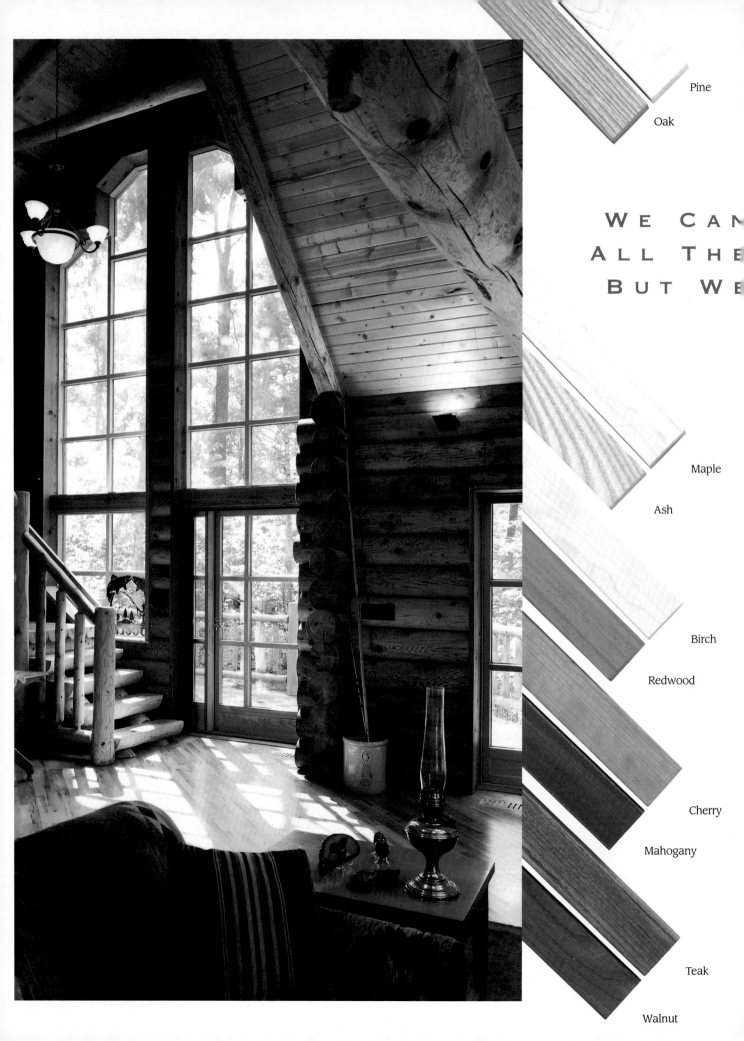

Pine

Oak

WE CAN
ALL THE
BUT WE

Maple

Ash

Birch

Redwood

Cherry

Mahogany

Teak

Walnut

SUNGLO®
SKYLIGHT PRODUCTS

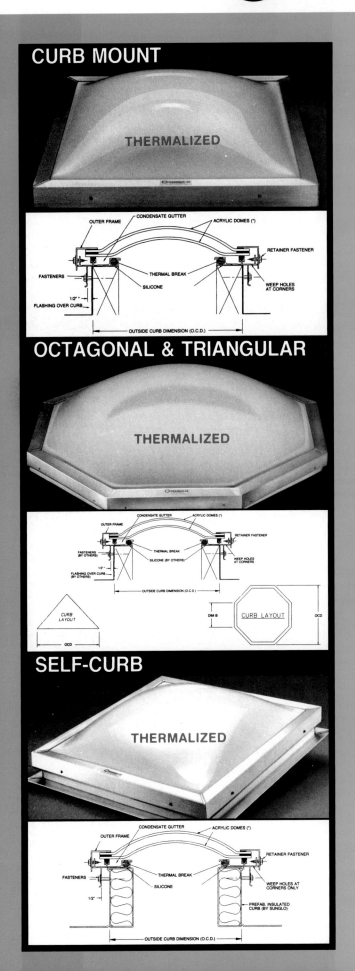

CURB MOUNT

CIRCULAR

OCTAGONAL & TRIANGULAR

VENTDOME

SELF-CURB

SELF-FLASHING

SUNGLO®
SKYLIGHT PRODUCTS
SINCE 1955

UNIT SKYLIGHTS SEE 07820/SUG FOR: **SLOPED** · **VAULTED** · **MODULAR** · **MONUMENTAL**

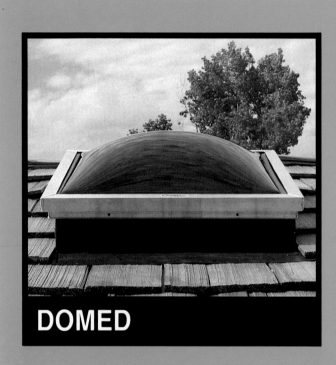

DOMED

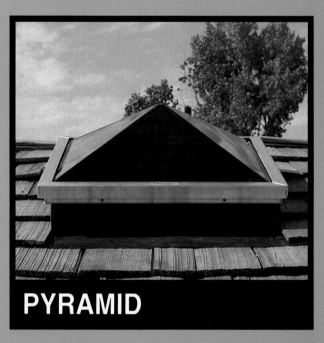

PYRAMID

TITELITE REFLECTIVE

LOW PROFILE

FOR UNMATCHED FLEXIBILITY
AND PERFORMANCE, JOIN THE
H WINDOW REVOLUTION.

FOR THE NAME OF THE
AUTHORIZED H WINDOW DEALER
NEAREST YOU, CALL:

1 - 8 0 0 - T H E - H - W A Y

(1 - 8 0 0 - 8 4 3 - 4 9 2 9)

WINDOW

H Window Company
P.O. Box 206
1324 East Oakwood Drive
Monticello, MN 55362
612/295-5305
Fax: 612/295-4656

FOR YOUR LOCAL AUTHORIZED DEALER, CONTACT:

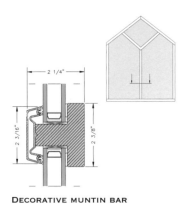

DECORATIVE MUNTIN BAR

SOURCES.
THE-H-WAY.

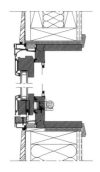

2 x 6 FRAME

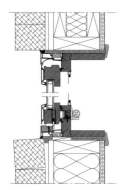

FRAME/BRICK VENEER

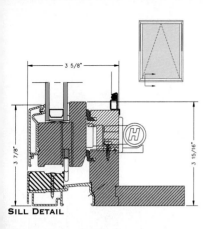

3 5/8"

3 7/8"

3 15/16"

SILL DETAIL

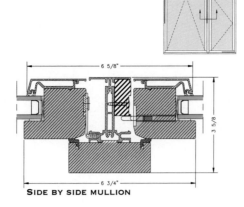

6 5/8"

6 3/4"

3 5/8

SIDE BY SIDE MULLION

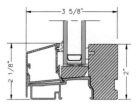

3 5/8"

2 1/8"

2"

GEOMETRIC STATIONARY

WE INVITE YOU TO
DRAW ON OUR RE
CALL 1-800

THE ONE THING
THAT'S MORE SOLID
THAN OUR WINDOWS.
OUR COMMITMENT TO
OUR CUSTOMERS.

Every H Window comes with a price-less bonus: H Window customer support. We treat all our customers as if our business depended on them...because it does.

We're waiting to help architects, contractors and homeowners with:

- Problem-solving
- Customization options/Design recommendations
- Detailed technical specifications
- AutoCAD files
- On-site installation/Retrofitting assistance
- Price quotes
- Copies of H Window materials
- Ongoing customer support

Schematic drawings for most applications are available free of charge, in printout form or digitally on 3 1/2" diskette, compatible with current version of AutoCAD. To order disks or printouts, call 1-800-THE-H-WAY, or fax your request to 612-295-4656.

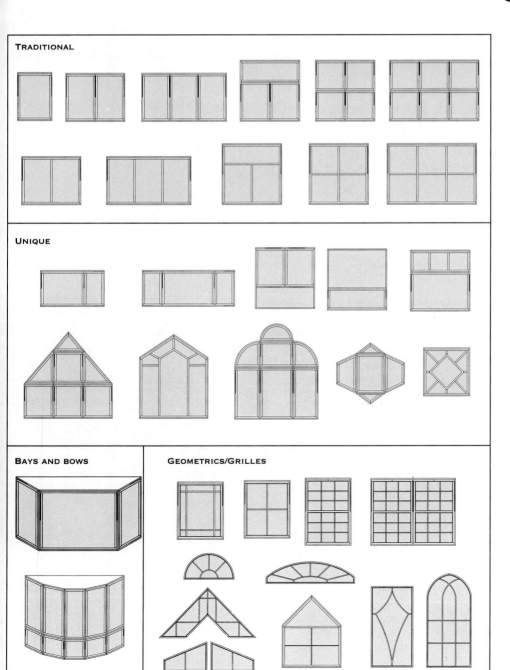

TRADITIONAL

UNIQUE

BAYS AND BOWS

GEOMETRICS/GRILLES

BUILD OLD STANDARDS, SPECIALIZE IN HELPING YOU SET NEW ONES.

EVERY WINDOW CUSTOM BUILT.

We never charge a premium on special sizes. Our manufacturing operation lets us build to your exact specifications as economically as we build standard sizes. Better yet, we can build your custom windows for you within twenty working days.

That makes H Windows the choice for both new construction and your most challenging remodeling projects.

After all, windows should be built to meet your exact size requirements, not just the closest standard size available.

CUSTOM EXTERIOR FINISHES (ANODIZED, POWDER COATINGS AND KYNAR™) IN A WIDE VARIETY OF COLORS.

OPERABLE MINI-BLIND IS SEALED BEHIND A GLASS PANEL AND IS REMOVABLE FOR WASHING OR SERVICING.

HANDCRAFTED DETAILING IS STANDARD ON EVERY WINDOW.

AIA AWARD WINNING DESIGN.

CLEAR/CLEAR

- MAXIMUM HEAT GAIN
- UNRESTRICTED LIGHT TRANSMISSION
- INCREASED GLARE

BRONZE/CLEAR

- RESTRICTED HEAT GAIN
- REDUCED GLARE
- MOST POPULAR COMBINATION

CLEAR/WHITE

- OPAQUE
- RESTRICTED VISION
- EVEN LIGHT DIFFUSION
- MAXIMUM GLARE REDUCTION
- INCREASED PRIVACY

U VALUES	WINTER HEAT LOSS 15 mph wind	SUMMER HEAT GAIN 7½ mph wind	ACRYLIC GLAZING COLORS	TRANSMITTANCE		SHADING COEFFICIENT	
				VISIBLE LIGHT	SOLAR ENERGY	SINGLE-GLAZED	DOUBLE-GLAZED*
SINGLE-GLAZED	1.2	0.8	COLORLESS	92%	85%	0.98	0.89
DOUBLE-GLAZED*	0.7	0.5	#2447 WHITE	56%	52%	0.56	0.46
			#2412 BRONZE	27%	35%	0.53	0.43
			#2094 GRAY	45%	55%	0.74	0.61

* Double-glazed coefficient is based on bronze outer dome, colorless inner dome. All figures are average and may vary with thickness of sheet.
SUNGLO SKYLIGHTS are not designed to support people. Where human safety is a consideration protective devices should be used.

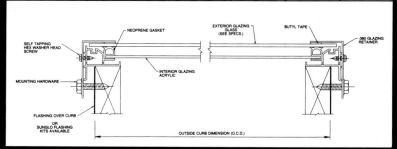

TITELITE

Use TITELITE **Reflective** and eliminate the need for **expensive shades,** costly customer call backs and blockage of the great free natural light.

	U-VALUE*		SHADING COEFFICIENT	RELATIVE HEAT GAIN
	WINTER	SUMMER		
TITELITE (Acrylglass with bronze outer)	.47	.50	.57	122
TITELITE (Acrylglass with **reflective** bronze outer)	.47	.50	.38	85

SKYLIGHT FLASHING KIT

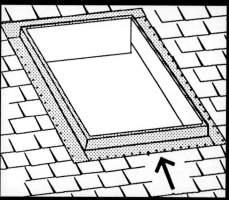

- Available in 9 sizes
- Color - Bronze finish aluminum
- Available in 4" and 6" curb application.

ACRYLIC REPLACEMENT DOMES AVAILABLE
FOR ANY SKYLIGHT MANUFACTURED

STANDARD SKYLIGHTS

CM	Curb Mount
SCM	Single Dome Curb Mount
PY-CM	Pyramid Curb Mount
LCM	Low Profile CM
G-CM	Glass CM
AVCM	Venting Curb Mount
TL	Titelite
SC	Self Curb
ISFAA	Aluminum Curb Attached
ISFAS	Aluminum Curb Separate
ISFGA	Galvanized Curb Attached
ISFGS	Galvanized Curb Separate

FRAME FINISHES

Standard Frame Finish
Bronze Finish
Clear Anodized
Dark Bronze Anodized

UNIT NO.	CURB MOUNT	VENTDOMES	LOW PROFILES	TITELITE	GLASS	PYRAMIDS	FLASHING KIT	"OCD" CURB MOUNT	"ICD" SELF CURB
1616	X		X		X	X		17½" x 17½"	14½" x 14½"
1624	X		X		X	X		17½" x 25½"	14½" x 22½"
1648	X		X	X	X		X	17½" x 49½"	14½" x 46½"
2424	X	X	X	X	X	X	X	25½" x 25½"	22½" x 22½"
2432	X	X	X	X	X	X	X	25½" x 33½"	22½" x 30½"
2448	X	X	X	X	X	X	X	25½" x 49½"	22½" x 46½"
2471	X		X	X	X		X	25½" x 72½"	22½" x 69½"
2492	X				X			25½" x 93½"	22½" x 90½"
3232	X	X	X	X	X	X	X	33½" x 33½"	30½" x 30½"
3248	X		X	X	X	X	X	33½" x 49½"	30½" x 46½"
3271	X	X			X			33½" x 72½"	30½" x 69½"
3939	X	X	X	X	X	X	X	40½" x 40½"	37½" x 37½"
3977	X				X			40½" x 78½"	37½" x 75½"
4545	X	X	X		X	X		46½" x 46½"	43½" x 43½"
4848	X	X	X	X	X	X	X	49½" x 49½"	46½" x 46½"
4871	X				X			49½" x 72½"	46½" x 69½"
4892	X				X			49½" x 93½"	46½" x 90½"
5757	X				X			58½" x 58½"	55½" x 55½"
6464	X				X			65½" x 65½"	62½" x 62½"
7171	X				X			72½" x 72½"	69½" x 69½"
7777	X				X			78½" x 78½"	75½" x 75½"
9292	X				X			93½" x 93½"	90½" x 90½"

Unless otherwise quoted the Standard SUNGLO Warranty period is 1 year.
Copies of this Standard Warranty are available upon request.

NON STANDARD SIZE SKYLIGHTS AVAILABLE

SUNGLO SKYLIGHTS ARE DISTRIBUTED BY:

SUNGLO®
SKYLIGHT PRODUCTS

3124 GILLHAM PLAZA
KANSAS CITY, MO 64109
816-561-1155
WATS: 1-800-821-6656
FAX: 816-561-5327

TUBULAR SKYLIGHT™

Let the Sun Shine In!

Open your home or office and let the sun shine in! A **TUBULAR SKYLIGHT**™ fills any room with bright sunshine without the problems of traditional skylights. And, a **TUBULAR SKYLIGHT**™ is more economical than a traditional skylight or artificial lighting.

*On your ceiling, a **TUBULAR SKYLIGHT**™ looks like an ordinary electric light fixture, but... what you see is not all that you get!*

TUBULAR SKYLIGHT™

A **TUBULAR SKYLIGHT**™ brings pleasant sunlight into any room. A small clear dome on the roof allows sunlight to enter a highly reflective tube that guides sunshine to your ceiling. A translucent diffuser lens gently disperses natural light throughout your room. And, only a **TUBULAR SKYLIGHT**™ produces clean light that has a 98.7 Color Rendering Index. That means, there are virtually no color distortions. For this reason, light produced by our product is more appealing than the "blue" light produced by our leading competitor's products or the "yellow" light produced by artificial lights.

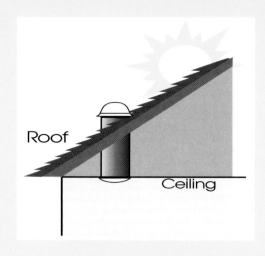

TUBULAR SKYLIGHT™ *versus* Traditional Skylights and Artificial Light

TUBULAR SKYLIGHT™ Reduces Your Electric Bill in Two Ways:

1. It reduces or eliminates the need for electric light during daylight hours.
2. Because a **TUBULAR SKYLIGHT**™ has a high insulation factor, it will not heat the room like traditional skylights or artificial light. That means that your air conditioner won't need to work so hard to cool your room. Likewise, a **TUBULAR SKYLIGHT**™ won't let heat escape when you're heating a room. A **TUBULAR SKYLIGHT**™ has a higher insulation rating than a standard constructed wall or roof. (Insulation Rating = R-22)

TUBULAR SKYLIGHT™ Delivers Soft, UV-Free Sunshine

With a **TUBULAR SKYLIGHT**™, bright sunlight is diffused to gently illuminate your whole room, while glaring harsh light and UV rays are blocked out. This is important because just as direct sunlight can damage your skin, direct sunlight can also damage and discolor carpeting and furnishings. To protect your inventory and furnishings, a **TUBULAR SKYLIGHT**™ is clearly the best choice.

When Properly Installed, **TUBULAR SKYLIGHT**™ is Leak Proof.

Natural Light is Better than Artificial Light.

People Prefer Natural Light

Our eyes use natural light more efficiently than artificial light. As our eyes strive to continually adjust to the excess glare that artificial light produces, we can experience eye strain that often leads to headaches and fatigue. Also, exposure to sufficient amounts of natural light can prevent illness such as SAD or winter blues. Soft, diffused natural light is healthier and more comfortable than artificial light.

Natural Light Saves Energy and Money

According to a recent article in the *Wall Street Journal* about studies of natural light in the work place, natural light has many advantages over artificial light:

- employees prefer natural light to artificial light, resulting in higher productivity and reduced absenteeism
- sales in retail outlets were significantly higher after natural light was introduced
- natural light cuts energy costs (both the lighting bill and the air conditioning bills are lowered significantly)

Natural Light Improves Air Quality by Reducing the Amount of Molds and Mildew

before

NASA's Kennedy Space Center Installed and Tested
TUBULAR SKYLIGHT™

TUBULAR SKYLIGHT™ was tested by NASA's Technology Outreach Program at Kennedy Space Center. They found:

Wind Load Analysis
- Withstands up to 140 miles per hour winds, far exceeding minimum national construction standards.

Thermographic Analysis
- Based on heat recordings from NASA, an R-22 insulation factor was calculated by an ASTM Certified Inspector.

Color Rendering Analysis
- 98.7 Color Rendering Index allows the beauty of the true colors of your room to stand out.

"Our employees enjoy working in the shop with the TUBULAR SKYLIGHT™ system."
Chuck Griffin, NASA's John F. Kennedy Space Center, Florida

"Our annual savings in energy costs have been over $2,560 per year. Because colors are so important in printing, this new lighting system has actually improved the quality of our work. Our employees really prefer it."
Matthew Combs,
American Southern Printing,
Sarasota Florida.

With **TUBULAR SKYLIGHT**™

With Electric Lighting

"With Tubular Skylights, the light level in this print shop increased by 225%. Each Tubular Skylight is the equivalent of 1,800 watts of conventional fluorescent. Tubular Skylights produce 68% less heat than the electrical lighting."
Al Othmer, Certified Energy Auditor,
Energy Conservation Assistance Program,
Florida Energy Office

With Electric Lighting

With **TUBULAR SKYLIGHT**™

*Webster Elementary School, Florida
Natural lighting creates a better learning environment and upgrades learning efficiency. A room lit with natural light requires only 1/3 as much brightness as standard fluorescent lights, so it's easier on your eyes.*

TUBULAR SKYLIGHT™
SPECIFICATIONS

The Dome
- Clear Acrylic
- High Impact Resistant
- UV Stable (non-yellowing)

Flashing
- Galvalume Flashing - 10 times more corrosive resistant than galvanized
- Adjustable to fit a variety of pitches (flat to 8/12 pitch). Other flashings are available for varied roof pitches

The Tube
- .020 Aluminum with a 95% Reflective Surface - creates light with a 98.7 Color Rendering Index
- Surface is bonded to aluminum with a highly effective patented thermoset adhesive process

Insulator Disk
- Creates dead air pocket.
- UV Stable Acrylic (non-yellowing)

Diffuser Lens
- Translucent White Acrylic
- Spreads Daylight Evenly
- UV Stable (non-yellowing)

Insulation Rating
- R-22 (Tested by an ASTM Certified Inspector)

Roof Types
- Shingle
- Metal
- Roll Roofing
- Cedar Shake
- Foam
- Rubber
- Tar & Gravel
- Torch Down
- Tile

Ceiling Types
- Acoustical
- Drywall
- Plaster
- Wood
- Flat
- Suspended
- Vaulted
- No Ceiling

10 Year Limited Warranty

*Locate Placement,
Cut Hole in Ceiling*

*Cut Hole in Roof,
Properly Seal Flashing*

*Insert Tube,
Measure, Cut & Secure*

*Attach Foam Seal,
Exterior Dome, Clamp &
Storm Collar*

*Attach Interior Seals,
Insulator Disk & Diffuser*

Three Sizes

Size	Typical Room Use	Max Recommended Tubing Length
8"	Bathrooms, Hallways, Closets	10'
13"	Living Room, Dining Room, Kitchen, Office	20'
21"	Industrial Warehouse	30'

Tile Roof

Tar & Gravel Roof

Rubber Roof

Made In the USA

Let the Sun Shine In with
TUBULAR SKYLIGHT™!

TUBULAR SKYLIGHT™

- Saves Energy
- Leak Proof
- Will Not Fade Furnishings
- Economical
- Higher Insulation Rating than a Standard Constructed Wall or Roof
- Non-Yellowing Acrylic Parts
- 10 Year Limited Warranty

Tubular Skylight, Inc.
Corporate Office
5704 Clark Road
Sarasota, FL 34233
(941) 927-TUBE (8823)
(941) 925-0500 Fax

Glass Shower Door Products

Hiawatha, Inc.

Contents

For over thirty years Hiawatha, Inc. has been manufacturing architectural door hardware including pulls, push bars and plates. In the last four years Hiawatha has added a variety of products including glass shower door hinges, towel bars and accessories for frameless shower enclosures. Hiawatha assures you prompt delivery and excellent service.

Starshower Series

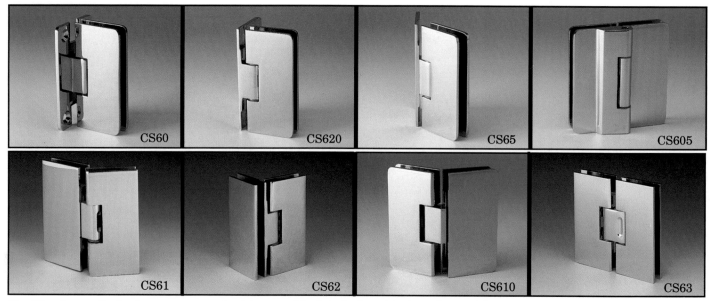

CS60   CS620   CS65   CS605

CS61   CS62   CS610   CS63

The Starshower Series is our most popular hinge model. It is designed for both $1/4$" and $3/8$" thick glass. This hinge features an automatic return to a true closed position from an arc of 20 degrees from center. The Starshower hinges are designed to hold a maximum weight of 80 lbs. per pair with a maximum width of 30". These hinges are stocked in polished brass and chrome.

Meridien Series

C170   C171

The Meridien Series is a brass self-closing hinge for $3/8$" thick glass. These hinges have an automatic return to 0 degrees within an arc of less than 85 degrees and have stops at 0 and 90 degrees . They are designed to hold a maximum weight of 85 lbs. per pair of hinges with a maximum width of 31" per pair. These hinges are stocked in polished brass and chrome.

Europa Series

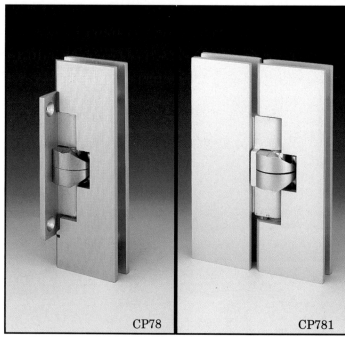

CP78   CP781

The Europa is an aluminum self-closing hinge for $3/8$" thick glass. These hinges are specially designed to hold up to 100 lbs. of glass per pair of hinges with a maximum width of 32" per pair. Available finishes include anodized aluminum, gold, bronze and black.

Featuring Hinges for 1/4", 3/8", and 1/2" Glass

Hiawatha stocks hinges in a variety of finishes including polished brass, polished chrome, white and black gloss. An array of finishes are available depending upon the hinge chosen and the custom finish desired. Hiawatha has the ability to meet your custom fabrications requirements.

Oceane Series

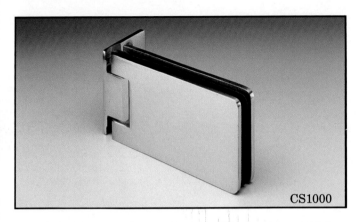

CS1000

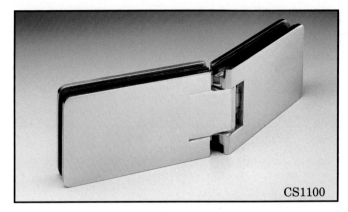

CS1100

Also available(not pictured): CS 1200 glass to glass at 90 degree angles and CS 1300 glass to glass at 135 degree angles.

The Oceane series of hinges are specially designed for 3/8" thick glass. The Oceane is designed to hold a maximum weight of 100 lbs. per pair and a maximum width of 36" per pair of hinges. These hinges can be both top and bottom and intermediate mounted. The Oceane Series hinge features an automatic return to a closed position from an arc of 20 degrees from center. These hinges are stocked in polished brass and chrome.

HSH Series

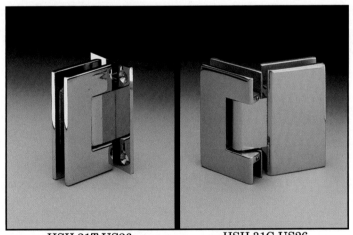

HSH 21T US26
HSH 22T US3

HSH 31G US26
HSH 32G US3

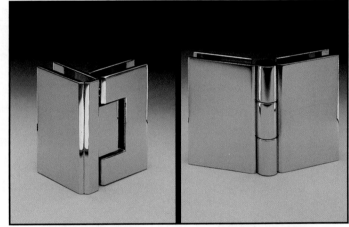

HSH 41 G9 US26
HSH 42 G9 US3

HSH 51 G5 US26
HSH 52 G5 US3

The HSH Series of hinges is designed for 1/2" or 3/8" thick glass. These self-centering hinges are created from a brass base and are stocked in polished brass and polished chrome. Other finishes are available upon request. The HSH Series is designed to hold up to 90 lbs. per pair of hinges with a maximum width of 28" per pair.

Edge Wipes & Seals

Hiawatha offers a complete line of edge wipes and seals manufactured from a clear polycarbonate material. These wipes and seals are used to prevent or reduce water leakage from shower enclosure.

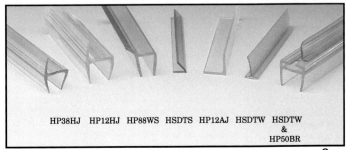

HP38HJ HP12HJ HP88WS HSDTS HP12AJ HSDTW HSDTW
&
HP50BR

3

Towel Bars, Pulls, and Shower Enclosure Accessories

Hiawatha offers a complete line of $^{3}/4$" diameter towel bars and door pulls for shower enclosures. The pulls and towel bars are available in a variety of polished and satin finishes including brass, aluminum, bronze, chrome, and stainless steel. Hiawatha has the ability to custom design pulls and towel bars according to your needs. Pulls and towel bars may be mounted together with a Figure-F mounting (as shown in Accessories picture below) at both free ends.

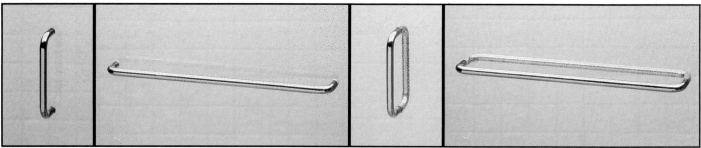

Single Pulls	Towel Bars		Pulls Back to Back	Towel Bars Back to Back	
523A 8"CTC	SD7518	18" CTC	523A x 523A 8"CTC	SD7518 x SD7518	18" CTC
523B 5½"CTC(Shown)	SD7520	20" CTC	523B x 523B 5½"CTC	SD7520 x SD7520	20" CTC
523C 10"CTC	SD7524	24" CTC	523C x 523C 10"CTC	SD7524 x SD7524	24" CTC
	SD7527	27" CTC		SD7527 x SD7524	27" CTC

Acrylic Towel Bars and Pulls

In addition to metal towel bars and pulls, Hiawatha provides a complete line of clear acrylic pulls with metal ends available in finishes such as brass, 24k plated gold, chrome, and stainless steel. These pulls are available in 3/4", 1" and 1½" diameters. Custom shapes and sizes are available.

HCP Series

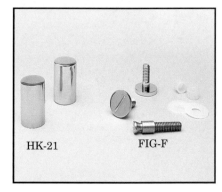

HD   HC   HJ   HS

Recessed Pull

This recessed pull is designed for use on sliding shower door enclosures. Pull can be mounted alone or as a towel bar mounting.

HRP5 - US 3
HRP26 - US26

Accessories

HK21-Knob available in all metal finishes. Fig F-Used for mounting single bars, HK21 knobs or for the free ends of pull and towel bar combinations.

Bushings, washers and shoulder bolts are included as required with each order.

HK-21   FIG-F

Warranty:

All company products are guaranteed to be free from defect in materials and workmanship for a period of one year from the date of purchase. The liability of Hiawatha, Inc. is strictly limited to the repair or replacement of units that are found to be defective, and no claims for consequential damages of any nature will be allowed. This warranty is in lieu of all other warranties, expressed or implied.

Cleaning of Metal Finishes:

All metal products should be kept free of dirt and dust. To clean use a soft cloth and a mild cleaner such as soapy water. Dry throughly with a soft cloth. Many commercial cleaners can damage finish.

Hiawatha, Inc. reserves the right to make engineering changes or other modifications at our discretion without notice.

Finished Lacquer On Products:

Lacquer finish on products cannot be guaranteed. Depending on local conditions, clean air standards, emissions of pollutants, and type of cleaning solution used, lacquer finishes will deteriorate over time.

Local Distributor:

ARDEN Architectural

wallwear™

NTEGRATED WALL PROTECTION SYSTEMS

▪ *Handrail Systems*

Arden Handrail Systems offer the best in performance and durability, flexibility and beauty. Every design features high-strength impact-resistant vinyl acrylic covers and sturdy aluminum frames – ideal for the abuse found in today's institutional and commercial buildings. With a wide range of styles and an array of standard and custom colors, Arden Handrails enhance any design motif.

MATERIALS
▪ Handrail covers are extended from high-impact vinyl acrylic with a minimum impact resistance of 1.2 inch-pounds per .001" of thickness when tested to ASTM D-4226.

▪ Vinyl acrylic extrusions are compounded with an anti-microbial additive and are chemical and stain resistant.

▪ Embossed pebble matte surfaces in many standard and custom colors.

▪ Aluminum extrusions are 6063-T5 mill finish alloy.

▪ End returns and corners are molded from tough, high-impact polymers.

FIRE RATING
▪ CLASS I: Flame spread is less than 25 and smoke is less than 450 when tested to UL 723, ASTM E-84, UBC 42-1, NFPA 255.

▪ ASTM D-635: Self extinguishing.

SPECIFICATIONS
GENERAL: Furnish as shown and specified Arden Series — Handrail System as manufactured by Arden Architectural, St. Paul, MN. INSTALLATION: Handrail System shall be permanently fastened to wall in accordance with manufacturer's approved details. Height above finished floor as required by applicable codes and contract documents.

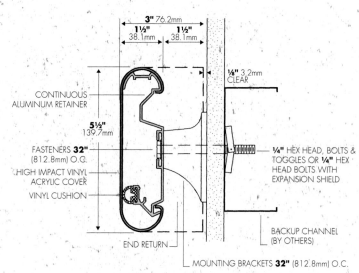

CONTINUOUS
ALUMINUM RETAINER

3" 76.2mm
1½" 38.1mm
1½" 38.1mm

⅛" 3.2mm
CLEAR

5½"
139.7mm

FASTENERS 32"
(812.8mm) O.C.

HIGH IMPACT VINYL
ACRYLIC COVER

VINYL CUSHION

¼" HEX HEAD, BOLTS &
TOGGLES OR ¼" HEX
HEAD BOLTS WITH
EXPANSION SHIELD

BACKUP CHANNEL
(BY OTHERS)

END RETURN

MOUNTING BRACKETS 32" (812.8mm) O.C.

SERIES HR – 55

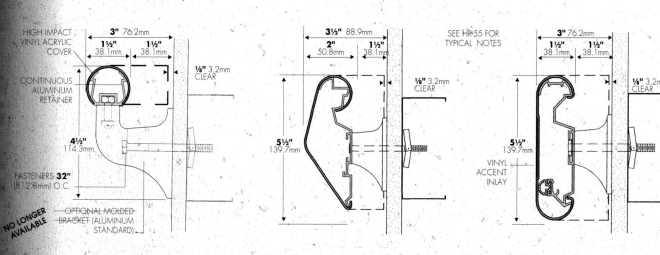

HIGH IMPACT
VINYL ACRYLIC
COVER

3" 76.2mm
1½" 38.1mm
1½" 38.1mm

⅛" 3.2mm
CLEAR

CONTINUOUS
ALUMINUM
RETAINER

4½"
114.3mm

FASTENERS 32"
(812.8mm) O.C.

OPTIONAL MOLDED
BRACKET (ALUMINUM
STANDARD)

NO LONGER
AVAILABLE

SERIES HRR – 150

3½" 88.9mm
2" 50.8mm
1½" 38.1mm

⅛" 3.2mm
CLEAR

5½"
139.7mm

SEE HR-55 FOR
TYPICAL NOTES

SERIES HRC – 55

3" 76.2mm
1½" 38.1mm
1½" 38.1mm

⅛" 3.2mm
CLEAR

5½"
139.7mm

VINYL
ACCENT
INLAY

SERIES HRI – 55

Each Handrail Series meets or exceeds the requirements of all national building codes including Life Safety, ANSI, BOCA, OSHA and UBC, and the Americans with Disabilities Act of 1990 (ADA). Each Handrail Series complies with Title 24, Part 2, of the Uniform Building Code as required by the State of California Office of Statewide Health Planning and Development (OSHPD).

▪ *Bumper Guard & Crash Rail Systems*

Rugged, yet attractive, Arden Bumper Guard and Crash Rail Systems afford the maximum in wall protection without sacrificing good looks. Designed especially for high abuse applications, they are mounted horizontally at points of impact. Bumper Guards mount to bumper cushions, providing maximum shock absorption. Crash Rails have a narrower profile and three mounting options.

MATERIALS

■ Bumper Guard & Crash Rail covers are extruded from high-impact vinyl acrylic with a minimum impact resistance of 1.2 inch-pounds per .001" of thickness when tested to ASTM D-4226.

■ Vinyl acrylic extrusions are compounded with an anti-microbial additive and are chemical and stain resistant.

■ Embossed pebble matte surfaces in many standard and custom colors.

■ Aluminum extrusions are 6063-T5 mill finish alloy.

■ End returns are molded from tough, high-impact polymers.

FIRE RATING

■ CLASS I: Flame spread is less than 25 and smoke is less than 450 when tested to UL 723, ASTM E-84, UBC 42-1, NFPA 255.

■ ASTM D-635: Self extinguishing.

SPECIFICATIONS

GENERAL: Furnish as shown and specified Arden Series — Bumper Guard & Crash Rail Systems as manufactured by Arden Architectural, St. Paul, MN. INSTALLATION: Shall be permanently fastened to wall in accordance with manufacturer's approved details. Height of system above finished floor as required by contract documents.

Crash Rails and Bumper Guards serve the same function while offering different aesthetic profiles. Crash Rails and Bumper Guards maybe used as stand alone protection or in tandem with Handrails and protective wall covering. For maximum protection use Crash Rails at floor level and Bumper Guards or Handrails at code heights.

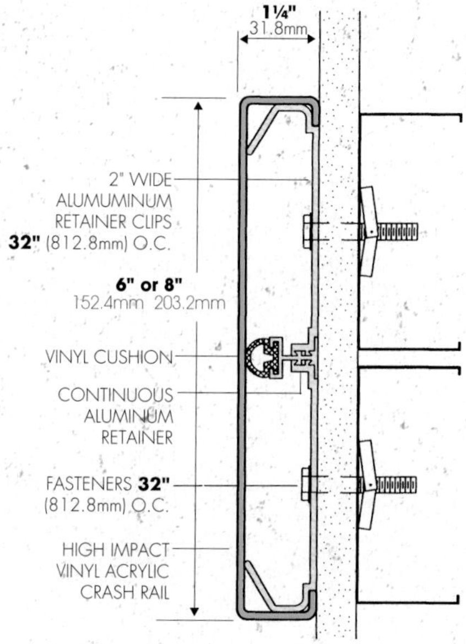

SERIES CRS – 6
SERIES CRS – 8
SERIES CRC – 8
(CONTINUOUS ALUMINUM RETAINER)

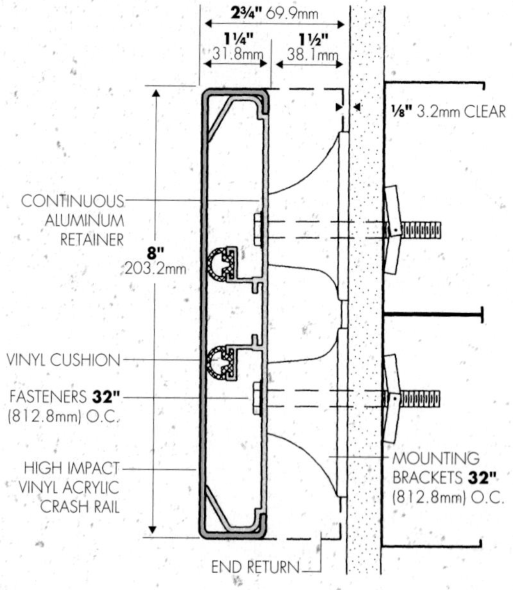

SERIES CRE – 8

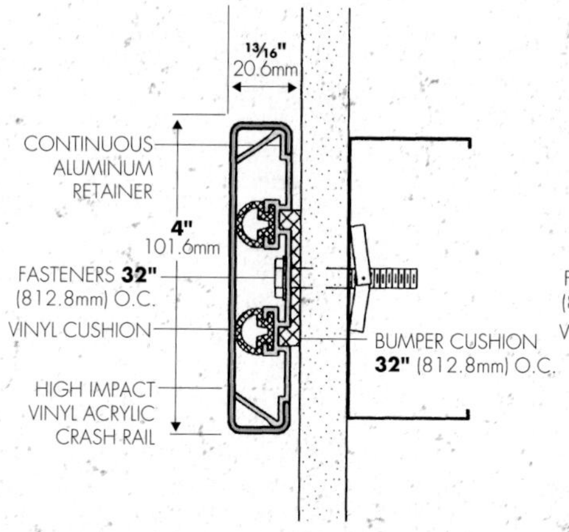

SERIES CRS – 4 (⅛" BUMPER)
SERIES CRB – 4 (⁵⁄₁₆" BUMPER)

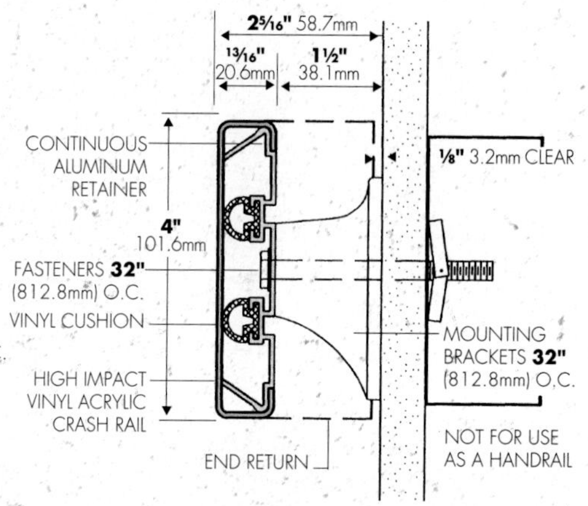

SERIES CRE – 4

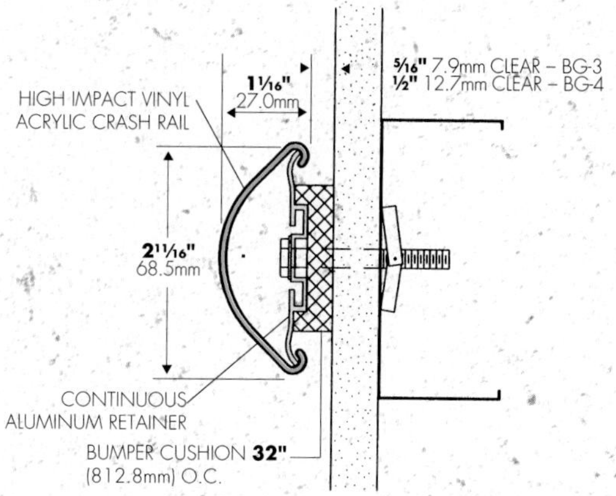

SERIES BG – 3 (2¹¹⁄₁₆" 68.5MM)
SERIES BG – 4 (4⅛" 104.8MM)

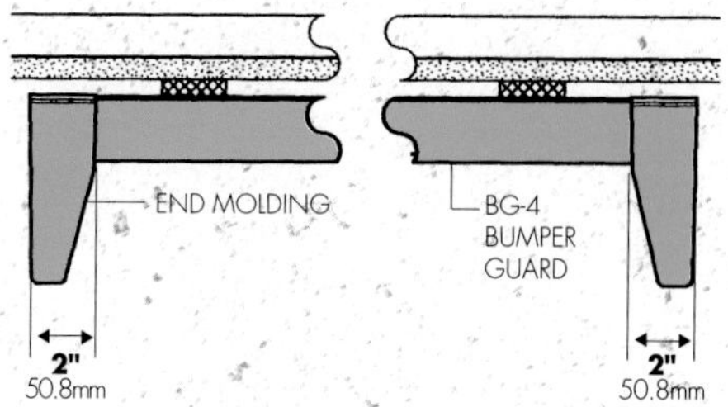

SERIES BGL – 4
BED LOCATOR
(SEE PHOTO OPOSITE)

5

▪ *Corner Guard Systems*

SURFACE MOUNT

Arden Architectural Surface Mounted Corner Guards are designed to protect the corners in existing buildings without marring the beauty of the interior decor. Our textured, high impact vinyl-acrylic covers snap onto durable aluminum retainers to give maximum impact protection. Thy are available in full, wainscot, or custom specified heights in our full range of standard and custom colors. Matching end caps are available to give a finished look.

MATERIALS
■ Corner Guard covers are extruded from high-impact vinyl acrylic with a minimum impact resistance of 1.2 inch-pounds per .001" of thickness when tested to ASTM D-4226.

■ Vinyl acrylic extrusions are compounded with an anti-microbial additive and are chemical and stain resistant.

■ Embossed pebble matte surfaces in many standard and custom colors.

■ Aluminum extrusions are 6063-T5 mill finish alloy.

■ End caps are molded from tough, high-impact polymers.

FIRE RATING
■ CLASS I: Flame spread is less than 25 and smoke is less than 450 when tested to UL 723, ASTM E-84, UBC 42-1, NFPA 255.

■ ASTM D-635: Self extinguishing.

SPECIFICATIONS
GENERAL: Furnish as shown and specified Arden Series — Flush Mount Corner Guards as manufactured by Arden Architectural, St. Paul, MN.
INSTALLATION: Shall be permanently fastened to wall in accordance with manufacturer's approved details.

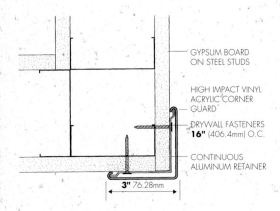

GYPSUM BOARD
ON STEEL STUDS

HIGH IMPACT VINYL
ACRYLIC CORNER
GUARD

DRYWALL FASTENERS
16" (406.4mm) O.C.

CONTINUOUS
ALUMINUM RETAINER

3" 76.28mm

SERIES CGS – 3S

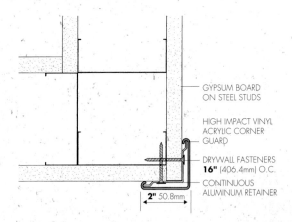

GYPSUM BOARD
ON STEEL STUDS

HIGH IMPACT VINYL
ACRYLIC CORNER
GUARD

DRYWALL FASTENERS
16" (406.4mm) O.C.

CONTINUOUS
ALUMINUM RETAINER

2" 50.8mm

SERIES CGS – 2S

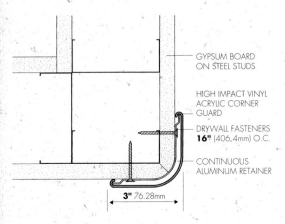

GYPSUM BOARD
ON STEEL STUDS

HIGH IMPACT VINYL
ACRYLIC CORNER
GUARD

DRYWALL FASTENERS
16" (406.4mm) O.C.

CONTINUOUS
ALUMINUM RETAINER

3" 76.28mm

SERIES CGS – 3R

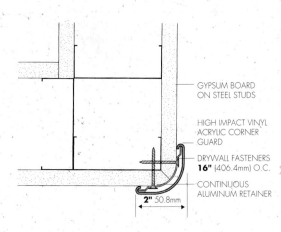

GYPSUM BOARD
ON STEEL STUDS

HIGH IMPACT VINYL
ACRYLIC CORNER
GUARD

DRYWALL FASTENERS
16" (406.4mm) O.C.

CONTINUOUS
ALUMINUM RETAINER

2" 50.8mm

SERIES CGS – 2R

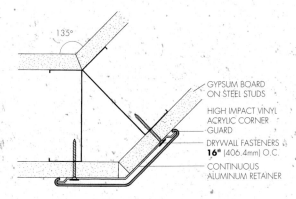

135°

GYPSUM BOARD
ON STEEL STUDS

HIGH IMPACT VINYL
ACRYLIC CORNER
GUARD

DRYWALL FASTENERS
16" (406.4mm) O.C.

CONTINUOUS
ALUMINUM RETAINER

SERIES CGS – 135

▪ *Corner Guard Systems*

FLUSH MOUNT

Arden Flush Mount and Fire-rated Corner Guards are designed to give inconspicuous wall protection for floor-to-ceiling applications. Available in both crisp and radius corners in a wide range of standard and custom colors, they transform wall protection systems into a creative element of the interior vocabulary.

MATERIALS

▪ Corner Guard covers are extruded from high-impact vinyl acrylic with a minimum impact resistance of 1.2 inch-pounds per .001" of thickness when tested to ASTM D-4226.

▪ Vinyl acrylic extrusions are compounded with an anti-microbial additive and are chemical and stain resistant.

▪ Embossed pebble matte surfaces in many standard and custom colors.

▪ Aluminum extrusions are 6063-T5 mill finish alloy.

FIRE RATING

▪ CLASS I: Flame spread is less than 25 and smoke is less than 450 when tested to UL 723, ASTM E-84, UBC 42-1, NFPA 255.

▪ ASTM D-635: Self extinguishing.

▪ Fire-Rated Construction (1 & 2 hour) – Flush Mount Systems for use in rated wall construction meet or exceed the requirements of UL 263 (ASTM E119, UBC 43-1, ANSI A2.1, & NFPA 251).

MECHANICAL JOINT ASSEMBLIES
CLASSIFIED BY
UNDERWRITERS LABORATORIES, INC.
FOR USE IN JOINT SYSTEMS
SEE UL FIRE RESISTANCE DIRECTORY
DESIGN NO.S CGS0005, CGS0006
1M98
ARDEN ARCHITECTURAL SPECIALTIES, INC.

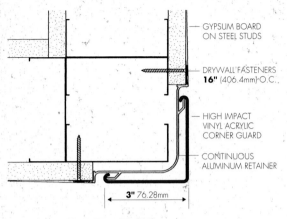

GYPSUM BOARD
ON STEEL STUDS

DRYWALL FASTENERS
16" (406.4mm) O.C.

HIGH IMPACT
VINYL ACRYLIC
CORNER GUARD

CONTINUOUS
ALUMINUM RETAINER

3" 76.28mm

SERIES CGF – 3S (3")
SERIES CGF – 2S (2")

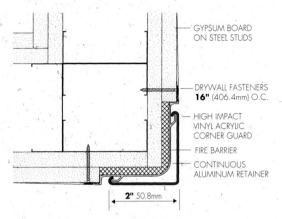

GYPSUM BOARD
ON STEEL STUDS

DRYWALL FASTENERS
16" (406.4mm) O.C.

HIGH IMPACT
VINYL ACRYLIC
CORNER GUARD

FIRE BARRIER

CONTINUOUS
ALUMINUM RETAINER

2" 50.8mm

SERIES CGR – 3S (3")
SERIES CGR – 2S (2")

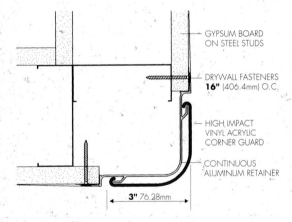

GYPSUM BOARD
ON STEEL STUDS

DRYWALL FASTENERS
16" (406.4mm) O.C.

HIGH IMPACT
VINYL ACRYLIC
CORNER GUARD

CONTINUOUS
ALUMINUM RETAINER

3" 76.28mm

SERIES CGF – 3R (3")
SERIES CGF – 2R (2")

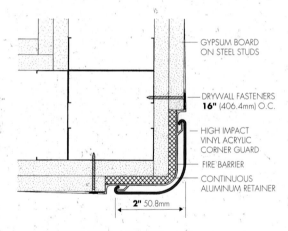

GYPSUM BOARD
ON STEEL STUDS

DRYWALL FASTENERS
16" (406.4mm) O.C.

HIGH IMPACT
VINYL ACRYLIC
CORNER GUARD

FIRE BARRIER

CONTINUOUS
ALUMINUM RETAINER

2" 50.8mm

SERIES CGR – 3R (3")
SERIES CGR – 2R (2")

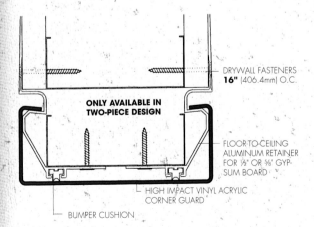

DRYWALL FASTENERS
16" (406.4mm) O.C.

**ONLY AVAILABLE IN
TWO-PIECE DESIGN**

FLOOR-TO-CEILING
ALUMINUM RETAINER
FOR ½" OR ⅝" GYP-
SUM BOARD

HIGH IMPACT VINYL ACRYLIC
CORNER GUARD

BUMPER CUSHION

SERIES CGF – 2SEW
SERIES CGR – 2SEW (FIRE RATED)

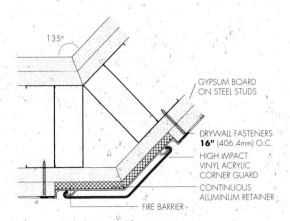

135°

GYPSUM BOARD
ON STEEL STUDS

DRYWALL FASTENERS
16" (406.4mm) O.C.

HIGH IMPACT
VINYL ACRYLIC
CORNER GUARD

CONTINUOUS
ALUMINUM RETAINER

FIRE BARRIER

SERIES CGR – 135
SERIES CGF – 135 (NON-RATED)

▪*Custom Color*

An exciting collection of handsome new standard colors and intriguing contemporary hues give Arden Architectural's Wallwear™ the broad palette to complement any decor or design motif. Standard Series colors are readily available for immediate shipment in most profiles. Custom Series colors require longer lead times and are subject to quantity minimums. For information on specific color matching, contact Arden Architectural. Actual colors may vary slightly from the printed swatches shown.

Arden Architectural's Wallwear wall protection systems are designed especially for the high-abuse environments found in institutions and commercial buildings. The high-strength and impact-resistant vinyl acrylic covers and sturdy aluminum frames offer maximum durability and flexibility. Our wall and corner protection products meet or exceed all major building codes as well as ADA requirements for handrails. Our materials meet Class 1/A requirements for flame spread and smoke. Our flush mount corner guards are available in 1 and 2 hour fire rated models.

#09, Moonlight*

#01, Parchment*

#18, Desert Beige*

#41, Sky Blue*

#03, Versailles*

#37, Misty Peach*

#26, Birchbark*

#23, Glacier Blue

#05, Mojave*

#21, Georgia Peach

#40, Taupe*

#27, Cornflower

#13, Silk*

#17, Jasmine*

#24, Putty

#31, Carribean

#02, Pueblo*

#22, Conch

#11, Winter Sky*

#35, Baltic

#33, Pecan

#25, Mauvelous

#30, Spanish Moss

#06, Morning Mist*

#10, Cappuccino

#29, Flamingo

#39, Teal

#04, Dolphin*

#14, Truffle

#07, Ming

#38, Nile

#15, London Smoke

#32, Cherokee

#12, Passion

#08, Neptune

#38, Rhino

#16, Windsor

#36, Pokeberry

#34, Mallard

#19, Black

**Matching wallwear acrylic vinyl sheet also available in most colors in .028",
.040" or .060" thicknesses.**
*Standard colors. All others are subject to slightly longer lead times and quantity minimums.
Custom color matching is available. Call or write Arden for color sample chips.

#20, Dragon

11

▪ Additional Corner Guard Systems

Stainless Steel Corner Guards are ideal where high abuse-resistance is required and coordination with the decor is not necessary.

Formed Surface Mount Corner Guards are an inexpensive alternative in areas where color match is important but the cushioning effect of a regular corner guard is not needed. They are extremely impact and scratch resistant, and meet Class 1/A fire code criteria when correctly applied.

Lexan® Corner Guards offer protection in areas where the wall finish needs to shine through.

	STAINLESS	VINYL	LEXAN
MATERIAL	#430 SS standard #304 SS optional	Acrylic Vinyl	Polycarbonate
THICKNESS	16 gauge	.078"	.062" or .093"
PROFILE	90° or 135°	90° or 135°	90° or 135°
SIZE	any	any size 3" or less	any
HEIGHT	10' maximum	18' maximum	8' maximum
EDGE	slight return	smooth	smooth
COLOR	natural	see chart	clear
APPLICATION	mastic	mastic, tape or drive nails	drive nails
FINISH	#4 satin	haircell	smooth

OTHER ARDEN PRODUCTS

- Entrance Flooring Systems – 12690/ARD
- Floor Access Systems – 05532/ARD

ARDEN Architectural
SPECIALTIES INC.

Arden Architectural Specialties, Inc.
1947 West County Road C-2
Saint Paul, Minnesota 55113
Toll-Free: **800.521.1826**
Tel: **612.631.1607**
Fax: **612.631.0251**

12

GLASS Blocks

WECK®

Glass Blocks

E

CAPTIVATE Them With Light

There is no more powerful design element than sparkling sunlight or evening light to make your designs soar. Capture the light and put it to work for you with WECK's glass blocks...available in the widest range of sizes, shapes and patterns.

WECK blocks combine the design flexibility that architects love, with the structural solidarity that blocklayers acknowledge as the superior option for your project. You can turn tight corners or use glass pillars, incorporate dramatic step-down walls, or end your block wall at any vertical or horizontal point you choose—with a smooth, finished edge. New WECK specialty shapes give you choices never before possible!

WECK blocks will make good designs great...great designs even better!

....Shapes

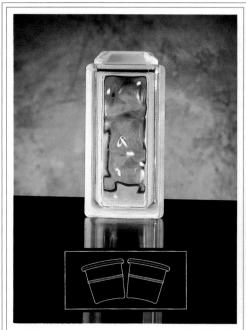

ALLBend

Smoothly curved 22 1/2° angle blocks combine to make curves and corners, or columns with as small as a 12" radius. May be used with other WECK blocks to give you the look and the angles you choose. Available in Clarity or the distorted Nubio patterns. Compared to blocks with exposed seams, AllBend installs more easily and beautifully.

K

With WECK's new Designer Shapes you can have it your way! The curves, the angles, the circular columns. The beautifully finished wall-ends, smooth corners, whatever your creativity demands for striking drama with light and structure! The most beautiful edges and corners ever known can now accent your designs. New for you from WECK's engineered superiority.

Blocks	AllBend	Outside Radius inches
1 piece 4" x 8" per	4	14.5
1 piece 4" x 8" per	2	16.7
1 piece 8" x 8" per	4	17.5
1 piece 4" x 8" per	1	21.6
1 piece 8" x 8" per	2	21.7
1 piece 8" x 8" per	1	31.9
2 pieces 4" x 8" per	1	32.5

AllBend
DoublEnd
WeckEnd
Corner Block

Specifications Thickness	Sizes	
AllBend (22 1/2°)	4"	8" high
WeckEnd	4"	8" x 8"
DoublEnd	4"	8" x 8"
Corner (90°)	4"	6" high
Corner (90°)	4"	8" high
Corner (90°)	3"	8" high

Notes:
- All dimensions nominal
- Designer Shapes available in Nubio and Clarity
- 3" thick corner also available in Nubio Goldtone

11 3/4"
AllBend
4 1/8"
3/8"
3"
3/16"
22 1/2°
3 7/8"
1/4"
8"
4 7/8"*
*3" thick version measures 4 1/8"

....Make Dark Spaces Great Places!

 D ark entries or hallways kill the spirit of your entire design. Lighten them up with sparkling WECK blocks. Paint them with glorious light, and they will become the dramatic centerpiece of the home.

For light and privacy choose the WECK Nubio to distort images. For pure light, clear vision, a temperature barrier and sound privacy, select the Clarity blocks. Or choose WECK's pattern blocks for exciting variety. With the new AllBend you can turn tight corners or use a skylit pillar. With the new WeckEnds or DoublEnds you can create dramatic planter areas, stub-walls, half-walls or any step-down configuration you choose. Their smooth, finished edges and corners are truly striking.

FIRESTOP Blocks

Setting new industry standards, WECK Firestop blocks offer new options for fire rated installations. Now both thinline and standard thickness blocks are 45 minute fire rated as protected openings in either masonry or gypsumboard walls. A labeled frame developed by Glashaus, Inc. is used for borrowed light applications in gypsumboard. For protected openings, Nubio-60, Clarity-60 or Fortress-60 blocks are 60 minute rated in either masonry or gypsumboard, and Clarity-90 is 90 minute rated in masonry.

Fire Rating	Block Thickness	Wall Type	Max Dimen	Max SqFt
45	4"	Masonry	12	120
45	3"	Masonry	10	88
45	4"	Gypsumboard	10	88
45	3"	Gypsumboard	10	88
60	4"	Masonry	10	100
60	4"	Gypsumboard	10	88
90	4"	Masonry	10	100

Tested by UL-9, a test for window assemblies.

Corner blocks, end blocks, metric blocks and 12 x 12 sizes are not fire rated.

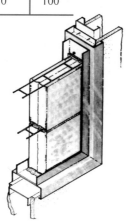

Fortress-60
Weck Firestop 60
Square Size: 8" x 8" x 3 7/8"
U.L. File R 11679-3

Clarity-90
Weck Firestop 90
Square Size: 6" x 6" x 3 7/8"
U.L. File R 11679-4

Clarity-60
Weck Firestop 60
Square Size: 8" x 8" x 3 7/8"
U.L. File R 11679-3

Nubio-60
Weck Firestop 60
Square Size: 8" x 8" x 3 7/8"
U.L. File R 11679-3

GOLDTONE Blocks

If you like the touch of soft, earthtone beauty, WECK's goldtone blocks offer you a truly distinctive option. Using no metallic elements or oxides which can discolor with time and sunlight exposure, goldtone blocks give you warmth and soft rays of golden light. Stark, contemporary designs can be muted and softened beautifully, turning cold spaces into warm and comfortable places.

GLASS BLOCK *Designs*

Nubio

Nubio Corner Block

WeckEnd

DoublEnd

AllBend

Aktis

Series	Size Nominal	Fire Rating minutes/ max. size sq. ft.	U/R Values	Light Trans- mission %	Shading Coeffi- cent	Sound Loss Decibels	Com- pressive Strength psi	Weight per block lbs	Installed Weight Per Sq. Ft.
NUBIO				**CLEAR**					
Intersecting random wave pattern, provides an attractive appearance and excellent privacy. Smooth exterior surface for easy cleaning.	**Standard and Firestop Series (3⅞" thick)**								
	4" x 8"	45/120	.48/2.08	72-74	.65	41	700	3.6	23.8
	6" x 6"	45/120	.48/2.08	72-74	.65	41	850	3.5	20.8
	8" x 8"	45/120	.48/2.08	72-74	.65	42	850	6.4	19.5
	8" x 8"	60/100	.45/2.22	57	.55	42	1000	7.7	22.7
	12" x 12"	—	.48/2.08	72-74	.63	42	850	15.3	18.7
Matching designer shapes provide beauty and flexibility to create angles, curves or finished jambs and/or heads. 45 and 60 minute fire ratings are available.	**Thinline Series (3⅛" thick)**								
	4" x 8"	45/120	.53/1.89	79	.66	41	700	2.9	18.6
	6" x 6"	45/120	.53/1.89	79	.66	40	850	3.1	17.2
	6" x 8"	45/120	.53/1.89	79	.66	41	850	4.5	17.9
	8" x 8"	45/120	.53/1.89	79	.66	41	850	5.4	15.9
	Corner (6" – 3⅞" thick) (8" – 3⅞" and 3⅛" thick)								
	6" High	—	.53/1.89	54	—	39	800	3.4	20.2
	8" High	—	.53/1.89	50	—	39	750	4.1	18.1
	WeckEnd and DoublEnd (3⅞" thick)								
	8" x 8"	—	—	70	.65	42	850	6.2	19.1
	AllBend (3⅞" thick)								
	8" High	—	.48/2.08	68	.65	41	700	3.6	23.8
				GOLDTONE					
	Standard Series (3⅞" thick)								
	8" x 8"	45/120	.48/2.08	52	.52	42	850	6.4	19.5
	Thinline Series (3⅛" thick)								
	6" x 6"	45/120	.53/1.89	52	.52	40	850	3.1	17.2
	6" x 8"	45/120	.53/1.89	52	.52	41	850	4.5	17.9
	8" x 8"	45/120	.53/1.89	52	.52	41	850	5.4	15.9
	Corner (3⅛" thick)								
	8" High	—	.53/1.89	32	.52	36	650	3.9	17.7
AKTIS				**CLEAR**					
Elegant crystalline pattern provides privacy and good light transmission, at reasonable cost. Smooth exterior surface.	**Standard Series (3⅞" thick)**								
	8" x 8"	45/120	.48/2.08	72-74	.65	42	700	6.4	19.5
	Thinline Series (3⅛" thick)								
	4" x 8"	45/120	.53/1.89	79	.66	41	700	2.9	18.6
	6" x 6"	45/120	.53/1.89	79	.66	40	850	3.1	17.2
	6" x 8"	45/120	.53/1.89	79	.66	41	850	4.5	17.9
	8" x 8"	45/120	.53/1.89	79	.66	41	850	5.4	15.9

Metric Blocks

Metric blocks are available in three distinctive patterns. Produced to metric dimensions, variable mortar joints will yield 7 3/4" or 8" rows. The blocks exterior measurements are 7 1/2" x 7 1/2" x 3 1/8".

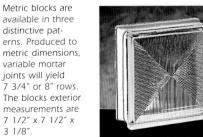

Metallic

Welle

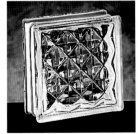

Regent

GLASS BLOCK *Designs*

Size Nominal	Fire Rating minutes/ max. size sq. ft.	U/R Values	Light Trans- mission %	Shading Coeffi- cent	Sound Loss Decibels	Com- pressive Strength psi	Weight per block lbs	Installed Weight Per Sq. Ft.	Series
CLEAR									**CLARITY**
Standard and Firestop Series (3⅞″ thick)									
4″ x 8″	45/120	.48/2.08	72-74	.65	41	700	3.6	23.8	
6″ x 6″	45/120	.48/2.08	72-74	.65	41	850	3.5	20.8	
6″ x 6″	90/100	.31/3.23	51	.53	43	3000	7.8	37.8	
8″ x 8″	45/120	.48/2.08	72-74	.65	42	850	6.4	19.5	
8″ x 8″	60/100	.45/2.22	57	.55	42	1000	7.7	22.7	
12″ x 12″	—	.48/2.08	72-74	.63	42	850	15.3	18.7	
Thinline Series (3⅛″ thick)									
4″ x 8″	45/120	.53/1.89	79	.66	41	700	2.9	18.6	
6″ x 6″	45/120	.53/1.89	79	.66	40	850	3.1	17.2	
6″ x 8″	45/120	.53/1.89	79	.66	41	850	4.5	17.9	
8″ x 8″	45/120	.53/1.89	79	.66	41	850	5.4	15.9	
Corner (6″ – 3⅞″ thick) (8″ – 3⅛″ and 3⅞″ thick)									
6″ High	—	.53/1.89	54	—	39	800	3.4	20.2	
8″ High	—	.53/1.89	50	—	39	750	4.1	18.1	
WeckEnd and DoublEnd (3⅞″ thick)									
8″ x 8″	—	—	70	.65	42	850	6.2	19.1	
AllBend (3⅞″ thick)									
8″ High	—	.48/2.08	68	.65	41	700	3.6	23.8	
GOLDTONE									
Standard Series (3⅞″ thick)									
8″ x 8″	45/120	.48/2.08	52	.52	42	850	6.4	19.5	
CLEAR									**FORTRESS**
Fire Stop Series (3⅞″ thick)									
8″ x 8″	60/100	.31/3.23	48	.54	48	2850	11.2	30.6	
CLEAR									**X-RIB**
Standard Series (3⅞″ thick)									
6″ x 6″	45/120	.48/2.08	72-74	.65	41	850	3.5	20.8	
8″ x 8″	45/120	.48/2.08	72-74	.65	42	850	6.4	19.5	
12″ x 12″	—	.48/2.08	72-74	.63	42	850	15.3	18.7	
Thinline Series (3⅛″ thick)									
8″ x 8″	45/120	.53/1.89	79	.66	41	850	5.4	15.9	
CLEAR									**SPRAY**
Standard Series (3⅞″ thick)									
8″ x 8″	45/120	.48/2.08	48-55	.41	42	850	6.4	19.5	

CLARITY

This see-through block provides a dramatic grid effect, undistorted vision, and maximum light transmission.

Matching designer shapes provide beauty and flexibility to create angles, curves or finished jambs and/or heads. 45, 60 and 90 minute fire ratings are available.

FORTRESS

Extra-heavy block; minimizes vandalism. Available with small line pattern or in Clarity.

X-RIB

Vertical ribs on one face and horizontal on the other for privacy.

SPRAY

Grid pattern offers privacy, reduces glare.

Clarity

Clarity Corner Block

Clarity WeckEnd

Fortress

X-Rib

Spray

INTRODUCING.................
BlokUp™ *Mortarless Systems*

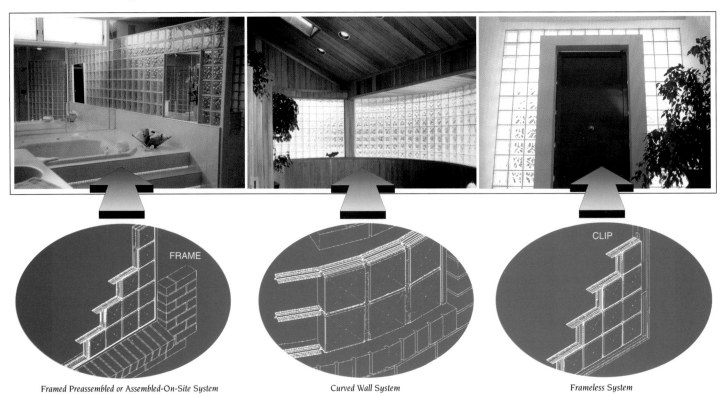

Framed Preassembled or Assembled-On-Site System

Curved Wall System

Frameless System

Metal Networks for Authentic WECK® Glass Block Walls and Windows...Save Time, Money and Labor.

Now there's a faster, easier way to enhance any project, large or small, with authentic glass block. Install genuine WECK glass blocks with any of three extruded metal BlokUp systems.

Full-frame extruded aluminum system adds strength, saves labor.

Now, WECK block windows can be preassembled off-site, like conventional windows. (Installed quickly with optional nailing fins.) Or you can construct a framed wall of blocks, on site, up to 150 sq. ft. – and still save much time and labor.

Framed curved-wall system for design versatility, increased strength, added security.

BlokUp's exclusive connectable radius sections permit any professional tradesman to create graceful curved walls of glass, indoors or out. Frame and horizontal metal sections provide added strength for additional home security. Hinged metal sections can be easily bent to fit any wall radius.

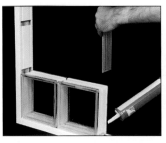

1 Glass block sealant is applied to the center seam of the vertical edge of the block. The vertical separator is inserted into the slot of the frame and against the glass block.

3 Sealant is applied to the center of the horizontal separator and on the sides of the frame, up to the next slot. Next, the first block of the second course is laid. Sealant is then applied to the vertical side of the block, and the next vertical separator is put in place.

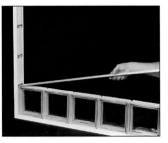

2 Sealant is next applied to the center seam of the top sidewalls of the first course. Next, the horizontal separator is laid on the blocks, extending from slot to slot at the sides. More than a spacer, the metal separator functions as a stiffener in every horizontal joint.

4 Smaller installations can be quickly erected by connecting horizontal separators with BlokUp clips.

WECK is a registered mark of J. Weck GmbH u. Co.
BlokUp is a trademark of Rawmaw Investment Pty Ltd.
TRADE MATE is a registered mark of Dow Corning Corp.

Frameless system provides clean-line walls of glass block, without aesthetic or structural compromise.

Special telescopic anchor clip permits unobstructed frameless installations without sacrificing strength or stabiltiy. System adapts to any-size opening. As with framed systems, frameless BlokUp adds the strength of horizontal metal beams.

BlokUp Advantages

- Design versatility: systems for curved, stepped or straight walls
- Ease of block assembly
- Predictable finished quality
- Faster installation
- Lower installed cost
- Mechanical connections
- Metal beams in all horizontal joints
- 3 ways weathertight: silicone inside, silicone front and rear seals
- Optional thermal break prevents energy-robbing conduction
- Optional sill drain system for automatic drainage

How to select the right BlokUp/WECK Glass Block System for your project...

Ask your dealer for a copy of the WECK Glass Block Catalog, to choose from the wide selection of high quality blocks for interior or exterior projects. Next consult the Dimensional Openings table below to determine the size and number of blocks you will need to complete your project. (Make certain that your "rough opening" is at least 1/4 inch larger [on the side and above] than the height and width of the combined blocks you select.)

Finally, consult the checklist below for options, tools and materials you will need to complete your WECK Glass Block project using BlokUp.

DIMENSIONAL WALL OPENINGS TABLE

Use this table with your predetermined exact panel dimensions (width and height) to determine the number of Weck glass blocks needed to complete your project. Follow this sequence:

(1) Select your BlokUp Installation System from one of the four column headings indicating "clip" or "frame" and block face dimension. (Also, decide both the width and the height of block you will use.)

(2) Looking down the appropriate column, find the *known width* of your panel; then, looking at the left-hand column, convert that dimension into the corresponding number of blocks you will need to lay one course of blocks.

(3) Next, looking down the appropriate column, find the *known height* of your panel; then, looking at the left-hand column, convert that dimension into the corresponding *number of courses* of blocks you will need to fill that opening.

(4) Now you can determine total blocks required by multiplying the *number of blocks* (width) by the *number of courses* (height).

(5) Finally, determine the *rough* opening by adding 1/4" to both the known height and width of the panel dimensions.

Note Wall Size Limitations: *Maximum width for BlokUp Frame System construction is 10 ft. Maximum height for Frame System is 20 ft. Maximum width for Clip System construction is 8 ft. Max. ht. for Clip System or curved wall construction is 12 ft.*

Example: When installing 4" x 8" or 6" x 8" blocks with the Clip System, use the 4" or 6" columns for one dimension and the 8" column for the other.

No. of Blocks	Frame: 8" Block	Clip: 8" Block	Clip: 6" Block	Clip: 4" Block
2	17-3/4"	15-3/4"	11-3/4"	7-3/4"
3	25-5/8"	23-5/8"	17-5/8"	11-5/8"
4	33-1/2"	31-1/2"	23-1/2"	15-1/2"
5	41-3/8"	39-3/8"	29-3/8"	19-3/8"
6	49-1/4"	47-1/4"	35-1/4"	23-1/4"
7	57-1/8"	55-1/8"	41-1/8"	27-1/8"
8	65"	63"	47"	30-7/8"
9	72-7/8"	70-7/8"	52-7/8"	34-3/4"
10	80-3/4"	78-3/4"	58-3/4"	38-5/8"
11	88-5/8"	86-5/8"	64-5/8"	42-1/2"
12	96-1/2"	94-1/2"*	70-1/2"	46-3/8"
13	104-3/8"	102-3/8"	76-3/8"	50-1/4"
14	112-1/4"	110-1/4"	82-1/4"	54-1/8"
15	120-1/8" *	118-1/8"	88"	55-7/8"
16	128"	126"	94-7/8" *	61-3/4"
17	135-7/8"	133-7/8"	99-3/4"	65-5/8"
18	143-3/4"	141-3/4"	105-5/8"	69-1/2"
19	151-5/8"	149-5/8"	111-1/2"	73-7/8"
20	159-1/2"	157-1/2"	117-3/8"	77-1/4"
21	167-3/8"	165-5/8"	123-1/4"	81-1/8"
22	175-1/4"		129-1/8"	85"
23	183-1/8"		135"	88-3/4"
24	191"		140-7/8"	92-5/8"
25	198-7/8"			96-1/2" *
26	206-3/4"			100-3/8"
27	214-5/8"			104-1/4"
28	222-1/2"			108-1/8"
29	230-3/8"			115-3/4"
30	238-1/4"			115-3/4"

* Maximum Panel Width Allowed

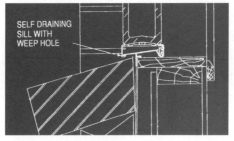

SELF DRAINING SILL WITH WEEP HOLE

Optional Integral Drain Sill
Sloped sill drain system provides automatic water drainage through weep hole in the base of the sill. Positively prevents undesirable water infiltration and potential damage.

Standard System Components

Slotted Aluminum Frame (Not shown; see photos on other side.)

Telescopic Anchor Clips (for frameless systems)

Vertical Separation Strips
"A" Strips for bottom and top courses in frame installations (slightly longer then "B" strips, so as to extend into frame slots) "B" Strips for vertical separation of middle courses in frames(or all courses in clip systems)

Horizontal Metal Separators (can be cut to full width of opening)

Radius Separators (can be linked to form curved wall sections)

Horseshoe Clips
(secure radius sections to frame at the jambs)

Optional Nailing Fin (allows framed glass blocks to be fastened directly to existing construction)

Required Glass Block Sealant
High-performance Dow Corning TRADE MATE Glass Block Sealant is the finest silicone rubber, designed specifically to connect sidewalls in glass block construction. Provides a permanent seal that resists water, air and sunlight (UV) degradation. (*Important: Do not substitute other sealant or Warranty will be void.*)

Required Paintable Glazing Sealant
Dow Corning TRADE MATE 100% White Silicone Sealant is ideal for BlokUp glass block sealing used along visible face joints. (Exception: For an all-glass look, Dow Corning TRADE MATE Glass Block Silicone Sealant may be substituted.) Provides excellent weatherability and durability. Easy to work with: makes for easy tooling with no stringing and excellent gunability. Simple clean-up. No noxious odor during curing.(*Important: Do not substitute other sealant than stated here or Warranty will be void.*)

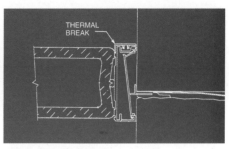

THERMAL BREAK

Thermal Break Option
Frame installations in cold climates require a thermal break frame, which includes an integral PVC vinyl extrusion. Clip-on vinyl sections prevent heat-robbing conduction between the metal and glass components.

Planning a Radius Wall
Order BlokUp connectable radius sections to construct curved wall designs using 8" WECK glass blocks. (4" and 6" sizes will be available in early 1996.)

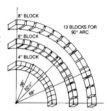

8" BLOCK 8" BLOCK 4" BLOCK
13 BLOCKS FOR 90° ARC

Tools/Supplies Checklist...
- Screwdriver
- Level
- Tape Measure
- Caulking Gun
- Electric Drill
- Empty Pail
- Closed Cell Sponge
- Optional Rivet Gun

Installation video available

Fast. Easy. Mortarless.

BLOKUP

Patents Pending PCT/AU94/00472

Glashaus Inc.
415 W. Golf Road Suite 13
Arlington Heights, Illinois 60005
708/640-6910 FAX: 708/640-6955

SPECIFICATIONS

PART 1 GENERAL

1.01 WORK INCLUDED
A. WECK GLASS BLOCKS
B. WECK GLASS BLOCKS with (45, 60 or 90) minute listed U.L. fire rating.
C. Integral joint reinforcing.
D. Miscellaneous metal anchors and/or fire rated hollow metal frames.
E. Mortars and sealants.

1.02 RELATED WORK
A. Section (_____-_____) Masonry.
B. Section (_____-_____) Lintels.
C. Section (_____-_____) Sealants.

1.03 REFERENCES
A. ASTM C153B2, Hot Dipped Zinc Coating.
B. ASTM C144, Aggregate for Masonry.
C. ASTM C150, Portland Cement.
D. ASTM C207, Hydrated Lime for Masonry.
E. ASTM C207, Mortar for Unit Masonry.
F. Underwriters Laboratories Building Materials Directory, 1992 Edition.

1.04 SUBMITTALS
A. Submit WECK Catalogue.
B. Submit _____ WECK GLASS BLOCK of each type for approval.

1.05 ENVIRONMENTAL REQUIREMENTS
A. Maintain materials and ambient air temperatures to a minimum of 40°F prior to, during and 48 hours after completion of work.
B. Protect WECK GLASS BLOCK from moisture prior to construction.

Technical drawings have been developed on disks for CAD systems.

WARRANTIES AND REMEDIES - LIMITATIONS

The products shall be free from defects relating to production for a period of 5 years after the date of purchase, but this warranty shall not extend to installation workmanship, accessory materials, or conditions of application, or the performance or results of an installation containing the product. The warranty described in this paragraph shall be IN LIEU OF any other warranty, express or implied, including but not limited to any implied warranty of MERCHANTABILITY OR FITNESS FOR A PARTICULAR PURPOSE. The buyer's sole and exclusive remedy against Glashaus Inc. and/or J. Weck GmbH u. Co. shall be for the replacement, but not installation, of defective products; Glashaus Inc. will also deliver the replacement products to the location where the defective products were originally purchased. The buyer agrees that no other remedy (including, but not limited to, incidental or consequential damages for lost profits, lost sales or injury to person or property) shall be available to the buyer, regardless of the theory of liability upon which any such damages are claimed. This warranty supersedes all prior warranties and representations regarding Weck Glass Block

PART 2 PRODUCTS

2.01 ACCEPTABLE MANUFACTURERS
A. J. WECK GmbH u. Co.

2.02 GLASS UNITS
A. _____ x _____ x _____ Inch.
B. _____ x _____ x _____ Inch with (45, 60 or 90) minute listed U.L. fire rating.
C. Color (Cleartone or Goldtone) _____
D. Pattern _____
E. Edge Coating – White latex based paint.

2.03 ACCESSORIES
A. Joint Reinforcing: Ladder type, hot dipped galvanized, 2-9 gauge parallel longitudinal wire at 2" o.c. for 3⅞" wide block or 1⅝" for 3⅛" wide block and cross rods welded at 8" o.c.
B. Panel Anchors: 20 gauge x 1¾" x 24" hot dipped galvanized steel with staggered perforations as supplied by Glass Masonry, Inc.
C. Perimeter Chase: Masonry recess, aluminum channel or steel channel.
D. Fire rated hollow metal frames as supplied by Glashaus, Inc.
E. Adjustable masonry anchors and wire ties.
F. Asphalt Emulsion: Karnac 100 or equal.
G. Expansion Strips: ⅜" x 3½" polyethylene plastic or glass fiber (for fire rating) as supplied by Glass Masonry, Inc.
H. Sealant: Silicone Type _____ Color.
I. Backer Rod: As recommended by sealant supplier.

2.04 MORTAR MATERIALS
A. Shall be prepared according to ASTM C270 for Type S Mortar. Mortar to have 1 part Portland Cement (Type 1), 1 part lime and 4½ to 6 parts of fine sand passing No. 20 sieve and free of iron compounds to avoid stains. Use white Portland Cement and silica sand for white joints. Mix mortar drier than normal and only an amount that will be used in ½ to 1 hour. Glass block will not absorb water the same as brick. Do not use retempered mortar. Do not use antifreeze compounds or accelerators.
B. Add _____ mortar color per manufacturer's instructions. Side walls of WECK GLASS BLOCK must be same color as mortar. If mortar is not white, strip paint and re-paint with colored latex paint.
C. Add Laticrete 8510 to increase waterproofing qualities of mortar.

Photo Credits:
Cover, C, D, E, H: Glass Block Warehouse, Westbury, NY
B, G: Photo: Rob McHugh, Installation: Glass Block Designs, San Francisco, CA
F, L: Orlando Sports Arena, Architect: Lloyd, Jones, Fillpot, Houston, TX Distributor: Glass Masonry Inc.
J: Photo: Terry Farmer, Springfield, IL
I, K: Distributor: Glass Block Source, Auburn, WA

PART 3 EXECUTION

3.01 PREPARATION
A. Verify that pocket recesses or chases provided under other sections are accurately located and sized.
B. Establish and protect lines, levels and coursing.

3.02 INSTALLATION
A. Arrange coursing pattern to provide consistent joint work throughout.
B. Locate and secure perimeter metal chase.
C. Coat sill under units with asphalt emulsion as a bond breaker.
D. Mortar joints must be solid. Furrowing not permitted. Neatly tool surface to a concave joint.
E. Place panel reinforcing in horizontal joint above first course of block and not more than 18" o.c. for Standard Series, every other course for Thinline Series and every course for Fire Stop Series. Panel anchors if used shall be installed in the same joints as reinforcing.
F. Isolate panel from adjacent construction on sides and top with expansion strips. Keep expansion joint voids clear of mortar.
G. Maintain uniform joint width of ¼" ± ⅛".
H. Maximum variation from plane of unit to next unit — 1/32".
I. Maximum variation of panel from plane — 1/16".
J. Do not use retempered mortar.
K. Do not tap glass block with steel tools.
L. When mortar has set, pack backer rod in jamb and head channels. Recess to allow for sealant. (Back-up for sealant at fire rated frames is mortar.)
M. Apply sealant.

3.03 CLEANING
A. Remove excess mortar from glass surfaces with a damp cloth before set occurs.
B. Number 4 steel wool can be used to remove remaining mortar.

For technical or installation information request our Design Guide.

Glass Blocks

Glashaus, Inc.
415 West Golf Road
Suite 13
Arlington Heights, IL 60005

TEL: 847/640-6910
FAX: 847/640-6955

C171
09300/AMF
Buyline 6862

American Olean Ceramic Tile

American Olean

Index

For additional information on products and services, or your closest American Olean service location call (215) 393-2828.

American Olean Ceramic Tile

All from one source

- Full line of residential glazed and unglazed floor tile with color coordinated wall tile
- Designer-styled floor/wall packages
- Easy to understand usage and application information. (See page 10 for details.)
- Good, Better, Best trade up selections

HOME COLORWAYS™

See our HOME Colorways program for color coordinations of every American Olean product, including floor and wall tile, plus plumbing fixture color recommendations.

Why choose the American Olean brand of ceramic tile for your customers?

1 American Olean is a leading name in home furnishings and has a strong, quality reputation.

2 We have rigid quality testing standards, and we refuse to sell our customers any tile that does not measure up. You should consider this fact when selecting tile suppliers... and the tile you will recommend to and install in your customers' homes. It is a reflection of you... and we take that fact very seriously.

3 As a U.S. manufacturer/marketer in business for over 70 years, you can trust that we are here and will stand behind our products. Foreign manufacturers simply cannot make the same offer or provide the level of service we can.

4 American Olean offers a full range of products - from the most popular stone look glazed floor tiles to elegant, decorated or value priced wall tiles - and all the enhancements in between. Also count on American Olean for tile for special installations like pools, patios and shower floors.

5 Whether you want to create a grand entrance or a slip resistant mudroom, we've got the tile you'll need - all from one source. Our local sales service centers stock a wide range of products - or can work with you to be sure you have what you need when you need it. You can even call in an order, and we'll have it wrapped and waiting for you to pick up. It's a one-stop shop!

6 Professional Selling Tools - No other manufacturer of ceramic tile provides the consumer-oriented sales tools that American Olean does. Based on consumer research, we've created a full range of literature and sample tools to increase visualization, support design and color coordination efforts, and help you close sales. The bottom line... we want to help your customers' visions become reality.

7 We want and will value your business. We understand your customers and can help you meet and exceed their expectations. And that's good business for you.

American Olean

The source you can trust... for all your ceramic tile needs.

Subtle Steps® II

GOOD

• 8" x 8", 12" x 12"

SS21	SS23	SS24	SS25

SS22	SS20

Designer Steps™

APPLICATION
F W C B

GOOD

• 8" x 8", 12" x 12"

DS31	DS32	DS37	DS33
DS34	DS36	DS35	DS40
DS39	DS38		

Integra™

APPLICATION
F W C B

GOOD

• 8" x 8", 12" x 12"

UP54	UP51	UP53	UP55
UP57	UP50	UP56	UP52
UP60	UP61		

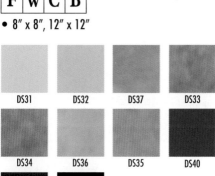

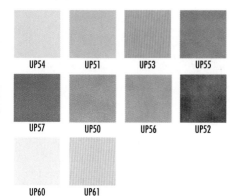

Solids/Fumés

Creekstones®

APPLICATION
F W C B

BEST

• 9" x 9"

H01	H05	H06
H03	H04	H07

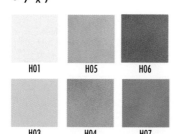

Mix & Matchables® Grandé and Pentagon Mixables

APPLICATION
F W C B

BETTER

• 10" Octagon+, 10" Pentagon*, 2-5/8" Dot

Dot Colors:

MM01	MM02	MM52
	MM07	MM16
	MM55	MM10
	MM03	MM19
	MM17	MM09

00DJ*   MM07*

00AL*   MM01+   MM02+

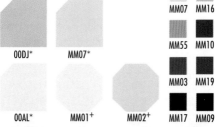

Shapes

Mix & Matchables®

APPLICATION
F W C B

BEST

• 6" Octagon, 6" Pentagon, 6" x 6", 1-3/8" Dot

Octagon/Pentagon Colors:

61	87	93

Dot Colors:

61	87	159	22	154	110	101
103	119	93	153	117	49	99

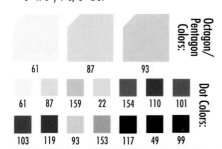

GLAZED FLOOR TILE

Subtle Steps® Stone

GOOD

APPLICATION
| F | W | C | B |

• 8" x 8", 12" x 12", 16" x 16"

 SS41
 SS42
 SS43
 SS45

 SS44

Pyrennes™

BETTER

APPLICATION
| F | W | C | B |

• 12" x 12"

 PR01
 PR02
 PR03
 PR04

Colorado™

BETTER

APPLICATION
| F | W | C | B |

• 12" x 12"

 CL01
 CL02
 CL03
 CL04

Stone Looks

Infinique™

BEST

APPLICATION
| F | W | C | B |

• 12" x 12"

 NF02   NF03

 NF01

 NF06   NF08

 NF04

NF07   NF09

 NF05

Stoneworks™

BETTER

APPLICATION
| F | W | C | B |

• 13" x 13"

 ST01
 ST02

 ST03
 ST04

 ST05

4

Porcelain Pavers

APPLICATION

F	W	C	B

• 12" x 12"

Some colors available in:
6" x 6", 6" x 12", 8" x 8",
12" x 24", 16" x 16", 24" x 24"

BEST — Terra Pavers
- W67
- TK10
- W77
- W73
- W61
- TK95
- W69
- TK93
- W64
- TK97
- TK17
- W66
- TK81
- W75
- W68
- TK14

• Polished and Unpolished

BEST — Imperial
- IG02
- IG06
- IG08
- IG07
- IG01

• Unpolished

BEST — Borgo Antico
- BA01
- BA05
- BA02
- BA06
- BA04

• Unpolished

BEST — Crystal Flame
- R104
- R107
- R102
- R106
- R105
- R108

• Polished and Unpolished

BEST — Quartz Crystal
- QC67
- QC61
- QC65
- QC68

• Polished and Unpolished

Stone Looks

Triad™ Granite

APPLICATION

F	W	C	B

• 8" x 8", 12" x 12"

BEST
- TR06
- TR02
- TR04
- TR03
- TR01
- TR33
- TR34
- TR32
- TR31
- TR22
- TR21
- TR20

Sandscapes™

APPLICATION

F	W	C	B

• 12" x 12"

BEST
- SC05
- SC10
- SC04
- SC09
- SC03
- SC08
- SC02
- SC07
- SC01
- SC06

Antiquity™

APPLICATION

F	W	C*	B

BEST

• 12" x 12", 18" x 18" x 6", 6" x 12"

- AN08
- AN09
- AN05
- AN06
- AN10
- AN11
- AN07
- AN01
- AN02
- AN03
- AN04

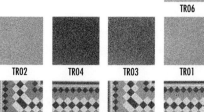
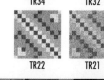

Subtle Steps® Marble

APPLICATION
F	W	C	B

GOOD

• 8″ x 8″, 12″ x 12″

SS50	SS51	SS52

Marble Looks

Triad™ Marble Look

APPLICATION
F	W	C	B

BEST

• 12″ x 12″, 16″ x 16″

TR11	TR26	TR13	TR28
TR12	TR24	TR10	TR23

TR14	TR30

Fresco

APPLICATION
F	W	C	B

BETTER

• 12″ x 12″

FR01	FR02	FR03

FR05	FR04

Overtures™

APPLICATION
F	W	C	B

BEST

• 12″ x 12″

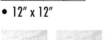

VT52	VT53	VT51	VT54

Softwinds™

APPLICATION
F	W	C	B

BETTER

• 12″ x 12″

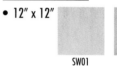

SW01	SW02	SW03

Marble 200

APPLICATION
F	W	C	B

BETTER

• 12″ x 12″

ML01	ML02	ML03

Traviata™

APPLICATION
F	W	C	B

BEST

• 12″ x 12″,
  16″ x 16″

TB01	TB02	TB03

GLAZED FLOOR TILE

6

Quarry Tile

APPLICATION
F W C B

- 6" x 6", 1-7/8" x 6",
  6" Pent., 1-7/8" Dot,
  3-7/8" x 8", 8" x 8"

(All colors not available in all sizes.)

Solids and Flashed Looks

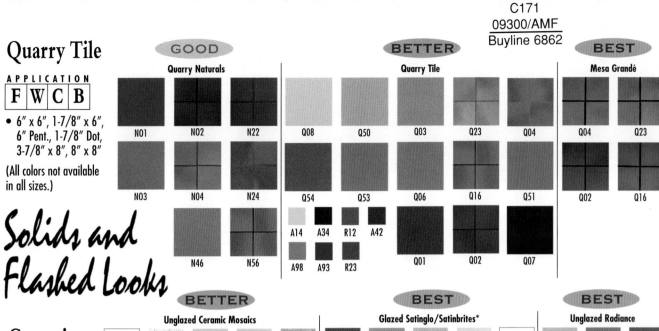

GOOD — Quarry Naturals
N01, N02, N22
N03, N04, N24
N46, N56

BETTER — Quarry Tile
Q08, Q50, Q03, Q23, Q04
Q54, Q53, Q06, Q16, Q51
A14, A34, R12, A42
A98, A93, R23
Q01, Q02, Q07

BEST — Mesa Grandé
Q04, Q23
Q02, Q16

Ceramic Mosaics

APPLICATION
F W C B

- 1" x 1", 2" x 2",
  1" Hex., 2" Hex.,
  2" Oct.

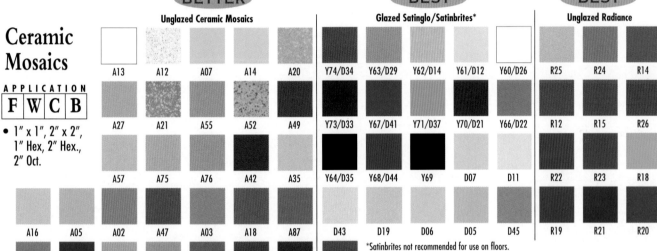

BETTER — Unglazed Ceramic Mosaics
A13, A12, A07, A14, A20
A27, A21, A55, A52, A49
A57, A75, A76, A42, A35
A16, A05, A02, A47, A03, A18, A87
A98, A93, A31, A32, A10, A19, A33
A34

BEST — Glazed Satinglo/Satinbrites*
Y74/D34, Y63/D29, Y62/D14, Y61/D12, Y60/D26
Y73/D33, Y67/D41, Y71/D37, Y70/D21, Y66/D22
Y64/D35, Y68/D44, Y69, D07, D11
D43, D19, D06, D05, D45
D46

*Satinbrites not recommended for use on floors.

BEST — Unglazed Radiance
R25, R24, R14
R12, R15, R26
R22, R23, R18
R19, R21, R20

Designer Accents®

APPLICATION
F W C B

- 4-1/4" x 4-1/4",
  4-1/4" Scored, 6" x 6"
+Only 4-1/4"

BEST
123
102, 101+, 113+, 110
103, 119, 117, 105

Decorated Accent Tiles

Personalities™

APPLICATION
F W C B

- 2" x 6"

BEST
PS01, PS02
PS03, PS04, PS05, PS06
PS07, PS08, PS09, PS10

Sizzle Strips®

APPLICATION
F W C B

- 6" x 1/2", 6" x 1",
  6" x 2", 4-1/4" x 2-1/8"

BEST
25, 13, 159, 36
22, 34, 154, 110
156, 119, 29, 103
32, 105, 117, 123
49

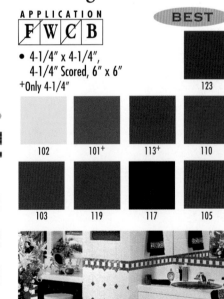

Starting Line™

| F | W | C | B |

GOOD

• 4-1/4" x 4-1/4", 6" x 6"

*SL10 SL20 *SL11 SL21
*SL12 SL22 *SL13 SL23
*SL14

* Walls only

Bright

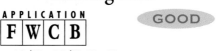

APPLICATION

| F | W | C* | B |

BETTER

• 4-1/4" x 4-1/4", 6" x 6"

25 05 48 13
45 07 46 24
18 22 20 21
43 49

Matte

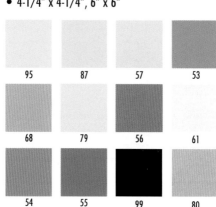

APPLICATION

| F* | W | C | B |

BETTER

• 4-1/4" x 4-1/4", 6" x 6"

95 87 57 53
68 79 56 61
54 55 99 80

Solids/Fumés

Marquee™

APPLICATION

| F | W | C* | B |

GOOD

• 6" x 8", 2" x 6"

MQ01 MQ02 MQ09

Mellowtones™

APPLICATION

| F* | W | C | B |

BETTER

• 4-1/4" x 4-1/4", 6" x 6"

J02 J04
J06 J05
J03 J01

Creekstones®

APPLICATION

| F | W | C* | B |

BEST

• 4" x 4" *Bath floors only

H01 H03
H05 H04 H06 H07

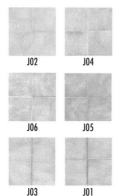

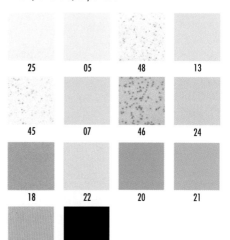

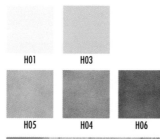

Colorado Peaks™

APPLICATION
| F | W | C* | B |

GOOD

• 6" x 8", 2-1/2" x 6"

| CP01 | CP02 | CP03 | CP09 |

Stone Looks

Softwinds™

APPLICATION
| F | W | C | B |

BETTER

• 8" x 10, 3" x 8"

| SW01 | SW02 | SW03 |

| SW04 | SW05 | SW06 |

| SW07 | SW08 | SW09 |

Traviata™

APPLICATION
| F | W | C* | B |

BEST

• 8" x 10, 2" x 8"

| TB01 | TB02 | TB03 |

| TB06 | TB07 |

| TB04 | TB05 |

Antiquity™

APPLICATION
| F* | W | C* | B |

BEST

• 4" x 4", 1" x 12"   *Bath floors only

| AN02 | AN01 | AN03 | AN04 |

| AN12 | AN13 | AN14 |

 AN15

 AN16

Marble Looks

Delancy™

APPLICATION
| F | W | C* | B |

GOOD

• 6" x 8", 2" x 6"

| DL01 | DL02 | DL03 | DL09 |

BETTER

Compri® and Compri Nouveau™

APPLICATION
| F | W | C* | B |

BEST

• 6" x 6", 2" x 6"

Compri

| 651 | 652 | 653 |

Compri Nouveau

| 656 | 657 | 658 |

| 654 | 655 |

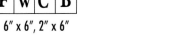
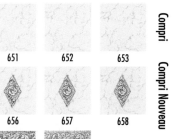

9

Crystalline®

APPLICATION

F*	W	C*	B

- 4-1/4" x 4-1/4", 4-1/4" Octagon*, 6" x 6", 1-3/8" Dot

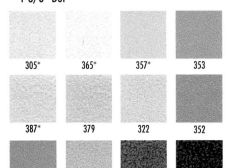

305*	365*	357*	353
387*	379	322	352
354	380*	345*	362

Tuscany®

APPLICATION

F	W	C	B

- 4-1/4" x 4-1/4", 6" x 6"
+4-1/4" only

965	935	912	907
909	911	916+	914

Textured Looks

Damask™

APPLICATION

F	W	C	B

- 8" x 10", 8" x 2-7/16"

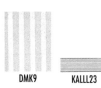

DMK9   KALLL23

Page Tabs
Indicates main usage applications.

∎∎∎∎∎∎∎ FLOOR TILE ∎∎∎∎∎∎∎

∎∎∎∎∎∎∎ WALL TILE ∎∎∎∎∎∎∎

∎∎ BATH FLOOR & WALL TILE ∎∎

Product Usage Bar
Represents general usage categories for each product line.

F	W	C	B

F = Floor   C = Countertop
W = Wall   B = Backsplash

For products with a ★, check details on special care or maintenance considerations in complete American Olean product literature.

Relative Pricing
Good, Better, Best ovals indicate relative pricing between products.

GOOD   BETTER   BEST

10

Ceramic tile helps you create extraordinary interiors!

Design Packages

Coordinating floor and wall tile packages that create unique, memorable rooms, adding value and enhancing design.

Matte/Bright Package

BETTER

- 6" or 4-1/4" Glazed Floor Tile (Matte)
- 6" or 4-1/4" Glazed Wall Tile (Bright)

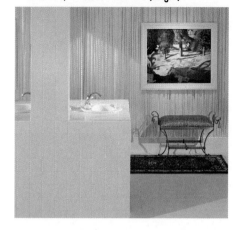

Crystalline/Bright Package

BETTER

- 6" x 6" Glazed Floor Tile (Crystalline)
- 6" x 6" Glazed Wall Tile (Bright)
- 6" x 1" Accent Strips (Sizzle Strips)

Softwinds Package

BETTER

- 12" x 12" Glazed Floor Tile
- 8" x 10" Glazed Wall Tile with Accent Wall Tile and Accent Strips

Mix & Matchables/ Bright Package

BEST   BETTER

- 6" Octagon Glazed Floor Tile (Mix & Matchables)
- 6" x 6" Glazed Wall Tile (Bright)
- 6" x 6" Glazed Wall Accent Tile (Designer Accents)
- 6" x 1" Accent Strips (Sizzle Strips)

Antiquity Package

BEST

- 12" x 12" Glazed Floor Tile and 12" x 12" Decorative Feature Floor Tile
- 4" x 4" Glazed Wall Tile
- 4" x 4" Decorative Wall Tile
- 1-5/16" x 12" Decorative Wall Tile Border

Creekstones Package

BEST

- 9" x 9" Glazed Floor Tile
- 4" x 4" Glazed Wall Tile

Overtures Package

BEST

- 12" x 12" Glazed Floor Tile
- 8" x 10" Glazed Wall Tile with Accent Wall Tile and Accent Strips

Traviata Package

BEST

- 12" x 12" Glazed Floor Tile
- 8" x 10" Glazed Wall Tile with Accent Wall Tile and Accent Strips

For additional information on products and services, call (215) 393-2828.

ON THE COVER:
Walls and Tub Surround: 8" x 10" Traviata, TB01 Pebble
Beige and TB06 Pebble Beige Accent Tile with 2" x 8" TB04
Pebble Beige Accent Strip
Floor: 12" x 12" Traviata, TB01 Pebble Beige

American Olean

Dallas, TX 75217

B1240 ©1996 American Olean Tile Co. Printed in the USA

products 1996

C173
09300/DAN
BuyLine 7585

daltile™

contents

timeless.

durable.

stylish.

vivid.

daltile is...

natural.

tasteful.

floortile

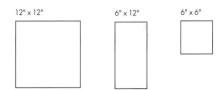

12" x 12" 6" x 12" 6" x 6"

frenchquarter™

If you're looking for the beauty of antique slate combined with the performance of ceramic tile, you'll want to come to French Quarter. Color variation and a unique slate-textured surface give this tile a natural look that brings the character and timelessness of New Orleans' French Quarter into any interior setting.

Application Recommended for commercial and residential use, on interior and exterior walls and heavy-duty interior floors.

Sizes 12" x 12", 6" x 12" and 6" x 6" sizes are 5/16" thick. See illustrations above.

Trim No trim is currently available for this line.

Test Results See below and page 43 for further information. ♿ Complies with A.D.A. recommendations for accessible routes. Manufactured in accordance with ANSI A-137.1 standards.

Wear Rating	4+
Wet-Dry C.O.F.	.060-.080
Glaze Hardness	9

Cobblestone 3114

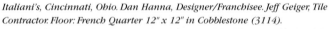
Italiani's, Cincinnati, Ohio. Dan Hanna, Designer/Franchisee. Jeff Geiger, Tile Contractor. Floor: French Quarter 12" x 12" in Cobblestone (3114).

Bourbon Street 3117

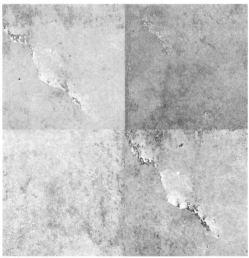
Mardi Gras 3103

12" x 12"   6" x 12"   6" x 6"

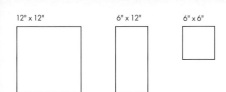

goldrush™

This rustic ceramic tile has a unique textured surface and rough-hewn appeal reminiscent of California's Gold Rush days. And this rough and tough tile is durable enough to keep looking great, year after year. In five contemporary color options and three sizes, Gold Rush can be mixed and matched to create striking designs and patterns on floors and walls.

Application Recommended for all commercial and residential floors, walls and countertops. Not recommended for areas subject to water or grease accumulation.

Sizes 12" x 12", 6" x 12" and 6" x 6" sizes are 5/16" thick. See illustrations above.

Trim Consult your Daltile representative for available trim.

Test Results See below and page 43 for further information.

♿ Complies with A.D.A. recommendations for accessible routes. Manufactured in accordance with ANSI A-137.1 standards.

Wear Rating	4+
Wet-Dry C.O.F.	.060-.080
Glaze Hardness	8.5

Texas Land and Cattle Company Steak House, Dallas, Texas. Susan Stipeck, Designer. Texas Tile and Stone, Tile Contractor. Floor and wall: Gold Rush Fargo Gray (5201).

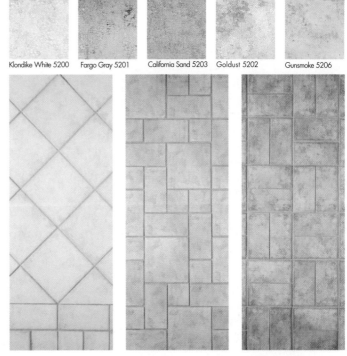

Klondike White 5200   Fargo Gray 5201   California Sand 5203   Goldust 5202   Gunsmoke 5206

Klondike White 5200   Goldust 5202   California Sand 5203

rustic.

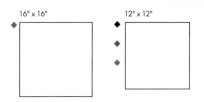

16" x 16"   12" x 12"

southwest

Now you can bring the glorious outdoor look inside with Southwest tile. The natural distressed earth tones and textures of these glazed, matte-finished pavers meet today's demand for a more naturalistic tile product. And since they're durable and easy to clean, these tiles are perfect for casual interiors.

Application Suitable for commercial and residential interior floors, walls, countertops and ceilings. Not recommended for areas subject to water or grease accumulation.

Size 12" x 12" size is 5/16" thick with cushioned edges. See illustration above.

Trim No trim is currently available for this line.

Test Results See below and page 43 for further information.

Wear Rating	4+
Wet-Dry C.O.F.	.060-.080
Glaze Hardness	8.5

Tempe 5704   Taos 5702   Pueblo 5701   Santa Fe 5703

wyoming™

The natural color and texture of these glazed ceramic pavers bring the rustic beauty of the American West inside. In addition to providing good slip, wear and stain resistance, these pavers come in a carefully-chosen color palette that will meet most any design requirement.

Application Suitable for residential and light commercial flooring applications. Not recommended for exterior use or areas subject to water or grease accumulation.

Size 12" x 12" size is 5/16" thick with cushioned edges. See illustration above.

Trim No trim is currently available for this line.

Test Results See below and page 43 for further information.

Wear Rating	4
Wet-Dry C.O.F.	0.50-0.80
Glaze Hardness	7-8

Sundance Beige 40   Casper Gray 41   Rock Springs Red 42   Green River 43

stone

In rich, natural colors and textures, this glazed ceramic tile has the romantic feel and appearance of French limestone. Use it to enrich all of your interior designs.

Application Suitable for interior floors, walls and countertops. Not recommended for areas subject to water or grease accumulation.

Sizes 16" x 16" and 12" x 12" sizes are 5/16" thick with cushioned edges. See illustrations above.

Trim No trim is currently available for this line.

Test Results See below and page 43 for further information.

Wear Rating	3
Wet-Dry C.O.F.	0.40-0.60
Glaze Hardness	5.5

Chalk Stone 5401   Coral Stone 5408

All glazed floor tile shown is manufactured in accordance with ANSI A-137.1 standards.

13" x 13"

vulcano

With a delicate gloss vein and granular texture, Vulcano marble floor tile erupts with natural beauty. Use this crystallized glazed paver wherever you want to add distinctive appeal. Vulcano boasts a PEI of three to four and carries a ten-year manufacturer's warranty.

Application Recommended for commercial and residential walls, floors, countertops and ceilings. Not recommended for exterior use or areas subject to water or grease accumulation.

Size 13" x 13" size is 5/16" thick with cushioned edges. See illustration above.

Trim No trim is currently available for this line.

Test Results See below and page 43 for further information.

Wear Rating	3-4
Wet-Dry C.O.F.	0.40-0.80
Glaze Hardness	7

St. Helen 51   Pinatubo 52   Poas 55   Aso 56

Etna 54   Kilauea 53

9

glazed floor tile

greatlakes

This versatile ceramic floor tile has the look and durability of natural stone. Choose from five shades that capture the open spirit of the Great Lakes. Thanks to high abrasion resistance, these pavers promise to keep their simple beauty through the years.

Application Recommended for interior floors, walls and countertops in residential and commercial areas. Not recommended for exterior use or areas subject to water or grease accumulation.

Size 13" x 13" size is 5/16" thick with cushioned edges. See illustration above.

Trim No trim is currently available for this line.

Test Results See below and page 43 for further information.

♿ Complies with A.D.A. recommendations for accessible routes.

Wear Rating	4
Wet-Dry C.O.F.	0.60-0.80
Glaze Hardness	5

All glazed floor tile shown is manufactured in accordance with ANSI A-137.1 standards.

Huron White 70   Michigan Almond 71   Erie Gray 72   Superior Taupe 73

Ontario Green 74

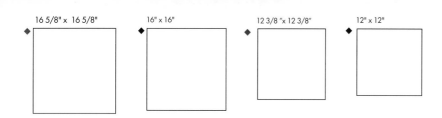

16 5/8" x 16 5/8" 16" x 16" 12 3/8 "x 12 3/8" 12" x 12"

◆ mission
◆ lithos

mission

This sophisticated tile captures the beauty of authentic saltillo. And with a durable, stain- and wear-resistant glaze that needs no sealing or waxing, you can be sure Mission tiles will keep their natural good looks for years to come.

Application Suitable for commercial and residential floors, walls and countertops. Not recommended for exterior use or areas subject to water or grease accumulation.

Sizes 16" x 16" and 12" x 12" sizes are 5/16" thick with cushioned edges. See illustrations above.

Trim No trim is currently available for this line.

Test Results See below and page 43 for further information.

Wear Rating	2
Wet-Dry C.O.F.	0.50-0.80
Glaze Hardness	4.6

Sand Beige 90   Blush Pink 92   Pink Salmon 93   Mist Green 96

Salmon 91

lithos

Lithos lets you bring the look of antique, weathered marble into your designs — at an affordable price. Combining the convenience and easy maintenance of ceramic tile with the look and feel of antique stone, this glazed ceramic paver is appropriate for even the most sophisticated interior settings. It also provides good slip, wear and stain resistance.

Application Recommended for most residential flooring applications. Not recommended for exterior use or areas subject to water or grease accumulation.

Sizes 16 5/8" x 16 5/8" and 12 3/8" x 12 3/8" sizes are 5/16" thick. See illustrations above. Listellos and Taco accents are also available.

Note Beige and Blanco are offered in 12 3/8" x 12 3/8" only, Gris in 16 5/8" x 16 5/8" only.

Trim No trim is currently available for this line.

Test Results See below and page 43 for further information.

Wear Rating	4
Wet-Dry C.O.F.	0.50-0.80
Glaze Hardness	7

Rosso   Verde   Beige   Blanco

Gris   Verde Listello 724112   Rosso Listello 724111   Verde Taco 724110

Rosso Taco 724109

All glazed floor tile shown is manufactured in accordance with ANSI A-137.1 standards.

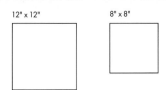

12" x 12"   8" x 8"

vitrestone

These rugged glazed pavers lend a natural, granite look to floors. That's fitting, since they also have the strength of stone — these naturally slip-resistant pavers pass the test of time with flying colors.

Application Recommended for commercial and residential floors, walls, countertops and exterior cladding. Not recommended for floors subject to water or grease accumulation.

Sizes 12" x 12" and 8" x 8" sizes are 5/16" thick with cushioned edges. See illustrations above.

Trim See page 15.

Test Results See below and page 43 for further information.

* When ordered with abrasive content, noted colors will comply with A.D.A. recommendations for accessible routes. Available in 8" x 8" size.

Manufactured in accordance with ANSI A-137.1 standards.

Wear Rating	3-4*
Wet-Dry C.O.F.	0.50-0.80**
Glaze Hardness	7.5

*colors 1914, 1918 rate 2
**"ABR" Finish tests 0.60+ Wet

Greystone 1917*   Rose Nugget 1901   Bluestone 1918*   Buffstone 1919

Ash Rose 1904*   Pink Granite 1920   Gray Granite 1921*   Black 1911*

Cordovan 1905*   Green Granite 1922   Agate 1914*   White Granite 1910*

McDonald's, Plainview, New York. Floor: Vitrestone Series 12" x 12" White Granite (1910) and 8" x 8" Black (1911).

practical.

12" x 12"   8" x 8"

sierra/desert

If you're looking for a tile that's as eye-catching as it is durable, try Sierra/Desert series. Subtle tone variation in these single-fired pavers produces a striking visual effect in area installations. Sierra has a soft matte glaze; the Desert series features an abrasive surface for extra slip resistance.

Application Recommended for commercial and residential floors, walls, countertops and exterior cladding. Not recommended for floors subject to water or grease accumulation.

Sizes 12" x 12" and 8" x 8" sizes are 5/16" thick with cushioned edges. See illustrations above.

Trim See page 15.

Test Results See below and page 43 for further information.

Wear Rating	3-4
Wet-Dry C.O.F.	0.50-0.80
Glaze Hardness	7

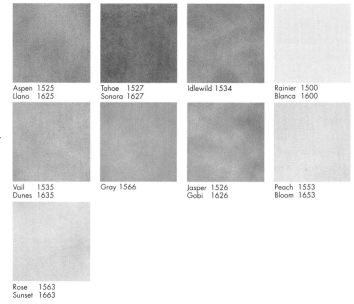

Aspen 1525
Llano 1625

Tahoe 1527
Sonora 1627

Idlewild 1534

Rainier 1500
Blanca 1600

Vail 1535
Dunes 1635

Gray 1566

Jasper 1526
Gobi 1626

Peach 1553
Bloom 1653

Rose 1563
Sunset 1663

mesa

An undulating surface and mottled coloration give this ceramic cobblestone tile an appealing, earthy look. Its permanently-fused, satin-matte glaze creates a flashed effect that actually disguises dirt.

Application Recommended for light-use commercial and residential floors, walls and countertops. Not recommended for exterior use or for areas subject to water or grease accumulation.

Size 8" x 8" size is 5/16" thick with rounded edges. See illustration above.

Trim See page 15.

Test Results See below and page 43 for further information.

Wear Rating	2-3
Wet-Dry C.O.F.	0.40-0.60
Glaze Hardness	6.5-8

All glazed floor tile shown is manufactured in accordance with ANSI A-137.1 standards.

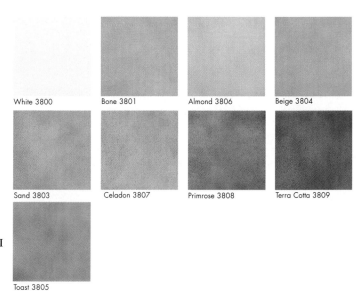

White 3800

Bone 3801

Almond 3806

Beige 3804

Sand 3803

Celadon 3807

Primrose 3808

Terra Cotta 3809

Toast 3805

12" x 12"   8" x 8"

◆ designer
◆ pastelle

designer

The rich, high-fashion hues and smooth, monochromatic glaze of these vitreous pavers give floors an unforgettable look. Most colors also match Kohler® plumbing fixtures as part of the Kohler Coordinates® program.

Application Recommended for commercial and residential floors, walls, countertops and exterior cladding. Not recommended for floors subject to water or grease accumulation.

Sizes 12" x 12" and 8" x 8" sizes are 5/16" thick with cushioned edges. See illustrations above.

Trim See page 15.

Test Results See below and page 43 for further information.

†Kohler colors shown complement Kohler plumbing fixtures as part of the Kohler Coordinates program.

* When ordered with abrasive content, noted colors will comply with A.D.A. recommendations for accessible routes. Available in 8" x 8" size.

Wear Rating	3-4*
Wet-Dry C.O.F.	0.50-0.80**
Glaze Hardness	6.5-7.5

*colors 2011, 2062, 2112, 2089 rate 1
**"ABR" Finish tests 0.60+ Wet

Biscuit 2075 †   Chamois™ 2080 †   Timberline™ 2112 †   Wild Rose™ 2088 †

Black 2011 †*   Almond 2009 †*   Tender™ Grey 2067 †   Creme 2027

Teal 2062 †   Navy 2089 †   Burgundy 2091 †   Desert Bloom™ 2053 †

Innocent Blush™ 2063 †

pastelle

This slate-textured floor tile creates a high-fashion look in rich, creamy solid colors. Its semi-gloss surface keeps Pastelle looking bright and new with minimal maintenance.

Application This tile is well-suited for light-use commercial and residential floors. Not recommended for use in areas subject to water or grease accumulation.

Size 12" x 12" size is 5/16" thick with cushioned edges. See illustration above.

Trim No trim is currently available for this line.

Test Results See below and page 43 for further information.

Wear Rating	3-4
Wet-Dry C.O.F.	0.40-0.80
Glaze Hardness	6.5

All glazed floor tile shown is manufactured in accordance with ANSI A-137.1 standards.

Cloud White 7261   Sand Dune 7262

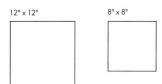

12" x 12"   8" x 8"

premier

This finely-textured, matte-glazed, vitreous paver has a look that works in virtually every design scheme. Aside from being scratch- and stain-resistant, Premier tile comes in an appealing selection of nine colors. And an extra-durable glaze, with a four-plus wear rating and a MOH's Scale hardness of eight to nine, makes it possible for us to offer a 15-year limited warranty with this tile.

Application Recommended for all high-traffic commercial floors, as well as residental floors, walls and countertops. Not recommended for floors subject to water or grease accumulation.

Sizes 12" x 12" and 8" x 8" sizes are 5/16" thick with cushioned edges. See illustrations above.

Trim See page 15.

Test Results See below and page 43 for further information.

* When ordered with abrasive content, noted colors will comply with A.D.A. recommendations for accessible routes. Available in 8" x 8" size.

Manufactured in accordance with ANSI A-137.1 standards.

Wear Rating	4+
Wet-Dry C.O.F.	0.50-0.70**
Glaze Hardness	9

***"ABR" Finish tests 0.60+ Wet

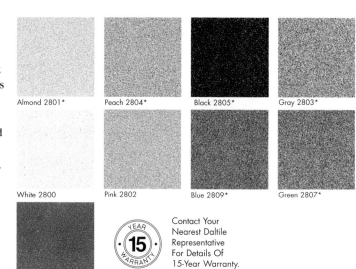

Almond 2801*   Peach 2804*   Black 2805*   Gray 2803*

White 2800   Pink 2802   Blue 2809*   Green 2807*

Rust 2808*

15 YEAR WARRANTY

Contact Your Nearest Daltile Representative For Details Of 15-Year Warranty.

◀ *McDonald's, Winnie, Texas. Jerry Kachel Builder, General Contractor. Cathie Ellis, J.B.I., Inc., Designers. Sonny Goode Tile Company, Tile Contractor. Floor: Premier Series 8" x 8" Gray Abrasive (2803) and Black Abrasive (2805) checkerboard.*

brillian

glazed floor tile trim shapes

Available Trim

Type	Number	Size	Desert	Sierra	Vitrestone	Designer	Premier	Mesa
Bullnose	*(for thinsetting bed installations)*							
	P-4889	8x8	•	•	•	•	•	•
	P-4129	12x12	•	•	•	•	•	
Thin Lip Bases	*(square top)*							
	P-3481	4H x 8L		•	•	•		
Thin Lip Bases	*(round top)*							
	P-3689	6H x 8L		•	•	•	•	
Beads								
	P-108	3/4 H x 8L		•	•	•		

Trim for other lines of floor tile is also available. Contact your Daltile representative for more information.

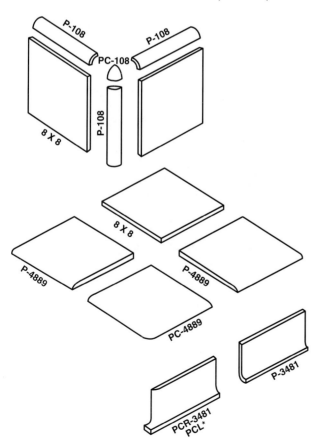

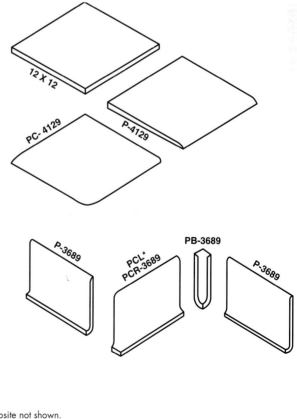

* Opposite not shown.

cultura™

This rustic, textured porcelain paver has the beauty and permanence of natural stone. In addition to resisting slip, wear, stains, and freeze/thaw cycles, Cultura features a subtly-detailed color-through body which ensures year after year of outstanding performance.

Application Recommended for commercial and residential floors, walls, countertops and exterior walls and floors.

Size 11 5/8" x 11 5/8" size is 5/16" thick with cushioned edges. See illustration above.

Trim No trim is currently available for this line.

Test Results See below and page 43 for further information.

♿ Complies with A.D.A. recommendations for accessible routes.

Slate 616

Leather 633

Copper 636

Rouge 634

Silver 631

Wear Rating	4+
Wet-Dry C.O.F.	.060-.080
Glaze Hardness	Impervious

quarry

State-of-the-art is how we describe our flawless Quarry tile. Mixed from the finest clays and raw materials available and manufactured under the strictest quality standards, Quarry is a vitreous, color-through tile that resists fading, staining and the effects of freezing. Contact your Daltile representative for current Quarry tile color and size availability.

Trim Consult your Daltile representative for available trim.

♿ Complies with A.D.A. recommendations for accessible routes.

All tile shown is manufactured in accordance with ANSI A-137.1 standards.

Sewell Lexus Dealership, Dallas, Texas. Wilson and Associates, Designer. Bussie-Dalworth Tile Company, Tile Contractor. J.R. Crownrich and Associates, General Contractor. Floor: Quarry.

6" x 6"   2 1/16" x 2 1/16"

◆ pavers/suretread
◆ det. warning

pavers and suretread

When it comes to safety, you can't beat Pavers. Even the most treacherous wet and greasy floor areas are no match for them. And with a vitreous body, our unglazed Pavers are more than just slip-resistant; they're durable. Choose from smooth surface or our raised Suretread for extra traction.

Application Recommended for commercial or industrial applications, such as kitchens, factories or any other area requiring added pedestrian safety.

Size 6" x 6" size is 3/8" thick. See illustration above.

Test Results See below and page 43 for further information.

Note Wide shade variation is characteristic of this product.

♿ Suretread surface also complies with A.D.A. recommendations for ramp access.

Red Suretread   Gray Suretread   Red Paver (Smooth Surface)   Gray Paver (Smooth Surface)

17

unglazed floor tile

Wear Rating	4+
Wet-Dry C.O.F.	.060-.080
Glaze Hardness	Vitreous

Suretread has a Wet C.O.F. of 0.80+.

detectable warning tile

Our Detectable Warning Tile complies with the requirements of The Americans with Disabilities Act Public Law 101-336. As a provision of the law, it is made in Daffodil (DK-310), Ebony (DK-311) and White (DK-317) to provide the safety of contrast with adjacent surfaces. Available in 2 1/16" x 2 1/16" size only.

♿ Complies with A.D.A. recommendations for visually-impaired.

Daffodil DK-310   Ebony DK-311   White DK-317

All tile shown is manufactured in accordance with ANSI A-137.1 standards.

durable.

12" x 12"

◆

granite

Formed by volcanic action, this igneous rock bursts with distinction. Flecks of quartz, feldspar and mica give Granite its own special character. Choose from polished, honed or flamed surfaces for an individual look.

Application Recommended for interior and exterior walls and heavy-duty interior floors. Polished finish not recommended for exterior or interior floors subject to water or grease accumulation.

Sizes 12" x 12" x 3/8" with slightly eased edges is stocked (see illustration above). Other sizes from 6" x 6" to 24" x 24", and custom shapes, are available by special order.

Notes Polished finish stocked in nine colors at selected locations. A wide variety of colors ranging from typical gray to blues, browns, blacks and reds are available by special order. Natural stone varies in pattern and tone from shipment to shipment and from tile to tile within a shipment.

Cambrian Black   Blue Pearl   Mahogany   Rosa Porrino

Balmoral Red   Autumn Brown   Stanstead Gray   Absolute Black

Caledonia

slate

This fine-grained metamorphic rock radiates a subtle, natural beauty. Slate also resists fading, abrasion and chemicals and is freeze/thaw stable, so it will look as beautiful as new for all its long life.

Application Suitable for both interior and exterior floor, wall and specialty uses, e.g., stairtreads, tabletops and cladding. Not recommended for floors subject to water or grease accumulation.

Sizes 12" x 12" x 1/4" gauged for thinset installation (see illustration above). Special-order sizes range from 6" x 6" to 24" x 24" with greater thickness and smooth sawed edges.

For more complete information, contact your nearest Daltile representative and ask for a copy of our *Stone Classics* catalog.

♿ Complies with A.D.A. recommendations for accessible routes.

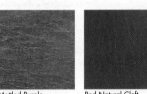
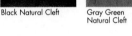

Mottled Purple Natural Cleft   Red Natural Cleft   Black Natural Cleft   Gray Green Natural Cleft

◀ *The Morikami Museum and Japanese Gardens, Delray Beach, Florida. Baretta & Associates, Architect. D.I.C. Commercial Construction Corporation, Builder/Developer. Progressive Tile & Marble, Tile Contractor. Lobby Floor: Slate Black Natural Cleft in random pattern.*

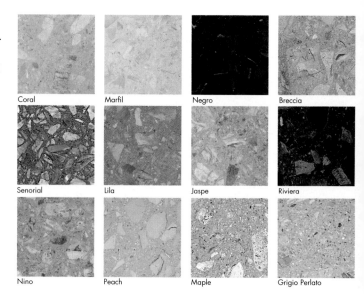

Coral   Marfil   Negro   Breccia

Senorial   Lila   Jaspe   Riviera

Nino   Peach   Maple   Grigio Perlato

marmitec

Marmitec has true personality with its artistic, marbleized effect. Because it is impervious (water absorption 0.2%), it is also practical. Natural marble stones, bonded with polyester resins (95% marble, 5% resin), create this unique product, available in stocked polished finish and special-order honed finish.

Application Suitable for interior commercial and residential floors, walls and vanities. Not recommended for exterior walls or floors subject to exposure to sunlight, water or grease accumulation.

Size 12" x 12" size is 3/8" thick. See illustration above.

Notes Variation in shade and veining is characteristic of natural stones within this product. Customer approval of order prior to installation is recommended. Darker colors tend to show visible abrasion in heavy traffic use. Polished finish can be slippery when wet–use caution in heavy traffic areas.

Additional colors available by special order.

Keystone at the Crossings Mall, Indianapolis, Indiana. P.R. Duke & Associates, General Contractor. Santarossa Mosaic & Tile, Tile Contractor. Mall Floor: Marmitec 12" x 12" in Marfil, Jaspe and Senorial.

12" x 12"

marble, travertine

Gathered from around the world, our quarried natural Marble and Travertine have the elegance and beauty of faraway places. And these timeless stone classics can make any of your interior spaces just as exquisite. Choose from a myriad of colors, in polished or satin-honed finish.

Application Suitable for interior walls, moderate-duty floors and exterior cladding in non-freeze/thaw areas. Not recommended for areas subject to water or grease accumulation.

Sizes 12" x 12" x 3/8" with eased edges is stocked (see illustration above). Other sizes from 6" x 6" to custom vanity top and dimensional stone sizes are available by special order.

Notes Marble varies in hardness, veining, color and finish, and shipments may vary from material shown on sample boards or showroom displays. For this reason, we recommend that the designer check material before installation. For more complete information, contact your nearest Daltile representative and ask for a copy of our *Stone Classics* catalog.

Test information concerning ASTM C241 is available upon request.

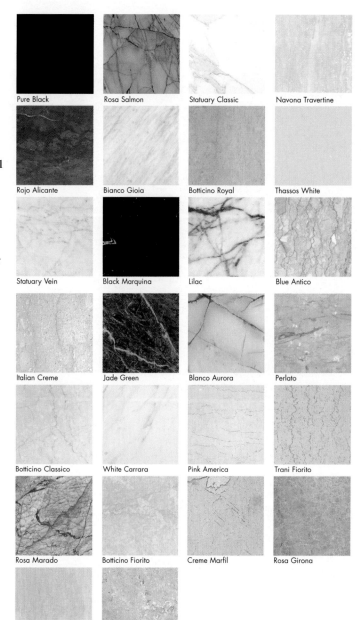

Pure Black — Rosa Salmon — Statuary Classic — Navona Travertine

Rojo Alicante — Bianco Gioia — Botticino Royal — Thassos White

Statuary Vein — Black Marquina — Lilac — Blue Antico

Italian Creme — Jade Green — Blanco Aurora — Perlato

Botticino Classico — White Carrara — Pink America — Trani Fiorito

Rosa Marado — Botticino Fiorito — Creme Marfil — Rosa Girona

Roman Classic Travertine — Cross-Cut Mexican Travertine

elegant.

wall*tile*

mosaictile

hand-painted murals

Mural art can turn any wall into a masterpiece. Watch basic tile transform when your own artwork or graphics are fired on with hand-painted ceramic glazes. Mural sizes can range up to large-scale architectural treatments, depending on your need. Tiles are shipped in cartons with a numerical setting guide, ready for standard installation. For more detailed information, request our *Ceramic Murals* catalog, showing a variety of styles and subjects.

Application Panels may be mounted permanently to interior walls or hung as panels in weather-protected areas.

Sizes Vary according to design and architectural area requirements.

Quotation Quotations are offered on an individual basis depending on original art development, size and complexity of design. Contact your nearest Daltile representative for further details. Daltile has the resources to offer fine architectural art in a variety of styles and ceramic material media. We welcome your inquiry.

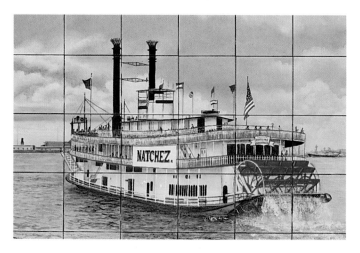

creative.

vating.

wall tile trim shapes

Available Trims

Type	Number	Size	Semi-Gloss	Matte	Crystaltex
Bullnose	*(for conventional mortar installation)*				
	A-3602	6H x 6L	• ◆	•	•
	A-4200	2H x 6L	•	•	•
	A-4402	4 1/4H x 4 1/4L	•	•	•
Bullnose	*(for thinset bed installations)*				
	S-2669	2H x 6L	•	•	•
	S-4449	4 1/4H x 4 1/4L	•	•	•
	S-4669	6H x 6L	•	•	•
Coves	*(for conventional mortar installation)*				
	A-3401	4 1/4H x 4 1/4L	•	•	
	A-3461	4 1/4H x 6L	• ◆	•	•
	A-3601	6H x 6L	• ◆	•	•
	surface-type cove angles (SCR-L) are available for thinset installation for D-1467 only.				
Sanitary Cove Base	*(round top)*				
	S-3419T	4 1/4H x 6L	•	•	•
	S-3401T	4 1/4H x 4 1/4L	•	•	•
	S-3619T	6H x 6L	• ◆	•	•
Beads					
	A-106	3/4H x 6L			

Type	Number	Size	Semi-Gloss	Matte	Crystaltex
Scored Tile Bullnose	*(for conventional mortar installation)*				
	A-4402D	4 1/4H x 4 1/4L	•		
Scored Tile Bullnose	*(for thinset bed installations)*				
	S-4449D	4 1/4H x 4 1/4L	•		
Scored Tile Cove	*(for conventional mortar installation)*				
	A-3401D	4 1/4H x 4 1/4L	•		
Curb Tile					
	A-7250*	2 1/2H x 6L	•	•	
	A-7350*	3 1/2H x 6L	•	•	
Counter Trim	*(for conventional mortar installation)*				
	A-8242*	2 1/2H x 2 1/8D x 4 1/4L		•	
	A-8262	2 1/2H x 2 1/8D x 6L	•	•	•

◆ Not available in colors DM-1, DM-7.

Surface Trim
4 1/4" x 4 1/4" typical installation

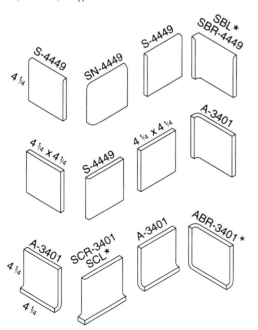

Conventional Trim
4 1/4" x 4 1/4" typical installation

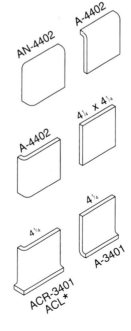

capt

* Opposite not shown. Available only in D-1467.

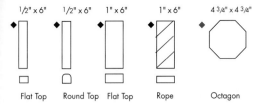

1/2" x 6"	1/2" x 6"	1" x 6"	1" x 6"	4 3/4" x 4 3/4"
Flat Top	Round Top	Flat Top	Rope	Octagon

octagon

Genuine ceramic-body tile in an octagon shape lets you create exciting designs. Octagon is available in a variety of colors and in Matte and Crystaltex finishes for an unconventional look with modern flair.

Application Recommended for commercial and residential walls and countertops. Crystaltex (1200 series) colors are also suitable for light commercial and residential floors. Not recommended for areas subject to water or grease accumulation.

Size 4 3/4" x 4 3/4" octagon is 5/16" thick with cushioned edges. See illustration above. 2" x 2" accent dot is 5/16" thick with cushioned edges.

Trim Consult your Daltile representative for available trim.

† Kohler colors shown complement Kohler plumbing fixtures as part of the Kohler Coordinates program.

KOHLER
COORDINATES

■ octagon colors
■ dot colors

Arctic White D-790 ■	Almond K-765 † ■	Arctic White D-1290 ■	Almond K-1265 † ■
White 6501 ■	Sable 6521 ■	Navy K-789 † ■	Teal K-762 † ■
Timberline™ K-711 † ■	Almond 6565 ■	Cypress D-752 ■	Burgundy D-799 ■

liners

Accent your tile designs with our full selection of liner tile. Available in a wide variety of colors and textures, liners are ideal for adding the finishing touch.

Sizes Liners are available in 1/2" x 6" Flat Top, 1/2" x 6" Round Top, 1" x 6" Flat Top and 1" x 6" Rope. See illustrations above.

† Kohler colors shown complement Kohler plumbing fixtures as part of the Kohler Coordinates program.

KOHLER
COORDINATES

All wall tile shown is manufactured in accordance with ANSI A-137.1 standards.

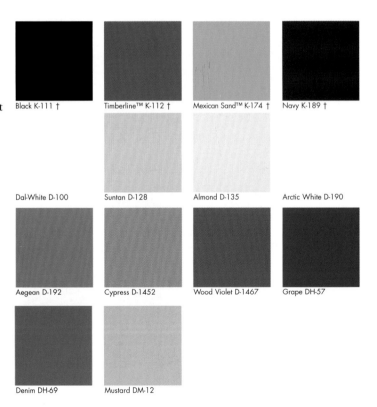

Black K-111 †	Timberline™ K-112 †	Mexican Sand™ K-174 †	Navy K-189 †
Dal-White D-100	Suntan D-128	Almond D-135	Arctic White D-190
Aegean D-192	Cypress D-1452	Wood Violet D-1467	Grape DH-57
Denim DH-69	Mustard DM-12		

8" x 10"   6" x 8"

nova

This tile gains its elegance from a high-gloss glaze with the look of natural marble. For added drama and coordination, pair Nova with one of four matching Listello tiles and our Marmol floor tile. The result is a room with exceptional style.

Application Interior walls, vanities and ceilings. Not recommended for floors, exteriors or surfaces subject to abrasive wear.

Size 8" x 10" size is 5/16" thick with cushioned edges. See illustration above.

Trim Consult your Daltile representative for available trim.

Note Coordinating Marmol 8" x 8" and 12" x 12" floor tile is available. Contact your nearest Daltile representative for further details.

 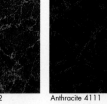

Alabaster 4100   Verde 4102   Anthracite 4111   Rosa 4133

Listello 75B   Listello 69   Listello 8N   Listello 22

classics

For a touch of retro elegance, choose Classics genuine ceramic tile in today's larger European size. The coordinated solids and marbles blush with delicate coloration, and feature a permanent sanitary glaze. Match them with Kohler® plumbing fixtures and a complete line of trim tile for a classic look.

Application Recommended for commercial and residential walls and countertops. Not recommended for areas subject to water or grease accumulation.

Size 6" x 8" size is 5/16" thick with cushioned edges. See illustration above.

Mounting See page 42.

Trim Consult your Daltile representative for available trim.

All wall tile shown is manufactured in accordance with ANSI A-137.1 standards.

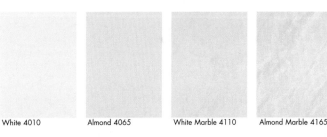

White 4010   Almond 4065   White Marble 4110   Almond Marble 4165

refined.

accentials

This small, glazed tile makes it possible to achieve perfect coordination between walls and floors. Use it as a wall tile to coordinate with similar, rustic floor tile, or use it alone on walls, countertops and floors. It is scratch- and impact-resistant, and comes in a variety of styles. Our Rustique colors, with their rustic finish, add warmth and character to any interior. Our Premier colors, with their granite-like appearance, possess an earthy charm. Accentials tile is also available in high-gloss solid colors, for dramatic contrasts and contemporary appeal.

Application Suitable for commercial and residential walls, countertops and backsplashes. Premier and Rustique colors are recommended for commercial interior floors (dry areas). Other lighter colors are suitable for interior residential floors in light-duty areas.

Size 3" x 3" size is 5/16" thick. See illustration above.

Mounting See page 42.

Trim See trim shapes below.

† Kohler colors shown complement Kohler plumbing fixtures as part of the Kohler Coordinates program.

KOHLER® COORDINATES

Manufactured in accordance with ANSI A–137.1 standards.

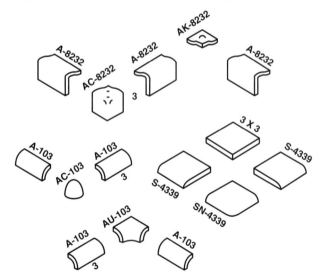

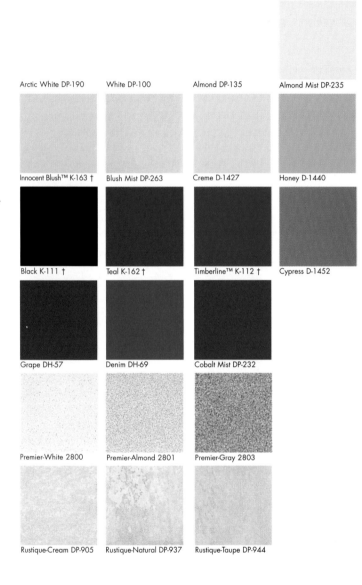

Arctic White DP-190 | White DP-100 | Almond DP-135 | Almond Mist DP-235
Innocent Blush™ K-163 † | Blush Mist DP-263 | Creme D-1427 | Honey D-1440
Black K-111 † | Teal K-162 † | Timberline™ K-112 † | Cypress D-1452
Grape DH-57 | Denim DH-69 | Cobalt Mist DP-232
Premier-White 2800 | Premier-Almond 2801 | Premier-Gray 2803
Rustique-Cream DP-905 | Rustique-Natural DP-937 | Rustique-Taupe DP-944

dramatic.

6" x 6"   4 1/4" x 4 1/4"

crystaltex

The appeal of this tile lies in the finely-textured crystal finish. Its striking appearance, combined with its light pastel color scheme, gives Crystaltex a dazzling, one-of-a-kind look that is also available in Kohler® Coordinates® colors.

Application Suitable for interior walls, vanities, kitchen countertops and ceilings. Also suitable for light-duty floors such as hotel guest room baths. Not recommended for exteriors. Use caution if water is present in light–duty floor areas.

Sizes 6" x 6" and 4 1/4" x 4 1/4" sizes are 5/16" thick with cushioned edges. See illustrations above.

Mounting See page 42.

Trim See page 30.

Numbers indicate price groups. No. 1 is the least expensive.

† Kohler colors shown complement Kohler plumbing fixtures as part of the Kohler Coordinates program.

KOHLER®
COORDINATES

Manufactured in accordance with ANSI A–137.1 standards.

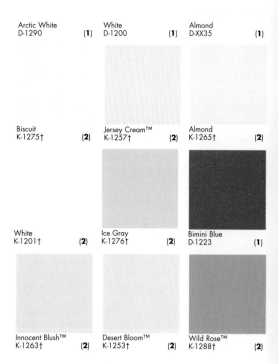

Arctic White D-1290 **(1)**	White D-1200 **(1)**	Almond D-XX35 **(1)**
Biscuit K-1275† **(2)**	Jersey Cream™ K-1257† **(2)**	Almond K-1265† **(2)**
White K-1201† **(2)**	Ice Gray K-1276† **(2)**	Bimini Blue D-1223 **(1)**
Innocent Blush™ K-1263† **(2)**	Desert Bloom™ K-1253† **(2)**	Wild Rose™ K-1288† **(2)**

alluring.

6" x 6"   4 1/4" x 4 1/4"

matte

The subdued, low-luster finish of this glazed interior tile sets it apart from other tiles. Tasteful colors also add to Matte's appeal; choose from a variety of gentle earth tones and Kohler® Coordinates® colors.

Application Recommended for interior walls, vanities, kitchen countertops and ceilings. Not recommended for floors, exteriors or surfaces subject to abrasive wear.

Sizes 6" x 6" and 4 1/4" x 4 1/4" sizes are 5/16" thick. See illustrations above.

Mounting See page 42.

Trim See page 30.

Numbers indicate price groups. No. 1 is the least expensive.

† Kohler colors shown complement Kohler plumbing fixtures as part of the Kohler Coordinates program.

Manufactured in accordance with ANSI A–137.1 standards.

Private Dining Area, Dallas, Texas. Walls: Kohler Coordinates 4 1/4" x 4 1/4" Almond (K-165), with 6" x 6" Timberline™ (K-112), Almond (K-165) and Mexican Sand™ (K-174) accent band. Floor: 2000 Designer Tile Series 12" x 12" Almond (2009) with hand-cut Timberline™ (2112) diamond accents.

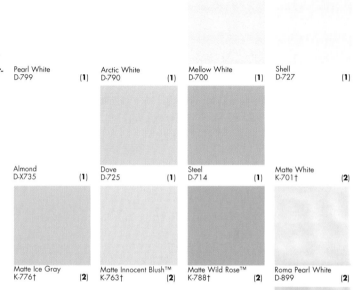

Pearl White D-799 **(1)**	Arctic White D-790 **(1)**	Mellow White D-700 **(1)**	Shell D-727 **(1)**
Almond D-X735 **(1)**	Dove D-725 **(1)**	Steel D-714 **(1)**	Matte White K-701† **(2)**
Matte Ice Gray K-776† **(2)**	Matte Innocent Blush™ K-763† **(2)**	Matte Wild Rose™ K-788† **(2)**	Roma Pearl White D-899 **(2)**
			Roma Almond D-X835 **(2)**

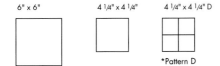

6" x 6"   4 1/4" x 4 1/4"   4 1/4" x 4 1/4" D

*Pattern D

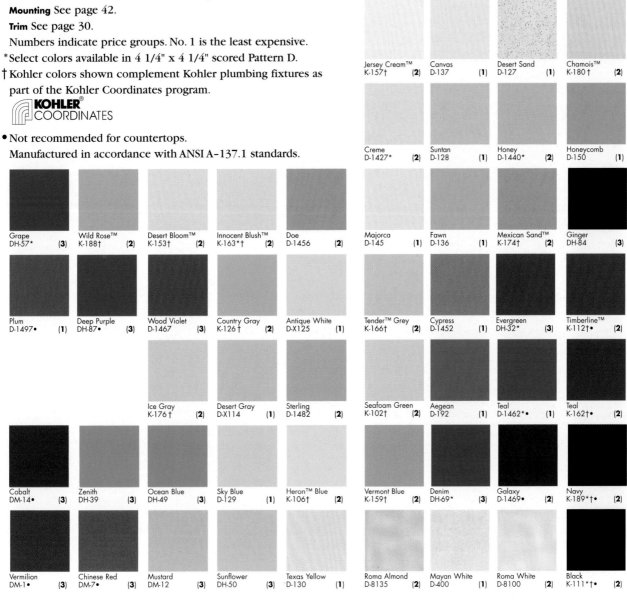

24

wall tile

semi-gloss

We know the challenge you face in integrating your design elements. That's why we've created Semi-Gloss, a striking medium-gloss wall tile in a wide range of colors. From muted pastels to Kohler® Coordinates®, a versatile series designed to match Kohler plumbing fixtures, the Semi-Gloss line will fill any design need. Some colors also coordinate with Keystones porcelain ceramic mosaics (see pages 36-37).

Application Recommended for interior walls, vanities, kitchen counter-tops and ceilings. Not recommended for floors, exteriors or surfaces subject to abrasive wear.

Sizes 6" x 6", 4 1/4" x 4 1/4" and 4 1/4" x 4 1/4" scored Pattern D sizes are 5/16" thick with cushioned edges. See illustrations above.

Mounting See page 42.

Trim See page 30.

Numbers indicate price groups. No. 1 is the least expensive.

*Select colors available in 4 1/4" x 4 1/4" scored Pattern D.

†Kohler colors shown complement Kohler plumbing fixtures as part of the Kohler Coordinates program.

KOHLER® COORDINATES

• Not recommended for countertops.

Manufactured in accordance with ANSI A–137.1 standards.

Color	Code	Group
Dal-White	D-100*	(1)
Arctic White	D-190*	(1)
White	K-101†	(2)
Pepperwhite	D-147	(1)
Golden Granite	D-138	(1)
Biscuit	K-175†	(2)
Almond	D-135*	(1)
Almond	K-165†	(2)
Jersey Cream™	K-157†	(2)
Canvas	D-137	(1)
Desert Sand	D-127	(1)
Chamois™	K-180†	(2)
Creme	D-1427*	(2)
Suntan	D-128	(1)
Honey	D-1440*	(2)
Honeycomb	D-150	(1)
Grape	DH-57*	(3)
Wild Rose™	K-188†	(2)
Desert Bloom™	K-153†	(2)
Innocent Blush™	K-163*†	(2)
Doe	D-1456	(2)
Majorca	D-145	(1)
Fawn	D-136	(1)
Mexican Sand™	K-174†	(2)
Ginger	DH-84	(3)
Plum	D-1497•	(1)
Deep Purple	DH-87•	(3)
Wood Violet	D-1467	(3)
Country Gray	K-126†	(2)
Antique White	D-X125	(1)
Tender™ Grey	K-166†	(2)
Cypress	D-1452	(1)
Evergreen	DH-32*	(3)
Timberline™	K-112†•	(2)
Ice Gray	K-176†	(2)
Desert Gray	D-X114	(1)
Sterling	D-1482	(2)
Seafoam Green	K-102†	(2)
Aegean	D-192	(1)
Teal	D-1462*•	(1)
Teal	K-162†•	(2)
Cobalt	DM-14•	(3)
Zenith	DH-39	(3)
Ocean Blue	DH-49	(3)
Sky Blue	D-129	(1)
Heron™ Blue	K-106†	(2)
Vermont Blue	K-159†	(2)
Denim	DH-69*	(3)
Galaxy	D-1469•	(2)
Navy	K-189*†•	(2)
Vermilion	DM-1•	(3)
Chinese Red	DM-7•	(3)
Mustard	DM-12	(3)
Sunflower	DH-50	(3)
Texas Yellow	D-130	(1)
Roma Almond	D-8135	(2)
Mayan White	D-400	(1)
Roma White	D-8100	(2)
Black	K-111*†•	(2)

keystones patterns, borders, murals and logos

You can see the versatility of Daltile porcelain mosaic tile in the wide variety of designs achieved through our special mounting services. Commercial patterns, borders, murals, logos and signage can be created by combining more than 65 colors and five unit sizes into custom-mounted designs from simple to intricate (within the limitations of standard unit sizes, shapes and colors).

Spell out your client's logo, or create a pictorial image by configuring different tile colors. The possibilities are endless and the results are nothing short of extraordinary.

Request our *Patterns, Borders, Murals & Logos* catalog for standard pattern selections, or create your own one-of-a-kind pattern. Daltile's mosaic designers are available to develop your ideas into mosaic art, mounted and ready for installation. Contract orders are quoted based on the size and complexity of your submitted design.

◀*Wizards, Universal City, California. Hirata Architect, Architect. BTS Co., Inc., Builder/Developer. Communication Arts, Boulder, Colorado, Designer. Pacific Tile, Tile Contractor. Bath Walls/Floor: Keystones 1" x 1" custom design in assorted colors.*

Tualitin Commons, Tualitin, Oregon. Walker/Macy, Designer/Architect. Silco Construction, Builder/Developer. Don P. Schonert Co., Inc., Tile Contractor. Crawfish Fountain Design: Keystones 1" x 1" Cinnamon Range (DK-07)

MGM Grand Hotel & Casino, Las Vegas, Nevada. Gateway Walls/Insets/Columns: Clear-Glazed Keystones 1" x 1" and 2" x 2" custom pattern in assorted colors.

Michael Jordan's Restaurant, Chicago, Illinois. Zackaspace, Architect/Designer. Keystones/Murals.

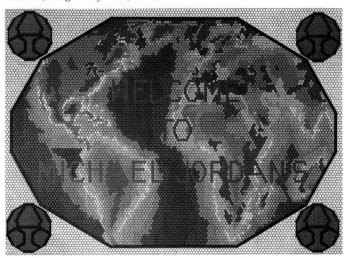

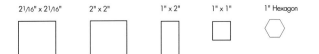

21/16" x 21/16"   2" x 2"   1" x 2"   1" x 1"   1" Hexagon

keystones

In a wide variety of colors ranging from earth tones to brights, Keystones ceramic mosaics borrow nature's beauty as well as its strength. These tiles will resist frost, weathering, staining and fading, and are virtually waterproof. Inorganic stains are precisely blended with porcelain raw materials and kiln fired to create Keystones' distinct look.

Application These tiles are suitable for interior walls, countertops, ceilings and floors in all types of residential or commercial buildings. Recommended for exterior walls and floors in any climate, as well as swimming pool linings and decking. Standard installation methods can be used.

Sizes 2 1/16" x 2 1/16", 2" x 2", 1" x 2", 1" x 1" and 1" Hexagon sizes are 1/4" thick with cushioned edges. See illustrations above. Diagonal halves are available for 1" x 1" and 2" x 2" sizes. Four-point and five-point halves are available in 1" Hexagon.

Mounting Available in three types of mounted sheet construction. See page 42.

Trim See page 41.

Notes Keystones are grouped by price. No. 1 is the least expensive. Clear glaze is available on all colors on a made-to-order basis (not recommended for floor use).

a. available in 2 1/16" x 2 1/16" on a made-to-order basis.

b. available with a 7 1/2% abrasive content in 1" x 1" and 2" x 2" sizes only.

c. standard hexagon color.

d. special pricing. Contact your Daltile representative for price listing.

Request our special *Patterns, Borders, Murals & Logos* catalog for more complete information.

 ♿ Complies with A.D.A. recommendations for accessible routes.

Manufactured in accordance with ANSI A-137.1 standards.

Michael Jordan's Restaurant. Keystones unglazed mosaics.

Brellas Cafe. Keystones unglazed mosaics.

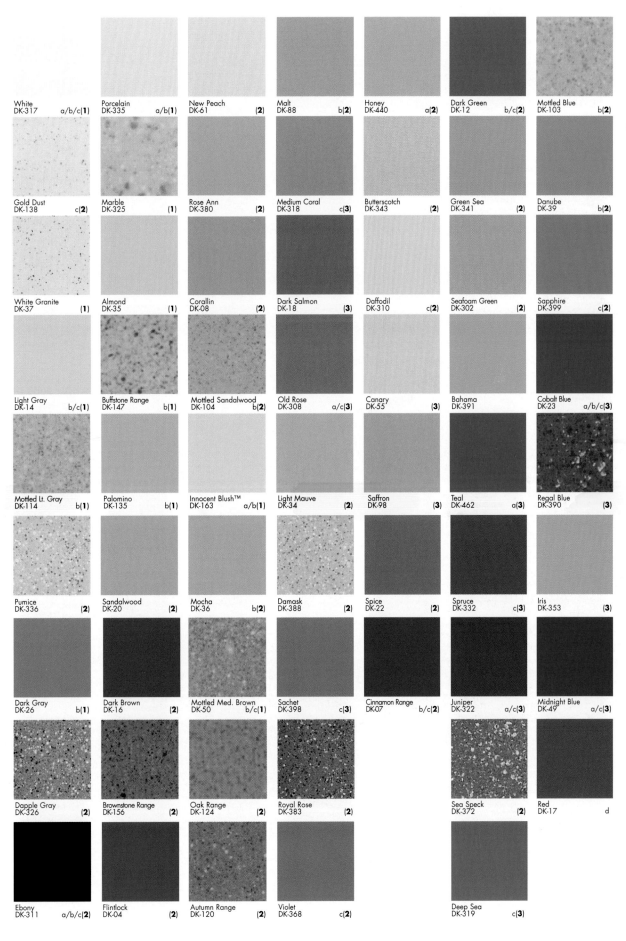

White DK-317 a/b/c**(1)**	Porcelain DK-335 a/b**(1)**	New Peach DK-61 **(2)**	Malt DK-88 b**(2)**	Honey DK-440 a**(2)**	Dark Green DK-12 b/c**(2)**	Mottled Blue DK-103 b**(2)**
Gold Dust DK-138 c**(2)**	Marble DK-325 **(1)**	Rose Ann DK-380 **(2)**	Medium Coral DK-318 c**(3)**	Butterscotch DK-343 **(2)**	Green Sea DK-341 **(2)**	Danube DK-39 b**(2)**
White Granite DK-37 **(1)**	Almond DK-35 **(1)**	Corallin DK-08 **(2)**	Dark Salmon DK-18 **(3)**	Daffodil DK-310 c**(2)**	Seafoam Green DK-302 **(2)**	Sapphire DK-399 c**(2)**
Light Gray DK-14 b/c**(1)**	Buffstone Range DK-147 b**(1)**	Mottled Sandalwood DK-104 b**(2)**	Old Rose DK-308 a/c**(3)**	Canary DK-55 **(3)**	Bahama DK-391	Cobalt Blue DK-23 a/b/c**(3)**
Mottled Lt. Gray DK-114 b**(1)**	Palomino DK-135 b**(1)**	Innocent Blush™ DK-163 a/b**(1)**	Light Mauve DK-34 **(2)**	Saffron DK-98 **(3)**	Teal DK-462 a**(3)**	Regal Blue DK-390 **(3)**
Pumice DK-336 **(2)**	Sandalwood DK-20 **(2)**	Mocha DK-36 b**(2)**	Damask DK-388 **(2)**	Spice DK-22 **(2)**	Spruce DK-332 c**(3)**	Iris DK-353 **(3)**
Dark Gray DK-26 b**(1)**	Dark Brown DK-16 **(2)**	Mottled Med. Brown DK-50 b/c**(1)**	Sachet DK-398 c**(3)**	Cinnamon Range DK-07 b/c**(2)**	Juniper DK-322 a/c**(3)**	Midnight Blue DK-49 a/c**(3)**
Dapple Gray DK-326 **(2)**	Brownstone Range DK-156 **(2)**	Oak Range DK-124 **(2)**	Royal Rose DK-383 **(2)**		Sea Speck DK-372 **(2)**	Red DK-17 d
Ebony DK-311 a/b/c**(2)**	Flintlock DK-04 **(2)**	Autumn Range DK-120 **(2)**	Violet DK-368 c**(2)**		Deep Sea DK-319 c**(3)**	

glassmosaics

These stunning — and weatherproof — opalized glass mosaics are available in both Venetian (molded) and Byzantine (hand-cut) styles, in a rainbow of colors. They are made from Silica sand and mineral colorants melted and blended at 2400° Fahrenheit.

Application Venetian mosaics are recommended for pools, kitchens, bathrooms or exteriors requiring a durable surface. The small unit size is perfect for graphics. **Byzantine** is recommended for artistic applications because of the irregular size and surface. Not recommended for commercial floor use.

Sizes Venetian: 3/4" x 3/4", 3/8" x 3/8".

Byzantine: 3/8" x 3/8" only.

Mounting Options Glass Mosaics are mounted on removable kraft paper sheets bonded to the face of the mosaics.

Trim No trim is currently available for this line.

Numbers indicate price groups. No. 1 is the least expensive.

Notes Byzantine glass mosaics are available in more than 200 colors. Request our *Glass Mosaics* catalog for more complete information on installation, delivery and ordering.

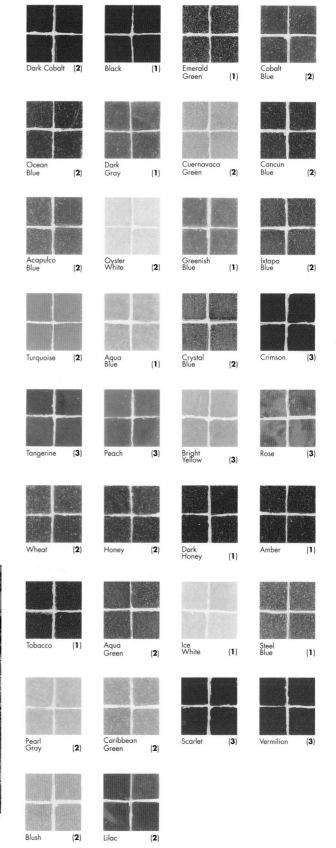

Dark Cobalt (2)	Black (1)	Emerald Green (1)	Cobalt Blue (2)
Ocean Blue (2)	Dark Gray (1)	Cuernavaca Green (2)	Cancun Blue (2)
Acapulco Blue (2)	Oyster White (2)	Greenish Blue (1)	Ixtapa Blue (2)
Turquoise (2)	Aqua Blue (1)	Crystal Blue (2)	Crimson (3)
Tangerine (3)	Peach (3)	Bright Yellow (3)	Rose (3)
Wheat (2)	Honey (2)	Dark Honey (1)	Amber (1)
Tobacco (1)	Aqua Green (2)	Ice White (1)	Steel Blue (1)
Pearl Gray (2)	Caribbean Green (2)	Scarlet (3)	Vermilion (3)
Blush (2)	Lilac (2)		

2" x 2"

permatones

These small-unit mosaic tiles enhance any design with the brilliant colors of the rainbow. And since they have a durable, matte finish, Permatones will resist fading and staining to always keep their vivid colors.

Application Suitable for light-duty commercial floors, interior and exterior walls and interior pool linings. Not recommended for exterior swimming pools where freeze/thaw cycles occur.

Size 2" x 2" size is 1/4" thick. See illustration above.

Mounting Dal-mounted 12" x 24" sheets provide an excellent bonding surface and faster, more efficient installation. See page 42.

Trim Complementary angles are available for trim shapes. Built-up cove base assemblies are available in both square and round top. See page 41.

Note Vitreous body and special grid-patterned backing ensure superior bonding characteristics. Permatones are expressly designed to coordinate with Keystones 2" x 2" and 1" x 1" porcelain ceramic mosaics.

Manufactured in accordance with ANSI A-137.1 standards.

Wall St. Deli, Houston, Texas. Gotsdiner, Architect. Gamble Tile, Tile Contractor. Permatones 2" x 2" White (6501), Sable (6521), Permabrites 2" x 2" Gloss White (6401), Gloss Sable (6421).

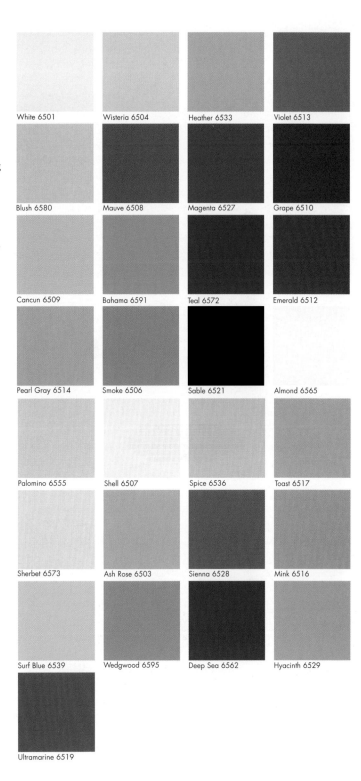

White 6501   Wisteria 6504   Heather 6533   Violet 6513

Blush 6580   Mauve 6508   Magenta 6527   Grape 6510

Cancun 6509   Bahama 6591   Teal 6572   Emerald 6512

Pearl Gray 6514   Smoke 6506   Sable 6521   Almond 6565

Palomino 6555   Shell 6507   Spice 6536   Toast 6517

Sherbet 6573   Ash Rose 6503   Sienna 6528   Mink 6516

Surf Blue 6539   Wedgwood 6595   Deep Sea 6562   Hyacinth 6529

Ultramarine 6519

2" x 2"   1" x 1"   1" Hexagon

40
glazed mosaics

permabrites

With a radiant high-gloss finish, these small-unit mosaic tiles enrich any design scheme. Use them to add the brilliance of a rainbow; since Permabrites resist fading and staining, their shining colors will last.

Application Suitable for interior and exterior walls and interior pool linings. Not recommended for exterior swimming pools where freeze/thaw cycles occur.

Size 2" x 2" size is 1/4" thick. See illustration above.

Mounting Dal-mounted 12" x 24" sheets provide an excellent bonding surface and faster, more efficient installation. See page 42.

Trim Complementary angles are available for trim shapes. Built-up cove base assemblies are available in both square and round top. See page 41.

Note Vitreous body and special grid-patterned backing ensure superior bonding characteristics. Permabrites are expressly designed to coordinate with Keystones 2" x 2" and 1" x 1" porcelain ceramic mosaics.

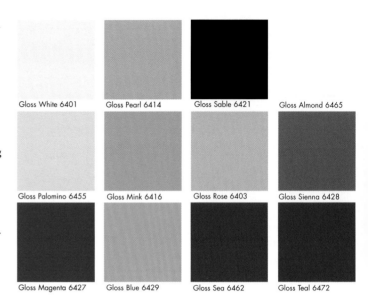

Gloss White 6401   Gloss Pearl 6414   Gloss Sable 6421   Gloss Almond 6465

Gloss Palomino 6455   Gloss Mink 6416   Gloss Rose 6403   Gloss Sienna 6428

Gloss Magenta 6427   Gloss Blue 6429   Gloss Sea 6462   Gloss Teal 6472

jewelstones

In its regal jewel colors, Jewelstones porcelain ceramic tile earns its name by adding polish and sophistication to any project. A high-gloss, acid-resistant glaze protects this tile from the elements.

Application Suitable for interior or exterior walls, ceilings and light-usage countertops in residential or commercial buildings. Ideal for random decorative accents blended into sheets of unglazed mosaics for wall installations. Not recommended for floors or surfaces subject to abrasive wear.

Sizes 2" x 2 ", 1" x 1" and 1" Hexagon sizes are 1/4" thick with cushioned edges. See illustrations above.

Mounting Fully impervious body tiles are "dot" back-mounted on 1' x 2' sheets.

Trim Surface bullnose with outside corners. Diagonal halves and four-point and five-point Hex halves are available. Colors GK-500 and GK-511 available in C-813, C-833 stretchers and complementary colors.

All glazed mosaics shown are manufactured in accordance with ANSI A-137.1 standards.

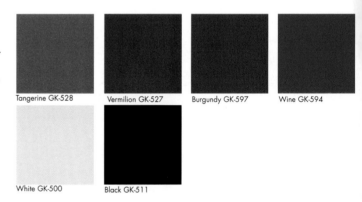

Tangerine GK-528   Vermilion GK-527   Burgundy GK-597   Wine GK-594

White GK-500   Black GK-511

mosaic trim chart

Available Trims

Section

1/4" R — 1" CAP — 1" — 1/4"

1/4" R — 2" — 2" CAP — 1/4"

1/4" — 1" — 3/4" R — 1" — 1" COVE

1" — 1/2" R — 1" — 1/4" — 1" CAP

Stretchers

1" — S-862

1" — S-866

1" — C-813

1" — S-812

2" — S-886

2" — C-833

2" — S-832

2¹/₁₆" — S-986

2¹/₁₆" — C-933

Round Outside Angle

SC-862

SC-886

SC-986

1" — 1" — 1/4" R — SCR-813 (SCL-813 AVAILABLE)

SCR-866 (SCL-866 AVAILABLE)

3/4" R — 1/4" R — 1" — 2¹/₁₆" — SCR-933 (SCL-933 AVAILABLE)

Butterfly

SM-862

Swimming Pool Nosing

2" — 1/4" — 1" — C-701

C-701 — 1"

Round Top Base

1x1 MDKB-5	2x2 MDKB-5B

1 ROW S-862 / 3 ROWS 1" x 1" / 1 ROW C-813

1 ROW S-886 / 1 ROW 2" x 2" / 1 ROW C-833

Square Top Base

1x1 MDKB-4C	2x2 MDKB-5A	21/16 x 21/16 MDKB-5C

3 ROWS 1" x 1" / 1 ROW C-813

2 ROWS 2" x 2" / 1 ROW C-833

2 ROWS 2¹/₁₆" x 2¹/₁₆" / 1 ROW C-933

Universal Trim

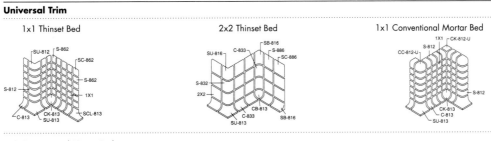

1x1 Thinset Bed — SU-812, S-862, SC-862, S-862, 1X1, S-812, C-813, CK-813, SU-813, SCL-813

2x2 Thinset Bed — SU-816, C-833, SB-816, S-886, SC-886, S-832, 2X2, CB-813, C-833, SU-813, SB-816

1x1 Conventional Mortar Bed — 1X1, CK-812-U, CC-812-U, S-812, S-812, CK-813, C-813, SU-813

2x2 Conventional Mortar Bed — CC-812U, C-833, CB-812-U, S-832, S-832, S-832, 2X2, CB-813, C-833, SU-813

mounted tile assemblies

Pre-mounted sheets speed up installation and make it easier, particularly on large unbroken wall areas.

* Self-Spacing

* Bridges Surface Irregularities

Pre-Grouted

Flexi-Set

Factory pre-grouted sheets of 16 units, 4 1/4" x 4 1/4" tiles are bonded into 17" x 17" sheets covering two sq. ft. using silicone sealant. This forms waterproof, flexible grout lines exceptionally resistant to stains, mildew, cracking and shrinking. Sheet perimeter joints should be job-site grouted with the same silicone (p.s.i. 631 sealant) to form an impervious area, e.g., operating suites (non-scored 4 1/4" x 4 1/4" tiles only).

Flexi-Set

E-Z Bond/Dal-Mount

Sheet-Mounted

Factory pre-mounted sheets of tile are assembled together in four different types of construction. Standard job-site procedures and materials are used to grout the tile joints.

E-Z Bond

4 1/4" x 4 1/4" tiles are "dot"-mounted into 17" x 17" sheets of 16.

Dal-Mount (Standard)

Tiles are edge- and back-mounted into sheets using a heat-cured polyvinyl chloride that is acid/alkaline resistant. Sheets are strong and flexible yet easily cut and fitted. Provides excellent bonding for most setting methods.

Keyramic (Special Order)

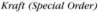
Kraft (Special Order)

Keyramic (Special Order)

Tiles are permanently back-mounted on sheets using a plasticized perforated paper. Not recommended for use in constantly wet areas, e.g., pools.

Kraft (Special Order)

Tiles are mounted on a removable kraft paper sheet bonded to the tile face.

Easy to Cut

Strong and Flexible

- Standard Production
S Special Order

	Unglazed Mosaics — Keystones (36-37)					Glazed Mosaics — Jewelstones (40)			Permatones (39)	Permabrites (40)	Accentials (24-27)	Crystaltex / Matte / Semi-Gloss (24-27)		
Unit Size (in.)	1 x 1	2 x 1	2 x 2	1" HEX	2 1/16 x 2 1/16	1 x 1	2 x 2	1" HEX	2 X 2	2 X 2	3 X 3	4 1/4 x 4 1/4	4 1/4 x 4 1/4	4 1/4 x 4 1/4
Pre-Grouted (Mounting Type)														
Flexi-Set 17 X 17 Sheet														•
Sheet-Mounted (Mounting Type)														
E-Z Bond 17 X 17 Sheet														•
Dal-Mount 12 X 12 Sheet											•			
12 X 24 Sheet	•	•	•				•		•	•				
12 7/8 X 25 3/4 Sheet					•									
11 1/2 X 25 1/4 Sheet				•				•						
Keyramic 12 X 12 Sheet	S					S								
12 X 24 Sheet		S	S				S							
11 1/2 X 25 1/4 Sheet				S				S						
Kraft 12 X 24 Sheet	S	S	S											
11 1/2 X 23 1/16 Sheet				S										

floor tile test results

"Honeycomb" flat back on our glazed floor tile promotes adhesion for thinset and mortar-set installations. Glaze durability varies by color. All glazed floor tile equals or exceeds applicable ASTM test requirements and ANSI A-137.1 specifications for ceramic tile.

Coefficient of Friction

Daltile products designed for commercial and institutional applications are tested for Coefficient of Friction (C.O.F.) in accordance with ASTM C1028 (American Society Testing Materials). Although there is no specific value requirement in ANSI standards (American Standards Institute), OSHA (Occupational Safety and Health Administration) has established a recognized industry standard of 0.50 (wet and dry) for slip-resistant surfaces.

The Ceramic Tile Institute of America (CTIOA) recommends a C.O.F. of 0.60 (wet and dry). The Americans with Disabilities Act (A.D.A.) recommends but does not require "a Static Coefficient of Friction of 0.60 for accessible routes and 0.80 for ramps." A.D.A. does not specifically state that 0.60 is both a dry and a wet requirement.

Abrasion Resistance

Durability of glazed tile can be measured, subjectively, by observing the visible abrasion to the tile surface when subjected to a Porcelain Enamel Institute (PEI) abrasion test. Daltile subjects all glazed tiles recommended for floor application to the European EN 154 abrasion test method. A rating of one through four is assigned, based on the following rating system:

Class One — Floor coverings in areas that are walked on essentially with soft-soled footwear or bare feet, without scratching dirt (e.g. domestic bathrooms and bedrooms without direct access from outside).

Class Two — Floor coverings in areas that are walked on by soft-soled or normal footwear with, at the most, occasional small amounts of scratching dirt (e.g. rooms in the living areas of homes except kitchens, entrances and other areas that may have a lot of traffic).

Class Three — Floor coverings in areas that, with normal footwear, are walked on more often with small amounts of scratching dirt (e.g. halls, kitchens and corridors).

Class Four — Floor coverings in areas that are walked on by considerable traffic with some scratching dirt so that the conditions are the most severe for which glazed tiles are suitable (e.g. entrances, workrooms, inns, and exhibition and salesrooms, as well as other rooms in public and private buildings not mentioned in classes one, two and three).

Floors should be adequately protected against scratching dirt at the entrances to buildings by interposing footwear-cleaning devices.

Glaze Hardness (MOH's Scale Ratings)

The relative hardness of glazed tile is an important issue that should be addressed when selecting tile. This test is performed by scratching the surface of the tile with different minerals and assigning a "MOH's Scale Hardness" number to the glaze. The softest mineral used is talc (a "1" rating if no scratch), the hardest is diamond (a "10" rating if no scratch). Other minerals of varying hardness provide MOH's Scale Hardness values of intermediate value. MOH's Scale Hardness values of four to six are suitable for most residential floor applications; a value of seven or greater is normally recommended for commercial applications.

Both abrasion resistance and glaze hardness should be addressed when considering using glazed tiles as floor products.

Contact your Daltile representative for specific color C.O.F., PEI and MOH's test results.

TECHNICAL DATA - GLAZED FLOOR TILE

TEST	RESULT	ANSI/ASTM Tests
Water Absorption	<3%	ASTM C373-72 (82)
Acid Resistance	Resistant	ASTM C650-83
Breaking Strength	365 lbs.	ASTM C648-84
Thermal Shock	Resistant	ASTM C484-66 (81)
Frost Resistance	Resistant	ASTM C1026-84
Bonding Strength	263 p.s.i.	ASTM C482-81
Modulus of Rupture	4357-4787 p.s.i.	ASTM C674
Crazing Resistance	Resistant	ASTM C424-75
*Coefficient of Friction	0.40-0.80 (wet-dry)	ASTM C1028
*Abrasion Resistance (Wear Rating)	2-4+	EN154
*Glaze Hardness	6-9	MOH's Scale

*see product page for series-specific information.

dal-quality brand installation products

Daltile offers a variety of excellent Dal-Quality Brand installation products. Your Daltile representative can explain the advantages of each in more detail, and answer any questions you might have.

Surface Preparation

Dal-Level Cementitious self-leveling underlayment levels and repairs interior floors up to 1/2" thick.

Dal-Patch Fast-setting, cement-based compound patches concrete or plywood floors up to 1/2" thick.

Dal-Elastofil Elastomeric crack isolation membrane protects tiles.

Dal-Multiboard Cementitious water-safe, multipurpose, interior/exterior backerboard, 36" x 60" x 1/2".

Thinset Mortars

High-quality dry-set mortars, multipurpose polymer-modified mortars and fast-setting systems work for every floor and wall tile application. Meet ANSI A118.1 and A118.4.

Grouts

Dal-Floor Tile Grout Sanded cementitious grout in 32 colors for joints over 1/8" wide. Meets ANSI A118.6.

Dal-Dry Wall Grout Unsanded cementitious grout in 30 colors for joints up to 1/8" wide. Meets ANSI A118.6.

Epoxy Grout & Mortar

Dal-Poxy Practical two-part, 100% solids epoxy system for interior use cleans up with water. Available in a variety of colors. ANSI A118.3.

Additives

Dal-Lastic Premium polymer mortar admix for difficult surfaces. Use with Dal-Bond. Meets ANSI A118.4.

Dal-Acrylmix Acrylic latex mortar admix for improved performance in all mortars. Meets ANSI A118.6.

Dal-Latex Acrylic latex grout admix for hard, dense joints. Meets ANSI A118.6.

Mastics

Dal-Stick-40 Economical Type II wall adhesive. Meets ANSI A136.1.

Dal-Stick-50 Multipurpose Type I wall and floor adhesive. Meets ANSI A136.1.

Dal-Stick-GOLD Premium bright white, multipurpose Type I wall and floor adhesive. Meets ANSI A136.1.

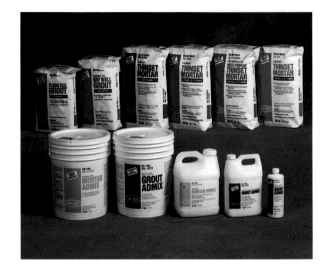

Availability Symbols

△ DQ-100 Wall Tile Grout

▼ DQ-200 Floor Tile Grout

● DQ-2000 Epoxy Grout

Grout Colors

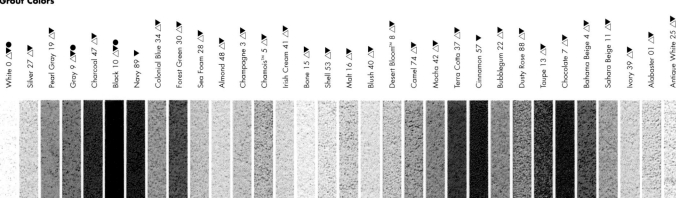

product selection guide

How to use this chart: Match condition, substrate and tile/stone type to product. Recommended products will have a dot in each area.

Stone Type			Tile Type				Substrates										Conditions					Product	
Granite and All Other Stable Stones	Green Marble, Rosso Levanto and Black Marquina	Light/Translucent Marbles and Agglomerates	Impervious (Porcelain)	Vitreous	Semi-Vitreous	Non-Vitreous	Clean Steel	Cutback Adhesive	Vinyl Floors	Existing Ceramic Tile (Exterior Floors)	Existing Ceramic Tile (Interior Floors or Walls)	Cementitious Backer Units (Exterior)	Cementitious Backer Units (Interior Floors or Walls)	Gypsum Wallboard (Interior Walls Only)	Plywood Floors & Counters (Interior Only)	Concrete Masonry Block	Other	Interior Walls	Interior Floors	Exterior Walls	Exterior Floors		
								†	†		†		•		•	•			•			Dal-Level	Prep
													•		•	•			•			Dal-Elastofil	Prep
															•	•			•			Dal-Patch	Prep
•	•		•	•	•	•	•				•		•		•	•		•	•			Dal-Poxy	Mortar
•		•		•	•	•					•		•		•				•			Dal-Medium Bed	Mortar
•			★	•	•	•					•	•	•					•	•			Dal-Poly Bond	Mortar
•			•	•	•	•						•	•		•			•	•	•	•	Dal-Set	Mortar
•		•	✓	•	•	•					•	•	•		•			•	•			Dal-Poly Quick	Mortar
				•	•	•							•		•				•		•	Dal-Floor	Mortar
•			•	•	•	•		•	•	•	•		•		•	•	•		•		•	Dal-Bond	Mortar
•			•	•	•	•		•	•	•	•		•		•			•	•	•	•	Dal-Lastic	Admix
•			•	•	•	•				•	•		•		•			•	•	•	•	Dal-Acrylmix	Admix
				•	•								•	•	•			•				Dal-Stick-40	Mastic
		•	•	•	•					•			•	•	•		•	•	•			Dal-Stick-50	Mastic
•			•	•	•					•	•		•		•			•	•			Dal-Stick-Gold	Mastic

▨ Shaded areas above indicate a mortar/additive combination is necessary for proper installation with these conditions or substrates.
† Primer U.P. must be used in conjunction with DAL-LEVEL. ★ Only for interior installations of porcelain tile sizes 8" x 8" or smaller.
✓ Only for interior installations of porcelain tile.

care and maintenance

Daltile products, for the most part, require minimal maintenance. Our glazed and unglazed tile, under normal situations, can be cleaned using clear water with a mild non-sudsing detergent. *Always* follow up with a rinse of clean water. It is a good idea once the floor has been rinsed to wipe the floor dry. Regular maintenance is recommended to avoid build-up of dirt, residue, grease, soap detergents, etc.

We do not recommend "acid cleaning" our tile products.

For all floor cleaning operations, follow these basic procedures:
1. Sweep or vacuum surface;
2. Mix water with cleaning solution per manufacturer's instructions;
3. Allow solution to sit for three to five minutes;
4. Agitate with sponge or synthetic mop;
5. Mop up dirty solution;
6. Rinse mop and change cleaning solution at least every 500 s.f.;
7. Rinse thoroughly with clean water;
8. Dry mop floor to remove moisture or pick up residue with a wet-vac.

For tile with coarse or abrasive type surfaces, maintenance will have to be performed more frequently. Agitation will need to be more vigorous and changing of water more frequent. Proper cleaning of these types of tile is necessary for the slip resistance value to be maintained. Grease or water accumulation can create slippery conditions. Use common sense to avoid introduction of grease from dirty mops to your floor surface.

Contact your Daltile office, or call 800-933-TILE, for more specific maintenance and cleaning instructions.

architectural services

Our commitment to being the best in the business extends to our service philosophy. Here are some of the "above and beyond" services you can expect every day from Daltile:

•Personal assistance, with the idea of helping you turn your design ideas into reality. Our architectural representatives are available to assist you with things like product specifications, usage and limitations, life-cycle costs, and installation procedures; our muralists can advise you on our custom-designed ceramic logos and murals.

•Product seminars, to keep you up-to-date on our innovative tile and stone products as they come to market. Other presentations help designers with topics such as installation and waterproofing. (Seminars can be arranged through our architectural representatives and Distribution Center managers.)

•Technical assistance, accessed through our Information Hot Line (800-933-TILE) can help with the latest data on industry standards, independent lab reports, special installation requirements and advice on how Daltile products can help you meet A.D.A.-suggested recommendations.

If you have any questions about our services or products, please call 800-933-TILE. Our representatives will be happy to assist you.

Product	Page	Application					Trim Page
		Interior			Exterior		
		Wall	Countertop	Floor	Wall/Cladding	Floor	
Glazed Floor Tile	6-15						
French Quarter™	6	•	•	•	•		N/A
Gold Rush™	7	•	•	•	•		*
Southwest	8	•	•	•	•		N/A
Wyoming™	8			•			N/A
Stone	8	•	•	•	•		N/A
Vulcano	9	•		•			N/A
Great Lakes	9	•		•			N/A
Mission	10	•		•			N/A
Lithos	10			•			N/A
Vitrestone	11	•	•	•	•		15
Sierra	12	•	•	•	•		15
Desert	12	•	•	•	•		15
Mesa	12	•	•	•	•		15
Designer	13	•	•	•	•		15
Pastelle	13			•			N/A
Premier	14			•			15
Unglazed Floor Tile	16-17						
Cultura™	16	•	•		•	•	N/A
Quarry	16	•	•	•	•	•	*
Pavers and Suretread	17	•	•		•	•	N/A
Detectable Warning Tile	17	•	•	•	•	•	N/A
Stone Classics	18-21						
Granite	19	•	•	•	•		N/A
Slate	19	•	•	•	•	•	N/A
Marmitec	20	•					N/A
Marble, Travertine	21	•	•	•	•		N/A
Wall Tile	24-31						
Semi-Gloss	24	•	•				30
Matte	25	•	•				30
Crystaltex	26	•	•				30
Accentials	27	•			•		27
Nova	28	•					*
Classics	28	•					*
Octagon	29	•					*
Liners	29	•					N/A
Hand-Painted Murals	31	•					N/A
Ceramic Mosaics	34-41						
Keystones	36-37	•	•	•	•	•	41
Glass Mosaics	38	•					*
Permatones	39	•	•	•			41
Permabrites	40	•	•		•		41
Jewelstones	40	•	•		•		41

*Consult your Daltile representative for information about product suitability for your specific application.

More Than 200 Company-Owned And Operated Office/Showroom/Warehouse Facilities Nationwide And In Canada.

Alabama

Birmingham
(205)941-1233

Mobile
(334)342-6977

Montgomery
(334)284-6234

Arizona

Flagstaff
(602)556-0583

Lake Havasu City
(520)855-4747

Mesa
(602)969-7297

Phoenix
(602)258-9390

Prescott
(520)778-5644

Scottsdale
(602)443-1057

Tucson
(602)748-7411

Arkansas

Fayetteville
(501)756-6970

Little Rock
(501)225-2700

California

Anaheim
(714)634-2546

Auburn
(916)888-7622

Bakersfield
(805)834-6714

Cerritos
(714)521-5224

Chico
(916)343-6425

Colton
(909)796-3466

Concord
(510)676-8222

Corona
(909)371-8181

El Cajon
(619)447-7700

Escondido
(619)743-7404

Fairfield
(707)429-4592

Fresno
(209)252-2909

Glendale
(213)257-7553

Irvine
(714)757-7060

Lancaster
(805)942-2968

Livermore
(510)449-0338

Long Beach
(310)427-7877

Modesto
(209)524-4711

Palm Springs
(619)324-4636

Rancho
(909)676-6881

Redding
(916)221-8453

Sacramento
(916)422-5400

Sacramento - North
(916)338-1170

Sacramento - East
(916)364-0741

Salinas
(408)758-9473

San Diego
(619)565-7767

San Francisco - South
(415)873-8526

San Jose
(408)435-1566

San Juan Capistrano
(714)661-3654

San Leandro
(510)635-7673

San Rafael
(415)454-8610

Santa Monica
(310)453-9112

Santa Rosa
(707)588-9015

Stockton
(209)948-4083

Thousand Oaks
(805)499-0073

Torrance
(310)323-4632

Upland
(909)949-1227

Van Nuys
(818)787-3224

Ventura
(805)642-2122

Victorville
(619)245-2060

Visalia
(209)739-8810

Whittier
(818)968-5022

Colorado

Colorado Springs
(719)260-7000

Denver
(303)744-1743

Denver - East
(303)373-2051

Fort Collins
(970)484-1244

Grand Junction
(970)241-9418

Connecticut

Hartford
(860)257-3333

Stamford
(203)323-9490

Delaware

Wilmington
(302)328-4266

Florida

Brandon
(813)621-9443

Clearwater
(813)546-0833

Daytona Beach
(904)767-9561

Destin
(904)837-5508

Fort Lauderdale
(305)735-5700

Fort Myers
(813)337-0444

Jacksonville
(904)262-0444

Melbourne
(407)951-8284

Miami
(305)477-3303

Naples
(813)649-1144

Ocala
(352)351-2922

Orlando
(407)297-8997

Pensacola
(904)433-6009

Port Charlotte
(813)255-0493

Port St Lucie
(407)871-0304

Sarasota
(813)355-2954

Tampa
(813)873-2403

West Palm Beach
(407)848-3507

Winter Haven
(941)294-8007

Georgia

Atlanta
(770)729-0902

Atlanta - South
(770)719-9333

Macon
(912)743-5459

Marietta
(770)955-3003

Savannah
(912)236-5516

Hawaii

Honolulu
(808)847-4684

Idaho

Boise
(208)375-4466

Illinois

Burr Ridge
(708)789-1400

Chicago
(708)228-9911

Springfield
(217)522-5801

Indiana

Evansville
(812)471-0019

Fort Wayne
(219)471-0033

Indianapolis
(317)841-0883

South Bend
(219)232-8933

Iowa

Des Moines
(515)252-0212

Quad-Cities
(319)388-6116

Kansas

Kansas City
(913)888-3557

Wichita
(316)941-9800

Kentucky

Erlanger
(606)371-7412

Lexington
(606)268-4196

Louisville
(502)968-0558

Louisiana

Baton Rouge
(504)291-3585

New Orleans
(504)885-9432

Shreveport
(318)687-5511

Maine

Portland
(207)878-8520

Maryland

Annapolis
(410)573-5791

Baltimore
(410)636-7012

Baltimore - North
(410)560-5990

Landover
(301)925-8444

Rockville
(301)948-2496

Massachusetts

Boston
(617)961-2223

Boston - North
(617)932-6622

Worcester
(508)842-4145

Michigan

Detroit
(810)471-7150

Detroit - East
(810)739-0370

Grand Rapids
(616)530-9090

Minnesota

Minneapolis
(612)593-7666

St Paul
(612)770-6643

Mississippi

Jackson
(601)853-2714

Missouri

Springfield
(417)883-4600

St Louis
(314)997-6970

Montana

Missoula
(406)721-3010

Nebraska

Omaha
(402)597-2800

Nevada

Carson City
(702)883-4200

Henderson
(702)565-9131

Las Vegas
(702)365-6265

Reno
(702)358-8720

New Hampshire

Manchester
(603)434-0507

New Jersey

Cranbury
(609)655-0333

Hackensack
(201)489-2505

Mt Laurel
(609)235-8822

New Mexico

Albuquerque
(505)884-0017

Las Cruces
(505)647-2001

New York

Albany
(518)452-4771

Buffalo
(716)684-2336

Hicksville
(516)933-2552

Mt Vernon
(914)667-2500

Rochester
(716)292-0870

Syracuse
(315)475-2364

North Carolina

Charlotte
(704)523-6980

Durham
(919)493-0090

Fayetteville
(910)323-3004

Greensboro
(910)274-7647

Raleigh
(919)878-5743

Wilmington
(910)792-0119

Winston - Salem
(910)661-9771

Ohio

Cincinnati
(513)791-7832

Cleveland
(216)661-4994

Cleveland - East
(216)464-4470

Columbus
(614)433-9181

Dayton
(513)294-0150

Oklahoma

Oklahoma City
(405)685-3526

Tulsa
(918)627-5381

Oregon

Bend
(503)317-9301

Eugene
(503)686-0217

Portland
(503)236-4585

Salem
(503)588-3333

Pennsylvania

Allentown
(610)266-6688

Harrisburg
(717)795-0154

Philadelphia
(215)441-4977

Pittsburgh
(412)787-2040

Scranton
(717)342-3381

Rhode Island

Providence
(401)944-1100

South Carolina

Charleston
(803)824-1970

Columbia
(803)252-4422

Greenville
(803)288-8090

Hilton Head
(803)689-3622

Tennessee

Chattanooga
(423)892-0605

Knoxville
(423)588-2155

Memphis
(901)794-1891

Nashville
(615)885-0440

Tri-Cities
(423)283-4875

Texas

Amarillo
(806)371-0982

Arlington
(817)640-5232

Austin
(512)837-7080

Beaumont
(409)840-9447

Carrollton
(214)245-3185

Corpus Christi
(512)855-4558

Dallas - North
(214)690-5724

Dallas - South
(214)398-8362

El Paso
(915)593-3161

Fort Worth
(817)332-4161

Houston - Clear Lake
(713)554-4575

Houston - North
(713)820-0900

Houston - South
(713)643-2631

Houston - Southwest
(713)774-2559

Laredo
(210)712-8453

Lubbock
(806)793-4484

McAllen
(210)618-3267

Midland
(915)520-0071

Plano
(214)578-1414

San Antonio
(210)342-9351

Waco
(817)751-1331

Utah

Ogden
(801)394-7701

Orem
(801)226-2170

Salt Lake City
(801)487-9901

St George
(801)634-9777

Virginia

Alexandria
(703)971-8485

Chantilly
(703)834-6064

Norfolk
(804)460-2900

Richmond
(804)359-8851

Roanoke
(703)563-4881

Washington

Everett
(206)355-1645

Seattle
(206)762-6620

Spokane
(509)534-0202

Tacoma
(206)581-1130

Wisconsin

Green Bay
(414)337-1887

Madison
(608)242-1816

Milwaukee
(414)781-4590

Canada

Calgary, AB
(403)255-2566

Toronto, Ontario
(905)660-9588

Vancouver, BC
(604)251-8995

Puerto Rico

Caribbean
(809)268-5029

7834 Hawn Freeway
Dallas, Texas 75217
214-398-1411
800-933-TILE

250M196.1HER

COLOR COORDINATION

A STUDY IN COLOR COORDINATION

Coordination is the key strength of Florida Tile® brand ceramic tile. This strength can be yours in a variety of tiles for every residential and commercial application. Floor, wall and accent tiles are designed to expand and enhance your creativity with an ever increasing selection of interchangeable color palettes and styles. This catalog is organized into sections highlighting the three basic groups of tiles (floor, wall and accent) and is color-keyed for easy reference and selection.

Florida Tile also makes it easy to choose coordinating tile colors from different lines by assigning common product identification numbers to each color. Even though the names of the tiles may be different, if the last two digits are the same, the colors coordinate - which means you can choose wall, floor and accent tiles that harmonize with confidence.

FLOOR TILE

Florida Tile is the number one recognized brand of floor tile among builders. The depth and versatility of this line provide tremendous creative possibilities - and when combined with our compatible wall tiles, the possibilities become even greater.

WALL TILE

More durable than most any other wallcovering, ceramic wall tile offers timeless beauty and the advantage of being easy to clean. Our wall tile lines provide an extraordinary range for you to choose from and have been designed to be compatible with our decorative accent tile and moldings, as well as with our floor tile lines.

ACCENT TILE

Express your individuality with accent tiles and moldings from Florida Tile. A multitude of murals, inserts and moldings offer unlimited decorative potential - in colors that go from bold and bright to soft and subtle. Whatever your personality, whatever your taste, Florida Tile accent tiles are the perfect choice.

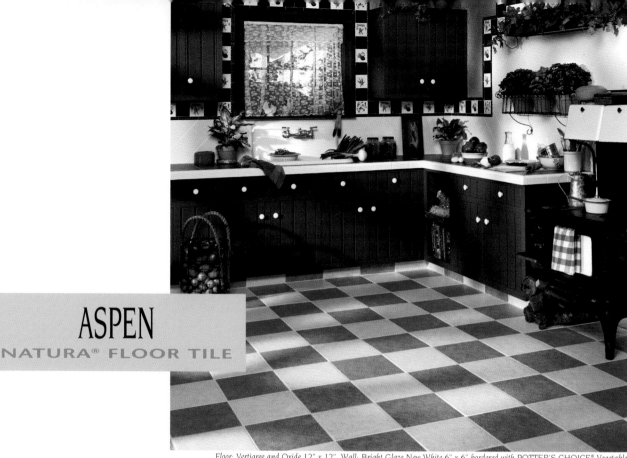

ASPEN
NATURA® FLOOR TILE

Floor: Vertigree and Oxide 12" x 12". Wall: Bright Glaze New White 6" x 6" bordered with POTTER'S CHOICE® Vegetable Inserts alternating with CONFETTI® Forest Green 4 3/8" x 4 3/8", accented by Rope Moldings in Forest Green. Countertop: NATURA® Tough One Forest Green 8" x 8" trimmed with Bright Glaze New White A8262.

FEATURES:

♦ Matte, rubbed stone glaze
♦ Rich, earthen colors
♦ Stain-resistant

USAGE:

♦ All commercial and residential wall, countertop and floor applications in dry pedestrian areas

TYPICAL PROPERTIES[1]:

Meets or exceeds A137.1 ANSI standard.

C.O.F.[2] Dry	Wet	Durability Classification	Glaze Hardness	Break Strength
0.63	0.55	Class IV	7.0 Mohs	300 lbs. avg.

[1] Refer to table of contents for explanation of tile properties.
[2] These values may vary from lot to lot.

♦ .34" thick
♦ 3.39 lbs. avg. weight/sq. ft.

Florida Tile's exclusive MONO-SIZED™ process ensures consistent squareness and size from tile to tile (8 x 8 and larger).

TRIM:

Surface Bullnose	Product #	Imperial	Metric (cm)
①	P-4489	4" x 8"	10 x 20
②	P-44C9	4" x 12"	10 x 30

SIZES:

8" x 8" (20 x 20 cm)

12" x 12" (30 x 30 cm)

16" x 16" (40 x 40 cm)

9704 Teakwood

9707 Oxide

9711 Ironstone

9722 Sand Pebble

9727 Clay Cavern

9750 Vertigree

Color reproductions in this printed piece will vary from the actual tile colors, final selection should be made from tile samples.

Floor: Canyon Clay 12" x 12" field and 12" x 12" Pentagon used with all four designs of accent tacos 4" x 4" in Azul-Clay.
Wall, Window sill, and step fronts: Accent tacos in all four designs Multi-Rose and Multi-Clay alternating with Desert Rose 4" x 4".

AZTECA
NATURA® FLOOR TILE

FLOOR TILE

TRIM:

Surface Bullnose	Product #	Imperial	Metric (cm)
①	① P-44C9	4" x 12"	10 x 30

Accent Tacos (4" x 4")

Galaxia

| 4460A/7682 Azul-Rose | 4460A/7679 Azul-Clay | 4460B/7682 Multi-Rose | 4460B/7679 Multi-Clay |

Escudo

| 4461A/7682 Azul-Rose | 4461A/7679 Azul-Clay | 4461B/7682 Multi-Rose | 4461B/7679 Multi-Clay |

Fuego

| 4462A/7682 Azul-Rose | 4462A/7679 Azul-Clay | 4462B/7682 Multi-Rose | 4462B/7679 Multi-Clay |

Flores

| 4463A/7682 Azul-Rose | 4463A/7679 Azul-Clay | 4463B/7682 Multi-Rose | 4463B/7679 Multi-Clay |

SIZES:

4" x 4"
(10 x 10 cm)

12" x 12"
(30 x 30 cm)

12" x 12" Pentagon
(30 x 30 cm)

Field Tiles (4" x 4", 12" x 12", 12" x 12" Pentagon)

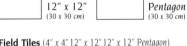

7623 Baja Beige

7624 Mesa Gold

7679 Canyon Clay

7682 Desert Rose

FEATURES:

- ♦ Mexican-style texture and finish
- ♦ Stain-resistant
- ♦ Modern, earthen colors
- ♦ Design versatility
- ♦ Modular with accent tacos

USAGE:

- ♦ All commercial and residential wall, countertop and floor applications in dry pedestrian areas

TYPICAL PROPERTIES[1]:

Meets or exceeds A137.1 ANSI standard.

C.O.F.[2]		Durability Classification	Glaze Hardness	Break Strength
Dry	Wet			
0.75	0.47	Class IV	6.5 Mohs	300 lbs. avg.

[1] Refer to table of contents for explanation of tile properties.

[2] These values may vary from lot to lot.

- ♦ .34" thick
- ♦ 3.36 lbs. avg. weight/sq. ft.

MONO-SIZED
UNIFORM SIZE
PRECISE CONTROL

Florida Tile's exclusive MONO-SIZED™ process ensures consistent squareness and size from tile to tile (8 x 8 and larger).

7

Color reproductions in this printed piece will vary from the actual tile colors, final selection should be made from tile samples.

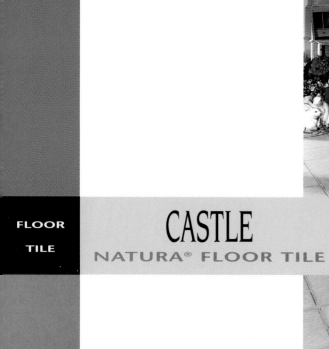

CASTLE
NATURA® FLOOR TILE

Ethan Allen Showroom, New Port Richey, FL. Floor: Camelot Beige 13" x 13"

FEATURES:

♦ Antique beauty of time-worn stone
♦ Durable, monocottura body with seven glaze applications
♦ Stain-resistant

USAGE:

♦ All commercial and residential wall, countertop and floor applications in dry pedestrian areas

TYPICAL PROPERTIES[1]:

Meets or exceeds A137.1 ANSI standard.

C.O.F.[2]		Durability Classification	Glaze Hardness	Break Strength
Dry	Wet			
0.67	0.55	Class IV+	8.5 Mohs	300 lbs. avg.

[1] Refer to table of contents for explanation of tile properties.
[2] These values may vary from lot to lot.

♦ .34" thick
♦ 3.68 lbs. avg. weight/sq. ft.

TRIM:

Surface Bullnose	Product #	Imperial	Metric (cm)
①	① P-43D9I	3" x 13"	8 x 33

SIZE:

13" x 13"
(33 x 33 cm)

7003 Camelot Beige   7016 Armor Gray   7074 Cobblestone Clay

Color reproductions in this printed piece will vary from the actual tile colors, final selection should be made from tile samples.

8

CORTINA
NATURA® FLOOR TILE

Residence, Charleston, SC. Floor: Natural 16" x 16" and 6" x 6", Wood Ash 6" x 12", and Tumblestone Marble Listello Cremo. Wall: Wood Ash 12" x 12" and Tumblestone Marble Listello.

Kitchen Backsplash: Natural 6" x 12" and Wood Ash 6" x 6". Countertop: Natural 12" x 12".

FEATURES:

♦ Natural stone appeal
♦ Mottled earthen colors
♦ Modular shapes to create unique patterns
♦ Extra durable rating
♦ Stain-resistant

USAGE:

♦ All commercial and residential wall, countertop and floor applications in dry pedestrian areas

TRIM:

Surface Bullnose	Product #	Imperial	Metric (cm)
①	① P-44C9	4" x 12"	10 x 30

SIZES:

12" x 12"
(30 x 30 cm)

6" x 6"
(15 x 15 cm)

16" x 16"
(40 x 40 cm)

6" x 12"
(15 x 30 cm)

For suggested patterns see p. 13

TYPICAL PROPERTIES[1]:

Meets or exceeds A137.1 ANSI standard.

C.O.F.[2]		Durability	Glaze	Break
Dry	Wet	Classification	Hardness	Strength
0.63	0.55	Class IV	7.0 Mohs	300 lbs. avg.

[1] Refer to table of contents for explanation of tile properties.
[2] These values may vary from lot to lot.

♦ .34" thick
♦ 3.36 lbs. avg. weight/sq. ft.

7907 Natural

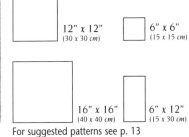

7915 Wood Ash

7924 Gold Dust

7951 Limestone

7977 Rust

MONO
UNIFORM
SIZE
PRECISE
CONTROL
SIZED

Florida Tile's exclusive MONO-SIZED™ process ensures consistent squareness and size from tile to tile (8 x 8 and larger).

Color reproductions in this printed piece will vary from the actual tile colors, final selection should be made from tile samples.

DESIGNER
NATURA® FLOOR TILE

Floor: White 12" x 12" accented with diagonally cut 12" x 12" pieces of Cobalt, Chicory, Winestone, Midori.

FEATURES:

♦ Bold, rich colors for stand-alone or accent statements
♦ Monochromatic semi-matte glaze
♦ 4" x 4" modular sizing ideal for transitioning from floor to wall
♦ Use 4" x 4" with Vento Coordinates Hexagon as dot (see page 25)
♦ Stain-resistant

USAGE:

♦ All light commercial and residential floors, interior walls, and countertops

TYPICAL PROPERTIES[1]:

Meets or exceeds A137.1 ANSI standard.

C.O.F.[2]		Durability	Glaze	Break
Dry	Wet	Classification	Hardness	Strength
0.73	0.41	Class III	6.5 Mohs	300 lbs. avg.

[1] Refer to table of contents for explanation of tile properties.
[2] These values may vary from lot to lot.

♦ .34" thick
♦ 3.53 lbs. avg. weight/sq. ft.

Florida Tile's exclusive MONO-SIZED™ process ensures consistent squareness and size from tile to tile (8 x 8 and larger).

TRIM:

Surface Bullnose	Product #	Imperial	Metric (cm)
①	P-4489	4" x 8"	10 x 20
①	P-44C9	4" x 12"	10 x 30
②	PN-4449	4" x 4"	10 x 10

SIZES:

4" x 4"
(10 x 10 cm)

8" x 8"
(20 x 20 cm)

12" x 12"
(30 x 30 cm)

8801 White   8805 Black   8817 Dove Gray   8824 Doeskin

8859N Midori   8865 Chicory   8868N Cobalt   8876 Adobe   8885 Winestone

Color reproductions in this printed piece will vary from the actual tile colors, final selection should be made from tile samples.

Countertop: Taupestone 6" x 6" trimmed with Brick A8262. Wall: Sandbar; Brick; and Taupestone 6" x 6".

EARTHSTONE®
FLOOR TILE

TRIM:

Surface Bullnose	Product #	Imperial	Metric (cm)
① S-4669	6" x 6"	15 x 15
② SN-4669	6" x 6"	15 x 15
③ Field	6" x 6"	15 x 15

Countertop Trim
Conventional & Thin Set

	Product #	Imperial	Metric (cm)
① A-8262	2¼" x 6"	6 x 15
② AC-8262	2¼" x 1⅛"	6 x 4
③ Field	6" x 6"	15 x 15
④ A-106	¾" x 6"	2 x 15
⑤ AZ-106	¾" x 1"	2 x 3

SIZES:

6" x 6"
(15 x 15 cm)

8" x 8"
(20 x 20 cm)

12" x 12"
(30 x 30 cm)

FEATURES:

♦ Slightly undulated surface with gently rounded corners
♦ Rustic appearance
♦ Unique color and shading create a distinctive movement

USAGE:

♦ All residential and light commercial floors, wall and counter applications.

TYPICAL PROPERTIES[1]:

Meets or exceeds A137.1 ANSI standard.

C.O.F.[2]		Durability Classification	Glaze Hardness	Break Strength
Dry	Wet			
0.66	0.33	Class III	7.0 Mohs	400 lbs. avg.

[1] Refer to table of contents for explanation of tile properties.
[2] These values may vary from lot to lot.

♦ .34" thick
♦ 3.6 lbs. avg. weight/sq. ft.

4101 Alabaster

4102 Sandbar

4122 Taupestone

4172 Clay Pink

4175 Canyon

4193 Brick

Color reproductions in this printed piece will vary from the actual tile colors, final selection should be made from tile samples.

EXCAVARE
NATURA® FLOOR TILE

Floor: Fossil 12" x 12" and 6" X 12", and Charcoal 6" x 6". Hearth: Charcoal 12" x 12". Wall: Fossil 12" x 12".

FEATURES:

♦ Semi-matte finish stone look

♦ Extra durable

♦ Modular sizes for design versatility and ease of transition from floor to wall applications

USAGE:

♦ All commercial and residential wall and floor applications in dry pedestrian areas

TYPICAL PROPERTIES[1]:

Meets or exceeds A137.1 ANSI standard.

C.O.F.[2]		Durability	Glaze	Break
Dry	Wet	Classification	Hardness	Strength
0.61	0.51	Class IV	7.0 Mohs	300 lbs. avg.

[1] Refer to table of contents for explanation of tile properties.

[2] These values may vary from lot to lot.

♦ .34" thick

♦ 3.42 lbs. avg. weight/sq. ft.

Florida Tile's exclusive MONO-SIZED™ process ensures consistent squareness and size from tile to tile (8 x 8 and larger).

TRIM:

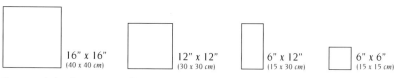

Surface Bullnose	Product #	Imperial	Metric (cm)
①	① P-44C9	4" x 12"	10 x 30

SIZES:

16" x 16"
(40 x 40 cm)

12" x 12"
(30 x 30 cm)

6" x 12"
(15 x 30 cm)

6" x 6"
(15 x 15 cm)

For suggested patterns, see pg. 13

9901 Talc

9906 Charcoal

9916 Fossil

9930 Shale Beige

9959 Chlorite

9977 Amber

Color reproductions in this printed piece will vary from the actual tile colors, final selection should be made from tile samples.

Residence, Tampa, FL. Floor: Natural 12" x 12".

LIBERTY
NATURA® FLOOR TILE

TRIM:

Surface Bullnose	Product #	Imperial	Metric (cm)
① P-4489	4" x 8"	10 x 20
① P-44C9	4" x 12"	10 x 30
② PN-4449	4" x 4"	10 x 10

Sanitary Cove Base & Outside Corner	Product #	Imperial	Metric (cm)
③ PCL/R-3689	6" x 8"	15 x 20
④ P-3689	6" x 8"	15 x 20

Sanitary Cove Base & Inside Corner	Product #	Imperial	Metric (cm)
④ P-3689	6" x 8"	15 x 20
⑤ PB-106	3/4" x 6"	2 x 15

FEATURES:

♦ Durable, textured glaze for high traffic

♦ Random fumé shading

♦ Stain-resistant

USAGE:

♦ All commercial and residential floor applications in dry pedestrian areas

TYPICAL PROPERTIES[1]:

Meets or exceeds A137.1 ANSI standard.

C.O.F.[2]		Durability	Glaze	Break
Dry	Wet	Classification	Hardness	Strength
0.93	0.77	Class IV	8.0 Mohs	300 lbs. avg.

[1] Refer to table of contents for explanation of tile properties

[2] These values may vary from lot to lot.

♦ .34" thick

♦ 3.20 lbs. avg. weight/sq. ft.

SIZES:

8" x 8" (20 x 20 cm)

12" x 12" (30 x 30 cm)

8601 Frost

8603 Parchment

8606 Ink

8607 Natural

8615 Stucco

8619 Pearl

8626 Adobe

8647 Old Gold

8659 Ivy

8664 Turquoise

8680 Cognac

8685 Garnet

Color reproductions in this printed piece will vary from the actual tile colors, final selection should be made from tile samples.

MONO SIZED
UNIFORM / SIZE / PRECISE / CONTROL

Florida Tile's exclusive MONO-SIZED™ process ensures consistent squareness and size from tile to tile (8 x 8 and larger).

MARBLE
NATURA® FLOOR TILE

Residence, Grasslands Project, Lakeland, FL. Floor: Capri Green 12" x 12". Countertop: Matte Glaze wall tile 6" x 6" accented with Rounded Moldings Forest Green.

FEATURES:

♦ Available in high-gloss glaze

♦ Delicate pastel veining on translucent white background

♦ Stain-resistant

USAGE:

♦ All residential and light commercial floor applications

TYPICAL PROPERTIES[1]:

Meets or exceeds A137.1 ANSI standard.

C.O.F.[2] Dry	Wet	Durability Classification	Glaze Hardness	Break Strength
0.75	0.36	Class III	5.0 Mohs	300 lbs. avg.

[1] Refer to table of contents for explanation of tile properties.
[2] These values may vary from lot to lot.

♦ .34" thick

♦ 2.88 lbs. avg. weight/sq. ft.

Florida Tile's exclusive MONO-SIZED™ process ensures consistent squareness and size from tile to tile (8 x 8 and larger).

TRIM:

Surface Bullnose	Product #	Imperial	Metric (cm)
①	P-4489	4" x 8"	10 x 20
②	P-44C9	4" x 12"	10 x 30

SIZES:

8" x 8"
(20 x 20 cm)

12" x 12"
(30 x 30 cm)

9112 Milan Gray

9124 Roman Haze

9156 Capri Green

9166 Venice Blue

9183 Lisbon Rose

Color reproductions in this printed piece will vary from the actual tile colors, final selection should be made from tile samples.

Wall: Perlato 12" x 12"; Floor and Wall: Perlato and Rosa Aurora 12" x 12" used with Tumblestone Marble Listello in Rosa.

TRIM:

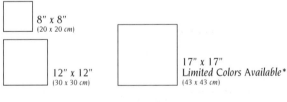

Surface Bullnose	Product #	Imperial	Metric (cm)
①	① P-3CL	3" x 12"	8 x 30

SIZES:

8" x 8"
(20 x 20 cm)

12" x 12"
(30 x 30 cm)

17" x 17"
*Limited Colors Available**
(43 x 43 cm)

7308 Crema Marfil*

7319 Pearl Carrara*

7316 Rosa Venezia

7320 Perlato*

7326 Alicante

7353 Verde Antico

7379 Rosa Aurora

*Also available in 17" x 17" (43 x 43 cm)

Color reproductions in this printed piece will vary from the actual tile colors, final selection should be made from tile samples.

FEATURES:

♦ Intricate look of stone
♦ Rich, soft sheen colors
♦ Multiple glaze shading
♦ Easy maintenance
♦ Stain-resistant

USAGE:

♦ All residential and commercial floor applications in dry pedestrian areas

TYPICAL PROPERTIES[1]:

Meets or exceeds A137.1 ANSI standard.

C.O.F.[2] Dry	Wet	Durability Classification	Glaze Hardness	Break Strength
0.72	0.47	Class IV	6.5 Mohs	300 lbs. avg.

[1] Refer to table of contents for explanation of tile properties.
[2] These values may vary from lot to lot.

♦ .33" thick
♦ 3.3 lbs. avg. weight/sq. ft.

19

RUSTICO II
NATURA® FLOOR TILE

Heritage Log Homes Project; <u>Mary Emmerling's Country Magazine</u>, Pagosa Springs, CO,
Countertop: Almond 8" x 8". Backsplash: Aspen Teakwood 12" x 12".

FEATURES:

♦ Soft sculptured edges and rounded corners

♦ Gentle undulated semi-matte glaze surface

♦ Stain-resistant

USAGE:

♦ All residential and light commercial floor applications

TYPICAL PROPERTIES[1]:

Meets or exceeds A137.1 ANSI standard.

C.O.F.[2]		Durability	Glaze	Break
Dry	Wet	Classification	Hardness	Strength
0.73	0.56	Class III	7.5 Mohs	300 lbs. avg.

[1] Refer to table of contents for explanation of tile properties.
[2] These values may vary from lot to lot.

♦ .34" thick

♦ 3.4 lbs. avg. weight/sq. ft.

Florida Tile's exclusive MONO-SIZED™ process ensures consistent squareness and size from tile to tile (8 x 8 and larger).

TRIM:

Surface Bullnose

	Product #	Imperial	Metric (cm)
① P-4489	4" x 8"	10 x 20
② P-44C9	4" x 12"	10 x 30

SIZES:

8" x 8"
(20 x 20 cm)

12" x 12"
(30 x 30 cm)

8901N Warm White   8903 Parchment   8911 Ironstone

8925 Mexican Sand   8935 Almond   8979 Sunset   8991 Leather   8995 Antique Red

Color reproductions in this printed piece will vary from the actual tile colors, final selection should be made from tile samples.

20

Residence, Boca Raton, FL. Floor: White Sand 12" x 12".

SHANNON
NATURA® FLOOR TILE

TRIM:

Surface Bullnose	Product #	Imperial	Metric (cm)
① P-4489	4" x 8"	10 x 20
① P-44C9	4" x 12"	10 x 30
② PN-4449	4" x 4"	10 x 10

SIZES:

8" x 8" (20 x 20 cm)

12" x 12" (30 x 30 cm)

 8301 Cotton

 8302 White Sand

 8304 Platinum

 8313 Clouds

 8322 Mushroom

 8324 Light Beige

 8335 Almond

8356 Oasis

8358 Clear Teal

8361 Blue Ice

8372 Clay Pink

8387 Tea Rose

Color reproductions in this printed piece will vary from the actual tile colors, final selection should be made from tile samples.

FEATURES:

♦ Distinctive mottled surface
♦ Semi-matte glaze
♦ Easiest of all floors to maintain
♦ Stain-resistant

USAGE:

♦ All residential and light commercial floor applications

TYPICAL PROPERTIES[1]:

Meets or exceeds A137.1 ANSI standard.

C.O.F.[2]		Durability	Glaze	Break
Dry	Wet	Classification	Hardness	Strength
0.74	0.33	Class III	6.5 Mohs	300 lbs. avg.

[1] Refer to table of contents for explanation of tile properties.
[2] These values may vary from lot to lot.

♦ .34" thick
♦ 3.4 lbs. avg. weight/sq. ft.

MONO
UNIFORM
SIZE
PRECISE
CONTROL
SIZED

Florida Tile's exclusive MONO-SIZED™ process ensures consistent squareness and size from tile to tile (8 x 8 and larger).

SIERRA

NATURA® FLOOR TILE

Sierra Floor: White 13" x 13".

FEATURES:

♦ Cleaved and honed slate appearance

♦ Unique texture creating movement

♦ Stain-resistant

♦ Soft monochromatic hues

USAGE:

♦ All residential and light commercial floor applications

TYPICAL PROPERTIES[1]:

Meets or exceeds A137.1 ANSI standard.

C.O.F.[2]		Durability	Glaze	Break
Dry	Wet	Classification	Hardness	Strength
0.72	0.52	Class III	7.0 Mohs	170 lbs. avg.

[1] Refer to table of contents for explanation of tile properties.

[2] These values may vary from lot to lot.

♦ .31" thick

♦ 2.76 lbs. avg. weight/sq. ft.

SIZES:

☐ 8" x 8"
(20 x 20 cm)

☐ 10" x 10"
(25 x 25 cm)

☐ 13" x 13"
(33 x 33 cm)

7201 White

7202 Beige

7204 Tan

7219 Gray

7250 Green

Color reproductions in this printed piece will vary from the actual tile colors, final selection should be made from tile samples.

Georgia Square Mall, Athens, GA. Floor: Oyster, Silver and Royal Blue 12" x 12" shown with 4" x 4" cut pieces of Burgundy and Oyster.

TRIM:

Surface Bullnose

	Product #	Imperial	Metric (cm)
①	P-4489	4" x 8"	10 x 20
①	P-44C9	4" x 12"	10 x 30
②	PN-4449	4" x 4"	10 x 10

Sanitary Cove Base & Inside Corner

	Product #	Imperial	Metric (cm)
④	P-3689	6" x 8"	15 x 20
⑤	PB-106	3/4" x 6"	2 x 15

Sanitary Cove Base & Outside Corner

	Product #	Imperial	Metric (cm)
③	PCL/R-3689	6" x 8"	15 x 20
④	P-3689	6" x 8"	15 x 20

FEATURES:

♦ Textured, semi-gloss glaze

♦ Extra durable, "10-Year Wear Warranty"

♦ Coordinates with Confetti wall tile

♦ Mix and match with Natura® Granite floor tile

♦ Stain-resistant

USAGE:

♦ All commercial and residential wall, countertop and floor applications in dry pedestrian areas

TYPICAL PROPERTIES[1]:

Meets or exceeds A137.1 ANSI standard.

C.O.F.[2]		Durability	Glaze	Break
Dry	Wet	Classification	Hardness	Strength
0.78	0.50	Class IV+	8.5 Mohs	300 lbs. avg.

[1] Refer to table of contents for explanation of tile properties.

[2] These values may vary from lot to lot.

♦ .34" thick

♦ 3.39 lbs. avg. weight/sq. ft.

SIZES:

8" x 8" (20 x 20 cm)

12" x 12" (30 x 30 cm)

8701 White

8703 Bone

8505 Black

8707 Oyster

8712 Silver

8722 Clay

8725 Mexican Sand

8559 Forest Green

8563 Teal Green

8568 Royal Blue

8580 Purple

8581 Coralstone

8584 Burgundy

Color reproductions in this printed piece will vary from the actual tile colors, final selection should be made from tile samples.

MONO SIZED
UNIFORM
SIZE
PRECISE
CONTROL

Florida Tile's exclusive MONO-SIZED™ process ensures consistent squareness and size from tile to tile (8 x 8 and larger).

VENTO
NATURA® FLOOR TILE

Residence, Grasslands Project, Lakeland, FL. Floor: White Sanibel Pattern 8" x 8".

FEATURES:

♦ Semi-matte glaze, subtle color variation

♦ Three decorative engraved patterns available

♦ Stain-resistant

USAGE:

♦ All residential and light commercial floor applications

TYPICAL PROPERTIES[1]:

Meets or exceeds A137.1 ANSI standard.

C.O.F.[2]		Durability	Glaze	Break
Dry	Wet	Classification	Hardness	Strength
0.70	0.37	Class III	6.5 Mohs	300 lbs. avg.

[1] Refer to table of contents for explanation of tile properties.
[2] These values may vary from lot to lot.

♦ .34" thick

♦ 3.5 lbs. avg. weight/sq. ft.

Florida Tile's exclusive MONO-SIZED™ process ensures consistent squareness and size from tile to tile (8 x 8 and larger).

TRIM:

Surface Bullnose

	Product #	Imperial	Metric (cm)
① P-4489	4" x 8"	10 x 20
① P-44C9	4" x 12"	10 x 30
② PN-4449	4" x 4"	10 x 10

SIZES:

8" x 8"
(20 x 20 cm)

12" x 12"
(30 x 30 cm)

*Patterns available in 8 x 8. **Captiva Pattern also available in 12 x 12 8401 White.

8401 White

8402 Cameo

8404 Putty

8414 Silver Gray

8422 Fawn Beige

8425 Mexican Sand

8435 Almond

8457 Jade

8466 Vermont Blue

8481 Coral

8489 Berry

NX8001
Sanibel Pattern*

NX8002
Captiva Pattern**

NX8003
Amelia Pattern*

Color reproductions in this printed piece will vary from the actual tile colors, final selection should be made from tile samples.

Condominium, Indian Shores, FL. Floor: Cameo 12" x 12" Hexagon with NATURA Verona Verde 4" x 4" dot.

VENTO COORDINATES
NATURA® FLOOR TILE

TRIM:

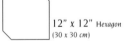

Surface Bullnose

	Product #	Imperial	Metric (cm)
① P-4489	4" x 8"	10 x 20
① P-44C9	4" x 12"	10 x 30
② PN-4449	4" x 4"	10 x 10

SIZES:

4" x 4"
(10 x 10 cm)

12" x 12" Hexagon
(30 x 30 cm)

Dots*

8801 White	8805 Black	8817 Dove Gray
8824 Doeskin	8859N Midori	8865 Chicory	8868N Cobalt
8876 Adobe	8885 Winestone	9305 Onyx	9359 Verde

Hexagon

12X12C2/8401 White   12X12C2/8402 Cameo

*Use care when cleaning dots. Abrasive cleaners will cause scratching to shiny surfaces.

Color reproductions in this printed piece will vary from the actual tile colors, final selection should be made from tile samples.

FEATURES:

♦ Semi-matte glaze, subtle color variation

♦ 4 x 4 dots for hexagon available in NATURA® Designer and Verona floor tile series

♦ Stain-resistant

USAGE:

♦ All residential and light commercial floor applications

TYPICAL PROPERTIES[1]:

Meets or exceeds A137.1 ANSI standard.

C.O.F.[2]		Durability Classification	Glaze Hardness	Break Strength
Dry	Wet			
0.70	0.37	Class III	6.5 Mohs	300 lbs. avg.

[1] Refer to table of contents for explanation of tile properties.
[2] These values may vary from lot to lot.

♦ .34" thick

♦ 3.4 lbs. avg. weight/sq. ft.

MONO
UNIFORM   SIZE
PRECISE   CONTROL
SIZED

Florida Tile's exclusive MONO-SIZED™ process ensures consistent squareness and size from tile to tile (8 x 8 and larger).

VERONA
NATURA® FLOOR TILE

Floor: Verde 12" x 12". Wall: Verona Opalescent White and Inserts 8" x 10"; Verona Listello; Rounded Moldings Verde; and Chair Rail Lumina White Matte. Countertops: Matte Glaze 6" x 6" trimmed with Chair Rail Lumina White Matte.

FEATURES:

♦ Rich marbling in classic colors

♦ High-gloss glaze

♦ Coordinates with Verona wall tile including decorative Listellos and Moldings

♦ Stain-resistant

♦ 4 x 4 size available for use as dot with Vento hexagon as well as being modular with other 8 x 8 and 12 x 12 Florida Tile® floor tile

USAGE:

♦ All residential and light commercial floor applications

TYPICAL PROPERTIES[1]:

Meets or exceeds A137.1 ANSI standard.

C.O.F.[2]		Durability Classification	Glaze Hardness	Break Strength
Dry	Wet			
0.66	0.33	Class III	5.0 Mohs	300 lbs. avg.

[1] Refer to table of contents for explanation of tile properties.
[2] These values may vary from lot to lot.

♦ .34" thick

♦ 2.80 lbs. avg. weight/sq. ft.

MONO SIZED
UNIFORM
SIZE
PRECISE
CONTROL

Florida Tile's exclusive MONO-SIZED™ process ensures consistent squareness and size from tile to tile (8 x 8 and larger).

TRIM:

Surface Bullnose	Product #	Imperial	Metric (cm)
①	① P-44C9	4" x 12"	10 x 30

SIZES:

◻ 4" x 4"
(10 x 10 cm)

◻ 12" x 12"
(30 x 30 cm)

9305 Onyx

9359 Verde

Color reproductions in this printed piece will vary from the actual tile colors, final selection should be made from tile samples.

Floor: Ecru, Mahogany, and Emerald Matte 8" x 8". Wall: Ecru Gloss 6" x 8", Emerald and Mahogany Gloss 8" x 8", Scroll Listello 2" x 6".

CARMEL
WALL TILE

WALL TILE

TRIM:

Surface Bullnose

	Product #	Imperial	Metric (cm)
①	S-4269*	2" x 6"	5 x 15
②	SN-4269*	2" x 2"	5 x 5
③	S-4289*	2" x 8"	5 x 20
③	S-42A9	2" x 10"	5 x 25
④	Field	6" x 8"	15 x 20

Conventional & Thin Set

	Product #	Imperial	Metric (cm)
①	A-106**	¾" x 6"	2 x 15
②	AC-106**	¾" x 6"	2 x 15
③	A-108**	1¼" x 8"	3 x 20
②	AC-108**	1¼" x 8"	3 x 20
④	Field	6" x 8"	15 x 20

* Gloss finish only; ** Gloss finish only, non-screen printed, coordinating color

SIZES:

▢ **2" x 6"** (5 x 15 cm)

▢ **3" x 8"** (8 x 20 cm)

▢ **6" x 8"** *Gloss* (15 x 20 cm)

▢ **8" x 8"** *Matte/Gloss* (20 x 20 cm)

▢ **8" x 10"** *Gloss* (5 x 25 cm)

FEATURES:

- ♦ Gloss and matte glaze available
- ♦ Classic marbling in elegant colors
- ♦ Large size format with coordinating, modular listellos
- ♦ Three decorative listello patterns
- ♦ Coordinates with Rounded and Chair Rail Moldings for further accenting

USAGE:

- ♦ All residential and commercial wall applications and residential bathroom floors

TYPICAL PROPERTIES[1] (MATTE):

Meets or exceeds A137.1 ANSI standard.

C.O.F.[2]		Durability	Glaze	Break
Dry	Wet	Classification	Hardness	Strength
0.72	0.45	Class III	6.0 Mohs	165 lbs. avg.

[1] Refer to table of contents for explanation of tile properties.
[2] These values may vary from lot to lot.

- ♦ .30" thick
- ♦ 2.82 lbs. avg. weight/sq. ft.

── Listellos not to scale to show detail ──

Scroll CL26A 2 x 6
Scroll CL38A 3 x 8

Patterns CL26B 2 x 6
Patterns CL38B 3 x 8

Diamonds CL26C 2 x 6
Diamonds CL38C 3 x 8

2810 Winterset Gloss
2710 Winterset Matte

2835 Ecru Gloss
2735 Ecru Matte

2859 Emerald Gloss
2759 Emerald Matte

2879 Quartz Gloss
2779 Quartz Matte

2893 Mahogany Gloss
2793 Mahogany Matte

Color reproductions in this printed piece will vary from the actual tile colors, final selection should be made from tile samples.

WALL TILE

CONFETTI/GEOS
WALL TILE

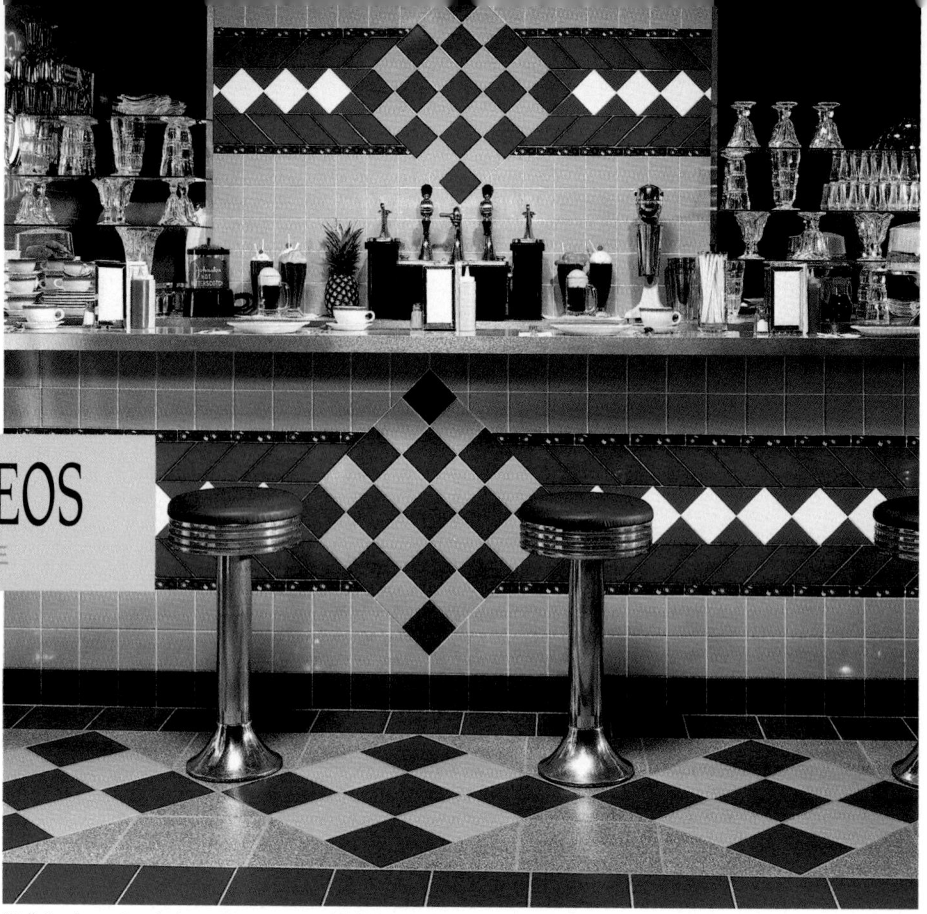

Wall: Coralstone, Royal Blue 4-3/8" x 4-3/8" with field Bright Glaze White; Burgundy Triangle, Royal Blue Parallelogram right and left; Memphis Deco Liner 2" x 6". Floor: Coordinating NATURA® Tough One and Granite colors 12" x 12" and 8" x 8".

FEATURES:

- ♦ High-gloss glaze in bold colors
- ♦ Decorative accent tiles and listellos
- ♦ Coordinates with wall tile moldings, and Natura® Granite and Tough-One floor tile
- ♦ "Geos" parallelogram and triangle shapes in selected colors

USAGE:

- ♦ All commercial and residential wall applications

TYPICAL PROPERTIES:

Meets or exceeds A137.1 ANSI standard.

- ♦ .30" thick
- ♦ 2.87 lbs. avg. weight/sq. ft.

GEOS[1]:

438X8R Right Parallelogram
4⅜" x 6⅛" (11 x 16 *cm*)

438X8L Left Parallelogram
4⅜" x 6⅛" (11 x 16 *cm*)

438T Triangle
4⅜" x 4⅜" x 6" (11 x 11 x 15 *cm*)

1 Geos available in White 100, French Provincial 2, Black 1005, Forest Green 1059, Royal Blue 1068, and Burgundy 1084

TRIM:

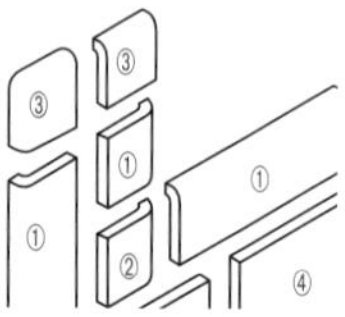

Bullnose	Product #	Imperial	Metric (cm)
	① A-4200[2]	2" x 6"	5 x 15
	② AM-4200[2]	2" x 2"	5 x 5
	③ AN-4200[2]	2" x 2"	5 x 5
	④ Field	4⅜" x 4⅜"	11 x 11

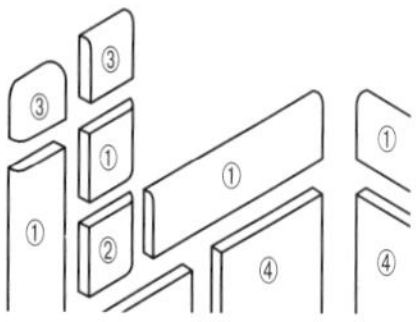

Bullnose-Thin Set	Product #	Imperial	Metric (cm)
	① S-4269[2]	2" x 6"	5 x 15
	② SM-4269[2]	2" x 2"	5 x 5
	③ SN-4269[2]	2" x 2"	5 x 5
	④ Field	4⅜" x 4⅜"	11 x 11

[2]Available in 1005 only

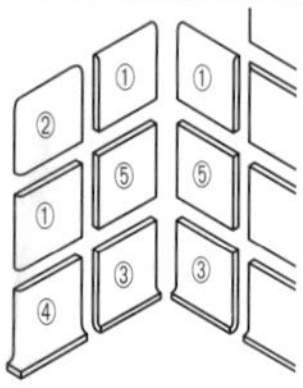

Bullnose & Cove Base-Thin Set	Product #	Imperial	Metric (cm)
	① S-4449	4⅜" x 4⅜"	11 x 11
	② SN-4449	4⅜" x 4⅜"	11 x 11
	③ A-3401[2]	3 15/16" x 4⅜"	10 x 11
	④ SCL/R-3401[2]	3 15/16" x 4 11/16"	10 x 12
	⑤ Field	4⅜" x 4⅜"	11 x 11

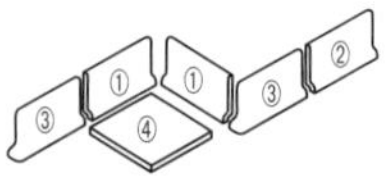

Sanitary Base-Thin Set	Product #	Imperial	Metric (cm)
	① S-3419[2]	3⅞" x 6"	10 x 15
	② SCL-3419	3⅞" x 6"	10 x 15
	③ SCR-3419	3⅞" x 6"	10 x 15
	④ Field	4-⅜" x 4-⅜"	11 x 11

SIZES:

1" x 6" (3 x 15 *cm*)
4⅜" x 4⅜" (11 x 11 *cm*)
2" x 2" (5 x 5 *cm*)

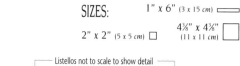

438909A/100 Daytona Deco

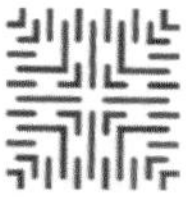

438909B/100 Daytona Multi

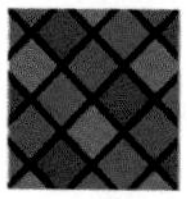

438910/1 Harlequin Deco

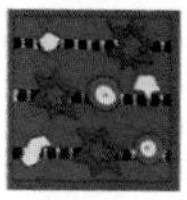

438911/1 Memphis Deco

Listellos not to scale to show detail

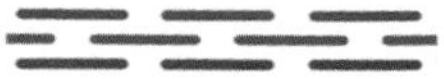

FX6109/100 Daytona

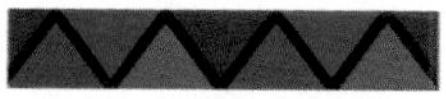

FX6110/1 Harlequin

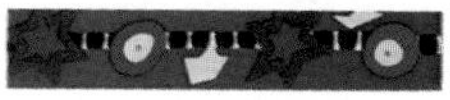

FX6111/1 Memphis

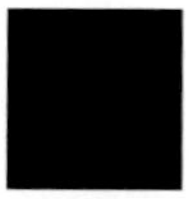

1005 Black

1059 Forest Green

1063 Teal

1068 Royal Blue

1080 Purple

1081 Coralstone

1084 Burgundy

1090 Harness

Color reproductions in this printed piece will vary from the actual tile colors, final selection should be made from tile samples.

Residence, Arvida Homes River Hills Project, Valrico, FL. Wall: Lumina White 8" x 8" accented with Rope Moldings in Lumina White and Sculptured Tulip Molding in French Provincial.

CURRENTS
WALL TILE

WALL
TILE

SIZES:

 2" x 6" Liners (5 x 15 cm)

6" x 8" Insert/Field
(15 x 20 cm)

8" x 8" Field
(20 x 20 cm)

Insert

6X8025F
Floral

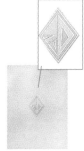

6X8026P
Profile

6X8027M
Motions

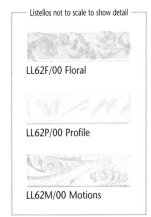

Listellos not to scale to show detail

LL62F/00 Floral

LL62P/00 Profile

LL62M/00 Motions

FEATURES

♦ High-gloss glaze, large size format
♦ Random undulation for depth and interest
♦ Decorative liners and inserts for design options
♦ Coordinates with Sculptured, Rope, Rounded and Chair Rail Moldings for walls

USAGE

♦ All residential and commercial wall applications

TYPICAL PROPERTIES[1]:

Meets or exceeds A137.1 ANSI standard.

♦ .30" thick
♦ 2.85 lbs. avg. weight/sq. ft.

TRIM:

See page 48 for trim isometrics.

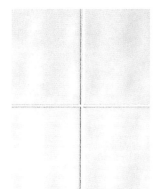

3500 Lumina White

3502 French Provincial

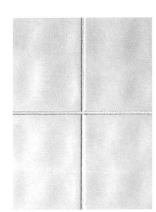

3519 Pearl

3582 Blush

Color reproductions in this printed piece will vary from the actual tile colors, final selection should be made from tile samples. Not shown to scale to show detail.

BRIGHT GLAZE
WALL TILE

New Southern Home, 1994, Orlando, FL. Countertop: New White 6" x 6" with alternating Bone and New White A8262 trim on counter front and S4669, SN4669 on backsplash.

FEATURES:

♦ High-gloss glaze
♦ Broad line of colors to coordinate with many wall tile moldings and Natura® floor tiles

USAGE:

♦ All commercial and residential wall and countertop applications

TYPICAL PROPERTIES:

Meets or exceeds A137.1 ANSI standard.

♦ .30" thick
♦ 2.80 lbs. avg. weight/sq. ft.

TRIM:

See page 48 for trim isometrics.

ALL COLORS AVAILABLE:

☐ 4⅜" x 4⅜"
(11 x 11 cm)

LIMITED COLORS AVAILABLE: (see notes)

☐ 2" x 2" (5 x 5 cm)

☐ 6" x 6" (15 x 15 cm)

100 New White*** | 1 White*** | 2 French Provincial*** | 3 Bone***

4 Parchment*** | 05 Onyx** | 7 Tender Grey | 12 Sterling Silver

20 Mink | 22 Fawn Beige | 24 Candlelyght | 35 Almond | 46 Lemon Chiffon | 54 Seafoam | 59 Verde**

66 Lt. Vermont Blue | 82 Blush* | 83N Dusty Rose | 101 Granite | 201 Gold Dust | 301 Pearl White | 302 Snow White

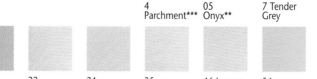

* Also available in 2" x 2"; ** **Only** available in 2" x 2"; *** 6" x 6" Tile available in these colors

Color reproductions in this printed piece will vary from the actual tile colors, final selection should be made from tile samples.

Countertop: Pearl 4-3/8" x 4-3/8" field with S4269 trim.

FEATURES:

- ♦ Delicate crystalline textured glaze
- ♦ Resistant to wear and water spots
- ♦ Large color palette to coordinate with many wall tile moldings and Natura® floor tiles

USAGE:

- ♦ All commercial and residential wall, residential countertop and bathroom floor applications

TYPICAL PROPERTIES[1]:

Meets or exceeds A137.1 ANSI standard.

C.O.F.[2]		Durability	Glaze	Break
Dry	Wet	Classification	Hardness	Strength
0.79	0.40	Class II	6.5 Mohs	150 lbs. avg.

[1] Refer to table of contents for explanation of tile properties.
[2] These values may vary from lot to lot.

- ♦ .30" thick
- ♦ 2.90 lbs. avg. weight/sq. ft.

SIZES:

- ☐ 2" x 2" (5 x 5 cm)
- ☐ 4⅜" x 4⅜" (11 x 11 cm)
- ⬡ 4¼" Hexagon (11 cm)

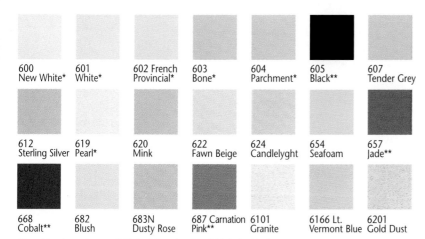

600 New White*	601 White*	602 French Provincial*	603 Bone*	604 Parchment*	605 Black**	607 Tender Grey
612 Sterling Silver	619 Pearl*	620 Mink	622 Fawn Beige	624 Candlelyght	654 Seafoam	657 Jade**
668 Cobalt**	682 Blush	683N Dusty Rose	687 Carnation Pink**	6101 Granite	6166 Lt. Vermont Blue	6201 Gold Dust

*Complete trim package available for full service; **Available in 2 x 2 only

Color reproductions in this printed piece will vary from the actual tile colors, final selection should be made from tile samples.

TRIM:

See page 48 for trim isometrics.

MATTE GLAZE
WALL TILE

Countertop: Lumina White 6" x 6" field with A3602 trim and Forest Green and Lumina White Rounded Moldings.

FEATURES:

♦ Soft matte sheen glaze
♦ Large color palette to coordinate with many wall tile moldings and Natura® floor tiles

USAGE:

♦ All commercial and residential wall, residential countertop and bathroom floor applications

TYPICAL PROPERTIES[1]:

Meets or exceeds A137.1 ANSI standard.

C.O.F.[2]		Durability	Glaze	Break
Dry	Wet	Classification	Hardness	Strength
0.81	0.44	Class II	6.5 Mohs	150 lbs. avg.

[1] Refer to table of contents for explanation of tile properties.
[2] These values may vary from lot to lot.

♦ .30" thick
♦ 2.81 lbs. avg. weight/sq. ft.

TRIM:

See page 48 for trim isometrics.

ALL COLORS AVAILABLE:

☐ 4⅜" x 4⅜" (11 x 11 cm)   ☐ 6" x 6" (15 x 15 cm)

LIMITED COLORS AVAILABLE: (see notes)

☐ 2" x 2" (5 x 5 cm)

☐ 6" x 6" Pentagon (15 x 15 cm)   ☐ 6" x 6" Hexagon (15 x 15 cm)

700 Lumina White*	701 Matte White	702 French Provincial*	703 Bone White	704 Parchment	705 Black**	712 Silver
719 Pearl	721 Vellum	735 Almond	755 Light Turquoise	760 Barely Blue	772 Coral Tone	782 Blush

* Also available in 2" x 2," 6" x 6" Hexagon, and 6" x 6" Pentagon; ** **Only** available in 2" x 2"

Color reproductions in this printed piece will vary from the actual tile colors, final selection should be made from tile samples.

HOTSPOTS
WALL TILE

Hot Spots Wall Tile: Red 6" x 6", 2" x 2", 1/2 x 6", Orange 4-3/8" x 4-3/8", 1/2" x 6", Yellow 2" x 2", 1/2" x 6".

FEATURES:

♦ High-gloss glaze in bright colors

♦ Suited for a variety of commercial wall applications

♦ 2" x 2" tiles are modular with 4-3/8" x 4-3/8"

♦ All sizes available in each brilliant color

♦ Molding stops available

USAGE:

♦ All commercial and residential wall applications

TYPICAL PROPERTIES:

Meets or exceeds A137.1 ANSI standard.

♦ .30" thick

♦ 2.72 lbs. avg. weight/sq. ft.

SIZES: 1/2" x 6" (1 x 15 cm) ▭   2" x 2" (5 x 5 cm) ☐   4⅜" x 4⅜" (11 x 11 cm) ☐   6" x 6" (15 x 15 cm) ☐

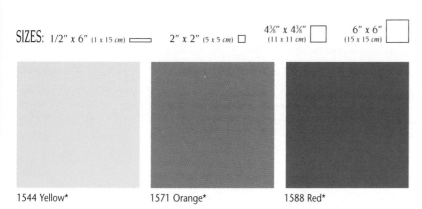

1544 Yellow*   1571 Orange*   1588 Red*

*These colors have a tendency to show slight crazing similar to the conditions found on fine china and pottery. This crazing has no effect on the structural integrity of the tile. Some shade variation is also inherent to these colors.

Color reproductions in this printed piece will vary from the actual tile colors, final selection should be made from tile samples.

33

IMAGERY II
WALL TILE

Floor: Green 6" x 6" (Matte) Wall: Green 6" x 8" field and Dogwood Inserts 6" x 8" accented with Green Dogwood 2" x 6" Listello, Celedon Green Rope Moldings, and Lumina White Chair Rail.

FEATURES

♦ Random marble pattern in pastel colors

♦ Available in both gloss and matte glaze

♦ Decorative inserts and listellos

♦ Coordinates with Natura® floor tile, Marble series, and decorative wall tile moldings

USAGE

♦ Gloss is appropriate for all residential and commercial wall applications

♦ Matte is appropriate for all residential and commercial wall applications and residential bathroom floors

TYPICAL PROPERTIES[1] (MATTE):

Meets or exceeds A137.1 ANSI standard.

C.O.F.[2]		Durability Classification	Glaze Hardness	Break Strength
Dry	Wet			
0.86	0.33	Class II	6.5 Mohs	150 lbs. avg.

[1] Refer to table of contents for explanation of tile properties.
[2] These values may vary from lot to lot.

♦ .30" thick

♦ 2.82 lbs. avg. weight/sq. ft.

TRIM:

See page 48 for trim isometrics.

SIZES:

☐ 2" x 6" *Listellos*
   (5 x 15 cm)

☐ 6" x 6" *Matte*
   (15 x 15 cm)

☐ 6" x 8" *Field/Insert*
   (15 x 20 cm)

Matte

Listellos not to scale to show detail

Listello-Dogwood

62DW/3124 Beige   62DW/3166 Blue

62DW/3112 Gray   62DW/3156 Green   62DW/3183 Rose

66/3712 Gray   66/3724 Beige   66/3756 Green   66/3766 Blue   66/3783 Rose

Field (Gloss)

68/3112 Gray   68/3124 Beige   68/3156 Green   68/3166 Blue   68/3183 Rose

Insert-Dogwood

68DW/3112 Gray   68DW/3124 Beige   68DW/3156 Green   68DW/3166 Blue   68DW/3183 Rose

Color reproductions in this printed piece will vary from the actual tile colors, final selection should be made from tile samples.

Countertop and Backsplash: Winter Mint field with S4269 trim accented with Crystal Glaze 2" x 2" Dots in New White and Black, and Rounded Moldings in Light Turquoise and Black.

SIZES:

4⅜" x 4⅜"
(11 x 11 cm)

1412 Silver Mist	1420 Touch of Mink

1430 Barely Beige   1456 Winter Mint   1462 Sheer Blue   1473 Peach Chiffon

Color reproductions in this printed piece will vary from the actual tile colors, final selection should be made from tile samples.

FEATURES:

♦ Updated color palette in gloss glaze
♦ Gentle mist of random color shading

USAGE:

♦ All residential wall and counter applications and commercial wall applications

TYPICAL PROPERTIES:

Meets or exceeds A137.1 ANSI standard.

♦ .30" thick
♦ 2.93 lbs. avg. weight/sq. ft.

TRIM:

See page 48 for trim isometrics.

MILANO
WALL TILE

Wall: Lumina White 6" x 6" and 6" x 6" Pentagon with Vine Dots 2" x 2" accented with 2" x 6" Vine Listello and Polished Silver Rounded Moldings. Floor: Lumina White 6" x 6" and 6" x 6" Pentagon with Vine Dots 2" x 2".

FEATURES

♦ Tone-on-tone, luminous glaze

♦ Glass relief designs on the accent listellos and 2" x 2" dots

♦ Listellos and dots to complement pentagon and 6" x 6" field

♦ Coordinates with Florida Tile® moldings and Natura® floor tile

USAGE

♦ Residential and commercial wall applications and residential bathroom floors and countertops (including 2" x 2" dots)

TYPICAL PROPERTIES[1]:

Meets or exceeds A137.1 ANSI standard.

C.O.F.[2]		Durability	Glaze	Break
Dry	Wet	Classification	Hardness	Strength
0.81	0.44	Class II	6.5 Mohs	110 lbs. avg.

[1] Refer to table of contents for explanation of tile properties
[2] These values may vary from lot to lot.

♦ .30" thick

♦ 2.80 lbs. avg. weight/sq. ft.

TRIM:

Bullnose-Thin Set	Product #	Imperial	Metric (cm)
① S-4269	2" x 6"	5 x 15
② SN-4269	2" x 2"	5 x 5

SIZES:

☐ 2" x 6" *Listello* (5 x 15 cm)

☐ 2" x 2" *Dot* (5 x 5 cm)

☐ 6" x 6" (15 x 15 cm)

⬠ 6" x 6" *Pentagon* (15 x 15 cm)

Field

3300
Lumina White

Dots

ML22A/3300
Vine

ML22B/3300
Floré

ML22C/3300
Crown

Listellos

ML26A/3300
Vine

ML26B/3300
Floré

ML26C/3300
Crown

Color reproductions in this printed piece will vary from the actual tile colors, final selection should be made from tile samples.

Wall: *Light Vermont Blue and Fruit Decorative Inserts 4-3/8" x 4-3/8", Decorative Fruit 3-tile border, 8-tile Fruit Mural, and Rope Moldings in Forest Green. Countertop: Light Vermont Blue 4-3/8" x 4-3/8" with 3-tile Fruit Border and Forest Green Rope Moldings on counter front.*

POTTER'S CHOICE®
WALL TILE

FEATURES:

♦ Rich, gloss glaze

♦ Popular, hand-sculptured surface

♦ Decorative tile inserts, borders and murals for design options

♦ Coordinates with many decorative wall tile moldings and Natura® floor tiles

USAGE:

♦ All residential wall and countertop and commercial wall applications

TYPICAL PROPERTIES:

Meets or exceeds A137.1 ANSI standard.

♦ .332" thick

♦ 2.97 lbs. avg. weight/sq. ft.

TRIM:

See page 48 for trim isometrics.

SIZES:

☐ 4⅜" x 4⅜"
(11 x 11 cm)

☐ 6" x 6"
(15 x 15 cm)

5500 New White

5501 White

5502 White Sand

5503 Bone

5519 Fashion Grey

5554 Seafoam

5566
Lt. Vermont Blue

5582 Blush

Color reproductions in this printed piece will vary from the actual tile colors, final selection should be made from tile samples.

37

PERFECT PARTNERS
WALL TILE

Floor: Lumina White Pentagon with Royal Blue Dot.
Wall: Lumina White Pentagon with Royal Blue Dot (front wall) and
Lumina White 6" x 6" (back wall), accented with alternating Royal Blue
and Lumina White 2" x 2" Dots, and Royal Blue Rounded Moldings;
Lumina White S4269 trim.

Wall: Lumina White Hexagon 6" x 6" with
Royal 2" x 2" Dots.

FEATURES:

♦ One and two off-corner field tiles for design options

♦ 2'" x 2" dot accent tiles with color coordinated moldings

♦ Wide range of colors in dots and moldings

♦ 2" x 2" dots are modular with all field tile

♦ Coordinates with Geos for additional interest and design options

♦ Stain-resistant

USAGE:

♦ All residential and commercial wall applications, residential countertops and residential bathroom floors

TYPICAL PROPERTIES[1] (MATTE):

Meets or exceeds A137.1 ANSI standard.

C.O.F.[2]		Durability	Glaze	Break
Dry	Wet	Classification	Hardness	Strength
0.81	0.44	Class II	6.5 Mohs	150 lbs. avg.

[1] Refer to table of contents for explanation of tile properties
[2] These values may vary from lot to lot.

♦ .30" thick

♦ Squares □ 3.02 lbs. avg. weight/sq. ft.

♦ Off Corners ◻ & ◻ 2.75 lbs. avg. weight/sq. ft.

TRIM:

See page 48 for trim isometrics.

SIZES:

▭ 1/2" x 6" Round (1 x 15 cm)

▭ 1" x 6" Rope (3 x 15 cm)

□ 2" x 2" (5 x 5 cm)

◻ 4⅜" x 4⅜" (11 x 11 cm)

◻ 6" x 6" (15 x 15 cm)

⬠ 6" x 6" Hexagon (15 x 15 cm)

⬠ 6" x 6" Pentagon (15 x 15 cm)

GEOS[1]:

438X8R Right Parallelogram
4⅜" x 6⅛" (11 x 16 cm)

438X8L Left Parallelogram
4⅜" x 6⅛" (11 x 16 cm)

438T Triangle
4⅜" x 4⅜" x 6" (11 x 11 x 15 cm)

1 Geos available in White 100, French Provincial 2, Black 1005, Forest Green 1059, Royal Blue 1068, and Burgundy 1084

Matte Glaze Floor/Wall Tile
(Available in 4⅜" x 4⅜" and 6" Square, 6" Hexagon and 6" Pentagon)

700	702
Lumina White	French Provincial

Bright Glaze Wall Tile
(Available in 4⅜" x 4⅜" and 6" Square)

100	02
New White	French Provincial

Color reproductions in this printed piece will vary from the actual tile colors, final selection should be made from tile samples.

Dots*

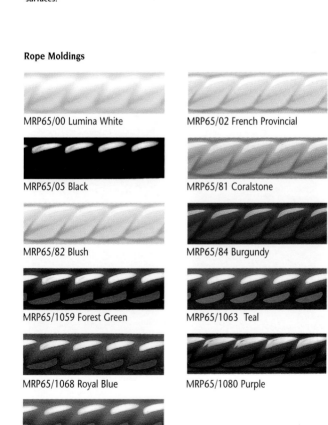

82 Blush	700 Lumina White Matte	702 French Provincial Matte	705 Black Matte

1005 Black	1059 Forest Green	1063 Teal	1068 Royal Blue	1080 Purple

1081 Coralstone	1084 Burgundy	1090 Harness	05 Onyx	59 Verde

*Use care when cleaning dots. Abrasive cleaners will cause scratching to shiny surfaces.

Rounded Moldings

MR65/00 Lumina White

MR65/02 French Provincial

MR65/05 Black

MR65/81 Coralstone

MR65/82 Blush

MR65/84 Burgundy

MR65/1059 Forest Green

MR65/1063 Teal

MR65/1068 Royal Blue

MR65/1080 Purple

MR65/1090 Harness

MRV65/05 Onyx*

MRV65/59 Verde*

*Also available in 1/2" x 8".

Rope Moldings

MRP65/00 Lumina White

MRP65/02 French Provincial

MRP65/05 Black

MRP65/81 Coralstone

MRP65/82 Blush

MRP65/84 Burgundy

MRP65/1059 Forest Green

MRP65/1063 Teal

MRP65/1068 Royal Blue

MRP65/1080 Purple

MRP65/1090 Harness

Color reproductions in this printed piece will vary from the actual tile colors, final selection should be made from tile samples.

POTTER'S TOUCH®
WALL TILE

Wall: French Provincial and Vermont Blue 4-3/8" x 4-3/8", Sculptured Moldings Tulip pattern French Provincial, and Rope Moldings French Provincial. Bathtub Front Surface: NATURA® Vento floor tile Vermont Blue 8" x 8" accented with Sculptured and Rope Moldings in French Provincial.

FEATURES:

♦ Rich, matte glaze finish

♦ Popular, undulated surface

♦ Coordinates with many decorative wall tile moldings and Natura® floor tiles

USAGE:

♦ All residential and commercial wall applications and residential bathroom floors

TYPICAL PROPERTIES[1]:

Meets or exceeds A137.1 ANSI standard.

C.O.F.[2]		Durability	Glaze	Break
Dry	Wet	Classification	Hardness	Strength
0.72	0.34	Class I	6.5 Mohs	150 lbs. avg.

[1] Refer to table of contents for explanation of tile properties.

[2] These values may vary from lot to lot.

♦ .332" thick

♦ 2.76 lbs. avg. weight/sq. ft.

TRIM:

See page 48 for trim isometrics.

SIZES:

◻ 4⅜" x 4⅜"
(11 x 11 cm)

◻ 6" x 6"
(15 x 15 cm)

500
Lumina White

501
White

502 French Provincial

503
Bone

505
Black

512
Sterling Silver

554
Seafoam

557
Jade

566
Vermont Blue

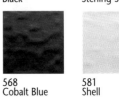
568
Cobalt Blue

581
Shell

587
Carnation Pink

Color reproductions in this printed piece will vary from the actual tile colors, final selection should be made from tile samples.

QUEBEC
WALL TILE

Wall: Pastille 6" x 6" accented with 2" x 6" Pastille Listello. Countertop: Pastille 6" x 6" trimmed with A8262.

FEATURES:

♦ Semi-matte glaze

♦ Natural fumé, tone-on-tone coloring

♦ Unique "Old World" mosaic wall listellos for design options

♦ Coordinates with Natura® floor tiles

SIZES:

☐ 2" x 6" *Listellos* (5 x 15 cm)

☐ 4⅜" x 4⅜"
(11 x 11 cm)

☐ 6" x 6"
(15 x 15 cm)

 2007 Natural

 2012 Flint

 2025 Mexican Sand

 2028 Claybec

 2035 Almond

 2050 Moss Green

2079 Pastille

Color reproductions in this printed piece will vary from the actual tile colors, final selection should be made from tile samples.

─ Listellos not to scale to show detail ─

LQ62/2007 Natural

LQ62/2028 Claybec

LQ62/2050 Moss Green

LQ62/2079 Pastille

USAGE:

♦ All residential and commercial wall applications, residential countertops, and residential bathroom floors

TYPICAL PROPERTIES[1]:

Meets or exceeds A137.1 ANSI standard.

C.O.F.[2]		Durability	Glaze	Break
Dry	Wet	Classification	Hardness	Strength
0.82	0.40	Class II	6.5 Mohs	150 lbs. avg.

[1] Refer to table of contents for explanation of tile properties.
[2] These values may vary from lot to lot.

♦ .30" thick

♦ 2.83 lbs. avg. weight/sq. ft.

TRIM:

See page 48 for trim isometrics.

41

SERENE
WALL TILE

Wall: Lumina White 6" x 8" with Floral Decorative Inserts, 2" x 6" Floral Listello and Rope and Rounded Moldings in Lumina White.
Bathtub Step-up: Blush 6" x 8" trimmed with S4269.

FEATURES:

♦ High-gloss glaze in soft colors
♦ Decorative listellos and inserts with color-coordinated motif
♦ Coordinates with Natura® floor tiles and Matte Glaze wall tile for countertops and decorative wall tile moldings

USAGE:

♦ All residential and commercial wall applications

TYPICAL PROPERTIES:

Meets or exceeds A137.1 ANSI standard.

♦ .30" thick
♦ 2.85 lbs. avg. weight/sq. ft.

TRIM:

See page 48 for trim isometrics.

SIZES:

2" x 6" *Listellos* (5 x 15 cm)

6" x 8" *Insert/Field*
(15 x 20 cm)

Insert

| 6X8025F | 6X8026P | 6X8027M |
| Floral | Profile | Motions |

Field

| 3201 | 3202 | 3219 | 3282 |
| Lumina White | French Provincial | Pearl | Blush |

Listellos not to scale to show detail

LL62F/00 Floral

LL62P/00 Profile

LL62M/00 Motions

Color reproductions in this printed piece will vary from the actual tile colors, final selection should be made from tile samples.

VERONA
WALL TILE

Wall:Opalescent White and Verona White Decorative Inserts 8" x 10" accented with 2" x 8" Verona Duotone Listello, Rounded Moldings in Polished Gold, and Black Matte Chair Rail. Wall and Floor: NATURA® Verona floor tile in Onyx 12" x 12".

FEATURES:

♦ Luminous silk screened tone on tone glaze

♦ Accent tiles and listellos with a unique diamond motif

♦ Coordinates with Natura® floor tile, Verona series and Florida Tile decorative wall tile moldings with Verona marble pattern

USAGE:

♦ All residential and commerical wall applications

TYPICAL PROPERTIES:

Meets or exceeds A137.1 ANSI standard.

♦ .30" thick

♦ 2.80 lbs. avg. weight/sq. ft.

TRIM:

Bullnose-Thin Set

	Product #	Imperial	Metric (cm)
① S-4289	2" x 8"	5 x 20
② S-42A9	2" x 10"	5 x 25
③ SN-4269	2" x 2"	5 x 5

SIZES:

1/2" x 6" *Molding* (1 x 15 cm)

1/2" x 8" *Molding* (1 x 15 cm)

2" x 6" *Listello* (5 x 15 cm)

8" x 10" *Insert/Field* (20 x 25 cm)

Listellos not to scale to show detail

LV8200/59
Verde (on White)

LV8200/05
Onyx (on White)

LV8202/59
Verde (on French Provincial)

LV8202/05
Onyx (on French Provincial)

LV82/59
Verona Duotone (on White)

Moldings

MRV65/05 Onyx

MRV65/59 Verde

Field

8XA02810/3400
Opalescent White

8XA02810/3402
French Provincial

Insert

8XA02959/3400
Verona
White Deco

8XA02959/3402
Verona French
Provincial Deco

43

Color reproductions in this printed piece will vary from the actual tile colors, final selection should be made from tile samples.

MOLDINGS
ACCENT TILE

Wall: Rope Moldings Lumina White with Tulip Sculptured Molding Luster French Provincial, Chair Rail French Provincial accenting Currents wall tile Lumina White 8" x 8" Countertop: NATURA® Vento floor tile Cameo 8" x 8" trimmed with Chair Rail French Provincial.

FEATURES:

♦ Wide range of colors, textures and patterns

♦ Colors compatible across all Florida Tile® ceramic tile lines for a wide range of decorating options

♦ Molding stops available on Rounded, Rope and Chair Rail

USAGE:

♦ All wall applications

SIZES:

▭ 1/2" x 6" *Round* (1 x 15 cm)

▭ 1" x 6" *Rope* (3 x 15 cm)

▭ 2" x 8" *Chair Rail* (5 x 20 cm)

LIMITED COLORS AVAILABLE: (see notes)

▭ 1/2" x 8" *Round* (1 x 20 cm)

Round

MR65/00 Lumina White	MR65/66 Vermont Blue	MR65/1068 Royal Blue
MR65/02 French Provincial	MR65/68 Cobalt	MR65/1080 Purple
MR65/05 Black	MR65/81 Coralstone	MR65/1090 Harness
MR65/12 Gray	MR65/82 Blush	MR65/10 Polished Silver*
MR65/19 Pearl	MR65/83 Dusty Rose	MR65/40 Polished Gold*
MR65/24 Beige	MR65/84 Burgundy	MRM65/95 Brick
MR65/54 Celedon Green	MR65/87 Carnation Pink	MRV65/05 Onyx*
MR65/55 Light Turquoise	MR65/1059 Forest Green	MRV65/59 Verde*
MR65/59 Jade	MR65/1063 Teal	

* Also available in 1/2" x 8" Round: MR85/10, MR85/40, MRV85/05, MRV85/59

Color reproductions in this printed piece will vary from the actual tile colors, final selection should be made from tile samples.

Chair Rail

MCR82I/00 Lumina White (gloss)
MCR82I/700 Lumina White (matte)

MCR82I/05 Black (gloss)
MCR82I/705 Black (matte)

MCR82I/02 French Provincial (gloss)
MCR82I/702 French Provincial (matte)

Rope

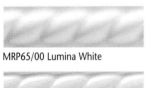

MRP65/00 Lumina White

MRP65/02 French Provincial

MRP65/05 Black

MRP65/12 Gray

MRP65/19 Pearl

MRP65/24 Beige

MRP65/54 Celedon Green

MRP65/55 Light Turquoise

MRP65/59 Jade

MRP65/66 Vermont Blue

MRP65/68 Cobalt

MRP65/81 Coralstone

MRP65/82 Blush

MRP65/83 Dusty Rose

MRP65/84 Burgundy

MRP65/87 Carnation Pink

MRP65/1059 Forest Green

MRP65/1063 Teal

MRP65/1068 Royal Blue

MRP65/1080 Purple

MRP65/1090 Harness

Color reproductions in this printed piece will vary from the actual tile colors, final selection should be made from tile samples.

SCULPTURED MOLDINGS
ACCENTS

FEATURES:

♦ Elegant accent tiles add the perfect finishing touch or focal point

♦ Wide range of regular and pearlized gloss finishes and multi-colored hand-painted glaze options

♦ Easily coordinated with all Florida Tile wall tile

♦ Corner pieces available

USAGE:

♦ All residential and light commercial wall applications

Walls: Multi colored, hand painted Culinary pattern shown with Potter's Touch Lumina White 4-3/8" x 4-3/8", Crystal Glaze New White, Candlelyght, and Jade 2" x 2", accented with Rope Moldings in Burgundy and Rounded Moldings in Burgundy, Harness, and Jade. Countertop: Potter's Touch Lumina White 6" x 6" trimmed with A8262.

Tulips Corner   **Tulips Molding**

LC25T/00 Lumina White   L825T/00 Lumina White   LC25T/02 French Provincial   L825T/02 French Provincial   LC25T/19 Pearl   L825T/19 Pearl

LC25T/82 Blush   L825T/82 Blush   LC25TP/00 Luster White   L825TP/00 Luster White   LC25TP/02 Luster French Provincial   L825TP/02 Luster French Provincial

Culinary Corner   **Culinary Molding**

LC33C/00 Lumina White   L83C/00 Lumina White   LC33C/02 French   L83C/02 French Provincial   LC33C/19 Pearl   L83C/19 Pearl

LC33C/82 Blush   L83C/82 Blush   LC33CP/00 Luster White   L83CP/00 Luster White   LC33CP/02 Luster French Provincial   L83CP/02 Luster French Provincial

LC33CH/00 Multi   L83CH/00 Multi

SIZES:

☐ 2-1/2" x 2-1/2" *Tulips Corner* (6 x 6 cm)

☐ 3" x 3" *Culinary Corner* (8 x 8 cm)

☐ 2½" x 8" *Tulips Molding* (6 x 20 cm)

☐ 3" x 8" *Culinary Molding* (8 x 20 cm)

Color reproductions in this printed piece will vary from the actual tile colors, final selection should be made from tile samples.

Residence, Lakeland, FL. Floor: Ermos shown with NATURA® Excavare floor tile Talc and Charcoal 16" x 16".

SIZES:

 2-1/2" x 11"
(6 x 30 cm)

Tumblestone Listellos

7407 Cremo (.394" 10 mm thick)

7448 Flaxen (.394" 10 mm thick)

7412 Ermos (.295" 7.5 mm thick)

7453 Verde (.295" 7.5 mm thick)

7426 Helena (.295" 7.5 mm thick)

7479 Rosa (.354" 9 mm thick)

Color reproductions in this printed piece will vary from the actual tile colors, final selection should be made from tile samples.

FEATURES:

♦ Real tumbled marble pieces, back-mounted for easy installation

♦ Coordinates with Florida Tile® ceramic stone floor tile products

♦ Natural colors and veining

USAGE:

♦ All residential and light commercial wall and floor applications

TYPICAL PROPERTIES:

Meets or exceeds A137.1 ANSI standard.

47

TRIM INFORMATION

BRIGHT GLAZE, CRYSTAL GLAZE, MATTE GLAZE, IMAGERY II, LUSTER, PERFECT PARTNERS, POTTER'S CHOICE, POTTER'S TOUCH, QUEBEC, SERENE, AND CURRENTS WALL TILE

Bullnose-Conventional

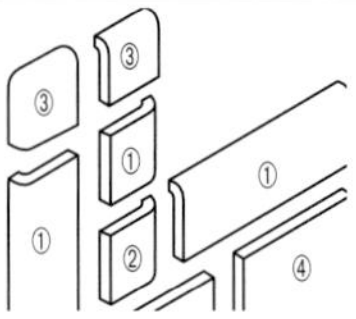

Product #	Imperial	Metric (cm)	Bright	Matte	Crystal	Currents	Imagery II	Luster	Perfect Partners	Potter's Choice	Potter's Touch	Quebec	Serene
① A-4200	2" x 6"	5 x 15	✓	✓	✓[1]	✓[2]	✓[7]	✓	✓	✓	✓	✓	✓
② AM-4200	2" x 2"	5 x 5	✓	✓	✓[1]	✓[2]	✓[7]	✓	✓	✓	✓	✓	✓
③ AN-4200	2" x 2"	5 x 5	✓	✓	✓[1]	✓[2]	✓[7]	✓	✓	✓	✓	✓	✓
④ Field	4⅜" x 4⅜"	11 x 11	✓	✓	✓				✓	✓	✓	✓	

Conventional-Square in Corners

Product #	Imperial	Metric (cm)	Bright	Matte	Crystal	Luster	Perfect Partners	Potter's Choice	Potter's Touch	Quebec
① A-4402	4⅜" x 4⅜"	11 x 11	✓	✓	✓[1]	✓	✓	✓	✓	✓
② AN-4402	4⅜" x 4⅜"	11 x 11	✓	✓	✓[1]	✓	✓	✓	✓	✓
③ ACL/R-3401	3 15/16" x 4 11/16"	10 x 12	✓	✓	✓[1]	✓	✓	✓	✓	✓
ACL/R-1663	3⅞" x 6 7/16"	9 x 16	✓	✓	✓[1]		✓			
④ ABL/R-4402	4⅜" x 4⅜"	11 x 11	✓	✓			✓			
⑤ A-3401	3 15/16" x 4⅜"	10 x 11	✓	✓	✓[1]	✓	✓	✓	✓	✓
⑥ AB-3401	3 15/16" x 4⅜"	10 x 11	✓	✓	✓[1]		✓			
⑦ AM-4402	4⅜" x 4⅜"	11 x 11	✓	✓	✓[1]	✓	✓	✓	✓	✓
⑧ Field	4⅜" x 4⅜"	11 x 11	✓	✓	✓		✓			
⑨ A-3601 (Not shown)	6" x 6"	15 x 15	✓	✓			✓			

Thin Set-Square in Corners

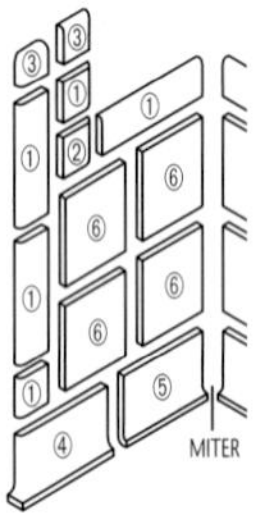

Product #	Imperial	Metric (cm)	Bright	Matte	Crystal	Currents	Imagery II	Luster	Perfect Partners	Potter's Choice	Potter's Touch	Quebec	Serene
① S-4269	2" x 6"	5 x 15	✓	✓	✓[1]	✓	✓[7]	✓	✓	✓	✓	✓	✓
① S-4289	2" x 8"	5 x 20				✓	✓[7]						✓
② SM-4269	2" x 2"	5 x 5	✓	✓	✓[1]		✓[7]	✓	✓	✓	✓	✓	
③ SN-4269	2" x 2"	5 x 5	✓	✓	✓[1]	✓	✓[7]	✓	✓	✓	✓	✓	✓
④ SCL/R-1663	3 7/16" x 6 7/16"	9 x 16	✓	✓	✓[1]				✓				
⑤ A-1663	3⅞" x 6"	10 x 15	✓	✓	✓[1]				✓				
⑥ Field	4⅜" x 4⅜"	11 x 11	✓	✓	✓			✓	✓	✓	✓	✓	

Bullnose & Cove Base-Thin Set

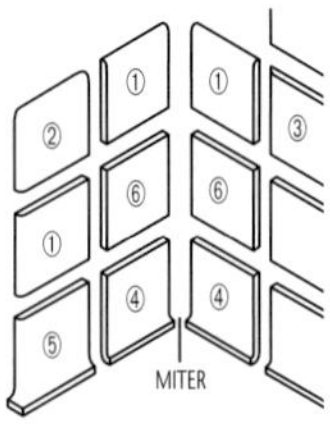

Product #	Imperial	Metric (cm)	Bright	Matte	Crystal	Luster	Perfect Partners	Potter's Choice	Potter's Touch	Quebec
① S-4449	4⅜" x 4⅜"	11 x 11	✓	✓	✓[1]	✓	✓	✓	✓	✓
S-4669	6" x 6"	15 x 15	✓[3]	✓	✓[1]		✓[3]	✓	✓	✓
② SN-4449	4⅜" x 4⅜"	11 x 11	✓	✓	✓[1]	✓	✓	✓	✓	✓
SN-4669	6" x 6"	15 x 15	✓	✓			✓	✓	✓	✓
③ SM-4449	4⅜" x 4⅜"	11 x 11	✓	✓	✓[1]	✓	✓	✓	✓	✓
④ A-3401	3 15/16" x 4⅜"	10 x 11	✓	✓	✓[1]	✓	✓	✓	✓	✓
⑤ SCL/R-3401	3 15/16" x 4 11/16"	10 x 12	✓	✓	✓[1]	✓	✓	✓	✓	✓
⑥ Field	4⅜" x 4⅜"	11 x 11								
	6" x 6"	15 x 15	✓[4]	✓			✓	✓	✓	✓

Sanitary Base-6" x 6" Conventional

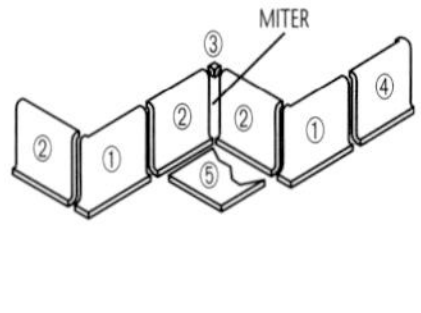

Product #	Imperial	Metric (cm)	Bright	Matte	Crystal	Perfect Partners
① ACR-3610	5 11/16" x 6 7/16"	14 x 16	✓	✓		✓
② A-3610	5 11/16" x 6"	14 x 15	✓	✓		✓
③ AK-106	¾" x ¾"	2 x 2	✓	✓	✓[1]	✓
④ ACL-3610	5 11/16" x 6 7/16"	14 x 16	✓	✓		✓
⑤ Field	6" x 6"	15 x 15	✓[4]	✓		✓[4]

Sanitary Base-Thin Set

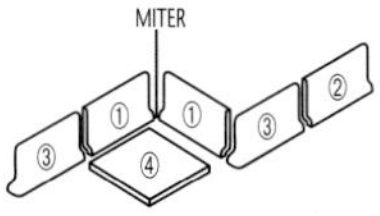

Product #	Imperial	Metric (cm)	Bright	Matte	Crystal	Currents	Imagery II	Luster	Perfect Partners	Potter's Choice	Potter's Touch	Quebec	Serene
① S-3419	3⅞" x 6"	10 x 15	✓	✓	✓	✓	✓[7]	✓	✓	✓	✓	✓	✓
② SCL-3419	3⅞" x 6"	10 x 15	✓	✓	✓			✓	✓	✓	✓	✓	
③ SCR-3419	3⅞" x 6"	10 x 15	✓	✓	✓			✓	✓	✓	✓	✓	
④ Field	4⅜" x 4⅜"	11 x 11	✓	✓	✓				✓	✓	✓		

FOOTNOTES: **1)** 600, 601, 602, 603, 604, 619 Only; **2)** No undulation on this trim piece; **3)** S-4669—100, 1, 3, 4 Only; **4)** 6" x 6"—100, 1, 3, 4 Only; **5)** Tapered; **6)** 601 and 603 Only; **7)** Available in gloss finish only.

Sanitary Base-Conventional

	Product #	Imperial	Metric (cm)	Bright	Matte	Crystal	Perfect Partners
①	SCR-3619T³	6" x 6"	15 x 15	✓	✓	✓⁶	✓
②	S-3619T³	6" x 6"	15 x 15	✓	✓	✓⁶	✓
③	SCL-3619T³	6" x 6"	15 x 15	✓	✓	✓⁶	✓
④	6" Floor	6" x 6"	15 x 15	✓⁴	✓		✓⁴

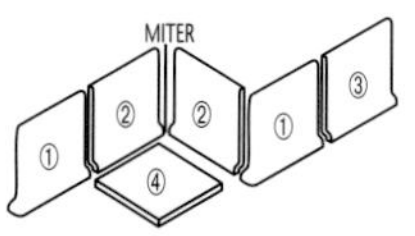

Countertop Trim Conventional & Thin Set

	Product #	Imperial	Metric (cm)	Bright	Matte	Crystal	Luster	Perfect Partners	Potter's Choice	Potter's Touch	Quebec
①	A-8262	2¼" x 6"	6 x 15	✓	✓	✓¹	✓	✓	✓²	✓²	✓
②	AC-8262	2¼" x 1⅝"	6 x 4	✓	✓	✓¹	✓	✓	✓²	✓²	✓
③	AM-8262	1⅝" x 1⅝"	4 x 4	✓	✓	✓¹	✓	✓	✓²	✓²	✓
④	A-106	¾" x 6"	2 x 15	✓	✓	✓¹	✓	✓	✓²	✓²	✓
⑤	AU-106	¾" x 1¹⁵/₁₆"	2 x 5	✓	✓	✓¹	✓	✓	✓²	✓²	✓
⑥	Field	6" x 6"	15 x 15	✓	✓			✓			
⑦	SC-8262	1⅝" x 2¼"	4 x 6	✓	✓	✓¹	✓	✓	✓²	✓²	✓
⑧	A-104 (Not shown)	¾" x 4"	2 x 10		✓			✓			

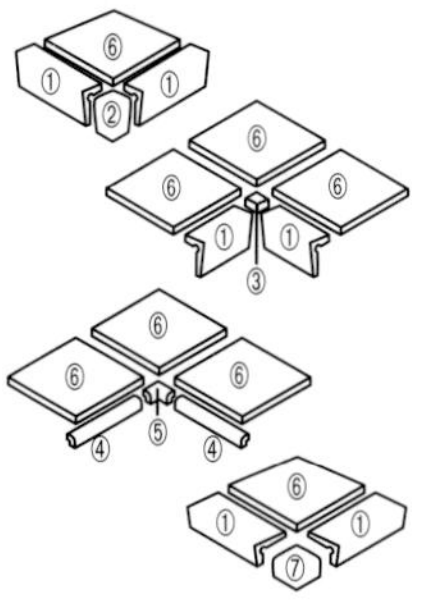

Shower Door Jams

	Product #	Imperial	Metric (cm)	Bright	Matte	Crystal	Luster	Perfect Partners	Potter's Choice	Potter's Touch	Quebec
①	A-7610	6" x 6"	15 x 15	✓	✓			✓			
②	A-3401	3¹⁵/₁₆" x 4⅜"	10 x 11	✓	✓	✓¹	✓	✓	✓	✓	✓
③	AK-106	¾" x ¾"	2 x 2	✓	✓	✓¹	✓	✓		✓²	✓
④	A-7250	2½" x 6"	6 x 15	✓	✓		✓		✓²	✓²	
⑤	AC-7250 (Not Shown)	2½" x 6"	6 x 15	✓	✓		✓		✓²	✓²	
⑥	AKC-7250 (Not Shown)	2½" x 2½"	6 x 6	✓	✓		✓	✓	✓²	✓²	
⑦	Field	4⅜" x 4⅜"	11 x 11	✓	✓	✓		✓	✓	✓	✓

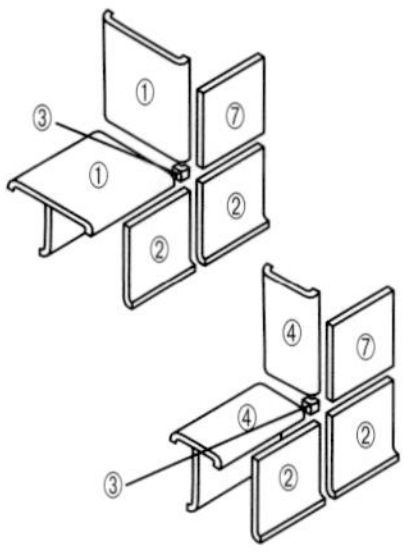

Bullnose-Conventional

	Product #	Imperial	Metric (cm)	Bright	Matte	Crystal	Luster	Perfect Partners	Potter's Touch	Quebec
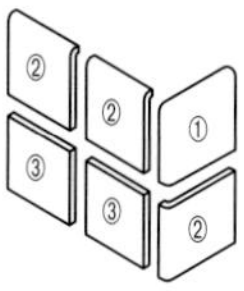 ①	AN-3602	6" x 6"	15 x 15	✓	✓	✓⁶		✓	✓	✓
②	A-3602	6" x 6"	15 x 15	✓	✓	✓⁶		✓	✓	✓
	A-3502	5" x 6"	13 x 15	✓				✓		
③	Field	6" x 6"	15 x 15	✓⁴	✓	✓		✓⁴	✓	✓

Beads

	Product #	Imperial	Metric (cm)	Bright	Matte	Crystal	Currents	Imagery II	Luster	Perfect Partners	Potter's Choice	Potter's Touch	Quebec	Serene
 ①	AC-106	¾" x 6"	2 x 15	✓	✓	✓¹			✓	✓	✓²	✓²	✓	
①	AC-108	1¼" x 8"	3 x 20				✓²	✓⁷						✓
②	A-108	1¼" x 8"	3 x 20				✓²	✓⁷						✓

CARE & MAINTENANCE

KEEPING YOUR CERAMIC TILE BEAUTIFUL IS AS EASY AS 1-2-3

1. IDENTIFY TYPE OF TILE

There are two basic types of ceramic tile-glazed and unglazed. The other surface which requires care is the tile grout, the material which is used when installing the tile. Each of these requires certain routine cleaning and may need heavy-duty cleaning, depending upon its use and the degree of traffic it gets.

Glazed tile is most often used on traditional walls, countertops and floors. It has a tough, glass-like surface produced by kiln firing at extremely high temperatures. Glazed tile can have a glossy, matte or textured finish.

Unglazed tile is composed of natural clays which are sometimes mixed with pigments. It can be used on floors, walls, countertops, window sills, fireplaces, swimming pools, etc. It may require more careful attention than glazed tile.

Tile grout is the material used to fill the spaces between tiles. It gives the installation its finished look. There are several types of grout, but all can be maintained by following the instructions listed.

2. ROUTINE CARE FOR YOUR TILE

Glazed-tile walls in your home will easily keep their lovely look with simple routine care. Just wipe regularly with a damp cloth or sponge, using a non-abrasive household cleaner. A window cleaner (such as Windex or Glass-Plus) is ideal for cleaning glossy tile surfaces.

For glazed-tile floors, vacuum regularly to remove dirt and gritty particles. Follow with a mop or sponge dampened with an approved household cleaner.

Tiled surfaces in your bathroom (tub, shower, vanity tops, etc.) may require a more thorough routine cleaning because of a build-up of soap scum, body oils or hard-water stains. Use the usual "clean, damp cloth or sponge" with an all-purpose cleaner, but allow it to stand for about five minutes before rinsing and drying. (You may also use a solution of equal parts of water and white vinegar* or a commercial cleaner available from your Florida Tile distributor.)

*Caution: Vinegar may damage some glazed tile. Be sure to test this solution first in a small area to see if it etches the tile or erodes the grout.

Here's a hint on how to keep shower walls mildew-free: clean regularly with tile cleaner or fungicide such as Lysol or ammonia. Dry with a towel after each use and leave curtain or door open between showers.

3. HEAVY-DUTY CLEANING

For high traffic areas or when tile has been neglected for a long time, heavy-duty cleaning may be required.

Glazed walls and countertops should be cleaned with a scouring powder, commercial tile cleaner or all-purpose cleaner applied with non-metallic or very fine stainless steel pad. Rinse and wipe dry.

To clean badly soiled countertops, cover with a solution of scouring powder and very hot water. Let stand for about five minutes, then scrub with a stiff brush. Rinse thoroughly. If stain remains, apply bleach and let stand. Rinse well with clean water and dry after all cleaning.

CARE & MAINTENANCE
(CONTINUED)

For glazed-tile floors, use a commercial tile cleaner, or apply a strong solution of all-purpose cleaner of scouring powder paste. Let stand for five minutes, brush and scrub. Then rinse with clean water and wipe dry.

Use chlorine bleach or hydrogen peroxide for stained shower surfaces. If badly stained, it's best to try a scouring powder containing a bleaching agent, such as Ajax or Comet. Let stand for four to six hours before scrubbing and rinsing thoroughly.

Remember, prompt clean-up of spills and regular cleaning will keep your ceramic tile surfaces looking their best.

DO'S AND DON'TS OF CERAMIC TILE CARE

- Do not combine ammonia and household bleaches.
- Do not use harsh cleaning agents (such as steel wool pads) which can scratch or damage the surface of your tile.
- Do not use a cleaning agent that contains color on unglazed tile. It has a relatively porous body and may absorb the color.
- Do test scouring powders in a small area before using on tile.
- Do use a silicone sealer on grout joints if continuous staining is a problem.
- Do read and follow label directions for all cleaners.
- Do keep this brochure and refer to it when necessary.
- Do see your nearest Florida Tile distributor for advice on special cleaning problems or if you have any questions.

REPAIRING DAMAGED OR LOOSE TILES

A damaged or broken tile should be removed and replaced by a good tile mechanic only. If the tile is simply loose, you should be able to repair it yourself. Just clean the back and sides of the tile of all grout and bonding material. Apply fresh mastic and set the tile into place. Let dry for 24 hours, then grout. If you have more than a few loose tiles, it's best to consult a professional tile mechanic to handle the job.

TILE GROUT

Grout may present a special cleaning problem because it is susceptible to many staining agents. It should be cleaned immediately if subjected to these substances. Our Stain Removal Guide on this page lists some typical causes of stains as well as the recommended method of removal for each.

After the counter has been cleaned and dried, grout joints should be treated with a silicone sealer to help keep them clean. (Apply the sealer several times a year for maximum protection.)

In addition to keeping the grout clean, be sure to keep grout joints in good repair. Scrape out loose, cracked or powdery joints and refill with a good grout.

One common grouting trouble spot is the joint between the tub and tile wall in your bathroom. As the house or tub settles, the grout may crack and crumble. It's relatively simple to remedy. Remove the old grout with a sharp pointed tool, watching out that you don't scratch the tile or tub. Then dry the joint thoroughly and fill with a flexible caulking compound, such as silicone rubber caulking. (This is available in an easy-to-use tube at your Florida Tile distributor or local hardware store.)

A WORD ABOUT CLEANERS

There are many excellent household cleaners on the market today. They should all do a good job for you, so use your favorite. Remember, read and follow the manufacturer's instructions and recommended usage. They will perform as promised, if you use them as directed.

Here is some general information about the cleaners which are mentioned in this brochure.

All-purpose cleaners include such products as Soft Scrub, Scrub Free, Mr. Clean, Top Job, Fantastik, Ajax Liquid, Liquid Comet, and Lestoil. You can find them at your supermarket.

"Soapless detergents" are also commonly found on supermarket shelves. They include such cleaners as Spic & Span.

Scouring powders which are readily available include Comet, Bon Ami, and Ajax. Nylon scouring pads may also be used (such as Scotch Brite), but steel wool pads are not recommended.

For bathrooms, several specialty cleaners may be used, such as Crew Bathroom Cleaner and Dow Bathroom Cleaner. They are very effective for routine maintenance.

Commercial cleaners such as Aqua Mix or Hillard's "Assurance", are suitable for heavy duty cleaning in commercial applications. These products are available from your Florida Tile distributor.

STAIN REMOVAL GUIDE

STAIN	REMOVAL AGENT
Grease and fats	Soda and water or commercial spot lifter
Inks and colored dyes	Household bleach
Mercurochrome	Ammonia
Blood	Hydrogen peroxide or household bleach
Coffee, tea, food, juices, fruit, lipstick	Neutral cleaner in hot water, followed by hydrogen peroxide or household bleach

TECHNICAL DATA

PRODUCT SPECIFICATIONS:

A. Glazed wall tile and glazed paver tile are Standard Grade complying with ANSI A137.1-1988 as manufactured by Florida Tile Industries, Inc., Lakeland, FL or approved equivalent.

B. Sizes, colors, textures and patterns as selected. See drawings and schedules.

C. Provide trim of the same color, size and finish of adjacent flat tile.

D. Accessories - Furnish cast vitreous china accessories to match or harmonize with color and finish of adjacent wall tile. Accessories required where shown on drawings.

SETTING MATERIALS:

Portland Cement Mortar Installation Materials: Provide materials to comply with ANSI A108.1 as required for installation method designated.

Cleavage Membranes: Polyethylene film 4 mil. ASTM C171 Type 1.1.2.

Reinforcing Mesh: Welded wire fabric 2" x 2" 16/16 gauge.

Dry-Set Portland Cement: ANSI 118.1 water-retentive Portland Cement, sand and special latex additives. Latices vary considerably. Follow manufacturer's directions explicitly.

Organic Adhesive: ANSI A136.1 Type 1 for areas requiring prolonged water resistance. Provide primer-sealer as recommended by the manufacturer.

Epoxy Mortar: ANSI 118.3 Formula AAR-11 or high-temperature resistance formula where indicated.

GROUTING MATERIALS:
Commercial Portland Cement Grout: Pre-blended compound composed of Portland Cement and additives formulated for the type tile installed.

Latex-Portland Grout: Use latex additive in grout compatible with Latex-Portland Cement Mortar.

Dry Set Grout: Portland Cement and additives formulated for type of tile installed.

INSTALLATION SPECIFICATIONS:

Before tile installation begins, substrate surfaces shall not show variations in excess of:

	Floor	Wall
Dry-Set Mortar	1/8" in 10'	1/8" in 8'
Organic Adhesive	1/16" in 3'	1/8" in 8'
Latex-Portland Cement Mortar	1/8" in 10'	1/8" in 8'
Epoxy	1/16" in 3'	

ANSI Installation Standard: Comply with applicable parts of ANSI A-108 Series for ceramic tile installation.

Extend tile work into recesses, and under and behind equipment and fixtures except where otherwise shown. Fit tile to electrical outlets, piping, fixtures and other penetrations so that plates, collars or covers overlap tile.

Joints shall align vertically and horizontally between trim and field tile. Grout tile to comply with reference installation standards using grout materials indicated.

Protection: Leave finished installation free of cracked, chipped, broken, unbonded or otherwise defective tile work. Protect all floor tile installations with kraft paper or other heavy covering during construction period to prevent staining or damage. No foot or wheel traffic permitted on floor for at least 7 days after grouting.

COEFFICIENT OF FRICTION:

ASTM C-1028-89 is the standard test method for determining the static coefficient of friction of ceramic tile and other like surfaces by the dynamometer pull meter method. Static coefficient of friction is a term used in physics to describe the amount of force required to cause an object (shoe sole material) to start moving across a surface (flooring material). A higher coefficient indicates increased resistance of shoe sole material to start moving across a flooring material. The ASTM procedure states that "the measurement made by this apparatus is believed to be one important factor relative to slip resistance. Other factors can affect slip resistance, such as the degree of wear on the shoe and flooring material; presence of foreign material, such as water, oil and dirt; the length of the human stride at the time of slip; type of floor finish; and the physical and mental condition of humans. Therefore, this test method should be used for the purpose of developing a property of the flooring surface under laboratory conditions, and should not be used to determine slip resistance under field conditions unless those conditions are fully described."

Please consult ASTM Standard Test Method C-1028-89 for a more detailed explanation of coefficient of friction and test methods.

Note that the precision of this test as described in the ASTM procedure indicates that the coefficient values can be expected to vary as much as 0.3. Since coefficient of friction is normally less than 1.0, test results will vary by more than 30%.

Also, the static coefficient of friction may vary within and between production runs because of the inherent characteristics of ceramic tile.

Although ANSI has not established a standard value for coefficient of friction, OSHA (Occupational Safety and Health Administration) has established a recognized industry of 0.5 (wet and dry) for slip-resistant surfaces. The Americans with Disabilities Act (ADA) recommends but does not require "a Static Coefficient of Friction of 0.60 for accessible routes and 0.80 for ramps" ADA does not specifically state that 0.60 is both a dry and a wet requirement.

It is important to note that any tile or other hard surface flooring can become slippery when wet or improperly maintained. The use of Florida Tile® ceramic tile is not recommended for exterior horizontal surfaces.

The coefficient of friction of all hard surface flooring materials, including ceramic tile, can be adversely effected by inadequate or improper maintenance, such as the use of unsuitable cleaning materials or procedures. The Florida Tile Care and Maintenance Brochure explains how to maintain your ceramic tile floor. For a copy of this brochure, see your Florida Tile Distributor or call Florida Tile at 1-800-FLA-TILE.

MOH'S HARDNESS

Scratch resistance of glazes is measured by scratching the glaze with a mineral of known hardness. Hardness of minerals is classified by Moh's Scale, which lists 10 minerals according to their hardness. Each mineral in this scale will scratch those with lower numbers in the scale, but will not scratch minerals with higher numbers. Talc is classified as number one on the Moh's Scales and diamond ten.

Resilient flooring materials, such as vinyl and asphalt tile, are relatively soft and can be scratched by talc, number one on the scale. White polished marble can be scratched by calcite, which is number three. Black marble rates a four and can be scratched by fluorite. Most glazes used on ceramic tile fall in the five to six range, which is also slightly harder than most steels. Case-hardened steel, such as what is used in drill bits used for drilling holes in steel, is approximately six and will scratch most glazes. Some glazes used on ceramic tiles, designed for floor use, cannot be scratched by a case-hardened drill bit.

Quartz, number 7 on Moh's Scale, will scratch most glazes and all but the hardest unglazed ceramic tiles. Sand is a common example of natural quartz.

BREAKING STRENGTH:

ASTM C-648 describes the standard test method for determining structural strength of ceramic tile. This test provides a means for establishing whether or not a lot of ceramic tile meets the strength requirements which may be required for a specific installation procedure and its ability to withstand load and impact. The ANSI standard requires an average breaking strength of 90 lbs. for wall tiles and 250 lbs. for floor tiles. Tiles installed on floors with adhesives may require higher breaking strengths.

ACID RESISTANCE:

ASTM C650 is the standard test method for determining resistance of ceramic tile to chemical substances. The glazed surface of Florida Tile products is resistant to virtually all caustic and corrosive liquids. Typical exceptions are: fluorides and concentrated hydrochloric acid.

FROST RESISTANCE:

ASTM C-1026 describes the standard test method for determining ceramic tile's ability to withstand repeated cycles of freezing and thawing.

Ability of tile to resist damage or deterioration when tested in freezing and thawing situations such as those found in central and northern sections of the United States.

MONO-SIZED:

Near perfect size control on all of our domestically manufactured 8" x 8" and larger floor tiles through our revolutionary MONO-SIZED process. Mono-sized tiles are:

• Virtually uniform in size (variation of linear size from piece to piece is always less than 0.5%)

• Consistently square

• Caliber-free (ordering tile lots by size range is not required) means improved service and delivery

• Easier to handle, cut and install

FLORIDA TILE® PRODUCT INFORMATION:

Florida Tile products are glazed, high-strength, flat-backed tiles. All Florida Tile floor tile products are made by the "single-fired" process, which generally impart superior impact resistance and superior breaking strength. All products are formulated using high quality clays, specifically designed for density and strength then pressed, glazed and fired.

Note that the data represented in this literature represents typical test results of randomly selected "standard" products.

FLORIDA TILE® RUSTIC PRODUCTS AND SHADE BLENDING:

Florida Tile's rustic products are: Aspen; Azteca; Cortina; Excavare; Formations; and Granite are designed to simulate natural surfaces by using a combination of ceramic processes. Shade and texture variations are inherent in these rustic products. These types of tiles are packed by *shade blends* and not *specific shades*. Products of a common shade blend type may be used together. Specific product lots are identified by the last letter of the shade code.

WARRANTY

LIMITED WARRANTIES - PRODUCT DEFECT WARRANTY:

Florida Tile Industries, Inc. ("Manufacturer") warrants to the original purchaser that it will replace with comparable products any standard grade products sold by it which fail to meet the requirements in American National Specifications Institute, Specification A137.1-1988 or of the ASTM tests noted above for durability, coefficient of friction, acid resistance, or frost resistance. Florida Tile Industries, Inc. will not be responsible for any costs of labor, installation or removal of tile.

TEN-YEAR GLAZE WEAR WARRANTY:

Manufacturer warrants that Natura Granite Series, and Natura Tough-One Series only, will be free of undue visible glaze wear caused by normal wear and tear from pedestrian foot traffic for a period of the (10) years from the date of original installation. Undue glaze wear is defined as wear in which the glaze is worn through to the body itself. Visibility of wear is measured from a standing height of not less than five feet looking down on the tile surface. This limited warranty is not intended to be a guarantee that glazed tiles will never show signs of wear. This warranty is for purchases made on or after May 1, 1992. It covers standard grade material manufactured by Florida Tile Industries, Inc.

GLAZE WEAR WARRANTY LIMITATIONS:

The Manufacturer specifically excludes from this glaze wear warranty glaze failures due to the following incidents:

• improper installation of the tile,

• acts of God,

• falling objects, abuse, misuse, negligence, vandalism, fire, exposure to extreme temperature, or accidents,

• failure to follow the Manufacturer's recommended installation, maintenance and care guidelines, including use of improper chemicals or compounds,

• non-foot traffic wear, or any act or omission which might be reasonably expected to damage a ceramic floor.

In the event of a valid claim, the Manufacturer will remove and replace the tile(s) in the affected area(s) at its own expense, FOB manufacturing plant. Color matching of the replacement material is restricted to the currently available production items or materials that is in the Manufacturer's existing inventory.

MAKING A CLAIM

The original purchaser must notify the Manufacturer in writing within sixty (60) days after delivery and prior to installation, of any defective tile: or for Natura Granite and Natura Tough-One within (60) days of the occurrence of any undue visible glaze wear. After notification of any defective tile or glaze wear, the Manufacturer, or authorized agent, will, as soon as reasonably practicable, inspect the tile. At Manufacturer's option, such inspection shall take place either on site, or by having samples of the allegedly defective tile sent to the Manufacturer's laboratories. No claim will be honored without the tile having been inspected by the manufacturer. Claims made beyond the above periods are void. "Nonstandard" and "substandard" tile are sold "as is" and "with all faults."

The original purchaser must provide Manufacturer with the following information in order to have a claim honored under these warranties - a copy of the sales invoice showing:

A. Date of Sale

B. Specific material and quantity purchased

C. Name and address of distributor

D. Name and address of buyer

Claims, or any questions about these warranties should be addressed in writing to: Vice President - Sales, Florida Tile Industries, Inc., P.O. Box 447, Lakeland, FL 33802

Your Florida Tile distributor has brochures for the care and maintenance of ceramic tile. If you do not have this maintenance brochure, contact your Florida Tile distributor or write to the manufacturer at the address listed above.

MANUFACTURER MAKES NO OTHER WARRANTIES, EXPRESS OR IMPLIED, INCLUDING MERCHANTABILITY OR FITNESS FOR A PARTICULAR PURPOSE. PURCHASER'S REMEDY IS LIMITED TO REPLACEMENT AS DESCRIBED ABOVE, AND UNDER NO CIRCUMSTANCES SHALL THE MANUFACTURER BE LIABLE FOR ANY LOSS OR DAMAGE ARISING FROM THE PURCHASE, USE, OR INABILITY TO USE THIS PRODUCT, OR FOR ANY SPECIAL, INDIRECT, INCIDENTAL, OR CONSEQUENTIAL DAMAGES. NO INSTALLER, DEALER, AGENT OR EMPLOYEE OF MANUFACTURER HAS THE AUTHORITY TO MODIFY THE OBLIGATIONS OR LIMITATION OF THIS WARRANTY.

These warranties give specific legal rights. Since some states have laws governing consumer rights and damages, some of the above limitations may not apply to you, and you may have other rights which vary from state to state. Except for these other rights, the remedy provided under these warranties state the limit of the Manufacturer's responsibilities.

FLORIDA TILE®
DISTRIBUTORS
& SHOWROOMS:

ALABAMA

BIRMINGHAM, 35202
Robert F. Henry Tile Co., Inc.
119-45th Place N.
AC 205/592-8615

DOTHAN, 36302
Whatley Supply Co.
230 Ross Clark Circle
AC 334/794-4173

HALEYVILLE, 35565
R & R Supply
Highway 5 North
AC 205/486-9966

MOBILE, 36617
Wade Tile Distributors
1150 N. Beltline
AC 334/476-1140

MONTGOMERY, 36102-2230
Roberty F. Henry Tile Co., Inc.
919 Bell Street
AC 334/269-2518

TUSCALOOSA, 35405
Robert F. Henry Tile Co., Inc
3100 Hargrove Rd. E.
AC 205/556-1900

ARIZONA

GLENDALE, 85308
Arizona Tile Supply, Inc.
5151 West Bell Road
AC 602/547-9838

PHOENIX, 85018
Arizona Tile Supply, Inc.
3535 E. Thomas Road
AC 602/279-4478

PRESCOTT, 86301
Arizona Tile Supply, Inc.
550 N. 6th Street
AC 602/776-1070

SCOTTSDALE, 85254
Arizona Tile Supply, Inc.
14046 N. Scottsdale Road,
Suite 1
AC 602/991-3288

SCOTTSDALE, 85260
Arizona Tile Supply, Inc.
7848 E. Redfield, Suite 112
AC 602/991-3066

TEMPE, 85283
Arizona Tile Supply, Inc.
7248 South Harl
AC 602/438-1324

TUCSON, 85719
Arizona Tile Supply, Inc.
1665 E. 18th Street, #122
AC 602/622-4671

ARKANSAS

FORT SMITH, 72901
Mussino Distributing Co.
801 South Zero
AC 501/646-5433

NORTH LITTLE ROCK, 72113
Elder Distributing Co., Inc.
9300 Maumelle Boulevard
AC 501/758-4170

TONTITOWN, 72770
Mussino Distributing Co.
Highway 412 W
AC 501/361-2551

CALIFORNIA

ANAHEIM, 92806
Florida Tile Ceramic Center
1330 S. State College Blvd.
AC 714/999-9575

BAKERSFIELD, 93307
Bill Ray Ceramic Tile Center
6301 E. Brundage Lane
AC 805/366-3255

CHICO, 95926
Tile City
359 East Park Avenue
AC 916/895-3455

CONCORD, 94520
Western Tile
1290 Diamond Way
AC 510/671-0145

FRESNO, 93702
Fresno Tile Supply
631 North Maple
AC 209/251-4268

LANCASTER, 93534
California Tile Supply
42704-10th Street
AC 805/945-3348

LONG BEACH, 90815
Ceramic Tile Center, Inc.
3945 Vernon Street
AC 310/498-2336

LOS ANGELES, 90025
Ceramic Tile Center, Inc.
2001 Westwood Blvd.
AC 310/470-6629

REDDING, 96002-0000
Tile City
1355-B2 Hartnell Avenue
AC 916/221-0826

SACRAMENTO, 95827
Florida Tile Ceramic Center
3170 Fite Circle
AC 916/854-9800

SAN DIEGO, 92110
Morena Tile Supply, Inc.
1065 W. Morena Blvd.
AC 619/276-5970

SAN DIEGO, 92121
Morena Tile Supply, Inc.
7415-A Caroll Rd.
AC 619/566-5970

SAN DIEGO, 92126
Morena Tile Distribution Center
9212 Miramar Rd., Suite A
AC 619/566-5970

SAN JOSE, 95131
Florida Tile Ceramic Center
1560 Montague Expressway
AC 408/432-8114

SAN LEANDRO, 94577
Florida Tile Ceramic Center
900 Doolittle Dr. #8A
AC 510/632-0887

SAN LUIS OBISPO, 93401
Tileco Distributors, Inc.
645 Tank Farm Road
AC 805/549-8453

SAN MARCOS, 92069
Morena Tile Supply, Inc.
696 Rancheros Drive
AC 619/744-1462

SANTA BARBARA, 93101
Tileco Distributors, Inc.
619 North Olive
AC 805-564-1868

SANTA MARIA, 93454
Tileco Distributors, Inc.
275 W. Betteravia Road
AC 805/925-8638

SANTA ROSA, 95401
Western Tile
3780 Santa Rosa Ave.
AC 707/585-1501

SEPULVEDA, 91343
Florida Tile Ceramic Center
16735 Roscoe Blvd.
AC 818/994-0466

TEMECULA, 92530
Morena Tile Supply, Inc.
27479 Enterprise Circle West
AC 909/676-3073

TORRANCE, 90501
Ceramic Tile Center, Inc.
525 Van Ness Avenue
AC 310/533-8231

VENTURA, 93003
California Tile Supply, Inc.
4350 Transport Street
AC 805/658-0677

VISALIA, 93277
Design Tile Center
2437 E. Main Street
AC 209/739-8453

YUBA CITY, 95993
Tile City
989 Klamath Lane
AC 916/671-7993

COLORADO

COLORADO SPRINGS, 80907
Florida Tile Ceramic Center
1096 Elkton Drive, Suite 200
AC 719/590-7227

DENVER, 80223
Florida Tile Ceramic Center
852 S. Jason, Unit 9
AC 303/744-2433

CONNECTICUT

EAST HARTFORD, 06108
Crest Tile & Marble Co.
262 Prestige Park Rd., Bay #9
AC 860/290-6622

DELAWARE

WILMINGTON, 19805
Mohawk Tile & Marble Dist.
Third & Greenhill Avenue
AC 302/655-7164

FLORIDA

BRADENTON, 35207
Gulf Tile Distributors of Florida
1215 50th Avenue Plaza West
AC 813/753-3545

BRANDON, 33511
Gulf Tile Distributors of Florida
305 West Robertson Street
AC 813/684-9945

SO. DAYTONA, 32119
Intercoastal Distributors, Inc.
1740 S. Segrave Avenue
AC 904/761-7454

FORT MYERS, 33907
West Florida Distributors, Inc.
2461 North Airport Road
AC 813/936-7676

FT. WALTON, 32548
Florida Tile Ceramic Center
30 Walter Martin Road
AC 904/243-0037

GAINESVILLE, 32606
Tile Contractors Supply Co. of Fla.
4005 N.W. 97th Blvd.
AC 904/332-5809

JACKSONVILLE, 32236
Fleming & Sons, Inc.
464 Cassat Avenue
AC 904/783-1240

JACKSONVILLE, 32211
Fleming & Sons, Inc.
9075 Atlantic Blvd.
AC 904/727-3553

LAKELAND, 33801
Florida Tile Ceramic Center
2635 Skyview Drive
AC 941/665-4646

LARGO, 34641
Gulf Tile Distributors of Florida
2200 Lake Avenue S.E.
AC 813/585-2816

LECANTO, (CRYSTAL RIVER) 34460
Tile Contractors Supply Co. of Fla.
4301 West Highway 44
AC 904/746-5475

MELBOURNE, 32901
East Coast Tile & Terrazzo Supplies
420 S. Neiman Avenue
AC 407/723-4353

MIAMI, 33126
Sikes Tile Distributors, Inc.
1601 N.W. 82nd Avenue
AC 305/591-0012

MIAMI, (KENDALL) 33176
Sikes Tile Distributors, Inc.
8725 S.W. 129th Terrace
AC 305/256-4190

NAPLES, 33942
West Florida Distributors, Inc.
2684 S. Horseshoe Drive
AC 941/643-3023

OAKLAND PARK, 33307
(Ft. Lauderdale)
Sikes Tile Distributors, Inc.
3484 NE 12 Avenue
AC 305/563-5666

OCALA, 34475
Tile Contractors Supply of Ocala
818 W. 27th Avenue
AC 904/629-5375

OLDSMAR, 34677
Gulf Tile Distributors of Florida
200 Scarlett Boulevard
AC 813/855-3399

ORANGE CITY, 32763
Intercoastal Distributors, Inc.
230 South Industrial Drive
AC 904/775-6262

ORMOND BEACH, 32174
Intercoastal Distributors, Inc.
11 Washington St.
AC 904/615-9100

PALM COAST, 32137
Intercoastal Distributors, Inc.
4894 Palm Coast Pkwy., NW
Suite #1
AC 904/445-9149

PANAMA CITY, 32405
Panama City Tile Distributors
1129 Highway 390
AC 904/769-5661

PENSACOLA, 32505
Florida Tile Ceramic Center
4200 N. Palafax
AC 904/434-1120

PINELLAS PARK, 34664-0690
Florida Ceramic Sales, Inc.
6669-96th Avenue N.
AC 813/546-5743

PORT RICHEY, 34668
Gulf Tile Distributors of Florida
5533 River Gulf Road
AC 813/842-3791

SANFORD, 32771
Watson Tile Distributors, Inc.
3625 Highway 46
AC 407/321-2958

SARASOTA, 34234
West Florida Distributors, Inc.
4500 Carmichael Avenue
AC 941/355-2704

SEBRING, 33870
Florida Tile Ceramic Center
6771 Hwy. 27 South
AC 813/382-4000

SPRING HILL, (BROOKSVILLE) 34609
Gulf Tile Distributors of Florida
11075 Hearth Road
AC 904/683-5888

ST. AUGUSTINE, 32086
Fleming & Sons, Inc.
2330 Dobbs Road
AC 904/824-5201

STUART, 34994
Sikes Tile Distributors, Inc
791 S.E. Monterey Road
AC 407/283-1362

TALLAHASSEE, 32301
Florida Tile Ceramic Center
1416 South Adams Street
AC 904/222-5184

TAMPA, 33607
Gulf Tile Distributors of Florida
2318 W. Columbus Drive
AC 813/251-8807

TAVARES, 32778
Watson Tile Distributors, Inc.
335 Duncan Drive
AC 904/343-0404

TITUSVILLE, 32780
East Coast Tile & Terrazzo Supplies
2880 South Hopkins Avenue
AC 407/267-7923

VERO BEACH, 32962
East Coast Tile & Terrazzo Supplies
450 Old Dixie Highway
AC 407/562-4164

WEST PALM BEACH, 33401
Sikes Tile Distributors, Inc.
425 Avon Road
AC 407/833-5727

WINTER HAVEN, 33880
Florida Tile Ceramic Center
158 Spirit Lake Road
AC 813/294-7522

WINTER PARK, 32789
(ORLANDO)
Watson Tile Distributors, Inc.
958 Orange Avenue
AC 407/644-9619

GEORGIA

ATLANTA, 30310
Tile Contractors Supply Co.
993-1001 Cox Avenue, S.W.
AC 404/753-4177

ATLANTA, 30305
Traditions in Tile, Ltd.
351 Peachtree Ave. N.E.
Suite 140
AC 404/239-9186

AUGUSTA, 30901
Tile Center, Inc.
1331 Reynolds Street
AC 706/722-6804

BOGART, 30622
Traditions in Tile, Ltd.
200 Cleveland Road
AC 706/543-0500

BRUNSWICK, 31520
Modern Builders Supply, Inc.
#1 Whittle Center
2933 Cypress Mill Road
AC 912/265-5885

COLUMBUS, 31909
The Tile Company
7505 C Hamilton Road
AC 706/327-0668

FAYETTEVILLE, 30214
Traditions in Tile, Ltd.
692 North Glynn Street
AC 404/461-8141

MACON, 31201
Tile Contractors Supply Co.
751 Fifth Street
AC 912/745-2319

MARIETTA, 30067
Florida Tile Distributors
4041 B Kingston Court
AC 404/951-1416

NORCROSS, 30093
Florida Tile Distributors
1256-F Oakbrook Drive
AC 404/448-8133

ROSWELL, 30076
Traditions in Tile, Ltd.
1495 Hembree Road, Suite 400
Ac 404/343-9104

SAVANNAH, 31405
Modern Builders Supply, Inc.
116 Central Junction Drive
AC 912/234-8224

STATESBORO, 30458
The Tile Center, Inc.
261 Northside Drive E.
AC 912/764-8453

WAYCROSS, 31502-0257
Modern Builders Supply, Inc.
U.S. Route 82 East
AC 912/283-5207

HAWAII

HONOLULU, 96819
Central Pacific Supply Co.
855 Ahua Street
AC 808/839-1952

IDAHO

BOISE, 83707
The Masonry Center
1424 North Orchard
AC 208/375-1362

ILLINOIS

ALSIP, 60658
Mid-America Tile, Inc.
4809 W. 128th Place
AC 708/388-4344

CHICAGO, 60610
Mid-America Tile, Inc.
440 North Wells
Suite 760
AC 312/467-0450

ELK GROVE VILLAGE, 60007
Mid-America Tile, Inc.
1650 Howard Street
AC 708/439-3110

MUNDELEIN, 60060
Mid-America Tile, Inc.
108 Terrace Drive
AC 708/566-5566

NORMAL, 61761
Keen Tile
801 East Pine Street
AC 309/454-1466

PEORIA, 61615
Keen Tile
8224 N. University St.
AC 309/689-6209

ROMEOVILLE, 60441
Mid-America Tile, Inc.
1404 Joliet Road
AC 708/972-1500

SPRINGFIELD, 62703
Keen Tile
2800-1 South 6th St.
AC 217/544-2137

INDIANA

EVANSVILLE, 47715
Louisville Tile Distributors
1417 N. Cullen Ave.
AC 812/473-0137

FT. WAYNE, 46808
Miles Distributing Co.
3922 N. Wells Street
AC 219/484-9649

INDIANAPOLIS, 46220
American Equipment Co., Inc.
7001 Hawthorne Park Dr.
AC 317/849-5400

SOUTH BEND, 46628
Miles Distributing Co.
2525 N. Foundation Drive
AC 219/234-4051

IOWA

DAVENPORT, 52806
Sunderland Bros. Co.
626 West 35th Street
AC 319/386-6151

URBANDALE, 50322
(DES MOINES)
Sunderland Bros. Tile Co.
4451 112th St.
AC 515/276-3600

KANSAS

LENEXA, 66219
Sunderland Bros. Tile Co.
10900 Lackman Road
AC 913/894-5515

WICHITA, 67202
General Distributors, Inc.
800 E. Indianapolis
AC 316/267-2255

KENTUCKY

ERLANGER, 41018
Florida Tile Ceramic Center
2744 Circle Port Dr., Bldg. C
AC 606/282-5400

LEXINGTON, 40509
Louisville Tile Distributors
2495 Palumbo Drive
AC 606/268-8373

LOUISVILLE, 40218
Louisville Tile Distributors
4520 Bishop Lane
AC 502/452-2037

LOUISIANA

BATON ROUGE, 70815
Bolick Distributors, Inc.
2055 North Airway Drive
AC 504/927-8016

HARAHAN, 70123 (NEW
ORLEANS)
Florida Tile Ceramic Center
5500 Jefferson Hwy.
AC 504/734-7911

MAINE

PORTLAND, 04104
Albert F. Fitzgerald, Inc.
12 Westfield Street
AC 207/772-1955

MARYLAND

BERLIN, 21811
Capitol Tile & Marble
10543 Ocean Gateway
AC 410/219-8453

LINTHICUM, 21090
Conestoga Tile of Maryland, Inc.
810A Oregon Avenue
AC 410/789-0700

ROCKVILLE, 20852
Capitol Tile & Marble Co.
5712 Wicomico Avenue
AC 301/881-8453

MASSACHUSETTS

WOBURN, 01888
Albert F. Fitzgerald, Inc.
120 Commerce Way
AC 617/935-7821

MICHIGAN

GRAND RAPIDS, 49508
Beaver Distributors, Inc.
4546 Roger B. Chaffee
AC 616/534-2883

FARMINGTON HILLS, 48335
Beaver Distributors, Inc.
24700 Drake Road
AC 810/476-2333

OKEMOS, 48864
Beaver Distributors, Inc.
1858 W. Grand River Ave.
AC 517/347-0708

ROCHESTER HILLS, 48309
Beaver Distributors, Inc.
2141 Austin Avenue
AC 810/299-8100

SAGINAW, 48603
Beaver Distributors, Inc.
2780 Enterprise Court
AC 517/790-5851

TROY, 48084
Beaver Distributors, Inc.
1700 Stutz Dive
Suite 37
AC 810/649-5552

MINNESOTA

BURNSVILLE, 55337
Rubble Tile Distributors
3220 West County Rd. 42
AC 612/882-8909

MINNETONKA, 55345
(MINNEAPOLIS)
Rubble Tile Distributors
6001 Culligan Way
AC 612/938-2599

WOODBURY, 55125
Rubble Tile Distributors
1830 Woodale Drive
AC 612/735-3883

MISSISSIPPI

HATTIESBURG, 39402
Bolick Distributors, Inc.
7028 Highway 49 N
AC 601/268-9001

JACKSON, 39208
BJ's Ceramic Tile Dist. Co.
512 Dexter Drive
AC 601/939-0111

MISSOURI

SPRINGFIELD, 65807
Mussino Distributing of
Missouri, Inc.
2414 E. West Battlefield Road
AC 417/889-8453

ST. LOUIS, 63108
AMC Tile Supply Co.
3905 Forest Park Blvd.
AC 314/371-2200

MONTANA

BILLINGS, 59107
Taylor Distributing
4141 State Avenue
AC 406/248-7737

MISSOULA, 59807
Taylor Distributing
2607 W. Railroad
AC 800/473-5749

NEBRASKA

OMAHA, 68127
Sunderland Bros. Co.
9700 J Street
AC 402/339-2220

NEVADA

CARSON CITY, 89706
Ceramic Tile Center
4388 N. Carson Street
AC 702/883-0833

LAS VEGAS, 89102
Designer Tile & Marble, Inc.
4525 Spring Mtn. Rd., Suite 110
AC 702/365-8453

SPARKS, 89431
Ceramic Tile Center
323 Freeport Blvd.
AC 702/359-6770

STATELINE, 89449
Ceramic Tile Center
290 Kingsbury Grade
AC 702/588-5408

NEW HAMPSHIRE

BEDFORD, 03110
Albert F. Fitzgerald, Inc.
Route 101 West
AC 603/472-3996

KEENE, 03431
Tilcon/AW
497 Winchester Street
AC 603/352-6680

NORTH SWANZEY, 03431
Tilcon/AW
25 Monadnock Highway
AC 603/352-0101

WEST LEBANON
Tilcon/AW
Block Plant, Inc.
Elm Street Extension
AC 603/298-9785

WEST LEBANON
Tilcon/AW
362 Miracle Mile
AC 603/448-0362

NEW JERSEY

BRICKTOWN, 08723
The Tile Place
720 Route 70
AC 908/477-4141

EAST HANOVER, 07936
Standard Tile Supply
320 Route 10
AC 201/884-4933

EDISON, 08817
Standard Tile Edison Corp.
810 Route 1
AC 908/248-0600

GREEN BROOK, 08812
Newark Tile Supply
Route 22
AC 908/968-0660

HAWTHORNE, 07506
John P. Fischer Tiles, Inc.
1064 Goffle Road
AC 201/427-7870

JERSEY CITY, 07307
Standard Tile Supply Co., Inc.
3527 Kennedy Blvd.
AC 201/653-0566

NEWARK, 07114
Newark Tile Supply Co.
19 Frelinghuysen Avenue
AC 201/824-5806

OAKHURST, 07755
The Tile Place
1604 Highway 35
AC 908/531-0500

PARAMUS, 07652
Standard Tile Supply Co., Inc.
137 West Route 4
AC 201/843-8119

RICHLAND, 08350
Orlandini Tile Supplies, Inc.
Route #40 Harding Hwy.
AC 609-697-2421

SUCCASUNNA, 07876
Standard Tile Supply Co., Inc.
159 Route 10
AC 201/584-4997

TOTOWA, 07512
Standard Tile Co., Inc.
255 Route 46
AC 201/256-6412

NEW MEXICO

ALBUQUERQUE, 87107
New Mexico Tile Supply
2513 Comanche Road, N.E.
AC 505/883-6076

NEW YORK

ALBANY, 12204
Albany Tile Supply, Inc.
452 N. Pearl Street
AC 518/434-0155

AMHERST, 14226-7888
Weinheimers, Inc.
1888 Niagara Falls Blvd.
AC 716/692-9000

ASTORIA, 11103
Parma Tile Company
2590 Steinway Street
AC 718/545-9393

BAYSIDE, 11361
Parma Tile Company
207-02 Northern Blvd.
AC 718/279-8500

LONG ISLAND CITY, 11102
Parma Tile Company
29-10 - 14th Street
AC 718/278-3060

NEW YORK, 10022
Parma Tile Company
241 East 58th Street
AC 212/751-9393

NEW YORK, 10029
Vedovato Bros., Inc.
246 E. 116th Street
AC 212/534-2854

PORT JEFFERSON STATION,
11776
Old Country Ceramic Tile
4679 Rt. 347 Nesconset Hwy.
AC 516/928-7722

POUGHKEEPSIE, 12603
Fitzgerald Tile Co.
15 Vassar Road
AD 914/462-2480

ROCHESTER, 14621
Tile Wholesalers of Rochester, Inc.
470 Hollenbeck Street
AC 716/544-3200

ROCKLAND COUNTY, 10982
Town & Country Ceramic Tile, Inc.
Rt. 59 & Airmont Rd.
(Tallman/Suffern)
AC 914/357-5553

SCARSDALE, 10583
Westchester Tile & Marble Corp.
178 Brook Street
AC 914/725-4355

SYRACUSE, 13211
Vestal Tile Distributors
6700 VIP Parkway
AC 315/454-0004

VESTAL, 13850
Vestal Tile Distributors
412 Prentice Road
AC 607/729-6128

WESTBURY, 11590
Old Country Ceramic Tile, Inc.
27 Urban Avenue
AC 516/334-6161

NORTH CAROLINA

ASHEVILLE, 28805
WNC Ceramic Tile, Inc.
508 Swannanoa River Rd.
AC 704/298-3251

CHARLOTTE, 28217
Florida Tile Ceramic Center
801 Pressley Road #106
AC 704/523-7615

HENDERSONVILLE, 28792
WNC Ceramic Tile, Inc.
203 Duncan Hill Road
AC 704/696-2408

RALEIGH, 27604
Florida Tile Ceramic Center
2640 Yonkers Road
AC 918/872-2903

WILMINGTON, 28405
Florida Tile Ceramic Center
6500 A-1 Windmill Way
AC 910/392-3072

WINSTON-SALEM, 27105
McCullough Ceramic Corp.
5272 Germanton Road
AC 910/744-0660

OHIO

BEACHWOOD, 44122
Ceramic Tile Distributors, Inc.
24000 Mercantile Road
AC 216/831-3867

CINCINNATI, 45242
Florida Tile Ceramic Center
10850 Millington Court
AC 513/891-1122

CLEVELAND, 44125
Ceramic Tile Distributors, Inc.
5400 Warner Road
AC 216/642-1117

COLUMBUS, 43229
Florida Tile Ceramic Center
7029 Huntley Road
AC 614/436-2511

HOLLAND, 43528
Beaver Distributors, Inc.
6561 Angola Road
AC 419/866-6122

MORAINE, 45439
Florida Tile Ceramic Center
2007 Springboro West
AC 513/293-5151

NORTH CANTON, 44720
Ceramic Tile Distributors, Inc.
7372 Whipple Ave. N.W.
AC 216/499-4900

OKLAHOMA

EDMOND, 73034
Paschal Tile Showroom
306-D S. Bryant
Bryant Square Shopping Center
AC 405/340-1091

OKLAHOMA CITY, 73106
John Paschal Tile Co., Inc.
1700 W. Reno
AC 405/232-9258

NORMAN, 73072
Paschal Tile Showroom
3700 W. Robinson
Brook Haven Village, Suite 144A
AC 405/321-8252

TULSA, 74146
Paschal Distributing Co.
10918 East 55th Place
AC 918/622-0017

OREGON

MEDFORD, 97504
Tile City
2560 Crater Lake Hwy., Unit C
AC 503/779-8453

PORTLAND, 97210
Florida Tile Ceramic Center
3259 N.W. Yeon Avenue
AC 503/226-6077

PENNSYLVANIA

ALLENTOWN, 18103
H. Winter & Company, Inc.
890 N. Gilmore Street
AC 610/434-4500

HARRISBURG, 17111-0585
Conestoga Ceramic Tile Dist.
4335 Lewis Road
AC 717/564-6860

KING OF PRUSSIA, 19406
Mohawk Tile & Marble Dist.
420 Swedeland Road
AC 610/279-2700

LESTER, 19029
Orlandini Tile Supply, Inc.
919-4th Avenue
AC 610/521-4621

PITTSBURGH, 15205
Fierst Distributing Co.
746 Trumbull
AC 412/429-9300

WILKES-BARRE, 18702
Tile Distributors of America
300 Mundy Street
AC 717/822-6123

RHODE ISLAND

CENTRAL FALLS, 02863
Crest Tile & Marble Co.
1136 Lonsdale Avenue
AC 401/723-9774

WARWICK, 02888
Crest Tile & Marble
319 Bald Hill Road
AC 401/737-0160

SOUTH CAROLINA

ANDERSON, 29625-9617
Clayton Tile Dist.
1718 Pearman Dairy Road
AC 803/225-0884

NORTH CHARLESTON, 29405
Melcer Tile Company, Inc.
2520 Oscar Johnson Drive
AC 803/744-5345

COLUMBIA, 29204
The Tile Center, Inc.
2517 Two Notch Road
AC 803/254-9338

GREENVILLE, 29606
Clayton Tile Dist. Corp.
Route 6, 535 Woodruff Road
AC 803/288-6290

HILTON HEAD, 29928
Modern Builders Supply, Inc.
116 Triangle Square
AC 803/681-3070

MYRTLE BEACH, 29577
Florida Tile Ceramic Center
3221 Old Socastee Road
AC 803/626-1758

SPARTANBURG, 29301
Clayton Tile Dist. Co.
530 S. Blackstock Rd.
AC 803/587-9732

TENNESSEE

CHATTANOOGA, 37404
Ceramic Tile Supply, Inc.
1601 East 27th Street
AC 615/698-1512

JOHNSON CITY, 37603
Winco Distributors, Inc.
1200 Indian Ridge Road
AC 615/929-1156

KNOXVILLE, 37921
Winco Distributors, Inc.
1740 Louisville Drive
AC 615/588-6522

MEMPHIS, 38134
Acme Brick Co.
5690 Summer
AC 901/387-4540

MEMPHIS, 38112
W.A. Oyler Distributing Co.
2636 Summer Avenue
AC 901/324-6143

NASHVILLE, 37204
Tile Contractors Supply Co.
of Tennessee
2548 Bransford Avenue
AC 615/269-9669

TEXAS

AUSTIN, 78758
American Tile Supply of Austin, Inc.
2020 G Rutland Drive
AC 512/837-2843

BROWNSVILLE, 78521
Diamond Ceramic Tile & Flooring
3220 FM 802
AC 210/544-4000

DALLAS, 75229
American Tile Supply, Inc.
2839 Merrell Road
AC 214/243-2377

DALLAS, 75238
American Tile Supply, Inc.
10550 Plano Road
AC 214/343-5733

DESOTO, 75115
American Tile Supply, Inc.
1707 Falcon Drive
AC 214/228-0066

EDINBURG, 78539
Mission Tile
4201 W. University Dr.
AC 210/383-0113

EL PASO, 79936
Florida Tile Ceramic Center
11333A Rojas
AC 915/591-5956

FT. WORTH, 76115
American Tile Supply, Inc.
200 E. Felix
AC 817/924-2232

HOUSTON, 77024
Master Tile Co., Inc.
10321-C Katy Freeway
AC 713/461-4297

HOUSTON, 77027
Master Tile Co., Inc.
3701 W. Alabama #160
AC 713/963-0084

HOUSTON, 77034
Master Tile Co., Inc.
10830 Kingspoint Drive
AC 713/947-1778

HOUSTON, 77074
Master Tile Co., Inc.
7075 Southwest Freeway
AC 713/772-0047

HOUSTON, 77092-8089
Master Tile Co., Inc.
2510 McAllister
AC 713/688-2271

LAREDO, 78041
Bricks International
6423 McPherson Rd., Suite 31
AC 210/722-5038

LONGVIEW, 75601
American Tile Suppply, Inc.
1612 East Whaley Street
AC 903/757-7762

LUBBOCK, 79414
Florida Tile Ceramic Center
5844-49th Street
AC 806/793-3688

MIDLAND, 79703
Anderson Tile Sales
1703 S. Midkiff
AC 915/683-5116

ODESSA, 79761
Anderson Tile Sales
1801 Kermit Highway
AC 915/337-0081

PLANO, 75074
American Tile Supply, Inc.
1701 Summit Ave., Suite 10
AC 214/516-4926

RICHLAND HILLS, 76118
American Tile Supply, Inc.
7412 Baker Blvd.
AC 817/589-1252

SAN ANGELO, 76902
Anderson Tile Sales
120 S. Madison
AC 915/655-0646

SAN ANTONIO, 78216
American Tile Supply
of San Antonio, Inc.
1130 Arion Parkway
AC 210/490-1927

SPRING, 77388
Master Tile Co., Inc.
100 Cypresswood Drive
Suite 1400
AC 713/350-3030

UTAH

SALT LAKE CITY, 84115
Florida Tile Ceramic Center
305 West 2880 South
AC 801/485-2900

VERMONT

BRATTLEBORO, 05301
Tilcon/AW
300 S. Main St.
AC 802/254-9488

EAST MONTPELIER, 05651
Tilcon/AW
Route 14
AC 802/229-5856

RUTLAND, 05701
Tilcon/AW
156 Ivy Street
AC 802/775-8037

SPRINGFIELD, 05156
Tilcon/AW
100 River Street
AC 802/885-3272

WINOOSKI, 05404
Tilcon/AW
2 East Street
AC 802/655-3747

VIRGINIA

CHESAPEAKE, 23320-2515
McCullough Ceramic Corp.
2129 Smith Avenue
AC 804/420-2020

RICHMOND, 23233
McCullough Ceramic Corp.
9878 Mayland Drive
Deep Run Gaskins Center
AC 804/747-8300

SALEM, 24153
Valley Tile Distributors
1510 Southside Drive
AC 540/387-0300

WASHINGTON

SEATTLE, 98108
Florida Tile Ceramic Center
665 South Orcas Street
AC 206/767-9819

SPOKANE, 99220
Floor Supply Distributing, Inc.
N. 1802 Langley
AC 509/535-9707

WEST VIRGINIA

CHARLESTON, 25301
Smith Floor Covering Dist.
1118 Smith Street
AC 304/344-2493

WISCONSIN

GREEN BAY, 54304
Jaeckle Wholesale, Inc.
820 Coronis Way
AC 414/337-0593

KENOSHA, 53144
Lexco Tile & Supply Co.
5915 52nd Street
AC 414/652-4800

LACROSSE, 54603
Jaeckle Wholesale, Inc.
2605 Hemstock
AC 608/781-4888

MADISON, 53704
Jaeckle Wholesale, Inc.
2310 Daniels Street
AC 608/221-8400

WEST ALLIS, 53214
Lexco Tile & Supply Co.
1616 S. 108th Street
AC 414/771-2900

BERMUDA

HAMILTON, HM05
Eurotile Bermuda
4 Mill Creek Lane
AC 809/292-6069

BRITISH VIRGIN ISLANDS

ROADTOWN TORTOLA
Drake's Traders Ltd.
AC 809/494-3282

CANADA

CALGARY, ALBERTA, T2H 2Y4
Centura
7360 12th Street S.E.
AC 403/259-0106

EDMONTON, ALBERTA, T5V 1H2
Centura
16427 118th Avenue
AC 403/454-8591

BURNABY, BRITISH COLUMBIA, V5G 1K7
Centura
4616 Canada Way
AC 604/298-8453

DARTMOUTH, NOVA SCOTIA, B3B 1H3
Tangram Surfaces, Inc.
66 Wright Avenue
AC 902/468-7679

HAMILTON, ONTARIO, L8H 6N6
Centura
469 Woodward Avenue North
AC 905/547-9300

LONDON, ONTARIO, N6E 1R5
Centura
993 Adelaide Street South
AC 519/681-1961

OTTAWA, ONTARIO, K2H 8K7
Centura
1070 Morrison Drive
AC 613/820-6622

PETERBOROUGH, ONTARIO, K9J 6W9
Centura
774 Rye Street
AC 705/743-2881

TORONTO, ONTARIO, M6A 2V6
Centura
53 Apex Road
AC 416/785-5165

WINDSOR, ONTARIO, N9A 6J3
Centura
3155 County Road 42
AC 519/966-3580

MONTREAL, QUEBEC, H4N 2S4
Centura
105 Deslauriers St. Laurent
AC 514/336-4311

STE-FOY, QUEBEC, GLP 3X3
Centura
2699 Watt Street
AC 418/653-5267

CARIBBEAN

ARUBA, ORANGESTAD
Antilliaanse Handel
Ferguson Straat 7
AC 011-297-8-204-040

NASSAU, BAHAMAS
Premier Imports Ltd.
St. Albans Dr. off W. Bay St.
AC 809/322-8396

BRIDGETOWN, BARBADOS
R & E Brancker
P.O. Box 419
AC 809/427-4347

BELIZE
Belize City
Benny's Hardware
AC 011-501-2-30550

CURACAO, N.A.
Mosaicos Samander
P.O. Box 111
AC 011-599-9-612587

DOMINICAN REPUBLIC
Santo Domingo
Mercantile Del Caribe
Ave. John F. Kennedy
AC 809/542-7766

EL SALVADOR
Ceramica Del Pacifico
Prolongacion Alameda
Juan Pablo II #333
AC 503/274-7844

GRAND CAYMAN, B.W.I.
Paramount Tile & Carpet
P.O. Box 236 Shedden Rd.
George Towne
AC 809/949-5000

JAMAICA, ST. ELIZABETH
House of Tile
Munro College PO
AC 809/966-2359

JAMAICA, KINGSTON
Tile Plus Ltd.
11 Derrymore Rd.
AC 809/960-0117

JAMAICA, KINGSTON 10
The Builders Arcade Ltd.
8 Red Hills Rd.
AC 809/926-2645

NETHERLAND ANTILLES
St. Maarten
A & A Supply, N.V.
18 Illidge Road
011-599-5-23002

TRINIDAD, TOBEGO
ACE Hardware
233 Western Main Rd.
Cocorite, Trinidad
628-4ACE

COSTA RICA

SAN JOSE
Eurodecoracion
Centro Comercial
Trejos Montealegre
Local #8 Escazu
011-506-897-7706

ENGLAND

SWEDECOR, LTD.
41-47 Scarborough Street
Hull HU3 4TG
(0482) 20691

GUAM

TAMUNING, GUAM, 96911
Benson Guam Enterprises, Inc.
477-4564

HONG KONG

HOPEWELL TRADING CO.
52 High Street
C/FL Sai Ying Poon
011-852-549-2568

IRELAND

DUBLIN 12
Rocca Tiles Ltd., Unit 4
Royal Live Retail Park
Naas Road
011-353-1-568-055

MEXICO

LOZETAS Y AZULEJOS SA
Justo Sierra #451
Mexicali-Baja California
AC 706/568-2101

TIJUANA

BAJA TILE
Blvd. Cuauhtemoc #125
Dessarrolo Urbano Rio
AC 170/668-81838

PANAMA

REP. DE PANAMA
Ceramica del Caribe SA
Via Argentina Edif Rattan
APTDO 108 Zona 9A
011-507-646-787

PUERTO RICO

CAROLINA, 00630
Commercial Adolfo S. Pagan, Inc.
272nd Street, Country Club
Industrial Park
AC 809/750-1650

SAUDI ARABIA

JEDDA-21492
P.A.M.A.S. Est.
Baladeyyah Street
966 266 56453

RIYADH-11484
P.A.M.A.S. Est.
Olaya Main Street
966-1-4653349

U.S. VIRGIN ISLANDS

ST. CROIX, 00851
U & W Industrial
Vitex Building
East Airport Road
Kings Hill
AC 809/778-0012

ST. THOMAS

MSI BUILDING SUPPLIES
AC 809/778-0012

55

Florida Tile Industries
Lakeland, Florida 33802
1-800-FLA-TILE

Summitville ®

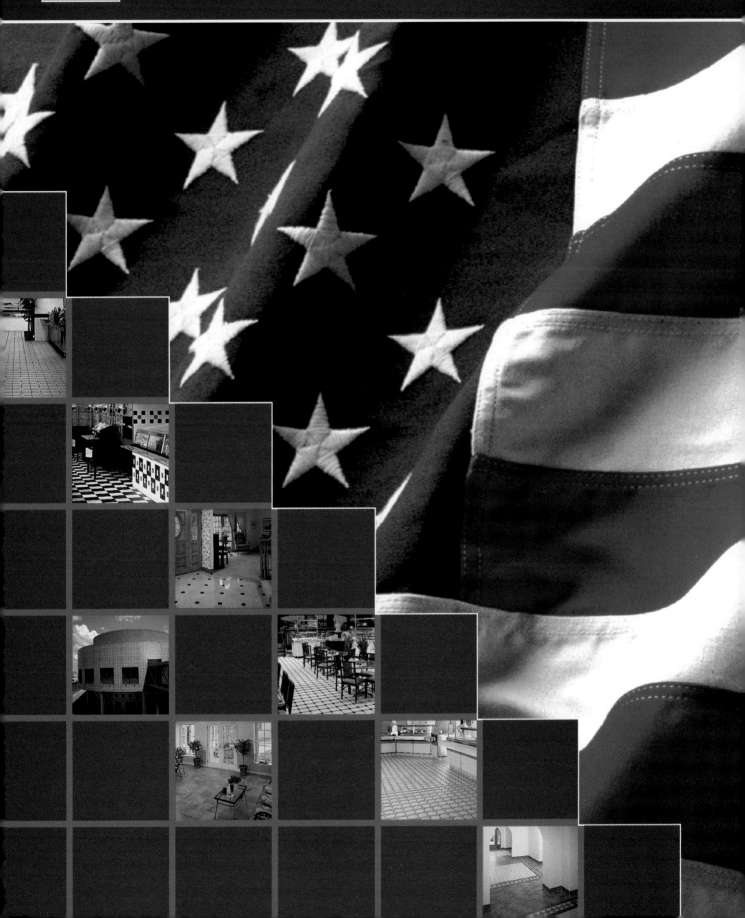

THE GREAT
AMERICAN
SHOWPLACE

Summitville's extensive collection of complementin colors, sizes and textures, for a broad range of commercial and residential installations, are currently on display at your local Distributor/Dealer.

Our knowledgeable representatives are available to show you our extensive selections, assist you wit

94 Dark Blend

95 Mixed Blend

94 Light Blend

95 Vintage Georgetown

94 Mixed Blend

97 Hickory Grove Standard

94 Ironspot

97 Dark Blend

95 Georgetown Standard

97 Light Blend

95 Dark Blend

97 Mixed Blend

95 Light Blend

Summitshades®

Summitshades are impervious glazed porcelain pavers with a delicate range of light and dark shading in each tile. Summitshades impervious body is suitable for commercial or residential settings, indoors or out.

Summitshades smooth or abrasive surface is easily cleaned with warm water and mild detergent.

Since Summitville's glazed porcelain pavers are impervious, we recommend a higher bond strength setting material such as latex modified mortars or epoxies.

All colors are available in 8″ x 8″ x $\frac{5}{16}$″ size. Abrasive surface and 12″ x 12″ are special order, contact factory for availability.

For trim units, see page 30; for specifications see page 43.

NOMINAL SIZE/SHAPE

8″ x 8″ x $\frac{5}{16}$″

WR Wear Rating; see page 12 for definition.

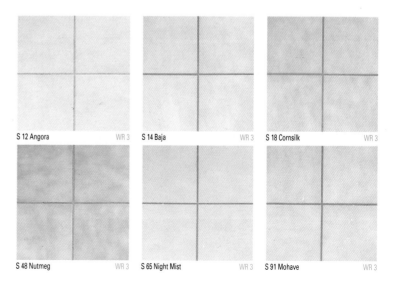

S 12 Angora   WR 3
S 14 Baja   WR 3
S 18 Cornsilk   WR 3
S 48 Nutmeg   WR 3
S 65 Night Mist   WR 3
S 91 Mohave   WR 3

Unmatched Physical Properties Give Summitville's Porcelain Pavers the Edge

Summitville's ability to meet the demanding specifications for jobs like tunnel projects are the result of innovating engineering and creative product development.

To demonstrate, to the Department of Transportation and the Cumberland Gap Tunnel engineering group, the feasibility of using 8"x 8" tile on the curved surface of a tunnel wall Summitville constructed the shortest tunnel in history. Although the mockup was built to the full scale dimensions of the tunnel, it was only 4 feet long.

The "short" tunnel did, however provide undeniable proof that Summitville's 8"x 8" porcelain pavers, grouted with S-400 Epoxy, offered a practical and less expensive solution than previously considered. This innovative demonstration eventually led to six major tunnel projects: the Cumberland Gap Tunnel in Middlesboro, Kentucky, Eisenhower Tunnel in

Four foot deep tunnel mock-up with 8"x 8" tile installed.

Silverstone, Colorado, McCarran Tunnel in Las Vegas, Knox County Tunnel in Tennessee, and the Lincoln and Brooklyn Battery Tunnels in New York City.

The Cumberland Gap project with radius walls used the traditional tile setters method of installing each tile to the wall of the tunnel. Over 250,000 sq. ft. of 8"x 8", dove tail back tile provided both a chemical and a physical bond to assure a successful installation.

Although both the Cumberland Gap and the Eisenhower tunnel projects used Summitville 8" impervious, porcelain, pavers the Eisenhower Tunnel used a panelized method of installing the tile. Panels were constructed with tile in a controlled, labor saving, environment then transported 30 miles to the site and installed on the tunnel walls.

Panalized method of tile installation, Eisenhower Tunnel

A recent installation using 8"x 8" Exterior Cladding. Charleston, WV

Summitville's Porcelain Pavers and epoxy were selected for their ability to withstand the harsh climate of the Continental Divide, 11,300 feet above sea level.

Summitville's environmental friendly, impervious, glazed, porcelain pavers have been specified and installed on building exteriors and tunnels in tile sizes ranging from $4^1/_4$" to 16"x 16" with smooth or textured finishes.

The manufacturing process that produces Summitville's impervious glazed porcelain pavers **benefits the environment in two ways.** First; feldspar tailings, **a post industrial waste product,** that has

Glaze to Body Comparisan Test

Summitville

Competitor

overloaded landfills for the past 100 years, is used as the primary raw material. Second; Summitville developed a closed system for solid waste accumulation and re-use at their North Carolina plant that resulted in a **manufacturing process that is virtually waste free.**

An additional benefit provided by the Summitville production process is the **superior fusion of glaze to body,** which results in a smoother, more continuous surface that is less prone to pitting, pinholes and other surface imperfections than those offered by other manufacturers. Laboratory tests have proven that **Summitville porcelain pavers offer superior durability and easier maintenance under extreme conditions.**

As it has throughout its 84-year history, Summitville is working today to provide a cleaner environment for tomorrow.

Recommended Use and Wear Rating Guide

1   LIGHT TRAFFIC: Very light-duty residential floors, such as slipper traffic.
2   MEDIUM TRAFFIC: Residential light-duty floors. Avoid pivot points, stairs or entryways where sand, gravel or other abrasives may be introduced.
3   MEDIUM HEAVY TRAFFIC: Suitable for most residential and light-duty commercial applications. Not recommended for heavy traffic areas.
4   HEAVY TRAFFIC: Suitable for all residential applications. Also for heavy duty commercial, retail and institutional use.
4+ EXTRA HEAVY TRAFFIC: Suitable for all residential and commercial applications. Use where maximum traffic and other circumstances require optimum durability.

Wear Ratings are listed on each page.

Morganmates®

Morganmates are impervious glazed porcelain pavers available with a smooth or abrasive surface for maximum adaptability, indoors and out.

Morganmates' impervious body is suitable for residential and commercial applications; its durable glazed surface is easily cleaned with warm water and mild detergent. We recommend wet-vacuum type cleaning for abrasive tile or when grease/oil combined with water are prevalent in commercial installations.

Morganmates are modular with all glazed porcelain products and Summitmates, for endless design possibilities. Complementing color ranges and modular sizes allow these products to be installed together with a common joint width for maximum design flexibility.

Since Summitville's glazed porcelain pavers are impervious, we recommend a higher bond strength setting material such as latex modified mortars or epoxies.

For trim units, see page 30; for specifications, see page 43.

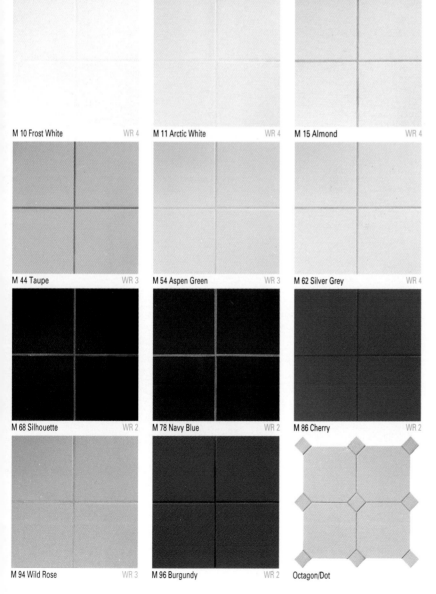

M 10 Frost White	WR 4	M 11 Arctic White	WR 4	M 15 Almond	WR 4
M 44 Taupe	WR 3	M 54 Aspen Green	WR 3	M 62 Silver Grey	WR 4
M 68 Silhouette	WR 2	M 78 Navy Blue	WR 2	M 86 Cherry	WR 2
M 94 Wild Rose	WR 3	M 96 Burgundy	WR 2	Octagon/Dot	

	SMOOTH			
	8 X 8 X 5/16	8 X 5/16 OCTAGON	2 X 2 X 5/16 DOT*	12 X 12 X 5/16
M 10	✔	✔	✔	✔
M 11	✔	✔	✔	✔
M 15	✔	✔	✔	✔
M 44	✔	●	✔	●
M 54	✔	●	✔	●
M 62	✔	●	✔	✔
M 68	✔	●	✔	✔
M 78	✔	●	✔	●
M 86	✔	●	✔	●
M 94	✔	●	✔	●
M 96	✔	●	✔	●

● Special order—check factory for available inventory, minimum quantity required.

✔ Stock readily available.

* Dots are extruded glazed quarry tile, same thickness and color range as field tile, but with different physical properties. Contact factory for test results if needed.

4¼" x 4¼", 4" x 8", 6" x 6" and 16" x 16" size available by special order; contact factory for availability, minimum quantity required.

WR Wear Rating; see page 12 for definition.

Imperva®

Imperva's heavy-duty commercial glaze combines with a body composition of superior density to form an extremely durable paver available in 11 colors and four sizes.

Imperva's impervious body is suitable for heavy traffic in commercial or residential settings, indoors or out. Imperva's smooth or abrasive surface is easily cleaned with warm water and mild detergent. We recommend wet-vacuum type cleaning for abrasive tile or when grease/oil combined with water are prevalent in commercial installations.

Imperva is modular with all porcelain products and Summitmates for maximum design flexibility. Complementing color ranges and modular sizes allow these products to be installed together for endless design possibilities.

Since Summitville's glazed porcelain pavers are impervious, we recommend a higher bond strength setting material such as latex modified mortars or epoxies.

For trim units, see page 30; for specifications, see page 43.

	SMOOTH				ABRASIVE			
	8 X 8 X 5/16	8 X 5/16 OCTAGON	2 X 2 X 5/16 DOT*	12 X 12 X 5/16	8 X 8 X 5/16	8 X 5/16 OCTAGON	2 X 2 X 5/16 DOT*	12 X 12 X 5/16
I 10	✔	✔	✔	✔	✔	✔	✔	✔
I 15	✔	✔	✔	✔	✔	✔	✔	✔
I 44	●	●	✔	●	✔	●	✔	●
I 54	●	●	✔	●	✔	●	●	●
I 58	●	●	✔	●	✔	●	●	●
I 62	✔	●	✔	✔	✔	●	✔	✔
I 68	✔	●	✔	✔	✔	✔	✔	✔
I 76	●	●	✔	●	✔	●	●	●
I 78	●	●	✔	●	✔	●	●	●
I 94	●	●	✔	●	✔	●	●	●
I 96	●	●	✔	●	✔	●	●	●

●   Special order—check factory for available inventory, minimum quantity required.

✔   Stock readily available.

*   Dots are extruded glazed quarry tile, same thickness and color range as field tile, but with different physical properties. Contact factory for test results if needed.

4¼" x 4¼", 4" x 8", 6" x 6" and 16" x 16" size available by special order; contact factory for availability, minimum quantity required.

WR   Wear Rating; see page 12 for definition.

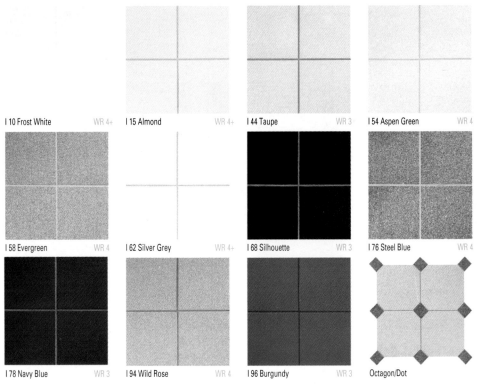

I 10 Frost White	WR 4+	I 15 Almond	WR 4+	I 44 Taupe	WR 3	I 54 Aspen Green	WR 4
I 58 Evergreen	WR 4	I 62 Silver Grey	WR 4+	I 68 Silhouette	WR 3	I 76 Steel Blue	WR 4
I 78 Navy Blue	WR 3	I 94 Wild Rose	WR 4	I 96 Burgundy	WR 3	Octagon/Dot	

Imperva® Granite

Imperva Granite is an impervious porcelain paver with a distinctive "granite-like" glazed surface which is color matched and modular with Imperva, Morganmates, Summit-shades, Summit-Tread, Marblesque, Stepping Stones and Summitmates.

Imperva Granite's smooth or abrasive surface is easily cleaned with warm water and mild detergent. We recommend wet-vacuum type cleaning for abrasive tile or when grease/oil combined with water are prevalent in commercial installations.

Imperva Granite's impervious body is suitable for heavy-duty commercial and residential applications, indoors or out.

Imperva Granite is available in 11 colors and four sizes.

Since Summitville's glazed porcelain pavers are impervious, we recommend a higher bond strength setting material such as latex modified mortars or epoxies.

For trim units, see page 30; for specifications, see page 43.

G 45 Sierra WR 4+   G 56 Allegheny WR 4+   G 57 Adirondack WR 4+   G 65 Smoky WR 4+

G 73 Shenandoah WR 4+   G 75 Appalachian WR 4+   G 77 Blue Ridge WR 4   G 92 Poconos WR 4+

Octagon/Dot
2" dot is available in Imperva and Morganmates for a variety of color options.

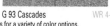

G 93 Cascades WR 4+   G 95 Rockies WR 4+   G 97 Piedmont WR 4

	SMOOTH			ABRASIVE		
	8 X 8 X 5/16	8 X 5/16 OCTAGON	12 X 12 X 5/16	8 X 8 X 5/16	8 X 5/16 OCTAGON	12 X 12 X 5/16
G 45	✔	•	✔	✔	•	✔
G 56	•	•	•	✔	•	•
G 57	•	•	•	•	•	•
G 65	✔	•	✔	✔	•	✔
G 73	•	•	•	•	•	•
G 75	•	•	•	•	•	•
G 77	•	•	•	•	•	•
G 92	•	•	•	•	•	•
G 93	✔	•	✔	•	•	✔
G 95	✔	•	✔	✔	•	✔
G 97	✔	•	✔	✔	•	✔

• Special order—check factory for available inventory, minimum quantity required.

✔ Stock readily available.

* Dots are extruded glazed quarry tile, same thickness and color range as field tile, but with different physical properties. Contact factory for test results if needed.

4¼" x 4¼", 4" x 8", 6" x 6" and 16" x 16" size available by special order; contact factory for availability, minimum quantity required.

WR Wear Rating; see page 12 for definition.

Summit-Tread

Summit-Tread is an impervious, stain-resistant porcelain paver with a raised grid pattern for added traction in commercial kitchens, stairways, and walkways; anywhere that improved slip-resistance is important. Summit-Tread's design improves traction by channeling water and grease away from the point of foot traffic. Summit-Tread has the same physical properties as Summitville's other porcelain pavers; see page 12 for details. Available in three colors and 8" x 8" x ⁵⁄₁₆" size in both tread and smooth surfaces. For smooth-surface trim units, see page 30; for specifications, see page 43.

NOMINAL SIZE/SHAPE

8" x 8" x ⁵⁄₁₆"

WR Wear Rating; see page 12 for definition.

T 10 Red Tread Surface
WR 4+

T 44 Tan Tread Surface
WR 4+

T 76 Blue Tread Surface
WR 4+

T 10 Red Smooth Surface
WR 4+

T 44 Tan Smooth Surface
WR 4+

T 76 Blue Smooth Surface
WR 4+

Stepping Stones® II

Stepping Stones are impervious glazed porcelain pavers that feature a subtle range of color shadings and a lightly textured surface. Stepping Stones are suitable for heavy-duty commercial and residential applications, indoors and out. Available in five color ranges; abrasive surface by special order. For trim units, see page 30; for specifications, see page 43.

NOMINAL SIZE/SHAPE

8" x 8" x ⁵⁄₁₆"
12" x 12" x ⁵⁄₁₆"

WR Wear Rating; see page 12 for definition.

P 10 Glacier   WR 4+

P 35 Desert Storm   WR 4+

P 39 Sandstone   WR 4+

P 65 Thunder Cloud   WR 4+

P 91 Sunset   WR 4+

17

Formalesque

The classic richness of the Formalesque selection of colors is suitable for a wide variety of decorating solutions.

With a heavy to extra heavy traffic wear rating, Formalesque is ideal for residential or heavy-duty commercial, retail and institutional areas.

A range of shades in each color adds to the beauty and interest of this selection in any installation.

Formalesque meets all A.N.S.I. standards for glazed porcelain paver tiles.

Abrasive surface available by special order, minimum quantity required. Contact factory for availability.

NOMINAL SIZE/SHAPE

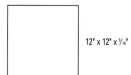

12" x 12" x 5/16"

WR Wear Rating; see page 12 for definition.

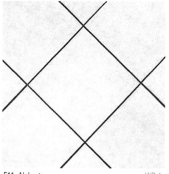

F11 Alabaster   WR 4+

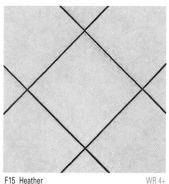

F15 Heather   WR 4+

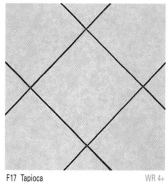

F17 Tapioca   WR 4+

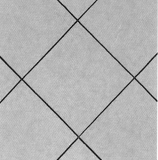

F62 Platinum   WR 4+

F94 Coral   WR 4

Pueblo Stones®II

Ten NEW porcelain colors have been created for the popular Pueblo Series, a continuation of the weathered colors reminiscent of the southwest.

A wide range of shades will be found in each color which deepens the visual interest of these tiles.

Random facial imperfections are a desirable and inherent characteristic which adds to the overall unique effect of Pueblo Stones II.

Pueblo Stones II meets all ANSI standards for glazed porcelain paver tiles.

Trim Shapes: 6″ X 12″ bullnose and bullnose corners are available in all colors.

NOMINAL SIZE/SHAPE

12" x 12" x ⅜"

WR Wear Rating; see page 12 for definition.

R12 Windswept   WR 4+

R21 Tipi   WR 4+

R31 Tumbleweed   WR 4+

R41 Coyote   WR 3

R47 Mesquite   WR 4

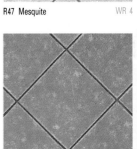

R51 Juniper   WR 3

R55 Blue Spruce   WR 4

R71 Blue Bell   WR 4+

R92 Adobe   WR 4

R97 Sedona   WR 3

Pueblo Shades

Pueblo Shades are reminiscent of the old west with a range of 5 colors that complement a relaxed, carefree decor that's always in style.

The natural look of Pueblo Shades is enhanced with a wide range of color shading and slight facial imperfections that are desirable and inherent characteristics.

Pueblo Shades are suitable for extra heavy traffic in all residential and commercial applications where maximum traffic and other circumstances require optimum durability.

Nominal 3" x 12" x 3/8" bullnose trim is available in all colors.

NOMINAL SIZE/SHAPE

6" x 6" x ³/₈"

6" x 12" x ³/₈"

12" x 12" x ³/₈"

V10 Maya   WR 4+

V20 Yuma   WR 4+

V30 Zuni   WR 4+

WR Wear Rating; see page 12 for definition.

V40 Pima   WR 4+

V50 Yaqui   WR 4+

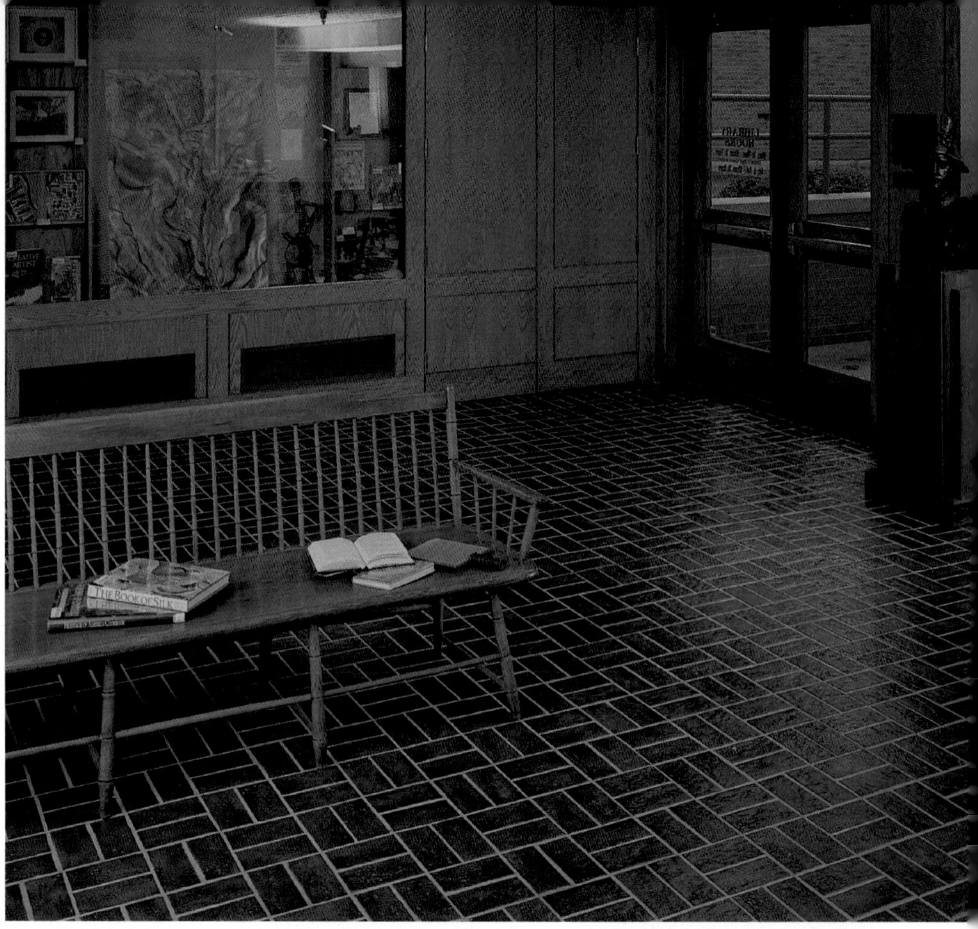

Olde Lombardic®

Olde Lombardic offers the hand-crafted look of irregular edge tile in 11 colors and four sizes.

A semi-vitreous glazed quarry tile, Olde Lombardic is suitable for residential and light-duty commercial floors.

Olde Lombardic complements the rustic decor of any room where architectural design calls for warmth and durability.

For interior walls and floors. Exterior applications only in temperate climates

For trim shapes, see page 30; for specifications, see page 43.

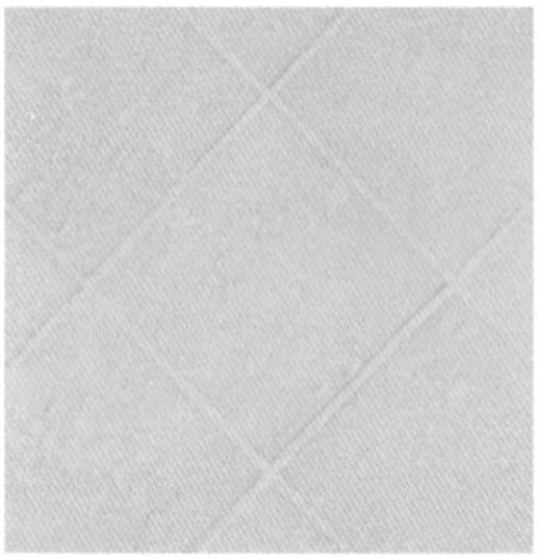

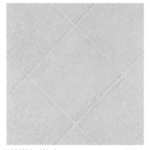

412 White Wash WR 3

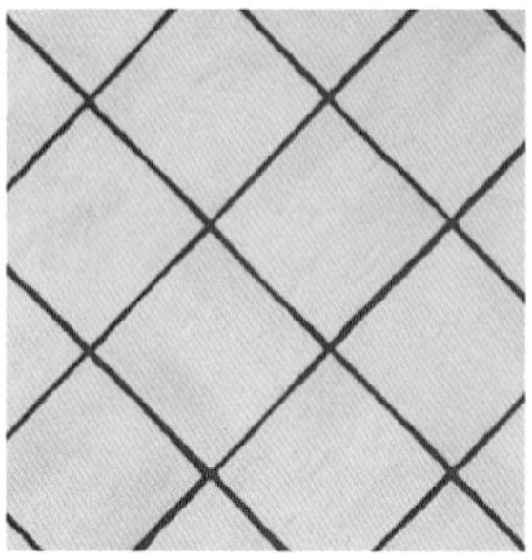

417 Buttermilk WR 3

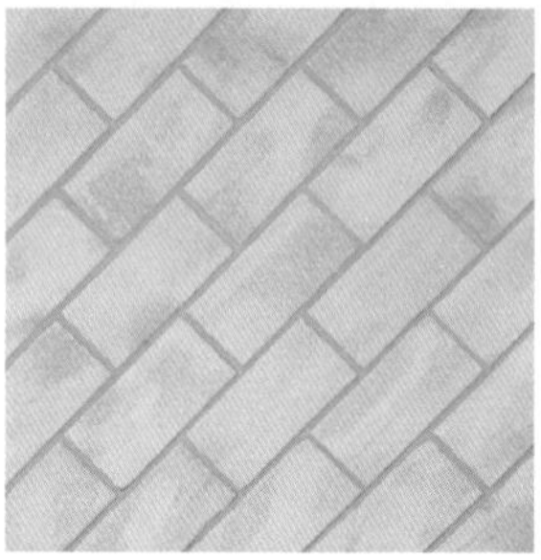

424 Oatmeal WR 3

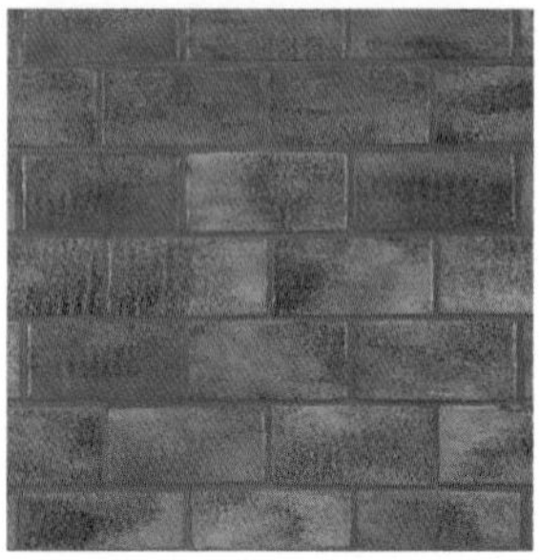

435 Burlap WR 3

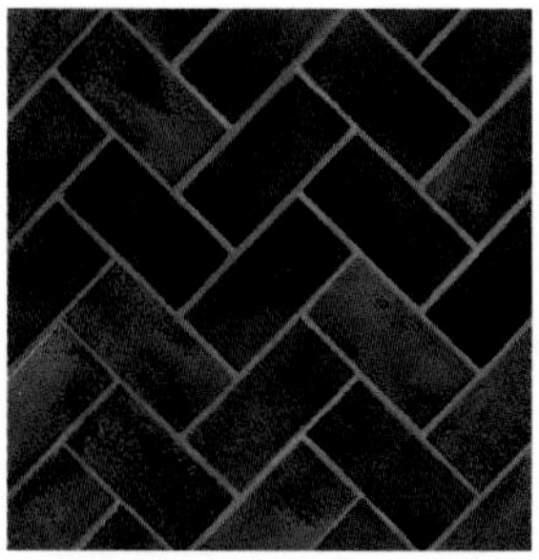

440 Bison Brown WR 3

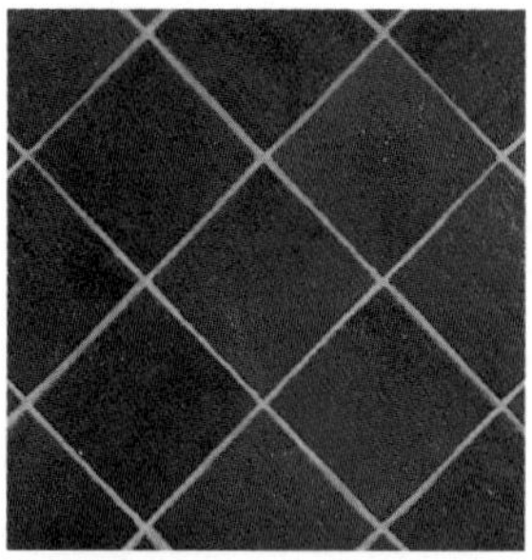

457 Village Green WR 3

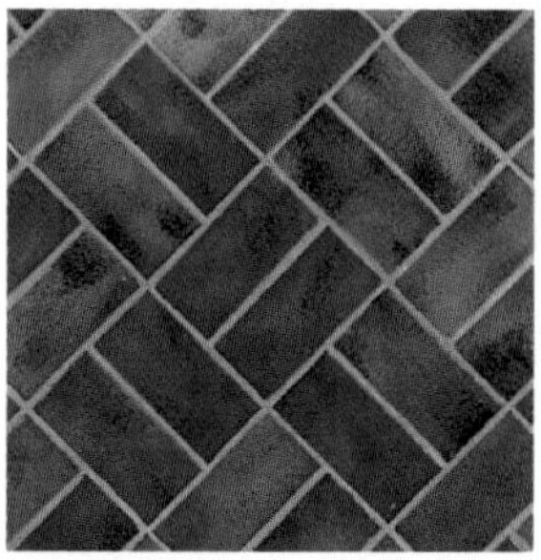

465 Silver Shadow WR 3

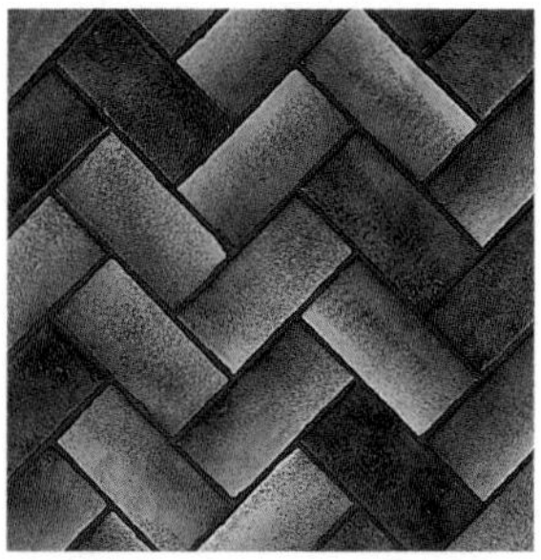

470 Steel Blue WR 3

NOMINAL SIZES/SHAPES

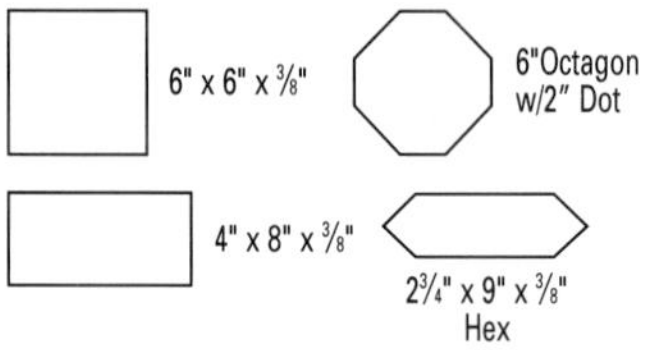
6" x 6" x 3/8"
6"Octagon w/2" Dot
4" x 8" x 3/8"
2 3/4" x 9" x 3/8" Hex

WR Wear Rating; see page 12 for definition.

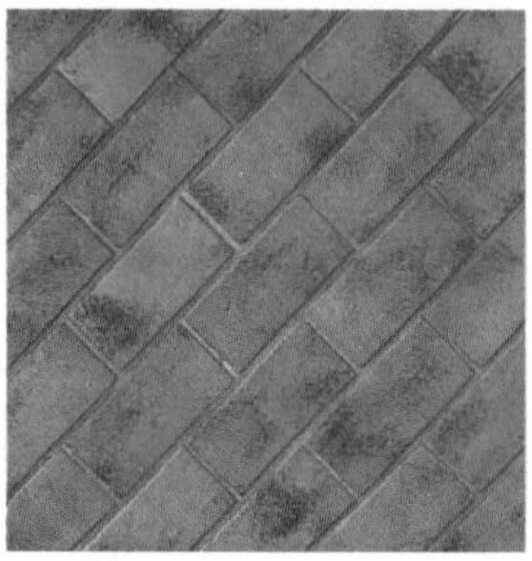

472 Blue Bonnet WR 3

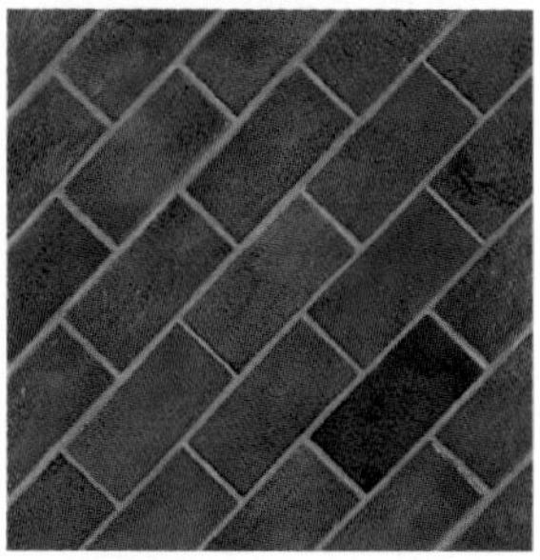

474 Nordic Blue WR 3

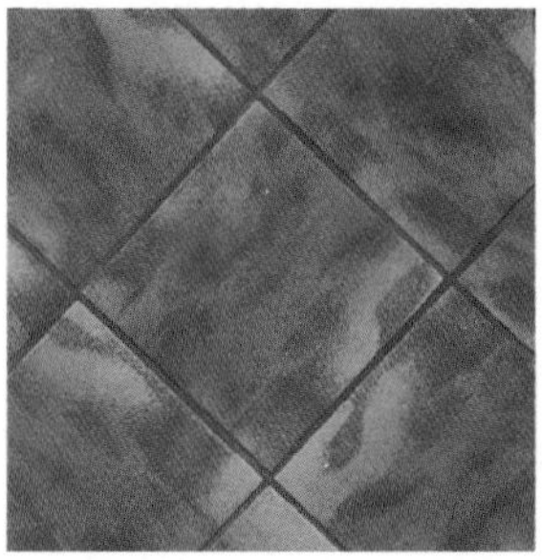

493 Dusky Rose WR 3

Country Classics

Country Classics are field tiles with decorative corners available in blue, green, red or brown. Decorative Inserts, shown on page 23, are also available with these rustic corner decorations.

Country Classics come in one size, 4" x 4" x ¼", and may be ordered in two background colors: 610 Frost White or 615 Almond, both with matte glaze finish. Trim shapes are available: 4" x 4" x ¼" Bullnose and Bullnose Corner.

See Summitmates trim, page 30; specifications, page 43.

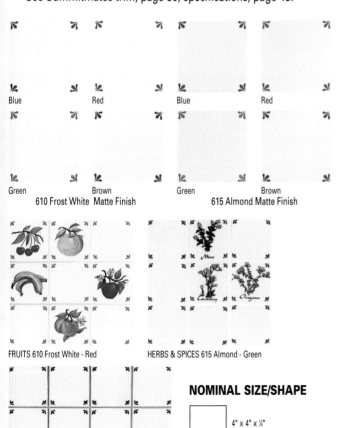

Blue   Red   Blue   Red

Green   Brown   Green   Brown
610 Frost White Matte Finish   615 Almond Matte Finish

FRUITS 610 Frost White - Red   HERBS & SPICES 615 Almond - Green

NOMINAL SIZE/SHAPE

4" x 4" x ¼"

FIELD TILE 615 Almond - Blue

Imperva-mates

NEW Imperva-mates are 2" x 2" x ⁵⁄₁₆" glazed mosaics suitable for commercial and residential floors, walls and countertops.

They are modular and color coordinated with Imperva, Imperva Granite, Morganmates and Summitmates.

Imperva-mates' glazed surface is easily cleaned with warm water and a mild detergent. We recommend wet vacuum type cleaning for abrasive tile or when grease/oil combined with water is prevalent in commercial installations.

Abrasive surface is available, minimum quantity required. Contact factory for availability.

Nominal 2"x 2" bullnose and bullnose corner trim is available in all colors.

NOMINAL SIZE/SHAPE

2" x 2" x ⁵⁄₁₆"

WR   Wear Rating; see page 12 for definition.

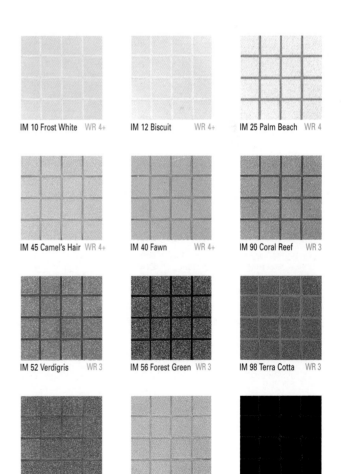

IM 10 Frost White   WR 4+   IM 12 Biscuit   WR 4+   IM 25 Palm Beach   WR 4

IM 45 Camel's Hair   WR 4+   IM 40 Fawn   WR 4+   IM 90 Coral Reef   WR 3

IM 52 Verdigris   WR 3   IM 56 Forest Green   WR 3   IM 98 Terra Cotta   WR 3

IM 80 Mason Blue   WR 3   IM 64 Gull Gray   WR 3   IM 68 Silhouette   WR 2

Summitmates®

Summitmates are semi-vitreous glazed quarry tiles in all sizes except 2" x 2", which is a glazed mosaic tile. Summitmates can be used in exterior applications only in temperate climates.

Tiles are back mounted to simplify installation; also available with custom mounting (Greek keys, checkerboards, etc.) by special order.

We do not recommend back mounted tiles in submerged areas without setting and/or grouting with epoxy such as S-300 or S-400. Contact the factory for detailed instructions.

Twenty-four colors are available in Bright Glaze and Matte Glaze, six colors in Designer Glaze.

Sizes 2" x 2" and 4" x 4" are stock items.

Abrasive surface, sizes 2"x 4" and 3"x 3" are special order, minimum quantity required. Contact factory for availability.

For trim shapes, see page 30; specifications, page 43.

NOMINAL SIZES/SHAPES

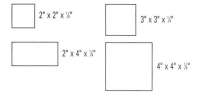

2" x 2" x ¼"

3" x 3" x ¼"

2" x 4" x ¼"

4" x 4" x ¼"

Groups 3 and 4 are premium priced colors.

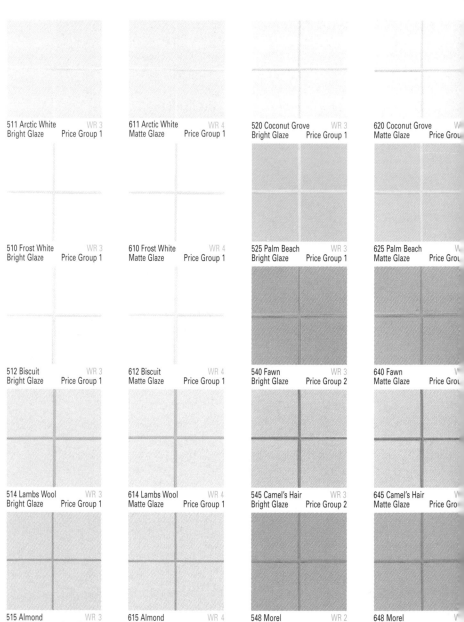

| 511 Arctic White | WR 3 | 611 Arctic White | WR 4 | 520 Coconut Grove | WR 3 | 620 Coconut Grove | W |
| Bright Glaze | Price Group 1 | Matte Glaze | Price Group 1 | Bright Glaze | Price Group 1 | Matte Glaze | Price Grou |

| 510 Frost White | WR 3 | 610 Frost White | WR 4 | 525 Palm Beach | WR 3 | 625 Palm Beach | W |
| Bright Glaze | Price Group 1 | Matte Glaze | Price Group 1 | Bright Glaze | Price Group 1 | Matte Glaze | Price Grou |

| 512 Biscuit | WR 3 | 612 Biscuit | WR 4 | 540 Fawn | WR 3 | 640 Fawn | W |
| Bright Glaze | Price Group 1 | Matte Glaze | Price Group 1 | Bright Glaze | Price Group 2 | Matte Glaze | Price Grou |

| 514 Lambs Wool | WR 3 | 614 Lambs Wool | WR 4 | 545 Camel's Hair | WR 3 | 645 Camel's Hair | W |
| Bright Glaze | Price Group 1 | Matte Glaze | Price Group 1 | Bright Glaze | Price Group 2 | Matte Glaze | Price Gro |

| 515 Almond | WR 3 | 615 Almond | WR 4 | 548 Morel | WR 2 | 648 Morel | W |
| Bright Glaze | Price Group 1 | Matte Glaze | Price Group 1 | Bright Glaze | Price Group 2 | Matte Glaze | Price Gro |

Designer Glaze

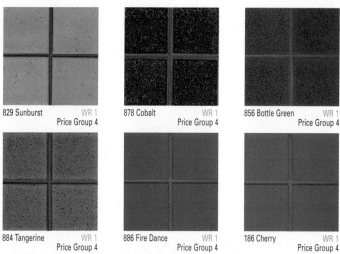

829 Sunburst WR 1 Price Group 4	878 Cobalt WR 1 Price Group 4	856 Bottle Green WR 1 Price Group 4
884 Tangerine WR 1 Price Group 4	886 Fire Dance WR 1 Price Group 4	186 Cherry WR 1 Price Group 4

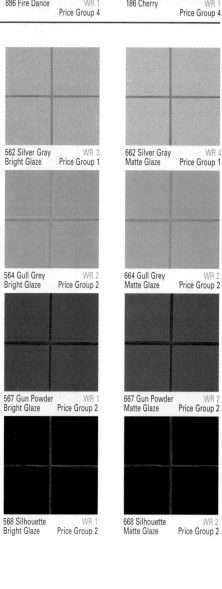

Spearmint ht Glaze WR 3 Price Group 2	649 Spearmint Matte Glaze WR 4 Price Group 2	569 Cerulean Bright Glaze WR 2 Price Group 2	669 Cerulean Matte Glaze WR 2 Price Group 2	562 Silver Gray Bright Glaze WR 3 Price Group 1	662 Silver Gray Matte Glaze WR 4 Price Group 1
Verdigris ht Glaze WR 1 Price Group 3	652 Verdigris Matte Glaze WR 2 Price Group 3	580 Mason Blue Bright Glaze WR 1 Price Group 2	680 Mason Blue Matte Glaze WR 2 Price Group 2	564 Gull Grey Bright Glaze WR 2 Price Group 2	664 Gull Grey Matte Glaze WR 2 Price Group 2
Forest Green ht Glaze WR 1 Price Group 2	656 Forest Green Matte Glaze WR 2 Price Group 2	577 Ocean Blue Bright Glaze WR 1 Price Group 2	677 Ocean Blue Matte Glaze WR 2 Price Group 2	567 Gun Powder Bright Glaze WR 1 Price Group 2	667 Gun Powder Matte Glaze WR 2 Price Group 2
Coral Reef nt Glaze WR 2 Price Group 2	690 Coral Reef Matte Glaze WR 2 Price Group 2	579 Mountain Majesties Bright Glaze WR 1 Price Group 3	679 Mountain Majesties Matte Glaze WR 2 Price Group 3	568 Silhouette Bright Glaze WR 1 Price Group 2	668 Silhouette Matte Glaze WR 2 Price Group 2
Terra Cotta t Glaze WR 1 Price Group 3	698 Terra Cotta Matte Glaze WR 2 Price Group 3	599 Cranberry Bright Glaze WR 1 Price Group 3	699 Cranberry Matte Glaze WR 2 Price Group 2		

24

Decorative Tiles

FLOWERS

FL 1
FL 3
FL 5
FL 7
FL 9
FL 11
FL 13
FL 15
FL 2
FL 4
FL 6
FL 8
FL 10
FL 12
FL 14
FL 16

FRUITS

FR 1
FR 3
FR 5
FR 7
FR 9
FR 11
FR 13
FR 15
FR 2
FR 4
FR 6
FR 8
FR 10
FR 12
FR 14
FR 16

VEGETABLES

VG 1
VG 3
VG 5
VG 7
VG 9
VG 11
VG 13
VG 2
VG 4
VG 6
VG 8
VG 10
VG 12
VG 14

GAME BIRDS

GB 1
GB 3
GB 5
GB 7
GB 9
GB 11
GB 13
GB 2
GB 4
GB 6
GB 8
GB 10
GB 12

HERBS & SPICES

HS 1 *Basil*
HS 3 *Caraway*
HS 5 *Dill*
HS 7 *Mint*
HS 9 *Rosemary*
HS 11 *Sage*
HS 2 *Borage*
HS 4 *Marjoram*
HS 6 *Oregano*
HS 8 *Saffron*
HS 10 *Tansy*
HS 12 *Chives*

HERITAGE SERIES

HT 1
HT 3
HT 5
HT 7
HT 9
HT11
HT13
HT 2
HT 4
HT 6
HT 8
HT10
HT12
HT14

BIRD DOGS

BD 1
BD 2
BD 3
BD 4
BD 5
BD 6

DECORATIVE INSERTS

Decorative Inserts are available on Country Classics or Summitmates, in Frost White or Almond backgrounds and matte glaze finishes.

All Decorative Inserts are 4" x 4" x ¼", suitable for walls and counters.

Country Classics are available on HT 1, HT 2 and HT 4 only.

Summitville invites you to explore the timeless design era of 18th-century America with its WILLIAMSBURG tile collection.

In cooperation with the curators of the Colonial Williamsburg Foundation, Summitville focuses on the colonial years 1760-1770 with four colorful series of ceramic tiles, all in 5" x 5" x ¼" size.

Summitville works closely with the Foundation to ensure design authenticity. Working from shards of colonial ceramics and antique tiles from the Foundation's collection, Summitville artists replicate the colors, styles and nuances of period ceramics. The result of this painstaking detail is four tile series: the Avian Whimsy, English Bouquet, Governor's Palace Delft and Macaroni.

Stretcher Tile

Not all fireplaces are designed the same. When the centerpiece spacing is larger than 5" x 5", use the 5" x 10" stretcher tile. Cut the appropriate amount from the left and right sides of the stretcher tile to accommodate the odd-size opening.

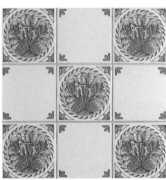

Tulip Tile Tulips, introduced to western Europe from Turkey in the 16th century, were an abiding passion of 17th-century Holland and England. These 6"x 6" x ⅜" tulip tiles shown with available field tile featuring decorative corners, are interpreted from late 17th-century delft dish made in London, which is part of the Colonial Williamsburg Foundation's extensive collection of English delft.

SUMMITVILLE'S
Williamsburg ®
TILE COLLECTION

Macaroni	Governor's Palace Delft	Avian Whimsy	English Bouquet

MAC 1   MAC 2

GPD 1   GPD 2

AW 1   AW 2

EB 1   EB 2

MAC 3   MAC 4

GPD 3   GPD 4

AW 3   AW 4

EB 3   EB 4

MAC 5   MAC 6

GPD 5   GPD 6

AW 5   AW 6

EB 5   EB 6

MAC 7   MAC 8

GPD 7   GPD 8

AW 7   AW 8

EB 7   EB 8

MAC 9   MAC 10

GPD 9   GPD 10

AW 9   AW 10

EB 9   EB 10

MAC 11   MAC 12

GPD 11   GPD 12

AW 11   AW 12

EB 11   EB 12

MAC 13   MAC 14

GPD 13   GPD 14

AW 13 Stretcher Tile

EB 13 Stretcher Tile

MAC 15   Field Tile
510 Frost White

GPD 15 Stretcher Tile

Field Tile 571 - Plain

Field Tile 571 - Plain

MAC 16 Stretcher Tile

Field Tile 570 - With Corners

Williamsburg ® and

FITZ AND FLOYD®
SCULPTURED TILES

The Fitz and Floyd tile series is a collection of sculptured, decorative tiles designed to complement Fitz and Floyd kitchen and bath accessories.

First in the series is Iris, a design dedicated to Spring's favorite flower. Fruit Fair, a second series, features six varieties of colorful fruit. And Vegetable Garden includes 12 fresh-cut images from Nature's bounty.

All Fitz and Floyd tiles are available in horizontal and vertical formats in three finishes: hand-painted, white glaze or terra cotta. All are suitable as running borders, chair rails, wainscotting or crown moldings.

Hand painted Fitz and Floyd giftware, serveware and decorative accessories add an artful touch to any decor. Summitville is proud of its association with Fitz and Floyd, internationally known for 33 years as the originators of contrasting yet complementary fine china.

IRIS

Hand Painted

05 Corner

04

01

02

03

06

Terra Cotta

11 Corner

10

07

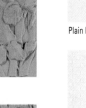
08

09

12

White Glaze

16

17 Corner

13

14

15

18

Plain Field Tile

Field Tile Wicker

Iris

Fruit Fair

Vegetable Garden
Sculptured murals are available for each of the series in handpainted, terra cotta and white glaze. Size 18" x 18".

Iris

Feel the warmth of Spring year 'round with Summitville's Iris sculptured tiles. Designed to complement Fitz and Floyd's bath accessories, these tiles are available in a running pattern of three vertical tiles and also in a repeating horizontal format. Iris tiles offer an excellent accent alternative for the bath.

Sizes: 3" x 6" (Iris design), 3" x 3" (corner) and 6" x 6" (field tile). All 3/8" thick.

Field Tile Plain

FRUIT FAIR
Hand Painted

01   02   03   04   05   09 Corner

Terra Cotta

10   11   12   13   14   18 Corner

White Glaze

20   21   22   23   27 Corner   06

07

08 End

Fruit Fair

01, 10, 19	Cherries	06, 15, 24	Lemon
02, 11, 20	Peaches	07, 16, 25	Leaves
03, 12, 21	Orange	08, 17, 26	Leaves End
04, 13, 22	Strawberries	09, 18, 27	Corner
05, 14, 23	Grapes		

15

16

24

25

17 End

Fruit Fair

Six fruit and a running leaf design make Fruit Fair an attractive motif in the kitchen. Mix and match grapes, lemons, cherries, peaches, oranges, and strawberries; leaf design is also available as an end-piece or corner-piece. These tiles can be used either horizontally or vertically.

Sizes: 3" x 6" (fruit design), 3" x 3" (corner) and 6" x 6" (field tile). All ⅜" thick.

Field Tile Plain

VEGETABLE GARDEN
Hand Painted

01   02   03   06 Corner

Terra Cotta

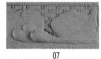  

07   08   09   12 Corner

04

10

11 End

White Glaze

14   15   18 Corner

05 End

16

17 End

Vegetable Garden

01, 07, 13	Tomato, Onion, Potato
02, 08, 14	Turnip, Corn, Peas
03, 09, 15	Carrots, Eggplant
04, 10, 16	Lettuce, Radish, Squash, Asparagus
05, 11, 17	Artichoke, End
06, 12, 18	Artichoke, Corner

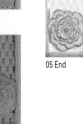

26 End

Field Tile Wicker

Vegetable Garden

This series features groups of vegetables on each of four sculptured tiles. Create your own pattern design by mixing tomatoes, onions and potatoes; lettuce, radishes, squash and asparagus; turnips, corn and peas; or carrots and eggplant. These tiles can be used either horizontally or vertically.

Sizes: 3" x 6" (vegetable design), 3" x 3" (corner) and 6" x 6" (field tile). All ⅜" thick.

Hand Painted

Terra Cotta   White Glaze

Wicker border, 3" x 6" can be used with Fruit Fair or Vegetable Garden.

Field Tile Wicker

Natural Stones

The natural, subtle color variations inherent in Marble, Agglomerated Marble and Granite makes the Summitville collection an attractive alternative for elegant interiors.

Slabs, sills and sizes other than 12"x 12" are also available for custom designs.

We recommend S-300 and S-400 Epoxy for setting and S-400, S-500, S-667 or S-687 for grouting these products.

Alabama White Cloud, an American marble available exclusively through Summitville. This domestic, highly polished marble provides architects and designers with a made-in-America option for any commercial or residential application.

AGGLOMERATED MARBLE

Lioz

Moleanos

Alpenia

Brecia St. Antonio

Ruivina

Brecha Algrave

Rosa Monte

Verde Viana

Verde Braganca

Preto Angola

MARBLE

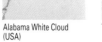
Alabama White Cloud (USA)

Travertine Navona

Bianco Venatino

Negro Marquina

Rosa Aurora

St. Thomas Lila

Honed CC Travertine

China Black

Travertine Roman

Botticino Classico

Rojo Alicante

Blanco Aurora

Black Monterey

Santa Helena

China White

Statuary Veined

Peruno Rosato

Emperador Marron

Rosa Salmon

Rosa Morado

French Vanilla

Thassos A

Crema Marfil

Trani Fiorito

Cafe Rosita

Jade Green Light

Jade Green Dark

GRANITE

SIZE/SHAPE

12" x 12" x ⅜"

Samoka Red

Iikai Red

Dark Black

Paradiso

Kashmiri White

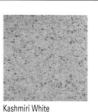

Pool Tile

Pool Tile is a durable porcelain paver glazed to provide an excellent surface for pool applications.

Available in 710 White, 775 Olympic Blue and 785 Black, in 2 sizes with smooth or abrasive surface. Depth markers are either plain or decorative. Custom colors are available by special order, minimum quantity required. Contact factory for availability.

NOMINAL SIZES/SHAPES

8" x 8" x ⅜"   6" x 6" x ⅜"

POOL TILE TRIM SHAPES

Bullnose
P 4669 (6")
P 4889 (8")

Bullnose Corner
PC 4669 (6")
PC 4889 (8")

Pool Coping (unglazed)
See Olde Towne Brick Trim page 30.

Cap   Q 4260 (6")
        Q 4280 (8")
Size: 2" x 6" x 3/8 "
Available in Blue, Black and White

Pool Nosing
Q 4665 (6")
Q 4885 (8")

Pool Nosing Corner
QC 4665 (6")
QC 4885 (8")

Trim units designated with the letter **P** are glazed porcelain pavers.
Trim units designated with the letter **Q** are matching glazed quarry tiles with different physical properties. Contact factory if additional information is needed.

ecorative
pth Marker

Plain Depth
Marker

710 White

775 Abrasive

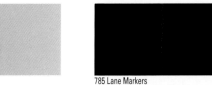

775 Smooth

785 Lane Markers

Trim Shapes

QUARRY TILE

1. **Q 6666 series are flat surface units.**
2. **Q 6665 series is a lip bullnose for concealing setting bed. In combination with standard tile and cove base units, there is unlimited flexibility for sill, stair tread and riser dimensions.**

***Golf Club colors available 10, 11, 33 only.**

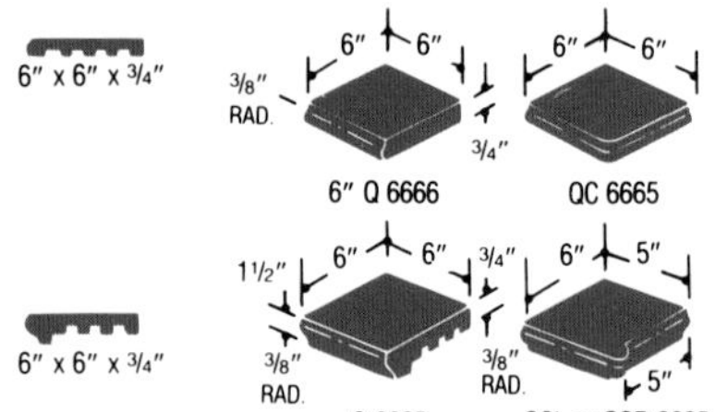

6″ x 6″ x 3/4″
3/8″ RAD.
6″ Q 6666
QC 6665
6″ x 6″ x 3/4″
3/8″ RAD.
Q 6665
QSL or QSR 6665

BULLNOSE

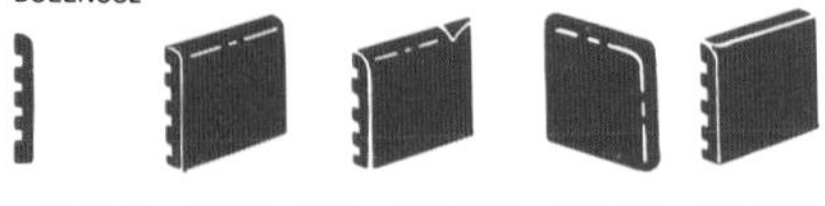

4 x 6 x ½	Q 1465	QKL or QKR 1445	QC 1465	QM 1445
*6 x 6 x ½	Q 1665	QKL or QKR 1665	*QC 1665	QM 1665
6 x 6 x ¾	Q 1660	QKL or QKR 1445	QC 1660	†QM 1660
3⅞ x 8 x ½	Q 1485	QKL or QKR 1445	QC 1445	QM 1445
8 x 3⅞ x ½	Q 1845		QC 1445	QM 1445

†Red only

COVE BASE (Square Top)

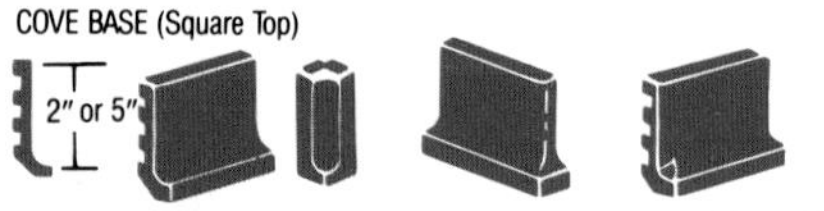

2″ or 5″

5 x 6 x ½	Q 3566	QB 3566	QCL or QCR 3566	QSL or QSR 3566
5 x 6 x ¾	Q 3561	QB 3561	QCL or QCR 3561	†QSL or QSR 3561
2 x 6 x ½	Q 3266	QB 3266	QCL or QCR 3266	QSL or QSR 3266
2 x 6 x ¾	Q 3261	QB 3261	QCL or QCR 3261	†QSL or QSR 3261

†Red only

DOUBLE BULLNOSE

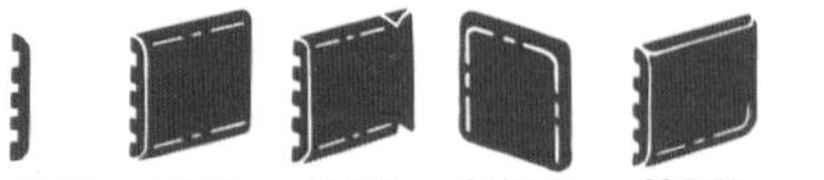

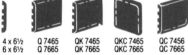

4 x 6½	Q 7465	QK 7465	QKC 7465	QC 7456
6 x 6½	Q 7665	QK 7665	QKC 7665	QC 7665

COVE BASE (Round Top)

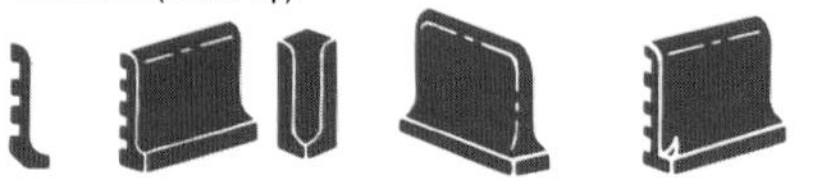

5 x 6 x ½	Q 3565	QB 3565	QCL or QCR 3565	QSL or QSR 3565
5 x 6 x ¾	Q 3560	QB 3560	QCL or QCR 3560	†QSL or QSR 3560

†Red only

OLDE TOWNE QUARRY

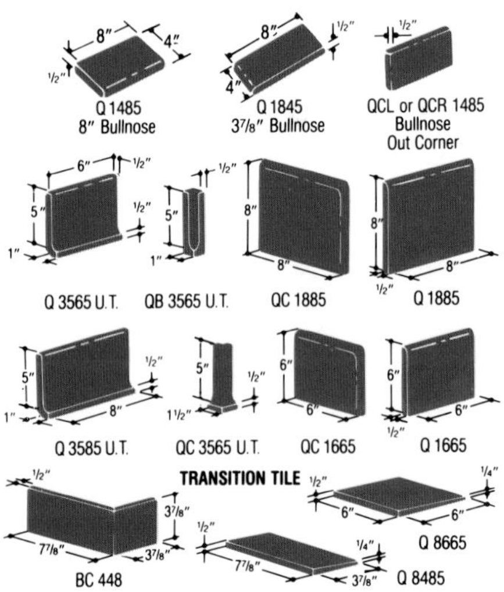

Q 1485
8″ Bullnose
Q 1845
3⅞″ Bullnose
QCL or QCR 1485
Bullnose
Out Corner
Q 3565 U.T.
QB 3565 U.T.
QC 1885
Q 1885
Q 3585 U.T.
QC 3565 U.T.
QC 1665
Q 1665
TRANSITION TILE
BC 448
Q 8665
Q 8485

DECORATIVE FRIEZE

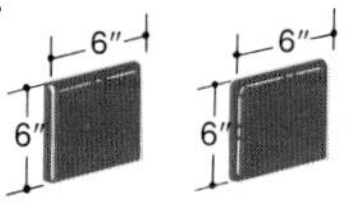

P 4669
BULLNOSE
PC 4669
BULLNOSE
CORNER

OLDE TOWNE BRICK

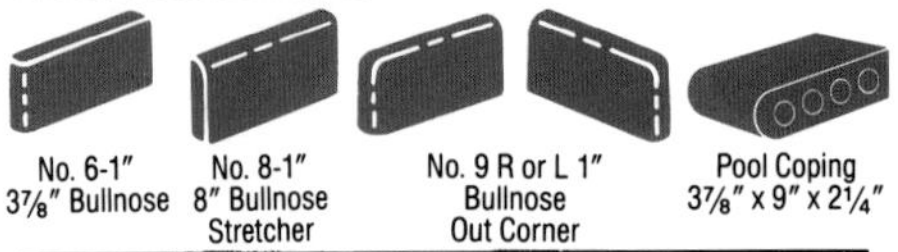

No. 6-1″
3⅞″ Bullnose
No. 8-1″
8″ Bullnose
Stretcher
No. 9 R or L 1″
Bullnose
Out Corner
Pool Coping
3⅞″ x 9″ x 2¼″

STRATA

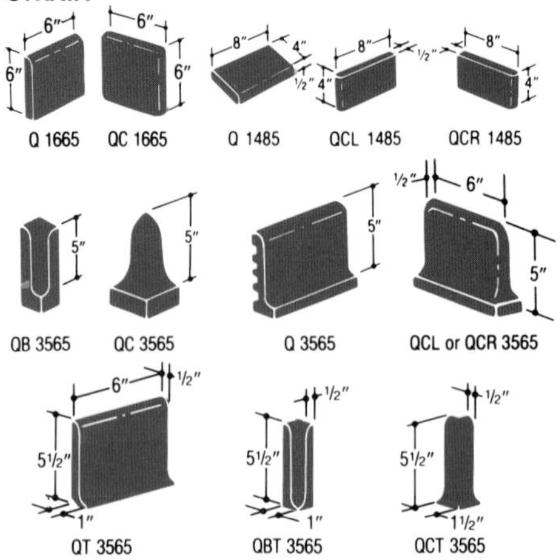

Q 1665
QC 1665
Q 1485
QCL 1485
QCR 1485
QB 3565
QC 3565
Q 3565
QCL or QCR 3565
QT 3565
QBT 3565
QCT 3565

SUMMITMATES

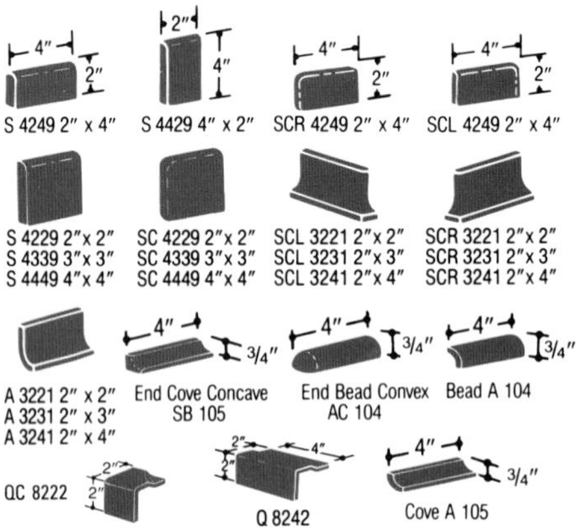

S 4249 2″ x 4″
S 4429 4″ x 2″
SCR 4249 2″ x 4″
SCL 4249 2″ x 4″
S 4229 2″x 2″
S 4339 3″x 3″
S 4449 4″x 4″
SC 4229 2″x 2″
SC 4339 3″x 3″
SC 4449 4″x 4″
SCL 3221 2″x 2″
SCL 3231 2″x 3″
SCL 3241 2″x 4″
SCR 3221 2″x 2″
SCR 3231 2″x 3″
SCR 3241 2″x 4″
A 3221 2″ x 2″
A 3231 2″ x 3″
A 3241 2″ x 4″
End Cove Concave
SB 105
End Bead Convex
AC 104
Bead A 104
QC 8222
Q 8242
Cove A 105

COUNTRY CLASSICS

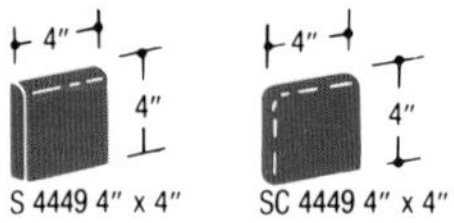

S 4449 4″ x 4″
SC 4449 4″ x 4″

IMPERVA-MATES

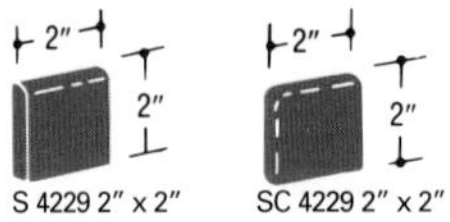

S 4229 2″ x 2″
SC 4229 2″ x 2″

IMPERVA / IMPERVA GRANITE / STEPPING STONES MORGANMATES / SUMMITSHADES / SUMMIT-TREAD

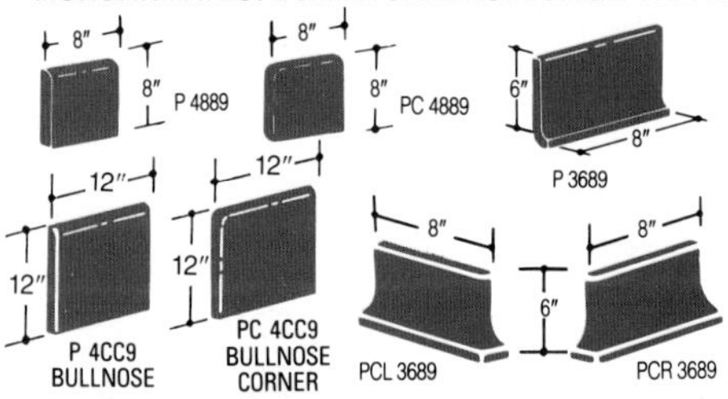

P 4889
PC 4889
P 3689
P 4CC9
BULLNOSE
PC 4CC9
BULLNOSE
CORNER
PCL 3689
PCR 3689

OLDE LOMBARDIC

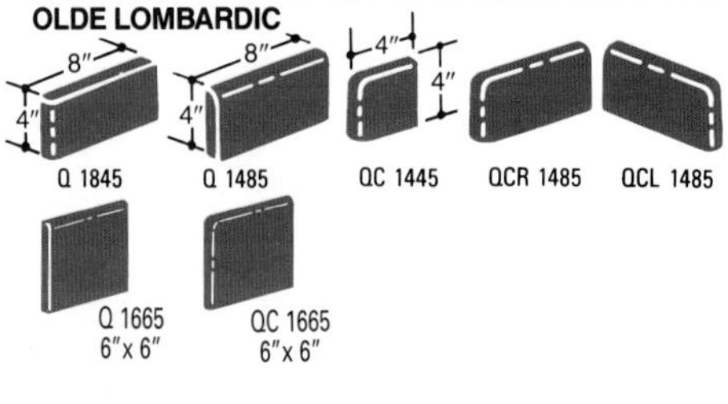

Q 1845
Q 1485
QC 1445
QCR 1485
QCL 1485
Q 1665
6″x 6″
QC 1665
6″x 6″

FLOOR BRICK

When ordering square top base, be sure to specify height.
Note: Where heavy duty trim is not required, Quarry Tile Trim Color No. 10 may be specified.

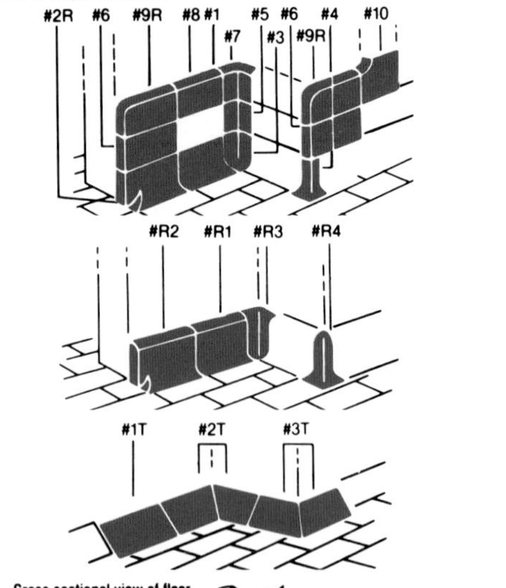

#2R
#6
#9R
#8
#1
#7
#5
#6
#3
#9R
#4
#10
#R2
#R1
#R3
#R4
#1T
#2T
#3T

Cross sectional view of floor brick turn-up base. For use where floor is to be laid against existing walls.

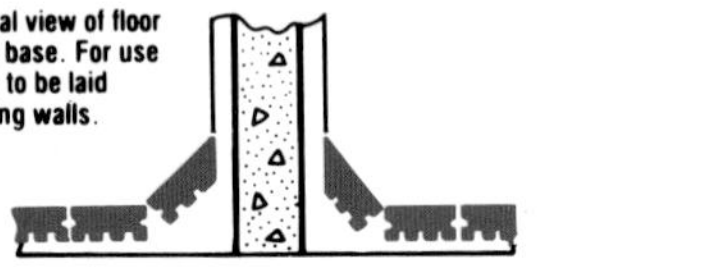

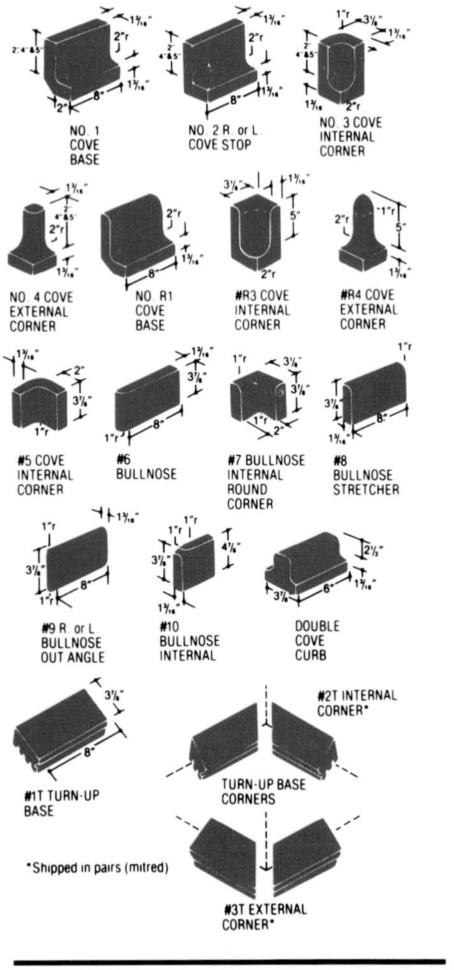

NO. 1
COVE
BASE
NO. 2 R. or L.
COVE STOP
NO. 3 COVE
INTERNAL
CORNER
NO. 4 COVE
EXTERNAL
CORNER
NO. R1
COVE
BASE
#R3 COVE
INTERNAL
CORNER
#R4 COVE
EXTERNAL
CORNER
#5 COVE
INTERNAL
CORNER
#6
BULLNOSE
#7 BULLNOSE
INTERNAL
ROUND
CORNER
#8
BULLNOSE
STRETCHER
#9 R. or L.
BULLNOSE
OUT ANGLE
#10
BULLNOSE
INTERNAL
DOUBLE
COVE
CURB
#1T TURN-UP
BASE
#2T INTERNAL
CORNER*
TURN-UP BASE
CORNERS
*Shipped in pairs (mitred)
#3T EXTERNAL
CORNER*

SUMMIT-BRICK

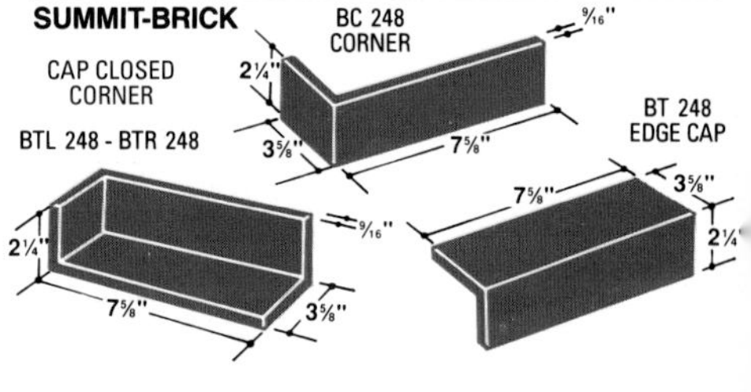

CAP CLOSED
CORNER
BTL 248 - BTR 248
BC 248
CORNER
BT 248
EDGE CAP

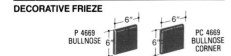

2

6 — DHN-A
0 — DHN-B
7 — DHN-C
2 — DHN-D

3 — DHN-E
4 — DHN-F
1 — DHN-G
5 — DHN-H

1

Ladies
7" x 4-3/4" oval

854
9" x 5" x 1/2" with frame

3 floral frieze

FF Corner FF 1 FF 2 FF 3 FF 4 FF 5 FF End

ivy frieze

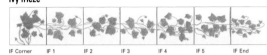

IF Corner IF 1 IF 2 IF 3 IF 4 IF 5 IF End

4

12311
Stag 15¼" x 8⅛" x 1"

9946
Tulip 12½" x 7⅜" x 1"

427
Chickadee 13¾" x 9" x 1"

636
Cardinal 14" x 18" x 1"

8001
Grape 15" x 8⅛" x 1"

9533
Pineapple 15⅛" x 9" x 1"

4 4 2
Wild Flowers 9⅞" x 13⅜" x 1"

1381
Primrose 13¾" x 9" x 1"

1830
Nuthatch 15⅛" x 8" x 1"

5

6

 60 Sunburst
 52 White
 51 Tangerine
 50 Lemon

 57 Fire Dance
 56 Sunburst
 54 Bronze
55 Black

 53 Black
 61 White
 59 Pewter
 58 Bronze

7

8

10

BRAINTREE

9

Sculptured Tiles

DECORATIVE SCULPTURED TILE
Three-dimensional sculptured ceramic designs range from address plaques to major relief sculptures. No limits in size, style, dimensions or colors; Summitville will design to your specifications.

1 DECORATIVE SIGNAGE
Handpainted plaques for house numbers, titles and directions. Available in either oval or rectangular; rectangular has optional solid walnut frame.

2 DECORATIVE HOUSE NUMBERS
Eight designs feature continuing motifs. Each 4" x 8" tile displays one numeral; available with or without solid cedar frame. Specify house number.

3 FRIEZES
Available in 6" x 6" x ³/₈" with 710 Frost White or 715 Almond background colors. Each frieze features a 5-tile running pattern, end- and corner-piece. Field tile is also available. Suitable for use as a chair rail, wainscoting, step riser, or as crown molding. For trim shapes, see page 30.

4 DECORATIVE ADDRESS PLAQUES
Handpainted, glazed address plaques in nine styles. Specify house number when ordering.

5 ZODIACS & COINS
6" x 6" x ½", available in 286 Fire Dance, 229 Sunburst, 249 Bronze and 294 Pewter. Matching field tile available.

6 SUMMITFORMS
These deep-sculptured tiles offer a contemporary appeal. Available in 6" x 6" x ½" size, Summitforms come in 12 designs and eight colors; custom colors by special order.

7 SUN
23" in diameter, shown in pewter. Custom colors by special order.

8 DEER
31¾" x 25½" Terra Cotta with Antique Flash.

9 PORTRAITS
3-dimensional portraits can be used as plaques or personal mementos.

10 TACTILE-TREAD
Tactile-Tread is specifically designed to comply with the Americans with Disabilities Act. Its truncated-dome surface warns of dangerous areas in transit stations and other public areas. Available in 6" x 6" and 12" x 12" sizes, ½" thick. Custom colors, by special order only.

CUSTOM DESIGNED MURALS, HAND PAINTED TO YOUR SPECIFICATIONS.

Summitville offers an unlimited range of hand-painted murals, each beginning with America's Tile, and ending with a unique personal statement. We also offer company logos, signage and custom plaques to fit any need.

Murals for interiors or exteriors in either residential or commercial settings, can be produced to any size, color or technique, depicting any subject.

Ceramic murals may be abstract designs or detailed representations, stylized or conventional renderings in traditional or contemporary formats.

CEMENTITIOUS SETTING PRODUCTS

S-759 Thin Set Mortar (TCA Formula 759)

S-759 Thin Set Mortar is recommended for setting most types of ceramic tile on floors. S-759 has a long open time, is easy to trowel and provides high bond strength.

S-759 is recommended for setting most types of ceramic tile floor installations. Formulated to provide high bond strength and high density for good compressive strength. S-759 is sag resistant, has a long open time even at high temperatures, and is easy to trowel. When setting and grouting, check the ANSI - TCA guidelines for proper substrate and cure conditions. Meets or exceeds ANSI A118.1 specifications. Available in 50-pound bags. Color: #960 Gray.

COVERAGE:
Sq. Ft. / Lb. at 3/32" to 1/8" bed thickness   2.0-2.5
Using a 1/4" x 1/4" square notched trowel

S-763 Thin Set For Walls (TCA Formula 763)

S-763 is recommended for setting most ceramic tile wall installations. This product is sag resistant and easy to trowel. It provides high bond strength and a long open time at high temperatures. When setting and grouting, check the ANSI / TCA guidelines for proper substrate and cure conditions. Meets or exceeds ANSI A118.1 specifications. Available in 50-pound bags. Color: #910 White.

COVERAGE:
Sq. Ft. / Lb. at 3/32" to 1/8" bed thickness   2.0-2.5
Using a 1/4" x 1/4" square notched trowel

S-777 Thin Set Mortar

S-777 is recommended for setting ceramic tile floor or wall installations. S-777 has good compressive strength, above average bond strength, and is sag resistant. S-777 has a long open time and is easy to trowel. When setting and grouting, check the ANSI/TCA guidelines for proper substrate and cure conditions. S-777 meets or exceeds ANSI A118.1 specifications. Available in 25-pound and 50-pound bags. Colors: #960 Gray; #910 White.

COVERAGE:
Sq. ft. / Lb. at 3/32" to 1/8" bed thickness.   2.0–2.5
Using a 1/4" x 1/4" square notched trowel

S-780 Floor Mortar
Thin Set Mortar for Floors

S-780 thin set floor mortar is designed to install all types of ceramic tile and paving brick on properly prepared, horizontal substrates, interior or exterior applications. S-780 can be mixed with water or with S-800 or S-810 for improved water resistance, tensile strength and flexural strength. If mixed with S-800 or S-810, S-780 can be used to set tile over exterior grade plywood in interior, dry applications. S-780 meets or exceeds the requirements of ANSI A 118.1. For more information consult Summitville's specification guide. Available in 50lb. bags. Colors: #910 White, #960 Gray.

COVERAGE:
Sq. ft. / Lb. at 3/32" to 1/8" bed thickness.   2.0–2.5
Using a 1/4" x 1/4" square notched trowel

S-1000 MP (Multi-Purpose) Thin Set Latex Mortar

S-1000 MP is formulated to set wall or floor tile in interior and exterior applications. It can be used to set tile over exterior-grade plywood, clean masonry surfaces, cementitious backer board, and gypsum board. This product contains a powdered latex which is activated by adding water. Since this product already contains a powdered latex, improper levels of latex additives are averted preserving the product's high bond strength and other characteristics. When setting and grouting, check the ANSI/TCA guidelines for proper substrate and cure conditions. S-1000 MP meets or exceeds ANSI A118.4.
Available in 25-pound and 50-pound bags. Colors: #910 White; #960 Gray.

COVERAGE:
Sq. Ft. / Lb. at 3/32" to 1/8" bed thickness   2.0–2.5
Using a 1/4" x 1/4" square notched trowel

S-1100 MP (Multi-Purpose) Premium Thin Set Latex Mortar

S-1100 MP is a premium high quality multi-purpose thin set mortar formulated with a special powdered latex designed to provide superior bond and shear strength, freeze-thaw resistance, impact-resistance, flexibility and reduced water absorption. The non-reemulsifying resin system in S-1100 MP also provides excellent workability. S-1100 MP meets or exceeds ANSI A118.4. S-1100 Premium Multi-purpose thin set mortar is designed for setting all types of tile, marble, slate and granite and can be used in both interior and exterior applications. Acceptable substrates include structurally sound fully cured masonry slabs, properly installed CBU, tile over tile, securely attached and properly cleaned vinyl tile, securely attached cutback adhesive and properly installed exterior grade plywood (interior, non-wet areas only).
S-1100 MP multi-purpose thin set mortar is available in 25 lb. and 50 lb. bags. Colors: #910 White and #960 Gray.

COVERAGE:
Sq. Ft. / Lb. at 3/32" to 1/8" bed thickness   2.0–2.5
Using a 1/4" x 1/4" square notched trowel

When a quick set latex is needed, S-2000 is the answer.

S-2000 Quick Setting Mortar

S-2000 is a quick setting thin-set latex mortar for walls and floors in interior and exterior applications. S-2000 is designed especially for installations which require a minimum amount of time. It can be used to set tile over plywood, clean masonry surfaces, cementitious backer board, and gypsum board. This product contains a powdered acrylic latex which is activated by water. The addition of water in the appropriate amounts is all that is required to attain proper working consistency. When setting and grouting, check the ANSI/TCA guidelines for proper substrate and cure conditions. S-2000 meets or exceeds ANSI A118.4. Available in 25-pound or 50-pound bags.

	Temperature		
	60 F (15 C)	70 F (21 C)	90 F (32 C)
Pot Life	40-50 min.	30-40 min.	20-30 min.
Open Time	20 min.	20 min.	10-15 min.
Clean Up Time	20-30 min.	20-30 min.	10-15 min.
Set Time	3 hrs.	2-3 hrs.	2 hrs.

COVERAGE:
Sq. Ft. / Lb. at 3/32" to 1/8" bed thickness   2.0–2.5
Using a 1/4" x 1/4" square notched trowel

CEMENTITIOUS GROUTING PRODUCTS

S-667 Unsanded Joint Filler

S-667 is especially formulated to be used on narrow joints.

S-667 unsanded wall grout is designed for narrow joints when using porous-bodied or glazed tile. S-667 has high compressive strength and is easy to clean. When setting and grouting, check the ANSI/TCA guidelines for proper substrate and cure conditions. S-667 unsanded wall grout is designed for narrow joints when using porous-bodied or glazed tile. S-667 has high compressive strength and is easy to clean. When setting and grouting, check the ANSI/TCA guidelines for proper substrate and cure conditions. Available in 5-pound and 25-pound bags. Available in 32 colors. Custom colors are available. Minimum quantity required.

COVERAGE for S-667 and S-687: Sq. Ft. / Lb.

Tile Size	1/8" Joint Width
1" x 1" x ¼"	2.4
2" x 2" x ¼"	4.8
2" x 4" x ¼"	6.8
3" x 3" x ¼"	7.2
4¼" x 4¼" x 5/16"	8.2
4" x 4" x ¼"	9.6
8" x 8" x 5/16"	15.4
12" x 12" x 5/16"	23.0
	1/16" Joint Width
4¼" x 4¼" x 5/16"	16

S-687 Fungus- and Mildew-Resistant Grout (TCA Formula MRG-82)

S-687 unsanded wall grout is recommended for narrow joints when using porous-bodied tile. This joint filler is formulated to resist the growth of most prevalent types of fungus and mildew, including black mold, which stain or discolor conventionally formulated grouts. The active ingredient in S-687 is registered with the EPA, No. 2204-19, and is ecologically safe. When setting and grouting, check the ANSI/TCA guidelines for proper substrate and cure conditions. Available in 5-pound and 25-pound bags. Colors: Available in same 32 colors as S-667.

TEST RESULTS

Tests performed by the Tile Council of America Research Center conclusively determined S-687 prevents mold, mildew and fungus growth on the grout as well as on a thin layer of growth-supporting medium poured onto the surface of the grout.

Tile grouted with S-687 shows no mold or mildew growth after 14 days immersion in growth-supporting medium.

Tile grouted with conventionally formulated grout immersed in the same substance for 14 days is covered with mold and mildew.

NOTE: We do not recommend sealing S-687. Sealing S-687 can encapsulate the fungicide that prevents mildew growth.

S-700 SummitChromes Sanded Joint Filler

S-700 SummitChromes provides a smooth, dense, color fast joint for wall or floor installations. S-700 has high bond strength, compressive strength and hardness, with improved workability and clean-up characteristics. Always wet cure according to ANSI standards; always slake 10-15 minutes to ensure complete moisture migration. When setting and grouting, check the ANSI / TCA guidelines for proper substrate and cure conditions; meets or exceeds ANSI A-118.6 specifications. S-700 may be mixed with clean potable water, with S-775 latex, S-776 latex accelerator, S-120 epoxy emulsion or S-600 100% epoxy admix. S-700 is available in 32 colors, custom colors are available in minimum quantities. S-700 SummitChromes is available in 9-lb, 25-lb. and 50-lb. bags.

S-710 PolyChromes Sanded Joint Filler Contains Powdered Latex

S-710 sanded grout features a premixed powdered latex formula. Simply mix with water for dense, color fast joints. S-710 is less expensive than adding liquid latex to S-700. It eliminates improper thinning (excessive water) of liquid latex. Liquid latex will freeze during shipment in winter months; powdered latex will not. Eliminates wet curing — DO NOT WET CURE. S-710 has higher compressive strength, greater flexibility (important over wood floors), greater bond strength and better color retentivity than S-700. It also provides improved protection from efflorescence (salts escaping from cementitious substrates) and improved shrinkage characteristics. Always slake 10-15 minutes to ensure complete moisture migration; when setting and grouting, check the ANSI / TCA guidelines for proper substrate and cure conditions; meets or exceeds ANSI A-118-6 specifications. *Available in the same 32 colors as S-700* with improved Physical Properties. Mix with water only; do not mix with S-775 or S-120. S-710 Polychrome available in 9-, 25- and 50-lb. units.

COVERAGE for S-700 and S-710:

Tile Size	⅛"	¼"	⅜"	½"
Sq. Ft. / Lb.		Joint Width		
1" x 1" x ¼"	1.7	0.8	0.5	0.4
2" x 2" x ¼"	3.4	1.6	1.0	0.8
4" x 8" x ½"	4.8	2.3	1.4	1.1
6" x 6" x ½"	5.1	2.4	1.5	1.2
4" x 8" x 1⅜"	1.7	0.8	0.5	0.4
8" x 8" x 5/16"	10.9	5.1	3.2	2.6
12" x 12" x ⅜"	13.6	6.4	4.0	3.2

S-700/S-710 Sanded Grout
S-667/S-687 Unsanded Grout Colors

914 Arctic White	935 Mexican Sand
911 Biscuit	929 Morel
909 Frost White	920 Palm Beach
916 Almond	999 Coral Reef
921 Fawn	940 Lilac
925 Buckskin	983 Cranberry
919 Coconut Grove	989 Terra Cotta
992 Peach	987 Clay Red
968 Mist Gray	931 Brownstone
964 Gull Gray	941 Cocoa*
963 Silver Gray	947 Walnut*
982 Mason Blue	962 Natural*
986 Cerulean	951 Camel's Hair*
973 Spearmint	966 Gun Powder*
974 Verdigris	984 Ocean Blue*
979 Forest Green	969 Silhouette*

The 32 colors shown above are available in both sanded and unsanded grout.

*Summitville recommends neutral colored grouts for heavy traffic floors. For superior stain resistance and color retentivity, use S-400 Epoxy.

NOTE: All colored grouts, when used on floors, will discolor over time due to normal foot traffic, etc. This will cause a graying of the original color. Keep this in mind when selecting a colored grout for floor application.

Always test your tile with colored grout for staining, especially with black grout, before proceeding with job. Use SL-90 grout release if necessary to prevent clean-up problems.

LATEX ADDITIVES

S-800 Setting Acrylic Latex Additive

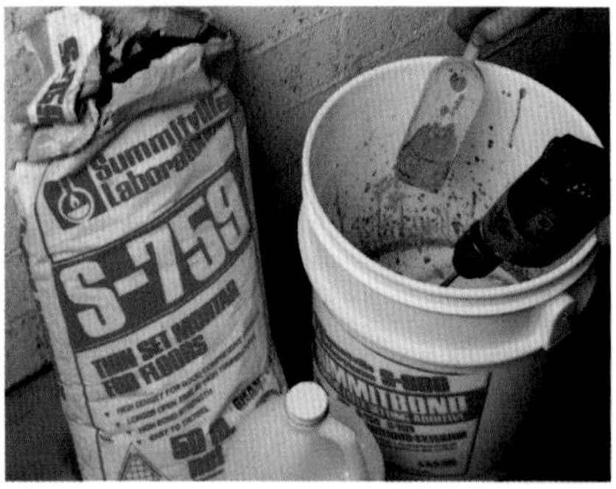

S-800 is a specially formulated and balanced acrylic latex additive for use with Summitville's S-759, S-763, S-777 and S-780 dry-set mortar formulas. Mortar made with S-800 after curing has excellent water and freeze thaw resistance. When mixed according to instructions, material will improve working, bonding and flexural characteristics of base product. When mixed properly with S-759, S-763, S-777 or S-780, S-800 can be used to set any type of ceramic tile over clean and dry masonry, concrete, brick, fiberglass reinforced backer board, exterior grade plywood, gypsum board, on interior or exterior floors or walls. When setting and grouting, check the ANSI/TCA guidelines for proper substrate and cure conditions. S-800 is available in 1-gallon containers, 5-gallon pails, and 55-gallon drums. Product meets or exceeds ANSI A 118.4.

COVERAGE:
Same as base product. Refer to base product data.

S-810 Flexible Mortar System

S-810 is a copolymer latex which, when mixed with S-777 or S-780 Thin Set Mortar, provides a flexible polymer mortar system for setting all types of ceramic tile and natural stones over various substrates. Use the S-810 /S-777 system for floors, walkways and ceilings in interior and exterior installations. Available in 2-gallon containers. Meets or exceeds ANSI A118.4. Color: #910 White only.

COVERAGE:
Same as base product. Refer to base product data.

S-775 Grouting Acrylic Latex Additive

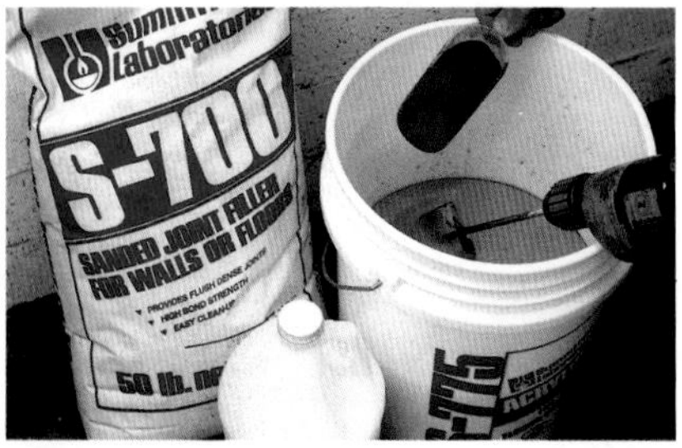

For easy mixing and better consistency, add powdered S-700 to liquid S-775 Acrylic Latex Additive.

S-775 is a specially formulated and balanced latex additive for use with Summitville's S-700, S-667 and S-687 grouts. S-775 improves workability, bonding and flexural characteristics of base product, and eliminates the need for damp curing. Has greater bond strength than S-700, 667, 687 mixed with water. Has greater flexibility (important over wood floors). Has improved protection from efflorescence (salts escaping from cementitious substrates). Better color retentivity. Improved shrinkage characteristics. DO NOT WET CURE. Always slake 10-15 minutes to ensure complete moisture migration; when setting and grouting, check the ANSI / TCA guide-lines for proper substrate and cure conditions.
S-775 is available in 1-quart containers, 1-gallon containers, 5-gallon pails and 55-gallon drums.

COVERAGE:
Same as base product. Refer to base product data.

S-776 Quick-Set Grout Additive

S-776 is a specially formulated and balanced acrylic latex additive designed to accelerate the curing of S-700, S-667 and S-687 grouts. S-776's quick-set formula is designed to speed up installation and job-site clean-up on applications that must be opened to traffic as quickly as possible. Grouts mixed with S-776 will set in about 3 hours at 75°F; use only where ambient or substrate temperatures are 50-90°F. Mix with grouts only; for quick-set mortars, use S-400 QS or S-2000.

COVERAGE:
Same as base product. Refer to base product data.

EPOXY ADHESIVES

S-120 Epoxy Emulsion Admixture

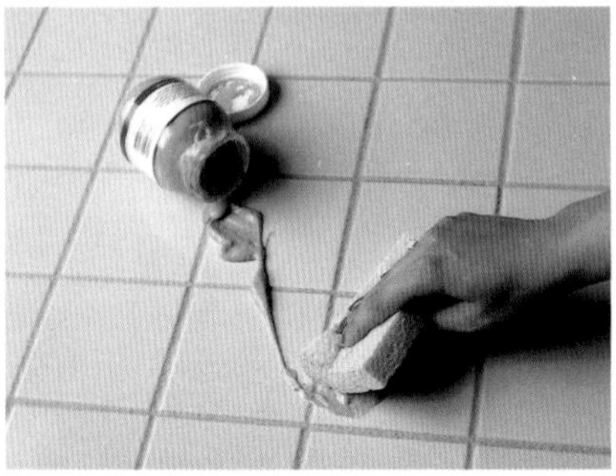

S-120 is a two-part epoxy admixture designed for use with S-700 Sanded Joint Filler to provide increased strength, durability and resistance to dilute acids and alkalies.
S-120/S-700 is used for setting or grouting quarry tile, ceramic mosaics, decorative tile, pavers and brick on floors and walls. S-120 is NOT stainproof; for improved stain resistance, use S-400, S-500 or S-600. S-120 is available in 6-lb. and 12-lb. units, and an industrial 79-lb. unit. Suitable for mixing with any S-700 color.

COVERAGE:

Setting: Trowel Size	**6 lb. Single Unit** Sq. Ft. / With S-700 Natural
5/32" V-Notch	65-80
1/4" x 1/4" sq. notch	35-55
3/8" x 3/8" sq. notch	25-33
1/2" x 1/2" sq. notch	15-30

Approximate Coverage: Sq. Ft. / Lb. of S-700

Grouting:

Tile Size:	Joint Width 1/8"	1/4"	3/8"	1/2"
1" x 1" x 1/4"	1.7	0.8	0.5	0.4
2" x 2" x 1/4"	3.4	1.6	1.0	0.8
4" x 8" x 1/2"	4.8	2.3	1.4	1.1
6" x 6" x 1/2"	5.1	2.4	1.5	1.2
4" x 8" x 1-3/8"	1.7	0.8	0.5	0.4
8" x 8" x 5/16"	10.9	5.1	3.2	2.6
12" x 12" x 3/8"	13.6	6.4	4.0	3.2

S-300 Epoxy Adhesive For Setting

S-300 epoxy adhesive is recommended for setting on horizontal or vertical surfaces. This product is recommended for installing marble or ceramic tile over existing ceramic tile, plastic laminates, vinyl floors, plywood, steel, and other surfaces that require high bond strength. This product will not bleed through marble. Available in 1-gallon units.

COVERAGE:
Sq. Ft./Unit Using a 5/32" V-Notch Trowel 40-60

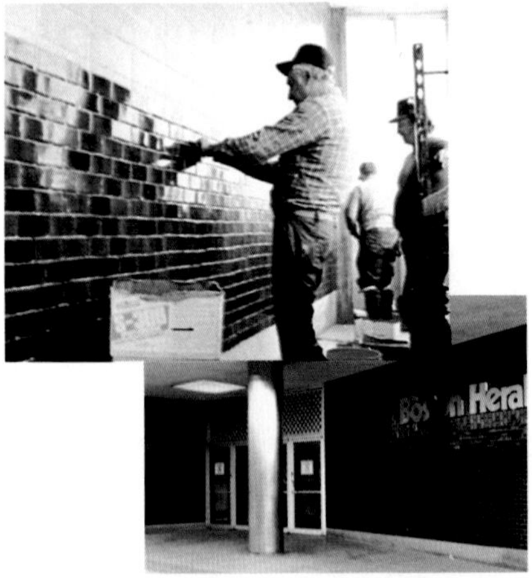

Ceramic tile was installed over concrete block for a striking new facade at the Boston Herald. S-300, used as the adhesive, provided exceptional bond strength. It is suitable for interior or exterior installations over most surfaces, and is especially recommended for tiling over tile.

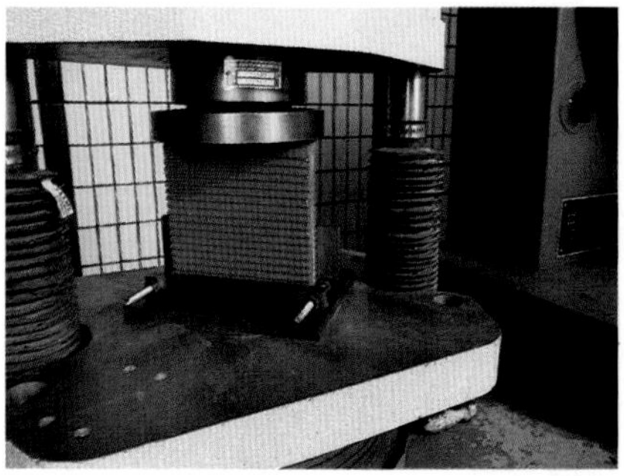

S-300 epoxy adhesive is tested for shear bond strength.

CHEMICAL RESISTANT EPOXIES

S-400 Setting and Grouting Epoxy
(TCA Formula AARII-HT epoxy mortar and grout)

Use S-400 where chemical resistance is important. Can be installed over floor brick, quarry, pavers and ceramic mosaics.

S-400 floor and wall (two-part) epoxy is ideal for setting and grouting floor brick, quarry tile, pavers and ceramic mosaics. This improved TCA AARII formula is recommended for use in distilleries, refineries, chemical laboratories, breweries, food processing plants, etc. S-400 is sag resistant and water cleanable. S-400 grout joints will be slightly concave. S-400 has exceptional bond strength (greater than 1,000 psi). It will remain rigid and cohesive at temperatures up to 350°F. This product meets or exceeds ANSI A118.3-1985 specifications. Available in 1-gallon and 3-gallon unit sizes. Also available in low-temperature formula for cold-weather installations (S-400 LT).

All light colored epoxies will yellow with exposure to ultraviolet light. Yellowing can be greatly reduced if washed with a mild acid solution (such as SL-7) in the first six months of installation.

917 Palomino	961 Gray
945 Moroccan Brown	991 Black
958 Confederate Gray	998 Red

COVERAGE:
Setting: Sq. Ft. / Gallon Unit
Using a ¼" x ¼" Sq. Notch Trowel 18-20

Grouting: Sq. Ft. / Gallon Unit

Tile Size:	Joint Width			
	⅛"	¼"	⅜"	½"
4" x 8" x ½"	65-80	32-40	23-26	16-20
6" x 6" x ½"	80-90	40-45	25-30	20-25
6" x 6" x ¾"	50-60	25-30	15-20	12-15
9" x 9" x ¾"	80-90	40-45	25-30	20-25
4" x 8" x 1-⅜"	25-30	12-15		

Chemical Resistance 28-day Immersion @ 72°F with Compressive Strength Greater than 4,000 psi and No Visual Deterioration

Acetic Acid 3%	Hydrochloric 10%
Aluminum Fluoride	Hydrochloric 37%
Ammonium Bromide	Hydrofluoric 10%
Amyl Alcohol	Hydrofluoric 48%
Barium Hydroxide	Hydriodic 20%
Beer	Nitric 10%
Bromine Water	Phosphoric 10%
Butanol	Potassium Hydroxide 5%
Calcium Chloride	Potassium Hypochlorite
Calcium Hydroxide	Sat. Sugar Solution
Calcium Tetrachloride	Sodium Carbonate
Citric 20%	Sodium Hypochlorite
Chlorine Water	Sodium Hydroxide
(Bleach)	Soy Sauce

Chromic 10%	Sulfuric 10%
Cooking Grease	Sulfuric 45%
Ferric Chloride	Trisodium Phosphate 5%
Household Ammonia	Vegetable Oil
Hydrobromic 10%	Wine

Compressive Strength Less Than 4,000 psi and No Visual Deterioration

Benzyl Acetate	Ethyl Alcohol
Carbon Disulfide	Pyridine 20%

Compressive Strength Less Than 4,000 psi with Visual Deterioration

Acetic Acid 10%	Ethyl Amine
Acetic Anhydride	Ethyl Bromide
Acetic Glacial	Formic Glacial
Acetone	Formic 10%
Aniline	Lactic 3%
Benzaldehyde	Lactic 10%
Benzene	Nitric 50%
Benzyl Alcohol	Nitrobenzene
Butyl Acetate	Nitrotoluene
Butyl Cellosolve	Phenol
Chloracetic 10%	Potassium Persulfate
Chloracetic 50%	Pyridine
Chlorobenzene	Sulfuric 95%
Cresol	Tetrahydrofuran

S-400 LT (Low Temperature) Setting and Grouting Epoxy

S-400 LT has the same physical properties and chemical resistance as S-400. Suited for installing between 32 and 50° F. S-400 LT is sag resistant and should be specified for setting or grouting ceramic tile on any wall or floor installation.

Floor brick, quarry tile, pavers and ceramic mosaics may be set and grouted with S-400 LT. For more information consult Summitville's specification guide. Available in 1 and 3 gallon sizes.
Colors: #961 Gray, and #991 Black.

S-400 EZ FLOW Setting/Grouting Epoxy

S-400 EZ Flow is self-leveling, easy to pour and convenient to use.

Recommended for horizontal surfaces.

S-400 EZ Flow has the same characteristics as S-400 except it is available in a self-leveling formula. It's recommended for horizontal surfaces and joints of ⅛" or less. It can also be used as epoxy topping to remodel and improve existing cement-based grout installations on horizontal surfaces when existing grout joint is ¼" below tile surface. Available in 1-, 3- and 9-gallon units.

S-400 QS (Quick Setting) Setting and Grouting Epoxy

S-400 QS has the same properties and characteristics as S-400 except for its quick-setting formula. S-400 QS allows installation to be opened to traffic as early as 4-6 hours. Available in 1-gallon and 3-gallon unit sizes.

	Temperature		
	60°F (16°C)	75°F (24°C)	90°F (32°C)
Pot Life	45-60 min.	35-45 min.	10-15 min.
Open Time	2 hrs.	1 hr.	1/2 hr.
Clean Up Time	45-6 min.	35-45 min.	10-15 min.
Set Time	3-4 hrs.	2-3 hrs.	1-2 hrs.

S-500 Setting and Grouting Epoxy

S-500 is a three-part epoxy system (resin, hardener and filler powder) which provides an easier cleaning version of 100% solids epoxies. S-500 contains a special blend of fillers which simplifies clean-up while retaining excellent chemical resistance.

902 Sierra	916 Almond
903 Allegheny	932 Sand
904 Adirondack	938 Saddle
905 Smoky	944 Chocolate
906 Blue Ridge	954 Green
907 Rockies	959 Cadet Gray
908 Piedmont	991 Black
913 Snow White	998 Summitville Red

This unique filler system also provides joints with deeper, richer color than traditional epoxies with better color retentivity during initial clean-up. Available in 16 colors, including seven which complement but do not exactly match Imperva Granite (see page 13). S-500 is available in 1.5 and 3 gallon unit sizes, which include resin and hardener; filler powder is sold separately.

COVERAGE:
Setting: Sq. Ft. / Gallon Unit
Using a ¼" x ¼" Sq. Notch Trowel 18-20

Grouting: Sq. Ft. / Gallon Unit

Tile Size:	Joint Width			
	⅛"	¼"	⅜"	½"
4" x 8" x ½"	65-80	32-40	23-26	16-20
6" x 6" x ½"	80-90	40-45	25-30	20-25
6" x 6" x ¾"	50-60	25-30	15-20	12-15
8" x 8" x ¾"				
9" x 9" x ¾"	80-90	40-45	25-30	20-25
12" x 12" x ¾"				
4" x 8" x 1-⅜"	25-30	12-15	—	—

S-500 WC (Wall & Counter) Setting & Grouting Epoxy

S-500 WC utilizes a fine filler for narrow joints and is recommended for walls and counter-tops from $1/32$" to $1/4$" joint width. S-500WC has the same physical properties and working characteristics as S-500. For more information consult Summitville's specification guide. Available in 1.5 and 3 gallon unit sizes, which include resin and hardener; filler powder is sold separately.

COLORS:
#913 Snow White, #916 Almond, #917 Palamino, #958 Confederate Gray, #991 Black.

S-600 100% Solids Epoxy Admix for S-700 Sanded Grout

S-600 is an epoxy admix that when added to a 25 lb. bag of S-700 sanded grout, gives a grout that meets the standards of a water cleanable, chemical resistant epoxy grout (ANSI A118.3). S-600 produces a high-performance, stain and chemical resistant grout while allowing a designer the flexibility of 32 colors. S-600 does not contain water like most epoxy admixes available today that meet ANSI A118.8. S-600 is more chemical resistant than A118.8 type epoxy admixes. S-600 / S-700 can be used in: commercial kitchens, fast food restaurants, schools, bathrooms and anywhere stain resistance and chemical resistance is of prime concern. Because the epoxy admix produces different color shades than water or latex in the S-700 grout, an S-700 / S-600 color chart should be consulted to determine the desired color choice.

S-600 is packaged in a pre-measured unit containing a part A (epoxy resin) and a part B (hardener). The A and B is mixed together then a 25 lb. bag of the desired color of S-700 sanded grout is added. This mixed unit produces 3 gallons of epoxy grout.

S-600 / S-700 is designed for joint widths 1/8" to 1/2" For joints less than 1/8" use S-500 WC, Wall and Counter grout.
(Coverage per gallon for S-600 is the same as S-500.)

S-700/S-600 Color Chart

914 Arctic White	935 Mexican Sand
911 Biscuit	929 Morel
909 Frost White	920 Palm Beach
916 Almond	999 Coral Reef

921 Fawn	940 Lilac
925 Buckskin	983 Cranberry
919 Coconut Grove	989 Terra Cotta
992 Peach	987 Clay Red
968 Mist Gray	931 Brownstone
964 Gull Gray	941 Cocoa*
963 Silver Gray	947 Walnut*
982 Mason Blue	962 Natural*
986 Ceruleen	951 Camel's Hair*
973 Spearmint	966 Gun Powder*
974 Verdigris	984 Ocean Blue*
979 Forest Green	969 Silhouette*

S-4500 Fura-Set® Epoxy Mortar

Fura-set is a 3-part 100% solid epoxy mortar system designed for outstanding chemical and moisture resistance. S-4500 Fura-set meets or exceeds ANSI A118.3 requirements for epoxy mortar. Furs-set will cure at low temperatures (40° F) and high humidity. Floor brick may be installed with Fura-set on sound damp concrete at temperatures as low as 40° F. Although Fura-set was designed primarily for floor brick installation, it will function well in other epoxy floor mortar applications. Fura-set meets USDA requirements for meat and poultry processing plants. S-4500 is available in a 12.8 gallon (164 lb.) unit consisting of a 6 gallon bucket of part A (48 lbs. net), 2 gallons of part B (16 lbs. net) and two 50 lb. bags of part C filler powder.

COVERAGE:
Setting: Sq. Ft. / Gallon Unit
Using a $1/4$" x $1/4$" Sq. Notch Trowel 18-20

Grouting: Sq. Ft. / Gallon Unit

Tile Size:	Joint Width			
	⅛"	¼"	⅜"	½"
4" x 8" x ½"	65-80	32-40	23-26	16-20
6" x 6" x ½"	80-90	40-45	25-30	20-25
6" x 6" x ¾"	50-60	25-30	15-20	12-15
9" x 9" x ¾"	80-90	40-45	25-30	20-25
4" x 8" x 1-⅜"	25-30	12-15	—	—

S-4000 Series Furan Chemical-Resistant Grouts

S-4000 Series is a 2-part (liquid resin and powder catalyst) grout system for use where chemical resistance is important. When prop-erly cured, S-4000 Series is resistant to most non-oxidizing acids, alkalies, solvents, oils, greases, salts, detergents and steam cleaning up to 350° F. Meets or exceeds ANSI A118.5 specifications. NOTE: Furan grouts require tile or brick to be waxed; installation requires special skills and procedures. Tile should be set with S-400 or S-4500. S-4000 Series is available in 50-lb. buckets of resin (S-4000A) and 50-lb. bags of powder/catalyst (S-4001B/4002B). Color: #991 Black.

Two types of powder catalyst are available: S-4001B, a silica/carbon filler, and S-4002B, a 100% carbon filler for optimum chemical resistance. Both fillers can be used to grout tile or brick using either the Tile Setter's method or the Bricklayer's method. Mixing ratios for each method are as follows:

Tile Setter's: 1 part liquid resin to 1.5 parts of powder/catalyst.

Bricklayer's: 1 part liquid resin to 1.8 parts of powder/catalyst.

S-4001B, when mixed with S-4000A liquid resin, is a 2-part system designed for tile setter's and bricklayer's method consisting of furan resin and silica/carbon and catalyst filler.

S-4002B, when mixed with S-4000A liquid resin, is a 2-part system designed for either tile setter's or bricklayer's method consisting of furan resin and 100% carbon/catalyst filler. S-4002B has superior chemical resistance and is resistant to most non-oxidizing acids, solvents and other chemicals as well as hot hydrofluoric acid and hot alkalies.

Chemical Resistance of S-4000 based on 28-day immersion @ room temperature.
R - Recommended
- Recommended to 80° F only.
N - Not Recommended

	S-4001B	S4002B
Acetic Acid, 3%	R	R
Acetic Acid, 10%	R	R
Acetic Acid, glacial	R	R
Acetic Anhydride	R	R
Acetone	N	N
Ammonia (household)	R	R
Ammonium Bromide	R	R
Amyl Alcohol	R	R
Aniline	N	N
Barium Hydroxide, 3%	R	R
Beer	R	R
Benzene	R	R
Benzyl Acetate	R	R
Benzyl Alcohol	R	R
Bromine Water	N	N
Butanol	R	R
Butyl Acetate	R	R
Calcium Chloride, 45%	R	R
Calcium Hydroxide	R	R
Carbon Disulfide	R	R
Carbon Tetra Chloride	R	R
Chlorine Water	N	N
Chloroacetic Acid, 10%	R	R
Chlorobenzene	R	R
Chromic Acid	N	N
Citric Acid	R	R
Cooking Grease	R	R
Cresol	N	N
Ethyl Alcohol	R	R

Ethyl Bromide	N	N
Ethylene Glycol Monobutanate	R	R
Ferric Chloride	R	R
Hydrobromic Acid	N	N
Hydrochloric Acid, 10%	R	R
Hydrochloric Acid, 37%	R	R
Hydrofluoric Acid, 10%	N	R
Hydrofluoric Acid, 48%	N	R
Lactic Acid, 3%	R	R
Lactic Acid, 10%	R	R
Nitrobenzene	R	R
Nitric Acid, 5%	N	N
Nitric Acid, 20% and over	N	N
Nitrotoluene	N	N
Phenol	R	R
Phosphoric Acid, 10%	R	R
Potassium Persulfate	R	R
Pyridine	N	#
Saturated Sugar Solution	R	R
Sodium Carbonate, 30%	R	R
Sodium Hydroxide, up to 30%	R	R
Sodium Hydroxide, over 30%	N	R
Soy Sauce	R	R
Sulfuric Acid, 10%	R	R
Sulfuric Acid, 45%	R	R
Sulfuric Acid, over 50%	N	R
Tetrafuran	N	N
Trisodium Phosphate	R	R
Vegetable Oil	R	R
Vinegar	R	R
Wine	R	R

FURAN ACCESSORIES

S-40 Primer (Asphaltum) and S-41 Corrosion Resistant Membrane

S-40 and S-41 are installed together as a system to form an acid-, alkali- and water-resistant barrier, as well as a flexible membrane, between Summitville floor brick and concrete substrates. This system protects concrete against highly corrosive chemical attack and isolates brick from structural movement of the concrete. The S-40/41 system provides long-term service in corrosive environments, such as concrete tank and floor construction in steel, chemical, pulp and paper, and refining industry applications. S-40 is available in 5-gallon pails; S-41 is available in 100-lb. drum.

COVERAGE:	Sq. Ft./Gallon	Sq. Ft./100-lb. drum
S-40:	*100*	*—*
S-41:	*—*	*67*

S-45 Textile Glass Cloth

S-45 is an asphalt-impregnated fiberglass cloth which provides additional structural reinforcement in corners, trenches, or areas where the substrate changes direction or is otherwise structurally weak. S-45 is available in 450-square-foot rolls.

COVERAGE:
110 Sq. Ft. of S-45 covers 100 Sq. Ft. of area.

SPECIALTY PRODUCTS

S-48 Expansion Joint Sealant

S-48 is a two-part compound (epoxy base compound and polysulfide accelerator) which provides a semi-rigid, durable joint filler that maintains excellent flexibility while evenly distributing loads to the substrate. S-48 is a pourable epoxy designed to absorb the shock and impact of heavy loads and steel-wheeled vehicles. S-48 is packaged in 11 lb., 4 oz. containers of base compound and 3 lb., 12 oz. containers of accelerator. Available in black, red and gray colors.

Coverage Chart for S-4001B and S-4002B

Per 1,000 square feet of tile. Use S-400 or S-4500 Epoxy as setting bed.

Method I – Tile setters (approx. 1 part Resin A to 1.5 parts Powder B by weight).

		S-4000A & S-4001B			S-4000A & S-4002B		
Tile Size	**Joint Width**	**Resin**	**Powder**	**Mixed Lbs./Sq. Ft.**	**Resin**	**Powder**	**Mixed Lbs./Sq. Ft.**
6" x 6" x ½"	¼"	123	184	0.31	111	167	0.28
6" x 6" x ¾"	¼"	184	277	0.46	167	251	0.42
4" x 8" x ½"	¼"	159	238	0.4	144	216	0.36
4" x 8" x 1³⁄₁₆"	¼"	374	562	0.94	339	509	0.85
4" x 8" x 1⅜"	¼"	434	650	1.08	393	589	0.98
4" x 8" x 1½"	¼"	461	692	1.15	376	668	1.04

Method II – Bricklayers (approx. 1 part Resin A to 1.8 parts Powder B by weight).

		S-4000A & S-4001B			S-4000A & S-4002B		
Tile Size	**Joint Width**	**Resin**	**Powder**	**Mixed Lbs./Sq. Ft.**	**Resin**	**Powder**	**Mixed Lbs./Sq. Ft.**
4" x 8" x 1⅜"	⅛"	195	347	0.54	177	314	0.49
4" x 8" x 1³⁄₁₆"	⅛"	169	300	0.47	153	271	0.42
4" x 8" x 1"	⅛"	142	252	0.39	129	229	0.36

COVERAGE:

Grouting: Lineal Feet Per Unit

Joint Depth	¼"	⅜"	½"	⅝"	¾"	⅞"	1"	1-¼"	1-⅜"	1-½"
Joint Width ¼"	308	205	154	123	102	88	77	61	56	51
Joint Width ⅜"	—	136	102	82	68	58	51	41	37	34

SP-888 Underlayment Primer

SP-888 is a copolymer emulsion designed for use with S-2200 Self-Leveling Underlayment. SP-888 seals the substrate and improves the bond strength of S-2200 to substrates. SP-888 is supplied at a high solids ratio and is diluted 1:1 (by vol.) with clean water at the job site. SP-888 is low foaming, non-toxic, non-flammable and easy to apply. Available in 1- and 5-gallon containers.

COVERAGE:
1 gallon SP-888 with 1 gallon of clean water will cover 400-600 sq. ft.

S-2200 Self-Leveling Underlayment (Interior Applications)

S-2200 is a self-leveling underlayment which contains hydraulic cements, aggregates and other materials. When mixed with water, S-2200 becomes a liquid material which will seek its own level and produce a smooth, flat surface. S-2200 sets fast, does not crack, shrink or spall and is water resistant. S-2200 has excellent adhesion, abrasion resistance, impact resistance, tensile strength and flexural strength. Can be walked on in 2-4 hours; floor coverings can be installed after 12-14 hours. Available in 50-lb. bags.
Color: #960 Gray.

COVERAGE:
One bag of S-2200 will cover approximately 60 sq. ft. at 1/8" thickness.

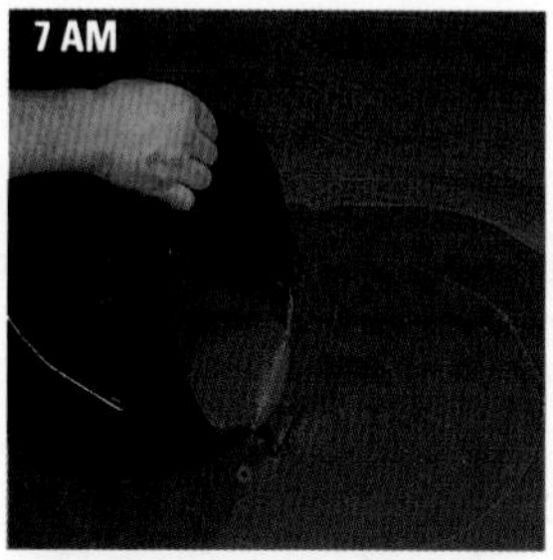

S-2200 Self-Leveling Underlayment can be poured from a pail or pumped into place using a hose.

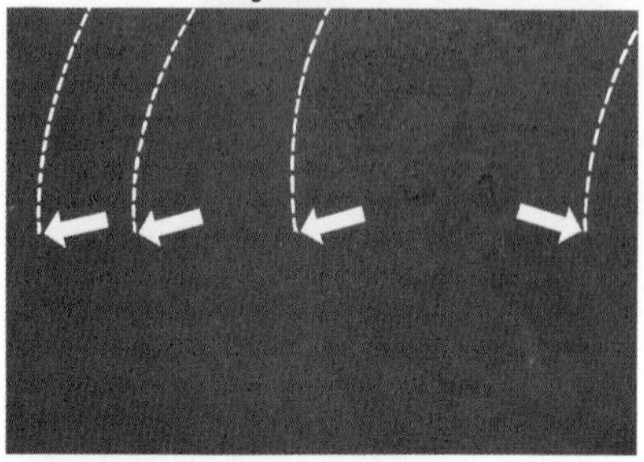
Arrows indicate 4 separate pours. Regardless of substrate, S-2200 will produce a flat, even surface.

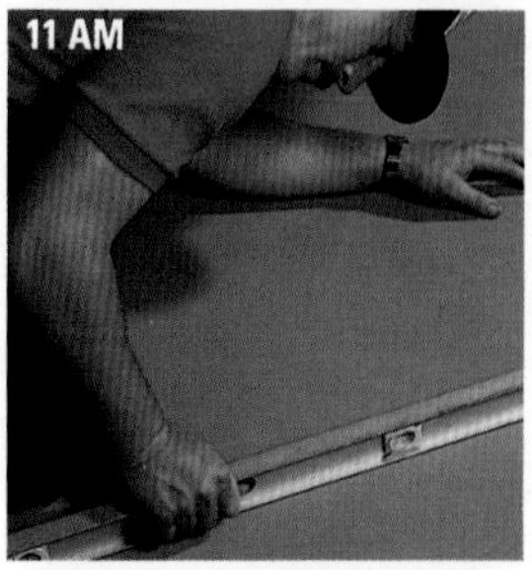

After only 4 hours, S-2200 can be opened to traffic. Using a bubble level, worker confirms the surface is level.

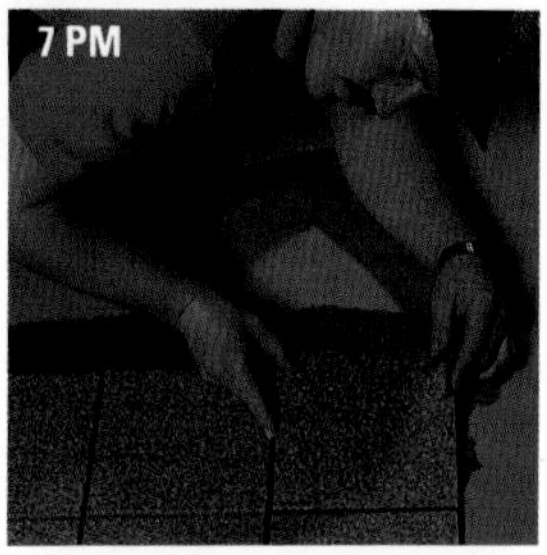

Twelve hours after applying S-2200, worker installs tile over a level, continuous, ready-to-work surface.

SETTING & GROUTING PRODUCTS

S-9000 Crack Isolation / Waterproof Liquid Membrane

S-9000 is an easy-to-apply liquid membrane which can be used for wither crack isolation or waterproofing. S-9000 meets or exceeds the requirements of ANSI A118.10 for load-bearing, bonded, waterproof membranes for thin-set ceramic tile and dimensional stone installations. S-9000 can be used vertically, horizontally, interior or exterior. S-9000 consists of a liquid polymer binder and a fiber mesh reinforcing fabric. It is easy to apply with a paint roller or brush. after proper installation and curing, ceramic tile can be installed over S-9000 with a Summitville latex modified mortar or epoxy mortar. The S-9000 when properly applied and cured, adds only about 20 mils to the thickness of the floor installation. S-9000 is chemical resistant and rated for Extra Heavy Traffic per ASTM C627 /TCA. S-9000 is formulated with a special color indicator which lets the installer know when the system is cured and ready to re-coat or apply tile. In the liquid stage the product is light pink and is brick red in the cured state. S-9000 will bond to concrete, plywood, CBU, gypsum board, clean tile and stone surfaces. S-9000 contains no organic solvents or harsh fumes and is safe and non-flammable. Available in 1 gallon and 6 gallon units. One S-9000 6 gallon unit contains enough liquid and fabric to cover approximately 225 to 250 sq. ft.

Color: #998 Red.

STATIC COEFFICIENT OF FRICTION RANGES*

QUARRY TILE	Diamond Tread	Abrasive	Abrasive	Tread
Smooth	Dry 0.75 to 0.85	Dry 0.65 to 1.0	Dry 0.70 to 0.90	Dry 0.75 to 0.95
Dry 0.70 to 0.95	Wet 0.65 to 0.75	Wet 0.60 to 0.90	Wet 0.60 to 0.90	Wet 0.60 to 0.90
Wet 0.60 to 0.90	Vertical Fiber	**MORGANMATES**	**PUEBLO STONES II**	**SUMMITMATES****
Abrasive	Dry 0.90 to 1.05	Smooth	Smooth	Bright Glaze
Dry 0.80 to 1.0	Wet 0.80 to 0.95	Dry 0.65 to 0.90	Dry 0.55 to 0.80	Dry 0.60 to 0.85
Wet 0.70 to 0.95	**STRATA / STRATA II**	Wet 0.40 to 0.70	Wet 0.50 to 0.70	Wet 0.30 to 0.65
OLDE TOWNE Quarry/Brick	Smooth	Abrasive	Abrasive	Abrasive
Smooth	Dry 0.60 to 0.90	Dry 0.65 to 0.95	Dry 0.70 to 0.90	Dry 0.70 to 0.90
Dry 0.70 to 0.95	Wet 0.60 to 0.80	Wet 0.60 to 0.85	Wet 0.60 to 0.90	Wet 0.60 to 0.90
Wet 0.65 to 0.90	Abrasive	**SUMMITSHADES**	**PUEBLO SHADES**	Matte Glaze
Abrasive	Dry 0.70 to 0.95	Smooth	Smooth	Dry 0.55 to 0.85
Dry 0.80 to 1.0	Wet 0.65 to 0.90	Dry 0.60 to 0.85	Dry 0.60 to 0.80	Wet 0.45 to 0.75
Wet 0.65 to 0.90	Wire Cut	Wet 0.50 to 0.65	Wet 0.60 to 0.75	Abrasive
Wire Cut	Dry 0.95 to 1.05	Abrasive	**OLDE LOMBARDIC**	Dry 0.70 to 0.90
Dry 0.95 to 1.05	Wet 0.85 to 0.95	Dry 0.65 to 0.90	Smooth	Wet 0.60 to 0.90
Wet 0.85 to 0.95	**IMPERVA**	Wet 0.60 to 0.90	Dry 0.70 to 1.0	Designer Glaze
FLOOR BRICK	Smooth	**STEPPING STONES II**	Wet 0.45 to 0.85	Dry 0.60 to 0.85
Smooth	Dry 0.60 to 0.90	Smooth	**IMPERVA-MATES**	Wet 0.30 to 0.65
Dry 0.70 to 0.85	Wet 0.50 to 0.75	Dry 0.65 to 0.85	Smooth	Abrasive
Wet 0.60 to 0.75	Abrasive	Wet 0.45 to 0.70	Dry 0.70 to 0.85	Dry 0.70 to 0.90
Abrasive	Dry 0.70 to 1.07	Abrasive	Wet 0.50 to 0.75	Wet 0.60 to 0.90
Dry 0.85 to 1.0	Wet 0.60 to 0.95	Dry 0.70 to 0.90	Abrasive	
Wet 0.80 to 1.05	**IMPERVA GRANITE**	Wet 0.60 to 0.90	Dry 0.70 to 0.90	
Double Abrasive	Smooth	**FORMALESQUE**	Wet 0.60 to 0.90	
Dry 0.88 to 1.05	Dry 0.60 to 0.90	Smooth	**SUMMIT-TREAD**	
Wet 0.80 to 1.05	Wet 0.50 to 0.75	Dry 0.60 to 0.90	Smooth	
		Wet 0.50 to 0.70	Dry 0.65 to 0.90	
			Wet 0.60 to 0.85	

** 2" x 2" C.O.F. are approximately 10% higher than 4" x 4" due to the grout joint.

* There is no ANSI standard for slip resistance. There are no ADA requirements for slip resistance. Static C.O.F. should be only one method to help you determine slip resistance. Other factors can affect slip resistance, such as the degree of wear on the shoe and flooring material; presence of foreign material, such as water, oil, and dirt; the length of the human stride at the time of slip; type of floor finish; and the physical and mental condition of humans. Therefore, this test method should be used for the purpose of developing a property of the flooring surface under laboratory conditions, and should not be used to determine slip resistance under field conditions unless those conditions are fully described. Static C.O.F. can vary from piece to piece with each production run.

SL-7 Super Cleanup Grout And Tile Cleaner

SL-7 is a blend of surfactants, acidic ingredients and inhibitors designed specifically for the removal of cementitious grout products from quarry tile, paver, brick, slate and other masonry surfaces. It may also be used to clean masonry surfaces in preparation of laying a mortar bed for a tile installation. SL-7 is normally safe with standard and colored grouts when used as directed. Always test a small area before general application. Available in 1-quart plastic bottles, 12 to a case, 1-gallon plastic bottles, 6 to a case.

SL-10 Waterless Hand Cleaner

SL-10 is a liquid hand cleaner, specifically designed to remove dirt, adhesives and stains from hands after installing ceramic tile. SL-10's environmentally-friendly formula removes grease, tar, uncured epoxies, organic adhesives, paints, varnishes and other stains associated with tile installations and other construction work. SL-10 may be used to clean tools, clothing and equipment. SL-10's formula features pumice powder for extra-strength cleaning, a citrus fragrance, plus emolients and lanolin to prevent dry hands. Available in 16-ounce plastic squeeze bottles, 12 to a case.

SL-15 Invisible Seal Penetrating Grout And Tile Sealer

SL-15 is a penetrating, below-surface sealer for unglazed ceramic tile, brick, concrete, stucco, clay and other masonry surfaces. It is non-flammable and does not change the surface appearance of the substrate. SL-15 requires a 24-hour cure period and will then protect tile and grout against water penetration and the

stains that come from ordinary use. SL-15 may also be used as a grout release by presealing over clean tile surfaces 16 to 24 hours prior to grouting. SL-15 is a penetrating sealer and should not be allowed to dry on glazed tile, glass or metal surfaces. Do not use SL-15 on wood. Available in 1-quart plastic bottles, 12 to a case, 1-gallon plastic bottles, 6 to a case and 5-gallon plastic buckets.

SL-33 Quarry Tile Floor Cleaner

SL-33 is a grease-cutting cleaner especially formulated for commercial kitchens and other food processing areas where grease and grime build-up can be a problem. The SL-33 formula helps reduce odor-causing bacteria while special grease cutters remove even ground-in grease and grime. Available in 1-qt. plastic bottles, 12 to a case, and 1-gallon plastic bottles, 6 to a case.

SL-44 Grout Cleaner And Mildew Remover

SL-44 is designed to remove mildew from tub and shower areas and to restore grout lines to their original color. SL-44 contains chlorine to help remove mildew stains and special cleaners to cut through soap scum and grease films. Available in 32-ounce spray bottles, 12 to a case.

SL-66 Adhesive Remover

SL-66 is a solvent-based, adhesive remover. It is designed to remove epoxy, mastics and latex adhesives from tile and tools after tile installations. SL-66 will soften cured epoxy and will allow its removal from tile by gently scraping off the residue. Available in 12-ounce aerosol cans, 12 to a case.

SL-70 Grout Residue Cleaner

SL-70 is a sulfamic acid-based product formulated to clean grout residue from ceramic tile installations. SL-70 water solution is recommended for the removal of grout residue from ceramic tile. It is an excellent cleaner for removing efflorescence from masonry surfaces. Muriatic acid is not recommended for grout stain removal. SL-70 is available in (4)- 6 lb. units and 40 lb. units - 5 gallon pail.

SL-80 Water Based Acrylic Floor Seal

SL-80 is a heavy-duty, long-wearing acrylic formula, designed to give the "wet look" to unglazed quarry tile, clay tile, slate, brick pavers and portland cement products. SL-80 needs no buffing and cleans easily with a damp mop. This product is not affected by hot cooking oils. SL-80 can be removed with SL-86 tile and floor stripper. SL-80 is not to be used in areas subjected to frequent or prolonged wetting. Available in 1-quart plastic bottles, 12 to a case and 1-gallon plastic containers, 6 to a case.

SL-86 Tile and Floor Stripper

SL-86 is a tile and floor stripper specially formulated for fast and efficient stripping of floor finishes without fumes or offensive odors. SL-86 is provided as a concentrate for value and convenience. For heavy build-up dilute 1:1 with water. For medium build-up use 1 part SL-86 with 3 parts water. For light build-up use 1 part cleaner with 5 parts water. For rotary or automatic floor scrubbers use 1 part SL-86 with 10 parts of water. SL-86 can be used with hot or cold water. SL-86 is available in 1 gallons and 5 gallons.

SL-90 Summit-Shield Grout Release

SL-90 is a water cleanable emulsion designed for jobsite application to unglazed ceramic tile and most types of paving brick. When properly applied, SL-90 will protect absorbent tile from the staining associated with highly colored cement grouts. SL-90 is fast-drying and non-toxic. Available in 1- and 5-gallon plastic containers.

SL-100 Grout / Tile and Epoxy Film Cleaner

SL-100 is a uniquely formulated grout and tile cleaner designed to clean dirt, epoxy film and other debris from the surface of grout and tile. This product will restore dirty grout back to a "like new" condition, even if the tile and grout has been in place for years. SL-100 is safe, effective and free of harsh mineral acids. SL-100 will work on any cementitious grout and epoxy grout. However, prolonged contact with epoxy grout surfaces is not recommended. Limit contact with epoxy grout surfaces to less than 30 minutes before removing. After the grout and tile has been cleaned SL-101 Grout Brightener should be applied. **Always test a small area first to see if the product performs satisfactorily.** SL-100 is available in 1 gallon, 5 gallon and 55 gallon.

SL-101 Grout Brightener

SL-101 is designed to be used to brighten the appearance of ceramic tile grout after it has been cleaned with SL-86 Tile and Floor Stripper or restored with SL-100 Grout and Tile Cleaner. SL-101 is safe and effective on all ceramic tile and grout. SL-101 contains no harsh mineral acids. After floor has been cleaned with SL-86 or restored with SL-100, allow to completely dry. Mix SL-101 1:1 with clean water and apply to floor using a sprayer. Agitate with a nylon brush or nylon pad and scrubber. Rinse with clean water. SL-101 is available in 1 gallon, 5 gallon and 55 gallon.

SPECIFICATIONS
SETTING & GROUTING PRODUCTS
Specifications shall include the following paragraph and appropriate product specification below:

Scope: The contractor shall be a qualified installer and shall furnish all labor, materials and equipment necessary to install setting and grouting materials described herein on floors and walls as indicated on specifications and architectural drawings. Installation and mixing techniques shall conform to Tile Council of America Hand Book for Ceramic Tile Installation and Mixing Instructions as listed on the manufacturer's product label.

Specification for S-40
Material: S-40 Primer shall be fast-drying liquid containing asphalt and a suitable solvent to be used with the S-41 hot melt membrane system. The primer shall be supplied by Summitville Tiles Inc., Summitville, Ohio.

Specification for S-41
Material: S-41 shall be used as chemical resistant membrane on which tile or floor brick may be set. S-41 Asphaltum shall be a hot melt oxidized asphaltic compound free from fillers or other adulterants. It shall contain no coal tar, phenol or naval store products. S-41 shall be used in conjunction with S-40 primer. S-41 shall be supplied by Summitville Tiles Inc., Summitville, Ohio.

Specification for S-45
Material: S-45 textile shall be used with S-40 and S-41 when a reinforcing fabric is specified in the chemical resistant membrane. S-45 shall be an open mesh, woven glass cloth made from inorganic glass fibers and lightly covered with a bituminous coating. S-45 shall be supplied by Summitville Tiles, Inc., Summitville, Ohio.

Specification for S-48
Material: S-48 Expansion joint sealant shall be a two-component system that when mixed together forms a pourable joint sealant. S-48 shall be flexible and resistant to attack by mild acids, alkalies, corrosive salts, alcohols and aliphatic hydrocarbons. S-48 is not recommended for joints wider than ⅜". S-48 shall be supplied by Summitville Tiles Inc., Summitville, Ohio. Color shall be #961 Gray, 991 Black or 998 Red as specified.

Specification for S-120
Material: Epoxy emulsion admixture as manufactured by Summitville Tiles, Inc., Summitville, Ohio. S-120 admixture mixed with S-700 shall be used for grouting quarry, ceramic mosaic decorative tile, pavers or brick on horizontal or vertical surfaces. S-120 parts A and B mixed according to instructions with S-700, when completely cured, shall be resistant to dilute acids and alkalies and other chemicals which normally break down concrete mortars and grouts. Color: S-120 may be mixed with any color S-700. S-120 shall be mixed with S-700 to provide dilute acid and alkali setting bed. Material meets or exceeds ANSI A118.8.

Specification for S-300
Material: Setting mortar shall be S-300 as manufactured by Summitville Tiles Inc., Summitville, Ohio. For setting all types of ceramic tile on horizontal surfaces and up to 4¼" x 4¼" ceramic tiles on vertical surfaces, where setting application requires high bond strength. When completely cured, S-300 shall be resistant to dilute acids, alkalies and exhibit superior physical properties.

Specifications for S-400, S-400LT, S-400QS, and (S-400 EZ Flow, where free-flowing and self-leveling grout is required for horizontal surfaces).
Materials: Setting mortar / grout shall be S-400, S-400LT, S-400QS and S-400 EZ Flow, a two component mix consisting of specially graded silica aggregate (#7 on the M.O.H. Scale of Hardness), color-fast pigments, a special blend of activating hardeners and liquid epoxy resin, and free of water and organic solvents; as manufactured by Summitville Tiles, Inc, Summitville, Ohio. The material in the mixed state shall not allow tile to sag on vertical surfaces and in the reacted state shall remain rigid and cohesive in temperatures up to 350° F. Acid and alkali resistant epoxy mortar and grout shall meet or exceed ANSI A118.3 and Tile Council of America AARII-HT, as approved by the United States Department of Agriculture. Color shall be color No._____.

Specification for S-500, S-500WC and S-600/S-700 System
Material: Setting mortar and tile grout shall be S-500, S-500WC, S-600/S-700, a three-component mix consisting of specially graded silica aggregate (#7 on M.O.H. Scale of Hardness), color-fast pigments, a special blend of activating hardeners and liquid epoxy resin, and free of water and organic solvents; as manufactured by Summitville Tiles, Inc., Summitville Ohio. The material in the mixed state shall not allow tile to sag on vertical surfaces and in the reacted state shall remain rigid and cohesive in temperatures up to 350° F. Acid and alkali resistant epoxy mortar and grout shall meet or exceed ANSI A118.3 and Tile Council of America AARII-HT, as approved by the United States Department of Agriculture. Color shall be color No._____.

Specification for S-667 (TCA Formula 567)
Material: Unsanded joint filler shall be S-667, a blended mixture of Type I portland cement, color-fast pigments and water retention aid; as manufactured by Summitville Tiles Inc., Summitville, Ohio. The material shall be used on porous-bodied or glazed ceramic tile for narrow joints (not to exceed ⅛") on vertical surfaces. Color shall be color No._____.

Specification for S-687 (TCA Formula MRG-82)
Material: Unsanded joint filler shall be fungus- and mildew-resistant S-687, consisting of a blended mix of Type I portland cement, Groutcide-75® as registered by E.P.A., and water retention aid; as manufactured by Summitville Tiles, Inc., Summitville, Ohio. Material shall be used for porous-bodied ceramic tile on vertical surfaces for narrow joints (less than ⅛"). Color shall be color No._____.

Specification for S-700
Material: Sanded ceramic tile joint filler for joints on vertical or horizontal surfaces shall be S-700, consisting of a blended mix of Type I portland cement, color-fast pigments, carefully graded quartz aggregate (#7 on M.O.H. Scale of Hardness), and other selected ingredients to assure superior density, compressive strength and hardness; as manufactured by Summitville Tiles, Inc., Summitville, Ohio. Color shall be color No._____.

Specification for S-710
Material: Sanded ceramic tile joint filler for joints on vertical or horizontal surfaces shall be S-710, consisting of a blended mix of Type I portland cement, color-fast pigments, carefully graded quartz aggregate (#7 on M.O.H. Scale of Hardness), dry powdered latex, and other selected ingredients to assure superior density, compressive strength and hardness; as manufactured by Summitville Tiles, Inc., Summitville, Ohio. Color shall be color No._____.

Specification for S-759 (TCA Formula 759)
Material: Thin-set mortar used for setting most types of ceramic tile on horizontal surfaces shall be S-759, consisting of Type I portland cement, specially graded silica aggregate (#7 on M.O.H. Scale of Hardness), water retention aid and anti-sag and anti-skinning aids; as manufactured by Summitville Tiles, Inc., Summitville, Ohio. Material shall conform to ANSI A118.1 and Tile Council of America Formula759. Color shall be color No._____.

Specification for S-763 (TCA Formula 763)
Material: Thin set mortar for setting most ceramic tile on vertical surfaces shall be S-763, consisting of Type I portland cement, specially graded silica aggregate (#7 on M.O.H. Scale of Hardness), water retention aid and anti-sag and anti-skinning aids; as manufactured by Summitville Tiles, Inc., Summitville, Ohio. Material shall conform to ANSI A118.1 and Tile Council of America Formula763. Color shall be color No._____.

Specification for S-775 and S-776
Material: S-775/776 shall be synthetic acrylic latex resin additive as manufactured by Summitville Tiles, Inc., Summitville, Ohio, and shall meet or exceed ANSI A118.1—and A118.4. S-775 Grouting Acrylic Latex Additive shall be added to Summitville S-667, S-687 and S-700 formulas at the rate of 1 gallon S-775/776 per 50-lb. bag of S-700, and 1 gallon S-775/776 diluted with 1 gallon clean, cool, potable water per 1-1/2 25-lb. bags (37.5 lbs. total) of S-667 or S-687. For grouting any type of ceramic tile on floors or walls as stated in base product specifications. Color shall be color #910 White.

Specification for S-777 and S-780
Material: Thin set mortar used for setting ceramic tile on vertical or horizontal surfaces shall be S-777/ thin set mortar for setting ceramic tile and paving brick on horizontal surfaces shall be S-780, consisting of Type I portland cement, specially graded silica aggregate (#7 on M.O.H. Scale of Hardness), water retention agents, anti-skinning agents, anti-sag agents and adhesion-promoting agents; as manufactured by Summitville Tiles, Inc., Summitville, Ohio. Material shall conform to ANSI A118. Color shall be #960 Gray.

Specification for S-800
Material: S-800 shall be synthetic acrylic latex resin additive as manufactured by Summitville Tiles, Inc., Summitville, Ohio, and shall meet or exceed ANSI A118.1 and A118.4. S-800 Setting Acrylic Latex Additive shall be added to Summitville S-759, S-763 and S-777 formulas at the rate of 2 gallons S-800 per 50-lb bag. For setting any type of ceramic tile on interior or exterior floors or walls as stated in base product specifications. Color shall be #910 White.

Specification for S-810
Material: S-810 shall be an acrylic copolymer latex resin system as manufactured by Summitville Tiles, Inc., Summitville, Ohio, and shall meet or exceed ANSI A118.4. S-777 shall be added to S-810 resin system at the rate of 50 lbs. to 2 gallons of S-810. For interior or exterior floor or wall applications as stated in base product specifications. Color shall be #910 White.

Specification for SP-888
Material: Copolymer emulsion manufactured by Summitville Tiles, Inc., Summitville, Ohio. SP-888 shall be used as a primer coat for substrates for S-2200 self-leveling underlayment. Cured SP-888 shall promote excellent adhesion of S-2200 to substrate. Color shall be #910 White.

Specification for S-1000 MP and S-1100 MP Premium
Material: Thin-set latex mortar for setting ceramic tile on vertical and horizontal surfaces shall be S-1000 MP/S-1100 MP Premium, consisting of Type I portland cement, specially graded silica aggregates (#7 on M.O.H. Scale of Hardness), water retention aid and anti-sag and anti-skinning aids, and a specially blended dry latex with protective colloids; as manufactured by Summitville Tiles, Inc., Summitville, Ohio. Material shall meet or exceed ANSI A118.4. Color shall be color No._____.

Specification for S-2000

Material: Thin-set latex mortar used for setting most types of ceramic tile on both horizontal and vertical surfaces, when rapid setting is required (can be grouted in 2-4 hour range depending on temperature), shall be S-2000. S-2000 consists of Type I portland cement, specially graded silica aggregate (#7 on M.O.H. Scale of Hardness), water retention aid and anti-sag and anti-skinning aids, special accelerators; as manufactured by Summitville Tiles, Inc., Summitville, Ohio. Material shall meet or exceed ANSI A118.4. Color shall be color No._____.

Specification for S-2200

Material: S-2200 shall be a self-leveling underlayment consisting of selected aggregates and hydraulic cements as manufactured by Summitville Tiles, Inc., Summitville, Ohio. For providing a smooth level surface for tile, carpet, resilient flooring, etc., installation, 7 day compressive strength shall be 3000 PSI (ASTM C-109). Color shall be #960 Gray.

Specification for S-4000 Series

Material: Furan chemical-resistant grout shall be S-4000, a two-part component mix consisting of: (Part A) a liquid component consisting of furfural alcohol-based resin and (Part B), 100% inert carbon or silica/carbon filler specially graded for optimum workability of the grout and minimum porosity which contains a special blend of activating hardeners. After curing, the material shall be resistant to most non-oxidizing acids, alkalies, solvents, oil, grease, salt and detergents up to 350° F. Color shall be #991 Black.

Specification for S-4500

Material: Fura-set mortar shall be S-4500, a three-part component mix consisting of an inert aggregate and a special blend of activating hardeners and liquid epoxy resin and free from organic solvents, as manufactured by Summitville Tiles, Inc., Summitville, Ohio. The material in the reacted state shall remain rigid and cohesive at temperatures up to 350° F.
Fura-set chemical resistant epoxy mortar shall meet or exceed ANSI A118.3 and Tile Council of America AAR 11-HT, and is approved by The United States Department of Agriculture for meat and poultry plants. Color shall be #998 Red.

Specification for S-9000

Material: A polymer liquid applied Crack isolation/waterproof membrane shall be S-9000, as manufactured by Summitville Tiles, Inc., Summitville, Ohio. The liquid membrane shall be used in conjunction with the reinforcing fabric. The material shall meet or exceed the requirements of ANSI A118.10. Color shall be #998 Red.

Limited Warranty

Summitville Tiles, Inc. products meet all of the rigid standards required of Summitville Tiles, Inc., with regard to quality. Any alleged failure to conform to this warranty shall be communicated to Summitville Tiles, Inc. immediately after purchaser takes delivery of the product, and Summitville Tiles, Inc., at its option, if any non-conformity exists, shall refund the purchase price or replace the product. This warranty is in lieu of all warranties of merchantability, fitness for purpose, or other warranties, expressed or implied, and correction of non-conformities in the manner above stated shall constitute fulfillment of all liability of Summitville Tiles, Inc., whether based on contract, negligence or otherwise.

Summitville Tiles, Inc. shall not be liable for special, indirect, or consequential damages, and the liability of Summitville Tiles, Inc., with respect to the sale or anything done in connection therewith, whether in contract, or tort, under any warranty, or otherwise, shall not exceed the price of the product.

Technical Assistance

Summitville Tiles, Inc. offers the technical assistance of a qualified staff to resolve problems or advise on a product application. Inquiries may be made through Summitville Tiles, Inc., Summitville, Ohio.

TILE PRODUCTS

Specifications / Extruded Quarry Tile / Strata / Terrain

Scope: The contractor for tile work shall furnish all labor, materials and equipment necessary to install Quarry Tile on floors and / or walls as specified and as indicated on architectural drawings. Installation techniques shall conform to Tile Council of America Handbook for Ceramic Tile Installation.

Quarry Tile shall be of standard grade quality and manufactured by the extrusion process as manufactured by Summitville Tiles, Inc., Summitville, Ohio.

Quarry tile shall conform to requirements of ANSI A137.1—1988.

TYPE: Tiles shall be _____. (Smooth surface, abrasive surface, etc.)
SIZE: Tiles shall be ground to specified size after firing and shall be furnished in size_____.
COLOR: Tiles shall be furnished in #10 Summitville Red or color range No._____.

Specifications /Olde Towne Quarry & Brick

Scope: The contractor for tile work shall furnish all labor, materials and equipment necessary to install Olde Towne Quarry and Brick on floors and/or walls as specified and as indicated on architectural drawings. Installation techniques shall conform to Tile Council of America Handbook for Ceramic Tile Installation.

Olde Towne Quarry and Brick shall be of standard grade quality and manufactured by the extrusion process, as manufactured by Summitville Tiles, Inc., Summitville, Ohio.

They shall conform to requirements of ANSI A137.1—1988.

TYPE: Tiles shall be _____ (Smooth, Smooth Flashed; Wire Cut or Wire Cut Flashed).
SIZE: Tiles shall be 3⅞" x 8", 6" x 6" and 8" x 8", in ½" and 1" thicknesses.
COLOR: Tiles shall be furnished in color range No. _____.

Specifications / Imperva / Imperva Granite / Morganmates / Summitshades / Summit-Tread / Stepping Stones II / Formalesque / Pueblo Stones II

Scope: The contractor for tile work shall furnish all labor, materials and equipment necessary to install _____ on floors or walls as specified and as indicated on architectural drawings. Installation techniques shall conform to Tile Council of America Handbook for Ceramic Tile Installation.

Tile shall be standard grade quality, produced by the dry press method as manufactured by Summitville Carolina, Inc., Morganton, NC.

They shall conform to requirements of ANSI A137.1—1988.

TYPE: Tiles shall be _____. (Smooth or abrasive surface.)
SIZE: Tiles shall be nominal 6" x 6", 8" x 8", 12" x 12" or 8" Octagon in 5⁄16" thickness.
COLOR: Tiles shall be furnished in color No._____ from price group No._____.

Specifications / Pool Tile / Tunnel Tile / Exterior Cladding

Scope: The contractor for tile work shall furnish all labor, materials and equipment necessary to install _____ on vertical or horizontal surfaces as specified and as indicated on architectural drawings. Installation techniques shall conform to Tile Council of America Handbook for Ceramic Tile Installation.

TYPE: Tiles shall be _____. (Smooth or abrasive surface, etc.)
SIZE: Tiles shall be 6" x 6" and 8" x 8" in ⅜" thickness.
COLOR: Tiles shall be furnished in color range No. ____, or in special order colors as specified.

Specifications / Extruded Summitmates / Summitstones / Olde Lombardic / Country Classics / Imperva-mates / Williamsburg / 2" Dot in Morganmates and Imperva

Scope: The contractor for tile work shall furnish all labor, materials and equipment necessary to install _____ on walls as specified and as indicated on architectural drawings. Installation techniques shall conform to Tile Council of America Handbook for Ceramic Tile Installation.

_____ shall be of standard grade quality, produced by the extrusion process as manufactured by Summitville Tiles, Inc., Summitville, Ohio.

They shall conform to requirements of ANSI A137.1—1988.

SIZE: Tiles shall be nominal (Size:_____) back mounted on sheets (except Olde Lombardic, Williamsburg and 2" Dot: all unmounted).
COLOR: Color range or ranges shall be No._____ from color group No._____.

Specifications / Floor Brick

Scope: The contractor responsible for brick work shall furnish all labor, materials and equipment necessary to install Floor Brick on floors as specified and as indicated on the architects' drawings.

Floor Brick shall be of standard grade quality and manufactured by the extrusion process, as manufactured by Summitville Tiles, Inc., Summitville, Ohio.

Brick shall conform to requirements of ASTM C410-60 TYPE H, ASTM C279-88 TYPE H.

TYPE: Brick shall have _____ surface (regular smooth, diamond tread smooth, abrasive). Bonding surface shall be scored. (Or) Brick shall be Vertical Fibre Floor Brick with end grain wearing surface, wire-cut top and bottom.
SIZE: Brick shall be furnished 3⅞" x 8" x 1³⁄16" or 3⅞" x 8" x 1", 3⅞" x 8" x 1⅜". Vertical Fibre Floor Brick shall be furnished in Summitville Red, No. 10 and shall be uniform in surface texture and color.

Specifications / Summit-Brick

Scope: The contractor responsible for brick work shall furnish all labor, materials and equipment necessary to install Summit-Brick on walls as specified and as indicated on the architects' drawings.

Summit-Brick shall be of standard grade quality and manufactured by the extrusion process, as manufactured by Summitville Tiles, Inc., Summitville, Ohio. Summit-Brick is tested in accordance with ASTM C1088, TYPE TBX (Select). TYPE: Summit-Brick shall have a wire-cut surface. SIZE: Summit-Brick shall be furnished 7⅝" x 2¼" x ⁹⁄16". COLOR: Tiles shall be furnished in color range No._____.

Specifications / Summitforms / Tactile-Tread

Ceramic tiles shall be Summitforms or Tactile-Tread tile as manufactured by Summitville Tiles, Inc., Summitville, Ohio. Summitforms shall be nominal 6" x 6"; Tactile-Tread shall be nominal 6" x 6" or 12" x 12". Design No. _____ (as specified). Color _____ (as specified).

Specifications / Pueblo Shades

Scope: The contractor for tile work shall furnish all labor, materials and equipment necessary to install Pueblo Shades on floors or walls as specified and as indicated on the architects' drawings. Installation techniques shall conform to Tile Council of America Handbook for Ceramic Tile Installation. COLOR: Tiles shall be furnished in color range No. _____. Size: _____.

DISTRIBUTORS & SHOWROOMS

ALABAMA
- Pelham 35124 — The Finish Line, 100 Commerce Ct. 205-322-3618
- Mobile 36609 — Craftsmen Supply, 1170-A South Beltline Highway 334-343-3398
- Montgomery 36102 — Robert F. Henry Tile Co. Inc., P.O. Box 2230 334-269-2518

ALASKA
- Anchorage 99502 — Pacific Tile Supply, 2000 W. International Airport Rd., #D2 907-248-8453

ARIZONA
- Glendale 85308 — Arizona Tile, Inc., 5151 W. Bell Road 602-507-9838
- Phoenix 85018 — Arizona Tile, Inc., 3535 E. Thomas Road 602-279-4478
- Prescott 86301 — Arizona Tile, Inc., 550 N. 6th Street 602-776-1070
- Scottsdale 85260 — Arizona Tile, Inc. – Warehouse, 7848 East Redfield 602-991-3066
- Scottsdale 85254 — Arizona Tile, Inc. – Showroom, 14046 N. Scottsdale Rd. 602-991-3288
- Tempe 85283 — Arizona Tile, Inc. – Warehouse, 7248 S. Harl Ave. 602-438-1324
- Tempe 85284 — Arizona Tile, Inc. – Showroom, 1245 W. Elliot Rd. 602-940-9555
- Tucson 85719 — Arizona Tile, Inc., 1665 E. 18th #123 602-622-4671

ARKANSAS
- N. Little Rock 72113 — Winburn Tile Supply Co., 8606 Riverwood Dr. 501-753-0220

CALIFORNIA
- Anaheim 92806 — Summitville Anaheim, Inc., 2050 S. State College Blvd. 714-978-1847
- Dublin 94568 — Terrastone Brick & Tile, 6500 Sierra Court 510-829-4600
- Sacramento 95827 — Unique Design Tile, 9891 A Horn Road 916-361-8773
- San Diego 92110 — Morena Tile, 1065 W. Morena Blvd. 619-276-3915
- San Diego 92121 — Morena Tile, 7415-A Carroll 619-566-5970
- San Marcos 92069 — Morena Tile, 696 Rancheros Dr. 619-744-1462
- Temecula 92592 — Morena Tile, 27479 Enterprise Circle W. 909-676-3073

COLORADO
- Denver 80223 — RBC of Colorado, 940 South Jason St. #5 303-777-1795

CONNECTICUT
- East Hartford 06108 — Crest Distributors, Inc., 258 Prestige Park Rd., Bay 9 860-290-6622

DELAWARE
- Wilmington 19805 — Bath/Kitchen & Tile Supply, 103 Greenbank Rd. 302-992-9220

FLORIDA
- Jacksonville 32236 — Fleming & Sons, Inc., 464 Cassat Avenue 904-783-1240
- Orlando 32811 — Summitville Orlando, Inc., 4210 L.B. McLeod Rd., Suite 101 407-849-5193
- Pompano Beach 33069 — Summitville Pompano, Inc., 1330 S. Andrews Ave. (S.W. 12th Ave.) 954-782-3522
- St. Augustine 32084 — Fleming & Sons, Inc., 2330 Dobbs Road 904-824-5201
- Tampa 33634 — Summitville Tampa, Inc., 7719 Anderson Road 813-887-3630

GEORGIA
- Dunwoody 30350 — Summitville Atlanta, Inc., 8607 Roswell Road 770-587-1744
- Savannah 31406 — Headlands Tile, 8114 White Bluff Rd. 912-920-2255

HAWAII
- Honolulu 96819 — Uniq. Distributing Corp., 2020 Auiki St. 808-847-6767

IDAHO
- Boise 83714 — Architectural Surface of Idaho, 5090 Sawyer Ave. 208-376-6691

ILLINOIS
- Elk Grove Village 60007 — Summitville Chicago, Inc., 1101 Lunt Avenue 708-439-8820
- Normal 61761 — Keen Tile, Inc., 801 East Pine Street 309-454-1466
- Peoria 61615 — Keen Tile, Inc., 8224 N. University 309-689-6209
- Springfield 62703 — Keen Tile, Inc., 2800-1 So. 6th. St. 217-544-2137

INDIANA
- Evansville 47715 — Evansville Tile, 1501 N. Cullen Ave. 812-473-8453
- Ft. Wayne 46808 — Miles Distributors, 3922 N. Wells Street 219-484-9649
- Indianapolis 46256 — Architectural Brick & Tile Inc., 7760 E. 88th. St. 317-842-2888
- South Bend 46628 — Miles Distributors, 2525 N. Foundation 219-234-4051

IOWA
- Des Moines 50325 — R.B.C. of Iowa, 2001 92nd Court, N.W. 515-224-1200

KANSAS
- Lenexa 66215 — Lowy Group, Inc., 9870 Pflumm 913-888-9444
- Wichita 67202 — General Dist., Inc., P.O. Box 11343 316-267-2255

KENTUCKY
- Bowling Green 42101 — Contractors Floor Covering, 1440 Campbell Lane 502-843-1542
- Florence 41042 — Reading Rock, 8252 Dixie Highway 606-371-0335
- Lexington 40508 — Mees Tile & Marble, 645 S. Broadway 606-252-4545
- Louisville 40213 — Mees Tile & Marble, 4536 Poplar Level Road 502-969-5858

LOUISIANA
- Baton Rouge 70815 — Bolick Distributors, Inc., 2055 Airway Drive 504-927-8016
- Harahan 70123 — Bolick Distributors, Inc., 5736 Blessey St. 504-734-8175
- Metairie 70010 — ABC Tile, 3105 18th Street 504-833-5543

MAINE
- Westbrook 04092 — Corriveau-Routhier, Inc., 1 Chabot 207-854-2077

MARYLAND
- Timonium 21093 — Summitville Baltimore, Inc., 8 West Aylesbury Road 410-252-0112

MASSACHUSETTS
- Sommerville 02145 — Crest Distributors, Inc., 128 Middlesex Ave. 617-666-3099

MICHIGAN
- Farmington Hills 48335 — Beaver Distributors, Inc., 24700 Drake Road 810-476-2333
- Grand Rapids 49508 — Beaver Distributors, Inc., 4546 R.B. Chaffee Drive 616-534-2883
- Okemos 48864 — Beaver Tile – Showroom, 1858 West Grand River Ave. 517-347-0708
- Rochester Hills 48309 — Beaver Distributors, Inc., 2141 Austin Avenue 810-299-8100
- Saginaw 48603 — Beaver Distributors, Inc., 2780 Enterprise Crt. 517-790-5852
- Troy 48084 — Beaver Distributors, Inc.–Design Center, 1700 Stutz, Suite 37 810-649-5552

MINNESOTA
- Plymouth 55441 — R.B.C. Tile & Stone, 1820 Berkshire Lane North 612-559-5531

MISSISSIPPI
- Jackson 39208 — J.T.M. Tile Dist. Co., Inc., 112 N. Layfair Drive 601-932-8689

MISSOURI
- St. Louis 63126 — Tile By Design, 9000 Watson Rd. 314-842-5440
- Springfield 65807 — Winburn Tile Supply Co., 1922 W. Woodland 417-886-3648

MONTANA
- Billings 59107 — Taylor Distributing Company, 4141 State Avenue 406-248-7737

NEBRASKA
- Omaha 68127 — RBC of Omaha, 9333 H Court 402-331-0665

NEVADA
- Hendersonville 89014 — Dal Tile, 1201 American Pacific Dr. #C 702-565-9131
- Las Vegas 89118 — Dal Tile, 4480 W. Hacienda Ave. 702-365-6265
- Sparks 89431 — R.M. Tile & Stone, 804 Packer Way 702-331-5203

NEW HAMPSHIRE
- Concord 03301 — Corriveau-Routhier, Inc., 375 No. State 603-465-3618
- Dover 03820 — Corriveau-Routhier, Inc., 71 Broadway 603-742-1901
- Keene 03431 — Tilcon-Arthur Whitcomb, 497 Winchester Street 603-352-6680
- Manchester 03103 — Corriveau-Routhier, Inc., 266 Clay St. 603-627-3805
- Nashua 03060 — Corriveau-Routhier, Inc., 159 Temple 603-889-2157

NEW JERSEY
- Berlin 08009 — Garden State Tile Dist., Inc., 231 Route 73 609-753-0300
- Dayton 08810 — Garden State Tile Dist., Inc., 1290 Route 130 908-329-0860
- Dover 07801 — Garden State Tile Dist., Inc., 267 Route 46 West 201-366-5035
- Newark 07105 — Tile Wholesalers of Newark, 659 Market Street 201-589-2080
- Roselle Park 07204 — Garden State Tile Dist., Inc., 472 E. Westfield Ave. & Rte. 28 908-241-4900
- Wall Township 07727 — Garden State Tile Dist., Inc., 5001 Industrial Rd. & Rte. 34 908-938-6663

NEW MEXICO
- Albuquerque 87107 — New Mexico Tile, 2513 Comanche Rd. N.E. 505-883-6076

NEW YORK
- Albany 12204 — Albany Tile Co., 452 N. Pearl Street 518-434-0155
- Bronx 10456 — Nemo Tile Supplies, 1349 Webster Avenue 718-538-6377
- Hicksville, L.I. 11802 — Nemo International, Inc., 277 Old Country Road 516-935-5300
- Jamaica, L.I. 11432 — Nemo Tile Company, Inc., 177-02 Jamaica Avenue 718-291-5969
- Mt. Kisco 10549 — Bedford Tile Corp., 510 Lexington Avenue 914-241-1755
- Newburgh 12550 — Sherwood Tile, Inc., 1102 Union Avenue 914-564-6710
- New York 10010 — Nemo Tile Company, Inc., 48 East 21st Street 212-505-0009
- Rochester 14615 — George Miller Brick, 734 Ridgeway Ave. 716-458-7745
- Rochester 14621 — Tile Wholesalers, 470 Hollenbeck Street 716-544-3200
- Scarsdale 10583 — Westchester Tile & Marble, 170 Brook Street 914-725-4355
- Syracuse 13211 — Vestal Tile Distributors Inc., 6700 V.I.P. Parkway 315-454-0004
- Tallman 10982 — Town & Country Ceramic Tile, Inc., Route 59 & Airmount Road 914-357-5553
- Tonawanda 14150 — Weinheimers, Inc., 1888 Niagara Falls Blvd. 716-692-9000
- Vestal 13850 — Vestal Tile Distributors Inc., 412 Prentice 607-729-6128
- Yorktown Hgts. 10598 — Bedford Tile Corp., 3333-6 Crompond Rd. 914-737-3200

NORTH CAROLINA
- Asheville 28805 — WNC Tile, 508 Swannanoa River Road 704-298-3251
- Charlotte 28209 — Summitville Charlotte, Inc., 4618 South Blvd. 704-525-8453
- Fayetteville 28301 — American Tile Dist., 927 Bragg Blvd. 910-433-2757
- Greenville 27834 — Byrd Tile, 3119 Bismarck Street 919-756-5997
- Hendersonville 28792 — WNC Tile, 203 Duncan Hill Rd., Suite 101 704-696-2408
- Raleigh 27609 — Byrd Tile Distributors, 3400 Tarheel Drive 919-876-5997
- Winston-Salem 27105 — McCullough Tile, 5272 Germantown Rd. 910-744-0660

OHIO
- Boardman 44512 — Summitville Boardman, Inc., 631 Boardman-Canfield Road 216-758-0835
- Cincinnati 45246 — Reading Rock, 4600 Devitt Drive 513-874-2345
- Columbus 43215 — Hamilton-Parker, P.O. Box 15217, 165 W. Vine St. 614-221-6593
- Dayton 45439 — Reading Rock, 2300 Arbor Blvd. 513-294-2345
- Holland 43528 — Beaver Distributors, Inc., 6561 Angola Road 419-866-6122
- Garfield Heights 44125 — Summitville Cleveland, Inc., 5350 Transportation Blvd., Suite 7 216-581-9900

OKLAHOMA
- Oklahoma City 73179 — Dal Tile Corp., 5417 S.W. 29th Street 405-685-3526
- Tulsa 74145 — Dal Tile, 7471 E. 46th Place 918-627-5381
- Tulsa 74146 — Laufen International, 5130 South 110th East Avenue 918-665-6205

OREGON
- Portland 97242 — United Tile Co., P.O. Box 42548 503-231-4959

PENNSYLVANIA
- Allentown 18103 — H. Winter Company, 890 N. Gilmore 610-434-4500
- Harrisburg 17111 — Conestoga Ceramic Tile Dist., Inc., 4335 Lewis Road 717-564-6860
- Philadelphia 19147 — Garden State Tile, 2712-C Grays Ferry Ave. 215-389-5001
- Pittsburgh 15233 — Architectural Clay Products, 1025-33 Beaver Ave. 412-322-0700
- Pittsburgh 15226 — Beechview Mantel & Tile Co., Inc., 1347 W. Liberty Avenue 412-531-0342
- Wilkes-Barre 18702 — Tile Distributors of America, Inc., 300 Mundy Street 717-822-6123

RHODE ISLAND
- Central Falls 02863 — Crest Distributors, Inc., 1136 Lonsdale Avenue 401-723-9774
- Warwick 02886 — Crest Distributors, Inc., 319 Bald Hill Road 401-737-0160

SOUTH CAROLINA
- Anderson 29625 — Clayton Tile Distributors, 1718 Pearman Dairy Road 803-225-0884
- Columbia 29204 — Tile Center, Inc., 2517 Two Notch Rd. 803-254-9338
- Florence 29504 — Florence Carpet & Tile, P.O. Box 13460 803-669-1851
- Greenville 29606 — Clayton Tile Distributors, 535 Woodruff Rd. 803-288-6290
- Hilton Head Island 29925 — Headland Tile, Inc., P.O. Box 23093 803-681-8453
- Spartanburg 29301 — Clayton Tile Distributor, 530 S. Blackstock Road 803-587-9732

SOUTH DAKOTA
- Rapid City 57709 — Gibson Tile, Inc., P.O. Box 3038 605-341-2113

TENNESSEE
- Johnson City 37603 — Winco, Inc., 1200 Indian Ridge Road 423-929-1156
- Knoxville 37921 — Winco, Inc., 1740 Louisville Drive 423-588-6522
- Memphis 38118 — Monarch Tile, 4072 Senator 901-363-5880
- Memphis 38111 — F.G. Whitt, 2520 Southern Avenue 901-458-1194
- Nashville 37203 — Ceramic Tile Distributors, Inc., 712 Fogg Street 615-255-6669

TEXAS
- Amarillo 79107 — William G. Sharp, 401 North Polk 800-843-0388
- Austin 78758 — American Tile Supply, 2020 G Rutland Drive 512-837-2843
- Dallas 75229 — American Tile Supply, 2839 Merrell Road 214-243-2377
- Dallas 75243 — American Tile Supply, 10550 Plano Road 214-343-5733
- DeSoto 75115 — American Tile Supply, 1707 Falcon Drive 214-228-0066
- El Paso 79935 — Dal Tile, 11185 Pelicand Dr. 915-593-3161
- Ft. Worth 76115 — American Tile Supply, 200 E. Felix 817-924-2232
- Houston 77007 — Summitville Houston, Inc., 7950 Washington Ave. 713-864-8453
- Longview 75601 — American Tile Supply, 1612 E. Whaley 903-757-7762
- Lubbock 79408 — Acme Brick, 2301 Avenue A 806-747-3181
- Richland Hills 76118 — American Tile Supply, 7412 Baker Blvd. 817-284-4787
- San Antonio 78216 — American Tile Supply, 1130 Arian Parkway 210-490-1927

UTAH
- Ogden 84404 — Dal Tile Corp., 860 Wall Avenue 801-394-7701
- Orem 84057 — Dal Tile Corp., 701 North, 1200 West 801-226-2170
- Salt Lake City 84115 — Dal Tile, 3037 South, 300 West 801-487-9901

VERMONT
- Rutland 05701 — Tilcon-Arthur Whitcomb, 2 Ivy Street 802-775-8037
- Springfield 05156 — Tilcon-Arthur Whitcomb, 100 River Street 802-885-3272
- N. Springfield 05150 — Tilcon-Arthur Whitcomb, Spooneville Road 802-886-2291
- Winooski 05404 — Tilcon-Arthur Whitcomb, 2 East St. 802-655-3747

VIRGINIA
- Lorton 22079 — Summitville Fairfax, Inc., 8245-G Backlick Road 703-541-1001
- Chesapeake 23320 — International Tile & Marble, Ltd., 828 Principal Lane 804-549-0055
- Newport News 23606 — International Tile & Marble, Ltd., 11761 Rock Landing Drive 804-873-13
- Richmond 23233 — McCullough Ceramic Corp., 9878 Mayland Drive 804-747-8300
- Salem 24153 — Valley Tile Distributors, 1510 Southside Drive 703-387-0300

WASHINGTON
- Seattle 98134 — Uniq Distributing Corp., 3807 Second Ave. South 206-682-9470
- Spokane 99212 — Uniq Distributing Co., North 509 Ella Road 509-922-1009

WEST VIRGINIA
- Charleston 25301 — Smith Floor Covering, 1118 Smith Street 304-344-2494

WISCONSIN
- LaCrosse 54603 — Jaeckle Wholesale, 2605 Hemstock St. 608-781-4888
- Madison 53704 — Jaeckle Wholesale, 2310 Daniels Street 608-221-8400
- Milwaukee 53051 — Childcrest Tile & Stone, W. 135 N5511 Campbell Drive 414-781-2551

FOREIGN DISTRIBUTORS

AUSTRALIA
- Sidney 2148 — Metz Pty. Ltd., P.O. Box 76, Marayong, NSW (02) 671-1311

BERMUDA
- Hamilton, 5 — Pool House Ltd., 54 Front Street, Box HM 1253-57 809-292-5522

CANADA
- Burnaby, British Columbia V5C 5N1 — Ames Bros. Distributors, Ltd., 2229 Beta Avenue 604-294-9690
- Calgary, Alberta T2G 3C1 — Ames Bros. Distributors, Ltd., 3405-9th Street SE 403-243-0434
- Dartmouth Nova Scotia B3B 1L3 — Select Ceramic Tile Centre Inc., 100 Isley Ave. Unit D 902-468-3416
- Edmonton, Alberta T5S 1JB — Ames Bros. Distributors, Ltd., 17203-102nd Avenue 403-483-8002
- Hamilton, Ontario L8W 2T7 — Summit Tile Canada Limited, 95 Unsworth Dr. 905-318-3348
- Longueil, Quebec J4K 3P9 — Cerodem, Ltd., 2650 Rue Delorimier 514-463-0815
- Winnipeg, Manitoba R2X 2P6 — Ames Bros. Distributors, Ltd., 26 Bunting Street 204-633-9491

KOREA
- Seoul — Dong Lim Homes Co., 113-1, Samsung-Dong, Knagnam-Ku (02) 553-6560

PUERTO RICO
- San Juan 00936 — Commercial A.S. Pagan, Inc., P.O. Box 364427 809-750-1650

FACTORY REPRESENTATIVES

CALIFORNIA
- Escondido 92029 — Fred W. Progner, 3161 Quiet Hills Dr. 619-489-5640
  TERRITORY AZ, So. CA, NM, NV, UT
- San Jose 95170 — Robert E. Dillon, P.O. Box 700355 415-309-8314
  TERRITORY OR, WA, Western & Central Canada, AK, Northern CA, Northern

GEORGIA
- Dunwoody 30350 — Roger Musgrove, 8607 Roswell Road 770-587-1744
  TERRITORY AL, FL, MS, NC, SC, VA

ILLINOIS
- Elk Grove Village 60007 — Robert R. Mau, 1101 Lunt Avenue 708-439-8820
  TERRITORY IA, ID, IL, MN, MO, MT, NE, SD, WI

INDIANA
- Fishers 46038 — Brian Renner, 12232 Parkview Lane 317-576-9943
  TERRITORY MI, IN, KY, TN

MASSACHUSETTS
- Marshfield 02050 — Bud Gill, 40 Christmas Tree Lane 617-834-9393
  TERRITORY New England & Eastern Canada

OHIO
- Summitville 43962 — Ewing Buta, Box 73, Summitville 216-223-1511
  TERRITORY DE, South NJ, Western NY, OH, PA, WV, Ontario

TEXAS
- Dallas 75229 — Joseph A. Hartzell, 3522 Duchess Trail 214-353-9372
  TERRITORY AR, CO, KS, LA, MO, OK, TX

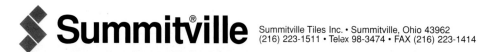

Summitville®

Summitville Tiles Inc. • Summitville, Ohio 43962
(216) 223-1511 • Telex 98-3474 • FAX (216) 223-1414

MADE IN USA
MEMBER: TILE COUNCIL OF AMERICA INC.

PRINTED IN U.S.A.
1-96

Factory Finished and Contract Unfinished Hardwood Floors

al Dente Restaurant — Bally's Las Vegas
WearMaster Maple EWM-3200 Maize with EWM-3204 Wild Walnut feature strip

Bruce®
hardwood floors
A division of Triangle Pacific Corp.

The Natural Choice™

SUPERIOR

WearMaster™ Acrylic

Universal Studios retail store — Orlando International Airport
WearMaster Oak EWM-3100 Golden Wheat

Introduction:

Bruce Hardwood Floors, a division of Triangle Pacific Corporation, is America's largest manufacturer of hardwood floors. For over 112 years, architects, builders and consumers have trusted Bruce to provide the best quality and value in hardwood floors.

With manufacturing facilities in Center, Texas; Nashville and Jackson, Tennessee; West Plains, Missouri; Port Gibson, Mississippi; and Beverly, West Virginia, Bruce provides our national and international, independent distributor network with a complete line of hardwood flooring products.

Contents:

The photography featured in this catalog is provided as a visual guide to the product pattern, not as an actual representation of the floor color itself.

Impregnated Hardwood Floors

EWM-3100 Golden Wheat

EWM-3101 Mocha Glaze

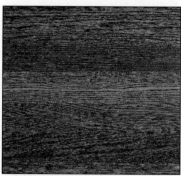

EWM-3104 Indian Brown

Description:

WearMaster floors are the culmination of over 112 years of Bruce innovation. Designed, engineered and manufactured specifically for commercial applications, every WearMaster performance feature represents state-of-the-art technology.

WearMaster floors are manufactured using a perfected acrylic impregnation process that makes them the toughest, most durable hardwood floors ever made. They are almost 50% harder than standard, unimpregnated hardwood floors.

WearMaster floors also feature a unique, pressurized ColorJet Infusion™ process that results in deep, penetrating colors for lasting appearance retention.

WearMaster floors have a low gloss, urethane surface that assures easy-care and superior stain resistance.

WearMaster floors are backed by the most comprehensive warranty in the hardwood flooring industry...your assurance of lasting beauty and durability in any commercial or residential application.

Technical Information:

WearMaster floors are factory-finished, 3-ply engineered plank floors. The planks are 3/8" thick (9.525 mm), 3" wide (76.20 mm) and are random in length ranging from 12" to 60" (304.80 - 1524.0 mm). WearMaster has tongue-and-groove side and end match construction, square end and side surface edges, and a smooth low gloss, commercial finish. WearMaster also carries a Class B Flame Spread rating, and exceeds the American's With Disabilities Act Recommendations for slip resistance. The impregnated wood surface and color layer is available in three wood species (oak, maple, and hickory).

Testing Standards:

ASTM D 2394, Sections 18-22 - Test Method for Indentation Resistance Using a Falling Ball. Indent depth (inches) Oak: 0.012 Maple: 0.011 Hickory: 0.0095

ASTM D 2394, Sections 33-37 - Test Method for Static Slip Resistance. Oak: 0.70 Maple: 0.072 Hickory: 0.069 Exceeds American's With Disabilities Acts Recommendations

ASTM D 4060-90 - Test Method for Abrasion Resistance of Organic Coatings by the Taber Abrader. Abrasion depth (inches) Oak: 0.011 Maple: 0.013 Hickory: 0.010

ASTM E 648 - Test Method for Critical Radiant Flux of Floor-Covering Systems Using a Radiant Heat Energy Source. Oak: 0.52 Maple: 0.50 Hickory: 0.52

ASTM E 84 - Test Method for Surface Burning Characteristics of Building Materials. Oak: Class B Maple: Class B Hickory: Class B

Product Usage:

WearMaster acrylic impregnated hardwood floors are designed for use in heavy and light commercial applications as well as residential use. WearMaster floors can be installed on, above, or below grade. They carry a Class B Flame Spread Rating and exceed the Americans With Disabilities Act Recommendations for slip resistance.

Note: WearMaster floors are not recommended for use in areas with high humidity, excessive moisture, or on concrete with compressive strength of less than 2000 psi.

WearMaster™ Acrylic

*"Store of the Future" Design by Chute Gerdeman, Columbus, OH
WearMaster Maple EWM-3200 Maize and EWM-3204 Wild Walnut*

Installation:

WearMaster floors can be installed on, above or below grade level, and over most existing SOUND, DRY AND LEVEL SUBFLOORS including; solid wood, exterior rated 5/8" (15.88mm) plywood or greater; underlayment grade particle board, wafer or chip board, and OSB; concrete - minimum 90 lb. density reinforced; resilient and sheet vinyl, VCT, terrazzo, or ceramic tile.

WearMaster can be installed over all radiantly heated concrete floors providing the concrete meets the requirements listed above.

• Bruce does not recommend installation over lightweight or acoustical concrete subfloors.

• All subfloors should be sound, clean, thoroughly dry, smooth, and level within 3/16" (4.763mm) in a 10' (3m) span.

• For a copy of WearMaster installation instructions, call toll free 1-800-722-4647.

• Adhesive required for warranted installations is Bruce Everbond LP adhesive. Trowel shall be pyramid notched 1/4" X 1/2" X 3/16" (6.350 X 12.70 X 4.763 mm) as required by Bruce Hardwood Floors.

EWM-3200 Maize

EWM-3202 Classic Cocoa

EWM-3204 Wild Walnut

Impregnated Hardwood Floors

EWM-3301 Sierra Brown

EWM-3302 Cordovan Brown

EWM-3304 Rustic Wood

EWM-3305 Violet Mist

EWM-3308 Cayenne

WearMaster Hickory EWM-3301 Sierra Brown with EWM-3304 Rustic Wood accents

Maintenance: WearMaster Acrylic Impregnated Products

WearMaster floors provide unprecedented ease of maintenance. The acrylic impregnated wear-layer features a tough, low gloss, commercial urethane surface that practically takes care of itself. It stops most spills and stains head-on. With prompt attention, most spills and stains wipe perfectly clean.

WearMaster floors require no special cleaning equipment or procedures. Routine maintenance is simply vacuuming to remove dirt and grit...and occasional light cleaning with WearMaster Commercial Cleaner Concentrate™.

Availability:

Bruce Hardwood Floors are sold through an international distribution network including; the United States, Canada, Mexico, Europe and Japan. For further information, please call the Sweet's BuyLine at 1-800-633-1180 or Bruce Hardwood Floors at 1-800-722-4647.

Warranty:

Bruce WearMaster products carry a Full Lifetime Warranty on Structural Integrity, Adhesive Bond and Subfloor Moisture Protection. Bruce includes a 25 Year Commercial Wood Wear Surface Warranty on WearMaster and a 25 Year Wood Wear Surface Warranty in residential applications.

How to Specify WearMaster Acrylic Impregnated Floors:

A. Flooring shall be Bruce 3/8" X 3" (9.525 mm X 76.20 mm) WearMaster flooring (specify product item number) in the (specify wood species) grade of wood as manufactured by Bruce Hardwood Floors, a division of Triangle Pacific Corporation.

B. Flooring shall be manufactured in a 3-ply, engineered construction that utilizes the Bruce ColorJet Infusion process to create a minimum 1/12" thick, pressurized wood color layer in the color (specify color name and number).

C. Flooring shall feature a minimum 1/12" thick acrylic impregnated wear surface utilizing the patent pending Bruce WearMaster impregnation process.

D. Factory finished, engineered WearMaster flooring shall be sanded to a smooth surface and provide a stain resistant, ultra-violet cured, low gloss, commercial urethane surface.

E. Factory finished, acrylic impregnated wood flooring will have no less than a Class B Flame Spread Rating (ASTM Test E-84).

F. Installed product will meet the Fuel Contribution and Smoke Density standards established for a product with a Class B Flame Spread Rating by the American Society for Testing and Materials (ASTM Test E-84).

G. Product to be installed will pass the Critical Radiant Flux test with a minimum Class I rating (ASTM Test E-648).

H. Installed flooring material will have a finish that exceeds the American's With Disabilities Act Recommendations of a minimum .620 coefficient of friction (slip resistance) rating (ASTM Test D-2394).

I. Installation of WearMaster floors shall be made in accordance with instructions provided in each carton.

J. Adhesive for WearMaster glue-down installation shall be Bruce® Everbond LP Adhesive® using a notched trowel as required by Bruce Hardwood Floors.

For additional product information, please call 1-800-722-4647.

Benchmark Collection:

Meridian Stone Custom Crafted Wood Tile —
H-4020 Sedona with H-316 Creme Diamond Accents

Description:

Bruce Dura-Luster urethane finish products are specifically designed for residential application only. These products receive the same multi-step sanding and stain process as all other Bruce products. Then they receive multiple coats of urethane cured with ultraviolet light between each coat. This produces a tough, durable finish that repels most household spills, requires no waxing, and is very easy to maintain. Dura-Luster finish floors are designed for use in all phases of residential areas, including the kitchen.

Maintenance: Dura-Luster® Urethane Finish Products

For the Dura-Luster urethane finish, Bruce recommends good general maintenance practices that include sweeping or vacuuming to remove dirt and grit. For a more thorough cleaning, simply clean with Dura-Luster cleaner made especially for Bruce. The Bruce Dura-Luster finish is a no-wax finish and does not require buffing. However, if buffing is desired after cleaning, use only a soft polishing attachment such as a lambs wool pad.

For additional product information, please call 1-800-722-4647.

Dura-Luster Urethane Finish

3/4" Solid Oak Strip and Plank

Sterling® Strip
Random lengths and a standard 2 1/4" width.
Square edges and ends. Tongue and groove.
Size: 3/4" X 2 1/4"

C-720 Natural	C-7220 Auburn
C-721 Gunstock	C-7221 Quartz
C-722 Spice	C-7222 Vintage Brown
C-723 Winter White	C-7223 Glacial White

Sterling Encore Plank®
Random lengths and alternate widths. Square
edges and ends. Tongue and groove.
Size: 3/4" X 2 1/4" - 3 1/4"

B-740 Natural	B-741 Gunstock

Devon® Plank
Random lengths and alternate widths. Eased
edges and square ends. Tongue and groove.
Size: 3/4" X 2 1/4" - 3 1/4"

B-640 Natural	B-642 Spice
B-641 Gunstock	B-643 Winter White

Windward® Strip
Random lengths and a standard 2 1/4" width.
Eased edges and square ends. Tongue and
groove. Size: 3/4" X 2 1/4"

C-620 Natural	C-623 Winter White
C-621 Gunstock	C-6220 Auburn
C-622 Spice	C-6224 Driftwood

Sterling Prestige Plank®
Random lengths and a standard 3 1/4" width.
Square edges and ends. Tongue and groove.
Size: 3/4" X 3 1/4"

C-730 Natural	C-732 Spice
C-731 Gunstock	C-733 Winter White

5/16" Solid Oak Strip

Natural Reflections™
Random lengths and a standard 2 1/4" width.
Square edges and ends. Tongue and groove.
Size: 5/16" X 2 1/4"

C-5010 Natural	C-5021 Quartz
C-5011 Gunstock	C-5028 Cherry
C-5012 Spice	C-5029 Mink Grey
C-5013 Ivory White	C-5030 Prairie
C-5014 Mellow	C-5031 Walnut
C-5016 Butterscotch	

3/8" Engineered Strip and Plank

Reunion® Plank
Random lengths and a standard 3" width. 5-ply
engineered oak. Square edges and ends. Tongue
and groove. Size: 3/8" X 3"

E-710 Toast	E-7120 Auburn
E-711 Gunstock	E-7121 Quartz
E-712 Mellow	E-7122 Vintage Brown
E-713 Ivory White	E-7123 Glacial White

LeClaire® Plank
Random lengths and a standard 3" width. 3-ply
engineered oak with eased edges and ends.
Tongue and groove.

E-820 Toast	E-824 Spice
E-821 Gunstock	E-8221 Quartz
E-823 Ivory White	E-8224 Driftwood

Charlemont® Plank
Random lengths and widths. 3-ply engineered
oak with eased edges and ends. Tongue and
groove. Size: 3/8" X 3" - 5" - 7"

E-840 Toast	E-841 Gunstock

Caruth® Plank
Random lengths and a standard 3" width. 5-ply
engineered maple with square edges and ends.
Tongue and groove. Size: 3/8" X 3"

E-910 Toast	E-913 Creme
E-911 Caramel	

Reunion Feature Strip®
Random lengths and a standard 1 1/2" width. 5-
ply engineered oak and ash with square edges
and ends. Tongue and groove. Size: 3/8" X 1 1/2"

TE-715 Natural	TE-718 Mauve
TE-716 Sable	TE-719 French Blue
TE-717 Dawn Gray	

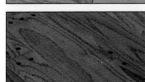

Antell® Plank
Random lengths and alternate widths. 3-ply
engineered oak with eased edges and ends.
Tongue and groove. Size: 3/8" X 3" - 5"

E-830 Toast	E-831 Gunstock

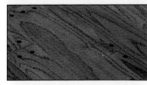

Hancock™ Plank
Factory installed pegs. Random lengths and
widths. 3-ply engineered oak with eased edges
and ends. Tongue and groove.
Size: 3/8" X 3" - 5" - 7"

E-851 Gunstock	E-854 Spice

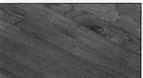

Stafford® Strip
Random lengths and a standard 2 1/4" width. 3-
ply engineered oak with square edges and ends.
Tongue and groove. Size: 3/8" X 2 1/4"

E-410 Toast	E-416 Butterscotch
E-410U Unfinished	E-417 Saddle
E-411 Gunstock	E-420 Auburn
E-413 Ivory White	E-421 Quartz

Installation:

Bruce Dura-Luster urethane products are recommended for
all phases of residential areas, including the kitchen.

Solid oak products can be installed on or above grade.
Engineered products can be installed on, above or below
grade level, including basements.

Detailed installation instruction sheets are provided in every
product carton.

For additional product information, please call 1-800-722-4647.

7

Benchmark Collection:
Dura-Luster Urethane Finish (continued)

3/8" Engineered Custom Wood Tile and Parquet

Debut®
3-ply engineered oak, single unit. Eased edges, tongue and groove. Size: 3/8" X 9" X 9"
K-2010 Toast   K-2011 Gunstock

Jeffersonian™ II
3-ply engineered oak, three piece construction. Eased, butt edges. Size: 3/8" X 8" X 8"
H-1710 Toast   H-1711 Gunstock

Sonata™
3-ply engineered maple center/oak pickets, five piece construction. Eased, butt edges.
Size: 3/8" X 12" X 12"
H-4621 Creme Center/Quartz Pickets
H-4625 Creme Center/Peachtree Pickets

Santa Fe Square
3-ply engineered oak, one unit with one diagonally cut corner to accept diamond insert. Eased edges, tongue and groove. Diamond inserts ordered separately. Size: 3/8" X 9" X 9"
K-2110 Toast   K-2111 Gunstock

Meridian Stone™
3-ply engineered maple, one unit with eased, butt edges. Four corners diagonally cut to accept diamond inserts. Diamond inserts ordered separately. Size: 3/8" X 12" X 12"
H-4016 Creme   H-4025 Parchment
H-4020 Sedona

Diamond Accents
3-ply engineered maple, one unit with eased, butt edges. For use with Santa Fe Square and Meridian Stone only. Size: 2 7/8" X 2 7/8"
H-310U Unfinished   H-325 Parchment
H-316 Creme   H-326 Sherwood
H-320 Sedona   H-327 Wood Violet
H-322 Espresso   H-328 Sahara
H-324 Charcoal

Herringstrip™
3-ply engineered oak, one unit with eased edges. Variety of pattern/design options. Tongue and groove. Size: 3/8" X 3" X 15"
H-1010 Toast   H-1022 Vintage Brown
H-1011 Gunstock

5/16" Solid Oak Custom Wood Tile and Parquet

Clairmont Elegancé™
Individual fillets assembled and joined into four groups, then glued to a backer. Eased, butt edges. Size: 5/16" X 12" X 12"
L-7310 Desert   L-7321 Quartz
L-7311 Chestnut   L-7324 Driftwood
L-7314 Mellow   L-7325 Peachtree

Oakmont®
Single unit contains oak fillets joined with a soft metal spline. Square edges. Tongue and groove. Size: 5/16" X 12" X 12"
L-70 Desert   L-77 Tudor
L-71 Chestnut   L-720 Auburn
L-72 Mellow   L-721 Quartz
L-76 Ivory White   L-724 Driftwood

Oakmont Feature Strip™
Square edges with tongues on both ends and grooves on both sides. Size: 5/16" X 2" X 26"
TL-70 Desert   TL-76 Ivory White
TL-71 Chestnut   TL-77 Tudor

Testing Standards:

ASTM D 968 - The falling sand test. Results represent the amount, in milliliters, of sand that falls on a controlled area before the finish is worn away. The higher the number, the better the finish.

Bruce Dura-Luster urethane finish - 88,000 milliliters per mil of finish.

Competitive urethane finish - 48,000 milliliters per mil of finish.

ASTM D 2394, Sections 33-37 - Test Method for Static Slip Resistance. Oak and Maple: Exceeds 0.60

Exceeds the American's With Disabilities Act Recommendations

ASTM E 648 - Test Method for Critical Radiant Flux of Floor Covering Systems Using a Radiant Heat Energy Source. Oak: 0.48

Color Fastness: Results represent in numerical value, the amount of shift from the original color toward a yellow coloration. The lower the number the better the color/finish.

Raw Oak Test Score: 8.055

Bruce Ivory White Test Score: 4.919

Bruce Desert/Natural Test Score: 3.003

Note: Bruce parquet products with a self-stik foam backing are available on a select basis. For acoustical rating data on these self-stik, foam backed hardwood floors, call: 1-800-722-4647.

Kensington™ Collection: Dura-Luster Urethane Finish

3/4" Solid Oak Strip and Plank

Laurel™ Strip
Random lengths and a standard 2 1/4" width. Eased edges with square ends. Tongue and groove. Size: 3/4" X 2 1/4"

CB-921 Natural	CB-924 Gunstock
CB-922 Spice	CB-926 Butterscotch
CB-923 Winter White	CB-927 Saddle

Valley View™ Plank
Random lengths and a standard 3 1/4" width. Eased edges with square ends. Tongue and groove. Size: 3/4" X 3 1/4"

CB-931 Natural	CB-934 Gunstock

5/16" Solid Oak Parquet

Sorrento® Parquet
Single unit contains oak fillets joined with a soft metal spline. Square edges.
Size: 5/16" X 12" X 12"

L-92 Mellow	L-94 Chestnut
L-93 Desert	L-95 Quartz

Glen Cove Plank — EB-880 Toast

3/8" Engineered Oak

Riverside™ Plank
Random lengths with a standard 3" width. 5-ply engineered oak with square edges and ends. Tongue and groove. Size: 3/8" X 3"

EB-720 Toast	EB-723 Ivory White
EB-721 Gunstock	EB-724 Spice

Glen Cove™ Plank
Random lengths and a standard 3" width. 3-ply engineered oak with eased edges and ends. Tongue and groove. Size: 3/8" X 3"

EB-880 Toast	EB-883 Ivory White
EB-881 Gunstock	EB-884 Spice

Sanford™ Plank
Random lengths with a standard 3" width. 3-ply engineered oak with square edges and ends. Tongue and groove. Size: 3/8" X 3"

E-320 Natural	E-326 Butterscotch
E-321 Gunstock	E-327 Saddle
E-325 Mellow	

Oceanside™ Strip
Random lengths and a standard 2 1/4" width. 3-ply engineered oak with square edges and ends. Tongue and groove. Size: 3/8" X 2 1/4"

E-100 Toast	E-106 Butterscotch
E-101 Gunstock	E-107 Saddle
E-105 Mellow	

Warranty:

All Bruce products carry a Full Lifetime Warranty on Structural Integrity, Adhesive Bond, and Subfloor Moisture Protection.

- First line Benchmark Dura-Luster urethane products carry a Full Five Year Finish Wear Layer Warranty for residential applications.
- Kensington Dura-Luster urethane products carry a Full Standard One Year Finish Wear Layer Warranty for residential applications.

How to Specify Dura-Luster Urethane Finish Floors:

A. Flooring shall be Bruce (state name, size and/or width) strip, plank, custom wood tile or parquet in the grade of (specify wood species) with a surface color/finish of (state color item number) as manufactured by Bruce Hardwood Floors, a division of Triangle Pacific Corporation.

B. Factory finished engineered strip, plank or parquet and solid strip, plank or parquet shall be sanded for a smooth finish and have an ultra violet cured urethane finish.

C. Installation must be made in accordance with the installation instruction sheets provided in each carton.

D. Adhesive for glue-down installation shall be Bruce Everbond LP adhesive. Bruce Everbond LP adhesive shall be used for all 3/8" strip, plank, and parquet. Adhesive for end fastening 3/4" random planks shall be Bruce Oakbond or PL-400 as recommended by Bruce Hardwood Floors.

E. Trowel for spreading Bruce Everbond LP adhesive shall be notched as required by Bruce Hardwood Floors.

F. Nailing Machines: 2" barbed fasteners or approved staples should be used for installing Bruce 3/4" strip or plank flooring, and nailing machines with 1 1/4" cleats should be used for nail-down installation of 3/8" strip or plank as required by Bruce Hardwood Floors.

Benchmark Collection:

Dillard's Department Store — Little Rock, Arkansas — Monterey Plank E-20 Gunstock

Description:

Bruce Dura-Satin® wax finish floors are specifically designed for light commercial and residential use, including high traffic areas. The Dura-Satin finish epitomizes the old-world richness and patina of soft, baked-in stain and wax. The exclusive Bruce 13-step penetrating stain and wax finish creates a protective barrier that provides lasting durability against traffic, wear, soil and stains. The Bruce Dura-Satin wax finish is an outstanding choice for beauty and durability in light commercial applications.

Testing Standards:

ASTM D 4060-90 - Test Method for Abrasion Resistance of Organic Coatings by the Taber Abrader. Oak: 0.011 Maple: 0.010

ASTM E 84 - Test Method for Surface Burning Characteristics of Building Materials. Oak: Class C Maple: Class C

Dura-Satin Wax Finish

Buy Line 4923

3/4" Solid Oak Strip and Plank

Westminster® Plank
Wrought iron nails for end fastening. Random lengths and widths. Beveled edges and ends. Tongue and groove. Size: 3/4" X 3" - 5" - 7"
A-3 Mellow Textured

Cathedral® Plank
Factory installed pegs. Random lengths and widths. Beveled edges and ends. Tongue and groove. Size: 3/4" X 3" - 5" - 7"
A-5 Toast   A-7 Gunstock

Ranch® Plank
Factory installed pegs. Random lengths and alternate widths. Beveled edges and ends. Tongue and groove. Size: 3/4" X 2 1/4" - 3 1/4"
B-3 Gunstock

Cambridge® Plank
Random lengths and widths. Beveled edges and ends. Tongue and groove. Size: 3/4" X 3" - 4" - 6"
A-20 Toast   A-21 Gunstock

Fireside® Plank
Random lengths and alternate widths. Beveled edges and ends. Tongue and groove.
Size: 3/4" X 2 1/4" - 3 1/4"
B-4 Gunstock   B-8 Toast

Country Oak® Plank
Factory installed pegs. Random lengths and widths. Beveled edges and ends. Tongue and groove. Size: 3/4" X 3" - 4" - 6"
A-25 Rustic

Homestead® Plank
Textured finish. Random lengths and alternate widths. Beveled edges and ends. Tongue and groove. Size: 3/4" X 2 1/4" - 3 1/4"
B-5 Mellow Textured

Prefinished Strip
Random lengths, standard 2 1/4" width. Beveled edges and ends. Tongue and groove.
Size: 3/4" X 2 1/4"
C-1 Natural   C-4 Gunstock
C-3 Bronzetone

3/4" Solid Oak Parquet

Monticello
Center square is 5 tongue and groove fillets joined with a soft metal spline. Four surrounding pickets are 2 1/4" wide. Beveled edges.
Size: 3/4" X 9 3/4" X 9 3/4"
F-1 Gunstock

Unit Block
Single unit with 6 tongue and groove fillets joined with a soft metal spline. Beveled edges.
Size: 3/4" X 9" X 9"
G-7 Natural   G-8 Gunstock

3/8" Engineered Plank

Village Plank®
Factory installed pegs. 3-ply engineered plank. Random lengths and widths. Beveled edges and ends. Tongue and groove. Size: 3/8" X 3" - 5" - 7"
E-1 Mellow   E-11 Gunstock

Villa Nova Plank®
3-ply engineered plank. Random lengths and widths. Beveled edges and ends. Tongue and groove. Size: 3/8" X 3" - 5" - 7"
E-12 Gunstock

Sierra Plank®
3-ply engineered plank. Random lengths and alternating widths. Beveled edges and ends. Tongue and groove. Size: 3/8" X 3" - 5"
E-30 Gunstock

Monterey™ Plank
3-ply engineered plank. Random lengths and standard 3" width. Beveled edges and ends. Tongue and groove. Size: 3/8" X 3"
E-20 Gunstock

Classic™ Plank
5-ply engineered plank. Square edges, random lengths and standard 3" width. Square edges and ends. Tongue and groove. Size: 3/8" X 3"
E-510 Toast   E-511 Gunstock

3/8" Engineered Parquet

Heritage Square®
3-ply engineered oak. One unit, with beveled edges. Tongue and groove. Size: 3/8" X 9" X 9"
K-25-TG Gunstock   K-27-TG Mellow
K-26-TG Toast   Textured

Kensington™ Collection:

Brookhollow Strip — CB-94 Gunstock

Installation:

Bruce Dura-Satin wax finish products are recommended for both residential and light commercial applications, including high traffic areas.

Solid oak products can be installed on or above grade. Engineered oak products can be installed on, above or below grade level, including basements.

Detailed installation instruction sheets are provided in every product carton.

Maintenance: Dura-Satin Wax Finish Products

Bruce recommends good general maintenance practices for Dura-Satin wax finish products.

Commercial Maintenance

• Sweep or vacuum daily to remove grit.

• Using a commercial floor buffer, buff daily with a fiber bristle polishing brush.

• Using a lamb's wool applicator or equivalent, apply Bruce floor care products once every two weeks or as required in extreme traffic areas. Follow with buffing.

Residential Maintenance

• Use quality solvent-based cleaners and waxes.

• Buffing between waxings will restore the floor's sheen.

• High traffic areas can be waxed without waxing the entire floor.

• Waxing too often may cause a wax build-up and dull the finish.

• Do not use water base waxes. Water may dull the finish and cause additional maintenance problems.

Dura-Satin Wax Finish

09550/BRU
Buy Line 4923

3/4" Solid Oak Strip and Plank

Madison™ Plank
Random lengths and widths. Beveled edges and ends. Tongue and groove. Size: 3/4" X 3" - 4" - 6"
A-51 Gunstock   A-52 Toast

Manchester® Plank
Random lengths and alternating widths. Beveled edges and ends. Tongue and groove.
Size: 3/4" X 2 1/4" - 3 1/4"
B-11 Toast   B-14 Gunstock

Prefinished Strip
Random lengths and standard 2 1/4" width. Beveled edges and ends. Tongue and groove.
Size: 3/4" X 2 1/4"
CB-21 Toast   CB-24 Gunstock

Brookhollow™ Strip
Random lengths and standard 2 1/4" width. Eased edges and square ends. Tongue and groove. Size: 3/4" X 2 1/4"
CB-91 Natural   CB-94 Gunstock

3/8" Engineered Oak Plank

Brookside™ Plank
Factory installed pegs. Random lengths and widths. Beveled edges and ends. Tongue and groove. Size: 3/8" X 3" - 5" - 7"
E-50 Gunstock Textured

Brandon™ Plank
Random lengths and widths. Beveled edges and ends. Tongue and groove. Size: 3/8" X 3" - 5" - 7"
E-52 Gunstock Textured

Sutton™ Plank
Random lengths and standard 3" width. Beveled edges and ends. Tongue and groove.
Size: 3/8" X 3"
E-51 Gunstock   E-55 Toast
Textured

3/8" Engineered Oak Parquet

Ridgewood™ Parquet
3-ply engineered oak. Center unit surrounded with 2 pickets. Beveled, butt edges.
Size: 3/8" X 8" X 8"
H-84 Gunstock Textured

Heritage Square®
3-ply engineered oak. One unit with beveled edges. Tongue and groove. Size: 3/8" X 9" X 9"
K-28-TG Gunstock Textured

Warranty:

All Bruce products carry a Full Lifetime Warranty on Structural Integrity, Adhesive Bond, and Subfloor Moisture Protection.

- First line Benchmark Dura-Satin wax products carry a Full Five Year Finish Wear Layer Warranty for residential applications and Full Standard One Year Finish Wear Layer Warranty in approved commercial applications.

- Kensington Dura-Satin wax products carry a Full Standard One Year Finish Wear Layer Warranty in residential applications and approved commercial applications.

How to Specify Dura-Satin Wax Finish Floors:

A. Flooring shall be Bruce (state name, size and/or width) strip, plank, custom wood tile or parquet in the grade of (specify wood species) with a surface color/finish of (state color item number) as manufactured by Bruce Hardwood Floors, a division of Triangle Pacific Corporation.

B. Factory finished engineered strip, plank, custom wood tile or parquet and solid strip, plank or parquet shall be sanded for a smooth finish or wire brushed for a textured surface, and have a baked-in Dura-Satin wax finish that includes a soya and linseed penetrating stain and carnauba wax.

C. Installation must be made in accordance with the installation instruction sheets provided in each carton.

D. Adhesive for glue-down installation shall be Bruce Everbond LP adhesive. Bruce Everbond LP adhesive shall be used for all 3/8" strip, plank, and parquet. Adhesive for end fastening 3/4" random planks shall be Bruce Oakbond or PL-400 as recommended by Bruce Hardwood Floors.

E. Trowel for spreading Bruce Everbond LP adhesive shall be notched as required by Bruce Hardwood Floors.

F. Nailing Machines: 2" barbed fasteners or approved staples should be used for installing Bruce 3/4" strip or plank flooring, and nailing machines with 1 1/4" cleats should be used for nail-down installation of 3/8" strip or plank as required by Bruce Hardwood Floors.

For additional product information, please call 1-800-722-4647.   13

Contract Unfinished

GOOD

Contract Unfinished CU-740. Custom finished in a Gunstock color.

Description:

Bruce manufactures a complete line of contract unfinished products for job site finishing. These products are kiln dried prior to milling and go through the identical manufacturing process as all other Bruce products with the exception of finishing. Contract unfinished floors are available in both solid and engineered oak.

Warranty:

Bruce Contract Unfinished products carry a Full Lifetime Warranty on Structural Integrity, Adhesive Bond, and Subfloor Moisture Protection.

How to Specify Contract Unfinished Floors:

A. Flooring shall be Bruce (state name, size and/or width) strip, plank, custom wood tile or parquet in the grade of oak/maple (state item number) as manufactured by Bruce Hardwood Floors, a division of Triangle Pacific Corporation.

B. Bruce CU unfinished strip, plank or parquet shall be installed and job site sanded and finished according to the job specification. Engineered strip, plank, and custom wood tile or parquet shall be presanded at the factory for minimum job site sanding.

C. Installation must be completed in accordance with the installation instruction sheets provided in each carton.

D. Adhesive for glue-down installation shall be Bruce Everbond LP adhesive. Everbond LP adhesive shall be used for all 3/8" strip, plank, and parquet. Adhesive for end fastening 3/4" random strip or planks shall be Bruce Oakbond or PL-400 as recommended by Bruce Hardwood Floors.

E. Trowel for spreading Everbond LP adhesive shall be notched as required by Bruce Hardwood Floors.

F. Nailing Machines: 2" barbed fasteners or approved staples should be used for installing Bruce 3/4" strip or plank flooring, and nailing machines with 1 1/4" cleats should be used for nail-down installation of 3/8" strip or planks as required by Bruce Hardwood Floors.

Products

3/4" Signature Series Solid Oak Plank

Available with square ends and edges or with beveled ends and edges, these planks provide exceptional quality and value. The 3/4" solid oak series is available in red or white oak, and in 3", 4", 5", 6" or 7" widths in random lengths. Sizes may be mixed to achieve alternate or random patterns.

Installation: Nail down, on or above grade level.

3" Plank	4" Plank	5" Plank	6" Plank	7" Plank
Item#				
CU-3RB	CU-4RB	CU-5RB	CU-6RB	CU-7RB
CU-3RS	CU-4RS	CU-5RS	CU-6RS	CU-7RS
CU-3WB	CU-4WB	CU-5WB	CU-6WB	CU-7WB
CU-3WS	CU-4WS	CU-5WS	CU-6WS	CU-7WS

R = Red Oak B = Beveled Edges S = Square Edges W = White Oak

Engineered Flooring

Engineered oak construction with square ends and edges and tongue and groove milling. Traditional red and white oak boards available in 2 1/4" and 3" widths and random lengths.

Installation: Nail down, or glue down, on above or below grade level.

1/2" Strip and Plank

Size	Select & Better Red Oak	Select & Better White Oak	#1 Common Red Oak	#1 Common White Oak
1/2" X 2 1/4"	CU-600	CU-610	CU-615	CU-625
1/2" X 3"	CU-640	CU-650	CU-635	CU-645

3/8" Strip and Plank

Size	Select & Better Red Oak	Select & Better White Oak	#1 Common Red Oak	#1 Common White Oak
3/8" X 2 1/4"	CU-700	CU-710	CU-715	CU-725
3/8" X 3"	CU-740	CU-750	CU-735	CU-745

3/4" Solid Oak Parquet

Solid, mixed red and white oak construction with square edges. Ideal for both commercial and residential application. Elegant patterns are adaptable to many different designs.

Installation: Glue down on or above grade level.

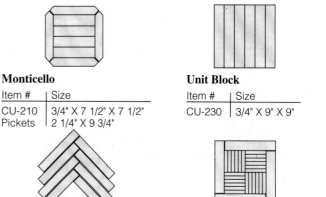

Monticello

Item #	Size
CU-210 Pickets	3/4" X 7 1/2" X 7 1/2" 2 1/4" X 9 3/4"

Unit Block

Item #	Size
CU-230	3/4" X 9" X 9"

Herringbone

Item #	Size
CU-240	3/4" X 1 1/2" X 9"

Breton

Item #	Size
CU-220	3/4" X 17 1/4" X 17 1/4"

5/16" Solid Oak Parquet

Solid oak construction with square edges provides a smooth, continuous surface that is ideal for both commercial and residential application. Unique patterns can be installed in various designs.

Installation: Glue down on or above grade level.

Finger Block (Paper Faced)

Item #	Size	Species
CU-310	5/16" X 17 1/2" X 17 1/2"	R & W Oak
CU-311	5/16" X 17 1/2" X 17 1/2"	White Oak

Monticello (Mesh Backed)

Item #	Size	Species
CU-320	5/16" X 12" X 12"	White Oak

Haddon Hall (Mesh Backed)

Item #	Size	Species
CU-330	5/16" 12" X 12"	White Oak

Clairmont® (Mesh Backed)

Item #	Size	Species
CU-340	5/16" X 12" X 12"	White Oak

Herringbone (Paper Faced)

Item #	Size	Species
CU-350	5/16" X 12 3/4" X 18 1/4"	White Oak

For additional product information, please call 1-800-722-4647.

Custom Color Feature Strips

Oakmont Tudor Parquet (L-77) with Oakmont Tudor Feature Strip (TL-77)

Bruce Custom Color Feature Strip gives any floor a handcrafted, custom designed appearance, making ordinary rooms, extraordinary. The custom accent colors can be coordinated to mix perfectly with room furnishings and accessories.

Oakmont Feature Strip

A 2" X 26" solid oak strip for use with Oakmont. This simple feature strip adds elaborate detail and design in many unique applications.

Reunion Feature Strip

This versatile 1 1/2" feature strip is designed specifically for use with Reunion Plank. This incredible feature strip allows you to incorporate borders or stunning corner treatments with a standard product.

Sterling Custom Combinations

This unique feature strip concept is designed to work with the entire Sterling family of products. By using different sizes and/or colors of these products, you can create unique borders and patterns. (not shown)

Reunion Plank E-713 Ivory White floor accented with TE-717 Dawn Gray Reunion Feature Strip.

Installation Products:

- **Adhesives.** Bruce Everbond LP adhesive is used for installation of all 3/8" strip, plank and custom wood tile or parquet, except when the parquet is self-stick, dry foam back or a vapor barrier is involved. Check adhesive label for trowel specifications.

  Bruce Oakbond Adhesive is required for end fastening some of the solid oak, random width nail-down strip or plank floors.

- **Trim and Molding.** Bruce's complete line of trim and molding products are available either factory-finished or unfinished for job site finishing.

- **Installation Accessories.** Bruce offers specially notched trowels for spreading adhesives to the proper specifications, cork expansion products, nails and other installation products to complete the job.

Maintenance/Repair Products

Bruce offers a complete line of maintenance products formulated specifically for each individual Bruce finish. In addition, a full line of repair products such as stains, fillers and finishes are available for routine maintenance and repair.

Sales and Specifier Support

Bruce has a complete library of sales and specifier support materials available, and a nationwide network of distributor representatives ready to assist you at the local level.

To order support materials, or for the name of the Bruce distributor in your area, call toll free: 1-800-722-4647.

Wood is a natural material containing distinctive differences in color and grain configuration. It is these differences caused by nature that create the warmth, beauty, and individuality of each hardwood floor. The printed room scenes in this catalog are intended as a guide for product pattern, not as an actual representation of the floor itself.

Bruce®

hardwood floors

A division of Triangle Pacific Corp.

The Natural Choice™

16803 Dallas Parkway Dallas, Texas 75248

Sweets brochure #102 8/95 © 1995, 1984 Bruce Hardwood Floors
A division of Triangle Pacific Corp.
Printed in U.S.A.

05532/ARD
BUYLINE 6402
C357

arden

FINEST IN FLOOR ACCESS SYSTEMS

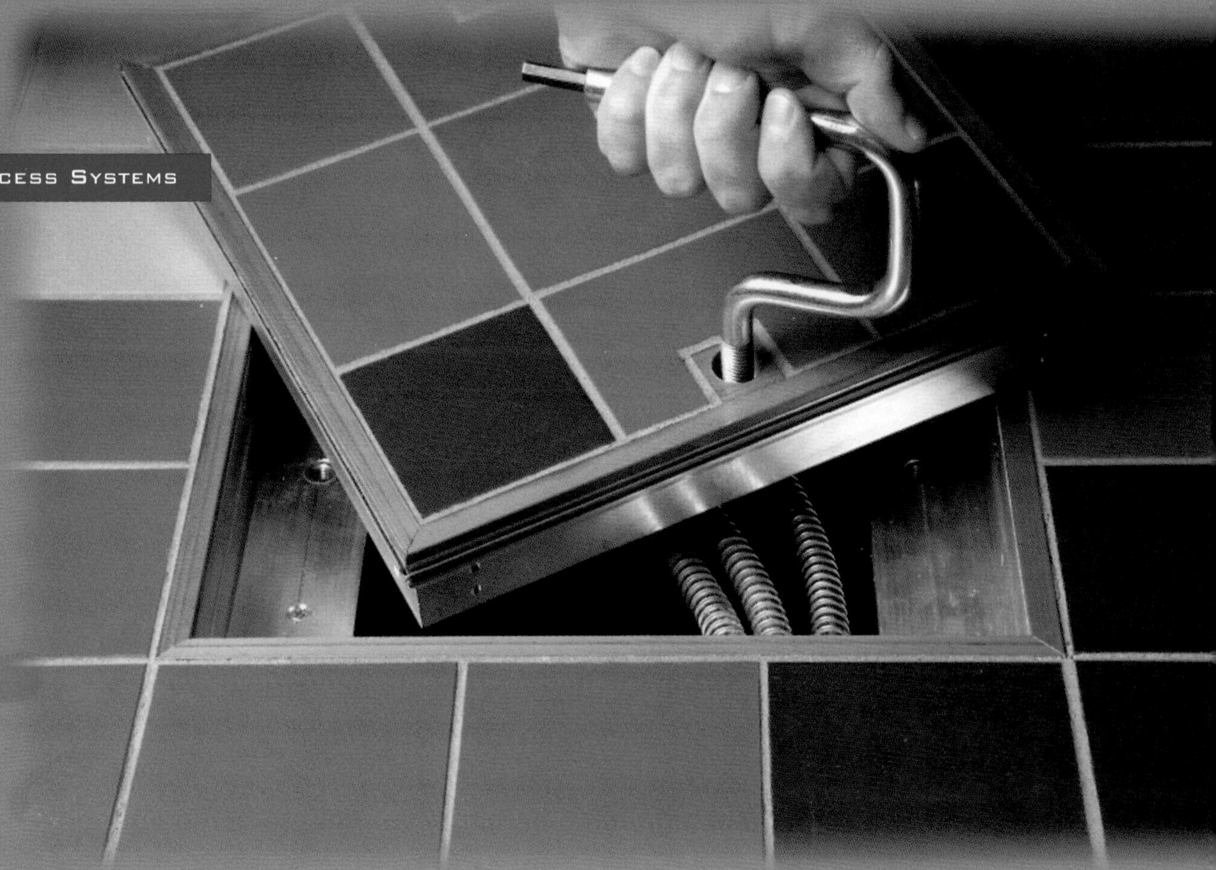

THE FINEST IN FLOOR ACCESS SYSTEMS...

- ENGINEERED FOR STRENGTH
- DESIGNED TO MATCH ANY FLOOR SURFACE
- CUSTOM-SIZED
- AFFORDABLY PRICED

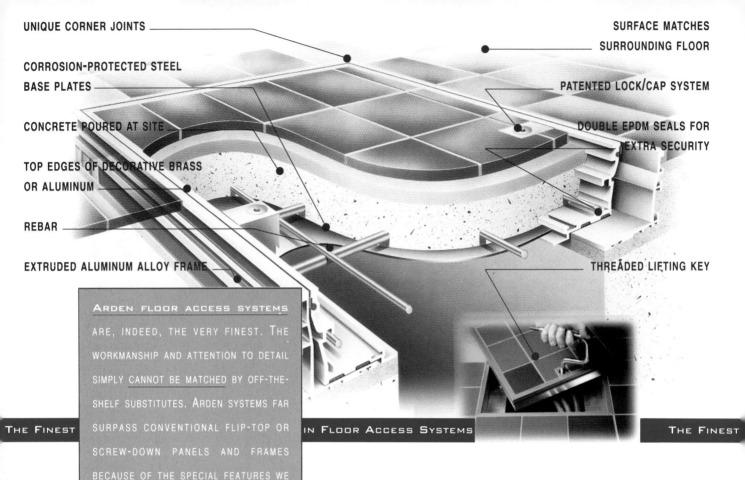

UNIQUE CORNER JOINTS

CORROSION-PROTECTED STEEL
BASE PLATES

CONCRETE POURED AT SITE

TOP EDGES OF DECORATIVE BRASS
OR ALUMINUM

REBAR

EXTRUDED ALUMINUM ALLOY FRAME

SURFACE MATCHES
SURROUNDING FLOOR

PATENTED LOCK/CAP SYSTEM

DOUBLE EPDM SEALS FOR
EXTRA SECURITY

THREADED LIFTING KEY

ARDEN FLOOR ACCESS SYSTEMS ARE, INDEED, THE VERY FINEST. THE WORKMANSHIP AND ATTENTION TO DETAIL SIMPLY CANNOT BE MATCHED BY OFF-THE-SHELF SUBSTITUTES. ARDEN SYSTEMS FAR SURPASS CONVENTIONAL FLIP-TOP OR SCREW-DOWN PANELS AND FRAMES BECAUSE OF THE SPECIAL FEATURES WE INCORPORATE TO MAKE OUR COVERS STRONGER, BETTER LOOKING, AND MORE AFFORDABLE.

ENGINEERING

With Arden floor access covers, all of the frames are made of 6063-T6 aluminum alloy. The rigid design of the section keeps frame and cover edges straight during pour and cure, which means that proper fit is insured. The strength of this alloy, and our anti-corrosion coating, assure long-lasting performance.

The unit comes completely ready to install — the entire reinforcement bar assembly is already snapped tightly into place, so after allowing for floor surface, you simply fill with concrete. This is without a doubt the best procedure for achieving a maximum load-bearing surface; the resulting strength exceeds anything that can be produced by on-site construction techniques.

Our exclusive method of corner joining also precludes distortion during assembly and installation. Therefore, the frame and hatch cover lie completely flat, eliminating any rocking as traffic passes over it.

Our standard vinyl top edge seal keeps water and dirt from wedging between the cover and the frame, thus preventing jamming when lifting, and protecting against moisture entering the recess. In addition, for extra security, covers can be provided with double EPDM seals to serve as a second line of defense against damaging moisture and dirt.

AESTHETICS

Arden covers are the right choice if you don't want to sacrifice aesthetics while insisting on a floor access system that is totally secure. The cover's surface can be finished to perfectly match the floor around it: whether of tile, terrazzo, stone, concrete, carpet, wood — whatever the surface, an Arden hatch cover blends beautifully into the surrounding floor.

Depending on the model, the top edges are available in either aluminum or brass — select whichever will be most attractive with the floor for which it's being custom-built. If floor grinding is necessary, up to 1/8" can be removed from the top edge surfaces. Again, the result will be a flush, precisely-fitting cover.

CUSTOM-SIZED

Arden floor access covers are available in any size from 6" square to 48" square, depending on the model, and can be installed individually or in multi-cover combinations [see pages 3 and 4 for details]. They are suitable for a wide variety of applications; basketball courts or gyms; in restaurants or commercial kitchens; in public traffic areas where intense scrubbing and rinsing from floor cleaning machinery places both weight and water pressure on the installation.

AFFORDABILITY

Our custom-designed, custom-sized systems are virtually incomparable — but, in terms of pricing and delivery, they can be compared very favorably with off-the-shelf products! They come complete and ready to install — there's no mess, no mistakes, and no time wasted in trying to invent a solution on site.

Builders of retail malls, institutional and commercial buildings, and sports facilities have recognized the economy of cost, efficiency of installation, and security of an Arden floor access system. Property owners as well as renovation contractors of existing commercial and industrial sites, appreciate the on-going low maintenance and trouble-free service. This enviable durability is ensured by the integrity of the aluminum frame and by the superb fit.

SAFETY

Pedestrian traffic is assured of safe footing, and rolling carts pass without obstruction. Because, when the hatch is closed and secured, the frame and access cover are flush with the floor — there are no visible gaps or uneven seams.

SECURITY

The patented lock/cap system guards the hatch against unwanted entry, making it almost impossible for anyone but designated staff to have assess to the recess. The factory supplied, threaded lifting keys serve to both secure the cover and to act as lifting handles.

VERSATILITY

Arden installations throughout the world provide access to plumbing, cables, drains, check valves, wires, and traps. Current installations, both indoors and out, include motels, malls, schools, prisons, kitchens, sport facilities, and office buildings.

So, whether you need access to data, power or communications lines, equipment pits, sewer, or other plumbing, remember that Arden hatches are the proven solution to any floor access problem.

arden

ARDEN OFFERS TWO SINGLE-COVER ACCESS OPTIONS — CHOOSE THE ONE THAT'S TAILORED TO YOUR NEEDS.

500 Series

750 Series

	500 Series	750 Series
• FRAME DEPTH	2"	3"
• AVAILABLE SIZES	6"sq. - 30"sq.	6"sq. - 48"sq.
• COVER WEIGHT PER SQ. FT. (AFTER CONCRETE INFILL)	18.5 lbs.	36 lbs.
• WEIGHT-BEARING CAPABILITIES	1ton pneumatic tire load or uniformly distributed load of up to 200 lbs/sq. ft. [pedestrian traffic and light hand trucks]	3 ton pneumatic tire load, or a uniformly distributed load of up to 300 lbs./sq. ft. [small vehicular traffic]
• TOP EDGE FINISH	aluminum	aluminum, with option for brass

• NOTE: BRASS TOP EDGES ARE PERMANENTLY SECURED TO THE ALUMINUM SUB-FRAME BY A PATENTED MECHANICAL JOINT. BECAUSE THIS METHOD USES NEITHER FASTENERS NO CLIPS, NO PARTS CAN COME LOOSE THROUGH WEAR AND TEAR. IN ADDITION, THE SPECIAL BRASS/ALUMINUM JOINT INCORPORATES A CONTINUOUS ISOLATION LAYER FOR PROTECTION AGAINST ELECTROLYTIC ACTION.

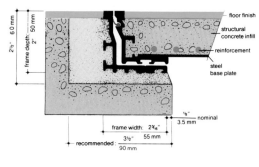

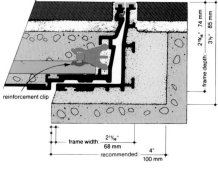

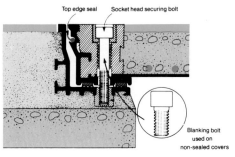

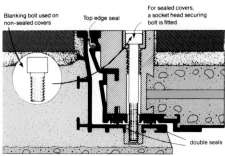

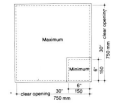

* Overall size = clear opening + $\frac{4\frac{5}{8}"}{117\ mm}$

** Overall size = clear opening + $\frac{5\frac{5}{8}"}{143\ mm}$

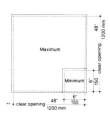

MULTI-COVER HATCHES

Arden access covers may be combined to form a trench or grid pattern. This system is remarkably versatile, affording considerable freedom of design: covers for trenches, faceted curves — even for complete access floors — can all be fabricated to meet your specific requirements. [Because of their technical complexity, we encourage you to consult with our technical department for guidelines.]

MAXIMUM SPANS FOR INDIVIDUAL COVERS USED IN MULTI-COVER CONFIGURATIONS ARE SLIGHTLY SMALLER THAN THOSE IN SINGLE-COVER SIZES, SPECIFICALLY,

MAXIMUM CLEAR OPENING	500 Series	750 Series
	24" [600 mm]	36" [900 mm]

SPECIFICATIONS

GENERAL CONSTRUCTION:

Furnish and install floor access hatch and cover system [specify 500 or 750], as manufactured by Arden Architectural Specialties, Inc., St. Paul, Minnesota, in sizes per plans and specifications. Frame and cover shall be fabricated from 6063-T6 aluminum alloy, with corners neatly mitred and keyed. Top edge shall be ——— [specify either 385 alloy bronze or aluminum.] Frames shall have factory applied coat of corrosion inhibitor. Covers shall be ——— [specify standard or double sealed]. [See Arden Guide Specifications for further details.]

INSTALLATION:

To ensure satisfactory performance, the manufacturer's instructions, included with each shipment must be precisely followed. Infill to be Portland Cement concrete with a minimum strength of 4,500 p.s.i., at 28 days with 3/8 inch [10 mm] maximum aggregate. [See Arden Guide Specificaitons for further details.]

WARRANTY:

Arden Architectural Specialties, Inc., warrants to its purchasers, for a period of two years from date of shipment, that any floor access hatch shall be free of defects in material or workmanship. The liability of Arden Architectural Specialties, Inc., is strictly limited to repair or replacement of units that, in our opinion, were properly installed and subsequently found to be defective. No claims for consequential damages of any nature will be allowed. This warranty is in lieu of all other warranties, expressed or implied.

layout examples

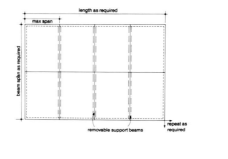
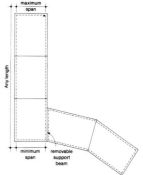

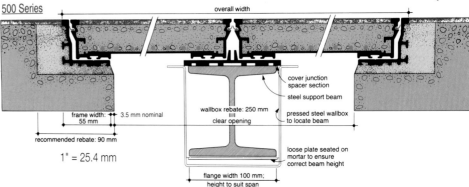

500 Series

overall width

cover junction spacer section
steel support beam
frame width: 55 mm
3.5 mm nominal
recommended rebate: 90 mm
wallbox rebate: 250 mm clear opening
pressed steel wallbox to locate beam
loose plate seated on mortar to ensure correct beam height
flange width 100 mm; height to suit span

1" = 25.4 mm

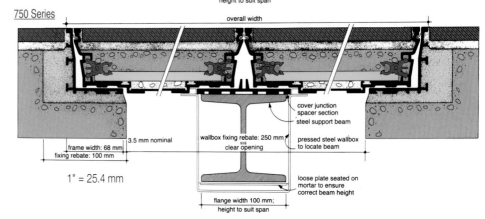

750 Series

overall width

cover junction spacer section
steel support beam
frame width: 68 mm
fixing rebate: 100 mm
3.5 mm nominal
wallbox fixing rebate: 250 mm clear opening
pressed steel wallbox to locate beam
loose plate seated on mortar to ensure correct beam height
flange width 100 mm; height to suit span

1" = 25.4 mm

The Howe Green hatch and trench system described in this brochure is manufactured under an exclusive licensing agreement with Howe Green Ltd., Hertford, Herts, Great Britain.

ARDEN ARCHITECTURAL SPECIALTIES, INC.

1947 West County Road C-2
Saint Paul, Minnesota 55113

Telephone: 612-631-1607
Facsimile: 612-631-0251
USA and Canada: 800-521-1826

Arden Architectural Specialties, Inc., reserves the right to make product changes, or withdraw any design without notice. ©Copyright Arden Architectural Specialties, Inc., 1993, Printed in USA. Manufactured under US patent #4,637,752. Other patents pending.

THE FINEST IN FLOOR ACCESS SYSTEMS   THE FINEST IN FLOOR ACCESS   SYST

IN ADDITION TO ACCESS COVERS, ARDEN OFFERS THE MOST COMPLETE LINE OF CUSTOM-MADE QUALITY ENTRANCE MATS AND GRATES. PLEASE CALL 1-800-521-1826 FOR INFORMATION

C379
06240/FOR
BuyLine 6388

FORMICA®

inviting

Laminate
Surfaces

from Formica Corporation

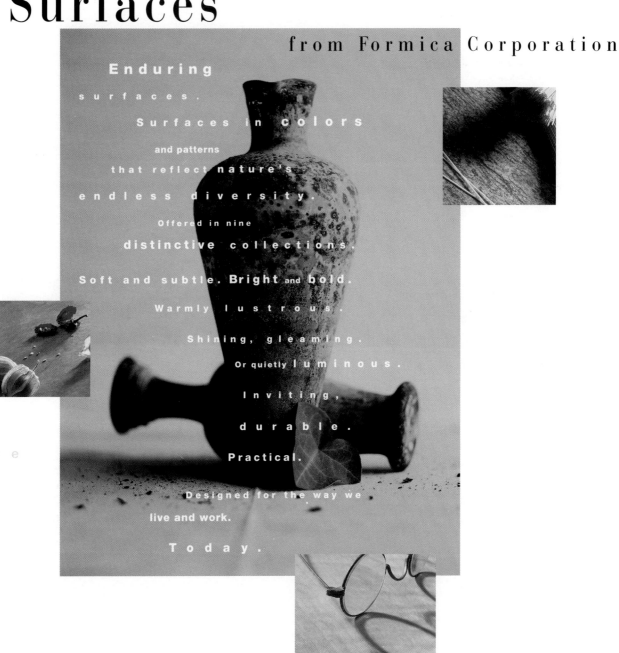

Enduring surfaces. Surfaces in **colors** and patterns that reflect nature's endless diversity. Offered in nine **distinctive collections**. Soft and subtle. **Bright** and bold. Warmly lustrous. Shining, gleaming. Or quietly **luminous**. Inviting, **durable**. Practical. Designed for the way we live and work. **Today**.

durable

practical

The Formica Corporation

offers its 1996 High Pressure Laminate

in nine collections,

living colors for the places

in which we live and work.

Choose from 375 colors,

High Pressure

patterns and textures in a durable,

Laminate

versatile and varied line.

All created by the world's

design leader in decorative surfacing.

The 1996 Laminate Collections

are available in a wide array

of thicknesses and sheet sizes

for commercial, institutional and

residential applications.

FORMICA® BRAND LAMINATE

For more than 80 years, Formica® brand laminate has served the places we live and work. As sparkling countertops and cabinet facings. As durable furniture and work surfaces in offices, hospitals and laboratories. And as inviting displays, counters and table tops in shops and restaurants. Created with melamine-impregnated decorative paper bonded to a phenolic treated kraft paper backing, Formica brand laminate offers a distinctive combination of economy, versatility and trend-leading design.

- Unparalleled choice of solids, patterns, woodgrains and pearlescents.
- Matte, polished and textured finishes.
- Postforming grades ranging from $\frac{3}{8}$" to $\frac{1}{2}$" minimum radius.
- Fire-rated, lab and flooring grades.
- NSF approved.

COLORCORE® SURFACING MATERIAL

Featuring the high-performance characteristics of standard laminate, ColorCore® surfacing material brings you the added dimension of solid-through color. Available in matte and polished finishes, ColorCore eliminates the familiar dark edge of standard laminate, creating a sense of mass versus surface.

- Unmatched color selection.
- Matte and polished finishes with matte appropriate for general purpose applications and polished for vertical and light-duty horizontal applictions.
- Concealed seams.

DECOMETAL™ COLLECTION AND SOLID METALS

DecoMetal™ Collection The crisp sheen of metal in 32 DecoMetal™ Collection items. Available in a wide variety of solids, natural patterns and geometrics. The DecoMetal Collection items are applied to a phenolic treated kraft paper backing to prevent creasing and to facilitate adhesion.

- Brushed, mirror, geometric and mottled finishes.
- Postformable from 4" to 10" minimum radius for metal laminate.

Solid Metals Choose from nine Solid Metals for gleaming accents in brushed and polished finishes.

- Postformable from to a $\frac{3}{32}$" minimum radius.

FORMICA® BRAND THICK STOCK LAMINATE

Formica® brand thick stock laminate, available in thicknesses up to one inch, delivers exceptional strength plus impact, humidity and water resistance. This material is available with or without laminate on one or both sides and can be cut, shaped and sanded with standard carbide tipped tools.

- Optional decorative laminate facings.
- Brown core standard: black core available.
- $\frac{1}{16}$" to 1" thicknesses.
- Impact, water and humidity-resistant.
- Standard Class 2(B) flame/smoke rating; Class 1(A) product available.

FORMICA® BRAND FIRE RATED LAMINATE

Formica® brand fire rated laminate meets Class 1(A) flame spread ratings and is available in a selection of solid colors, patterns and woodgrains. It is listed by Underwriters Laboratory Inc., and meets the following standards: U.S. Coast Guard, Subpart 164.012: MIL-P-17171 D (SH), MIL-STD-1623 D (SH). With two grades suitable for general purpose, non-postforming applications, this laminate is ideal for most military applications. For more information, including a complete Codes and Specifications list, see *Tech Data–Fire Rated Laminate* (Form No. 01-059) and *Data Sheet–Fire Rated Laminate/Ship Building* (Form No. 01-078).

GRADE SELECTION GUIDE

Consult this chart to determine the recommended grades for typical applications.

	Horizontal							Vertical								Metal Laminates and Solid Metals
	General Purpose					General Purpose Postform		General Purpose	General Purpose Postform		Cabinet Liner	Backing Sheet				
NEMA	GP50	HW62	HW62	FR50	GP50	PF42	PF42	FR32	PF30	PF42	CL20	BK30	BK50	BK20	BK50	
ISO	HGS	HCS	HCS	HGF	HGS	HGP	HGP	VGF	VGP	VGP	CLS	BLF	BGF	BLS	BGS	
Formica Brand Product /Grade	Grade 10	Grade 41	Grade 43	Grade 50	Grade 51	Grade 12	Grade 52	Grade 32	Grade 20	Grade 30/31	Grade 72	Grade 87	Grade 89	Grade 91	Grade 92	•
Nominal Thickness	.048"	.051"	.062"	.062"	.050"	.038"	.039"	.028"	.028"	.039"	.020"	.028"	.050"	.020"	.050"	
Commercial Work Surfaces: Teller Stations, Desks, Conference Tables, Nurses Stations, Restaurant Tables, Bar Tops	•	•		•	•	•	•							•	•	
Commercial Cabinetry and Furniture: Store Fixtures, Study Carrels, Dormitory Furniture, Library Equipment, Bookcases, Column Covers	•	•	•	•	•	•	•	•	•	•	•	•	•	•	•	•
Commercial Doors and Partitions: Interior Passage Doors, Toilet Compartments, Elevator Cabs, Moveable Partitions	•	•	•	•	•	•	•									
Residential Work Surfaces: Kitchen Countertops, Bar Tops, Vanity Tops, Windowsills	•	•		•	•	•	•									
Residential Cabinetry and Furniture: Kitchen Cabinets, Bookcases, Occasional Furniture, Tables, Case Goods	•	•	•		•	•	•		•	•	•			•	•	•
Laboratory Work Surfaces						• 840 only										

How to specify Formica Brand Laminate

PART I – GENERAL

Contractor shall supply and install high pressure laminate as shown on drawings and specified herein.

1.1 Product Delivery and Storage High pressure laminate to be stored with top face-down and a caul board on top to protect material from damage and from warping. Laminate to be protected from moisture and from contact with floors or outside walls.

1.2 Preconditioning Laminate and substrate to acclimate for at least 48 hours at same ambient condition. Optimum conditions being approximately 75° F and relative humidity of 45 to 55%. Air circulation to be provided around product.

PART II – PRODUCTS

2.2 High Pressure Laminates High pressure laminates should be Formica brand laminate from Formica Corporation, Cincinnati, Ohio.

PL-1 Color Number   PL-2 Color Number
Color Name   Color Name
Grade (Name/Number)   Grade (Name/Number)
Finish (Name/Number)   Finish (Name/Number

2.2 Adhesives (for standard and postforming grade laminates) Contact, semi-rigid (PVAc) or rigid (Urea Resorcinol) adhesives are recommended. Fabricator to follow adhesive manufacturer's recommendations.

2.3 Adhesives (ColorCore® surfacing material) Semi-rigid (PVAc) or non-pigmented contact adhesives are recommended. Fabricator to follow adhesive manufacturer's recommendations.

2.4 Substrates Laminate to be bonded to a suitable substrate such as medium-density fiber board (MDF) or a 45# density particle board (CS 236-66; Type 1, Grade B, Class 2). The following materials are not recommended for use: plywood, plaster, gypsum board, concrete.

2.5 Backing Sheets Backing sheets to be provided as necessary to balance assembly and prevent warping.

PL-1 Color Number   Grade (Name/Number)
Color Name

PART III – EXECUTION

3.1 Inspection All surfaces to be laminated are to be inspected to determine if they are sound, clean and free of surface defects. All defects found are to be corrected.

3.2 Preparation Surfaces to be sanded and prepared as required to provide a surface that is smooth, clean, free of oil or grease and uniform in thickness.

3.3 Installation

A. Material equipment and workmanship should conform to industry-standard practices, conditions, procedures and recommendations as specified by ANSI/NEMA LD3-1991 Section 4, Architectural Woodwork Quality Standards, National Association of Plastic Fabricators and ANSI 161.2-1979 standards.

B. Panel assemblies should be laminated with suitable backer sheets to minimize warping.

C. Maximum panel widths to be 24" for Grade 55 and 20.

D. All inside corners of cutouts to be radiused as large as possible (⅛" minimum). All edges and corners to be filed smooth, free of chips and nicks. Surface shall be Formica brand laminate, manufactured by Formica Corporation.

For detailed specification information, refer to *SweetsSource* CD-ROM.

Choose from the Complete Line of Formica Brand Decorative Surfacing

Beyond Formica Ligna™ wood surfacing material, choose from a complete line of versatile, durable surfacing materials including:

SURELL® SOLID SURFACING MATERIAL

The elegant look and feel of natural granites and marbles for virtually seamless surfaces. Available with a complete line of sheet stock, kitchen sinks, lavatory bowls, vanities, windowsills, shower bases, wall surrounds and complete shower kits. See Section 06650/FOS for more information.

FORMICA® BRAND HIGH PRESSURE LAMINATE

The Formica Corporation offers its 1996 High Pressure Laminate in nine collections, living colors for the places in which we live and work. Choose from 375 colors, patterns and textures in a durable, versatile and varied line. See Section 06240/FOR for more information.

NUVEL® SURFACING MATERIAL

Nuvel® surfacing material offers a distinctive new combination of remarkable flexibility, virtually seamless surfaces. Compatible with the Surell line of kitchen sinks, lavatory bowls, sheet stock and shower bases. See Section 06650/FOR for more information.

GRANULON® SPRAY-ON SURFACING MATERIAL

A spray-on particle-filled polyester coating that may be applied in variable thicknesses for surfaces with virtually invisible seams. Available in neutral solids and in neutral and jewel-toned granites, Granulon can be finished to a matte or polished surface.

For Complete Information

Complete information on all Formica® brand decorative surfaces, including *Surface Level 1996* – the complete laminate surfaces catalog – sample sets, fabrication guides, care and maintenances guides, warranty information and technical data, are available through Zip Chip, our sample and literature fulfillment hotline. Call, toll free, **1-800-FORMICA.** Or, contact your nearest Formica Corporation regional sales office.

Nuvel, Formica, the Formica Logo, Surell and Granulon are registered trademarks of Formica Corporation or its subsidiaries. Formica Ligna is a trademark of Formica Corporation or its subsidiaries.

REGIONAL OFFICES

CANADA

Formica Canada, Inc.
25 rue Mercier
St. Jean sur Richelieu
Quebec J3B 6E9
514-347-7541 phone
514-347-5065 fax

CENTRAL

Formica Corporation
10155 Reading Road
Cincinnati OH 45241
513-786-3525 phone
513-786-3566 fax

EASTERN

Formica Corporation
One Stanford Road
Piscataway NJ 08854
908-469-1559 phone
908-469-5917 fax

FLORIDA

Formica Corporation
2981 W. State Road 434
Suite 300
Longwood FL 32779
407-682-0331 phone
407-682-5560 fax

MEXICO

Formica de Mexico S.A. de C.V.
Viaducto Miguel Aleman No. 55
06780 **Mexico D.F.**
525-530-3135 phone
525-530-4248 fax

MIDWEST

Formica Corporation
1400 East Touhy Avenue
Suite 430
Des Plaines IL 60018
708-390-9500 phone
708-390-9507 fax

NORTHEAST

Formica Corporation
131 Stedman St. #1
Chelmsford MA 01824
508-458-4666 phone
508-458-2999 fax

NORTHWEST

Formica Corporation
3500 Cincinnati Avenue
Sunset Whitney Ranch CA 95765
916-645-0390 phone
916-645-1577 fax

PUERTO RICO

Formica Corporation
Calle B, Lote 6
Amelia Industrial Park
Guaynabo PR 00968
809-793-1230 phone
809-792-2925 fax

SOUTHERN

Formica Corporation
5525 Westfield Dr. SW
Atlanta GA 30336
404-349-9909 phone
404-349-2995 fax

SOUTHWEST

Formica Corporation
1245 Viceroy Drive
Dallas TX 75247
214-688-0671 phone
214-630-1228 fax

WESTERN

Formica Corporation
2601 Saturn, Suite 103
Brea CA 92621
714-993-0393 phone
714-993-0182 fax

Fountainhead by Nevamar®

C467
06600/NEV
BuyLine 7632

NEVAMAR®
DECORATIVE SURFACES

As tough as they are beautiful.

INTERNATIONAL Ⓐ PAPER
DECORATIVE PRODUCTS DIVISION
8339 TELEGRAPH ROAD
ODENTON MD 21113-1397

The solid surface alternative.

The first true alternative to Corian,® elegant Fountainhead by Nevamar® solid surfacing is a wise investment that can increase the value of your home now and at resale. Extremely durable and easy to care for, Fountainhead is available in a wide range of colors and patterns. Fountainhead sinks and bowls complete the look in bath or kitchen. A 10-year limited warranty is standard on all Fountainhead products.

Because it's non-porous, most spills can simply be wiped away from Fountainhead with a damp cloth or sponge. Stains from wine, vinegar, coffee, even grape juice can be removed, although some may require more aggressive cleaning with household bleach. *

When properly fabricated, Fountainhead's outstanding heat resistance makes it ideal for use around rangetops.

Fountainhead resists most household chemicals.

Fountainhead resists the impact of falling objects.

Fountainhead will not burn. Brown nicotine stains or scorch marks can be removed from the matte finish by using an abrasive cleanser or buffing with a wet Scotch Brite® pad.

Because the color runs throughout, scuffs, scratches and even accidental cuts can be easily repaired on the matte finish by buffing with a Scotch Brite pad or 320-350 grit sand-paper. If your countertop has a polished (gloss) appearance which requires more complicated finishing techniques, damage must be repaired by a professional. *

Fountainhead offers a wide selection of kitchen and bar/utility sinks and vanity bowls. These products provide all the beauty and performance of Fountainhead sheet goods. Fountainhead sinks and bowls have been tested and approved by IAPMO/UPC. They are also certified by the National Association of Home Builders Research Foundation, Inc. Color choices include a range of solid colors as well as Nevamar's exclusive Matrix pattern on vanity bowls and bar/utility sinks. An extra deep (9-1/2") kitchen sink is available to accommodate large pots and pans.

Mounting Options and Installation.

Fountainhead kitchen and bar/utility sinks offer three mounting options: Flush, Seamed, and Undermount. All three options are installed level with or below the counter surface, facilitating easy cleanup. Fountainhead vanity bowls can be seamed or undermounted.

The monolithic appearance of an integral bowl can be achieved by seaming sinks or bowls to sheet goods of the same color. Thanks to their unique design, all Fountainhead sinks and bowls can be positioned on the sheet anywhere the installation requires. Two or more bowls can even be installed in the same sheet. The special design also makes installation faster and easier than most other solid surface sinks and bowls to save time and money!

 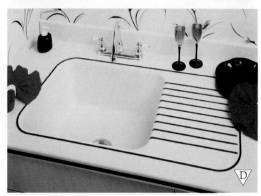

A. *Material Used: Parchment Fountainhead sink (K026 - Seam mount) in Parchment Fountainhead top with custom inlay*
B. *Material Used: Architectural White Fountainhead vanity bowl (B052 - Seam mount) in Aegean Mist Fountainhead top*
C. *Material Used: Medium Gray Matrix Fountainhead vanity bowl (B022 - Seam mount) in Architectural White Fountainhead top*
D. *Material Used: Classic White Fountainhead sink (K013- Seam mount) in Classic White Fountainhead top with Black Matrix accents and drainboard inlay*
E. *Material Used: Sand Beige Fountainhead bar/utility sink (B031- Flush mount) in Verde Matrix Fountainhead top*

Edges and Inlays for a customized look

Fountainhead can be fabricated to give your designs a truly personalized effect. Edges can be left at just the thickness of the Fountainhead sheet or built up to create a greater thickness and unique edge appearance. These edges represent just a few of the looks which can be achieved. Another way your designs can be given that custom look is with Fountainhead inlay kits. Using these, your Nevamar Accredited Fabricator can create inlaid designs ranging from simple geometrics to elegant works of art. Any color choice is possible!

Fountainhead has met the requirements for a Class I fire rating. It has been classified by Underwriters Laboratories (UL) as safe for use in all public and private spaces. Fountainhead sheets have met all requirements of and been certified by NSF International.

A: *Material Used:* Parchment combined with Fawn Mist.
B: *Material Used:* Mystic White Matrix with routed grooves
C: *Material Used:* Architectural White with quarter round Verde Matrix accent
D: *Material Used:* Custom Color inlay in Architectural White and White Matrix top
E: *Material Used:* Sand Beige Fountainhead shower wall with custom inlay

NEVAMAR®
DECORATIVE SURFACES

As tough as they are beautiful.

INTERNATIONAL Ⓐ PAPER
DECORATIVE PRODUCTS DIVISION
8339 TELEGRAPH ROAD
ODENTON MD 21113-1397

SPECIFYING CORIAN

CORIAN®
SURFACES
Created For Life.™

DUPONT

Corian®.
A world apart from other materials.

CORIAN is an advanced composite of natural minerals and pure acrylic polymer*, developed for one purpose: to create an ideal surface for living.

CORIAN is *the original solid surface material*. With a track record of more than 25 years, CORIAN has proven itself to be a remarkably durable, versatile material that's easy to live with in both residential and commercial environments.

Color and pattern run all the way through and cannot wear away. CORIAN cannot delaminate. Joints are seamless, unobtrusive, impermeable and hygienic.

CORIAN has a *rich, natural translucence*, like fine stone. Yet CORIAN is *warm and inviting to the touch*, like fine wood.

CORIAN offers *design versatility, function and durability far beyond the scope of conventional materials*. Yet CORIAN surfaces can be fabricated with conventional tools.

CORIAN. CREATED FOR LIFE.™

CORIAN gives architects and designers the freedom to create beautiful interior and exterior designs that stand up to the most demanding conditions.

CORIAN is created to stand up to the hard knocks life can dish out. As a result, CORIAN makes any environment easy to live with.

Easy to clean
Everyday stains clean up with just soapy water and cleanser.**

Resists stains
CORIAN resists stains because liquids can't penetrate. CORIAN has no pores, seams or voids like ceramic tile, granite or marble. It is unaffected by food stains and common disinfectants. Stubborn stains from cigarette burns, marking pens and hair dyes can be removed easily with abrasive cleanser and a scouring pad.**

Resists impacts
CORIAN resists fracture, chipping and cracking better than most marble, stone or polyester products. Minor cuts and scratches can be removed with fine sandpaper.**

* Methyl methacrylate
** For more information, refer to *DuPont CORIAN Care & Maintenance* (H-56461)

Resists heat
CORIAN resists heat better than many other surface materials. However, the use of a hot pad under hot cookware or electrical appliances is recommended.**

Class I flammability rating
All colors of CORIAN have Class I flammability ratings, making them suitable for any private, public, commercial or military application.

NSF compliance
The National Sanitation Foundation has accepted all colors of CORIAN for "food contact" applications under the *NSF Standard 51: Plastic Materials and Components Used In Food Equipment.* This approval means CORIAN can be used anywhere food is prepared or served, including areas where food will routinely come into contact with the surface of CORIAN. This makes CORIAN ideal for use in food service areas such as restaurants, healthcare and educational facilities, office buildings and public buildings.

Hygienic
Independent laboratory tests clearly show that nonporous CORIAN will not support the growth of fungi, mildew and bacteria such as staph or other germs.

Additional information on radioactive compounds and HIV (AIDS) cleanup is available through a series of bulletins issued by DuPont.

Renewable
CORIAN surfaces are completely *renewable*, usually with ordinary abrasive cleansers and a scouring pad**. Renewability and durability make CORIAN inherently environmentally friendly: In effect, CORIAN recycles itself as time goes by. Or, when needed, CORIAN can be recycled to create new materials.

Inert, nontoxic, chemically nonreactive, hypoallergenic
There is virtually no off-gassing from CORIAN at normal room temperatures. Even when exposed to direct flame, CORIAN is one of the least toxic materials available. No wonder CORIAN is the material of choice for such sensitive applications as museum archival storage and display cases, and for walls and work surfaces in hospital operating rooms and intensive care facilities.

Barrier-free design
The versatility of CORIAN lends itself to barrier-free design. Whether in ADA-compliant vanity tops, unobtrusive thresholds, or accessible shower pans, CORIAN allows design for any lifestyle need.

APPLICATIONS

The versatility of CORIAN is almost limitless in scope. So it is impossible to list every conceivable use for CORIAN. Some typical applications for Healthcare, Hospitality, Institutions, Public Spaces, Corporate Environments, Shopfitting, and Residential, Public & Military Housing are listed below:

- Countertops ▪ Vanity tops ▪ Lavatories ▪ Sinks ▪ Shower & bath surrounds ▪ Wall cladding ▪ Work surfaces ▪ Windowsills ▪ Wainscotting ▪ Signage ▪ Indoor & outdoor shop fronts ▪ Furniture ▪ Display cases ▪ Elevators ▪ Shelves ▪ Trash receptacles ▪ Bar tops ▪ Service areas

FABRICATION

CORIAN products can be fabricated in the shop or on-site, because CORIAN has working characteristics similar to those of fine hardwood. Unlike marble or granite, CORIAN can be thermoformed to any shape and easily cut or joined to create smooth, seamless surfaces of any size. CORIAN may be combined with wood, brass, tile, acrylics and other CORIAN colors to create a wide variety of unique designs and edge treatments. Surface effects, logos and graphics can be routed, sandblasted or laser-etched. And the translucent quality of CORIAN means it can be backlit for visual impact.

Wilsonart® Laminate

Manufacturer

Wilsonart International
2400 Wilson Place
P.O. Box 6110
Temple, Texas 76503-6110
Phone: (817) 778-2711
FAX: (817) 770-2384

For more information and delivery of samples,
just call: (800) 433-3222.

Short Specification Form

Type:	(specify 107, 335 or 350)	
Surface:	Color Number:	
	Color Name:	
Finish:	Number:	Name:
Edge Trim:	Color Number:	
	Color Name:	
Adhesive:	Name:	
	Grade/Type:	
	Brand: Lokweld®	

Care and Maintenance

1. To clean the surface, use a damp cloth or sponge and a mild soap or detergent.
2. Difficult stains such as coffee or tea can be removed using a mild household cleaner/detergent and a soft bristle brush, repeating as necessary.
3. If a stain persists, use a paste of baking soda and water and apply with a soft bristled brush. Light scrubbing for 10 to 20 strokes should remove most stains. Although baking soda is a low abrasive, excessive scrubbing or exerting too much force could damage the decorative surface, especially if it has a gloss finish.
4. Stubborn stains that resist any of the above cleaning methods may require the use of undiluted household bleach or nail polish remover. Apply the bleach or nail polish remover to the stain and let stand no longer than two minutes. Rinse thoroughly with warm water and wipe dry. This step may be repeated if the stain appears to be going away and the color of the laminate has not been affected. WARNING: Prolonged exposure of the laminate surface to bleach will cause discoloration.

Your area sales representative will provide free copies of the "Care and Maintenance Guide," which covers care and maintenance of most Wilsonart products, for your own information, for project manuals and for provision to clients and contractors involved with interior construction and finishing.

Limited Warranty

Wilsonart International warrants that, under normal use and service, the material and workmanship of its products shall conform to the standards set forth on the applicable technical data sheets for a period of twelve (12) months from the date of sale to the first consumer purchaser. Dealers and distributors are provided with the technical data sheets which contain specific standards of performance for the products. In the event that a Wilsonart International product does not perform as warranted, the first purchaser's sole remedy shall be limited to repair or replacement of all or any part of the product which is defective, at the manufacturer's sole discretion.

This warranty applies only to product:

1. In its original installation; and
2. Purchased by the first consumer purchaser.

This warranty is not transferable, and expires upon resale or transfer by the first consumer purchaser.

This warranty shall not apply to defects or damage arising from any of the following:

1. Accidents, abuse or misuse;
2. Exposure to extreme temperature;
3. Improper fabrication or installation; or
4. Improper maintenance.

No other warranties, expressed or implied, are made. Under no circumstances shall the manufacturer be liable for any loss or damage arising from the purchase, use or inability to use this product, or for any special, indirect, incidental or consequential damages. No fabricator, installer, dealer, agent or employee of Wilsonart International has the authority to modify the obligations or limitation of this warranty.
This warranty gives you specific legal rights, and you may also have other rights which vary from state to state; therefore, some of the limitations stated above may not apply to you. It is to your benefit to save your documentation upon purchase of a product.

Availability Summary

Sheet Widths:	30", 36", 48", 60"
	(762mm, 914mm,
	1219mm, 1524mm)
Sheet Lengths:	96", 120", 144"
	(2438mm, 3048mm, 3658mm)
Sheet Thicknesses:	
	General Purpose Type 107:
	0.048" ± 0.005"
	(1.219mm ± 0.127mm)
	Vertical Surface Type 335:
	0.028" ± 0.004"
	(0.711mm ± 0.101mm)
	Postforming Type 350:
	0.039" ± 0.005"
	(.990mm ± 0.127mm)

For information on product,
samples or literature,
call toll free (800) 433-3222.

Recommended Uses

Wilsonart® Laminate is suitable for use on fine quality residential and contract furniture and casework; and for architectural application on columns, wainscoting, valances, cornices, interior doors and divider systems.

General Purpose Type 107 is most frequently used for work surfaces on counters, islands, vanities, desks and tables. Typical vertical uses include surfacing for wall panels, teller cages and the front panels of work stations, such as those in hospitals, airports and restaurants.

Vertical Surface Type 335 is the usual choice to surface cabinet walls, doors and drawer panels. It often appears on the vertical surfaces of desks, restaurant booths and maitre d' stations, and as architectural cladding.

Postforming Type 350 adds the decorative capability of the soft edge to any typical laminate use. Formed edges for counters and desk tops and for cabinet doors and drawer panels are familiar applications of postforming laminates.

Basic Limitations

Wilsonart Laminate is for interior use only, and is not recommended for direct application to plaster or concrete walls or gypsum wallboard. This laminate is not a structural material, and must be bonded to a suitable substrate.

Do not subject these laminates to extremes in humidity, or to temperatures of over 275°F (135°C) for sustained periods of time, or to intense, continuous, direct sunlight.

Fabrication and Assembly

Wilsonart Laminate must be bonded to a substrate of reliable quality, such as particleboard, medium-density fiberboard, or plywood with one A face. Recommended substrate material is 45-lb. industrial-grade particleboard. High pressure laminate, plaster, concrete and gypsum board should not be considered suitable substrates. Basic Types laminate may not be used as structural members.

Bond with adhesives and follow the techniques recommended by the adhesive manufacturer.

Recommended adhesives are permanent types, such as urea and polyvinyl acetate (PVA); and contact types. Lokweld® Adhesives are recommended for most bonding conditions.

Take care to ensure an appropriate moisture balance between the laminate and the substrate prior to fabrication. The face and backing laminates and the substrate should be conditioned in the same environment for 48 hours before fabrication.

Recommended conditioning temperature is about 75°F (24°C). Laminates should be conditioned at about 45% relative humidity.

With postforming machinery, a sheet will form, throughout its thickness, at a nominal temperature of 325°F (163°C) in 20 ± 5 seconds.

Tools: Carbide-tipped saw and router blades should be used for cutting. High tool speed and low feed speed are advisable. Cutting blades should be kept very sharp, and use a hold-down to prevent any vibration.

Methods: Fabrication should follow approved methods. Assembled pieces should meet the specifications of DLPA (Decorative Laminate Products Association), ANSI A-161.2-1995, and "Architectural Woodwork Quality Standards, Guide Specifications and Quality Certification Program" guidelines of the Architectural Woodwork Institute where applicable.

To avoid stress cracking, do not use square-cut inside corners. All inside corners should have a minimum of 1/8" (3.175mm) radius and all edges should be routed smooth.

Drill holes for bolts or screws oversized. Screws or bolts should be slightly countersunk into the face side of a laminate-clad substrate.

Optional Finishes

Wilsonart Laminate may be specified in other optional designer finishes. Contact your local representative for availability.

#1 High Gloss. A mirror sheen finish which gives a smooth, brilliant appearance.

Glossometer reading: MD and CD 90 minimum.

#7 Textured Gloss. A textured finish which reproduces the high sheen of waxed wood furniture.

Glossometer reading: MD and CD 36 ± 3.

#41 Gloss Diagonal. Semigloss diagonal finish.

Glossometer reading: MD and CD 75 ± 5.

#50 Touchstone. A pebbled texture with the look and feel of coarse-grained sand.

Glossometer reading: MD and CD 10 ± 2.

#60 Matte. A textured finish with a moderate reflective quality.

Glossometer reading: MD and CD 10 ± 1.

#81 Cathedral Grain. An embossed finish that offers the look and feel of true flatcut wood.

Glossometer reading: MD and CD 25 ± 6.

#90 Crystal. A very finely beaded texture which minimizes smudges and finger marks and improves scratch resistance.

Glossometer reading: MD and CD 13 ± 3.

NOTE: Glossometer readings made at 60° angle of incidence. MD means the machine direction of a laminate sheet, and CD refers to the cross direction.

For information on product, samples or literature, call toll free (800) 433-3222.

Wilsonart® Solid Surfacing Veneer
Wilsonart® Gibraltar® Solid Surfacing

Care And Maintenance

1. Wilsonart Gibraltar Solid Surfacing and Solid Surfacing Veneer offer exceptional beauty and durability. Routine care is as simple as wiping the surface with a damp cloth.

2. Most stains will wash away with soap and water. For tougher stains (on a matte finish*), apply an abrasive cleanser and buff with a Scotch-Brite® pad using a circular motion.

3. Minor burns (on a matte finish*) may also be removed using an abrasive cleanser and buffing the surface with a Scotch-Brite pad.

4. Hot pans and heat-producing appliances should be placed on heat shields or hot pads.

* If you have a high-gloss finish, contact your dealer or fabricator before attempting repairs.

Recommended Uses

Wilsonart Solid Surfacing Veneer and Gibraltar Solid Surfacing panels are recommended for interior and exterior decorative and functional applications where a prestigious appearance, high stain resistance, ease of maintenance and extensive customizing capabilities are beneficial.

Wilsonart Solid Surfacing Veneer is also fire-rated to a code compliance Class II per ASTM-E-84.

Gibraltar Solid Surfacing panels are Class 1 (A) fire-rated, which further enhances their usefulness in high-end contract, commercial and institutional applications.

Appropriate horizontal applications include tops for counters, tables, vanities, bars and laboratory work surfaces.

These materials may also be used to create windowsills and store fixtures, as well as fine custom furniture.

Typical vertical applications include paneling for walls, elevators, counter facades; partitions for toilets and dressing rooms; and interior signage.

Because of their chemical makeup, panels are appropriate for many hospital surfaces. Gibraltar Solid Surfacing panels may be bonded to each other with watertight seals.

Watertight seals can be created with Wilsonart Solid Surfacing Veneer by using Lokweld® 8215 Adhesive (see corresponding tech data).

Basic Limitations

Gibraltar Solid Surfacing sheet goods are designed for interior and exterior use. When specifying Gibraltar Solid Surfacing for exterior applications, the design, fabrication and installation procedures must consider extreme concurrent temperature contrasts which could result in seam failure. Gibraltar Solid Surfacing is not recommended for building facade and facia applications.

Wilsonart Solid Surfacing Veneer is designed for interior use. It should be bonded to particleboard, medium-density fiberboard or plywood (please refer to Fabrication Manual for details regarding substrate selection).

Gibraltar Solid Surfacing panels do not require bonding to substrates, and should not be bonded to solid wood, plaster, concrete, gypsum wallboard or other brands of solid surfacing. They do, however, require a supporting material or framework.

Wilsonart® Solid Surfacing Veneer

Availability Summary

Panel Widths:	30", 36"*	(762mm, 914mm)
Panel Lengths:	96", 144"	(2438mm, 3658mm)
Thickness:	Product Type 013	0.115" ± 0.010"

*Available in limited colors

Wilsonart® Gibraltar® Solid Surfacing

Short Specification Form

Type:	See specific types under Product Description/Product Definition
Surface:	Color/Design Number:
	Color/Design Name:
Finish:	(specify desired texture of completed application)
Sink Type:	Color/Design Name/Model Number:
Decorative Functional Treatments:	
Adhesive:	Gibraltar Seam Kit Adhesive, color-matched to panels to be seamed.
	Color/Design Number:
	Color/Design Name:
Caulk/Sealant:	Gibraltar Color-Matched Silicone Sealant
	Color/Design Number:
	Color/Design Name:
	Fastening System:
Certification:	Surface shall be UL rated, Class 1 (A)

Availability Summary

Panel Widths:	30", 36"	(762mm, 914mm)
Panel Lengths:	96", 144"	(2438mm, 3658mm)
Thickness:	Product Types 050, 051	1/2" (13mm) Nominal
Strips:	Width - 1 3/4", 5 3/4"	(44mm, 146mm)
	Length - 144"	(3658mm)

Shaped Goods:	
(inside dimensions only)	
BK128-Round Sink	16 1/4" x 16 1/4" x 7 3/4"
BK222-Square Sink	16 3/4" x 16 3/4" x 7 3/4"
BK323-Rectangle Sink	10 1/4" x 16 3/4" x 8"
BK324-Rectangle Sink	21 1/4" x 15 3/4" x 7 1/2"
BK325-Bar Sink	8 3/4" x 11 3/4" x 5 1/2"
BK327-Disposal Sink	8" x 15 1/2" x 5 1/2"
BK426-D Bowl	20 3/4" x 16 1/2" x 7 1/2"
BV111, BV121-Vanity Bowl (BV111 is a drop-in)	12 3/4" x 15 3/4" x 6"
BV122-Vanity Bowl (ADA)	12 3/4" x 15 3/4" x 4"
BV123-Vanity Bowl	13 1/2" x 16 1/4" x 5 1/2"
BD321-Offset Double Sink	29 1/2" x 17 1/2" x 8"
BD322-Double Sink	30" x 18" x 8"
BD323-Double Sink	34" x 19" x 8 1/2"

Wilsonart® Gibraltar® Solid Surfacing

Warranty Information

Wilsonart International warrants to the consumer in the U.S. and Canada that Gibraltar Solid Surfacing, when installed by a recognized Gibraltar Solid Surfacing fabricator in the Gibraltar Fabricators Guild program, shall be free from defects in material, workmanship, fabrication and installation under normal use and service, for a period of ten years from date of sale to the consumer.

This warranty shall not apply to damage arising from any of the following:

1. Accidents, abuse or misuse;
2. Exposure to extreme heat;
3. Improper maintenance; or
4. Alteration or repair by anyone other than a recognized Gibraltar Solid Surfacing fabricator.

This warranty applies only to installations in which the Gibraltar Solid Surfacing product is affixed to the location (e.g. kitchen and bath countertops, vanity tops). This warranty extends to the original purchaser and may be transferred to the new purchaser of the location, provided the new purchaser submits a warranty registration card and provides proof of purchase. A warranty registration card can be obtained by notifying the manufacturer at the address listed below. The transferred warranty shall apply only for the remainder of the original ten year period.

No other warranties, expressed or implied, are made, including merchantability or fitness for a particular purpose. Under no circumstances shall Wilsonart International be liable for any loss or damage arising from the purchase, use or inability to use this product, or for any special, indirect or consequential damages.

To make a claim under this warranty, the consumer must contact Wilsonart International at the following address: 2400 Wilson Place, P.O. Box 6110, Temple, Texas 76503-6110.

This warranty gives you specific legal rights, and you may also have other rights which may vary from state to state. Some states do not allow the exclusion of implied warranties or of incidental or consequential damages, so the above limitation or exclusion may not apply to you. Return of owner registration card is not a condition precedent to warranty coverage. No fabricator, installer, dealer, agent or employee of Wilsonart International has the authority to increase or alter the obligation or limitation of this warranty.

Wilsonart® Solid Surfacing Veneer

Warranty Information

Wilsonart International warrants that, under normal use and service, Wilsonart Solid Surfacing Veneer products, for a period of one (1) year from the date of sale to the original consumer purchaser, shall be free of defect. In the event that the product does not perform as warranted, the first consumer's sole remedy shall be limited to repair or replacement of all or any part of the product which is defective, at the manufacturer's sole discretion.

This warranty applies only to product:

1. In its original installation; and
2. Purchased by the first consumer purchaser.

This warranty shall not apply to defects or damages arising from any of the following:

1. Accidents, abuse or misuse;
2. Exposure to extreme temperature;
3. Improper fabrication or installation; or
4. Improper maintenance.

No other warranties, expressed or implied, are made, including merchantability or fitness for a particular purpose. Under no circumstances shall the manufacturer be liable for any loss or damage arising from the purchase, use or inability to use this product, or for any special, indirect, incidental or consequential damages. No fabricator, installer, dealer, agent or employee of Wilsonart International has the authority to modify the obligations or limitations of this warranty.

This warranty gives you specific legal rights, and you may also have other rights which may vary from state to state; therefore, some of the limitations stated above may not apply to you. It is to your benefit to save your documentation upon purchase of a product.

To receive a warranty registration form, call toll free (800) 433-3222.

Corporate Headquarters
2400 Wilson Place
P.O. Box 6110
Temple, TX 76503-6110
Toll Free: (800) 433-3222
Mon.-Fri. 7:00 am-7:00 pm CST
Phone: (817) 778-2711
Fax: (817) 770-2384 (24 hours)

THE SMART SOURCE

C484
11452/BRO
BuyLine 8612

$3 00
1996

BROAN®
Range
Hoods

Introducing Finesse.™
Performance dramatically
styled for today's
kitchens.

Finesse
By **BROAN**

Finesse is an innovative vision of what range hoods are meant to be. Graceful, contoured lines beautifully complement today's popular new range and cooktop designs. Yet its form follows function.

■ Powerful, quiet dual centrifugal blower — 250 CFM (81000 Series) and 400 CFM (83000 Series) models available.

■ Select horizontal or vertical exhausting.

■ Convertible to vent-free operation with exclusive Microtek® System filters that are 25 times more effective than vent-free filters of other manufacturers (available separately).

■ Smoked, tempered-glass visor elegantly accentuates the clean, sweeping lines of this range hood, while improving overall performance.

■ Infinite-speed touch controls are color-matched to the hood and form-fitted for a clean, stylish appearance.

■ Indicator light lets you know the blower is on.

■ Dual 75-watt lights provide 150-watts of illumination (bulbs not included); dual prismatic lenses help eliminate harsh glare.

■ Fully enclosed underside is easy to keep clean.

■ Dishwasher-safe filters run the full width of the range hood; filters lift out easily with no tools necessary.

■ Duct connector with built-in damper included (vented models only).

■ Available in 30" and 36" widths.

■ Choose white, almond, black or stainless steel finish.

When your customers step beyond simple "remodeling" to dream kitchens with facilities for serious cooking... Rangemaster® by Broan.

High-performance, restaurant ranges are one of the hottest trends in kitchen remodeling today. When your customers select one of these commercial-look, high B.T.U. units, show them the range hood designed for these ranges: Rangemaster.

Top line features in all Rangemaster hoods include:

- Heavy-gauge, double-wall steel construction for years of service.

- Easy-to-clean stainless steel interior with no sharp edges.

- Two, 15" fluorescent tubes for two-level, cooktop lighting (bulbs not included).

- Two, 250-watt infrared food warming lamps "hold" one dish while you finish preparing others (bulbs not included).

- Extra large, easily removable, dishwasher-safe grease filters.

- Exclusive Heat Sentry™ automatically turns blower to high speed when excess heat is detected.

- Infinite, solid-state speed control with blower memory "remembers" last setting selected.

Custom options fit Rangemaster to any range; any kitchen.

- Select eight sizes (widths) from space-saving 30" to spacious 72".

- Select HVI-certified 600 CFM or 1200 CFM interior blowers, or 600 CFM or 900 CFM exterior blowers for maximum ventilation performance. See page 14 for blower choices.

- Restaurant quality stainless steel backsplash with fold-down food warming shelves provides the ultimate in "commercial" looks and ease of cleaning.

- Matching soffit chimneys for kitchens with higher "cathedral" ceilings; vertical ducting only, two soffit maximum.
- Select horizontal or vertical exhausting.

- Select stainless steel, white, almond or black.

Optional backsplash with condiment shelves that fold down for food warming.

When customers demand a hood with a disappearing act ... show them our Eclipse® or Silhouette® Series.

Eclipse downdraft ventilator.

Silhouette slide-out range hood.

Eclipse downdraft system for island and peninsula cooking where updraft venting is impractical.

Features of all Eclipse ventilators:

- Sleek, trim line styling complements any cooktop style or color.

- Compatible with virtually all cooktops.

- Discreet, integral, easy-to-reach blower control.

- Blower discharges to right, left or down and side-to-side to avoid floor joists.

- Space-saving design saves valuable under-counter cabinet space.

- Access panel allows easy cleaning.

Eclipse options to suit any kitchen layout:

- Select 30" or 36" wide models (fits all standard kitchen cabinets).

- Powerful, quiet 500 CFM internal or 900 CFM external blower.

- Stainless steel cover standard. White or black optional.

Silhouette hoods fit under kitchen cabinets, and slide out of sight when not in use.

Features found in all Silhouette Series range hoods:

- Powerful performance – HVI- certified 300 CFM. For vented installations only.

- Ultra-quiet performance – HVI-certified 4.5 Sones.

- Compact, trim line styling maximizes kitchen cabinet space.

- Dramatic glass visor slides out to turn on blower; slides in to turn off.

- 24" fluorescent light with prismatic glass lens provides bright cooktop lighting (bulb not included).

- Easy to reach, "up-front" infinite blower control.

- Exclusive Heat Sentry automatically turns blower to high speed when excess heat is detected.

- Dual connector with built-in damper.

Options available in Silhouette Series:

- 30" or 36" width hoods (fits all standard kitchen cabinets).

- Available in white or black. Fits any contemporary kitchen decor.

ee page 14 for all performance specifications and installation requirements.

90000 Series deluxe hood.

Industry-leading, exclusive features make Broan Deluxe Range Hoods the obvious choice for your preferred customers.

Heat Sentry™, Auto Temp, Blower Memory, Microtek® System filters…they're the features that define deluxe range hoods today and only Broan has them.

Broan 90000 Series. Take control of every cooking task with the most technologically advanced conventional range hood in North America.

Deluxe features in all 90000 Series range hoods:

■ Powerful, quiet 360 CFM / 5.5 Sone (vertical discharge) or 350 CFM / 6.0 Sone (horizontal discharge) performance (HVI certified).

■ Also available vent-free with exclusive Microtek System filter that's 65 times more effective than vent-free filters of other manufacturers (available separately).

■ Popular 30", 36" and 42" widths.

■ Advanced function electronic touchpad controls, flush-mounted for easy cleaning.

■ LED indicators signal all operating functions whenever hood is operating.

■ Exclusive Heat Sentry automatically turns blower to high speed when excess heat is detected.

■ Auto Temp continuously monitors cooking conditions; automatically adjusting blower to appropriate ventilation levels.

■ High Heat Signal sounds alarm whenever overheating occurs on cooktop (Heat Sentry and High Heat Signal activate at all times; even when blower is off).

■ Two 75-watt bulbs offer three light settings, including "night light" (bulbs not included).
■ Test function enables monitoring of all features.

■ Broan's dual blower system is the quietest, high-performance system available in a conventional range hood.

■ Choose white-on-white, white, almond, black or stainless steel finish.

88000 Series deluxe hood.

89000 Series deluxe hood.

Broan 88000 Series. A top-performing, great-looking hood that would be the top of anyone else's line.

These features are found in all Broan 88000 Series range hoods:

- Powerful, quiet 360 CFM/5.5 Sone (vertical discharge) or 350 CFM/6.0 Sone (horizontal discharge) performance (HVI certified).

- Convertible to vent-free operation with exclusive Microtek® System filter that's 65 times more effective than vent-free filters of other manufacturers (available separately).

- Popular 30", 36" and 42" widths.

- Convenient, contemporary slide controls.

- Exclusive Blower Memory automatically returns to last setting selected.

- Exclusive Heat Sentry automatically turns blower to high speed when excess heat is detected.

- Two 75-watt bulbs offer bright cooktop lighting and night-light settings (bulbs not included).
- Infinite blower controls.

- Choose white-on-white, white, almond, black or stainless steel finish.

Broan 89000 Series. Perfect for high-performance cooktops or indoor gas or electric grilles.

Same great feature complement as Broan 88000 Series, plus:

- Super-performing 460 CFM/6.0 Sone (vertical discharge) or 440 CFM/7.0 Sone (horizontal discharge) dual centrifugal blowers (HVI certified).

- Available in 30", 36", 42" and 48" widths (and additional special order sizes).

- Choose white, almond, black, or stainless steel finish (additional special order colors available).

See page 14 for all performance specifications and installation requirements.

76000 Series intermediate hood.

Broan offers more intermediate hoods than anyone because step-up sales come in all shapes, sizes and colors.

Broan 76000 Series. More performance, quality and value than any hood in its class.

All these great features are found in every 76000 Series hood:

- Powerful, quiet 200 CFM/5.5 Sone (vertical discharge) or 200 CFM/6.0 Sone (horizontal discharge) performance (HVI certified).

- Convertible to vent-free operation with exclusive Microtek® System filter that's 25 times more effective than vent-free filters of other manufacturers.

- 11-5/8" by 6-5/8" dishwasher safe aluminum grease filters (vented models).

- Popular 24", 30", 36" and 42" widths.

- Infinite rotary blower speed control.

- 75-watt cooktop lighting with polymeric lens.

- Duct connector with built-in damper.

- Choose white-on-white, white, almond, black or stainless steel finish.

75000 Series intermediate hood.

68000 Series intermediate hood.

48000 Series intermediate hood.

Broan 75000 Series. Same great features as 76000 Series with more powerful blowers.

■ Powerful, quiet 250 CFM/6.5 Sone (vertical discharge) or 250 CFM/6.0 Sone (horizontal discharge) performance (HVI certified).

■ Popular 30", 36" and 42" widths.

■ Choose white-on-white, white, almond, black or stainless steel finish.

Broan 68000 and 67000 Series. Simple, understated elegance in range hood design.

Features common to 68000 (7" round vented) and 67000 (vent-free) Series range hoods:

■ 230 CFM/7.0 Sone (vertical discharge) performance (68000 only) (HVI certified).

■ Simple, elegant, easy-to-clean black or white "glass look" styling.

■ Popular 30", 36" and 42" widths.

■ Two-speed control inside hood presents clean, uncluttered front.

■ 75-watt cooktop lighting with lens (bulb not included).

■ Dishwasher safe aluminum grease filter and damper (68000 only).

■ Combination vent-free filter (67000 only).

■ Choose monochromatic white or black finish.

Broan 48000 and 47000 Series. Straight side styling offers that subtle difference preferred by many consumers.

Features common to 48000 (7" round vented) and 47000 (vent-free) Series range hoods:

■ 230 CFM/7.0 Sone (vertical discharge) performance (HVI certified).

■ Popular 30", 36" and 42" widths.

■ 75-watt cooktop lighting with lens (bulb not included).

■ Dishwasher safe aluminum grease filter and damper (48000 only).

■ Combination vent-free filter (47000 only).

■ Choose white, almond or stainless steel finish.

See pages 14 and 15 for all performance specifications and installation requirements.

46000 Series with optional, matching backsplash.

Simple. Dependable. Affordable. No wonder Broan economy range hoods lead the category.

Broan 46000 Series. When performance, profits and value are critical, you can rely on this great, step-up economy model.

Standard features of 46000 Series include:

■ 180 CFM/7.0 Sone (vertical discharge) and 180 CFM/6.5 (horizontal discharge) performance (HVI certified).

■ Convertible to vent-free operation with exclusive Microtek® System filter that's 10 times more effective than vent-free filters of other manufacturers.

■ Microtek System filter included.

■ Popular 30", 36" and 42" widths.

■ Infinite rotary fan speed control.

■ 75-watt cooktop lighting with polymeric lens (bulb not included).

■ Duct connector with built-in damper included (vented models).

■ Choose white, almond or stainless steel finish.

41000 Series economy hood with optional, matching backsplash.

40000/42000 Series economy hood with optional, matching backsplash.

Broan 42000, 41000 and 40000 Series. The industry's best-featured economy hoods.

Standard features of 42000, (7" round vented) 41000 (vent-free) and 40000 (vented) Series range hoods:

■ 190 CFM/5.5 Sone (vertical discharge) performance (42000 Series) (HVI certified).

■ 160 CFM/5.5 Sone (vertical discharge) or 160 CFM/6.5 Sone (horizontal discharge) performance (40000 Series) (HVI certified).

■ 10-1/2" diameter dishwasher safe aluminum grease filter (42000 Series).

■ Requires Broan #87 damper (available separately) (42000 Series).

■ Microtek® System filter included that's 9 times more effective than vent-free filters of other manufacturers (41000 Series).

■ 75-watt cooktop lighting with polymeric lens (bulb not included).

■ Duct connector with built-in damper included (40000 Series).

■ 10-1/2" by 8-3/4" dishwasher safe aluminum grease filter (40000 Series).

■ Popular 24", 30" and 36" widths (41000 and 40000 Series); 30" and 36" widths (42000 Series).

■ Choose white, almond or stainless steel finish.

See page 15 for all performance specifications and installation requirements.

For customers who want a custom look in kitchen ventilation, look to Broan.

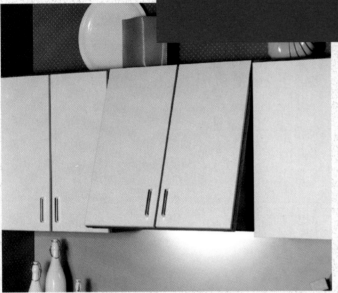

Hideaway Hood (inside cabinets)-Model 113023.

Hideaway...great ventilation performance. Great flush look.

■ Expandable 24"-30" height accommodates 30" face frame with cabinet doors.

■ Powerful, quiet 360 CFM/4.5 Sone (vertical or horizontal discharge) performance (HVI certified).

■ Blower and light automatically turn on when hood is pulled out.

■ Exclusive Heat Sentry™ automatically turns blower to high speed when excess heat is detected.

■ Bright cooktop lighting (bulb not included).

■ For vented installations only; not available vent-free.

■ Requires rough-in kit Model 113123.

Wood Hood Kit-Model 103023.

Wood Hood...high-performance ventilation in a rich, traditional look.

■ Fits into wood hoods from 28-1/4" to 28-7/8" wide (and adapts to hoods up to 42" in width).

■ Powerful, quiet 360 CFM/5.0 Sone (vertical discharge) or 360 CFM/4.5 Sone (horizontal discharge) performance (HVI certified).

■ Exclusive Heat Sentry automatically turns blower to high speed when excess heat is detected.

■ 24" fluorescent tube lighting (bulb not included).

■ Duct connector with built-in damper for 3-1/4" by 10" vents.

■ For vented installations only; not available vent-free.

■ Requires rough-in kit Model 103123.

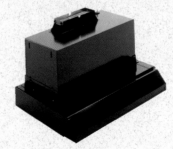

See page 15 for all performance specifications and installation requirements.

Micromate™. A powerful range hood. A place for your microwave. In one unit.

- Accommodates virtually any brand microwave oven.

- Installs vented or vent-free (Microtek® filter sold separately).

- Powerful, quiet 300 CFM/4.5 Sone (vertical discharge) performance (HVI certified).

- Bright cooktop lighting (bulb not included).

Micromate-120000 Series.

Canopy Hood. A warm, traditional, "heart-of-the-home" look.

- 190 CFM/6.0 (vertical discharge) or 200 CFM/6.5 Sone (horizontal discharge) performance (HVI certified).

- Convertible to vent-free operation with exclusive Microtek System filter that's 10 times more effective than vent-free filters of other manufacturers (available separately).

- Cooktop lighting with your choice of 100-watt bulb or 150-watt flood lamp (lamps sold separately).

- Textured, hammered finish in white, almond, harvest, avocado and coffee.

11000 Series Wall Canopy Hood.

See page 15 for all performance specifications and installation requirements.

Range Hood Accessories and Blower Systems

Accessories

Model #	Description
634	Roof cap with backdraft damper and safety screen, 3-1/4" x 10" or up to 8" round duct
644	Aluminum roof cap with backdraft damper and safety screen, 3-1/4" x 10" or up to 8" round duct
639	Wall cap 3-1/4" x 10" duct with backdraft damper with safety screen
641	Aluminum wall cap with backdraft damper with safety screen fits 6" round duct
643	Aluminum wall cap fits 8" round duct
647	Aluminum wall cap fits 7" round duct
649	Aluminum wall cap fits 3-1/4" x 10" duct with backdraft damper with safety screen
87	7" vertical discharge damper
97	7" spring-loaded, in-line damper
99	9" spring-loaded, in-line damper
401	3-1/4" x 10" duct, 2' section
406	6" round duct, 2' section
407	7" round duct, 2' section
410	10" round duct, 2' section
411	3-1/4" x 10" to 6" round transition
412	3-1/4" x 10" to 7" round transition
413	3-1/4" x 10" to 8" round transition
414	8" to 10" expander
415	7" adjustable elbow (carton of four)
418	10" adjustable elbow (individual)
419	6" adjustable elbow (individual)
421	10" round section with in-line damper
423	Vertical transition, 4-1/2" x 18-1/2" to 10" round
424	Rear transition, 4-1/2" x 18-1/2" to 10" round
425	Horz. left transition, 4-1/2" x 18-1/2" to 10" round
426	Horz. right transition, 4-1/2" x 18-1/2" to 10" round
453	Right end boot
454	Left end boot
428	3-1/4" x 10" vertical elbow
429	3-1/4" x 10" horizontal elbow
430	Short eave elbow for 3-1/4" x 10" duct with backdraft damper and grille
431	Long eave elbow for 3-1/4" x 10" duct with backdraft damper and grille
437	High capacity roof cap – up to 1200 CFM exhaust
441	Wall cap with gravity damper, 13-1/8" sq. fits 10" round duct
35	Wall hanging kit (for mounting hoods to wall when not hung from overhead cabinets)

Broan 331 (600 CFM) and 332 (900 CFM) exterior blowers.

Broan's new 600 CFM and 900 CFM exterior blowers offer your customers powerful ventilation performance with all the benefits of exterior mounting (roof or wall), and one benefit they won't find anywhere else... Broan quality.

- Reduce kitchen noise by locating range hood blowers on roof or outside walls.

- Select either Model 331 or the 332 exterior blower with 332K rough-in kit for Rangemaster® depending on cooking style and ventilation needs; the 332 is recommended for the Eclipse® downdraft.

- New, low-profile design fits unobtrusively with all home exterior styles.

- Durable, weather-resistant all aluminum construction.

- Safety screen keeps small animals and debris away from blower and motor.

Broan splash plates.

Stock and display splash plates for add-on sales:

- Durable 19-gauge enamel finish (appliance colors) or 24-gauge stainless steel.

- Select white, almond, black, stainless steel, avocado, coffee or harvest wheat.

- Available in 24", 30", 36" or 42" widths; all 24" high.

- Simplifies kitchen clean-up.

- Easily installed with four screws.

- See Broan price list for colors, models and prepacked display/dispenser.

RANGEMASTER®...see page 4

Width	Stainless Steel	White	Black	Almond
30"	603004	603001	603023	603008
36"	603604	603601	603623	603608
42"	604204	604201	604223	604208
48"	604804	604801	604823	604808
54"	605404	+	+	+
60"	606004	+	+	+
66"	606604	+	+	+
72"	607204	+	+	+

Options Selection Table

	Backsplash	Soffit Chimney			
Width	Stainless Steel	Stainless Steel	White	Black	Almond
30"	RP3004	RN3004	RN3001	RN3023	RN3008
36"	RP3604	RN3604	RN3601	RN3623	RN3608
42"	RP4204	RN4204	RN4201	RN4223	RN4208
48"	RP4804	RN4804	RN4801	RN4823	RN4808
54"	RP5404	RN5404	+	+	+
60"	RP6004	RN6004	+	+	+
66"	RP6604	RN6604	+	+	+
72"	RP7204	RN7204	+	+	+

+ Available as special order

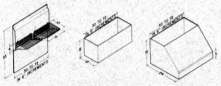

Blower Selection Table and Specifications

Model	Mounting	CFM	Volts	Hz	Amps*	Vent Size
325	Interior	600	120	60	7.6	7" Round
326	Interior	1200	120	60	8.1	4-1/2" x 18-1/2" **
331	Exterior	600	120	60	2.3	10" Round
332++	Exterior	900	120	60	5.8	10" Round

++ Model 332K rough-in kit required for mounting.
   Model no. 421 10' in-line damper recommended.
 * Includes 4.5 Amps representing all lights.
 ** Transitions to 10" round available. (see accessory section on page 13)

Replacement bulbs:
Fluorescent: F14T12/SW (Soft White) Any F14T8 or F14T12 15" long preheat fluorescent lamp will fit.
Heat Lamps: 250-Watt, R40 Infrared (Bulbs and lamps not included).

ECLIPSE®...see page 5

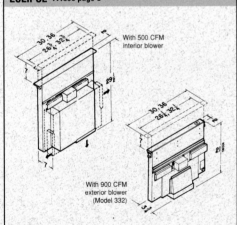

With 500 CFM interior blower

With 900 CFM exterior blower (Model 332)

To Fit Nominal Cooktop Size	Model	Description	Cover Color
30"	273003	Interior Blower Unit	Stainless Steel
36"	273603	Interior Blower Unit	Stainless Steel
30"	283003	Exterior Blower Unit*	Stainless Steel
36"	283603	Exterior Blower Unit*	Stainless Steel
30"	273001C	Optional Cover	White
36"	273601C	Optional Cover	White
30"	273023C	Optional Cover	Black
36"	273623C	Optional Cover	Black

* Exterior unit utilizes Model 332 Exterior-Mounted Blower, available separately.

Specifications**

Model	Volts	Amps	CFM	Vent
27000	120	4.0	500	3-1/4" x 10"
28000	120	4.0	900	3-1/4" x 10"

** Cooktops, countertops and cabinets vary in dimension and support systems depending upon manufacturer. These factors may impact the Eclipse's ability to fit with every worktop/cabinet combination. Specifications subject to change without notice.

SILHOUETTE®...see page 5

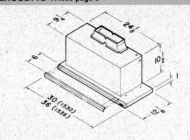

Width	White	Black
30"	153001	153023
36"	153601	153623

Allow 18 inches minimum from cooking surface to bottom of hood.

Specifications

Volts	Amps	Sones	CFM	Vent
120	3.7	4.5	300	3-1/4" x 10" (vertical)

Fluorescent Tube - 24", F20T12 (not included).

EXTERIOR BLOWERS...see page 13

For use with Rangemaster and Eclipse models.

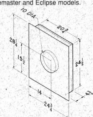

Specifications

Model	Volts	Amps	CFM	Vent
331	120	2.3	600	10" round
332	120	5.8	900	10" round

90000 SERIES...see page 6

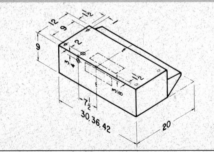

Width	White	Almond	White on White	Black	Stainless
30"	903001	903008	903011	903023	903004
36"	903601	903608	903611	903623	903604
42"	904201	904208	904211	904223	904204

Order Microtek® System IV filter 97007662 for vent-free operation.

Specifications

Volts	Amps	Sones		CFM		Vent-Free RHP Index	Vent
		Ver.	Hor.	Ver.	Hor.		
120	4.5	5.5	6.0	360	350	59.09	3-1/4" x 10"

89000 SERIES...see page 7

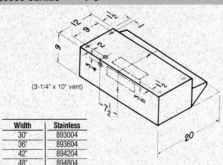

(3-1/4" x 10" vent)

Width	Stainless
30"	893004
36"	893604
42"	894204
48"	894804

Specifications

Volts	Amps	Sones		CFM		Vent
		Ver.	Hor.	Ver.	Hor.	
120	6.0	6.0	7.0	460	440	3-1/4" x 10"

88000 SERIES...see page 7

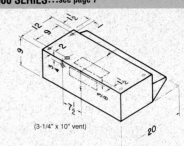

(3-1/4" x 10" vent)

Width	White	Almond	White on White	Black	Stainless
30"	883001	883008	883011	883023	883004
36"	883601	883608	883611	883623	883604
42"	884201	884208	884211	884223	884204

Also available in Harvest, Avocado and Coffee.

Specifications

Volts	Amps	Sones		CFM		Vent-Free RHP Index	Vent
		Ver.	Hor.	Ver.	Hor.		
120	4.5	5.5	6.0	360	350	59.09	3-1/4" x 10"

76000 SERIES...see page 8

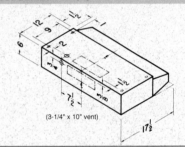

(3-1/4" x 10" vent)

Width	White	Almond	White on White	Black	Stainless
24"	762401	762408	762411	762423	762404
30"	763001	763008	763011	763023	763004
36"	763601	763608	763611	763623	763604
42"	764201	764208	764211	764223	764204

Also available in Harvest, Avocado and Coffee.

Specifications

Volts	AMPS	Sones		CFM	Vent-Free RHP Index	Vent
		Ver.	Hor.			
120	3.0	5.5	6.0	200	22.73	3-1/4" x 10"

75000 SERIES...see page 9

Width	White	Almond	Stainless
30"	753001	753008	753004
36"	753601	753608	753604
42"	754201	754208	754204

Specifications

Volts	AMPS	Sones		CFM	Vent-Free RHP Index	Vent
		Ver.	Hor.			
120	3.6	6.5	6.0	250	25.0	3-1/4" x 10"

68000 SERIES...see page 9

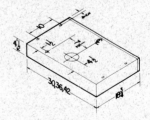

7" Round Vent

Width	White	Black
30"	683001	683023
36"	683601	683623
42"	684201	684223

Specifications

Volts	AMPS	CFM	Sones
120	2.5	230	7.0

67000 SERIES...see page 9

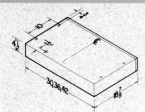

Vent-Free

Width	White	Black
30"	673001	673023
36"	673601	673623
42"	674201	674223

Specifications

Volts	AMPS	CFM	Sones
120	2.0	Vent-Free	Vent-Free

48000 SERIES...see page 9

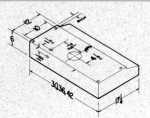

7" Round Vent

Width	White	Almond	Stainless
30"	483001	483008	483004
36"	483601	483608	483604
42"	484201	484208	484204

Specifications

Volts	AMPS	CFM	Sones
120	2.5	230	7.0

47000 SERIES...see page 9

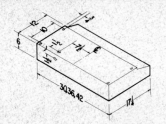

Vent-Free

Width	White	Almond	Stainless
30"	473001	473008	473004
36"	473601	473608	473604
42"	474201	474208	474204

Specifications

Volts	AMPS	CFM	Sones
120	2.0	Vent-Free	Vent-Free

FINESSE...see page 3

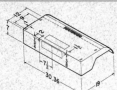

1000 Series (250 CFM)

Width	White	Almond	Black	Stainless
30"	813011	813018	813025	813004
36"	813611	813618	813625	813604

3000 Series (400 CFM)

Width	White	Almond	Black	Stainless
30"	833011	833018	833025	833004
36"	833611	833618	833625	833604

46000 SERIES...see page 10

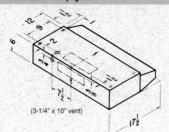

(3-1/4" x 10" vent)

Width	White	Almond	Stainless
30"	463001	463008	463004
36"	463601	463608	463604
42"	464201	464208	464204

Also available in Harvest, Avocado and Coffee.

Specifications

Volts	AMPS	Sones Ver.	Sones Hor.	CFM	Vent-Free RHP Index	Vent
120	2.5	7.0	6.5	230	7.0	3-1/4" x 10"

42000 SERIES...see page 11

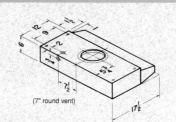

(7" round vent)

7" Round Vent

Width	White	Almond	Stainless
30"	423001	423008	423004
36"	423601	423608	423604

Also available in Harvest, Avocado and Coffee.

Specifications

Volts	AMPS	Sones Ver.	Sones Hor.	CFM	Duct-Free RHP Index	Vent
120	2.5	5.5	–	190	–	7" Round

Economy hoods are not convertible.

41000/40000 SERIES...see page 11

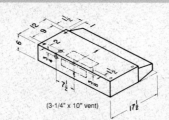

(3-1/4" x 10" vent)

41000 Vent-Free

Width	White	Almond	Stainless
24"	412401	412408	412404
30"	413001	413008	413004
36"	413601	413608	413604

Also available in Harvest, Avocado and Coffee.

41000 Specifications

Volts	AMPS	Sones Ver.	Sones Hor.	CFM	Vent-Free RHP Index
120	2.0	Vent-Free		Vent-Free	8.70

40000 Vented

Width	White	Almond	Stainless
24"	402401	402408	402404
30"	403001	403008	403004
36"	403601	403608	403604

Also available in Harvest, Avocado and Coffee.

40000 Specifications

Volts	AMPS	Sones Ver.	Sones Hor.	CFM	Vent-Free RHP Index	Vent
120	2.0	5.5	6.5	160	–	3-1/4" x 10"

Economy hoods are not convertible.

HIDEAWAY-Model 113023...see page 12

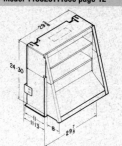

Specifications

Volts	Amps	Sones	CFM	Vent
120	3.7	4.5	360	3-1/4" x 10"

WOOD HOOD-Model 103023...see page 12

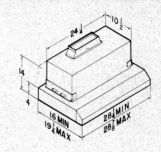

Specifications

Volts	Amps	Sones Ver.	Sones Hor.	CFM	Vent
120	3.7	5.0	4.5	360	3-1/4" x 10"

MICROMATE™-120000 Series...see page 13

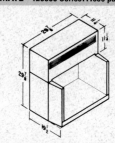

Specifications

Volts	Amps	Sones	CFM	Vent-Free RHP Index	Vent
120	2.7	4.5	300	9.8	3-1/4" x 10"

11000 SERIES...see page 13

Traditional Wall Canopy Hood

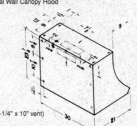

(3-1/4" x 10" vent)

11000 Series

Width	Hammered White	Hammered Almond	Hammered Harvest	Hammered Avocado	Hammered Coffee
30"	113036	113042	113047	113048	113049

Specifications

Volts	AMPS	Sones Ver.	Sones Hor.	CFM Ver.	CFM Hor.	Vent-Free RHP Index	Vent
120	3.0	6.0	6.5	190	200	9.80	3-1/4" x 10"

15

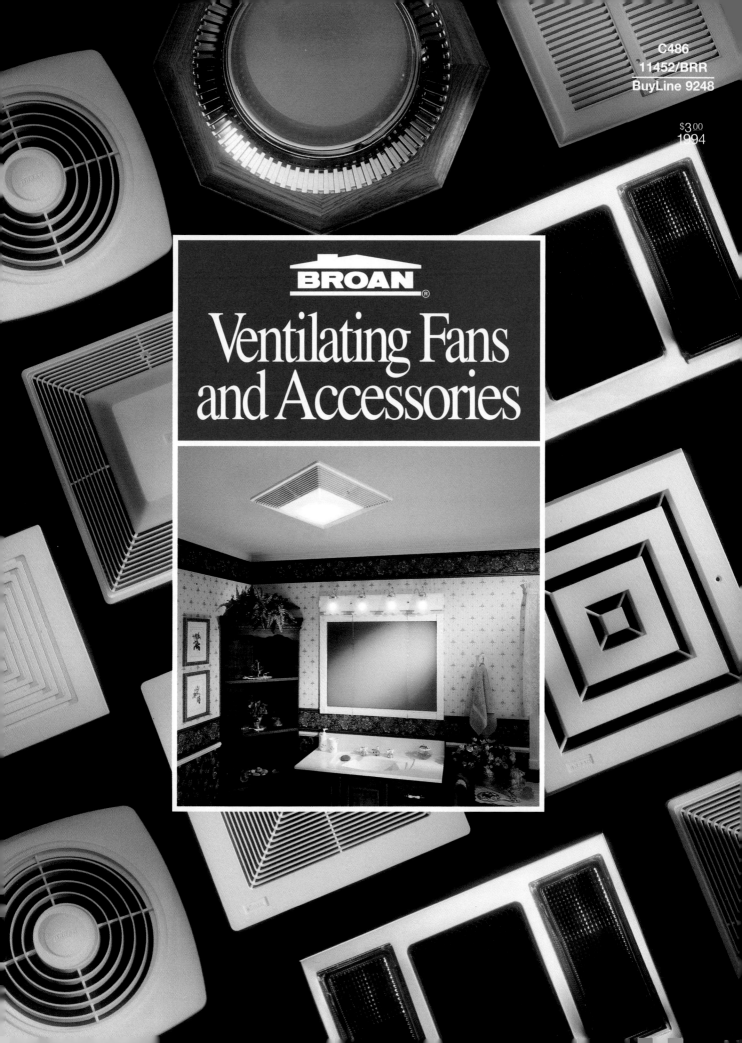

C486
11452/BRR
BuyLine 9248

$3.00
1994

BROAN®

Ventilating Fans and Accessories

Why homes need ventilation

Take a moment to consider areas of your home that occasionally need extra ventilation—what the industry refers to as *intermittent ventilation.* For instance, high moisture levels generated in the bathroom. Or dampness in laundry or utility rooms. Maybe cooking odors and grease from the kitchen spring to mind.

Now consider the consequences if excess moisture or cooking fumes aren't dealt with promptly and properly.

Moisture from a steamy shower, for instance, will do more than just saturate bathroom air. Left unchecked, lingering moisture will provide an ideal breeding ground for mold and mildew. Excess moisture will infiltrate plaster and drywall. Or seep through ceiling fixtures into attic insulation. And ultimately, moisture will be absorbed into your home's framework, and into the woodwork of doors and furnishings, resulting in warping, paint peeling and even wood rot.

In the kitchen, smoke or fumes from cooking spread odors throughout your entire home. Suspended grease particles can also drift through the air and settle on countertop and cabinet surfaces where they will attract dust and add more work to your routine housecleaning chores.

Protect your home and add comfort inexpensively
Problems such as those described above are identified as *point-source* contaminants. And ridding your home of problems like these is really very simple. In fact, it's as easy as installing readily available intermittent ventilation products such as bath fans, utility fans or range hoods.

Effective point-source ventilation products make your home more comfortable by providing a concen-

trated level of ventilation where it's needed most.

Just as importantly, ventilation products help protect your home investment by eliminating many of the factors that compromise your home's structural integrity.

Why more homes choose Broan

Broan is the residential ventilation leader. We have been since 1932 when Henry Broan introduced the through the wall ventilating fan – the first fan specifically engineered for residential room ventilation.

With hundreds of easy-to-install products to choose from, Broan offers the industry's most comprehensive selection of quality ventilation products. So it's easy to find solutions that precisely match your needs.

Like the hands-free convenience of our SensAire® fans and fan/lights. The extended performance life of our HD Series™ fans and fan/lights. Or the remarkably quiet

Broan Ventilating Fans

performance of our remotely-mounted Single-Port and Multi-Port ventilators.

Choosing the ventilation solution that's right for you

First decide what features you'd like to have; a fan only, a fan/light combination, or a unit with a fan, light and built-in heater. Some models even feature a built-in night-light. Our top-of-the-line units come equipped with state-of-the-art motion and/or humidity sensors for the ultimate in convenience and effective ventilation.

Then, use the chart at the right to determine cubic feet per minute (CFM), and the recommended ventilation capacity for a particular size and type of room.

Sones – how sound levels are measured.

A key consideration when choosing a ventilation unit is sound level. That's measured by an industry standard called a "sone." One sone roughly equals the sound the average refrigerator makes when operating in a quiet kitchen. The higher the sone rating, the louder the fan. For example, a 4.0 sone fan is twice as loud as a 2.0 sone fan, and so on.

CFM – How Exhaust Capacity Is Measured

Air changes per hour recommended by the Home Ventilating Institute (HVI)

Wall and Ceiling Fans	Recommended Air Changes/ Hour	Formula (8 ft. ceiling)
Kitchen	15	L x W x 2 = CFM (i.e. 100 sq. ft. x 2 = 200 CFM)
Bathroom	8	L x W x 1.07 = CFM (i.e. 55 sq. ft. x 1.07 = 60 CFM, rounded)
Recreation Room, Utility or Laundry Room, Basement, etc.	6	L x W x 0.8 = CFM (i.e. 150 sq. ft. x 0.8 = 120 CFM)

L = Room Length   W = Room Width

TABLE TO MATCH CFM TO ROOMS

CFM-to-Room Area for Recommended HVI Ventilation

	Bathroom		Kitchen	Laundry, Family or Recreation
CFM	Sq. ft.	CFM	Sq. ft.	Sq. ft.
50	45	60	–	75
60	55	80	–	100
70	65	100	–	125
80	75	120	60	150
90	85	140	70	175
100	95	160	80	200
110	105	180	90	225
120	110	200	100	250
130	120	250	125	310
140	130	300	150	375
150	140	350	175	435
200	185	400	200	500
		450	225	560
		500	250	625
		550	275	685

Typical CFM ratings are shown above. Ceiling height of 8 feet is assumed.

Broan fan units are tested and certified by the Home Ventilating Institute. This is your assurance that each Broan fan has been tested by an independent agency, and found to consistently deliver the air and sound performance specified on the following pages.

On the following pages you'll find brief descriptions of the many products we offer for effective, efficient and reliable residential and light commercial ventilation. Please refer to back cover for specifications.

Table of Contents

& Accessories

Hands-free convenience with automatic response to rising humidity, motion ... or both.

The innovative use of advanced sensor technology helps you fight the battle against bathroom mold and mildew – automatically. That's because SensAire® fans and fan/lights utilize sensors that automatically trigger operation in response to motion, rapid rises in humidity, or both.

Once a rapid change in humidity is detected, the humidity sensing SensAire® starts automatically and remains running for a user adjustable 5 to 60 minute time period. Structural problems associated with mold and mildew are quickly and effortlessly eliminated.

A convenient toggle feature lets you bypass the humidity sensor mechanism temporarily. This feature allows you to operate the humidity sensing SensAire® units manually or automatically — with just one switch. This means faster and less-expensive installation for do-it-yourself remodelers and professional contractors.

Our motion response SensAire® fans or fan/lights turn on the moment someone enters the room – and remain on for a user adjustable 5 to 60 minutes after the motion stops.

SensAire® is ideal for light commercial or institutional applications such as

public restrooms or nursing homes. The exclusive sensing capability can even eliminate the need for a wall switch altogether.

SensAire® also features a super-quiet centrifugal blower. So you enjoy hands-free convenience in one of the quietest high performance fans in the industry.

- Easy installation
  - Uses standard 4" round duct
  - 7⅝" high housing mounts directly to ceiling joists
  - Alternately, slide bar brackets span up to 24"
  - Pre-wired outlet box for plug-in motor plate
- Reliable
  - Balanced blower wheel
  - Permanently lubricated motor
  - Resilient neoprene motor mounts isolate vibration
- UL listed for use over bathtubs and showers when connected to a GFCI protected branch circuit
- Type IC (Fan/Lights)
- AMCA licensed for both air and sound*

*See Broan Catalog #99850138 for complete AMCA licensed ratings

77W Three Switch Control
(for fan/light units)

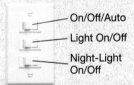

— On/Off/Auto
— Light On/Off
— Night-Light On/Off

Sensor Technology

Products	Motion	Humidity	Motion & Humidity
90 CFM Fan 1.5 Sones	MS90	HS90	–
130 CFM Fan 2.5 Sones	MS130	HS130	–
120 CFM Fan/Light/ Night-Light 2.5 Sones	MS120L	HS120L	MHS120L

Three Exclusive Sensing Control Options

Using advanced sensor technology, only Broan offers you the simplicity, luxury and convenience of "hands-free" bath fan operation.

Motion Sensing

Motion activated SensAire® units provide automatic solutions for problem areas where hands-free lighting and/or ventilation is a must. Adjustable "field of view" lets you adjust sensor response area to your specific application needs.

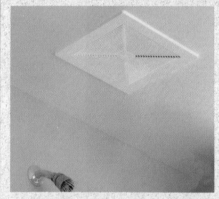

Humidity Sensing

The moisture activated SensAire® units sense rapid increases in humidity brought on by the bath or shower and turn on automatically. The unit shuts itself off after a user-adjustable period of 5 to 60 minutes.

Motion & Humidity Sensing

Utilizing both motion and humidity sensors, this top-of-the-line SensAire® provides the ultimate in convenience and user-friendly operation. As illustrated below, the motion sensor controls the light, while the humidity sensor controls the fan.

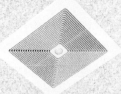

MS130/MS90 Fan

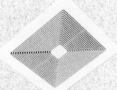

HS130/HS90 Fan

HS120L Fan/Light/Night-Light

MS120L/MHS120L Fan/Light/Night-Light

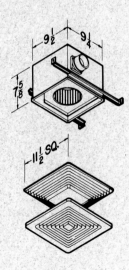

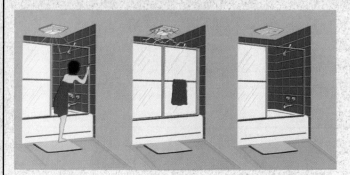

Enter shower. Motion sensor turns on light.

Humidity sensor turns on fan.

Lack of motion- turns off light. Fan turns off after pre- set time period.

S E N S A I R E ® F A N S & F A N / L I G H T S

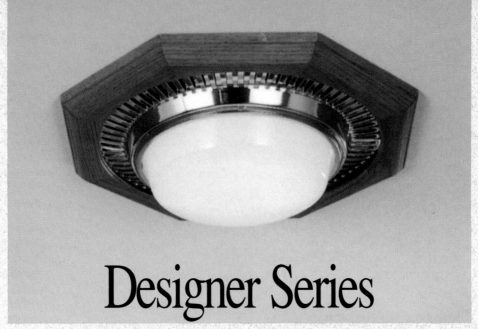

Designer Series

Fan/light/night-light combinations that quietly deliver style, quality & performance.

Surround the soft glow of a genuine glass lens with your choice of designer frames trimmed with decorator finishes. Choose aluminum frames with a polished brass, polished chrome or satin white finish. Or durable oak frames with multi-layer moisture protection, so they stand up to the high humidity of bathroom environments. Each features a durable, centrifugal blower wheel delivering superior, yet quiet, ventilation (100 CFM, 3.5 Sones). Each Designer Series Fan/Light also offers outstanding reliability with a plug-in, permanently lubricated motor surrounded by a rugged steel housing. Bright 100 watt light capacity combines with a 7 watt night-light for added security and safety (bulbs not included).

1.   2.   3.   4.   5.   6.

1. *Model 722 Fan/Light/Night-Light*
- Solid oak frame
- Handsome polished brass finished grille

2. *Model 721 Fan/Light/Night-Light*
- Solid oak frame
- Round design eliminates squaring with bathroom walls

3. *Model 720 Fan/Light/Night-Light*
- Solid oak frame
- Polished brass finished grille

4. *Model 714 Fan/Light/Night-Light*
- Rich, polished chrome finished grille
- Round design eliminates squaring with bathroom walls
- UL listed for use over bathtubs and showers when connected to a GFCI protected branch circuit

5. *Model 712 Fan/Light/Night-Light*
- Soft white painted aluminum grille
- Round design eliminates squaring with bathroom walls
- UL listed for use over bathtubs and showers when connected to a GFCI protected branch circuit

6. *Model 710 Fan/Light/Night-Light*
- Handsome polished brass finished grille
- Round design eliminates squaring with bathroom walls
- UL listed for use over bathtubs and showers when connected to a GFCI protected branch circuit

Three-Function Decorator Controls Available

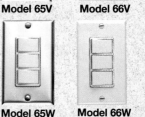
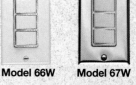

Model 65V   Model 66V   Model 67V

Model 65W   Model 66W   Model 67W

Heater/Fan/Light With Night-Light

On cold mornings, you'll appreciate fan/lights that also deliver the instant comfort of a powerful 1500 watt fan-forced heater. Choose from two models delivering 70 CFM of ventilation at a quiet 3.5 Sones. Both feature non-glare light-diffusing glass lenses with capacity for 120 watt lighting, as well as a 7 watt night-light (bulbs not included).

Quality construction includes plug-in permanently lubricated motors. A polymeric damper eliminates metallic clatter while preventing cold backdrafts. Installation is simplified with four-point adjustable mounting brackets with keyhole slots, and torsion spring grille mounting that requires no tools. A four-function wall control that fits a single-gang opening is included. Both models are suitable for use with insulation.

Model 735 Heater/Fan/Light/ Night-Light

■ Polished brass finished grille with solid oak frame
■ Four-funtion wall control with coordinating wall plate included – fits single-gang opening

Model 730 Heater/Fan/Light/ Night-Light

■ Polished chrome stainless steel grille
■ Four-funtion wall control with coordinating wall plate included – fits single-gang opening

Fan/Light And Fan

A whisper quiet centrifugal blower, delivering 80 CFM of ventilation at just 3.0 Sones, combines with the elegant simplicity of a solid oak frame. A polymeric damper quiets metallic clatter while preventing backdrafts.

Model 709 Fan/Light

■ 100 watt light capacity (bulb not included)
■ Shatter-resistant light lens
■ Type IC

Model 708 Fan

■ Solid oak fan face – an industry exclusive

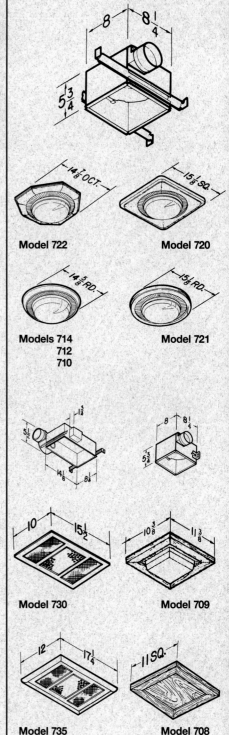

Model 722

Model 720

Models 714 712 710

Model 721

Model 730

Model 709

Model 735

Model 708

Solitaire® Series

Humidity emitted by whirlpools and spas in today's larger bathrooms creates a special ventilation challenge for ordinary fans. Solitaire® fans and fan/lights respond to this challenge beautifully and quietly.

Inside sleek and stylish white grilles we've installed high capacity fans. Each features a balanced centrifugal blower wheel, a permanently lubricated motor and resilient neoprene motor mounts for remarkably quiet operation.

Installation is simplified through the use of standard 4" ductwork. Plus, our 7⅝" high housing mounts directly to ceiling joists as small as 2" x 8". Or use the easily adjustable slidebar brackets to span up to 24".

Multi-Function Fan/Light/Night-Light Controls (Available separately)

A multi-function control in your choice of decorator face plates features three independent 120V, 15A rated switches that fit in a single-gang opening.

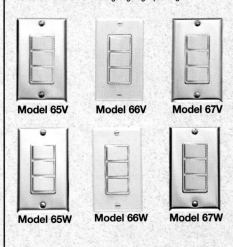

Model 65V Model 66V Model 67V

Model 65W Model 66W Model 67W

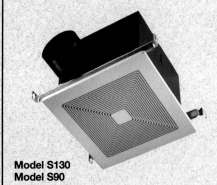

Model S130
Model S90

Fans

Model S130

- 130 CFM 2.5 Sones
- Pre-wired outlet box for plug-in motor plate
- Torsion spring-mounted grille
- Durable damper quietly eliminates backdrafts with no metallic clatter
- UL listed for use over bathtubs and showers when connected to a GFCI protected branch circuit
- AMCA licensed for both air and sound*

Model S90

- 90 CFM 1.5 Sones
- All other features same as S130

*See Broan Catalog #99850138 for complete AMCA licensed ratings.

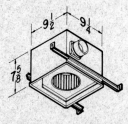

Models S130
S90

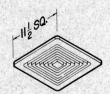

Model S120L

Fan/Light/Night-Light

Model S120L

- 120 CFM 2.5 Sones
- 100 watt lighting with separate built-in 7 watt night-light (bulbs not included)
- Durable damper quietly eliminates backdrafts with no metallic clatter
- Plug-in receptacles for fan and lights
- UL listed for use over bathtubs and showers when connected to a GFCI protected branch circuit
- Type IC
- Grille mounts securely with two screws
- AMCA licensed for both air and sound*

*See Broan Catalog #99850138 for complete AMCA licensed ratings.

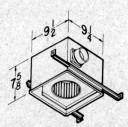

Models S120L
S120FL

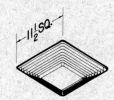

Model S120FL

Fluorescent Fan/Light/Night-Light

Model S120FL

- 120 CFM 2.5 Sones
- Energy-saving 18 watt twin-tube fluorescent bulb produces the equivalent of 75 watts of incandescent lighting. Separate 7 watt night-light (bulbs not included)
- Fluorescent bulb lasts up to 13 years in normal use (based on 2 hrs. use daily)
- Uses 75% less electricity than incandescent bulbs
- Replacement bulb available locally or through Broan (Part #97010730)
- Other features same as S120L

Savings of over 55% over the life of the bulb with a Broan Fluorescent Fan/Light	Life-cycle savings with an 18 watt Broan Fluorescent Fan/Light*	
	75 watt Incandescent	**18 watt Compact fluorescent**
Bulb Purchase Price	13 @ $.50 = $6.50	1 @ $15.00 = $15.00
Electricity cost	75 watts for 10,000 hours @ $.08 KWH = $60.00	18 watts for 10,000 hours @ $.08 KWH = $14.40
Total cost	**$66.50**	**$29.40**

*Costs and savings may differ based on local cost of electricity.

ENERGY REBATES

This model may qualify for an energy savings rebate from your local electric company. Check with your utility for confirmation.

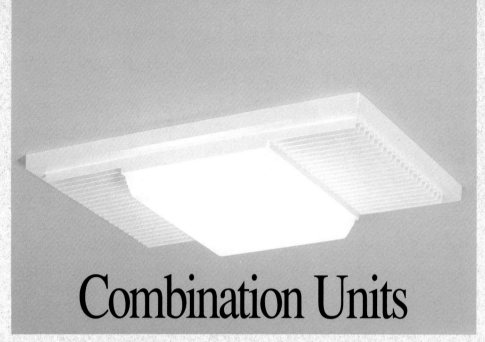

Combination Units

Choose from a wide selection of compact, easy-to-install combination units featuring any two or all three of the most desirable bathroom comfort conveniences. It might be an incandescent or fluorescent light protected by a shatter-resistant lens. Or on cold mornings, the added comfort and energy-saving efficiency of a fan-forced heater. Or a high performance bath fan that removes moisture and odors for a fresher, cleaner bathroom. Just pick the features and Broan will have the unit that satisfies your needs.

Deluxe Heater/Fan/Light Combination Units

Units feature the quiet performance and high efficiency of two blower wheels, each powered by its own permanently lubricated plug-in motor. A polymeric 4" round duct features a 2" long tapered sleeve for easy, positive ducting. A built-in damper prevents backdrafts and eliminates annoying metallic clatter.

Our 1300 watt heater units provide efficient and even heat distribution. Each is suitable for use with insulation.

Installation is simplified with adjustable slotted mounting brackets that span up to 24". And all models are available in single packs or Project Paks except where noted.

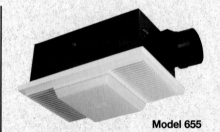

Model 655

Model 655 Heater/Fan/Light
- 70 CFM 3.5 Sones
- 20 amp circuit required
- Fan and heater function independently or together
- Use with Model 66W, 66V, 65W, 65V, 67W, 67V three-function control (available separately) — Page 24
- Up to 100 watt light with light diffusing lens (bulb not included)

Model 659 Heater/Fan/Light
- 50 CFM 2.5 Sones
- All other features same as Model 655

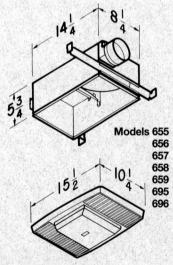

Models 655 656 657 658 659 695 696

Model 695 Heater/Fan/Light
- 100 CFM 4.0 Sones
- Housing lined with 1/2" acoustic insulation
- 20 amp circuit required
- Fan and heater function independently or together
- Use with Model 66W, 66V, 65W, 65V, 67W, 67V three-function control (available separately) — Page 24
- Up to 100 watt light with light diffusing lens (bulb not included)
- For AMCA licensed performance ratings see Broan catalog #99850138
- Single packs only

Model 696 Fan/Light
- 100 CFM 4.0 Sones
- Housing lined with 1/2" acoustic insulation
- Does not include heater
- Up to 100 watt light with light diffusing lens (bulb not included)
- Type IC
- Use with Model 68W or 68V control (available separately) — Page 24
- For AMCA licensed performance ratings see Broan catalog #99850138
- Single packs only

Model 657 Fan/Light
- 70 CFM 3.5 Sones
- UL listed for use over bathtubs and showers when connected to GFCI protected branch circuit
- Type IC
- Use with Model 68W or 68V control (available separately) — Page 24

Model 658 Heater/Fan
- 70 CFM 3.5 Sones
- Does not include light
- Use with Model 68W or 68V control (available separately) — Page 24
- Other features same as Model 655

Model 656 Heater/Light
- Does not include fan
- Use with Model 68W or 68V Control (available separately) — Page 24
- Other features same as Model 655

Fan/Light Combination Units

This popular and easy-to-install series features a plug-in, permanently lubricated motor driving an efficient polymeric impeller. Mounting ears are provided for quick, sturdy installation. UL listed for use over bathtubs and showers when connected to a GFCI protected branch circuit.

Models 679FL 679 678

Uses Model 68W and 68V two-function control (available separately). And features polymeric duct connectors with tapered sleeves for easier, positive ducting. All are available in single packs and Project Paks.

Model 679 Fan/Light
- 70 CFM 3.5 Sones
- Type IC
- Shatter-resistant light diffusing lens
- Up to 100 watt bulb capacity (bulb not included)

Model 678 Fan/Light
- 50 CFM 2.5 Sones
- Other features same as Model 679

Model 679FL Fluorescent Fan/Light
- 70 CFM 3.5 Sones
- Type IC
- 13 watt double twin-tube fluorescent bulb provides the equivalent of 60 watts of incandescent light (bulb not included)
- Bulb lasts up to 13 years in normal use (based on 2 hrs. use daily)
- Uses 75% less energy than incandescent bulb
- Replacement available locally or from Broan (part # 97010729)

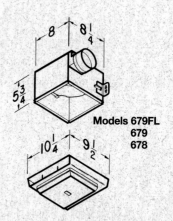

Models 679FL 679 678

Savings of over 50% with a Broan Fluorescent Fan/Light	Life-cycle savings with a 13 watt Broan Fluorescent Fan/Light*	
	60 watt Incandescent	**13 watt Compact fluorescent**
Bulb Purchase Price	13 @ $.50 = $6.50	1 @ $15.00 = $15.00
Electricity cost	60 watts for 10,000 hours @ $.08 KWH = $48.00	13 watts for 10,000 hours @ $.08 KWH = $10.40
Total cost	**$54.50**	**$25.40**

*Costs and savings may differ based on local cost of electricity.

ENERGY REBATES

This model may qualify for an energy savings rebate from your local electric company. Check with your utility for confirmation.

Bath Fans

Quiet high performance bath fans for every need and every budget

For fresher, cleaner bathrooms there's nothing like Broan bathroom fans. From Economy to Premium models, Broan offers one of the widest selections in the industry. Plus, all Broan bath fans are manufactured in the USA to the highest quality standards. So you can be sure the bath fan you choose will deliver quiet, high performance ventilation and great looks that add up to extraordinary value.

Motor/blower assemblies designed for quiet, high performance ventilation & easy installation

Behind attractively styled white polymeric grilles, durable fan and blower assemblies are encased in sturdy housings. Permanently lubricated motors drive specially designed blowers to deliver high exhaust performance at low sound levels. And each fan features quiet, durable dampers to prevent cold backdrafts.

Installation is simplified with built-in mounting ears. Plus, polymeric duct connectors feature long tapered sleeves for easier, positive ducting.

All Broan bath fans are UL listed for use over bathtubs and showers when connected to a GFCI protected branch circuit.

Premium

Models 676 684

- Centrifugal blower wheels and 4-pole motors for high capacity at low sound levels
- Built-in mounting ears for quick, sturdy installation
- Torsion spring grille mounting — no tools required
- Single packs and Project Paks
- Metal grille kits available separately — Page 27

Model 676 Ceiling Fan
- 110 CFM 4.0 Sones

Model 684 Ceiling Fan
- 80 CFM 2.5 Sones

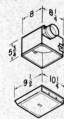

Models 676 684

Deluxe

Models 671 670

- Durable Broan-designed blower wheels
- Torsion spring grille mounting — no tools needed
- Compact housings fit easily between wall studs
- Double strength steel mounting flanges with keyhole slots for fast installation
- Single packs and Project Paks
- Covered by U.S. and foreign patents
- Metal grille kits available separately — Page 27

Model 671 Ceiling/Wall Fan
- 70 CFM 3.0 Sones

Model 670 Ceiling/Wall Fan
- 50 CFM 1.5 Sones

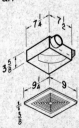

Models 671 670

Economy

Models 689 688

- Torsion spring grille mounting — no tools required
- Compact housings fit easily between wall studs
- Single packs and Project Paks
- Covered by U.S. and foreign patents
- Metal grille kits available separately — Page 27

Model 689 Ceiling/Wall Fan
- 60 CFM 3.5 Sones

Model 688 Ceiling/Wall Fan
- 50 CFM 2.0 Sones

Vertical

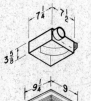

Models 689 688

Model 673

Model 673 Vertical Discharge Ceiling Fan
- 60 CFM 4.0 Sones
- Durable polymeric fan blade
- Spin-on, white-white polymeric grille
- Galvanized steel housing
- Double strength steel mounting brackets with keyhole slots for fast installation
- Single packs only

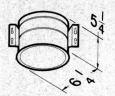

Model 673

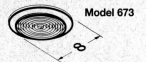

Model 673

Duct-Free Fans & Fan/Light
Easy to install, no duct work required. Perfect for applications where ducting is impossible or impractical.

- Attractive, white molded grilles
- Single packs and Project Paks (fans)

Model 686 Duct-Free Fan/Powered Air Freshener

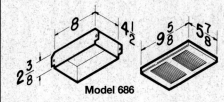

- Mounts in ceiling or wall
- Includes steel housing, polymeric grille, and replaceable air freshener
- Fan circulates air past readily available air-freshener that snaps in behind grille

Model 686

Model 682 Duct-Free Fan
- Patented, fast snap-in metal housing installation
- Whisper quiet fan circulates air past replaceable activated charcoal filter
- ICBO ES, BOCA ES, and SBCCI PST and ESI recognized. See NES report No. NER-367

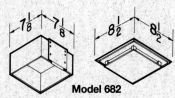

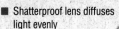

Model 682

Model 682L Duct-Free Fan/Light
Perfect for closets — provides needed lighting and eliminates musty smells.

- Shatterproof lens diffuses light evenly
- Bright 100 watt bulb capacity (bulb not included)
- Type IC
- Other features same as Model 682

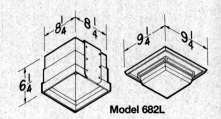

Model 682L

BATH FANS / DUCT-FREE FANS AND FAN/LIGHTS

13

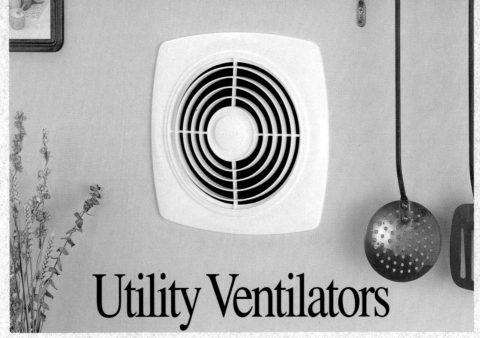

Utility Ventilators

High Efficiency Ventilation for Kitchens, Laundry Rooms, Rec Rooms & Workshops

Eliminate cooking fumes, tobacco smoke or humidity in rooms throughout the house with utility ventilators from Broan. All feature powerful, permanently lubricated motors encased in rugged steel housings. Attractive low profile white-white polymeric grilles can be painted to match the surrounding wall color. Metal grille kits and filters for all models (except Model 509S) are also available. See pages 26–27.

Model 506 10" Chain-Operated Wall Fan

- 480 CFM 6.5 Sones
- Specially designed polymeric fan blade
- Housing features foam insulated door for energy efficiency
- Pull chain opens door and turns on fan — no wall switch to wire
- Housing adjusts to fit walls from 4-1/2" to 9-1/2" thick

Model 507 8" Chain-Operated Wall Fan

- 250 CFM 4.5 Sones
- 8-3/8" diameter sleeve
- All other features same as Model 506

Model 508 10" Automatic Wall Fan

- 270 CFM 6.0 Sones
- Specially designed polymeric fan blade
- Rugged steel housing with slim profile
- Housing adjusts to fit walls from 4-1/2" to 9-1/2" thick
- Built-in damper minimizes backdrafts

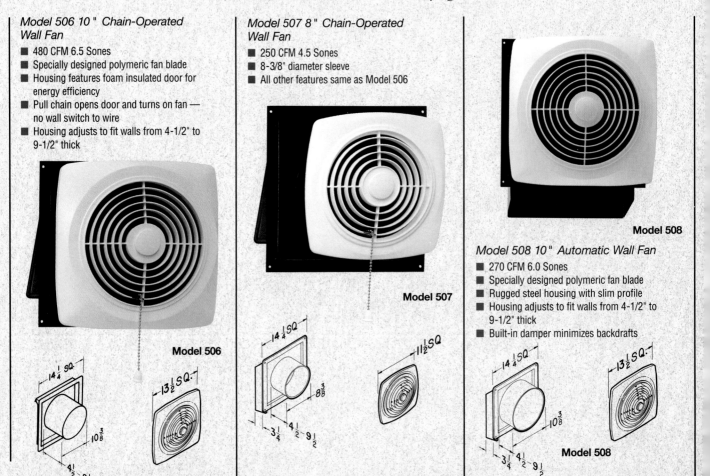

Model 506

Model 507

Model 508

Model 508

Models 509
509S

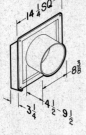

Model 509 8 " Automatic Wall Fan

- 180 CFM 5.0 Sones
- 8-3/8" diameter sleeve
- All other features same as Model 508

Model 509S 8 " Automatic Wall Fan

- Includes on-off rotary switch —
  no wall switch to wire
- All other features same as Model 509

Motordor®

Model 12C Motordor® 10 " Wall Fan

- 380 CFM 5.5 Sones
- Housing features foam insulated door for
  energy efficiency
- Separate motor opens door when fan is turned
  on, closes door when turned off
- Housing adjusts to fit walls from 5-1/2" to
  9-7/8" thick

Model 12C

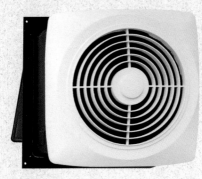

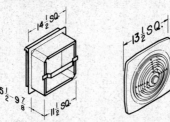

Models 502
503

Wall/Ceiling Mount

Model 502 10 " Side Discharge Fan

- 270 CFM 7.0 Sones
- Installs easily between ceiling joists or
  wall studs
- Built-in damper prevents backdrafts
- Fits 3-1/4" x 10" duct

Model 503 8 " Side Discharge Fan

- 160 CFM 5.0 Sones
- All other features same as Model 502

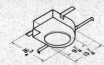

Model 502   **Model 503**

Vertical

Models 504
505

Model 504 10 " Vertical Discharge Fan

- 350 CFM 6.5 Sones
- Installs easily between ceiling joists
- Fits 10" round duct — use Model 472
  transition/damper for 8" round duct (available
  separately) — Page 26

Model 505 8 " Vertical Discharge Fan

- 180 CFM 5.0 Sones
- Housing features built-in backdraft damper
- 8-1/4" diameter housing
- Fits 8" round duct
- All other features same as Model 504

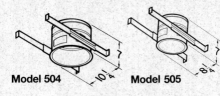

Model 504   **Model 505**

NEW! **Through The Wall Ventilator**

Model 512M

- 70 CFM 3.5 Sones,
- Easy to install –
  features white
  polymeric interior
  grille and attractive
  louvered exterior wall cap with
  built-in bird screen
- Flexible aluminum duct included
- Accommodates walls from 5-1/4" to 10"
- Use with remotely mounted wall switch or speed
  control (Model 57W/57V) – Page 24

Model 512M

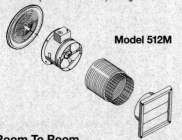

Model 512M

Room To Room

Broan Room To Room Fans Feature:

- Easy interior wall installation
- Quiet, high performance fan – permanently
  lubricated motor
- High strength reinforced polymeric fan blade
- Two attractive white-white polymeric grilles can be
  painted to match any decor

Model 512 6 " Room To Room Fan

- 90 CFM 3.5 Sones
- Use with Model 57W,
  57V Variable Speed
  Control (available
  separately)
  — Page 24
- Housing fits walls up to 5-
  1/8" thick

Model 512

Model 510 10 " Room To Room Fan

- 380 CFM 5.0 Sones
- Built-in variable speed
  control
- Housing adjusts to fit walls
  from 3" to 5-1/2" thick

*Model 511 8 " Room
To Room Fan*

- 180 CFM 3.5 Sones
- Built-in variable speed control
- Housing adjusts to fit walls
  from 3" to 5-1/2" thick

Models 510
511

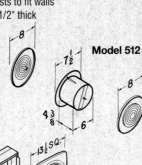

Model 512

Models 510
511

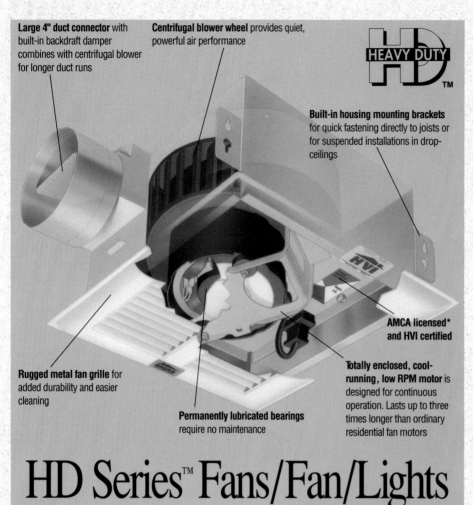

Large 4" duct connector with built-in backdraft damper combines with centrifugal blower for longer duct runs

Centrifugal blower wheel provides quiet, powerful air performance

HEAVY DUTY HD™

Built-in housing mounting brackets for quick fastening directly to joists or for suspended installations in drop-ceilings

AMCA licensed* and HVI certified

Rugged metal fan grille for added durability and easier cleaning

Permanently lubricated bearings require no maintenance

Totally enclosed, cool-running, low RPM motor is designed for continuous operation. Lasts up to three times longer than ordinary residential fan motors

Fan/Lights

Model HD80L
- 80 CFM 3.5 Sones
- 100 watt lighting capacity (bulb not included)
- White molded polymeric grille with unbreakable light diffusing lens
- Plug-in receptacles for fan and light
- Type IC
- AMCA licensed for both air and sound*

Model HD50L
- 50 CFM 2.5 Sones
- Other features same as HD80L

Models HD80L HD50L

HD Series™ Fans/Fan/Lights

A Long-Term Solution for Light Commercial Applications

For heavy-duty ventilation in light commercial or public restroom applications, choose the fan engineered to last *up to three times longer* than ordinary residential bath fans. Follow-up costs associated with service or replacement calls are virtually eliminated.

A broad certified performance spectrum from AMCA* and HVI means you can choose the HD Series™ for light commercial or institutional applications such as:

- Restaurants
- Taverns
- Convenience stores
- Gas stations
- Office buildings
- Care facilities

Choose a fan-only model or a fan/light with 100 watt light capacity (bulb not included). All are UL listed for use over bathtubs or showers when connected to GFCI protected branch circuit.

Models HD80 HD50

Fans

Model HD80
- 80 CFM 2.5 Sones
- Torsion spring-mounted metal fan grille for easy installation
- Pre-wired outlet box for plug-in motor plate
- AMCA licensed for both air and sound*

Model HD50
- 50 CFM 2.0 Sones
- Other features same as HD80

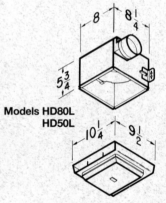

Models HD80L HD50L

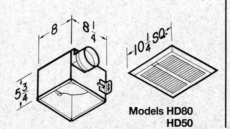

Models HD80 HD50

*See Broan Catalog #99850138 for complete AMCA licensed ratings.

Model 164

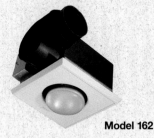

Model 162

Model 162 One-Bulb Heater/Fan
- ■ 70 CFM 3.5 Sones
- ■ Overall housing dimensions 6-3/8" x 11-5/8" x 8-1/8"
- ■ Uses one infrared bulb (not included) — all other features same as Model 164
- ■ UL listed for 60° wiring (retrofits)
- ■ Use with Broan Models 68W, 68V Two-function Control (available separately) — Page 24

Model 161 One-Bulb Heater
- ■ Same features as Model 162, without ventilating fan
- ■ Overall housing dimensions 6" x 12-1/4" x 8-1/8"
- ■ UL listed for 75° wiring (retrofits)

Bulb Heaters & Heater Fans

Energy-Saving Warmth...

Infrared bulb heaters provide instant warmth and comfort in the bathroom... without turning up the central thermostat.

- ■ Use 250 watt R40 size infrared bulbs (not included)
- ■ Attractive, white-white polymeric grilles
- ■ Compact steel housings
- ■ Adjustable mounting brackets with keyhole slots span up to 24"
- ■ Suitable for use with insulation

...Plus the Option of Quiet Bathroom Ventilation

- ■ Ventilators feature polymeric blower wheels
- ■ Quiet polymeric dampers prevent backdrafts
- ■ Polymeric 4" round duct connectors with tapered sleeves
- ■ Bulbs and ventilating fans may be operated independently or in combination
- ■ Single packs and Project Paks (Heater/Fans)

Model 164 Two-Bulb Heater/Fan
- ■ 70 CFM 3.5 Sones
- ■ Overall housing dimensions 6-3/8" x 11-5/8" x 14-1/4"
- ■ UL listed for 60° wiring (retrofits)
- ■ Use with Broan Models 68W, 68V, 67W, 67V, 66W, 66V, 65W, 65V, Multi-function Controls (available separately) — Page 24

Model 163 Two-Bulb Heater
- ■ Same features as Model 164, without ventilating fan
- ■ Overall housing dimensions 6" x 10-1/8" x 14-1/4"
- ■ UL listed for 60° wiring (retrofits)

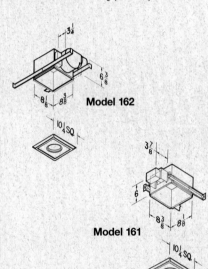

Model 162

Model 161

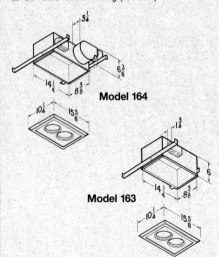

Model 164

Model 163

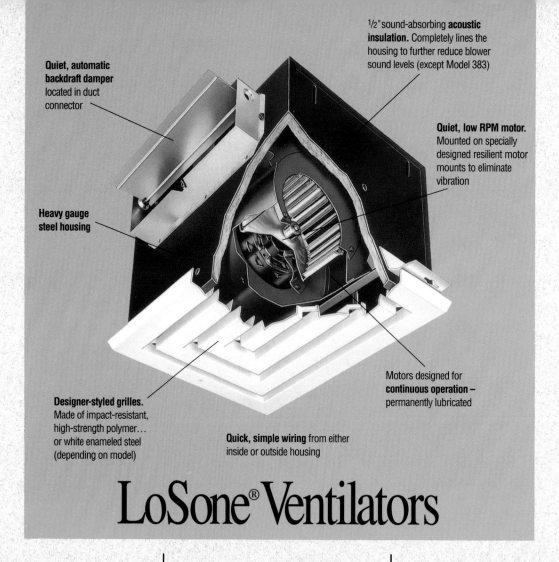

Quiet, automatic backdraft damper located in duct connector

¹⁄₂″ sound-absorbing acoustic insulation. Completely lines the housing to further reduce blower sound levels (except Model 383)

Quiet, low RPM motor. Mounted on specially designed resilient motor mounts to eliminate vibration

Heavy gauge steel housing

Designer-styled grilles. Made of impact-resistant, high-strength polymer… or white enameled steel (depending on model)

Quick, simple wiring from either inside or outside housing

Motors designed for **continuous operation** – permanently lubricated

LoSone® Ventilators

The Industry's Best Value in Super-Quiet Specification Grade Ventilators

Broan LoSone® ventilators are designed to give quality conscious architects, design engineers, builders and specifiers the ultimate in quiet heavy-duty ventilation.

Available from 100 to 3300 CFM, all units use centrifugal blower wheels and low RPM neoprene-mounted motors designed for continuous operation. Then we surround the entire assembly with acoustic insulation and rugged, heavy-duty

housings. Motors and blower wheels are also dynamically balanced to achieve extremely low sound levels. The result: noise and vibration are kept to the absolute minimum.

Handsomely styled grilles of either impact-resistant white polymer or white enameled steel (depending on model) complement any surroundings. So LoSone® ventilators are perfect for offices, conference rooms, bathrooms, hospitals… anywhere attractively designed fan units delivering continuous, quiet, high-capacity ventilation are needed.

LoSone® ventilators may be ducted horizontally or vertically and can even be installed as in-line blowers. LoSone® ventilators are also AMCA licensed for both air and sound.*

*See Broan Catalog #99850138 for complete AMCA licensed ratings.

Models 360 361

100/160 CFM

Model 360

- 100 CFM 1.5 Sones
- 120 volts, 0.7 amps
- 5-1/4" dia. x 3" deep blower wheel
- Fits 3-1/4" x 10" duct
- Variable blower speed and sound level selection with Broan Model 57W or 57V Electronic Speed Control (available separately) — Page 24
- Metal grille kit (Model 88) and in-line adapter kit (Model 94) available separately — Page 20

Model 360MG

- Same as Model 360 except furnished with white enamel finished metal grille — Page 20

Model 361

- 160 CFM 3.0/3.5 Sones
- 120 volts, 1.2 amps
- Other features same as Model 360

Model 361MG

- Same as Model 361 except furnished with white enamel finished metal grille — Page 20

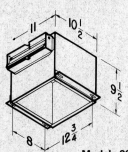

Models 360(MG) 361(MG)

Polymeric

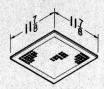

Metal

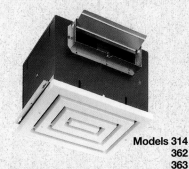

Models 314 362 363 383

120/310 CFM

Model 314

- 120/140 CFM 1.5 Sones
- 120 volts, 0.9 amps
- High capacity, dual 5-1/4" dia. x 3" deep blower wheels
- Fits 3-1/4" x 10" duct
- Variable blower speed and sound level selection with Broan Model 57W or 57V Electronic Speed Control (available separately) — Page 24
- Metal grille kit (Model 89) and in-line adapter kit (Model 94) available separately — Page 20

Model 314MG

- Same as Model 314 except furnished with white enamel finished metal grille — Page 20

Model 362

- 200 CFM 2.0/2.5 Sones
- 120 volts, 1.3 amps
- Other features same as Model 314

Model 362MG

- Same as Model 362 except furnished with white enamel finished metal grille — Page 20

Model 363

- 300 CFM 4.0/4.5 Sones
- 120 volts, 2.3 amps
- Other features same as Model 362

Model 363MG

- Same as Model 363 except furnished with white enamel finished metal grille — Page 20

Model 383

- 310 CFM 4.5/5.0 Sones
- 120 volts, 2.3 amps
- May be installed over cooking equipment (does not include insulation in housing)
- Aluminum filter (Part #99010137) available separately
- Other features same as Model 363

Model 383MG

- Same as Model 383 except furnished with white enamel finished metal grille — Page 20

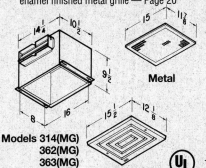

Metal

Models 314(MG) 362(MG) 363(MG) 383(MG)   **Polymeric**

Models 365 375

460/750 CFM

Model 365

- 460 CFM 4.5 Sones
- 120 volts, 3.0 amps
- Fits 7" duct
- Use with Broan Model 57W or 57V Electronic Speed Control for variable blower speed and sound level selection (available separately) — Page 24
- White enamel finished steel grille
- In-line adapter kit (Model 94) available separately — Page 20

Model 375

- 750 CFM 6.5/7.0 Sones
- 120 volts, 3.9 amps
- Use with Broan Model 72W or 72V Electronic Speed Control for variable blower speed and sound level selection (available separately) — Page 24
- Other features same as Model 365

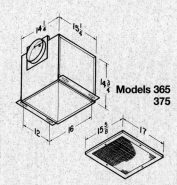

Models 365 375

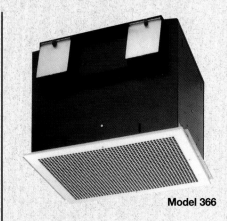

Model 366

940/960 CFM

Model 366

- 940/960 CFM 6.0 Sones
- 120 volts, 5.6 amps
- White enamel finished steel grille
- Fits 6" x 18" duct
- Use with Broan Model 72W or 72V Electronic Speed Control for variable blower speed and sound level selection (available separately) — Page 24
- In-line adapter kit (Model 96) available separately — see next column

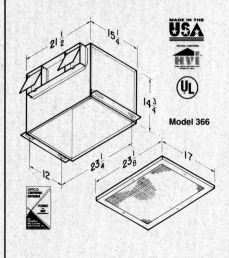

Model 366

Accessory In-Line Adapter Kits

Convert Broan LoSone® or equivalent units to in-line capability quickly and easily. Allow ventilator to be installed in a location remote from the air intake. The kit installs in place of the ceiling grille utilizing either two or four mounting screws.

Model 93

- For 3-1/4" x 10" duct
- Galvanized steel construction
- 10-1/4" x 11"
- For use with LoSone® Models 360, 360MG, 361, 361MG

Model 94

- For 3-1/4" x 10" duct
- Galvanized steel construction
- 10-1/4" x 14-1/2"
- For use with LoSone® Models 314, 314MG, 362, 362MG, 363, 363MG, 383, 383MG

Model 95

- For 7" round duct
- Black finish
- 15-1/4" x 14-1/4"
- For use with LoSone® Models 365, 375

Model 96

- For 6" x 18" duct
- Black finish
- 15-1/4" x 21-1/2"
- For LoSone® Model 366

*In-Line Adapters were tested on appropriate units at 0.1" static pressure. CFM reductions are noted in the table below.

MODEL	CFM REDUCTION
Model 360/360MG	0%+
Model 314/314MG	0%+
Model 361/361MG	7%
Model 362/362MG	0%+
Model 363/363MG	17%
Model 383/383MG	17%
Model 365	20%
Model 375	20%
Model 366	0%

+Motor RPM increased slightly.

Accessory Metal Grilles

Model 88

- Fits LoSone® Models 360 & 361
- 11-7/8" square

Model 89

- Fits LoSone® Models 314, 362, 363 & 383
- 11-7/8" x 15"

Model G102

- Fits LoSone® Model 367
- 16-1/4" x 39-5/8"

Model G103

- Fits LoSone® Model 368
- 18-3/8" x 47-1/4"

TABLE 2 – SONES / AMPS

Model Number & Discharge	HVI Sones @ 0.1" S.P.*	AMCA Sones @ 0.0" S.P.*	Amps
360/360MG Ver.	1.5	2.9	0.7
360/360MG Hor.	1.5	2.7	0.7
314/314MG Ver.	1.5	3.2	0.9
314/314MG Hor.	1.5	3.0	0.9
361/361MG Ver.	3.0	4.6	1.2
361/361MG Hor.	3.5	4.3	1.2
362/362MG Ver.	2.0	3.1	1.3
362/362MG Hor.	2.5	3.9	1.3
363/363MG Ver.	4.5	5.2	2.3
363/363MG Hor.	4.0	5.1	2.3
383/383MG Ver.	5.0	6.4	2.3
383/383MG Hor.	4.5	6.5	2.3
365 Ver.	4.5	5.6	3.0
365 Hor.	4.5	5.2	3.0
375 Ver.	7.0	11.3	3.9
375 Hor.	6.5	10.3	3.9
366 Ver.	6.0	8.0	5.6
366 Hor.	6.0	7.5	5.6

*There is a difference between Sone values certified by HVI for residential use and by AMCA for commercial/industrial use. Exact comparison of these values is not possible. This difference is mainly due to the procedures used to convert measured sound to perceived sound. ANSI S3.4, used by both HVI and AMCA, specifies a procedure for calculating loudness as perceived by a typical listener under specific conditions. HVI establishes values at a distance of 5 feet from the fan in a "spherical free field"; AMCA established values at a distance 5 feet in a "hemispherical free field." HVI results are rounded to the nearest 0.5 Sone, AMCA to the nearest 0.1 Sone.

TABLE 1 – AMCA LICENSED PERFORMANCE

Model Number & Discharge	AMCA Sones @ 0.0" S.P.*	CFM At Static Pressure (Ps–inches of H$_2$0)						Volts	Total Watts	RPM	Duct Size	Model Number & Discharge
		0.0" Ps	0.1" Ps	.125" Ps	.250" Ps	.375" Ps	.500" Ps					
360/360MG Ver.	2.9	120	110	107	90	55	—	120	80	1200	3¼"x10"	360/360MG Ver.
360/360MG Hor.	2.7	127	113	109	84	32	—	120	80	1325	3¼"x10"	360/360MG Hor.
314/314MG Ver.	3.2	140	128	124	106	46	—	120	70	1000	3¼"x10"	314/314MG Ver.
314/314MG Hor.	3.0	160	148	145	120	52	—	120	70	1050	3¼"x10"	314/314MG Hor.
361/361MG Ver.	4.6	180	166	162	146	126	—	120	100	1600	3¼"x10"	361/361MG Ver.
361/361MG Hor.	4.3	174	158	155	134	106	—	120	100	1625	3¼"x10"	361/361MG Hor.
362/362MG Ver.	3.1	220	204	200	178	138	—	120	115	1150	3¼"x10"	362/362MG Ver.
362/362MG Hor.	3.9	236	221	216	182	122	—	120	115	1250	3¼"x10"	362/362MG Hor.
363/363MG Ver.	5.2	330	310	304	276	232	—	120	165	1575	3¼"x10"	363/363MG Ver.
363/363MG Hor.	5.1	330	308	300	268	216	—	120	165	1625	3¼"x10"	363/363MG Hor.
383/383MG Ver.	6.4	340	319	312	280	236	144	120	165	1575	3¼"x10"	383/383MG Ver.
383/383MG Hor.	6.5	344	324	316	282	236	120	120	165	1625	3¼"x10"	383/383MG Hor.
365 Ver.	5.6	485	460	450	410	360	300	120	255	1050	7" Round	365 Ver.
365 Hor.	5.2	505	455	445	395	350	240	120	240	1100	7" Round	365 Hor.
375 Ver.	11.3	770	750	740	700	670	630	120	420	1600	7" Round	375 Ver.
375 Hor.	10.3	775	750	745	705	675	650	120	435	1600	7" Round	375 Hor.
366 Ver.	8.0	960	940	935	895	815	710	120	440	1050	6"x18"	366 Ver.
366 Hor.	7.5	1010	960	950	880	780	660	120	440	1050	6"x18"	366 Hor.

The performances shown are with inlet grille, backdraft damper and outlet duct. RPM shown is nominal and the performance is based on actual speed of test.

LoSone® Cabinet Ventilators

For large meeting room or institutional applications requiring up to 3300 CFM. LoSone® Cabinet Ventilators are quiet-running, heavy-duty, specification grade ventilators. Permanently lubricated ball bearing motors are designed for continuous operation. Resilient motor mounts and 1/2" acoustic insulation surrounding a 20-gauge galvanized steel housing result in exceptionally quiet operation for ventilators of these capacities.

May be installed as either a right angle or in-line ventilators. Unique mounting brackets permit easy mounting in any of eight different positions.

Cabinet Ventilator Accessories

Model D100	Damper Kit for Model 367 Cabinet Ventilator. Twin damper flaps and mounting hardware included.
Model D101	Damper Kit for Model 368 Cabinet Ventilator. Twin damper flaps and mounting hardware included.
Model V104	Vibration Dampening Hangers. Fits both Models 367 and 368 Cabinet Ventilators. Set of four required for each ventilator.

Broan Mfg. Co., Inc. certifies that the cabinet ventilators shown hereon are licensed to bear the AMCA seal. The ratings shown are based on tests made in accordance with AMCA standard 210 and comply with the requirements of the AMCA Certified Ratings Program.

Model 367
- 120 volts, 5.8 amps
- Fits 7-3/4" x 33-3/4" duct
- Use Model G102 Grille Kit for ceiling applications (available separately) — Page 20
- Use Model 72W or 72V (6 amp, 120V) Electronic Speed Control for variable blower speed and sound level selection (available separately) — Page 24
- Use Model D100 Damper Kit for applications where unit will be ducted to outside (available separately) — twin damper flaps prevent backdrafts

Model 368
- 240 volts, 5.4 amps
- Fits 9-3/4" x 41-3/8" duct
- Use Model G103 Grille Kit for ceiling applications (available separately) — Page 20
- Use Model 75V (6 amp, 240V) Electronic Speed Control for variable blower speed and sound level selection (available separately) — Page 24
- Use Model D101 Damper Kit for applications where unit will be ducted to outside (available separately) — twin damper flaps prevent backdrafts

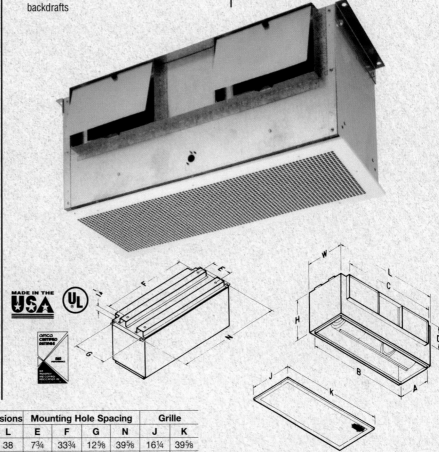

MADE IN THE USA

Model	Inlet		Outlet		Outside Dimensions			Mounting Hole Spacing				Grille	
	A	B	C	D	H	W	L	E	F	G	N	J	K
367	12⅜	35¾	33¾	7¾	14⅝	14⅝	38	7¾	33¾	12⅝	39⅝	16¼	39⅝
368	14½	43½	41⅜	9¾	16¾	16¾	45¾	10¼	41¾	12⅝	47⅜	18⅜	47¼

See catalog #99850138 for complete AMCA licensed ratings.

Typical Fan Performance as Installed

Model	RPM	CFM @ Various Static Pressure – (Ps-in. of H_2O)				
		0.100Ps CFM	0.250Ps CFM	0.375Ps CFM	0.625Ps CFM	0.750Ps CFM
367 (Rt. Angle Discharge)	950	1900	1750	1650	1400	1050
367 (In-Line Discharge)	1000	1750	1650	1550	1250	900
368 (Rt. Angle Discharge)	1080	3300	3100	2950	2550	2250
368 (In-Line Discharge)	1080	3300	3100	3000	2400	2200

RPM shown is nominal and performance is based on actual speed of test.

Theoretical Fan Capacity @ 1100 RPM

Model	CFM @ Various Static Pressures – (Ps-in. of H_2O)					Nominal Bhp
	0.100Ps	0.250Ps	0.375Ps	0.625Ps	0.750Ps	
367 (Rt. Angle Discharge)	2390	2100	1900	1450	700	.45 hp
367 (In-Line Discharge)	2000	1900	1750	1250	700	.45 hp
368 (Rt. Angle Discharge)	3390	3150	2690	2510	2100	1.35 hp
368 (In-Line Discharge)	3500	3250	3050	2300	2050	1.35 hp

AMCA Certified Ratings Seal applies to air capacities only.   Sone ratings are in accordance with AMCA Bulletin 300-67.

Performance does not include the effect of an inlet screen or backdraft damper.

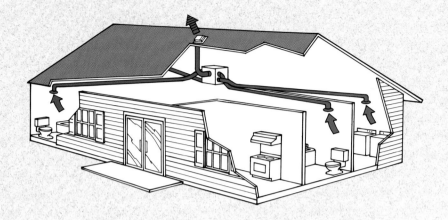

Remote In-Line
Multi-Port Ventilators

A Remotely Mounted Ventilator That Delivers Quiet, High Performance Ventilation Throughout The House

Now you can enjoy the benefit of super-quiet high-capacity ventilation throughout the house — all from a single remotely-mounted ventilator.

Energy efficient, permanently lubricated motors drive high static pressure blowers. That means each unit can easily accommodate extended duct runs from numerous inlet locations. So a number of rooms — specifically bathrooms — can be ventilated simultaneously.

Easy Installation

Like our other ventilation products, the Multi-Port is designed to install quickly and easily. Using the built-in mounting brackets, the Multi-Port can be installed in virtually any orientation. You can use 2, 3 or all 4 inlet ports for installation ease and application flexibility. Ducting T's and Y's can be used for even greater installation flexibility — Page 26.

Service has been simplified, too, with removable panels that give you quick access to the motor without disturbing the ductwork. A removable plug-in blower also contributes to fast service.

■ HVI certified and AMCA licensed* air performance to ensure consistent operating performance
■ UL listed/CSA certified
■ 6" round outlet, 4" round inlets
■ Two inlet duct covers furnished

*See Broan Catalog #99850138 for complete AMCA licensed ratings.

Model MP280

Specifications

Model	MP100	MP140	MP200	MP280
Rated Airflow @ 0.25" S.P. - CFM	107	145	208	284
Airflow @ 0.1" S.P. - CFM	115	157	217	297
Sones*	1.0	1.5	2.0	3.0
When used for continuous, whole house ventilation: Max Area of Home - SQ FTG		Assumes airflow at 0.25" S.P.		
0.3 AC/HR	2675	3625	5200	7100
0.35 AC/HR	2293	3107	4457	6085
0.5 AC/HR	1605	2175	3120	4260
When used for intermittent, point-source ventilation: Max Area - SQ FTG		Assumes airflow at 0.25" S.P.		
15 AC/HR (kitchens)	54	73	104	142
8 AC/HR (bathrooms)	100	136	195	266
6 AC/HR (rec rooms, utility rooms, etc.)	134	181	260	355

All SQ FTG numbers assume 8' ceilings.

*No HVI sound test procedure currently exists for remotely mounted fans. These products were tested using sound test procedures similar to those used by HVI for other exhaust fans.

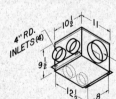

Models MP100
MP140
MP200

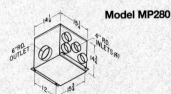

Model MP280

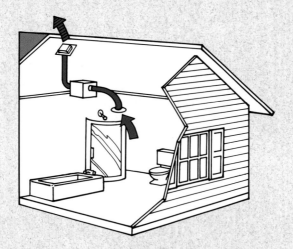

Remote In-Line Single-Port Ventilators

Single-Port Simplicity and the Quiet of Remote Installation

Our Single-Port Ventilator is one of the quietest and most efficient methods of residential ventilation on the market. Remote installation means you have the flexibility of installing the housing in the attic, the basement, or even in an adjacent room. And because the Single-Port utilizes high pressure centrifugal blowers, it accommodates long duct runs. Ducting "Ts" and "Ys" are also available separately permitting multiple intake locations for more application flexibility — Page 26.

Easy Installation & Service

Our Single-Port Ventilator features built-in mounting brackets to simplify installation. It also features a long-life, permanently lubricated motor for years of trouble-free service. Plus, quick-remove panels allow for fast mechanical service access without disturbing attached ductwork.

- 6" round outlet and inlet for easy duct connections
- Air performance is HVI certified and AMCA licensed*
- UL listed/CSA certified
- Plug-in blower removes easily

*See Broan Catalog #99850138 for complete AMCA licensed ratings.

**Models SP100
SP140
SP200**

Specifications

Model	SP100	SP140	SP200
Rated Airflow @ 0.25" S.P. - CFM	107	145	207
Airflow @ 0.1" S.P. - CFM	115	157	217
Sones*	1.0	1.5	2.0
When used for continuous, whole house ventilation: Max Area of Home - SQ FTG	Assumes airflow at 0.25" S.P.		
0.3 AC/HR	2675	3625	5175
0.35 AC/HR	2293	3107	4435
0.5 AC/HR	1605	2175	3105
When used for intermittent, point-source ventilation: Max Area - SQ FTG	Assumes airflow at 0.25" S.P.		
15 AC/HR (kitchens)	54	73	104
8 AC/HR (bathrooms)	100	136	194
6 AC/HR (rec rooms, utility rooms, etc.)	134	181	259

All SQ FTG numbers assume 8' ceilings.

*No HVI sound test procedure currently exists for remotely mounted fans. These products were tested using sound test procedures similar to those used by HVI for other exhaust fans.

Decorator Wall Controls

Model 57W   **Model 57V**

3 Amp Electronic Variable Speed Controls*

- Positive on/off action – dial for variable selection of air speeds and sound levels
- 120V, 3A capacity
- Fit single-gang box
- Built-in radio noise suppressor
- Can be used with all Broan fans within amp rating except Models 682, 682L, 686, 688, 689, 670, 678 and ceiling paddle fans
- Blister packs available (P57W, P57V)

Model 59W   **Model 59V**   **Model 71V**

60 Minute & 12 Hour Time Controls

- Operate continuously or for any set period up to 60 minutes (59W, 59V) or 12 hours (71V)
- Fit single-gang box
- 120V, 20A capacity
- 240V, 10A capacity
- For all Broan heaters and fans within amp ratings
- Blister packs available (P59W, P59V)

Model 61W   **Model 61V**

15 Minute Time Controls

- Operate for any set period up to 15 minutes (no "continuous on" position)
- Fit single-gang box
- 120V, 20A capacity
- 240V, 10A capacity
- For all Broan heaters and fans within amp ratings
- Blister packs available (P61W, P61V)

Model 62W   **Model 62V**

60 Minute Time Controls with Two Rocker Switches

- Timer operates continuously or for any set period up to 60 minutes
- Two separate on/off rocker switches
- Fit two-gang box
- 120V, 20A or 240V, 10A timer/15A rockers
- For all Broan heaters and fans within amp ratings

Model 63W   **Model 63V**

60 Minute Time Controls with Single Rocker Switch

- Timer operates continuously or for any set period up to 60 minutes
- Separate on/off rocker switch
- Fit two-gang box
- 120V, 20A or 240V, 10A timer/15A rocker
- For all Broan heaters and fans within amp ratings

Model 64V

Fan/Light Control with Off-Delay

- Fan and light operate together when control is turned on. Fan continues to operate for a user adjustable time period from 5-60 minutes after light is turned off
- Center position bypasses timer and turns fan and light off immediately
- Fits single-gang box
- 120V, 60 cycle, 4A fan and 4A light capacity
- For use with any Broan fan or fan/light
- Requires hot and neutral wires in the switch box

Model 65W   **Model 65V**

Brass Finished Three-Function Controls

- Polished brass finished wall plate
- Three independent, 120V, 15A rocker switches (20A total)
- Fit single-gang opening
- For all Broan heaters and fans within amp ratings
- Blister packs available (P65W, P65V)

Model 66W   **Model 66V**

Three-Function Controls

- Three independent, 120V, 15A rocker switches (20A total)
- Fit single-gang opening
- For all Broan heaters and fans within amp ratings
- Blister packs available (P66W, P66V)

Model 67W   **Model 67V**

Chrome Finished Three-Function Controls

- Polished chrome finished wall plate
- Three independent, 120V, 15A rated rocker switches (20A total)
- Fit single-gang opening
- For all Broan heaters and fans within amp ratings
- Blister packs available (P67W, P67V)

Model 68W   **Model 68V**

Two-Function Controls

- Two independent, 120V, 15A rocker switches (20A total)
- Fit single-gang box
- For all Broan heaters and fans within amp ratings
- Blister packs available (P68W, P68V)

Model 72V   **Model 72W**   **Model 75V**

6 Amp Electronic Variable Speed Controls*

- 120V, 6A capacity – Models 72W, 72V
- 240V, 6A capacity – Model 75V
- Other features same as 57W/57V
- Can be used with all Broan fans within amp rating except Models 682, 682L, 688, 689, 670, 678, 699 and ceiling paddle fans

Model 77W

Three Switch Control

- Specially designed for use with SensAire® Fan/Lights — Pages 2-3
- Top switch provides three settings for fan sensor (On-Auto-Off)
- Remaining switches control light/night-light
- White wall plate and switches
- Fits single-gang opening
- Blister packs available (P77W)

Do not use with impedance protected motor.

Broan Wall Control Selection Guide – Ventilation

How to use this chart:
Find your desired ventilator in the border column and match with your desired wall control model.
An "x" indicates the control can be used with the listed ventilator.

Broan Model Number	57W 57V	59W 59V	61W 61V	62W 62V	63W 63V	64V	65W 65V	66W 66V	67W 67V	68W 68V	72W 72V	75V	77W	Broan Model Number
12C	X	X	X			X					X			12C
161		X	X			X					X			161
162	X	X	X		X					X	X			162
163		X	X		X					X				163
164	X	X	X		X		X	X	X	X	X			164
314/MG	X	X	X			X					X			314/MG
360/MG	X	X	X			X					X			360/MG
361/MG	X	X	X			X					X			361/MG
362/MG	X	X	X			X					X			362/MG
363/MG	X	X	X			X					X			363/MG
365	X	X	X			X					X			365
366		X	X								X			366
367		X	X								X			367
368		X	X									X		368
375		X	X			X					X			375
383/MG	X	X	X			X					X			383/MG
502	X	X	X			X					X			502
503	X	X	X			X					X			503
504	X	X	X			X					X			504
505	X	X	X			X					X			505
506	X	X	X			X					X			506
507	X	X	X			X					X			507
508	X	X	X			X					X			508
509	X	X	X			X					X			509
509S		X	X			X								509S
510		X	X			X								510
511	X	X	X			X					X			511
512	X	X	X								X			512
512M	X	X	X								X			512M
655	X	X	X	X			X	X	X		X			655
656		X	X		X					X				656
657	X	X	X		X	X				X	X			657
658	X	X	X		X	X				X	X			658
659	X	X	X	X			X	X	X		X			659
670		X	X			X					X			670
671	X	X	X			X					X			671
673	X	X	X			X					X			673
676	X	X	X			X					X			676
678		X	X		X	X				X				678
679	X	X	X		X	X				X	X			679
679FL	X	X	X		X	X				X	X			679FL
681		X	X			X								681
682		X	X			X								682
682L		X	X		X	X				X				682L
684	X	X	X			X					X			684
686		X	X			X								686
688		X	X			X								688
689		X	X			X								689
695	X	X	X	X			X	X	X		X			695
696	X	X	X		X	X				X	X			696
708	X	X	X			X					X			708
709	X	X	X		X	X				X	X			709
710	X	X	X	X		X	X	X	X		X			710
712	X	X	X	X		X	X	X	X		X			712
714	X	X	X	X		X	X	X	X		X			714
720	X	X	X	X		X	X	X	X		X			720
721	X	X	X	X		X	X	X	X		X			721
722	X	X	X	X		X	X	X	X		X			722
730	FOUR-FUNCTION CONTROL INCLUDED													730
735	FOUR-FUNCTION CONTROL INCLUDED													735
HD50	X	X	X			X	X	X	X		X			HD50
HD50L	X	X	X		X	X				X	X			HD50L
HD80	X	X	X			X					X			HD80
HD80L	X	X	X		X	X				X	X			HD80L
HS120L							X	X	X				X	HS120L
HS130														HS130
HS90														HS90
MHS120L								X	X	X			X	MHS120L
MS120L								X	X	X			X	MS120L
MS130														MS130
MS90														MS90
S120FL	X	X	X	X		X	X	X	X		X			S120FL
S120L	X	X	X	X		X	X	X			X			S120L
S130	X	X	X			X					X			S130
S90	X	X	X			X					X			S90
Broan Model Number	57W 57V	59W 59V	61W 61V	62W 62V	63W 63V	64V	65W 65V	66W 66V	67W 67V	68W 68V	72W 72V	75V	77W	Broan Model Number

Roof Caps

Model 611 Roof Cap
- For flat roof installation
- Aluminum natural finish
- For up to 8" round duct

Model 611

Model 611CM Roof Cap
- With curb mount
- Other features same as Model 611

Model 611CM

Model 612 Roof Cap
- For flat roof installation
- Aluminum natural finish
- For up to 12" round duct

Model 612

Model 612CM Roof Cap
- With curb mount
- Other features same as Model 612

Model 612CM

Model 634 Roof Cap
- For 3-1/4" x 10" or up to 8" round duct
- Built-in backdraft damper and bird screen
- Steel baked black enamel finish

Models 634 634M 644

Model 634M Roof Cap
- For 6" round duct
- Other features same as Model 634

Model 644 Roof Cap
- Aluminum, natural finish
- Other features same as Model 634

Model 636 Roof Cap
- For 3" or 4" round duct
- Built-in backdraft damper and bird screen
- Steel baked black enamel finish

Models 636 636AL

Model 636AL Roof Cap
- Same as Model 636 except aluminum natural finish

Ducting

Model 401 Duct
- 3-1/4" x 10" duct
- 2' galvanized section

Model 401

Model 403 Round Duct
- 3" round duct
- 2' galvanized section

Model 403

Model 404 Round Duct
- 4" round duct
- 2' galvanized section

Model 406 Round Duct
- 6" round duct
- 2' galvanized section

Model 407 Round Duct
- 7" round duct
- 2' galvanized section

Model 410 Round Duct
- 10" round duct
- 2' galvanized section

Models DT4C, DT6C, DT7C Non-Insulated Flexible Duct
- For 4" (DT4C), 6" (DT6C), 7" (DT7C). (DT4C is a 4-pack)
- 25' standard length

Models DT4C DT6C DT7C

Models DT4W, DT6W, DT7W Insulated Flexible Duct
- For 4" (DT4W), 6" (DT6W), 7" (DT7W)
- 25' standard length

Models DT4W DT6W DT7W

Ducting "Ts" and "Ys"
- 30-gauge galvanized steel construction
- Choice of a variety of duct diameters
- "Ts" include:
  T446 – 4"x4"x6"; T466 – 4"x6"x6"
  T666 – 6"x6"x6"; T777 – 7"x7"x7"
- "Ys" include:
  Y446 – 4"x4"x6"; Y466 – 4"x6"x6";
  Y666 – 6"x6"x6"; Y777 – 7"x7"x7"
- Individually packaged

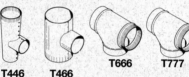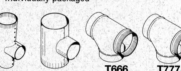
T446   T466   T666   T777

Y446   Y466   Y666   Y777

Transitions

Model 411 Transition
- Converts 3-1/4" x 10" duct to 6" round duct

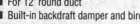
Model 411

Model 412 Transition
- Converts 3-1/4" x 10" duct to 7" round duct

Model 413 Transition
- Converts 3-1/4" x 10" duct to 8" round duct

Model 472 Transition
- Converts 10" round duct to 8" round duct
- Includes damper

Wall Caps

Model 613 Wall Cap
- For 12" round duct
- Built-in backdraft damper and bird screen
- Aluminum natural finish

Model 613

Model 645 3" Louvered Wall Cap

Model 646 6" Louvered Wall Cap
- Standard package – 6 to a carton
- White polymeric

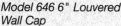
Model 645 (3" dia.)

Model 639 Wall Cap
- For 3-1/4" x 10" duct
- Spring-loaded backdraft damper
- Steel baked black enamel finish

Model 649 Wall Cap
- Aluminum, natural finish
- Other features same as Model 639

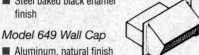
Models 639 649

Model 640 Wall Cap
- For 3" round duct
- Built-in bird screen
- Steel baked black enamel finish
- Standard package – 6 to a carton

Model 640

Model 641 Wall Cap
- For 6" round duct
- Built-in backdraft damper and bird screen
- Aluminum, natural finish

Model 647 Wall Cap
- For 7" round duct
- Other features same as Model 641

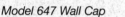
Models 641 647

Model 642 Wall Cap
- For 3" or 4" duct
- 4" to 3" transition included
- Built-in damper
- Aluminum, natural finish
- Standard package – 4 to a carton

Model 642

Model 643 Wall Cap
- For 8" round duct
- Aluminum, natural finish

Ducting Kits

Model 443 Flexible Roof Ducting Kit
- Includes Model 636 Roof Cap
- 4" diameter metal duct connector
- 2 duct clamps
- 4" to 3" reducer
- 8' of 4" flexible ducting

Model 443

Model 450 Flexible Wall Ducting Kit
- Includes white polymeric louvered wall cap
- 4" diameter metal duct connector
- 2 duct clamps
- 4" to 3" reducer
- 5' of 4" flexible ducting

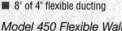
Model 450 (4" dia.)

Filters

Model 99010042 Aluminum Filter
- Fits Utility Ventilator Models 503, 505, 509, and 509S
- Model 51AF – same as 99010042, except 6 to a carton

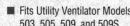
Model 99010042

Model 99010271 Aluminum Filter
- Fits Utility Ventilator Models 12C, 502, 504, 508, 510, and 511
- Model 52AF – same as 99010271, except 6 to a carton

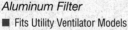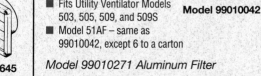

Elbows

Model 417
Adjustable Elbow
■ Fits 3" round duct

Models 415
416
417
418
419

Model 416 Adjustable Elbow
■ Fits 4" round duct

Model 418 Adjustable Elbow
■ Fits 10" round duct

Model 419 Adjustable Elbow
■ Fits 6" round duct

Model 415 Adjustable Elbow
■ Fits 7" round duct

Model 428 Vertical Elbow
■ Fits 3-1/4" x 10" duct

Model 428

Model 429 Horizontal Elbow
■ Fits 3-1/4" x 10" duct

Model 430 Short Eave Elbow
■ For 3-1/4" x 10" duct
■ Includes backdraft damper and grille

Model 429

Model 431 Long Eave Elbow
■ For 3-1/4" x 10" duct
■ Includes backdraft damper and grille

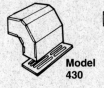
Model 430

Model 431

Metal Grille Kits

Model 97008485 Metal Grille Kit
■ Fits fan Models 688, 689, 670, 671, 684 and 676
■ Anodized aluminum

Model 97007378
■ Fits Utility Ventilator Models 12C, 502, 504 and 508
■ Anodized aluminum
■ Model 50MG – same as 97007378, except 6 to a carton

Model 97007377
■ Fits Utility Ventilator Models 503, 505 and 509
■ Anodized aluminum

Model 97008068
■ Fits Utility Ventilator Model 506
■ Anodized aluminum

Model 97008069
■ Fits Utility Ventilator Model 507
■ Anodized aluminum

Broan Ducting Accessory Selection Guide – Ventilation Fans

How to use these charts:
1) Look for your model number in the Duct Size Reference chart.
2) Match that model's duct size to the appropriate row in the Accessory Application Matrix.
3) Choose your desired accessories from the choices listed.

Duct Size Reference

Model #	Duct Size	Model #	Duct Size	Model #	Duct Size	Model #	Duct Size	Model #	Duct Size
162	4"	503	3¹/₄" x 10"	679	4"	720	4"	MHS120L	4"
164	4"	504	10"	679FL		721	4"	MS120L	4"
314	3¹/₄" x 10"	505	8"	684	4"	722	4"	MS130	4"
360	3¹/₄" x 10"	655	4"	688	3"	730	4"	MS90	4"
361	3¹/₄" x 10"	657	4"	689	3"	735	4"	S120FL	4"
362	3¹/₄" x 10"	658	4"	695	4"	HD50	4"	S120L	4"
363	3¹/₄" x 10"	659	4"	696	4"	HD50L	4"	S130	4"
365	7"	670	3"	708	4"	HD80	4"	S90	4"
366	12"	671	3"	709	4"	HD80L	4"		
375	7"	673	6"	710	4"	HS120L	4"		
383	3¹/₄" x 10"	676	4"	712	4"	HS130	4"		
502	3¹/₄" x 10"	678	4"	714	4"	HS90	4"		

Broan Accessory Application Matrix

Duct Size	Roof Caps	Wall Caps	Ducting	Transitions
3" Round	636 636AL 443 (kit)	640 642 645 450 (kit)	403 417	
4" Round	636 636AL 443 (kit)	642 450 (kit)	404 416 DT4C DT4W	
6" Round	634 634M 644	641 646	406 419 DT6C DT6W	411 (3¹/₄" x 10")
7" Round	634 644	647	407 415 DT7C DT7W	412 (3¹/₄" x 10")
8" Round	611 611CM 634 644	643		413 (3¹/₄" x 10") 472 (10" Rd.)
10" Round	612 612CM 437	441	410 418	472 (8" Rd.)
12" Round	612 612CM	613		
3¹/₄" x 10"	611 611CM 634 644	639 649	401 428 429 430 431	411 (6" Rd.) 412 (7" Rd.) 413 (8" Rd.)

Specifications

	Model No.	Description	Housing H x W x D	CFM / Sones	Amps*	Duct
SENSAIRE® SERIES (pgs. 4–5)	HS90	Humidity-Sensor Fan	7⅝ x 9¼ x 9½"	90 / 1.5	0.70	4" Round
	HS120L	Humidity-Sensor Fan / Light / Night-Light	7⅝ x 9¼ x 9½"	120 / 2.5	1.80	4" Round
	HS130	Humidity-Sensor Fan	7⅝ x 9¼ x 9½"	130 / 2.5	0.90	4" Round
	MHS120L	Motion/Humidity-Sensor Fan / Light / Night-Light	7⅝ x 9¼ x 9½"	120 / 2.5	2.10	4" Round
	MS90	Motion-Sensor Fan	7⅝ x 9¼ x 9½"	90 / 1.5	0.70	4" Round
	MS120L	Motion-Sensor Fan / Light / Night-Light	7⅝ x 9¼ x 9½"	120 / 2.5	1.80	4" Round
	MS130	Motion-Sensor Fan	7⅝ x 9¼ x 9½"	130 / 2.5	0.90	4" Round

	Model No.	Description	Housing H x W x D	CFM / Sones	Heater Watts	Amps*	Duct
DESIGNER SERIES (pgs. 6–7)	708	Fan - oak grille	5¾ x 8¼ x 8"	80 / 3.0	—	1.50	4" Round
	709	Fan / Light - square oak frame	5¾ x 8¼ x 8"	80 / 3.0	—	2.50	4" Round
	710	Polished brass finished metal grille	5¾ x 8¼ x 8"	100 / 3.5	—	2.00	4" Round
	712	Soft white painted metal grille	5¾ x 8¼ x 8"	100 / 3.5	—	2.00	4" Round
	714	Polished chrome finished metal grille	5¾ x 8¼ x 8"	100 / 3.5	—	2.00	4" Round
	720	Square oak frame	5¾ x 8¼ x 8"	100 / 3.5	—	2.00	4" Round
	721	Round oak frame	5¾ x 8¼ x 8"	100 / 3.5	—	2.00	4" Round
	722	Octagonal oak frame	5¾ x 8¼ x 8"	100 / 3.5	—	2.00	4" Round
	730	Heater / Fan / Light / Night-Light	6½ x 10 x 14⅛"	70 / 3.5	1500	15.50	4" Round
	735	Heater / Fan / Light / Night-Light	6½ x 10 x 14⅛"	70 / 3.5	1500	15.50	4" Round
SOLITAIRE® SERIES (pgs. 8–9)	S90	Fan	7⅝ x 9¼ x 9½"	90 / 1.5	—	0.50	4" Round
	S120FL	Fluorescent Fan / Light / Night-Light	7⅝ x 9¼ x 9½"	120 / 2.5	—	1.20	4" Round
	S120L	Fan / Light / Night-Light	7⅝ x 9¼ x 9½"	120 / 2.5	—	1.50	4" Round
	S130	Fan	7⅝ x 9¼ x 9½"	130 / 2.5	—	0.70	4" Round
COMBINATION UNITS (pgs. 10–11)	655	Heater / Fan / Light	5¾ x 8¼ x 14¼"	70 / 3.5	1300	12.75	4" Round
	656	Heater / Light	5¾ x 8¼ x 14¼"	—	1300	11.90	—
	657	Fan / Light	5¾ x 8¼ x 14¼"	70 / 3.5	—	2.00	4" Round
	658	Heater / Fan	5¾ x 8¼ x 14¼"	70 / 3.5	1300	11.90	4" Round
	659	Heater / Fan / Light	5¾ x 8¼ x 14¼"	50 / 2.5	1300	12.00	4" Round
	678	Fan / Light	5¾ x 8¼ x 8"	50 / 2.5	—	2.00	4" Round
	679	Fan / Light	5¾ x 8¼ x 8"	70 / 3.5	—	2.00	4" Round
	679FL	Fluorescent Fan / Light	5¾ x 8¼ x 8"	70 / 3.5	—	1.50	4" Round
	695	Heater / Fan / Light	5¾ x 8¼ x 14¼"	100 / 4.0	1300	12.75	4" Round
	696	Fan / Light	5¾ x 8¼ x 14¼"	100 / 4.0	—	2.00	4" Round

	Model No.	Description	Housing H x W x D	CFM/Sones	Amps*	Duct
BATHROOM FANS (pgs. 12–13)	670	Wall / Ceiling	3⅝ x 7½ x 7¼"	50 / 1.5	0.80	3" Round
	671	Wall / Ceiling	3⅝ x 7½ x 7¼"	70 / 3.0	1.15	3" Round
	673	Ceiling	5¼"H x 6¼" Rd.	60 / 4.0	1.00	6" Round
	676	Ceiling	5¾ x 8¼ x 8"	110 / 4.0	1.30	4" Round
	684	Ceiling	5¾ x 8¼ x 8"	80 / 2.5	0.75	4" Round
	688	Wall / Ceiling	3⅝ x 7½ x 7¼"	50 / 2.0	0.70	3" Round
	689	Wall / Ceiling	3⅝ x 7½ x 7¼"	60 / 3.5	1.10	3" Round
DUCT-FREE FANS (pg. 13)	682	Fan	3¾ x 7⅛ x 7⅛"	—	1.00	Duct-free
	682L	Fan / Light	6¼ x 8¼ x 8¼"	—	1.50	Duct-free
	686	Fan	2⅜ x 4½ x 8"	—	0.30	Duct-free
UTILITY VENTILATORS (pgs. 14–15)	12C	Wall	11½" Sq.	380 / 5.5	1.70	Direct Discharge
	502	Wall / Ceiling	3¼ x 13⅞ x 16¾"	270 / 7.0	1.70	3¼" x 10"
	503	Wall / Ceiling	3¼ x 12 x 14"	160 / 5.0	1.75	3¼" x 10"
	504	Ceiling / Vertical Discharge	7"H x 10¼" Rd.	350 / 6.5	1.70	10" Round
	505	Ceiling / Vertical Discharge	7"H x 8¼" Rd.	180 / 5.0	1.50	8" Round
	506	Wall / Chain Operated	10⅜" Rd.	480 / 6.5	1.70	Direct Discharge
	507	Wall / Chain Operated	8⅜" Rd.	250 / 4.5	1.50	Direct Discharge
	508	Wall	10⅜" Rd.	270 / 6.0	1.70	Direct Discharge
	509	Wall	8⅜" Rd.	180 / 5.0	1.50	Direct Discharge
	509S	Wall / Built-in Switch	8⅜" Rd.	180 / 5.0	1.50	Direct Discharge
	510	Room-to-Room	11½" Sq.	380 / 5.0	1.70	—
	511	Room-to-Room	11½" Sq.	180 / 3.5	1.50	—
	512	Room-to-Room	6" Round	90 / 3.5	1.00	—
	512M	Wall	6" Round	70 / 3.5	1.00	Direct Discharge
HD SERIES™ VENTILATORS (pg. 16)	HD50	Fan	5¾ x 8¼ x 8"	50 / 2.0	0.40	4" Round
	HD50L	Fan / Light	5¾ x 8¼ x 8"	50 / 2.5	1.30	4" Round
	HD80	Fan	5¾ x 8¼ x 8"	80 / 2.5	0.60	4" Round
	HD80L	Fan / Light	5¾ x 8¼ x 8"	80 / 3.5	1.70	4" Round
BULB HEATERS (pg. 17)	161	Ceiling (One Bulb)	6 x 12¼ x 8⅛"	—	2.10	—
	162	Ceiling (One Bulb, Fan)	6⅜ x 11⅝ x 8⅛"	70 / 3.5	2.50	4" Round
	163	Ceiling (Two Bulb)	6 x 10⅛ x 14¼"	—	4.30	—
	164	Ceiling (Two Bulb, Fan)	6⅜ x 11⅝ x 14¼"	70 / 3.5	4.50	4" Round
LOSONE® VENTILATORS		See pgs. 18–21 for specifications – also see Broan catalog #99850138				

*Total Connected Load   Specifications subject to change without notice.

BROAN®

A NORTEK COMPANY

P.O. Box 140, Hartford, WI 53027 1-800-548-0790
In Canada: Broan Limited 905-670-2500

ALL THE COMFORTS OF HOME™

Printed in the U.S.A.

DACOR PREFERENCE
The cooktop of distinction

A reflection of your good taste.™

Preference (SGM-464EM) in Satin with EM-5 module and Pinnacle RV 46

One glance at the DACOR "Preference"* and you know it's the look you love.

The elegance of the Preference begins with its neo-classical styling in a luxurious "Satin" finish or one of three rich lustrous porcelainized colors of White, Black, or Almond. Complementing these finishes is the sophisticated matte black texture of the uniquely designed grates which are gracefully curved at the front and rear providing more useable cooking surface area. Most important—these grates form a platform with a continuous surface to allow easy sliding of pots and pans across the cooktop. The very sleek low profile of the Preference is an added touch of class.

Easy-to-Clean

A second glance at the DACOR Preference reveals how easy it is to clean. The cooktop surface is totally sealed with the absence of any cracks or areas for spills to hide. Because the spill areas are extra large with radius sides and corners, they can be easily cleaned. There is only one grate for each pair of burners. Simply remove a grate and wipe with a damp sponge.

Commercial-Type Cooking Performance

The DACOR Preference has been designed specifically for residential kitchens with user-friendly features and it gives you the performance preferred by serious cooks. The gas burners are high output for a complete range of cooking needs. The 46" Preference has three burners that deliver 12,500 BTU's and three that deliver 8,500 BTU's. Two of the burners on the 36" Preference deliver 12,500 BTU's and the other two, 8,500 BTU's. The 30" model has two 11,000 BTU and two 8,000 BTU burners. The high BTU burners are staggered for convenience when cooking with large containers.

The controls are also ergonomically designed. Burners are ignited when the control is turned to any position. Precise flame level is maintained by brass valving. And DACOR's Perma-Flame feature promises that your gas flame will automatically restart instantly if it goes out.

*Patent pending

Gas or Electric—Your Preference

Some cooks prefer a gas cooktop, others electric. And many cooks wish they could have both. The DACOR Preference offers you the best of both fuels.

Our 36" and 46" EM models combine gas burners with electric cooking modules which offer a selection of different type elements. Interchangeable barbecue and wok/canning modules enable you to change your cooking capability quickly. Talk about flexibility! The barbecue even has griddle and rotisserie accessories.

All DACOR cooking appliances are made in America

Preference (SGM-362EM) in Black with EM-4 module and Pinnacle RV 36

The perfect complement to your Preference cooktop

CPS 127 ovens in Stainless

DACOR Convection Plus built-in ovens, combined with your DACOR Preference, distinguish your kitchen with world-class cooking performance and design excellence.

These double or single self-cleaning ovens are available in 27" and 30" sizes in stainless steel or colors which harmonize with those of your cooktop. Featuring an elegant frameless design with a gracefully curved control panel and handle, the innovative Convection Plus ovens offer many value-added benefits—electronic touch pad controls…pure convection with a third element for extra-delicious baked goods and roasts…the largest pure convection and non-convection capacities of any 27" oven…and a deactivation mode to provide child safety.

CPD 227 oven in white   Patent pending

Cutout Dimensions For SGM Cooktop

	Cutout Width		Cutout Depth		Overall Width		Overall Depth	
	inches	cm	inches	cm	inches	cm	inches	cm
SGM304	27½	70	19⅞	51	30	77	21	54
SGM364	33¾	86	19⅞	51	36	92	21	54
SGM362EM*	33¾	86	19⅞	51	36	92	21	54
SGM466	44½	113	19⅞	51	46	117	21	54
SGM464EM*	44½	113	19⅞	51	46	117	21	54
SGM304 w/RV	27½	70	22⁵⁄₁₆	57	30	77	23⅛	59
SGM364 w/RV	33¾	86	22⁵⁄₁₆	57	36	92	23⅛	59
SGM362EM w/RV*	33¾	86	22⁵⁄₁₆	57	36	92	23⅛	59
SGM466 w/RV	44½	113	22⁵⁄₁₆	57	46	117	23⅛	59
SGM464EM w/RV*	44½	113	22⁵⁄₁₆	57	46	117	23⅛	59

Note: The height of the chassis is 4."

*Maximum connected load 3.6 K.W.@ 20A. 240V.
Specify natural or L.P gas when ordering.

For the most current specifications, call Dimension Express at (702) 833-3600 from a fax machine. Enter "9003" for instructions and a directory of Dacor products.

All DACOR Preference cooktops carry a one year full warranty.

LISTED

dacor

950 South Raymond Avenue, Pasadena, California 91109
Telephone: (818) 799-1000 Fax: (818) 441-9632
Mexico: Telephone: 011-525-211-7055 Fax: 011-525-211-7063

Lit No. L-85436A   © September, 1995, DACOR   Printed in U.S.A.

A Touch of Glass

A reflection of your good taste.™

Touch Top in Black (ETT 365B)   **Cabinetry by Snaidero**

DACOR Touch Top

Cooking precision is at your fingertips with the innovative command center on the new DACOR "Touch Top." Touch an element control twice and a slender red ribbon illuminates to ascend or descend according to your need for higher or lower heat. From slow heating delicate sauces to a rolling boil for pasta, you are in control. It's fun and easy to operate.

Precaution is at your fingertips too. Press the DACOR logo and the cooktop is secured against accidental operation by children or during cleaning. Another safety feature is heat indicator lights which remain illuminated until the cooktop surface is cool to the touch.

The distinctive styling of the new cooktop offers 21st century design combined with the quality and performance that have been DACOR hallmarks for over thirty years.

All DACOR cooking appliances are made in America

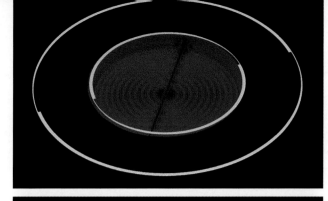

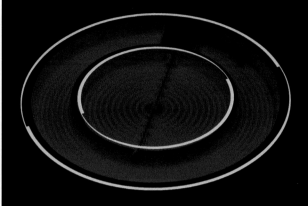

Dual circuit ribbon elements

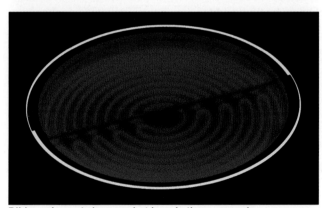

Ribbon elements become hot in only three seconds

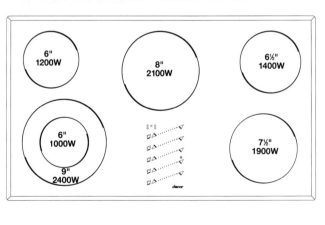

The DACOR Touch Top contributes to the pleasure and performance of all kinds of cooks. Whether you cook a little or a lot, its uncomplicated easy operation frees you to prepare something quick and easy or complex and elegant with equal confidence. Its versatility appeals to those who are seriously involved in the craft of cooking as well as the beginning cook. Equally important for all of the cooks at your house, the smooth surface of the Touch Top allows cookware to be moved safely and easily across the top. Clean up is a snap…just wipe away spills.

The superiority of the Touch Top's cooking capability begins with the five elements on the 36″ model. Most other electric glass cooktops have only four. Another feature of both the 30″ and 36″ models is the dual circuit radiant element which offers the option of two sizes with the touch of a finger. The other elements are a unique combination so you can match your different size pans to the same size element. This is quick and efficient, saving time and money.

Developed from a new technology, the radiant elements deliver a three-second response with very uniform heat distribution on the cooking surface. The heat is transmitted directly upward so that only the cooking zone becomes hot; the rest of the cooktop surface remains cool. A limiter on each element prevents empty pots and pans from melting or damaging the cooking surface.

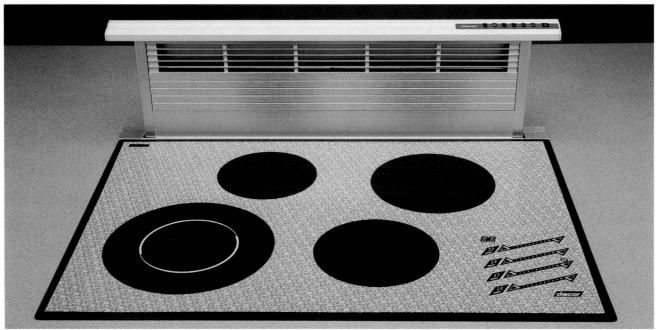

Touch Top in White (ETT 304W) with Pinnacle Raised Vent (RV 30)

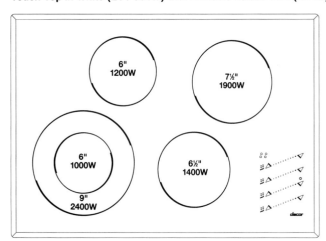

The DACOR Touch Top is the ultimate in design sophistication becoming an elegant centerpiece of the countertop. The surface is just one smooth piece of glass with a beautiful bevelled perimeter which interfaces with the countertop. There is no separate control panel or protruding knobs to disturb the smooth symmetry of the glass.

An important feature of the Touch Top is its shallow depth of only 2¾." This provides extra space for cabinet drawers or storage underneath the cooktop.

In addition to a one-year full warranty the DACOR Touch Top carries an additional four-year limited warranty on glass and an additional limited one-year warranty on elements and controls.

DACOR ETT Cabinet Planning Details

	Cutout Dimensions*	Overall Dimensions*	Electrical Requirements
ETT304	28½W x 19½D	30W x 21D x 2¾H	240V., 30 amp
ETT365	34½W x 19½D	36W x 21D x 2¾H	240V., 40 amp
ETT304 w/RV	28½W x 21½D	30W x 23D x 2¾H	240V., 30 amp
ETT365 w/RV	34½W x 21½D	36W x 23D x 2¾H	240V., 40 amp

*Note: These dimensions are not intended for use as final installation specifications. Refer to installation instructions packed with unit for complete information. Constant product improvement makes some features and specifications subject to change without notice.

For the most current specification, call Dimension Express at (702) 833-3600 from a fax machine. Enter "9003" for instructions and a directory of all DACOR products.

A reflection of your good taste.™

950 South Raymond Avenue, Pasadena, California 91109
Telephone: (818) 799-1000 Fax: (818) 441-9632

Mexico
Telephone: 011-525-211-7055
FAX: 011-525-211-7063

 LISTED c

The perfect complement to your DACOR Touch Top is a DACOR Convection Plus 27" or 30" self-cleaning single or double oven. The Convection Plus offers "pure convection," extra-large capacity, and cooking flexibility. The single oven may be placed under your Touch Top or in the wall.

Lit. No. L-85121 © July 1995 DACOR Printed in U.S.A.

THE *Art* & SCIENCE OF COOKING

dacor

Epicure Ovens

FIRST THERE'S SCIENCE

DACOR has been on the leading edge of creating superb cooking appliances for over 25 years. Leaders in convection technology, our design and development teams invite you to compare other convection ovens with the Epicure — the best you can buy.

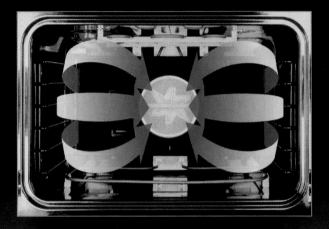

Pure Convection

DACOR's pure convection is a total system approach to cooking. Other convection ovens simply heat air with the elements in the chamber, but DACOR's pure convection uses a third element outside the cooking area, behind a "baffle". The baffle not only separates the food from the heat source, but also channels the air from the convection fan evenly into the oven, eliminating any hot or cool spots.

This system allows multi-rack cooking with even results from one rack to another. This unique process also eliminates transfer of flavors and aromas from one dish to another (and helps the oven stay cleaner).

The externally heated air moving vigorously through the oven saves you time and money by cooking foods in 10% less time at the same temperature, or at a 25° lower temperature in the same time. If you're not familiar with convection cooking, relax! We include a booklet that spells it out simply and quickly.

Easy To Use Control Panel

Easy to read, understand, and use, the control panel of the Epicure Pure Convection Oven is activated by the touch of a finger. Select Pure Convection, Convection Bake, Convection Broil, Standard Bake, Standard Broil or Self-Clean.

Let's talk about safety. Only Dacor ovens have a deactivation mode which prevents accidental use by children and also permits cleaning of the control panel without activating the oven. The Epicure broils with the door closed, which is a safe and efficient way to keep the kitchen cooler and energy consumption lower. And not only does the self cleaning feature allow you to relax about spills or splatters, but it is safe. After the latch is automatically closed and locked for self-cleaning at 875°, the oven door cannot be opened until the interior oven temperature cools down to 390°.

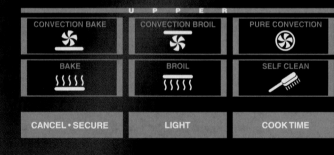

Time Keeping / Temperature Control

More than just a time piece, the digital electronic clock on the new Epicure Convection Oven performs all time-keeping and temperature control functions. It displays the selected temperature setting and cooking mode as well as shows the actual oven temperature in 5-degree increments as the oven heats. When the oven is heated to the set temperature, a pleasant audible tone announces the oven is ready.

When two ovens are used, each has its own light...think about it...have you seen this feature on any other oven? And whether the oven is single or double, there are two minute-timers for your convenience.

Epicure 30" Double Oven
Model #ECPD 230S

Epicure Ovens

Display courtesy of Cooper-Pacific Kitchens, Inc., Pacific Design Center, Los Angeles

THEN THERE'S *Art*

Whether you follow your favorite recipes to the letter, or delight in adding your own innovative touches, you can trust Epicure to perform flawlessly . . . every time. Indulge in the exhilaration of accomplishment when you serve an intimate meal for two, a family dinner, or a feast for friends. Epicure gives you the capacity and capability to do just that, with dependable, consistent, unparalleled results. Which is, after all, the criteria by which we judge a great oven.

The DACOR Epicure Pure Convection Oven makes it a pleasure to create extraordinary meals for family or friends. Even a banquet can be prepared in less time than ever before.

Prepare a meal of meat, poultry and vegetables simultaneously without flavors and aromas being transferred from one dish to another.

Bake as many as six racks of cookies simultaneously in the Epicure and the cookies will be the same.

The Epicure cooking chamber is surrounded by a remarkable ceramic fiber insulation, the same material used by NASA on the re-entry tiles of the space shuttle. **This insulation is only 3/4″ thick!** Other oven manufacturers use 2-1/2″ to 3″ of bulky fiberglass insulation that costs them less, but is less efficient. What happens to that extra 1-3/4″ to 2-1/4″ of space? We add it to the interior dimension of your oven, for an increased capacity of 3.17 cu.ft. in the 30″ oven. **No other convection oven with the same capacity of the DACOR, offers as much usable width.**

THE PROFESSIONAL GOURMET 36" RANGE SERIES

For many years, chefs all over the world have been using Jade Equipment to achieve the ultimate in all types of food preparation. Now for the first time, these unique products are available in domestic models.

The Dynasty range series has been developed for home use by the domestic division of Jade Range, Inc., one of the world's largest manufacturers of commercial cooking and refrigeration equipment for over fifty years.

EXCLUSIVE FEATURES:

- **Exclusive** Dedicated Simmer Burner (located at right rear)
- **Exclusive** Stainless steel oven interiors
- **Exclusive** Rigid stainless steel oven gasket
- **Exclusive** Power control system
- **Exclusive** Heavy duty metal knobs
- **Exclusive** Conduction chamber wok with 20,000 BTU
- **Exclusive** All welded construction

STANDARD FEATURES:

- Commercial styling and appearance
- Heavy duty commercial welded construction
- Designed and AGA certified for residential installation
- Heavy-duty adjustable commercial legs
- Convenient, slide out control panel for easy seviceability
- Stainless steel front
- Removable stainless steel drip trays
- Commercial oven controls and indicator light system
- Full 14" high useable oven capacity
- Heavy-duty cast iron grates
- Chefs oven 28" W x 23" D x 14" H
- Commercial oven racks and supports
- Commercial infra-red broiler
- Electronic ignition

OPTIONS:

- Convection oven (not available with infra-red broilers)
- High back w/ shelf
- Base kit
- Mid back
- Cutting board
- Chrome grate supports
- Casters
- Brass trim kit

A DIVISION OF JADE RANGE, INC.
7355 E. Slauson Ave., Commerce, CA 90040
(213)728-5700 • Fax (213)728-2318

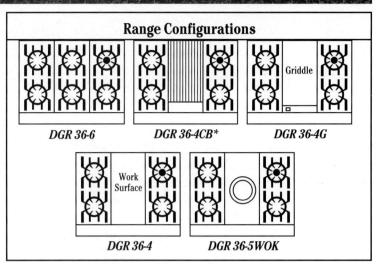

Range Configurations

DGR 36-6   DGR 36-4CB*   DGR 36-4G (Griddle)

DGR 36-4 (Work Surface)   DGR 36-5WOK

*DGR 36-4CB Does not have an in oven infra-red broiler.

Specifications	36" Series
Simmer Burner	500 - 10,000 BTU
Top Burner Rating	1,000 - 15,000 BTU
Chefs Oven Burner Rating	30,000 BTU
Oven Infra-Red Burner Rating	17,000 BTU
Wok Burner Rating	1,000 – 20,000 BTU
12" Griddle Rating	16,000 BTU
12" Charbroiler Rating	24,000 BTU
Electrical Requirements	120V / 60HZ / 8 AMPS
Electrical With Convection	120V / 60HZ / 12 AMPS
Manifold Pipe Size	3/4" NPT

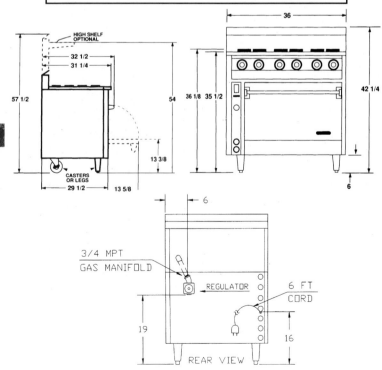

For the client who is interested in the ultimate range, call your local Dynasty dealer.

Note: In line with its policy to continually improve its products, Jade Range, Incorporated reserves the right to change materials and specifications without notice.

C491
BuyLine 7540

THE
PROFESSIONAL
GOURMET
36" RANGE
SERIES

*E*xtra heavy duty, all-welded construction.

*E*xclusive stainless steel oven interiors.

*H*igh performance burners with low simmer capability.

Dynasty
The Benchmark of Quality

A DIVISION OF JADE RANGE, INC.

PROFESSIONAL CHEF 30" GAS RANGE

The Perfect 30" Replacement Range.
Ideal for Replacing Existing Ranges, Remodeling and New Construction.

For many years, chefs all over the world have been using Jade Equipment to achieve the ultimate in all types of food preparation. Now for the first time, these unique products are available in domestic models.

The Dynasty range series has been developed for home use by the domestic division of Jade Range, Inc., one of the world's largest manufacturers of commercial cooking and refrigeration equipment for over fifty years.

The new Dynasty range series incorporates all the finest features of our commercial ranges plus the newest technology available in the domestic market.

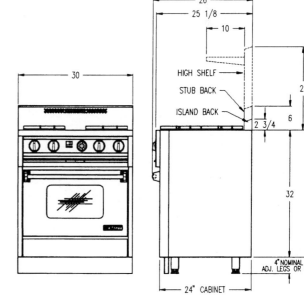

500-10,000 BTU
SIMMER BURNER

15,000 BTU
STANDARD BURNER

DGRS 30-4

E X C L U S I V E   F E A T U R E S :

- **Exclusive** Oversized oven cavity with 4.56 cubic feet. Useable area of 4.13 cubic feet is the largest available
- **Exclusive** Dedicated simmer burner with a low 500 BTU setting
- **Exclusive** Dual oven lights located at front for maximum visibility, without glare
- **Exclusive** Lifetime stainless steel door gaskets
- **Exclusive** Commercial infrared broiler burner
- **Exclusive** Wraparound, heavy duty oven racks
- **Exclusive** Stainless steel oven interior
- **Exclusive** Largest viewing glass window
- **Exclusive** State of the art, heavy duty GEOGRATES™

Specifications	30" Range
Top Burner Rating	**1,000 - 15,000 BTU**
Simmer Burner	**500 - 10,000 BTU**
Oven Burner	**27,500 BTU**
Infra-Red Burner	**17,000 BTU**
Electrical Requirements	**120V / 60HZ / 4 AMPS**
Manifold pipe connection	**1/2" NPT**
Oven size	**25" X 16 1/4" X 19 3/8"**
Cubic Volume	**4.56 CF**
Useable Volume	**4.13 CF**

S T A N D A R D   F E A T U R E S :

- Commercial styling and appearance
- Heavy duty welded construction
- Designed and AGA certified for residential installation
- Removable stainless steel drip trays
- Power indicator light
- Stainless steel stub back and curb base
- Electronic ignition
- Commercial size burners

O P T I O N S :

- Stainless steel high shelf
- Island back
- Stainless side panels

The Benchmark of Quality

A DIVISION OF JADE RANGE, INC.
7355 E. Slauson Ave., Commerce, CA 90040
(213)728-5700 • Fax (213)728-2318

For the client who is interested in the ultimate range, call your local Dynasty dealer.

Note: In line with its policy to continually improve its products, Jade Range, Incorporated reserves the right to change materials and specifications without notice.

PROFESSIONAL

CHEF

30" GAS

RANGE

*T*he largest 30" oven available.

*P*rofessional performance burners with simmer capability.

*O*nly 24" deep for flush cabinet installation.

Dynasty
The Benchmark of Quality

A DIVISION OF JADE RANGE, INC.

Epicure Ovens

Available in a single oven style for mounting side-by-side or in undercounter, island or peninsular installation. We invite you to compare the features and benefits of the DACOR Epicure Convection Oven with any comparable product in the world.

Pure convection

Five cooking modes

Self Cleaning

Extra large capacity of 3.17 cu.ft.

Six rack positions

Reverse air flow

Closed door broiling

Delay timed cooking

5° increment temperature setting

Temperature "count up"

Temperature span of 135° to 555°

Special ceramic fiber insulation

Two minute timers

144 square-inch offset viewing window

**Epicure 30˝ Single Oven
Model #ECPS 130S**

OUR COMMITMENT TO QUALITY AND INNOVATION

We are proud of our impressive array of "firsts", a tradition of technological breakthroughs and our recognized leadership in the industry. But, as a family operation, our greatest commitment is intensely focused on designing and producing superior quality cooking appliances for other families. A great part of Dacor's success can be attributed to not just a willingness, but a desire to implement our customers' needs and preferences in the development of Dacor products. This is a family tradition that we will continue to honor.

**Anthony Joseph, President
and Michael Joseph, Chairman**

For the most current specifications, call Dimension Express at (702) 833-3600 from a fax machine. Enter "0993" for instructions and a directory of DACOR products. DACOR offers a two year parts and labor warranty. MADE IN USA

Distinctive Appliance Corporation™

USA
950 South Raymond Avenue
Pasadena, California 91109
Telephone: (818) 799-1000
Fax: (818) 441-9632
Mexico
Telephone: 011-525-211-7055
Fax: 011-525-211-7063

And you never have to worry about the Epicure being too hot to touch or the kitchen too warm for comfort. The insulation and the three panels of glass in the viewing window keep the exterior cool to the touch even at the self cleaning temperature.

However, the real value of any oven is measured by its cooking performance. The technology is fascinating, but it's results that count. The DACOR Epicure produces flaky pastries, golden brown light breads, roasts and poultry with crispy outside and juicy flavors sealed inside, that you cannot hope to create in a conventional oven.

Bake as many as six racks of cookies simultaneously in the Epicure and the cookies will be the same. Try this with ovens which do not use "pure convection" and you will get cookies that are underdone, overdone, and many shades in between. The large 144 square-inch viewing window means that you don't have to open the door to check those cookies. But if you can't resist, the handle will be cool to the touch because of DACOR's unique reverse air flow.

The Epicure's performance is matched by its convenience. The "Delay Timed" mode allows you to preset the time for the beginning and ending of the cooking cycle. If the family is late for dinner, the Epicure has a "Hold" mode which keeps the food warm at 150° for two hours after it has finished cooking. The "Delay Timed" mode will also save you money because you can self-clean the oven overnight when the kitchen is not in use and energy costs are lower.

DACOR products have been distinguished for superior design, and the new Epicure showcases this excellence. The sleek, frameless styling of the Epicure is complemented by the handsome design of the control panel and handle. The tailored 45° handle end permits corner installation for space efficiency. The finishing touch is the mellow glow of stainless steel. Reminiscent of finishes found in the kitchens of fine restaurants and hotels, this surface is easy to keep clean and resists finger prints and smudges.

What you see is what you get! The DACOR Epicure looks beautiful. The superb design and elegant appearance imply state-of-the-art excellence — and it delivers. The Epicure is available in 27″ and 30″ sizes in Stainless Steel.

DACOR Epicure...Serious cooking equipment for people who love and enjoy cooking.

The DACOR Epicure produces flaky pastries, golden brown light breads, and roasts and poultry with crispy outside and juicy flavors sealed inside that you cannot hope to create in a conventional oven.

THE

PROFESSIONAL

GOURMET

48" DOUBLE OVEN

RANGE SERIES

*E*xtra heavy duty, all-welded construction.

*E*xclusive stainless steel oven interiors.

*H*igh performance burners with low simmer capability.

Dynasty
The Benchmark of Quality

A DIVISION OF JADE RANGE, INC.

THE PROFESSIONAL GOURMET 48" DOUBLE OVEN RANGE SERIES

For many years, chefs all over the world have been using Jade Equipment to achieve the ultimate in all types of food preparation. Now for the first time, these unique products are available in domestic models.

The Dynasty Double Oven Range Series has been developed for home use by the domestic division of Jade Range, Inc., one of the world's largest manufacturers of commercial cooking and refrigeration equipment for over fifty years.

EXCLUSIVE FEATURES:

- **Exclusive** Dedicated Low Simmer Burner (located at right rear)
- **Exclusive** Stainless steel oven interiors
- **Exclusive** Rigid stainless steel oven gasket
- **Exclusive** Power control system
- **Exclusive** Heavy duty metal knobs
- **Exclusive** Conduction chamber wok with 20,000 BTU
- **Exclusive** All welded construction

STANDARD FEATURES:

- Standard oven 20" W x 23" D x 14" H
- Classic oven 16" W x 23" D x 14" H
- Commercial styling and appearance
- Heavy duty commercial welded construction
- Designed and AGA certified for residential installation
- Heavy-duty adjustable commercial legs
- Convenient, slide out control panel for easy seviceability
- Commercial oven controls and indicator light system
- Stainless steel front
- Removable stainless steel drip trays
- Full 14" high useable oven capacity
- Heavy-duty cast iron grates
- Commercial oven racks and supports
- Commercial infra-red broiler
- Electronic ignition

OPTIONS:

- Convection oven (on right side)
- Mid back
- High back w/ shelf
- Base kit
- Cutting board
- Chrome grate supports
- Casters
- Brass trim kit

A DIVISION OF JADE RANGE, INC.
7355 E. Slauson Ave., Commerce, CA 90040
(213)728-5700 • Fax (213)728-2318

Range Configurations

DGR 248-8   DGR 248-6G   DGR 248-4G

DGR 248-6CB   DGR 248-5GWOK   DGR 248-4GCB

Specifications	48" Series
Simmer Burner	500 - 10,000 BTU
Top Burner Rating	1,000 - 15,000 BTU
Standard Oven	24,000 BTU
Classic Oven	20,000 BTU
Oven Infra-Red Burner Rating	17,000 BTU
Wok Burner Rating	1,000 – 20,000 BTU
12" Griddle Rating	16,000 BTU
12" Charbroiler Rating	24,000 BTU
Electrical Requirements	120V / 60HZ / 12 AMPS
Electrical With Convection	120V / 60HZ / 16 AMPS
Manifold Pipe Size	3/4" NPT

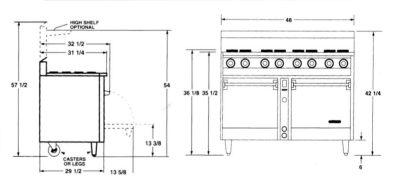

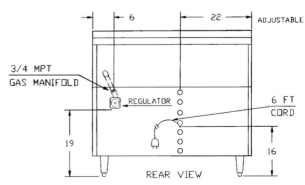

For the client who is interested in the ultimate range, call your local Dynasty dealer.

Note: In line with its policy to continually improve its products, Jade Range, Incorporated reserves the right to change materials and specifications without notice.

THE

PROFESSIONAL

GOURMET

60" DOUBLE OVEN

RANGE SERIES

*E*xtra heavy duty, all-welded construction.

*E*xclusive stainless steel oven interiors.

*H*igh performance burners with low simmer capability.

Dynasty
The Benchmark of Quality

A DIVISION OF JADE RANGE, INC.

THE PROFESSIONAL GOURMET 60" DOUBLE OVEN RANGE SERIES

For many years, chefs all over the world have been using Jade Equipment to achieve the ultimate in all types of food preparation. Now for the first time, these unique products are available in domestic models.

The Dynasty Double Oven Range Series has been developed for home use by the domestic division of Jade Range, Inc., one of the world's largest manufacturers of commercial cooking and refrigeration equipment for over fifty years.

EXCLUSIVE FEATURES:

- **Exclusive** Dedicated Low Simmer Burner (located at right rear)
- **Exclusive** Stainless steel oven interiors
- **Exclusive** Rigid stainless steel oven gasket
- **Exclusive** Power control system
- **Exclusive** Heavy duty metal knobs
- **Exclusive** Conduction chamber wok with 20,000 BTU
- **Exclusive** All welded construction

STANDARD FEATURES:

- Chef's oven 28" W x 23" D x 14" H
- Deluxe oven 20" W x 23" D x 14" H
- Commercial styling and appearance
- Heavy duty commercial welded construction
- Designed and AGA certified for residential installation
- Heavy duty adjustable commercial legs
- Convenient, slide out control panel for easy seviceability
- Commercial oven controls and indicator light system
- Stainless steel front
- Removable stainless steel drip trays
- Full 14" high useable oven capacity
- Heavy duty cast iron grates
- Commercial oven racks and supports
- Commercial BTU oven bake / roast burners
- Electronic ignition

OPTIONS:

- Convection oven (on right side)
- High back w/ shelf
- Base kit
- Cutting board
- Gold trim
- Casters
- Back splash
- Chrome grate supports

Dynasty
The Benchmark of Quality

A DIVISION OF JADE RANGE, INC.

7355 E. Slauson Ave., Commerce, CA 90040

(213)728-5700 • Fax (213)728-2318

Range Configurations

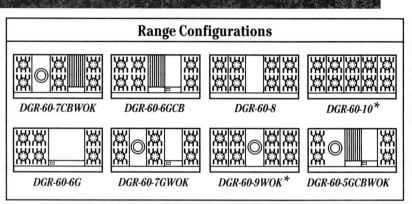

DGR-60-7CBWOK DGR-60-6GCB DGR-60-8 DGR-60-10*

DGR-60-6G DGR-60-7GWOK DGR-60-9WOK* DGR-60-5GCBWOK

Subject to special order

Specifications	60" Series
Simmer Burner	500 - 10,000 BTU
Top Burner Rating	15,000 BTU
Chef's Oven Burner Rating	30,000 BTU
Deluxe Oven Burner Rating	24,000 BTU
Oven Infra-Red Burner Rating	17,000 BTU
Wok Burner Rating	20,000 BTU
12" Griddle Rating	16,000 BTU
12" Charbroiler Rating	24,000 BTU
Electrical Requirements	120V / 60HZ / 12 AMPS
Electrical With Convection	120V / 60HZ / 16 AMPS
Manifold Pipe Size	3/4" NPT

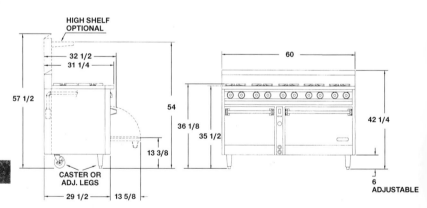

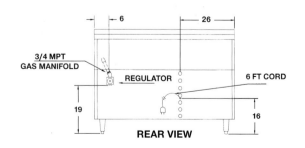

REAR VIEW

For the client who is interested in the ultimate range, call your local Dynasty dealer.

Note: In line with its policy to continually improve its products, Jade Range, Incorporated reserves the right to change materials and specifications without notice.

DYNASTY

GAS COOKTOPS

30", 36", 48", 59"

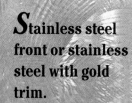

*S*tainless steel front or stainless steel with gold trim.

*H*igh performance burners with simmer capability.

*R*emovable stainless steel drip trays.

*E*xtra heavy duty, all-welded construction.

Dynasty
The Benchmark of Quality

A DIVISION OF JADE RANGE, INC.

DYNASTY GAS COOKTOPS 30", 36", 48", 59"

The Dynasty line of Gas Cooktops was developed to offer cooks the same great features that chefs the world over have used to achieve the ultimate culinary delight for years.

The Dynasty Cooktops are designed and engineered for home use by the domestic division of Jade Range, Inc. For over a half century, Jade Range has been an innovator in the manufacturing of premier restaurant cooking and refrigeration equipment.

Quality and customer satisfaction are our goals. Quality will never be compromised for economic reasons. The Dynasty company stands firm in our belief of strict adherence to quality as the fundamental, irreplaceable ingredient in successful performance. That quality is there for everyone to see, experience and enjoy. "Dynasty still cares about quality," is more than a slogan to our dedicated employees, it's a way of life.

The new Dynasty Cooktops incorporate all the finest features of our commercial cooking products plus the newest technology available on the market today.

EXCLUSIVE FEATURES:

- **Exclusive** Stay cool metal knobs
- **Exclusive** 20,000 BTU Wok system
- **Exclusive** All welded construction

STANDARD FEATURES:

- Dedicated low simmer burner (located at right rear)
- Commercial styling and appearance
- Heavy duty, commercial welded construction
- Designed and AGA certified for residential installation
- Stainless steel island trim
- Push-to-turn brass control valves
- Stainless steel front
- Removable stainless steel drip trays
- Heavy duty, cast iron grates
- 15,000 BTU open-top burners

OPTIONS:

- 11" backguard
- Butcher block cutting board
- Gold trim
- Geo grates
- Chrome grate supports

A DIVISION OF JADE RANGE, INC.

7355 E. Slauson Ave., Commerce, CA 90040

(213)728-5700 • Fax (213)728-2318

DCT 30

DCT 36

DCT 48

DCT 59

DCT-30-4

DCT-36-6

DCT-36-4G

DCT-36-4CB   DCT-36-5W

DCT-48-6CB   DCT-48-6G

DCT-48-4GCB   DCT-48-5GW

DCT-59-7CBW   DCT-59-6GCB

DCT-59-5GCBW   DCT-59-7GW

DCT-59-10 *   DCT-59-9W *

DCT-59-8 *   DCT-59-6G

* Subject to special order.

Specifications	All Series
Simmer Burner	500 – 10,000 BTU
Top Burner Rating	15,000 BTU
Wok Burner Rating	20,000 BTU
11" Griddle Rating	16,000 BTU
11" Charbroiler Rating	24,000 BTU
Electrical Requirements	120V / 60HZ 1 ph / 4 AMPS
Manifold pipe connection	1/2" NPT

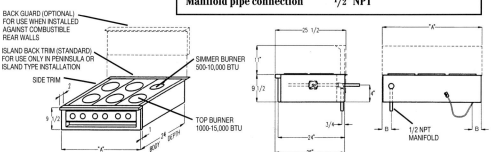

BACK GUARD (OPTIONAL) FOR USE WHEN INSTALLED AGAINST COMBUSTIBLE REAR WALLS

ISLAND BACK TRIM (STANDARD) FOR USE ONLY IN PENINSULA OR ISLAND TYPE INSTALLATION

SIDE TRIM

SIMMER BURNER 500-10,000 BTU

TOP BURNER 1000-15,000 BTU

1/2 NPT MANIFOLD

Model	Dim. "A"	Dim. "B"
DCT-30	30	2 1/4
DCT-36	36	2 1/4
DCT-48	48	2 3/4
DCT-59	59	2 3/4

For the client who is interested in the ultimate range, call your local Dynasty dealer.

Note: In line with its policy to continually improve its products, Jade Range, Incorporated reserves the right to change materials and specifications without notice.

DYNASTY

HI PERFORMANCE

SMOKER /

BROILER

*C*aptures true smoke flavor with exclusive, wood chip smoke-ejector system.

*H*ighest BTU-rated burners offer optimal cooking capacity.

*D*ynasty-proven commercial construction assures even, grilling temperature.

Dynasty
The Benchmark of Quality

A DIVISION OF JADE RANGE, INC.

DYNASTY HI PERFORMANCE SMOKER / BROILER

For many years, chefs all over the world have been using the Jade Smoke Broiler to achieve the ultimate in true wood flavoring. Now, for the first time, this unique product is available in domestic models.

The Jade Smoke Broiler has been developed for domestic use by the Dynasty Division of Jade Range, Inc., one of the world's largest manufacturers of commercial cooking and refrigeration equipment for over 50 years.

The new Dynasty Hi Performance Smoker / Broiler is the only broiler that incorporates woodsmoke flavoring through the use of the exclusive Smoke-Ejector System. Through this unique feature, aromatic smoke is generated by placing a few wood chips (Hickory, Mesquite, Oak, etc.) into the smoke system, and with the use of the three-in-one smoke hood, you are able to maximize the flavor of any food being prepared.

The Dynasty Hi Performance Smoker / Broiler has all of the features of our commercial line with such quality features as 14-gauge heavy duty stainless steel construction, one 25,000 BTU cast-iron burner per 12 inches, heavy duty cast-iron grates with porcelain finish removable 16-gauge drip tray for ease of cleaning and a 1 to 5 year warranty.

The Dynasty Hi Performance Smoker / Broiler has a capacity of almost 400 hamburger patties per hour in the 36" model.

STANDARD FEATURES:

- Stainless steel hood with durable handle and three positions of operation
- Enclosed stainless steel stand allows for wood and accessory storage. (open stainless steel stand also available)
- Broilers are available in 4 sizes
- Heavy duty 14-gauge construction
- Insulated body for maximum safety and fuel efficiency
- Heavy duty cast-iron grill grates
- Ceramic briquettes provide even heat and virtually eliminate grease flame-ups. Drippings vaporize, providing more of that true barbecue flavor.
- Heavy duty cast-iron grates hold the briquettes and maximize heat distribution
- Heavy duty 12-gauge fire box construction
- Cast-iron burners with Heavy duty stainless steel radiants, rated at 25,000 BTU's each
- Heavy duty, one-piece knobs
- Exclusive Dynasty smoke-ejector system is state-of-the-art. The smoke is transferred through a series of beveled 1/2 inch tube ejectors to provide maximum smoke to the grill surface.
- Heavy duty rotisserie
- Lift off griddle
- Stainless steel shelf
- Heavy duty vinyl cover
- 6" N.S.F. casters

Dynasty
The Benchmark of Quality

A DIVISION OF JADE RANGE, INC.
7355 E. Slauson Ave., Commerce, CA 90040
(213)728-5700 • Fax (213)728-2318

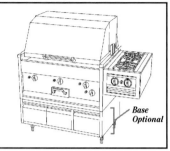 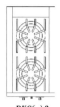

DKC 36-2 (specify if base to be included)

Base Optional

ATTACHED COOKTOPS

DKC( )-2   DKC( )-1

( ) - Width of Outdoor Cook Center
24", 36", 48", 60"

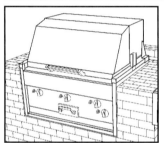

DKC 36-2C (base always included)

ATTACHED COOKTOPS WITH CABINETS

DKC( )-2C   DKC( )-1C

( ) - Width of Outdoor Cook Center
24", 36", 48", 60"

DETACHED COOKTOPS

DOCT-2
(2 Burners)

DOCT-1
(1 Burner),
not shown

DKC 36

All models may be ordered for natural or liquid propane gas.

Specifications	DKC-24	DKC-36	DKC-48	DKC-60 *
Burners	Two	Three	Four	Five
BTU Rating	57,000 BTU	82,000 BTU	114,000 BTU	139,000 BTU
Smoke Ejectors	One	One	Two	Two
Width	24"	36"	48"	60"
Height	48 1/2"	48 1/2"	48 1/2"	48 1/2"
Depth	26 1/2"	26 1/2"	26 1/2"	26 1/2"

* *Not available with rotisserie or vinyl cover*

 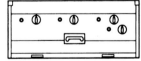

DKC 24   *DKC 36*

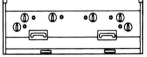 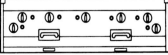

DKC 48   *DKC 60*

For your client that is interested in the ultimate in an outdoor cook center that will make any cook a chef, it's called DYNASTY.

Note: In line with its policy to continually improve its products, Jade Range, Incorporated reserves the right to change materials and specifications without notice.

This year, the Frigidaire Gallery™ Collection will be an even bigger success than it was last year.

(Turn the page to see what an understatement this is.)

These three exciting new features are found only on Frigidaire Gallery™ Collection appliances.

(People everywhere will be asking, "why didn't someone think of this years ago?")

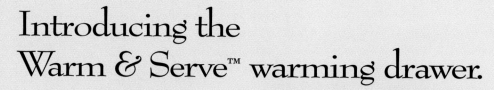

Introducing the Warm & Serve™ warming drawer.

This exclusive Frigidaire Gallery feature has its own heating element that holds meals at serving temperature. It assures everyone will get a warm meal, even late-comers, and it assures everything will be warm at serving time. It's the hottest new feature in ranges this year. And it's one of many terrific features found in Frigidaire Gallery Collection ranges.

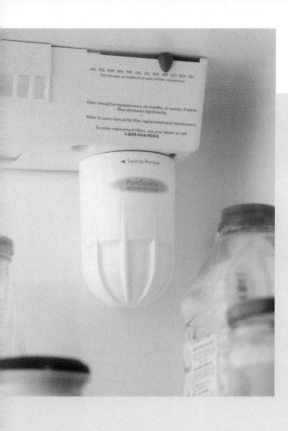

Introducing the Frigidaire PureSource Ice & Water Filter.

This is a built-in filter that reduces lead, chlorine, particulates and germs* to reduce odor and give ice and water better taste and clarity. It's right inside to make access and changing easy. It's another smart feature found on select Frigidaire Gallery and Frigidaire Gallery Professional Series™ refrigerators.

Introducing the Flip & Slide™ shelf.

The Flip & Slide shelf adds even more storage flexibility to refrigerators already loaded with features. A divided shelf, one of its sides flips up to accommodate tall bottles; the other slides out to make it easier to reach items in the back. It's a unique feature found only on select Frigidaire Gallery Collection refrigerators.

* 3-4 microns in size in accordance with ANSI/NSF standards 42 and 53.

Looking for one more good reason to call Frigidaire?

(We'll give you three.)

Contour Concept™ (Yet another Frigidaire exclusive.)

This is not marketing talk. Contour Concept is our guiding principle: sculpted design that looks and works better. It translates into appliances that look more attractive on the outside and work smarter on the inside.

ISO 9000 Series Registration. (Another way of saying world-class quality standards.)

Our nine factories, making products in every category, have received ISO 9000 series quality assurance registration. Our national parts distribution center has, too.

This assures Frigidaire products are made in facilities that have world-class quality procedures. It's part of our commitment to quality in everything we do.

The Frigidaire Gallery™ and Frigidaire Gallery Professional Series™ Warranty.
(For two years, an appliance problem is our problem, not yours.)

 When you build with Frigidaire Gallery™ appliances, you can rest easy. Here's why: Our Full Two-Year Warranty: Every Frigidaire Gallery and Frigidaire Gallery Professional Series™ appliance is guaranteed to be free of material defects or component malfunctions. We will repair, without charge, any problem that occurs during the first two years after original date of purchase.*

Across the U.S.A., our national network of Factory Service Centers and authorized independent services provide prompt, professional repair service. To maintain warranties, always ask for Frigidaire Company Genuine Renewal Parts.

To learn more about the Frigidaire Gallery Professional Series appliances, call our Builder Source Line at 1-800-685-6005. Or see us on the Internet at http://www.frigidaire.com.

FRIGIDAIRE®

THE LOOK OF BETTER PERFORMANCE

*For complete warranty details, please refer to your Owner's Guide. Some restrictions apply for Alaska and Hawaii.

High standards of quality at Frigidaire mean we are constantly working to improve our products. We reserve the right to change specifications or discontinue models without notice.

6000 Perimeter Drive Dublin, OH 43017   © 1996 White Consolidated Industries, Inc.   (Stylemaster # B96FL0602)

Full Line Product Specifications

C493
11452-FRI

Frigidaire

The look of better performance.

INTRODUCING THE
FRIGIDAIRE GALLERY PROFESSIONAL SERIES.

The commercial look of stainless steel will add distinction to any kitchen as well as enhance the value of your homes. That's the Frigidaire Gallery Professional Series. The first full line of stainless steel appliances that are remarkably affordable. Freestanding and built-in appliances that match and perform brilliantly. Refrigerators with the Frigidaire PureSource™ Ice and Water Filter and Flip & Slide™ SpillSafe™ adjustable shelves. Self-cleaning wall ovens. Ranges with our new Warm & Serve™ Drawer and convection cooking. A dishwasher with an UltraPower wash system. Gas cooktops with five sealed burners. Electric smoothtops with halogen elements. Everything you need to create a culinary look that really performs.

FRIGIDAIRE®

The look of better performance.

The Look of Better Performance in Stainless Steel
Frigidaire Gallery Professional Series

FRS26ZSE • PureSource Filter • Flip & Slide Shelf • Variable crushed ice • 5 adjustable gallon-plus door bins

FGF379WEC • Warm & Serve Drawer • Self-cleaning oven • European-style sealed burners • 2 Power Burners • Full coverage cast iron grates

FEF389WEC • Warm & Serve • EvenCook convection oven • Self-cleaning oven • Ceramic smoothtop surface • 2 expandable & 2 radiant elements

FDB768GC • UltraPower wash system • Solid food disposer • Continuous self-cleaning wash system • Ultra-Quiet insulation system

FEB789WCC • EvenCook convection oven • Self-cleaning oven • Electronic touchpad controls • AutoSet controls

FEB798WCC • 2 EvenCook convection ovens • 2 Self-cleaning ovens • Electronic touchpad controls • AutoSet controls

FEC6X9XCC • 36" Ceramic smoothtop surface • 1-6" & 1-9" elements • 1 radiant & 2 expandable radiant elements

FGC6X9XCC • 36" easy-to-clean glass cooktop • 5 sealed gas burners • Porcelain burner pans • Linear flow burner controls

Frigidaire Side by Side & Top Mount Refrigerators

FRS26ZGE *Gallery* • PureSource Filter • SpillSafe sliding shelves • Micro-Serv dishes • Variable crushed ice • 5 adjustable gallon-plus door bins

Built-in Frigidaire PureSource Ice and Water Filter reduces lead, chlorine, particulates and cysts* to give ice and water better taste, odor and clarity.

FRS22PRC • 3 adjustable glass shelves • 5 fixed door shelves • Glacier Blue adjustable temperature meat keeper

Flip & Slide™ SpillSafe shelf opens to make room for tall bottles or slides forward for easy access to items stored on the back of the shelf. Both sides are SpillSafe.

FRT26XGC *Gallery* • Variable crushed ice • SpillSafe shelves • Micro-Serv dishes • 3 adjustable gallon deep door bins

FRT18NNC • 3 Full Width Glass Shelves • Gallon Door Bins • 2 Clear Crispers

Encapsulated, lighted, extra-large crisper drawers feature perfectly clear fronts that show the way to your favorite foods.

Adjustable temperature meat keeper keeps various types of meat refrigerated at just the right temperature.

For more space, put big and tall containers on the door inside one of these gallon-size, adjustable bins.

* 3-4 microns in size. In accordance with ANSI/NSF Standards 42 and 53. Features vary by model. See feature specifications sheet for more information.

Frigidaire Electric & Gas Freestanding Ranges

FEF389CES *Gallery* • Warm & Serve Drawer • EvenCook convection oven • Self-cleaning oven • Ceramic smoothtop surface

FEF385CCT • Self-cleaning oven • 2-6" & 2-8" high density multi-wrap coil elements

FEF350BAW • Self-cleaning oven • High density multi-wrap coil elements • Seamless upswept cooktop

New Warm & Serve Drawer

New granite pattern top

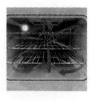

EvenCook convection oven - allows for gentle, even cooking and reduces cooking time.

FGF374CCT *Gallery*
• Self-cleaning oven • European-style sealed burners • 2 Power Burners • Cast iron grates with porcelain pans

FGF353CAS • Self-cleaning oven • European-style sealed burners • Cast iron grates with porcelain pans

FGF350BBW • Self-cleaning oven • Conventional easy-to-clean dual burners • Cast iron grates with porcelain pans

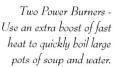

Two Power Burners - Use an extra boost of fast heat to quickly boil large pots of soup and water.

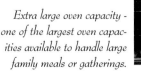

Extra large oven capacity - one of the largest oven capacities available to handle large family meals or gatherings.

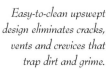

Easy-to-clean upswept design eliminates cracks, vents and crevices that trap dirt and grime.

Frigidaire Electric Wall Ovens

FEB386CCS *Gallery*
- 30" EvenCook convection oven • Self-cleaning
- Electronic touch-pad controls
- Electronic clock & timer

FEB374CCT
- 30" Self-Cleaning oven
- Electronic touch-pad controls
- Electronic clock & timer
- 2 oven racks

FEB796CBS • Self-cleaning lower oven • Electronic touch-pad controls • Microwave upper oven • Electronic clock & timer • 2 oven racks

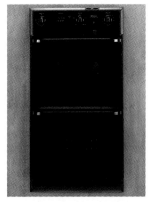

FEB755BBB • 27" Self-cleaning upper oven • Manual-clean lower oven • Automatic upper oven control • Electronic clock & timer

FEB789CCT *Gallery*
- 27" EvenCook convection oven
- Self-cleaning oven • Electronic touch-pad controls • Electronic clock & timer

FEB798CCS *Gallery*
- 2 - 27" EvenCook convection ovens • 2 self-cleaning ovens
- Electronic touch-pad controls
- Electronic clock & timer

FEB702CBS • 27" Manual cleaning porcelain oven • Side-swing oven door • Automatic oven control • Electronic clock & timer

FEB556BBB • 24" Self-cleaning oven • Electronic touch-pad controls • Electronic clock & timer • Dual-Radiant baking & roasting

EvenCook convection oven - allows for gentle, even cooking and reduces cooking time up to 30%.

Frigidaire Electric Cooktops

FEC6X9XCS *Gallery* • 36" Ceramic smoothtop surface • 1-6" & 1-9" halogen elements • 1 radiant & 1 expandable radiant elements • 1 expandable warmer

FEC3X9XCS *Gallery* • 30" Ceramic smoothtop surface • 1-6" & 1-9" halogen elements • 1 radiant & 1 expandable radiant element

FEC9X8XAB • 36" modular downdraft cooktop • Self-contained downdraft venting system • Dual coil element module • Heavy-duty grill module

FEC3X7XAB • 30" Ceramic smoothtop surface • 1 expandable radiant element • 1-8" radiant element • 2-6" radiant elements

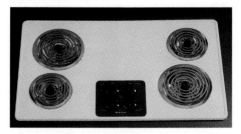

FEC6X6XAD • 36" spill control porcelain cooktop • 2-6" & 2-8" coil elements • Chrome drip bowls • Surface indicator light

FEC3X5XAD • 30" spill control porcelain cooktop • 2-6" & 2-8" coil elements • Chrome drip pans • Surface indicator light

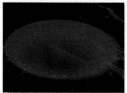

Halogen heating elements heat up instantly.

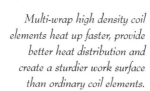

Multi-wrap high density coil elements heat up faster, provide better heat distribution and create a sturdier work surface than ordinary coil elements.

FEC3X2XAD • 32" spill control porcelain cooktop • 2-6" & 2-8" coil elements • Chrome drip pans • Surface indicator light

Frigidaire Electric Slide-Ins & Drop-Ins

FES387CCS *Gallery* • 30"
Slide-in EvenCook convection oven
• Self-cleaning oven • Ceramic
smoothtop surface

FED387CCS *Gallery* • 30"
Drop-in EvenCook convection oven
• Self-cleaning oven • Ceramic
smoothtop surface

Granite pattern top

FES355CCB • 30" Slide-in
self-cleaning oven • 2-6" & 2-8"
plug-in coil elements • Electronic
touch-pad controls

FES353CCD • 30" Slide-in
self-cleaning oven • 2-6" & 2-8"
plug-in coil elements • Automatic
clock with timer

*EvenCook convection
oven - allows for gentle,
even cooking and reduces
cooking time up to 30%.*

*Electronic Oven Controls -
Precise oven temperature
settings and convenient
features at the touch
of a button.*

Frigidaire Microwaves

FMT116U1W • 10 power levels • 6 one-touch
convenience pads • Auto-weight defrost • Keep
warm pad

FMS062E1W • 10 power levels • Turntable
• 3 one-touch convenience pads • Auto-weight
defrost

Frigidaire Gas Built-Ins

FGC9X8XAB • 36" modular downdraft cooktop
• Self-contained downdraft venting system
• Dual gas burner module • Heavy-duty grill module

FGC6X9XCS *Gallery* • 36" gallery cooktop
• 5 sealed gas burners • Easy-to-clean glass cooktop
• Porcelain burner pans

FGC3X8XCB *Gallery* • 30" gallery cooktop
• 4 sealed gas burners • Easy-to-clean glass cooktop
• Porcelain burner pans

FGB557CBS • Self-cleaning oven • Electronic
touch-pad controls • Electronic clock & timer
• Vari-Broil

FGC3X4XAD • 30" cooktop • 4 sealed
gas burners • Easy-to-clean porcelain cooktop
• Porcelain burner pans

Frigidaire Disposers & Compactors

D3000, D5000, D5500, D7501 • E-Z mount
• Dishwasher drain connection
• Replacement warranty • 1/3 to 3/4 HP

**MTC500RBS/
MTC500RBM**
• Easy open toe bar
• Sound conditioned
• 2300lb ram force
• Deodorant system

Frigidaire Dishwashers

FDB898GC *Gallery*
• UltraPower wash system
• Solid food disposer
• Continuous fine-mesh
filtered system • Ultra-Quiet
insulation system

FDB643RBR • 3 wash levels
• Soft food disposer • Self-cleaning filter • Quiet II sound pack

FDB232RBR • 2 wash levels
• Soft food disposer
• Quiet insulation

FDP652RBR • Almond
cabinet with wood veneer top
• 3 wash levels • Soft food disposer
• Quiet insulation

MDR251RER • 18" Built-in
• 2 wash levels • Soft food disposer
• 3-sided insulation

*Self-cleaning filter and disposer
handles hard foods like popcorn
and traps fine particles like coffee
grounds so you always get the
cleanest dishes without pre-rinsing.*

*Features like space-
saving cup shelf,
removable silverware
basket and fold-down
divider give you extra
cleaning flexibility.*

*Convenient-rinse
aid dispenser features
a new clear cap
indicator to show
you when to refill.*

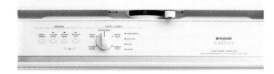

Easy-to-clean and easy-to-use electronic controls, with 5 year warranty, make cycle selection fast and easy.

Frigidaire Laundry Products

FWS845GC *Gallery*
• Loadsaver super capacity
• Tri-action agitation • 12 wash
cycles • 4 wash/rinse temperature
combinations

FDE/FDG847GE *Gallery*
• Exclusive two-way tumble dry
• Balanced dry system • 4 time/
3 auto dry cycles • Press saver
• Interior drum light

*Tri-action wash system
tub and agitation work
together for optimal water
and cleaning action.*

FLSE/FLSG72GC *Gallery*
• Loadsaver super capacity
• Tri-Action agitation • 10 wash
cycles • 4 wash/rinse temperature
combinations • 4 time/3 auto
dry cycles • Balanced dry system
• Press Saver • Interior drum light

*The Titan 25 washtub
is guaranteed not to
rust, chip or crack for
25 years, plus it's made
of recyclable material.*

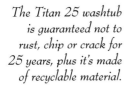

YEAR FULL WARRANTY   YEAR FULL WARRANTY   YEAR LIMITED WARRANTY

The Frigidaire Warranties

Full Two-Year Warranty: Every Frigidaire <u>Gallery</u> and Frigidaire <u>Gallery Professional</u> appliance is guaranteed to be free of material defects or component malfunctions. We will repair, without charge, any problem that occurs during the first two years after original date of purchase.*

Full One-Year Warranty: Every Frigidaire appliance is guaranteed to be free of defects or component malfunctions. We will repair, without charge, any problem that occurs during the first year after original date of purchase.*

Refrigerators:

Limited Five-Year Warranty: Cabinet Liner, Refrigerating System. During the second through fifth years, Frigidaire Company will repair, without charge, any defect or malfunction in the cabinet liner and/or refrigerating system.

Limited Ten-Year Compressor Warranty: Every Frigidaire Gallery and Frigidaire Gallery Professional refrigerator compressor is covered for 10 years.*

Full Two-Year Warranty: Through-the-Door Ice Dispenser. During the second year, Frigidaire Company will repair, without charge for parts or labor, any defect or malfunction in the Through-the-Door Ice and/or Water dispensers. *

Smoothtop Ranges and Cooktops:

Limited Five-Year Warranty: Glass Smoothtop. During the third through fifth years, Frigidaire will furnish, free of charge, a replacement for any defective surface heating element, deteriorated rubberized-silicon seals (upswept models only), or glass smoothtop that cracks due to thermal breakage (not customer abuse).

Microwaves:

Limited Two-Year Warranty: Every Frigidaire microwave oven is guaranteed to be free of materials defects or component malfunctions. We will replace parts, without charge, during the first two years after original date of purchase.*

Limited Ten-Year Warranty:** Frigidaire guarantees the magnetron tube in your microwave oven to be free of defects or malfunctions for a minimum of 10 years.
**Excluding model FMS062E1S

Disposers:

Free replacement warranty. See printed warranty for details.

Trash Compactors:

Every Frigidaire trash compactor is guaranteed to be free of materials defects or component malfunctions. We will repair, without charge, any problem that occurs during the first year after original date of purchase.*

Dishwashers:

Limited Five-Year Warranty: Electronics/Nylon Racks. Frigidaire will repair, without charge, any defects or malfunctions occurring in the electronic controls or nylon-coated racks through the fifth year (parts only).

Limited Ten-Year Warranty: Polytub/Door Liner. Frigidaire will repair or replace, without charge, any polytub or door liner that fails to contain water due to a manufacturing defect for a minimum of ten years (parts only).

Full Twenty-Year* Warranty: Polytub/Door Liner.** Frigidaire will repair or replace, without charge, any polytub or door liner that fails to contain water due to a manufacturing defect for a minimum of twenty years.
*** Applies to models FDB898GC, FDB878GC, FDB874RC, FDG768GC, FDB765RB and FDB765RCR

Washers/Dryers/Laundry Centers:

Limited Five-Year Warranty: Washer Transmission. During the second through fifth years, Frigidaire will furnish replacement parts for your washer transmission.

Full Twenty-Five-Year Warranty: Titan 25 Washtub. Frigidaire will repair or replace, without charge any Titan 25 washtub that does not stand up to normal daily wear and tear for a minimum of 25 years.

*For complete warranty details, please refer to your Owner's Guide. Some restrictions apply for Alaska.

High standards of quality at Frigidaire mean we are constantly working to improve our products. We reserve the right to change specifications or discontinue models without notice.

Parts and Service

Wherever you live or move in the U.S.A., our national network of Factory Service Centers and authorized independent services provide prompt, professional repair service. To maintain warranties, always ask for Frigidaire Company Genuine Renewal Parts.

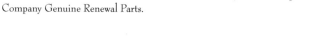

1·800·685·6005

The look *of* better performance.

6000 Perimeter Drive
Dublin, Ohio 43017

BLUE CREEK™
BY JENN-AIR®

JENN-AIR PRODUCT INFORMATION

Designer Line

Pro-Style™

Expressions® Collection

▼▼▼®JENN-AIR
THE SIGN OF A GREAT COOK®.

BLUE CREEK™

BY JENN-AIR®

It's time to say hello to color—thanks to a bright line of professional-style products from Blue Creek™ Appliances.

The Blue Creek Watercolors™ Collection offers a full palette of brilliant, colorful appliances to let you make a dramatic change.

Pick one color for all your appliance choices. Or mix and match. Blue Creek gives you the freedom to create just the effect you want.

**27" DOUBLE ELECTRIC
WALL OVEN**
(model WW27210P)
The Electric Double Wall Oven
features an upper self-cleaning convection oven for even
baking with up to three racks
and a lower bake/broil oven.

48″ Triple-Bay Gas Downdraft Cooktop

(model CVG4380P)

48″Triple-Bay Gas Downdraft Cooktop, shown here in gleaming Bordeaux Red, gives you practically unlimited options in both style and function. Professional-style knobs enhance the distinctive look of this versatile cooktop.

Dual-Fuel™ Range

(model SVD8310S)

Crisp, jewel-toned copper, featured here on the Dual-Fuel Range, adds bold drama to any decor. Range features a modular gas cooking surface with self-cleaning electric convection and bake/broil oven. Comes with interchangeable grill and 2 two-burner modules. Shown with optional backsplash.

BLUE CREEK ™

BY JENN-AIR®

ELECTRIC RANGE

(model S156P)

Electric Range, shown in shimmering Jade with optional backsplash, brings warmth and richness to the kitchen, along with a wealth of professional features. Creative cooks will love the advantages of the convection and bake/broil oven and downdraft ventilation as much as they love the color!

Optional gleaming brass accents add a dash of distinction to knob rings and handles.

ULTIMATE QUIET DISHWASHER

(model DW860UQP)

Shown in striking Sapphire Blue, this Ultimate Quiet Built-In Dishwasher has pizazz and practicality. This model features a Deep Flex Rack loading system and triple-level quiet action wash system for outstanding performance.

BLUE CREEK

BY JENN-AIR®

For fresh new ideas in kitchen appliances, look to Blue Creek. For more information, call **800-244-1491.**

S U N C A S T S E R I E S™ C O O K T O P S

CRESCENT

(model CCE9300)

The shape of the Crescent cooktop is ideal for both traditional and corner applications. The versatile, flush-to-the-counter design of Crescent features three Ultra-Quick radiant elements, and one Ultra-Quick dual radiant element for fast start-up and even heating.

BASICS

(model CCE9200)

Basic is beautiful with the Basics rectangular-shaped cooktop. Three Ultra-Quick radiant elements, and one Ultra-Quick dual radiant element combine with split side-mounted recessed controls for a smooth, seamless appearance.

PROFORM

(model CCE9100)

The ProForm cooktop extends beyond the counter profile for a unique look. Side-mounted recessed controls keep a low profile for a perfect blend of form and function.

The Suncast Series™ explores a full spectrum of choices with a fascinating array of textured and solid color cooktops. Each works with virtually any cabinet or countertop material imaginable. Cooktop material is cool to the touch, thanks to Nustone III,™ a specially engineered material that dissipates heat.

Nustone III is a trademark of IDI.

For fresh new ideas in kitchen appliances, look to Blue Creek. For more information, call **800-244-1491**.

EXPRESSIONS® COLLECTION

With its award-winning flush design and appealing features, the Jenn-Air Expressions® Collection is perfect for those who appreciate great style as well as great cooking. Let's begin with the Expressions modular cooktop system. It enables you to design your own personal cooktop by mixing and matching a variety of innovative cooking cartridges. The smooth lines and top performance of Expressions wall ovens and refrigerators round out the collection to create a beautifully coordinated look for the kitchen. No matter how you serve it up, the Expressions Collection is the ideal choice for today's home.

While a conventional oven uses radiant heat to warm the food, oven interior and air, convection uses a fan inside the oven cavity to circulate that warm air. The moving air strips away a layer of cooler air that surrounds the food, thus speeding up the baking or roasting process. So you'll spend less time cooking and more time enjoying juicier roasts and golden brown baked goods.

30"/27" EXPRESSIONS® COLLECTION
DOUBLE ELECTRIC

(models WW30430 and WW27430)

The Double Electric Wall Oven features upper dual mode convection which lets you choose between Convect Bake and Convect Roast, as well as conventional baking, roasting and temperature-controlled broiling. The lower oven offers bake/broil capabilities. Large Panaview™ oven windows give you a clear look at what's cooking inside.

30"/27" EXPRESSIONS® COLLECTION
MICROWAVE/ELECTRIC COMBO

(models WM30460 and WM27460)

This Combination Wall Oven features a sleek outline backed by effortless efficiency, all in one versatile package. Electronic touch controls, curved handles and flush design give this combo its streamlined appearance, while upper microwave and lower dual mode convection oven with temperature probe help streamline its performance as well.

30" EXPRESSIONS® COLLECTION SINGLE ELECTRIC

(model W30400)
(shown with **model CCG2422**)
The sleek, flush design of the 30" Single Electric Wall Oven is designed for the consumer who demands that an appliance look as good as it performs. The curved designer handle and electronic touch controls complete the look. Extra-large, dual mode convection and bake/broil oven ensures top performance. Choose in-wall or under-counter installation.

30 ¹⁵/₁₆" EXPRESSIONS® COLLECTION DOUBLE ELECTRIC

(model CVEX4720W)
This electric cooktop features the Expressions® Collection award-winning flush-to-the-counter design with side-mounted, backlit controls. Energy-Saver grill with Jenn-Air's Excalibur® non-stick finish grill grates makes grilling indoors easy and enjoyable anytime of the year. Shown with optional cartridge.

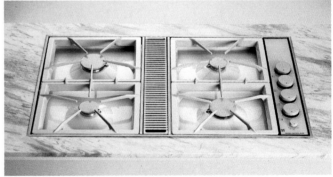

34 ¹/₈" EXPRESSIONS® COLLECTION DOUBLE GAS *

(model CVG2420, white shown)
Flush-to-the-counter design offers a smooth appearance enhanced by the low contour of its backlit controls. Four sealed burners with porcelain-enameled cast-iron burner grates make clean-up easy. Add a single Expressions® Collection grill to either side to increase your cooking options.

20 CU. FT. EXPRESSIONS® COLLECTION
COUNTER DEPTH SIDE-BY-SIDE

(model JRSD209T)

This 20 cubic foot refrigerator offers a sleek, counter depth design for built-in look without a built-in price. The extended front door panel with concealed hinge and factory installed perimeter door trim extends up to 1/4" to easily accept custom wood and decorator panels to suit any decor. Spill-proof shelves roll out for convenience.

PRO-STYLE™

The Pro-Style™ Collection gives you the best of both worlds—the sleek styling of professional appliances plus the innovative features of Jenn-Air appliances.

Our self-cleaning oven, modular downdraft cooktop and convection baking system are but a few of the Pro-Style Collection offerings. And best of all, the professional look of the Pro-Style Collection is available without the professional price.

24 CU. FT. PRO-STYLE™
REFRIGERATOR
(model JRSD2490T)
This side-by-side crushed
ice/chilled water dispenser
model accepts optional
custom stainless steel panels
that give it the same sleek,
professional look as the rest
of the Pro-Style™ Collection.
Its Crystal White interior
features spill-proof roll-out
shelves to afford you easy
access.

27" PRO-STYLE™ DOUBLE
ELECTRIC WALL OVEN
(model WW27210P)
The Pro-Style™ Electric
Double Wall Oven features
an upper self-cleaning convection oven for even baking
with up to three racks and a
lower bake/broil oven. It's
no wonder more homes have
chosen Jenn-Air convection
ovens over any other brand.

DESIGNER LINE

The Jenn-Air Designer Line offers a full selection of appliances featuring sophisticated design and innovative features. From convertible cooktop systems to high-performance wall ovens and ranges to feature-rich refrigerators and dishwashers, the Jenn-Air Designer Line has it all. Turn to the Designer Line for incomparable versatility and streamlined good looks. With Jenn-Air reliability and innovation built into every model, the Designer Line is sure to be a perfect fit for any kitchen. Looking at our unique cooking products, you can understand why Jenn-Air is the #1 preferred brand of cooking appliances.*

* Based on consumer surveys.

30" DUAL-FUEL™ PRO-STYLE™

(model SVD8310S)
*(shown with optional
30" lighted A518S backsplash)*

*The 30" Pro-Style™ self-
cleaning range combines the
versatility of a gas cooktop with
the performance of a convection
and bake/broil oven. The
modular design allows you to
choose from a variety of
accessories to customize your
cooking surface. And our downdraft ventilation system lets you
grill right in your kitchen.*

ULTIMATE QUIET SERIES PRO-STYLE™

(model DW860UQP)

*The Ultimate Quiet Series Dishwasher combines superb
cleaning power with virtually silent operation. The Quiet
Action Multi-Fan Jet wash system can handle anything you
dish out. This is the Quietest Dishwasher made in America.†*

48" PRO-STYLE™ TRIPLE GAS

(model CVG4380P)

*The modular design of the Pro-Style™ Cooktop enables you to change
cooking surfaces in seconds. Its downdraft ventilation system allows you
to grill indoors. Install in countertop or island/peninsula for a professional style downdraft cooktop anywhere in the kitchen.*

†Based on consumer sound evaluations of leading manufacturers' wash actions.

For the most current specification sheets, call Dimension Express from your fax machine at (702)833-3600. Enter code #9018 for Jenn-Air products. You will receive
information on how to use the system, along with the corresponding model code numbers. Or, for a complete Jenn-Air full line catalog, call 1-800-JENN-AIR.

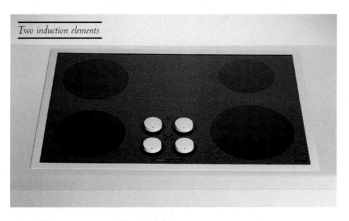

Two induction elements

30" DESIGNER LINE CONVENTIONAL MAGNETIC INDUCTION AND ULTRA QUICK-START™ RADIANT

(model CCE3450)
This 30" Designer Line Cooktop features two Ultra Quick-Start™ radiant elements, and two magnetic induction elements for responsive results. The hot surface indicator light is a stylish way of showing at-a-glance if heating elements are on.

36" DESIGNER LINE FRAMELESS RADIANT COOKTOP

(model CCE3531)
The unique frameless design of this Jenn-Air Cooktop smooths the way to performance and style. Ultra Quick-Start™ radiant elements make cooking easy, while smooth, polished radiused edges and glass-ceramic surface make clean-up a breeze.

30" DESIGNER LINE DOWNDRAFT ELECTRIC

(model CVE3400)
30" Downdraft Electric Cooktop features a variable-speed fan that pulls smoke and odors down and out for a fresher, cleaner kitchen. Ultra Quick-Twin™ dual radiant element, and three Ultra Quick-Start™ radiant elements make cooking easy.

48" DESIGNER LINE DOWNDRAFT TRIPLE GAS

(model CVG4380)
The Downdraft Triple Gas Cooktop offers the ultimate in flexibility for creative cooking. Three bays can accommodate up to six burners and accepts gas accessories. E-ven Heat™ grill and two-speed downdraft ventilation continue Jenn-Air's tradition of excellence in indoor grilling.

Haloring™ is a trademark of Ceramaspeed Limited.

30" ELECTRIC

(model SVE47600) (shown with A126W
Haloring™ halogen element cartridge)

Designed for countertop, island or peninsula installation, the slide-in range provides the elegant built-in look that today's consumer's prefer. With its sleek, electronic keypad controls, extra-large dual mode convection and bake/broil oven, and Energy Saver grill, it's the natural choice.

30" DUAL-FUEL™

(model SVD48600)

The Dual-Fuel™ Range combines a modular gas cooking surface with electric dual mode convection and bake/broil oven for maximum versatility. Along with Jenn-Air's extra-large 3.8 cu. ft. oven size, you'll find that no other range gives you so much performance in so little space.

30" RADIANT

(model SCE30600)

Jenn-Air ranges serve up the perfect combination—contemporary designer styling and a variety of creative cooking features. Like this model's three Ultra Quick-Start™ radiant elements, the Ultra Quick-Twin™ dual radiant element, and a dual mode convection and bake/broil oven.

24 CU. FT. DESIGNER LINE

(model JRSD2490T)

This 24 cubic foot refrigerator gives you more of what every kitchen needs—space. With three spill-proof roll-out cantilevered shelves, a temperature-controlled cold storage drawer, lift-out storage trays and deep storage shelves, you can always make room for more. Comes with perimeter door trim which extends to 1/4" to easily accept custom wood and decorator panels to suit any decor.

27" DESIGNER LINE MICROWAVE/ ELECTRIC COMBO

(model WM27260)

The 27" Wall Oven/Microwave Electric Combo brings microwave and oven together in a streamlined design. The lower dual mode convection and bake/broil oven means superior baking and roasting results, while the upper microwave offers the perfect match in Designer Line styling and convenience.

ULTIMATE QUIET SERIES

(model DW960UQ)

The Ultimate Quiet Series dishwasher brings you the quiet efficiency of Jenn-Air's UQ insulation system, along with all the features you depend on for easy loading and clean, sparkling dishes every time.

ULTIMATE QUIET SERIES

(model DW860UQ)

This Ultimate Quiet Series dishwasher features the complete UQ series insulation system. With features like the Quiet Liner™ Tub and SoundGuard™ insulation package, the only thing you'll hear in the kitchen is compliments.

QUIETEST DISHWASHER MADE IN AMERICA[†] AND HERE'S THE PROOF

| JENN-AIR |
| GE |
| WHIRLPOOL |
| FRIGIDAIRE |
| KITCHENAID |

▲ SOFT   ▲ LOUD

†Based on consumer sound evaluations of leading manufacturers' wash actions. Applies to Jenn-Air Ultimate Quiet Series Dishwashers only.

CARTRIDGES AND ACCESSORIES

Customize your own modular cooktop or range with these cartridges and accessories.
(Expressions® Collection models shown, except for gas module and cooker-steamer)

SOLID ELEMENT

GAS TWO-BURNER
MODULE

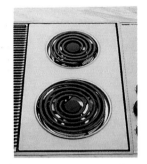

CONVENTIONAL COIL

HALOGEN ELEMENT

RADIANT ELEMENT

GRIDDLE

WOK

ENERGY SAVER
GRILL ASSEMBLY

COOKER-STEAMER

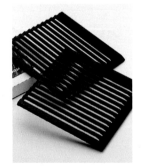

EXCALIBUR® FINISH
GRILL GRATES

BIG POT ELEMENT

ROTISS-KEBAB

EXPRESSIONS®
COLLECTION
GRILL COVERS

▼▼▼ JENN-AIR

THE SIGN OF A GREAT COOK®.

C503
Buyline 8625

FULL LINE
PRODUCT CATALOG

FOR THE WAY IT'S MADE.™

The new series of KitchenAid® Dishwashers with Sculptura™ family-look styling continues our reputation for premium quality. A stylish six-inch high control panel matches cabinet drawer height, so cabinets and dishwasher flow together in an uninterrupted line. Rounded corners and your choice of monochromatic White, Almond or Black styling combine with a Satin Finish™ Stainless Steel Interior to complete the Sculptura look. You'll also like the appearance of your clean dishes. A multi-level HYDRO SWEEP™ washing system and UltraFine filtration system ensure that dishes are washed clean without prerinsing. Features such as a DELAY WASH option and automatic water heating help you save water and energy. 100% usable space in the upper and lower racks include many quality conveniences for true random loading. Model KUDR24SE features electronic controls that let you select the correct cycle and options for every load at a touch. Select Black (shown right), White or Almond.

2

DISHWASHERS

All KitchenAid dishwashers feature a Satin Finish™ Stainless Steel interior composed of 18 gauge stainless steel. Not only do you get a surface with lasting good looks, the stainless steel finish actually assists you in getting first-rate performance.

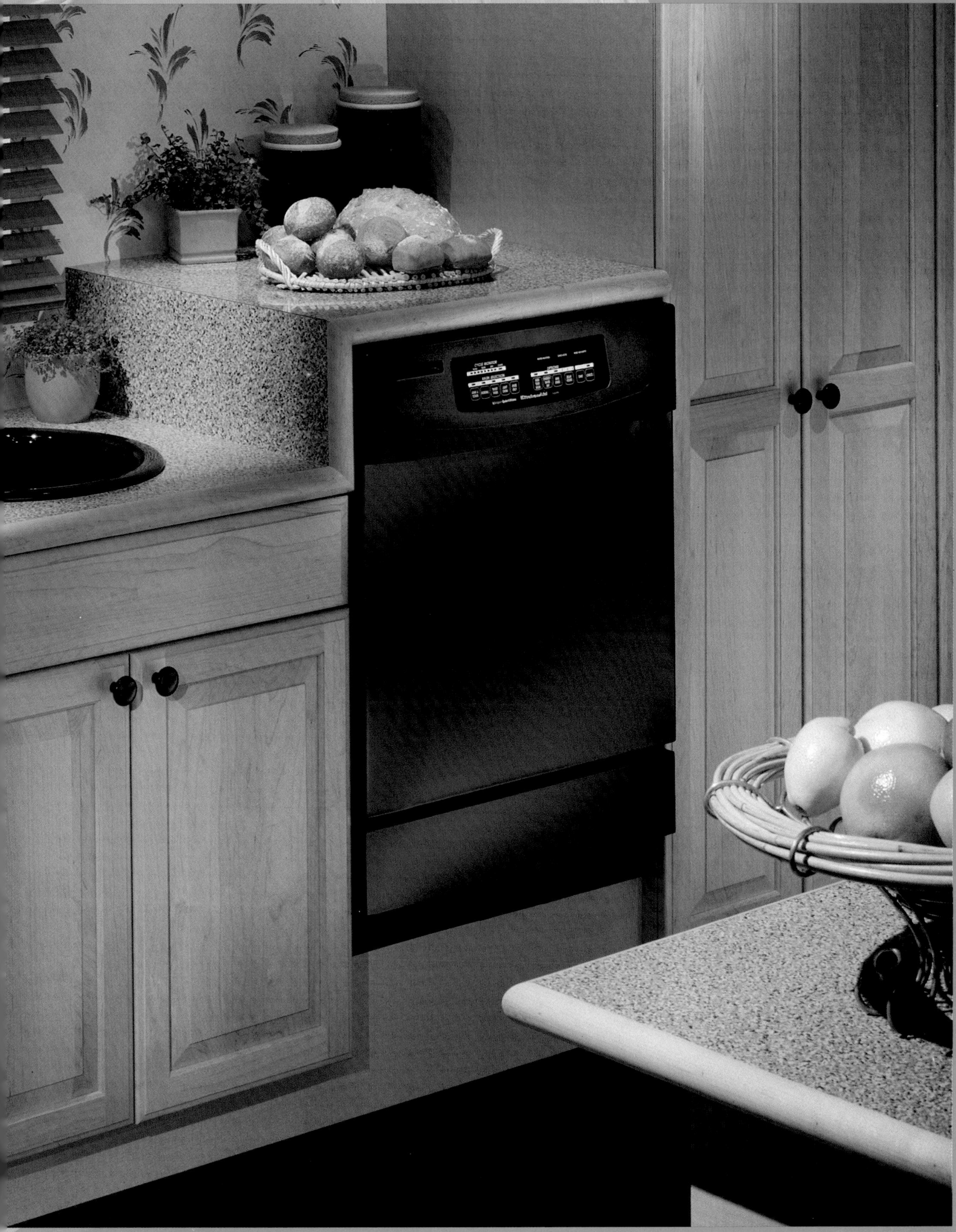

BEHIND THE HANDSOME PANELED DOORS OF THIS
KITCHENAID® BUILT-IN REFRIGERATOR IS HOME REFRIGERATION
THAT IS CONVENIENT, FUNCTIONAL AND ENERGY EFFICIENT.
THE EXCLUSIVE EXTENDFRESH™ TEMPERATURE MANAGEMENT
SYSTEM PROVIDES ACCURATE CONTROL OF
TEMPERATURE VARIATIONS — SO YOU'LL NEVER HAVE TO BE
CONCERNED ABOUT FOOD PRESERVATION. AND, KITCHENAID
BUILT-IN REFRIGERATORS CARRY THE CONCEPT OF FRESHNESS
THROUGHOUT THE REFRIGERATOR. THE ADJUSTABLE
FRESHCHILL™ MEAT LOCKER HELPS PROLONG FRESH MEAT
STORAGE AND THE LARGE CLEARVUE™ CRISPERS ARE
HUMIDITY-CONTROLLED TO HELP KEEP PRODUCE FRESH.
DRAWERS AND BASKETS MOVE IN AND OUT SMOOTHLY EVEN
WHEN FULLY LOADED ON THE EXCLUSIVE ROLLERTRAC™ PLUS
SYSTEM. A THROUGH-THE-DOOR ICE AND WATER DISPENSER
PROVIDES CRUSHED ICE, ICE CRESCENTS AND CHILLED WATER
NEATLY AND EFFICIENTLY. DISPENSERS ARE AVAILABLE IN
COLOR-COORDINATED BLACK OR WHITE TO MATCH YOUR
REFRIGERATOR DOOR.

4

BUILT-IN REFRIGERATORS

48-inch Model KSSS48QDW (shown right) offers the convenience of ice and water through-the-door. A 28.9 cubic foot total capacity with a 10.5 cubic foot freezer is large enough to handle the needs of any household.

42-inch Model KSSS42MDX (shown with decorative custom panels) provides 24.7 cubic feet of total food storage capacity including a 9.1 cubic foot freezer.

Three sizes...36-inch, 42-inch and 48-inch – with or without ice and water through-the-door – satisfy every space, capacity and convenience requirement. Totally hidden hinges help create a seamless flush look with existing cabinetry. You can install custom panels to match kitchen cabinets, or select factory precut panels in your choice of Almond, White, Black-Glass Look or Stainless Steel.

KitchenAid® Side-by-Side and Top-Mount
Refrigerators are a good illustration of how
form follows function. Sculptura™ styling accents
the seamless lines and monochromatic colors that
add elegance to any kitchen. Inside, brilliant lighting
dances off the all-white interior making it easy to
see all the conveniences: humidity-controlled crispers,
temperature-controlled meat pan, RollerTrac™ Plus
Shelves, gallon door storage and through-the-door
ice and water — these are just a few of the quality
touches you can expect. And because of our exclusive
ExtendFresh™ Temperature Management System,
you get accurate control of temperature variations —
so you'll never have to be concerned about food
preservation. Model KSRS25QD (shown right) has
all the features described and adds an innovative
ClearVue™ Carousel Pan for a fresh approach to
delicate item storage. Available in White, Almond
or with an All-Black cabinet, $^{1}/_{8}$-inch thick factory-
installed trim kit and color-coordinated door panels.

REFRIGERATORS

6

*Model KSBS20QE comes
with a factory-installed
trim kit and accepts
custom panels to give
your freestanding
refrigerator a built-in
appearance.*

*This is not your average
top-mount refrigerator.
Model KTRS25QD features
a through-the-door ice
and water dispenser with
crushed or cubed ice. Provides
24.9 cubic feet of total food
storage capacity including
a 7.7 cubic foot freezer.*

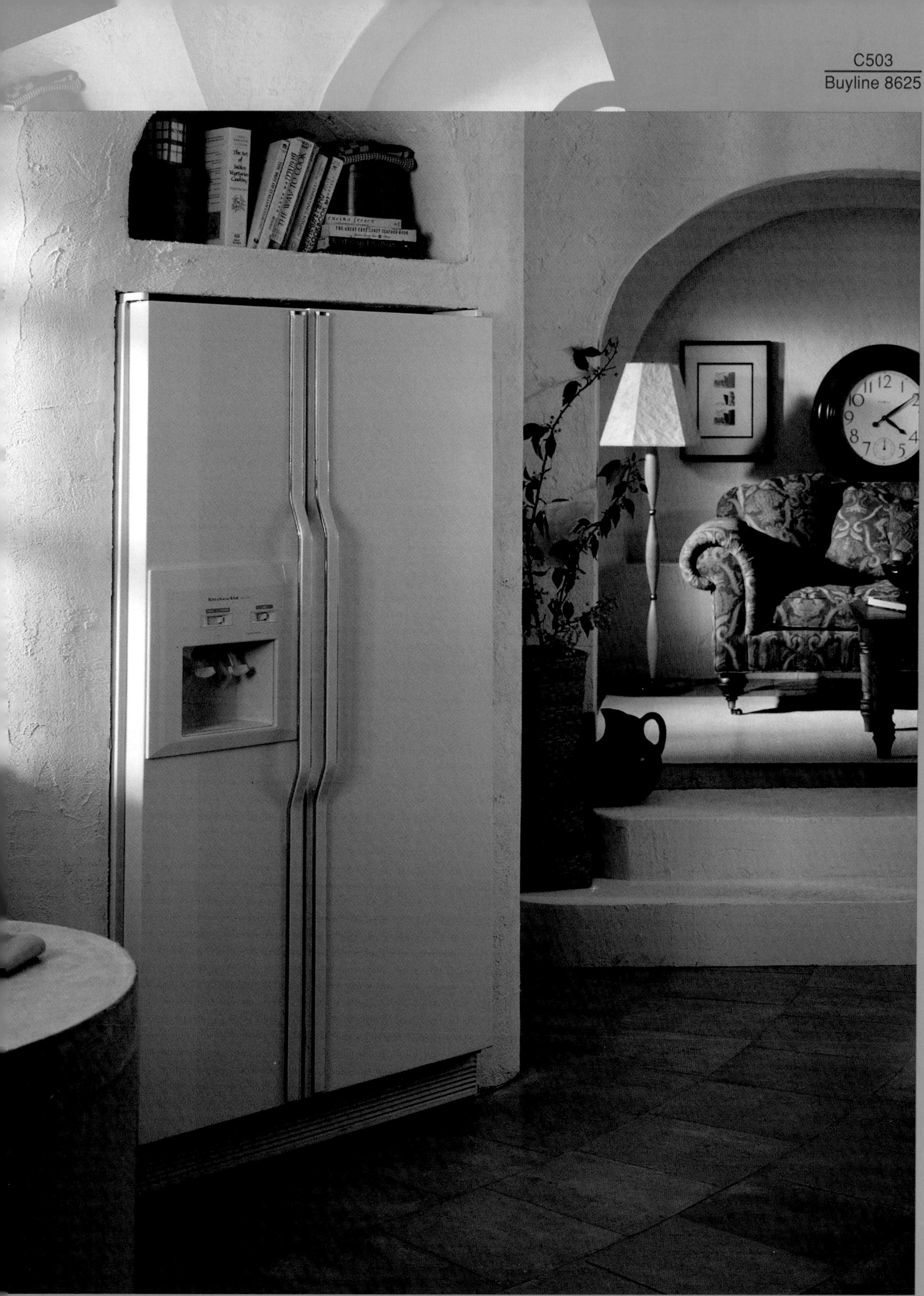
THE WAY TO COOK

KitchenAid® Ranges strike the perfect balance between style and performance. Whether your choice is free-standing or slide-in, electric or gas — there's a model that's right for you.

The Sculptura™ family look* makes a stylish impression in any kitchen. Monochromatic White, Almond or Black styling matches your kitchen decor. All gas ranges offer sealed gas burners for easy cleanup.

KitchenAid ranges give you virtually unlimited cooking options as well. Choose a range with a conventional thermal oven or, for more convenience, try a THERMAL-CONVECTION™ oven with EasyConvect™ Conversion. It will change the way you think about convection cooking. Electric ranges with the T.H.E. (Third Hidden Element) Convection System take convection one step further. In this system, heated air is circulated without exposing foods to direct radiant heat — which can create undesired hot spots.

*Available on freestanding and slide-in gas ranges and slide-in electric ranges.

8

FREESTANDING/ SLIDE-IN RANGES

KitchenAid gas range Model KGST307B features state-of-the-art styling and a superior range of cooking options including our EasyConvect Conversion feature.

KitchenAid freestanding electric range Model KERH507Y has a 24¹/₂" depth for a flush appearance with kitchen cabinets. An easy-cleaning ceramic-glass cooktop and convection cooking options are sure to please.

Even-heating radiant elements, easy-cleaning ceramic-glass cooktop, and versatile cooking options add to the attractive styling of electric range Model KESC307B. Choose monochromatic White or Almond styling.

Model KGRT507B (shown far right) adds the convenience of a THERMAL-CONVECTION oven to the attractive styling available on this gas range. Choose monochromatic White, Almond or Black styling.

KitchenAid® Built-In Ovens deliver both superlative cooking performance and enduring aesthetic appeal.

Ovens are available in single or double oven configurations with a 24-, 27- or 30-inch width. All ovens feature two-element balanced baking and roasting, variable temperature broiling and variable time self-cleaning. It's the kind of quality performance you expect from the KitchenAid brand name.

Built-in ovens with THERMAL-CONVECTION™ options let you enjoy both conventional and convection cooking. In the KitchenAid true-convection system, heated air is pulled into the fan then circulated back throughout the oven cavity with the aid of a series of baffles. The result of this fan-driven circulation is gently, evenly cooked foods at lower temperatures and shorter cooking times.

And KitchenAid offers the widest variety of combination ovens, giving you unlimited flexibility for your kitchen.

10

BUILT-IN OVENS

Choose Model KEMS378B 27-Inch SUPERBA™ Microwave-Convection/ THERMAL-CONVECTION oven for microwave speed, convection versatility and thermal baking and roasting all in one elegant oven. Available in monochromatic White, Almond or Black styling.

30-inch Model KEBS208B provides THERMAL-CONVECTION Cooking capability in the upper and lower ovens for maximum convenience and versatility. Choose monochromatic White, Almond or Black styling. Also available in a 27-inch size (Model KEBS278B).

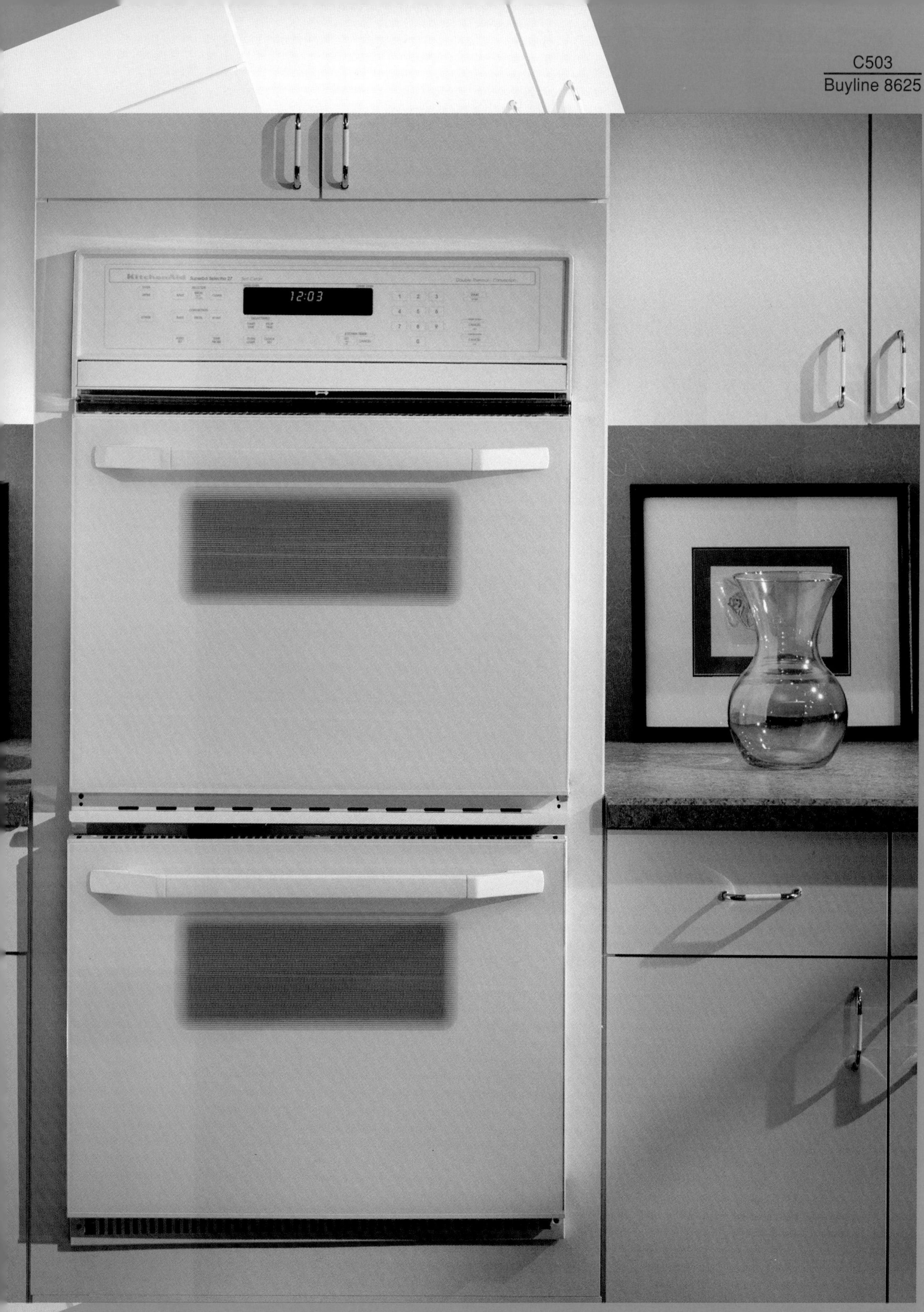

WANT TO STAY ON TOP OF YOUR COOKING?
KITCHENAID® CERAMIC-GLASS COOKTOPS ARE EXCEP-
TIONALLY PRACTICAL YET DESIGNED TO BLEND SMOOTHLY
INTO ALMOST ANY COUNTERTOP SETTING, IN EITHER
TRADITIONAL OR MODERN KITCHENS. COMPONENTS
ARE SEALED INTO THE COOKTOP SO CLEANUP IS SIMPLE!
JUST WIPE THE SURFACE WITH A DAMP CLOTH OR
SPONGE. COOKTOPS ARE AVAILABLE IN GAS OR ELECTRIC,
30-INCH OR 36-INCH SIZE AND WITH YOUR CHOICE
OF WHITE, ALMOND OR BLACK STYLING. OPTIONAL
DOWNDRAFT SYSTEMS MAKE IT POSSIBLE TO CONVERT
COOKTOPS TO SELF-VENTILATING OPERATION.

BUILT-IN COOKTOPS

*Model KGCT365E 36-inch
Gas Cooktop (shown right)
fits in virtually any 33- or 36-
inch cutout. Color-coordinated
cast-iron grates accent the easy-
cleaning tempered-glass White
cooktop which is also available
in Almond or Black.*

*Model KECC502B
30-inch Electric
Cooktop features
single- and dual-circuit
radiant elements and
a durable ceramic-
glass surface that
resists scratches and
stains. Infinite-heat
controls allow you to
"fine-tune" the level
of heat you need from
rapid boiling to slow
simmering.*

*Gas burners are sealed
into the tempered-glass
surface of Model KGCT305E
30-inch Cooktop which is
sized to fit virtually any
30-inch cutout.*

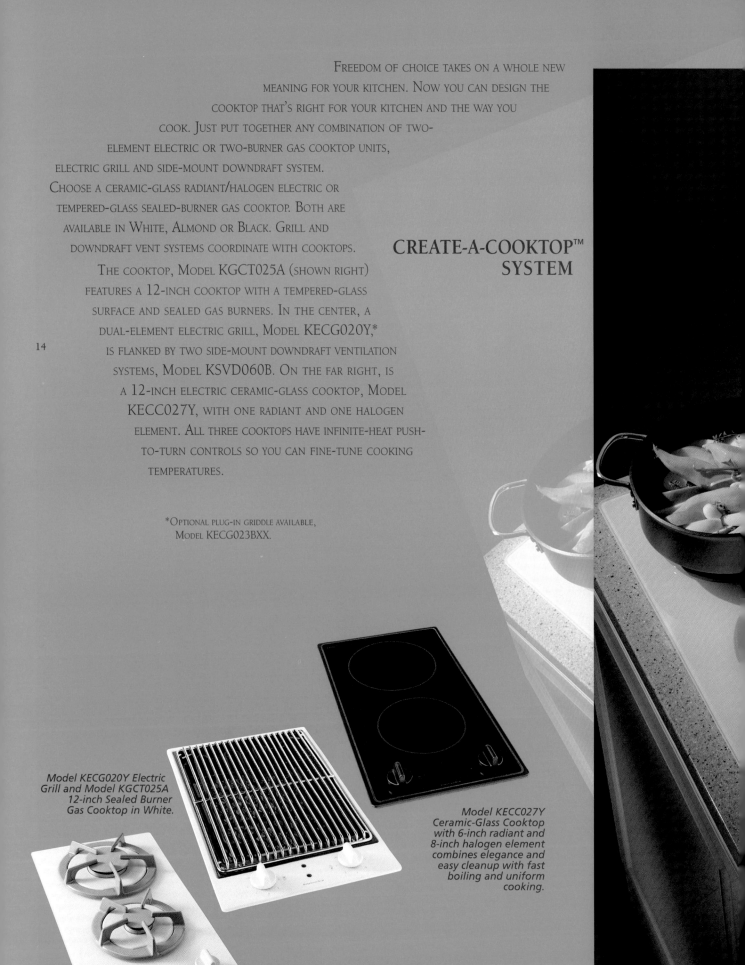

FREEDOM OF CHOICE TAKES ON A WHOLE NEW MEANING FOR YOUR KITCHEN. NOW YOU CAN DESIGN THE COOKTOP THAT'S RIGHT FOR YOUR KITCHEN AND THE WAY YOU COOK. JUST PUT TOGETHER ANY COMBINATION OF TWO-ELEMENT ELECTRIC OR TWO-BURNER GAS COOKTOP UNITS, ELECTRIC GRILL AND SIDE-MOUNT DOWNDRAFT SYSTEM. CHOOSE A CERAMIC-GLASS RADIANT/HALOGEN ELECTRIC OR TEMPERED-GLASS SEALED-BURNER GAS COOKTOP. BOTH ARE AVAILABLE IN WHITE, ALMOND OR BLACK. GRILL AND DOWNDRAFT VENT SYSTEMS COORDINATE WITH COOKTOPS.

CREATE-A-COOKTOP™ SYSTEM

THE COOKTOP, MODEL KGCT025A (SHOWN RIGHT) FEATURES A 12-INCH COOKTOP WITH A TEMPERED-GLASS SURFACE AND SEALED GAS BURNERS. IN THE CENTER, A DUAL-ELEMENT ELECTRIC GRILL, MODEL KECG020Y,* IS FLANKED BY TWO SIDE-MOUNT DOWNDRAFT VENTILATION SYSTEMS, MODEL KSVD060B. ON THE FAR RIGHT, IS A 12-INCH ELECTRIC CERAMIC-GLASS COOKTOP, MODEL KECC027Y, WITH ONE RADIANT AND ONE HALOGEN ELEMENT. ALL THREE COOKTOPS HAVE INFINITE-HEAT PUSH-TO-TURN CONTROLS SO YOU CAN FINE-TUNE COOKING TEMPERATURES.

14

*OPTIONAL PLUG-IN GRIDDLE AVAILABLE, MODEL KECG023BXX.

Model KECG020Y Electric Grill and Model KGCT025A 12-inch Sealed Burner Gas Cooktop in White.

Model KECC027Y Ceramic-Glass Cooktop with 6-inch radiant and 8-inch halogen element combines elegance and easy cleanup with fast boiling and uniform cooking.

WHEN YOU CHOOSE THE KITCHENAID®
BRAND, VENTILATION SYSTEMS DON'T HAVE TO
BE AN AFTERTHOUGHT. STYLISH OPTIONS ABOUND
TO MATCH WHATEVER ARCHITECTURAL STYLE YOU HAVE.
ISLAND CANOPY AND WALL-MOUNT CANOPY RANGE
HOODS PROVIDE A DRAMATIC FLAIR TO ANY KITCHEN
SETTING. RETRACTABLE OR STATIONARY DOWNDRAFT
SYSTEMS AND SLIDE-OUT VENTILATION HOODS PROVIDE
SUBTLE ELEGANCE TO YOUR KITCHEN DESIGN.
MICROWAVE OVENS COME IN COUNTERTOP AND
OVER-THE-RANGE VARIATIONS. ALL KITCHENAID
MICROWAVE OVENS FEATURE GENEROUS OVEN SIZE
CAPACITIES WITH GREAT PERFORMANCE FEATURES
TO MATCH.

16

VENTILATION SYSTEMS AND MICROWAVES

30-Inch Retractable Downdraft Ventilation System Model KIRD801XSS provides a great solution to kitchen ventilating problems in installations where an overhead exhaust hood is not practical.

Complement your kitchen in truly exquisite fashion with this Island Canopy Range Hood Model KICU265B in your choice of White, Almond or Stainless Steel styling.

Model KWVU265YBA gives eye-catching appeal to your kitchen design. When it's not in use, it slides out of sight and rests flush to overhead cabinets.

Microwave/Hood Model KHMC107B combines overhead/cooktop venting with all the conveniences of microwave cooking. Available in White, Almond or Black styling.

For exceptional style that carries even into the laundry room, look for the KitchenAid® brand name. Our SUPERBA® Clothes Washers and Clothes Dryers provide elegant styling inside and out. Restyled monochromatic consoles provide a clean look for any kitchen. Inside, the TriDura® Wash Basket Finish resists rust, stains and scratches to keep its good looks for years. KitchenAid dryers feature a PowderKote™ Finish that makes it easy to find stray socks and other small items. Some models include a drum light and door window for even easier viewing.

But the real proof is in the performance. KitchenAid laundry products give you an ideal blend of cycles and cycle options to custom-tailor washing and drying for special load requirements.

18

LAUNDRY PRODUCTS

SUPERBA® Model KAWE977B Electronic Clothes Washer offers eight automatic cycles, a three-speed 1/2 HP motor and a stylish monochromatic white console with cycle status lights. The matching Electronic Clothes Dryer, Model KEYW977B, has seven automatic cycle selections, CUSTOM DRY Control which senses the amount of moisture in the load and the SMOOTH GUARD™ System for extended tumbling. Also available as a gas model, Model KGYW977B.

Choose this KitchenAid laundry pair, Model KAWE670B clothes washer with Model KEYE670B clothes dryer. Shown left with black console, this model is also available in monochromatic White or Almond.

KITCHENAID® TRASH COMPACTORS TAKE
THE UNPLEASANTNESS OUT OF THE JOB NO ONE WANTS
TO TAKE ON: TAKING OUT THE TRASH. COMPACTING ACTION
REDUCES A WEEK'S WORTH OF TRASH FOR AN AVERAGE
FAMILY OF FOUR TO A SMALL, EASY-TO-HANDLE PACKAGE.
THE ACTIVATED CHARCOAL FILTER AND ODOR CONTROL
FAN EFFECTIVELY DEAL WITH UNPLEASANT TRASH
ODORS. KITCHENAID TRASH COMPACTORS ARE
15 INCHES WIDE TO ACCOMMODATE MOST BUILT-IN
KITCHEN REQUIREMENTS. CONVERTIBLE COMPACTORS
ARE AVAILABLE FOR ADDED CONVENIENCE. OPTIONAL
COLOR-COORDINATED CONTROL PANELS AND THE
VARI-FRONT™ DOOR PANELS LET YOU MATCH
YOUR TRASH COMPACTOR TO OTHER APPLIANCES. THE
INSTALLED TRIM KIT CAN ALSO ACCEPT CUSTOM PANELS.
SHOWN ON THE RIGHT IS MODEL KUCC151DWH
15-INCH TRASH COMPACTOR WITH MONOCHROMATIC
WHITE STYLING AND TOE-BAR DRAWER OPENER.

20

TRASH
COMPACTORS
ICE CUBE MAKER
INSTANT-HOT®
WATER DISPENSER
FOOD WASTE
DISPOSERS

*The heat's on – at the turn of a tap. The INSTANT-HOT®
Water Dispenser, Model KHWS160V, available in
White, Almond or Chrome, delivers up to 60 cups
of 190°F water an hour. A great convenience in
both kitchen and bathroom.*

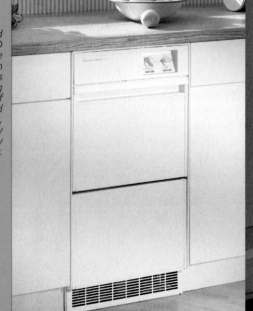

*With the KitchenAid
Model KUIS185D
Automatic Ice Cube
Maker, the iceman
cometh – and keeps
on coming, producing
up to 51 pounds of
clear ice daily. A lighted
bin holds 35 pounds,
refills automatically
when the ice supply
runs low.*

*A must in the kitchen, a KitchenAid food waste
disposer grinds away even bones and nut shells
quickly and quietly. Choose from batch-feed
or continuous-feed models, with motors up to
one HP. Optional flange and stopper kits for
continuous-feed models are available in White,
Almond or Brass.*

Dishwasher Optional Custom Front Panels

You may want to install a custom front panel on your dishwasher to match your kitchen cabinetry or laminate countertop. Installing a custom front panel requires a custom panel kit. The kit includes dimensions for constructing a custom panel and installation instructions. Unframed (trimless) and framed kits are available.

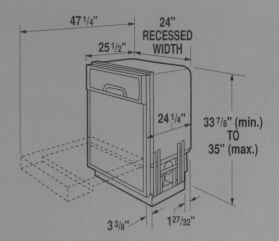

	Unframed	Framed*
White	4378861	4378864
Black	4378862	4378865
Almond	4378863	4378866

*A 1/4-in. panel can slide directly into the framed kit. If custom panel is thicker than 1/4 in., refer to detailed installation instructions for routing front panels.

NOTE: The kits contain heavy-duty door springs which hold panels weighing up to 10 pounds. The heavy-duty door springs must be used for panels weighing more than 4 pounds.

Built-In Refrigerator Dimensions.
Shown in inches (centimeters).

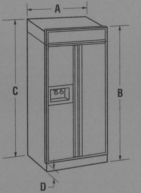

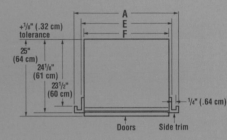

	Dispenser and Non-Dispenser Models			
	KSSS36QDW KSSS36QDX KSSS36MDX	KSSS42QDW KSSS42QDX KSSS42MDX	KSSS48QDW KSSS48QDX KSSS48MDX	KSBS20QE
A - Width	36 (91)	42 (106)	48 (122)	35¾ (91)
B - Overall Height	83⅜* (212.4)	83⅜* (212.4)	83⅜* (212.4)	67½* (172)
C - Recessed Height	83¼ (211.5)	83¼ (211.5)	83¼ (211.5)	N/A
D - Floor to Door	3½* (9)	3½* (9)	3½* (9)	3½* (9)
E - Width Allowing for Spaces and Tolerance	35½ (90)	41½ (105)	47½ (120)	N/A
F - Recessed Width	35 (89)	41 (104)	47 (119)	N/A

*Dimensions shown are for levelers extended 1/8" below rollers.
For levelers fully extended 1¼" below rollers, add 1⅛" to this dimension. Additional upper panel adjustment kit available.

Built-In Refrigerator Door Panel Kits

	Glass Look			Stainless Steel
	White	Almond	Black	
KSSS36QDX, QDW	4378650	4378656	4378653	4378659
KSSS36MDX	4318635	4318638	4318632	4318641
KSSS42QDX, QDW	4378651	4378657	4378654	4378660
KSSS42MDX	4318636	4318639	4318633	4318642
KSSS48QDX, QDW	4378652	4378658	4378655	4378661
KSSS48MDX	4318637	4318640	4318634	4318643

NOTE: Panels should be 1/4-in. (.64-cm) thick, with 5/16-in. (.80-cm) offset. Tolerance plus or minus 1/16 in. (.16 cm). Dimensions of door and ventilation panels shown are with routed edges. If custom door panels greater than 1/4-in. (.64-cm) thick are used, it may be necessary to rout the handle side of the panel a minimum of 3 in. (7.6 cm) in from the panel edge to provide a 2-in. (5.1-cm) min. access to the door handle. Either the full length of the panel or a selected area(s) can be routed. Check with your builder.

Built-In Refrigerator Panel Dimensions. Shown in inches (centimeters).

	KSSS36QDX, QDW	KSSS36MDX	KSSS42QDX, QDW	KSSS42MDX	KSSS48QDX, QDW	KSSS48MDX	KSBS20QE
Adjustable Ventilation Panel	6 (15) h x 32⅜ (82) w	6 (15) h x 32⅜ (82) w	6 (15) h x 38⅜ (97) w	6 (15) h x 38⅜ (97) w	6 (15) h x 44⅜ (113) w	6 (15) h x 44⅜ (113) w	N/A
Freezer Door Panel (no dispenser)	—	70⁷/₁₆ (179) h x 14¼ (36) w	—	70⁷/₁₆ (179) h x 16¾ (43) w	—	70⁷/₁₆ (179) h x 19¼ (49) w	—
Freezer Upper Door Panel (w/dispenser)	23⁷/₁₆ (60) h x 14¼ (36) w	—	23⁷/₁₆ (60) h x 16¾ (43) w	—	23⁷/₁₆ (60) h x 19¼ (49) w	—	18⅜ (47) h x 13¾ (35) w
Freezer Lower Door Panel (w/dispenser)	34⁷/₁₆ (87) h x 14¼ (36) w	—	34⁷/₁₆ (87) h x 16¾ (43) w	—	34⁷/₁₆ (87) h x 19¼ (49) w	—	31⅜ (80) h x 13¾ (35) w
Refrigerator Door Panel	70⁷/₁₆ (179) h x 19¼ (49) w	70⁷/₁₆ (179) h x 19¼ (49) w	70⁷/₁₆ (179) h x 22¾ (58) w	70⁷/₁₆ (179) h x 22¾ (58) w	70⁷/₁₆ (179) h x 26¼ (67) w	70⁷/₁₆ (179) h x 26¼ (67) w	63¹/₁₆ (160) h x 19⅜ (49) w

Kit includes refrigerator and freezer door panels and upper ventilation panel.

Dimensions are for planning purposes only. For complete details, see installation instructions packed with product. Specifications subject to change without notice.

Side-by-Side Refrigerator Dimensions. Shown in inches.

	KSRS27QD KSRB27QD	KSRS25QD KSRB25QD	KSRS22QD KSRB22QD	KSFS20QE KSBS20QE
Height (A)	$68^7/_8$	$68^7/_8$	$65^7/_8$	$67^1/_2$
Width (B)	$35^1/_2$	$35^1/_2$	$32^3/_4$	$35^3/_4$
Depth (C)*	$34^1/_4$	33	33	$27^7/_8$
Depth w/o Door & Grille (D)	$29^3/_4$	$29^3/_4$	$29^3/_4$	$23^1/_2$
Depth Door Open 90° (E)	$49^7/_8$**	$49^7/_8$**	$49^7/_8$**	$45^3/_4$

*Subtract $^1/_8$" for factory-installed trim kits – (KSRBxxxx models only).
  Add $^1/_4$" for custom door panels (available on most side-by-side models).
**Add $^1/_8$" for factory-installed trim kits – (KSRBxxxx models only).

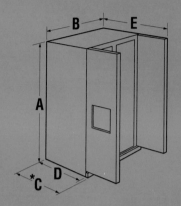

Top-Mount/Bottom-Mount Refrigerator Dimensions. Shown in inches.

	KTRS25QD KTLS25QD	KTRS25KD	KTRS22QD KTLS22QD	KTRS22KD KTRS22MD	KTRS21KD KTRS21MD	KTRS19KE	KBRS21KD
Height (A)	$68^7/_8$	$68^7/_8$	$65^7/_8$	$65^7/_8$	$65^1/_2$	$65^1/_2$	$65^7/_8$
Width (B)	$35^1/_2$	$35^1/_2$	$32^3/_4$	$32^3/_4$	$32^1/_2$	$29^1/_2$	$32^3/_4$
Depth (C)*	$32^7/_8$	$32^7/_8$	$32^7/_8$	$32^7/_8$	$32^5/_8$	$32^5/_8$	$32^7/_8$
Depth w/o Door & Grille (D)	$29^5/_8$	$29^3/_8$	$29^5/_8$	$29^5/_8$	$27^5/_8$	$27^5/_8$	$29^5/_8$
Depth Door Open 90° (E)	$65^1/_8$	$65^1/_8$	$62^3/_8$	$62^3/_8$	$62^1/_4$	$59^1/_4$	$62^3/_8$

*Dimension illustrates overall depth (including handles).

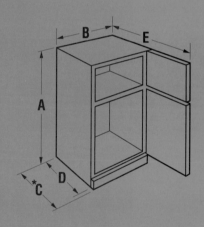 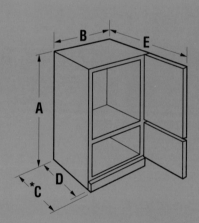

Dimensions for $^1/_4$-Inch Thick Custom Door Panels. Shown in inches.

Refrigerator Model		Refrigerator Door	Freezer Door	
			Upper	Lower
Side-by-Side				
KSRS27QD KSRB27QD*	KSRS25QD KSRB25QD*	$19^9/_{16}$ W x $63^3/_8$ H	$14^{13}/_{16}$ W x $20^3/_8$ H	$14^{13}/_{16}$ W x $28^7/_{16}$ H
KSRS22QD	KSRB22QD*	$19^9/_{16}$ W x $60^7/_{16}$ H	$12^1/_{16}$ W x $17^3/_8$ H	$12^1/_{16}$ W x $28^7/_{16}$ H
KSBS20QE		$19^3/_8$ W x $63^1/_{16}$ H	$13^3/_4$ W x $18^3/_8$ H	$13^3/_4$ W x $31^5/_8$ H
KSFS20QE		$19^3/_8$ W x $61^{15}/_{16}$ H	$13^3/_4$ W x $17^1/_4$ H	$13^3/_4$ W x $31^5/_8$ H
Top-Mount				
KTRS25KD		$35^1/_{16}$ W x $40^7/_{16}$ H	$35^1/_{16}$ W x $22^5/_8$ H	—
KTRS25QD KTLS25QD	KTRS22QD KTLS22QD	N/A	N/A	N/A
KTRS22KD	KTRS22MD	$32^5/_{16}$ W x $40^7/_{16}$ H	$32^5/_{16}$ W x $19^5/_8$ H	—
KTRS21KD	KTRS21MD	$32^{11}/_{16}$ W x $40^5/_{32}$ H	$32^{11}/_{16}$ W x $21^3/_8$ H	—
KTRS19KE		$29^{11}/_{16}$ W x $40^5/_{32}$ H	$29^{11}/_{16}$ W x $21^3/_8$ H	—
Bottom-Mount				
KBRS21KD		$32^5/_{16}$ W x $37^1/_{16}$ H	—	$32^5/_{16}$ W x $22^7/_8$ H

*Factory-installed trim kits will accept $^1/_8$" panels only.   N/A = Not Available

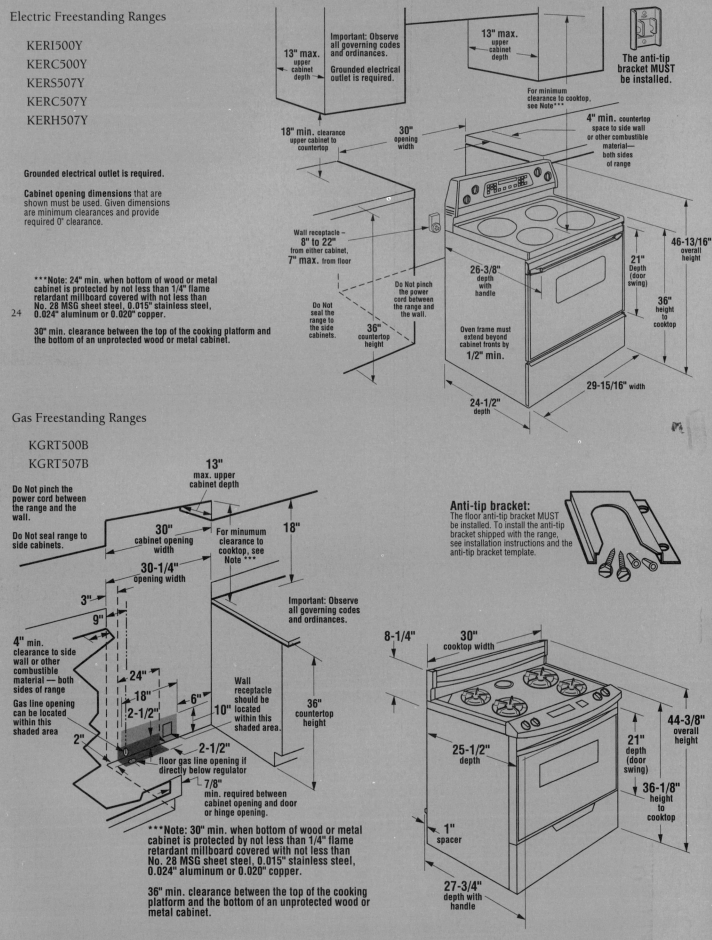

Electric Freestanding Ranges

KERI500Y
KERC500Y
KERS507Y
KERC507Y
KERH507Y

Grounded electrical outlet is required.

Cabinet opening dimensions that are shown must be used. Given dimensions are minimum clearances and provide required 0" clearance.

***Note: 24" min. when bottom of wood or metal cabinet is protected by not less than 1/4" flame retardant millboard covered with not less than No. 28 MSG sheet steel, 0.015" stainless steel, 0.024" aluminum or 0.020" copper.

30" min. clearance between the top of the cooking platform and the bottom of an unprotected wood or metal cabinet.

24

13" max. upper cabinet depth

Important: Observe all governing codes and ordinances.
Grounded electrical outlet is required.

13" max. upper cabinet depth

The anti-tip bracket MUST be installed.

For minimum clearance to cooktop, see Note***

18" min. clearance upper cabinet to countertop

30" opening width

4" min. countertop space to side wall or other combustible material—both sides of range

Wall receptacle – 8" to 22" from either cabinet, 7" max. from floor

Do Not seal the range to the side cabinets.

Do Not pinch the power cord between the range and the wall.

36" countertop height

26-3/8" depth with handle

Oven frame must extend beyond cabinet fronts by 1/2" min.

24-1/2" depth

21" Depth (door swing)

36" height to cooktop

46-13/16" overall height

29-15/16" width

Gas Freestanding Ranges

KGRT500B
KGRT507B

Do Not pinch the power cord between the range and the wall.

Do Not seal range to side cabinets.

4" min. clearance to side wall or other combustible material — both sides of range

Gas line opening can be located within this shaded area

13" max. upper cabinet depth

30" cabinet opening width

30-1/4" opening width

For minimum clearance to cooktop, see Note***

18"

Important: Observe all governing codes and ordinances.

3"
9"
24"
18"
2-1/2"
2"
6"
10"
2-1/2"
floor gas line opening if directly below regulator

Wall receptacle should be located within this shaded area.

36" countertop height

7/8" min. required between cabinet opening and door or hinge opening.

***Note: 30" min. when bottom of wood or metal cabinet is protected by not less than 1/4" flame retardant millboard covered with not less than No. 28 MSG sheet steel, 0.015" stainless steel, 0.024" aluminum or 0.020" copper.

36" min. clearance between the top of the cooking platform and the bottom of an unprotected wood or metal cabinet.

Anti-tip bracket:
The floor anti-tip bracket MUST be installed. To install the anti-tip bracket shipped with the range, see installation instructions and the anti-tip bracket template.

8-1/4"

30" cooktop width

25-1/2" depth

1" spacer

27-3/4" depth with handle

21" depth (door swing)

44-3/8" overall height

36-1/8" height to cooktop

Dimensions are for planning purposes only. For complete details, see installation instructions packed with product. Specifications subject to change without notice.

Electric Slide-In Ranges

KESS300B
KESC300B
KESC307B
KESH307B

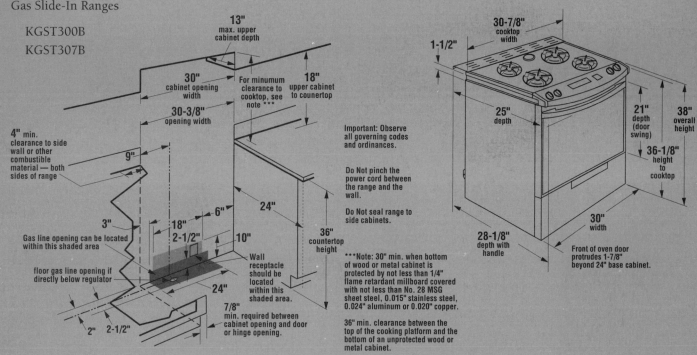

For minimum clearance to the top of cooktop, see Note***

13" max. upper cabinet depth

1/2" radius both corners

18" upper cabinet to countertop

22-3/4" opening depth

30-3/8" opening width

4" min. clearance to side wall or other combustible material — both sides of range.

Important: Observe all governing codes and ordinances.

junction box— 8" to 22" from either cabinet, 7" max. from floor

7/8" min. required between cutout and cabinet door or hinge.

36" countertop height

Anti-tip bracket:
The floor anti-tip bracket MUST be installed. To install the anti-tip bracket shipped with the range, see installation instructions and the anti-tip bracket template.

30-7/8" cooktop width

1-1/2"

1"

22-5/8" depth

Do Not pinch the power supply cord between the range and the wall.

Do Not seal range to side cabinets.

21" depth (door swing)

36" countertop height

25-3/4" depth with handle

29-15/16" width

***Note: 24" min. when bottom of wood or metal cabinet is protected by not less than 1/4" flame retardant millboard covered with not less than No. 28 MSG sheet steel, 0.015" stainless steel, 0.024" aluminum or 0.020" copper.

30" min. clearance between the top of the cooking platform and the bottom of an unprotected wood or metal cabinet.

Gas Slide-In Ranges

KGST300B
KGST307B

13" max. upper cabinet depth

30" cabinet opening width

30-3/8" opening width

For minumum clearance to cooktop, see note ***

18" upper cabinet to countertop

4" min. clearance to side wall or other combustible material — both sides of range

9"

3"

18"

2-1/2"

6"

10"

24"

Gas line opening can be located within this shaded area

floor gas line opening if directly below regulator

Wall receptacle should be located within this shaded area.

36" countertop height

24"

2"   2-1/2"

7/8" min. required between cabinet opening and door or hinge opening.

Important: Observe all governing codes and ordinances.

Do Not pinch the power cord between the range and the wall.

Do Not seal range to side cabinets.

***Note: 30" min. when bottom of wood or metal cabinet is protected by not less than 1/4" flame retardant millboard covered with not less than No. 28 MSG sheet steel, 0.015" stainless steel, 0.024" aluminum or 0.020" copper.

36" min. clearance between the top of the cooking platform and the bottom of an unprotected wood or metal cabinet.

30-7/8" cooktop width

1-1/2"

25" depth

21" depth (door swing)

38" overall height

36-1/8" height to cooktop

28-1/8" depth with handle

30" width

Front of oven door protrudes 1-7/8" beyond 24" base cabinet.

Countertop Preparation

FRONT EDGES: You may need to shave or cut the trim of formed, tiled or metal front-edged countertops to clear the 30" width of cooktop.

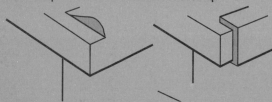

If countertop extends more than 1-1/8" beyond cabinet front, additional notching of edge is required to clear step of end cap.

1-1/8"

Countertop must be level. Place level on countertop, first side to side; then front to back. If countertop is not level, range will not be level. Oven must be level for satisfactory baking conditions.

Built-In Oven Dimension and Installation Data. Shown in inches, weights in pounds.

Model	Overall Dimensions					Cutout Dimensions			Electrical Data			Weights (approx.)	
	Width (side to side) (A)	Height (bottom to top) (B)	Depth (back to front)			Width (side to side) (E)	Height (bottom to top) (F)	Depth (min.) (back to front) (G)	KW 240V	KW 208V	Circuit Amps (min.)	Net	Shipping
			Door Closed (to edge of door) (C)	Door Closed (to edge of handle) (D)	Door Open								
Electric*													
KEBS177B	26	28⅝	26½	28¼	43¾	24½	27⅞	23⅝	3.1	2.3	30	152	173
KEBS107B	29⅝	33⁷⁄₁₆	25¼	27⅜	46½	28½	31⅝	23	3.1	2.3	30	147	167
KEBS277B	26	49⅞	26½	28¼	43¾	24½	49	23⅝	6.1	4.6	40	260	290
KEBS278B	26	49⅞	26½	28¼	43¾	24½	49	23⅝	6.3	4.8	40	270	300
KEBS207B	29⅝	59⅜	25¼	27⅜	46½	28½	56⁹⁄₁₆	23	6.1	4.6	40	227	257
KEBS208B	29⅝	59⅜	25¼	27¾	46½	28½	56⁹⁄₁₆	23	6.3	4.8	40	230	260
KEMS377B	26	50⅞	26½	28⅝	43¾	24½	49	23⅝	5.9	5.1	40	236	266
KEMS378B	26	50⅞	26½	28⅝	43¾	24½	49	23⅝	6.3	5.5	40	241	271

*Separate 3-wire with ground circuit required. 4-foot flexible steel conduit with product. Dual Rated 240-208/120 Volts AC, 60 Hertz.
Minimum distance between cutout and cabinet doors: 24-in. and 27-in. models, 2½ in.; 30-in. models, 1¼ in.

26

Built-In Oven Cavity Dimensions. Shown in inches.

Size, Style	Width	Height	Depth (door closed)
24-in. Thermal Oven (Electric)	17½	15	17¾
27-in. Thermal Oven (Electric)	19½	15	17¾
27-in. Thermal Oven (Gas)	19¼	16	17
27-in. THERMAL-CONVECTION™ Oven (Electric)	19½	15	16⅛
30-in. Thermal Oven (Electric)	22	16¾	18¼
30-in. THERMAL-CONVECTION™ Oven (Electric)	22	16¾	16½
Microwave Oven – 27-in. Combination	16⁷⁄₁₆	9⅞	13⅞
Microwave-Convection Oven – 27-in. Combination	14¾	10	15⅛
Microwave-Convection Oven – 30-in. Combination	14¾	10	15⅛

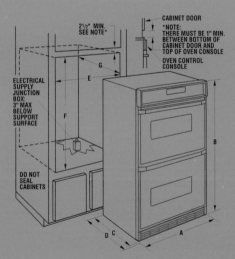

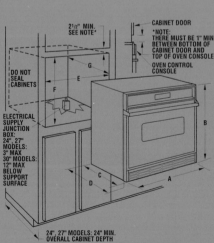

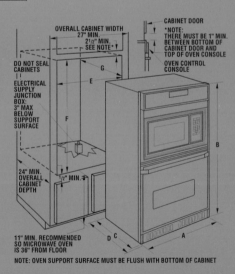

Dimensions are for planning purposes only. For complete details, see installation instructions packed with product. Specifications subject to change without notice.

Microwave/Hood
KHMS105B
KHMC107B

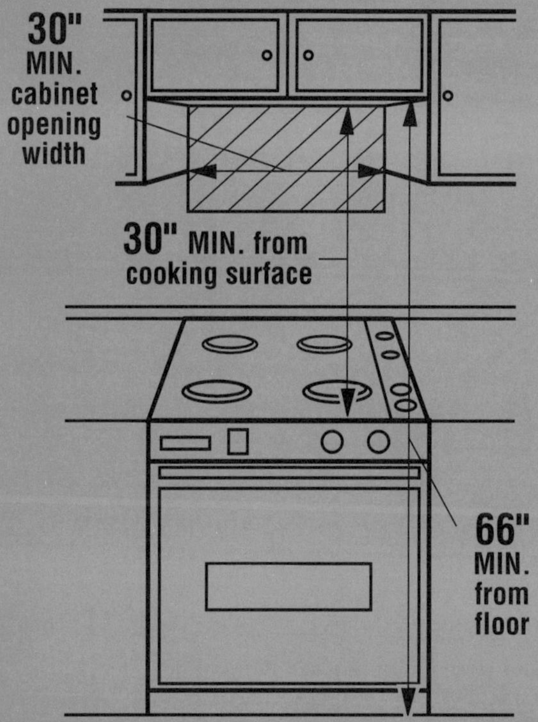
30" MIN. cabinet opening width
30" MIN. from cooking surface
66" MIN. from floor

Microwave Oven
KCMS122Y
KCMS125Y

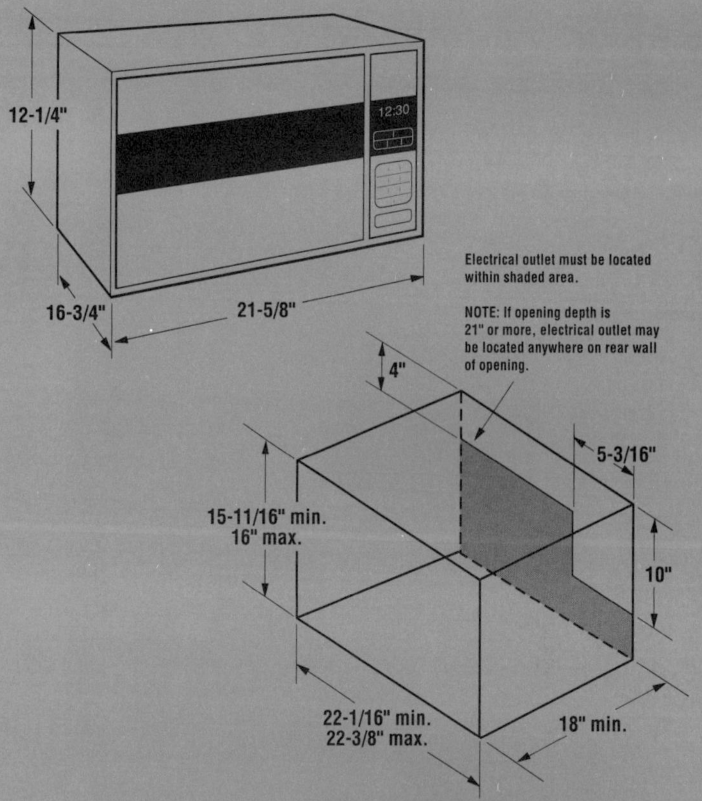
12-1/4"
16-3/4"
21-5/8"
12:30
Electrical outlet must be located within shaded area.
NOTE: If opening depth is 21" or more, electrical outlet may be located anywhere on rear wall of opening.
4"
5-3/16"
15-11/16" min.
16" max.
10"
22-1/16" min.
22-3/8" max.
18" min.

Ventilation Hoods –
Island Canopy Hood
KICU265B

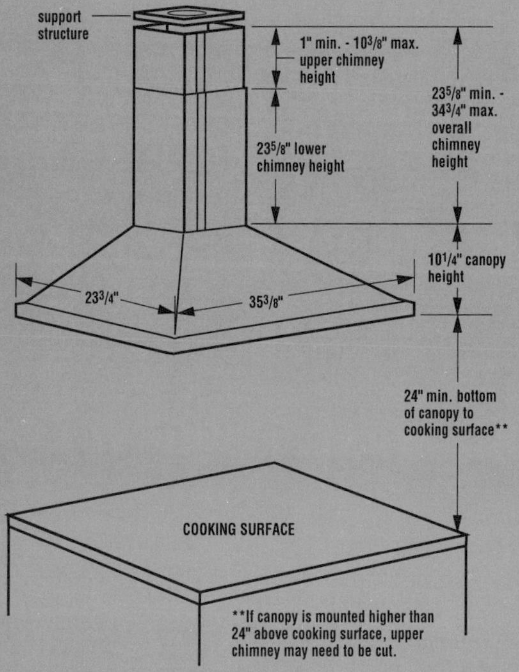
support structure
1" min. - 10 3/8" max. upper chimney height
23 5/8" min. - 34 3/4" max. overall chimney height
23 5/8" lower chimney height
10 1/4" canopy height
23 3/4"
35 3/8"
24" min. bottom of canopy to cooking surface**
COOKING SURFACE
**If canopy is mounted higher than 24" above cooking surface, upper chimney may need to be cut.

Ventilation Hoods –
Wall-Mount Canopy Hood
KWCU265B

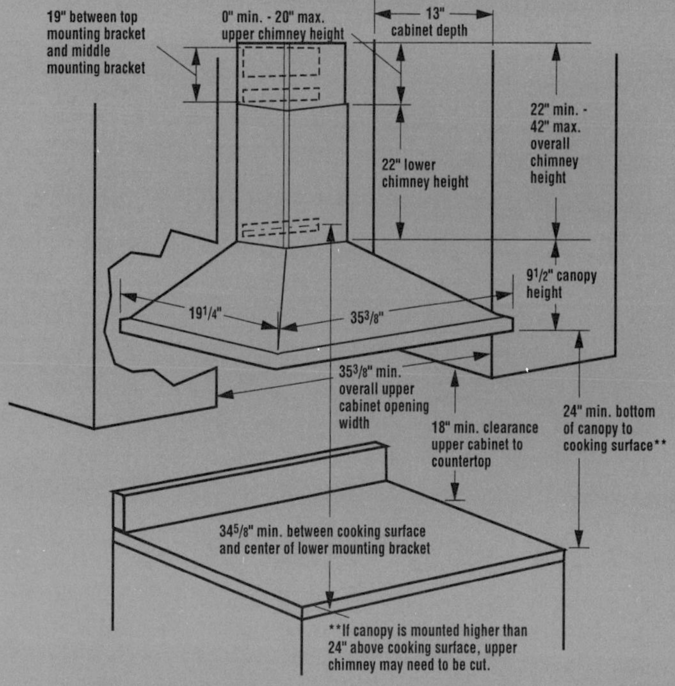
19" between top mounting bracket and middle mounting bracket
0" min. - 20" max. upper chimney height
13" cabinet depth
22" min. - 42" max. overall chimney height
22" lower chimney height
9 1/2" canopy height
19 1/4"
35 3/8"
35 3/8" min. overall upper cabinet opening width
18" min. clearance upper cabinet to countertop
24" min. bottom of canopy to cooking surface**
34 5/8" min. between cooking surface and center of lower mounting bracket
**If canopy is mounted higher than 24" above cooking surface, upper chimney may need to be cut.

Cooktop Dimensions. Shown in inches, weights in pounds.

	36" Electric Cooktops**		30" Electric Cooktops**		36" Gas Cooktop	30" Gas Cooktop
	KECC567B	KECG260S	KECC507B	KECC502B	KGCT365E‡	KGCT305E‡
Cooktop						
Width (A)	36	36	30	30	36	30³⁄₄
Depth (B)	21	21³⁄₄	21	21	21³⁄₄	21³⁄₄
Burner Box Height* (C)	2⁷⁄₈	4	2⁷⁄₈	2⁷⁄₈	3	3
Cabinet Countertop						
Cutout Width (D)	35¹⁄₂	33	29¹⁄₂	29¹⁄₂	33⁷⁄₁₆	27³⁄₁₆
Cutout Depth (E)	20¹⁄₂	18⁷⁄₈	20¹⁄₂	20¹⁄₂	18¹⁵⁄₁₆	18¹⁵⁄₁₆
Min. Space to Backsplash or Vertical Wall (F)	—	—	—	—	1	1
Countertop Space Both Sides of Cutout from a Combustible Surface (G)	6	3	6	6	4⁵⁄₈	5¹⁄₄
Min. to Countertop Front Edge (H)	1⁷⁄₈	2⁷⁄₈	1⁷⁄₈	1⁷⁄₈	2³⁄₈	2³⁄₈
Electrical						
KW 240V	8.7	9.0	7.3	7.2	—	—
KW 208V	—	6.8†	—	—	—	—
Circuit Amps	40	40	40	40	15***	15***
Conduit	3	4	3	3	3¹⁄₂	3¹⁄₂
Approx. Weights						
Net	45	50	35	35	56	50
Shipping	51	64	40	40	70	62

28

*Power/Fuel supply connections extend below cooktop and are not included in
  Burner Box Height dimensions.
**Separate 2-wire with ground circuit required.
***3¹⁄₂ ft. (106.7 cm) 120 Volts AC, 60 Hz., 3-wire cord, 3-prong plug with product (for ignition).
†Special higher wattage 208-Volt open-coil elements are available:
  6-in., Part No. 3177639
  8-in., Part No. 3177292
  8-in. POWER™ burner Part No. 3177296
  Grill (Model KECG260S only), Part No. 3177526
‡LP Conversion Kit 4173627

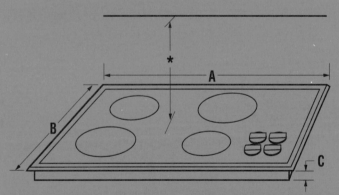

*GAS MODELS: 30" MIN., ELECTRIC MODELS: 24" MIN. CLEARANCE WHEN BOTTOM
OF WOOD OR METAL CABINET IS PROTECTED BY NOT LESS THAN 1/4" FLAME
RETARDANT MILLBOARD COVERED WITH NOT LESS THAN NO. 28 MSG SHEET STEEL,
.015" STAINLESS STEEL, OR .024" ALUMINUM OR .020" COPPER.
GAS MODELS: 36" MIN., ELECTRIC MODELS: 30" MIN. CLEARANCE BETWEEN TOP OF
COOKING PLATFORM AND BOTTOM OF UNPROTECTED WOOD OR METAL CABINET.

Dimensions are for planning purposes only. For complete details, see installation instructions packed with product. Specifications subject to change without notice.

Retractable Downdraft Ventilation Systems – Cutout Dimensions

When Installed With	KIRD801X/KIRD802X		KIRD861X/KIRD862X		
	KGCT305	KECC502, KECC507	KECG260	KGCT365	KECC567
See Figure	2	1	2	2	1
Size	30"	30"	36"	36"	36"
A Min.	18³/₄"	—	18³/₄"	18³/₄"	—
A Max.	20⁵/₈"	20¹/₂"	20⁵/₈"	20⁵/₈"	19¹/₄"
B	1³/₄"	2"	1³/₄"	1³/₄"	2¹/₈"
C for A Min.	1¹/₂"	—	1¹/₂"	1¹/₂"	—
C for A Max.	⁹/₁₆"	—	⁹/₁₆"	⁹/₁₆"	—
X	27¹/₂"	27¹/₂"	27¹/₂"	33¹/₂"	33¹/₂"

Dimension A:
If just a "Max" dimension is given, that dimension must be used.
If dimension A is between the "Min." and "Max":
1. Subtract actual dimension from "A Max."
2. Divide by 2
3. Add to "C for A Max." for required C dimension
Example: KGCT305 with 19¹/₈" cutout
"A" Max.   20⁵/₈
Actual "A"   -19¹/₈
           1¹/₄ ÷ 2 = ⁵/₈"
C for A Max. ⁹/₁₆" + ⁵/₈" = 1³/₁₆" (required C dimension)

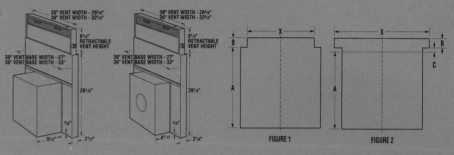

Interior-Mounted Motor   Exterior-Mounted Motor

FIGURE 1   FIGURE 2

Retractable Downdraft Ventilation Systems – Basic Dimensions and Installation Data

	Interior-Mounted Motors*		Exterior-Mounted Motors**	
	KIRD801X – 30"	KIRD861X – 36"	KIRD802X – 30"	KIRD862X – 36"
Base Width	27"	33"	27"	33"
Vent Width	26⁵/₈"	32⁵/₈"	26⁵/₈"	32⁵/₈"
Retractable Height	8¹/₄"	8¹/₄"	8¹/₄"	8¹/₄"
Base Height	26¹/₈"	26¹/₈"	26¹/₈"	26¹/₈"
Base Depth	2¹/₈"	2¹/₈"	2¹/₈"	2¹/₈"
Base to Motor	⁵/₈"	⁵/₈"	⁵/₈"	⁵/₈"
Depth of Motor	9³/₈"	9³/₈"	4"	4"
Voltage/Hz.	115/60	115/60	115/60	115/60
Circuit Amps	15	15	15	15

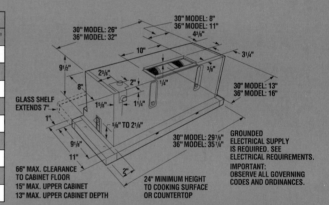

Slide-Out Ventilation System

Stationary Downdraft Ventilation Systems – Basic Dimensions and Installation Data

	Intake/Plenums		Power Units	
	KIVD860T – 36-in.*	KIVD800T – 30-in.**	KPID850T – Interior	KPED890T – Exterior
Base Depth	2¹/₂"	2¹/₂"	—	—
Vent Cover Depth	2³/₈"	2³/₈"	—	—
Overall Width	35"	28³/₄"	—	—
Vent Cover Height	1¹/₄"	1¹/₄"	—	—
Base Width	33¹/₄"	27"	—	—
Cutout Width	33¹/₄"	27"	—	—
Cutout Depth	22¹/₄"	22¹/₄"	—	—
Voltage/Hz.	115/60	115/60	—	—
Circuit Amps	15	15	—	—
Net Weight – Lbs.	24	22	25	27
Shipping Weight – Lbs.	26	23	22	24

*36-in. intake/plenums for models KECC567, KECG260, KGCT365
**30-in. intake/plenums for models KECC502, KECC507, KGCT305

Slide-Out Ventilation Systems – Basic Dimensions and Installation Data

	KWVU265YBA – 36"	KWVU205YBA – 30"
Overall Width	35⁷/₈"	29⁷/₈"
Centerline	16"	13"
Opening Side to Edge	11"	8"
Recessed Width	32"	26"
Min. Height to Cooking Surface or Countertop	24"	24"
Max. Clearance to Cabinet Floor	66"	66"
Cutout Depth	9³/₁₆"	9³/₁₆"
Cutout Width	32⁷/₈"	26¹/₈"
Voltage/Hz.	115/60	115/60
Circuit Amps	15	15
Net Weight – Lbs.	34	32
Shipping Weight – Lbs.	38	34

Maximum length of ductwork is 26 feet.
Non-vent kit Part No. 883140 is available.

Create-A-Cooktop™ System Dimensions and Installation Data.
Shown in inches (centimeters).

	Cooktops KECC027Y KGCT025A	Electric Grill KECG020Y	Downdraft Ventilation System KSVD060B
Overall Dimensions			
Width (side to side)	11¹⁵⁄₁₆ (30.3)	13¹⁵⁄₁₆ (35.4)	5¹⁵⁄₁₆ (15.1)
Depth (front to back)	21¾ (55.2)	21¾ (55.2)	21¾ (55.2)
Height (top to bottom)	4¼ (10.8)	4¼ (10.8)	4¼ (10.8)
Cutout Dimensions			
Width (side to side)	11 (27.9)	13 (33.0)	4½ (11.4)
Depth (front to back)	20½ (52.1)	20½ (52.1)	20½ (52.1)
Height (top to bottom)	4¼ (10.8)	4¼ (10.8)	4¼ (10.8)*

2 Cooktops
- Width (side to side) 23 (58.4)
- Depth (front to back) 20½ (52.1)
- Height (top to bottom) 4¼ (10.8)

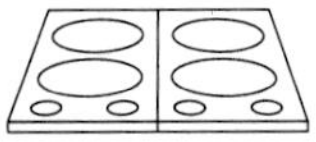

3 Cooktops
- Width (side to side) 35 (88.9)
- Depth (front to back) 20½ (52.1)
- Height (top to bottom) 4¼ (10.8)

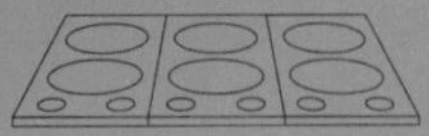

4 Cooktops
- Width (side to side) 47 (119.4)
- Depth (front to back) 20½ (52.1)
- Height (top to bottom) 4¼ (10.8)

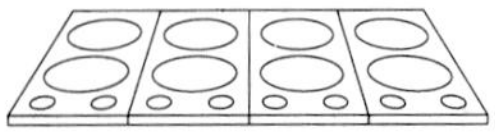

1 Cooktop with Vent
- Width (side to side) 16⅞ (42.9)
- Depth (front to back) 20½ (52.1)
- Height (top to bottom) 4¼ (10.8)*

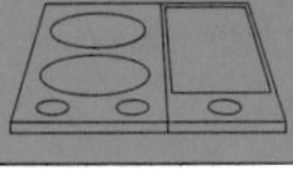

2 Cooktops with Vent
- Width (side to side) 29 (73.7)
- Depth (front to back) 20½ (52.1)
- Height (top to bottom) 4¼ (10.8)*

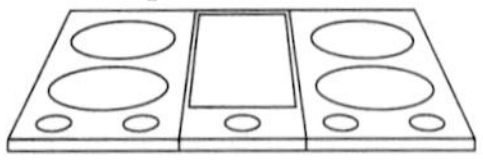

3 Cooktops with 2 Vents
- Width (side to side) 47 (119.4)
- Depth (front to back) 20½ (52.1)
- Height (top to bottom) 4¼ (10.8)*

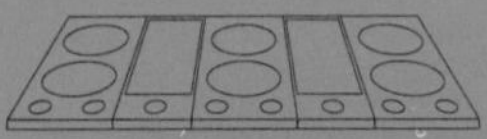

1 Grill with Vent
- Width (side to side) 18⅞ (47.9)
- Depth (front to back) 20½ (52.1)
- Height (top to bottom) 4¼ (10.8)*

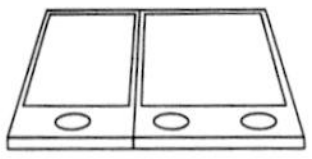

2 Grills with Vent
- Width (side to side) 33 (83.8)
- Depth (front to back) 20½ (52.1)
- Height (top to bottom) 4¼ (10.8)*

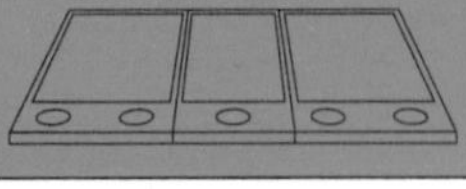

3 Grills with 2 Vents
- Width (side to side) 53 (134.6)
- Depth (front to back) 20½ (52.1)
- Height (top to bottom) 4¼ (10.8)*

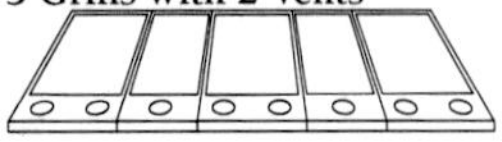

1 Cooktop, 1 Vent, 1 Grill
- Width (side to side) 31 (78.7)
- Depth (front to back) 20½ (52.1)
- Height (top to bottom) 4¼ (10.8)*

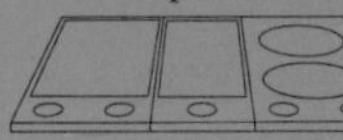

2 Cooktops, 2 Vents, 1 Grill
- Width (side to side) 49 (124.5)
- Depth (front to back) 20½ (52.1)
- Height (top to bottom) 4¼ (10.8)*

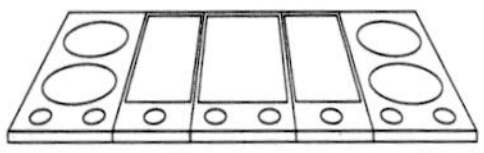

NOTE: For installations with gas units: *Plus Ductwork
If a downdraft vent is to be installed next to a gas unit, the downdraft vent must use the interior-mounted vent motor only. A gas unit cannot be located between two downdraft vents.

Create-A-Cooktop™ Feature Comparison

	Cooktops Electric KECC027Y	Cooktops Gas† KGCT025A	Electric Grill KECG020Y	Plug-In Griddle KECG023BXX	Side-Mount Downdraft Ventilation System KSVD060B*
Front Controls Push-to-Turn Infinite-Heat	•	•	•	•	—
Variable Speed	—	—	—	—	•
Radiant/Halogen Elements	6-in, 1400W 8-in, 1800W	—	—	—	—
Sealed Gas Burners	—	Front, 6000 BTU Rear, 10,000 BTU	—	—	—
Heating Elements	—	—	Front, 1100W Rear, 1000W	1200W	—
Power "ON" Light(s)	2		2	1	
Hot-Surface Indicator(s)	2				
Glass Surface	SmoothTop Ceramic	Tempered	—	—	—
KW @ 240V	3.2	–	2.2	2.2	–
Min. Circuit Amps	20	15	20	20	15
Colors Black White Almond	• • •	• • •	• • •	— — —	• • •

*Rated 450 CFM when used with Interior Power Unit KPID850T, 900 CFM with Exterior Power Unit KPED890T.
†LP Gas Conversion Kit available for Model KGCT025A, Part No. 4175444.

"T" Adapter Kit
For use with two KSVD060B and one external power system, KPED890T. Includes "T" adapter, backdraft damper and top stamping with no switch opening.

Color	Part No.
White	4319251
Almond	4319252
Black	4175456

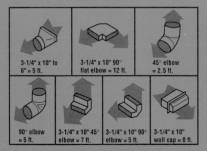

3-1/4" x 10" to 6" = 5 ft.   3-1/4" x 10" 90° flat elbow = 12 ft.   45° elbow = 2.5 ft.
90° elbow = 5 ft.   3-1/4" x 10" 45° elbow = 7 ft.   3-1/4" x 10" 90° elbow = 5 ft.   3-1/4" x 10" wall cap = 0 ft.

Recommended Standard Fittings
To calculate the length of system you need, add the equivalent feet for each duct piece used in the system. Flexible metal ductwork is not recommended. If it is used, calculate each foot of flexible metal ductwork as two feet of straight metal ductwork. Flexible metal elbows count twice as much as standard elbows. Use only metal ductwork. To see what fittings are recommended for your specific vent system, refer to the Installation Instructions.

30

Dimensions are for planning purposes only. For complete details, see installation instructions packed with product. Specifications subject to change without notice.

Compactor Electrical Requirements

	KUCC151DBL/WH (15-in.)	KCCC151DBL/WH (15-in.)
Volts (AC)	120	120
Hertz	60	60
Rated Load (Maximum Amps)	6.5	6.5
Electrical Circuit Requirements	Special 15 Amp. 3-Wire – Grounded Circuit	

Compactor Dimensions for $\frac{1}{4}$-Inch Thick Custom Front Panels. Shown in inches.

Model	Width	Height
KUCC151DBL/WH KCCC151DBL/WH	$14\frac{5}{8}$	$21\frac{7}{8}$

When Custom Panels are thicker than $\frac{1}{4}$ in., refer to detailed installation instructions for routing front panels.

Compactor Dimensions. Shown in inches.

Model	A	B	C	D	E	F
KUCC151DBL/WH	$34\frac{1}{8}$ to $34\frac{1}{2}$	$14\frac{15}{16}$	24	$34\frac{1}{2}$ min.	15	24 min.*
KCCC151DBL/WH	$34\frac{1}{8}$ to $34\frac{1}{2}$	15	$24\frac{1}{4}$	$34\frac{1}{2}$ min.	$15\frac{1}{8}$	24 min.*

*Recommend outlet must be recessed $\frac{3}{4}$-in. into wall.

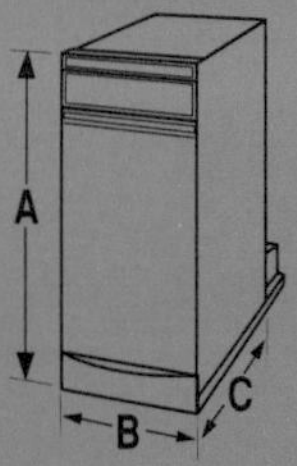

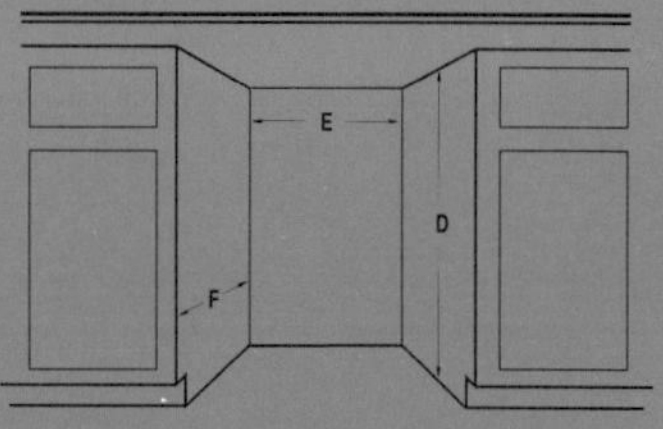

Compactor Door and Control Panel Inserts

Model	Door Panels			Control Panels	
	Almond/ Harvest	White/ Black	Brushed Stainless Steel	Almond	Brushed Stainless Steel
15-In. KU/CCC151DBL	4151462	4151463	882675	9871143	9871144
15-In. KU/CCC151DWH	N/A	N/A	882675	N/A	9871144

N/A – Not available

Food Waste Disposer Installation Data. Shown in inches.

Model No.	A	B*	C*	D	E
KBDS250X	$16\frac{1}{16}$	$9\frac{7}{16}$	4	$10\frac{1}{16}$	$7\frac{1}{8}$
KCDS250X	$13\frac{11}{16}$	$6\frac{13}{16}$	4	$10\frac{1}{16}$	$7\frac{1}{8}$
KCDI250X	$13\frac{7}{16}$	$6\frac{13}{16}$	4	$9\frac{1}{16}$	$5\frac{3}{4}$
KCDC250X	$12\frac{3}{4}$	$6\frac{11}{16}$	4	$7\frac{25}{32}$	$5\frac{3}{4}$
KCDC150X	$12\frac{3}{4}$	$6\frac{11}{16}$	4	$8\frac{1}{16}$	$5\frac{3}{4}$
KCDB250S	$12\frac{5}{8}$	$5\frac{15}{16}$	4	$6\frac{5}{16}$	5
KCDB150S	$11\frac{3}{8}$	$5\frac{15}{16}$	4	$6\frac{5}{16}$	5

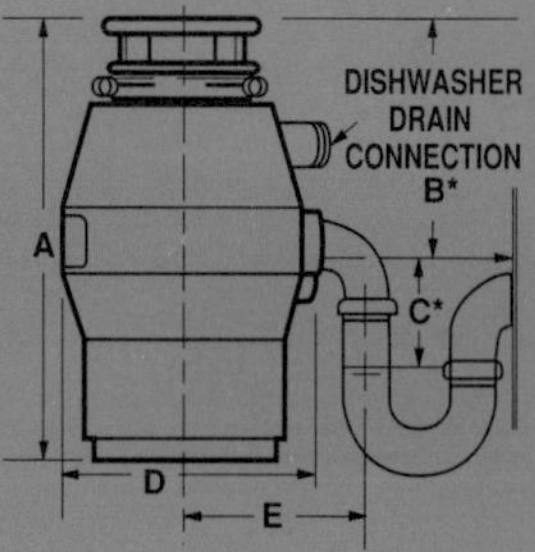

Drawing shows just one model type.

B* – Distance from bottom of sink to center line of disposer outlet. Add $\frac{1}{2}$ inch when stainless steel sink is used.
C* – Length of waste line pipe from center line of disposer outlet to end of waste line pipe.
IMPORTANT: Plumb waste line to prevent standing water in the disposer motor housing.

Automatic Ice Cube Maker Custom Panel Dimensions

	Width	Height
Upper	17 in.	$11\frac{1}{4}$ in.
Lower	17 in.	$11\frac{15}{16}$ in.

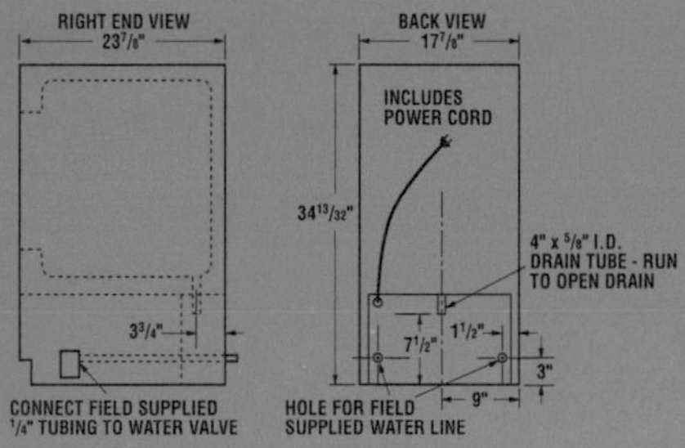

Automatic Ice Cube Maker Accessories

Accessory	Part No.
Stainless Steel Exterior Trim	819421
Stainless Steel Door Panels	819419
Hardwood Top (for free-standing installations only)	4178026
Drain	$\frac{5}{8}$" I.D. rubber tube**
Approx. Weights (lbs./kg) Net	103/46.4
Shipping	116/52.2

**Subject to local codes.
For installations where no drain is available, a condensate pump able to maintain a flow rate of 0.4 gpm @ 12 ft. lift or greater is required.

Automatic Ice Cube Maker Specifications

Cube Size	($\frac{3}{8}$" to $\frac{3}{4}$") x $\frac{3}{4}$" x $\frac{3}{4}$"
Capacity per 24 Hrs.* Production	Up to 51 Lbs.
Storage Rating	35 Lbs.
Electrical Requirements	115V, 60 Hz
Water Supply	$\frac{1}{4}$" O.D. copper tube**

*Based on 70°F ambient and 50°F water temperatures.
**Subject to local codes.

Hot Water Dispenser Dimensions. Shown in inches.

	Height	Width	Depth
Faucet	$3\frac{1}{2}$	$2\frac{1}{2}$	$6\frac{3}{8}$
Tank	$11\frac{1}{8}$	$6\frac{3}{4}$	$7\frac{13}{16}$
Approximate Weight – Net, $7\frac{1}{2}$ lbs.; Shipping, 9 lbs.			

- Mounting hole $1\frac{1}{16}$ in. to $1\frac{3}{8}$ in. diameter.
- Counter thickness up to $1\frac{1}{8}$ in.
- Saddle valve* accommodates $\frac{5}{8}$-in. to $1\frac{3}{8}$-in. O.D. copper cold water line.
- $\frac{1}{4}$-in. O.D. copper tubing* to connect to saddle valve.
- Mount tank so clear tube from spout will reach tank tube.

*Must be obtained locally.

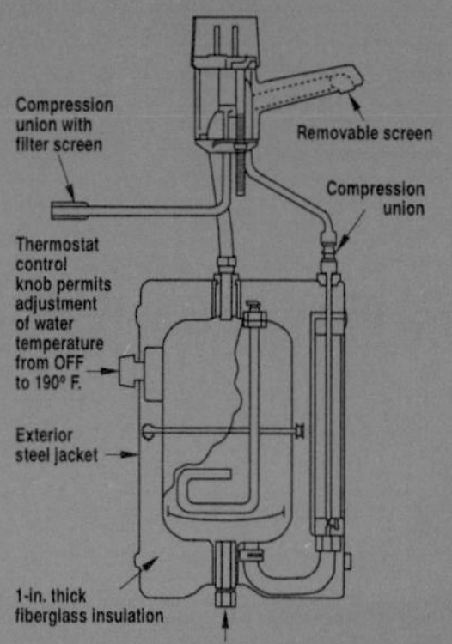

KitchenAid® For the way it's made.™

KitchenAid® Brand Promise

"KitchenAid appliances have everything you would expect of a superior appliance, plus the distinct style and thoughtful details of design which contribute to the overall look of your home and your enjoyment of it."

From our initial dishwasher offering in 1949, to today's SUPERBA® dishwasher line, KitchenAid has led the industry in combining innovative technology with stylish features. This blend of style and substance keeps the KitchenAid brand name synonymous with superior dishwasher quality.

WHISPER QUIET® sound protection is a feature found on many KitchenAid appliances. From the kitchen to the laundry room, we design KitchenAid dishwashers, refrigerators and washers to operate at exceptionally low sound levels.

KitchenAid was the first U.S. manufacturer to develop True-Convection cooking. Over a decade later, KitchenAid offers the greatest diversity of True-Convection products in the industry.

The style and substance of KitchenAid appliances mirrors the elegant beauty of nature. And, all KitchenAid appliances are designed to provide consumers with the highest level of energy efficiency to help conserve valuable resources.

Warranty key:

- ♥ FULL WARRANTY Parts and Labor (1st year)
- ●◆ FULL WARRANTY Parts and Labor (1st – 2nd year)
- ✳ FULL WARRANTY Parts and Labor (2nd – 5th year)
- ⁙ FULL WARRANTY Parts and Labor (3rd – 25th year)
- ■ FULL WARRANTY Parts and Labor (2nd – 25th year)
- ◆ LIMITED WARRANTY Parts Only (2nd year)
- ✚ LIMITED WARRANTY Parts Only (2nd – 5th year)
- ★ LIMITED WARRANTY Parts Only (6th – 10th year)
- ✿ LIMITED WARRANTY Parts Only (7th – 12th year)
- ⁙ LIMITED WARRANTY Parts Only (2nd – 10th year)
- ✲ LIFETIME WARRANTY Parts Only

Product	Col 1	Col 2	Col 3	Col 4
Dishwashers	♥ Entire product	✚ Gold Seal Motor DURAKOTE™ nylon racks Electronic controls	■ TriDura® tub and inner door	
Trash Compactors	♥ Entire product			
Freestanding Refrigerators	♥ Entire product	✳ Refrigerator/ Freezer liner Sealed refrigeration system*	★ Sealed refrigeration system*	✲ Slide 'N' Lock™ can racks Slide 'N' Lock™ door bins
Built-In Refrigerators	●◆ Entire product	⁙ Sealed refrigeration system* Automatic ice maker	✿ Sealed refrigeration system*	
Clothes Washers	♥ Entire product	◆ Entire product	✚ Cabinet 1/2 HP Gold Seal motor Electronic controls	✲ Gearcase assembly Outer tub
Clothes Dryers	♥ Entire product	◆ Entire product	✚ Cabinet 1/3 HP Gold Seal motor Electric element or Gas burner Electronic controls	✲ Drum
Built-In Ovens	♥ Entire product	✚ Electric elements/ Gas burners Magnetron tube in combination ovens Convection element Electronic control	✲ Porcelain liner and Inner door	
Built-In Cooktops	♥ Entire product	✚ Electric elements/ Gas burners Ceramic-glass cooktop		
Freestanding Ranges	♥ Entire product	✚ Electric elements/ Gas burners Ceramic-glass cooktop Electronic control	✲ Porcelain liner and Inner door	
Slide-In Ranges	♥ Entire product	✚ Electronic elements/ Gas burners Ceramic-glass cooktop Electronic control	✲ Porcelain liner and Inner door	
Microwave Ovens	♥ Entire product	✚ Electronic control Magnetron tube		
Microwave/Hoods	♥ Entire product	✚ Convection element Electronic control Magnetron tube		
Ventilation Hoods	♥ Entire product			
Downdraft Vent Systems	♥ Entire product	✚ Power system motor		
Ice Cube Maker	♥ Entire product	✳ Sealed refrigeration system*		
INSTANT-HOT® Water Dispenser	♥ Entire product			

Food Waste Disposers – All models carry FULL Warranties, Parts and Labor. Length of warranty varies with model.
SUPERBA® – 7 years. IMPERIAL™ – 5 years. KCDC250 – 4 years. KCDC150 – 3 years. KaDette™ – 1 year.

*Sealed refrigeration system includes compressor, evaporator, condenser, dryer/strainer and connecting tubing.
Complete warranty details are included in the Use & Care Guide for each product or ask your dealer.

KitchenAid • Benton Harbor, Michigan 49022 U.S.A.
For additional information, call us at: 1-800-422-1230

(CA296)
Printed in U.S.A

C507
11452/May
BuyLine 7564

YOUR HELPFUL GUIDE TO
KITCHEN DESIGN

MAYTAG

MAYTAG

WELCOME

The kitchen is truly the hub of activity for the family of the '90s. Besides being the primary spot where household meals are prepared, the kitchen is the place family members plan their day, where kids tackle homework, where Mom often pays the bills, and where Dad and daughter discuss the fundamentals of T-ball.

Such a special room needs a versatile design—one that will allow family members ample room to move around, that offers surfaces of different heights to accommodate all who use it, and that brings many functions into a central space without feeling crowded.

Planning the ideal kitchen requires information that is dependable, that you can count on. We at Maytag—the dependability people—understand your concerns, and we're here to help. We know that for many of you, your home is your greatest investment. As one of the most recognized brand name appliances in North America, Maytag and its full line of appliances add to the value of your investment, just as they add to the quality of your life. So, if you're considering building a new house or remodeling your current kitchen, plan to customize your kitchen to fit your family needs—and plan to use Maytag appliances to add lasting value.

Your Helpful Guide to Kitchen Design provides an imaginative array of exciting, inspirational ideas to help you meet that goal. It also offers two bonus sections: one on planning a utility room that will do more than just meet your laundry needs, and one on the latest in kitchen trends and technology.

We at Maytag want to help you—and the kitchen professionals you choose—create the ideal plan for your family's needs and lifestyle.

YOUR HELPFUL GUIDE TO KITCHEN DESIGN

C507
11452/May
BuyLine 7564

Your Helpful Guide to KITCHEN DESIGN

Table of Contents

©1995 Maytag/Admiral Products, Newton, Iowa.
Published for Maytag by Meredith Publishing Services, a division of Meredith Corp.

YOUR HELPFUL GUIDE TO KITCHEN DESIGN
TWO

THE RIGHT STUFF

Designing a Kitchen that Works for You

As the nerve center of the home, the kitchen is the place you and your family play together, work together, eat together and ponder some of life's biggest decisions. It's where your kids struggle with algebra problems, where friends gather to share a cup of coffee and neighborhood news and where holiday meals are created.

For all its uses, the kitchen needs to be the most accommodating room in your house. It should encourage fluid movement, offer dependable appliances and suggest an atmosphere that buoys your spirits.

If you're dreaming of a new kitchen or a new home, read on. You'll learn how to plan your project so that when the sawdust has been swept away, you can relax at the table knowing there's nothing you would change.

WHAT'S IN IT FOR ME?

Start by holding a heart-to-heart talk with family members. Ask how each person uses the kitchen—and how each person *wants* to use the kitchen. Kitchen designers recommend that your kitchen be a series of activity areas rather than one free-for-all space.

Don't forget to think about your future, too.

Will an elderly parent likely be living with you down the road? Are your kids leaving home in the next few years? Imagine what lifestyle changes might lie ahead, and how the kitchen layout and features you plan today can help accommodate those lifestyle changes now and in the future.

As you draw up your plan, think about how you move around the kitchen as you prepare meals. Typically, a cook moves from the refrigerator to the sink to cooking and serving areas. Arrange major appliances so you will be able to move smoothly from one point to the next without backtracking.

GO WITH THE FLOW

Think also about your family's traffic flow through the kitchen. You won't want family members—as much as you love them—trooping through your work space at the busiest stage of meal preparation. Consider adding a small second sink where the children can get a drink of water, or purchase a refrigerator with an ice and water dispenser in the door. Either way, place it on the outside edge of the work core.

Plan doorways carefully, and route traffic around the work core with an island or

continued on page five

Smart design ideas in the kitchen shown opposite include appliances from Maytag— your full-line kitchen manufacturer. A microwave is located conveniently close to the refrigerator and dishwasher and opposite the island sink. The oven lies outside the main work area.

The all-Maytag kitchen above serves as heart of the home by offering a cozy, intimate table where two can share a meal. A wing chair nearby can be pulled up for a third person or can simply provide a cozy planning spot.

MAYTAG

PROVEN 25 TIPS FOR SMART KITCHEN DESIGN

Time-tested tips to help you plan your dream kitchen.

1. Before you start, figure out how much you can spend.

2. Work with a certified kitchen designer who can help you best utilize your space while staying within your budget.

3. Consider the needs of the entire family to create a kitchen that functions well and fits your lifestyle.

4. Involve all members of the family in planning. Consider how each person uses the kitchen.

5. Share ideas; make a list of your priorities.

6. Aim for a kitchen that is attractive, efficient, comfortable, labor-saving and well-equipped—not just big.

7. Avoid gadgets and fads that add expense but don't simplify day-to-day life.

8. Create the look of custom cabinetry while saving money. Use stock cabinetry in imaginative ways or mix stock with custom cabinetry.

9. Spend the money saved on cabinetry to buy appliances that save time and energy.

10. Don't scrimp on counter space or adequate storage; they make a kitchen function well. Plan to have stretches of continuous countertop.

11. Store items as near the appliance or spot where you will use them most often.

12. Store heavy items at a height between your hip and shoulder and light articles above your head.

13. Install vertical pullouts, rollouts and lazy Susans on full extension slides for maximum accessibility.

14. Plan counters and work stations of different heights according to the tasks to be performed there and the height of the user.

15. Shield the cooking area from the eating area by installing a multilevel island.

16. For a safer kitchen, use non-skid flooring.

17. Choose surface materials that are easy to maintain and aren't likely to chip or dent.

18. Replace outdated appliances with newer, energy-efficient models to save on utility bills.

19. To avoid back strain, situate dishwashers 6 to 18 inches above the floor.

20. Install ovens at convenient heights.

21. Position your dishwasher close to dish storage for easier unloading.

22. Add a second microwave at a height accessible to children.

23. Incorporate a recycling center.

24. Plan to locate your laundry in or near your kitchen.

25. Be sure to include enough electrical outlets for smaller appliances.

Unload your dishwasher with ease while doing your back a favor. When installing your Maytag dishwasher, raise it from 6 to 18 inches off the floor, as shown above.

continued from page three

Install a Maytag stacked washer and dryer next to the ~cling center, top, to make good use of ~ce. The desk below ~rs a place to work; ~e built-in Maytag ~rowave in the back-ground saves space.

Monotonous? Vary the heights of ceilings and floors to add visual interest and define parameters.

Losing identity? Create a feel of separate areas with columns, pocket doors and partial walls.

Jumbled? Install separate lighting systems for each activity area. Then you'll be able to turn out your sink lights, for example, so you're not spotlighting dirty dishes.

continued on page seven

peninsula. If you include a countertop in your island or peninsula, other family members can chat with you, do homework, have a snack or engage in other activities without getting in your way.

DEFINE AN OPEN PLAN

If you're planning a kitchen that's adjacent to the family room, consider the following solutions to problems you could encounter:

Too gaping? Break up open spaces with angled walls, alcoves or nooks.

The side-by-side Maytag refrigerator, left, is conveniently near the kitchen table. The Maytag cooktop, below, is located at a convenient height for a person in a wheelchair.

MAYTAG

WHAT'S AMISS
IN YOUR PRESENT KITCHEN

Early in the planning process, use this checklist to pinpoint major and minor problems in your present

kitchen. Taking this step will ensure that these problems do not reappear in your new kitchen. Also, keep notes

about the features you dislike most in your existing kitchen.

- ☐ Inadequate countertop space
- ☐ Broken-up space
- ☐ Counter space in wrong locations
- ☐ Inadequate lighting
- ☐ Cabinetry too dark
- ☐ Room decorated in dark colors
- ☐ Appliances outdated aesthetically
- ☐ Appliances outdated functionally
- ☐ Insufficient storage
- ☐ Cabinets scratched, gouged and worn
- ☐ Sink chipped or difficult to clean
- ☐ Traffic aisles too narrow
- ☐ Not enough room for extra cooks
- ☐ No room to socialize in kitchen

- ☐ Countertop worn or color no longer appropriate
- ☐ Poor use of floor and wall space
- ☐ Doors and windows poorly located
- ☐ Too many doors and windows
- ☐ Ventilation nonexistent or inadequate
- ☐ Family dining area too small or nonexistent
- ☐ Electrical outlets inadequate
- ☐ Dishwasher does poor job or no dishwasher
- ☐ Not enough daylight
- ☐ It's seen better days
- ☐ It's ugly
- ☐ Floor covering outdated or worn

- ☐ Cook isolated from family
- ☐ Poor work triangle
- ☐ Doors interfere with work counters
- ☐ Too few drawers
- ☐ No efficiency/convenience features
- ☐ No recycling center
- ☐ No landing counter next to refrigerator
- ☐ No landing counter next to oven
- ☐ No good location for microwave
- ☐ Traffic goes through work area

☐ **NUMBER OF ITEMS CHECKED**

SCORING
Total up the number of checked items.

SCORE 5 OR LESS
You have a pretty good kitchen.

SCORE 6-14
Can use improvement, but not a disaster.

SCORE 15-24
You should start remodeling your kitchen now.

SCORE 25-30
Gut the kitchen and start from scratch.

SCORE 31-36
Evacuate. Your kitchen is hazardous to your health.

continued from page five

PUT APPLIANCES IN THEIR PLACE

Avoid hassles and enjoy your kitchen more by thoughtfully deciding where to place appliances. Here are a few tried-and-true tips.

DISHWASHER

Designers are beginning to realize that the dishwasher doesn't have to be located under a counter. Consider placing yours 6 to 18 inches above the floor to minimize bending when you load and unload. You can plan cabinets or drawers above and below. Since you lose counter space when you raise the dishwasher, leave at least 18 inches of counter space between the sink and the raised dishwasher so you'll have a landing spot for dirty and just-cleaned dishes. In any installation, you'll probably want the dishwasher no more than 36 inches from the edge of a sink.

Because so many important activities take place in your kitchen, shop around for a dishwasher that is designed to work quietly.

Also consider whether a dishwasher is easy to load, what its capacity is and how it performs. A good dishwasher will clean your

continued on page nine

As you plan, think about how you live and cook. In the kitchen at left, an island offers an additional landing pad for hot dishes from the nearby Maytag wall ovens. In the kitchen below, kids can snack at the table and help themselves to water from the Maytag refrigerator without bothering the cook.

MAYTAG

The Work Triangle Revisited

The classic foundation of kitchen design has been the work triangle—the three points being the refrigerator, cooktop (or range) and sink.

But as appliances get better and better and lifestyles get busier and busier, the evolution of kitchen design has speeded up. While traditional design principles remain valuable tools, designers are adding new twists to target the needs of individual homeowners. The old rules are no longer dictates—but instead serve as starting points for creating a customized kitchen.

Conventional wisdom has long held that the distance from refrigerator to cooktop to sink should total 12 to 22 feet. Any less, the kitchen will feel cramped; any more, extra mileage will be added to kitchen chores. Standard distances in the triangle: four to seven feet from refrigerator to sink, four to six feet from sink to cooktop and four to nine feet from cooktop to refrigerator.

Using these rules as a springboard, kitchen designers now encourage families to consider their own needs and shape the kitchen accordingly. For example:

✗ Consider designing a kitchen within a kitchen. On weekdays, when you're making quick, simple meals, you'll use the scaled-down space. On weekends, when you cook for a crowd, you'll use the entire kitchen.

✗ If two members of your family like to work in the kitchen simultaneously, you could create two separate work triangles. Both might include the refrigerator, but don't overlap or

The old rules no longer dictate— but instead serve as starting points for creating a customized kitchen.

you'll likely be in one another's way. The secondary triangle might include a microwave oven and small sink.

✗ Kitchen islands are especially useful in large kitchens, because they can keep the work triangle down to a manageable size.

✗ Today's dishwasher, which can be plumbed directly into the water line and can handle unrinsed dishes, does not have to be right next to the sink, though you'll probably still want a sink nearby. But for easier loading, consider putting the dishwasher a few steps closer to the dining area—perhaps in a peninsula.

✗ Dual appliances may be worth the investment. For example, consider a second microwave under a countertop near the eating area so the kids can make popcorn and other snacks. If you entertain on a large scale, two wall ovens will help you cook for a crowd. If you entertain often or have a large family, consider one dishwasher near the sink and another near the table to make after-meal clean-up more efficient.

✗ You may want to incorporate a stacked washer and dryer into your kitchen design. For busy people and those with limited mobility, this is an efficient way to bring major household tasks to a central location.

✗ Place a wall oven, which may be used infrequently, outside your main work space to save prime locations for your workhorses: the microwave oven and cooktop.

If you're busy and like to combine tasks, or if you have limited mobility and want to avoid stairs, include a Maytag stacked washer and dryer, right, in or near the kitchen.

continued from page seven

dishes without prerinsing, once large food scraps have been removed.

REFRIGERATOR/FREEZER

Place your refrigerator/freezer so that it's near the kitchen area but also as close to the table as possible. You'll have to decide between a side-by-side or a top-freezer unit. Side-by-side models offer freezer access to children and to people in wheelchairs; top freezers usually cost less.

MICROWAVE OVEN

Microwave ovens are used frequently, so place them in the main work area. Because their doors hinge left, plan counter space to the right of your microwave. For children, it's safest to install the microwave oven at countertop level or lower.

WALL OVEN

It's a kitchen staple. But designers often place it outside the main work area because most people don't use the oven daily. For safety's sake, a wall oven should be installed in an area where its open door is three inches below the user's bent elbow and won't hinder passersby.

Another rule of thumb: Install a single wall oven so the bottom is at countertop level or about 36 inches off the floor. With two wall ovens, the top one should open at countertop height; the second oven should be placed directly below the top oven.

RANGE OR COOKTOP

It's one of the most used kitchen appliances, and should be placed for easy access next to the microwave oven and the refrigerator, the kitchen's other hard-working equipment. Make sure you plan at least 12 inches of counter space on either side of the

continued on page eleven

In the white kitchen, below left, a Maytag wall oven is located outside the main work triangle. This arrangement makes the second Maytag oven available for parties, but leaves the prime space to meet the demands of everyday living.

A Maytag drop-in range, below, serves as one point in the traditional triangle.

GETTING THE MOST FOR
YOUR REMODELING DOLLAR

Don't be afraid to dream of creating your fantasy kitchen, even if your building or remodeling budget is modest. With creativity and wise planning, you can hold down costs. The money you save can buy design touches, wonderful appliances and other items you've longed for.

Here are some inside tips from today's top designers:

✖ Save on cabinetry, which can account for more than half the cost of a major kitchen remodeling project, by finding someone who can add a few details to customize sturdy, ready-made cabinets. You could add a plate rack, display nook or perhaps decorative cutouts to fashion a great look while holding costs down.

✖ Ask your builder for the cost of creating a built-in pantry. Building one may cost less than a cabinetry pantry unit.

✖ Fit an island with recessed wheels so it can double as a serving counter or be moved to provide an extra work surface anywhere in the kitchen.

✖ If you're trying to add storage space on a budget, consider the space between studs. It's about 3½ inches deep and can house spices and canned goods. You can create a pantry that's about 30 inches wide if you remove a stud and

A rolling island with recessed wheels can double as a serving counter or an extra work surface wherever it's needed.

With creativity and planning, you can hold down costs. The money you save can buy design touches, wonderful appliances and other items you've longed for.

add a header and full-width storage shelves. Finish off with face frame and doors to match other cabinets.

✖ Place wall cabinets on the back or far side of an island. The cabinets will provide foot-deep storage, and if you use 42-inch-high units behind a 36-inch-high island, they will conceal the work area.

✖ To create a recycling center, place two wastebaskets in one pull-out cabinet.

✖ Combine two inexpensive mouldings to create the look of high-end decorative moulding.

✖ Create the clean look of a built-in refrigerator by pulling adjacent base cabinets forward to match the front line of the refrigerator. This provides extra-deep countertops as a bonus. You also can build an enclosure for the refrigerator with plywood panels.

✖ Another way to make your refrigerator look like a built-in is to bump it into the wall behind it, if it's not a weight-bearing interior wall. To do this, remove the drywall behind the refrigerator and frame the area. Then remove the studs between the frame and install a new header. Move the refrigerator into the recess and install cabinetry around it. This is far less expensive than purchasing special cabinetry and a shallower built-in appliance.

continued from page nine

cooktop to make room for pan handles and to serve as landing areas for hot pots.

FINISHING TOUCHES

The colors, patterns and materials you choose will set the tone in your kitchen. If you don't know where to start, try letting a lovely set of dishes or a favorite picture inspire the color scheme.

Cabinets have a major impact on a kitchen's look. Choose a set that's compatible with your home's overall design.

Select materials that unify the design and make your kitchen inviting. To lend continuity, repeat a design element, material or motif from elsewhere in your home—perhaps a few items from a set of collectibles displayed in your living room can be shown off in your new kitchen.

Exhibit an item or two near and dear to your heart to complement the warmth your family brings to this very special room.

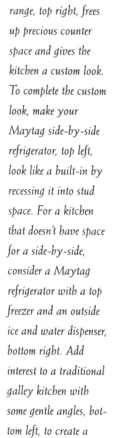

Tucking a Maytag microwave above the range, top right, frees up precious counter space and gives the kitchen a custom look. To complete the custom look, make your Maytag side-by-side refrigerator, top left, look like a built-in by recessing it into stud space. For a kitchen that doesn't have space for a side-by-side, consider a Maytag refrigerator with a top freezer and an outside ice and water dispenser, bottom right. Add interest to a traditional galley kitchen with some gentle angles, bottom left, to create a zig-zag effect.

UTILIZING THE UTILITY ROOM

Imagine a first-floor room near the kitchen in which you could do your laundry, store soft drinks, work on a special hobby, drop off muddy boots, locate a recycling center and stow bulk food items. Imagine having places for your roasting pans and serving platters and a handy spot for mops and brooms.

If you find this appealing, you're not alone. Yesterday's laundry room is evolving into the ultimate utility room.

CENTER OF ATTENTION

When located near the kitchen, such a room centralizes work areas near the hub of home activity. It enables working parents to tackle laundry chores in the evening hours without sacrificing family time. And being next to the kitchen offers the money-saving benefit of tapping into existing plumbing lines.

Every laundry room should include a few basics. Besides the washer and dryer, you'll need adequate storage space for detergents and dirty laundry. You will want places to hang up your damp clothes and garments fresh from the dryer. The utility room will need a drain and plumbing line, and the dryer will need to be vented to the outdoors.

YOUR DREAMS ARE THE LIMITS

But there's no reason to stop with the basics when the room can do so much more to accommodate your family. Consider these additional ideas:

✗ **Plan for the storage space of your dreams.** Use it for paper goods purchased in bulk, large pots, party goods, platters, roasting pans, soft drinks and snacks.

✗ **Establish a recycling center.** You can simply plan floor space for stackable plastic bins, or design a more elaborate cabinetry system with containers on pull-out shelves.

✗ **Include space for a large freezer.** Stocks of frozen foods are a great convenience.

continued on page fourteen

A stacked Maytag washer and dryer, opposite page, leaves plenty of room for storage and counter space for bathroom necessities. A rolling worktable near the Maytag pair, above, offers a landing pad for freshly folded clothes. Or it can be scooted off to be used as a hobby table or work surface.

continued from page thirteen

✗**Make way for work or play.** Incorporate a sewing or hobby table, a desk for paying bills or a place for your computer.

✗**Raise the dryer.** Position it 15 inches off the floor to reduce back strain. A drawer below offers additional storage space.

Stacked Maytag washers and dryers make efficient use of space in these utility rooms. A pull-out ironing board adds to an efficient laundry center at top right. The room at bottom left doubles as a sewing and potting center. The raised Maytag dryer in the cheery room at bottom right eliminates stooping.

✗**Keep the noise down.** Consider Maytag's Quiet-Pak™ feature, especially in an open plan or if you'll be using the utility room as a home office. Offered to lessen the level of sound emitted by appliances, it's available on all Dependable Care™ "Plus" washers and dryers.

✗**Aim for the right height.** Install cabinets, shelves and countertops that accommodate your height.

✗**Figure on a folding zone.** Consider including easy-to-clean countertop or tabletop space for folding. You could also locate a shelf below to hold laundry baskets; label with each family member's name to simplify putting clothes away.

✗**Store cleaning agents away from little hands.** If you have young children, you'll want wall cabinets to keep detergents and bleach out of their reach.

✗**Shelve it.** Open shelving, pull-out drawers or tilt bins will simplify laundry collection and sorting.

✗**Designate a drip-dry area.** Plan a place for drip-drying clean clothes as well as wet snow gear and swimwear. Include a drip pan or drain.

✗**Include an entry door from the garage or yard.** That way, you and your kids can peel off wet or muddy clothes as you enter the house and toss them right into the washer.

✗**Short on space? Install stacked washer and dryer units.** They use about 27 inches of floor space instead of the 54 inches needed for installation of traditional side-by-side models.

✗**Try a wandering worktable.** A worktable on casters can be positioned where you need it most. Roll it near the dryer for folding clothes, place it beside the desk when doing computer work or roll it into

the kitchen to transport groceries or soft drinks to the refrigerator.

✗**Hide the ironing corner.** Consider installing an ironing board that pulls down or slides out.

✗**Create a place for potting plants.** Add a deep pull-out drawer for your potting tools and include racks for wet items.

✗**Isolate the laundry.** If you're planning a utility room that's adjacent to your kitchen, be sure to shield the laundry function from direct contact with the area where food is prepared. A folding door, a standard door or a peninsula can help accomplish that separation.

Remember the days when doing the laundry meant descending to a shadowy basement? In contrast, the room above, featuring a stacked Maytag washer and dryer, suggests a summer garden—a delightful place to start a load of laundry, catch up on ironing or spend some time sewing.

MAYTAG

WHAT'S HOT

A dishwasher that does the thinking for you, an oven that improves the quality of your food while letting you cook more of it, a grill that allows you to enjoy the taste of outdoor cooking in the dead of winter, gas burners that won't let the boilover seep down—and more!

ADVANCED BUT SIMPLE

The Maytag IntelliSense™ Plus dishwasher, directly below, simplifies your life by choosing the right settings for each load it wash-

es. It's the first dishwasher that makes a mental note of your dishwashing habits, and then does the thinking for you, adjusting water temperature, cycle times, even drying time with each load. And, the IntelliSense dishwasher saves you up to 21 percent in energy, 27 percent in water and 19 percent in wash time.

CONVECTION EASE

The Dependable Bake™ Plus Convection Oven, bottom left, is available as a wall oven or a freestanding electric range. The freestanding unit comes in

monochromatic white, almond or black. It circulates hot air over, under and around food, improving the quality of food and increasing the quantity you can bake at one time.

ISLAND COOKING

Maytag's grill-range, bottom right, lets you enjoy the flavor of outdoor cooking without leaving the comfort of your kitchen. The grill-range's powerful surface-ventilation system eliminates the need for an overhead exhaust hood, so you can install the grill-range in a freestanding island.

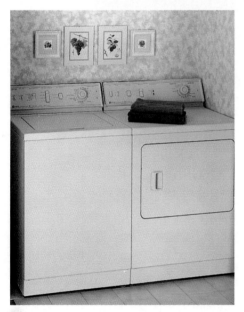

THE BUILT-IN LOOK

Get the look of a built-in refrigerator without paying the price of one. Maytag's counter-depth, side-by-side refrigerator, top left, is shallower than standard models, so it doesn't stick out beyond standard cabinets. But its 20-cubic feet of storage space provides ample room. Available in monochromatic white or black, it offers two sealed humidity controlled crisper drawers, temperature adjustable meat and cheese drawer, adjustable easy-glide Spill-Catcher™ sealed shelves, covered dairy compartment and deep door bins.

STEP-SAVING LAUNDRY

In a two-story home, an upstairs laundry eliminates the chore of lugging clothes from floor to floor. The washer and dryer at left are tucked neatly into an upstairs alcove.

THE DISHWASHER GETS A RAISE

Reduce the amount of stooping you do when unloading the dishwasher by installing it 6 to 18 inches off the floor, as shown top right.

A HOT NEW OPTION: SEALED GAS BURNERS

"Boilovers" won't seep under the gas burners shown below because they're sealed into the cooktop. The newest technological and design advancement in gas cooking, they save you from the task of cleaning the burner box.

Mrs. Gampl has always had the same husband and washer, but only one gives her any trouble.

Mrs. Ruth Gampl of McHenry, Illinois, can remember the day she began what has turned out to be a truly wonderful relationship. In all the years since that special day, she's raised a family, moved that family three times and, of course, done thousands and thousands of loads of laundry.

She has no regrets about that choice she made all those years ago. The fact is, during all that time, for better and for worse, through thick and through thin, she's hardly had a single problem.

And you will be happy to hear that, like her washer, Mrs. Gampl's marriage is still going as strong as ever.

We can't promise your Maytag washer will last as long as Mrs. Gampl's, but we vow to build every one of our washers to last longer and need fewer repairs.

So when you're ready to make a long-term commitment, make your next washer a Maytag. Chances are, like Mrs. Gampl, you'll end up spending many happy years together.

MAYTAG
THE DEPENDABILITY PEOPLE ™

SHARP®

C512
11452/SHA
BuyLine 8637

Carousel®
MICROWAVE OVENS

AS ALWAYS, SHARP REMAINS FOCUSED ON EASE AND EXCELLENCE FOR TODAY'S CONSUMER

The challenge in designing microwave ovens is to come up with innovative ideas, yet still "keep it simple". Sharp expands the limits of timesaving technology with new ways to make microwaving easy and efficient.

Sharp is "Simply the best" with higher wattages for faster cooking, more Over The Range options than ever before, the revolutionary Interactive Cooking System and the most versatile features on the market... Convection Microwave Ovens.

INTERACTIVE COOKING SYSTEM

This industry-changing innovation "walks" the user through the programming and cooking process for easy, customized microwaving.

The exclusive Custom Help™ key spells out programming steps for special options and cooking tips on a 7-digit display. Easy-to-read full word prompts roll vertically, telling everything from how to set the clock to when to use a paper towel.

SELECT FOOD NUMBER
HOW MANY PRESS NUMBER
PLACE ON PAPER TOWEL
PRESS START

POTATO

This easy-to-follow, "customized" help is ready whenever it's needed.

Custom Help guides the user through Demo Mode, child lock, audible signal elimination, Auto Start, and language/weight options.

CONVECTION & MORE

The Sharp design team has engineered the most advanced 4-way system on the market. Brown, bake, broil and crisp with Convection Microwave Ovens...the ultimate in ease and versatility.

Sharp also offers an expanded selection of Over The Range options. Each is a marvel of form and function with easy-fitting flexibility.

Interactive Cooking System "walks" the user through each step for customized microwaving.

Simply press Custom Help key. Follow the step-by-step programming for use with special options.

It's easy!

INTERACTIVE™
COOKING SYSTEM

OVER THE RANGE

R-1471
R-1470

R-1471

INTERACTIVE COOKING SYSTEM OFFERS "CUSTOM HELP"

Now the consumer can enjoy a new generation of ease. The revolutionary Interactive Cooking System and Smart & Easy™ Sensor give help every step of the way.

The advanced 7-digit Interactive display spells out programming steps, cooking hints and other options. Full word prompts roll vertically rather than scroll horizontally.

Turntable "On / Off" option provides greater versatility.

EASY-TO-INSTALL DESIGNS LEAVE THE COUNTER CLEAR

Sharp Over The Range microwave ovens offer superb quality and top performance, with flexibility that leaves the countertop free for workspace. R-1471 is a white-on-white model; R-1470 is all black. Each has a 1.1 cu. ft. capacity with 12" diameter turntable. "On/Off" option provides the choice of opting for turntable "Off" position for oblong dishes or cooking for a crowd. Output power: 850 watts.

FEATURES

Smart & Easy Sensor automatically "senses" when favorite foods are done. Popcorn Sensor is one-touch easy. No guesswork!

Custom Help key walks the user through Demo Mode, child lock, audible signal elimination, Auto Start, language and weight options and cooking hints.

7-digit Interactive display even tells the user how to set the clock!

CompuCook™ computes times and power levels for automatic cooking. CompuDefrost™ yields quick, even defrosting of meats, poultry.

Programmable 4-stage cooking, 10 Variable Power levels, Minute Plus™, kitchen timer, clock. "Touch On" operates microwave while finger touches key.

Built-in exhaust system with powerful 2-speed fan and hood lamp.

R-1470

SENSOR

OVER THE RANGE

R-1462

R-1462

R-1462
R-1461
R-1460

INTERACTIVE COOKING SYSTEM

This innovative system is like having a "tour guide" always on call. The 7-digit Interactive display spells out programming steps, cooking hints and options. Custom Help key walks the user through Demo Mode, child lock, audible signal elimination, Auto Start, language and weight options and handy tips. Over The Range 1.1 cu. ft. capacity microwave with 12" turntable. R-1462 is a new almond-on-almond design; R-1461 is white-on-white; R-1460 is black-on-black. Output power: 850 watts.

Spacious 1.1 cu. ft. interior is roomy enough for a party-size 4-quart 15"x10" oblong dish.

18⅜"

FEATURES

Turntable On/Off lets the user opt for the "Off" position for oblong dishes or cooking for a crowd.

CompuCook, Breakfast and Snacks & Reheat settings automatically calculate times/power levels for frequently microwaved foods.

CompuDefrost is a safe, easy way to defrost meats, poultry. Popcorn key offers one-touch convenience.

Also features Minute Plus, 10 Variable Power levels, kitchen timer, clock and 4-stage programmable cooking.

"Touch On" operates microwave while finger touches key.

Built-in exhaust system with powerful 2-speed fan and hood lamp. Space-efficient Over The Range styling in 3 colors, including the designer's choice: almond.

R-1460

R-1830B

OVER THE RANGE

R-1831B
R-1830B

4-WAY COOKING PLUS EASY-TO-INSTALL, FLEXIBLE DESIGN

Brown, bake, broil or crisp with this remarkable system. Microwave, convection, combination and broil options add up to the most advanced, top-performing system on the market.

The R-1831B and R-1830B maximize space and leave the countertop free and clear. Installation is simple, offering a welcome measure of flexibility for home improvement projects or new home designs.

Every Sharp Microwave and Convection Microwave Oven offers 360° cooking for excellent results without hot or cold spots.

NO SYSTEM OUTPERFORMS SHARP CONVECTION COOKING

This system merges the speed and convenience of microwave cooking and the browning and baking capabilities of conventional cooking. Choice of sleek black (R-1830B as shown), or all white (R-1831B). Output power: 800 watts.

FEATURES

Generous 0.9 cu. ft. capacity with 13" diameter turntable provides a comfortable fit for family meals.

Includes hood lamp and powerful fan; built-in exhaust system offers horizontal or vertical discharge or ductless recirculation.

4-way system makes it easy to brown, bake, broil or crisp. Also features Slow Cook, Sensor Temp, CompuCook, CompuDefrost.

ESP™ Sensor Cook "senses" when food is done for no-guesswork, automatic cooking. Pizza, Popcorn, Beverage and Reheat keys are one-touch easy.

Auto-Touch® controls highlighted by 2-color digital display; clock, 99 min 99 sec timer, Auto Start.

Worksavers: Timer/Pause, Minute Plus, 10 Variable Power levels, programmable 4-stage cooking.

R-1830B

CONVECTION • SENSOR

5

R-9H94B
R-9H84B

FLEXIBLE DESIGN, EASY ACCESS AND 4-WAY COOKING

Sharp has mastered the art of bringing together the best in design excellence and cooking expertise. The R-9H94B (white-on-white) and R-9H84B (metallic charcoal) feature a pull-down door design.

R-9H84B

R-9H94B

Pull-down door design offers easy access from right or left. The door doubles as a convenient shelf to hold food.

R-9H94B

Each of these full size units sits on the counter or installs as a wall oven using optional Built-in Kit RK-90/90W. Output power: 900 watts.

Choice of two consumer favorites: all white or metallic charcoal.

FEATURES

Advanced system browns, bakes, broils, crisps. Two combination settings for roasting and baking.

ESP Sensors offer automatic, no-guesswork cooking, reheating and defrosting. No mistakes!

Loaded with "extras" that save time and work: Cook & Simmer setting, Slow Cook, CompuCook, CompuDefrost, programmable 4-stage cooking, 10 Variable Power levels and Instant Start keys.

Auto-Touch controls make it easy to achieve ultimate precision. Features Auto Start, clock, Timer/Pause, 99 minute 99 second timer, Minute Plus and Memory Plus.

Large 1.5 cu. ft. capacity with 15³⁄₈" diameter turntable. No need for manual turning.

Flexible placement... each unit sits on the counter or installs as a wall oven with optional built-in kit.

S E N S O R

R-9H76
R-9H66

CONVECTION

ONE OVEN Can DO IT ALL! HERE'S THE PROOF...

Everything's possible and it's all so easy. Brown, bake, broil or crisp with microwave, convection, combination and broil options. This top-performing system bridges the gap between microwave and conventional cooking. Breads, cakes, roasts, casseroles, appetizers and more turn out perfectly.

Smart & Easy Sensors further enhance the capabilities, taking the guesswork out of microwave cooking and reheating. Full size 1.5 cu. ft. capacity with 15^{3}/$_{8}$" turntable. R-9H66 is white-on-white; R-9H76 is metallic charcoal. Optional Built-in Kits RK-66WB/RK-66A for in-the-wall installation. Output power: 900 watts.

A choice of colors, plus easy flexibility. Use as a countertop unit...

R-9H66

R-9H76

FEATURES

◼ Styled with side-opening door and the flexibility to use as a countertop unit or built-in using an optional trim kit.

◼ 4-way system seals in moisture, flavor. Low mix/bake and high mix/roast settings; broil key automatically preheats oven, signals when ready.

◼ Sensor Cook and Instant Start Sensor keys take the guesswork out of everyday microwaving.

◼ CompuCook computes cooking times/temperatures for favorite foods. CompuDefrost is a no-fail way to defrost meats, poultry.

◼ Programmable 4-stage cooking; Cook & Simmer setting, 10 Variable Power levels.

◼ Auto-Touch controls offer precision and ease. Auto Start, Timer/Pause key, time-of-day clock, Memory Plus and Minute Plus.

R-9H76

...or install as a wall oven with optional Built-in Kit RK66WB/RK66A.

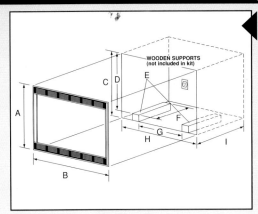

WOODEN SUPPORTS
(not included in kit)

Your Sharp Microwave Oven can be built into your kitchen wall or cabinet using the appropriate Sharp Built-in Kit. Complete hardware and easy-to-follow instructions are included. Prepare cabinet or wall opening according to the illustration at left, providing access to a separate 3-pronged, 120V AC outlet, 15 amps. or larger.

Each Sharp Over The Range microwave oven can be easily adapted for either outside ventilation (vertical or horizontal) or nonvented, ductless recirculation. Make sure top of oven will be at least 66" from the floor and at least 30" from the cooking surface. A separate 15 amp. or greater electrical receptacle must be located in the cabinet directly above the microwave oven.

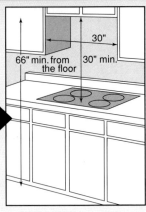

	A	B	C	D	E	F	G	H	I
RK-90W, RK-90	19⁷⁄₈"	26⁷⁄₈"	17³⁄₈" (+ height of wood)	17³⁄₈"	nominal 2"x 2"; actual 1⁹⁄₁₆" x 1⁹⁄₁₆" x 16"	16"	18³⁄₈" ± ¹⁄₈"	25¹⁄₄" ± ¹⁄₈"	min. 20½"
RK-66WB, RK-66A	19⁷⁄₈"	26⁷⁄₈"	17¹⁄₈" (+ height of wood)	17¹⁄₈"	nominal 2"x 2"; actual 1⁹⁄₁₆" x 1⁹⁄₁₆" x 15"	15"	18³⁄₈" ± ¹⁄₈"	25¹⁄₄" ± ¹⁄₈"	min. 19½"

SPECIFICATIONS	R-1471, R-1470	R-1462, R-1461, R-1460	R-1831B, R-1830B	R-9H94B, R-9H84B	R-9H66, R-9H76
Oven Capacity:	1.1 cu. ft.	1.1 cu. ft.	0.9 cu. ft.	1.5 cu. ft.	1.5 cu. ft.
Cooking Uniformity:	Turntable or stirrer system; 12" diameter glass turntable	Turntable or stirrer system; 12" diameter glass turntable	Carousel system; 13" diameter porcelain enamel turntable	Carousel system: 15³⁄₈" diameter porcelain enamel turntable	Carousel system: 15³⁄₈" diameter porcelain enamel turntable
Display:	7-digit Interactive	7-digit Interactive	2-color lighted digital	2-color lighted digital	2-color lighted digital
Convection Oven Temperature Control:			100°, 150,° 275°-450°F in 25° increments	100°, 150,° 275°-450°F in 25° increments	100°, 150,° 275°-450°F in 25° increments
Design:	R-1471: White-on-white R-1470: Black-on-black	R-1462: Almond-on-almond R-1461: White-on-white R-1460: Black-on-black	R-1831B: White-on-white R-1830B: Black-on-black	R-9H94B: White-on-white R-9H84B: Metallic charcoal	R-9H66: White-on-white R-9H76: Metallic charcoal
Output Power:	850W	850W	800W	900W	900W
Outside Dimensions: (WHD)	29⁷⁄₈" x 15³⁄₄" x 14"	29⁷⁄₈" x 15³⁄₄" x 14"	29⁷⁄₈" x 16¹⁄₂" x 15"	24⁵⁄₈" x 14⁷⁄₈" x 20⁵⁄₈"	24⁵⁄₈" x 14⁷⁄₈" x 18³⁄₄"
Oven Dimensions: (WHD)	18¹⁄₈" x 7³⁄₄" x 13¹⁄₄"	18¹⁄₈" x 7³⁄₄" x 13¹⁄₄"	13⁵⁄₈" x 8³⁄₈" x 13¹⁄₂"	16¹⁄₈" x 9⁵⁄₈" x 16¹⁄₈"	16¹⁄₈" x 9⁵⁄₈" x 16¹⁄₈"
Oven Interior:	Acrylic with light	Acrylic with light	Stainless steel with light	Stainless steel with light	Stainless steel with light
Approx. Weight:	Net: 57 lbs., Shipping: 65 lbs.	Net: 57 lbs., Shipping: 65 lbs.	Net: 74 lbs., Shipping: 87 lbs.	Net: 62 lbs., Shipping: 70 lbs.	Net: 60 lbs., Shipping: 68 lbs.
AC Line Voltage:	120V, single phase, 60Hz, AC only	120V, single phase, 60Hz, AC only	120V, single phase, 60Hz, AC only	120V, single phase, 60Hz, AC only	120V, single phase, 60Hz, AC only
AC Power Required:	1.68kW, 14.0A	1.68kW, 14.0A	1.6kW, 13.0A	1.55kW, 13.0A	1.55kW, 13.0A
Safety Compliance:	FCC, DHHS, UL listed	FCC, DHHS, UL listed	FCC, DHHS, UL listed	FCC, DHHS, UL listed	FCC, DHHS, UL listed
Supplied Accessories:			Broiling trivet, baking rack, temperature probe	Broiling trivet, baking rack	Broiling trivet, baking rack
Optional Accessories: (Available at extra cost)	RK-220 Charcoal Filter for non-ducted installations†	RK-220 Charcoal Filter for non-ducted installations†	RK-210 Charcoal Filter for non-ducted installations†	R-9H94B: Built-in kit RK-90W (white) R-9H84B: Built-in kit (black) for in-the-wall installation†	R-9H66: Built-in kit RK-66WB (white) R-9H76:Built-in kit RK-66A (black) for in-the-wall installation†

Specifications subject to change without notice. †Refer to Operation Manual for installation recommendations. Output wattage based on IEC-705 1988 Test Procedure.
Models R-9H66/76 have UL approval to build-in over General Electric brand 27" electric wall oven model ZEK735WP or ZEK734GP.

**Sharp Electronics Corporation
in New Jersey**

**Sharp Manufacturing Company of America
Memphis, Tennessee**
A Division of Sharp Electronics Corporation

Sharp Electronics Corporation
Corporate Headquarters and Executive Offices • Sharp Plaza, Mahwah, New Jersey 07430-2135
1-800-BE-SHARP
© 1996 Sharp Electronics Corporation

Printed in USA
MW-06-037

To receive the most current specifications, call Dimension Express at (702) 833-3600 from a fax machine. Enter code 8026 for a directory of Sharp microwave oven products.

Built~in Home Refrigeration
Designed for Beauty and Performance

The first choice in kitchens of distinction

In remodeling and new construction, the look of distinction in kitchens begins with the beauty of built-in appliances and built-in refrigeration by Sub-Zero. That's why leading custom kitchen designers choose Sub-Zero first. Classic in styling and unequaled for storage, convenience and quality, Sub-Zero true built-ins are the ultimate in elegant home refrigeration.

Enjoy the elegance of built-in refrigeration

Sub-Zero home refrigeration is designed to enhance the beauty of any decor by blending compatibly with other kitchen furnishings. This is possible because of its simple design...removable decorative panels and the fact it is the same 24″ depth as most base kitchen cabinets. A Sub-Zero is designed with a minimum of external hardware, making it hardly noticeable when built into a kitchen. It also has an exclusive toe-base feature, important in kitchen appliances, which lines up with kitchen cabinets.

All units are constructed with the 24″ depth which enables the face to fit flush with most standard base cabinets. A typical free-standing refrigerator protrudes into the room 4 to 6 inches beyond cabinets, creating an unsightly appearance and takes up valuable space in the room.

Sub-Zero built-ins are designed to accept removable exterior panels of any material on the front and sides. In doing so, the unit practically disappears into the overall kitchen, blending completely into the decor instead of dominating the kitchen appearance, as a free-standing unit does. And, because the panels are removable, they can be changed, should the room decor change.

These true built-in features mean your home refrigeration need not be an unattractive standout but can now complement the over-all style of the kitchen and function as an integral part of the total kitchen design. They allow individual styling and expression of your personal taste.

Built-in work savers

Truly an accent to the kitchen of distinction, Sub-Zero built-in refrigeration offers all of the time and work saving features that today's lifestyles require...like convenient usable storage, easy up-keep, simplified cleaning, automatic defrosting and automatic ice maker.

The shallow depth makes it easier to find what you are looking for, eliminating the need to search for items that have found their way to the back shelf area (as in other refrigerators). This, along with the fact that all shelves are fully adjustable, gives even greater flexibility for storage arrangements.

Easy up-keep is achieved because of the quality materials and craftsmanship used in the construction of a Sub-Zero, ...interior, exterior and mechanical.

Cleaning is simplified because of two reasons: First the unit's built-in feature eliminates cracks and crevices that would normally collect dust and also eliminates the chore of pulling the refrigerator out to clean behind it.

Secondly, all shelves in Sub-Zero full-size units are removable to allow for ease of cleaning.

The automatic defrost feature is standard on all full-size models as well as the undercounter models (except

Model 550

249R). This eliminates the need to shut down the refrigerator to defrost and clean the unit.

Another standard feature of the full-size units is the automatic ice maker which produces an adequate supply of ice automatically without the need to handle awkward ice trays.

Many models to choose from

Whatever your space or usage requirements, Sub-Zero offers a selection of over 12 models to fit your needs and specifications. Choose from the popular side-by-side, the over-n-under (freezer on the bottom), the all-freezer and all-refrigerator units, compact undercounter refrigerators and an ice maker. Ranging in width from 18″ to 48″, Sub-Zero units offer capacities to 30.0 cubic feet. The combination all-refrigerator and all-freezer together provide as much as 40.0 cubic feet of food storage.

Sub-Zero 12-Year Protection Plan

Sub-Zero has always backed what it has manufactured, and offers a warranty package no one can match — the Sub-Zero 12-Year Protection Plan. From the day your Sub-Zero is installed, you have a full five-year (parts and labor) warranty and limited sixth through twelfth-year (parts) warranty on the sealed system, consisting of the compressor, condenser, evaporator, drier and all connecting tubing. You also have a full two-year (parts and labor) warranty on the entire product. (See warranty for non-residential use and other exceptions). Sub-Zero stands behind every refrigerator and freezer they manufacture, ensuring you of the finest in service and trouble-free maintenance.

Outstanding performance and craftsmanship

Sub-Zero is a leader in the industry in engineering functional refrigeration. Because Sub-Zero full-size units use a refrigerant in both the refrigerator and freezer compartments, proper and even temperatures are maintained more consistently throughout. This is the same type system used in some commercial refrigerators and is a standard feature in Sub-Zero home units, to insure top performance and operation. Complete factory testing of every Sub-Zero unit is your assurance of quality workmanship.

More than just refrigeration, Sub-Zero quality craftsmanship is a tradition, custom designed to enhance the value and elegance of your home for years to come.

Maximum storage with the
500 SERIES Models 501R and 501F

For large families or those people who need maximum storage, Sub-Zero offers the convenience of its new Eurostyled all-refrigerator (Model 501R) and all-freezer (Model 501F) with a total storage capacity of 40 cubic feet. The "all-refrigerator's" 20 cubic foot capacity makes this exclusive unit the largest built-in all-refrigerator on the market. One of the advantages of these units is the flexibility of planning your kitchen. The units can be installed side-by-side or with a convenient counter between them or at opposite ends of the room, depending on your kitchen layout. Adjustable shelving in both the refrigerator and freezer gives even more storage versatility. The 501F has an automatic ice maker. The "all-refrigerator" Model 501R is also ideal for people who have existing freezer storage. **Separate detailed specification sheets on models 501R and 501F available upon request.**

501F   501R

ALL FREEZER
Model 501F—Automatic defrost. Freezer is equipped with automatic ice maker.
ALL REFRIGERATOR
Model 501R—Automatic defrost refrigerator.

Model	501F	501R
Capacity	20.0 cu. ft.	20.0 cu. ft.
Dimensions	Height 73″ Width 36″ Depth 24″	Height 73″ Width 36″ Depth 24″
Finished Roughing-In Dimensions	35½″x72¾″	35½″x72¾″
Weight (lbs.)	363 crated	376 crated

* Additional shelves available at extra cost.

←— 23⅞″ —→
BEHIND FLANGE

←———— 36 ————→

73

4

|←— 3 —→|

PANEL
SIZE
34⅛″ W.
x 58¹⁵/₁₆″ H.

NOTE: Roughing-in width is 71½″ when these models are installed side by side. If mullion is used to separate cabinets, add mullion width to 71½″ dimension. Filler must be used when installed hinge to hinge.

One 115 volt, 60 cycle single phase, 15 amp. wall outlet must be provided.

Refer to 500 series "Installation Instruction" booklet for detailed installation and panel requirements.

Minimum height required (when levelers in) is 72⁷/₁₆″

Model 561

Model 561 Interior

SUB-ZERO ®

Side by Side Combination
Models 561 and 532

The new 500 series incorporates exciting engineering innovations, with built-in beauty and elegant Eurostyled interiors. This series also features the new satin-brushed aluminum exterior trim and simplicity of design. The elegant combination of white and clear interiors, together with the built-in appearance, offers breathtaking beauty.

Sub-Zero's model 561 features an 8.9 cu. ft. freezer and 12.5 cu. ft. refrigeration in convenient top-to-bottom, side-by-side storage. Its two compressors provide independent temperature control of the freezer and refrigerator compartments. The freezer compartment has four pull-out storage baskets, automatic ice maker with removable ice storage drawer and adjustable door storage.

Model 561

COMBINATION REFRIGERATOR-FREEZER
Model 561 — Automatic defrost model. Freezer compartment equipped with automatic ice maker.

Capacity:	12.5 cu. ft. Refrigerator 8.9 cu. ft. Freezer
Dimensions:	Height 84″ Width 36″ Depth 24″
Finished Rough-In Dimensions	35½″x83¾″
Weight (lbs.):	480 lbs. crated

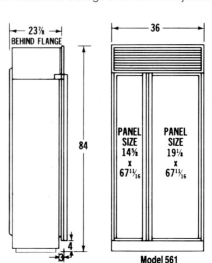

← 23⅞ →
BEHIND FLANGE

← 36 →

84

4
3

PANEL SIZE 14⅝ x 67¹¹⁄₁₆

PANEL SIZE 19¼ x 67¹¹⁄₁₆

One 115 volt, 60 cycle single phase, 15 amp. wall outlet must be provided.

Minimum height required (when levelers in) is 82⅞″ (smaller grille recommended).

Refer to 500 series "Installation Instruction" booklet for detailed installation and panel requirements.

Model 561

4

Model 532   Model 532 Interior

Sub-Zero's huge 30 cu. ft. combination refrigerator/freezer model 532 is one of the largest home built-in units made. It incorporates new engineering innovations and Eurostyled interior. It has an 11.2 cu. ft. freezer and 18.8 cu. ft. refrigerator with convenient top-to-bottom storage.

The freezer compartment has four pull-out storage baskets, an automatic ice maker with roll-out removable ice storage drawer and adjustable door storage. The refrigerator has four self-sealing crispers, each with independent humidity control. It also features an adjustable roll-out utility drawer, adjustable door storage shelves and adjustable glass shelves. This model also has two compressors to provide independent temperature control in both the freezer and refrigerator compartments.

This unit is available in the 48 inch format with water and ice dispensed through the refrigerator door. This is not an option but another addition to our full line called the Model 590.

Detailed specification sheets on model 532, 561 and 590 are available on request.

Optional solid panel grilles that accept matching panels are available for 532 and 561. The panel grille is standard on the 590. Detailed specification sheets on the three units and grilles available upon request.

Model 532

COMBINATION REFRIGERATOR-FREEZER
Model 532—Automatic defrost model Equipped with automatic ice maker.

Capacity:	18.8 cu. ft. Refrigerator 11.2 cu. ft. Freezer
Dimensions:	Height 84″ Width 48″ Depth 24″
Finished Rough-In Dimensions:	47½″ x 83¾″
Weight (lbs.):	563 crated

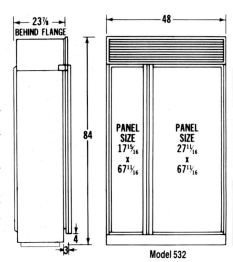

Model 532

One 115 volt, 60 cycle single phase, 15 amp. wall outlet must be provided.

Minimum height required (when levelers in) is 82⅞″ (smaller grille recommended).

Refer to 500 series "Installation Instruction" booklet for detailed installation and panel requirements.

Model 550

Model 550 Interior

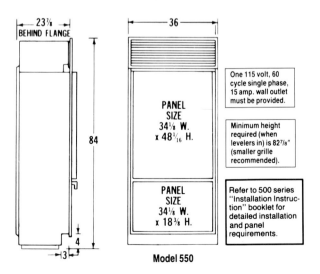

SUB-ZERO ®

Over-N-Under (freezer on bottom)
Models 550 and 511

For those who prefer, Sub-Zero offers a convenient arrangement with freezer on the bottom. This design was prompted by the fact that the refrigerator section is used more often than the freezer, thereby providing the greatest convenience and best accessibility. The refrigerated top half offers full width storage on adjustable shelves while frozen foods below are easily accessible with a pull-out drawer.

The over-n-under units in the 500 series also incorporate exciting engineering innovations with built-in beauty and elegant Eurostyled interiors. These units also feature the new satin-brushed aluminum exterior trim and simplicity of design.

Sub-Zero's 22.1 cu. ft. model 550 over-n-under combination unit has a 6.4 cu. ft. slide-out, double-tier freezer drawer in the

Model 550

COMBINATION REFRIGERATOR-FREEZER
Model 550 — Automatic defrost model. Freezer compartment equipped with automatic ice maker.

Capacity:	15.7 cu. ft. Refrigerator
	6.4 cu. ft. Freezer
Dimensions:	Height 84"
	Width 36"
	Depth 24"
Finished Rough-In Dimensions	35½"x83¾"
Weight (lbs.):	468 crated

23⅞
BEHIND FLANGE

36

84

PANEL SIZE
34⅛ W.
x 48¹/₁₆ H.

PANEL SIZE
34⅛ W.
x 18⅜ H.

4

3

One 115 volt, 60 cycle single phase, 15 amp. wall outlet must be provided.

Minimum height required (when levelers in) is 82⅞" (smaller grille recommended).

Refer to 500 series "Installation Instruction" booklet for detailed installation and panel requirements.

Model 550

(Optional panel grille shown)   Model 511

Model 511 Interior

bottom. The freezer has an automatic ice maker with removable ice storage container. The top pull freezer handle and double-tier design provide easy access. The refrigerator has two self-sealing crispers, each with independent humidity control. It has a roll-out utility drawer, adjustable glass shelves and fully adjustable door storage.

The model 511 features a 5.2 cu. ft. slide-out double-tier freezer drawer and a 12.7 cu. ft. refrigerator compartment. Again the freezer has an automatic ice maker with removable ice storage container. Like the model 550, easy freezer access is provided by top pull handle and roll-out double-tier design.

These over-n-under models are extremely versatile for kitchen designs used alone or in various combinations, such as the kitchen shown on the cover of this brochure.

Both units have two compressors which provides independent temperature control in both the refrigerator and freezer compartments. These units are backed by Sub-Zero's exclusive Twelve-Year Protection Plan.

Optional solid panel grilles that accept matching panels also available. Specification sheet available upon request. Detailed specification sheets on models 550 and 511 are available upon request.

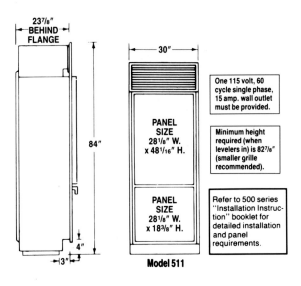

23⁷/₈″ BEHIND FLANGE

84″

4″

3″

30″

One 115 volt, 60 cycle single phase, 15 amp. wall outlet must be provided.

PANEL SIZE 28¹/₈″ W. x 48¹/₁₆″ H.

Minimum height required (when levelers in) is 82⁷/₈″ (smaller grille recommended).

PANEL SIZE 28¹/₈″ W. x 18³/₈″ H.

Refer to 500 series "Installation Instruction" booklet for detailed installation and panel requirements.

Model 511

COMBINATION REFRIGERATOR-FREEZER
Model 511 — Automatic defrost model. Freezer compartment equipped with automatic ice maker.

Capacity:	12.7 cu. ft. Refrigerator 5.2 cu. ft. Freezer
Dimensions:	Height 84″ Width 30″ Depth 24″
Finished Rough-In Dimensions	29¹/₂″ x 83³/₄″
Weight (lbs.):	375 crated

Model 511

Features of full-size, built-in units

1. Convenient Storage

All Sub-Zero units are 24″ in depth to conform to most kitchen base cabinet units. This not only improves appearance of finished installation but provides more accessible storage on interior shelves.

2. Sub-Zero 12-Year Protection Plan

Full five-year (parts and labor) warranty and limited sixth through twelfth-year (parts) warranty on the sealed system, consisting of the compressor, condenser, evaporator, drier and all connecting tubing; and a full two-year (parts and labor) warranty on the entire product from the date of installation. (Does not include installation.) (See warranty for non-residential use and other exceptions.)

3. Automatic Ice Maker

Makes and stores crescent-shaped ice pieces. Although several conditions affect the amount of ice that is produced in a given period of time, an adequate supply is provided. (Model 532 and 561 icemaker shown)

4. Automatic Defrosting

Automatically eliminates frost accumulation in both refrigerator and freezer sections.

5. Accepts Removable Decorative Door Panels

Front panels of virtually any material, not exceeding 1/4″ in thickness are easily installed. Raised panels may also be used when perimeter edge does not exceed 1/4″. **(We recommend routing, recessing or optional extended handles for finger clearance when using raised panels.) Refer to Installation Instruction Guide for detailed information. Only colored and stainless steel panels are available from the factory. (50# per door panel weight limit.)**

6. Side Panels

Unit is made to accept side panels if sides are exposed. Only colored and stainless steel panels are available from the factory.

7. Front-Vented

Allows for true built-in installation and eliminates over heating.

8. Removable and Adjustable Shelves

Cantilever type glass shelves in the refrigerator and wire shelves in the freezer for easy cleaning and flexible storage.

9. Deluxe Crispers

Spacious, self-sealing crispers have easy-glide roller design and adjustable, independent humidity control to assure food freshness.

10. Interiors

Award-winning Eurostyled white and clear interior.

11. Magnetic Door Gasket

Surrounds entire door with a pull that assures a positive seal. **NOTE** — Because of a perfect seal, allow a slight delay before reopening door.

12. Right or Left Door Swing

Available, when specified, on all over-n-under and single door units (all side-by-side units are hinged on outside). Doors are not reversible.

13. Portable Egg Trays

Convenient and versatile, they may be carried to the table or preparation area.

14. Adjustable Dairy Compartment

Versatile, positive sealing compartment for dairy items.

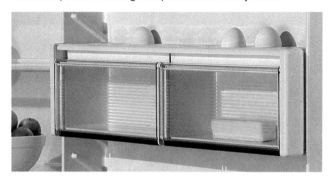

15. Adjustable Utility Basket

Adjustable roll-out refrigeration basket offers handy storage for small items.

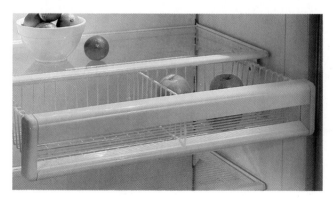

16. Clean Trim

No visible screws.

17. Colored Panels

Decorator front and side steel panels are available from Sub-Zero in the following colors: Harvest Gold, Almond, Avocado, Coffee, Stainless Steel and White.

18. Grilles

Standard grille height is 11″. Other available grille heights range from 10″ to 15″ in 1″ increments. Optional decorative, solid panel grilles that accept matching panels also available in these sizes.

Panel grille

19. Toe Space Base

Integral part of cabinet. Inset is 4″ high by 3″ deep — meeting specifications of American Institute of Architects and conforming with most bases of kitchen cabinets.

20. Door Handles

Standard as shown in photographs throughout this literature.

21. Door Closers

All models equipped with door closers.

22. Door Stops

Although most installations do not require a door stop (door opens to 130°), an optional kit is available if needed. The Door Stop Kit allows the door to open to 90°.

23. Rollers

Unit has rollers and convenient leveling system for ease of installation.

24. Additional Shelves

Available at additional cost.

IMPORTANT: For proper operation and use, the door must open at least a full 90°. A minimum 2″ filler should be used in corner installations to assure a 90° door opening. Remember to allow enough clearance in front of unit for full door swing.

Undercounter models

Sub-Zero undercounter refrigerators, freezers, combinations and ice makers are ideal for the bar, den, family room, yacht or office. They are designed to be installed under a counter. However, some may also be used as free-standing units.

All under-counter models are self-venting, have foamed-in-place insulation, have durable ABS easy to clean interiors and accept front door panels of practically any material to harmonize with cabinets or other equipment. They also have right to left door swings which are interchangeable in the field (kit required except model 245). All of these features and more are backed by Sub-Zero's 12-Year Protection Plan – providing a full five-year (parts and labor) warranty and limited sixth through twelfth year (parts) warranty on the sealed system, consisting of the compressor, condenser, evaporator, drier and all connecting tubing; and a full two year (parts and labor) warranty on the entire product from the date of installation. (Does not include installation.) (See warranty for non-residential use and other exceptions.)

The Sub-Zero combination model 245 provides automatic defrost, refrigerator storage, freezer storage and automatic ice making.

Sub-Zero also offers "all-refrigerator" and "all-freezer" undercounter units. The model 249RP "all-refrigerator" features automatic defrost, door storage and adjustable compartment shelving. Our model 249FF "all-freezer" features automatic defrost, adjustable compartment shelving and can be equipped with an automatic ice maker, but it must be installed at the factory.

A unit for those who desire primarily refrigerator storage with some freezer storage is the model 249R. This unit is a manual defrost, with a small full-width freezer, door storage and adjustable compartment shelving.

We also offer a built-in ice maker for those who entertain in style. Requirements for clear ice can be satisfied with the model 506, which provides an abundance of crystal-clear cubes in a unit that requires only an 18″ width. Featuring a drop-down hopper-type door, this unit stores up to 35 pounds of 3/4″ cubes. This unit requires a drain or pump.

Separate specification sheet on each undercounter model is available upon request.

Undercounter Model	249R	249RP	249FF	245	506
Capacity	4.4 cu. ft. Refrigerator .7 cu. ft. Freezer	4.9 cu. ft. Refrigerator	4.6 cu. ft. Freezer	3.0 cu. ft. Refrigerator 1.9 cu. ft Freezer	Stores 35 lbs. of ice
Unit Dimensions [Levelers in] (H x W x D in inches)	$33^{13/16}$ x $23^{7/8}$ x 24	$33^{13/16}$ x $23^{7/8}$ x 24	$33^{13/16}$ x $23^{7/8}$ x 24	34 x $23^{7/8}$ x 24	$34^{13/32}$ x $17^{7/8}$ x $23^{7/8}$
Weight (lbs.)	120 crated	117 crated	135 crated	139 crated	110 crated

Note: Refer to "Installation Instruction" booklet for detailed water, electrical and other installation requirements.

Model 249R

Model 249RP

Model 249FF
(ICEMAKER OPTIONAL)

Model 245

Model 506

Installation specifications

Following are the installation specifications for all Sub-Zero full-size and undercounter models. The dimensions shown in the chart correlate with the schematic drawings. For further details refer to the **Installation Instruction Booklet.**

Schematic drawing

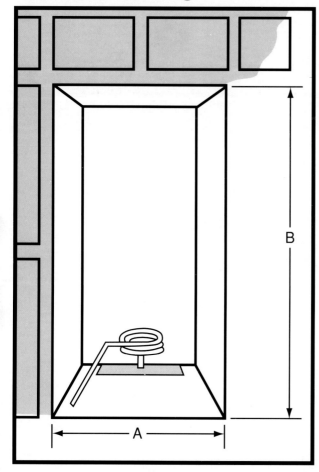

Door Clearance Schematic Drawing Top View

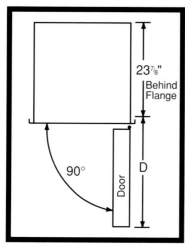

Wood grille not available from Sub Zero.

Model No.	Finished Rough Opening Dimensions		Door Panel Dimensions (width x height)	Minimum Door Clearance Requirement at 90°
	A	B	C	D
550	35½″	83¾″	34⅛″ x 48¹/₁₆″ & 34⅛″ x 18⅜″	36¹/₁₆″
511	29½″	83¾″	28⅛″ x 48¹/₁₆″ & 28⅛″ x 18⅜″	30⅛″
561	35½″	83¾″	14⅝″ x 67¹¹/₁₆″ & 19⅛″ x 67¹¹/₁₆″	20¾″
532	47½″	83¾″	17¹⁵/₁₆″ x 67¹¹/₁₆″ & 27¹¹/₁₆″ x 67¹¹/₁₆″	29¼″
501R	35½″	72¾″	34⅛″ x 58¹⁵/₁₆″	36¹/₁₆″
501F	35½″	72¾″	34⅛″ x 58¹⁵/₁₆″	36¹/₁₆″
590	47½″	83¾″	15⅛″ x 67¹¹/₁₆″ & 20⁹/₁₆″ x 67¹¹/₁₆″	29¼″
245	24″	34½″	23½″ x 28⅛″	25¹³/₁₆″
249R	24″	34½″	23⅝″ x 30″	25⅜″
249RP	24″	34½″	23⅝″ x 30″	25⅜″
249FF	24″	34½″	23⅝″ x 30″	25⅜″
506	18″	34½″	17″ x 13³/₁₆″ & 17″ x 11¹⁵/₁₆″	11¾″

(Optional panel grille shown)

How to buy

Sub-Zero home refrigeration can be seen and purchased at top custom kitchen dealers and appliance stores in all major cities across the United States and many Canadian cities. If not available in your area, feel free to contact Sub-Zero direct for the distributor nearest you. Call 800-222-7820.

Service

There are hundreds of authorized service centers throughout the country to provide warranty service and perform other service functions. These centers maintain a stock of Sub-Zero approved parts and a staff of qualified repair technicians. The service center nearest you may be found in the yellow pages or by contacting the dealer you purchased the unit from. If service cannot be found, contact Sub-Zero direct: 800-356-5826.

SUB-ZERO FREEZER CO., INC.
Post Office Box 44130
Madison, Wisconsin 53744-4130
608/271-2233

SUB-ZERO ®

Model 590
Ice & Water Refrigerator-Freezer

Innovative Excellence

SUB-ZERO ®

Sub-Zero has led the built-in home refrigeration industry for years with product enhancements which have set trends. Sub-Zero continues to redefine the art of built-in refrigeration for the 90's with the introduction of the distinctive Model 590 with its innovative version of ice and water through the refrigerator door.

The convenient placement and inconspicuous appearance of the ice and water dispenser and its controls were designed with you in mind.

And the ability to match your kitchen design has been assured with the Model 590. Like all Sub-Zero units, the Model 590 will fit flush with virtually all 24-inch cabinets and accept decorative side and front panels. Another exclusive feature of the Model 590 is the complementary color handle trim panels and glasswells which are offered at no charge.

Craftsmanship, a Sub-Zero trademark, is also built into each of these features:

•**Ice & Water Dispenser**– designed and practically placed for your convenience. A new industry feature, the water is <u>constantly</u> chilled within its huge 51 oz. reservoir.

•**Bulk Ice Dispenser**– conveniently located inside the refrigerator door when larger quantities are needed. This new industry feature is activated at the touch of a button.

•**Two Refrigeration Systems**– ensures independent, accurate freezer and refrigerator temperature control.

•**Decorative Door Panels**– front panels of virtually any material not exceeding 1/4" perimeter thickness are accommodated. Only color and stainless steel panels are available from the factory. (50# per door panel weight limit)

•**Automatic Defrosting**– freezer and refrigerator have own systems.

•**Adjustable Shelves**– cantilever type, easy to move and clean.

•**Spacious Crispers with Humidity Control**– four self-sealing crispers have clear view and individual controls.

•**Adjustable Door Shelves**– easy to adjust shelves provide complete flexibility on both doors.

•**Automatic Ice Maker**– an adequate supply of cresent-shaped ice is ensured.

•**Dairy Module**– a moveable, sealed environment for freshness.

•**Master Switch**– quick practical access is offered to shut unit off.

•**Rollers**– provides easy installation.

•**Positive Sealing Doors**– magnetic gaskets guarantee a tight seal.

•**Brushed Satin Trim**– offers clean design so there's no distraction from the beauty of your kitchen.

•**Portable Egg Containers**– easy access and convenient storage.

•**Panel Grille**– 11"panel grille is standard. Other sizes from 10" to 15" are available in one inch increments.

•**Solid Toe Plate**– allows custom finishing.

Refrigeration System Control and Bulk Ice Dispenser.

Ice & Water Dispenser with Night Light.

Model 590 shown with optional bright white handle trim panel and glasswell.

Sub-Zero 12 Year Protection Plan—full five-year (parts and labor) warranty and limited sixth through twelfth-year (parts) warranty on the sealed system, consisting of the compressor, condenser, evaporator, drier and all connecting tubing; a full two-year (parts and labor) warranty on the entire product from the date of installation. (Does not include installation. See warranty for other exceptions.)

Beauty—our award-winning interior is beautiful to the eye, but more importantly it is spacious with nearly 30 cubic feet of flexible storage for all your needs.
Refrigerator – 18.2 cubic feet.
Freezer – 11.2 cubic feet.

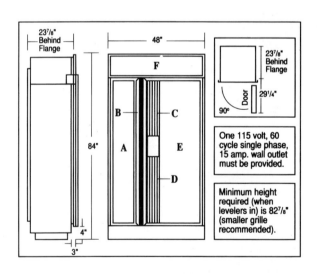

One 115 volt, 60 cycle single phase, 15 amp. wall outlet must be provided.

Minimum height required (when levelers in) is 82^7/$_8$" (smaller grille recommended).

Capacity: Refrigerator 18.2 cu. ft. Freezer 11.2 cu. ft.	Dimensions: Height 84" Width 48" Depth 24"
Two Compressors	Finished Roughed-in Dimensions: 47^1/$_2$ x 83^3/$_4$

Weight: 598 lbs. crated

| Door Panel Dimensions: A 15 ^{1}/$_8$ w x 67 ^{11}/$_{16}$ h B 2 ^{9}/$_{16}$ w x 67 ^{11}/$_{32}$ h C 6 ^{7}/$_8$ w x 25 ^{7}/$_{32}$ h | D 6 ^{7}/$_8$ w x 31 ^{7}/$_{32}$ h E 20 ^{9}/$_{16}$ w x 67 ^{11}/$_{16}$ h Grille Panel Dimension: F 46 ^{3}/$_{16}$ w x 9 ^{3}/$_{16}$ h |

B,C & D may not exceed .050" thickness

Due to our continuous improvement program, models and specifications are subject to change without notice.

Color Selection Guide
for model 590 only

Complete Flexibility

Your Sub-Zero Model 590 will be shipped with handsome pin-striped pewter gray handle trim panels and glasswell. But an exclusive feature from Sub-Zero allows you to change this color scheme to accent your kitchen.

Model 590 shown with standard pin-striped pewter gray handle trim panels and glasswell.

Ask your local dealer about specific color combinations. The eight glasswell and laminate handle trim panel alternatives we offer at no charge are:

P1/G1 — Bright White

P2/G2 — Almond Buff

P3/G3 — Camel

P4/G4 — Adobe

P5/G5 — Pewter Gray

P6/G6 — Smoke Gray

P7/G7 — Charcoal

P8/G8 — Port Brown

P9/G9 — Black Slate

The colors illustrated here are only meant to give you an idea of the shades available and you should contact your dealer for more accurate color combinations and shading.

Note: Metal handle trim panels to match Sub-Zero supplied metal door and side panels are also available in white, almond, avocado, coffee, harvest gold and stainless steel at no charge.

Sales

In addition to the Model 590, Sub-Zero features a full line of built-in home refrigeration units with side-by-side, over-and-under and undercounter models which vary in size from 4.5 to 30 cubic feet of storage. For the dealer near you look in the yellow pages or call Sub-Zero at **800/222-7820** for your nearest distributor.

Service

Sub-Zero has an extensive service network throughout the United States and Canada to meet your needs. You can find them in the yellow pages or call us at **800/356-5826.**

SUB-ZERO ®

SUB-ZERO FREEZER CO., INC.
P.O. Box 44130
Madison, WI 53744 - 4130
(608) 271-2233

*I*t takes vision to create a revolutionary new system of refrigeration.

SUB-ZERO

Close other refrigerators, and the light disappears. Close these, and the refrigerator disappears. Our new integrated refrigerators and freezers don't just complement the decor. They seamlessly blend into it — better than

𝒯hen again, it takes even better vision to find it.

any other built-ins ever designed. They appear, in all their eminent beauty, to be just another cabinet or drawer. But swing open the cabinet, or pull out the drawer, and you'll discover the most flexible, most sophisticated refrigeration system ever created. And the advantages of that are obvious. Even if the refrigerators aren't.

𝒥ntroducing the Integrated 700 Series from Sub-Zero. The flexible refrigeration system that not only blends in. It disappears.

▲ Spice cabinets. China
cabinets. Now Sub-Zero
introduces orange juice
and pork chop cabinets.

Tuck a freezer into the ▶
island and you'll never be
stranded there.

cabinet by the kitchen table. And a separate freezer drawer near the back door for the kids. The advantages of our integrated refrigerators and freezers go well beyond aesthetics. Measuring just 27 inches wide, they allow you to put refrigeration in places never before possible. Instead of being limited to a single, centralized refrigerator, you can now utilize several. (Hence, when your teenager complains there's nothing good in the refrigerator, you can reply, "Which refrigerator?") With five different configurations, you can mix and match our tall units with additional base units. Or use them to supplement a 500 Series Sub-Zero. (In fact, who says you have to limit them to the kitchen? Imagine hiding a refrigerator in the living room, bedroom or entertainment area.) And rest assured, each features Sub-Zero's legendary, uncompromising craftsmanship. Which is why we're confident enough to back them with the 12-Year Sub-Zero Protection Plan. So the only unknown you will ever face with our new refrigerators is how many places to put them.

▲ How's this for a reminder to wash the fruits and vegetables? Store them near the sink.

With its inconspicuous looks, you could misplace the refrigerator. But thanks to its brilliant halogen lighting,

*I*ts advanced features are fresher than anything you are likely to put inside it.

you'll never misplace the food inside. All units also feature a microprocessor control panel that lets you program specific temperatures. In one tall refrigerator, for instance, you could store fresh meat at 30 degrees, while storing your vegetables at the optimal 32 degrees — and the milk and leftovers at 38 degrees. Leave any door or drawer ajar and an alarm will sound. (It can be disengaged for loading groceries.) And like all Sub-Zeros, our tall units offer the ultimate in adjustable, drip-proof shelving.

▲ A see-through, humidity-controlled crisper cover provides easy access to fresh fruits and vegetables.

◄ The tall unit comes with spill-proof shelves and a deli drawer for handy storage.

▲ The microprocessor control panel uses "fuzzy logic," which helps save energy by continuously adapting to usage and climates.

All the doors and compartment shelves are adjustable, providing exceptional flexibility. ►

700TR-All Refrigerator

DIMENSIONS
H 80" W 27" D 24"
Door Swing Clearance: 25½"

ENERGY USAGE
553 kwh/$46/Annually*

STORAGE INFORMATION

Refrigerator:
15.0 cu. ft. of Storage
   9.8 cu. ft. upper cabinet
   5.2 cu. ft. combined drawers
3 Adjustable Glass Shelves
1 Stationary Glass Shelf
3 Adjustable Door Shelves
1 Adjustable Dairy Compartment
1 Adjustable Deli-Drawer
1 Removable Crisper Cover
2 Removable Drawer Dividers
1 Egg Tray

CRATED WEIGHT
360 pounds

700TC-Refrigerator/Freezer

DIMENSIONS
H 80" W 27" D 24"
Door Swing Clearance: 25½"

ENERGY USAGE
672 kwh/$56/Annually*

STORAGE INFORMATION

Refrigerator (Top Cabinet):
9.8 cu. ft. of Storage
3 Adjustable Glass Shelves
1 Stationary Glass Shelf
1 Adjustable Crisper/Deli Drawer
3 Adjustable Door Shelves
1 Adjustable Dairy Compartment

Freezer (Combined Drawers):
5.4 cu. ft. of Storage
2 Removable Drawer Dividers
(1 Removable Divider when Ice Maker ordered)
Ice Maker Optional (700TCI)

CRATED WEIGHT
360 pounds

700TF-All Freezer

DIMENSIONS
H 80" W 27" D 24"
Door Swing Clearance: 25½"

ENERGY USAGE
782 kwh/$65/Annually*

STORAGE INFORMATION

Freezer:
15.2 cu. ft. of Storage
   9.8 cu. ft. upper cabinet
   5.4 cu. ft. combined drawers
4 Adjustable Door Shelves
3 Adjustable Glass Shelves
1 Stationary Glass Shelf
2 Removable Drawer Dividers
(1 Removable Divider when Ice Maker ordered)
Ice Maker Optional (700TFI)

CRATED WEIGHT
360 pounds

700BR-All Refrigerator

DIMENSIONS
H 34½" W 27" D 24"
Drawer Clearance: 19½"

ENERGY USAGE
449 kwh/$37/Annually*

STORAGE INFORMATION

Refrigerator (Combined Drawers):
4.9 cu. ft. of Storage
2 Removable Drawer Dividers
1 Removable Crisper Cover

CRATED WEIGHT
190 pounds

700BF-All Freezer

DIMENSIONS
H 34½" W 27" D 24"
Drawer Clearance: 19½"

ENERGY USAGE
522 kwh/$43/Annually*

STORAGE INFORMATION

Freezer (Combined Drawers):
5.1 cu. ft. of Storage
2 Removable Drawer Dividers
(1 Removable Divider when Ice Maker ordered)
Ice Maker Optional (700BFI)

CRATED WEIGHT
190 pounds

*Annual energy costs are based on 8.3 cents per kilowatt hour.
Consultant: Jerome Caruso Design, Inc.

We've shown you the beautiful exteriors and features. Now take a look at the nuts and bolts.

Our Integrated 700 Series offers five different configurations, to fit any lay-out. In addition to a tall refrigerator/freezer combination unit, we offer both the tall and base models in all-refrigerator or all-freezer models. You also have a choice of left or right-hand door swing, as well as an optional ice maker. And all units can accept most any style of cabinetry panels. Additional accessories, such as stainless steel fronts and handles, are also available. For more details, review our Planning and Installation Guide with your designer, architect or dealer.

**Sub-Zero Freezer
Company, Inc.**

Post Office Box 44130

Madison, Wisconsin
53744-4130

800-200-7820 or
608-271-2233

This book represents

Sub-Zero's Integrated

700 Series. To see our

full line, including our

classic 500 Series,

call us for the

dealer nearest you.

[RDDS3OVQS: Stainless Steel, Downdraft, Drop-In Model]

[RES30QW: White, Updraft, Slide-In Model]

Choosing Thermador proves your taste in great appliance design and function is as sharp as your appetite for good food. The Thermador 30" Built-In Ranges offer a full span of cooking modes, in a choice of finishes, from black to white to stainless.

Thermador's Built-In Range with Gas Cooking Surface and Electric Oven Features:

- XLO® simmer and hold burners on select models provide the lowest possible heat settings (375 BTU/HR) for simmering temperature-sensitive foods and sauces.

- Quick, high-power heat is provided by powerful 11,000 BTU/HR burners.

- Single-piece cast-iron grates that span two burners allow for easier movement of heavy pots and pans.

- A completely sealed cooking surface simplifies cleaning, and automatic ignition/reignition eliminates pilot lights and accidental "blow-outs."

Thermador's Built-In Range with Electric Ceran® Cooking Surface Features:

- A single-piece ceramic cooktop, sealed for ease of cleaning. Radiant ribbon heating elements hidden below provide quick heat-up.

- A variety of heating element sizes and their staggered configuration accommodate a variety of cooking needs.

- Hot surface indicator lights that stay on even after the element has been turned off, as a reminder that the surface is still hot to-the-touch.

Both models include:

- 3.4 cu. ft. electric, convection, self-cleaning oven.

- An enlarged oven window for easy viewing.

- Drop-In models feature an integrated Cook'n'Vent® downdraft ventilation system. Slide-In models can be integrated with Thermador updraft ventilation systems.

Thermador®
When cooking is its own reward.™

Thermador 30" Built-In Ranges

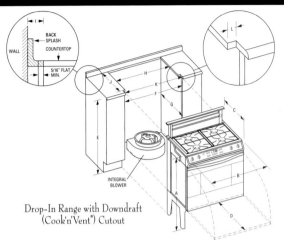

Drop-In Range with Downdraft
(Cook'n'Vent®) Cutout

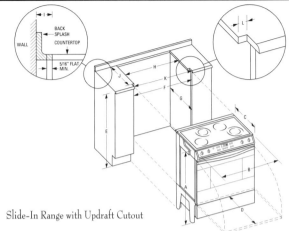

Slide-In Range with Updraft Cutout

MODEL NO.	ELECTRICAL SPECIFICATIONS	OVERALL DIMENSIONS (inches)				CUTOUT DIMENSIONS*		COUNTER TOP CUTOUT DIMENSIONS***					BTU/HR FRONT		REAR		APPROX. SHIP. WT.
		A	B	C**	D	E	F	G	H	I	J	K	L	LEFT	RIGHT	LEFT	RIGHT	
DUAL-FUEL MODELS																		
RDSS30Q Updraft	120/240 Volts, 3 wire, 60 HZ Single Phase A.C., 20 AMP Circuit	36– 37-1/2	29-15/16	25-3/16	17-7/8	35-1/2– 37	30	24	29-1/4	3-1/8	21-9/16	30	3/8	300– 9,100	1,650– 11,000	365– 11,000	1,300– 9,100	260 lb
RDDS30VQ* Downdraft	120/240 Volts, 3 wire, 60 HZ Single Phase A.C., 30 AMP Circuit	36– 37-1/2	29-15/16	26-7/8	17-7/8	35-1/2– 37	30	24	29-1/4	1-3/4	23-3/16	30	3/8					265 lb
ELECTRIC MODELS														WATTAGE				
RES30Q Updraft	120/240 Volts, 3 wire, 60 HZ Single Phase A.C., 40 AMP Circuit	36– 37-1/2	29-15/16	25-3/16	17-7/8	35-1/2– 37	30	24	29-1/4	3-1/8	21-9/16	30	3/8	1,800 Watts 7" Radiant Ribbon	1,000– 2,500 6"–9" Dual Circuit Radiant Ribbon	1,000– 2,200 5"–8" Dual Circuit Radiant Ribbon	1,500 Watts 6" Radiant Ribbon	255 lb
RED30VQ* Downdraft	120/240 Volts, 3 wire, 60 HZ Single Phase A.C., 50 AMP Circuit	36– 37-1/2	29-15/16	26-7/8	17-7/8	35-1/2– 37	30	24	29-1/4	1-3/4	23-3/16	30	3/8					270 lb

* Cutout dimensions account for Cook'n'Vent® clearance.
**Dimension measures from rear of Cook'n'Vent® to front of control panel end cap. ***Dimensions are based on a standard 24" cabinet. Please refer to installation instructions prior to making cutout.
Notes: 1) Oven interior dimensions: 23 1/2" W x 15 1/2" H x 16" D (3.4 cu. ft.). 2) LP Conversion kit available (NLPKIT3) for dual-fuel models. 3) Venting requirements: Cook'n'Vent® hoodless downdraft ventilation system or an overhead hood must be vented to outside. 4) The Thermador Cook'n'Vent® range with hoodless downdraft ventilation system consists of the range (with the downdraft intake included) and the blower which must be ordered separately. Either a remote blower (model VTR1000Q) with a duct attachment box, (model RD310 or RD7), or an integral blower (model VTN30RQ) may be used. 5) A toe kick accessory can be installed on drop-in models to achieve a slide-in look. Model# RKPQ_ (indicate Black, White or Stainless).

Ventilation Ducting Options†

Integral Ventilator Installation: Blower may be rotated to achieve right/left side, rear or floor venting.

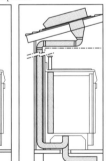

Remote Ventilator Installation: 3-1/4"x 10" ducting below floor to front or to rear and up wall.

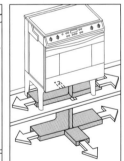

3-1/4"x 10" ducting above or below floor, to left, right, front or rear.

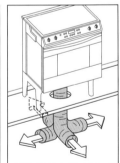

7" round duct below floor, to left, right, front or rear.

†See installation instructions for full details on ventilation and ducting options for the model you choose. Ducting and blower instructions included in range carton.

Warranty: Gas cooking surface models have full one-year parts and labor warranty. Electric cooking surface models have full one-year parts and labor warranty plus an additional three-year limited warranty on the glass-ceramic surface. See your distributor or dealer or write Thermador® for full warranty details. We reserve the right to change specifications or design without notice. Thermador, 5119 District Blvd., Los Angeles, CA 90040

Thermador®

For the dealer nearest you, call 1-800-656-9226, ext. 66
or visit us at http://www.thermador.com
For immediate critical installation dimensions by fax, use your fax handset and call (702) 833-3600. Use code #8030

©1996, Masco Corporation
Form: 30SD Litho date: 1/96

  Ranges and blowers are UL and CUL approved.

EXPECT THE BEST...
DON'T SETTLE FOR THE ORDINARY

Eurodesign offers the panache and sophistication of custom European cabinet design plus the assurance and cost advantage of local manufacturing. Our myriad of door styles are designed to serve a wide spectrum of needs - from the entry level home builders all the way up to high-end custom estate builders. Let us show you how other leading builders are taking advantage of the latest technology being utilized by Eurodesign.

Corporate Headquarters and 106,000 square foot manufacturing facility in Chino, California.

MANUFACTURING PLANT AND SHOWROOM:

13428 Benson Avenue
Chino, CA 91710
Telephone: 909.590.4300
FAX: 909.590.4677

euro design INC.

international styling, european technology, manufactured in america

CHANTILLY
Euro 317
Honey Maple

MONTREAL
Euro 410
Mocha Maple

VIENNA
Euro 253
White Polymeric Foil

MONET
Euro 505
Mocha Maple

NAPOLI
Euro 363
White Polymeric Foil

KENT
Euro 208
Honey Maple Laminate

FLORENCE
Euro 309
Natural Limed Oak

SONORA
Euro 500
Faux Finish

Richmond - 200
(honey maple laminate)

Kent - 208
(white laminate)

Vienna - 253
(white matte PLF)

Chateau - 258
(pearl white PLF)

Milano - 308
(natural oak)

Florence - 309
(white wash maple)

Napoli - 363
(white matte PLF)

Logano - 402
(natural limed oak)

Del Mar - 404
(high gloss PLF)

Montreal - 410
(fruitwood on maple)

Montreal - 410
(honey maple)

Hamilton - 451
(birds eye maple PLF)

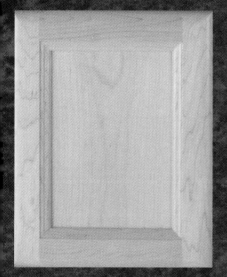

Lexington - 457
(honey maple)

Sheffield - 465
(natural oak)

Sonora - 500
(natural oak)

Elegantè - 501
(white wash maple)

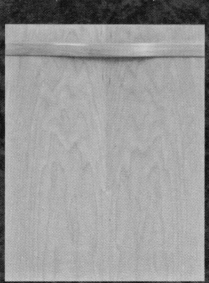

Ertè - 502
(plain slice-honey maple)

Picasso - 503
(plain slice-honey maple)

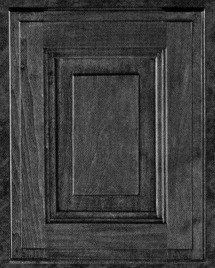

Monet - 505
(fruitwood on maple)

Sicily - 508
(white lacquer)

Newport - 533
(white semi-gloss
lacquer)

Roma - 563
(high gloss PLF)

Elegantè Supreme 601
(white wash maple)

Cambridge - 603
(rift-natural limed oak)

Victoria - 604
(white lacquer)

Divinci - 703
(anigre veneer)

Windsor - 707
(honey maple)

Specifications

Liberty - euro 100: 3/4" Low or High Pressure Laminated MDF Panel. Square Edges Banded With PVC.

Richmond - euro 200: 3/4" Low or High Pressure Laminated MDF Panel. Vertical Edges Banded With PVC. Solid Oak Or Maple Continuous Pull.

Kent - euro 208: 3/4" Low or High Pressure Laminated MDF Panel. Square Vertical Edges Banded With PVC. 1/2" Solid Oak Or Maple Continuous Pull.

Hanover - euro 251: 3/4" MDF Panel Laminated With White Matte Polymeric Foil Bullnose On All Four Sides. (Available In Mother Of Pearl Foil And White Wash Maple Foil. See Upgrade Chart.)

Catalina - euro 252: 7/8" MDF Panel Laminated With White Matte Polymeric Foil, Ingrooved 1-1/2" From All Bullnose Edges. (Available In Mother Of Pearl Foil And White Wash Maple Foil - See Upcharge Chart.)

Vienna - euro 253: 3/4" MDF Panel W/Routered Raised Center Panel Laminated In White Matte Polymeric Foil. Bullnose Edges.

Salzburg - euro 254: 3/4" MDF Panel W/Routered Cathedral Arch Raised Center Panel Laminated In White Matte Polymeric Foil. Bullnose Edges.

Chateau - euro 258: 3/4" MDF Panel Laminated In White Matte Polymeric Foil, Bullnose On Top and Bottom Edges Only. Sides Are Flat Eased Vertical Edged. (Available In Mother Of Pearl Foil And White Wash Maple Foil - See Upgrade Chart.)

Elika - euro 300: 3/4" MDF Panel With Wood Veneer. Veneered Square Edges.

Milano - euro 308: 5/8" MDF Panel With Rift Oak Wood Veneer. 5/8" Solid Wood Radiused Horizontal Edges. Veneered Vertical Square Edges.

Florence - euro 309: 13/16" Solid Wood Frame With 1/4" Veneered Center Panel.

Chantilly - euro 317: In Wood 13/16" Wide Frame With 5/16" Thick Central Panel In Plain Slice Book Matched Hardwood Veneer. Available in Polymeric Foil.

Napoli - euro 363: 13/16" Square Raised Panel With 2 1/2" Beveled Frame Laminated In White Matte Polymeric Foil.

Carmel - euro 401: 3/4" MDF Panel Laminated With High Gloss White Polymeric Foil. Bullnose Edges.

Logano - euro 402: 7/8" Solid Wood Frame With 1/4" Recessed Veneered Center Panel.

Del Mar - euro 404: 3/4" MDF Panel With Routered Raised Center Panel Laminated With High Gloss Polymeric Foil. Bullnose Edges.

Montreal - euro 410: 13/16" Solid Wood Frame With 9/16" Thick Veneered Raised Center Panel.

Barcelona - euro 435: 5/8" Hardwood Veneer Center Square Raised Panel With 2 1/2" Beveled Solid Wood Frame.

Cortina - euro 448: 3/4" MDF Panel Prefinished In White Semi-Gloss Lacquer. Bullnose On Top And Bottom Edges.

Hamilton - euro 451: 3/4" MDF Panel Laminated In .4mm Thick Matte Birds Eye Maple Polymeric Foil Or White High Gloss Polymeric Foil. Bullnose Edges.

Lexington - euro 457: 7/8" Solid Oak Frame With 1/4" Recessed Veneered Center Panel. Railing System Door.

Marquesa - euro 458: 3/4" MDF Panel Laminated In White High Gloss Polymeric Foil Or Birds Eye Maple Polymeric Foil. Bullnose On Top And Bottom Edges Only. Sides Are Flat Eased Vertical Edged. Available In Railing System.

Sheffield - euro 465: 2-3/4" Wide Solid Wood Frame, 45 Degree Mitered And Doweled At Each Corner, Central Panel Is Made Of 5/16" Thick Plain Slice Book Matched Hardwood Veneer.

Sonora - euro 500: 13/16" Solid Wood Square Raised Panel. Companion to E600.

Elegante - euro 501: 3/4" Rift Cut Veneer Panel With 1-1/4" Thick Radiused Solid Wood Horizontal Edges. Veneered Vertical Square Edges. Railing System Door.

Erte - euro 502: 3/4" MDF Panel Finished With White Semi-Gloss Lacquer. Beveled On Four Edges. Ingrooved Handles Of Veneered Hard Bent Wood. Chrome Or Gold - Plate Handles @ 20% Upcharge.

Picasso - euro 503: 3/4" Plain Slice Veneer Panel. 1/4" Solid Wood On All Four Edges. Railing System Door.

Monet - euro 505: 7/8" MDF Frame With 5/8" Thick Semi-Raised Center Panel Finished In White Semi-Gloss Lacquer.

Sicily - euro 508: 7/8" MDF Frame With 3/8" Thick Recessed Center Panel Finished In White Semi-Gloss Lacquer. Railing System Door.

Linea - euro 509: 3/4" Plain Slice Veneer Center Panel With Eased Edge On All Four Sides. 1-1/4" Thick Top Edge With 45 Degree Angle Finger Pull (No Hardware Required).

Newport - euro 533: 7/8" MDF Frame With 1/4" Thick Recessed Center Panel Finished In White Semi-Gloss Lacquer.

Georgetown - euro 553: 3/4" MDF Frame With Routered Raised Center Panel Finished In White Semi-Gloss Lacquer.

Espana - euro 557: 7/8" Solid Oak Frame With 9/16" Thick Veneer Raised Central Panel. Railing System Door.

Roma - euro 563: 3/4" Square Raised Panel With 2-1/2" Beveled Frame Laminated In White High Gloss Polymeric Foil.

Modesto - euro 600: 13/16" Solid Wood Cathedral Arch Raised Panel. Companion To E500.

Elegante Supreme - euro 601: 3/4" Rift Cut Veneer Panel Inlaid With .3mm Black Walnut. 1-1/4" Thick Radiused Solid Wood Horizontal Edges And 1/4" Thick Vertical Edges. Railing System Door.

Cambridge - euro 603: 13/16" Solid Wood Square Raised Panel With 2-1/2" Beveled Wood Frame.

Victoria - euro 604: 13/16" MDF Square 5 Piece Raised Panel With 2-1/2" Beveled Frame Finished In Semi-Gloss White Lacquer.

Venice - euro 614: 11/16" MDF Square Raised Panel Finished In White Semi-Gloss Lacquer. Companion To E714.

Madrid - euro 702: 3/4" MDF Cathedral Raised Panel. Finished In White Semi-Gloss Lacquer.

Divinci Supreme - euro 703: 3/4" Birds Eye Maple Veneered Panel . 1/4" Solid Maple On All Four Edges. Railing System Door.

Windsor - euro 707: 7/8" Solid Wood Raised Panel. Railing System Door.

Monaco - euro 708: 7/8" Raised Panel Finished With White Semi-Gloss Lacquer. Railing System Door.

Madrid - euro 714: 11/16" MDF Cathedral Arch Raised Panel. Finished In White Semi-Gloss Lacquer. Companion To E614.

INSTALLATION/SOUTHERN CALIFORNIA

A team of project managers measures every individual unit to ensure proper fit of all cabinets in each and every home. Eurodesign cabinets are installed by factory trained installers under the supervision of field managers who ensure consistency in quality of workmanship.

NATIONAL/INTERNATIONAL:

Our export division is staffed with experienced professionals to support national and international residential project developments outside of Southern California and the U.S. We continuously explore the international life-style and endeavor to provide a product line designed specifically to serve the needs and requirements of our long distance clients.

DESIGN:

Eurodesign has professional kitchen designers/sales consultants to assist the Architect and the home builder in selecting Eurodesign cabinets for their projects.

MANUFACTURING:

Eurodesign cabinets are produced using the 32mm system of case construction. All components that compromise the finished product are manufactured under one roof. This provides for quality control unparalleled in the industry. Our state of the art facility enables us to deliver superior quality at surprisingly affordable prices.

euro
design INC.

WELLBORN
CABINET, INC.

Elite Series

Founded in 1961, Wellborn Cabinet, Inc. produces high quality lines of stock cabinetry in a 900,000 square feet manufacturing facility employing 1,100 people. Wellborn is fully integrated, operating its own timber processing mill, dry kilns and state-of-the-art production equipment to craft fine kitchen and bath cabinetry. Cabinets are built on four levels of construction – Elite, Premium, Deluxe and Advantage Series – to satisfy every budget. Every facet of building Wellborn cabinets is accomplished in one facility helping to insure the highest quality craftsmanship in the industry.

Monaco

Elite Series
Wall Cabinet Construction

3¹/₂" x ³/₄" white laminated fiberboard hanging rails

¹/₂" white laminated particle board top

¹/₈" white printed hardboard back

⁵/₈" white laminated particle board adjustable shelves with edgebanding; White dual locking shelf clips

¹/₂" white laminated particle board bottom

1³/₄" x ³/₄" kiln-dried solid hardwood frames; mortised and tenoned, glued and stapled

Hanging rail dadoed to receive cabinet floor

¹/₂" white laminated particle board end panels with edgebanding

Elite Series
Base Cabinet Construction

Plastic corner braces stapled into sides and frame

3¹/₂" x ³/₄" white laminated fiberboard hanging rails

¹/₈" white printed hardboard back

⁵/₈" white laminated particle board adjustable shelves with edgebanding; White dual locking shelf clips

3¹/₂" x ³/₄" solid hardwood center mullion

¹/₂" white laminated particle board bottom (solid wood brace on 30" wide and larger cabinets)

Hanging rail dadoed to receive cabinet floor

1³/₄" x ³/₄" kiln-dried solid hardwood frames; mortised and tenoned, glued and stapled

¹/₂" white laminated particle board end panels

Depth 3¹/₈"

4¹/₂" x ⁵/₈" particle board toe board

Monaco, Brighton and Sea Spray represent the Elite Series, all white with full overlay designs and concealed hinges. Monaco is a white painted door featuring a Roman Arch design on wall cabinets and a square one-piece design on base cabinets. Brighton is a thermafoil door with a square 90° corner decorative profile. Sea Spray features a thermafoil door with a radius corner profile. All three are made of fiberboard and have an all white interior.

Sea Spray

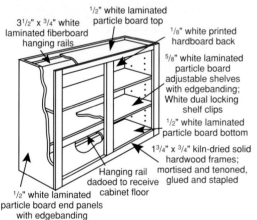

Elite Series
Drawer Construction

⁵/₈" white laminated particle board drawer sides tenoned to accept sub-front and back

¹/₈" white printed hardboard bottom

³/₄" thick fiberboard drawer front

75 lb. white epoxy coated captive self-closing drawer slides

Capri

OXFORD

Premium Series
Wall Cabinet Construction

$3^1/2$" x $^3/4$" wood grain laminated fiberboard hanging rails

$^1/2$" wood grain laminated particle board top

$^1/8$" wood grain printed hardboard back

$^5/8$" wood grain laminated particle board adjustable shelves with edgebanding; Dual locking shelf clips

$^1/2$" wood grain laminated particle board bottom

$1^3/4$" x $^3/4$" kiln-dried solid cherry, oak, maple or hickory face frames; mortised and tenoned, glued and stapled

Hanging rail dadoed to receive cabinet floor

$^1/2$" cherry, oak, maple or hickory finished matching plywood end panels with laminated interior

Premium Series
Base Cabinet Construction

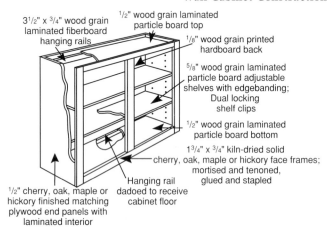

$3^1/2$" x $^3/4$" wood grain laminated fiberboard hanging rails

Plastic corner braces stapled into sides and frame

$^1/8$" wood grain printed hardboard back

$3^1/2$" x $^3/4$" solid cherry, oak, maple, or hickory center mullion

$^5/8$" wood grain laminated particle board adjustable shelves with edgebanding; Dual locking shelf clips

$^1/2$" wood grain laminated particle board bottom (solid wood brace on 30" wide and larger cabinets)

$1^3/4$" x $^3/4$" kiln-dried solid cherry, oak, maple or hickory frames; mortised and tenoned, glued and stapled

Hanging rail dadoed to receive cabinet floor

$^1/8$" cherry, oak, maple or hickory finished matching plywood end panels with laminated interior

Depth $3^1/8$"

$4^1/2$" x $^5/8$" particle board toe board

Premium Series
Drawer Construction

$^3/4$" solid hardwood drawer sides, sub-front and back with dovetail construction

$^1/4$" finished plywood drawer bottom

$^3/4$" solid cherry, oak, maple or hickory drawer front

75 lb. undermount epoxy coated captive self-closing drawer slides

Manor House Cherry

Wellborn offers 84 contemporary and traditional door styles in oak, maple, hickory and cherry with finish selections ranging from sparkling white to deep, rich burgundy. Over 70 accessory cabinets are available for modern convenience and efficient space planning. Wellborn has a semi-custom program featuring extended stiles, increased or decreased wall cabinet depths and full height base cabinet doors.

The Premium Series cabinet construction is available on the following door styles:

Oak	Ashley Natural, Light and Pickle
	Oxford Cathedral Natural, Light, Medium and Pickle
	Oxford Natural, Light, Medium and Pickle
Hickory	Cheyenne Cathedral Natural and Medium
	Cheyenne Natural and Medium
Maple	Capri Arch Natural, Light, Pickle and Burgundy
	Capri Natural, Light, Pickle and Burgundy
Cherry	Manor House Cherry Light
	Mt. Vernon Cherry Dark
	Manor House Cherry Square Light
	Mt. Vernon Cherry Square Dark

Deluxe Series

Wellborn offers our customers Warehouse on Wheels, a quick delivery transportation program designed to meet delivery of 43 inventoried door styles on a 5-10 day work schedule. A nationwide cycle shipment program provides a tremendous advantage to our customers by eliminating warehousing costs and insuring on-time delivery of orders. Contact your nearest dealer for complete information.

The Deluxe Series cabinet construction is available in these door styles:

Maple	Avalon Natural and Light
	Seville Arch Light and Pickle
	Seville Light and Pickle
	Essex Natural, Light, Pickle and Burgundy
	Rose Hall Cathedral Natural, Light, Pickle and Burgundy
	Rose Hall Natural, Light, Pickle and Burgundy
Oak	Sierra Arch Light and Pickle
	Sierra Light and Pickle
	Waverly Cathedral Natural, Light, Medium and Pickle
	Waverly Natural, Light, Medium and Pickle
	Pioneer Cathedral Light, Medium and Pickle
	Pioneer Square Light, Medium and Pickle
	Highland Natural, Light, Medium and Pickle
	Shady Oak Light, Medium and Pickle

Waverly

Rose Hall

Sierra Arch

Deluxe Series
Wall Cabinet Construction

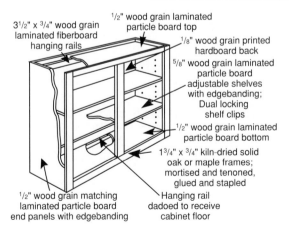

3½" x ¾" wood grain laminated fiberboard hanging rails

½" wood grain laminated particle board top

⅛" wood grain printed hardboard back

⅝" wood grain laminated particle board adjustable shelves with edgebanding; Dual locking shelf clips

½" wood grain laminated particle board bottom

1¾" x ¾" kiln-dried solid oak or maple frames; mortised and tenoned, glued and stapled

½" wood grain matching laminated particle board end panels with edgebanding

Hanging rail dadoed to receive cabinet floor

Deluxe Series
Base Cabinet Construction

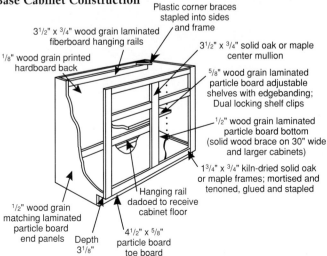

Plastic corner braces stapled into sides and frame

3½" x ¾" wood grain laminated fiberboard hanging rails

3½" x ¾" solid oak or maple center mullion

⅛" wood grain printed hardboard back

⅝" wood grain laminated particle board adjustable shelves with edgebanding; Dual locking shelf clips

½" wood grain laminated particle board bottom (solid wood brace on 30" wide and larger cabinets)

1¾" x ¾" kiln-dried solid oak or maple frames; mortised and tenoned, glued and stapled

½" wood grain matching laminated particle board end panels

Depth 3⅛"

Hanging rail dadoed to receive cabinet floor

4½" x ⅝" particle board toe board

Deluxe Series
Drawer Construction

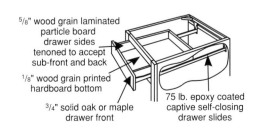

⅝" wood grain laminated particle board drawer sides tenoned to accept sub-front and back

⅛" wood grain printed hardboard bottom

¾" solid oak or maple drawer front

75 lb. epoxy coated captive self-closing drawer slides

Advantage Series

Advantage series offers two choices of wood in oak and maple. Sheffield is available in light or medium oak and has a raised panel door. Oak Crest, with its flat center panel comes in light, medium or pickle oak. Both Sheffield and Oak Crest feature a self-closing, fully adjustable knife hinge. Silverton and Bellemeade are made of maple and feature a flat center panel. Silverton is exclusively in the pickle finish while Bellemeade is available in our burgundy finish.

With all the many styles and finish choices, Wellborn pleases the most discriminating tastes. Design with Wellborn and be assured of high quality, beautiful cabinetry.

Sheffield

Oak Crest

Advantage Series Wall Cabinet Construction

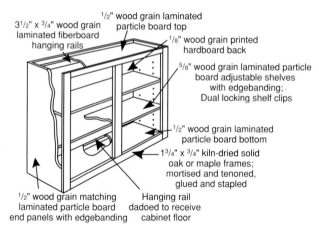

- $3^1/2$" x $3/4$" wood grain laminated fiberboard hanging rails
- $1/2$" wood grain laminated particle board top
- $1/8$" wood grain printed hardboard back
- $5/8$" wood grain laminated particle board adjustable shelves with edgebanding; Dual locking shelf clips
- $1/2$" wood grain laminated particle board bottom
- $1^3/4$" x $3/4$" kiln-dried solid oak or maple frames; mortised and tenoned, glued and stapled
- $1/2$" wood grain matching laminated particle board end panels with edgebanding
- Hanging rail dadoed to receive cabinet floor

Advantage Series Drawer Construction

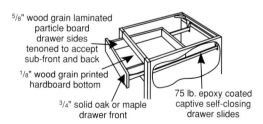

- $5/8$" wood grain laminated particle board drawer sides tenoned to accept sub-front and back
- $1/8$" wood grain printed hardboard bottom
- $3/4$" solid oak or maple drawer front
- 75 lb. epoxy coated captive self-closing drawer slides

Advantage Series Base Cabinet Construction

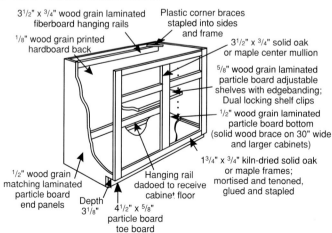

- $3^1/2$" x $3/4$" wood grain laminated fiberboard hanging rails
- Plastic corner braces stapled into sides and frame
- $1/8$" wood grain printed hardboard back
- $3^1/2$" x $3/4$" solid oak or maple center mullion
- $5/8$" wood grain laminated particle board adjustable shelves with edgebanding; Dual locking shelf clips
- $1/2$" wood grain laminated particle board bottom (solid wood brace on 30" wide and larger cabinets)
- $1^3/4$" x $3/4$" kiln-dried solid oak or maple frames; mortised and tenoned, glued and stapled
- $1/2$" wood grain matching laminated particle board end panels
- Hanging rail dadoed to receive cabinet floor
- Depth $3^1/8$"
- $4^1/2$" x $5/8$" particle board toe board

KITCHEN CABINET **KCMA** MANUFACTURERS ASSOCIATION

NATIONAL KITCHEN **NKBA** & BATH ASSOCIATION

WELLBORN
W
People Who Care

Wellborn Cabinet, Inc.
38669 Hwy. 77, P.O. Box 1210
Ashland, AL 36251
(205) 354-7151   Fax (205) 354-7022

B8652

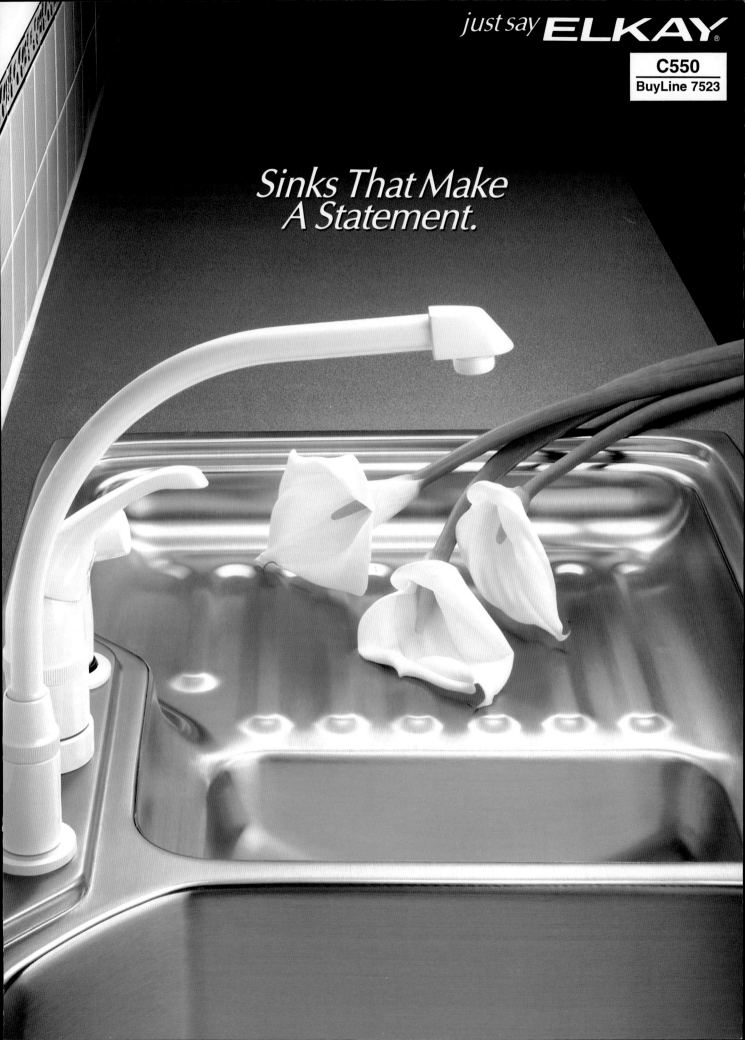

just say **ELKAY**

C550
BuyLine 7523

Sinks That Make A Statement.

TRADITIONAL

To reflect the true elegance and beauty of your kitchen, choose our Traditional Gourmet Collection in shining stainless steel. As America's leading designer of stainless steel sinks, Elkay offers you the ultimate in quality. Each sink is carefully crafted from durable 18-gauge material and is machine ground and meticulously hand buffed to our exclusive Lasting Beauty™ finish that resists scratching, chipping, fading or cracking and is more forgiving to dropped glassware.

Our Traditional Gourmet Collection also features classic styling in single-, double- and triple-bowl configurations with large, 10" deep bowls and optional ribbed areas. With so much to choose from, you're bound to find a brilliant complement to brighten your kitchen.

EGPI-4322-R

Elkay's Gourmet Cuisine Centre makes food preparation a joy! Our exclusive design includes an innovative bi-level food preparation area, with a ribbed area, convenient disposer bowl and spacious 10" deep bowl. Choose either a left- or a right-bowl model (EGPI-4322-R or L). Components separately: Faucet (LK-4381-F-BK), Soap/Lotion Dispenser (LK-313-BK), Hot Water Machine (LKH-180).

DIMENSIONS IN INCHES. TO CONVERT TO MILLIMETERS, MULTIPLY BY 25.

EGPI-4322-R

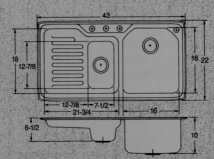

ILGR-6022-L-C

Featuring a ribbed area and over-sized bowls, this triple-bowl sink has a Hi-Arc™ faucet with contemporary spout styling, swivel aerator and retractable spray and hose. Shown here with left-side sink bowl, the package is also available with a right-side sink bowl. Components separately: Triple-bowl Sink (ILGR-6022-R or L), Faucet (LK-4124-F).

LGR-4322-C

A compact and efficient design makes this triple-bowl sink package ideal for multiple cooking tasks. The Hi-Arc™ faucet allows quick and easy access to all bowls, while the retract-able spray and hose make rinsing effortless. Components separately: Sink (LGR-4322), Faucet (LK-4124-F).

ILFGR-5422-L

Make big chores into small work with our extra-wide, double-bowl sink, featuring our exclusive Lasting Beauty finish and a handy 19 3/4" ribbed area. Shown here with left-side sink bowls, this model is also avail-able with right-side sink bowls. Components separately: Sink (ILFGR-5422-L or R), Faucet (LK-4324-F-BK), Soap/Lotion Dispenser (LK-313-BK).

ILGR-6022-L-C

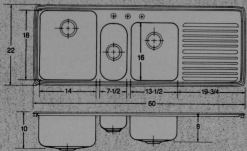

LGR-4322-C

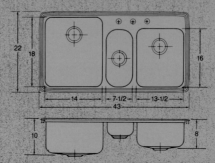

ILFGR-5422-L

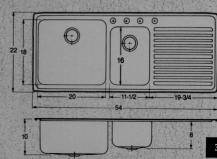

ILGR-5422-L

The two large sink bowls and expansive 19 7/8" ribbed area offer ample room for so many tasks. Shown here with left-side sink bowls, this design is also available with right-side sink bowls. Components separately: Sink (ILGR-5422-L or R), Faucet (LK-4324-F-AL), Soap/Lotion Dispenser (LK-313-AL) and Strainer (LK-35-AL).

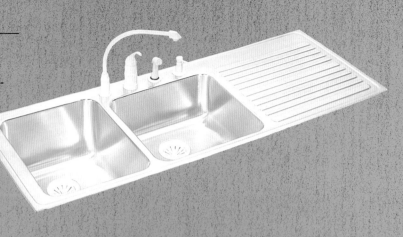

ILFGR-4822-L

For maximum versatility and unmatched durability, try this Elkay design featuring large and small bowls with a 17 1/2" ribbed area. Shown with left-side bowls, it's also available with right-side bowls. Components separately: Sink (ILFGR-4822-L or R), Faucet (LK-4340-F-CR), Soap/Lotion Dispenser (LK-313-CR), Hot Water Machine (LKH-180).

ILGR-4822-L

If you have limited space, this sink offers unlimited options. Two large bowls make work comfortable and convenient, while the ribbed area is ideal for rinsing, drying and food preparation. Shown here with left-side sink bowls, it's also available with right-side sink bowls. Components separately: Sink (ILGR-4822-L or R), Faucet (LK-4324-F-WH), Soap/Lotion Dispenser (LK-313-WH).

DIMENSIONS IN INCHES. TO CONVERT TO MILLIMETERS, MULTIPLY BY 25.4

ILGR-5422-L

ILFGR-4822-L

ILGR-4822-L

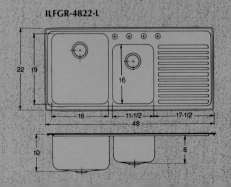

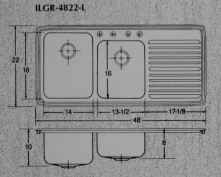

LFGR-3722

Featuring a large and small bowl, this Elkay design offers virtually unlimited flexibility; clean and rinse in one bowl, prepare food in the other. Components separately: Sink (LFGR-3722), Faucet (LK-4350-F-BK), Soap/Lotion Dispenser (LK-313-BK), Hot Water Machine (LKH-180) and Strainer (LK-35-BK).

LGR-3722

An all-time favorite, this double sink with 10″ deep bowl, Hi-Arc faucet and retractable spray and hose makes cleaning large pots and pitchers easier than ever. Components separately: Sink (LGR-3722), Faucet (LK-2453).

LFGR-3322

With a large and small bowl, this sparkling sink is great for smaller work spaces. And, for years of lasting brilliance, this model features our exclusive Lasting Beauty finish. Components separately: Sink (LFGR-3322), Faucet (LK-4361), Hot Water Machine (LKH-180).

LFGR-3722

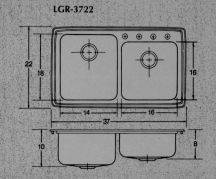

LGR-3722

LFGR-3322

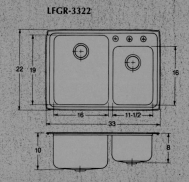

LGR-3322

One look at this shiny, compact sink and you'll know you've discovered the perfect addition to a small work area. Fits traditional kitchen counter areas. Components separately: Sink (LGR-3322), Faucet (LK-4324-F-BK), Soap/Lotion Dispenser (LK-313-BK).

ILGR-4322-L

Simple and convenient, this Elkay model is the first choice for those who need one spacious, durable sink bowl and a handy 20" ribbed area. Shown with left-side bowl, it's also available with a right-side bowl. Components separately: Sink (ILGR-4322-L or R), Faucet (LK-4391-F-WH) and Escutcheon (LK-2725-WH).

DIMENSIONS IN INCHES. TO CONVERT TO MILLIMETERS, MULTIPLY BY .25.4.

LGR-3322

ILGR-4322-L

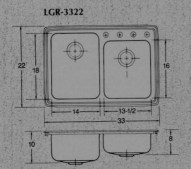

CONTEMPORARY

Soft and elegant, yet durable and tough — that's Elkay's Contemporary Gourmet Collection. Like all our stainless steel sinks, the Contemporary Gourmet Collection won't chip, crack or fade. And our Lasting Beauty finish gives a soft, satin look that resists scratching.

Featuring a sleek, round-bowl design and European styling, these sinks will give your kitchen a fresh, modern look while performing radiantly well into the future. The optional left or right placement of the smaller bowl and the handy ribbed area provide customized convenience and unmatched efficiency. Once you've owned an Elkay stainless steel sink, you'll see it's as beautiful as it is durable.

ILCGR-5322-L

Neatness and efficiency are the key advantages of this stainless steel sink. Featuring a large, double bowl, it also has a wide ribbed area for drying dishes quickly and easily. Components separately: Sink (ILCGR-5322-L or R), Faucet (LK-4391-F-BK), Hot Water Machine (LKH-180), Strainer (LK-35-BK).

ILCGR-5322-L

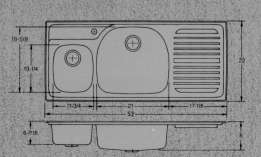

18-5/8

13-1/4

22

11-3/4   21   17-1/8

53

6-7/16

LCGR-3822-L

With a smaller yet functional bowl on the left, and a larger bowl on the right, this sink affords the busy cook ample work space. If you prefer the smaller bowl on the right, it's also available. Components separately: Sink (LCGR-3822-L or R), Faucet (LK-4381-F-CR), Soap/Lotion Dispenser (LK-313-CR).

ILCGR-4822-L

Need more space to create enticing entrees? Choose this Elkay design, with double-bowl configuration and spacious 16 15/16″ right-side ribbed area for cutting, rinsing and preparing food. Also available with left-side ribbed area. Components separately: Sink (ILCGR-4822-L or R), Faucet (LK-4381-F-BK), Soap/Lotion Dispenser (LK-313-BK), Hot Water Machine (LKH-180).

LCGR-3322-L

Shown with our sophisticated Regency faucet, this stainless steel sink features a smaller bowl on the left or right side for added ease in food preparation. Components separately: Sink (LCGR-3322-L or R), Faucet (LK-4391-F-WH), Soap/Lotion Dispenser (LK-313-WH).

DIMENSIONS IN INCHES. TO CONVERT TO MILLIMETERS, MULTIPLY BY 25.4

LCGR-3822-L

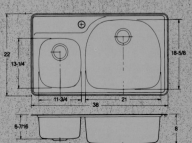

ILCGR-4822-L

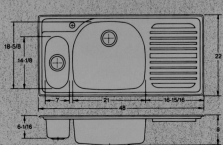

LCGR-3322-L

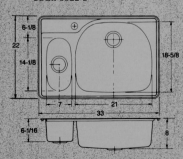

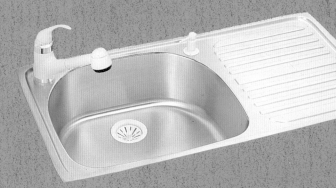

ILCGR-4022-L

Rinse, clean, cut and slice! Our single-bowl sink provides you with the perfect bowl and 17″ ribbed area to do it all. Shown with left-side bowl, it's also available with right-side bowl. Components separately: Sink (ILCGR-4022-L or R), Faucet (LK-4350-F-AL), Soap/Lotion Dispenser (LK-313-AL) and Strainer (LK-35-AL).

LCGR-2522

Few sinks can offer the spacious and modern styling of our large, single-bowl sink. This single bowl provides the capacity for cleaning large pots and pans easily. Components separately: Sink (LCGR-2522), Faucet (LK-4350-F-WH) and Soap/Lotion Dispenser (LK-313-WH).

ILCGR-4022-L

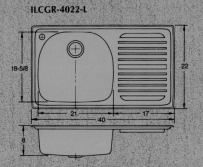

LCGR-2522

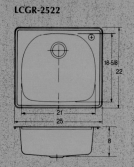

NOUVEAU GOURMET™

Elkay celebrated it's 75th anniversary with the introduction of a new collection of sinks to complement the Traditional and Contemporary Gourmet series. The Nouveau Gourmet™ sinks, a beautiful blend of quality and style, are crafted and polished to a brilliant, lasting finish that won't stain, fade or rust. The clean lines and cool texture of stainless steel also reflect the colors and decor around it, complementing and enhancing literally any kitchen—whether modern or vintage.

The versatile Nouveau Gourmet sinks have especially helpful features, from the bowl shapes that range from traditional square and rectangles to contemporary curves and even the spacious trapezoids to the double-bowl model with ribbed area for added space and convenient stacking and drying of pots and pans.

NG-3322

NG-3322

Attractive, contemporary-style Diamond Jubilee sink is a double-bowl model that mixes European styling with common-sense functionality. Made of heavy 20-gauge stainless steel, this sink features two different sized bowls for added convenience. Bowls are 7 1/2" deep. Components separately: Sink (NG-3322), Faucet (LK-4371-F-CR), and Hot Water Machine (LKH-180).

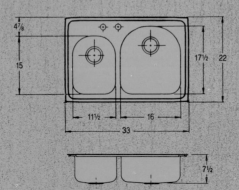

DIMENSIONS IN INCHES. TO CONVERT TO MILLIMETERS, MULTIPLY BY 25.4.

NG-3722

Symmetrical, contemporary design optimizes the appearance and maximizes the space in this double-bowl sink. Bowls are 7 1/2" deep. Components separately: Sink (NG-3722), Faucet (LK-4350-F-WH) and Hot Water Machine (LKH-190-WH).

NGA-3322

This double bowl Nouveau Gourmet sink offers traditional styling using two different but complementary bowl designs. Bowl depths are 7 1/2". Left bowl is 11 1/2"×16" and right bowl is 16"×18". Components offered separately: Sink (NGA-3322), Faucet (LK-4371-F-CR), Hot Water Machine (LKH-180).

NGR-4822-L

Designed with the busy cook in mind, this sink has traditional style bowls with a right side ribbed area to simplify food preparation. Components separately: Sink (NGR-4822-L), Faucet (LK-4324-F-WH), and Soap/Lotion Dispenser (LK-313-WH).

NG-3722

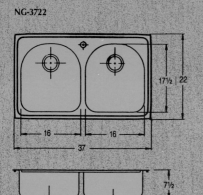

NGA-3322

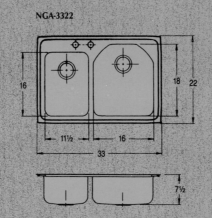

NGR-4822-L

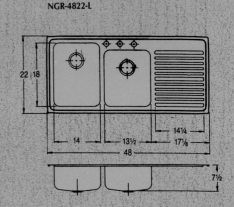

UNDERMOUNT

Elkay gives you the freedom to design your own kitchen, entertainment area or custom bath with its Undermount Sink components. Make a statement of personal style by choosing one of the contemporary designs from the industry's largest collection of shapes and sizes. There are eleven individual single-bowl designs and three double-bowl combinations. The single bowls allow you to mix and match your favorite shapes, while the double-bowl sinks help keep water in the sink area, and off the countertop, when moving the faucet between bowls.

Whichever style you choose, you can be sure it's as durable as it is beautiful. All of our Undermount Sinks are crafted from the highest quality 18-gauge stainless steel—hand buffed to an exclusive scratch-resistant Lasting Beauty finish.

Each sink has been carefully designed to fit tightly under any solid surface for a clean, integrated look. And because they're mounted neatly under the counter, they won't interrupt your kitchen's design—giving you more options for working with color.

ELU-3621

This beautiful design brings contemporary styling to the double-bowl collection. The larger bowl handles all your largest pots and pans, while the attached smaller bowl is perfect as a disposal area. And the rounded corners add flair to any kitchen design.

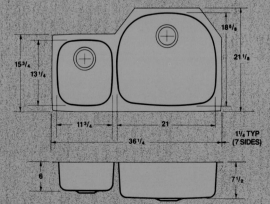

DIMENSIONS IN INCHES. TO CONVERT TO MILLIMETERS, MULTIPLY BY 25.4.

ELU-3118

Double your work space with the perfect combination of two large bowls. The double-bowl style lets you swing the faucet from bowl to bowl without splashing on the counter. And the durable stainless steel construction will stay beautiful through years of use.

ELU-3120

If extra capacity is what you need, this is the double-bowl design for you. The combination of one large and one extra-large bowl means you'll have plenty of room for even the largest kitchen cleanups. Plus the left bowl is extra-deep, to accommodate tall pots, vases, etc. And like all our sinks, it's crafted from durable, beautiful stainless steel.

ELU-2118

Add contemporary styling to extra-large capacity and you've got it all. This unique design offers ultrarounded corners to easily fit even the biggest of pots and pans. Pair it with any of the smaller components to create the ultimate kitchen work area.

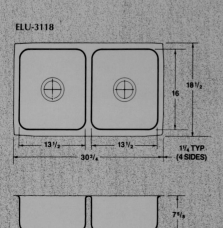

ELU-3118

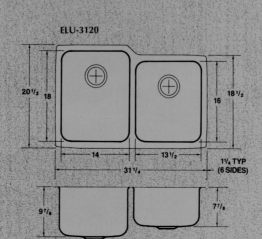

ELU-3120

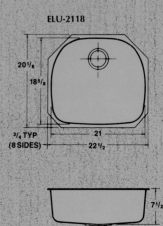

ELU-2118

ELU-2115

When it comes to big kitchen work, this sink can take whatever you dish out — featuring a spacious rectangular bowl and an offset drain. The longer width design fits perfectly in narrower countertops.

ELU-1618

This full-capacity sink, with its 9 1/2" deep bowl, features unique beveled back corners. And the heavy-duty 18-gauge steel construction helps make it as durable as it is functional. Choose a small companion sink for simple food preparation and cleanup.

ELU-1316

A versatile design, small enough to fit in tight spaces yet large enough to handle the big chores. Couple it with a larger sink for ultimate capacity.

ELU-2816

The longer width design of this sink with it's 7 1/2" deep bowl fits perfectly in narrower countertops.

ELU-1418

The added size makes handling larger pots and pans easy. Pair it with a smaller sink to enhance the food preparation area.

DIMENSIONS IN INCHES. TO CONVERT TO MILLIMETERS, MULTIPLY BY 25.4.

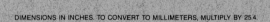

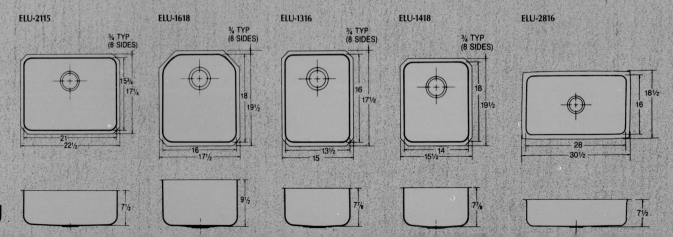

ELU-1113

Contemporary, sophisticated styling. Use it as a second sink, or pair it with a larger bowl for the kitchen area.

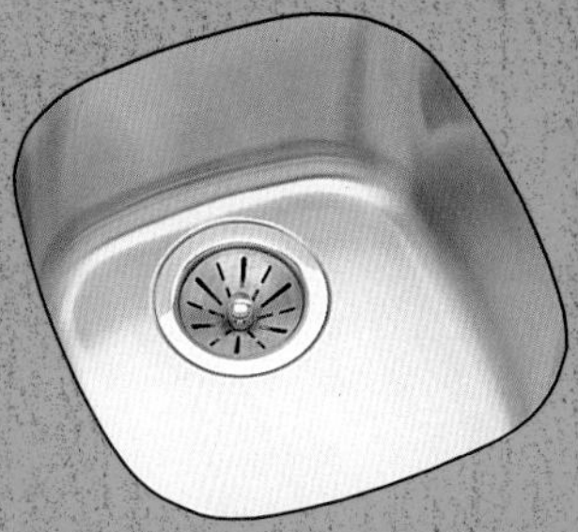

ELU-1111

This uniquely stylish design is ideal as a corner sink for the kitchen or bar. The hand-ground satin finish makes it scratch-resistant, to keep it looking showroom-new for years.

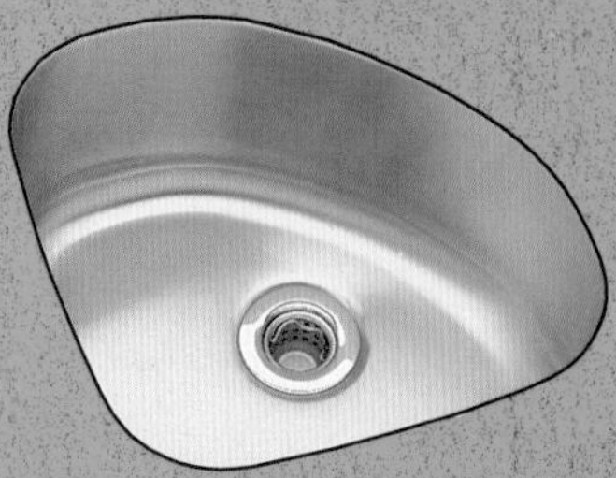

ELU-715

This handy utility sink is a perfect companion to a spacious main sink. Ideal for cleaning fruits and vegetables.

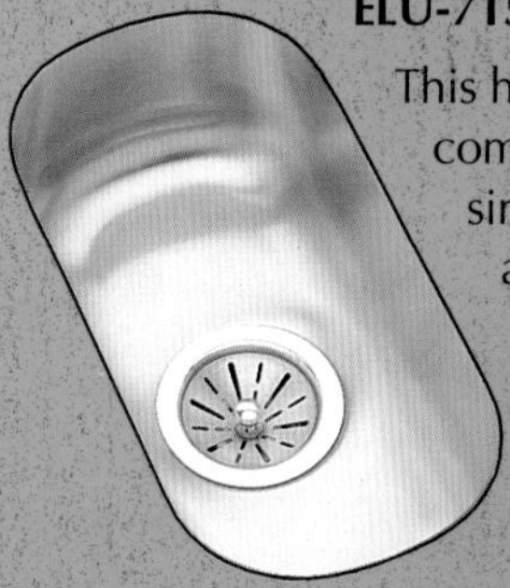

ELU-714

Perfect as a side sink to accompany a larger bowl. And, like all of Elkay's durable stainless designs, it will never chip, fade or crack.

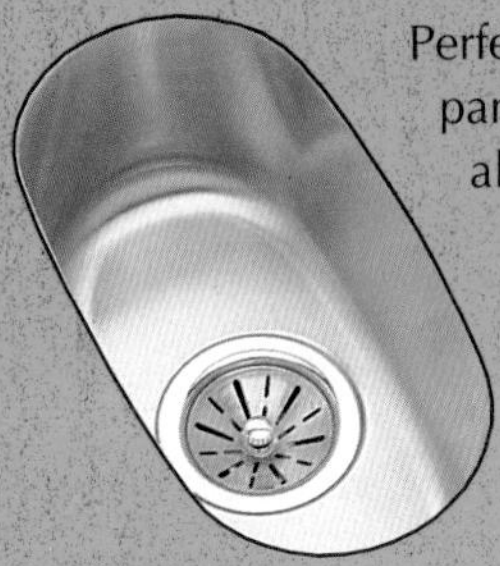

ELU-1511

Elegant in form, this oval design is perfect as a stand-alone for the bath. As always, the vibrant stainless steel reflects and enhances the color of its environment.

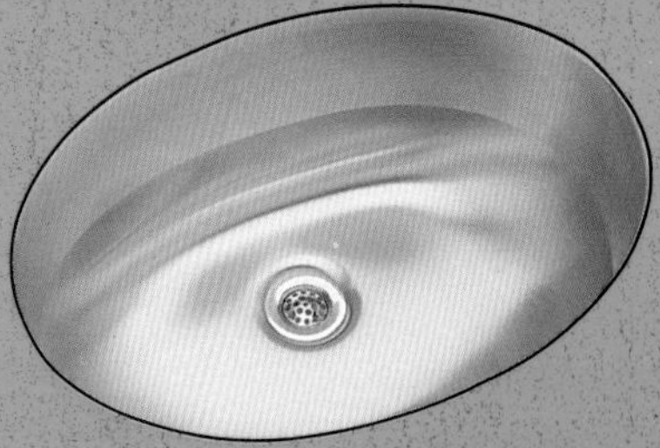

ELU-1113

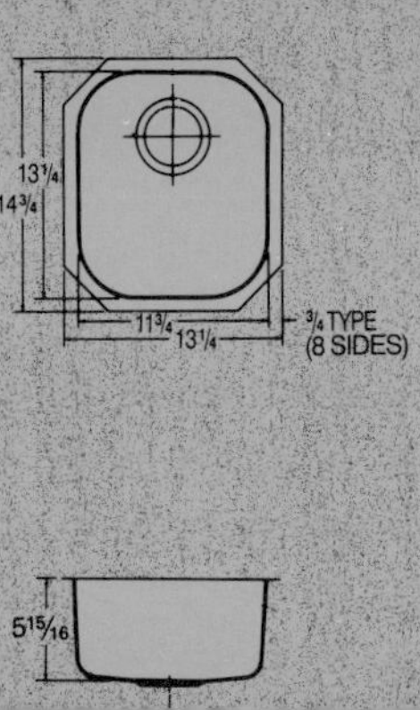

13¾
14¾
11¾
13¼
¾ TYPE (8 SIDES)
5¹⁵⁄₁₆

ELU-1111

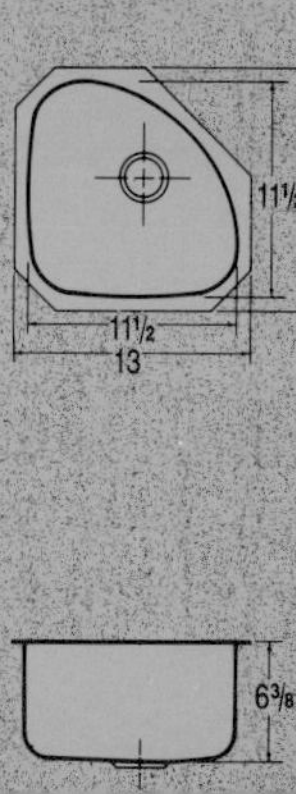

13
11½
11½
13
6⅜

ELU-715

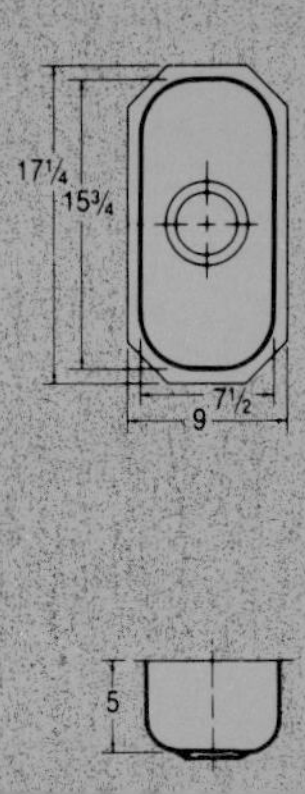

17¼
15¾
7½
9
5

ELU-714

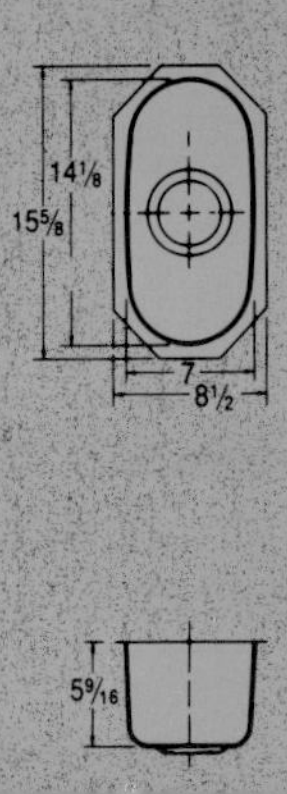

14⅛
15⅝
7
8½
5⁹⁄₁₆

ELU-1511

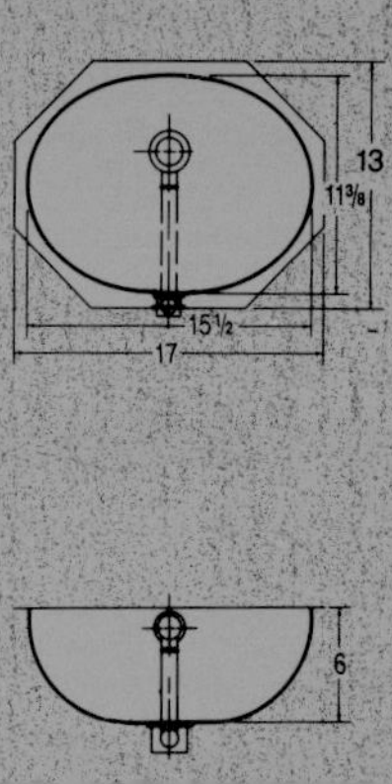

13
11⅜
15½
17
6

LUSTERTONE®

Deep, warm, classic tones. Elegant styling and a luxurious glow —that's Lustertone®. Polished to a deep patina, our Lustertone sinks reflect your own good taste. And, like all our high-quality 18-gauge stainless steel sinks, the Lustertone Collection resists scratching and won't chip, crack or peel.

From versatile triple-bowl sinks to double-bowl sinks that make work equally easy from either side, to single-bowl sinks with spacious bowls with straight sides, our Lustertone sinks will stand up to any culinary wizardry you may cook up. These sinks blend beautifully with any decor, are easy to clean and are built to last. With Elkay Lustertone, you can make a classic statement and bask in the glow of Lustertone.

LCR-4322

For doing so many different tasks, you need a sink with many different options — like this triple-bowl design from Elkay. Components separately: Sink (LCR-4322), Faucet (LK-4301-F), Soap/Lotion Dispenser (LK-313-CR).

LCR-4322

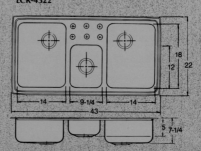

DIMENSIONS IN INCHES. TO CONVERT TO MILLIMETERS, MULTIPLY BY 25.4.

LR-3322

Overflow won't be a problem with this Elkay design, featuring a 7/16" drop-ledge and a raised faucet deck. Two large sink bowls offer all the room you need to clean and rinse dishes. Components separately: Sink (LR-3322), Faucet (LK-2433).

LMR-3322

Get double performance from this double-bowl sink. For cleaning and rinsing larger food items, use the right-side bowl. The bowl on the left is perfect for tasks that require less space, but easy access to water. Components separately: Sink (LMR-3322), Faucet (LK-4324-F-WH), Soap/Lotion Dispenser (LK-313-WH).

LR-250

These big bowls can accommodate any pot, pan, large roast or turkey with ease, making cleanup a snap. Components separately: Sink (LR-250), Faucet (LK-4391-F-AL), Soap/Lotion Dispenser (LK-313-AL).

LR-3322
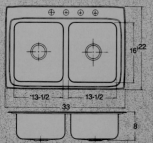

LMR-3322
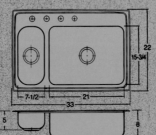

LR-250
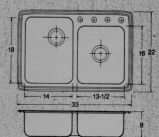

STLR-3322

Unlimited flexibility and efficient clean-up is available in this sink and tray combination of one regular and one deep bowl. Components separately: Sink (STLR-3322) and Faucet (LK-4124-F).

LCCR-3232

Now you can take full advantage of your kitchen work space — with Elkay's unique corner sink. Faucet with swivel aerator, soap dispenser and pop-up drain outlets complete the design and add to your cleaning ease. Components separately: Sink (LCCR-3232), Faucet (LK-4301-F), Soap/Lotion Dispenser (LK-313-CR), Pop-up Drain Outlet (LK-94).

LR-2522

This single-bowl design is large enough to handle the biggest tasks. The straight sides and tight-radius corners maximize bowl space. Components separately: Sink (LR-2522), Faucet (LK-4391-F-BK), Soap/Lotion Dispenser (LK-313-BK).

DIMENSIONS IN INCHES. TO CONVERT TO MILLIMETERS, MULTIPLY BY 25.4.

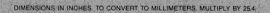

STLR-3322

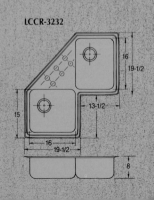

LCCR-3232

LR-2522

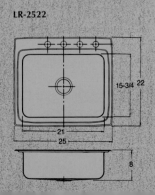

18

DLH-2222-10-C

This single-bowl sink really cleans up! Specially designed for laundry rooms and work areas, this Elkay model has a 10″ deep bowl but is also available with 12″ deep bowl (DLH-2522-12-C). Components separately: Sink (DLR-2222-10, 10″ deep bowl or DLR-2522-12, 12″ deep bowl), Faucet (LK-2432).

LH-1722-C

Here's another single-bowl sink that stands up to the toughest hospitality and gardening jobs. Shown here as a package with a 22″ wide bowl (LH-1722-C) with Faucet (LK-2432). This sturdy sink is also available with a 20″ wide bowl (LH-1720-C). Components separately: Sink (LR-1722 or LR-1720), Faucet (LK-2432).

DLH-2222-10-C

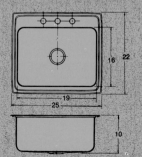

LH-1722-C

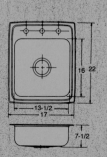

STARLITE™

Only Elkay's Starlite sink combines the lasting beauty and durability of CORIAN® * with the versatility of a top-mount design.

CORIAN is exceptionally strong and resilient. It cleans easily, resists chips, scratches, burns and stains, including coffee and tea. Starlite carries a 10-year guarantee against defects. CORIAN resists impacts that can dent, crack or shatter other surfaces.

Starlite opens nearly unlimited design possibilities. Available in Almond, Glacier White, and Cameo White, it offers a variety of new opportunities to highlight or contrast with any countertop color or material.

True functionality is built into both single- and double-bowl models. The 9″ deep bowls handle even the largest pots and pans. The ribbed area is handy for soap and detergent bottles. A raised rim keeps water in the sink and off the countertop.

Starlite can be installed quickly and easily where you'd use any top-mount sink. No special tools or techniques are required.

CORIAN is a product of DuPont.

ELC-3322-AL

Featuring a contemporary look, with smooth rounded lines, the Starlite sink has 9″ deep double bowls. It's a popular size for ease in replacement of existing kitchen sinks. Components separately: Sink (ELC-3322-AL), Faucet (LK-4324-F-AL), and Soap/Lotion Dispenser (LK-313-AL).

ELC-3322

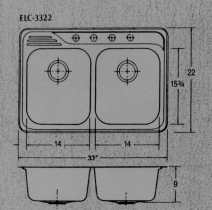

DIMENSIONS IN INCHES. TO CONVERT TO MILLIMETERS, MULTIPLY BY 25.4.

ELC-3322-GW

Beautiful styling is clear in every Starlite sink. Shown is the double bowl model in Glacier White. Components separately: Sink (ELC-3322-GW), Faucet (LK-4340-F-WH), Soap/Lotion Dispenser (LK-313-WH), Hot Water Machine (LKH-190-WH) and Aqua Chill Cold Water Dispenser (LK-2156-WH).

ELC-2522-CW

The remarkable material of CORIAN has been the choice of discriminating homeowners for countertops and vanities. Starlite is also available in a single bowl model in all three color choices. Components separately: Sink (ELC-2522-CW), Faucet (LK-4391-F-BK), and Hot Water Machine (LKH-190-BK).

Add more work space to your sink with a CORIAN work surface, available in matching colors: Almond (CBC-1714-AL); Cameo White (CBC-1714-CW); and Glacier White (CBC-1714-GW). Fits both the single and double bowl sinks.

Starlite Colors

Almond   **Cameo White**   **Glacier White**

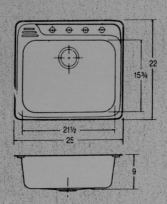

22
15¾
21½
25
9

HOSPITALITY

When it's your turn to relax, or to throw the party of the year, who better to turn to than Elkay to assist you with all your entertaining needs. And, because Elkay stainless steel coordinates so beautifully with any decor, it never looks out of place. Even if you change your decor, you never have to change your sink. And Elkay's Hospitality Collection sinks are specially crafted to make you feel comfortable while you entertain...with extra-deep bowls, far-reaching Hi-Arc faucets, handy swing spouts and compact design. Make sure one of our Hospitality sinks gets invited to your next party.

BILGR-2115-L

Add polish to your bar area with our Contemporary Gourmet bar sink and Brass-finish faucet. Available with sink bowl on the right or left, it features 7 3/4" ribbed area for food preparation. Components separately: Sink (BILGR-2115-L or R), Polished Brass Faucet (LK-2088-13-D), Strainer (LK-36).

BILGR-2115-L

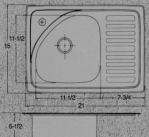

DIMENSIONS IN INCHES. TO CONVERT TO MILLIMETERS, MULTIPLY BY 25.4.

BLGR-1515

This compact Contemporary Gourmet sink can make any entertainment area much more inviting. Components separately: Sink (BLGR-1515), Faucet (LK-2223), Strainer (LK-36).

BLR-150-C

This Hospitality sink package features a Hi-Arc bar faucet with two solid brass wing handles and strainer. Faucet height: 12 3/8". Components separately: Sink (BLR-15-1), Faucet (LK-2223), Strainer (LK-36).

BLH-15-C

Choose this elegant Hospitality sink package with Hi-Arc faucet for contemporary styling. Shown here with Crystalac handles and strainer. Components separately: Sink (BLR-15-3), Faucet (LKA-2438), Strainer (LK-36).

BLGR-1515 **BLR-150-C** **BLH-15-C**

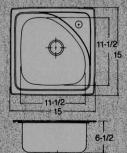
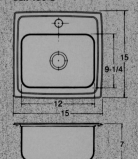
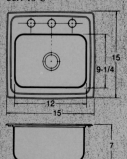

BPSH-15-C

This gleaming sink shown here as a package, is complemented by our Hi-Arc faucet with traditional spout styling, sparkling Crystalac handles and strainer. Components separately: Sink (BPSR-15-3), Faucet (LKA-2437), Strainer (LK-36).

BPSRA-150-C

Another brilliant sink from Elkay! Shown here as a package with our 8" Hi-Arc faucet bar, two forged brass wing handles and strainer. Components separately: Sink (BPSR-15-1), Faucet (LK-2088-8), Strainer (LK-36).

BCRA-150-C

One of our most efficient sinks…shown here as a package, with Elkay's deluxe faucet and decorative Crystalac handles. Components separately: Sink (BCR-15-2), Faucet (LKA-2479-8), Strainer (LK-58).

NGT-2022

The Nouveau Gourmet Single Bowl design has traditional style but an untraditional size for optimum function in entertainment and kitchen areas. Shown with deluxe two-handle deck mount faucet and Soap/Lotion Dispenser. Components separately: Sink (NGT-2022-2), Faucet (LK-2223), Soap/Lotion Dispenser (LK-313-CR).

DIMENSIONS IN INCHES. TO CONVERT TO MILLIMETERS, MULTIPLY BY 25.4.

BPSH-15-C

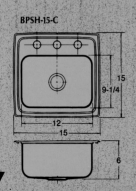

15
9-1/4
12
15
6

BPSRA-150-C

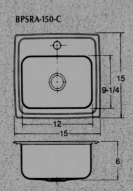

15
9-1/4
12
15
6

BCRA-150-C

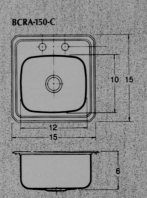

10 15
12
15
6

NGT-2022

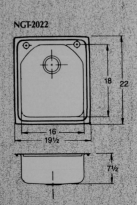

18 22
16
19½
7½

F A U C E T S

Elkay offers you three superb choices: the elegant Regency Collection, the colorful Hi-Arc Collection, and the Decorator Faucet Collection.

The Regency Collection, in polished chrome or colored epoxy, combines exclusive detailing with advanced technology. The Regency Pull-Out features an innovative pull-out spray and single-lever design.

The Hi-Arc Collection blends color and functionality. With it's 10" reach and 9" height, the Hi-Arc faucet makes it easy to fill large pots or vases. And you can select from four distinctive designer colors.

REGENCY PULL-OUT

Elegant lines and graceful design combine to make the Regency Pull-Out faucet. The single-lever design gives you a full temperature range with the touch of a finger. Regency Pull-Out faucets are available in a full range of decorative colors including solid White, Almond and Black, or White, Almond and Black with Brass accents, or Chrome with Black accents. Or choose Chrome with an Almond, Black or White Spray head.

LK-4350-F-AL*

LK-4350-F-BK*

LK-4350-F-CR*

LK-4350-F-WH*

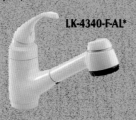

LK-4340-F-AL*

LK-4340-F-BK*

LK-4340-F-CR*

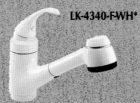

LK-4340-F-WH*

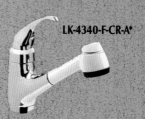

LK-4340-F-CR-A*

LK-4340-F-CR-W*

*Feature water saving flow restrictor: 2.5 gallons per minute (G.P.M.) or 9.5 liters per minute (L/min) at 80 psig supply pressure.

REGENCY SINGLE-LEVER

Sophisticated and distinctive, our Regency Collection of faucets features a selection of colors and accents. Faucet shown here, Glossy Black with Brass accents, may also be ordered in White, Almond or Chrome with Brass accents.

LK-4381-F-BK*

LK-4381-F-CR*

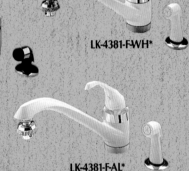

LK-4381-F-WH*

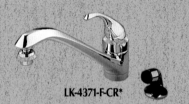

LK-4381-F-AL*

REGENCY SINGLE-LEVER

Another fine faucet from our Regency Collection, this time in White epoxy. As with all our Regency faucets, this comes in a variety of solid color options with a 10" cast-brass swing spout. May also be ordered with or without a handy spray hose.

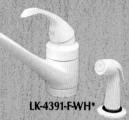

LK-4391-F-WH*

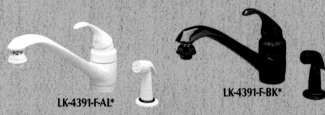

LK-4391-F-AL*

LK-4391-F-BK*

LK-4371-F-CR*

HI-ARC SINGLE-LEVER

Cleaning big kitchen items is easy with this faucet's 10" reach and 9" height. Hi-Arc single-lever faucet shown in Black. Also available in White, Almond and Brass.

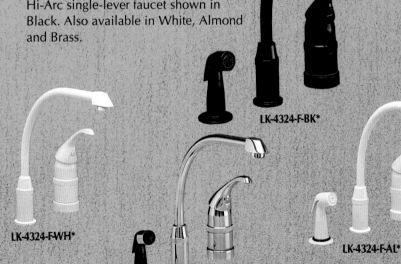

LK-4324-F-BK*

LK-4324-F-WH*

LK-4324-F-D*

LK-4324-F-AL*

26

DECORATOR SINGLE-LEVER

Yet another fine faucet from Elkay. Choose from a variety of solid color options, with an 8" swing spout which can be ordered with or without a handy spray hose.

LK-4161-AL*

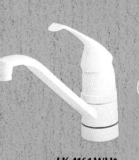

LK-4161-BK*

LK-4161-WH*

LK-4161*

HI-ARC SINGLE-LEVER

This Hi-Arc single-lever faucet has added convenience with a swivel aerator and retractable spray and hose.

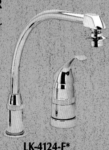

LK-4124-F*

HI-ARC TWO-HANDLE

Easy to clean and use, this attractive faucet features chrome metal wing handles and a handy swing spout with an extended 10" reach. Available with our hose/spray option (LK-2453) or without hose/spray (LK-2452).

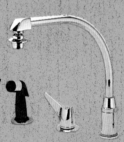

LK-2453*

DELUXE SINGLE-LEVER POST MOUNT

Our deluxe Post Mount features a 9" reach, swing spout, swivel aerator and hose/spray to make your kitchen chores easier. The single-lever faucet provides volume and water temperature control at your fingertips.

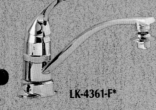

LK-4361-F*

HI-ARC TWO-HANDLE

With its contemporary spout styling and 10" height, Elkay's Hi-Arc kitchen faucet adds efficiency to your space. Filling larger pots, vases and pitchers is a snap! Wing handles complement its sleek design.

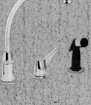

LK-2433*

27

*Feature water saving flow restrictor: 2.5 gallons per minute (G.P.M.) or 9.5 liters per minute (L/min) at 80 psig supply pressure.

ACCESSORIES

Details, details...it's all in the details. And with these fine Elkay accessories you'll give your kitchen that final touch of class right down to the details, while making food preparation and cleanup virtually effortless! With our handy Hot Water Machine™ and Aqua Chill®, and our useful cutting boards, drain trays, colanders, rinsing baskets, soap/lotion dispensers and strainers, you'll look forward to working in the kitchen, and your kitchen will have that final polished look.

HOT WATER MACHINE AND AQUA CHILL

The convenience of instant hot or refreshing chilled water is now available in decorator colors and features our No-Lead design. With waterway systems designed to be completely free of lead-containing materials, the LKH-180, LKH-190 and LK-2156 dispensers ensure you that no lead is being added to your drinking water. Our Hot Water Machine heats water to 190°F for hot drinks, soups or gelatins, while our Aqua Chill refrigerates water to 40°F for fast refreshment. Order both the dispenser (LK-2156) and chiller ERS-1 for the Aqua Chill.

LKH-190-AL†/LK-2156-AL††

LKH-180†/LK-2156††

LKH-190-BK†/LK-2156-BK††

LKH-190-WH†/LK-2156-WH††

† Flow Rate - 1.0 gallons per minute (G.P.M.) or 3.8 liters per minute (L/min) at 80 psig supply pressure.
†† Flow Rate - 1.6 gallons per minute (G.P.M.) or 6.3 liters per minute (L/min) at 80 psig supply pressure.

COLANDER

If you own an Elkay Contemporary Gourmet sink, this colander is a must! It's great for straining, draining or storing vegetables and fruits. Available in White (SC-1407-WH) and Almond (SC-1407-AL). Fits models LCGR-3322 and ILCGR-4822.

COLANDER

This colander fits our larger Contemporary Gourmet sinks for those with larger kitchen tasks. Available in White (LC-1412-WH) or Almond (LC-1412-AL). Fits LCGR-3822 and ILCGR-5322 models.

DRAIN TRAY

For our Elkay Contemporary Gourmet sink, make sure you own an Elkay drain tray, too. Perfect for rinsing and draining, it actually expands your counter work surface. Comes in two ever-popular colors: White (DT-2215-WH) and Almond (DT-2215-AL).

RINSING BASKET/TEAK CUTTING BOARD

With these special Elkay accessories, kitchen work becomes much more pleasurable. Our bright White, top-fitting rinsing basket measures 17 3/4" x 15 3/4" x 3 1/2". Simply order VB-1816. Our specially designed teak cutting board fits over the larger bowls of our Gourmet sinks and brings unique style and efficiency to your kitchen work area. Choose from two popular sizes: our large 17" x 13 1/2" model (CBT-1713) or our smaller 16 3/4" x 13 1/2" model (CBT-1613). Order rinsing basket and teak cutting board with all Traditional Gourmet sinks except ILFGR and LFGR models.

RINSING BASKET

Durable and roomy, this vinyl-covered rinsing basket fits our Contemporary Gourmet sinks and is ideal for draining dishes or other items. It features a removable plate rack as well. Available in White (DB-1420-W) or Almond (DB-1420-A), it measures 14" x 20" x 4 5/8".

TEAK CUTTING BOARD

This carefully crafted teak cutting board adds natural beauty to your work area and is designed to fit over the large bowl of our Contemporary Gourmet sinks. It measures 22″×13″ (CBT-2213).

CUTTING SURFACE

Standard with every Gourmet Cuisine Centré, our custom designed cutting surface fits neatly into the Centre's ribbed area. The cutting surface is 11″ × 16 1/2″ and fits right- or left-side sinks (CBP-1116). Or choose our optional counter-top cutting surface, shown here. It measures 13″×19″ and fits flush with our Gourmet Cuisine Centré and your countertop. (Model CBP-1319-L fits EGPI-4322-L; CBP-1319-R fits EGPI-4322-R.) Both cutting surfaces are made from the same tough high-density polymer.

STRAINERS

Specially designed as a fashionable finish to your Elkay sink: our newest strainers. We offer spicy colors to suit your personal tastes—White (LK-35-WH), Almond (LK-35-AL), Black (LK-35-BK), Gray (LK-35-GR), or Chrome (LK-35).

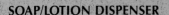

STARLITE WORK SURFACE

Add work space to your countertop with the handy Starlite Work Surface, made with the same CORIAN material as the Starlite sinks. The work surface—measuring 17 1/4″ ×14 1/2″×1/2″—is available in matching colors— Almond (CBC-1714-AL), Cameo White (CBC-1714-CW), and Glacier White (CBC-1714-GW).

SOAP/LOTION DISPENSER

Creatively designed as an attractive complement to your sink area, our soap and lotion dispensers are always there when you need them. Choose from Chrome (LK-313-CR), White (LK-313-WH), Almond (LK-313-AL) and Black (LK-313-BK).

POP-UP DRAIN OUTLET

Elkay's remote-control drain outlets (LK-94) allow you to empty the sink bowls without putting your hands in the water. Fits 3 1/2″ opening; 4 1/2″ top diameter. Be sure to order extra drilling hole on sink ledge.

SINK SPECIFICATIONS

	MODEL NUMBER	MINIMUM CABINET SIZE	HOLE DRILLINGS
TRADITIONAL	EGPI-4322 — L or R	48"*	1, 3 or 4
	ILGR-6022 L-C or R-C	48"	3 (package)
	ILGR-6022 — L or R	48"	3 or 4
	LGR-4322-C	48"	3 (package)
	LGR-4322	48"	4
	ILFGR-5422 — L or R	42"	3 or 4
	ILGR-5422 — L or R	42"	3 or 4
	ILFGR-4822 — L or R	36"	3 or 4
	ILGR-4822 — L or R	36"	3 or 4
	LFGR-3722	42"	3
	LGR-3722	42"	3 or 4
	LFGR-3322	36"	3
	LGR-3322	36"	3 or 4
	ILGR-4322 — L or R	30"	3 or 4
CONTEMPORARY	ILCGR-5322 — L or R	42"	1, 3 or 4
	LCGR-3822 — L or R	42"	1, 3 or 4
	ILCGR-4822 — L or R	36"	1, 3 or 4
	LCGR-3322 — L or R	36"	1, 3 or 4
	ILCGR-4022 — L or R	30"	1 or 2
	LCGR-2522	30"	1 or 2
NOUVEAU GOURMET	NG-3322	36"	1, 2 or 3
	NG-3722	42"	1 or 2
	NGA-3322	36"	1, 2 or 3
	NGR-4822-L	36"	1, 2, 3 or 4
UNDERMOUNT	ELU-714	24"	
	ELU-715	24"	
	ELU-1111	24"	
	ELU-1113	24"	NOTE: Undermount cabinet sizes are based on stand alone individual models. If models are combined or faucet/accessories are placed at side locations, larger minimum cabinet sizes will be required.
	ELU-1316	24"	
	ELU-1418	24"	
	ELU-1511	24"	
	ELU-1618	24"	
	ELU-2115	30"	See Undermount section for sink size specifications, p. 12-15.
	ELU-2118	30"	
	ELU-2816	36"	
	ELU-3118	36"	
	ELU-3120	36"	
	ELU-3621	42"	
LUSTERTONE	LCR-4322	48"	6
	LR-3322	36"	3 or 4
	LMR-3322	36"	3 or 4
	LR-250	36"	3 or 4
	STLR-3322	36"	1, 2 or 3
	LCCR-3232	36"	4
	LR-2522	30"	3 or 4
	DLH-2222-10-C/DLH-2522-12-C	30"	3 (package)
	LH-1720/1722-C	30"	3 (package)
STARLITE	ELC-3322-AL	36"	0, 3 or 4
	ELC-3322-CW	36"	0, 3 or 4
	ELC-3322-GW	36"	0, 3 or 4
	ELC-2522-AL	30"	0, 3 or 4
	ELC-2522-CW	30"	0, 3 or 4
	ELC-2522-GW	30"	0, 3 or 4
HOSPITALITY	BILGR-2115 — L or R	24"	1
	BLGR-1515	24"	1
	BLR-150-C	24"	1 (package)
	BLH-15-C	24"	3 (package)
	BPSH-15-C	24"	3 (package)
	BPSRA-150-C	24"	1 (package)
	BCRA-150-C	24"	2 (package)
	NGT-2022	24"	1 or 2

*Can be installed in 30" cabinet with modifications to adjoining cabinet.

Elkay Manufacturing Company
2222 Camden Court
Oak Brook, Illinois 60521
708.574.8484
(After August 3, 1996, area code will be 630.)

The Beauty
Runs Deep In Every
Elkay Stainless Steel Sink.

ELKAY®
A Tradition of Quality
75th ANNIVERSARY 1920-1995

Introducing The Nouveau Gourmet™ Sinks.

A Beautiful Blend of Quality and Style — at a value price.

We're celebrating our 75th anniversary the best way we know. With an elegant new collection of sinks to complement our Traditional and Contemporary Gourmet Series.

Tough 20-gauge stainless steel — with the Elkay quality touch.

Now you can order Elkay sinks in durable 20-gauge stainless steel that offers high quality.

It's the Nouveau Gourmet line of sinks crafted and polished to a brilliant, lasting finish that won't stain, fade or rust.

Nouveau Gourmet sinks clean easily, yet keep their sheen. They won't chip or crack, and have a little extra "give" to reduce dish chipping and breakage. Underside insulation helps reduce sink sound.

A sink for every kitchen design.

Nouveau Gourmet sinks offer all the design versatility of our other sink lines, which are preferred by architects, remodelers and homeowners alike.

Only stainless steel offers all these unique benefits:	
Won't stain, rust or fade	✓
Cleans easily to a brilliant luster	✓
Won't chip, crack or dent	✓
"Gives" to resist dish chipping	✓
Undercoating reduces sink noise and prevents condensation	✓

The Nouveau Gourmet Model NG-2522.

The Nouveau Gourmet Model NG-3322.

The Nouveau Gourmet Model NGR-4822L.

NG-3322 — Our Diamond Jubilee design combines Euro styling with common sense function at a reasonable price.

NG-3722 — Symmetrical, contemporary design optimizes appearance and maximizes space use.

NGA-3322 — Traditional styling, using two different, but complementary bowl designs.

NGA-3722 — Spacious and appealing. Designed to accommodate the extra capacity needed for large pots and pans.

NGT-3722 — Traditional design with spacious twin bowls. Extra wide compartments provide additional capacity.

NG-2522 — Contemporary design uses minimum space, but maximizes function.

NG-2022 — Ideal for hospitality areas, or as a second kitchen sink.

NGT-2022 — Single bowl design has traditional style, but an untraditional size for optimum function in entertainment and kitchen areas.

NGR-4822L — Traditional style bowls with a ribbed work surface.

Bar Sink To Food Prep Center. A Complete Line.

With so many Nouveau Gourmet choices, you're sure to find the sink configuration to fit your kitchen and entertainment area planning.

You'll find nine designs, from handy 20" bar sinks to an elegant 48" double bowl model with ribbed work surface. That's an exceptionally wide selection for even the most discriminating buyers.

Nouveau Gourmet. Elkay's reputation for quality, style, value and innovation shines through as bright as ever. Visit your Elkay dealer/distributor today.

NOUVEAU GOURMET SINK CHART

Model Number	Over All		Inside Each Bowl						Number Faucet Holes
			Left			Right			
	L	W	L	W	D	L	W	D	
NG-3322	33	22	11 1/2	15	7 1/2	16	17 1/2	7 1/2	1, 2 & 3
NG-3722	37	22	16	17 1/2	7 1/2	16	17 1/2	7 1/2	1 & 2
NGA-3322	33	22	11 1/2	16	7 1/2	16	18	7 1/2	1, 2 & 3
NGA-3722	37	22	16	16	7 1/2	16	18	7 1/2	1, 2 & 3
NGT-3722	37	22	16	18	7 1/2	16	18	7 1/2	1 & 2
NG-2522	25	22	21	18 5/8	7 1/2	-	-	-	1 & 2
NG-2022	19 1/2	22	16	17 1/2	7 1/2	-	-	-	1 & 2
NGT-2022	19 1/2	22	16	18	7 1/2	-	-	-	1 & 2
NGR-4822L	48	22	14	18	7 1/2	13 1/2	16	7 1/2	1, 2, 3 & 4

Dimensions in inches. Length (L) is left to right. Width (W) is front to back.

ELKAY MANUFACTURING COMPANY
2222 Camden Ct.
Oak Brook, IL 60521
Phone 708/574-8484
Fax 708/574-5012
© 1995 Elkay Manufacturing Company
Printed in USA
F-2815 (4/95)

just say

Introducing Starlite™

Only Elkay combines the lasting beauty and durability of CORIAN® with the versatility of a top-mount design.

Now, Elkay brings the rich enduring elegance of CORIAN® to the heart of the kitchen: the sink.

This remarkable material is a patented blend of natural minerals and pure acrylic resin. For years, its been the choice of discriminating homeowners for countertops and vanities.

Beauty with built-in strength.
CORIAN is exceptionally strong and resilient. It cleans easily, resists chips, scratches, burns and stains, including coffee and tea. We're so confident of its durability, we've given our new Starlite™ sinks a 10-year warranty.

A color and style for every kitchen.
The Starlite™ opens nearly unlimited design possibilities. Available in Almond, Glacier White, and Cameo White, it offers a variety of new opportunities to highlight or contrast with any countertop color or material.

True functionality is built into both single- and double- bowl models. The 9" deep bowls handle even the largest pots and pans. The ribbed area is handy for soaps and detergent bottles. A raised rim keeps water in the sink and off the countertop. And of course, Starlite™ will accommodate any Elkay faucet, plus accessories.

The Starlite™ can be installed quickly and easily where you'd use any top-mount sink. No special tools or techniques are required.

CORIAN® surfaces offer these exclusive benefits:	
Resists chips, scratches, burns, cuts	✓
Won't crack, bend, or dent	✓
Resists coffee, tea and fruit stains	✓
Cleans easily	✓
10-year warranty	✓

Starlite™ double bowl sink shown in Almond.

Glacier White

Cameo White

Almond

Starlite™ single bowl sink shown in Cameo White.

Design And Technology Only From Elkay.

Beautiful styling is clear in every sink we build. From classic to contemporary, these are the sinks that bring fresh individuality to any kitchen.

But CORIAN,® like stainless steel, requires far more than the stylist's skill. Our experienced designers teamed up with specialists from CORIAN® in materials and manufacturing technology to create this industry first for Elkay.

One glance at our new Starlite™ sinks and you'll agree we've reached a beautiful balance of art and science.

Starlite™ Single Bowl,
Model ELC-2522

Starlite™ Double Bowl,
Model ELC-3322

Starlite™ Sinks

Model Number	Over All		Inside Each Bowl			Number Faucet Holes
	L	W	L	W	D	
ELC-2522	25	22	21 1/2	15 3/4	9	0, 3 & 4
ELC-3322	33	22	14	15 3/4	9	0, 3 & 4

Dimensions in inches. Length (L) is left to right. Width (W) is front to back.

Add versatility with a CORIAN® work surface available in matching colors.
Size: 17 1/4 x 14 1/2 x 1/2"
Model CBC-1714

CORIAN is a registered trademark of E.I. duPont de Nemours and Company.
© 1995 Elkay Manufacturing Company
Printed in USA.

ELKAY MANUFACTURING COMPANY
2222 Camden Ct.
Oak Brook, IL 60521
Phone 708/574-8484
Fax 708/574-5012

F-2814 (4/95)

just say **ELKAY**®

■ Technology   ■ Quality   ■ Design

■■■ Contents

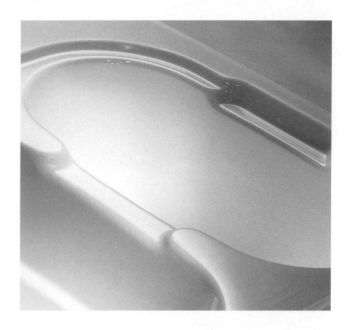

■■■ It's Almost Like Being in Love

■■■ At the heart of your home is your kitchen. It's estimated that one spends 75% of kitchen time at or near the sink. <u>That</u> is a lot of togetherness. Your sink choice should not be an afterthought.

■■■ Franke appreciates how much time you spend with your sink, and we understand that taste and work patterns are very personal. That's why we offer so many carefully considered options, from materials to styles and colors, faucets to accessories.

■■■ Your sink will lead a busy life. That's the reason to buy the best. Franke selects materials for beauty and reliable performance, because a good relationship is built on a solid foundation.

■■■ Stainless Steel
Franke uses only heavy-gauge type 304 stainless with the industry's highest percentages of chromium (18%) and nickel (10%) for a deep rich glow and corrosion resistance. Our shine and flawless finish have never been duplicated. A lifetime investment, Franke stainless improves with use, developing a patina like fine sterling silver.

■■■ Quartz Composite
No ordinary material, this. Innovative technology produces a durable, practical sink composed of 66% quartz, nature's hardest common mineral, bonded in a resin composite. Its color is clear through with no surface coating to chip or peel. It will please you for years with warm, neutral color and functional sculptural detail.

■■■ Franke Granite™
is a harmonious blend of strength and beauty with the enduring characteristics of stone. Composed of 75% fired granite in a resin composite, it easily withstands the toughest everyday wear and resists stains, scratches, and chips. It is a superior sink material in subtle unpolished natural tones.

■■■ Select your material, then choose a design that suits your work pattern and kitchen layout. Finish your system with your choice of faucet styles, lotion and water dispensers, filtration systems, and waste disposers. Add custom-fitted, color-coordinated accessory options for the perfect union of style and function.

■■■ You'll see it all, and how it works, in this book. To really fall in love, see the Franke product line in person at your nearest kitchen professional. It could be the start of something beautiful. Soon, you'll wonder…

■■■ What Would I Do Without My Franke?

PRX 110-21 and CP 110

ER 110

■■■ A sink should be fun. Really. Franke Elements® are wonderful shapes that mount beneath granite, marble, or man-made solid surfaces, alone, in pairs, or in any combination. You're the designer, so your sink will fit your work style perfectly... and look great too, because there's more to life than work, work, work.

■■■ Details, pp. 32-35.

Elements photographed in Avonite.®

4

■■■ Opposite: A favorite Franke design in undermount components. You might opt for two large bowls or the smaller compartment placed on the left. The beauty of Elements is flexibility. Opposite below: Salad sink, large enough for kitchen chores, elegant enough for a bar.

■■■ Right: Two complementary shapes cleverly undermounted with a fabricated water spill. Elements are meticulously manufactured for perfect fit to the countertop without hard-to-clean gaps.

■■■ **A Franke Feature:** Because they are individual components, Elements allow complete freedom of faucet and accessory placement on the countertop.

RG 110 and CP 110

PR 110-7 and NA 110

■■■ Stainless Elements® Components

Two RG 110s

■■■ Above: Smaller Elements fit when space is limited. There are sizes and shapes for any kitchen layout, any cabinetry style.

■■■ The distinctive Franke finish reflects the colorful rays of your kitchen decor. And, like the best of us, stainless improves with age. Right: Two deep and roomy rectangular Elements paired.

5

■■■ The creative fun of Franke Elements® includes custom-fitted sink accessories that can merge your sink and countertop into a perfect prep and clean-up center. Left: Stainless colander fits into countertop, as will cutting board.

■■■ Details, pp. 32-35.

AR 110-6 and AR 110-14

■■■ Double Undermounts

■■■ We've made two of Franke's most popular Prestige™ sink designs into undermounts. They are created to mount flush with the underside of the countertop for a precise fit without gaps.

PRX 160

PRQ 120

■■■ Choose double undermount models with either of two right-hand compartment sizes. Stainless steel or quartz composite, white, biscuit, or black. Stainless models are also available with small compartment on left.

■■■ Details, pp. 32-35.

RGQ 110-13 and PRQ 110

■■■ Color Elements®

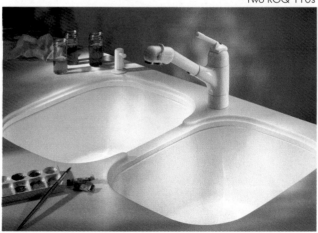

Two RGQ 110s

■■■ Picture Elements in color. Choose from a collection of undermount Elements to mix, pair, or use alone, in pure white, biscuit, or dramatic black.

■■■ We know a sink is seldom a "still life." That's why Franke color components are durable, chip- and stain-resistant quartz composite. You will appreciate your composition for many years to come.

■■■ Details, pp. 33-35.

Patent pending.

PRX 660

■■■ Prestige™ Stainless

■■■ Only Franke can form stainless steel with a sculptured shelf. Above, our new enhanced **Prestige Plus™** that can suspend a grid drainer across the main compartment for a contemporary approach to food prep, rinsing, and draining. The grand compartment has been deepened so that submerging a roaster or filling a tall pan is easier than ever.

■■■ A Franke Feature: Accessory options, left, add to the joy of cooking. Above: grid drainer raises work surface; coated-chrome prevents scratching. See pp. 30-35.

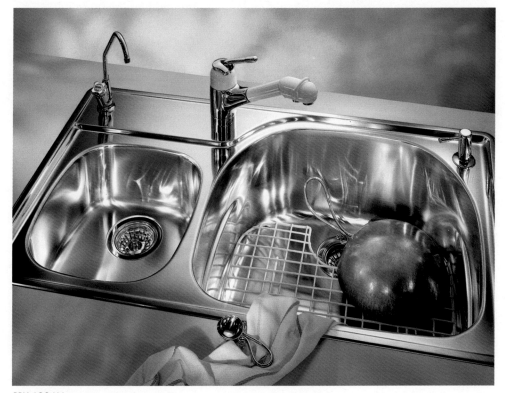

■■■ Left: The functional **Prestige Plus**™ bowl with large side compartment makes it simple to do several things at once. A waste disposer may be placed in either compartment. Accessory options make it easy to clean up as you progress through meal preparation.

PRX 620 LH

PR 660

■■■ Below: The **Prestige Plus**™ single bowl does a big job. Franke sinks feature flat bottoms and rear drains to give you more room for stacking dishes, and also more under-sink cabinet space since plumbing is at the back.

PRX 610

■■■ Above: **Prestige Classic**,™ the original Franke design that changed the look of kitchen sinks, is still available. The large sink compartment, with straight sides and standard depth, may be accessorized with a footed custom-fitted grid drainer for the bottom of the sink as well as a complete array of work- and time-saving options.

■■■ Details, pp. 33-35.

PRQ 620

■■■Prestige Color™

PRQ 660

■■■ Dinner at 8:00. It's 7:30. Take-out won't tempt when Franke's great styling and time-saving accessories ease you into a fresh, quickly prepared meal. Models feature the grand size and shape of Prestige, plus delicious color. White, biscuit, or black.

■■■ **A Franke Feature:** Our color material is bonded quartz. Unlike traditional color materials, it can be formed with functional sculptural details like a shelf for the optional grid drainer and the matte skid-free bottom, shaped for easy draining.

■■■ Right: A single-bowl Prestige Color™ can be a complete food-prep center. Sculpted hand recesses make it easy to place and remove accessories.

■■■ Details, pp. 33-35.

PRQ 610

■■■ Regatta Color™

RGQ 620

■■■ Right: The practical, warm look of bonded quartz in Regatta™ styling. Rounded corners for a contemporary look and two compartments for great work space. The wide deck accepts color-coordinated accessories. White, biscuit, or black.

■■■ Details, pp. 32-35.

PRG 660

■■■ Franke Granite™

■■■ This material takes a beating and is fearless in the face of food processor blades or hot skillets. Forgive the pun, but you can really take these sinks for granite. Formed of fired granite in a resin composite, no matter what crashes or clatters into it, under normal kitchen conditions, it does not chip, scratch, or stain. Above in classic Prestige™ styling.

■■■ Four subtle, unpolished natural tones enhance decors, from rustic country to bold contemporary, in any counter-top surface.

■■■ Details, pp. 32-35.

Iceberg

Sand

Boulder

Flint

■■■ Right: A Franke Granite™ triple compartment is a durable, practical assistant for any project. Two deep compartments plus a large center, in Artisan™ design, will hold a full complement of Franke accessories for additional convenience. There's nothing like it when several tasks are going at once. (Model not available in Sand.)

■■■ **A Franke Feature:** Sinks, faucets, and drain baskets can be color coordinated or contrasted.

ARG 670

RTG 110

■■■ Left: A Franke Granite Rotondo® as a second sink fields flying utensils and helps keep the mess contained as you work. The main sink stays free for larger tasks. Franke sprayer faucets can be easily reconfigured for use with small bowls (pictured).

13

■■■ **Nobel**®

■■■ Above: A great family sink. Two large compartments and a wide deck for accessory options. Deck accessories, below left to right, dispense hot, and chilled or filtered water, empty the bowl from the sink deck, and dispense soap or lotion without messy bottles. Add a versatile Franke faucet with pull-out sprayer for everyone's convenience.

■■■ Sink details, p. 33. Faucet and accessories, pp. 22-35.

NA 660

■■■ Left: This Nobel® model has compartments of two ample sizes. The deck is designed for accessories. Here, Value Line™ pull-out faucet and Uniflow™ System.

■■■ **A Franke Feature:** Filtered water is available at the sink where it is most convenient, either with individual taps or, below, incorporated into our Triflow® faucet system. See pp. 24-25.

RG 620

■■■ Regatta™

■■■ When the little squirts take off, the mess is easy to fix. Regatta™ features two large bowls, plus a deep drop-ledge that helps contain water. Pop-up waste strainer releases water from the deck. And, water play won't use up Franke's Triflow water filter because it's operated by a separate handle on the faucet.

AR 670

■■■ The Artisan™ Collection

■■■ In the still of the night or the hustle of a hectic day, your sink should be there for you. An Artisan sink is an extra pair of hands. Above: A full triple model with large, deep bowls washes, rinses, drains at one time with the assistance of the optional colander and drain basket. Artisan model shown above is also available in Franke Granite.™

■■■ **A Franke Feature:** Artisan models may be fitted with semi-professional stainless steel accessories or with Franke color accessories.

■■■ Details, pp. 32-35.

■■■ A most luxurious Artisan™ design. Inevitably, there will be days when you will especially appreciate its large center compartment as well as its practical main bowls. A busy kitchen requires a capable sink.

AR 630

AR 621 RH

■■■ No matter what your kitchen layout, it's always hard to find a place to land a hot pot. The drainboard, left, gives you the perfect spot. And, it's your baby. As with all Franke sinks, the faucets and accessories can be matched for a personal look.

SL 660

■■ Specialty Sinks

■■■ Above: A sink can be romantic. The Sunline™ glows beautifully in the most sophisticated kitchens and hospitality areas. Only Franke artisans have perfected the technique required to sculpt stainless steel. Gold, shown, or chrome Decor Panel is optional.

PN 671

■■■ Progresso™… and suddenly an unused corner comes to life! A creative design solution with three compartments plus handy drainboard.

■■■ Details, pp. 33-35.

AB 110

■■■ Ambiance™ Brass Sinks

■■■ For warm moments shared, the perfect hospitality sinks, designed to be under-mounted or inset. Franke Ambiance brass has a unique golden radiance with no lacquer finish that can peel away leaving an uneven color. Pictured above with Old-Fashioned™ Biflow™ faucet.

■■■ A Franke Feature:
Biflow bar faucets, in NuBrass® finish, exquisitely match Ambiance sinks. Biflow faucets are also available in other finishes.

AB 610-14

■■■ Right: Classic bar sink styling, shown with Traditional™ Biflow faucet.

■■■ Details, pp. 32-35.

Two ER 110s

■■■ Specialty Sinks and Faucets for Around the Home

■■■ Two sparkling sinks on a kitchen island enhance simple tasks. (Also pictured on page 4 as undermount Element.™) We show them here with a Corinthian™ Triflow® faucet featuring a handle option that matches the counter surface.

ES 110

■■■ Frankie Fish demonstrates that even pets create water needs. A well-placed sink makes life much easier. Left: Euroset® has a flat bottom and corner drain for good work space.

MH 280

FC 610

■■■ Above: The Manor House™ faucet has an elegant Edwardian appearance that looks so right in today's eclectic kitchens. It may be installed on a sink deck or countertop. And it also converts for wall mounting. Chrome, pewter, pewter/ NuBrass,® or NuBrass® finishes with simple white porcelain handles.

■■■ Franke Classic™ oval with off-center faucet. Works in family rooms and on patios. Have you thought about a sink for your second floor for easy access to water?

RSN 110

■■■ The Rotondo® is perfect for the mud room, laundry, or in a butler's pantry. Ideal in a baking center or as a second kitchen sink, as well.

■■■ **A Franke Feature:** Our versatile little sinks have helpful accessories too.

■■■ Details of sinks, faucets, and accessories begin on p. 32. (Faucet style left is discontinued.)

FF 310

■■■ **A Franke Feature:** Dual aerators. Two flow modes, aerated stream and spray, are controlled with a flip of the lever. Mode stays on until you change it. Soft spray remains on, even under low water pressure.

■■■ Select a Franke faucet for years of perfect operation. Solid brass construction with dependable ceramic disc cartridge.

■■■ **Safety** To prevent accidents, an internal anti-scald dial allows regulation of water temperature through a wide comfort zone.

■■■ **Water-Saving** Six-setting dial adjusts water pressure to your preferred flow rate. It's an anti-splash feature too.

■■■ **Styling** Top- and side-lever models with single-post construction for flexible placement. Side-lever faucets mount for right- or left-handed operation. Cast spout or pull-out sprayer.

■■■ **Sprayer flexibility** Unique two-part handle. The palm-sized end unit pulls out for most jobs and for extra maneuverability (opposite), or both parts can be used together (right). Hose extends a full two feet.

■■■ Color and finish details, p. 34.

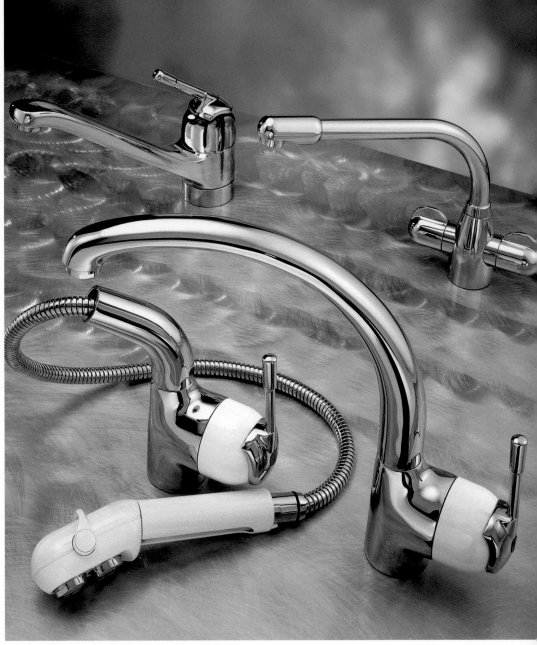

Clockwise from lower left: FF 601, FF 400, FF 500, FF 801

■■■Franke Faucets. Dependable, Safe, Water-Saving

#512

■■■ Accessibility handle. Franke single-handle faucets may be adapted with easy-to-operate special-access handle.

FF100

■■■ Franke's **Value Line** faucet features a convenient pull-out stream head. Solid brass with either nickel-chrome or epoxy-color finish.

U.S. patent 5417348

TFT 309

■■■ Triflow® Water Filtration System

■■■ Remember when you felt comfortable drinking water from your kitchen faucet? You can again.

■■■ Touch the third handle. Incorporating an advanced filtration system within an elegant kitchen faucet, Franke's patented Triflow eliminates the need for bottled water or a separate filtered water tap.

■■■ An independent waterway runs through the faucet body and continues through the spout. Beneath the sink it connects to a compact filtration unit containing a replaceable ceramic cartridge. There is no possibility of contamination from hot and cold supplies.

■■■ The cartridge removes microscopic particles, Cryptosporidium, lead, and chlorine, releasing the flavor of coffee, tea, juices, and the water itself. The life of the cartridge is extended since only drinking or cooking water is filtered. You may also connect the filter to refrigerated water and ice cube supply lines, or to a Little Butler™ dispensing unit.

■■■ Above, Traditional™ design in chrome and NuBrass.®

24

DW 100

■■■ Uniflow™ is the water filtration system that installs as easily as a faucet on a sink deck or a countertop. The solid brass faucet features a swivel spout and quarter-turn ceramic valve. This ultimate deck accessory connects to the Franke cartridge beneath the counter, has all the fine filtration benefits of Triflow,™ yet works with any faucet.

■■■ The filter is also available separately for use with in-door refrigerated water and with ice makers.

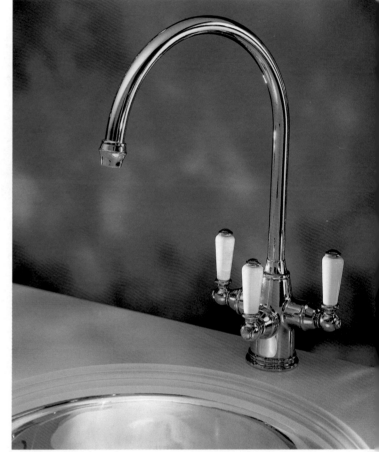

TFC 390

TFC 389

■■■ Above: Corinthian™ in golden tarnish-resistant NuBrass® with standard white porcelain handles. Corinthian handle options include: chrome, NuBrass,® and pictured at far left, popular solid-surface materials. Left: Pewter/NuBrass® finish for Corinthian and Traditional Triflow™ models.

■■■ Color and finish details, p. 34.

Avonite® and Corian® are registered trademarks.

Avonite Black Ice
Avonite Polar White
Corian Sierra Dusk
Corian Sierra Sandstone
Corian Sierra Pink Coral
Corian Sierra Sunset
Corian Sierra Oceanic
Corian Sierra Evergreen
Corian Sierra Burnt Amber
Corian Sierra Midnight

LB 110

■■■ Silently available on your sink deck, the Little Butler can serve up hot, hot/chilled, or filtered water, instantly.

■■■ Of solid brass construction, this handsome unit is available in durable white, biscuit, black, chrome, or NuBrass,® as well as in combinations of chrome/NuBrass,® white/NuBrass,® or pewter/NuBrass® finishes, to coordinate with Franke faucets. Installs on sink or countertop.

■■■ Little Butler® Dispensing Systems

LB 100   LB 209

■■■ **Hot only** Dispenses up to sixty cups of 190° (approx.) water per hour for instant beverages and food, pre-boiling, thawing, and mixing. Control handle may be positioned to left or right of spout for convenient operation.

■■■ **Hot/cold** The same great features as the hot-only system, plus a drinking water tap that can bypass a water softener, or connect to a chiller or Franke's filter unit.

■■■ In fact, we consider water quality to be so important that we include our filtration system with every hot/cold Little Butler™ unit.

■■■ Details, p. 35.

■■■ Your Franke custom sink system can be expanded with the highest quality waste disposers. Powerful, dependable, quick, and quiet.

■■■ Batch- or continuous-feed models are powered by 1 HP or 3/4 HP high-torque induction motors. All have automatic reversing action for jam-free operation and long life.

■■■ Right: Continuous-feed disposers can be operated by an air-activated control switch (button at upper right) mounted on deck or countertop. Also shown, flange and stopper options. All colors match sink lines.

■■■ Details, p. 35.

■■■ Little Butler® Waste Disposers

■■■ Chromed wall racks, a necessity in professional kitchens, are designed for mounting above the cooktop, sink, or wherever utensils must be handy.

■■■ Racks are available in three sizes. Each unit includes paper towel dispenser, saucepan lid holder, and two loose hooks. Utensil holder option pictured.

■■■ **A Franke Feature:** Racks placed above cooktops swing up for easy wall cleaning.

■■■ Details, p. 35.

RS 975-33

■■■ Wall Racks and Waste Bin

AE E17

■■■ The professional chef's countertop waste bin collects recyclable bottles and cans or food scraps destined for composting. Stainless steel lid seals to stop odors. Choose removable 3½-gallon synthetic or optional 2-gallon stainless steel container, both with lift handle. Unit may be undermounted. Synthetic container may be trimmed for use as waste chute.

■■■ Convenient dispensing for detergent, liquid hand soap, or lotion. Gentle-touch brass dispenser head connects to a 17-oz. container that refills from above the sink. All Franke colors.

■■■ Nice Touches: Soap/Lotion Dispensers, Strainer Baskets, Pop-Ups

■■■ Strainer baskets have the tightest seal possible with a replaceable sealing gasket linked to a positive-lock ball bearing fixing system. All Franke colors.

■■■ Drain your sink from the deck. Pop-up strainer system puts an end to dipping your hands in hot messy water. All Franke colors.

■■■ Details, p. 35.

■■■Franke Sinks and Accessories Are Made for Each Other. And for You!

■■■ On previous pages, you've seen accessories featured with all of our sink lines. We believe in them. From food preparation to cleanup, the amount of time you spend at your sink, and your enjoyment of it, can be influenced by your accessory options.

■■■ Franke accessories, made from the finest materials, are custom fitted and color coordinated to all sink lines. They are multifunctional and work in perfect harmony with our faucets and our deck accessories. After you've worked with them, you'll wonder what you did without them.

■■■ Colanders
Fit small bowls. Rinse, drain, defrost, strain, air-dry silverware. Dishwasher safe.

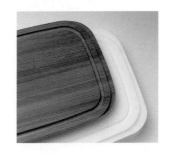

■■■ Cutting boards
Specialty hardwoods or synthetic. Reversible. Some with integral colander. Lock into sink for steady chopping. (Some require drain trays.)

■■■ Drain baskets
Rinse food or air-dry fine crystal and china. Some with removable or integral plate racks.

■■■ Drain trays
Portable drainboards extend work surface across or next to sink. They can support drain baskets and/or cutting boards.

■■■ Grid drainers
For all Prestige models. Grid fits across integral shelf for rinsing or drying. Also available in footed version.

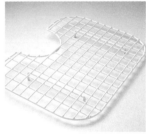

■■■ Accessory options
Available for your sink choice. See pp. 32-33.

Unless otherwise indicated, sinks are in stainless steel; accessories are available in white, biscuit, or black; and cutting boards are wood. Dimensions are approximate.

■■■ Ambiance™ Brass

AB 110 18" Dia.

AB 610-14 14"x16"

■■■ Artisan™

AR 670 available in **Granite**. Order **ARG 670**. Specify Iceberg, Flint, or Boulder. (Sand not available in this model.)

AR 670 39"x20"

AR 630 46"x20"

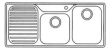

AR 621 LH 46"x20"

AR 621 RH

Cutting Boards
AR 40S, AR 40W (synthetic)
Colander AR 70* (for AR 630 and AR 621 order tandem cutting board AR 40C for use with colander)
Drain Basket AR 50*
Drain Tray AR 60*
Accessories not available in biscuit.
*Also available in stainless steel.

■■■ Classic™

FC 610 22"x19"

Cutting Board FC 40S

■■■ Double Undermounts

All **Prestige Plus**™ **(PRX)** models are also available as **Prestige Classic**™. Specify **PR** prefix.

PRX 160 30"x19"

PRX 160 LH

PRX 120 34"x19"

PRX 120 LH

PRQ 160 31"x19"

PRQ 120 37"x19"

Specify white, biscuit, or black.

Drain Basket PR 50
Drain Tray PR 61
Grid Drainers PR 31†, PR 36†
Colanders CP 80 (for small bowl in PR 620) PR 70 (for small bowl in PR 660)

†Also available in coated chrome.

■■■ Elements® Stainless

All **Prestige Plus**™ **(PRX)** models are also available as **Prestige Classic**™. Specify **PR** prefix.

PRX 110-21 21"x19"

CP 110 12"x13"

NA 110 17"x17"

PR 110-7 7"x14"

AR 110-14 14"x17"

AR 110-6 7"x13"

AR 110-13 13"x14"

ER 110 16" Dia.

RG 110 15"x19"

PRX/PR 110-21:
Cutting Boards
PR 40S** PR 40W (synthetic)
PR 40C (w/integral colander–not available in biscuit)
Drain Basket PR 50
Drain Tray PR 61
Grid Drainers PR 31†, PR 36†

NA 110: Cutting Board
NA 40C (w/integral colander)
Drain Basket CP 50
Drain Tray CP 60
Accessories not available in biscuit.

AR 110-14: Cutting Boards
AR 40S, AR 40W (synthetic)
Drain Basket AR 50*
Drain Tray AR 60
Accessories not available in biscuit.

AR 110-13: Cutting Board and tandem **Colander** AR 40C w/AR 70
Not available in biscuit.

CP 110: Colander CP 80

PR 110-7: Colander PR 70

AR 110-6: Colander AR 70*
Not available in biscuit.

ER 110: Cutting Boards
ER 40W (synthetic)
Drain Basket ER 50S (stainless only)

*Also available in stainless steel.
**Requires Drain Tray PR 61.
†Also available in coated chrome.

■■■ Elements,® Color

Specify white, biscuit, or black.

PRQ 110 21"x19"

RGQ 110 16"x19"

RGQ 110-13 13"x17"

PRQ 110: Cutting Boards
PR 40S** PR 40W (synthetic)
PR 40C (w/integral colander–not
available in biscuit)
Drain Basket PR 50
Drain Tray PR 61
Grid Drainers PR 31†, PR 36†

RGQ 110-13: Cutting Board
CP 40S, CP 40W (synthetic)
Drain Basket CP 50
Drain Tray CP 60
Accessories not available in biscuit.
**Requires Drain Tray PR 61.
†Also available in coated chrome.

■■■ Euroset®

ES 110 16"x15"

■■■ Nobel®

NA 620 38"x22"

NA 660 33"x22"

Cutting Board NA 40C (w/inte-
gral colander)
Drain Basket CP 50
Drain Tray CP 60
Colander CP 80 (for small bowl in
NA 660 only)
Accessories not available in biscuit.

■■□ Prestige™ Stainless

All **Prestige Plus™ (PRX)**
models are also available as
Prestige Classic.™
Specify **PR** prefix.

PRX 620 38"x22" **PRX 620 LH**

PRX 610 25"x22"

PRX 660 33"x22" **PRX 660 LH**

Cutting Boards
PR 40S** PR 40W (synthetic)
PR 40C (w/integral colander–not
available in biscuit)
Drain Basket PR 50
Drain Tray PR 61
Grid Drainers PR 31†, PR 36†
Colanders CP 80 (for small bowl
in PR 620) PR 70 (for small bowl
in PR 660)

**Requires Drain Tray PR 61.
†Also available in coated chrome.

■■■ Prestige Color™

Specify white, biscuit, or black.

PRQ 620 39"x22"

PRQ 610 26"x22"

PRQ 660 34"x22"

PR 660 available in **Granite**. Order
PRG 660. Specify Iceberg, Flint,
Boulder, or Sand.

Cutting Boards
PR 40S** PR 40W (synthetic)
PR 40C (w/integral colander–not
available in biscuit)
Drain Basket PR 50
Drain Tray PR 61
Grid Drainers PR 31†, PR 36†
Colanders CP 80 (for small bowl
in PRQ 620) PR 70 (for small bowl
in PRQ 660)
**Requires Drain Tray PR 61.
†Also available in coated chrome.

■■■ Regatta™

RG 620 available in **Quartz**. Order
RGQ 620. Specify white,
biscuit, or black.

RG 620 33"x22"

Cutting Board CP 40S,
CP 40W (synthetic)
Drain Basket CP 50
Drain Tray CP 60
Accessories not available in biscuit.

■■■ Progresso™

PN 671 33"x20"

Cutting Board PN 40S
Drain Basket PN 50W (white only)
Colander PN 70 (for small bowl,
white only)

■■■ Rotondo®

RSN 110 available in **Granite**.
Order **RTG 110**. Specify Iceberg,
Flint, Boulder, or Sand.

RSN 110 17" Dia.

Stainless:
Cutting Board RBN 40S
Drain Basket RBN 50W (white
only)
Granite: Same as above,
order with RTG prefix.

■■■ Sunline™

SL 660 34"x20"

Cutting Board SL 40S
Colander SL 65S (smoke only)
Decor Panel SL 20C (chrome)
SL 20G (gold)

■■■ Faucets, Dispensers, and Nice Touches

■■■ Faucets

All 300, 400, 500 and 800 series faucets are IAPMO listed (file #2994).

FF 600 chrome

Also available in:
FF 601 chrome/white
FF 603 chrome/black
FF 604 chrome/biscuit
FF 610 white
FF 630 black
FF 640 biscuit
FF 690 gold/black*

FF 300 chrome

Also available in:
FF 301 chrome/white
FF 303 chrome/black
FF 304 chrome/biscuit
FF 310 white
FF 330 black
FF 340 biscuit

FF 800 chrome

Also available in:
FF 801 chrome/white
FF 803 chrome/black
FF 804 chrome/biscuit
FF 810 white
FF 830 black
FF 840 biscuit
FF 890 gold/black*

*Gold-finish sprayhead and/or cap (custom order)

FF 400 chrome

Also available in:
FF 410 white

Accessibility Handle #512

FF 100 chrome

Also available in:
FF 110 white
FF 130 black
FF 140 biscuit

FF 500 chrome

Also available in:
FF 510 white

■■■ Manor House

MH 200 chrome

Also available in:
MH 280 pewter
MH 289 pewter/NuBrass®
MH 290 NuBrass®

Wall mount kit (to convert deck mount to wall mount)
WMK 80 pewter
WMK 90 NuBrass®

■■■ Biflow™ Faucets

BFT 200 chrome

Also available in:
BFT 209 chrome/NuBrass®
BFT 289 pewter/NuBrass®
BFT 290 NuBrass®

BFO 200 chrome

Also available in:
BFO 290 NuBrass®

■■■ Triflow® Filtration System

All models include **FRXH1** filtration unit. (Also available separately.)

FRXO2 Replacement Cartridge now with lead removal
FRXO3 Nitrate
FRXO4 Pre-filter (5 micron)
FRXSH Specialty Housing (for FRX03 or FRX04)

Meets NSF 53 (Full Compliance) and 42 (Class One Rating) in every test conducted. Summary of test results available on request.

TFT 300 chrome

Also available in:
TFT 309 chrome/NuBrass®
TFT 310 white
TFT 319 white/NuBrass®
TFT 389 pewter/NuBrass®
TFT 390 NuBrass®

TFC 300 chrome

Also available in:
TFC 389 Pewter/NuBrass®
TFC 390 NuBrass®

Handle Options
for TFC 300 series

Chrome	OPT-CHR
NuBrass®	OPT-BRS
Avonite Black Ice	OPT-ABI
Avonite Polar White	OPT-APW
Corian Sierra Dusk	OPT-CSD
Corian Sierra Sandstone	OPT-CSS
Corian Sierra Pink Coral	OPT-CSP
Corian Sierra Sunset	OPT-CSU
Corian Sierra Oceanic	OPT-CSO
Corian Sierra Evergreen	OPT-CSE
Corian Sierra Burnt Amber	OPT-CSB
Corian Sierra Midnight	OPT-CSM

Avonite® and Corian® are registered trademarks.

DW 100 chrome

Also available in:
DW 110 white
DW 130 black
DW 140 biscuit
DW 190 NuBrass®

■■■ Little Butler® Water Dispensers

All LB 200 series models include water filtration system, FRXH1.

LB 100 chrome

Also available in:
LB 109 chrome/NuBrass®
LB 110 white
LB 119 white/NuBrass®
LB 130 black
LB 140 biscuit
LB 189 pewter/NuBrass®
LB 190 NuBrass®

LB 200 chrome

Also available in:
LB 209 chrome/NuBrass®
LB 210 white
LB 219 white/NuBrass®
LB 230 black
LB 240 biscuit
LB 289 pewter/NuBrass®
LB 290 NuBrass®

■■■ Little Butler® Waste Disposers

3/4 HP

WD 750
Continuous Feed

WD 750B
Batch Feed

1 HP

WD 1000
Continuous Feed

WD 1000B
Batch Feed

Disposer Options:
(Available in all Franke colors.)

Continuous Feed:
Air Switch WD 3428
Controller WD 9088
(Must be ordered with air switch.)
Stopper WD 7001
Flange WD 7026

Batch Feed:
Flange WD 7026

■■■ Wall Racks

RS 975-22 22" x 13"

RS 975-33 33" x 13"

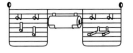

RS 975-38 38" x 13"

RS 905

RS 910
Set of additional hooks

■■■ Waste Bin

AE E17
Includes synthetic container

AE 81
Stainless container option

■■■ Soap/Lotion Dispensers

902C chrome

Also available in:
902 W white
902 BT biscuit
902 BK black
902 BRS brass

■■■ Strainer Baskets

900 chrome
Strainer Basket Unit

Available in:
900 W white
900 BT biscuit
900 BK black
900 G gold
900 BRS brass

900P chrome
Pop-up Unit

Available in:
900 PW white
900 PBT biscuit
900 PBK black
900 PG gold

Due to our continuing interest in product development, dimensions and specifications are subject to change without notice. Colors shown in this brochure are printed in ink. Colors of actual products may vary slightly.

■■■ What Would I Do Without My Franke?

Franke, Inc.
Kitchen Systems Division
212 Church Road
North Wales, PA 19454
800-626-5771

FRANKE®

Kitchen Sinks
Faucets
Water Dispensing Systems
Disposers
Custom Accessories

■ Technology   ■ Quality   ■ Design

The Finishing Touches

C561
15440/OPE
BuyLine 6942

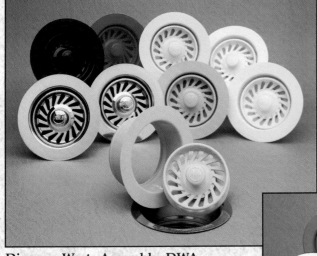

Disposer Waste Assembly: DWA

Color coordinate your kitchen decor
with these designer kitchen
accessories made of Celcon®,
guaranteed not to crack, chip or peel.

Soap Lotion Dispenser: SLD

Strainer Waste Assembly: STW

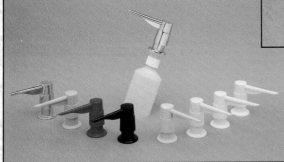

Remote Control Strainers: STR 1 or STR 2

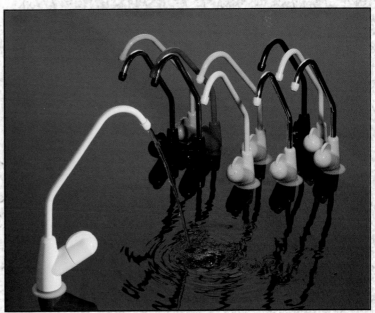

Drinking Dispenser Faucet: DDF
Also available: DDF with an Air Gap: ADF

Also available for the complete kitchen or bath: Pop-up Waste, Air Gap, Hole Covers, Sprayer Hose, Aerators and more.

OPELLA, Inc. For information on our complete line, call us at (800) 969-0339 Fax (800) 867-3552

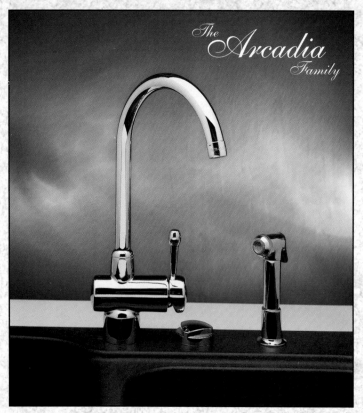

The Arcadia Family

OPELLA ®

SUPERGRIF

Arcadia Kitchen   Arcadia Bar

This sleek contemporary European designed faucet makes a bold statement in any surrounding. Our solid brass kitchen or bar faucet with single lever hot and cold cartridge will provide years of dependable service and is available with a matching solid brass sprayer.

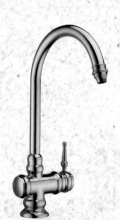 

Colonial Kitchen   Colonial Bar

The Colonial Family

Classic elegance to complement any decor with the old world style of the Colonial family. These single lever hot and cold, bar and kitchen faucets are offered in 12 different finishes and are available with matching soap lotion dispenser and sprayer.

OPELLA, Inc. For information on our complete line, call us at (800) 969-0339 Fax (800) 867-3552

SWANSTONE®

THE REINFORCED SOLID SURFACE

C562
15440/SWB
BuyLine 7502

Swanstone is a revolutionary and thoroughly proven solid surface material that combines affordable luxury with durability and permanence. Because Swanstone is nonporous and uniformly solid, it is virtually impervious to stains, burns, scratches and gouges.

Kitchen & Bar Sinks

The luxurious appearance, durability, and convenience found in each of these sinks make them a surprisingly economical investment. Swanstone sinks are offered in eight bowl styles for the kitchen and two for the bar. Swanstone sinks are available in solid, aggregate, and galaxy colors. All kitchen and bar sinks are backed with a 10-year limited warranty. Optional cutting boards, wire baskets, and drain grids are available in a variety of sizes and styles making each a practical and distinctive additional to the Swanstone kitchen sink.

SWANSTONE 10 YEAR LIMITED WARRANTY

Double Bowl Model
KSDB-3322
22" x 33

Large Double Bowl
Model KSLB-2233
22" x 33"

Large & Small Bowl
Model KSLS-3322
22" x 33"

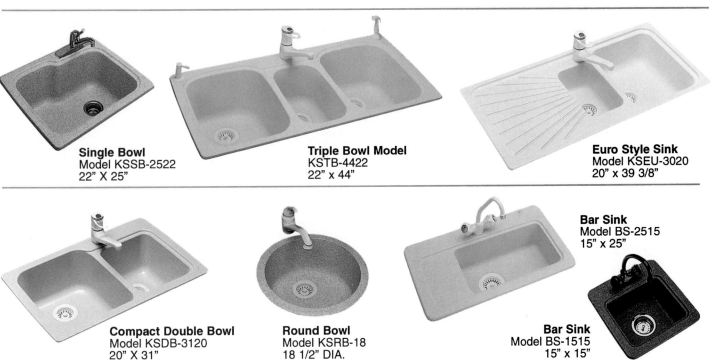

Single Bowl
Model KSSB-2522
22" X 25"

Triple Bowl Model
KSTB-4422
22" x 44"

Euro Style Sink
Model KSEU-3020
20" x 39 3/8"

Compact Double Bowl
Model KSDB-3120
20" X 31"

Round Bowl
Model KSRB-18
18 1/2" DIA.

Bar Sink
Model BS-1515
15" x 15"

Bar Sink
Model BS-2515
15" x 25"

SWANSTONE®

THE REINFORCED SOLID SURFACE

Vanity Tops & Bowls

Exclusively Swanstone, this line of one-piece, solid surface vanity lavatories will highlight any bath. Available in single, double, offset and Neo-Angle bowl models.

SWANSTONE BOWL SELECTIONS
POSITION OF BOWLS

Size	Center	Offset	Double Bowl	Neo Angle
17" x 19"	x	—	—	—
19" x 25"	x	—	—	—
19" x 31"	x	—	—	—
19" x 37"	x	—	—	—
22" x 25"	x	—	—	—
22" x 31"	x	—	—	—
22" x 37"	x	—	—	—
22" x 43"	x	—	—	—
22" x 49"	x	x	—	x
22" x 55"	x	x	—	—
22" x 61'	x	x	x	—
22" x 67"	—	x	—	—
22" x 68"	x	—	—	—
22" x 73"	x	x	—	—
22" x 85"	x	x	—	—

Custom Contrasts Vanity Tops & Bowls

Choose any color top and combine it with any color bowl for a custom look with either a smooth seam or overlap mounting treatment.

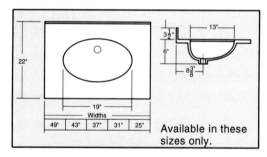

Available in these sizes only.

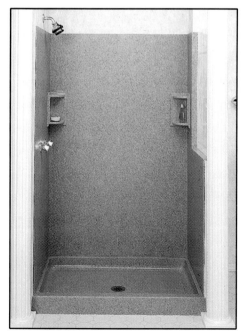

Bathtub & Shower Wall Panel System

The Swanstone bathtub and shower wall panel system allows the opportunity to create a totally luxurious environment. And Swanstone shower floors make an excellent companion to the Swanstone shower wall panels. Sizes are available to accommodate standard shower area applications.

Shower Floors

Designed to be used with Swanstone wall panel systems. Eight sizes are available to accommodate the more popular shower areas.

Color Selection

Solid Colors - White, Bone, Dove Gray, Shell Rose, Blue Mist
Aggregate Colors - Midnight Galaxy, Bermuda Sand, Gray Granite, Rose Granite, Country Blue Granite, Arctic Granite
Galaxy Colors - Mocha Galaxy, Almond Galaxy, Gray Galaxy, Rose Galaxy, Blue Galaxy, Jade Galaxy, Black Galaxy

The Swan Corporation
One City Centre
St. Louis, Missouri 63101
(314) 231-8148

SWANSTONE Patent
25 YEAR Pending
WARRANTY
AGAINST CRACKING Printed in USA

FORM #540-3-96-5M

Kitchen&Bar
DECORATOR FAUCETS

C563
BUYLINE 7430

G E R B E R

Decorator Kitchen Faucets

All Gerber Kitchen faucets feature Ceramaflow™ ceramic disk cartridges with 20 year warranty for years of trouble free operation.
2.0 gpm (7.6 L/min) Maximum Aerator

CX-82-349 Undercounter Mount
with E-Z Filler Spout-
Chrome and Polished Brass
85-739 Handle Pack:
Ultamira Facet Ring-Chrome & Polished Brass

CX-A2-341 Undercounter Mount
with E-Z Filler Spout-Almond
A5-271 Handle Pack:
Almond China Lever-Almond

CX-82-345 Undercounter Mount
with E-Z Filler Spout-Antique Brass
85-105 Handle Pack:
Small Metal Cross-Antique Brass

CX-82-347 Undercounter Mount
with E-Z Filler Spout-Polished Brass
85-107 Handle Pack:
Small Metal Cross-Polished Brass

CX-82-367 Undercounter Mount
with 10" D Tube-Polished Brass
85-237 Handle Pack:
White China Lever-Polished Brass

CX-W2-361 Undercounter Mount
with 10" D Tube-White
W5-741 Handle Pack:
Ultamira Rope Ring-White

Used on
Polished
Brass

Used on
Antique
Brass

Used on
Chrome &
Polished
Brass

Used on
Almond

Used on
Chrome

Used on
White

Bar Faucets

CX-88-987 Bar Faucet-Polished Brass
85-277 Handle Pack:
Almond China Lever-Polished Brass

CX-W8-981 Bar Faucet-White
W5-101 Handle Pack:
Small Metal Cross-White

CX-88-985 Bar Faucet-Antique Brass
85-247 Handle Pack:
Small Round Crystaline-Antique Brass

CX-A8-981 Bar Faucet-Almond
A5-211 Handle Pack:
Crystalite Lever-Almond

CX-88-989 Bar Faucet-Chrome & Polished Brass
85-209 Handle Pack:
Metal Lever-Chrome & Polished Brass

GERBER
PROFESSIONALLY MADE • PROFESSIONALLY SOLD
Gerber Plumbing Fixtures Corp. 4600 W. Touhy Avenue, Chicago, IL 60646
(847) 675-6570, FAX 1-800-5GERBER (Illinois FAX (847) 675-5192)

MADE IN USA

Quality Within Reach

Form And Function For Your Kitchen. GROHE pull-out spray kitchen faucets do more than deliver water, they transform your kitchen sink into a functional work space. Whether rinsing dishes or vegetables, or filling large pots, you bring the water where you need it. Choose from three distinctive styles: EuroPlus, timelessly contemporary to fit any kitchen; Eurowing, sleek and modern; and the original pull-out, Ladylux. The GROHE quality difference is functional design and meticulous engineering backed by the highest manufacturing standards. Ensure your satisfaction by reaching for the best. Experience GROHE...Ultimate Quality, Timeless Design.

Send $3.00 for a complete set of literature: Grohe America, Inc. • 241 Covington Drive • Bloomingdale, IL 60108 • 708.582.7711 • Fax 708.582.7722

© 1994 Grohe America, Inc.

Quality Within Reach

Relexa Plus...Innovative, Distinctive Shower Products. Let quality distinguish your shower designs with the best in functional and aesthetic European innovations. Softly contoured ergonomic form is only the beginning. Relexa Plus' unique *Speedclean*™ system eliminates limescale build-up...a wipe of the hand restores *like new* performance instantly. And, the integrated shower arm design of Relexa Plus shower heads creates a wide range of shower positioning options. Add to these innovations multiple spray functions and the new integrated *Grohclick*™ snap coupling. Experience GROHE...Ultimate Quality, Timeless Design.

Write or call us for a complete set of literature: Grohe America, Inc. • 241 Covington Drive • Bloomingdale, IL 60108 • 708.582.7711 • Fax 708.582.7722

GROHMIX THERMOSTAT VALVES

Protect your family from accidental scalding in the shower or bath with a Grohmix Thermostat Valve...the ultimate in safety, comfort, luxury, and quality. Dial your water termperature just as you would the heat or air conditioning in your home – it's that simple, that worry-free.

The Grohmix thermal element automatically controls the flow of hot and cold water to accurately deliver the desired water temperature for your shower or bath. Manual adjustments to correct water temperature fluctuations are completely eliminated. Should the hot or cold water fail, Grohmix cuts off the waterflow to protect from scalding or thermal shock. Grohmix also features a safety stop at 100°F; maximum temperature 110°F.

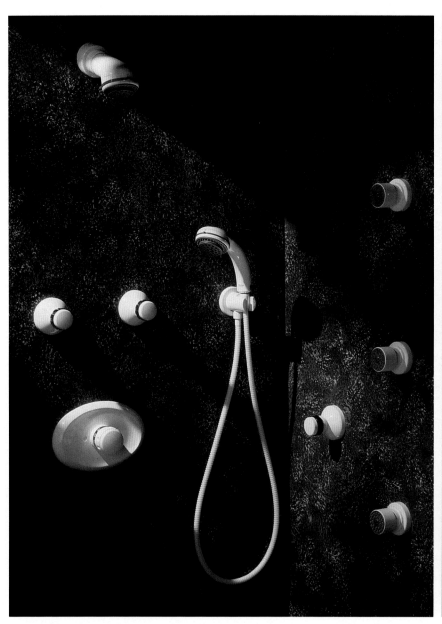

34.436
1/2" Integrated
Grohmix Thermostat
with Lever Handle
Volume Control

34.458
1/2" Integrated
Grohmix Thermostat
with Lever Handle
Volume and Temperature
Controls

34.419
3/4" Grohmix Thermostat
34.493
1/2" Grohmix Thermostat

34.457
3/4" Grohmix Thermostat
34.456
1/2" Grohmix Thermostat
each with Lever Handle
Temperature Control

Temperature Control for Custom Shower Systems

Custom shower installations require ample water volume and the 3/4" Grohmix delivers. Given adequate water pressure, the 3/4" Grohmix can supply enough water to simultaneously power a shower head, a personal hand shower, and body sprays, and maintain a specific water temperature as well! Grohmix Tub and Shower Combinations are available in chrome, 23-karat gold, white, and polished brass. Consult GROHE's Price List for complete details on Grohmix products, options and available finishes. (GROHE shower products featured have a maximum flow rate of 9.4 l/min or 2.5 gpm).

Write or call for Grohe's complete product literature file.

Grohe America, Inc. • Subsidiary of Friedrich Grohe AG, Germany • 241 Covington Drive, Bloomingdale, IL 60108 • TEL: 1.708.582.7711 • FAX: 1.708.582.7722

BELVEDERE™ COLLECTION

Belvedere™ Pedestal and Whirlpool

The Belvedere™ Collection captures the essence of grand luxury
with a suite of bathroom fixtures that command admiring glances.
Designed by Axel Enthoven for Absolute℠, the fixtures are enhanced by
a unique 24 karat gold integrated faucet that sends water cascading
into the basin and tub.

ABSOLUTE℠
by
American Standard Inc.

A WORLD OF BATHROOMS
1-800-359-3261

Description:

Vitreous china pedestal with rear overflow and integrated 24 karat gold plated faucet with brushed chrome escutcheon plate. Designed by Axel Enthoven for Absolute℠ by Ideal Standard™, Italy.

Colors:

Exclusively in white. May be coordinated with American Standard™ #020 White fixtures.

Dimensions:

31 ½" wide x 23⅝" front to back x 35¾" high

To be specified:

❏ The faucet finish is available only in 24 karat gold plate with brushed chrome escutcheon plate. Drain assembly and pop-up included.

❏ Other:

Description:

Vitreous china pedestal with rear overflow and integrated 24 karat gold plated faucet with brushed chrome escutcheon plate. Designed by Axel Enthoven for Absolute℠ by Ideal Standard™, Italy.

 ADA compliant.

Colors:

Exclusively in white. May be coordinated with American Standard™ #020 White fixtures.

Dimensions:

31½" wide x 23⅝" front to back x 21¼" high

To be specified:

❏ The faucet finish is available only in 24 karat gold plate with brushed chrome escutcheon plate. Drain assembly and pop-up included.

❏ Other:

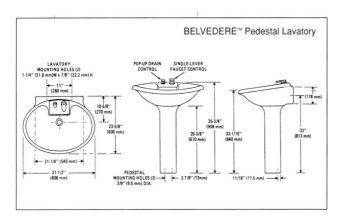

BELVEDERE™ Pedestal Lavatory

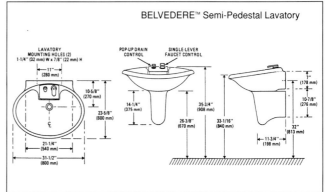

BELVEDERE™ Semi-Pedestal Lavatory

2626.394 **Belvedere™ Whirlpool**
2626.028 **Belvedere™ Whirlpool with System II**
2626.294 **Belvedere™ Bathing Pool**

Description: Whirlpool

Acrylic construction; textured tub bottom; 3/4 HP self-draining pump/motor with DRY RUN seal; supplied with drain, integral bath filler valve and waterfall spout*; six multi-directional and individually flow adjustable jets; one 24 karat gold air volume control; ON/OFF air switch; U.L. approved whirlpool system. Manufactured in the USA for Absolute℠ by American Standard™.

Description: Whirlpool with System II

Same as above plus 1HP two-speed pump, electronic on/off switch with 20 minute built-in timer and chrome bezel. Factory installed in-line electric water heater available.

Description: Bathing Pool

Same as above less whirlpool.

Colors:

Shown in white which coordinates with American Standard™ #020 White fixtures. The whirlpools or tub may be ordered in any American Standard™ acrylic color.

Specifications:

Tub size:	72" long x 33¼" wide x 22¾" deep
Whirlpool weight:	105 lbs.
Bathing pool weight:	95 lbs.
Whirlpool weight with water:	639 lbs.
Bathing pool weight with water:	584 lbs.
Gallons to overflow:	65 gallons
Sump Dimensions:	28" x 17" x 22¾"

Electrical specifications-pump:

System I: 3/4 HP, 9.2 Amps., 115V

System II: 1 HP, 10.2 Amps., 115 V

To be specified:

❏ System II In-Line Water Heater: American Standard™ #9870.100

*Tub Filler Finish:

Tub filler finish available only in 24 karat gold plate with brushed chrome escutcheon plate.

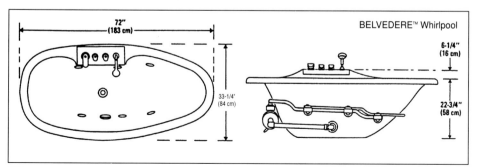

BELVEDERE™ Whirlpool

72" (183 cm)

33-1/4" (84 cm)

6-1/4" (16 cm)

22-3/4" (58 cm)

Belvedere™ integrated tub filler with waterfall spout.

Notes:
1. Bath can be installed above or below floor line as pier, island or peninsula type installation. Rim support for bath and enclosing material by contractor.
2. Provide access to bath filler pump and electrical connections.
3. Installer: Refer to installation instructions supplied with pool for additional information.
These measurements are subject to change or cancellation. No responsibility is assumed for use of superseded or voided pages.

Description:

Self-rimming vitreous china countertop with rear overflow and integrated 24 karat gold plated faucet with brushed chrome escutcheon plate. Designed by Axel Enthoven for Absolute℠ by Ideal Standard™, Italy. Template included.

Colors:

Exclusively in white. May be coordinated with Amercian-Standard™ #020 White fixtures.

Dimensions:

27½" wide x 20⅝" front to back x 7" deep

To be specified:

❏ Faucet finish: available only in 24 karat gold plate with brushed chrome escutcheon plate. Drain assembly and pop-up included.

❏ Other:

Suggested Coordinates:

2028.035 Enthoven™ One-Piece Water Closet
2288.016 Enthoven™ Two-Piece Water Closet
5026.028 Enthoven™ Bidet
See Axel Enthoven™ Collection for descriptions and specifications.

Notes:

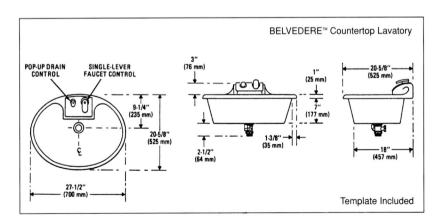

BELVEDERE™ Countertop Lavatory

Template Included

For more information call: 1-800-359-3261

CLASSIC™ COLLECTION

Reprise™ Whirlpool, Classic™ Pedestal and Water Closet

Escape the stress of today's busy world and surround yourself
with the grand European design of the Classic™ Collection by Absolute℠.
Classic™, with its timeless beauty and grace, will never go out of style.

ABSOLUTE℠
by
American Standard Inc.

A WORLD OF BATHROOMS
1-800-359-3261

0215.803   Classic™ Pedestal

Description:
Vitreous china pedestal with rear overflow and faucet ledge. Available in 8" centers only. From Absolute℠ by Ideal Standard™, Italy. Shown with Sottini Azimuth lavatory fitting in mixage with lever handles by American Standard™.

Colors:
Exclusively in white. May be coordinated with American Standard™ #020 White fixtures.

Dimensions:
$30^{11}/_{16}$" wide x $23^{1}/_{4}$" front to back x 33" high

To be specified:
❏ Faucet:

❏ Faucet finish:

❏ Other:

Description:
Vitreous china, two-piece, elongated bowl with concealed trapway, 1.6 gallons per flush, gravity flush, 12" rough. Includes either polished chrome or polished brass trip lever as well as a white toilet seat with either polished chrome or polished brass hinges. Made exclusively for Absolute℠ by Ideal Standard™.

Colors:
Exclusively in white. May be coordinated with American Standard™ #020 White fixtures.

Dimensions:
$17^{1}/_{4}$" wide x 29" front to back x $30^{1}/_{8}$" high

To be specified:
❏ **2047.039.002**
   Classic™ Two-Piece Water Closet
   with polished chrome trip lever and hinges
❏ **2047.039.099** (shown at right)
   Classic™ Two-Piece Water Closet
   with polished brass trip lever and hinges

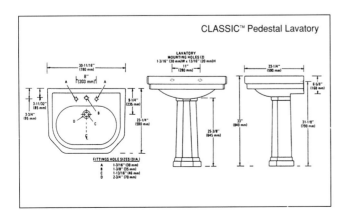

CLASSIC™ Pedestal Lavatory

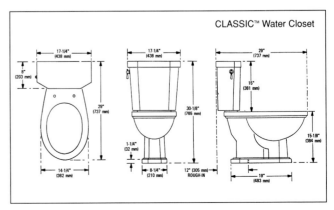

CLASSIC™ Water Closet

2615.302 Reprise™ Whirlpool
2615.028 Reprise™ Whirlpool with System II
2615.202 Reprise™ Bathing Pool

Description: Whirlpool

Acrylic construction; textured tub bottom; 3/4 HP self-draining pump/motor with DRY RUN seal; six multi-directional and individually flow adjustable jets; two air volume controls; ON/OFF air switch; U.L. approved whirlpool system. Shown with Amarilis Jasmine Tub Filler. Manufactured in the USA for Absolute℠ by American Standard™.

Description: Whirlpool with System II

Same as above plus 1 HP two-speed pump, electronic on/off switch with 20 minute built-in timer and chrome bezel. Factory installed in-line electric water heater available.

Description: Bathing Pool

Same as above less whirlpool.

Colors:

Available in American Standard™ #020 White to coordinate with the Classic™ Suite. May also be ordered in any other American Standard™ acrylic color.

To be specified:

❏ Drain: American Standard™ #1573.170
  (.002 for Chrome, .099 for Brass, .094 for Gold, .020 for White)
❏ Air Control Kit (if other than #020 White):
  2 per kit, 1 kit required; American Standard™ #9850.200
  (.002 for Chrome, .099 for Brass, .094 for Gold)
❏ Jet Trim Ring Kit (if other than #020 White):
  2 per kit, 3 kits required; American Standard™ #9860.200
  (.002 for Chrome, .099 for Brass, .094 for Gold)
❏ Tub Filler:
❏ Personal Shower:
❏ System II In-Line Heater: American Standard™ #9870.100

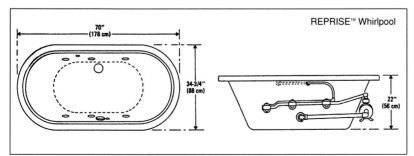

REPRISE™ Whirlpool

Specifications:

Tub size:	70" long x 34¾" wide x 22" deep
Whirlpool weight:	111 lbs.
Bathing pool weight:	96 lbs.
Whirlpool weight with water:	665 lbs.
Bathing pool weight with water:	640 lbs.
Gallons to overflow:	66 gallons
Sump Dimensions:	39" x 18" x 22"
Electrical specifications-pump:	

System I: 3/4 HP, 9.2 Amps., 115V
System II: 1 HP, 10.2 Amps., 115V

Notes:
1. Bath can be installed above or below floor line as pier, island or peninsula type installation. Rim support for bath and enclosing material by contractor.
2. Provide access to bath filler pump and electrical connections.
3. Installer: Refer to installation instructions supplied with pool for additional information.
These measurements are subject to change or cancellation. No responsibility is assumed for use of superseded or voided pages.

Description:

Self-rimming vitreous china countertop with front overflow and faucet ledge. Available in 8" centers only. From Absolute℠ by Ideal Standard™, Italy. Shown with Olympia™ faucet with porcelain cross handles by Ideal Standard™, Italy. Template included.

Colors:

Exclusively in white. May be coordinated with American Standard™ #020 White fixtures.

Dimensions:

25" wide x 21¼" front to back x 8½" deep

To be specified:

❏ Faucet:

❏ Faucet finish:

❏ Other:

Description:

Vitreous china bidet with single hole, for over-the-rim spray. Made by Ideal Standard™, Italy for Absolute℠. Shown with Olympia™ monoblock bidet fitting with porcelain cross handles from Absolute℠ by Ideal Standard™, Italy.

Colors:

Exclusively in white. May be coordinated with American Standard™ #020 White fixtures.

Dimensions:

15¾" wide x 24⅛ front to back x 15³⁄₁₆" high

To be specified:

❏ Single-hole, over-the-rim bidet fitting

❏ Other:

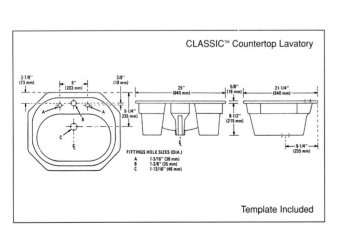

CLASSIC™ Countertop Lavatory

Template Included

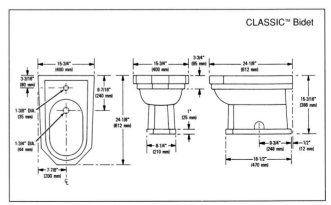

CLASSIC™ Bidet

For more information call: 1-800-359-3261

Enthoven™ Asymmetrical Right Hand Tall Pedestal, Water Closet, Bidet and Asymmetrical Left Hand Regular Pedestal

Perhaps it's the way it appeals to the eye—the delicacy of contour,
the sublety of form. Designed in Belgium by Axel Enthoven,
this collection evokes a distinct sensation of balance. Enthoven's constant theme
of total integration has resulted in fixtures that blend naturally
and unobtrusively into the bathroom environment.

ABSOLUTE℠
by
American Standard Inc.

A WORLD OF BATHROOMS
1-800-359-3261

0063.803 (regular) **0064.803** (tall)
Enthoven™ Asymmetrical Right Hand Pedestal

0060.803 (regular) **0061.803** (tall)
Enthoven™ Asymmetrical Left Hand Pedestal

Enthoven™ Asymmetrical Right Hand Tall Pedestal

Enthoven™ Asymmetrical Left Hand Regular Pedestal

Description:

Asymmetrical right or left hand vitreous china pedestal with rear overflow and faucet ledge. Available in 8" centers only. From American Standard™, Canada. Designed by Axel Enthoven. Great for corner installations. Shown with the Amarilis faucet with Lexington spout and Fabian handles from American Standard™. Pedestals must be corner mounted.

Colors:

Exclusively in white. May be coordinated with American Standard™ #020 White fixtures.

Dimensions:

Regular: 28½" wide x 20 ½" front to back x 31½" high
Tall: 28 ½" wide x 20 ½" front to back x 35 ½" high

To be specified:

❏ Right hand or left hand

❏ Regular or tall

❏ Faucet:

❏ Faucet finish:

❏ Other:

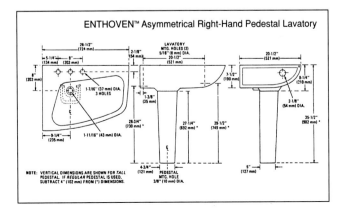

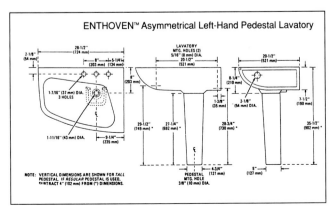

Description:

One-piece or two-piece, vitreous china water closet, 12" rough, elongated siphon-flushing action bowl with design-matched integrated toilet seat cover, 24 karat gold plated hinges and two bolt hole covers. Flushes 1.6 gallons per flush. Ceramic side-mounted flush actuator. Manufactured exclusively for Absolute℠ by Ideal Standard™.

Dimensions:

2028.035 One-Piece Water Closet
18" wide x 29½" front to back x 25" high

2288.016 Two-Piece Water Closet
18" wide x 29½" front to back x 28¼" high

Colors:

Exclusively in white. May be coordinated with American Standard™ #020 White fixtures.

Description:

Vitreous china bidet with rim wash and douche spray, integral overflow, concealed bolt covers, design-integrated cover with 24 karat gold plated hinges. Factory installed 24 karat gold plated and vitreous china color-matched control handles are concealed under cover when not in use. Includes wall-mounted vacuum breaker, and vitreous china vacuum breaker cover which can be used as an integral soap holder and towel holder. From American Standard™, Canada.

Colors:

Exclusively in white. May be coordinated with American Standard™ #020 White fixtures.

Dimensions:

17" wide x 28½" front to back x 17½" high

To be specified:

❏ Other:

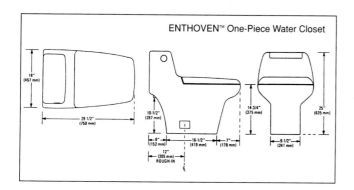

ENTHOVEN™ One-Piece Water Closet

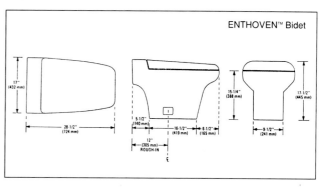

ENTHOVEN™ Bidet

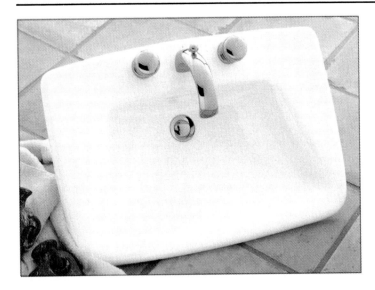

Colors:

Exclusively in white. May be coordinated with American Standard™ #020 White fixtures.

Dimensions:

26¾" wide x 18¾" front to back x 7⁵⁄₁₆" deep

To be specified:

❏ Faucet:

❏ Faucet finish:

❏ Other:

Suggested Coordinates:

Whirlpool/Bathing Pools	Faucets
Belvedere™	Cesello™
Sensorium Collection	Amarilis
Symphony Collection	

Description:

Self-rimming vitreous china countertop with rear overflow and faucet ledge. Available in 8" centers only. From American Standard™, Canada. Shown with the Amarilis faucet with Lexington spout and Fabian handles from American Standard™. Template included.

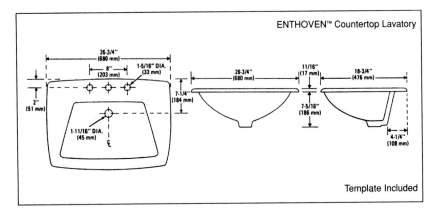

ENTHOVEN™ Countertop Lavatory

Template Included

Notes:

3.0895

KIMERA™ COLLECTION

Kimera™ Semi-Pedestal, Wall Hung Bidet and Wall Hung Water Closet

The Kimera™ Collection, featuring European-styled wall hung fixtures,
is an exquisite combination of ingenuity and practicality.
Elimination of the visible water closet tank offers unlimited and attractive
solutions for today's universal bathroom designs.

ABSOLUTE℠
by
American Standard Inc.

A WORLD OF BATHROOMS
1-800-359-3261

0285.001   Kimera™ Pedestal Lavatory

Description:
Vitreous china pedestal with rear overflow and faucet ledge. Available in center hole only. Manufactured by Ideal Standard™, Germany, for Absolute℠. Shown with Ceramix lavatory faucet in polished chrome by American Standard™.

Colors:
Exclusively in white. May be coordinated with American Standard™ #020 White fixtures.

Dimensions:
33½" wide x 22½" front to back x 33" high

To be specified:
❑ Faucet:

❑ Faucet finish:

❑ Other:

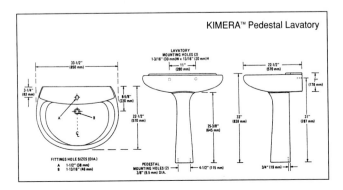

KIMERA™ Pedestal Lavatory

0265.601   Kimera™ Petite Pedestal Lavatory

Description:
Vitreous china pedestal with rear overflow and faucet ledge. Available in center hole only. Manufactured by Ideal Standard™, Germany, for Absolute℠. Shown with Ceralux lavatory faucet in chrome with edelmessing by Absolute℠.

Colors:
Exclusively in white. May be coordinated with American Standard™ #020 White fixtures.

Dimensions:
25½" wide x 21" front to back x 33" high

To be specified:
❑ Faucet:

❑ Faucet finish:

❑ Other:

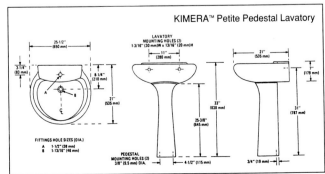

KIMERA™ Petite Pedestal Lavatory

3213.032
Kimera™ Semi-Pedestal Lavatory

3235.037
Kimera™ Petite Semi-Pedestal Lavatory

Description:

Vitreous china semi-pedestal with rear overflow and faucet ledge. Available in center hole only. Manufactured by Ideal Standard™, Germany, for Absolute℠. Shown with Ceralux lavatory faucet in chrome with edelmessing by Absolute™.

 ADA compliant

Colors:

Exclusively in white. May be coordinated with American Standard™ #020 White fixtures.

To be specified:

❏ Faucet:

❏ Faucet finish:

❏ Other:

Dimensions:

Semi-pedestal:
33½" wide x 22½" front to back x 20¼" high
Petite semi-pedestal:
25½" wide x 21" front to back x 20¼" high

Kimera™ Wall Hung Water Closet with Pre-Wall Installation and Kimera™ Petite Semi-Pedestal

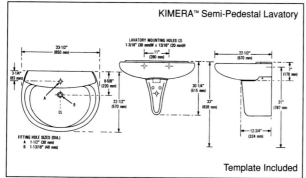

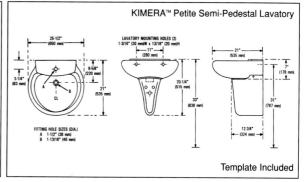

2051.019
Kimera™ Wall Hung Water Closet Pre-Wall Installation

2066.024
Kimera™ Wall Hung Water Closet In-Wall Installation

5031.039
Kimera™ Wall Hung Bidet

Description:

Vitreous china, 1.6 gallons per flush, one-piece wall hung bowl with ergonomically designed matching seat and cover. Concealed tank and bowl carrier for either pre-wall or in-wall installation. Actuator and access cover plate included. Manufactured in the USA by American Standard™ for Absolute℠.

 ADA compliant

Colors:

Exclusively in white. May be coordinated with American Standard™ #020 White fixtures.

Dimensions:

14⅜" wide x 21⅞" front to back x 13¾" high
Rim height may be mounted at 15" min. to 19" max.

To be specified:

❏ **2051.019** Pre-Wall   ❏ **2066.024** In-Wall

❏ Other:

Description:

Vitreous china wall hung bidet, single hole for over-the-rim spray. Manufactured by Ideal Standard™, Germany, for Absolute℠. Shown with Ceralux bidet fitting in chrome with edelmessing by Absolute℠.

Colors:

Exclusively in white. May be coordinated with American Standard™ #020 White fixtures.

Dimensions:

14½" wide x 23¹³⁄₁₆" front to back x 13¾" high
Rim height may be mounted at 15" min. to 19" max.

To be specified:

❏ Fitting:

❏ Fitting finish:

❏ Other:

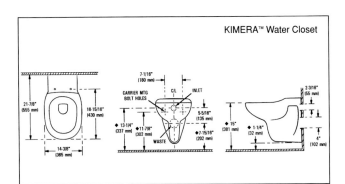

KIMERA™ Water Closet

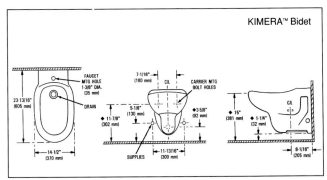

KIMERA™ Bidet

 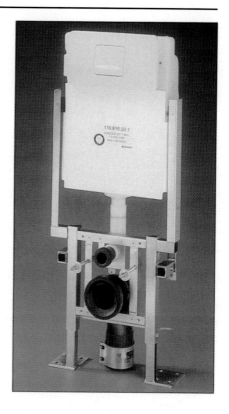

Kimera™ Petite Pedestal and Kimera™ Wall Hung Water Closet with In-Wall Installation

Description:

The Geberit Concealed Tank and Bowl Carrier, shipped with each Kimera™ Wall Hung Water Closet, is a fully factory assembled unit ready for easy installation at the job site. An instructional video on the installation of the Kimera™ Water Closet and Geberit System ships with every unit.

Geberit, with 30 years of experience in concealed tank and bowl carrier technology, is the market leader in Europe and the USA. The Geberit concealed tank is made of an impact resistant, high density polyethylene material that is insulated to eliminate condensation. The Geberit bowl carrier is made of structured galvanized steel and is designed to support both the flushing tank and the wall hung bowl.

The Geberit concealed tank is designed to be

mounted into a 2" x 6" stud wall. The *in-wall* unit mounts into an existing wall. The *pre-wall* unit mounts into a wall built in front of an existing wall. The tank, supply line, supply stop valve and flush pipe are, therefore, invisible. Only the attractive white access cover with the integrated trip lever indicates the presence of a flushing system. The flushing mechanism can be easily serviced through the access cover without having to shut off the main water supply.

The benefits of a concealed tank and wall hung bowl are: a quieter flush than conventional water closets, floor space savings of up to 6" on the in-wall installation, the ability to adjust the rim height from 15" to 19", ease of cleaning and improved aesthetics.

The Kimera™ Wall Hung Bidet comes with the Geberit concealed bowl carrier only.

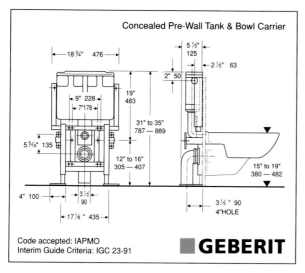

Concealed Pre-Wall Tank & Bowl Carrier

Code accepted: IAPMO
Interim Guide Criteria: IGC 23-91

GEBERIT

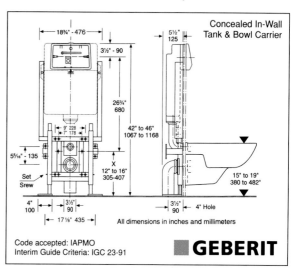

Concealed In-Wall Tank & Bowl Carrier

All dimensions in inches and millimeters

Code accepted: IAPMO
Interim Guide Criteria: IGC 23-91

GEBERIT

Colors:

Exclusively in white. May be coordinated with American Standard™ #020 White fixtures.

Dimensions:

19¾" wide x 19¾" front to back x 7½" deep

To be specified:

❏ **3209.015** Center hole

❏ **0482.803** 8" centers

❏ Faucet:

❏ Faucet finish:

❏ Other:

Description:

Vitreous china countertop lavatory with rear overflow and faucet ledge. Available in center hole and 8" centers. Manufactured by Ideal Standard™, Germany, for Absolute℠. Shown with Ceralux lavatory faucet in chrome with edelmessing.

Suggested Coordinates:

Whirlpool/Bathing Pools	Faucets
Sensorium Collection	Class™
Symphony Collection	Ceralux
	Amarilis

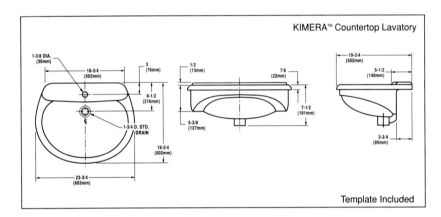

KIMERA™ Countertop Lavatory

Template Included

Notes:

4.0895

Bedminster™ Pedestal, Whirlpool with Apron Panel, Water Closet and Bidet

The Bedminster™ Collection is an entire suite of traditional fixtures
inspired by the graceful Victorian Era. The collection, manufactured in England
exclusively for Absolute℠, features a crisply defined sculpted rope decoration
which carries beautifully across every fixture. Bedminster's exceptional strength
of character adds an extra touch of period distinction to any bathroom.

ABSOLUTE℠
by
American Standard Inc.

A WORLD OF BATHROOMS
1-800-359-3261

0206.803 Bedminster™ Pedestal Lavatory

Description:
Vitreous china pedestal with decorative rear overflow, sculpted rope detailing, faucet ledge and backsplash. Available in 8" centers only. Made in England exclusively for Absolute℠. Shown with Jasmine lavatory fitting in polished brass with porcelain cross handles from American Standard™.

Colors:
Exclusively in white. May be coordinated with American Standard™ #215 Euro White fixtures.

Dimensions:
26½" wide x 21" front to back x 32¼" high + 3¾" backsplash

To be specified:
❏ Faucet:

❏ Faucet finish:

❏ Other:

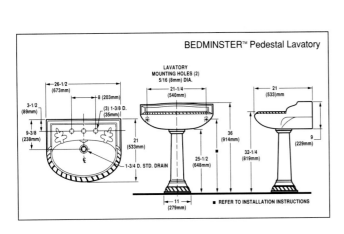

BEDMINSTER™ Pedestal Lavatory

REFER TO INSTALLATION INSTRUCTIONS

0212.403 Bedminster™ Pedestal Lavatory 4" Centers
0202.100 Bedminster™ Pedestal Lavatory Center Hole

Description:
Vitreous china pedestal with decorative rear overflow, sculpted rope detailing, faucet ledge and backsplash. Available in 4" centers or center hole. Made in England exclusively for Absolute℠. Shown with Cadet Prestige lavatory fitting in polished brass with porcelain cross handles from American Standard™.

Colors:
Exclusively in white. May be coordinated with American Standard™ #215 Euro White fixtures.

Dimensions:
23" wide x 19¼" front to back x 32" high + 2¾" backsplash

To be specified:
❏ 0202.403   4" centers

❏ 0202.100   Center hole

❏ Faucet:

❏ Faucet finish:

❏ Other:

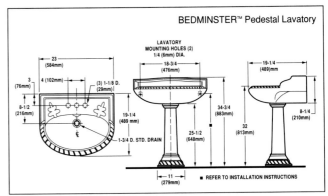

BEDMINSTER™ Pedestal Lavatory

REFER TO INSTALLATION INSTRUCTIONS

0212.403 **Bedminster™ Cloakroom Pedestal Lavatory 4" Centers**
0212.100 **Bedminster™ Cloakroom Pedestal Lavatory Center Hole**

2079.030.002 **Bedminster™ Two-Piece Water Closet Polished Chrome Trip Lever**
2079.030.099 **Bedminster™ Two-Piece Water Closet Polished Brass Trip Lever**

Description:
Vitreous china pedestal with decorative rear overflow, sculpted rope detailing, faucet ledge and backsplash. Available in 4" centers or center hole. Made in England exclusively for Absolute℠. Shown with Cadet Prestige lavatory fitting in polished brass with procelain cross handles from American Standard™.

Colors:
Exclusively in white. May be coordinated with American Standard™ #215 Euro White fixtures.

Dimensions:
19½" wide x 16⅜" front to back x 31" high + 1¾" backsplash

To be specified:
❏ **0212.403** 4" centers
❏ **0212.100** Center hole
❏ Faucet:
❏ Faucet finish:
❏ Other:

Description:
Vitreous china, two-piece, elongated bowl with concealed trapway, 1.6 gallons per flush, gravity flush, 12" rough. Sculpted rope detailing. Includes either polished chrome or polished brass and ceramic trip lever and matching seat. Made by Ideal Standard™ exclusively for Absolute℠.

Colors:
Exclusively in white. May be coordinated with American Standard™ #215 Euro White fixtures.

Dimensions:
17½" wide x 29" front to back x 30½" high + 2¼" backsplash

To be specified:
❏ **2079.030.002** Bedminster™ Two-Piece Water Closet with polished chrome trip lever and hinges
❏ **2079.030.099** Bedminster™ Two-Piece Water Closet with polished brass trip lever and hinges

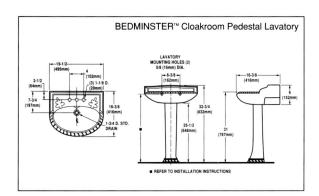

BEDMINSTER™ Cloakroom Pedestal Lavatory

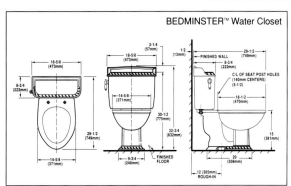

BEDMINSTER™ Water Closet

0212.004 Bedminster™ Wall Hung Basin 4" Centers
0212.001 Bedminster™ Wall Hung Basin Center Hole

0484.803 Bedminster™ Countertop Lavatory

Description:

Vitreous china countertop lavatory with decorative rear overflow, sculpted rope detailing and faucet ledge. Available in 8" centers only. Made in England exclusively for Absolute℠. Shown with Jasmine lavatory fitting in polished brass with perfume bottle handles by American Standard™.

Colors:

Exclusively in white. May be coordinated with American Standard™ #215 Euro White fixtures.

Dimensions:

22" wide x 17⅝" front to back x 8¼" deep

To be specified:

❏ Other:

Description:

Vitreous china wall hung lavatory with decorative rear overflow, sculpted rope detailing, faucet ledge and backsplash. Available in 4" centers or center hole. Made in England exclusively for Absolute℠. Shown with Cadet Prestige lavatory fitting in polished brass with porcelain cross handles from American Standard™.

Colors:

Exclusively in white. May be coordinated with American Standard™ #215 Euro White fixtures.

Dimensions:

19½" wide x 16⅜" front to back x 4½" high + 1¾" backsplash

To be specified:

❏ **0212.004** 4" centers
❏ **0212.001** Center hole
❏ Faucet:
❏ Faucet finish:
❏ Other:

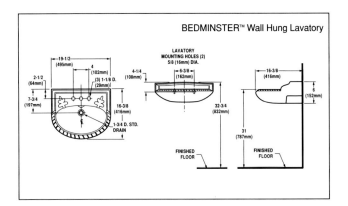

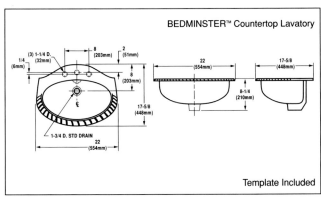

2737.018   **Bedminster™ Whirlpool**
2737.028   **Bedminster™ Whirlpool with System II**
2737.002   **Bedminster™ Bathing Pool**
2762.018   **Bedminster™ Apron Panel**

Description: Whirlpool

Acrylic construction with textured tub bottom. 3/4 HP self-draining pump/motor with DRY RUN seal; six multi-directional and individual flow adjustable jets, jet rings, two air volume controls; ON/OFF air switch; U.L. approved whirlpool system. Manufactured in the USA by American Standard™ for Absolute℠. Shown with American Standard™ Amarilis Jasmine deck mount tub filler in polished brass with porcelain handles.

Description: Whirlpool with System II

Same as above plus 1HP two-speed pump, electronic on/off switch with 20 minute built-in timer and chrome bezel. Factory installed in-line electric water heater available.

Description: Bathing Pool

Same as above less whirlpool.

Description: Apron Panel

For use with Bedminster™ whirlpool or bathing pool.

Colors:

Available in any American Standard™ acrylic color. Whirlpool shown may be coordinated with American Standard™ #215 Euro White fixtures.

To be specified:

- ❏ Drain: American Standard™ #1553.170 (.002 for Chrome, .099 for Brass, .094 for White)
- ❏ Tub Filler:
- ❏ Bath/Shower Valve:
- ❏ Shower Head:
- ❏ Body Sprays:
- ❏ Grab Bars:
- ❏ Air Control Kit (if other than #215 Euro White): 2 per kit, 1 kit required American Standard™ #9850.200 (.002 for Chrome, .099 for Brass, .094 for Gold)
- ❏ Jet Trim Ring Kit (if other than #215 Euro White): 2 per kit, 3 kits required American Standard™ #9860.200 (.002 for Chrome, .099 for Brass, .094 for Gold)
- ❏ Universal Tile Bead Kit: American Standard™ #751-755-100
- ❏ System II In-Line Heater: American Standard™ #9870.100

Specifications:

Tub size:	59¾" long x 31¾" wide x 20" deep
Whirlpool weight:	97 lbs.
Bathing pool weight:	82 lbs.
Whirlpool weight with water:	564 lbs.
Bathing pool weight with water:	549 lbs.
Gallons to overflow:	56 gallons
Sump dimensions:	42" x 18" x 20"

Electrical specifications-pump:

System I pump: 3/4 HP, 9.2 Amps., 115V
System II pump: 1 HP, 10.2 Amps., 115V

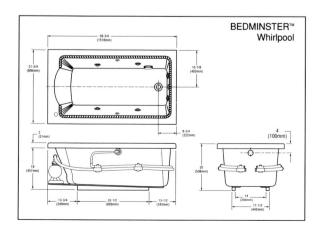

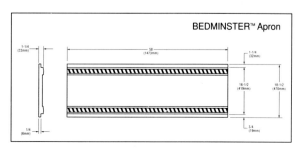

ABSOLUTE℠
by
American Standard Inc.

Description:

Vitreous china bidet with sculpted rope detailing. Available in single hole for over-the-rim spray. Made in England exclusively for Absolute℠. Show with Olympia bidet fitting in polished brass with porcelain cross handles by Absolute℠.

Colors:

Exclusively in white. May be coordinated with American Standard™ #215 Euro White fixtures.

Dimensions:

16⅜" wide x 24¼" front to back x 16" high + 1¾" ledge

To be specified:

❏ Single hole over-the-rim bidet fitting:

❏ Other:

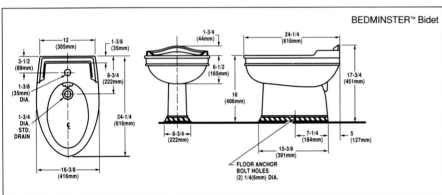

BEDMINSTER™ Bidet

Notes:

5.0895

DECO™ COLLECTION

Deco™ Water Closet, Pedestal and Whirlpool with Apron Panel

Deco™ awakens the Jazz Age in an "Art Deco" inspired suite perfectly suited
for smaller bathrooms. The clean, hexagonal forms of the traditional basin
are echoed in the design of the water closet, bidet and whirlpool.
The Deco™ Collection is ideal for renovation where space is limited,
but luxurious fixtures are desired.

ABSOLUTE℠
by
American Standard Inc.

A WORLD OF BATHROOMS
1-800-359-3261

0223.018 Deco™ Pedestal Lavatory

Description:

Vitreous china, rear overflow, pedestal lavatory. Available with 8" centers only. Manufactured in England for Ideal Standard™. Offers traditional styling in a compact size well suited for the small bath or renovation. Shown with the American Standard™ Amarilis goose neck, wide spread lavatory faucet with Iris metal cross handles in mixage.

Colors:

Exclusively in white. May be coordinated with American Standard™ #215 Euro White fixtures.

Dimensions:

22¾" wide x 18⅛" front to back x 31⅝" high

To be specified:

❏ Faucet: Wide spread lavatory faucet

American Standard™ fittings that can be mounted on the Deco™ Pedestal:
Amarilis Lexington spout (8871.000)
Amarilis Fabian spout (8811.000)
Heritage Gooseneck spout (7831.000)
Cadet Prestige/Porcelain cross handles (2272.232)
Cadet Prestige/Acrylic lever handles (2272.221)
Cadet Prestige/Clear acrylic handles (2272.310)
Cadet Prestige/Metal knob handles (2272.110)
Cadet Prestige Crescent spout/Porcelain cross handles (2290.232)
Cadet Prestige Crescent spout/Acrylic lever handles (2290.221).

❏ Faucet finish:

❏ Other:

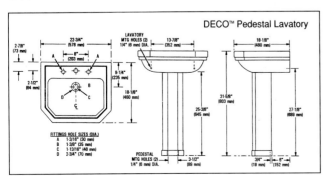

DECO™ Pedestal Lavatory

NOTE: Do not use faucet spouts with base diameter larger than 2" (51mm).

2059.147.002 Deco™ Two-Piece Water Closet Polished Chrome Trip Lever
2059.147.099 Deco™ Two-Piece Water Closet Polished Brass Trip Lever

Description:

Vitreous china, two-piece, round front bowl with exposed trapway, 1.6 gallons per flush, gravity flush, 12" rough. Includes either a polished chrome or polished brass and ceramic trip lever and matching seat. Manufactured exclusively for Absolute℠ by Ideal Standard™.

Colors:

Exclusively in white. May be coordinated with American Standard™ #215 Euro White fixtures.

Dimensions:

17" wide x 27" front to back x 29⅜" high

To be specified:

❏ **2059.147.002** Deco™ Two-Piece Water Closet with polished chrome trip lever and hinges
❏ **2059.147.099** Deco™ Two-Piece Water Closet with polished brass trip lever and hinges

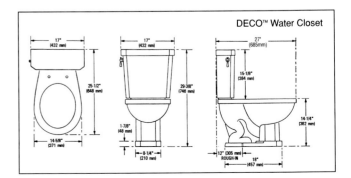

DECO™ Water Closet

2695.302   **Deco™ Whirlpool**
2695.028   **Deco™ Whirlpool with System II**
2695.202   **Deco™ Bathing Pool**
9035.019   **Deco™ Apron Panel**

Description: Whirlpool

Acrylic construction with textured tub bottom. 3/4 HP self-draining pump/motor with DRY RUN seal; six multi-directional and individual flow adjustable jets, jet rings, two air volume controls; ON/OFF air switch; U.L. approved whirlpool system. Manufactured in the USA for Absolute℠ by American Standard™. Shown with American Standard™ Amarilis Jasmine tub filler with Iris metal cross handles in mixage.

Description: Whirlpool with System II

Same as above plus 1 HP two-speed pump, electronic on/off switch with 20 minute built-in timer and chrome bezel. Factory installed in-line electric water heater available.

Description: Bathing Pool

Same as above less whirlpool.

Description: Apron Panel

For use with the Deco™ Whirlpool or Bathing Pool.

Colors:

Available in any American Standard™ acrylic color. Whirlpool shown may be coordinated with American Standard™ #215 Euro White fixtures.

To be specified:

- ❏ Drain: American Standard™ #1553.170
  (.002 for Chrome, .099 for Brass, .094 for Gold, .215 for Euro White)
- ❏ Tub Filler:
- ❏ Bath/Shower Valve:
- ❏ Shower Head:
- ❏ Body Sprays:
- ❏ Grab Bars:
- ❏ Air Control Kit (if other than #215 Euro White): 2 per kit, 1 kit required
  American Standard™ #9850.200
  (.002 for Chrome, .099 for Brass, .094 for Gold)
- ❏ Jet Trim Ring Kit (if other than #215 Euro White):
  2 per kit, 3 kits required. American Standard™ #9860.200
  (.002 for Chrome, .099 for Brass, .094 for Gold)
- ❏ Universal Tile Bead Kit: American Standard™ #751755-100
- ❏ System II In-Line Heater: American Standard™ #9870.100

Specifications:

Tub size:	59¾" long x 31¾" wide x 20" deep
Whirlpool weight:	97 lbs.
Bathing pool weight:	82 lbs.
Whirlpool weight with water:	580 lbs.
Bathing pool weight with water:	565 lbs.
Gallons to overflow:	58 gallons
Sump dimensions:	42" x 18" x 20"
Electrical specifications-pump:	System I: 3/4 HP, 9.2 Amps., 115V
	System II: 1 HP, 10.2 Amps., 115V

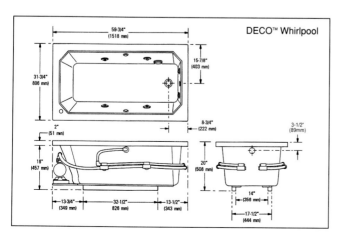

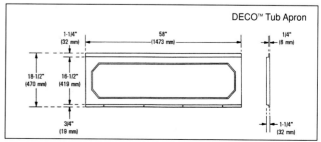

Description:
Vitreous china bidet with single hole for over-the-rim spray. Manufactured in England by Ideal Standard™ for Absolute℠. Shown with American Standard™ Amarilis over-the-rim bidet fitting with Heritage cross handles in polished chrome.

Colors:
Exclusively in white. May be coordinated with American Standard™ #215 Euro White fixtures.

Dimensions:
13¾" wide x 21⅝" front to back x 15⅜" high

To be specified:
❑ Single hole, over-the-rim bidet fitting

❑ Other:

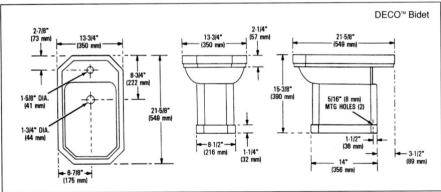

DECO™ Bidet

Notes:

For more information call: 1-800-359-3261

6.0895

SIENA™

Pedestal Lavatory

Siena™ Pedestal

Siena™ by Absolute℠– an exquisite pedestal lavatory. For those who love
the beauty and grace of a pedestal lavatory but hate to give up precious counterspace,
Absolute℠ offers a unique solution. Measuring a spectacular 61" wide,
Siena™ is sure to make a striking addition to any bath.

ABSOLUTE℠
by
American Standard Inc.

A WORLD OF BATHROOMS
1-800-359-3261

Description:

Manufactured for Absolute℠ by Ideal Standard™, Germany, Siena™ reflects ingenuity and grace in its design. Manufactured of fine fireclay, Siena™ features a generous bowl with rear overflow and faucet ledge.

Siena™ is shown with the Class™ chrome lavatory faucet from Absolute℠.

Colors:

Exclusively in white. May be coordinated with American Standard™ #020 White fixtures.

Special:

Due to the extra large size of the basin, a properly reinforced wall for mounting is required.

Dimensions:

Pedestal: 61" wide x 21 ¼" front to back x 33⅝" high
Bowl size: 21" wide x 13" front to back x 8" deep

To be specified:

❏ Faucet:

❏ Faucet finish:

❏ Other:

Suggested Coordinates:

Faucets	Toilets/Bidets	Whirlpools/Baths
Class™	Enthoven™	Sensorium Collection
Ceralux™	Kimera™	Symphony Collection
Olympia™	Fontaine	Scala

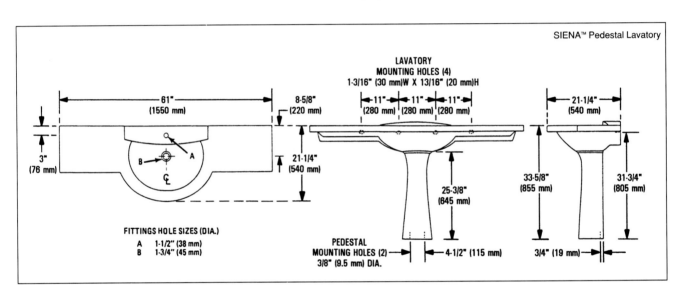

SIENA™ Pedestal Lavatory

LAVATORY MOUNTING HOLES (4)
1-3/16" (30 mm)W X 13/16" (20 mm)H

61" (1550 mm)
8-5/8" (220 mm)
3" (76 mm)
21-1/4" (540 mm)

FITTINGS HOLE SIZES (DIA.)
A   1-1/2" (38 mm)
B   1-3/4" (45 mm)

11" (280 mm)   11" (280 mm)   11" (280 mm)
25-3/8" (645 mm)

PEDESTAL MOUNTING HOLES (2)
3/8" (9.5 mm) DIA.
4-1/2" (115 mm)

21-1/4" (540 mm)
33-5/8" (855 mm)
31-3/4" (805 mm)
3/4" (19 mm)

8.0895

THE CHRISTINE BELFOR COLLECTION

Hand Painted Countertops

Hey! Diddle, Diddle!™

The Owl & The Pussycat™

Hey! Diddle, Diddle!™ and The Owl & The Pussycat™ hand painted children's basins
feature classic nursery rhyme designs which are timely, beautiful
and will become a family heirloom to be passed on for generations.

ABSOLUTE℠
by
American Standard Inc.

A WORLD OF BATHROOMS
1-800-359-3261

❏ **2344.200 Leopard**™
Hand Painted
Spread Lavatory Faucet
Available in polished brass
with the hand painted lever
handles (mechanical
drawings available upon
request).

0475.318   Leopard™

3196.110   Damask™

Absolute℠ offers a distinguished
collection of hand painted
lavatory designs. Choose the
exotic Leopard™ basin and add
a touch of the Safari to your
bathroom. Damask™ is a
traditional tone-on-tone design
reminiscent of treasured linens
and will easily coordinate with
any decor. The Indian Block
Print™ is a rich, natural design
available in three luxurious
color options.

❏ **0042.211**
Rain Forest
Green

❏ **0042.209**
Indigo Blue

0042.018   Indian Block Print™ **in Berry**

9019.004　Hibiscus™

Add a splash of color to your bath with the Harlequin™ and Hibiscus™ hand painted basins. Harlequin™ and Hibiscus™ are self-rimming vitreous china bowls manufactured in Costa Rica. Available in 4" centers only, they are shown with the Cadet Prestige™ centerset lavatory faucet in polished brass from American Standard™.

Mosaic™ evokes an old world European feeling which ccordinates with today's most popular floor and wall tile designs. This undercounter mount lavatory is shown with the Jasmine lavatory fitting in polished brass from American Standard™. Mosaic™ is available in a variety of color options.

9021.104　Harlequin™

3185.224　Mosaic™ **in Black and Cream**

❏ **3115.174**
Black and Grey

❏ **3122.094**
Terra Cotta and Cream

If you're looking for dramatic bowl designs, Absolute℠ offers Fishbowl™, Galaxy™ and Grapevine™. All basins are hand painted on vitreous china bowls and require a deck mounted faucet. Fishbowl™ is a colorful, whimsical design with a tropical theme.

3187.210   Fishbowl™

Galaxy™ features 22 karat gold stars set against an elegant cobalt blue bowl. Grapevine™ is a sophisticated design available in purple, green or autumn. All hand painted basins are extremely durable and ideal for individuals looking to create a one-of-a-kind bathroom.

3194.134   Galaxy™

3182.169   Grapevine™ in Purple

❏ **3179.127** Green

❏ **3183.114** Autumn

THE CHRISTINE BELFOR COLLECTION

Hand Painted Countertops

Absolute℠, A World of Bathrooms, is proud to present
The Christine Belfor Collection. These exiting hand painted vitreous china
countertop lavatories are available in a dramatic color palette.
This opulent, exotic collection was designed by New York artist
Christine Belfor exclusively for Absolute℠ and represents the ultimate
in luxury and sophistication for the discriminating client.
Christine Belfor's use of innovative glazing and firing techniques
produces decorative products of lasting durability and timeless beauty.

0164.013   Tassels™ in Royal Blue

❏ **0164.173** Magenta

❏ **0164.202** Gold

On front cover:

❏ **9456.803** Hey! Diddle, Diddle!™
Hey! Diddle, Diddle!™ is shown with the Jasmine
lavatory fitting with perfume bottle handles in polished
brass from American Standard™.

❏ **0023.015** The Owl & The Pussycat™
The Owl & The Pussycat™ is shown with the Jasmine
lavatory fitting in polished brass with porcelain cross
handles from American Standard™.

Mechanical drawings:

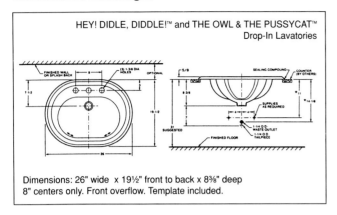

HEY! DIDLE, DIDDLE!™ and THE OWL & THE PUSSYCAT™
Drop-In Lavatories

Dimensions: 26" wide x 19½" front to back x 8⅜" deep
8" centers only. Front overflow. Template included.

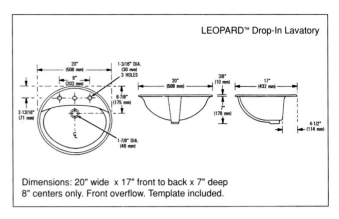

LEOPARD™ Drop-In Lavatory

Dimensions: 20" wide x 17" front to back x 7" deep
8" centers only. Front overflow. Template included.

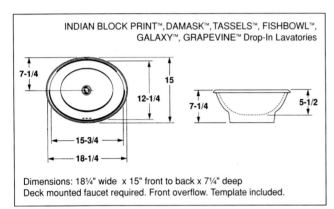

**INDIAN BLOCK PRINT™, DAMASK™, TASSELS™, FISHBOWL™,
GALAXY™, GRAPEVINE™ Drop-In Lavatories**

Dimensions: 18¼" wide x 15" front to back x 7¼" deep
Deck mounted faucet required. Front overflow. Template included.

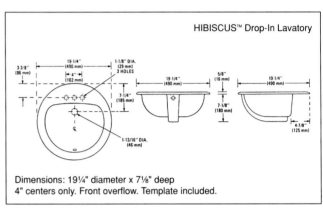

HIBISCUS™ Drop-In Lavatory

Dimensions: 19¼" diameter x 7⅛" deep
4" centers only. Front overflow. Template included.

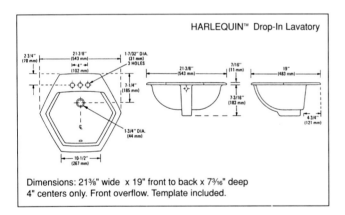

HARLEQUIN™ Drop-In Lavatory

Dimensions: 21⅜" wide x 19" front to back x 7³⁄₁₆" deep
4" centers only. Front overflow. Template included.

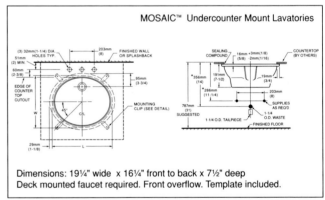

MOSAIC™ Undercounter Mount Lavatories

Dimensions: 19¼" wide x 16¼" front to back x 7½" deep
Deck mounted faucet required. Front overflow. Template included.

Description:

All basins are hand painted on vitreous china lavatories and have front overflow holes. Templates are included with all basins.

Colors:

Exclusively in white with hand painted designs in colors as shown. May be coordinated with American Standard™ #020 White fixtures. Galaxy™ available exclusively in cobalt blue.

Use and care:

Clean with a non-ammoniated, non-abrasive, pure liquid soap and warm water. Wipe with a soft cotton cloth. Abrasives are not recommended. An occassional application of glass wax will help maintain the lustrous finish of the hand painted basin.

To be specified:

❏ Faucet:
❏ Faucet finish:
❏ Other:

For more information call: 1-800-359-3261

American Standard

C566
BuyLine 7300

THE BATHROOM BOOK
— now everybody wants in —

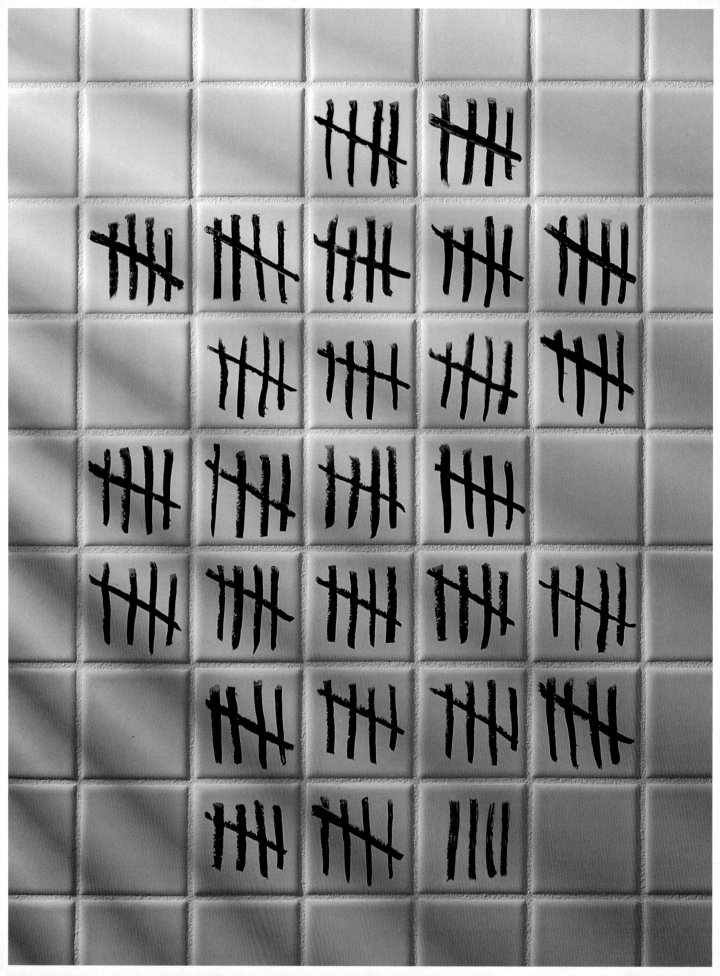

We've been in the bathroom for 134 years

That's a long time to make funny faces in the chrome faucet spout. But all those years mean more than a lot of towels on the floor. We know for a fact our toilets last and last because we've been here to see it. It follows that our faucets are just as safe as they are stunning. And we're sure our whirlpools can wash away your troubles because our tubs have been washing away troubles since the Great Depression. That really made you want to sit and soak. Still, there's one thing we've noticed lately. People talk about their bathrooms more and more. Some actually refer to them as "an investment." They're finally coming around to our point of view. A bathroom can be a pretty nifty place. If we didn't believe that, we'd have come out the first time someone pounded on the door

Life once took longer than it does today. Once,

rapid transit meant the merry-go-round at the park.

People couldn't help but relax. Men

smoked pipes. Women wore pearls to

the supermarket. Children

washed up before dinner.

heritage

That's the era that inspired

our Heritage suite. It's a real classic.

Sculpted lines. Brass handles. An air of

refinement. Not that you'll notice all of this in the mad

dash to the carpool. But at least you'll know it's there.

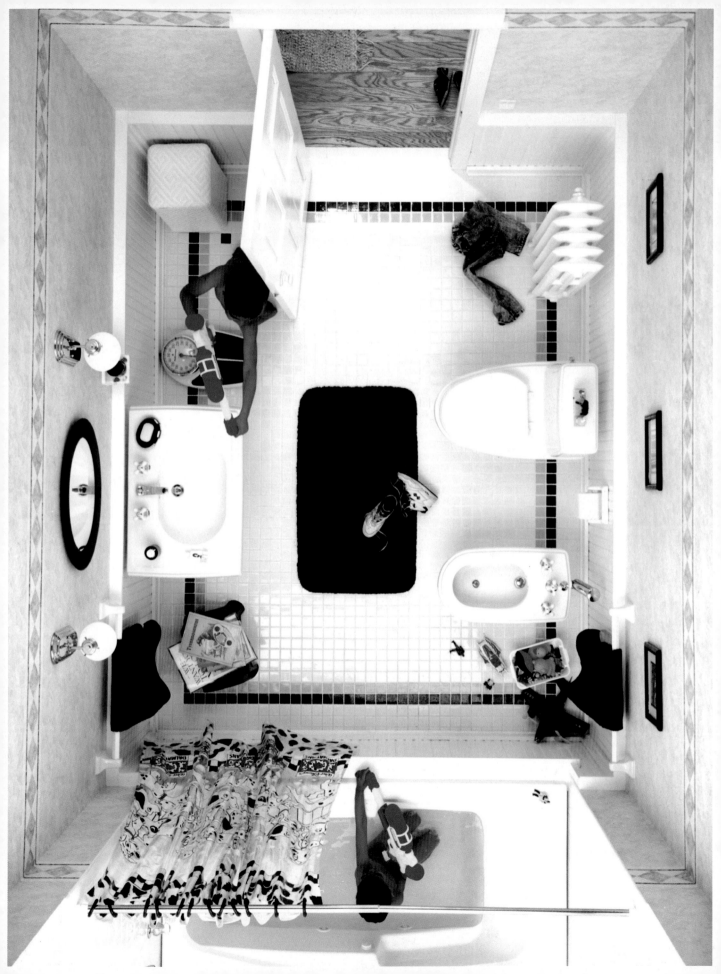

A Heritage EL 1.6/PA
Low-profile, vitreous china toilet. Traditional styling. Uses pressure-assisted flushing action. Design-matched elongated seat and cover. Elegant chrome-plated side trip lever, other finishes available.

B Pallas EL 1.6
Contemporary low-profile design. Vitreous china. Uses gravity-fed flushing action. Design-matched elongated contoured seat for comfort. Side push-button actuator.

C Ellisse EL 1.6
Sleek, low-profile design. Vitreous china. Uses gravity-fed flushing action. Design-matched elongated contoured seat. Color-matched side push-button actuator.

D High Hamilton EL 1.6
Exclusive space-saving low profile design. Vitreous china. Elongated front for comfort. Elongated bowl fits into the same space as most round bowls. Extra height meets ADA requirements. Includes Rise-and-Shine seat for easy cleaning. Gravity-fed flushing action. Color-matched trip lever.

E Hamilton EL 1.6
Exclusive space-saving low-profile design. Vitreous china. Elongated front for comfort. Elongated bowl fits into the same space as most round bowls. Includes Rise-and-Shine toilet seat for easy cleaning. Gravity-fed flushing action. Color-matched trip lever, other finishes available.

F Heritage 2-pc EL 1.6
Traditional styling. Vitreous china two-piece toilet. Uses gravity-fed flushing action. Design-matched seat and cover. Chrome-plated side trip lever, other finishes available.

Fontaine™ EL 1.6/PA
One-piece design with Rise-and-Shine toilet seat for easy cleaning. Vitreous china. Uses
pressure-assisted flushing action. Elongated front for comfort. Chrome-plated top button actuator, other finishes available.

A Ellisse 2-pc EL 1.6
Sculpted tank design. Vitreous china.
Elongated front for comfort. Gravity-fed
flushing action. Color-matched trip lever.

B Cascada EL 1.6
Elegantly styled two-piece design.
Vitreous china. Gravity-fed flushing action.
Elongated front for comfort. Also available
in round front to conserve space. Color-
matched trip lever, other finishes available.

C Antiquity EL 1.6
Turn-of-the-century detailing. Vitreous
china. Gravity-fed flushing action. Elongated
bowl. Smooth-sided concealed trapway.
Chrome-plated trip lever. Available in White.

D Calais 2-pc EL 1.6
Elegant European styling. Vitreous china.
Elongated front for comfort. Gravity-fed
flushing action. Color-matched trip lever.

E Antiquity RF 1.6
Turn-of-the-century detailing.
Vitreous china two-piece toilet. Space-saving
round-front bowl. Available in White.
Gravity-fed flushing action.

F Clarion
Contemporary styling. Vitreous
china, two-piece toilet. Elongated front for
comfort. Gravity-fed flushing action.
Color-matched trip lever.

New Lexington EL 1.6
Elegant low-profile design. Vitreous china. Gravity-fed flushing
action. Elongated front for comfort. Color-matched side push button actuator.

Infinity EL 1.6

Contemporary style. Vitreous china two-piece toilet. Gravity-fed flushing action.
Elongated front for comfort. Also available in round front to conserve space. Color-matched trip lever.

Cadet II 1.6

Choice of elongated front for comfort or round front to conserve space. Gravity-fed flushing action. Color-matched trip lever.
Exclusive Speed Connect™ for rapid installation. Also available for 10" or 14" roughing in. Optional Aquaguard liner to reduce tank sweating.

A Chloe 2-pc EL 1.6
Curving, European design. Vitreous china two-piece toilet. Elongated front for comfort. Gravity-fed flushing action. Color-matched trip lever.

B Cadet 1.6/PA
Vitreous china two-piece toilet with option of elongated front for comfort or round front to conserve space. Pressure-assisted flushing action. Exclusive Speed Connect™ system for rapid installation. Side-mounted trip lever.

C Linear RF 1.6
Vitreous china two-piece toilet. Space-saving round-front bowl. Available in White, Bone, Silver and Peach Blossom. Gravity-fed flushing action.

D Cadet II 16⅜" H 1.6/PA
Extra height for comfort and accessibility. Vitreous china two-piece toilet with elongated bowl. Gravity-fed flushing action. Exclusive Speed Connect™ for rapid installation. Side-mounted trip lever.

E Renaissance 1.6
Vitreous china two-piece toilet. Option of either elongated front for comfort or space-saving round front. Available in White, Bone, Silver, Peach Blossom, and Black. Gravity-fed flushing action.

F Yorkville EL 1.6/PA
Vitreous china two-piece back-outlet toilet. Elongated front for comfort. Pressure-assisted flushing action. Exclusive Speed Connect™ for rapid installation. Side-mounted trip lever.

A Heritage Bidet
Traditional styling. Vitreous china.
Vertical cleansing spray. Deck-mounted
faucet. Shown with Amarilis faucet and
Porcelain Cross handles.

B Ellisse Bidet
Vitreous china. Deck-mounted
faucet. Vertical cleansing spray. Shown with
Amarilis faucet and Fabian handles.

C Roma Bidet
Vitreous china. Deck-mounted
faucet. Option of vertical cleansing spray or
over-the-rim spray. Shown with Amarilis
faucet and Lexington handles.

D Pallas Bidet
Vitreous china. Deck-mounted
faucet. Option of vertical cleansing spray or
over-the-rim spray. Shown with Amarilis
faucet and Fabian handles.

E Madval Bidet
Vitreous china. Available with
option of deck-mounted or wall-mounted
faucet. Option of vertical cleansing spray
or over-the-rim spray.

F Lexington Bidet
Vitreous china. Deck-mounted
faucet. Option of vertical cleansing spray or
over-the-rim spray. Shown with Amarilis
faucet and Triune Cross handles.

Heritage Pedestal Lavatory (shown) and Heritage Petite Pedestal Lavatory
Traditional styling. 31" high. Choose from 30" x 20" or the Petite at 24" x 20." Vitreous china. Available with faucet holes at 8." Shown with Amarilis Jasmine faucet and Jasmine Perfume Bottle handles.

Antiquity Pedestal Lavatory
Turn-of-the-century styling with delicate pattern on deck. 33" high x 24½" x 19." Vitreous china. Available with faucet holes at 8," 4," and center only. Available in White. Shown with Cadet Prestige Porcelain Cross handles.

Roma Pedestal Lavatory
Clean lines. 31" high x 30" x 20½." Vitreous china. Available with faucet holes at 8," 4," and center only. Shown with Amarilis Iris faucet and Iris Cross handles.

Pallas Pedestal Lavatory
Contemporary design. 31" high x 30½" x 19." Vitreous china. Available with faucet holes at 8," 4," and center only. Shown with Amarilis Lexington spout and Heritage Wrist Blade handles.

Ellisse Pedestal Lavatory (shown) and Ellisse Petite Pedestal Lavatory
Graceful design. 31½" high. Vitreous china. Available with faucet holes at 8," 4," and center only.
Choose from 26¾" wide or the Petite at 24½" wide. Shown with Amarilis Iris faucet with Iris Metal Lever handles.

Seychelle

Sculptured shell patterned bowl. 34" high x 23½" x 19." Vitreous china. Available with faucet holes at 8," 4," and center only. Shown with Amarilis Iris faucet with Metal Lever handles.

Repertoire

Classically sculptured. 34" high x 24" x 20." Vitreous china. Available with faucet holes at 8," 4," and center only. Shown with Amarilis Iris faucet with Metal Lever handles.

Hydra Pedestal Lavatory

Vitreous china. 30½" high x 21¾" x 17¾." Available with faucet holes at 4." Available in White and Bone. Shown with Cadet Prestige faucet.

Renaissance Pedestal Lavatory

Large deck area. Vitreous china. 31½" high x 23" x 18¼." Available with faucet holes at 8" and 4." Shown with Cadet Prestige faucet.

Tilche Pedestal Lavatory
Choose either 31½" or 34" high x 22" x 21".
Vitreous china. Available with faucet holes at 8", 4", and center only.
Shown with Ceramix faucet.

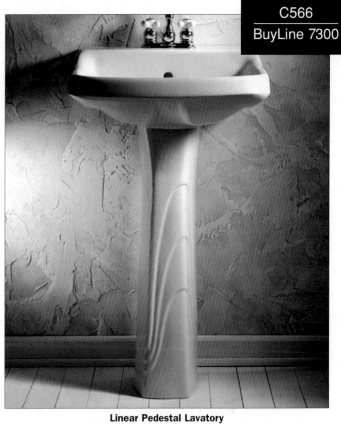

Linear Pedestal Lavatory
Unique sculpted design. Fits in compact spaces. 32¼" high
x 20½" x 18½". Vitreous china. Available with faucet holes at 8" and 4".
Shown with Cadet Prestige faucet.

Lexington Pedestal Lavatory
Choose either 31½" or 34" high x 24" x 18".
Vitreous china. Available with faucet holes at 8", 4", and center only.
Shown with Ceratop faucet.

Cadet Pedestal Lavatory
Full size pedestal lavatory with generous 24" x 20" basin.
Vitreous china. 31½" high. Available with faucet holes at 8" and 4".
Shown with Reliant+ faucet.

Heritage Countertop Lavatory
Traditional styling. 26" wide x 19½." Vitreous china. Available
with faucet holes at 8." Shown with Amarilis Jasmine faucet and Jasmine Perfume Bottle handles.

Pallas Countertop Lavatory and Pallas Petite Countertop Lavatory
Self-rimming. Offered in both 26" x 18" (shown) and 24" x 18." Vitreous china.
Available with faucet holes at 8," 4," and center only. Shown with Amarilis Iris faucet and Iris Cross handles.

Roma Countertop Lavatory
Self-rimming. Vitreous china. 26" x 20." Available with faucet holes
at 8," 4," and center only. Shown with Amarilis Lexington spout and Lexington handles.

Ellisse Countertop Lavatory
Self-rimming. Vitreous china. Choose from 24" wide x 20" or the Petite at 24" x 18½."
Available with faucet holes at 8," 4," and center only. Shown with Amarilis Iris faucet and Iris Cross handles.

Lexington Countertop Lavatory
Self-rimming. Vitreous china. 22" x 19." Available
with faucet holes at 8," 4," and center only. Shown with Sottini
Azimuth faucet and Lever handles.

Ovalyn™ Countertop Lavatory
Dramatic undermount (shown) or flush-to-counter
installation. Vitreous china. Two sizes: 19¼" x 16¼" or 21¼" x 17¼."
Shown with Cadet Prestige faucet.

Ceramica Decorativa French Tulip™
Elegant self-rimming design. Vitreous china. 18¾" wide x 15½." Available
with 8" x 8" tiles in White, matching patterns or matching border design.
Shown with Amarilis Jasmine faucet and Jasmine Cross handles.

Ceramica Decorativa White
Self-rimming. Vitreous china. 20¼" wide x 16½."
Shown with Amarilis Iris faucet and Iris Cross handles.

Shapes Trapezoid
Unique geometric shape allows faucet placement to the side or
back for design interest and accessibility. Self-rimming. Vitreous china.
21" wide x 14." Shown with Reliant faucet.

Shapes Oval
Unique geometric shape allows faucet placement to the side or
back for design interest and accessibility. Self-rimming. Vitreous china.
20" wide x 14." Shown with Ceramix faucet.

Shapes Rectangle
Unique geometric shape allows faucet placement to the side or back for
design interest and accessibility. Self-rimming. Vitreous china. 21" wide x 14". Shown with Reliant faucet.

Antiquity™ Countertop Lavatory
Traditional design. Self-rimming. Vitreous china. 24½" wide x 18", fits standard
20" x 17" cutout in countertop. Available with faucet holes at 8" and 4". Shown with Cadet Prestige faucet.

Tulip™ Countertop Lavatory
A space-saver, measuring 19" x 16." Unique detailing. Self-rimming.
Vitreous china. Available with faucet holes at 4" and center only. Shown with Cadet Prestige faucet.

Chloe Countertop Lavatory
Curved, European design. Self-rimming. Vitreous china. 22" x 18½."
Available with faucet holes at 8," 4," and center only. Shown with Sottini Azimuth faucet and Lever handles.

Hexalyn™ Countertop Lavatory

Geometric design. Self-rimming. Vitreous china. 22" x 19."
Available with faucet holes at 8," 4," and center only. Shown with
Heritage faucet and Wrist Blade handles.

Lily™ Countertop Lavatory

Generous bowl for washing and shampooing. Self-rimming. Vitreous
china. 22" x 19." Available with faucet holes at 8," 4," and center only. Shown
with Amarilis Lexington faucet and Heritage Wrist Blade handles.

Rondalyn™ Countertop Lavatory

Self-rimming. Vitreous china. 19" diameter. Available
with faucet holes at 8," 4," and center only. Shown with Sottini
Azimuth faucet and Cross handles.

Linear™ Countertop Lavatory

Unique sculpted design with option of round or oval design.
Self-rimming. Vitreous china. Two sizes: 19" diameter or 20" wide x 17."
Available with faucet holes at 8" and 4." Shown with Cadet faucet.

Renaissance Countertop Lavatory

Self-rimming. Vitreous china. Two sizes: 19" diameter
or 20" wide x 17." Available with faucet holes at 8" and 4."
Shown with Cadet faucet.

Aqualyn™ Countertop Lavatory

Self-rimming. Vitreous china. 20" wide x 17."
Available with faucet holes at 8," 4," and center only. Shown with
Cadet wide-spread faucet.

Ascencia™ Countertop Lavatory

Self-rimming. Durable Americast® material with glossy porcelain finish.
Sloped front wall, perfect for shampooing. 23¾" wide x 19¼". Available
with faucet holes at 8," 4," and center only. Shown with Amarilis
Heritage faucet and Heritage Wrist Blade handles.

Acclivity™ Ivy Countertop Lavatory

Self-trimming. 19" diameter. Americast material, with traditional
ivy pattern fired into porcelain surface. Also available with Brush Strokes
pattern or without decoration. Choice of faucet holes at 8," 4," and
center only. Shown with Cadet Prestige with cross handles.

Affinity™ Countertop Lavatory

Self-rimming. 20¾" x 17½". Americast material with contemporary
Brush Strokes pattern fired into porcelain surface. Also available with Ivy
pattern or without decoration. Choice of faucet holes at 8," 4," or
center only. Shown with Cadet Prestige with cross handles.

Ashmont Lavatory

Option of self-rimming or (as shown) dramatic undermount installation.
Durable Americast material with glossy porcelain finish. Large
bowl area. 18¾" diameter. Shown with Amarilis Iris faucet
and Iris Cross handles.

Horizon™ Countertop Lavatory

Space-saver for smaller bathrooms. 19" diameter.
Self-rimming. Enameled cast iron. 4" faucet holes. Shown with Amarilis
Heritage faucet and Heritage Cross handles.

La Terrasse™ Countertop Lavatory

Contoured sides step down into generous bowl.
Self-rimming. Enameled cast iron. Flexibility of
faucet placement to back or sides. 20" wide x 16½". Shown with
Amarilis Heritage faucet and Heritage Lever handles.

Delicacy™ Countertop Lavatory
Delicately contoured sides spiral into a generous bowl. Self-rimming. Enameled cast iron. Flexibility
of faucet placement to back or sides. 20" wide x 16½." Shown with Amarilis Heritage faucet and Heritage Cross handles.

Oval Horizon™ Countertop Lavatory
Self-rimming. Enameled cast iron. 19¼" wide x 16¼."
8", 4" faucet holes. Shown with Amarilis Heritage faucet and Heritage Cross handles.

Promenade Lavatory

Self-rimming. Enameled cast iron. Softly rounded bowl and front wall slope down to deep well in center. For shampooing hair or washing delicates without filling entire bowl. Flexibility of faucet placement left or right. 30" wide x 18½." Shown with Ceramix Lift faucet.

Ovation™ Tulip Countertop Lavatory

Self-rimming. Enameled steel. 20" wide x 17." Faucet holes at 4." Available in White or Bone. Shown with Amarilis Heritage faucet and Heritage Cross handles.

Highlyn™ Countertop Lavatory

Enameled cast iron. For mounting frame installation. Dual soap depressions. 20" wide x 18" front to back. Available with faucet holes at 8" and 4." Shown with Amarilis Heritage faucet and Heritage Lever handles.

Vanette Poppy™ Countertop Lavatory

Self-rimming. Enameled steel. 19" diameter. Faucet holes at 4." Available in White or Bone. Shown with Amarilis Heritage faucet and Heritage Lever handles.

Spacelyn™ Countertop Lavatory

Perfect for tight spaces at 20" wide x 12." Corner faucet installation option of right or left. Faucet holes at 4." Enameled cast iron. For mounting frame installation. Shown with Amarilis Heritage faucet and Heritage Lever handles.

Ledgelyn™ Countertop Lavatory

Enameled cast iron. For mounting frame installation. 19" wide x 16." Available with faucet holes at 8" and 4." Shown with Amarilis Heritage faucet and Heritage Lever handles.

Circlyn™ Countertop Lavatory
Enameled cast iron. For mounting frame installation.
18" diameter. Available with faucet holes at 8" and 4". Shown
with Reliant+ faucet.

Corner Minette™ Wall-Hung Lavatory
Perfect for tight spaces. Only 11" by 16¼." Unique corner installation.
Vitreous china. 4" faucet holes only. Shown with Reliant+ faucet.

Lucerne™ Wall-Hung Lavatory
Wall-hung for accessibility. Vitreous china. 20" x 18."
Available with faucet holes at 8", 4." Shown with Reliant+ faucet.

Comrade™ Wall-Hung Lavatory
Wall-hung for accessibility. Soap depression on deck. Vitreous
china. 20" wide x 18." 4" faucet holes only. Shown with Reliant faucet.

Ellisse ADA Semi-Pedestal Lavatory
Spacious wall-mounted lavatory with drop front for easier access.
Meets ADA requirements. Vitreous china. 26¾" x 21¼". Available with faucet
holes at 8" and 4." Shown with Amarilis Heritage faucet and
Heritage Wrist Blade handles.

Declyn™ Wall-Hung Lavatory
Wall-hung for accessibility. Soap depression on deck. Vitreous
china. 19" wide x 17." 4" faucet holes only. Shown with Reliant faucet.

Water when it gurgles puts an orchestra to shame.

Our Symphony whirlpools look smashing and new, but,

oh, the music in your mind when you slink down in. The

shape of the tub envelops you. The curves cling to your

body. Even wet. There are tubs for two,

symphony

tubs for all shapes of bathrooms. Plus, the

accessories are in total harmony. Grab bars wrap around.

Headrests fit snuggly. And the hand spray, when not in

use, makes a fine baton for conducting.

Rondo Whirlpool

Idealcast™. 72" x 42" x 21½". Oval. Two-person bathing. 1hp two-speed pump. Eight jets. Wave grab bar. Also available in tub only.

Symphony Accessories

 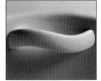 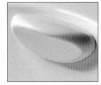 

| **Grab Bar - Twist and Rotary Drain** | **Grab Bar - Wave** | **Bath Filler - Integral** | **Bath Filler - Deck Mounted** | **Fittings with Hand Shower** | **Headrest - Large & Small** |

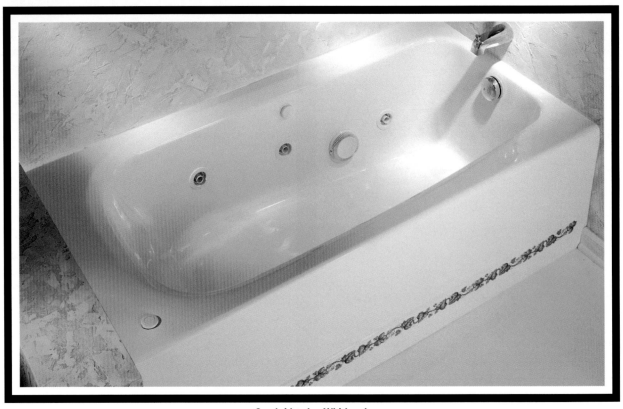

Cambridge Ivy Whirlpool
Americast® with traditional Ivy pattern fired into glossy porcelain finish. Fits existing tub recess. Integral apron.
60" x 32" with 17¾" depth. ¾ hp, single-speed pump/motor with deck-mounted controls. Six directional and flow adjustable jets.
Two air volume controls. Integral headrest and lumbar support. Optional grab bars. Also available without pattern or in tub only.

Cambridge Brush Strokes Whirlpool
Americast with contemporary Brush Stroke pattern fired into glossy porcelain finish. Fits existing tub recess. Integral
apron. 60" x 32" with 17¾" depth. ¾ hp, single-speed pump/motor with deck-mounted controls. Six directional and flow adjustable jets.
Two air volume controls. Integral headrest and lumbar support. Optional grab bars. Also available without pattern or in tub only.

Heritage 6' Whirlpool

Idealcast™. 72" x 36" x 21½". Integral faucet deck. Dual integral arm rests. Grab bar. Four multi-directional,
individually flow-rate adjustable body massage jets and two multi-directional, flow-rate adjustable ideal-flow jets. Center drain outlet.
Whirlpool control options. Optional grab bars. New for 1996.

Heritage 5' Whirlpool

Idealcast. 60" x 42" x 21½". Integral faucet deck. Grab bar. Four multi-directional, individually flow-rate
adjustable body massage jets and two multi-directional, individually flow-rate adjustable ideal-flow jets. Center drain outlet.
Whirlpool control options. Optional apron panel and grab bars. New for 1996.

Sensorium Corner Whirlpool
Acrylic. 62" x 62" x 22". Two person bathing. 1hp two-speed pump. Integral bath filler.
Fittings include hand shower. Eight jets. One grab bar. Rotary drain and overflow. Integrated seat. Also available in tub only.

Sensorium Whirlpool
Acrylic. 72" x 44" x 20". Two person bathing. 1hp two-speed pump. Integral bath filler.
Fittings include hand shower. Six jets. Two grab bars. Rotary drain and overflow. Also available in tub only.

Heritage 5' Built-In Whirlpool
Idealcast." 60" x 32" x 21½." Six directional
and flow adjustable jets. Left or right hand drain outlet. Whirlpool
control options. Optional apron panel. New for 1996.

Ellisse 6' Whirlpool
Idealcast. 72" x 48" x 21½." Built-in seat/step. Three lumbar
support positions. Three multi-directional, individually flow-rate adjustable
body massage jets and three multi-directional, individually flow-rate
adjustable ideal-flow jets. Whirlpool control options. Center drain outlet.
Optional grab bar. New for 1996.

Ellisse Whirlpool
Acrylic. 72" x 44" x 20". Two-person bathing.
Two whirlpool control options. 1hp two-speed pump. Six jets. Two grab
bars. Also available in tub only.

Lexington Whirlpool
Idealcast. 60" x 32" x 20". One-person
bathing. Two whirlpool control options. ¾ hp pump. Six jets.
Also available in tub only.

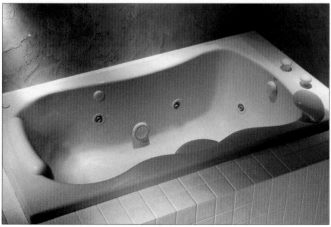

Concertino Whirlpool
Idealcast, 66" x 36" x 21½." One-person
bathing. System II 1hp two-speed pump. Six jets. Wave grab bar.
Also available in tub only.

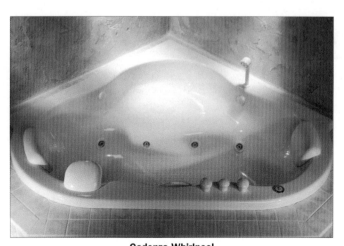

Cadenza Whirlpool
Idealcast. 60" x 60" x 21½." corner. Two-person
bathing. System II 1hp two-speed pump. Eight jets. Wave grab bar.
Also available in tub only.

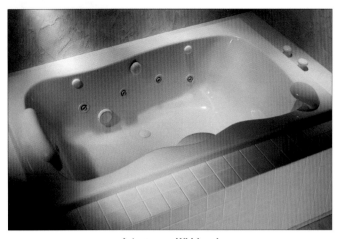

Intermezzo Whirlpool
Idealcast™ 72" x 44" x 21½". Two-person
bathing. System II 1hp, two-speed pump. 10 jets. Wave grab bar.
Also available in tub only.

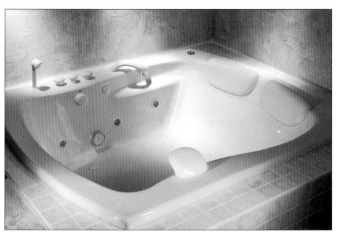

Romanza Whirlpool
Acrylic. 74" x 62" x 21½". Two-person
bathing. System II 1hp, two-speed pump. 10 jets.
Also available in tub only.

Impromptu Whirlpool
Acrylic. 60" x 42" x 21½". Two-person
bathing. System II 1hp, two-speed pump. Six jets.
Also available in tub only.

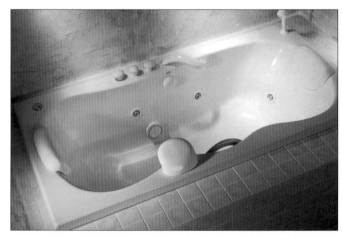

Virtuoso Whirlpool
Acrylic, 72" x 36" x 21½". One-person bathing.
System II 1hp, two-speed pump. Six jets. Wave grab bar.
Also available in tub only.

Aria Whirlpool
Idealcast, 60" x 34" x 21½". One-person
bathing. System II 1hp, two-speed pump. Six jets. Wave grab bar.
Also available in tub only.

Scala Corner Whirlpool
Acrylic. 60" x 60" x 20" depth.
Two-person bathing. ¾ hp pump. Six jets. Integral seat.
Also available in tub only.

Ellisse Built-In

Idealcast™ 60"x 32"x 21½." Dual integral arm rests. Six directional and flow-rate adjustable jets. Whirlpool control options. Optional apron panel and grab bars.

Ellisse Oval Whirlpool

Acrylic. 70" x 38½" x 20½." One-person bathing. 1hp pump.
Six jets. Two optional grab bars. Two whirlpool control options. Also available in tub only.

Scala 6' Whirlpool
Acrylic. 72" x 36" x 20". One-person bathing. Dual, molded arm rests.
Six directional and flow-rate adjustable jets. End drain outlet. ¾ hp pump.
Optional grab bar and apron panel. Also available as tub only.

Scala II 6' Whirlpool
Acrylic. 72" x 44" x 20". Two-person bathing. Molded back support.
Six directional and flow-rate adjustable jets. Center drain outlet. ¾ hp pump.
Optional apron panel. Also available as tub only.

Scala II 5½' Whirlpool
Acrylic. 66" x 44" x 20". Two-person bathing. Molded back support.
Six directional and flow-rate adjustable jets. Center drain outlet. ¾ hp pump.
Optional apron panel. Also available as tub only.

Scala Oval 5½' Whirlpool
Acrylic. 66" x 36" x 20". One-person bathing. Molded back support.
Six directional and flow-rate adjustable jets. End drain outlet. ¾ hp pump.
Optional apron panel. Also available as tub only.

Scala Oval 5' Whirlpool
Acrylic. 60" x 42" x 20". One-person bathing. Molded back support.
Six directional and flow-rate adjustable jets. End drain outlet. ¾ hp pump.
Optional grab bar and apron panel. Also available as tub only.

Scala 5' Whirlpool
Acrylic. 60" x 32" x 20". One-person bathing. Molded back support.
Six directional and flow-rate adjustable jets. End drain outlet. ¾ hp pump.
Optional grab bar and apron panel. Also available as tub only.

Scala Renaissance

Acrylic. 60" x 32" x 20". One-person bathing. Molded back support. Six directional and flow-rate adjustable jets. End drain outlet. Dual grab bars. ¾ hp pump. Optional apron panel. Also available as tub only.

Monarch Whirlpool

Idealcast™ 66" x 36" x 20". One-person bathing. ¾ hp pump. Six jets. Also available in tub only.

Piermont Whirlpool

Idealcast. 72" x 36" x 20". One-person bathing. ¾ hp pump. Six jets. Also available in tub only.

Stratford Whirlpool

66" x 32", with 18" depth. ¾ hp, single-speed pump/motor with deck-mounted control. Six jets. Two air volume controls. Beveled headrest. Optional grab bars. Durable Americast® material with glossy porcelain finish.

Princeton™ Bathtub

60" x 30" bathtub for recessed installations. Integral lumbar support for comfort. Option of wider Luxury ledge for storing toiletries, 60" x 34" as shown. Available with right or left hand outlet. Above floor rough-in. Durable Americast material with glossy porcelain finish.

Oxford Whirlpool

72" x 36", with 20" depth. 1hp, single-speed pump/motor with deck-mounted control. Eight jets. Two air volume controls. Integral headrest and lumbar support. Optional grab bars. Durable Americast material with glossy porcelain finish.

Scala Wide 5' Whirlpool
Acrylic. 60" x 36" x 20." One-person bathing. Dual, molded arm rests. Six directional
and flow-rate adjustable jets. End drain outlet. ¾ hp pump. Optional apron panel. Also available as tub only.

Scala Oval 6' Whirlpool
Acrylic. 72" x 42" x 20." Two-person bathing. Molded back support. Six directional
and flow-rate adjustable jets. End drain outlet. ¾ hp pump. Optional apron panel. Also available as tub only.

Neo Angle Shower Bases
Idealcast™ Double water retention. Tiling flange.
Integral threshold water dam. Metal shower drain. Available in sizes
42" x 42" and 38" x 38", plus 36" x 36" new for 1996.

Single Threshold Shower Bases
Idealcast. Double water retention. Tiling
flange. Integral threshold water dam. Metal shower drain.
Available in two sizes: 60" x 34", 48" x 34".

Single Threshold Shower Bases
Idealcast. Double water retention. Tiling flange.
Integral threshold water dam. Metal shower drain. Available in sizes
36" x 36" and 32" x 32", plus 42" x 42" new for 1996.

Clarion Bathware Products

WHIRLPOOLS AND SOAKERS

TUB/SHOWERS

SHOWER MODULES

ASSISTED CARE UNITS

CFM, INC.

larion's whirlpool and soaker tub collection offers both acrylic and fiberglass models. President's Series acrylic models are vacuum formed from a one-piece solid sheet of cast acrylic to provide years of care free use. Each whirlpool is engineered and manufactured to meet the most demanding specifications. Clarion's acrylic is the tub of choice for many families. Clarion's gel-coated fiberglass whirlpools and soaker tubs are manufactured with the same exacting standards as our acrylic products.

Multiple laminates of fiberglass and 16-18 mills of gel-coat make our products among the strongest in the industry. All whirlpools are manufactured using custom formed PVC pipe, 3/4 H.P. motors with a 5 year warranty, and matching trim. The air control, suction outlet, and on/off switch are all factory installed. Clarion pressure water tests each whirlpool before it is delivered. A host of options such as 6 jets, brass or chrome trim, mood lites, and heaters are among some of the upgrades available for your new whirlpool.

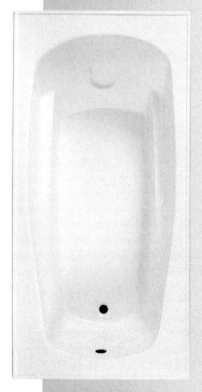

ACRYLIC

MODEL# AC6060SO
59$\frac{1}{2}$" x 59$\frac{1}{2}$" x 26$\frac{1}{2}$" x 26$\frac{1}{2}$" x 21$\frac{3}{4}$"H

VAN BUREN

ACRYLIC

MODEL# AC7236SO
71$\frac{1}{2}$"L x 36"W x 21$\frac{1}{2}$"H

BUCHANON

ACRYLIC

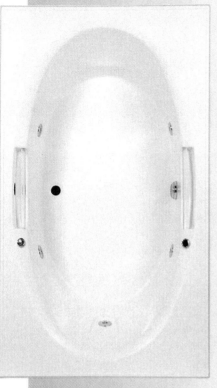

MODEL# AC7242SO
70³/₄"L x 41¹/₂"W x 21¹/₂"H

LINCOLN

ACRYLIC

MODEL# AC7248SO
71³/₄"L x 47³/₄"W x 21¹/₂"H

TAFT

ACRYLIC

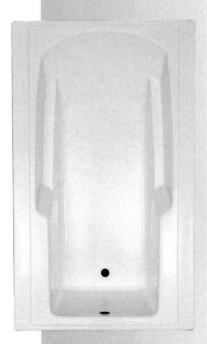

MODEL# AC6036SO
60¹/₂"L x 36"W x 21¹/₂"H

WASHINGTON I

ACRYLIC

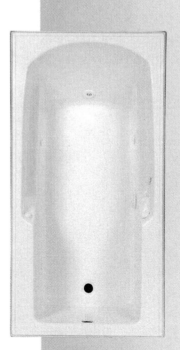

MODEL# AC6032SO
60"L x 31³/₄"W x 21¹/₂"H

WASHINGTON II

Lucite XL

Clarion Bathware uses LUCITE XL cast acrylic sheet in all of its acrylic modules. LUCITE XL is beautiful, durable and will not mildew and stain. Its hard, non-porous surface is scratch resistant. Its rich colors go all the way through the thickness of the material to ensure color fastness and its high gloss finish wipes to a shine without scrubbing. LUCITE XL, easy to maintain with common household non-abrasive cleaning products, is your assurance of quality.

Freight Information

Clarion ships product on our own fleet of air-ride trailers with new tractors and company drivers. Assisted care products ship on Clarion's trucks or on any number of LTL companies contracted with CFM.

Limited Warranty

Clarion Bathware offers a Three-Year Limited Warranty against defects in material and workmanship on fiberglass and acrylic products. Whirlpool systems carry a Full Three-Year Limited Warranty.

For More Information

For sales information, service, technical support or ordering information call your Clarion Bathware distributor or the corporate office below.

CFM, Inc.

CORPORATE AND SALES OFFICE

CLARION BATHWARE

| 205 AMSLER AVENUE | PHONE | 814-226-5374 |
| SHIPPENVILLE, PA 16254 | FAX | 814-226-5568 |

MANUFACTURING PLANT

CLARION BATHWARE

| STAR ROUTE BOX 20 | PHONE | 814-782-3011 |
| MARBLE, PA 16334 | FAX | 814-782-3434 |

ENVIRO SUITES

**Complete
Showerbathing
Environments**

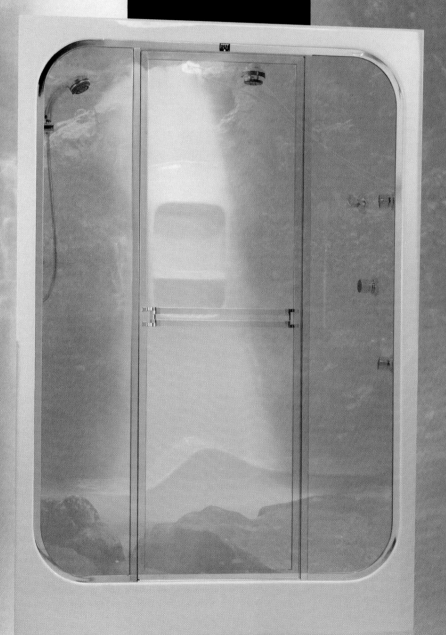

CRANE PLUMBING **FIAT** *by*

SHOWERBATHING

Today's fast and active pace combined with the pressures of our daily routine has turned what used to be merely a utilitarian function into an enjoyable, depressurizing, and on occasion, social activity.

The regular routine of bathing or showering as we now know it will become a thing of the past as the desire to re-energize and relax allows showerbathing to gain popularity with people of all ages.

Showerbathing is a new phenomenon that not only embodies the practical benefits of having a shower or a bath, but also allows you to create any one of a number of atmospheres that will suit the mood or sensation you desire.

And the best way to fully enjoy shower-bathing is in an Enviro Suite by CRANE Plumbing/ FIAT Products.

Feel the exhilaration of clean clear water jetting from multiple shower heads aimed in various directions.

Pamper your feet with an invigorating foot massage.

Let whirlpool and bubbler jets swirl the water around mood-creating underwater lights.

Inhale the haunting aroma of eucalyptus, or your favourite fragrance.

And when you really need to turn off the stress and adjust an attitude, turn on the steam, relax on a recliner seat and dream away a few minutes... or more.

In developing Enviro Suites, we took the best of our popular acrylic bathware line, added some new models, and adapted them all to the new showerbathing concept.

The basis of all Enviro Suites is a high quality pre-plumbed multiple shower head system. Every system comes complete with a thermostatic mixing valve that can be preset to a temperature just as you would the heat or air conditioning in your home. Then, depending on the system, a combination of body massage and hand held shower heads provide you with a variety of spray patterns. Each is accompanied by a fully sealed exquisitely-designed door enclosure. Then, a host of options and accessories may be added - all geared to providing the ultimate showerbathing experience.

And they all look absolutely gorgeous!

Showerbathing in an Enviro Suite is convenient, healthy, enjoyable, relaxing and practical.

There's an Enviro Suite for every situation, home or cottage, bathroom or fun room, there's a model and size that's sure to appeal to you. There's even a corner model that will knock your socks off. In fact these sensational units will make you want to take everything off... and jump right in.

Showerbathing is the best and it's even better in an Enviro Suite by CRANE Plumbing/FIAT Products.

C 567
15440/CRC
BUYLINE 7453

NOTIONS

*Designed to accommo-
date decorating
challenges, Notions
tucks neatly into a
corner and gives you
the option of
showerbathing
under the dome.*

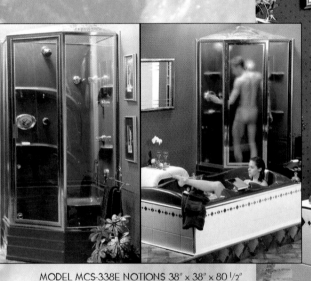

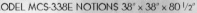

MODEL MCS-338E NOTIONS 38" x 38" x 80 1/2"

STANDARD FEATURES

es338 shower system with the following components:
- shower head with four spray settings: normal, jet, champagne, and pulsating
- three body massage heads
- thermostatic valve
- chrome, white or polished brass finish

D-38 shower door with clear or patterned glass, in chrome or gold finish

Integrally molded seat

OPTIONS

Steam package (-S): with generator, air switch, and steam head in chrome or gold finish • Foot massage (-FM): deluxe bubbler system with 10 air injectors, variable speed heated blower, digital display timer switch and filler spout. • Acrylic dome (standard feature for steam option) available in smoked or crystal finish • Fold up seat - factory-installed • Fragrance injection system (steam option required) • Padded vinyl head rest (white only)

Sensations

THE PERFECT COMPLEMENT

Sensations offers a complete deep-soaking experience. It combines the enjoyment of a traditional whirlpool bath with contemporary mood lights, bubbler system and head rest.

With Sensations as a complement to one of the four Enviro Shower models, showerbathing is truly sensational.

MODEL IW-380E SENSATIONS 71 3/4" × 41 7/8" × 22"

STANDARD FEATURES

- Deluxe 8 jet whirlpool system with 3-speed 1HP pump motor
- Deluxe bubbler system with 10 air injectors and variable speed heated blower
- Digital display timer switch with temperature readout and probe, and low water detector
- 2 underwater mood lights with interchangeable lenses, air switch

OPTIONS

Padded vinyl head rest (white only)

5

ENCOUNTERS

SHOWERBATHING WITH MORE THAN STANDING-ROOM-ONLY.

Select your seating arrangements for this beautiful roomy Enviro Suite. Seats can be molded into left corner, right corner, or both. Either way, there's plenty of room for two.

MODEL MS-305E ENCOUNTERS 62" × 34" × 88 1/2"

STANDARD FEATURES

es305 shower system with the following components:
- hand shower with showerbar-mounted soap dish, champagne/regular/jet/pulsating spray
- ceiling shower head with champagne/regular spray
- four body massage heads
- thermostatic valve
- chrome, white, or polished brass finish

D-57-2 shower door with clear glass, in chrome or gold finish
Two integrally-molded seats

OPTIONS

Steam package (-S): with generator, air switch, and steam head in chrome or gold finish • Fragrance injection system (steam option required) • Canopy light kit (for field installation) • Canopy mood lights with interchangeable lenses (for field installation) • Padded vinyl head rest (white only) • Optional left or right side single integrally-molded seat

$\mathcal{I}$NCLINATIONS

So Comfortable You'll Almost Feel Guilty

Almost but not quite.
A recliner seat in a
shower suite?
Why not?
That's showerbathing.
Comfort comes first -
your comfort.

Inclinations is similar
to Encounters with one
important difference:
a very comfortable
recliner seat integrally
molded into the unit.
It's ideal for when you
have the inclination
and the time.

MODEL MS-306E INCLINATIONS 62" x 34" x 88 ½"

STANDARD FEATURES

es306 shower system with the following components:
- hand shower with showerbar-mounted soap dish, champagne/regular/jet/pulsating spray
- ceiling shower head with champagne/regular spray
- three body massage heads
- thermostatic valve
- chrome, white, or polished brass finish

D-57-2 shower door with clear glass, in chrome or gold finish

OPTIONS

Steam package (-S): with generator, air switch, and steam head in chrome or gold finish • Fragrance injection system (steam option required) • Canopy light kit (for field installation) • Canopy mood lights with interchangeable lenses (for field installation) • Padded vinyl head rest (white only)

7

ELATIONS

This spacious one-person enclosure has been designed for exceptional comfort. A left or right hand seat option makes it suitable for almost any situation. Elations - it's the way you'll feel.

Seat not exactly as shown

MODEL MS-348E ELATIONS 50" x 34" x 88 1/2"

STANDARD FEATURES

es348 shower system with the following components:
- hand shower with showerbar-mounted soap dish, champagne/regular/jet/pulsating spray
- three body massage heads
- thermostatic valve
- chrome, white or polished brass finish

D-58-2 shower door with clear glass, in chrome or gold finish
Left or right hand side integrally-molded seat

OPTIONS

Steam package (-S): with generator, air switch, and steam head in chrome or gold finish • Fragrance injection system (steam option required). • Canopy light kit (for field installation) • Canopy mood lights with interchangeable lenses (for field installation) • Padded vinyl head rest (white only)

8

ENTITY

SHOWERBATHING ELEGANCE

Take a shower, bath, steam, whirlpool - or all four. Entity leaves all the choices to you. The extra depth of this beautifully-designed Enviro Suite makes it especially suitable for the whirlpool and bubbler systems.

Then, add steam and other exciting options to complete the picture.

MODEL 2010E ENTITY 62" x 34" x 90"

STANDARD FEATURES

es2010 shower system with the following components:
- hand shower with showerbar-mounted soap dish, champagne/regular/jet/pulsating spray
- three body massage heads
- thermostatic valve
- chrome, white or polished brass finish

D-72-2 shower door with clear glass, in chrome or gold finish

OPTIONS

Whirlpool package (-W): deluxe 4 jet whirlpool system with 3-speed 1HP pump motor, digital display timer switch • Bubbler package (-B): deluxe bubbler system with 10 air injectors, variable speed heated blower, digital display timer switch • Steam package (-S): with generator, air switch, and steam head in chrome or gold finish • Canopy light kit (for field installation) • Canopy mood lights with interchangeable lenses (for field installation) • Underwater mood lights with interchangeable lenses (factory-installed) with air switch • Fragrance injection system (steam option required) • Padded vinyl head rest (white only)

ESSENCE

IT JUST DOESN'T GET ANY BETTER THAN THIS.

Showerbathing is the ultimate experience. Now, experience the ultimate in shower-bathing. Essence is everything. It's roomy - a full twelve inches longer than conventional bathing suites. It's comfortable, and it's designed for total relaxation. Its standard equipment puts Essence in a class by itself. And the available options make it even better.

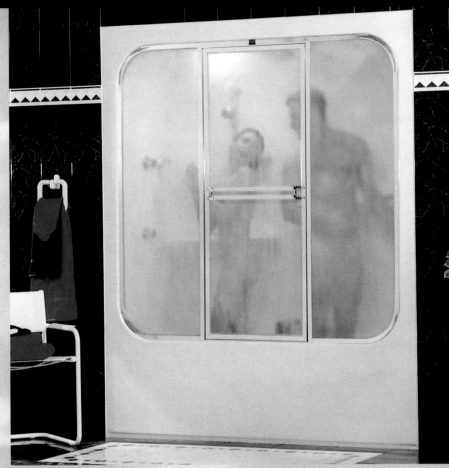

MODEL MTS-377E ESSENCE 72" x 36 1/4" x 84"

STANDARD FEATURES

es377 shower system with the following components:
- hand shower with showerbar-mounted soap dish, champagne/regular/jet/pulsating spray
- ceiling shower head with champagne/regular spray
- four body massage heads
- thermostatic valve
- chrome, white, or polished brass finish

D-77-2 shower door with clear glass in chrome or gold finish

OPTIONS

Whirlpool package (-W): deluxe 7 jet whirlpool system with 3-speed 1HP pump motor, digital display timer switch • Bubbler package (-B): deluxe bubbler system with 10 air injectors, variable speed heated blower, digital display timer switch • Steam package (-S): with generator, air switch, and steam head in chrome or gold finish • Acrylic seat(s) • Teakwood seat(s) • Canopy light kit (for field installation) • Canopy mood lights with interchangeable lenses (for field installation) • Two (2) underwater mood lights with interchangeable lenses and air switch (factory-installed) • Fragrance injection system (steam option required) • Padded vinyl head rests (white only)

Shower Bathing at a Glance

	NOTIONS MS-338E	SENSATIONS IW-380E	ENCOUNTERS MS-305E	INCLINATIONS MS-306E	ELATIONS MS-348E	ENTITY 2010-E	ESSENCE MS-377E
SHOWER SYSTEM							
Ceiling shower	n/a	n/a	S	S	n/a	n/a	S
Wallmount shower head	S	n/a	n/a	n/a	n/a	n/a	n/a
Hand shower/showerbar mounted soap dish	n/a	n/a	S	S	S	S	S
Body massage heads	3	n/a	4	3	3	3	4
Thermostatic valve	S	n/a	S	S	S	S	S
Filler spout	n/a	supplied by others	n/a	n/a	n/a	S	S
SHOWER SYSTEM FINISHES							
Polished chrome	O	n/a	O	O	O	O	O
Polished brass	O	n/a	O	O	O	O	O
White	O	n/a	O	O	O	O	O
DOOR FINISHES							
Polished chrome	O	O	O	O	O	O	O
Polished brass	O	O	O	O	O	O	O
DOOR GLASS FINISHES							
Clear	O	S	S	S	S	S	S
Striped pattern	O	n/a	n/a	n/a	n/a	n/a	n/a
OPTIONS							
Deluxe whirlpool system	n/a	O	n/a	n/a	n/a	O	O
Deluxe bubbler system	n/a	O	n/a	n/a	n/a	O	O
Foot massage system	O	n/a	n/a	n/a	n/a	n/a	n/a
Mood lights	n/a	S(2)	n/a	n/a	n/a	O	O
Steam	O	n/a	O	O	O	O	O
* Fragrance injection system	O	n/a	O	O	O	O	O
Dome	O	n/a	n/a	n/a	n/a	n/a	n/a
Head rest (white only)	O	O	O	O	O	O	O
Seats standard	integral	n/a	two integral	integral recliner seat	integral (LH or RH side)	integral	n/a
Seats optional	fold-up	n/a	one integral (LH or RH side) or no seat	n/a	n/a	n/a	teak wood or acrylic bench style (LH and/or RH)
Canopy lights	n/a	n/a	O	O	O	O	O
Canopy mood lights	n/a	n/a	O	O	O	O	O

* available late 1995

Standard acrylic colors: White, bone, sterling silver

Optional colors: Innocent Blush, Desert Bloom, Teal, Wild Rose, Dresden Blue, Red.
Other colors may be available by special request

CRANE
PLUMBING

1235 Hartrey Avenue
Evanston, IL 60202
708-864-9777

C568

15440/DOR

BuyLine 8636

KULTUR IM BAD

CULTURE IN THE BATHROOM   CULTURA E BAGNO   CULTURA EN EL BAÑO

Pure country love. The naturalness of an original language of material as a rejection of the age of fast- living.

L'amore per la natura allo stato puro. La naturalezza di un linguaggio primordiale del materiale come rifiuto a un'epoca della vita febbrile.

Amor puro a lo campestre. La naturalidad de un lenguaje material original como rechazo de una época de prisas.

OBINA

SIEGER DESIGN

Country look.

Back to the roots, back to nature. Following footsteps - in terracotta and wood. A harmonious ambience that is a reminder of nice times. The fitting: simple, discreet, harmonious.

As the perfect example of pluralistic style and striving towards individuality, OBINA succeeds against all attempts to impose restrictions on design. Anything goes. A fitting that is as varied as the personalities who use it.

Country look.

Back to the roots, ritorno alle radici, alla natura. Seguire le tracce sulla terracotta o sul legno. Un ambiente armonioso che ricorda i bei vecchi tempi. La rubinetteria: semplice, decente, armoniosa.

Come quintessenza del pluralismo dello stile e della ricerca dell'individualità, OBINA si impone contro ogni dettato stilistico. Tutto è possibile. Una rubinetteria versatile come la personalità dei suoi utilizzatori.

Country look.

Back to the roots, regreso a la naturaleza. Seguir las huellas - sobre terracota y madera. Un ambiente armonioso que evoca buenos y viejos tiempos. La grifería: simple, discreta, armoniosa.

Como síntesis de pluralidad estilística y aspiración hacia lo individual OBINA se opone a todo clase de dictado en el diseño. Todo es posible. Una grifería - tan polifacética como las personalidades de sus usuarios.

The country style in the bathroom. Trips to the bathroom become as pleasurable as country outings. The fitting to go with it: OBINA. Naturally.

Lo stile Country nel bagno. Il soggiornarvi si rivela riposante come una gita in campagna. La rubinetteria adeguata: OBINA, naturalmente.

El estilo country en el baño. La estancia en él se vuelve tan relajante como una excursión al campo. La grifería correspondiente: OBINA. Naturalmente.

TARA

SIEGER DESIGN

Reduction to essentials.
The quality of the material and the function of the form as the highest standards. TARA - an archetypal design. With convincing simplicity, but not without extravagance.

La riduzione all'essenziale.
Criterio supremo, la qualità del materiale e la funzionalità della forma. Tara, un design archetipo. Di una semplicità convincente, ma non senza stravaganza.

Reducción a lo esencial.
Calidad del material y función de la forma como normas máximas. La TARA - un diseño arquetípico. Con sencillez persuasiva, pero no sin extravagancia.

Clear striking shapes develop their own characteristic independence within the interaction. The curve and cross make the source of water in the bathroom stand out: the fitting.

Il gioco delle forme chiare e pregnanti fa nascere una autonomia caratteristica. L'arco e la croce caratterizzano la sorgente del bagno: la rubinetteria.

Formas claras y concisas desarrollan en conjunto una autonomía caracteristica. Arco y cruz caracterizan la fuente del baño: la grifería.

TARA CLASSIC
SIEGER DESIGN

TARA CLASSIC - an original design with various combinations. From the classic bathroom furnishing to an expressive production - TARA CLASSIC blends in everywhere and still makes a decisive point.

TARA CLASSIC - una variante autonoma dalle molteplici possibilità di combinazione. Dal decoro classico alla messa in scena espressiva: TARA CLASSIC si integra dappertutto, ma la sua presenza non è per questo meno dominante.

La TARA CLASSIC - una variación formal autónoma con posibilidades de combinación variables. Desde una instalación de baño clásica hasta una escenificación de baño expresiva - la TARA CLASSIC encaja en todas partes y pone el acento decisivo.

The simple lever releases creative ideas in bathroom design - and also sets new standards in functionality. TARA CLASSIC is not only nice to look at, it is easy to use.

La semplicità della leva libera idee creative per l'arredamento del bagno fissando nuove norme in materia di funzionalità, in quanto TARA CLASSIC non è solo bella da vedere, ma anche facile da usare.

El grifo-palanca simple libera ideas creativas para la configuración del baño - y fija nuevas normas de funcionalidad. Porque la TARA CLASSIC no es solamente un placer visual, sino también fácil de manejar.

Always the centre of attention in bathrooms: TARA CLASSIC. Contrasts can be established and an interesting tension created between them.

TARA CLASSIC non passa mai inosservata in un bagno: nascono contrasti, si creano interessanti tensioni.

Siempre un punto atractivo del baño: la TARA CLASSIC. De aquí resultan contrastes y tensiones interesantes.

A highlight in bathroom creation: valuable materials and sophisticated crafts-manship allow the aesthetics of design come into their own.

Clou della messa in scena del bagno: i materiali pregiati e una lavorazione di alta qualità fanno emergere l'estetica dello stilismo.

Un punto culminante de la escenificación del baño: sólo unos materiales valiosos y una elaboración exigente llegan a poner en relieve la estética de la formación.

FINO
SIEGER DESIGN

Straight lines and soft curves create a clear form. A blending of cool reduction and sensual appearance that corresponds to the bathroom's language of shape. Tension that is timeless.

Una forma chiara nasce dall'unione di linee dritte e di archi morbidi. La fusione di una riduzione fredda e di una sensualità apparente corrispondente al linguaggio formale del bagno. Una tensione che prosegue atemporalmente.

La forma clara se compone de líneas rectas y arcos suaves. Es la fusión de una reducción reservada y un aspecto sensual que corresponde con el lenguaje formal del baño. Una tensión que continúa intemporalmente.

POINT
SIEGER DESIGN

POINT brings movement into the bathroom. The basic geometric shapes - cones, cylinders and triangles - go well together. Bathroom use is declared a sensual experience. A lively fitting that triggers aesthetic pleasure.

POINT mette movimento nel bagno. Le forme di base della geometria, il cono, il cilindro ed il triangolo tramano un bel complotto. L'uso del bagno diviene un avvenimento sensuale. Una rubinetteria che ama il contatto e che conferisce un piacere estetico.

POINT trae movimiento al baño. Las formas básicas de la geometría - cono, cilindro y triángulo - forman un complot bello. El uso del baño es declarado experiencia sensual. Una grifería jovial con la cual se tiene un placer estético.

The accessories are like the fitting: an ensemble of different configurations that aesthetically comment a trip to the bathroom.

Rubinetterie e accessori: un insieme di figurazioni diverse, commento estetico della visita del bagno.

Tal como la grifería así también los accesorios: un conjunto de figuraciones diferentes que comentan estéticamente la visita en el baño.

POINT. The lever effect always looks different. Various combinations of colour underline this aspect.

POINT. Il gioco della leva lo fa sembrare sempre diverso. Diverse combinazioni di colore accentuano questo effetto.

La POINT. El juego del efecto de palanca siempre le da un aspecto diferente. Las diferentes combinaciones de colores favorecen este efecto.

Fascination created by the elegance of shape and the value of the materials. The MADISON charm is always impressive.

Fascino dell'eleganza della forma e del valore del materiale. Lo charme di MADISON è sempre seducente.

Fascinación gracias a la elegancia de la forma y al valor del material. Siempre la MADISON seduce con su encanto.

MADISON

A fitting with a past - and future. The historic cross-head fitting is rediscovering its future. Influenced by the post modern it has become a source of an individual style of design. Twenty years ago, the original from the American "Golden Twenties" was discovered by - and for - Dornbracht. Today, a whole range of fittings and accessories bears the name MADISON, the original.

Una rubinetteria che ha un passato - e un avvenire. In effetti la rubinetteria con le manopole a crociera riscopre il proprio avvenire. Sotto il segno del Postmoderno diviene sorgente di stile d'arredamento individuale. Sono passati vent'anni da quando nell'America dei "golden twenties" fu scoperto l'originale da (e per) Dornbracht. Oggi una gamma completa di rubinetterie e di accessori porta il nome MADISON, l'originale.

Una grifería con pasado - y futuro. Porque la grifería de grifos cruciformes descubre de nuevo su futuro. Con motivo del postmodernismo se convierte en la fuente de un estilo de instalación individual. Hace 20 años el original de los "Golden Twenties" americanos fue descubierto por - y para - Dornbracht. Hoy un programa de griferías y accesorios completo lleva el nombre MADISON, el original.

Manopole a crociera con bianche placchette di porcellana e rubinetti spigolosi, ecco i caratteri tipici dell'originale. Un classico del re-design. Spesso imitato, mai superato.

The originals can always be recognized by their cross-head handles with white porcelain inlays and square spouts. A classic of redesign. Frequently copied - never equalled.

Grifos cruciformes con plaquitas de porcelana blancas y salidas angulares · en eso se conoce el original. Un clásico del re-diseño. A menudo copiado - nunca alcanzado.

A clear harmonious line defines the pleasing-to-use lever handles, the historic appearance of the spout lends a flair of nostalgia.

Leve di facile uso, dalle linee chiare e armoniose. Il rubinetto dall'aspetto graziosamente antico, le conferisce un profumo nostalgico.

Un trazado de la linea claro y armonioso determina los grifos-palanca de manejo agradable, el caño de salida de aspecto histórico le da un aire nostálgico.

The glass holder. Its shape is typical for MADISON FLAIR: transparency of function and origin define its appearance.

Il portabicchiere. La sua forma è tipica per MADISON FLAIR: in materia di funzionalità e di origine, la trasparenza determina il suo look.

El apoyo del vaso. Su forma es típica para la MADISON FLAIR: la transparencia respecto al origen y a la función determinan su aspecto.

MADISON FLAIR

Madison Flair - the union of nostalgic charm and functional design. The simple while elegant lever handles stylize the classic-historical original. Traditional design in harmony with highest technical perfection.

Madison Flair - il matrimonio di uno charme nostalgico e di uno stilismo funzionale. Le leve, semplici ed eleganti, stilizzano il suo modello classico-storico. Un design ricco di tradizioni in armonia con la più alta perfezione tecnica.

La Madison Flair - la unión de encanto nostálgico y forma funcional. Los grifos-palanca simples y a la vez elegantes estilizan el modelo clásico histórico. Diseño de mucha tradición en armonía con la más alta perfección técnica.

JEFFERSON

SIEGER DESIGN

JEFFERSON. A fitting, whose name is linked to one of the most important periods of American history. A fitting whose form writes its own history: Nostalgia as a sign of modernity. The conveniently arched lever handles invite your touch. A timeless esthetic, which recalls the past. Even tomorrow.

JEFFERSON. Le rubinetterie il cui nome ricorda una grande epoca della storia americana. Le rubinetterie il cui disegno scrive da sè la sua storia: nostalgia improntata allo spirito moderno. Le sue impugnature a leva, bombate e maneggevoli, sono un invito al contatto. Un'estetica atemporale, che ricorda il passato. Ma anche l'avvenire.

JEFFERSON. Una grifería cuyo nombre va unido a una gran época de la historia americana. Una grifería cuya forma escribe su propia historia: nostalgia bajo el signo de la modernidad. Los grifos-palanca manejablemente arqueados invitan a tocarlos. Una estética intemporal que recuerda a antes. Aún mañana.

The combination of materials, formed by the ceramic handles, is an expression of nostalgia. And yet, it has an look that never wears out: JEFFERSON.

La combinazione di materiali, che viene creata dalle impugnature di ceramica, si presenta con una punta nostalgica. Una manifestazione, tuttavia, che non si logora mai: JEFFERSON.

La combinación de material que forman los grifos de cerámica está bajo el signo de la nostalgia. Y, no obstante, es de un aspecto que nunca se gasta: la JEFFERSON.

A faithful fitting, an object to which one always returns with pleasure. Because, who wash themselves here, experience pure design: A pure form - for a clean function.

Rubinetterie da affidare in buone mani, oggetti a cui piace tornare di continuo. Perché chi si lava con essi, vive un'esperienza di puro design: una forma pura - per una funzionalità pulita.

Una grifería en manos seguras, un objeto al cual siempre se regresa con mucho gusto. Pues quien se lave aquí experimentará un diseño puro: una configuración pura - para una funcionalidad limpia.

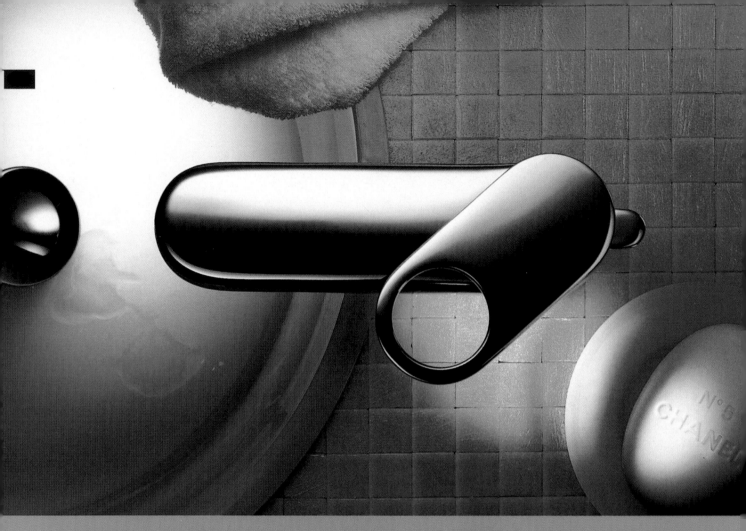

A shape abstracted as a striking symbol. Factual, but not stark. As topical today as it will be tomorrow. The feature of a classic.

Una forma, astratta in un segno marcato. Sobria senza essere severa. Così attuale oggi come domani. Ecco ciò che contraddistingue questo classico.

Una forma, reducida a una señal pronunciada. Objetiva, pero no rigida. Hoy tan actual como mañana. En esto sobresale este clásico.

The accessories in the DOMANI range. Timeless sophisticated shape - ennobled by high-quality finishes.

Gli accessori della serie DOMANI. Uno stilismo maturo che li rende atemporali, superfici pregiate che li rendono nobili.

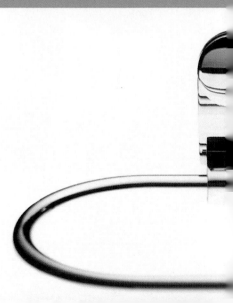

DOMANI
SIEGER DESIGN

The appearance of a classic design today: contemporary while timeless. The round handle hole is a declaration: less is more. DOMANI - a fitting as perfect as its basic shape: the circle. - No other fitting has received so many awards.

Ecco che cosa contraddistingue un classico del design di oggi: moderno, ma nello stesso tempo atemporale. Il foro rotondo della manopola diviene una professione di fede: meno diventa più. DOMANI, una rubinetteria altrettanto perfetta quanto la sua forma di base: il cerchio. Nessun'altra rubinetteria è stata tanto premiata.

Así se presenta un clásico del diseño de hoy: contemporáneo - y a la vez intemporal. El agujero redondo del tirador se convierte en confesión: menos es más. La DOMANI - una grifería tan perfecta como su forma fundamental: el círculo. - Ninguna otra grifería ha sido premiada tantas veces.

Los accesorios de la serie DOMANI. Intemporales gracias a una formación madura - ennoblecida por superficies de primera calidad.

BELLEVUE

The ring closes, the design is completed. The different decorative possibilities can be combined until the absolutely perfect solution has been found.

Il cerchio si chiude, la creazione è perfetta. Le più diverse possibilità di decorazione possono essere provate fino al raggiungimento della soluzione migliore.

El anillo se va cerrando, la creación llega a su perfección. Las posibilidades de decoración más diversas pueden ser ideadas hasta que se encuentre la solución redonda.

Sweeping elegance runs through the entire BELLEVUE series providing a positive outlook towards a perfect bathroom design.

L'eleganza slanciata che percorre tutto lo spettro della serie BELLEVUE apre nuove prospettive in materia di perfezione del decoro.

Elegancia con brío se manifiesta en la serie BELLEVUE entera. Eso ofrece una bonita perspectiva para una instalación de baño perfecta.

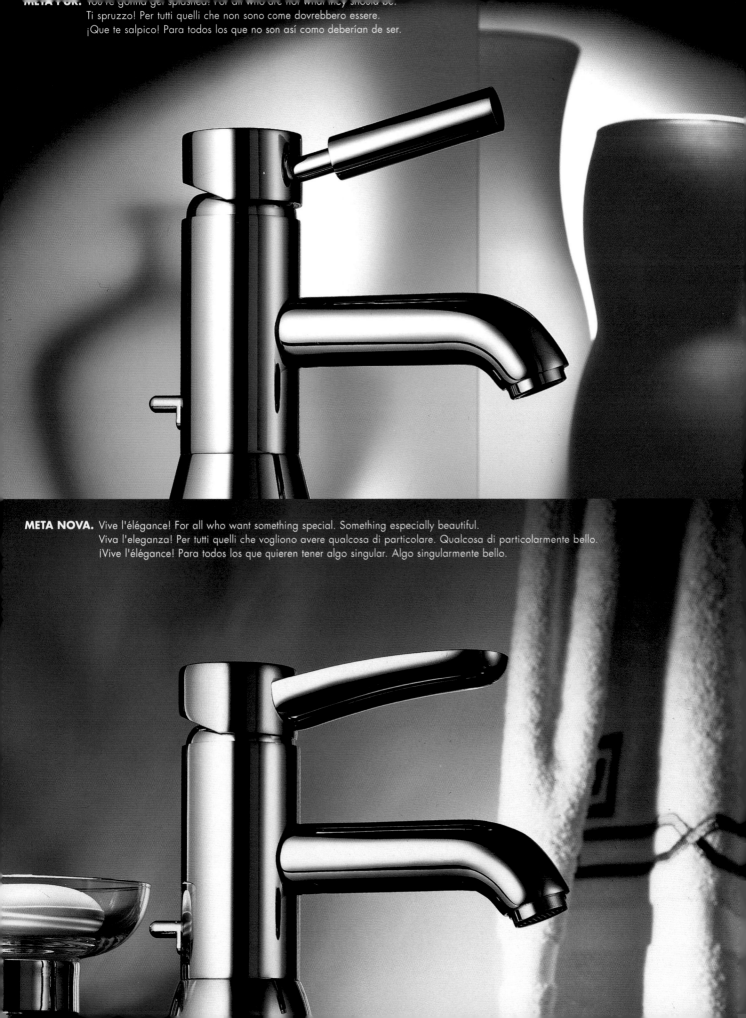

META FOR. You're gonna get splashed! For all who are not what they should be.
Ti spruzzo! Per tutti quelli che non sono come dovrebbero essere.
¡Que te salpico! Para todos los que no son así como deberían de ser.

META NOVA. Vive l'élégance! For all who want something special. Something especially beautiful.
Viva l'eleganza! Per tutti quelli che vogliono avere qualcosa di particolare. Qualcosa di particolarmente bello.
¡Vive l'élégance! Para todos los que quieren tener algo singular. Algo singularmente bello.

META

SIEGER DESIGN

Meta means "right in the middle" and Meta is right in the middle - in the middle of transformation. Because it is based on an innovative modular system. And that is why it can be adapted to the individual assumptions of style.

Meta significa "nel bel mezzo", e Meta si trova nel bel mezzo - della metamorfosi. In quanto Meta si basa su un sistema modulare innovativo ed è per questo che essa tiene conto delle concezioni più individuali di stile.

Meta significa "estar en el centro". Por eso Meta esta ahi, en el centro - de la metamorfosis. Porque Meta esta pasada por un innovador sistema de modulos. Y es por eso que tiene en cuenta las concepciones mas individuales en materia de estilos.

META CLASSIC. You've got to have style. And because META has style, you should have META.
Bisogna avere stile. E siccome META ha stile, dovreste possedere META.
Hay que tener estilo. Y porque META tiene estilo, Vd. debería tener META.

REPRESENTED EXCLUSIVELY BY

International Corporation

6687 JIMMY CARTER BLVD.   NORCROSS, GEORGIA 30071   TEL. 404/416-6224   FAX 404/416-6239

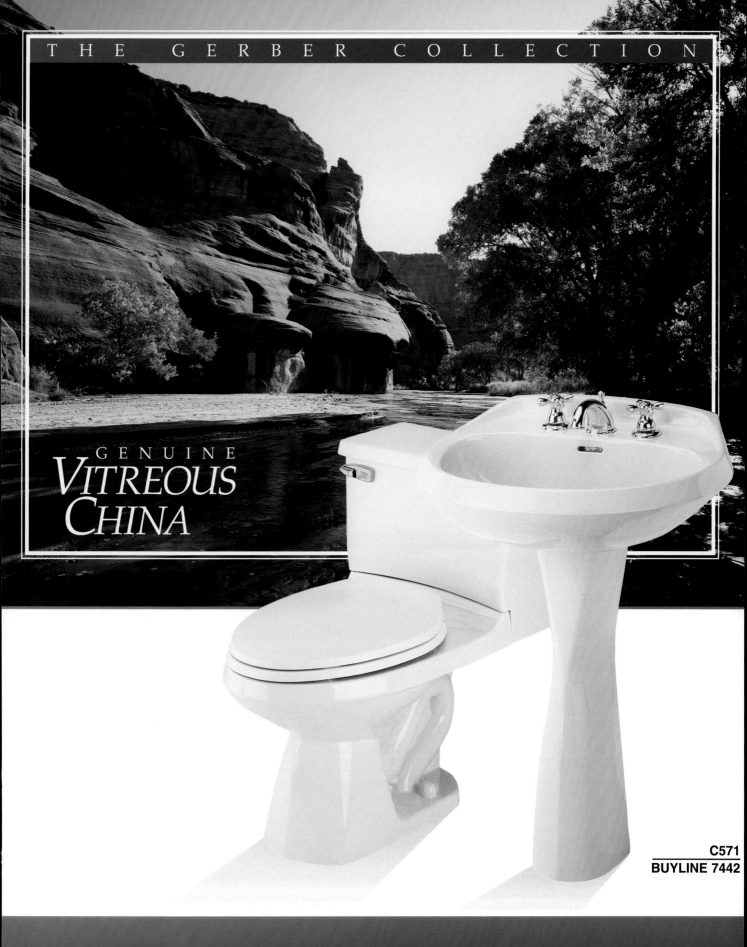

THE GERBER COLLECTION

GENUINE
VITREOUS
CHINA

C571
BUYLINE 7442

GERBER

Pedestal Lavatories and Toilets

22-534-09
La Mer Petite Pedestal Lavatory - Biscuit

22-558-15
La Mer Pedestal Lavatory - Almond

21-702-21
Aqua Saver - Round Front
Bahama Pink

21-712-14
Aqua Saver - Elongated
Powder Blue

22-598-25
La Rive Petite Pedestal Lavatory - Bone

22-578-23
La Rive Pedestal Lavatory - Silver

21-302-25
Ultra Flush
Round Front
Bone

21-312-23
Ultra Flush - Elongated
Silver

Room Set:
21-122-15 Mirage Almond
22-578-15 La Rive Almond

Drop in Lavatories, Bidets and Lavanities

12-844-11
Oval Lavatory - Blush

12-868-29
Hex Lavatory - Dawn Blue

12-898-19
Round Lavatory - Rose

27-511
Bidet-White

22-206
Lavanity - White

22-408-15
Lavanity - Almond

GERBER
PROFESSIONALLY MADE • PROFESSIONALLY SOLD
Gerber Plumbing Fixtures Corp. 4600 W. Touhy Avenue, Chicago, IL 60646
(847) 675-6570, FAX 1-800-5GERBER (Illinois FAX (847) 675-5192)

© 1996 G.P.F. Printed in U.S.A.

MADE IN USA

Hastings

IL BAGNO COLLECTION

The Essence of Design

Hastings
TILE & IL BAGNO COLLECTION

TAIFUN/EUCLIDE

TAIFUN-A wall mounted polished chrome column with a large pivoting mirror, moveable shelves, complete with towel bars, light and magnifying mirror. Choice of perforated metal or glass shelf inserts for trays.
Dimensions: 81 7/8" H

EUCLIDE-A free standing space saving, floor mounted conical wash basin in polished stainless steel or painted metal with enameled basin and Hi-Fi faucet.
Dimensions: 19 1/2" W x 19 1/2" D x 33" H

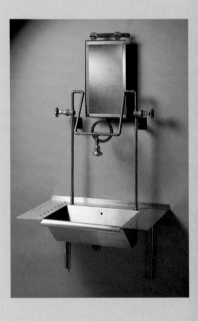

LASER/RAPSODY

LASER-A wall or floor mounted polished chrome accessory column with large mirror, 2 shelves, 4 towel bars, light and magnifying mirror. All accessories pivot on pole. Large mirror can be made to order.
Dimensions: 33 1/2" W x 81 7/8" H

RAPSODY-Unit consists of wall mounted wash basin with polished stainless steel finish. Available with optional tempered glass contoured countertop in 3 sizes (24", 32", 39 1/2"). Unit comes with Hi-Fi faucet and drain cover.
Dimensions: 24" D x 32" W x 8" H

PROLOGUE 2000

A wall hung stainless steel basin countertop, with exposed copper tubing. Industrial handles and spout create structural framework. Unit comes with rectangular mirror and towel ring.
Dimensions: 30" W x 19 1/2" D

STARCK

A free standing tubular chrome polished stainless steel basin with side mounted soap holders and Hi-Fi faucet.
Dimensions: 20" W x 21" D x 33" H
Design: Philippe Starck

WASHMOBIL "S"

A free standing wash basin with towel bars, shelf, soap and tumbler holder. Available in red, white, black or chrome with stainless steel basin.
Dimensions: 26 1/2" W x 23 3/4" D x 72" H

COVER PHOTO
AMERICA'S CUP

A free standing floor mounted polished stainless steel basin. The countertop is made of tempered glass. Available with mirror and shelf, made in enamel glass and stainless steel.
Dimensions of Mirror: 31 1/2" D
Dimensions of Shelf: 31 1/2" W x 8" D
Dimensions of Basin: 25" D x 23 5/8" W x 33 3/4" H

NOST

A wall mounted wash basin all in tempered glass cantilevered off wall through supplied support bracket. The wall mounted faucet spout is designed with low volume output.
Dimensions: 24" D x 32" W

OLIMPIA 70

A wall mounted wash basin with a conical brass pedestal support finished in brushed copper or polished chrome. The frosted or blue glass basin is mounted to the pedestal and floats above a clear tempered glass countertop with faucet.
Dimensions: 23 5/8" D x 27 1/2" W x 33 1/2" H (with Basin)

ETA BETA

RETA-Wall mounted beveled mirror with contoured intrical glass shelf with chrome railing.

RBETA-Wall mounted chrome plated frame which supports a contoured tempered glass countertop with stainless steel basin. Complete with faucet and drain.
Dimensions of Mirror: 13 3/4" W x 27 1/2" H
Dimensions of Shelf: 24 1/2" W x 5 3/4" D x 3/8" H
Dimensions of Beta: 18 1/2" D x 41" W x 26 3/8" H

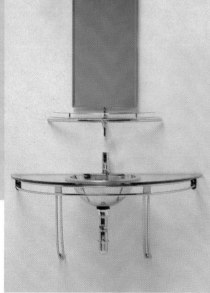

OLIMPIA

A free standing tempered glass console with chrome wall mounted faucet. The glass basin is mounted on a conical pedestal finished in brushed copper or polished chrome. Basin available in frosted or blue glass.
Dimensions: 23 1/2" D x 39 1/2" W x 33 1/2" H (with basin)

PUTMAN

A wall mounted stain-less steel wash basin with chrome plated tubular support legs. Available with mirror, faucet and accessories.
Dimensions of Basin: 20" D x 16" W x 35" H
Dimensions of Mirror: 14" W / 20" W x 32" H

MIRO

A range of basins made in polished stainless steel, w/overflow. Basin also available in 12", 14" and 15.5" diameter with single hole for deck faucet.

Dimensions for Miro 47 = 18 1/2" O.D.

Dimensions for Miro 40 = 16" O.D.

Dimensions for Miro 54 = 21 " O.D.

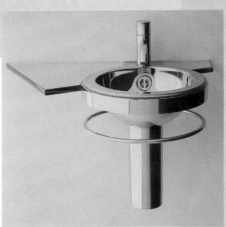

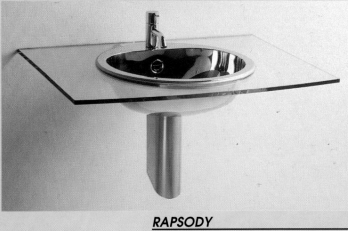

RAPSODY

Unit consists of wall mounted wash basin with polished stainless steel finish. Available with optional tempered glass contoured countertop in 3 sizes (24", 32", 39 1/2"). Unit comes with Hi-Fi faucet and drain cover.
Dimensions: 24" D x 32" W x 8" H

HANDAQUA

A free floating polished stainless steel basin with towel ring and Hi-Fi faucet. Available with optional tempered glass countertop.
Dimensions: 23 1/2" W x 14 5/8" D x 14 1/2" H

STOOL

Sitting stool in radius tubular chrome steel.
Dimensions: 19 3/4" D x 17 7/8" W x 18 3/8" H

NEO-CLASSICA PEDESTAL BASIN

Dimensions: Lg. 26" W
x 19 1/2" D x 32 5/8" H
Dimensions: Sm. 24" W
x 19 11/16" D x 32 5/8" H

SPOLETO VANITY

A chrome or gold leg stand with china
undermount basin. The marble counter-
top is stocked in White Carrara,
Calacatta Oro and Verde Campello.
Other marble available by special order.
Available with pivoting mirror, towel bars
and glass tray.
Dimensions of Vanity: 37 1/2" W x 23" D
x 32 3/4" H
Dimensions of Mirror: 25" W x 35 1/2" H

MARBLE CONSOLE WITH LEGS

Custom Sizes available.
Dimensions: 36" W x 23" D
Hgt. is adjustable from
31"-36".

PITTI & TOPAZIO BASINS

Pitti Dimensions: 29 3/4" W x
22 1/8" D x 32 1/2" H
Topazio Dimensions: 20 1/4" W
x 15 7/8" D x 32 5/8" H

PALLADIO WITH LEGS

Dimensions: 28 1/2" W x
21" D x 36" H

PALLADIO PEDESTAL BASIN

Dimensions: Lg. 28 1/2" W x 21" D x
33 3/4" H
Dimensions: Sm. 22 1/4" W x 18" D x
33" H

ELSA SEMINCASSO BASIN

25 1/2" W x 19 1/2" D x 8 1/4" H
Recessed back-10 3/4"

5

ELENALI PEDESTAL BASIN
Custom made to order

ELENALI WALL HUNG or DROP-IN BASIN
CODE: HE3000
CODE: HEBMFC for wall mount frame
DIMENSIONS: 17 1/2" D

ELENALI PEDESTAL BASIN
CODE: HE3004
DIMENSIONS: 17 1/2" W x 20" D x 33" H

ELENALI MIRROR
CODE: HEM2
DIMENSIONS: 30" D

ELENALI WALL HUNG BASIN
CODE: HE3001 for basin
CODE: HEBMFC for wall mount frame
DIMENSIONS: 17 1/2" W x 20" D

ELENALI MIRROR
CODE: HEM3
DIMENSIONS: 36" x 37"

ELENALI PEDESTAL BASIN
CODE: HE1501 for 1 hole faucet
CODE: HE1503 for 3 hole faucet
DIMENSIONS: 32" W x 23 1/4" D x 34" H

ELENALI PEDESTAL BASIN
With wall mounted accessories.
CODE: HE1001 for 1 hole faucet
CODE: HE1003 for 3 hole faucet
DIMENSIONS: 32" L x 23" W x 33" H
Countertop also available with round basin (23" L x 23" W x 33" H)

DESCRIPTION FOR ITEMS:
Elenali features 3/4" thick molded glass with smooth top and textured underside. The basin can be clear or textured and is press molded directly from the countertop drawn to 5/8" thick. Countertops are supported by a steel pedestal column wrapped with 3/8" thick silver back molded glass. Manufacturer can make any and all special sizes, 3-5 week delivery.

MANOVELLA
Code: VM4

PRINCIPE FAUCET
Code: V701

HI-FI FAUCET
Code: VH204

I BALOCCHI

CALIBRO FAUCET
Code: VC104

MT. BLANC FAUCET
Code: N1608

MCKINLEY FAUCET
Code: N2609

MEDITERRANEO FAUCET
Code: VME4

GIROTONDO FAUCET
Code: VG4

I BALOCCHI
Code: VB888

COPERNICO FAUCET
Code: VC1104

BIJOUX FAUCET
Code: V2001

SIMBOLO FAUCET
Code: V1001

SPAZIO FAUCET
Code: V8001

MCKINLEY FAUCET
Code: N2609

ZEUS FAUCET
Code: ZEUS

SHOWER BAR & HEAD
Code: V785, V784

MISURA FAUCET
Code: VM553

DAMES ANGLAISES
Code: N1409

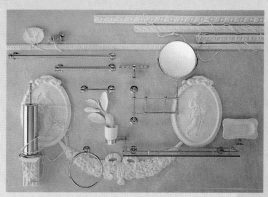

OLD ENGLAND ACCESSORIES

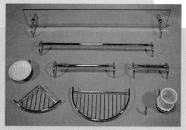

TRIS ACCESSORIES

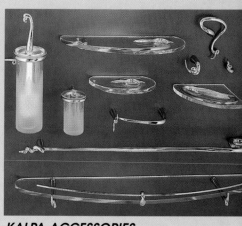

KALPA ACCESSORIES

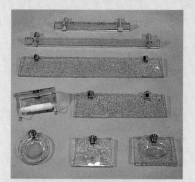

ELENALI ACCESSORIES

AMANDA ACCESSORIES

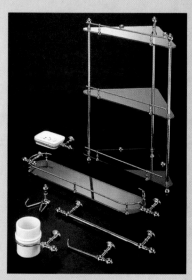

I BALOCCHI ACCESSORIES

KENSINGTON ACCESSORIES

TREVI ACCESSORIES

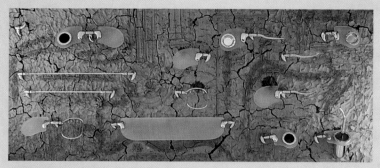

ELECTRAGLIDE ACCESSORIES

Hastings

TILE & IL BAGNO COLLECTION

CORPORATE OFFICE
30 Commercial St. / Freeport, NY 11520
516-379-3500 Fax 516-379-3187

SHOWROOMS
230 Park Ave. So. / New York, NY 10003
212-674-9700 Fax 212-674-8083

404 Northern Blvd. / Great Neck, NY 11021
516-482-1840 Fax 516-482-5350

1802 E. Jericho Tpke. / Huntington, NY 11743
516-493-1111 Fax 516-493-1874

13-100 Mdse. Mart / Chicago, IL 60654
312-527-0565 Fax 312-527-2537

More than

100 ways to take

a shower™*!*

For over 25

years.

ADLON the full-sized,

high-performance brass showerhead.

Ondine makes it easy to combine the InTouch II showerheads with a complementary line of valves and accessories for an installation that really serves your needs. And, for perfect design coordination, the entire system is available in Ondine's exciting colors, in addition to chrome and several special finishes.

Strong lines, high performance and prudent use of resources are hallmarks of Ondine's InTouch Series

InTouch II

A powerful line of showerheads, systems & accessories

Building on its extensive experience and its very successful InTouch Shower System, Ondine now offers InTouch II: shower systems that combine InTouch styling with new generation technology to deliver the ultimate in shower performance at low flow rates now mandated across the country.

Featuring 10 dial settings and eight spray selections, the InTouch II takes advantage of just 2.5 gallons / 9.5 liters water flow per minute to deliver shower patterns that range from wide to narrow sprays, strong to soft, as well as pulsating massage sprays and any combination of these. Each spray setting is clearly marked by a click in the dial that feels just right.

hold

full cone & massage

slow massage

turbo massage

massage

Inside InTouch II, water is directed through three separate channels. The center jet with adjustable intensity delivers a concentrated stream of water that removes shampoo quickly and easily. The outer spray delivers a drenching full-cone shower. The variable speed massage has 3 settings – soft, normal and turbo. Combination sprays add more choices yet. All channels are kept clean with an integral filter which captures sediment before it reaches the spray mechanisms.

Since few people can agree on what in a shower feels just right to them, InTouch II has been designed to allow a user to fine-tune both the outer and the center sprays from forceful needle to soft flows. It's easy and fast with the special tool provided.

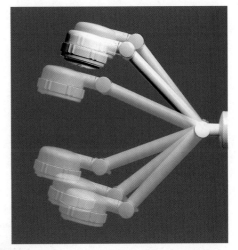

*The Hi-Lo Showerhead is
adjustable by up to 17 inches*

Spray mechanisms are self-cleaning. Minor spray adjustments help with flushing out water-borne impurities. There are two temporary shut-off positions on the InTouch II shower dial, one at each end for convenience and additional help in saving water. Ondine's InTouch II showers are part of a system designed to make installation easy and to have a shower within convenient reach of any user. Included are the patented 3-Position wall mount and the Hi-Lo Slide Bar – an accessory that allows instant shower height adjustment of 24 inches or as much as 48 inches. Even small children can now take their own shower!

InTouch II combines new generation technology with unique styling performance for complete shower systems that really serve your needs.

*Fine-tune the inner and outer spray patterns
with the InTouch Tool, included with all
InTouch II showers*

*Ondine Colors
add excitement*

center & massage

center jet

full cone & center

full cone

hold

Elite II

A refined line of showerheads, systems & accessories

Refinement beyond where most would say good enough. It's Elite II. Our top-of-the-line model to please those who want it all. Solid brass finished to a fine polish. The crystal look. Engineered for performance at 2.5 gpm; 9.5 L/m, Elite II delivers a drenching full cone spray to a combination with pulsating massage and slow to fast massage sprays, all selected with a turn of the outer dial.

Elite II shower spray mechanisms need little or no maintenance. Made of a specially formulated elastomer, the spray ring resists accumulation of mineral deposits. It is designed to allow water-borne impurities to be simply flushed out. Carefully selected engineering polymers guarantee proper fit and function, free from corrosion.

Refinement beyond

where most would

say good enough.

Elite II.

The Elite II mechanism directs water through two separate channels. The outer channel delivers a full cone spray. As the dial is turned, water begins to flow through the massage channel.

coarse spray

needle spray

combination spray

slow massage spray

massage spray

fast massage spray

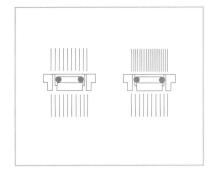

A turbine rotor mechanism delivers a pulse of water to each massage port giving a soothing and invigorating massage pulse. All of these settings are designed for highest shower performance at water and energy saving flow rates.

Unlike conventional showers which use rigid flow restrictors to limit water flow, Ondine's Flow Controller senses incoming water pressure and automatically adjusts flows to 2.5 gallons / 9.5 liters per minute for highest performance at any pressure level up to 80 PSI (550 KPa).

Ondine's Elite II showers are part of a complete system designed to make installation easy and to have a shower within convenient reach of any user. Ondine's Deckmount System, for instance, allows installation of a handshower with a free-standing tub, sunken tub or spa. Now you can have a shower where once there was none!

Elite II Deckmount System

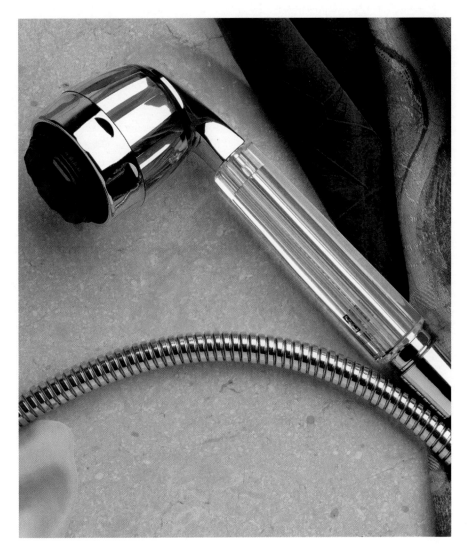

Pressure Balancing Valve

Available in combination with most Ondine showers or as a separate unit.

The Ondine No-Scald Pressure Balancing Valve is designed to complement all Ondine shower systems. Its safety features are a valuable addition to any tub or shower installation.

This high quality extension of the Ondine product line will upgrade and enhance any tub and shower installation.

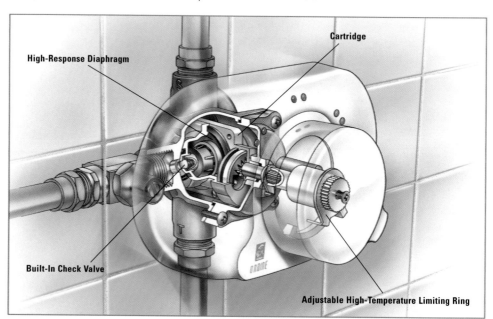

High-Response Diaphragm

Cartridge

Built-In Check Valve

Adjustable High-Temperature Limiting Ring

A high response diaphragm engineered into a cartridge containing a mixing chamber automatically and continuously balances pressures of incoming hot and cold water flows. **A consistent water temperature is maintained** despite pressure fluctuations caused by intermittent use of other water outlets nearby.

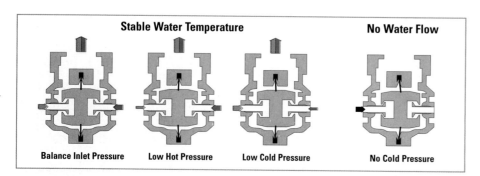

Stable Water Temperature

Balance Inlet Pressure Low Hot Pressure Low Cold Pressure

No Water Flow

No Cold Pressure

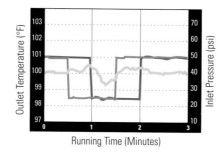

Outlet Temperature (°F)

Inlet Pressure (psi)

Running Time (Minutes)

Inlet Temperatures

HOT   140°F
COLD   50°F
OUTLET   100°F

Graph Legend

Supply Pressure HOT
Supply Pressure COLD
Outlet Temperature

Rotating the handle counter-clockwise turns on the water flow with the temperature increasing gradually.

A large 70° "comfort zone" in the rotation of the handle represents water temperatures from 90° to 110°F, 32° to 43°C. This "Comfort Zone" allows fine-tuning to easily select temperatures that are just right. Should hot or cold pressure be lost entirely, the valve will restrict water flow entirely to prevent cold shock or scalding. There is also an adjustable stop to allow setting a high-temperature limit.

The pressure balancing cartridge is engineered with a high response elastic diaphragm which prevents calcium build-up and seizing of the control common in piston style valves. The cartridge is accessible after installation for easy serviceability. Back-to-back installations are made possible by rotating the cartridge 180°.

The cartridge also contains a **built-in check valve**. It provides 100% protection against cross connection within the valve and can significantly reduce or eliminate noise due to water hammer in homes with quick closing faucets.

The Pressure Balancing Valve integrates with all Ondine showers and accessories for complete design coordination. It will upgrade and enhance any tub and shower installation where ease of installation and reliable performance are a priority.

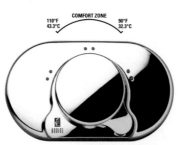

COMFORT ZONE
110°F 43.3°C — 90°F 32.3°C

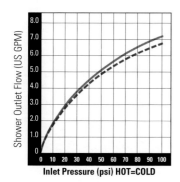

Inlet Temperatures
HOT 140°F
COLD 50°F
OUTLET 100°F

Graph Legend
——— *Flow Rate for valve "WITHOUT STOPS"*
- - - *Flow Rate for valve "WITH STOPS"*

Shower Outlet Flow (US GPM)
Inlet Pressure (psi) HOT=COLD

Inlet Temperatures		Inlet Pressure	
HOT	140°F	HOT	50 psi
COLD	50°F	COLD	50 psi

Outlet Temperature (°F)
Handle Rotation from Off to Full Hot (°)
Shower Range

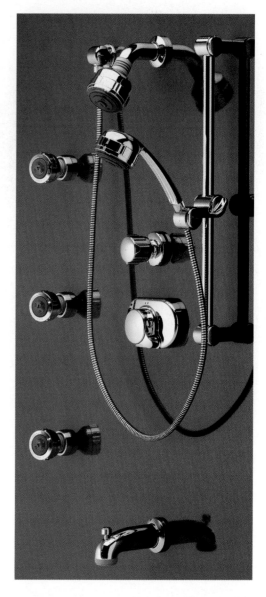

INTOUCH II INCOLOR

In addition to traditional finishes, InTouch II is available in split finishes and in Ondine's exciting colors.

All White

White

Chrome-on-White

Chrome-on-Mist Grey

Chrome

Polished Brass

Tropicals

New Naturals

Basic Primaries

Pastels

Gold-on-White

Gold-on-Chrome

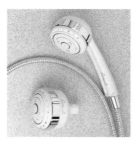

Gold-on-Ivory

Gold-on-Apricot

To specify a different finish for a model shown in this brochure, replace the "WW" suffix with the appropriate suffix on this page.

Finish	Suffix		
All White	W	1	
White	W	W	
Chrome-on-White	C	W	
Chrome-on-Mist Grey	C	G	*
Chrome (omit suffix)			
Polished Brass	P	B	
Tropicals	T	R	1
New Naturals	N	N	1

Finish	Suffix		
Basic Primaries	B	P	1
Pastels	P	A	1
Gold-on-White	G	W	*
Gold-on-Chrome	G	C	*
Gold-on-Ivory	G	I	*
Gold-on-Apricot	G	A	*

* Australian Market Only.

Call or write for a complete catalog.

Interbath Inc.
665 North Baldwin Park Blvd.
City of Industry, CA 91746
800 800 2132
fax 818 369 3316

ONDINE
INTERBATH

IB402.1194

C573A
15440/JAS
BuyLine 4168

Ahhh…the luxury of Jason

Behind Every JASON® Product Stands A Jacuzzi

Our family name, Jacuzzi, has come to mean more than kinship. It began in 1915 when my father and his six brothers formed a business called Jacuzzi Brothers, Inc. But in the 1950s my family name became a household word when my uncle, Candido, invented the whirlpool bath.

For many years, I worked for the family business. Then in 1982, after all family members sold their respective interests in the business, I formed Jason International, Inc. Many experienced family members and employees have since joined us.

Today, JASON whirlpool baths combine therapy with luxury and convenience to bring you the absolute state-of-the-art in whirlpool bathing. We've put complete, and incredibly quiet, operation at your fingertips. Our rich acrylic finishes are long lasting and so very easy to clean. Your back, indeed every part of your body, is considered in our designs. Integrated lumbar supports and armrests, recessed therapy jets...everything we do is designed to make your bathing experience more soothing and pleasurable. The new JASON collection within these pages is a testament of how far we've come.

We appreciate this opportunity to tell you about our heritage and our products, and for making us the first family of luxury bathing.

Remo Jacuzzi
President
JASON International, Inc.

Foreground: Remo Jacuzzi, President. Standing from left to right: Remo V. Jacuzzi, Vice President of Manufacturing; Matthew Jacuzzi, Manufacturing Projects Coordinator; Paulo Jacuzzi, Product Coordinator; Jennifer Jacuzzi Peregrin, Vice President of Finance.

2

THE ANABELLA™

A Bold Affirmation

This exciting new Signature Series bath is a bold affirmation of Remo Jacuzzi's prolific design spirit. With its unique shape, the ANABELLA opens the imagination to a variety of placement possibilities…island, corner, or a most creative bay. Of the five therapy jets, one is a recessed Ultrassage™ back jet for a thoroughly relaxing massage of your back. The JASON digital control puts complete state-of-the-art whirlpool operation at your fingertips. Welcome the ANABELLA, one of our most luxurious and exciting baths. And one of our most distinctive as well.

42" (107 cm)

78" (198 cm)

height: 20-1/2" (52 cm)

Full selection of colors with complementing fittings. Lumbar support and armrests. One hp pump (120V, 20A). JASON digital control with programmable timer. Low water level and temperature sensors. Five therapy jets including an Ultrassage™ back jet. Two silent air controls. Textured floor. Shown in large photo with optional trim kit with two grip handles and bath spout in polished chrome. See pages 24-26 for other options. Individually factory tested, IAPMO and UL listed.

3

THE CASARSA ™

The Perfect Circle

This exciting bath is named after Casarsa, Italy, site of the ancestral home built by Remo Jacuzzi's grandfather, Giovanni. The circular shape is ideal for installation in a corner, platform, or island setting. There's ample room for two and a choice of four bathing positions, each with lumbar support. For the greatest relaxation, there are six therapy jets including two recessed Ultrassage™ back jets and two recessed opposing end jets. So a simultaneous back and foot massage can be enjoyed by both you and your bathing partner. As in all Signature Series baths, two silent air controls allow whisper-quiet operation. And the JASON digital control puts complete state-of-the-art whirlpool operation at your fingertips while you bathe in luxury.

72" (183 cm) diameter
height: 23" (58 cm)

Full selection of colors with complementing fittings. Lumbar supports and armrests. One hp pump (120V, 20A). JASON digital control with programmable timer. Low water level and temperature sensors. Six therapy jets including two recessed Ultrassage™ back jets and two recessed opposing end jets. Two silent air controls. Textured floor. Shown in large photo with optional metal trim kit and two Double Cascade Spout® & faucet sets in bright brass. See pages 24-26 for other options. Individually factory tested, IAPMO and UL listed.

4

Roman Goddess of Flowers

We named this bath the FLORA because it is internally shaped like the cup of a flower. And because it exudes a warm and gracious feeling like Remo Jacuzzi's sister, Flora. Designed for corner place- ment, the dimensions of the FLORA provide generous space for two. To ensure the greatest relaxation, there are six therapy jets including a recessed Ultrassage™ back jet and a recessed opposing end jet. Thus, you can enjoy a soothing lower back and foot massage at the same time. Two silent air controls bring life to a whisper. And, as in all Signature Series baths, the JASON digital control puts complete whirlpool operation at your fingertips. Could life be better?

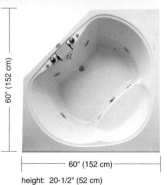

60" (152 cm)

60" (152 cm)

height: 20-1/2" (52 cm)

Full selection of colors with complementing fittings. Lumbar supports. One hp pump (120V, 20A). JASON digital control with programmable timer. Low water level and temperature sensors. Six therapy jets including a recessed Ultrassage™ back jet and a recessed opposing end jet. Two silent air controls. Textured floor. Shown in large photo with optional metal trim kit and Double Cascade Spout® & faucet set in gold. See pages 24-26 for other options.

Ultimate Luxury Resort

Just off the coast of Venice and not far from the Jacuzzi ancestral home, lies la isola Lido, one of Europe's most fashionable and relaxing island resorts. And as one of our most fashionable and relaxing baths, we have named this the LIDO. This bath features five therapy jets including a recessed Ultrassage™ jet to provide you with a most soothing lower back massage. Also for your comfort are raised shoulder supports, armrests, and lumbar support. The JASON digital control puts complete whirlpool operation at your fingertips. Finally, two silent air controls let you calm the roar of the world.

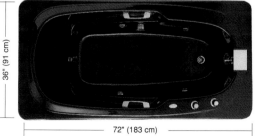

height: 23" (58 cm)

36" (91 cm)

72" (183 cm)

Full selection of colors with complementing fittings. Lumbar support and armrests. One hp pump (120V, 20A). JASON digital control with programmable timer. Low water level and temperature sensors. Five therapy jets including a recessed Ultrassage™ back jet. Two silent air controls. Textured floor. Shown in large photo with optional metal trim kit with grip handles, Double Cascade Spout® & faucet set, and hand held shower in bright brass. See pages 24-26 for other options. Individually factory tested, IAPMO and UL listed.

THE BON JOUR™

For A Good Day, Every Day

Here is yet another reason why JASON whirlpool baths are so esteemed. Elegant European styling with raised shoulders and sweeping armrests. The BON JOUR gives you room enough for two. The BON JOUR PETITE™ is a roomy, though more narrow bath, well-suited for remodeling installations. For the greatest relaxation, both baths feature six therapy jets including a recessed Ultrassage™ back jet and a recessed opposing end jet. You can enjoy a soothing lower back and foot massage at the same time. Two silent air controls. JASON digital control puts whirlpool operation at your finger tips. Should you start the day or end the day in the luxury of your JASON BON JOUR? Why not both?

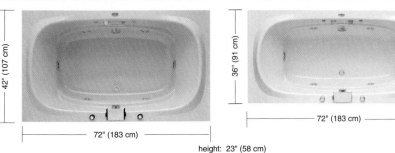

42" (107 cm)

72" (183 cm)

36" (91 cm)

72" (183 cm)

height: 23" (58 cm)

Full color selection, complementing fittings. Lumbar supports and armrests. One hp pump (120V, 20A). JASON digital control with programmable timer. Low water level and temperature sensors. Six therapy jets including a recessed Ultrassage™ back jet and a recessed opposing end jet. Two silent air controls. Textured floor. Large photo shows optional metal trim kit with grip handle, headrests, and Double Cascade Spout® & faucet set in gold. See pages 24-26 for other options. Individually factory tested, IAPMO and UL listed.

THE MIA ™

Two Can Say "It's Mine"

In Italian, mia means "mine." And that might suggest to you that this is a personal-sized bath. But such is not the case, and we can explain. As in other Signature Series baths, the MIA provides you with a recessed Ultrassage™ back jet and a recessed opposing end jet for simultaneous back and foot massage. Yet, in the MIA, these jets are offset from the center so that two of you can relax with a back massage while stretching out in comfort to enjoy the MIA's full length and shoulder room. Not to mention all the Signature Series features. Such as JASON digital control and two silent air controls. So yes, mia means "mine." And in this case, it means "mine" for two.

48" (122 cm)

72" (183 cm)

height: 23" (58 cm)

Full selection of colors with complementing fittings. Lumbar supports and armrests. One hp pump (120V, 20A). JASON digital control with programmable timer. Low water level and temperature sensors. Six therapy jets including a recessed Ultrassage™ back jet and a recessed opposing end jet, both offset from center. Two silent air controls. Textured floor. Shown in large photo with optional metal trim kit with grip handle, and Double Cascade Spout® & faucet set in bright brass. See pages 24-26 for other options. Individually factory tested, IAPMO and UL listed.

8

As Spacious As The Heavens

One of our most spacious baths, the ANGELICA is as wide as many baths are long. And here is a bath to set your mind free. With two optional Double Cascade Spouts® flowing, it's easy to imagine yourself (and your partner) in a hot spring with twin waterfalls at your feet. Of the six therapy jets, there are two recessed Ultrassage™ back jets so that each of you can enjoy a most therapeutic lower back massage. Each of you can also enjoy a foot massage from the therapy jets at your feet. Shoulder supports, armrests, lumbar supports, silent air controls, and JASON digital control...the ANGELICA gives you all the features that set the standards for luxury bathing.

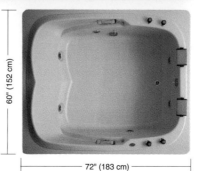

60" (152 cm)

72" (183 cm)

height: 23" (58 cm)

Full selection of colors with complementing fittings. Lumbar supports and armrests. One hp pump (120V, 20A). JASON digital control with programmable timer. Low water level and temperature sensors. Six therapy jets including two recessed Ultrassage™ back jets and two recessed opposing end jets. Two silent air controls. Textured floor. Shown in large photo with optional metal trim kit with grip handles, and two Double Cascade Spout® & faucet sets in gold. See pages 24-26 for other options. Individually factory tested, IAPMO and UL listed.

Pure Enchantment

The graceful design of this bath is only part of its true beauty. Thanks to the exclusive new RippleWall™, the MATISSA serenades you with the melodic sound of falling water. Besides full body massage, and back massage from one of two JASON Ultrassage™ back jets, this bath offers specially-placed rotating jets for a luxurious massage of your neck. Proportions are generous – there's even extra depth – providing ample room for two. And the built-in accessory compartment is the perfect place to neatly tuck away an optional recessed hand held shower. These luxury features, of course, are in addition to the many others that come standard with the MATISSA. Silent air controls, lumbar supports, digital whirlpool control... The JASON MATISSA. Yes, this is pure enchantment.

54" (137 cm)

72" (183 cm)

height: 26" (66 cm)

Full selection of colors with complementing fittings. Lumbar supports and armrests. One hp pump (120V, 20A). JASON digital control with programmable timer. Low water level and temperature sensors. Eight therapy jets including two recessed Ultrassage™ back jets and two rotating neck jets. RippleWall™. Two silent air controls. Textured floor. Shown in large photo with optional metal trim kit in polished chrome and a recessed hand held shower set. See pages 24-26 for other options. Individually factory tested, IAPMO and UL listed.

The Music of Nature

This beautiful corner bath is one of our most luxurious for several reasons. You can enjoy a soothing back massage from one of two Ultrassage™ back jets. You can enjoy a neck massage from our special rotating neck jets. And all this, of course, is in addition to full body massage from the four remaining therapy jets. Ahhh. Thanks to JASON's exclusive new RippleWall™, the CAMPANA brings the soothing and sensory experience of sound. As water cascades over the RippleWall, it's easy to imagine yourself in a babbling brook. The generous proportions and greater depth provide ample room for two, with lumbar support and a recessed Ultrassage™ back jet for each. And as a member of the JASON Signature Series, the list of luxury features goes on and on.

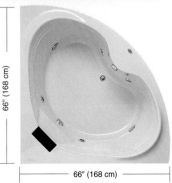

66" (168 cm)

66" (168 cm)

height: 25-1/2" (65 cm)

Full selection of colors with complementing fittings. Lumbar supports and armrests. One hp pump (120V, 20A). JASON digital control with programmable timer. Low water level and temperature sensors. Eight therapy jets including two recessed Ultrassage™ back jets and two rotating neck jets. RippleWall™. Two silent air controls. Textured floor. Shown in large photo with optional metal trim kit in bright brass. See pages 24-26 for other options. Individually factory tested, IAPMO and UL listed.

THE HANNAH ™

Artist's Rendering of Luxury

Named after Remo Jacuzzi's youngest granddaughter, this exciting Signature Series design is so new that it was not yet in production at press time. Yet even in this illustration, the stunning beauty of the HANNAH is easy to see. With its rounded sides and offset bathing well, this bath is certainly one of our most unique. Its gracefully flowing lines work beautifully in an island setting or, as shown, with matching skirt. Besides full body and back massage, the HANNAH has special rotating jets for a soothing massage of your neck. The generous proportions and depth provide room for two. There's lumbar support and a recessed Ultrassage™ back jet for each of you. Welcome the new JASON HANNAH. Ahhh...the luxury.

48" (122 cm)
72" (183 cm)
height: 26" (66 cm)

Full selection of colors with complementing fittings. Lumbar supports and armrests. One hp pump (120V, 20A). JASON digital control with programmable timer. Low water level and temperature sensors. Eight therapy jets including two recessed Ultrassage™ back jets and two rotating neck jets. Two silent air controls. Textured floor. Shown in large illustration with optional wall skirt and Double Cascade Spout® & faucet set in chrome. See pages 24-26 for other options. Individually factory tested, IAPMO and UL listed.

12

An Oval In An Oval

Designed as an oval within an oval, it's not just a matter of style that makes the MADELINE so unique. The sculpted design brings comfort to your shoulders while the lumbar support brings relaxation to your back. Six therapy jets surround you with whirlpool action. Opposing, recessed end jets simultaneously provide you with soothing foot and back massage. The flat deck is more than ample for mounting your favorite faucet. There's even room for two. Also offered as a soaking bath without whirlpool features (see page 23).

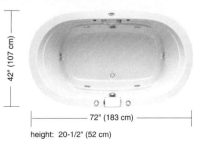

42" (107 cm)

72" (183 cm)

height: 20-1/2" (52 cm)

Full selection of colors with complementing fittings. Lumbar supports and armrests. 3/4 (.75) hp pump (120V, 20A). Variety of control options. Six therapy jets including two opposing recessed end jets. Two silent air controls. Textured floor. Shown in large photo with optional metal trim kit with grip handle, and Double Cascade Spout® & faucet set in bright brass. See pages 24-26 for other options. Individually factory tested, IAPMO and UL listed.

THE BRITTANY™

High Sophistication Without A High Price

Brittany is a region of France and one of the most sophisticated areas of the world. We chose to name this bath the BRITTANY because of its sophisticated (and French influenced) design. We offer the BRITTANY in your choice of two sizes, the BRITTANY V and the BRITTANY VI. Both are spacious enough for two. Both feature a host of standard equipment such as built in lumbar support and sweeping armrests. And both have recessed therapy jets at your back to comfortably massage you. In addition, the BRITTANY VI provides opposing recessed end jets for a most relaxing massage of your back and feet at the same time. Both baths are also offered as BRITTANY LX Luxury Bathing Systems (see page 22) and as soaking baths without whirlpool features (see page 23).

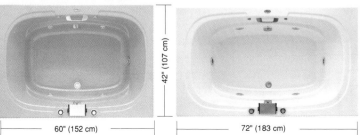

60" (152 cm)   72" (183 cm)   42" (107 cm)

Full selection of colors with complementing fittings. Lumbar supports and armrests. 3/4 (.75) hp pump (120V, 20A). BRITTANY V has 60" length, five therapy jets (one recessed back jet). BRITTANY VI has 72" length, six therapy jets (two opposing recessed end jets). Both have two silent air controls, textured floor. Variety of control options. Shown in large photo with optional metal trim kit with grip handle, and Double Cascade Spout® & faucet set in bright brass. See pages 24-26 for other options. Individually factory tested, IAPMO and UL listed.

14

Song of Joy

In Italy, a canto is a song. And singing is what you'll do when you experience the exceptional value in this fine bath. Because there are so many places to sit in the CANTO, each of the four therapy jets is recessed and located so that they can comfortably massage your back and feet at the same time. There's room for two, of course, and each of you can enjoy your own built-in lumbar support. Also offered as a soaking bath without whirlpool features (see page 23).

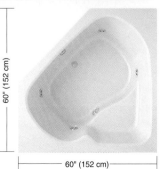

60" (152 cm)
60" (152 cm)
height: 20-1/2" (52 cm)

Full selection of colors with complementing fittings. Lumbar supports. 3/4 (.75) hp pump (120V, 20A). Four therapy jets, all recessed. Two silent air controls. Textured floor. Variety of control options. Shown in large photo with optional metal trim kit and Double Cascade Spout® & faucet set in bright brass. See pages 24-26 for other options. Individually factory tested, IAPMO and UL listed.

Extra Shoulder Room

A recent JASON design, the ASHLEY has become one of our most popular baths. It incorporates a bit more width for extra shoulder room. And it offers you recessed therapy jets on each end so you can enjoy simultaneous back and foot massage. Plus, these jets are offset from center so that two can stretch out in comfort and relaxation. Other superb JASON features remain – built in lumbar supports and sweeping armrests.

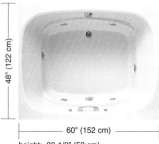

48" (122 cm)

60" (152 cm)

height: 20-1/2" (52 cm)

Full selection of colors with complementing fittings. Lumbar supports and armrests. 3/4 (.75) hp pump (120V, 20A). Six therapy jets including two opposing recessed back jets. Two silent air controls. Textured floor. Variety of control options. Shown in large photo with optional metal trim kit with grip handle, and Double Cascade Spout® & faucet set in bright brass. See pages 24-26 for other options. Individually factory tested, IAPMO and UL listed.

Spacious Elegance

One of the most spacious baths of our Decorator Series, the distinctive design of the LORELLE imparts an undeniable elegance to any decor. Here you'll find an abundance of JASON luxury features. Lumbar support sweeps the entire width. Of the six therapy jets, two are recessed for a very soothing back massage. There's even room for two. Also offered as a soaking bath without whirlpool features (see page 23).

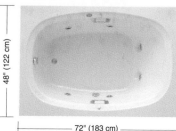

48" (122 cm)

72" (183 cm)

height: 20-1/2" (52 cm)

Full selection of colors with complementing fittings. Lumbar support. 3/4 (.75) hp pump (120V, 20A). Six therapy jets including two recessed back jets. Two silent air controls. Textured floor. Variety of control options. Shown in large photo with optional metal trim kit with grip handles in polished chrome. See pages 24-26 for other options. Individually factory tested, IAPMO and UL listed.

A Big Idea For Small Space

In Italy, nina means "little girl." Like a little girl, this little bath can bring you great joy. Remo Jacuzzi was mindful of that when he named this bath after his granddaughter. Its small dimensions (and price) make it ideal for replacing a conventional 5' bathtub with the lasting luxury of a JASON whirlpool bath. Yes, this bath is small, but it's hardly short on "big bath" features. Built-in lumbar support and gracefully flowing armrests. Five therapy jets, one of which is recessed for complete massage of your back. Two silent air controls for whisper quiet operation. Also offered as a NINA LX Luxury Bathing System (see page 22) and as a soaking bath without whirlpool features (see page 23).

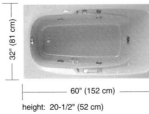

32" (81 cm)

60" (152 cm)

height: 20-1/2" (52 cm)

Full selection of colors with complementing fittings. Lumbar support and armrests. 3/4 (.75) hp pump (120V, 20A). Five therapy jets including one recessed back jet. Two silent air controls. Textured floor. Variety of control options. Shown in large photo with optional metal trim kit with grip handles in polished chrome. See pages 24-26 for other options. Individually factory tested, IAPMO and UL listed.

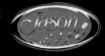

As Big Or As Small As You Want

With the ENCORE, you can choose from three sizes to fit your needs and space. All are classically designed. All are of the quality you expect from JASON. And all offer you many features you don't expect at this price. Built in armrests and lower back lumbar support. Five therapy jets for full whirlpool relaxation, one of which is positioned and recessed for soothing massage of your back. Two silent air controls for whisper quiet operation. The ENCORE V and VI are also offered as soaking baths without whirlpool features (see page 23).

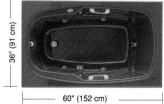

60" (152 cm)

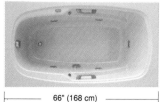

66" (168 cm)

height: 20-1/2" (52 cm)

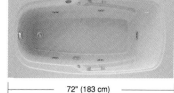

72" (183 cm)

36" (91 cm)

ENCORE V, V-1/2, VI have 60', 66", and 72" lengths, respectively. Full selection of colors with complementing fittings. Lumbar support and armrests. 3/4 (.75) hp pump (120V, 20A). Five therapy jets including one recessed back jet. Two silent air controls. Textured floor. Variety of control options. Shown in large photo with optional metal trim kit with grip handles in bright brass. See pages 24-26 for other options. Individually factory tested, IAPMO and UL listed.

THE EMILY ™

Our Most Adaptable Design

The special design of the EMILY, with its end-drain configuration and reduced length, allows a beautiful installation in a corner, wall, platform, or island setting. Its flat deck is ideal for mounting your favorite faucet. Though compact in overall dimensions, this bath will surprise you with its very large bathing well. Of the five therapy jets, one is recessed for a comfortable massage of your back. Two others are positioned for a soothing massage of your feet. One of our most distinctive baths, certainly our most adaptable of the Decorator Series. Also offered as a soaking bath without whirlpool features (see page 23).

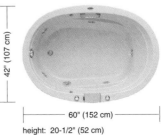

42" (107 cm)

60" (152 cm)

height: 20-1/2" (52 cm)

Full selection of colors with complementing fittings. Lumbar support and armrests. 3/4 (.75) hp pump (120V, 20A). Variety of control options. Five therapy jets including one recessed back jet. Two silent air controls. Textured floor. Shown in large photo with optional trim kit with grip handle and Double Cascade Spout® in bright brass. See pages 24-26 for other options. Individually factory tested, IAPMO and UL listed.

So Graceful

Even at first glance, you're certain to admire the gracefully flowing armrests and cameo-like oval design of the JACQUELINE. This beautiful bath literally invites you into its bathing well. And once there, be assured that you'll enjoy all the luxury and quality you expect from JASON. Four therapy jets comfortably massage your body at its sides. And from a recess in the lumbar support behind you, yet another therapy jet massages your back. There are two sizes to choose from. The JACQUELINE V is a personal-sized bath. The JACQUELINE VI provides extra length. With either size, you'll long enjoy one of our most distinctive and enduring designs. Both baths are also offered as JACQUELINE LX Luxury Bathing Systems (see page 22) and as soaking baths without whirlpool features (see page 23).

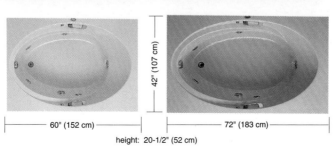

60" (152 cm) — 72" (183 cm) — 42" (107 cm) height: 20-1/2" (52 cm)

JACQUELINE V and VI are 60" and 72" in length, respectively. Full selection of colors with complementing fittings. Lumbar support. 3/4 (.75) hp pump (120V, 20A). Five therapy jets including one recessed back jet. Two silent air controls. Textured floor. Variety of trim options. Shown in large photo with optional trim kit with two grip handles in bright brass. Individually factory tested, IAPMO and UL listed.

THE LX SYSTEMS

All The Things That Are Wonderful About Bathing

Welcome to the height of luxury bathing, our new LX Luxury Bathing Systems. Here is the transformation of a JASON Bath into a very luxurious and personal home health spa. Fully featured, a JASON LX System combines all the things that are wonderful about bathing – whirlpool, steam, and full body shower. Standard equipment is lavish. There's even a special device that releases fragrance while you bathe. From there, options will take you to an even higher level of luxury. An adjustable hand held shower, a dome light, plus a variety of digital controls that let you run the entire system with the touch of a finger. Ahhh...the luxury of JASON.

For more information, see the separate literature on JASON LX Luxury Bathing Systems.

SOAKING BATHS

The same construction quality and fine acrylic surfaces found in JASON whirlpool baths are also available in JASON soaking baths without whirlpool features.

	MADELINE™	BRITTANY™ V, VI	CANTO™	LORELLE™	NINA™	ENCORE™ V,VI	EMILY™	JACQUELINE™ V,VI
CONSTRUCTION								
Fully pigmented acrylic surface, full color selection.	S	S	S	S	S	S	S	S
Fiberglass reinforced structure.	S	S	S	S	S	S	S	S
Built-in lumbar support(s).	S	S	S	S	S	S	S	S
Built-in armrests.	S	S	–	–	S	S	S	S
Textured floor.	S	S	S	S	S	S	S	S
Tile flange kit	–	O+	O+	O+	O+	O+	–	O+
ACCESSORIES								
Plated brass grip handle(s); polished chrome/bright brass/gold.	O	O	–	O	O	O	O	O
Powder coated brass grip handle(s); white/bone/quicksilver.	O	O	–	O	O	O	O	O
Metal overflow drain assembly or overflow drain kit.	O+	O+	O+	O+	O+	O+	O+	O+
Hand held shower kit; polished chrome/bright brass/gold.	O+	O+	O+	O+	O+	O+	O+	O+
Removable headrest; white.	O+	O+	O+	O+	O+	O+	O+	O+
Tile flange kit.	–	O+	O+	O+	O+	O+	–	O+
Lateral skirt.	–	O+	O+	O+	O+	O+	–	O+
For additional information, refer to page...	13	14	15	17	18	19	20	21

S = standard   O = optional   O+ = field installable option

NOTE: Soaking bath surfaces may subtly reveal the location where hydrotherapy fittings would be installed if the bath was constructed for whirlpool application. Field plumbing of a soaking bath to convert it to a whirlpool bath will void its warranty.

THE ALEXIA™
Brazilian Shower/Bath

In Brazil, Remo Jacuzzi discovered the concept of a combination shower base and small bath. The stylish ALEXIA is the embodiment of this concept. In a small space, it provides a shower base, a small bath, and a seat.

Molded seat. Left or right hand drain. Textured bottom. Shown in large photo with optional tempered glass enclosure. Overflow drain kit, optional.

48" (122 cm)

36" (91 cm)

height: 12" (30 cm)

SHOWER BASES

JASON offers a beautiful selection of shower bases to match your JASON bath. Ask your dealer for the separate literature.

23

While some baths are designed to simply look good, JASON baths are designed to feel good as well. JASON combines enduring aesthetics with baths of high therapeutic value. This is a noteworthy distinction between JASON whirlpool baths and competitive products.

Our overall goal is to provide you with a luxurious bath of soothing, therapeutic comfort. Many unique design details* aid us in this goal.

- Built-in lumbar supports and recessed back jets for comfortable support and massage of your lower back.
- Opposing end jets for simultaneous massage of your back and feet.
- Ultrassage™ therapy jets for the deepest, most therapeutic whirlpool massage. This feature is standard in Signature Series baths, optional in most Decorator Series baths.
- Built-in armrests for greater relaxation.
- Bathing wells that are spacious relative to the outside bath perimeter. This allows greater comfort, even in our smaller baths.
- Rotating neck jets for a comforting massage of your neck are standard equipment on some of our Signature Series models.

Trust The Quality

Besides the details mentioned above, each JASON bath is appointed with other standard features that you'll long appreciate. Rich, deep acrylic colors

for lasting beauty. Three layers of fiberglass reinforcement for high strength and rigidity. Self draining pumps and plumbing for better sanitation. Directionally adjustable jets, specially designed to never freeze in place. Quality fittings and components for years and years of reliable service.

The pump has a run-dry seal for protection if accidentally run without water. Every whirlpool bath is factory tested to assure that everything works exactly as it should. Every whirlpool bath arrives on an exclusive, fully supporting thermoformed base for a simple and solid installation.

The Signature Series

Signature Series designs represent the state-of-the-art in whirlpool bathing. Each Signature Series bath has a more powerful one hp whirlpool pump. Whirlpool operation is programmable and at your fingertips with the JASON digital control. A low water level sensor helps protect your bath and your bathroom. A temperature sensor aids your

comfort by monitoring the water temperature of your bath. All are standard Signature Series features.

Many luxury options are available only in our Signature Series baths. A bather-operated heater, for example, can be incorporated into the JASON digital control – allowing you to set and maintain your desired water temperature. The digital control itself is available in a multi-speed version so you can select your favorite whirlpool action.

Options For All JASON Whirlpool Baths

For both Signature and Decorator Series models, there are many options which help you transform your bath into a very personal luxury.

To determine the standard and optional equipment for each bath, refer to the chart on page 26. Some options are pictured here.

With the help of your JASON dealer, and your imagination, your JASON bath can be equipped just about any way you want.

Programmable JASON Digital Control. On Signature Series baths, a one-speed digital control is standard and a multi-speed digital control is optional. With either, a button at your fingertips lets you set the desired whirlpool time. Then, while you bathe, a digital display informs you of the water temperature and remaining whirlpool time. With the optional programmable in-line heater, a separate button lets you set and maintain the desired water temperature.

JASON Touch Control. Available on all JASON whirlpool baths. The whirlpool "touch" control button is incorporated into the JASON emblem affixed to the bath. Includes a built-in 20-minute timer and protective sensor that shuts off pump if water level is too low. Choose either a single-speed or multi-speed version.

& LUXURY

JASON Ultrassage™ Jet. Standard on Signature Series baths, optional on most others. Jet orifice rotates for deeper, soothing, therapeutic massage over your entire back. Color coordinated assembly. Escutcheon optionally available in polished chrome, bright brass, or gold.

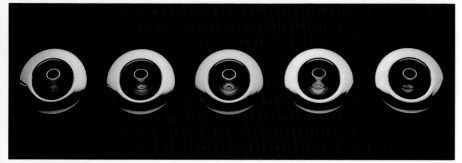

Metal trim package colors. A variety of attractive metal trim options to complement other bathroom fixtures. Photo shows escutcheon and jet nozzle combinations available to replace standard color-coordinated jet nozzles. Choose polished chrome, bright brass, or gold finish. Two-color trim packages are also available – either "polished chrome dominant" or "bright brass dominant." Jet escutcheons and grip handles are provided in the dominant color, with air control knobs and jet nozzles in the highlight color. It is suggested that other bath options be selected in the dominant color.

JASON Double Cascade Spout® & faucet set. This patented spout is an example of the JASON knack for combining technology and luxury. A beautiful option for most JASON whirlpool baths. Used to fill bath and/or provide aesthetic recirculation of water. Metal finished in polished chrome, bright brass or gold. Also available in white, bone, and quicksilver powder-coated finishes.

Metal Grip Handles. An attractive and useful option for most models. Choose polished chrome, bright brass, or gold plated finish; white, natural bone, or quicksilver powder-coated finishes.

* Some design details are not available on some models.

Removable headrests. Add comfort to your bathing experience. Raised shoulder model (HR100, black only) fits all Signature Series baths except FLORA and ANABELLA. Ultrasoft model (HR200, white only) fits all JASON baths.

Hand held shower. A luxury option for all models. Mounts at deck. Provided with extension hose and diverter. Facilitates bath cleaning. Choose polished chrome, bright brass, or gold.

Underwater light with mood lenses. Sets the perfect mood for luxury bathing. An option for all models. 12V

25

BATH FEATURES, OPTIONS & ACCESSORIES

	SIGNATURE SERIES											DECORATOR SERIES								
	ANABELLA™	CASARSA™	FLORA™	LIDO™	BON JOUR™	BON JOUR PETITE™	MIA™	ANGELICA™	MATISSA™	CAMPANA™	HANNAH™	MADELINE™	BRITTANY™ V, VI	CANTO™	ASHLEY™	LORELLE™	NINA™	ENCORE™ V, V-1/2, VI	EMILY™	JACQUELINE™ V, VI
CONSTRUCTION:																				
Fully pigmented acrylic surface, full color selection	S	S	S	S	S	S	S	S	S	S	S	S	S	S	S	S	S	S	S	S
Fiberglass reinforced structure.	S	S	S	S	S	S	S	S	S	S	S	S	S	S	S	S	S	S	S	S
Pre-leveled thermoplastic full-support base.	S	S	S	S	S	S	S	S	S	S	S	S	S	S	S	S	S	S	S	S
Color coordinated high fashion suction, jet & air fittings.	S	S	S	S	S	S	S	S	S	S	S	S	S	S	S	S	S	S	S	S
Individually factory assembled & tested to exacting standards.	S	S	S	S	S	S	S	S	S	S	S	S	S	S	S	S	S	S	S	S
Built-in lower back lumbar support(s).	S	S	S	S	S	S	S	S	S	S	S	S	S	S	S	S	S	S	S	S
Built-in armrests.	S	S	—	S	S	S	S	S	—	S	S	S	S	—	S	—	S	S	S	S
Textured floor.	S	S	S	S	S	S	S	S	S	S	S	S	S	S	S	S	S	S	S	S
Integral tile-in lip.	—	—	O	—	—	—	—	—	—	—	—	—	—	—	—	—	—	—	—	—
Factory plumbed for Double Cascade Spout® & faucet set.	S	S	S	S	S	S	S	S	S	S	S	S	S	S	S	—	—	—	S	S
Available as soaking bath, except Encore V-1/2. Requires grouting.	—	—	—	—	—	—	—	—	—	—	—	O	O	O	—	O	O	O	O	O
PUMP and BATH CONTROLS:																				
3/4 Hp single-speed pump and 30-minute wall timer.	—	—	—	—	—	—	—	—	—	—	—	O	O	O	O	O	O	O	O	O
3/4 Hp single-speed pump and air switch with 20-minute timer.	—	—	—	—	—	—	—	—	—	—	—	O	O	O	O	O	O	O	O	O
3/4 Hp single-speed pump and electronic touch control with 20-minute timer & low water level sensor.	—	—	—	—	—	—	—	—	—	—	—	S	S	S	S	S	S	S	S	S
3/4 Hp multi-speed pump and electronic touch control with 20-minute timer & low water level sensor.	—	—	—	—	—	—	—	—	—	—	—	O	O	O	O	O	O	O	O	O
1 Hp single-speed pump, digital control with programmable timer, low water level and temperature sensors.	S	S	S	S	S	S	S	S	S	S	S	—	—	—	—	—	—	—	—	—
1 Hp six-speed pump, digital control with programmable timer, low water level and temperature sensors	O	O	O	O	O	O	O	O	O	O	O	—	—	—	—	—	—	—	—	—
1 Hp multi-speed pump and electronic touch control with 20-minute timer & low water level sensor.	O	O	O	O	O	O	O	O	O	O	O	—	—	—	—	—	—	—	—	—
1 Hp one-speed pump and electronic touch control with 20-minute timer & low water level sensor.	O	O	O	O	O	O	O	O	O	O	O	—	—	—	—	—	—	—	—	—
In-line bath heater, 1.5 kw/120V, (temp. settings programmable with digital controls above).	O	O	O	O	O	O	O	O	O	O	O	O	O	O	O	O	O	O	O	O
HYDROTHERAPY SYSTEM:																				
Full size JASON directionally adjustable jets for gentle massage.	S	S	S	S	S	S	S	S	S	S	S	S	S	S	S	S	S	S	S	S
Super quiet JASON air volume controls for optimal relaxation.	S	S	S	S	S	S	S	S	S	S	S	S	S	S	S	S	S	S	S	S
IAPMO & UL listed JASON hi-flow suction fitting protects bather.	S	S	S	S	S	S	S	S	S	S	S	S	S	S	S	S	S	S	S	S
Water lines plumbed in rigid PVC to assure self draining and hygenic operation time after time.	S	S	S	S	S	S	S	S	S	S	S	S	S	S	S	S	S	S	S	S
Recessed back jet(s) for more comfortable hydrotherapy.	S	S	S	S	S	S	S	S	S	S	S	S	S	S	S	S	S	S	S	S
Opposing back and foot jets (except BRITTANY V).	—	S	S	—	S	S	S	S	S	S	S	S	S	S	S	—	—	—	S	—
Integral RippleWall™.	—	—	—	—	—	—	—	—	S	S	S	—	—	—	—	—	—	—	—	—
Rotating neck jets.	—	—	—	—	—	—	—	—	S	S	S	—	—	—	—	—	—	—	—	—
ACCESSORIES: (For available finishes see pages 24 & 25)																				
Decorative metal trim kits.	O	O	O	O	O	O	O	O	O	O	O	O	O	O	O	O	O	O	O	O
Solid metal grip handle(s).	O	O	—	O	O	O	O	O	O	—	O	O	O	—	O	O	O	O	O	O
Metal overflow drain assembly or overflow drain kit.	O+	O+	O+	O+	O+	O+	O+	O+	O+	O+	O+	O+	O+	O+	O+	O+	O+	O+	O+	O+
Double Cascade Spout® & faucet set.	O+	O+	O+	O+	O+	O+	O+	O+	O+	O+	O+	O+	O+	O+	O+	—	—	—	O+	O+
JASON Ultrassage™ jet for back massage.	S	S	S	S	S	S	S	S	S	S	S	Ø	Ø	O	O	Ø	O	O	—	O
Hand held shower kit with diverter.	O+	O+	O+	O+	O+	O+	O+	O+	O+	O+	O+	O+	O+	O+	O+	O+	O+	O+	O+	O+
Recessed hand held shower with a valve set.	—	—	—	—	—	O+	—	—	—	—	—	—	—	—	—	—	—	—	—	—
Bath light with mood lenses, 12V.	O+	O+	O+	O+	O+	O+	O+	O+	O+	O+	O+	O+	O+	O+	O+	O+	O+	O+	O+	O+
Locationally adjustable and removable head rest	O+	O+	O+	O+	O+	O+	O+	O+	O+	O+	O+	O+	O+	O+	O+	O+	O+	O+	O+	O+
JASON Heat Saver — maintains water temp. non-electrically, (except for BRITTANY V and all multi-speed units or if unit is an ENCORE V, V-1/2, or NINA equipped with an Ultrassage).	O	O	—	O	O	O	O	O	O	O	O	O	O	O	—	O	O	—	O	O
Tile flange kit.	—	—	O+	—	—	—	—	—	—	—	—	—	O+	O+	O+	O+	O+	O+	—	O+
Lateral skirt.	—	—	—	O+	O+	O+	—	—	—	—	—	O+	—	O+	O+	O+	O+	O+	—	O+

NOTE: Above options must be factory installed unless otherwise noted and therefore must be specified with bath order.
LEGEND: S = Standard, O = Optional, — = Not available, O+ = Option available for field installation only, Ø = Location on end opposite pump only
Most baths and components are also offered for the electrical requirements of countries other than U.S.A., consult factory.

26

COLORS THAT GLOW WITH QUALITY

With JASON, you're assured of acrylic colors that are rich, deep, and lasting. Care is easy, too. Just wipe with a soft cloth and the finish will return to a high-gloss shine. And just look at the color selection JASON offers you.

Basic Colors

 **Classic White 001(WT)**

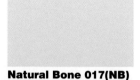 **Natural Bone 017(NB)**

Standard Colors

Quicksilver 007(QS) **Morning Blue 011(GB)** **Rose 012(RS)** **Smoke Grey 014(SG)** **Blush 016(SH)**

Coral Shell 018(CS) **Ice Blue 019(IB)** **Rouge 021(RG)** **Sea Green 022(SN)** **Peach 027(PH)**

   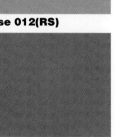 

Rose Bloom 029(RB) **Classic Beige 031(CB)** **Almond Bone 036(AB)** **Glacier Grey 038(GG)** **Bisquite 040(BQ)**

High Fashion Colors

 **Raspberry 013(RP)**

 **Black 015(BK)**

 **Ruby Red 020(RY)**

 **Navy Blue 025(NY)**

 **Teal Green 026(TL)**

Verde Green 035(VE)

Unless optional metal fittings are specified, baths are shipped with fittings of complementary color. This color chart should be used as a preliminary reference only. Due to printing process, exact colors may vary from those presented here. To determine exact color, refer to your JASON dealer for an acrylic sample.

JASON LUXURY BATHING SYSTEMS

JASON INTERNATIONAL INC. • 8323 MACARTHUR DRIVE • NORTH LITTLE ROCK, ARKANSAS 72118
1-800-255-5766 (ORDER DESK) / 501-771-4477 / 501-771-2333 (FAX)

*A vital contributor to JASON quality is your JASON dealer.
We stake our reputation on these fine people.*

New products

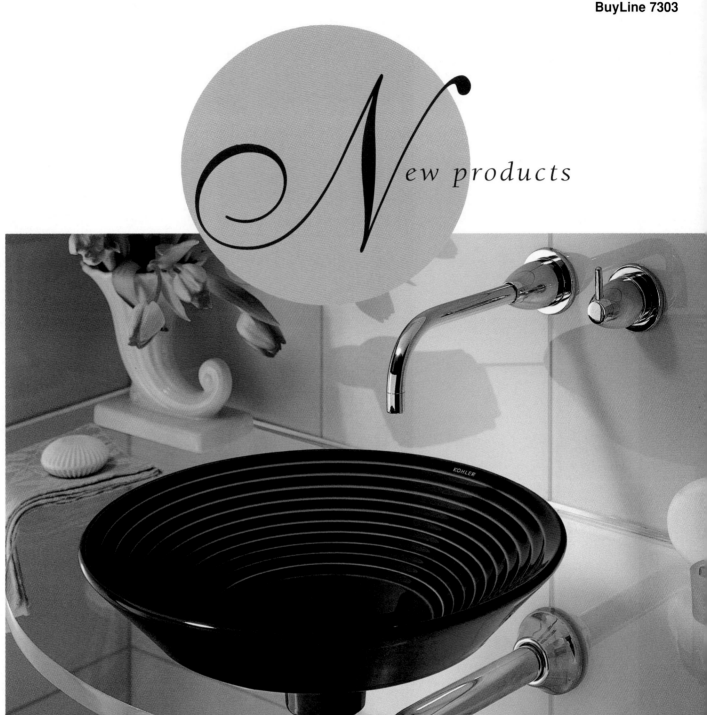

THE BOLD LOOK
OF **KOHLER**®

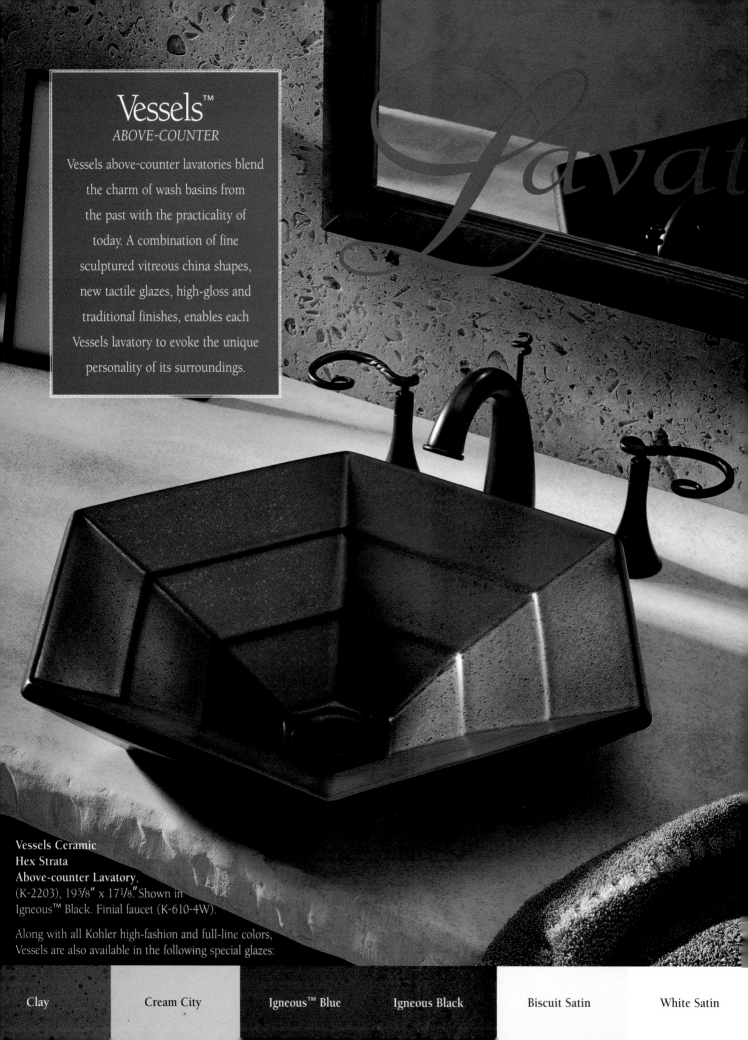

Vessels™
ABOVE-COUNTER

Vessels above-counter lavatories blend the charm of wash basins from the past with the practicality of today. A combination of fine sculptured vitreous china shapes, new tactile glazes, high-gloss and traditional finishes, enables each Vessels lavatory to evoke the unique personality of its surroundings.

**Vessels Ceramic
Hex Strata
Above-counter Lavatory**,
(K-2203), 19⅝″ x 17⅛″. Shown in
Igneous™ Black. Finial faucet (K-610-4W).

Along with all Kohler high-fashion and full-line colors,
Vessels are also available in the following special glazes:

| Clay | Cream City | Igneous™ Blue | Igneous Black | Biscuit Satin | White Satin |

ories

Vessels™ Ceramic Conical Bell Above-counter Lavatory
(K-2200), 16¼″ diameter. Shown in Igneous™ Blue. Falling Water faucet (K-199).

Vessels Ceramic Turnings Above-counter Lavatory
(K-2191), 16¼″ diameter. Shown in Cream City.

Kohler® Cast Iron Lavatories

Compact designs with ample basin areas, timeless styling, and solid Kohler Cast Iron construction, are the signatures of Kohler's five new lavatories. Each will fit into standard 30″ wide stock cabinetry and is available with a choice of 8″, 4″ or single-hole faucet drillings.

Lavat

Thoreau™ Self-rimming Lavatory (K-2907-1), 24″ x 18″ with single-hole faucet drilling. Kohler Cast Iron. Shown in Seafoam Green. Provence™ faucet (K-14513-1).

Larkspur™ Self-rimming Lavatory (K-2908-8), 24″ x 18″ with 8″ centers. Kohler Cast Iron. Shown in Innocent Blush.™ Revival™ faucet (K-16102-4A).

Thoreau Undercounter Lavatory (K-2909-8), 18″ x 11.″ Kohler Cast Iron. Shown in Ice™ Grey. Provence faucet (K-14513-1).

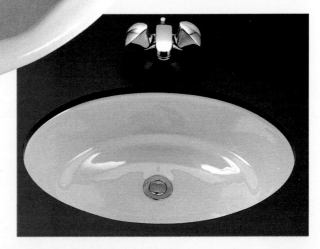

ories & Colors

Ellington™ Self-rimming Lavatory (K-2906-8), 19¼″ x 16¼″ with 8″ centers. Kohler® Cast Iron. Shown in Timberline™. Revival™ faucet (K-16102-4A).

Providence™ Self-rimming Lavatory (K-2929-4), 22″ x 19″ with 4″ centers. Kohler Cast Iron. Shown in Almond. Coralais™ Decorator faucet (K-15810-K/K-15850-4N).

Brilliance

White Brilliance, Blue Brilliance, and Black Brilliance open a new realm of Kohler color. The result of a high-gloss glaze treatment, Brilliance colors owe their subtle beauty to the delicate play of light that radiates from beneath layers of sheen. Responsive to changes in light, Brilliance colors enhance the sculptural qualities of select Kohler lavatories.

Black Brilliance, White Brilliance, and Blue Brilliance. Shown on Linia™ self-rimming lavatories (three K-2217).

Pheasant™

Inspired by sketches circa 1900, Pheasant features pairs of Oriental pheasants and a basketweave pattern drawn from a fisherman's creel on a Biscuit background. Pheasant includes countertop and undercounter lavatories with an optional single-letter monogram, ceramic faucet trim, decorative tile, floor container and countertop accessories.

Arti

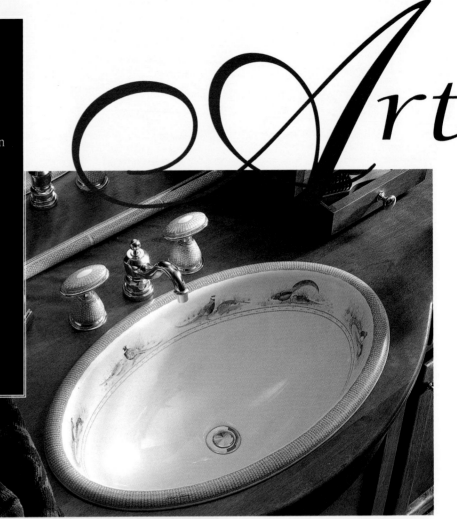

Pheasant Floor Container (K-14317-PH-96), 12″ diameter x 13″ with plastic liner.

Pheasant Vintage™ Countertop Lavatory (K-14272-P-96), 24″ x 15″. Antique™ faucet (K-280-9B) with Pheasant ceramic trim (K-258-PH-96). Pheasant decorative tile. Also available with a single-letter monogram.

Pheasant Vintage Undercounter Lavatory with optional single-letter monogram (K-14273-PH-96), 24¼″ x 12¼″. Antique faucet (K-280-9B) with Pheasant ceramic trim (K-258-PH-96). Also available without monogram.

Pheasant Decorative Field Tile with pheasant design with basketweave border (K-14200-PH-96) and pheasant design with Biscuit border (K-14200-PF-96). Packed 6 tiles per carton — approximately .66 square feet. Nominal dimensions 4¼″ x 4¼″.

Pheasant Decorative Half-round Tile with basketweave pattern (K-14204-PH-96). Packed 6 tiles per carton — approximately 3 linear feet. Nominal dimensions 1″ x 6″.

st Editions

Classic Oak

Classic Oak features oak leaves, acorns and squirrels on a White background, rendered in an architectural style popular in 18th century France. Classic Oak includes countertop and undercounter lavatories, ceramic faucet trim, decorative tile, floor container and countertop accessories. Lavatories are available with an optional single-letter monogram in a choice of charcoal, silver or gold.

Classic Oak Vintage™ Undercounter Lavatory (K-14254-C-0), 21¹/4″ x 12¹/4″. Antique™ faucet (K-280-9B) with Classic Oak ceramic trim (K-258-CX-0). Classic Oak decorative tile. Also available with a single-letter monogram.

Classic Oak Countertop Accessories (K-14181-CX-0). Includes three decorative ceramic containers with covers (6″, 4″ and 2″ high) and soap dish.

Classic Oak Decorative Strip Tile with squirrels on White (K-14208-CS-0) and with acorns and oak leaves on White (K-14208-CX-0). Packed 4 tiles per carton — approximately 4 linear feet. Nominal dimensions 4″ x 12″.

Classic Oak Vintage Countertop Lavatory (K-14253-CN-0), 24″ x 15″ with optional single-letter monogram in charcoal. Antique faucet (K-280-9B) with Classic Oak ceramic trim (K-258-CX-0). Also available without monogram.

Ankara™ & Carnivale

Ankara draws its inspiration from a 14th century water vessel unearthed near the Euphrates River in Turkey. A delicate filigree and diamond pattern is worked in tones of blue on a Biscuit background. Ankara includes pedestal, self-rimming and undercounter lavatories, a toilet, ceramic faucet trim, decorative tile and accessories. Carnivale was inspired by an 18th century Minton teacup with a harlequin pattern. It's subtle White Brilliance on White pattern flirts with the eye, reflecting the fun and trickery of the harlequin.

Artist Editions

CONTINUED

Ankara Revival Lite™ One-piece Toilet (K-14230-TF-96), 31″ x 21¼″ x 28⅝″.

Ankara Floor Container (K-14317-TF-96), 12″ diameter x 13″ with plastic liner.

Ankara Vintage™ Countertop Lavatory (K-14272-TF-96), 24″ x 15″. Antique™ faucet (K-280-9B) with Ankara ceramic trim (K-258-TF-96).

Carnivale Parigi™ Pedestal Lavatory (K-14219-CN-0), 19¾″ x 14″ x 32⅞″, with Trocadero™ faucet (K-15000).

Carnivale Decorative Strip Tile with diamond pattern (K-14203-CN-0) and with triangle pattern (K-14203-CV-0). Packed 6 tiles per carton — approximately 3 linear feet. Nominal dimensions 2″ x 6″.

Gravity-fed Lite™ Toilets

Expanding on Kohler's popular one-piece toilet line, the new San Raphael™ Lite and Rialto™ Lite toilets feature seamless, space-saving designs that are perfect for today's contemporary homes. A large 2″ trapway and ample 9″ x 8″ water surface help to ensure these new Lite toilets flush cleanly and completely with just 1.6 gallons of water.

Toilets

San Raphael Lite Toilet (K-3384), 28$7/8$″ x 20$3/8$″ x 22$1/4$″. Elongated bowl. Gravity-fed operating system that flushes with 1.6 gallons of water. Shown in Mexican Sand™ with polished brass trip lever (K-9430). Includes French Curve™ seat and cover. **San Tropez™ Bidet** (K-4854), 24$3/8$″ x 15$1/2$″ x 15$1/2$″. Shown in Mexican Sand. Antique™ faucet (K-142-4). Pheasant™ decorative tile.

Rialto Lite Toilet (K-3386), 25$1/4$″ x 21$1/8$″ x 22$3/4$″. Round-front bowl. Gravity-fed operating system that flushes with 1.6 gallons of water. Shown in White. Includes Lustra™ seat and cover. **Amaretto™ Bidet** (K-4864), 24$3/8$″ x 15$3/8$″ x 15$1/2$″. Shown in White. Revival™ faucet (K-16131-4A). Classic Oak decorative tile.

Undermount Installation

Kohler opens a new avenue of installation with Undermount Whirlpool Installation Kits. Available for select Kohler® Cast Iron whirlpools and baths, the kits allow sturdy, water-tight installation beneath a surrounding deck. The result is a harmonious blending of the enduring strength of cast iron with the intrinsic beauty of solid surface deck materials.

Whir

Pristine® Bath Whirlpool
(K-772-N) installed under a wood deck using undermount installation kit (K-583), 60″ x 42″ x 20³/8.″ Kohler Cast Iron. Shown in Jersey Cream.™ Finial faucet (K-T614-4W/K-301-K).

Maestro™ Bath Whirlpool (K-845-H) installed under a marble deck using undermount installation kit (K-585), 66″ x 32″ x 18¹/4.″ Kohler Cast Iron. Shown in Almond. IV Georges Brass™ faucet (K-6905-4) with riser tubes (K-126).

pool Baths

Caribbean Bath Whirlpool
(K-812-N) installed under a solid surface deck using undermount installation kit (K-581), 72″ x 36″ x 18¼.″ Kohler® Cast Iron. Shown in Skylight. Grip rails (K-9616) and Finial faucet (K-T614-4S/K-301-K).

Ellery™ System I Whirlpool

Designed to fit into a standard 5-foot bath alcove, the high-gloss acrylic Ellery Whirlpool is perfect for remodeling. Previously offered as a Kohler Whirlpool System II, it is now also available in a System I version with standard features of a 3/4 hp, one-speed pump and factory-installed, color-matched Flexjet whirlpool jets. Its front-mounted whirlpool pump is easily accessed by simply removing the factory-installed apron.

Ellery Whirlpool (K-1273), 60″ x 32″ x 20½.″ High-gloss acrylic. Shown in Innocent Blush.™ Features five Flexjet whirlpool jets. Clearflo drain (K-7161-AF) required. Flair Rite-Temp™ faucet (K-6213-4).

Undertone™

UNDERCOUNTER

Three new additions join the popular Undertone sink line. These new 18-gauge stainless steel sinks are 5¹/2″ to 9¹/2″ deep and feature Hushcoat undercoating on the entire underside of each basin to minimize noise. Fitted cutting boards, wire rinse baskets and colanders are also available to create a custom workstation.

These symbols indicate which custom accessories are available for the individual sink with which they are shown:

 Cutting Board

 Colander

 Vinyl Covered Wire Rinse Basket

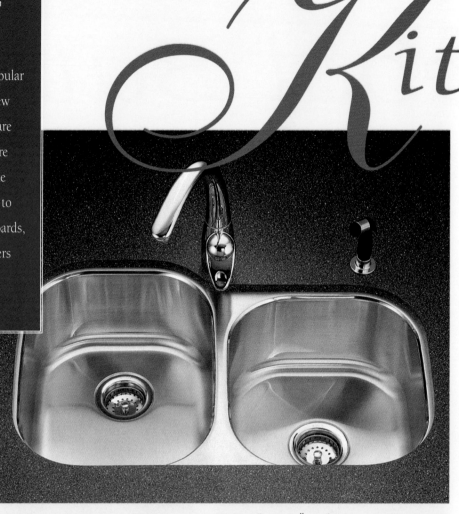

Undertone Large/Medium Kitchen Sink (K-3354), 31″ x 20¹/8″. 7¹/2″ left and right basin depths. Avatar™ faucet (K-6356).

Undertone High/Low Kitchen Sink (K-3355), 30³/4″ x 20¹/8″. 9¹/2″ left and 5¹/2″ right basin depths. Coralais™ faucet (K-15170).

Undertone Extra Large/Medium Kitchen Sink (K-3356), 35¹/8″ x 20¹/8″. 9¹/2″ left and 7¹/2″right basin depths. Avatar faucet (K-6352).

hen Sinks

Iron/Tones™

SELF-RIMMMING/ UNDERCOUNTER

Combine the benefits of Kohler® Cast Iron and the versatility of self-rimming or undercounter installation with Iron/Tones. Mix and match one, two or more of these sinks to create a custom food preparation, utility, dishwashing or multi-functional area. A fitted cutting board is also available for selected models.

Iron/Tones Sinks (K-6587) and (K-6584). Shown in Skylight. Provence™ faucet (K-14502).

Iron/Tones Sink (K-6588), 14 1/2″ diameter exterior; 11 1/2″ diameter x 5″ deep interior. Shown in Jersey Cream™.

Iron/Tones Sink (K-6585), 24 1/4″ x 18 3/4″ exterior; 21 1/4″ x 15 3/4″ x 7 1/2″ deep interior. Shown in Jersey Cream.

Iron/Tones Sink (K-6586), 12″ x 18 3/4″ exterior; 9″ x 15 3/4″ x 5 1/2″ deep interior. Shown in Jersey Cream.

Iron/Tones Sink (K-6587), 20 7/8″ x 20 7/8″ exterior; 17 7/8″ x 17 7/8″ x 9″ deep interior. Shown in Jersey Cream.

Iron/Tones Sink (K-6584), 17″ x 18 3/4″ exterior; 14″ x 15 3/4″ x 7 1/2″ deep interior. Shown in Jersey Cream.

Color Guide

Colors shown are illustrated in ink. There may be variations in color fidelity between these samples and actual plumbing fixtures.

	WHITE 0	FULL LINE														HIGH FASHION											LIMITED EDITION		
		HERON BLUE 68	SKYLIGHT 6	ICE GREY 95	TENDER GREY 56	SEAFOAM GREEN 71	WILD ROSE 45	INNOCENT BLUSH 55	DESERT BLOOM 89	MEXICAN SAND 33	CHAMOIS 98	JERSEY CREAM 12	BISCUIT 96	ALMOND 47	WHITE BRILLIANCE 7W	BLACK BRILLIANCE 7B	BLUE BRILLIANCE 7U	BLACK BLACK 7	THUNDER GREY 58	MERLOT 85	RASPBERRY PUREE 53	NAVY 52	TEAL 17	TIMBERLINE 97	LEMON TWIST 70	COBALT BLUE C9	CRACKLE 81	BUTTERED RUM 82	PEPPER 'N SALT 84
VESSELS																													
Ceramic Conical Bell K-2200	•													•															
Ceramic Hex Strata K-2203	•													•															
Ceramic Turnings K-2191	•													•															
LAVATORIES — KOHLER CAST IRON																													
Ellington K-2906-1/06-4/06-8 (K-2906-04 not available in High Fashion/Limited Ed. Colors)	•																												
Larkspur K-2908-1/08-4/08-8 (K-2908-4 not available in High Fashion/Limited Ed. Colors)	•																												
Providence K-2929-1/29-4/29-8 (K-2929-4 not available in High Fashion/Limited Ed. Colors)	•																												
Thoreau K-2907-1/07-4/07-8/Thoreau Undercounter K-2909-4/-8 (K-2907-4, 2909-4 not available in High Fashion/Limited Ed. Colors)	•																												
TOILETS																													
Rialto Lite K-3386 With K-4662 Seat	•																												
San Raphael Lite K-3384 With Seat	•													•															
WHIRLPOOLS																													
Ellery Whirlpool K-1273/74	•																												
KITCHEN SINKS — KOHLER CAST IRON																													
Iron/Tones K-6584/85/86/87/88	•																												

For a complete set of full-color Kohler product catalogs including baths, whirlpools, showers, lavatories, toilets, bidets, kitchen and entertainment sinks, and faucets, send $8 to Kohler Co., Dept. WP1, Kohler, WI 53044 or call 1-800-4-KOHLER, ext. WP1.

1 9 9 6

N ew products

THE BOLD LOOK
OF **KOHLER.**

The *Magna* Family

C575
15440/OPF
BuyLine 6965

Magna Rings

Magna Dorica

Magna Crystal

The Magna family is offered in four different finishes and four beautiful handle styles Rings, Dorica, Crystal, and Magna Plus (not shown). The Magna features solid brass construction to combine beauty with durability in creating a sheer and stunning elegance.

The *Miami* Family

Miami Tara

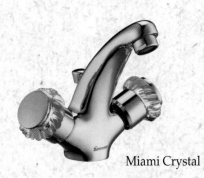

Miami Crystal

The Miami offers six beautiful finishes with four distinctly different handle designs, the Miami Rings, Miami Crystal, Miami Tara and the Miami Quadra (not shown). All the faucets are made of a solid brass construction with a 1/4-turn ceramic cartridge providing long-term operation. These cleverly designed faucets can be accented with a full line of matching designer accessories for a very distinct appearance.

Miami Ring

OPELLA, Inc. For information on our complete line, call us at (800) 969-0339 Fax (800) 867-3552

The *Golden* *Family*

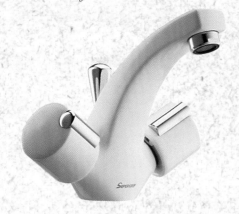

SUPERGRIF

The magnificence of the Golden family is captured in all the different models. From the daring and durable centerset through the 8" widespread lavatory faucet, bidets fittings, Roman tub filler, elegant shower systems to the beautifully coordinated line of accessories. The touch of gold makes the Golden design one of our most popular faucets. No less than 11 different, splendidly rich finishes are available, in this solidly constructed, all brass range. Don't forget your bathroom accessories, the Golden series can complete your bathroom furnishing with rob hooks to matching shelves. Why settle for less?

The *Concord* *Family*

The Concord family features a dynamic design, quality, style, and a first class valve. It is crafted in solid brass with 1/4-turn ceramic cartridges for a long and trouble-free life. The Concord family also includes a 8" widespread faucet, roman tub filler, and shower system.

The **Niagara** *Family*

C575
15440/OPF
BuyLine 6965

Niagara Roman Tub

Niagara provides the appearance of a cascading waterfall. Contemporary, sophisticated and superbly finished with all the matching Supergrif handles styles, Niagara reduces the time to fill a tub. To coordinated the bathroom, the Niagara is available with a matching widespread lavatory faucet. For easy cleaning the Niagara features a removable cylinderical screen.

12" Niagara Roman Tub

Niagara Roman Tub with Hand Shower

Widespread Lavatory Faucet

Coordinated Pressure Balance Tub/Shower

OPELLA, Inc. *For information on our complete line, call us at* (800) 969-0339 *Fax* (800) 867-3552

The Diva Family

OPELLA®

SUPERGRIF

Classic

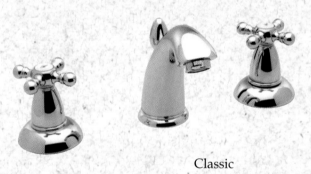
Classic

Using modern technology, the Diva series revives the old world style in todays bathrooms. This solid brass faucet line is available in eight color choices and three handle styles, Neo, Classic and Futura (lever handle - not shown). The Diva line includes the bath tub filler, shower system, bath tub filler with shower and the bidet faucet.

Neo

The Hand Shower Accessories

C575
<u>15440/OPF</u>
BuyLine 6965

Shower Systems

- State-of-the-art design
- Easy-to-install 24" rail
- Adjusts to any height instantly
- Handset easily detaches for convenience
- Flexible 59-inch spiral hose
- Contemporary soap dish in matching colors
- Available in white, almond and chrome

Also Available:
- Handsets
- Wall Bracket Adjustable or Fixed
- Stop Valve
- Flexible Spiral Hose 59" or 69"
- Chrome Tub Spout
- Diverter Unit
- Supply Elbow

The Supergrif Coordinated Accessories

The Supergrif Bathroom Accessories are available in five decorator design lines to match all the Supergrif Bathroom faucets and handle styles, as well as, many color combinations to match your bathroom decor.

The Golden Family

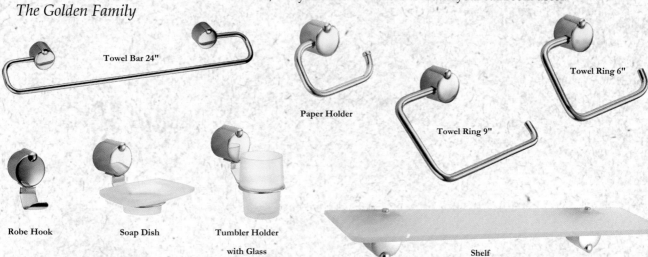

Towel Bar 24"

Paper Holder

Towel Ring 9"

Towel Ring 6"

Robe Hook

Soap Dish

Tumbler Holder
with Glass

Shelf

OPELLA, Inc. *For information on our complete line, call us at* (800) 969-0339 *Fax* (800) 867-3552

The Omega *Family*

The Oasis *Family*

The Omega, Oasis, Duna, and Hydra families are extremely practical single lever faucets that are offered in a range of different finishes. They have a high quality 1/4 turn ceramic cartridge for dependable, trouble free performance. These sleek designed faucets are stylish, extremely price competitive and make a beautiful addition to any bathroom. Each series is available with a matching single lever roman tub and shower system.

The Duna *Family*

The Hydra *Family*

Duna Roman Tub with Hand Shower

Hydra two-handle

OPELLA, Inc. For information on our complete line, call us at (800) 969-0339 Fax (800) 867-3552

Zoeller Pump Co.
"Quality Pumps Since 1939"

Qwik Jon Sewage Removal Systems

INSTALL A QWIK JON JUST ABOUT ANYWHERE.

- Designed to accommodate a toilet, lavatory and a bathtub
- Use with a variety of toilet styles (1.6 Gallon residential flush; other installations should use over 3 gallon flush)
- Perfect for basements, family rooms, warehouse, factories, room additions.
- No need to destroy concrete floors.
- Reduces construction cost.
- Pumps any direction.
- Fits just about anywhere.

MODELS:
Model 100 UL Listed 262 Pump
Model 102 UL Listed 266 Pump
Patent No. 5,038,418

TYPICAL INSTALLATIONS
Versatile installation enables the pump compartment and piping to be concealed by the installation of a wall.

NOTE: Access must be maintained to the pump compartment.

NOTE: The Qwik Jon is designed to fit flush with any elevated floor made of standard 2" x 6" material (actual dimensions 1½" x 5½"). And you can add a Lavatory - Bathtub - Shower with the installation of the 2" adapt-a-flex seal (provided). Tub or shower requires built in installation. See Installation Instructions.

BOCA ES

UPC FOUNDED 1926 IAPMO

Built In Installation
Toilet, Fixtures and Piping Not Included

Basic Installation
Toilet, Fixtures and Piping Not Included

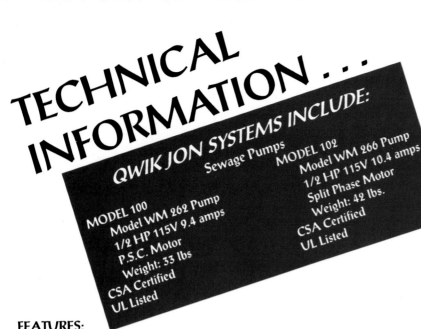

TECHNICAL INFORMATION . . .

QWIK JON SYSTEMS INCLUDE:

Sewage Pumps

MODEL 100
Model WM 262 Pump
1/2 HP 115V 9.4 amps
P.S.C. Motor
Weight: 33 lbs
CSA Certified
UL Listed

MODEL 102
Model WM 266 Pump
1/2 HP 115V 10.4 amps
Split Phase Motor
Weight: 42 lbs.
CSA Certified
UL Listed

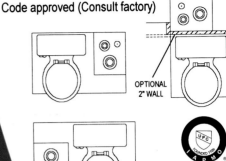

Code approved (Consult factory)

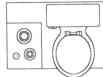

OPTIONAL 2" WALL

BOCA ES

FEATURES:
- Automatic level control switch.
- Thermal overload protected motor.
- Stainless steel screws, bolts & handle.
- Non-clogging vortex impeller.
- Passes 2" solids (sphere).
- UL listed 3-wire neoprene 10 ft. cord & plug.
- Maximum temperature rating - 130° F. (54° C).

Tank
MODEL 100/102 (Patented)
- Polyethylene
- Lt. gray finish
- Lightweight
- Wt. 26 lbs.

2" Back Flow Device and Union
- 2" back flow device (check local codes) required to prevent backflow of water and sewer gas.
- No threading of pipe required.
- Fits ABS, PVC and steel pipe.
- Rated at 25 PSI.
- Weight: 2 lbs.

ALL IN ONE CARTON
- Tank, lid & gasket.
- 1/2 HP sewage pump.
- Back flow device (check local codes).
- 2" Discharge & 3" Vent with adapt-a-flex seals.
- 2" adapt-a-flex seal for additional fixtures.
- Floor Flange Extender Kit for 1/2" & 5/8" thick floors.
- Hardware pack and floor anchor kit.
- Installation instructions.
- Shipping weight:
  100 System - 85 lbs.
  102 System - 94 lbs.

ITEMS NEEDED BY INSTALLER
- Supply fittings & waste pipe.
- Toilet fixture and/or other fixtures.
- Electrical source with ground fault interrupter protected receptacle.
- Water source.
- Waste Line per code.
- Vent Line per code.
- Tools.

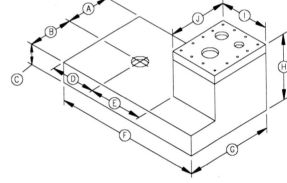

MODEL NO.	A	B	C	D	E
100/102	12¼	12¼	5½	12¼	14 ⅛
	F	G	H	I	J
100/102	41	24½	17	14	17

Model		262(100)		266(102)	
Feet	Meters	Gal.	Ltrs.	Gal.	Ltrs.
5	1.52	102	386	100	379
10	3.05	60	227	89	223
15	4.57	11.5	44	34	129
Lock Valve:		16 ft.		18.4 ft.	

NOTE:
Recommended for installations up to 16' total dynamic head. Consult factory if installation is above 15' vertical height in 2" pipe.

NOTE:
Sewage Pumps WM262 & WM266 are designed for use in Qwik Jon units only. They are not designed for use in any other application.

CAUTION
All installation of controls, protection devices and wiring should be done by a qualified licensed electrician. All electrical and safety codes should be followed including the most recent National Electric Code (NEC) and the Occupational Safety and Health Act (OSHA).

ZOELLER PUMP COMPANY
MAIL TO: P.O. BOX 16347 • Louisville, KY 40256-0347
SHIP TO: 3649 Cane Run Road • Louisville, KY 40211-1961
(502) 778-2731 • 1 (800) 928-PUMP • FAX (502) 774-3624

CONCEPT FOUR
DECORATOR FAUCETS

C578
BUYLINE 7414

GERBER

CONCEPT FOUR WIDESPREAD LAVATORY FAUCETS

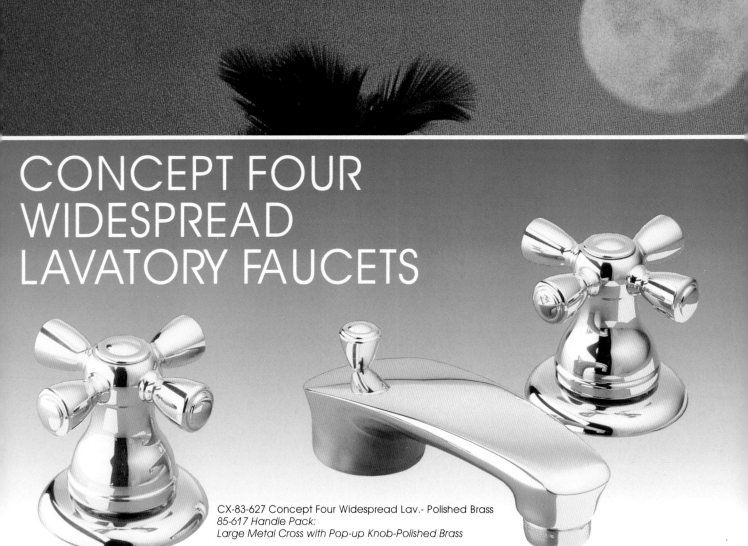

CX-83-627 Concept Four Widespread Lav.- Polished Brass
85-617 Handle Pack:
Large Metal Cross with Pop-up Knob-Polished Brass

CX-83-627 Concept Four Widespread Lav.- Polished Brass
85-037 Handle Pack:
White China Lever with Pop-up Knob-Polished Brass

CX-A3-621 Concept Four Widespread Lav.- Almond
A5-071 Handle Pack:
Almond China Lever with Pop-up Knob-Almond

CX-83-623 Concept Four Widespread Lav.- Chrome
85-683 Handle Pack:
Large White China Cross with Pop-up Knob-Chrome

CX-83-625 Concept Four Widespread Lav.- Antique Brass
85-655 Handle Pack:
Large Round Crystaline with Pop-up Knob-Antique Brass

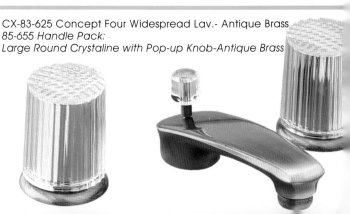

All Gerber Concept Four Lavatory faucets feature Ceramaflow™ ceramic disk cartridges with 20 year warranty for years of trouble free operation.

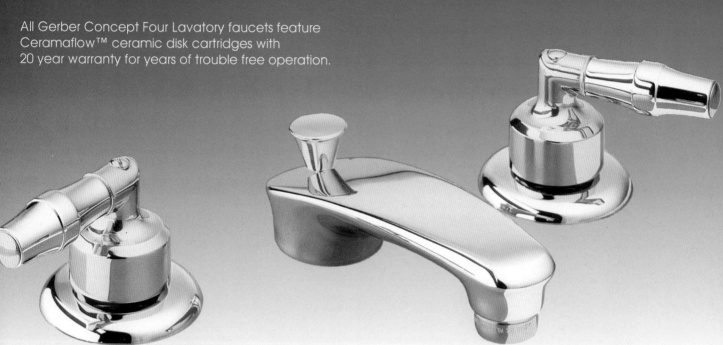

CX-83-629 Concept Four Widespread Lav.- Chrome and Polished Brass
85-009 Handle Pack:
Metal Lever with Pop-up Knob- Chrome and Polished Brass

CX-83-623 Concept Four Widespread Lav.- Chrome
85-013 Handle Pack:
Crystalite Lever with Pop-up Knob-Chrome

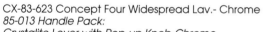

CX-83-625 Concept Four Widespread Lav.- Antique Brass
85-035 Handle Pack:
White China Lever with Pop-up Knob-Antique Brass

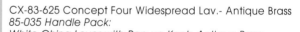
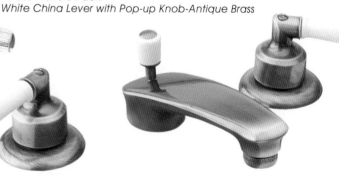

CX-83-627 Concept Four Widespread Lav.- Polished Brass
85-687 Handle Pack:
Large White China Cross with Pop-up Knob-
Polished Brass

CX-W3-621 Concept Four Widespread Lav.- White
W5-611 Handle Pack:
Large Metal Cross with Pop-up Knob-White

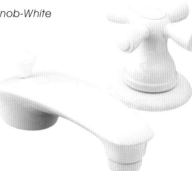

CONCEPT FOUR FAST FILL ROMAN TUB FILLERS

At 60 PSI Gerber Fast Fill Valves deliver over 22 gallons per minute – one of the fastest flow rates available.

X-88-803 Concept Four Final Fit 11" Roman Tub Filler-Chrome
85-719 Handle Pack:
Large Metal Cross-Chrome and Polished Brass

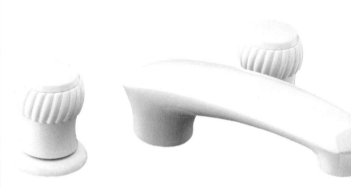

X-W8-801 Concept Four Final Fit 11" Roman Tub Filler-White
W5-741 Handle Pack:
Ultamira Rope Ring-White

X-88-807 Concept Four Final Fit 11" Roman Tub Filler-Polished Brass
85-737 Handle Pack:
Ultamira Facet Ring-Polished Brass

X-88-805 Concept Four Final Fit 11" Roman Tub Filler-Antique Brass
85-757 Handle Pack:
Large Round Crystaline-Polished Brass

X-A8-801 Concept Four Final Fit 11" Roman Tub Filler-Almond
A5-771 Handle Pack:
Large Almond China Cross- Almond

X-88-803 Concept Four Final Fit 11" Roman Tub Filler-Chrome
85-723 Handle Pack:
Ultamira Triple Ring-Chrome

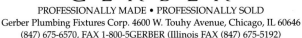

GERBER
PROFESSIONALLY MADE • PROFESSIONALLY SOLD
Gerber Plumbing Fixtures Corp. 4600 W. Touhy Avenue, Chicago, IL 60646
(847) 675-6570, FAX 1-800-5GERBER (Illinois FAX (847) 675-5192)

© 1996 G.P.F. Printed in U.S.A.

MADE IN USA

THE GERBER COLLECTION

The Sea Spouts
DECORATOR FAUCETS

C579
BUYLINE 7426

GERBER

BEAUTY BORN

SEA SPOUT WIDESPREAD LAVATORY FAUCETS

All Gerber Sea Spout lavatory faucets feature Ceramaflow™ ceramic disk cartridges with 20 year warranty for years of trouble free operation.

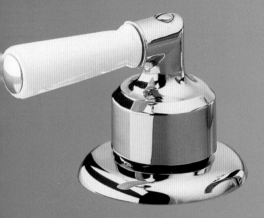

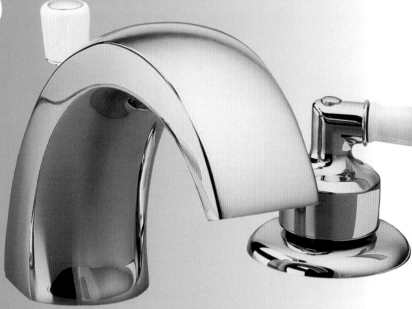

CX-83-743 Sea Spout Widespread Lav.- Chrome
85-033 Handle Pack:
White China Lever with Pop-up Knob-Chrome

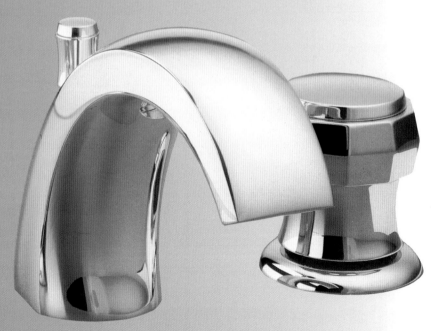

CX-83-747 Sea Spout Widespread Lav.- Polished Brass
85-637 Handle Pack:
Ultamira Facet Ring with Pop-up Knob Polished Brass

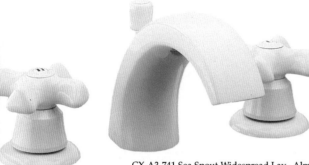

CX-A3-741 Sea Spout Widespread Lav.- Almond
A5-671 Handle Pack:
Large Almond China Cross with Pop-up Knob-Almond

CX-83-747 Sea Spout Widespread Lav.- Polished Brass
85-017 Handle Pack:
Crystalite Lever with Pop-up Knob-Polished Brass

CX-83-743 Sea Spout Widespread Lav.- Chrome
85-653 Handle Pack:
Large Round Crystaline with Pop-up Knob-Chrome

CX-83-745 Sea Spout Widespread Lav.- Antique Brass
85-075 Handle Pack:
Almond China Lever with Pop-up Knob-Antique Brass

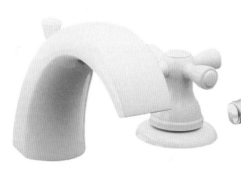

CX-W3-741 Sea Spout Widespread Lav.- White
W5-611 Handle Pack:
Large Metal Cross with Pop-up Knob-White

CX-83-749 Sea Spout Widespread Lav.- Chrome and Polished Brass
85-009 Handle Pack:
Metal Lever with Pop-up Knob-Chrome and Polished Brass

CX-83-745 Sea Spout Widespread Lav.- Antique Brass
85-685 Handle Pack:
Large White China Cross with Pop-up Knob-Antique Brass

CX-83-747 Sea Spout Widespread Lav.- Polished Brass
85-037 Handle Pack:
White China Lever with Pop-up Knob-Polished Brass

SEA SPOUT FAST FILL ROMAN TUB FILLERS

At 60 PSI Gerber Fast Fill Valves deliver over 22 gallons per minute – one of the fastest flow rates available.

X-88-547 Sea Spout Final Fit 10" Roman Tub Filler-Polished Brass
85-757 Handle Pack:
Large Round Crystaline-Polished Brass

X-88-543 Sea Spout Final Fit 10" Roman Tub Filler-Chrome
85-713 Handle Pack:
Large Metal Cross-Chrome

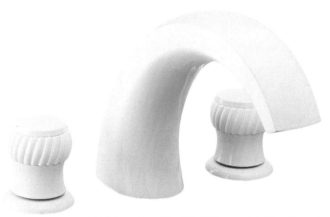

X-A8-541 Sea Spout Final Fit 10" Roman Tub Filler-Almond
A5-741 Handle Pack:
Ultamira Rope Ring-Almond

X-88-545 Sea Spout Final Fit 10" Roman Tub Filler-Antique Brass
85-785 Handle Pack:
Large White China Cross-Antique Brass

X-88-543 Sea Spout Final Fit 10" Roman Tub Filler-Chrome
85-739 Handle Pack:
Ultamira Facet Ring- Chrome and Polished Brass

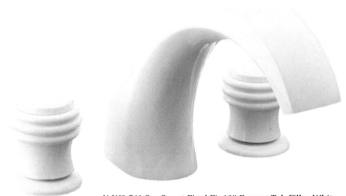

X-W8-541 Sea Spout Final Fit 10" Roman Tub Filler-White
W5-721 Handle Pack:
Ultamira Triple Ring-White

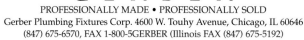

GERBER
PROFESSIONALLY MADE • PROFESSIONALLY SOLD
Gerber Plumbing Fixtures Corp. 4600 W. Touhy Avenue, Chicago, IL 60646
(847) 675-6570, FAX 1-800-5GERBER (Illinois FAX (847) 675-5192)

MADE IN USA.

Bristol & Chadwick

CLASSIC FAUCETS

C580
BUYLINE 7440

GERBER

Bristol
Widespread, Kitchen and Centerset Faucets

CX-83-277 Bristol Widespread Lav.
Polished Brass
*85-157 Handle Pack: Large Belmont Levers
with Pop-up Knob-Polished Brass*

CX-A3-271 Bristol Widespread
Lav. - Almond
*A5-611 Handle Pack: Large
Metal Cross with Pop-up
Knob-Almond*

XX-43-273 Bristol Widespread
Lav. - Chrome
*85-153 Handle Pack:
Large Belmont Levers with
Pop-up Knob-Chrome*

CX-82-189 Bristol Deck Mount
Kitchen - Chrome and
Polished Brass
*85-179 Handle Pack: Small
Belmont Levers*

CX-A2-381 Bristol Under-Counter
Mount Kitchen - Almond
*A5-261 Handle Pack: Small
Almond China Cross*

XX-43-173 Bristol
Centerset Lav. - Chrome
*85-163 Handle Pack:
Small Belmont
Levers with
Pop-up Knob-
Chrome*

CX-A3-171 Bristol
Centerset Lav. - Almond
*A5-161 Handle Pack:
Small Belmont Levers
with Pop-up Knob-
Almond*

CX-W3-171 Bristol
Centerset Lav. - White
*W5-081 Handle Pack:
Small Metal Cross
with Pop-up Knob-
White*

Chadwick
Widespread
Lavatory Faucets

CX-83-807 Chadwick Widespread Lav.
Polished Brass
*85-617 Handle Pack: Large Metal Cross
with Pop-up Knob-Polished Brass*

CX-W3-801 Chadwick Widespread Lav.
White
*W5-611 Handle Pack: Large Metal Cross
with Pop-up Knob-White*

CX-83-803 Chadwick Widespread Lav.
Chrome
*85-153 Handle Pack: Large Belmont Levers
with Pop-up Knob-Chrome*

Roman Tub Fillers

At 60 PSI Gerber Fast Fill Valves release over 22 gallons per minute – one of the fastest flow rates available.

Bristol
TUB FILLERS

X-W8-441 Bristol Fast Fill Roman Tub Filler- White
W5-251 Handle Pack: Large Belmont Levers

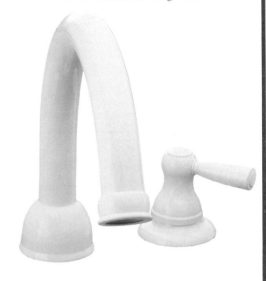

X-88-447 Bristol Fast Fill Roman Tub Filler- Polished Brass
85-777 Handle Pack: Large Almond China Cross

Chadwick
TUB FILLERS

X-88-619 Chadwick Fast Fill Roman Tub Filler
Chrome and Polished Brass
85-719 Handle Pack: Large Metal Cross

X-88-613 Chadwick Fast Fill Roman
Tub Filler Chrome
85-253 Handle Pack: Large Belmont Levers

GERBER
PROFESSIONALLY MADE • PROFESSIONALLY SOLD
Gerber Plumbing Fixtures Corp. 4600 W. Touhy Avenue, Chicago, IL 60646
(847) 675-6570, FAX 1-800-5GERBER (Illinois FAX (847) 675-5192)

MADE IN
USA.

© 1996 G.P.F. Printed in U.S.A.

C581
15445/KOH
BuyLine 7301

1 9 9 6

*N*ew products

KOHLER
FAUCETS

Finial Art

Finial Art offers faucet designs that fly in the face of presumption with playful handle shapes, gold coined and rich colored accents, and a new Teflon* finish. All designed to enable the bath or powder room to be transformed into a gallery of personal expression.

Finial deck-mount bath faucet with wrought swirl handles (K-T614-4W/K-301-K) in Teflon* black.

Finial deck-mount bath faucet with scroll handles (K-T614-4S/K-301-K) in polished chrome with blueberry accents.

* Teflon is a registered trademark of E.I. du Pont de Nemours and Company.

cets

Finial widespread lavatory faucet with scroll handles (K-610-4S) in satin chrome with gold coined accents.

Finial widespread lavatory faucet with Kudu handles (K-610-4T) in polished nickel with gold coined accents.

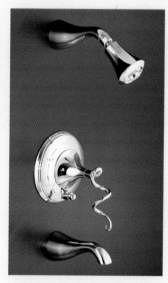

Finial widespread lavatory faucet with wrought swirl handles (K-610-4W) in Teflon* black with gold coined accents.

Finial bidet faucet with vertical spray, fixture-mount vacuum breaker/transfer valve and scroll handles (K-616-4S) in polished nickel with raspberry accents.

Finial Rite-Temp™ bath and shower faucet with Kudu handle (K-612-4T) in polished chrome.

Wrought Swirl

Kudu

Teflon Black

Teflon Black/Gold Coin

Pol. Chrome/ Teflon Black

Pol. Nickel/Gold Coin

Pol. Chrome

Scroll

Pol. Chrome/ Raspberry

Pol. Nickel/Raspberry

Pol. Chrome/Blueberry

Pol. Nickel/Blueberry

Pol. Chrome/Mocha

Pol. Nickel/Mocha

Satin Chrome/Gold Coin

Finial
Fundamentals

Finial Fundamentals represent art at its simplest, a showcase of sleek, sculptured pieces that emphasize flawless artistry. Three handle styles and a selection of unique finish combinations blend to create functional art for a room that's as individual as its owner.

Finial widespread lavatory faucet with tee handles (K-310-6) in polished chrome.

Finial widespread lavatory faucet with lever handles (K-310-4) in polished chrome with polished brass accents.

cets

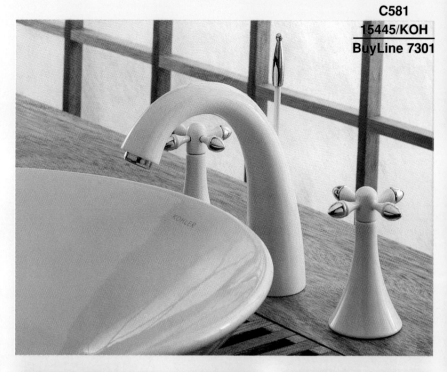

Finial widespread lavatory faucet with cross handles (K-310-3) in White with polished brass accents.

Finial bidet faucet with vertical spray, fixture-mount vacuum breaker/transfer valve and lever handles (K-316-4) in polished chrome with polished brass accents.

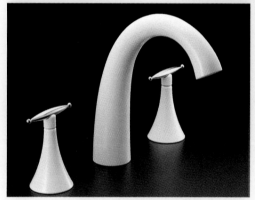

Finial deck-mount bath faucet with tee handles (K-T314-6/K-301-K) in White with polished chrome accents.

Finial Rite-Temp™ pressure-balancing bath and shower faucet with cross handle (K-312-3) in polished chrome with polished brass accents.

Tee (-6)

Pol. Chrome/ Pol. Brass	White/Pol. Brass	Pol. Chrome	Satin Chrome/ Pol. Chrome	White/ Pol. Chrome	Teflon* Black/ Pol. Brass

Finial deck-mount bath faucet with lever handles (K-T314-4/K-301-K) in White with polished brass accents.

Lever (-4)　　　　　　　　　　　　**Cross (-3)**

Pol. Chrome/ Pol. Brass	White/Pol. Brass	Pol. Chrome	Pol. Chrome/Pol. Brass	White/Pol. Brass

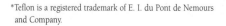

Falling Water

Falling Water faucets are striking in their simplicity; smooth and serene with total functionality. Offered exclusively in polished chrome, Falling Water is available with a choice of 6", 9" or 12" spout lengths and features convenient single-control operation. Washerless ceramic valving and solid brass construction ensure years of reliable performance.

Falling Water
wall-mount faucet with 12" spout (K-199). Also available with 9" spout (K-197) or with 6" spout (K-195).*

* Spout lengths are measured from wall to center of outlet.

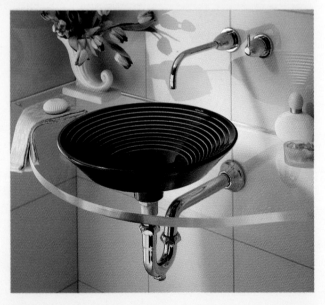

cets

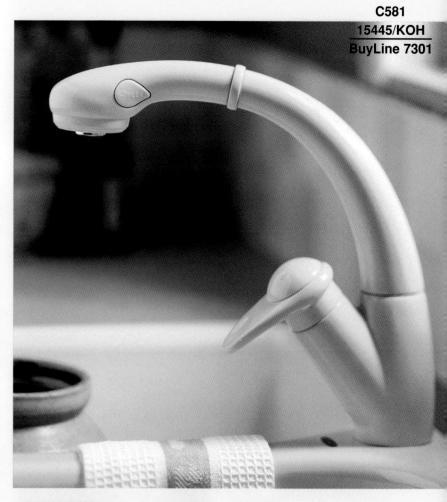

Avatar™

Avatar brings break-through design to pull-out spray faucets. Modeled around the natural motion of the hand and wrist, the Avatar pull-out spray fits comfortably in the palm of your hand. To use, simply place your hand around the sprayhead and pull. There's no need to twist the wrist. A selection of four models and five finishes ensure aesthetic satisfaction as well.

Avatar kitchen sink faucet with pull-out spray and front lever handle (K-6350) in Almond.

Avatar kitchen sink faucet with cast spout and front lever handle (K-6356) in polished chrome.

Avatar kitchen sink faucet with pull-out spray and right side lever handle (K-6352) in White.

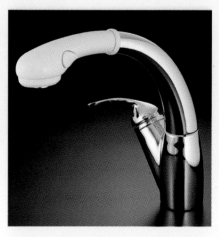

Avatar kitchen sink faucet with pull-out spray and left side lever handle (K-6353-MP) in polished chrome with Almond sprayhead.

For a complete set of full-color Kohler product catalogs including baths, whirlpools, showers, lavatories, toilets, bidets, kitchen and entertainment sinks, and faucets, send $8 to Kohler Co., Dept. WP1, Kohler, WI 53044 or call 1-800-4-KOHLER, ext. WP1.

THE BOLD LOOK
OF KOHLER.

C584
15445/STR
BuyLine 8653

Strom Plumbing

■ ■ ■ ■ ■

P0150

P0146

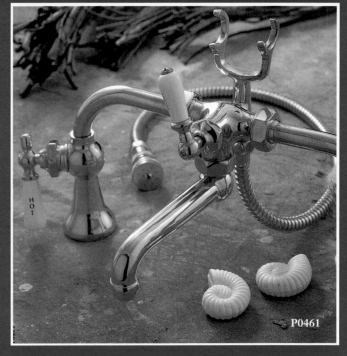

P0461

BY

Sign of 🦀 the Crab

Sign of the Crab, Ltd.
3756 Omec Circle, Dept. 214
Rancho Cordova, CA 95742

Telephone (916) 638-2722
FAX (916) 638-2725

SIGN OF THE CRAB specializes in solid brass plumbing and decorative accessories. Through years of product development, our products include authentic reproduction items and new, designer-oriented products. Also available is the service that is necessary to see your project through to completion. We have custom made many items to include stainless steel and brass products for the Sheraton Palace Hotel in San Francisco and the Beverly Wilshire Hotel in Beverly Hills.

Enclosed is a sampling of some of our items. Please write to us or call us for our complete catalog available at no charge to the trade. We welcome you to the world of STROM PLUMBING.

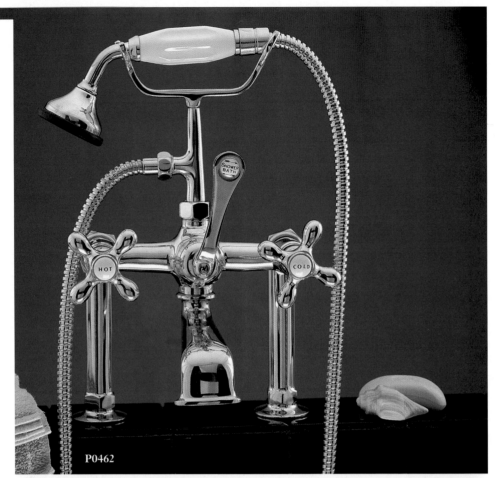

P0462

P0460

P0467

This photograph indicates how towel bars and other bath accessories can be modified with different escutcheons to create a bath "suite", thereby coordinating an entire room with matching faucets and accessories.

P0034 – Leg Tub Shower Enclosure Set.

Includes: P0006, P0008, P0009, P0010.

P0006 – Leg Tub Faucet with Diverter. Porcelain handles marked "Hot", "Cold" and "Shower", 33/8" centers.

P0008 – Shower Enclosure with Adjustable Ceiling 36" and Wall 12" Braces. 5/8" (1/4" IPS) heavy gauge polished brass tubing, 45" long, 25" wide.

P0009 – Shower Riser (2 piece). 3/8" brass pipe size, 5' total height, 1/2" iron pipe size shower head fitting extends 9" from vertical.

P0010 – Shower Head. Polished brass, 47/8" diameter, 1/2" IPS connection.

All items may be purchased separately.

P0034P – Leg Tub Enclosure Set. *Same as P0034, but with P0051 porcelain shower head instead of P0010.*

For gooseneck spout order P0400 faucet or P0403 enclosure set

P0008-1

P0087

P0051

GB0215

P0147

P0008-1 – C Clamp only.

Extra braces include c-clamp, brace & escutcheon:

P0008 – 12
P0008 – 24
P0008 – 36
P0008 – 48

P0034 – Shower Enclosure
P0034P – Shower Enclosure with P0051 Porcelain Shower Head

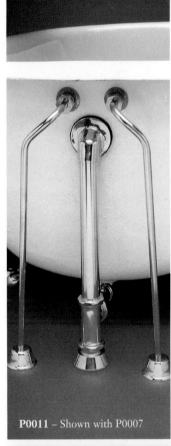

P0011 – Shown with P0007

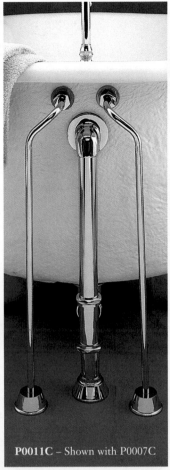

P0011C – Shown with P0007C

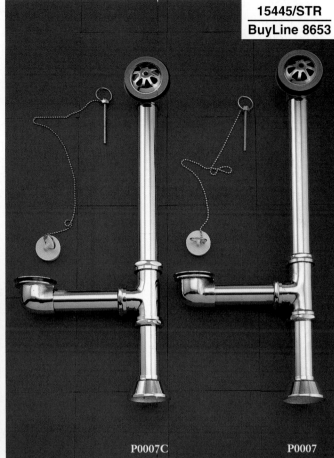

P0007C   **P0007**

P0149-1 and P0398

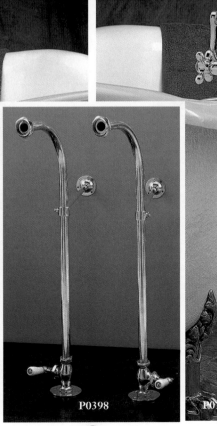

P0398

P0146 and P0398

P0140

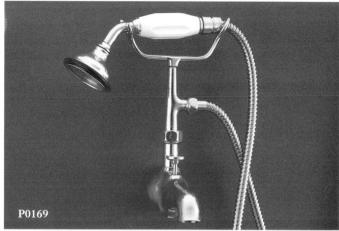

P0169

P0402

P0400C

P0499C

P0460

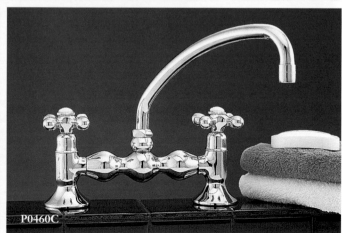

P0460C

P0353C

P0354C

P0355C

P0356C

P0357C

P0353C on P0081 Pedestal Lav

P0359C – Roman Tub Set
P0362C – Roman Spout Only

P0360C – Tub & Shower Set
P0408C – Tub Only Set
P0409C – Shower Only Set

P0188

P0188C

P0188X

P0188XC

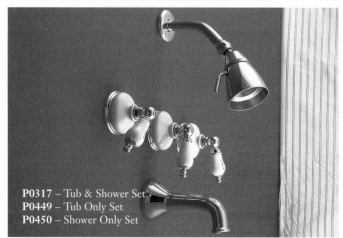

P0317 – Tub & Shower Set
P0449 – Tub Only Set
P0450 – Shower Only Set

P0317C – Tub & Shower Set
P0449C – Tub Only Set
P0450C – Shower Only Set

P0444

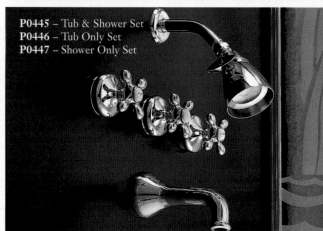

P0445 – Tub & Shower Set
P0446 – Tub Only Set
P0447 – Shower Only Set

AQUASTYL
SANITAIRE
M-K-F METKLEN FRANCE

C584A
BuyLine 9660

Europe's Finest Selection of Elegant Bath Accessories

The Emeraude Collection —
its beautiful Neo-Classical Design, will add charm and elegance to any bath decor. This collection is quality constructed of Zamak with 24 karat gold overlay.

The Concorde Collection —
adds a distinctive Ultra Contemporary Style to all modern bath decors. This collection is made of Zamak with choice of chrome or white epoxy overlay.

MENAGER INTERNATIONAL

Europe's Finest Selection c

AQ

M-K-F-M

The Soleil Collection — available in a variety of finishes, the impressive 17th Century French Design will enhance all bath decors.

The Marguerite Collection — with a French Country Floral Design, will add warmth and charm to any bath.

The Megeve Collection — is the ultimate in Transitional Style. The attractive polished brass with white porcelain inset will blend with any decor.

MENAGER IN

f Elegant Bath Accessories

JASTYL

The Dauphin Collection —
its European styling and symbol of
"Prosperity", will add elegance and
sophistication to any bath decor.

The Porcelain Concorde Collection —
adds beauty and grace to any bath decor,
with its hand-painted floral porcelain inset from 'Limoges'.

The Aleria Collection —
the ultimate in beauty and elegance. Superb styling and quality
craftsmanship with a 24 karat gold overlay have been
combined to create this exciting new look.

ERNATIONAL

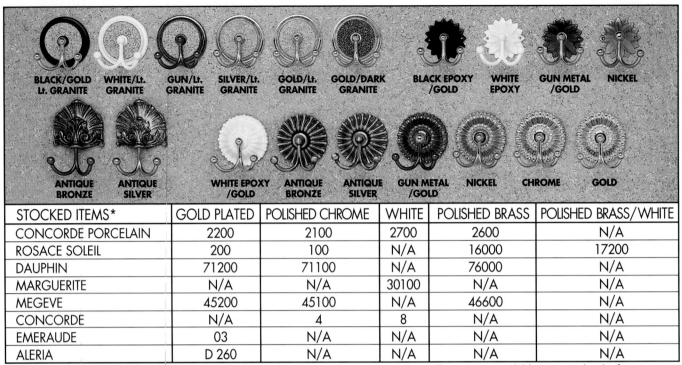

STOCKED ITEMS*	GOLD PLATED	POLISHED CHROME	WHITE	POLISHED BRASS	POLISHED BRASS/WHITE
CONCORDE PORCELAIN	2200	2100	2700	2600	N/A
ROSACE SOLEIL	200	100	N/A	16000	17200
DAUPHIN	71200	71100	N/A	76000	N/A
MARGUERITE	N/A	N/A	30100	N/A	N/A
MEGEVE	45200	45100	N/A	46600	N/A
CONCORDE	N/A	4	8	N/A	N/A
EMERAUDE	03	N/A	N/A	N/A	N/A
ALERIA	D 260	N/A	N/A	N/A	N/A

*All above items are stocked and available for direct shipment from North Carolina. Other collections are available on special order from France. All collections are cast of solid Zamak, a strong alloy, with quality chrome, brass, and/or 24 karat gold plating, and/or baked-on epoxy finishes.

M.K.F., France is France's leading manufacturer of bath accessories made of Zamak. Incorporating more than 25 years of experience in this industry, and recognized worldwide for superb quality, and craftsmanship, M.K.F. manufactures products for such famous brand names as Cartier, Christophle, Yves Saint Laurent, and Boucheron.

MENAGER INTERNATIONAL • Post Office Box 6097 • Raleigh, North Carolina 27628 • USA • Fax: 919 / 821-8091 • Phone: 919 / 832-3554

Printed in the U.S.A.

BALDWIN®
CABINET HARDWARE

NEW LINES

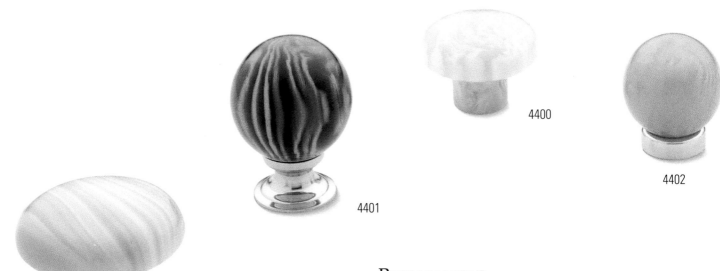

4400

4401

4402

4403

RESIN MARBLE
Bring the stately look of marble to your kitchen and bath projects with this new series of cabinet knobs from Baldwin. Available in four colors: Ivory, Malachite, Greystone, and Rose.

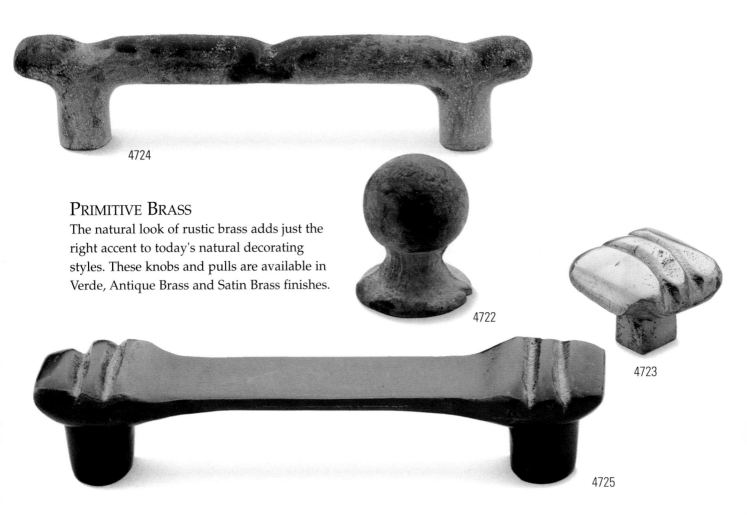

4724

PRIMITIVE BRASS
The natural look of rustic brass adds just the right accent to today's natural decorating styles. These knobs and pulls are available in Verde, Antique Brass and Satin Brass finishes.

4722

4723

4725

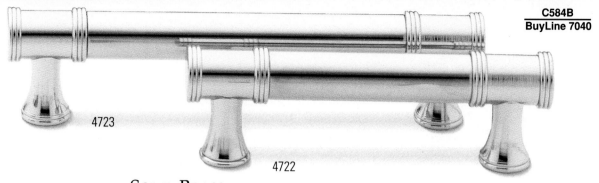

4723

4722

SOLID BRASS

The sleek look of polished brass along with chrome or brushed stainless steel adds new dimension and depth to your furniture and cabinets. Knobs are available in polished brass or polished brass/polished chrome. Pulls are available in polished brass/brushed stainless steel.

4721

4721

4720

4720

4454

SOLID BRASS

If your decorating scheme calls for color you'll want to choose these solid brass knobs and pulls available in striking shades of rose, white and black.

4450

4451

4452

4418
4417
4416

ACRYLIC ACCENTS

The beauty of crystal is captured in these sophisticated acrylic knobs and pulls. Every style in this group is offered in clear acrylic. To further complement the decor of your room, styles 4413, 4414 and 4415 are also available in pink, blue and smoke.

4412
4411
4410

4415   4414
4413   4413

4419

4420

BALDWIN QUALITY

For 50 years, Baldwin has been recognized as a leading manufacturer of superior architectural hardware. Solid brass, exceptional design, time-honored craftsmanship and refined elegance are the standards of excellence that go into every product Baldwin offers.

For more information call 1-800-566-1986 or visit your local dealer.
© 1995 BALDWIN Hardware Corp. P.O. Box 15048, Reading, PA 19612

The Estate Collection™
by Baldwin®

CRYSTAL CABINET HARDWARE

BALDWIN®

The choice is . . .

SWAROVSKI

 Regarded as fine collectible art, Swarovski crystal from Austria has attracted innumerable admirers because of its extraordinary beauty and brilliance. World-renowned for its elegance, superior quality and craftsmanship, Swarovski crystal is now available as part of The Estate Collection™ by Baldwin®. This exceptional crystal line complements our Estate Collection of solid brass hardware, providing the ultimate selection of decorative accessories for the home. Baldwin's Swarovski crystal cabinet knobs are also available in gold plate. A Swarovski crystal latchset coordinates with this offering to provide continuity of design (see back page).

crystal clear.

Crystal cabinet hardware in The Estate Collection by Baldwin also includes fine crafted knobs and pulls in many faceted designs and colors. Designs in this offering are ideal for restoration projects.

FACING PAGE: SWAROVSKI *crystal, top row from left to right* 4336.S, 4341.S, 4337.S; *Next to copy* 4338.S; *Enlargement* 4336.S.

THIS PAGE: *Crystal knobs, top row left to right* 4302, 4311, 4322, 4319; *Second row left to right* 4314, 4305, 4316, 4328, 4325; *Third row* 4330; *Pulls top to bottom* 4344, 4347, 4350; *Coat hook* 0790.

Art and function.

Our new latchsets combine the best of Baldwin with beautiful high quality crystal, enabling you to bring the elegance of crystal throughout your home. These latchsets from The Estate Collection are available in passage, privacy and dummy functions.

THIS PAGE: *Crystal Melon knobset 5007; Crystal Ball knobset 5001; SWAROVSKI Faceted Crystal knobset 5009; Brass Crown knobset 5008; Crystal leverset 5160.*

BALDWIN QUALITY

For nearly 50 years, Baldwin has been recognized as a leading manufacturer of superior architectural hardware. The Baldwin name is synonymous with quality. Solid brass, exceptional design, time-honored craftsmanship and refined elegance are the standards of excellence that go into every product Baldwin offers.

For more information call 1-800-566-1986 or visit your local dealer.

BALDWIN

BRASS®

C584B
BuyLine 7040

EPIC™ BATH ACCESSORIES

BALDWIN BRASS

EPIC™ BATH ACCESSORIES

First Impressions Last a Lifetime . . .

For over forty years, Baldwin has been building a worldwide position of leadership in solid brass products for the home: architectural hardware, lighting and home furnishing accessories that are unmatched for design integrity and brilliance of finish. This same excellence of design and uncompromising Baldwin quality can be used in the bath...from the most classic to the most contemporary.

Baldwin Bath Accessories are produced in the USA from solid brass through a forging process to yield a denser, stronger, heavier product. The smooth, blemish-free surface of each piece is meticulously polished to a brilliant luster and carefully protected by a clear baked-on coating for durability and ease of maintenance. All designs feature concealed mounting to eliminate visible fasteners and provide a tamper-proof installation.

Every imaginable detail including distinctively designed packaging has been considered to offer the highest standard of service. Each box includes all required fasteners for any condition, installation tools and simple step by step instructions.

Elegant Designs. Uncompromising Quality. Reliable Performance. Baldwin Bath Accessories...a tradition for the most exciting baths in residential and commercial installations.

LEXINGTON®

WARM. INVITING. THE OPEN, GENEROUS STYLING OF LEXINGTON
ACCESSORIES CREATES A CHARM THAT IS NOTABLY AMERICAN.

3054-030 Towel Ring, 3051-030 Towel Bar, 3055-030 Robe Hook

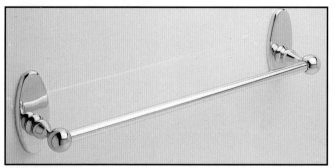

3051-030 Towel Bar

3053-030 Tissue Roll Holder

3054-030 Towel Ring

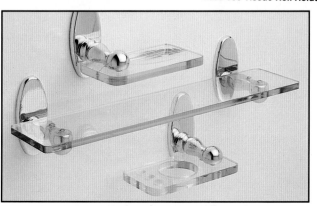

3056-030 Soap Dish, 3058-030 Glass Shelf, 3057-030 Thbrsh/ Tmblr Holder

3055-030, -260, Robe Hooks

LOS ANGELES®

DISTINCTIVE. MASCULINE. A MASTERFUL COMBINATION OF POLISHED AND SATIN METAL MAKES A COMMANDING STATEMENT IN THE LOS ANGELES BATH.

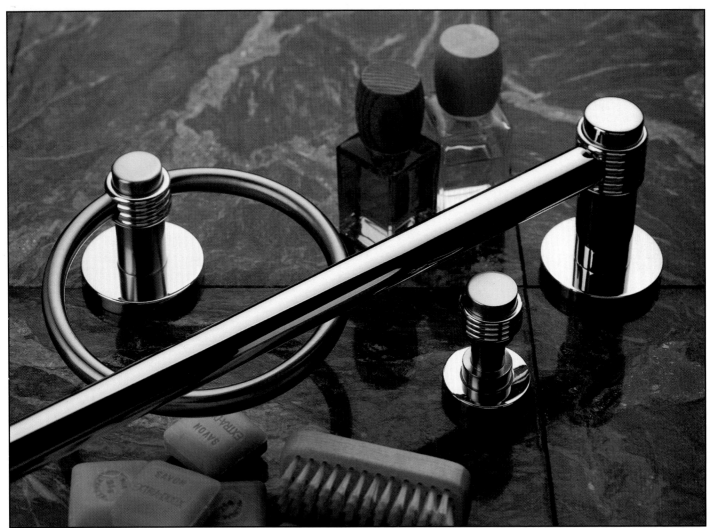

3284-153 Towel Ring, 3281-263 Towel Bar, 3285-153 Robe Hook

3281-263 Towel Bar

3284-153 Towel Ring

3285-263, 3285-153, 3285-030, 3285-260 Robe Hooks

3283-263, 3283-153 Tissue Roll Holders

GEORGETOWN®

GRACE. CHARM. UNDERSTATED ELEGANCE REFLECTED IN THE
TRADITIONAL STYLE OF GEORGETOWN BATH APPOINTMENTS.

3011-030 Towel Bar, 3014-030 Towel Ring

3011-030 Towel Bars

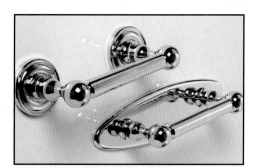

3013-030, 3013-030-BP Tissue Roll Holders

3015-030 Robe Hook

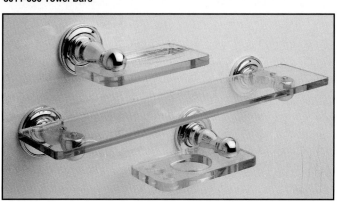

3016-030 Soap Dish, 3018-030 Glass Shelf, 3017-030 Thbrsh/Tmblr Holder

3012-030-H Tissue Roll Holder/Hood

DALLAS®

3221-030-A, 3221-030 Towel Bars

3221-030 Towel Bar

3224-030 Towel Ring

3224-030-A Towel Ring

3223-030, 3223-030-BP Tissue Roll Holders

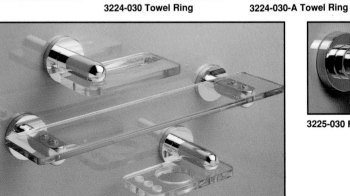

3226-030 Soap Dish, 3228-030 Glass Shelf, 3227-030 Thbrsh/Tmblr Holder

3225-030 Robe Hook

VICTORIA/WILSHIRE®

C584B
BuyLine 7040

GRACIOUS. DIGNIFIED. VICTORIA WHITE LIMOGES PORCELAIN. WILSHIRE
REFLECTS ITS OWN REFINED ELEGANCE IN BOLD CONTRASTS OF POLISHED METALS.

3121-263 Towel Bar, 3121-030 Towel Bar, 3104-030 Towel Ring

3121-263, 3101-030, 3121-030 Towel Bars

3123-263, 3103-030, 3123-260 Tissue Roll Holders

3125-263, 3105-260,
3105-030 Robe Hooks

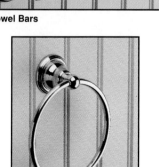

3104-030 Towel Ring

3124-263 Towel Ring

3107-030 Toothbrush/Tumbler Holder, 3106-030 Soap Dish

CHESAPEAKE™

EASY GOING LUXURY HALOS THE SPARKLING AND REFRESHING CHESAPEAKE FOR THE TRADITIONALLY-STYLED BATH.

3065-030 Robe Hook, 3061-030 Towel Bar, 3064-030 Towel Ring

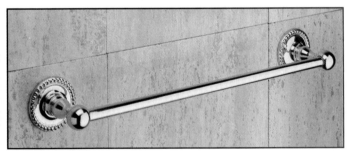

3061-030 Towel Bar

3064-030 Towel Ring

3063-030 Tissue Roll Holder

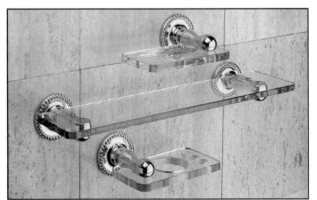

3066-030 Soap Dish, 3068-030 Glass Shelf, 3067-030 Thbrsh/Tmblr Holder

ATLANTA®

ANTEBELLUM HERITAGE. IN HOME AND BATH THERE ARE CONTRASTS AS WELL, FURTHER ACCENTED BY THE BRILLIANT ATLANTA CONTEMPORARY DESIGN.

C584B
BuyLine 7040

3245-326 Robe Hook, 3244-326 Towel Ring

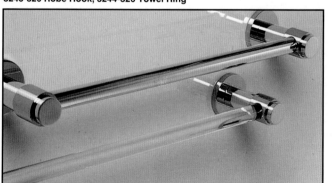

3241-326, 3241-326-A Towel Bars

3244-326-A Towel Ring

3245-326 Robe Hook

3243-326 Tissue Roll Holder

3243-326-BP Tissue Roll Holder

CAMBRIDGE™

WORLDLY. A HINT OF NAUTICAL. A BATH TASTEFULLY APPOINTED WITH CAMBRIDGE ACCESSORIES CREATES AN IMPRESSION OF UNPRETENTIOUS LUXURY.

3043-030 Tissue Roll Holder, 3041-030 Towel Bar

3041-030 Towel Bars

3044-030 Towel Ring

3045-030 Robe Hook

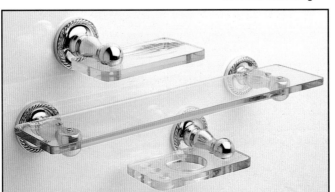

3046-030 Soap Dish, 3048-030 Glass Shelf, 3047-030 Thbrsh/Tmblr Holder

NEW YORK®

METROPOLITAN. URBANE. THE SLEEK LINES OF NEW YORK BATH
ACCESSORIES SIGNIFY TASTE FOR CONTEMPORARY LIVING.

3261-030, 3261-260 Towel Bars

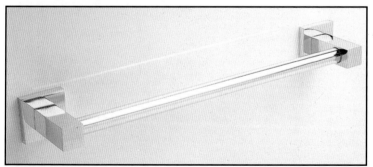

3261-030 Towel Bar

3264-030 Towel Ring

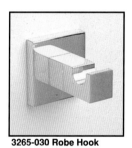

3265-030 Robe Hook

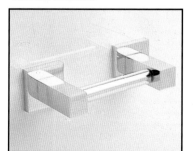

3263-030 Tissue Roll Holder

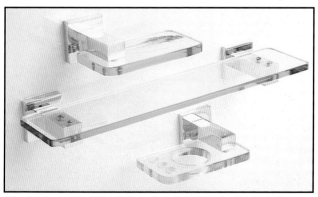

3266-030 Soap Dish, 3268-030 Glass Shelf, 3267-030 Thbrsh/Tmblr Holder

NEW ORLEANS.

UNHURRIED LIFESTYLES. IN COOL, HALF-SHUTTERED BATHS, THE AIR IS PERFUMED AND EXOTIC FLOWERS SET THE TONE FOR THE GENTLY SCULPTED New Orleans DESIGN.

3023-030 Tissue Roll Holder

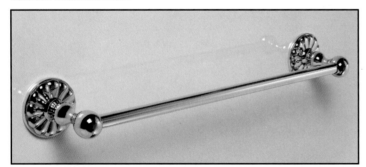

3021-030 Towel Bar

3024-030 Towel Ring

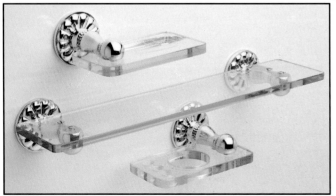

3026-030 Soap Dish, 3028-030 Glass Shelf, 3027-030 Thbrsh/Tmblr Holder

3025-030 Robe Hook

LAFAYETTE™

SLEEK YET DISTINCTIVE. LAFAYETTE'S SHIMMERING ELEGANCE REFLECTS
EVERY DETAIL OF A TRADITIONAL BATH AS WELL AS THE CONTEMPORARY SPA.

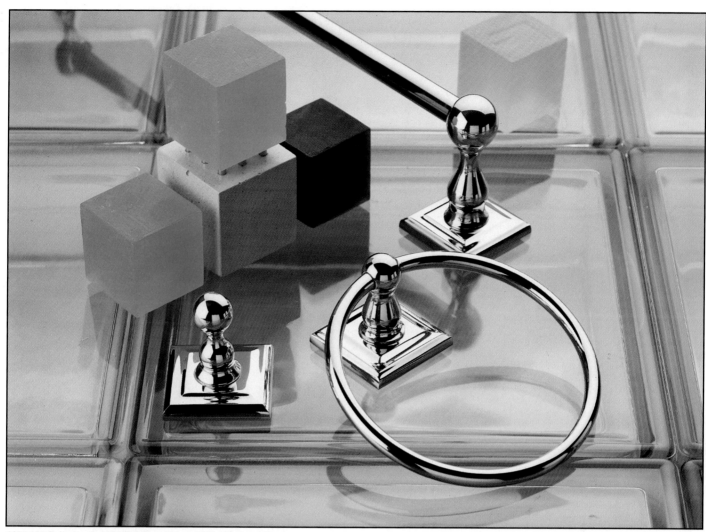

3075-326 Robe Hook, 3074-326 Towel Ring, 3071-326 Towel Bar

3071-030, 3071-326, 3071-260 Towel Bars

3074-326 Towel Ring

3075-030, -326, -260 Robe Hooks

3076-326 Soap Dish, 3077-326 Thbrsh/Tmblr Holder, 3078-326 Glass Shelf

3072-326-H Tissue Roll Holder

3073-326 Tissue Roll Holder

PALM SPRINGS.

INFORMALITY IN ENTERTAINMENT AND DRESS CREATES AN ATMOSPHERE OF CONTEMPORARY LIVING.
STYLISH AND SOPHISTICATED DOWN TO THE FINEST DETAILS OF PALM SPRINGS BATH DECOR.

3211-030, 3211-260, 3211-250 Towel Bars

3211-030 Towel Bar

3214-030 Towel Ring

3215-030 Robe Hook

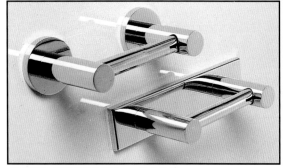

3213-030, 3213-030-BP Tissue Roll Holders

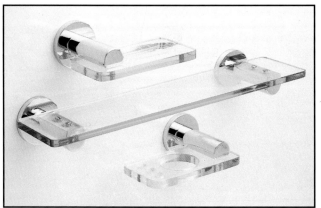

3216-030 Soap Dish, 3218-030 Glass Shelf,
3217-030 Thbrsh/Tmblr Holder

ACCESSORIES

Complementary accessories include solid brass towel bars, 16" or 24" lengths, and single post tissue roll holders, with or without a hood. Both items are available in various finishes.

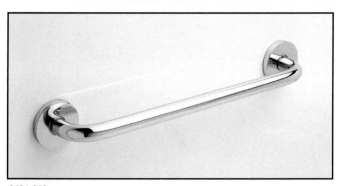

3421-260

3012-030-H

FINISHES

Highly polished brass. Subtle antique brass. Sparkling chrome, polished brass and chrome combined. Contemporary polished black nickel. The richest, most requested finishes are available from Baldwin.

The first step to the perfect finish of Baldwin Bath Accessories is Baldwin's manufacturing process. Formed by hot forging, each piece of brass has a surface superior to those produced by casting. Free from the blemishes inherent in cast products, the

smooth surface of Baldwin brass bath accessories is carefully polished by skilled craftsmen to bring out the deep warm luster of the brass and to create a mirror-like brilliance.

With respect for your investment, Baldwin has protected each brass piece with a unique, clear enamel. Using the latest technology, the enamel is bonded onto Baldwin Bath Accessories to provide a lasting beauty with minimum care.

030- Polished Brass

060- Antique Brass

250- Polished Black Nickel

260- Polished Chrome

153- Satin Nickel/
Polished Brass

263- Polished Chrome/
Polished Brass

326- Polished Brass/
Polished Chrome

Available Finishes and Coordinates

Series / Finishes

Finishes	Lexington	Los Angeles	Georgetown	Dallas	Victoria	Wilshire	Chesapeake	Atlanta	Cambridge	New York	New Orleans	Lafayette	Palm Springs	Solid Towel Bars
Polished Brass (030)	•	•	•	•	•	•	•	•	•	•	•	•	•	•
Polished Chrome (260)	•	•	•	•	•	•		•	•	•		•	•	
Antique Brass (060)			•						•					
Polished Brass/ Polished Chrome (326)								•				•		
Polished Chrome/ Polished Brass (263)		•				•		•						
Polished Black Nickel (250)													•	
Satin Nickel Polished Brass (153)		•						•						

Coordinate Options

	Lexington	Los Angeles	Georgetown	Dallas	Victoria	Wilshire	Chesapeake	Atlanta	Cambridge	New York	New Orleans	Lafayette	Palm Springs	Solid Towel Bars
18", 24" or 30" Towel Bar	•	•		•	•	•	•	•	•	•	•	•	•	
18" or 24" Glass Shelf	•		•	•		•		•	•	•	•	•		
Single Post Tissue Roll Hldr. w/wo Hood			•								•			
Double Post Tissue Roll Holder	•	•	•	•	•	•	•	•	•	•	•	•		
Towel Ring	•	•	•	•	•	•	•	•	•	•	•	•		
Robe Hook	•	•	•	•	•	•	•	•	•	•	•	•		
Soap Dish	•		•	•	•	•		•	•			•	•	
Toothbrush/ Tumbler Holder	•		•	•	•	•	•	•	•	•		•		
Acrylic Towel Bar			•					•					•	
Acrylic Towel Ring			•					•					•	

NOTE: We recommend the Palm Springs soap dish, toothbrush/tumbler holder, 18" or 24" glass shelf accessories to complement the Los Angeles and Atlanta Series designs.

- All Baldwin Accessories in brass finishes are protected with a unique, clear, baked-on coating.

- All Baldwin Accessories have concealed mounting. Installation instructions and mounting hardware are supplied.

Items in this brochure are covered by one or more of the following patents: 293,867; 294,905; 296,006; 296,175; 296,637; 298,710; 299,096; 299,097; 299,098; 301,293; 303,333. Other patents pending.

Baldwin Hardware Corporation
841 E. Wyomissing Blvd.
Reading, PA 19612, USA
Phone (215) 777-7811
FAX (215) 777-7256

BALDWIN BATH

Accessories are the perfect companions for today's popular faucet designs. From traditional to contemporary, Baldwin suites your style.

First Impressions Last a Lifetime

IMAGES™

by Baldwin®

The Images Bath Collection

Laguna

Agean

Seacrest

Edgewater

*T*he Images Bath Collection by Baldwin offers four distinctive styles. Each style is available in your choice of two popular finishes: polished brass or polished chrome. Laguna is also available in polished chrome/polished brass.

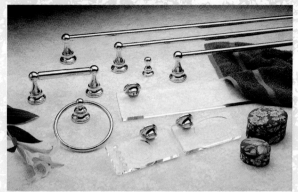

Edgewater®   *Polished Brass or Polished Chrome*

Seacrest®   *Polished Brass or Polished Chrome*

Aegean™   *Polished Brass or Polished Chrome*

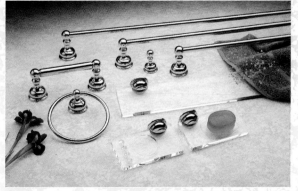

Laguna™   *Polished Brass/Polished Chrome or
All Polished Brass or All Polished Chrome*

Inspired designs. Beautiful detailing. Exceptional craftsmanship. These are the qualities that make the Images Bath Collection by Baldwin the perfect choice for your bath.

From the elegant and traditional to the bold and contemporary, the solid brass Images Bath Collection offers four distinctive designs to complement any decor. Each design is available in seven fashionable yet functional accessories: towel bars, towel ring, soap dish, toothbrush/tumbler holder, 24" shelf, tissue roll holder, and robe hook.

Crafted in America, the Images Bath Collection is made of solid brass, then carefully polished and protected with a clear baked-on coating. Each piece also features Baldwin's patent pending two-step mounting system ensuring quick and easy installation, and concealing the mounting hardware to preserve the integrity of the design.

To distinguish your bath with timeless quality, don't compromise. Select from the Images Bath Collection by Baldwin.

Towel Bar
18", 24" and 30" lengths

Robe Hook

Shelf
24" length

Tissue Roll Holder

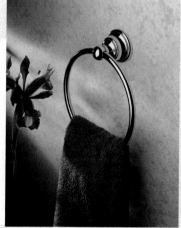

Towel Ring

Soap Dish

*Toothbrush/Tumbler
Holder*

Nothing more elegantly reflects your appreciation of quality than solid brass hardware from Baldwin. Each decorative element is crafted from a piece of solid brass. Then it is polished to a lustrous sheen and protected with a clear baked-on coating.

To carry this elegant look throughout your home, look for other fine brass products from Baldwin. Choose complementary entrance sets and interior latchsets from Baldwin's Images Hardware Collection. Or open a whole world of decorating possibilities with Baldwin's extensive selection of cabinet hardware. All coordinate beautifully to lend timeless elegance to your home.

The Images Collection

Made in the USA
Made by the craftspeople of Baldwin Hardware
Reading, Pennsylvania 19612 USA

©1996 Baldwin Hardware Corporation
Toilet Tissue Holder-U.S. Patent Nos. 362,361/357,840/362,360
Ring Towel Holder-U.S. Patent Nos. 357,838/357,839/357,378
Towel Holder Bar-U.S. Patent Nos. 357,379/357,841
Other Patents Pending

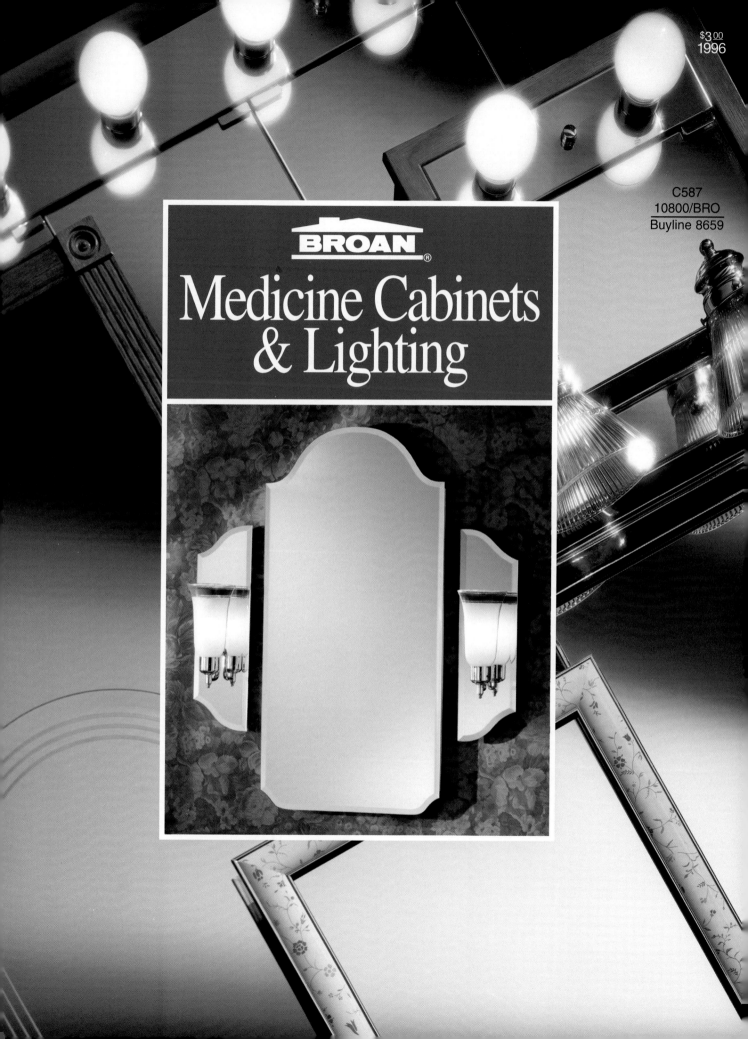

3^{00}
1996

C587
10800/BRO
Buyline 8659

BROAN®

Medicine Cabinets & Lighting

This Broan catalog has more styles and sizes than ever before... Over 500 models in all. To help you review this large assortment and find the products you need, the book is divided into product sections as shown in the Table of Contents below. The specification list at the end of the book will help you compare products and choose the right models for your needs.

Throughout the line, no detail is overlooked. From genuine oak frames to the jewel-like finish of our beveled-edge mirrors, Broan cabinets display quality and craftsmanship.

Broan uses high quality plate glass mirrors for distortion-free viewing. And all lighting products are UL approved so they can be installed with confidence.

Most cabinet bodies are made of high quality, heavy-duty steel with a white baked powder coat paint process for exceptional durability. Cabinets with molded polystyrene bodies are noted and cabinets with wood bodies are detailed in a separate section (pp. 24–27).

Broan selection, quality and value ... a nice reflection on you.

Table of Contents

Frameless
Expressions OF LUXURY

The Expressions Series is elegantly crafted so each cabinet sparkles like a precious gem. These exquisite beveled-edge designs feature the sophisticated quality touches and materials that redefine luxury in the bath.

Large, 8" diameter magnifying make-up mirror for the inside door can be mounted at any height, on the single-door style or on the center door of the Tri-View style.

Heavy-gauge stainless steel cabinets are hand-crafted one at a time for a lifetime of use. Stainless steel interiors are accented with fully adjustable ¼"-thick, smoked glass shelves and fully mirrored back walls.

Fully concealed, 6-way adjustable hinges open 110° for easy access, and a full 150° on doors with magnifying make-up mirrors for convenient viewing.

All edges of the distortion-free plate mirrors are either polished or beveled to a jewel-like luster.

LBC10 Cabinet

LE BACCARAT
Expressions

Like fine cut crystal, Le Bacarrat brings the bath to life with a rich kaleidoscope of light. This arched-top beveled mirror is framed in your choice of clear or smoked finish mirror mosaic trim with a clear mirror single-door in the center. Matching wall mirrors echo the arched motif and the mosaic beveled glass design.

Style	Clear Mirror Model	Overall Size W H D	Wall Opening W H D
Single-Door Recessed Cabinet	LBC10	24 x 35⅝	16½ x 25¼ x 3⅞
Single-Door Surface Mount Cabinet	LBC10SM	24 x 35⅝	None
Wall Mirror Only	LBM15	24 x 35⅝	None

PRC2160 Cabinet with PRL2060 Soffit Light

PRIMEVÉRE
Expressions

Tasteful design on a grand scale, our leader in luxury options features a polished-edge, clear tri-view mirror framed with beveled mirror trim in clear or smoked finish. Matching soffit light with mirror trim sold separately; features instant-on, warm-tone, color correct fluorescent light (included). Parabolic diffuser softens the light for a decidedly elegant atmosphere.

Style	Clear Mirror Model	Smoked Mirror Model	Overall Size W H D	Wall Opening W H D
Tri-View Recessed Cabinets	PRC1148 PRC1160	PRC2148	48 x 37⅝ 60 x 37⅝	36⅞ x 32⅞ x 3⅞ 48⅞ x 32⅞ x 3⅞
Tri-View Surface Mount Cabinets	PRC1148SM PRC1160SM	PRC2148SM	48 x 37⅝ 60 x 37⅝	None None
Matching Soffit Light for Tri-View Surface Mount or Recessed Cabinets	PRL1048 PRL1060	PRL2048	48 x 4¼ x 5⅜ 60 x 4¼ x 5⅜	None None

See pages 32–39 for detailed specifications.

Cabinet 655236

SATURN

The distinctive look of the industry's first beveled-edge, tri-view mirror designed for new warm-tone fluorescent light tubes (not included). These lights provide true-color reflections making them ideal for cosmetic lighting, while offering substantial energy savings compared to incandescent bulbs. Electrical outlets inside cabinet add convenience and glass shelves add elegance.

Style	Brass End Cap Model	Chrome End Cap Model	Overall Size W H D	Wall Opening W H D
Tri-View Recessed Cabinets	655036	655036CRM	36 x 30	33¾ x 24¾ x 3½
	655048	655048CRM	48 x 30	45¾ x 24¾ x 3½
Tri-View Surface Mount Cabinets	655236	655236CRM	36 x 30	None
	655248	655248CRM	48 x 30	None

See pages 32–39 for detailed specifications.

OPUS

Dramatically styled art deco cabinets with beveled-edge mirrors and hand-fitted mirror appliques. Each cabinet is truly a work of art in itself that makes it the focal point of any bath.

Style	Model	Overall Size W H D	Wall Opening W H D
Tri-View	165230	30 x 28¼ x 5¼	None
Surface Mount	165236	36 x 28¼ x 5¼	None
Cabinets	165248	48 x 28¼ x 5¼	None
Top Lights for	HO33090	30 x 4¼ x 5⅞	None
Tri-View Surface	HO33690	36 x 4¼ x 5⅞	None
Mount Cabinets	HO34890	48 x 4¼ x 5⅞	None
Single-Door	260	16 x 26	14 x 18 x 3½
Recessed Cabinets	268	16 x 26	14 x 24 x 3½
Top Lights for Single-Door Recessed Cabinets	73290	16 x 4½ x 2	None

Cabinet 165248; Light HO34890

Cabinet 268;
Light 73290

MIRROR-ON-MIRROR

Stunning beveled-edge, mirror-on-mirror designs create a sophisticated, upscale look even in small-space environments. Each features a clear center mirror with contrasting grey smoke background mirror for an all-glass, picture-frame effect.

Style	Oval Model	Rectangular Model	Overall Size W H D	Wall Opening W H D
Single-Door	1452	1450BC	16 x 26	14 x 18 x 3½
Recessed Cabinets	1457	1458	16 x 26	14 x 24 x 3½
Top Lights for Single-Door Recessed Models	73290	73290	16 x 4½ x 2	None
Side Light for Single-Door Recessed Models	73190*	73190*	5 x 12 x 6½	None

*Packed in pairs.

Cabinet 1452; Light 73290

Cabinet 1450BC; Light 73190

FRAMELESS

Cabinet 5528; Lights 73591

Cabinet 5518; Lights 73591

TORINO

Classic beauty with frosted cut-glass teardrop motif or all clear glass design, both with beveled-edge. Ideal for use with "his-n-hers" vanity sinks or pedestal lavatories. Matching side light fixtures feature beveled-edge mirror backplates and frosted glass shades.

Style	Teardrop Model	Clear Glass Model	Overall Size W H D	Wall Opening W H D
Single-Door Recessed Cabinets	5520 5528	5510 5518	16½ x 34½ 16½ x 34½	14 x 18 x 3½ 14 x 24 x 3½
Side Light for All Single-Door Recessed Cabinets	73591*	73591*	5⅜ x 13¾ x 6½	None

*Packed in pairs.

Cabinet 5410, Light 73690

Cabinet 5418

ADANTE

A distinctive arched top, beveled-edge mirror. Adante is also reversible for use with optional arched top light, creating a dramatic 2-piece oval ensemble. Door is hinged at the right when arch is at the top.

Style	Model	Overall Size W H D	Wall Opening W H D
Single-Door Recessed Cabinets	5410 5418	16½ x 26 16½ x 31	14 x 18 x 3½ 14 x 24 x 3½
Top Light for Single-Door Recessed Cabinets	73690	16½ x 6¼ x 2	None

See pages 32–39 for detailed specifications.

MIRAGE

Faceted like a gemstone, this octagonal, beveled-edge mirror cabinet teams nicely with side lights featuring beveled-edge mirror backplates and tinted glass shades.

Style	Model	Overall Size W H D	Wall Opening W H D
Single-Door Recessed Cabinets	1454	18 x 27	14 x 18 x 3½
	1456	17⅜ x 32	14 x 24 x 3½
	1413†	16 x 24	14 x 18 x 2½
Side Light for Single-Door Recessed Cabinets	73190*	5 x 12 x 6½	None

*Packed in pairs.
†Molded body.

Cabinet 1454; Lights 73190

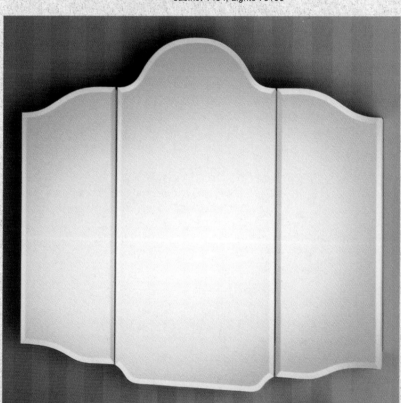

Cabinet 205236

SOÑATA

Graceful curves, top and bottom, on these beveled-edge cabinets and lights make an elegant and unusual ensemble in single-door and tri-view designs.

Matching side light fixtures feature beveled-edge mirror backplate and distinctive frosted glass shades with grey accent and chrome-plated fittings.

Surface mount tri-view cabinets and matching lights feature bright stainless steel side panels.

Style	Model	Overall Size W H D	Wall Opening W H D
Tri-View Surface Mount Cabinets	205230	30 x 32 x 5¼	None
	205236	36 x 32 x 5¼	None
Side Light for Tri-View Surface Mount Cabinets	72152*	5 x 17½ x 10	None
Single-Door Recessed Cabinets	250	16 x 28	14 x 18 x 3½
	258	16 x 32	14 x 24 x 3½
Side Light for Single-Door Recessed Cabinets	72052*	5 x 17½ x 6⅛	None

*Packed in pairs.

DECORAH

Plate glass mirror with soft gold-tone and soft-white floral design lends a unique decorator touch that beautifully completes an overall floral motif.

Style	Model	Overall Size W H D	Wall Opening W H D
Single-Door Recessed Cabinets	1420FL	16 x 26	14 x 18 x 3½
	1428FL	16 x 26	14 x 24 x 3½
Top Light for Single-Door Recessed Cabinets	735FL	16 x 4⅜ x 2	None

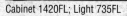

Cabinet 1420FL; Light 735FL

Cabinet 258; Lights 72052

See pages 32–39 for detailed specifications.

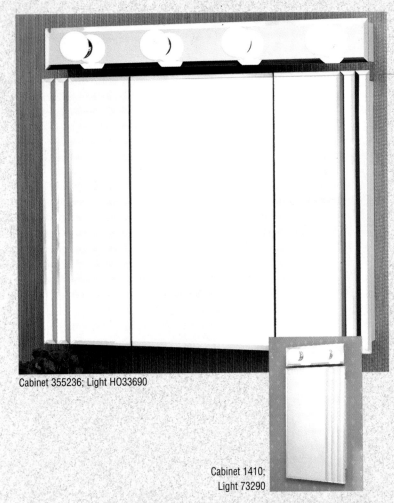

AURORA

Deep-cut, beveled-edge design mirrors fill the bath with shimmering reflections, adding a new dimension to a classic style.

Style	Model	Overall Size W H D	Wall Opening W H D
Tri-View Recessed Cabinets	355030	30 x 28¼	27¾ x 24¾ x 3½
	355036	36 x 28¼	33¾ x 24¾ x 3½
	355048	48 x 28¼	45¾ x 24¾ x 3½
Tri-View Surface Mount Cabinets	355230	30 x 28¼ x 5¼	None
	355236	36 x 28¼ x 5¼	None
	355248	48 x 28¼ x 5¼	None
Top Lights for Tri-View Recessed Cabinets	HO43090	30 x 4½ x 2¼	None
	HO43690	36 x 4½ x 2¼	None
	HO44890	48 x 4½ x 2¼	None
Top Lights for Tri-View Surface Mount Cabinets	HO33090	30 x 4½ x 5⅞	None
	HO33690	36 x 4½ x 5⅞	None
	HO34890	48 x 4½ x 5⅞	None
Single-Door Cabinets	1410	16 x 26	14 x 18 x 3½
	1418	16 x 26	14 x 24 x 3½
Top Lights for Single-Door Recessed Cabinets	73290	16 x 4½ x 2	None

Cabinet 355236; Light HO33690

Cabinet 1410;
Light 73290

HORIZON

Our most popular style, Horizon features the understated elegance of beveled-edge design. A wide selection of tri-view and single-door models and optional matching light bars means this classic is right at home in any size bath.

Style	Model	Overall Size W H D	Wall Opening W H D
Tri-View Recessed Cabinets	255024	24 x 24	21¾ x 20½ x 3½
	255030	30 x 28¼	27¾ x 24¾ x 3½
	255036	36 x 28¼	33¾ x 24¾ x 3½
	255048	48 x 28¼	45¾ x 24¾ x 3½
Tri-View Surface Mount Cabinets	255224	24 x 24 x 5¼	None
	255230	30 x 28¼ x 5¼	None
	255236	36 x 28¼ x 5¼	None
	255248	48 x 28¼ x 5¼	None
Top Lights for Tri-View Recessed Cabinets	HO42490	24 x 4½ x 2¼	None
	HO43090	30 x 4½ x 2¼	None
	HO43690	36 x 4½ x 2¼	None
	HO44890	48 x 4½ x 2¼	None
Top Lights for Tri-View Surface Mount Cabinets	HO32490	24 x 4½ x 5⅞	None
	HO33090	30 X 4½ x 5⅞	None
	HO33690	36 x 4½ x 5⅞	None
	HO34890	48 x 4½ x 5⅞	None
Single-Door Recessed Cabinets‡	1451	16 x 26	14 x 18 x 3½
	1459	16 x 26	14 x 24 x 3½
	1459MOD**	16 x 26	14 x 24 x 3½
	1453†	16 x 20	14 x 18 x 2½
Side Lights for Recessed Cabinets	73190*	5 x 12 x 6½	None
Top Lights for Single-Door Recessed Cabinets	73290	16 x 4½ x 2	None

*Packed in pairs — See page 7 for picture.
**Modular shelf storage — See page 29 for details.
†Molded body.
‡For stainless steel body cabinets see page 29.

Cabinet 255236; Light HO33690

Cabinet 1451;
Light 73290

See pages 32–39 for detailed specifications.

FOCUS

Simple, clean polished-edge design enables this tri-view mirror with built-in top lights to complement a diverse range of decorating styles.

Style	Model	Overall Size W H D
Tri-View Surface Mount Cabinets	295224	24 x 30 x 5¼
	295230	30 x 34 x 5¼
	295236	36 x 34 x 5¼

Cabinet 295236

QUANTUM

Beveled-edge elegance with the softened radius corner design; ideal for the curvaceous, flowing lines of many of today's vanity tops and bath fixtures.

Style	Model	Overall Size W H D
Tri-View Surface Mount Cabinets	455230	30 x 36½ x 5¼
	455236	36 x 36½ x 5¼
	455248	48 x 36½ x 5¼

Cabinet 455248

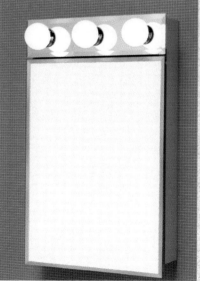

LAFAYETTE

A choice of beveled-edge mirror cabinets to suit your decorating tastes. Both square corner and radius corner styles feature built-in top lights. Optional side mirror kit adds elegance. Includes mirrors for both sides of the cabinets.

Style	Model	Overall Size W H D
Single-Door Surface Mount Cabinets	1402	18⅛ x 32⅜ x 6
	1462	18⅛ x 28⅜ x 6
Side Mirror Kit for Cabinet	SMK1002	

Cabinet 1462

Cabinet 1402

See pages 32–39 for detailed specifications.

FRAMELESS

BEL AIRE

This series features our largest size tri-view. Clean contemporary lines, with stainless steel trim top and bottom and polished vertical edges, make this series a big favorite with builders and designers. No cabinet behind center mirror. Often used in high rise buildings. (Allows for plumbing behind the center panel.) Choice of 2 matching strip lights with candelabra-base bulbs or medium-based bulbs.

Style	Model	Overall Size (A)	Dist. (B)	Wall Opening (C) x (D) x (E)
Tri-View	131D	36 x 36	18¼	8 x 33¼ x 3½
Recessed	151D	48 x 36	23¾	11¼ x 33¼ x 3½
Cabinets	171D	58 x 36	33¾	11¼ x 33¼ x 3½
Tri-View Surface	136H	36 x 36 x 5⅜	None	None
Mount Cabinets	148G	36 x 36 x 5⅜	None	None
Top Lights for	CL73629*	36 x 3¼ x 1¾	None	None
Tri-View	CL74829*	48 x 3¼ x 1¾	None	None
Recessed	BA93629†	36 x 3¼ x 3	None	None
Cabinets	BA94829†	48 x 3¼ x 3	None	None
Top Lights for	CL73729*	36 x 3¼ x 5	None	None
Tri-View Surface	CL74929*	48 x 3¼ x 5	None	None
Mount Cabinets	SB63629†	36 x 3¼ x 6½	None	None
	SB64829†	48 x 3¼ x 6½	None	None

*Uses candelabra-base bulbs.
†Uses standard medium-based bulbs.

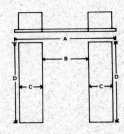

Cabinet 151B; Light CL74829

BEL AIRE 2

Modern Bel Aire styling for the cost-conscious buyer. Offers easy mounting with deluxe features: stainless steel trim. Model 151224 has two doors.

Style	Model	Overall Size W H D
Tri-View Surface	151230	29 x 30 x 5
Mount Cabinets	151236	35 x 30 x 5
Top Lights for	SB23029	29 x 3 x 5¾
Tri-View Surface	SB23629	35 x 3 x 5¾
Mount Cabinets		
Bi-View Surface	151224	23⅜ x 30 x 5
Mount Cabinets		
Top Lights for	SB22429	23⅜ x 3 x 5¾
Bi-View Surface		
Mount Cabinets		

Cabinet 151224; Light SB22429

Cabinet 151230; Light SB23029

See pages 32–39 for detailed specifications.

VIENNA

Most cost-effective steel body tri-view cabinet series. Contemporary elegance trimmed in polished chrome finish. Matching top lights have polished stainless steel faceplates.

Style	Model	Overall Size W H D
Tri-View Surface	155124	24 x 26 x 5½
Mount Cabinets	155130	30 x 26 x 5½
	155136	36 x 26 x 5½
Top Lights for	SB22529	24 x 4 x 5½
Tri-View Surface	SB23129	30 x 4 x 5½
Mount Cabinets	SB23729	36 x 4 x 5½

Cabinet 155136; Light SB23729

STYLELINE 2

Stainless steel trim top and bottom; polished vertical edges. Built-in top light features stainless steel faceplate.

Style	Single-Door Model	Overall Size W H D
Single-Door Surface Mount Cabinet	565	18 x 28 x 6

Cabinet 565

See pages 32–39 for detailed specifications.

Cabinet 471236; Light CT53618

COUNTRY FLORAL

Innovative decorator styling with light, airy floral pattern. Incorporates popular china colors and bright brass accent trim to beautifully complement today's rich, colorful bath fixtures.

Cabinet 4710; Light 705CT

Style	Model	Overall Size W H D	Wall Opening W H D
Tri-View Surface or Recessed Cabinets	471230	30 x 29¾ x 4	27½ x 27 x 3½*
	471236	36 x 29¾ x 4	33½ x 27 x 3½*
Top Lights for Tri-View Surface Mount Cabinets	CT53018	30 x 8 x 9¾	None
	CT53618	36 x 8 x 9¾	None
Single-Door Recessed Cabinets	4710	18 x 27½	14 x 18 x 3½
	4718	18 x 27½	14 x 24 x 3½
Single-Door Surface Mount Cabinets	4712	18 x 27½ x 5	None
Top Lights for Single-Door Recessed Cabinets	705CT	18 x 8 x 7½	None
Top Lights for Single-Door Surface Mount Cabinets	706CT	18 x 8 x 11	None

*Optional Wall Opening

See pages 32–39 for detailed specifications.

MESA

Captures the essence of the Great Southwest, bringing one of today's most popular decorating styles to your bath. Hand-carved design in a durable, moisture-resistant polymeric frame material. Tri-view and single-door models and matching top lights enable you to create this distinctive look in any size bath.

Style	Model	Overall Size W H D	Wall Opening W H D
Tri-View Surface	714230	30 x 28⅜ x 5½	None
Mount Cabinets	714236	36 x 28⅜ x 5½	None
Top Lights for	ME73048	30 x 11¼ x 8⅛	None
Tri-View Surface	ME73648	36 x 11¼ x 8⅛	None
Mount Cabinets			
Single-Door	7140BC	18 x 27½	14 x 18 x 3½
Recessed Cabinets	7148BC	18 x 27½	14 x 24 x 3½
Single-Door Surface Mount Cabinets	7142BC	18 x 27½ x 5½	None
Top Lights for Single-Door Recessed Cabinets	71848	18 x 11¼ x 8	None
Top Lights for Single-Door Surface Mount Cabinets	71948	18 x 11¼ x 11½	None

Cabinet 7142BC; Light 71948

Cabinet 714236; Light ME73648

See pages 32–39 for detailed specifications.

Cabinet 3230WH; Light SP132WH

SPECTRUM WHITE TRI-VIEW

Tri-View cabinets with matching top light are available in gloss white only. Same Enduro frame material as other styles.

Style	Model	Overall Size W H D	Wall Opening W H D
Tri-View Surface or	3230WH	30 x 30 x 4¼	27½ x 27 x 3½*
Recessed Mount Cabinets,	3236WH	36 x 30 x 4¼	33½ x 27 x 3½*
White Only	3248WH	48 x 30 x 4¼	45⅜ x 26⅞ x 3½*
Top Lights for Tri-View	SP132WH	30 x 6½ x 5¼	None
Surface Mount Cabinets,	SP133WH	36 x 6½ x 5¼	None
White Only	SP134WH	48 x 6½ x 5¼	None

*Optional Wall Opening.

SPECTRUM WHITE AND COLORS

Spectrum bath cabinets are created to match the popular colors of bathroom plumbing fixtures for dramatic, colorful bathrooms. "Enduro" frame with "hardshell" acrylic finish on a molded core offers long life in high moisture atmosphere. Matching top light fixtures feature bright chrome faceplate.

Style	Model	Overall Size W H D	Wall Opening W H D
Tri-View Surface or	3330 Series	31 x 30⅜ x 5	28¾ x 27½ x 3½*
Recessed Cabinets w/Built-In Top Lights	3336 Series	37 x 30⅜ x 5	34¾ x 27½ x 3½*
Single-Door Surface or Recessed Cabinets w/Built-In Top Lights	2009 Series	19⅛ x 32¼ x 5	16¾ x 28¾ x 3½*
Single-Door Recessed Cabinets	350 Series	18 x 27½	14 x 18 x 3½
	358 Series	18 x 27½	14 x 24 x 3½
Single-Door Surface Mount Cabinet	352 Series	18 x 27½ x 5	None
Top Lights for Single-Door Recessed Cabinets	745 Series	18 x 6½ x 3	None
Top Lights for Single-Door Surface Mount Cabinets	746 Series	18 x 6½ x 5½	None

*Optional Wall Opening.

SPECTRUM ORDERING INFORMATION

When ordering Spectrum bath cabinets and top lights, indicate color by including color code after model number. For example, to order a surface mounted 352 series cabinet in Rose (WR), ask for 352WR.

COLORS AVAILABLE

Teal(TL)

Rose(WR)

Almond(AL)

Black(BL)

White(WH)

See pages 32–39 for detailed specifications.

Cabinet 350AL (3); Light 745AL (3)

Cabinet 3336TL

Cabinet 2009WR

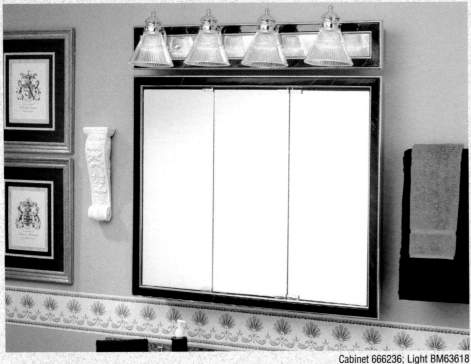

Cabinet 666236; Light BM63618   Cabinet 660BC; Light 76668

MAXIM

Classic formal design featuring an inlay of polished black marble-stone with bright brass trim. Tri-view features brass-tone side panels. Matching top light features bright brass finish fittings and clear prismatic glass shades.

Style	Model	Overall Size W H D	Wall Opening W H D
Tri-View Surface or	666230	30 x 29¾ x 5½	27½ x 27 x 3½*
Recessed Cabinets	666236	36 x 29¾ x 5½	33½ x 27 x 3½*
Top Lights for Tri-View	BM63018	30 x 17¼ x 11½	None
Surface Cabinets	BM63618	36 x 7¼ x 11½	None
Single-Door	660BC	18 x 27½	14 x 18 x 3½
Recessed Cabinets	668BC	18 x 27½	14 x 24 x 3½
Single-Door Surface Mount Cabinets	662BC	18 x 27½ x 5	None
Top Lights for Single-Door Recessed Cabinets	76668	18 x 7¼ x 9¼	None
Top Lights for Single-Door Surface Mount Cabinets	76768	18 x 7¼ x 12½	None

*Optional Wall Opening.

TREASURES

Distinctive, Euro-styled cabinet. High-gloss frame available in White, Black and Almond, with color coordinated side panels. Glass shelves. Striking gold accent stripe and faceplate. Upscale design features back-to-back mirror doors and mirrored interior for 3-way viewing from a 2-door cabinet.

Style	Model	Overall Size W H D	Wall Opening W H D
Bi-View Surface or	3130 Series	31 x 30⅜ x 5	28¾ x 27½ x 3½*
Recessed Mount Cabinets w/Built-In Top Lights	3136 Series	37 x 30⅜ x 5	34¾ x 27½ x 3½*

*Optional Wall Opening.

Cabinet 3130BL

WHITE (WH)   ALMOND (AL)   BLACK (BL)

TREASURES ORDERING INFORMATION
When ordering, indicate color after model number. For example, to order a cabinet in black (BL), ask for 3130BL.

See pages 32–39 for detailed specifications.

Cabinet 113930

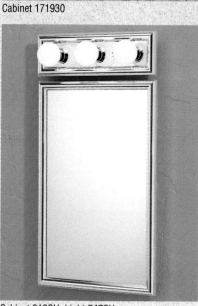

Cabinet 171930

Cabinet 2012BR

CASPAR

Sculptured, extruded aluminum frame features a rich, silver lustre finish. A brass finish, center accent strip offers added drama. Includes built-in top light with matching faceplate.

Style	Silver & Brass Model	Overall Size W H D	Wall Opening W H D
Tri-View Surface or	113930	30 x 29⅜ x 5½	28¾ x 27½ x 3½*
Recessed Cabinets	113936	36 x 29⅜ x 5½	34¾ x 27½ x 3½*

*Optional Wall Opening.

VICEROY

Bright brass or chrome metallic-look framing on a molded core complement today's bathroom accessories.

Style	Brass Model	Chrome Model	Overall Size W H D	Wall Opening W H D
Tri-View Surface or	171924	172924	23¾ x 29⅝ x 4¼	22¾ x 27¾ x 3½*
Recessed Cabinets	171930	172930	30 x 29⅝ x 4¼	28¾ x 27¾ x 3½*
w/Built-In Top Lights	171936	172936	36 x 29⅝ x 4¼	34¾ x 27¾ x 3½*
	171948	172948	48 x 29⅝ x 4¼	46¾ x 27¾ x 3½*
Single-Door Surface or Recessed Cabinets w/Built-In Top Lights	2012BR	2022CH	18 x 31 x 5	16¾ x 29 x 3½*

*Optional Wall Opening.

VERONA

Reflective, glossy metallic-framed mirror in fixture-matching brass finish. Molded frame core is designed for the bath.

Style	Model	Overall Size W H D	Wall Opening W H D
Single-Door	310BR	17¼ x 27¼	14 X 18 x 3½
Recessed Cabinets	318BR	17¼ x 27¼	14 x 24 x 3½
	318BRMOD**	17¼ x 27¼	14 x 24 x 3½
	313BR†	16 x 20	14 x 18 x 2½
Top Lights for All Single-Door Recessed Models	747BR	17¼ x 5½ x 3	

**Modular Shelf Storage — See page 29 for details.
†Molded body.

Cabinet 318CH; Light 747CH

See pages 32–39 for detailed specifications.

17

DECORATOR FRAMES

Cabinet 842236;
Light BS84623

Cabinet 820; Light 70323

Cabinet 872;
Light 70173

BAKER STREET

Charming Victorian detail lends a distinctive period touch to practical bathroom storage. Choose from classic colonial white painted hardwood or warm honey finish solid oak frames. Matching light fixtures feature frosted glass shades and bright brass fittings. Side lights have towel rings.

Tri-View cabinets are often used over pedestal lavatories. See Mesa cabinet, page 13, for this look.

Style	Colonial White Model	Honey Oak Model	Overall Size W H D	Wall Opening W H D
Tri-View Surface Mount Cabinets	842230	847230	30 x 28½ x 5½	None
	842236	847236	36 x 28½ x 5½	None
Top Lights for Tri-View Surface Mount Cabinets	BS84023	BS84073	30 x 6 x 6½	None
	BS84623	BS84673	36 x 6 x 6½	None
Single-Door Recessed Cabinets	820	870	18 x 27	14 x 18 x 3½
	828	878	18 x 27	14 x 24 x 3½
Single-Door Surface Mount Cabinets	822	872	18 x 27 x 5	None
Side Lights for Recessed Cabinets	70123*	70173*	6½ x 13½ x 9½	None
Top Lights for Single-Door Recessed Cabinets	70323	70373	18 x 8 x 9	None
Top Lights for Single-Door Surface Mount Cabinets	70223	70273	18 x 8 x 13½	None

*Packed in pairs.

See pages 32–39 for detailed specifications.

Cabinet 182248; Light SE24828

CANTERBURY

Traditional cathedral arch design. Available in solid oak with honey oak finish or hardwood painted colonial white, both with matching finish sides. Matching top lights feature clear ribbed prismatic glass shades and bright brass fittings for a warm, inviting look.

Style	Honey Oak Model	White Model	Overall Size W H D	Wall Opening W H D
Tri-View Surface	187230	182230	30 x 28½ x 5½	None
Mount Cabinets	187236	182236	36 x 28½ x 5½	None
	187248	182248	48 x 28½ x 5½	None
Top Lights for Tri-View	SE23078	SE23028	30 x 8 x 11	None
Surface Mount Cabinets	SE23678	SE23628	36 x 8 x 11	None
	SE24878	SE24828	48 x 8 x 11	None
Single-Door	8570	8520	18¼ x 27¼	14 x 18 x 3½
Recessed Cabinets	8578	8528	18¼ x 27¼	14 x 24 x 3½
Single-Door Surface Mount Cabinets	8572	8522	18¼ x 27¼ x 5½	None
Top Lights for Single-Door Recessed Cabinets	76378	76328	18 x 8 x 8	None
Top Lights for Single-Door Surface Mount Cabinets	76478	76428	18 x 8 x 11½	None

Cabinet 8578; Light 76378

See pages 32–39 for detailed specifications.

Cabinet 562248; Light WH54873

WHITE MARBLE

Solid oak frame, honey oak finish with white onyx cultured marble inlay. White accent brightens the room, oak frame blends with most wood vanities. Also looks great over white pedestal lavatory. Matching wood-tone sides.

Style	Model	Overall Size W H D	Wall Opening W H D
Tri-View Surface	562230	30 x 28½ x 5¼	None
Mount Cabinets	562236	36 x 28½ x 5¼	None
	562248	48 x 28½ x 5¼	None
Top Lights for	WH53023	30 x 7¼ x 12¼	None
Tri-View Surface	WH53623	36 x 7¼ x 12¼	None
Mount Cabinets	WH54823	48 x 7¼ x 12¼	None
Single-Door	5620	17⅛ x 27⅛ x 2	14 x 18 x 3½
Recessed Cabinets	5628	17⅛ x 27⅛ x 2	14 x 24 x 3½
Single-Door Surface Mount Cabinet	5622	17⅛ x 27⅛ x 5½	None
Top Lights for Single-Door Recessed Cabinets	707WH	17⅛ x 7¼ x 6¾	None
Top Lights for Surface Mount Cabinet	708WH	17⅛ x 7¼ x 10⅛	None

Cabinet 5620; Light 707WH

See pages 32–39 for detailed specifications.

Cabinet 816236; Light OK81668

Cabinet 8120; Light 70928

PRAIRIE

Genuine ¾" solid oak or white painted hardwood frames with traditional detailing and matching wood-tone sides. Choose from the warmth of honey oak, the sophistication of blonde oak or the simple elegance of colonial white. Matching top light fixtures feature clear prismatic glass shades and bright brass finish fittings.

Cabinet 8178; Light 71078

Style	Colonial White Model	Blonde Oak Model	Honey Oak Model	Overall Size W H D	Wall Opening W H D
Tri-View	812230	816230	817230	30 x 28½ x 5½	None
Surface Mount Cabinets	812236	816236	817236	36 x 28½ x 5½	None
Top Lights for Tri-View	OK81028	OK81068	OK81078	30 x 8 x 11	None
Surface Mount Cabinets	OK81628	OK81668	OK81678	36 x 8 x 11	None
Single-Door	8120	8160	8170	18 x 27½	14 x 18 x 3½
Recessed Cabinets	8128	8168	8178	18 x 27½	14 x 24 x 3½
Single-Door Surface Mount Cabinet	8122	8162	8172	18 x 27½ x 5	None
Top Lights for Single-Door Recessed Cabinet	70928	70968	70978	18 x 8 x 8	None
Top Lights for Single-Door Surface Mount Cabinets	71028	71068	71078	18 x 11½ x 8	None

Cabinet 797236

AUTUMN

Warm solid oak, honey finish frame with matching wood-tone sides. Canopy design shields bulbs and provides close-up make-up light, yet delivers plenty of subdued lighting for the whole bath.

Style	Model	Overall Size W H D	Wall Opening W H D
Tri-View Surface	197230	30 x 29 x 5½	28¾ x 27½ x 3½*
or Recessed	197236	36 x 29 x 5½	34¾ x 27½ x 3½*
Cabinets	197248	48 x 29 x 5½	46¾ x 27½ x 3½*

*Optional Wall Opening.

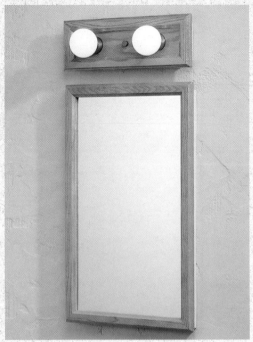

Cabinet 277930; Light SG33079

Cabinet 8778; Light 74279

GRAND OAK II

GRANT

Solid oak frame, honey finish tri-view cabinet for surface or recessed installation. Top light has matching frame and oak finish faceplates. Light is designed for use with surface mount cabinet.

Solid oak, honey finish frame cabinet. Top light has matching frame and oak finish faceplate.

Style	Model	Overall Size W H D	Optional Wall Opening W H D
Tri-View Surface or Recessed Cabinets	277924	24 x 25	22¼ x 23 x 3½*
	277930	29 x 28⅞	27½ x 27 x 3½*
	277936	35 x 28⅞	33½ x 27 x 3½*
	277948	47 x 28⅞	45½ x 27 x 3½*
Top Lights for Tri-View Surface Mount Cabinets	SG32479	24 x 5⅝ x 5¼	None
	SG33079	29 x 5⅝ x 5¼	None
	SG33679	35 x 5⅝ x 5¼	None
	SG34879	47 x 5⅝ x 5¼	None

*Optional Wall Opening.

Style	Model	Overall Size W H D	Wall Opening W H D
Single-Door Recessed Cabinets	8770	16¼ x 24¼	14 x 18 x 3½
	8778	16¼ x 26¼	14 x 24 x 3½
	8778MOD*	16¼ x 26¼	14 x 24 x 3½
	8773†	16¼ x 22	14 x 18 x 2½
	973BC†	16 x 20	14 x 18 x 2½
Single-Door Surface Mount Cabinet	8772	16¼ x 24¼ x 5½	None
Top Lights for Single-Door Recessed Cabinets	74279	16¼ x 5½ x 3	None
Top Lights for Single-Door Surface Mount Cabinets	74379	16¼ x 5½ x 6½	None

*Modular Shelf Storage — See page 29 for details.
†Molded body.

Cabinet 1370

DUNHILL

Solid oak oval with honey finish frames your face in cameo style. Add side lights from Adante Series for added styling.

Style	Model	Overall Size W H D	Wall Opening W H D
Single-Door Recessed Cabinets	1370	21 x 31	14 x 18
	1378	24 x 35¾	14 x 24
Wall Mirror Only	1375	21 x 31	None

Cabinet 5470; Light 73679

ADANTE

Arched beveled-edge mirror is framed in solid oak. Matching side lights.

Style	Model	Overall Size W H D	Wall Opening W H D
Single-Door Recessed Cabinets	5470	18¾ x 33⅛	14 x 18 x 3½
	5478	18¾ x 33⅛	14 x 24 x 3½
Side Lights	73679*	5⅝ x 13¼ x 7¼	None

*Packed in pairs.

See pages 32–39 for detailed specifications.

Cabinet 2072

Cabinet 177930

OAKDALE

Style	Model	Overall Size W H D	Wall Opening W H D
Single-Door Surface or Recessed Cabinet	2072	18 x 31 x 5½	16¾ x 28¾ x 3½*

*Optional Wall Opening.

OAKHILL

Style	Model	Overall Size W H D	Optional Wall Opening W H D
Tri-View Surface or Recessed Cabinets w/Built-In Top Lights	177924	23¼ x 29⅝ x 4¼	22¾ x 27½ x 3½*
	177930	30 x 29⅝ x 4¼	28¾ x 27½ x 3½*
	177936	36 x 29⅝ x 4¼	34¾ x 27½ x 3½*
	177948	48 x 29⅝ x 4¼	46¾ x 27½ x 3½*

*Optional Wall Opening.

Classically-shaped edges on this solid oak, honey finish frame make it a traditional style. Built-in lights make installation easier for surface or recessed mounting.

Cabinet 8278; Light 75719

CHAPEL HILL

Solid oak honey finish frame has contemporary rounded edge styling.

Style	Model	Overall Size W H D	Wall Opening W H D
Single-Door Recessed Cabinet	8278	17¼ x 27¼	14 x 24 x 3½
Top Lights for Single-Door Recessed Cabinet	75719	17¼ x 5½ x 3	None

KINGSTON

Honey oak frame with beveled-edge mirror has a shadowbox effect.

Style	Model	Overall Size W H D	Wall Opening W H D
Single-Door Recessed Cabinets	8370	16½ x 26½	14 x 18 x 3½
	8378	16½ x 26½	14 x 24 x 3½
Top Lights for Single-Door Recessed Cabinets	71829	16½ x 5½ x 2¼	None

Cabinet 8378; Light 71829

See pages 32–39 for detailed specifications.

Cabinet 917236; Light CF93679

DELUXE OAK FRAME

Handsome cabinet with solid oak frame and beveled-edge mirror. Matching top light has bright chrome finish faceplate.

Style	Model	Overall Size W H D
Tri-View Surface	917224	24 x 26 x 4¾
Mount Cabinets	917230	30 x 30 x 4¾
	917236	36 x 30 x 4¾
	917248	48 x 30 x 4¾
Top Lights for Tri-View	CF92479	24 x 7 x 5½
Surface Mount Cabinets	CF93079	30 x 7 x 5½
	CF93679	36 x 7 x 5½
	CF94879	48 x 7 x 5½

Cabinet 907236; Light CR93679

SOLID OAK OR WHITE FRAME

Our most popular wood body tri-view cabinet. Features solid oak or white painted hardwood frames with matching finish cabinet body. Matching top light for oak model has brass finish faceplate, and white model has bright chrome finish faceplate.

Style	Solid Oak Model	White Model	Overall Size W H D
Tri-View Surface	907224	902224	24 x 26 x 4¾
Mount Cabinets	907230	902230	30 x 30 x 4¾
	907236	902236	36 x 30 x 4¾
	907248	902248	48 x 30 x 4¾
Top Lights for Tri-View	CR92479	CR92429	24 x 5⅞ x 5½
Surface Mount Cabinets	CR93079	CR93029	30 x 5⅞ x 5½
	CR93679	CR93629	36 x 5⅞ x 5½
	CR94879	CR94829	48 x 5⅞ x 5½
Bulk Pack Tri-View Cabinet			
(24 - bulk pack)	907224BP*		24 x 26 x 4¾
(20 - bulk pack)	907230BP*		30 x 30 x 4¾
(18 - bulk pack)	907236BP*		36 x 30 x 4¾

*Bulk pack models have open face cartons with top and bottom banded carton caps.

Cabinet 902236

Cabinets on these two pages are all in our Prestique Series featuring:
• Cabinet-maker wood box styling
• Sturdy glue-and-nail butt-joint construction
• Classic designs at affordable prices

See pages 32–39 for detailed specifications.

Cabinet 928

SOLID OAK FRAME
WITH WHITE INLAY

White laminate material coordinates beautifully with white bath fixtures… a little extra decorating idea at a very affordable price. Coordinating light fixture (not shown) has theatre-style lights like those shown on facing page with matching white inlay frame and bright chrome finish faceplate.

Style	Model	Overall Size W H D
Tri-View Surface	927230	30 x 30 x 4¾
Mount Cabinets	927236	36 x 30 x 4¾
	927248	48 x 30 x 4¾
Top Lights for	CW93079	30 x 5⅞ x 5½
Tri-View Surface	CW93679	36 x 5⅞ x 5½
Mount Cabinets	CW94879	48 x 5⅞ x 5½
Single-Door Surface	922	16 x 20 x 4¾
Mount Cabinets	928	16 x 26 x 4¾

Cabinet 927236

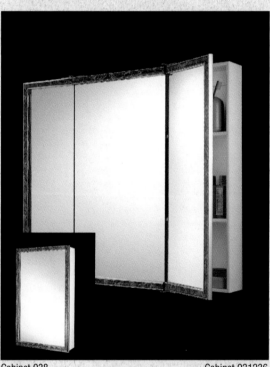

Cabinet 938   Cabinet 931236

Cabinet 905236; Light CR93690

BRASS FINISH FRAME
WITH BLACK INLAY

Marble-like laminate adds a rich dimension to a basic wood-body cabinet. Coordinating top light available (not shown) with theatre-style lights like other Prestique lights, matching frame, and bright brass finish faceplate.

Style	Model	Overall Size W H D
Tri-View Surface	931230	30 x 30 x 4¾
Mount Cabinets	931236	36 x 30 x 4¾
Top Lights for Tri-View	CB93019	30 x 5⅞ x 5½
Surface Mount Cabinets	CB93619	36 x 5⅞ x 5½
Single-Door Surface	932	16 x 20 x 4¾
Mount Cabinets	938	16 x 26 x 4¾

FRAMELESS BEVELED-EDGE

Frameless tri-view cabinet with beveled-edge glass mirrors and matching light. Simple elegance at a wood-body price.

Style	Model	Overall Size W H D
Tri-View Surface	905224	24 x 26 x 4¾
Mount Cabinets	905230	30 x 30 x 4¾
	905236	36 x 30 x 4¾
	905248	48 x 30 x 4¾
Top Lights for Tri-View	CR92490	24 x 5⅞ x 5½
Surface Mount Cabinets	CR93090	30 x 5⅞ x 5½
	CR93690	36 x 5⅞ x 5½
	CR94890	48 x 5⅞ x 5½

See pages 32–39 for detailed specifications.

Cabinet 9472

WOOD FRAME WITH BUILT-IN TOP LIGHT

All-in-one frame style offers upscale look in a value-priced cabinet.
Available in tri-view and single-door models in oak or white finish.
Lights have bright chrome finish faceplate.

Style	Oak Model	White Model	Overall Size W x H x D
Tri-View Surface Mount Cabinets	947224	942224	24 x 28⅞ x 4⅛
	947230	942230	30 x 28⅞ x 4⅛
	947236	942236	36 x 28⅞ x 4⅛
	947248	942248	48 x 28⅞ x 4⅛
Single-Door Surface Mount Cabinets	9472	9422BC	15¾ x 23⅝ x 4⅛

Cabinet 947230

Prestique
Bathroom Cabinets

Cabinets on these two pages are all in our
Prestique Series featuring:
• Cabinet-maker wood box styling
• Sturdy glue-and-nail butt-joint construction
• Classic designs at affordable prices

See pages 32–39 for detailed specifications.

Cabinet 977225

Cabinet 972225

PERFUME & MEDICINE CABINETS

Add color and variety to any bath with one of Broan's distinctive two-compartment cabinets. Narrow compartment features a clear beveled-edge glass window with delicate stenciled pattern and three shelves. It's perfect for displaying today's elegant designer fragrance and colorful health and beauty product packaging. The larger compartment has a framed, beveled-edge mirror door and two shelves.

Style	Oak Model	White Model	Overall Size W H D
2-Door Surface Mount Cabinet	977225	972225	25½ x 28 x 4¾

Cabinet 967224; Light CR92475

WOOD FRAME TRI-VIEW

These value-priced tri-view cabinets are standardized on a 25½" height. Available in oak or white finish. Matching top lights with bright chrome finish faceplate. Single-door versions available individually or in easily merchandised bulk packs.

Style	Oak Model	White Model	Overall Size W x H x D
Tri-View	967224	962224	24 x 25½ x4¾
Surface Mount	967230	962230	30 x 25½ x4¾
Cabinets	967236	962236	36 x 25½ x4¾
	967248	962248	48 x 25½ x4¾
Top Lights for	CR92475	CR92425	24 x 7 x 5½
Tri-View Cabinets	CR93075	CR93025	30 x 7 x 5½
	CR93675	CR93625	36 x 7 x 5½
	CR94875	CR94825	48 x 7 x 5½
Single-Door Surface	902	902WH	16 x 20 x 4¾
Mount Cabinets	982	982WH	16 x 26 x 4¾
Bulk Pack			
(38 - bulk pack)	902BP		16 x 20 x 4¾
(38 - bulk pack)	982BP		16 x 26 x 4¾

Cabinet 962230; Light CR93025

Cabinet 902

Cabinet 902WH

See pages 32–39 for detailed specifications.

OBSCURA

Auxiliary storage with frameless polished-edge mirror doors. Special low-profile (1/4" projection from wall) designed to fit flush with adjacent wall mirrors.

Style	Model	Overall Size W H D	Wall Opening W H D
Recessed Cabinets	629	15 x 36	14 x 34 x 4
	639BC	13 x 36	12 x 34 x 4

Hide cabinet storage in a flat wall mirror area.

Cabinet 629

AVANTI CORNER CABINET

Triangular shape ideal for 3-way viewing with a simple wall mirror makes small corner areas look larger. See "CL" Series strip lights on facing page and page 10.

Style	Model	Trim	Overall Size W H D
Surface Mount	631	Stainless Steel	13 x 36 x 7¼
Corner Cabinets	632	Gold Aluminum	13 x 36 x 7¼

Dimensions for models 631/632

7¼"
5¾"
Wall Mirror
12"
13"
1⅜"

Triangular Shaped

Cabinet 631 (2); Mirror PEM3636; Light Strip CL73629 (See pg. 10)

CENTERED CORNER CABINET

For use over corner vanity.

Style	Model	Trim	Overall Size W H D
Surface Mount	672	Oak Frame	19½ x 33½ x 10½
Corner Cabinets	672SS	Stainless Steel Frame	17¼ x 31 x 9⅞

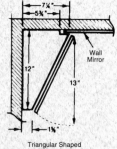

Cabinet 672

See pages 32–39 for detailed specifications.

BEL AIRE AUXILIARY

Ideal in combination with wall mirror and light strips to provide extra storage and 3-way viewing. Stainless steel trim top and bottom with polished vertical mirror edges. See lights on pp. 10 and 28.

Style	Model	Overall Size W H D	Wall Opening W H D
Recessed Cabinets	625	13 x 36	11¼ x 33¼
Surface Mount Cabinets	626	13 x 36 x 4¼	None
Strip lights for use with wall mirror	CL72429* CL73029*	24 x 2¾ x 1¾ 30 x 2¾ x 1¾	

*Use candelabra-base bulbs.
Note: Additional size lights can be found on page 10.

Cabinet 626 (2); Mirror PEM3036

STAINLESS STEEL BODY

Easy to clean, rust-resistant swing-door cabinet. High lustre type 304 stainless steel with bright #4 satin finish and choice of two mirror styles. Beveled-edge mirror looks like Horizon Series on page 8. Stainless steel looks like Styleline on page 31.

Style	Model	Description	Overall Size W H D	Wall Opening W H D
Recessed Cabinets	1448	Beveled-Edge	16 x 26	14 x 24 x 3½
	448BC	Stainless Steel Frame	16 x 26	14 x 24 x 3½
Surface Mount Cabinets	1442	Beveled-Edge	16 x 26	None
	442	Stainless Steel Frame	16 x 26	None

Cabinet 1448

MODULAR SHELF

Our unique cabinet design provides maximum storage capacity. Six modular half-shelves can be positioned in a number of configurations utilizing four snap-in center posts. This flexible design means shelves can quickly be adjusted without tools to accommodate various container sizes.

The modular shelf design is available with any of four distinctive frames. All deliver more storage flexibility with no wasted space!

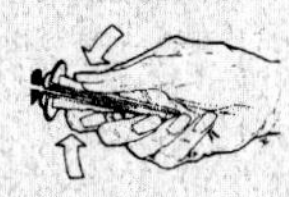

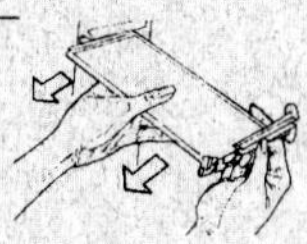

Model	Frame	Overall Size W H D	Wall Opening W H D	See Frame Styles On Page...
8778MOD	Oak	16¼ x 26¼	14 x 24 x 3½	22
318BRMOD	Brass Finish	17¼ x 27¼	14 x 24 x 3½	17
1459MOD	Frameless	16 x 26	14 x 24 x 3½	8
468MOD	Stainless Steel	16 x 26	14 x 24 x 3½	31

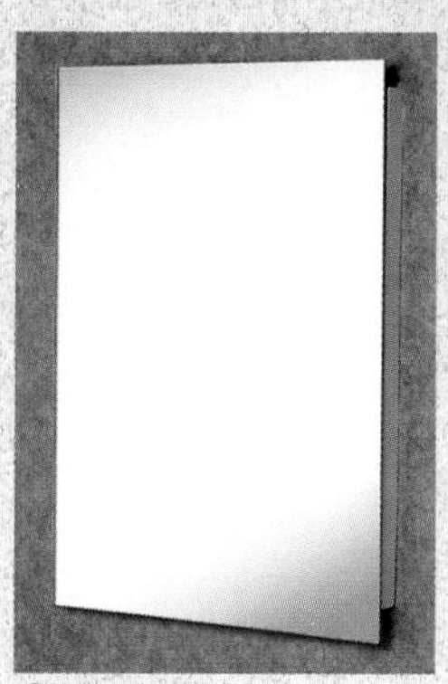

Cabinet 1430

FOCUS

Polished-edge plate mirror.

Style	Model	Overall Size W H D	Wall Opening W H D
Single-Door Recessed Cabinets	1430	16 x 22	14 x 18 x 3½
	1438†	16 x 26	14 x 24 x 3½
	1433†	16 x 20	14 x 18 x 2½

†Molded body.

Cabinet 1430

See pages 32–39 for detailed specifications.

Cabinet 247IL

OAK HOLLYWOOD

Honey solid oak frame and matching wood-tone sides. Built-in top light, grounded outlet, on-off switch and gold-tone door pulls.

Style	Model	Overall Size W H D
Surface Mount Cabinets	2471IL	24¾ x 24½ x 9
	2871IL	28¾ x 24½ x 9

Cabinet 2472

HOLLYWOOD STANDARD

Oak finish frame and chrome door pulls. Built-in top light and on-off switch.

Style	Model	Overall Size W H D
Surface Mount Cabinets	2472	24¾ x 20½ x 9
	2872	28¾ x 20½ x 9

Cabinet SDL25

BEAUTY GLIDE

Stainless steel shadow box frame with chrome door pulls. Grounded outlet and on-off switch. Models with built-in top light include fluorescent tube.

Style	Model	Overall Size W H D	Wall Opening W H D
Recessed Cabinets Unlighted	SD15	24 x 18¾	21½ x 17 x 3½
	SD41	27½ x 19¼	26¼ x 17¼ x 3½
Recessed Cabinets w/Top Light	SDL25	24 x 21¼	21½ x 16½ x 3½
	SDL82	27½ x 22	26¼ x 18¼ x 3½

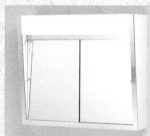

Cabinet 128LP

ENSIGN

Stainless steel trim with built-in light. Includes convenient grounded outlet and on-off switch.

Style	Model	Overall Size W H D
Surface Mount Cabinets	124LP	24 x 23½ x 8¼
	128LP	28 x 23½ x 8¼

Cabinet 323LP

FLAIR

Our economy leader, with incandescent built-in top light. Stainless steel trim and on-off switch.

Style	Model	Overall Size W H D
Surface Mount Cabinets	323LP	24 x 19½ x 8
	327LP	28 x 19½ x 8

CABINET 455FL-G

One-piece steel storage cabinet. Attached fluorescent side lights (tubes included). Grounded outlet and on-off switch.

Style	Model	Overall Size W H D	Wall Opening W H D
Recessed Storage Cabinet	455FL-G	22¼ x 20½ x 3¾	14 x 18 x 3½

CABINET 555IL

Surface mounted steel cabinet. Stainless steel frame and trim. Grounded outlet and on-off switch.

Style	Model	Overall Size W H D
Surface Mount Cabinet	555IL	16 x 24 x 8

See pages 32–39 for detailed specifications.

STYLELINE

Cabinet 451

Classic one-piece mirrored storage cabinet in a variety of sizes. Steel or molded body. Window glass mirror models are not guaranteed distortion-free.

Style	Model	Mirror	Overall Size W H D	Wall Opening W H D
Recessed	401BC†	Window	16 x 20	14 x 18 x 2½
Cabinets	449BC†	Plate	16 x 22	14 x 18 x 2½
Molded	407BC†	Window	16 x 22	14 x 18 x 2½
	Bulk Packs			
	405BP	(407BC in a 2-Pack)		
	405BP27	(407BC in a Bulk Pack of 30)		
Recessed	410BC	Window	16 x 22	14 x 18 x 3½
Steel	420BC	Window	16 x 22	14 x 20 x 3½
Cabinets‡	421BC	Plate	16 x 22	14 x 20 x 3½
	451	Plate	16 x 22	14 x 18 x 3½
	458	Plate	16 x 26	14 x 24 x 3½
	468	Window	16 x 26	14 x 24 x 3½
	468MOD*	Window	16 x 26	14 x 24 x 3½
	490	Plate	18 x 24	16 x 21½ x 3½
	471FS**	Plate	16 x 22	14 x 18 x 3½
	478FS**	Plate	16 x 26	14 x 24 x 3½
	495	Plate	20 x 30	17¼ x 26¼ x 3½
Surface	412SM	Window	16 x 22 x 4¾	None
Mount	422SM	Window	14 x 20 x 5	None
Steel	452SM	Plate	16 x 22 x 4¾	None
Cabinets				

*Modular storage. See page 29 for details.
†Molded Body
**Meets Federal spec #WW-P-541/8B
‡For stainless steel body cabinets see page 29.

WHITE FRAME

Cabinet 313WH

Molded polystyrene body with white finish molded frame.

Model	Overall Size W H D	Wall Opening W H D
313WH	16 x 20	14 x 18 x 2½

HIDEAWAY

Steel single-door can be wallpapered to blend with wall for hidden storage. Reversible for left or right hand opening. Door has tension latch.

Cabinet 622

Style	Model	Overall Size W H D	Wall Opening W H D
Single-Door Recessed Cabinet	622	17⅛ x 21½	14 x 18 x 3½

LOUVER DOOR

Cabinets 606, 607, 609

Cabinet 603

Cabinets 602, 605, 608

Versatile auxiliary cabinets for added storage. Available in white molded polystyrene or unfinished pine which can be painted or stained.

Style	Model	Overall Size W H D	Wall Opening W H D
Arch Top Door	602	16 x 24	14 x 18 x 3½
(Unfinished)	608	16 x 28	14 x 24 x 3½
Recessed Cabinet	605†	16 x 24	14 x 18 x 2½
Flat Top Door	606	16 x 22	14 x 18 x 3½
(Unfinished)	609	16 x 26	14 x 24 x 3½
Recessed Cabinet	607†	16 x 22	14 x 18 x 2½
White Molded Recessed Cabinet Door	603†	16 x 22¼	14 x 18 x 2½

†Molded body.

COMMODORE

Combination VM230M

Light IL36; Mirror PEM3624; Cabinet V36

Choose convenient combination unit or match individual components to suit your needs. Components channeled for easy installation. Light fixture includes grounded outlet and switch. Mirrors feature polished-edges and copper backing. Stainless steel trim.

Style	Model	Mirror Door Model	Styrene Door Model	Overall Size W H D
Combination		VM224M	VM218P	18¼ x 32 x 4⅛
Mirror&Cabinet		VM224M	VM224P	24¼ x 32 x 4⅛
		VM230M	VM230P	30¼ x 32 x 4⅛
		VM236M	VM236P	36¼ x 32 x 4⅛
Storage Cabinets	V24			24¼ x 8¾ x 4¼
	V30			30¼ x 8¾ x 4¼
	V36			36¼ x 8¾ x 4¼
	V48			48¼ x 8¾ x 4¼
Incandescent	IL24			24 x 4 x 7½
Light Fixtures	IL30			30 x 4 x 7½
	IL36			36 x 4 x 7½
	IL48			48 x 4 x 7½
Wall Mirrors	PEM2424			24 x 24
	PEM3024			30 x 24
	PEM3624			36 x 24
	PEM4824			48 x 24
	PEM3036			30 x 36
	PEM3636			36 x 36
	PEM4836			48 x 36
	PEM6036			60 x 36

See pages 32–39 for detailed specifications.

MEDICINE CABINET SPECIFICATIONS

Page	Model No.	Style Name	Frame	Style (T-Tri-View, B-BiView, S-Single, SB-Slide-by, L-Light, WM-Wall Mirror)	Overall Size W"H"D"	Mount Type (S-Surface, R-Recessed, S/R-Surface or Recessed, WM-Wall Mirror)	Wall Opening W"H"D"	Hinge Type (P-Piano, C-Con., L-Leaf, PN-Pin, B-Butt)	Single Door Hinge (L-Left, R-Right, RV-Rev.)	Cabinet Body (S-Steel, SS-Stainless, P-Polystyrene, W-Wood)	Shelves: Quantity *	Shelves: G-Glass, S-Steel, P-Polystyrene, AL-Aluminum	Shelves: F-Fixed, A-Adjustable	Matching Light Fixture	Recommended Bulbs Qty-Type
17	113930	Caspar	Aluminum	T	30x29⅜x5½	S/R	28¾x27½x3½	PN	-	S	2	S	F	Built-in	4-60W G25/G40
17	113936	Caspar	Aluminum	T	36x29⅜x5½	S/R	34¾x27½x3½	PN	-	S	2	S	F	Built-in	5-60W G25/G40
30	124LP	Ensign	Stainless Steel Trim	SB	24x33½x8¼	S	None	None	-	S	1	S	F	Built-in	4-60W Std. MB
30	128LP	Ensign	Stainless Steel Trim	SB	28x23½x8¼	S	None	None	-	S	1	S	F	Built-in	4-60W Std. MB
10	131D	Bel Aire	Stainless Steel Trim	2-Door, T	36x36	R	See pg. 10	L	-	S	6**	P	A	See pg. 10	-
10	136H	Bel Aire	Stainless Steel Trim	2-Door, T	36x36x5⅜	S	None	L	-	S	6**	P	F	See pg. 10	-
22	1370	Dunhill	Solid Oak, Honey	S	21x31	R	14x18x3½	P	RV	S	2	P	A	73679	-
22	1375	Dunhill	Solid Oak, Honey	WM	21x31	WM	None	P	-	-	-	-	-	-	-
22	1378	Dunhill	Solid Oak, Honey	S	24x35¾	R	14x24x3½	P	RV	S	3	P	A	73679	-
9	1402	Lafayette	Frameless	S	18⅛x32⅜x6	S	None	P	R	S	3	S	F	Built-in	3-60W G25/G40
8	1410	Aurora	Frameless	S	16x26	R	14x18x3½	P	RV	S	2	P	A	73290	-
7	1413	Mirage	Frameless	S	16x24	R	14x18x2½	P	RV	P	2	P	F	-	-
8	1418	Aurora	Frameless	S	16x26	R	14x24x3½	P	RV	S	3	P	A	73290	-
7	1420FL	Decorah	Frameless	S	16x26	R	14x18x3½	P	RV	S	2	P	A	735FL	-
7	1428FL	Decorah	Frameless	S	16x26	R	14x24x3½	P	RV	S	3	P	A	735FL	-
29	1430	Focus	Frameless	S	16x22	R	14x18x3½	P	RV	S	2	P	A	-	-
29	1433	Focus	Frameless	S	16x20	R	14x18x2½	P	RV	P	2	P	F	-	-
29	1438	Focus	Frameless	S	16x26	R	14x24x3½	P	RV	S	3	P	A	-	-
29	1442	Horizon	Frameless	S	16x26	S	None	P	RV	SS	3	SS	F	73290	-
29	1448	Horizon	Frameless	S	16x26	R	14x24x3½	P	RV	SS	2	P	A	73290	-
5	1450BC	Mirror-on-Mirror	Frameless	S	16x26	R	14x18x3½	P	RV	S	2	P	A	See pg. 5	-
8	1451	Horizon	Frameless	S	16x26	R	14x18x3½	P	RV	S	2	P	A	73290	-
5	1452	Mirror-on-Mirror	Frameless	S	16x26	R	14x18x3½	P	RV	S	2	P	A	73290	-
8	1453	Horizon	Frameless	S	16x20	R	14x18x2½	P	RV	P	2	P	F	73290	-
7	1454	Mirage	Frameless	S	18x27	R	14x18x3½	P	RV	S	2	P	A	73190	-
7	1456	Mirage	Frameless	S	17⅜x32	R	14x24x3½	P	RV	S	3	P	A	73190	-
5	1457	Mirror-on-Mirror	Frameless	S	16x26	R	14x24x3½	P	RV	S	3	P	A	See pg. 5	-
5	1458	Mirror-on-Mirror	Frameless	S	16x26	R	14x24x3½	P	RV	S	3	P	A	See pg. 5	-
8	1459	Horizon	Frameless	S	16x26	R	14x24x3½	P	RV	S	3	P	A	73290	-
8	1459MOD	Horizon	Frameless	S	16x26	R	14x24x3½	P	RV	S	6†	P	A	73290	-
9	1462	Lafayette	Frameless	S	18⅛x28⅜x6	S	None	P	R	S	3	S	F	Built-in	3-60W G25/G40
10	148G	Bel Aire	Stainless Steel Trim	2-Door T	48x36x5⅜	S	None	L	-	S	6**	P	F	See pg. 10	-
10	151224	Bel Aire 2	Stainless Steel Trim	B	23⅜x30x5	S	None	PN	-	S	2	S	F	SB22429	-
10	151230	Bel Aire 2	Stainless Steel Trim	T	29x30x5	S	None	PN	-	S	2	S	F	SB23029	-
10	151236	Bel Aire 2	Stainless Steel Trim	T	35x30x5	S	None	PN	-	S	2	S	F	SB23629	-
10	151B	Bel Aire	Stainless Steel Trim	2-Door T	48x36	R	See pg.10	L	-	S	6**	P	A	See pg. 10	-
11	155124	Vienna	Chrome Finish Trim	T	24x26x5½	S	None	L	-	S	2	S	F	SB22529	-
11	155130	Vienna	Chrome Finish Trim	T	30x26x5½	S	None	L	-	S	2	S	F	SB23129	-
11	155136	Vienna	Chrome Finish Trim	T	36x26x5½	S	None	L	-	S	2	S	F	SB23729	-
5	165230	Opus	Frameless	T	30x28¼x5¼	S	None	C	-	S	2	S	F	HO33090	-
5	165236	Opus	Frameless	T	36x28¼x5¼	S	None	C	-	S	2	S	F	HO33690	-
5	165248	Opus	Frameless	T	48x28¼x5¼	S	None	C	-	S	2	S	F	HO34890	-
17	171924	Viceroy	Molded, Brass Finish	T	23¾x29⅝x4¼	S/R	22¾x27¾x3½	PN	-	S	2	S	F	Built-in	3-60W G25/G40
17	171930	Viceroy	Molded, Brass Finish	T	30x29⅝x4¼	S/R	28¾x27¾x3½	PN	-	S	2	S	F	Built-in	4-60W G25/G40
17	171936	Viceroy	Molded, Brass Finish	T	36x29⅝x4¼	S/R	34¾x27¾x3½	PN	-	S	2	S	F	Built-in	5-60W G25/G40
17	171948	Viceroy	Molded, Brass Finish	T	48x29⅝x4¼	S/R	46¾x27½x3½	PN	-	S	2	S	F	Built-in	6-60W G25/G40
10	171B	Bel Aire	Stainless Steel Trim	2-Door, T	58x36	R	See pg. 10	L	-	S	6**	P	A	See pg. 10	-
17	172924	Viceroy	Molded, Chrome Fin.	T	23¾x29⅝x4¼	S/R	22¾x27¾x3½	PN	-	S	2	S	F	Built-in	3-60W G25/G40
17	172930	Viceroy	Molded, Chrome Fin.	T	30x29⅝x4¼	S/R	28¾x27¾x3½	PN	-	S	2	S	F	Built-in	4-60W G25/G40
17	172936	Viceroy	Molded, Chrome Fin.	T	36x29⅝x4¼	S/R	34¾x27¾x3½	PN	-	S	2	S	F	Built-in	5-60W G25/G40
17	172948	Viceroy	Molded, Chrome Fin.	T	48x29⅝x4¼	S/R	46¾x27¾x3½	PN	-	S	2	S	F	Built-in	6-60W G25/G40
23	177924	Oakhill	Solid Oak, Honey	T	23¼x29⅝x4¼	S/R	22¾x27½x3½	PN	-	S	2	S	F	Built-in	3-60W G25/G40
23	177930	Oakhill	Solid Oak, Honey	T	30x29⅝x4¼	S/R	28¾x27½x3½	PN	-	S	2	S	F	Built-in	4-60W G25/G40
23	177936	Oakhill	Solid Oak, Honey	T	36x29⅝x4¼	S/R	34¾x27½x3½	PN	-	S	2	S	F	Built-in	5-60W G25/G40
23	177948	Oakhill	Solid Oak, Honey	T	48x29⅝x4¼	S/R	46¾x27½x3½	PN	-	S	2	S	F	Built-in	6-60W G25/G40
19	182230	Canterbury	Hardwood, White	T	30x28½x5½	S	None	L	-	S	2	S	F	SE23028	-
19	182236	Canterbury	Hardwood, White	T	36x28½x5½	S	None	L	-	S	2	S	F	SE23628	-
19	182248	Canterbury	Hardwood, White	T	48x28½x5½	S	None	L	-	S	2	S	F	SE24828	-
19	187230	Canterbury	Solid Oak, Honey	T	30x28½x5½	S	None	L	-	S	2	S	F	SE23078	-

*Cabinet bottom always provides an additional storage level.

† Modular half shelves.

**3 shelves in each side.

Page	Model No.	Style Name	Frame	Style T-Tri-View B-BiView S-Single SB-Slide-by L-Light WM-Wall Mirror	Overall Size W"H"D"	Mount Type S-Surface R-Recessed S/R-Surface or Recessed WM-Wall Mirror	Wall Opening W"H"D"	Hinge Type P-Piano C-Con. L-Leaf PN-Pin B-Butt	Single Door Hinge L-Left R-Right RV-Rev.	Cabinet Body S-Steel SS-Stainless P-Polystyrene W-Wood	Shelves Quantity *	Shelves G-Glass S-Steel P-Polystyrene AL-Aluminum	Shelves F-Fixed A-Adjustable	Matching Light Fixture	Recommended Bulbs Qty-Type
19	187236	Canterbury	Solid Oak, Honey	T	36x28½x5½	S	None	L	-	S	2	S	F	SE23678	-
19	187248	Canterbury	Solid Oak, Honey	T	48x28½x5½	S	None	L	-	S	2	S	F	SE24878	-
21	197230	Autumn	Solid Oak, Honey	T	30x29x5½	S/R	28¾x27½x3½	PN	-	S	2	S	F	Built-in	4-60W Std. MB
21	197236	Autumn	Solid Oak, Honey	T	36x29x5½	S/R	34¾x27½x3½	PN	-	S	2	S	F	Built-in	5-60W Std. MB
21	197248	Autumn	Solid Oak, Honey	T	48x29x5½	S/R	46¾x27½x3½	PN	-	S	2	S	F	Built-in	5-60W Std. MB
15	2009 Series	Spectrum	Molded Acrylic Fin.	S	19⅛x32¼x5	S/R	16¾x28¾x3½	PN	R	S	3	S	F	Built-in	3-60W G25/G40
17	2012BR	Viceroy	Molded Brass Finish	S	18x31x5	S/R	16¾x29x3½	PN	R	S	3	S	F	Built-in	3-60W G25/G40
17	2022CH	Viceroy	Molded Chrome Fin.	S	18x31x5	S/R	16¾x29x3½	PN	R	S	3	S	F	Built-in	3-60W G25/G40
7	205230	Sonata	Frameless	T	30x32x5¼	S	None	C	-	S	2	S	F	-	-
7	205236	Sonata	Frameless	T	36x32x5¼	S	None	C	-	S	2	S	F	-	-
23	2072	Oakdale	Solid Oak, Honey	S	18x31x5½	S/R	16¾x28¾x3½	PN	R	S	3	S	F	Built-in	3-60W G25/G40
30	2471IL	Oak Hollywood	Solid Oak, Honey	SB	24¾x24½x9	S	None	-	-	S	1	S	F	Built-in	4-60W Std. MB
30	2472	Hollywood Standard	Oak Finish	SB	24¾x20½x9	S	None	-	-	S	1	S	F	Built-in	4-60W Std. MB
7	250	Sonata	Frameless	S	16x28	R	14x18x3½	-	R	S	2	P	A	75052	-
8	255024	Horizon	Frameless	T	24x24	R	21¾x20½x3½	C	-	S	2	S	A	HO42490	-
8	255030	Horizon	Frameless	T	30x28¼	R	27¾x24¾x3½	C	-	S	2	S	A	HO43090	-
8	255036	Horizon	Frameless	T	36x28¼	R	33¾x24¾x3½	C	-	S	2	S	A	HO43690	-
8	255048	Horizon	Frameless	T	48x28¼	R	45¾x24¾x3½	C	-	S	2	S	A	HO44890	-
8	255224	Horizon	Frameless	T	24x24x5¼	S	None	C	-	S	2	S	F	HO32490	-
8	255230	Horizon	Frameless	T	30x28¼x5¼	S	None	C	-	S	2	S	F	HO33090	-
8	255236	Horizon	Frameless	T	36x28¼x5¼	S	None	C	-	S	2	S	F	HO33690	-
8	255248	Horizon	Frameless	T	48x28¼x5¼	S	None	C	-	S	2	S	F	HO34890	-
7	258	Sonata	Frameless	S	16x32	R	14x24x3½	P	R	S	3	P	A	75052	-
5	260	Opus	Frameless	S	16x26	R	14x18x3½	P	RV	S	2	P	A	73290	-
5	268	Opus	Frameless	S	16x26	R	14x24x3½	P	RV	S	3	P	A	73290	-
22	277924	Grand Oak II	Solid Oak, Honey	T	24x25	S/R	22¼x23x3½	PN	-	S	2	S	F	SG32479	-
22	277930	Grand Oak II	Solid Oak, Honey	T	29x28⅞	S/R	27½x27x3½	PN	-	S	2	S	F	SG33079	-
22	277936	Grand Oak II	Solid Oak, Honey	T	35x28⅞	S/R	33½x27x3½	PN	-	S	2	S	F	SG33679	-
22	277948	Grand Oak II	Solid Oak, Honey	T	47x28⅞	S/R	45½x27x3½	PN	-	S	2	S	F	SG34879	-
30	2871IL	Oak Hollywood	Solid Oak, Honey	SB	28¾x24½x9	S	None	-	-	S	1	S	F	Built-in	4-60W Std. MB
30	2872	Hollywood Standard	Wood Oak Finish	SB	28¾x20½x9	S	None	-	-	S	1	S	F	Built-in	4-60W Std. MB
9	295224	Focus	Frameless	T	24x30x5¼	S	None	C	-	S	2	S	F	Built-in	3-60W G25/G40
9	295230	Focus	Frameless	T	30x34x5¼	S	None	C	-	S	2	S	F	Built-in	4-60W G25/G40
9	295236	Focus	Frameless	T	36x34x5¼	S	None	C	-	S	2	S	F	Built-in	5-60W G25/G40
17	310BR	Verona	Brass Finish	S	17¼x27¼	R	14x18x3½	P	RV	S	2	P	A	747BR	-
16	3130AL	Treasures	High Gloss Almond	B	31x30⅜x5	S/R	28¾x27½x3½	PN	-	S	3	G	A	Built-in	4-60W G25/G40
16	3130BL	Treasures	High Gloss Black	B	31x30⅜x5	S/R	28¾x27½x3½	PN	-	S	3	G	A	Built-in	4-60W G25/G40
16	3130WH	Treasures	High Gloss White	B	31x30⅜x5	S/R	28¾x27½x3½	PN	-	S	3	G	A	Built-in	4-60W G25/G40
16	3136AL	Treasures	High Gloss Almond	B	37x30⅜x5	S/R	34¾x27½x3½	PN	-	S	3	G	A	Built-in	5-60W G25/G40
16	3136BL	Treasures	High Gloss Black	B	37x30⅜x5	S/R	34¾x27½x3½	PN	-	S	3	G	A	Built-in	5-60W G25/G40
16	3136WH	Treasures	High Gloss White	B	37x30⅜x5	S/R	34¾x27½x3½	PN	-	S	3	G	A	Built-in	5-60W G25/G40
17	313BR	Verona	Molded, Brass Finish	S	16x20	R	14x18x2½	B	RV	P	2	P	F	747BR	-
31	313WH	White Frame	Molded, White Finish	S	16x20	R	14x18x2½	B	RV	P	2	P	F	-	-
17	318BR	Verona	Molded, Brass Finish	S	17¼x27¼	R	14x24x3½	P	RV	S	2	P	A	747BR	-
17	318BRMOD	Verona	Molded, Brass Finish	S	17¼x27¼	R	14x24x3½	P	RV	S	6†	P	A	747BR	-
30	323LP	Flair	Stainless Steel Trim	SB	24x19½x8	S	None	-	-	S	1	S	F	Built-in	4-60W Std. MB
14	3230WH	Spectrum	Molded, Acrylic Fin.	T	30x30x4½	S/R	27½x27x3½	PN	-	S	2	S	F	SP132WH	-
14	3236WH	Spectrum	Molded, Acrylic Fin.	T	36x30⅜x4½	S/R	33½x27x3½	PN	-	S	2	S	F	SP133WH	-
14	3248WH	Spectrum	Molded, Acrylic Fin.	T	48x30x4½	S/R	45⅜x27x3½	PN	-	S	2	S	F	SP134WH	-
30	327LP	Flair	Stainless Steel Trim	SB	28x19½x8	S	None	-	-	S	1	S	F	Built-in	4-60W Std. MB
15	3330 Series	Spectrum	Molded, Acrylic Fin.	T	31x30⅜x5	S/R	28¾x27½x3½	PN	-	S	2	S	F	Built-in	4-60W G25/G40
15	3336 Series	Spectrum	Molded, Acrylic Fin.	T	37x30⅜x5	S/R	34¾x27½x3½	PN	-	S	2	S	F	Built-in	5-60W G25/G40
15	350 Series	Spectrum	Molded, Acrylic Fin.	S	18x27½	R	14x18x3½	P	RV	S	2	P	A	745 Series	-
15	352 Series	Spectrum	Molded, Acrylic Fin.	S	18x27½x5	S	None	P	RV	S	3	P	F	746 Series	-
8	355030	Aurora	Frameless	T	30x28¼	R	27¾x24¾x3½	C	-	S	2	S	A	HO43090	-
8	355036	Aurora	Frameless	T	36x28¼	R	33¾x24¾x3½	C	-	S	2	S	A	HO43690	-
8	355048	Aurora	Frameless	T	48x28¼	R	45¾x24¾x3½	C	-	S	2	S	A	HO44890	-
8	355230	Aurora	Frameless	T	30x28¼x5¼	S	None	C	-	S	2	S	F	HO33090	-
8	355236	Aurora	Frameless	T	36x28¼x5¼	S	None	C	-	S	2	S	F	HO33690	-

*Cabinet bottom always provides an additional storage level.

† Modular half shelves.

MEDICINE CABINET SPECIFICATIONS

Page	Model No.	Style Name	Frame	Style T-Tri-View B-BiView S-Single SB-Slide-by L-Light WM-Wall Mirror	Overall Size W"H"D"	Mount Type S-Surface R-Recessed S/R-Surface or Recessed WM-Wall Mirror	Wall Opening W"H"D"	Hinge Type P-Piano C-Con. L-Leaf PN-Pin B-Butt	Single Door Hinge L-Left R-Right RV-Rev.	Cabinet Body S-Steel SS-Stainless P-Polystyrene W-Wood	Shelves Quantity *	Shelves G-Glass S-Steel P-Polystyrene AL-Aluminum	Shelves F-Fixed A-Adjustable	Matching Light Fixture	Recommended Bulbs Qty-Type
8	355248	Aurora	Frameless	T	48x28¼x5¼	S	None	C	-	S	2	S	F	HO34890	-
15	358 Series	Spectrum	Molded, Acrylic Fin.	S	18x27½	R	14x24x3½	P	RV	S	3	P	A	745 Series	-
29	401BC	Styleline	Stainless Steel ■	S	16x20	R	14x18x2½	B	RV	P	2	P	F	-	-
31	405BP	Styleline	Stainless Steel ■	S	16x22	R	14x18x2½	B	RV	P	2	P	F	-	-
31	405BP27	Styleline	Stainless Steel ■	S	16x22	R	14x18x2½	B	RV	P	2	P	F	-	-
31	407BC	Styleline	Stainless Steel ■	S	16x22	R	14x18x2½	B	RV	P	2	P	F	-	-
31	410BC	Styleline	Stainless Steel ■	S	16x22	R	14x18x3½	P	RV	S	2	P	A	-	-
31	412SM	Styleline	Stainless Steel ■	S	16x22x4¾	S	None	P	RV	S	2	S	F	-	-
31	420BC	Styleline	Stainless Steel ■	S	16x22	R	14x20x3½	P	RV	S	2	P	A	-	-
31	421BC	Styleline	Stainless Steel	S	16x22	R	14x20x3½	P	RV	S	2	P	A	-	-
31	422SM	Styleline	Stainless Steel ■	S	14x20x5	S	None	P	RV	S	2	P	F	-	-
29	442	Styleline	Stainless Steel	S	16x26	S	None	P	RV	SS	3	SS	F	-	-
29	448BC	Styleline	Stainless Steel	S	16x26	R	14x24x3½	P	RV	SS	3	SS	A	-	-
31	449BC	Styleline	Stainless Steel	S	16x22	R	14x18x2½	B	RV	P	2	P	F	-	-
31	451	Styleline	Stainless Steel	S	16x22	R	14x18x3½	P	RV	S	2	P	A	-	-
31	452SM	Styleline	Stainless Steel	S	16x22x4¾	S	None	P	RV	S	2	S	F	-	-
30	455FL-G	Styleline	Stainless Steel	S	22¼x20½x3¾	R	14x18½x3½	P	R	S	2	P	A	Built-in	Fluorescent (incl.)
9	455230	Quantum	Frameless	T	30x36½x5¼	S	None	C	-	S	2	S	F	Built-in	4-60W G25/G40
9	455236	Quantum	Frameless	T	36x36½x5¼	S	None	C	-	S	2	S	F	Built-in	5-60W G25/G40
9	455248	Quantum	Frameless	T	48x36½x5¼	S	None	C	-	S	2	S	F	Built-in	6-60W G25/G40
31	458	Styleline	Stainless Steel	S	16x26	R	14x24x3½	P	RV	S	3	P	A	-	-
31	468	Styleline	Stainless Steel ■	S	16x26	R	14x24x3½	P	RV	S	3	P	A	-	-
31	468MOD	Styleline	Stainless Steel ■	S	16x26	R	14x24x3½	P	RV	S	6†	P	A	-	-
12	4710	Country Floral	Molded, Patterned	S	18x27½	R	14x18x3½	P	RV	S	2	P	A	705CT	-
12	4712	Country Floral	Molded, Patterned	S	18x27½x5	S	None	P	RV	S	3	P	F	706CT	-
12	471230	Country Floral	Molded, Patterned	T	30x29¾x4	S/R	27½x27x3½	PN	-	S	2	S	F	CT53018	-
12	471236	Country Floral	Molded, Patterned	T	36x29¾x4	S/R	33½x27x3½	PN	-	S	2	S	F	CT53618	-
12	4718	Country Floral	Molded, Patterned	S	18x27½	R	14x24x3½	P	RV	S	3	P	A	705CT	-
31	471FS	Styleline	Stainless Steel •	S	16x22	R	14x18x3½	P	RV	S	2	A	A	-	-
31	478FS	Styleline	Stainless Steel •	S	16x26	R	14x24x3½	P	RV	S	3	A	A	-	-
31	490	Styleline	Stainless Steel	S	18x24	R	16x21½x3½	P	RV	S	3	P	A	-	-
31	495	Styleline	Stainless Steel	S	20x30	R	17¼x26¼x3½	P	RV	S	3	P	A	-	-
6	5410	Adante	Frameless	S	16½x26	R	14x18x3½	P	RV	S	2	P	A	73690	-
6	5418	Adante	Frameless	S	16½x31	R	14x24x3½	P	RV	S	3	P	A	73690	-
22	5470	Adante	Arched Oak	S	18¾x33⅛	R	14x18x3½	P	R	S	2	P	A	73679	-
22	5478	Adante	Arched Oak	S	18¾x33⅛	R	14x24x3½	P	R	S	3	P	A	73679	-
6	5510	Torino	Frameless	S	16½x34½	R	14x18x3½	P	R	S	2	P	A	73591	-
6	5518	Torino	Frameless	S	16½x34½	R	14x24x3½	P	R	S	3	P	A	73591	-
6	5520	Torino	Frameless	S	16½x34½	R	14x18x3½	P	R	S	2	P	A	73591	-
6	5528	Torino	Frameless	S	16½x34½	R	14x24x3½	P	R	S	3	P	A	73591	-
30	555IL	Styleline	Stainless Steel	S	16x24x8	S	None	P	R	S	2	S	F	Built-in	-
20	5620	White Marble	Solid Oak & White	S	17⅛x27⅛x2	R	14x18x3½	P	RV	S	2	P	A	707WH	-
20	5622	White Marble	Solid Oak & White	S	17⅛x27⅛x5½	S	None	P	RV	S	3	P	F	708WH	-
20	562230	White Marble	Solid Oak & White	T	30x28½x5¼	S	None	L	-	S	2	S	F	WH53023	-
20	562236	White Marble	Solid Oak & White	T	36x28½x5¼	S	None	L	-	S	2	S	F	WH53623	-
20	562248	White Marble	Solid Oak & White	T	48x28½x5¼	S	None	L	-	S	2	S	F	WH54823	-
20	5628	White Marble	Solid Oak & White	S	17⅛x27⅛x2	R	14x24x3½	P	RV	S	3	P	A	707WH	-
11	565	Styleline 2	Stainless Steel	S	18x28x6	S	None	P	R	S	3	S	F	Built-in	3-60W G25/G40
31	602	Louver Door	Unfinished Pine	S	16x24	R	14x18x3½	B	R	S	2	P	A	-	-
31	603	Louver Door	White Molded	S	16x22¼	R	14x18x2½	P	RV	P	2	P	F	-	-
31	605	Louver Door	Unfinished Pine	S	16x24	R	14x18x2½	P	R	P	2	P	F	-	-
31	606	Louver Door	Unfinished Pine	S	16x22	R	14x18x3½	B	RV	S	2	P	A	-	-
31	607	Louver Door	Unfinished Pine	S	16x22	R	14x18x2½	P	RV	P	3	P	F	-	-
31	608	Louver Door	Unfinished Pine	S	16x28	R	14x24x3½	P	R	S	3	P	A	-	-
31	609	Louver Door	Unfinished Pine	S	16x26	R	14x24x3½	P	RV	S	3	P	A	-	-
31	622	Hideaway	Steel Door	S	17⅛x21½	R	14x18x3½	P	RV	S	2	P	A	-	-
29	625	Bel Aire Auxiliary	Stainless Steel Trim	S	13x36	R	11¼x33¼x3½	P	RV	S	3	S	A	-	-
29	626	Bel Aire Auxiliary	Stainless Steel Trim	S	13x36x4¼	S	None	P	RV	S	3	P	F	-	-
28	629	Obscura	Frameless	S	15x36	R	14x34x4	C	RV	S	3	S	A	-	-

*Cabinet bottom always provides an additional storage level. † Modular half shelves. ■ Economy window glass mirror. • Meets federal spec., see page 31.

Page	Model No.	Style Name	Frame	Style T-Tri-View B-BiView S-Single SB-Slide-by L-Light WM-Wall Mirror	Overall Size W"H"D"	Mount Type S-Surface R-Recessed S/R-Surface or Recessed WM-Wall Mirror	Wall Opening W"H"D"	Hinge Type P-Piano C-Con. L-Leaf PN-Pin B-Butt	Single Door Hinge L-Left R-Right RV-Rev.	Cabinet Body S-Steel SS-Stainless P-Polystyrene W-Wood	Shelves			Matching Light Fixture	Recommended Bulbs Qty-Type
											Quantity *	G-Glass S-Steel P-Polystyrene AL-Aluminum	F-Fixed A-Adjustable		
28	631	Avanti Corner	Stainless Steel Trim	S	13x36x7¼	S	None	P	RV	S	3	G	F	-	-
28	632	Avanti Corner	Gold Aluminum Trim	S	13x36x7¼	S	None	P	RV	S	3	G	F	-	-
28	639BC	Obscura	Frameless	S	13x36	R	12x34x4	C	RV	S	3	S	A	-	-
4	655036	Saturn	Frameless	T	36x30	R	33¾x24¾x3½	C	-	S	2	G	A	Built-in	2-17 W Fluor.
4	655048	Saturn	Frameless	T	48x30	R	45¾x24¾x3½	C	-	S	2	G	A	Built-in	2-17 W Fluor.
4	655236	Saturn	Frameless	T	36x30	S	None	C	-	S	2	G	A	Built-in	2-17 W Fluor.
4	655248	Saturn	Frameless	T	48x30	S	None	C	-	S	2	G	A	Built-in	2-17 W Fluor.
4	655036CRM	Saturn	Frameless	T	36x30	R	33¾x24¾x3½	C	-	S	2	G	A	Built-in	2-17 W Fluor.
4	655048CRM	Saturn	Frameless	T	48x30	R	45¾x24¾x3½	C	-	S	2	G	A	Built-in	2-17 W Fluor.
4	655236CRM	Saturn	Frameless	T	36x30	S	None	C	-	S	2	G	A	Built-in	2-17 W Fluor.
4	655248CRM	Saturn	Frameless	T	48x30	S	None	C	-	S	2	G	A	Built-in	2-17 W Fluor.
16	660BC	Maxim	Brass Finish & Black	S	18x27½	R	14x18x3½	P	RV	S	2	P	A	76668	-
16	662BC	Maxim	Brass Finish & Black	S	18x27½x5	S	None	P	RV	S	3	P	F	76768	-
16	666230	Maxim	Brass Finish & Black	T	30x29¾x5½	S/R	27½x27x3½	PN	-	S	2	S	F	BM63018	-
16	666236	Maxim	Brass Finish & Black	T	36x29¾x5½	S/R	33½x27x3½	PN	-	S	2	S	F	BM63618	-
16	668BC	Maxim	Brass Finish & Black	S	18x27½	R	14x24x3½	P	RV	S	2	P	A	76668	-
28	672	Avanti Corner	Solid Oak, Honey	S	19½x33½x10½	S	None	PN	RV	S	3	S	F	-	-
28	672SS	Avanti Corner	Stainless Steel	S	17¼x31x9⅞	S	None	PN	RV	S	3	S	F	-	-
18	70123	Baker Street	Hardwood, White	L▲	6½x13½x9½	For R Cab.	None	-	-	-	-	-	-	-	1-60W Std. MB
18	70173	Baker Street	Solid Oak, Honey	L▲	6½x13½x9½	For R Cab.	None	-	-	-	-	-	-	-	1-60W Std. MB
18	70223	Baker Street	Hardwood, White	L	18x8x13½	For S Cab.	None	-	-	-	-	-	-	-	2-60W Std. MB
18	70273	Baker Street	Solid Oak, Honey	L	18x8x13½	For S Cab.	None	-	-	-	-	-	-	-	2-60W Std. MB
18	70323	Baker Street	Hardwood, White	L	18x8x9	For R Cab.	None	-	-	-	-	-	-	-	2-60W Std. MB
18	70373	Baker Street	Solid Oak, Honey	L	18x8x9	For R Cab.	None	-	-	-	-	-	-	-	2-60W Std. MB
12	705CT	Country Floral	Molded, Patterned	L	18x8x7½	For R Cab.	None	-	-	-	-	-	-	-	2-60W Std. MB
12	706CT	Country Floral	Molded, Patterned	L	18x8x11	For S Cab.	None	-	-	-	-	-	-	-	2-60W Std. MB
20	707WH	White Marble	Solid Oak & White	L	17⅛x7¼x6¾	For R Cab.	None	-	-	-	-	-	-	-	2-60W Std. MB
20	708WH	White Marble	Solid Oak & White	L	17⅛x7¼x10⅛	For S Cab.	None	-	-	-	-	-	-	-	2-60W Std. MB
21	70928	Prairie	Hardwood, White	L	18x8x8	For R Cab.	None	-	-	-	-	-	-	-	2-60W Std. MB
21	70968	Prairie	Solid Oak, Blonde	L	18x8x8	For R Cab.	None	-	-	-	-	-	-	-	2-60W Std. MB
21	70978	Prairie	Solid Oak, Honey	L	18x8x8	For R Cab.	None	-	-	-	-	-	-	-	2-60W Std. MB
21	71028	Prairie	Hardwood, White	L	18x11½x8	For S Cab.	None	-	-	-	-	-	-	-	2-60W Std. MB
21	71068	Prairie	Solid Oak, Blonde	L	18x11½x8	For S Cab.	None	-	-	-	-	-	-	-	2-60W Std. MB
21	71078	Prairie	Solid Oak, Honey	L	18x11½x8	For S Cab.	None	-	-	-	-	-	-	-	2-60W Std. MB
13	714230	Mesa	Molded, Patterned	T	30x28⅜x5½	S	None	L	-	S	2	S	F	ME 73048	-
13	714236	Mesa	Molded, Patterned	T	36x28⅜x5½	S	None	L	-	S	2	S	F	ME 73648	-
13	7140BC	Mesa	Molded, Patterned	S	18x27½	R	14x18x3½	P	RV	S	2	P	A	71848	-
13	7142BC	Mesa	Molded, Patterned	S	18x27½x5½	S	None	P	RV	S	2	P	A	71948	-
13	7148BC	Mesa	Molded, Patterned	S	18x27½	R	14x24x3½	P	RV	S	2	P	A	71848	-
23	71829	Kingston	Solid Oak, Honey	L	16½x5½x2¼	For R Cab.	None	-	-	-	-	-	-	-	3-60W G25/G40
13	71848	Mesa	Molded, Patterned	L	18x11¼x8	For R Cab.	None	-	-	-	-	-	-	-	2-60W Std. MB
13	71948	Mesa	Molded, Patterned	L	18x11¼x11½	For S Cab.	None	-	-	-	-	-	-	-	2-60W Std. MB
7	72052	Sonata	Frameless	L▲	5x17½x6⅛	For R Cab.	None	-	-	-	-	-	-	-	2-75W Std. MB
7	72152	Sonata	Frameless	L▲	5x17½x10	For S Cab.	None	-	-	-	-	-	-	-	2-75W Std. MB
7	73190	Mirage	Frameless	L▲	5x12x6½	For R Cab.	None	-	-	-	-	-	-	-	2-60W Std. MB
8	73290	Horizon	Frameless	L	16x4½x2	For R Cab.	None	-	-	-	-	-	-	-	2-60W G25/G40
6	73591	Torino	Frameless	L▲	5⅜x13¾x6½	For R Cab.	None	-	-	-	-	-	-	-	2-75W Std. MB
7	735FL	Decorah	Frameless	L	16x4⅜x2	For R Cab.	None	-	-	-	-	-	-	-	2-60W G25/G40
22	73679	Adante (Oak)	Solid Oak, Honey	L▲	5⅜x13¼x7¼	For R Cab.	None	-	-	-	-	-	-	-	2-60W Std. MB
6	73690	Adante (Beveled)	Frameless	L	16½x6¼x2	For R Cab.	None	-	-	-	-	-	-	-	2-60W G25/G40
22	74279	Grant	Solid Oak, Honey	L	16¼x5½x3	For R Cab.	None	-	-	-	-	-	-	-	2-60W G25/G40
22	74379	Grant	Solid Oak, Honey	L	16¼x5½x6½	For S Cab.	None	-	-	-	-	-	-	-	2-60W G25/G40
15	745 Series	Spectrum	Molded, Acrylic Fin.	L	18x6½x3	For R Cab.	None	-	-	-	-	-	-	-	3-60W G25/40
15	746 Series	Spectrum	Molded, Acrylic Fin.	L	18x6½x5½	For S Cab.	None	-	-	-	-	-	-	-	3-60W G25/40
17	747BR	Verona	Molded, Brass Fin.	L	16x20	For R Cab.	None	-	-	-	-	-	-	-	3-60W G25/40
23	75719	Chapel Hill	Solid Oak, Honey	L	17¼x5½x3	For S Cab.	None	-	-	-	-	-	-	-	3-60W G25/40
19	76328	Canterbury	Hardwood, White	L	18x8x8	For R Cab.	None	-	-	-	-	-	-	-	2-60W Std. MB
19	76378	Canterbury	Solid Oak, Honey	L	18x8x8	For R Cab.	None	-	-	-	-	-	-	-	2-60W Std. MB
19	76428	Canterbury	Hardwood, White	L	18x8x11½	For S Cab.	None	-	-	-	-	-	-	-	2-60W Std. MB

*Cabinet bottom always provides an additional storage level.

▲ Packed in pairs.

MEDICINE CABINET SPECIFICATIONS

Page	Model No.	Style Name	Frame	Style T-Tri-View B-BiView S-Single SB-Slide-by L-Light WM-Wall Mirror	Overall Size W"H"D"	Mount Type S-Surface R-Recessed S/R-Surface or Recessed WM-Wall Mirror	Wall Opening W"H"D"	Hinge Type P-Piano C-Con. L-Leaf PN-Pin B-Butt	Single Door Hinge L-Left R-Right RV-Rev.	Cabinet Body S-Steel SS-Stainless P-Polystyrene W-Wood	Shelves			Matching Light Fixture	Recommended Bulbs Qty-Type
											Quantity *	G-Glass S-Steel P-Polystyrene AL-Aluminum	F-Fixed A-Adjustable		
19	76478	Canterbury	Solid Oak, Honey	L	18x8x11½	For S Cab.	None	-	-	-	-	-	-	-	2-60W Std. MB
16	76668	Maxim	Brass Finish & Black	L	18x7¼x9¼	For R Cab	None	-	-	-	-	-	-	-	2-60W Std. MB
16	76768	Maxim	Brass Finish & Black	L	18x7¼x12½	For S Cab	None	-	-	-	-	-	-	-	2-60W Std. MB
21	8120	Prairie	Hardwood, White	S	18x27½	R	14x18x3½	P	RV	S	2	P	A	70928	-
21	8122	Prairie	Hardwood, White	S	18x27½x5	S	None	P	RV	S	3	P	F	71028	-
21	812230	Prairie	Hardwood, White	T	30x28½x5½	S	None	L	-	S	2	S	F	OK81028	-
21	812236	Prairie	Hardwood, White	T	36x28½x5½	S	None	L	-	S	2	S	F	OK81628	-
21	8128	Prairie	Hardwood, White	S	18x27½	R	14x24x3½	P	RV	S	3	P	A	70928	-
21	8160	Prairie	Solid Oak, Blonde	S	18x27½	R	14x18x3½	P	RV	S	2	P	A	70968	-
21	8162	Prairie	Solid Oak, Blonde	S	18x27½x5	S	None	P	RV	S	3	P	F	71068	-
21	816230	Prairie	Solid Oak, Blonde	T	30x28½x5½	S	None	L	-	S	2	S	F	OK81068	-
21	816236	Prairie	Solid Oak, Blonde	T	36x28½x5½	S	None	L	-	S	2	S	F	OK81668	-
21	8168	Prairie	Solid Oak, Blonde	S	18x27½	R	14x24x3½	P	RV	S	3	P	A	70968	-
21	8170	Prairie	Solid Oak, Honey	S	18x27½	R	14x18x3½	P	RV	S	2	P	A	70978	-
21	8172	Prairie	Solid Oak, Honey	S	18x27½x5	S	None	P	RV	S	3	P	F	71078	-
21	817230	Prairie	Solid Oak, Honey	T	30x28½x5½	S	None	L	-	S	2	S	F	OK81078	-
21	817236	Prairie	Solid Oak, Honey	T	36x28½x5½	S	None	L	-	S	2	S	F	OK81678	-
21	8178	Prairie	Solid Oak, Honey	S	18x27½	R	14x24x3½	P	RV	S	3	P	A	70978	-
18	820	Baker Street	Hardwood, White	S	18x27	R	14x18x3½	P	RV	S	2	P	A	See p. 18	-
18	822	Baker Street	Hardwood, White	S	18x27x5	S	None	P	RV	S	3	P	F	See p. 18	-
23	8278	Chapel Hill	Solid Oak, Honey	S	17¼x27¼	R	14x24x3½	P	RV	S	3	S	F	75719	-
21	828	Baker Street	Hardwood, White	S	18x27	R	14x24x3½	P	RV	S	3	P	A	See p. 18	-
23	8370	Kingston	Solid Oak, Honey	S	16½x26½	R	14x18x3½	P	RV	S	2	S	A	71829	-
23	8378	Kingston	Solid Oak, Honey	S	16½x26½	R	14x24x3½	P	RV	S	3	S	A	71829	-
21	842230	Baker Street	Hardwood, White	T	30x28½x5½	S	None	L	-	S	2	S	F	BS84023	-
21	842236	Baker Street	Hardwood, White	T	36x28½x5½	S	None	L	-	S	2	S	F	BS84623	-
21	847230	Baker Street	Solid Oak, Honey	T	30x28½x5½	S	None	L	-	S	2	S	F	BS84073	-
21	847236	Baker Street	Solid Oak, Honey	T	36x28½x5½	S	None	L	-	S	2	S	F	BS84673	-
19	8520	Canterbury	Hardwood, White	S	18¼x27¼	R	14x18x3½	P	R	S	2	P	A	76328	-
19	8522	Canterbury	Hardwood, White	S	18¼x27¼x5½	S	None	P	R	S	3	P	F	76428	-
19	8528	Canterbury	Hardwood, White	S	18¼x27¼	R	14x24x3½	P	R	S	3	P	A	76328	-
19	8570	Canterbury	Solid Oak, Honey	S	18¼x27¼x5½	R	14x18x3½	P	R	S	2	P	A	76378	-
19	8572	Canterbury	Solid Oak, Honey	S	18¼x27¼	S	None	P	R	S	3	P	F	76378	-
19	8578	Canterbury	Solid Oak, Honey	S	18¼x27¼	R	14x24x3½	P	R	S	3	P	A	76378	-
21	870	Baker Street	Solid Oak, Honey	S	18x27	R	14x18x3½	P	RV	S	2	P	A	See p. 18	-
21	872	Baker Street	Solid Oak, Honey	S	18x27x5	S	None	P	RV	S	3	P	F	See p. 18	-
22	8770	Grant	Solid Oak, Honey	S	16¼x24¼	R	14x18x3½	P	RV	S	2	P	A	74279	-
22	8772	Grant	Solid Oak, Honey	S	16¼x24¼x5½	S	None	P	RV	S	2	P	F	74379	-
22	8773	Grant	Solid Oak, Honey	S	16¼x22	R	14x18x2½	B	RV	P	2	P	F	74279	-
22	8778	Grant	Solid Oak, Honey	S	16¼x26¼	R	14x24x3½	P	RV	S	3	P	A	74279	-
22	8778MOD	Grant	Solid Oak, Honey	S	16¼x26¼	R	14x24x3½	P	RV	S	6†	P	A	-	-
21	878	Baker Street	Solid Oak, Honey	S	18x27	R	14x24x3½	P	RV	S	3	P	A	See p. 18	-
27	902	Prestique	Wood, Oak Finish	S	16x20x4¾	S	None	B	RV	W	1	Wood	F	-	-
27	902BP	Prestique	Wood, Oak Finish	S	16x20x4¾	S	None	B	RV	W	1	Wood	F	-	-
27	902WH	Prestique	Wood, White Finish	S	16x20x4¾	S	None	B	RV	W	1	Wood	F	-	-
24	902224	Prestique	Hardwood, White	T	24x26x4¾	S	None	L	-	W	2	Wood	F	CR92429	-
24	902230	Prestique	Hardwood, White	T	30x30x4¾	S	None	L	-	W	2	Wood	F	CR93029	-
24	902236	Prestique	Hardwood, White	T	36x30x4¾	S	None	L	-	W	2	Wood	F	CR93629	-
24	902248	Prestique	Hardwood, White	T	48x30x4¾	S	None	L	-	W	2	Wood	F	CR94829	-
25	905224	Prestique	Frameless	T	24x26x4¾	S	None	C	-	W	2	Wood	F	CR92490	-
25	905230	Prestique	Frameless	T	30x30x4¾	S	None	C	-	W	2	Wood	F	CR93090	-
25	905236	Prestique	Frameless	T	36x30x4¾	S	None	C	-	W	2	Wood	F	CR93690	-
25	905248	Prestique	Frameless	T	48x30x4¾	S	None	C	-	W	2	Wood	F	CR94890	-
24	907224	Prestique	Solid Oak, Honey	T	24x26x4¾	S	None	L	-	W	2	Wood	F	CR92479	-
24	907224BP	Prestique	Solid Oak, Honey	T	24x26x4¾	S	None	L	-	W	2	Wood	F	CR92479	-
24	907230	Prestique	Solid Oak, Honey	T	30x30x4¾	S	None	L	-	W	2	Wood	F	CR93079	-
24	907230BP	Prestique	Solid Oak, Honey	T	30x30x4¾	S	None	L	-	W	2	Wood	F	CR93079	-
24	907236	Prestique	Solid Oak, Honey	T	36x30x4¾	S	None	L	-	W	2	Wood	F	CR93679	-
24	907236BP	Prestique	Solid Oak, Honey	T	36x30x4¾	S	None	L	-	W	2	Wood	F	CR93679	-

*Cabinet bottom always provides an additional storage level.

† Modular half shelves.

Page	Model No.	Style Name	Frame	Style T-Tri-View B-BiView S-Single SB-Slide-by L-Light WM-Wall Mirror	Overall Size W"H"D"	Mount Type S-Surface R-Recessed S/R-Surface or Recessed WM-Wall Mirror	Wall Opening W"H"D"	Hinge Type P-Piano C-Con. L-Leaf PN-Pin B-Butt	Single Door Hinge L-Left R-Right RV-Rev.	Cabinet Body S-Steel SS-Stainless P-Polystyrene W-Wood	Shelves Quantity *	Shelves G-Glass S-Steel P-Polystyrene AL-Aluminum	Shelves F-Fixed A-Adjustable	Matching Light Fixture	Recommended Bulbs Qty-Type
24	907248	Prestique	Solid Oak, Honey	T	48x30x4¾	S	None	L	-	W	2	Wood	F	CR94879	-
24	917224	Prestique	Solid Oak, Honey	T	24x26x4¾	S	None	L	-	W	2	Wood	F	CF92479	-
24	917230	Prestique	Solid Oak, Honey	T	30x30x4¾	S	None	L	-	W	2	Wood	F	CF93079	-
24	917236	Prestique	Solid Oak, Honey	T	36x30x4¾	S	None	L	-	W	2	Wood	F	CF93679	-
24	917248	Prestique	Solid Oak, Honey	T	48x30x4¾	S	None	L	-	W	2	Wood	F	CF94879	-
25	922	Prestique	Solid Oak & White	S	16x20x4¾	S	None	B	RV	W	1	Wood	F	-	-
25	927230	Prestique	Solid Oak & White	T	30x30x4¾	S	None	L		W	2	Wood	F	CW93079	-
25	927236	Prestique	Solid Oak & White	T	36x30x4¾	S	None	L	-	W	2	Wood	F	CW93679	-
25	927248	Prestique	Solid Oak & White	T	48x30x4¾	S	None	L	-	W	2	Wood	F	CW94879	-
25	928	Prestique	Solid Oak & White	S	16x26x4¾	S	None	B	RV	W	2	Wood	F	-	-
25	931230	Prestique	Brass Finish & Black	T	30x30x4¾	S	None	L	-	W	2	Wood	F	CB93019	-
25	931236	Prestique	Brass Finish & Black	T	36x30x4¾	S	None	L	-	W	2	Wood	F	CB93619	-
25	932	Prestique	Brass Finish & Black	S	16x20x4¾	S	None	B	RV	W	1	Wood	F	-	-
25	938	Prestique	Brass Finish & Black	S	16x26x4¾	S	None	B	RV	W	2	Wood	F	-	-
26	9422BC	Prestique	Wood, White Finish	S	15¾x23⅝x4⅛	S	None	PN	R	W	2	Wood	F	Built-in	2-60W G25/G40
26	942224	Prestique	Wood, White Finish	T	24x28⅞x4⅛	S	None	PN	-	W	2	Wood	F	Built-in	3-60W G25/G40
26	942230	Prestique	Wood, White Finish	T	30x28⅞x4⅛	S	None	PN	-	W	2	Wood	F	Built-in	4-60W G25/G40
26	942236	Prestique	Wood, White Finish	T	36x28⅞x4⅛	S	None	PN	-	W	2	Wood	F	Built-in	5-60W G25/G40
26	942248	Prestique	Wood, White Finish	T	48x28⅞x4⅛	S	None	PN	-	W	2	Wood	F	Built-in	5-60W G25/G40
26	9472	Prestique	Wood, Oak Finish	S	15¾x23⅝x4⅛	S	None	PN	R	W	2	Wood	F	Built-in	2-60W G25/G40
26	947224	Prestique	Wood, Oak Finish	T	24x28⅞x4⅛	S	None	PN	-	W	2	Wood	F	Built-in	3-60W G25/G40
26	947230	Prestique	Wood, Oak Finish	T	30x28⅞x4⅛	S	None	PN	-	W	2	Wood	F	Built-in	4-60W G25/G40
26	947236	Prestique	Wood, Oak Finish	T	36x28⅞x4⅛	S	None	PN	-	W	2	Wood	F	Built-in	5-60W G25/G40
26	947248	Prestique	Wood, Oak Finish	T	48x28⅞x4⅛	S	None	PN	-	W	2	Wood	F	Built-in	5-60W G25/G40
27	962224	Prestique	Wood, White Finish	T	24x25½x4¾	S	None	L	-	W	2	Wood	F	CR92425	-
27	962230	Prestique	Wood, White Finish	T	30x25½x4¾	S	None	L	-	W	2	Wood	F	CR93025	-
27	962236	Prestique	Wood, White Finish	T	36x25½x4¾	S	None	L	-	W	2	Wood	F	CR93625	-
27	962248	Prestique	Wood, White Finish	T	48x25½x4¾	S	None	L	-	W	2	Wood	F	CR94825	-
27	967224	Prestique	Wood, Oak Finish	T	24x25½x4¾	S	None	L	-	W	2	Wood	F	CR92475	-
27	967230	Prestique	Wood, Oak Finish	T	30x25½x4¾	S	None	L	-	W	2	Wood	F	CR93075	-
27	967236	Prestique	Wood, Oak Finish	T	36x25½x4¾	S	None	L	-	W	2	Wood	F	CR93675	-
27	967248	Prestique	Wood, Oak Finish	T	48x25½x4¾	S	None	L	-	W	2	Wood	F	CR94875	-
27	972225	Prestique	Wood, White Finish	2-Door	25½x28x4¾	S	None	D‡	-	W	5	Wood	F	-	-
22	973BC	Grant	Solid Oak, Honey	S	16x20	-	14x18X2½	B	RV	P	2	P	F	74279	-
27	977225	Prestique	Wood, Oak Finish	2-Door	25½x28x4¾	S	None	D‡	-	W	5	Wood	F	-	-
27	982	Prestique	Wood, Oak Finish	S	16x26x4¾	S	None	B	RV	W	2	Wood	F	-	-
27	982BP	Prestique	Wood, Oak Finish	S	16x26x4¾	S	None	B	RV	W	2	Wood	F	-	-
27	982WH	Prestique	Wood, White Finish	S	16x26x4¾	S	None	B	RV	W	2	Wood	F	-	-
10	BA93629	Bel Aire	Stainless Steel Trim	L	36x3¼x3	For R Cab	None	-	-	-	-	-	-	-	5-60W G25/G40
10	BA94829	Bel Aire	Stainless Steel Trim	L	48x3¼x3	For R Cab	None	-	-	-	-	-	-	-	6-60W G25/G40
16	BM63018	Maxim	Brass Finish & Black	L	30x7¼x11½	For S Cab	None	-	-	-	-	-	-	-	3-60W Std. MB
16	BM63618	Maxim	Brass Finish & Black	L	36x7¼x11½	For S Cab	None	-	-	-	-	-	-	-	4-60W Std. MB
21	BS84023	Baker Street	Hardwood Wh. Paint	L	30x6x6½	For S Cab	None	-	-	-	-	-	-	-	3-60W Std. MB
21	BS84073	Baker Street	Solid Oak, Honey	L	30x6x6½	For S Cab	None	-	-	-	-	-	-	-	3-60W Std. MB
21	BS84623	Baker Street	Hardwood Wh. Paint	L	36x6x6½	For S Cab	None	-	-	-	-	-	-	-	4-60W Std. MB
21	BS84673	Baker Street	Solid Oak Honey	L	36x6x6½	For S Cab	None	-	-	-	-	-	-	-	4-60W Std. MB
25	CB93019	Prestique	Brass Finish & Black	L	30x5⅞x5½	For S Cab	None	-	-	-	-	-	-	-	4-60W G25/G40
25	CB93619	Prestique	Brass Finish & Black	L	36x5⅞x5½	For S Cab	None	-	-	-	-	-	-	-	5-60W G25/G40
24	CF92479	Prestique	Solid Oak, Honey	L	24x7x5½	For S Cab	None	-	-	-	-	-	-	-	3-G25/G40
24	CF93079	Prestique	Solid Oak, Honey	L	30x7x5½	For S Cab	None	-	-	-	-	-	-	-	4-G25/G40
24	CF93679	Prestique	Solid Oak, Honey	L	36x7x5½	For S Cab	None	-	-	-	-	-	-	-	5-G25/G40
24	CF94879	Prestique	Solid Oak, Honey	L	48x7x5½	For S Cab	None	-	-	-	-	-	-	-	6-G25/G40
29	CL72429	Bel Aire Auxiliary	Stainless Steel Trim	L	24x2¾x1¾	For WM	None	-	-	-	-	-	-	-	-
29	CL73029	Bel Aire Auxiliary	Stainless Steel Trim	L	30x2¾x1¾	For WM	None	-	-	-	-	-	-	-	-
10	CL73629	Bel Aire	Stainless Steel Trim	L	36x3¼x1¾	For R Cab	None	-	-	-	-	-	-	-	6-60W G-16½CL
10	CL73729	Bel Aire	Stainless Steel Trim	L	36x3¼x5	For S Cab	None	-	-	-	-	-	-	-	6-60W G-16½CL
10	CL74829	Bel Aire	Stainless Steel Trim	L	48x3¼x1¾	For R Cab	None	-	-	-	-	-	-	-	8-60W G-16½CL
10	CL74929	Bel Aire	Stainless Steel Trim	L	48x3¼x5	For S Cab	None	-	-	-	-	-	-	-	8-60W G-16½CL
27	CR92425	Prestique	Wood, White Finish	L	24x7x5½	For S Cab	None	-	-	-	-	-	-	-	4-60W G25/G40

*Cabinet bottom always provides an additional storage level.

‡ Decorative exposed.

MEDICINE CABINET SPECIFICATIONS

Page	Model No.	Style Name	Frame	Style T-Tri-View B-BiView S-Single SB-Slide-by L-Light WM-Wall Mirror	Overall Size W"H"D"	Mount Type S-Surface R-Recessed S/R-Surface or Recessed WM-Wall Mirror	Wall Opening W"H"D"	Hinge Type P-Piano C-Con. L-Leaf PN-Pin B-Butt	Single Door Hinge L-Left R-Right RV-Rev.	Cabinet Body S-Steel SS-Stainless P-Polystyrene W-Wood	Shelves: Quantity *	Shelves: G-Glass S-Steel P-Polystyrene AL-Aluminum	Shelves: F-Fixed A-Adjustable	Matching Light Fixture	Recommended Bulbs Qty-Type
24	CR92429	Prestique	Hardwood, White	L	24x5⅞x5½	For S Cab	None	-	-	-	-	-	-	-	3-60W G25/G40
27	CR92475	Prestique	Wood,Oak Finish	L	24x7x5½	For S Cab	None	-	-	-	-	-	-	-	3-60W G25/G40
24	CR92479	Prestique	Solid Oak, Honey	L	24x5⅞x5½	For S Cab	None	-	-	-	-	-	-	-	3-60W G25/G40
25	CR92490	Prestique	Frameless	L	24x5⅞x5½	For S Cab	None	-	-	-	-	-	-	-	3-60W G25/G40
27	CR93025	Prestique	Wood, White Finish	L	30x7x5½	For S Cab	None	-	-	-	-	-	-	-	4-60W G25/G40
24	CR93029	Prestique	Hardwood, White	L	30x5⅞x5½	For S Cab	None	-	-	-	-	-	-	-	4-60W G25/G40
27	CR93075	Prestique	Wood, Oak Finish	L	30x7x5½	For S Cab	None	-	-	-	-	-	-	-	4-60W G25/G40
24	CR93079	Prestique	Solid Oak, Honey	L	30x5⅞x5½	For S Cab	None	-	-	-	-	-	-	-	4-60W G25/G40
25	CR93090	Prestique	Frameless	L	30x5⅞x5½	For S Cab..	None	-	-	-	-	-	-	-	4-60W G25/G40
27	CR93625	Prestique	Wood, White Finish	L	36x7x5½	For S Cab.	None	-	-	-	-	-	-	-	5-60W G25/G40
24	CR93629	Prestique	Hardwood, White	L	36x5⅞x5½	For S Cab.	None	-	-	-	-	-	-	-	5-60W G25/G40
27	CR93675	Prestique	Wood, Oak Finish	L	36x7x5½	For S Cab.	None	-	-	-	-	-	-	-	5-60W G25/G40
24	CR93679	Prestique	Solid Oak, Honey	L	36x5⅞x5½	For S Cab.	None	-	-	-	-	-	-	-	5-60W G25/G40
25	CR93690	Prestique	Frameless	L	36x5⅞x5½	For S Cab.	None	-	-	-	-	-	-	-	5-60W G25/G40
27	CR94825	Prestique	Wood, White Finish	L	48x7x5½	For S Cab.	None	-	-	-	-	-	-	-	4-60W G25/G40
24	CR94829	Prestique	Hardwood, White	L	48x5⅞x5½	For S Cab.	None	-	-	-	-	-	-	-	6-60W G25/G40
27	CR94875	Prestique	Wood, Oak Finish	L	48x7x5½	For S Cab.	None	-	-	-	-	-	-	-	6-60W G25/G40
24	CR94879	Prestique	Solid Oak, Honey	L	48x5⅞x5½	For S Cab.	None	-	-	-	-	-	-	-	6-60W G25/G40
25	CR94890	Prestique	Frameless	L	48x5⅞x5½	For S Cab.	None	-	-	-	-	-	-	-	6-60W G25/G40
12	CT53018	Country Floral	Molded Patterned	L	30x8x9¾	For S Cab.	None	-	-	-	-	-	-	-	3-60W MB
12	CT53618	Country Floral	Molded Patterned	L	36x8x9¾	For S Cab.	None	-	-	-	-	-	-	-	4-60W MB
25	CW93079	Prestique	Solid Oak & White	L	30x5⅞x5½	For S Cab.	None	-	-	-	-	-	-	-	4-60W G25/G40
25	CW93679	Prestique	Solid Oak & White	L	36x5⅞x5½	For S Cab.	None	-	-	-	-	-	-	-	5-60W G25/G40
25	CW94879	Prestique	Solid Oak & White	L	48x5⅞x5½	For S Cab.	None	-	-	-	-	-	-	-	6-60W G25/G40
8	HO32490	Horizon	Frameless	L	24x4½x5⅞	For S Cab.	None	-	-	-	-	-	-	-	3-60W G25/G40
8	HO33090	Horizon	Frameless	L	30x4¼x5⅞	For S Cab.	None	-	-	-	-	-	-	-	4-60W G25/G40
8	HO33690	Horizon	Frameless	L	36x4¼x5⅞	For S Cab.	None	-	-	-	-	-	-	-	4-60W G25/G40
8	HO34890	Horizon	Frameless	L	48x4¼x5⅞	For S Cab.	None	-	-	-	-	-	-	-	5-60W G25/G40
8	HO42490	Horizon	Frameless	L	24x4½x2¼	For R Cab.	None	-	-	-	-	-	-	-	3-60W G25/G40
8	HO43090	Aurora	Frameless	L	30x4½x2¼	For R Cab.	None	-	-	-	-	-	-	-	4-60W G25/G40
8	HO43690	Aurora	Frameless	L	36x4½x2¼	For R Cab.	None	-	-	-	-	-	-	-	4-60W G25/G40
8	HO44890	Aurora	Frameless	L	48x4½x2¼	For R Cab.	None	-	-	-	-	-	-	-	5-60W G25/G40
31	IL24	Commodore	Stainless Steel Trim	L	24x4x7½	For S Cab.	None	-	-	-	-	-	-	-	4-60W MB
31	IL30	Commodore	Stainless Steel Trim	L	30x4x7½	For S Cab.	None	-	-	-	-	-	-	-	4-60W MB
31	IL36	Commodore	Stainless Steel Trim	L	36x4x7½	For S Cab.	None	-	-	-	-	-	-	-	4-60W MB
31	IL48	Commodore	Stainless Steel Trim	L	48x4x7½	For S Cab.	None	-	-	-	-	-	-	-	6-60W MB
3	LBC 10	Le Baccarat	Frameless	S	24x35⅜	R	16½x25¼x3⅞	C	R	SS	3	G	A	-	-
3	LBC 10SM	Le Baccarat	Frameless	S	24x35⅜	S	None	C	R	SS	3	G	A	-	-
3	LBM 15	Le Baccarat	Frameless	WM	24x35⅜	WM	None	-	-	-	-	-	-	-	-
13	ME73048	Mesa	Molded, Patterned	L	30x11¼x8⅛	For S Cab.	None	-	-	-	-	-	-	-	3-60W Std. MB
13	ME73648	Mesa	Molded, Patterned	L	36x11¼x8⅛	For S Cab.	None	-	-	-	-	-	-	-	4-60W Std. MB
21	OK81028	Prairie	Hardwood, White	L	30x8x11	For S Cab.	None	-	-	-	-	-	-	-	3-60W MB
21	OK81068	Prairie	Solid Oak, Blonde	L	30x8x11	For S Cab.	None	-	-	-	-	-	-	-	3-60W MB
21	OK81078	Prairie	Solid Oak, Honey	L	30x8x11	For S Cab.	None	-	-	-	-	-	-	-	3-60W MB
21	OK81628	Prairie	Hardwood, White	L	36x8x11	For S Cab.	None	-	-	-	-	-	-	-	4-60W MB
21	OK81668	Prairie	Solid Oak, Blonde	L	36x8x11	For S Cab.	None	-	-	-	-	-	-	-	4-60W MB
21	OK81678	Prairie	Solid Oak, Honey	L	36x8x11	For S Cab.	None	-	-	-	-	-	-	-	4-60W MB
31	PEM2424	Commodore	Stainless Steel	WM	24x24	S	None	-	-	-	-	-	-	-	-
31	PEM3024	Commodore	Stainless Steel	WM	30x24	S	None	-	-	-	-	-	-	-	-
31	PEM3036	Commodore	Stainless Steel	WM	30x36	S	None	-	-	-	-	-	-	-	-
31	PEM3624	Commodore	Stainless Steel	WM	36x24	S	None	-	-	-	-	-	-	-	-
31	PEM3636	Commodore	Stainless Steel	WM	36x36	S	None	-	-	-	-	-	-	-	-
31	PEM4824	Commodore	Stainless Steel	WM	48x24	S	None	-	-	-	-	-	-	-	-
31	PEM4836	Commodore	Stainless Steel	WM	48x36	S	None	-	-	-	-	-	-	-	-
31	PEM6036	Commodore	Stainless Steel	WM	60x36	S	None	-	-	-	-	-	-	-	-
3	PRC1148	Primevère	Clear Mirror	T	48x37⅜	R	36⅞x32⅞x3⅞	C	-	SS	3	G	A	PRL1048	-
3	PRC1148SM	Primevère	Clear Mirror	T	48x37⅜	S	None	C	-	SS	3	G	F	PRL1048	-
3	PRC1160	Primevère	Clear Mirror	T	60x37⅜	R	48⅞x32⅞x3⅞	C	-	SS	3	G	A	PRL1060	-

*Cabinet bottom always provides an additional storage level.

Page	Model No.	Style Name	Frame	Style T-Tri-View B-BiView S-Single SB-Slide-by L-Light WM-Wall Mirror	Overall Size W"H"D"	Mount Type S-Surface R-Recessed S/R-Surface or Recessed WM-Wall Mirror	Wall Opening W"H"D"	Hinge Type P-Piano C-Con. L-Leaf PN-Pin B-Butt	Single Door Hinge L-Left R-Right RV-Rev.	Cabinet Body S-Steel SS-Stainless P-Polystyrene W-Wood	Shelves			Matching Light Fixture	Recommended Bulbs Qty-Type
											Quantity *	G-Glass S-Steel P-Polystyrene AL-Aluminum	F-Fixed A-Adjustable		
3	PRC1160SM	Primevère	Clear Mirror	T	60x37⅜	S	None	C	-	SS	3	G	F	PRL1060	-
3	PRC2148	Primevère	Smoked Mirror	T	48x37⅜	R	36⅞x32⅞x3⅞	C	-	SS	3	G	A	PRL2048	-
3	PRC2148SM	Primevère	Smoked Mirror	T	48x37⅜	S	None	C	-	SS	3	G	F	PRL2048	-
3	PRL1048	Primevère	Clear Mirror	L	48x4¼x5⅜	For S/R Cab.	None	-	-	S	-	-	-	-	Flourescent Incl.
3	PRL1060	Primevère	Clear Mirror	L	60x4¼x5⅜	For S/R Cab.	None	-	-	S	-	-	-	-	Flourescent Incl.
3	PRL2048	Primevère	Smoked Mirror	L	48x4¼x5⅜	For S/R Cab.	None	-	-	S	-	-	-	-	Included
10	SB22429	Bel Aire 2	Stainless Steel Trim	L	23⅜x3x5¾	For S Cab.	None	-	-	-	-	-	-	-	4-60W G25/G40
11	SB22529	Vienna	Chrome Trim	L	24x4x5½	For S Cab.	None	-	-	-	-	-	-	-	3-60W G25/G40
10	SB23029	Bel Aire 2	Stainless Steel Trim	L	29x3x5¾	For S Cab.	None	-	-	-	-	-	-	-	4-60W G25/G40
11	SB23129	Vienna	Chrome Trim	L	30x4x5½	For S Cab.	None	-	-	-	-	-	-	-	4-60W G25/G40
10	SB23629	Bel Aire 2	Stainless Steel Trim	L	35x3x5¾	For S Cab.	None	-	-	-	-	-	-	-	5-60W G25/G40
11	SB23729	Vienna	Chrome Trim	L	36x4x5½	For S Cab.	None	-	-	-	-	-	-	-	5-60W G25/G40
10	SB63629	Bel Aire	Stainless Steel Trim	L	36x3¼x6½	For S Cab.	None	-	-	-	-	-	-	-	5-60W G25/G40
10	SB64829	Bel Aire	Stainless Steel Trim	L	48x3¼x6½	For S Cab.	None	-	-	-	-	-	-	-	6-60W G25/G40
30	SD15	Beauty Glide	Stainless Steel Trim	SB	24x18¾	R	21½x17x3½	-	-	S	1	S	A	-	-
30	SD41	Beauty Glide	Stainless Steel Trim	SB	27½x19¼	R	26¼x17¼x3½	-	-	S	1	S	A	-	-
30	SDL25	Beauty Glide	Stainless Steel Trim	SB	24x21¼	R	21½x16½x3½	-	-	S	1	S	A	Built-in	Flourescent Incl.
30	SDL82	Beauty Glide	Stainless Steel Trim	SB	27½x22	R	26½x18¼x3½	-	-	S	1	S	A	Built-in	Flourescent Incl.
19	SE23028	Canterbury	Hardwood, White	L	30x8x11	For S Cab.	None	-	-	-	-	-	-	-	3-60W Std. MB
19	SE23078	Canterbury	Solid Oak, Honey	L	30x8x11	For S Cab.	None	-	-	-	-	-	-	-	3-60W Std. MB
19	SE23628	Canterbury	Hardwood, White	L	36x8x11	For S Cab.	None	-	-	-	-	-	-	-	4-60W Std. MB
19	SE23678	Canterbury	Solid Oak, Honey	L	36x8x11	For S Cab.	None	-	-	-	-	-	-	-	4-60W Std. MB
19	SE24828	Canterbury	Hardwood, White	L	48x8x11	For S Cab.	None	-	-	-	-	-	-	-	5-60W Std. MB
19	SE24878	Canterbury	Solid Oak, Honey	L	48x8x11	For S Cab.	None	-	-	-	-	-	-	-	5-60W Std. MB
22	SG32479	Grand Oak II	Solid Oak, Honey	L	24x55x5¼	For S Cab.	None	-	-	-	-	-	-	-	3-60W G25/G40
22	SG33079	Grand Oak II	Solid Oak, Honey	L	29x5⅝x5¼	For S Cab.	None	-	-	-	-	-	-	-	4-60W G25/G40
22	SG33679	Grand Oak II	Solid Oak, Honey	L	35x5⅝x5¼	For S Cab.	None	-	-	-	-	-	-	-	5-60W G25/G40
22	SG34879	Grand Oak II	Solid Oak, Honey	L	47x5⅝x5¼	For S Cab.	None	-	-	-	-	-	-	-	6-60W G25/G40
14	SP132WH	Spectrum	Molded, Acrylic Fin.	L	30x6½x5¼	For S Cab.	None	-	-	-	-	-	-	-	4-60W G25/G40
14	SP133WH	Spectrum	Molded, Acrylic Fin.	L	36x6½x5¼	For S Cab.	None	-	-	-	-	-	-	-	5-60W G25/G40
14	SP134WH	Spectrum	Molded, Acrylic Fin.	L	48x6½x5¼	For S Cab.	None	-	-	-	-	-	-	-	6-60W G25/G40
31	V24	Commodore	Stainless Steel Trim	SB	24¼x8¾x4¼	S	None	-	-	Cosmetic Box, Mirrored Door					
31	V30	Commodore	Stainless Steel Trim	SB	30¼x8¾x4¼	S	None	-	-	Cosmetic Box, Mirrored Door					
31	V36	Commodore	Stainless Steel Trim	SB	36¼x8¾x4¼	S	None	-	-	Cosmetic Box, Mirrored Door					
31	V48	Commodore	Stainless Steel Trim	SB	48¼x8¾x4¼	S	None	-	-	Cosmetic Box, Mirrored Door					
31	VM218P	Commodore	Stainless Steel Trim	SB	18¼x32x4⅛	S	None	-	-	Cosmetic Box & Mirror, Styrene Door					
31	VM224M	Commodore	Stainless Steel Trim	SB	24¼x32x4⅛	S	None	-	-	Cosmetic Box & Mirror, Mirrored Door					
31	VM224P	Commodore	Stainless Steel Trim	SB	24¼x32x4⅛	S	None	-	-	Cosmetic Box & Mirror, Styrene Door					
31	VM230M	Commodore	Stainless Steel Trim	SB	30¼x32x4⅛	S	None	-	-	Cosmetic Box & Mirror, Mirrored Door					
31	VM230P	Commodore	Stainless Steel Trim	SB	30¼x32x4⅛	S	None	-	-	Cosmetic Box & Mirror, Styrene Door					
31	VM236M	Commodore	Stainless Steel Trim	SB	36¼x32x4⅛	S	None	-	-	Cosmetic Box & Mirror, Mirrored Door					
31	VM236P	Commodore	Stainless Steel Trim	SB	36¼x32x4⅛	S	None	-	-	Cosmetic Box & Mirror, Styrene Door					
20	WH53023	White Marble	Solid Oak & White	L	30x7¼x12¼	For S Cab.	None	-	-	-	-	-	-	-	3-60W MB
20	WH53623	White Marble	Solid Oak & White	L	36x7¼x12¼	For S Cab.	None	-	-	-	-	-	-	-	4-60W MB
20	WH54823	White Marble	Solid Oak & White	L	48x7¼x12¼	For S Cab.	None	-	-	-	-	-	-	-	5-60W MB

*Cabinet bottom always provides an additional storage level.

A NORTEK COMPANY

P.O. Box 140, Hartford, WI 53027 1-800-548-0790 In Canada: Broan Limited 1-905-670-2500
Broan reserves the right to change product and specifications without notice.
Printed in the U.S.A.

ALL THE COMFORTS OF HOME™

99850016D
B69

C588
BuyLine 8620

COLLECTIONS

LUXURY BATHROOM FAUCETS AND ACCESSORIES

By **JADO**

Dear JADO friends,

We are pleased to present you with this showcase of continuing refinements in our line of luxury bath fixtures. The products featured in this brochure once again demonstrate JADO's commitment to provide you with the highest quality available in the industry in both design and performance.

JADO remains at the forefront in the development of new design. The addition of Wyndemere Series and Telluride Series represent our latest achievements in coordinated design. The Crystal Collection offers design versatility with the radiance of crystal levers. A brilliant silver finish, with the durability of our UltraBrass® finish, is now available in the Platinum Nickel Collection. And as always, the beauty of our design is complemented by JADO's precision engineering to make sure the beauty lasts.

We invite you to visit an authorized JADO dealer to fully appreciate the beauty and craftsmanship of our luxury bath plumbing and hardware. We are confident you will agree that JADO's commitment to the finest in design and engineering continue to be unmatched in the industry.

Dennis D. Dickover
President
JADO, U.S.A.

Available Finishes

Gold

UltraBrass®

Polished Chrome

Brushed Nickel

Platinum Nickel

Brushed Nickel/ Gold

SiNi/Gold

Available Finishes Not Pictured:
Polished Chrome/Gold
Polished Chrome/UltraBrass®

Warranties

JADO Bathroom & Hardware Manufacturing Corp. provides the finest warranties in the industry.

A LIFETIME MECHANICAL WARRANTY is provided against defects in materials and workmanship.

The GENERAL FINISH WARRANTY is a full 10 years from the date of purchase, against manufacture related defects in materials and workmanship.

ULTRABRASS carries a full LIFETIME WARRANTY against tarnishing.

PLATINUM-NICKEL, the newest line, also carries a LIFETIME WARRANTY against tarnishing.

JADO warranties carry the normal limitations regarding proper installation, abuse or mishandling. Contact your authorized JADO dealer who has all the details and conditions on JADO plumbing and hardware warranties. JADO means integrity throughout the world.

030/010
Robe hook

030/145
Tissue holder with
cover

030/133
Soap dish

030/150
Towel ring 6"

030/141
Tumbler clear

SERIES
TELLURIDE

030/600
Towel bar 24"

833/018
Widespread lavatory
set - flat spout

834/448
Roman tub set
with hand shower

833/008 Widespread lavatory set

3

027/141
Tumbler clear

027/612
Clear shelf 24"

027/150
Towel ring 6"

027/600
Towel bar 24"

027/911
Toilet brush set
wall mounted

027/132
Soap dish clear

807/875
Roman tub set
with hand shower

027/145
Tissue holder
with cover

SERIES
AMADEA

807/003 Widespread lavatory set

4

016/145
Tissue holder with
cover

016/911
Toilet brush set -
wall mounted

016/121
Soap dish - clear

016/150
Towel ring 6"

016/612
Clear shelf 24"

016/010
Robe hook

016/600
Towel bar 24"

016/141
Tumbler clear

The
Wyndemere
Collection

816/003 Widespread lavatory set

Crystal knob
handle selection

033/145
Tissue holder
with cover

891/650
Pressure balanced
shower set

033/150
Towel ring 6"

891/903
Single hole
lavatory set

Series
Oriental

033/141
Tumbler clear

033/600
Towel bar 24"

894/933
Roman tub set
with hand shower

893/933 Widespread lavatory set

Cross handle
selection

Crystal handle
selection

Curved lever handle
selection

Porcelain handle
selection

THE
CLASSIC
COLLECTION

853/948 Widespread lavatory set

820/751
Mirror

508/010
Robe hook

508/146
Tissue holder

855/948
3-Valve tub and
shower set

7

SERIES
EVERGREEN

855/927 Widespread lavatory set

Lever handle selection

014/600
Towel bar 24"

855/927
Roman tub set with hand shower

875/907
Single control thermostatic shower set

037/010
Robe hook

037/145
Tissue holder with cover

037/600
towel bar 24"

837/011
Widespread lavatory set

Series
Vogue

837/001 Widespread lavatory set

508/150
Towel ring 6"

508/010
Robe hook
508/145
Hooded tissue holder

THE
SANTA FÉ
COLLECTION

853/948 Widespread lavatory set

181 series-cabinet knob
611 series-ball cabinet knob
754 series-cabinet knob

508/600 Towel bar 24"
853/948 Spread set

Crystal knob handle
selection

030/150
Towel ring 6"

030/145
Tissue holder
with cover

030/010
Robe hook

859/925
Complete personal
hand shower set

The
Rainbow
Collection

030/612
Clear shelf 24"

030/600
Towel bar 24"

830/405
Widespread lavatory set-
flat spout - rope rings

833/905 Widespread lavatory set

033/141
Tumbler clear

033/140
Tissue holder

Lever handle
selection

033/010
Robe hook

033/600
Towel bar 24"

875/908
Single control thermostatic
shower set

Series
Colonial

853/998 Widespread lavatory set

892/928
3-Hole bidet set

033/612
Clear shelf 24"

031/010
Robe hook

843/992
3-Valve tub and
shower set

Lever handle
selection

843/912
Widespread lavatory
set-flat spout

The
Golden Gate
Collection

843/412 Widespread lavatory set

031/145
Tissue holder
with cover

031/600
Towel bar 24"

031/150
Towel ring 6"

843/903
Widespread lavatory
set - C spout - levers

501/150
Towel ring 6"

501/600
Towel bar 24"

501/145
Tissue holder with
cover

501/185
Shaving mirror

Series

Perlrand

893/902 Widespread lavatory set

Swan

896/302 Roman tub set

Rhapsody crystal lever
handle selection

Solid knob handle
selection

Curved handle
selection

862/102
Wet Bar faucet

508/010
Robe hook

508/150
Towel ring 6"

508/145
Tissue holder with
cover

508/600
Towel bar 24"

853/998
Widespread lavatory
set - low sprout - cross
handles

853/968
Widespread lavatory
set - Porcelain handles

853/938
Widespread lavatory
set - cross handles

855/993
Roman tub set

The
Platinum Nickel
Collection

853/948 Widespread lavatory set

14

Perlrand

894/815
Widespread lavatory set

Oriental

893/934
Widespread lavatory set

Crystal Collections

CLASSIC

853/868
Widespread lavatory set

Perlrand

893/902
Widespread lavatory set

15

LUXURY BATHROOM FAUCETS AND ACCESSORIES FORGED FROM BRASS

Products Available

Single Hole LAV Sets
Widespread LAV Sets
Wet Bar Faucets
Single Hole Bidet Sets
3-Hole Bidet Sets
Roman Tub Sets
Roman Tub with Hand Shower
Pressure Balanced Tub and Shower Sets
Pressure Balanced Shower Sets
3 Valve Tub and Shower Sets
2 Valve Shower Sets
Single Control Thermostatic Shower Sets
3/4" Thermostatic Mixing Valve Sets
5-Port Diverters
4-Port Diverters
1/2" and 3/4" Wall Valves
Body Sprays
Wall Angle Stops

Hand Shower Systems
Robe Hooks
6" Towel Rings
8" Towel Rings
12" Towel Rings
18" Towel Bars
24" Towel Bars
30" Towel Bars
Tissue Holders
Tumbler Holders
Soap Dish Holders
24" Shelves
Mirrors
Facial Tissue Box
Waste Paper Baskets
Wire Soap Trays

1/4 Turn Ceramic Disc Cartridge-LIFETIME WARRANTY

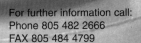
For further information call:
Phone 805 482 2666
FAX 805 484 4799

P.O. BOX 1329 CAMARILLO, CA 93011

17

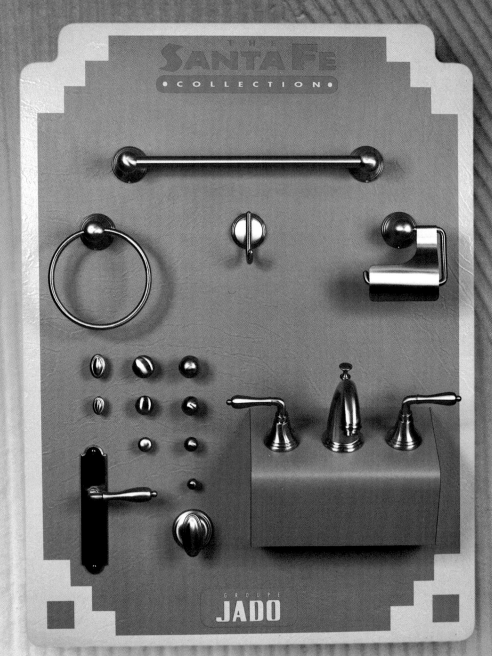

Elegant brushed nickel products inspired by the tradition of the Southwest.

PRODUCTS AVAILABLE

Lavatory Faucets

Bar Faucets

Shower Sets

Roman Tub Sets

Tub & Shower Sets

Hand Shower Systems

Body Sprays

Towel Bars

Towel Rings

Robe Hooks

Tissue Holders

Tumbler Holders

Soap Dish Holder

Shelves

Mirrors

Door Hardware

Cabinet Hardware.

- Lifetime limited mechanical warranty
- Ten year finish warranty
- Lifetime 1/4 turn ceramic disc cartridge warranty.

JADO®

P.O. BOX 1329 CAMARILLO, CA 93011
Phone 805.482.2666 FAX 805.484.4799

Topline TAMARAC

Topline Tamarac, finished in gleaming chrome or polished brass, is timeless and traditional with its understated elegance and choice of cross or lever handles. Coordinating a complete JADO look are accessories that include a robe hook, towel ring, tumbler holder, shower set and single-control tub and shower combination.

Topline PHOENIX

Cleanly modern in design, the graceful curve of the Topline Phoenix faucet creates a superb accent compatible with almost any style of bath. Topline Phoenix can be paired with lever, knob or cross handles and is available in chrome and polished brass. The product line consists of the tissue holder, robe hook, towel ring, soap dish, tumbler holder and shower set.

WATERMASTER SERIES™

Put JADO quality and design to work in your kitchen.

JADO®

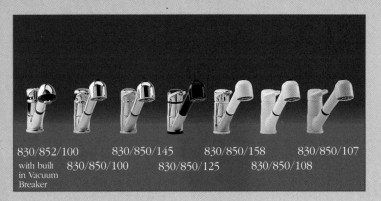

830/852/100
with built
in Vacuum
Breaker
830/850/100

830/850/145

830/850/125

830/850/158

830/850/108

830/850/107

The 830/850 and 830/852 single-lever kitchen faucet sets combine simplicity, versatility and contemporary European design. The choice of spray or stream at the touch of a button and the pull-out faucet head give you complete control over water flow. The single lever ceramic disc cartridge carries a lifetime mechanical warranty, and the 830/852 includes a non-drip integral vacuum breaker that conforms to IAPMO code approvals. The 830/850 and 830/852 sets are available in a wide selection of colors and finishes, including Almond, White, Polished Chrome, Chrome/Black split finish, Polished Chrome/White split finish, or Brushed Chrome/Chrome split finish. Includes 10" cover plate.

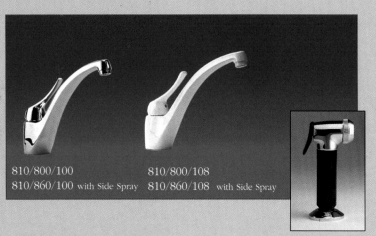

810/800/100
810/860/100 with Side Spray

810/800/108
810/860/108 with Side Spray

The 810/800 and 810/860 single-lever kitchen faucet sets add a touch of international flair with a gracefully sculpted solid cast swing spout. The long, arched spout of either the 810/800 or 810/860 set easily accommodates larger cookware, and the 810/860 includes a companion side sprayer to provide additional reach and utility. The single lever ceramic disc cartridge carries a lifetime mechanical warranty. The 810/800 and 810/860 sets are available in Polished Chrome, White, and Polished Chrome/White split finish. Includes 10" cover plate.

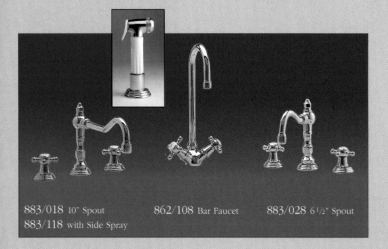

883/018 10" Spout
883/118 with Side Spray

862/108 Bar Faucet

883/028 6 1/2" Spout

The 883 series kitchen faucet sets with separate spout and hot/cold valves inherit a warm, traditional look from our Classic Series design. A choice of spout length (10" or 6-1/2") and an available companion side spray offer the versatility to meet both your functional requirements and design tastes. The 1/4-turn ceramic disc cartridge carries a lifetime mechanical warranty. The 883/018, 883/028 and 883/118 sets are available in Polished Chrome, UltraBrass or Brushed Nickel finish and accented with hot and cold trim buttons. The 862/108 bar faucet set (shown) is one of several designs available from our collective series of bath fixtures. One can attractively be incorporated with any of the sets listed above. The 862/108 set is available in Polished Chrome, UltraBrass, Brushed Nickel, Platinum Nickel or Chrome/UltraBrass split finish.

JADO WaterMaster Series kitchen faucet sets are manufactured under the same demanding specifications for design, engineering and quality as those used to create our luxury bath fixtures and accessories. All WaterMaster sets are engineered to comply with 2.2 gpm water-conserving flow rate codes.

JADO®

P.O. Box 1329   Camarillo, CA 93011
Phone 805.482.2666   Fax 805.484.4799

JADO

JADO Introduces their exclusive "Diamond Finish"… with a Lifetime Warranty!

DIAMOND FINISH WARRANTY: A Lifetime **warranty** against tarnishing is offered on all "Diamond Finish" products.

FEATURES: TARNISH & CORROSION RESISTANT
Special high technology coatings, initiated in a computer controlled environment, are applied to meticulously cleaned brass surfaces of the product, resulting in a simulation of polished brass finish that will resist tarnishing due to UV rays or humidity.

BENEFIT: JADO products subjected to Diamond Finishing can successfully be placed in situations of high humidity or intense sun with no concern to tarnishing-ever! Salt air, high humidity, direct UV rays, and chemical influences of household cleaners will not tarnish JADO Diamond Finish products.

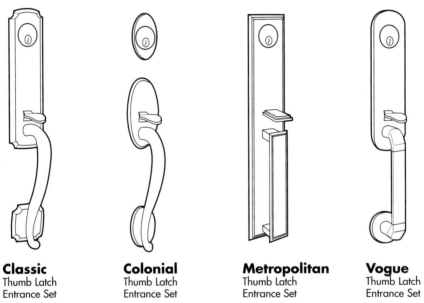

Classic
Thumb Latch
Entrance Set

Colonial
Thumb Latch
Entrance Set

Metropolitan
Thumb Latch
Entrance Set

Vogue
Thumb Latch
Entrance Set

FEATURE: POLISHED BRASS APPEARANCE

BENEFIT: The Diamond Finish simulated polished brass color has been so closely matched to actual polished brass that there is no cause for concern in placing the two finishes in close proximity. Interior door hardware sets of traditional polished brass finish can be used as a coordinate to Diamond Finish entry sets.

CARE OF PRODUCTS:
Diamond Finish requires no scrubbing or heavy polishing. Just a simple light polishing with a soft cloth will remove dust and fingerprints, and restore the high luster to the product.

ALSO AVAILABLE IN COORDINATING DIAMOND FINISH INTERIOR HARDWARE

Traditional   SouthWest

"Naturally Aging Finish"
THE
· PATINA ·
COLLECTION™
JADO

25

"Naturally Aging Finish"

THE ·PATINA· COLLECTION™
JADO

754/032

416/353

422/451

422/446

272/040

424/446

754/096

26

THE
·PATINA·
COLLECTION

C588
BuyLine 8620

422/451

416/354

754/096

754/032

272/040

420/446

27

The Patina Collection is the original "Naturally Aging Finish" manufactured exclusively by JADO. Its dramatic design is true to the heritage of quality craftsmanship that is JADO's world-wide trademark. As the newest member of the TopLine Series, the Patina Collection is competitively priced, yet unmistakably JADO.

Patina's precision craftsmanship is backed by a lifetime mechanical warranty. Known by many as JADO's personal seal of approval, this warranty is by far the most respectable in the industry.

JADO's Patina Finish is guaranteed to age gracefully. Classic warmth and elegance combine to make this one of the most sought after finishes in the country. The Patina Collection entry set is accompanied by a wide variety of passage and dummy sets, as well as cabinet hardware.

To learn more about all the precision engineering and incomparable design of JADO hardware and plumbing products, we invite you to visit an authorized JADO designer showroom.

The Patina Collection by JADO

JADO®

P.O. Box 1329, Camarillo, CA 93011

For further information call:
Phone 805 482 2666
FAX 805 484 4799

28

Topline™

Hardware
Collections

By **JADO**

422/451

416/354

422/353

419/446

420/446

424/446

444/446

445/446

Topline

422/446

423/446

426/446

Topline II

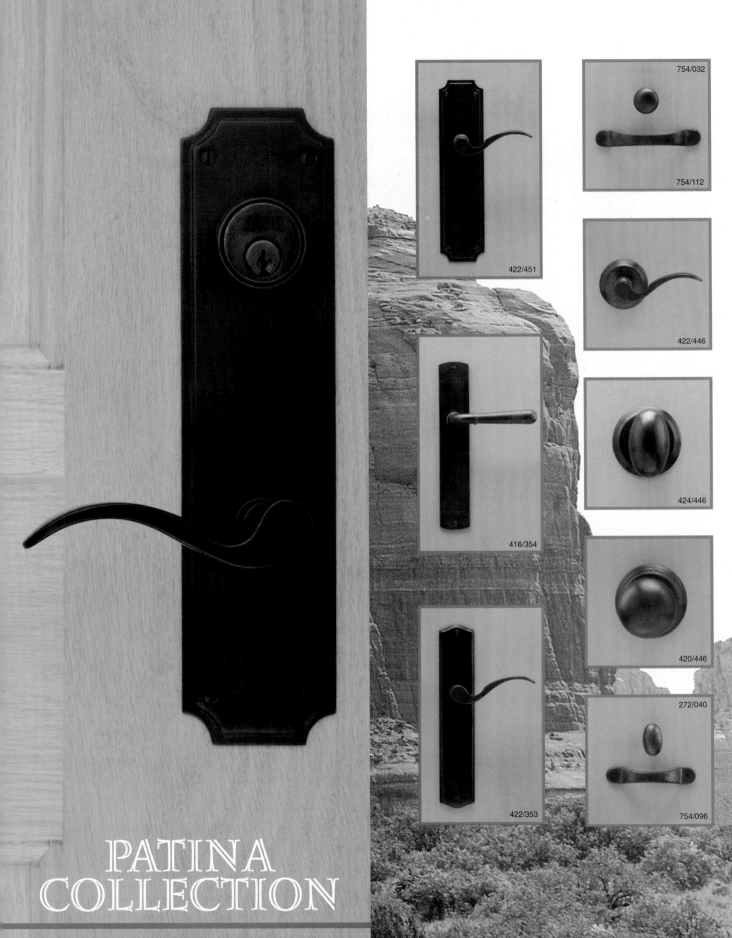

754/032

754/112

422/451

422/446

416/354

424/446

420/446

272/040

422/353

754/096

PATINA
COLLECTION

NuTone®

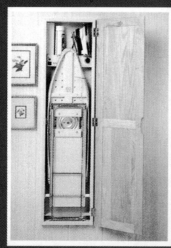

Door Chimes • Pushbuttons • Exhaust Fans • Central Ventilation
Electric Heaters • Attic Cooling Fans • Whole House Ventilators
Kitchen Ventilation • Ceiling Fans • Central Cleaning • Ironing Centers
Food Center • Lighting • Intercoms • Music Distribution Systems
Video Door Answering • Bath Cabinets & Hardware

NuTone®
BUILDING SOLUTIONS

SmartSense™ Automatic Fans

Fans that give user-friendly a new meaning!

NuTone's SmartSense Fans are a must for the modern home. Automatic activation provides convenience while protecting the bathroom from the damaging effects of excess humidity.

- The fan is automatically activated by humidity – helps fight mold and mildew
- The light is automatically activated by motion – provides bright, safe lighting
- Fan can be set on automatic or can be manually operated if desired
- Convenient night light
- White polymeric grille

NuTone's SmartSense™ Timer provides a choice of programmed operating profiles to provide powerful ventilation automatically.

- Ideal for use in businesses or small offices where regular exchanges of air are required
- Improves indoor air quality by supplying continuous makeup air
- Choose from several operational time profiles to meet any indoor air quality needs

Imagine being able to walk into a room and have it lighted for you or have the bathroom fan automatically activated when taking a shower! (Available unlighted version.) ℗℗℗

VS-95 Switch
- With auto/off switch
- 3 on-off switches for vent, light and night light
- For two-gang outlet box

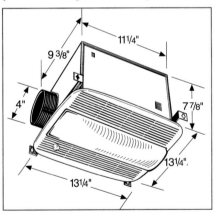

QT100LH, QT100LM, QT100LHM

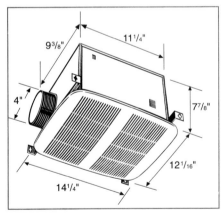

QT110H, QT90T

Model No.	Description	For Baths Up To	Other Rooms Up To	Duct Size	Lamp Watts	Amp Rating	Certified Test Data Air Delivery	Sound Level
SmartSense Fans								
QT90T	Ceiling Fan (Timer)	85 sq ft	115 sq ft	4"	–	.5	90 CFM	1.5 sones
QT110H	Ceiling Fan (Humidity Sensor)	105 sq ft	135 sq ft	4"	–	.65	110 CFM	2.0 sones
QT100LH	Ceiling Fan/Light (Humidity Sensor)	95 sq ft	125 sq ft	4"	100/7	.65	100 CFM	1.5 sones
QT100LM	Ceiling Fan/Light (Motion Sensor)	95 sq ft	125 sq ft	4"	100/7	.65	100 CFM	1.5 sones
QT110LHM	Ceiling Fan/Light (Hum./Mot. Sensor)	95 sq ft	125 sq ft	4"	100/7	.65	100 CFM	1.5 sones

2

NuTone

NEW!

Imagine an efficient ventilation fan that can hardly be heard at all! *mpp*

Ultra-quiet and energy efficient all in one!

NuTone has developed a ventilation fan that can hardly be heard at all! The Ultra-QuieTTest fan series provides efficient, powerful ventilation while being very unobtrusive to its environment.

- Highly energy efficient – consumes half the energy of standard fans
- Perfect for any room where ventilation is desired – bathroom, powder room, den or office
- Suitable for continuous ventilation applications
- Meets specific ventilation requirements of
  - Good Cents Program
  - Washington State Ventilation and Indoor Air Quality Code
- Easy hanger bar mounting

Model No.	Description	For Baths Up To	Other Rooms Up To	Duct Size	Watts	Amp Rating	Certified Test Data Air Delivery	Sound Level
Ultra-QuieTTest Fans								
LS50	Ceiling Fan	45 sq ft	60 sq ft	4"	21	.15	50 CFM	0.3 sones
LS80	Ceiling Fan	75 sq ft	100 sq ft	4"	24	.22	80 CFM	0.8 sones
LS100	Ceiling Fan	95 sq ft	125 sq ft	4"	38	.30	110 CFM	1.5 sones

9³/₈"   11¹/₄"
4"   7⁷/₈"
12¹/₁₆"
14¹/₄"

LS50, LS80, LS100

NuTone Fans Are Rated by Sones and CFM

- *A sone is an internationally recognized unit of loudness which tells in a single number the total sound output of the device being tested. One Sone, for example, is equivalent to the sound of a modern refrigerator operating in a quiet kitchen.*
- *CFM = Cubic Feet per Minute of air delivery*

NuTone

QuieTTest®
Fan-Lights

NuTone QuieTTest™ powerful ventilation

NuTone QuieTTest fans combine powerful air movement with very quiet operation.

- A selection of 10 QuieTTest models let you freshen rooms of every size – powder rooms, dressing rooms, even today's largest baths.
- Rounded, low-profile grilles add distinction to your room.
- Six models let you bring QuieTTest performance to your tub or shower – install with GFI branch circuit wiring.
- All QuieTTest Fans include prewired outlet boxes with plug-in receptacles for easy installation.

NuTone QuieTTest™ Fan-Lights. Three models to choose!

Now you can choose an energy saving fluorescent or incandescent ceiling light in conjunction with QT ventilation and a convenient night light.

Fan-light packages

- Triple-function units
  - Quiet ventilation
  - Bright ceiling light
  - Convenient night light
- Easy installation
- Operate singly, any combination or all together
- Glass lens

QT100L – 100 CFM/Incandescent light
QT100FL – 100 CFM/Fluorescent light
QT140L – 150 CFM/Incandescent light

QT100FL, QT100L QuieTTest Fan-Lights - Choose fluorescent or incandescent ceiling light combined with 100 CFM ventilation and energy-saving night light

HVI Certified

NuTone Fans are designed to deliver the number of air changes per hour recommended by the Home Ventilating Institute (HVI). This insures a fresher atmosphere throughout your home, exhausting the heat, smoke, humidity, odors and other airborne contaminant's generated by everyday living.

QT140L QuieTTest Fan-Light – Ideal for larger baths, up to 140 sq. ft.

NuTone

Deluxe Fan-Lights

High performance, triple function!

Choose from wood-framed fans, white polymeric or polished metal models.

- 100 CFM to quietly ventilate baths up to 95 sq. ft.
- 100W ceiling light or energy-saving fluorescent light
- 7W night light – great convenience
- Patented snap-on grille assembly

UL Listed for tub/shower with GFI branch circuit wiring. (Wood and fluorescent models not recommended).

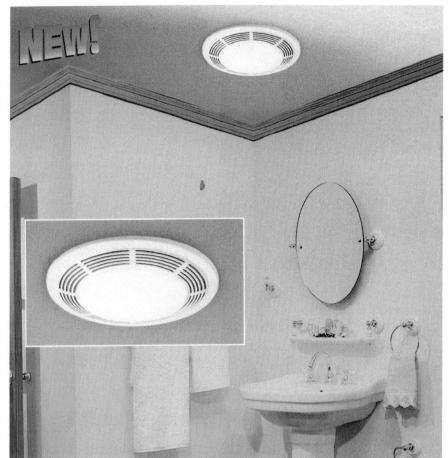

NEW!

8673P Fan-Light mpp

New! Graceful and sleek 8663 fan series 8663P, 8664P, 8663F mpp

8663MAB Fan-Light – Antique Brass
8663MBR Fan-Light – Polished Brass
8663MSA Fan-Light – Satin Aluminum
mpp

Patented snap-together assembly allows user to adjust fan from square (8673) to round

NuTone Designer Grilles

Use NuTone Designer Grilles with 8663/73 fan series to complement bathroom decor (Housing sold separately) Available in April.

8663LG Fan-Light – Bleached Wood mpp

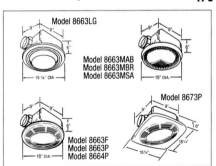

Model 8663LG

Model 8663MAB
Model 8663MBR
Model 8663MSA

Model 8663F
Model 8663P
Model 8664P

Model 8673P

Model No.	Description	Grille Finish	For Baths Up To	Other Rooms Up To	Duct Size	Amp Rating	Lamp Watts	Certified Test Data Air Delivery	Sound Level
Deluxe Bath Fan-Light Combinations (lamps not included)									
8663LG	Ceiling Fan-Light	Bleached Wood	95 sq. ft.	125 sq. ft.	4"	1.7	100/7	100 CFM	3.5 sones
8663F	Fluor. Ceiling Fan-Light	White Polymeric	95 sq. ft.	125 sq. ft.	4"	1.7	26	100 CFM	3.5 sones
8663MSA		Satin Aluminum							
8663MAB	Ceiling Fan-Light	Ant. Brass Anod. Alum.	95 sq. ft	125 sq. ft.	4"	1.7	100/7	100CFM	3.5 sones
8663MBR		Pol. Brass Anod. Alum.							
8663P	Ceiling Fan-Light	White Polymeric	95 sq. ft.	125 sq. ft.	4"	1.7	100/7	100 CFM	3.5 sones
8664P	Ceiling Fan-Light	White Polymeric	95 sq. ft.	125 sq. ft.	4"	1.7	100	100 CFM	3.5 sones
8673P	Ceiling Fan-Light	White Polymeric	95 sq. ft.	125 sq. ft.	4"	1.7	100/7	100 CFM	3.5 sones

NuTone

QuieTTest™ Heat-A-Ventlite®

Four great benefits in one simple installation!

- Soothing heat
- Powerful ventilation
- Bright ceiling light
- Convenient night light

Now you can select the QuieTTest® model for extra-quiet operation, the new Deluxe incandescent or the Deluxe fluorescent for energy-saving lighting.

A fluorescent Deluxe Heat-A-Ventlite – Model 9093FWH
Provides energy-savings, high light output and 10,000 hour-life.
Models 9093WH and QT9093WH are incandescent *mpp*

QT-9093CH and 9093CH Heat-A-Ventlites® and 9013NL Heat-A-Lite® in Chrome finish *mpp*

QT-9093BR, 9093BR
Polished Brass grille surrounds the high-quality glass lens. (Antique Brass finish available in 9093 model) *mpp*

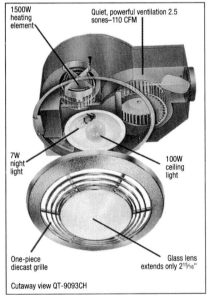

1500W heating element
Quiet, powerful ventilation 2.5 sones–110 CFM
7W night light
100W ceiling light
One-piece diecast grille
Glass lens extends only 2¹⁵⁄₁₆"
Cutaway view QT-9093CH

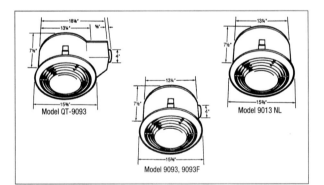

Model QT-9093

Model 9013 NL

Model 9093, 9093F

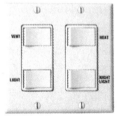

Each Heat-A-Ventlite includes a wall switch with separate on-off controls for all four functions.

Since NuTone invented the Heat-A-Ventlite more than 30 years ago, it has been providing comfort, convenience and long-lasting dependability to countless homes.

Model No.	Description	Finish	Housing Dimensions	Fan Forced or Radiant Heat	Total Connected Load in Watts	Element Watts	Lamp Watts	Exhaust Motor Watts	Htg. Motor Watts	Cooling Motor Watts	BTU	Certified Test Data Air Delivery (CFM)	Sound Level (Sones)
Built-In Ceiling Heaters													
9013NL	Heat-A-Lite	Chrome	13¼" dia. x 7½"	FF	1662	1500	100/7	–	55	–	5118	–	–
QT-9093BR	QuieTTest Heat-A-Ventlite	Polished Brass	13¼" x 18⅛" x 7½"	FF	1717	1500	100/7	55	55	–	5118	110	2.5
QT-9093CH		Chrome											
QT-9093WH		White Enamel											
9093AB	Deluxe Heat-A-Ventlite	Antique Brass	13¼" dia. x 7½"	FF	1717	1500	100/7	55	55	–	5118	70	3.5
9093BR		Polished Brass											
9093CH		Chrome											
9093WH		White Enamel											
9093FWH	Fluorescent Heat-A-Ventlite	White Enamel	13¼" dia. x 7½"	FF	1717	1500	26/7	55	55	–	5118	70	3.5

NuTone

V-91 Designer
Range Hoods

400 CFM twin blower hood with micro-processor controls and night light

The style of tomorrow ... today! Gently rounded corners and seamless patent-pending design are the ideal complement for the best-looking kitchens! Textured finish hides fingerprints and is easy to clean. Microprocessor touchpad gives you precise, easy control for fan and light. Powerful 400 CFM twin blowers provide excellent ventilation for every cooking situation.

- Seamless, patent-pending design features rounded corners
- Textured finish coordinates with other kitchen appliances and is easy to clean
- Low profile – just 8" high
- Variable speed controls
- Simple-to-use Touchpad gives you precise air delivery needed
- Auto-off control gradually reduces fan speed until complete shut-off is reached
- Programmable night light
- Two 60W lamps illuminate cooking surface (bulbs not included)
- Two 11¾" x 7" permanent grease filters. 164 sq. in. of washable aluminum mesh
- Energy-efficient motor
- 3¼" x 10" duct or 7" round (using 886 transition)
- 30" and 36" widths
- V-91 400 CFM: 5.5 sones horizontal, 6.0 sones vertical – HVI Certified

V-9130BL *Rounded corners and seamless design provide upscale elegance for the contemporary kitchen*

Automated Touchpad Makes Cooking Easier

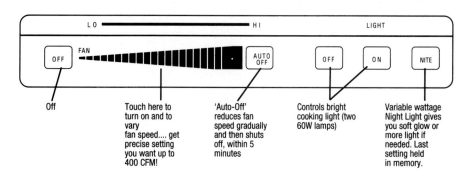

Off	Touch here to turn on and to vary fan speed.... get precise setting you want up to 400 CFM!	'Auto-Off' reduces fan speed gradually and then shuts off, within 5 minutes	Controls bright cooking light (two 60W lamps)	Variable wattage Night Light gives you soft glow or more light if needed. Last setting held in memory.

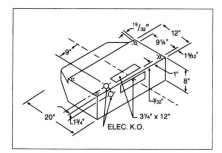

Finish	30" Model	36" Model
V-91 Deluxe 400 CFM Twin Blower Hood		
Almond Enamel w/Almond trim	V-9130AA	V-9136AA
Almond Enamel w/Black trim	V-9130ALN	V-9136ALN
Black Enamel w/Black trim	V-9130BL	V-9136BL
White Enamel w/White trim	V-9130WW	V-9136WW
White Enamel w/Black trim	V-9130WHN	V-9136WHN

MAXIMUM PERFORMANCE PRODUCTS –GUARANTEED FOR AS LONG AS YOU OWN YOUR HOME.

7

NuTone

NEW!

TN8300 Convertible Twin Blower Hood – Enjoy superior performance from twin-blowers that provide 250 CFM air movement. mp̄ḇ

Simply reposition Power Unit to convert for rear, top or non-duct.

Top ducting

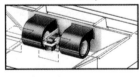

Non-ducted

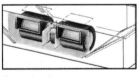

Rear ducting

Finish	30" Model	36" Model
TN8300 Convertible 3¼" x 10" Ducted or Non-Ducted		
All White Enamel	TN8330WW	TN8336WW
Almond Enamel	TN8330AL	TN8336AL
Black Enamel	TN8330BL	TN8336BL
White Enamel w/black trim	TN8330WH	TN8336WH
Stainless Steel	TN8330SS	TN8336SS
All Almond	TN8330AA	TN8336AA

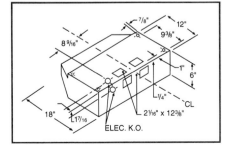

Convertible twin blower hood with night light

TN8300 BL mp̄ḇ

TN8300 WH mp̄ḇ

TN8300 AL mp̄ḇ

This handsome Decorator Range Hood with front mitred corners and powerful twin-blowers efficiently clears the air ... with exceptional quietness. Use with 3¼" x 10" ducting ... or as a Non-Duct! No special kit is needed! Simply reposition blower unit to exhaust the air for horizontal or vertical ducting through back or top knockouts. . . or to recirculate the filtered air through the front vent.

- Solid-state speed control lets you adjust air-movement gradually from quietest low-speed to whatever level is needed
- 75W light (lamp not included) with easily removable lens
- Night Light setting for extra convenience. Rotary control switches are located in an easy-to-reach area
- Two 9¹/₁₆" x 8⁷/₁₆" permanent grease filters: 152 sq. in. of washable aluminum mesh
- Two activated charcoal filters included for non-duct installations
- Duct adapter with damper included for ducted installations
- Prewired with plug-in power unit
- Ready for quick and easy installation with conveniently located wiring knockouts and keyhole mounting slots
- TN8300 – 250 CFM: 5.5 sones horizontal, 6.5 sones vertical.UL and CSA Listed – HVI Certified

NuTone

Decorator SM Series Range Hoods

Non-ducted hood

3¼" x 10" Ducted. Use either horizontally or vertically – duct adapter and damper included

7" Round Ducted. Adapter included

Good looks! Decorator mitred front. A variety of finishes complement the color scheme of any kitchen decor. Infinite speed control gives you quiet operation with back-up power when you need it.

- 3¼" x 10" duct either horizontally or vertically
- 7" round duct
- Non-duct – no special kit is needed! Purchase FKM65 filter separately for maximum odor absorption
- Handy up front rotary controls for infinite speed and light
- 75W light (lamp not included) illuminates cooking surface
- Night Light setting for extra convenience
- Lens easily removed for relamping
- 8¼" x 11¼" permanent grease filter included (92 sq. in. of washable aluminum mesh)
- Electronically balanced polymeric blades for quiet operation
- Easy to install: prewired with keyhole mounting slots
- Plug-in motor
- 30", 36" and 42" widths
- SM6500 – 190 CFM: 7.0 sones vertical, 200CFM: 7.5 sones horizontal with 3¼" x 10" duct. 220 CFM: 6.5 sones vertical with 7" round
- UL and CSA Listed – HVI Certified *mpp*

SM6500 Series – Infinite speed control, convenient night light and four ducting options make this handsome range hood a great choice for any kitchen. *mpp*

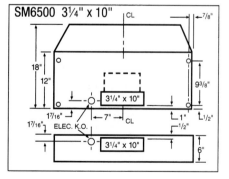

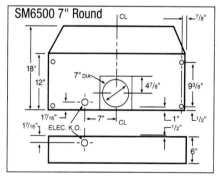

Finish	30" Model	36" Model	42" Model
SM6500 3¼" x 10" Ducted or 7" Round Ducted or Non-Ducted			
All White Enamel	SM6530WW	SM6536WW	SM6542WW
Almond Enamel	SM6530AL	SM6536AL	SM6542AL
All Almond Enamel	SM6530AA	SM6536AA	SM6542AA
Black Enamel	SM6530BL	SM6536BL	SM6542BL
White Enamel w/black trim	SM6530WH	SM6536WH	SM6542WH
Stainless Steel	SM6530SS	SM6536SS	SM6542SS

NuTone

IM-4406 Intercom with CD Player and Radio
Available 2nd Qtr, 1996

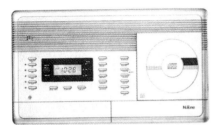

IM-4406L Biscuit Intercom

IM-4406BL Black Intercom

PLUS PERFORMANCE PRODUCT

IM-4406WH Radio Intercom with CD Player

Excellent Fidelity plus Compact Disc Player, AM/FM Radio

- The clear sound of compact disc
- Control CD/radio on/off and radio memory channels/CD tracks from any remote station
- Powerful 20 watt amplifier
- 12 radio station memory, battery backup
- "Wake to music" feature functions as alarm clock
- CD pauses when intercom or chime is used so you never miss a beat!
- Separate bass and treble control
- Optional door or gate release
- Smoked window allows view of CD in player

IMA-4006 and IM-4406
Intercom
- 'Hands-free' answering at all Stations
- One-button talk/listen: push to speak, release to hear reply
- Programming is muted during intercom calls
- 'Listen-in' (Monitor) baby's room, sick room, etc.
- LEDs show function selected
- Control up to 9 Remote Stations and 3 Door Speakers from Master – to control more, order Expansion Module
- Optional chime module and video door answering

FM/AM Radio
- Electronic scan tuning finds nearest strong signal
- Digital display of time and radio frequency shown at Master Station; battery backup
- Store favorite radio stations in memory

Remote Stations
- Remote Stations feature one-button talk/listen operation with 'Inside/Patio,' 'Door Talk,' 'Private,' and 'End Call' buttons, volume controls
- Available in Square or Rounded profile
- Control radio or CD (on IM-4406 only) from remote stations; On/Off, select radio station, select CD track
- Answer the door from any station

IMA-4006 Intercom with Cassette Player and Radio

IMA-4006WH Radio-Intercom
- Available in Bright White or Light Walnut

NuTone

IS-445 Inside Speaker – 5"
- IS-445WH Bright White
- IS-445D Sable Brown
- IS-445BL Black
- IS-445L Biscuit
- IR-50 Rough-in (or surface-mount with IA-60)
- Available 2nd Qtr, 1996

IS-448 Inside Speaker – 8"
- IS-448WH Bright White
- IS-448D Sable Brown
- IS-448BL Black
- IS-448L Biscuit
- IR-80 Rough-in
- Available 2nd Qtr, 1996

IS-449WH Outdoor Speaker – 5"
- Surface-mounts
- IS-449WH Bright White
- Available 2nd Qtr, 1996

IC-441WH Inside Remote Control
- IC-441WH Bright White
- Use with IS-75, IS-76 and ISA-78 Speakers
- IR-91 Rough-in
- Available 2nd Qtr, 1996

IC-441WHW Outside Remote Control
- IC-441WHW Bright White
- Use with ISA-77 and IS-79 Speakers
- Surface-mounts
- Available 2nd Qtr, 1996

IS-405 Inside Speaker – 5"
- IS-405WH Bright White
- IS-405D Walnut
- IS-405L Biscuit
- IR-50 Rough-in (or sur-face-mount with IA-60)

IS-408 Inside Speaker – 8"
- IS-408WH Bright White
- IS-408D Walnut
- IS-408L Biscuit
- IR-80 Rough-in

IS-409 Outdoor Speaker – 5"
- Surface-mounts
- IS-409WH Bright White
- IS-409L Biscuit

IC-401L Inside Remote Control
- IC-401L Biscuit
- IC-401WH Bright White
- Use with IS-75, IS-76 and ISA-78 Speakers
- IR-81 Rough-in

IC-401LW Outside Remote Control
- IC-401LW Biscuit
- Use with ISA-77 and IS-79 Speakers
- Surface-mounts

IS-419 Outdoor Speaker – 5"
- IS-419WH Bright White
- IS-419AB Antique Brass
- IS-419PB Polished Brass
- Use IR-50 Rough-in or, for stucco or brick, IR-55 Rough-in

IM-4406 and IMA-4006 System Components — Order rough-in PLUS finish kit to make a complete unit

Finish Kit Model No.	Description	Finish	Width	Height	In-Wall Depth	Projects	Rough-In Model No.
IMA-4006D IMA-4006WH	Master Station (9-station capacity — plus 3 Door Speakers)	Light Walnut Bright White	17"	9"	3⅛"	1½"	IR-103
IM-4406BL IM-4406L IM-4406WH	Master Station (9 station capacity — plus 3 Door Speakers)	Black Biscuit Bright White	17¾"	10⅛"	3½"	1⅞"	IR-105
IA-410	Expansion Kit for IMA-4006 (Up to 19 stations)						
IA-440	Expansion Kit for IM-4406 (Up to 15 stations)						
IS-405D IS-405L IS-405WH	5" Inside Speaker with controls (Square corners)	Walnut Biscuit Bright White	6¼"	8³⁄₁₆"	1⁷⁄₁₆"	⅞"	IR-50
IS-445BL IS-445D IS-445L IS-445WH	5" Inside Speaker with controls (Rounded corners)	Black Sable Brown Biscuit Bright White	6⁵⁄₁₆"	8¼"	1⁷⁄₁₆"	1³⁄₁₆"	IR-50
IS-408D IS-408L IS-408WH	8" Inside Speaker with controls (Square corners)	Walnut Biscuit Bright White	10"	11¼"	2¼"	⅞"	IR-80
IS-448BL IS-448D IS-448L IS-448WH	8" Inside Speaker with controls (Rounded corners)	Black Sable Brown Biscuit Bright White	10"	11¼"	2¾"	⅞"	IR-80
IC-401L IC-401WH	Inside Remote Control for IS-75, IS-76, ISA-78 (see Pg. E11) (Square corners)	Biscuit Bright White	6⅞"	4⅞"	⅝"	—	IR-81
IC-401LW	Outdoor Remote Control for ISA-77, IS-79 (see Pg. E11)	Biscuit	6⅞"	4⅞"	2⅞"	—	—
IC-441WH	Inside Remote Control for IS-75, IS-76, ISA-78 (see page E11) (Rounded corners)	Bright White	7"	4"	1¹⁄₁₆"	1³⁄₁₆"	IR-91
IC-441WHW	Outside Remote Control for ISA-78, IS-79. Surface mount	Bright White	7"	4"	2⅞"	—	—
IS-409L IS-409WH	5" Outdoor Speaker with controls — Surface-Mounted Square corners	Biscuit Bright White	6⅝"	8⁹⁄₁₆"	3⅛"	—	—
IS-449WH	5" Outdoor Speaker with controls — Surface-Mounted Rounded corners	Bright White	6⅝"	8⁹⁄₁₆"	3⅛"	—	—
IS-419AB IS-419PB IS-419WH	5" Outdoor Speaker with controls — Recessed	Antique Brass Polished Brass Bright White	6¼"	8³⁄₁₆"	1⅞"	⁷⁄₁₆"	IR-50 or IR-55

INSTALLATION WIRE: NuTone 3-twisted-pair (6-wire) Cable: 1000 ft. — IW-6-1000; 200 ft. — IW-6-200. NuTone Twisted Pair (22/2) Cable: 100 ft. — IW-2-100; 500 ft. — IW-2-500. S-143-500 Twisted Pair (18/2). For installation where UL Listed wire is specified, add 'UL' suffix to model number when ordering.

NuTone

3430BE Clearview TriVista
- Pure and simple all glass TriVista
- Provides all-round viewing and easy access to lots of storage through its trio of beveled edge mirror doors
- Surface mount cabinet; two fixed steel shelves
- Door swing: RH/LH/LH
- Choose from four sizes: 24", 30", 36" or 48"

Model	Overall Size	Rough Opening
3424BE	24" x 31⅜" x 4¾"	Surface Mount
3430BE	30" x 31⅜" x 4¾"	Surface Mount
3436BE	36" x 31⅜" x 4¾"	Surface Mount
3448BE	48" x 31⅜" x 4¾"	Surface Mount

1030BE Bevel-edge Unframed TriVista
- The beauty of beveled glass ... the convenience of all-round viewing
- Three adjustable glass shelves
- Recesses, can be surface mounted with SMK-30 Surface Mount Kit
- Door swing: RH/LH/LH
- Available in 30" and 36" sizes

Model	Overall Size	Rough Opening
1030BE	30" x 30" x 4½"	29¼" x 27½" x 3¼"
1036BE	36" x 30" x 4½"	35¼" x 27½" x 3¼"

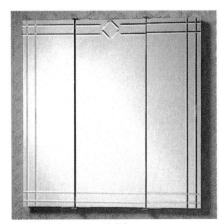

3530BE Minuet TriVista
- Delightfully different octagonal shape all-glass TriVista cabinet
- Beveled-edge mirror doors open for ample storage and all-round viewing
- Cabinet surface mounts for easy installation
- Two fixed steel shelves
- Door swing: RH/LH/LH

Model	Overall Size	Rough Opening
3530BE	30" x 34½" x 4⅞"	Surface Mount
3536BE	36" x 34½" x 4⅞"	Surface Mount

3351-30 Splendor TriVista
- Stunning all glass TriVista with beveled edge mirror doors, polished V-grooves and diamond shaped accent
- Cabinet recesses or can be surface mounted with SMK-30 Surface Mount Kit
- Three adjustable glass shelves
- Door swing: RH/LH/LH

Model	Overall Size	Rough Opening
3351-30	30" x 30" x 4½"	29¼" x 27½" x 3¼"
3352-36	36" x 30" x 4½"	35¼" x 27½" x 3¼"

3630BE Clarity TriVista
- Pure and simple all-glass TriVista with radius corners, beveled-edge mirrors
- Enjoy all-round viewing and storage too
- surface mount cabinet has two fixed, steel shelves plus concealed self-closing hinges
- Door swing: RH/LH/LH
- Matching toplight: NTLD1132-36, NTLD1131-30

Model	Overall Size	Rough Opening
3630BE	30" x 30⅞" x 4⅞"	Surface Mount
3636BE	36" x 30⅞" x 4⅞"	Surface Mount

3930LPB Park Avenue TriVista

- Exquisite polished brass half-round frame surrounds three beveled mirrored doors
- Built-in lights have reflective backplate to enhance brilliance and illumination; UL Listed
- Door swing: RH/LH/LH
- Surface mount cabinet; two adjustable glass shelves and push-to-release magnetic catches
- Available in 24" and 30" sizes

Model	Overall Size	Rough Opening	Lamps*
3924LPB	23¾" x 30½" x 5"	Surface Mount	(4) G16½ 40W
3930LPB	29¾" x 30½" x 5"	Surface Mount	(5) G16½ 40W

• Lamps not included

4010-30LPC Regent TriVista

- Surface mount lighted TriVista cabinet with mirrored doors
- Polished chrome frame with brass inlay
- Two adjustable glass shelves
- Door swing: RH / LH / LH
- Available in 30" and 36" sizes
- UL Listed

Model	Overall Size	Rough Opening	Lamps*
4010-30LPC	31½" x 32¼" x 5¼"	Surface Mount	(4) G25 60W
4011-36LPC	37½" x 32¼" x 5¼"	Surface Mount	(5) G25 60W

*Lamps not included

NTCX981-30 Scottsdale Tri-View

- Square corner unframed beveled mirror doors
- Two fixed, steel shelves
- Concealed self-closing hinges
- Surface mount cabinet

Model	Overall Size	Matching Light
NTCX980-24	24" x 30⅞" x 4⅞"	NTLD-974-24
NTCX981-30	30" x 30⅞" x 4⅞"	NTLD-975-30
NTCX982-36	36" x 30⅞" x 4⅞"	NTLD-976-36
NTCX983-48	48" x 30⅞" x 4⅞"	NTLD-977-48

* Lamps not included

2250-30BE Monterey TriVista with DL2250-30BE Toplight

- Polished V-grooves on beveled mirror doors add interest to this all glass TriVista and matching toplight; toplight is UL Listed
- Cabinet recesses or can be surface mounted using SMK-30 Surface Mount Kit
- Three adjustable glass shelves; Door swing: RH/LH/LH

Model	Overall Size	Rough Opening	Lamps*
2250-30BE	30¼" x 30½" x 4¼"	29¼" x 27½" x 3¼"	—
2251-36BE	36¼" x 30½" x 4¼"	35¼" x 27½" x 3¼"	—
DL2250-30BE	30" x 5¼" x 1½"	Surface Mount	(3) G25 60W
DL2251-36BE	36" x 5¼" x 1½"	Surface. Mount	(4) G25 60W
DL2260-30BE	30" x 5¼" x 4¾"	Surface Mount	(3) G25 60W
DL2261-36BE	36" x 5¼" x 4¾"	Surface Mount	(4) G25 60W

*Lamps not included

For recessed cabinet, use DL2250/51 light bar. For surface mount, use DL2260/61 light bar.

3830LBE Encore TriVista

- Squared-corners enhance contemporary styling on beveled edge mirror doors
- Built-in toplight adds perfect illumination
- Surface mount cabinet; two fixed steel shelves and convenience outlet
- Concealed self-closing hinges
- Door swing: RH/LH/LH
- UL Listed

Model	Overall Size	Rough Opening	Lamps*
3824LBE	24" x 33⅛" x 4¾"	Surface Mount	(4) G16½ 40W
3830LBE	30" x 33⅛" x 4¾"	Surface Mount	(5) G16½ 40W
3836LBE	36" x 33⅛" x 4¾"	Surface Mount	(6) G16½ 40W
3848LBE	48" x 33⅛" x 4¾"	Surface Mount	(8) G16½ 40W

* Lamps not included

NuTone

Steel Body
Swing Door

Swing Door Cabinets offer many decorating options...
genuine wood, mirror-on-mirror, polished brass and more!

NTCSL1714-18
- Beveled mirror door with Polished Brass finish PVC frame
- Built-in light & convenience outlet; UL Listed
- Push to release magnetic catch
- Right hand door swing
- Two adjustable glass shelves

Model	Overall Size	Lamps*
NTCSL1714-18	17¾" x 30½" x 5⅛"	(3) G16½

* Lamps not included

NTCSL1390-17
- Unframed beveled mirror cabinet
- Built-in light, plus convenience outlet and switch on exterior of cabinet; UL Listed
- Right hand door swing
- Two adjustable glass shelves

Model	Overall Size	Lamps*
NTCSL1390-17	16½" x 26" x 4¾"	(2) G25

* Lamps not included

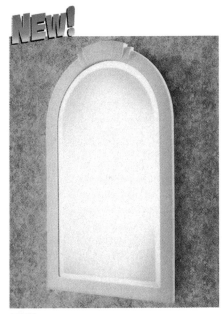

D195-18
- Natural limestone in molded frame
- The look of tied reeds
- Recessed cabinet with two adjustable plastic shelves
- RH or LH door swing
- Available 2nd QTR, 1996

Model	Overall Size	Rough Opening
D195-18	17¼" x 27¼" x 5½"	14" x 18" x 3½"
D195-24	17¼" x 27¼" x 5½"	14" x 24" x 3½"

D196-18
- Natural limestone in molded frame
- "Prairie" look of cut stone
- Recessed cabinet with two adjustable plastic shelves
- RH or LH door swing
- Available 2nd QTR, 1996

Model	Overall Size	Rough Opening
D196-18	18" x 27¾" x 5½"	14" x 18" x 3½"
D196-18	18" x 27¾" x 5½"	14" x 24" x 3½"

D197
- Natural limestone in molded arched frame
- Deco arch fits any bath
- Recessed cabinet with two adjustable plastic shelves
- RH door swing
- Available 2nd QTR, 1996

Model	Overall Size	Rough Opening
D197	19⅜" x 32" x 4⅞"	14" x 18" x 3½"

NuTone

D171 Continental
DL171 Continental Toplight
- Beveled mirror door with polished brass look half-round frame
- Recessed cabinet; 18" cabinet has two adjustable plastic shelves, 24" cabinet has three shelves
- Matching surface mount toplight features mirror chrome backplate; UL Listed

Model	Overall Size	Rough Opening	Lamps*
D171	16½" x 26½" x 5½"	14" x 18" x 3½"	—
D171-24	16½" x 26½" x 5½"	14" x 24" x 3½"	—
DL171	16" x 4¼" x 2½"	Surface Mount	(3) G16½ 40W

*Lamps not included

D169N Deauville
- The look of polished brass makes a stylish statement in the decorator bath
- A single band of seamless extruded aluminum tubing elegantly finished in polished brass frames a tasteful arched mirror
- Recessed cabinet with two adjustable plastic shelves
- RH door swing

Model	Overall Size	Rough Opening
D169N	17¾" x 29¾" x 5⅝"	14" x 18" x 3½"

D168 Elegance
- Beveled edge arched mirror door... clean, simple styling at its best
- Recessed cabinet
- Two adjustable plastic shelves; RH door swing
- Also available as Decorator Mirror – Model 790N
- Can be surface mounted with SM-1418 Converter Sleeve

Model	Overall Size	Rough Opening
D168	16½" x 29" x 4¾"	14" x 18" x 3½"
790N Mirror	16½" x 29" x 3/16"	—

D179 Reflections
- Graceful arched mirror-on-mirror cabinet
- Full bevel around both mirrors
- Two adjustable plastic shelves; left hand door swing
- Also available as Decorator Mirror – Model 780

Model	Overall Size	Rough Opening
D179	18" x 30" x 5"	14" x 18" x 3½"
780 Mirror	18" x 30" x ½"	—

D142-18 Reflections
- Stunning mirror-on-mirror design, each mirror beveled a full inch
- Clear "looking glass" with bronze framing mirror
- Recessed cabinet in 18" and 24" sizes
- 18" size: two adjustable plastic shelves; 24" size: three adjustable shelves

Model	Overall Size	Rough Opening
D142-18	16½" x 26" x 5"	14" x 18" x 3½"
D142-24	16½" x 26" x 5"	14" x 24" x 3½"

D146-18 Reflections
- Distinctive octagonal shape beveled-mirror-on-beveled-mirror design
- Recessed cabinet reverses for right or left hand door swing
- 18" cabinet features two adjustable plastic shelves; 24" has three shelves

Model	Overall Size	Rough Opening
D146-18	18" x 30" x 4¾"	14" x 18" x 3½"
D146-24	18" x 30" x 4¾"	14" x 24" x 3½"

NuTone

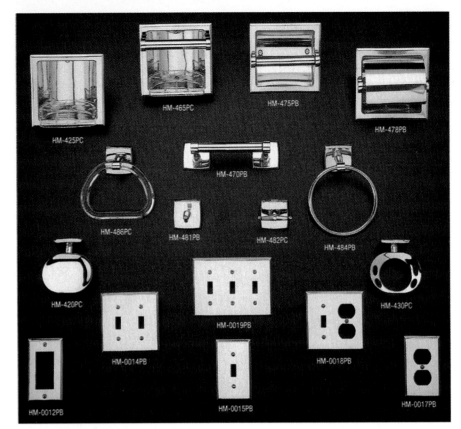

HM-425PC
HM-465PC
HM-475PB
HM-478PB
HM-470PB
HM-486PC
HM-481PB
HM-482PC
HM-484PB
HM-420PC
HM-0019PB
HM-430PC
HM-0014PB
HM-0018PB
HM-0012PB
HM-0015PB
HM-0017PB

When only the finest will do, AristoChrome solid brass accessories in two finishes!

NuTone meets the demands of the most discriminating with the craftsmanship of AristoChrome. Clean, simple elegance in fine forged solid brass! Choose from two beautiful finishes – Polished Brass or Polished Chrome.

Polished Brass AristoChrome accessories are ordered by adding the suffix PB to the model number. For Polished Chrome, add PC.

- Surface mounted AristoChrome back-plates can be locked into a square or diamond position
- Screw-mounted wall plate(s) included with surface mounted accessories
- Recessed units fit into 5¼" square openings, with direct screw mount through back of accessory, or with HM-800CN Spring Clamp. For easy wall installation, or vanity and tile installations, use Recessed Mounting Clamp HM-600CN (for Polished Chrome finish) or HM-600PBN (for Polished Brass); includes 2" screws for wall thickness from ¼" to 1¼".

Coordinating Switchplates

For an elegant finishing touch select solid brass NuTone switchplates in Polished Brass (PB) or Polished Chrome (PC) to coordinate with your NuTone Bath Accessories. Or they're perfect in any room of the house. All are UL Listed.

Model No.	Description
HM-0012	GFI Switch Plate
HM-0014	Double Switch Plate
HM-0015	Single Switch Plate
HM-0017	Duplex Receptacle Plate
HM-0018	Duplex Receptacle and Switch Plate
HM-0019	Triple Switch Plate. (Available in Polished Brass only)

Model No.	Description
HM-420	Soap Holder
HM-425	Recessed Soap/Tumbler Holder with removable polystyrene tray.
HM-430	Toothbrush & Tumbler Holder
HM-465	Recessed Soap and Bar with removable polystyrene tray.
HM-470	Surface mounted Paper Holder
HM-475	Recessed Paper Holder
HM-478	Recessed Paper Holder with Hood
HM-481	Single Hook
HM-482	Double Hook
HM-484	Towel Ring - 4½" diameter
HM-486	Towel Ring with clear Lucite™ ring
HM-488	Towel Tree - available in PC only. 15½" wide x 24" high
HM-489	Triple Towel Ring 24" high - Available in PC only.
HM-492	Towel Bar - ¾" Hexagonal Stainless steel bar. 18" & 24" lengths. Available in PC only.
HM-495	Towel Bar - ¾" round bar. 18", 24", 30" & 36" lengths.
HM-499	Towel Ladder - 16 ¾" x 32". Available in PC only.

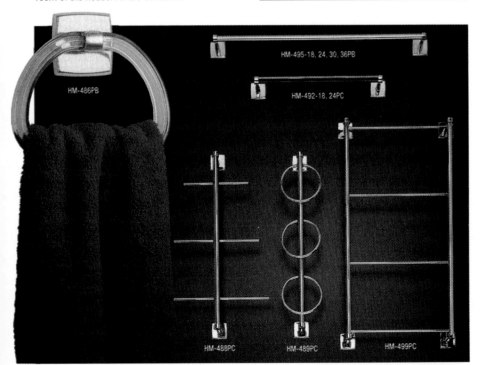

HM-486PB
HM-495-18, 24, 30, 36PB
HM-492-18, 24PC
HM-488PC
HM-489PC
HM-499PC

Surface Fixtures Specifications: To be NuTone AristoChrome No. _____. All exposed metal parts to be solid brass* and provide positive attachment to metal mounting bracket that can be fixed to wall or supporting surface by use of wood screws, toggle bolts, expansion bolts. Finish to be (specify) Polished Chrome (PC) over a nickel plate base or Polished Brass (PB).
*HM-492 Hexagonal Towel Bar to be stainless steel finished in Polished Chrome.

Recessed Fixtures Specifications: To be NuTone AristoChrome No. _____. All metal parts to be solid brass, measuring 6⅛" x 6⅛" overall to fit wall opening 5¼" x 5¼" x 2", and permitting installation by wood screws or machine screws with clamps. Finish to be (specify) Polished Chrome (PC) over a nickel plate base or Polished Brass (PB).

NuTone

256N Food Processor shown on Designer White Power Unit 251WH

- Performs variety of food preparation including chopping, grating, shredding and slicing
- Exclusive design creates double action inside bowl moving and folding ingredients
- Includes clear plastic bowl with handle, precision-ground steel cutter blade, slicer disk, shredder disk, french-fry disk, tamper and base adapter
- 1-quart capacity

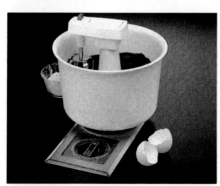

271 Mixer

- Exclusive center tube mixing bowl keeps mix constantly in the path of the beater
- Motor turns bowl automatically one way, beater turns the opposite way
- Includes bowl, turntable, beater and beater head
- Big 4-quart bowl is lightweight melamine. Extra Mixing bowl available Model 286

276 Coffee Grinder

- Grinds coffee beans to the exact texture you require
- Stainless steel blades and specially designed grinder hopper circulate beans and grounds for uniform texture

272 Blender

- Pitcher is clear break-resistant plastic
- Blender lid has removable insert for adding liquids during processing
- Graduated markings on side in cups, ounces and metric equivalents
- 1½ quart capacity

173N Fruit Juicer

- Makes fresh juice in a hurry
- Bowl holds up to 3 quarts
- Strainer lets pulp through, catches seeds
- Includes strainer and reamer
- Use with Mixer Bowl and Turntable from Model 271

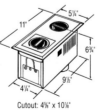

Cutout: 4⅝" x 10⅛"

Specifications: 1/3 horsepower variable speed motor, 650W maximum, 120v AC: high speed, 14,000 RPM for center shaft, and down to approx. 750 RPM of the drive clutch at low speed. Current draw 5.42A at 120VAC Max. Size of cutout: 4⅝" x 10⅛" (⅞" Radius). Shipping weight: 9.8 lbs. Easily installed even in existing homes. In new homes, wiring provision should be made for electrical connection during rough-in wiring at proposed location. Allow enough free wire to reach the front of cabinet when installed. Allow 18" clearance between countertop and any wall cabinet above ... and 3¾" clearance to adjacent walls at back or sides. Unit must be grounded in accordance with local wiring codes.

Built-In Food Center

Quality performance...and an end to counter clutter!

Whether you're designing your dream kitchen or remodeling an existing one, don't forget to build in a NuTone Food Center!

When installed, all you see is the Power Unit Surface Plate. Food Center appliances – Blender, Mixer, Food Processor, Fruit Juicer, Coffee Grinder attach to Power Unit with a simple twist. When not in use, appliances store out of sight in a cabinet.

251 Power Unit
Model 251WH – Designer White
Model 251SS – Stainless Steel

- Highly efficient motor – designed to handle light to heavy loads
- Compact, it installs beneath countertop
- You see only the surface-plate ... in your choice of Designer White or classic Stainless Steel
- The surface-plate is virtually flush with your countertop so you have complete use of your counter when not using appliances
- Appliances lock on to Power Unit with just a twist. Won't hop around no matter how heavy the load.

Solid-State Variable Speed Control

- Graduated markings on the dial make it easy to operate the Power Unit at the correct speeds for various appliances and needs
- Motor accelerates smoothly, gradually as needed
- A reverse twist slows down speed if necessary

Food Center Cookbook
featuring recipes for your NuTone Food Center is included with Models 251SS, 251WH, and 262

Model	Description
251SS	Power Unit – Stainless Steel surface plate
251WH	Power Unit – Designer White surface plate
262	Starter Package including: 251SS Power Unit and Blender
173N	Fruit Juicer (requires Mixer Bowl and Turntable from Model 271)
256N	Food Processor
271	Mixer
272	Blender
276	Coffee Grinder
286	Extra Mixing Bowl

NuTone®

Build in time-saving convenience and added value to your home with a NuTone Ironing Center. A variety of models available to fit your needs and your lifestyle.

Deluxe Ironing Center Cabinet AVC-40NDR

Strong and Reliable
- Sturdy steel recessed cabinet
- Heavy-gauge steel ironing board perforated for ventilation

Fully electric!
- Prewired, includes convenience outlet for iron (iron not included)
- Work light. Uses R-20, 50 watt bulb (not included)
- Automatic timer shuts off iron even if you forget
- UL Listed

Completely adjustable!
- Adjust the board the way you want it!
- Board swivels full 180° for comfort and convenience
- Adjusts to three heights – a full 6" difference between top and bottom position

Stores all your ironing supplies!
- Special shelf to store iron – even when it's hot
- Room for spray starch, sprinkler, and other ironing supplies
- Garment hook for door

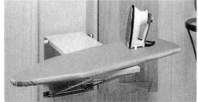

AVC-40NDR board swivels 180°

Optional accessories available
- AVC-SM Frame Kit for surface mount installation. See page D14
- AVC-DHK Door Hinge Kit for mounting your own door
- AVC-SL1 Sleeve Board
- AVC-CP Replacement Ironing Board Cover Pad. Fits securely with sewn-in nose pocket

AVC-40NDR Deluxe Cabinet with AVC-RP Door mpp

LOOK FOR THIS SYMBOL

GUARANTEED FOR AS LONG AS YOU OWN YOUR HOME

NuTone®

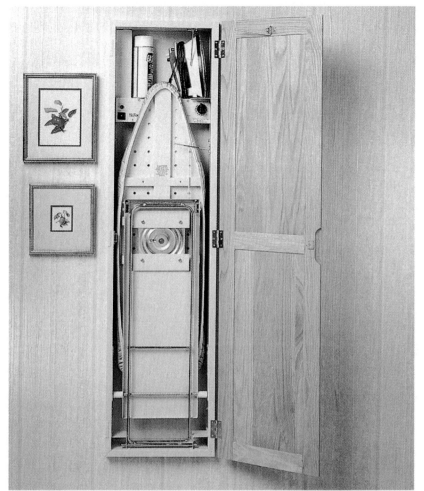

AVC-40NDR offers space-saving convenience!

Deluxe Ironing Center and Doors

AVC-40NDR

Installs easily in existing homes or new construction

- Sturdy recessed steel cabinet
- Heavy-gauge steel ironing board perforated for ventilation
- Recesses between 16" o.c. studs
- Fits wall opening 14¼"W x 60¼"H x 3¾"D
- Cabinet is 16"W x 62"H x 5½"D
- Projects 2⅝" from finished wall
- Overall ironing board size is 12"W x 42"L
- Board extends 45½" from wall when in down position
- Suggested mounting height 22" from floor to bottom of cutout – provides heights of 32", 35" and 38" for the ironing board. Other heights possible
- Includes non-stick ironing board cover/pad with sewn-in nose pocket

Customize your Ironing Center Cabinet with a choice of doors!

Order AVC-40NDR Ironing Center Cabinet, then select the door of your choice from models shown at left. Hinge kit included with door. Doors can be hinged for right or left opening.

- **AVC-M** Attractive mirror door with pencil edge. 16" x 62" x ⅜" *mpp*
- **AVC-RP** Traditional style unfinished raised panel door in genuine oak. 16" x 62" x ¾" *mpp*
- **AVC-W** Smooth unfinished wood door can be painted, stained or wallpapered. 16" x 62" x ¾" *mpp*
- **AVC-DHK** Door Hinge Kit Includes all necessary mounting hardware, magnetic catch and garment hook for mounting your own door for a truly custom look

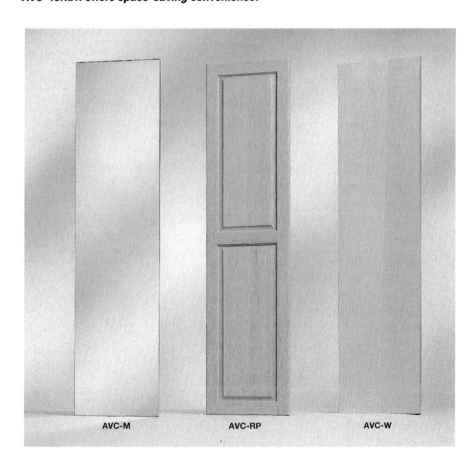

AVC-M   AVC-RP   AVC-W

NuTone®

Additional Products

OP Overall Product Data

Let NuTone add more convenience and comfort to your home

Central Vacs

NuTone Central Vac is quiet, yet very powerful for better clean-ability. Just insert the hose in a nearby inlet and the system is on. Heavy duty Power Unit is outside your living area. All you carry from room to room is a lightweight t hose and cleaning tools. It makes cleaning drapes, furniture, blinds and stairs so much easier. Choose from four systems.

mpp

Door Chimes

Since 1936, NuTone Door Chimes have been announcing visitors to homes across the country. Today, NuTone pro-vides the finest selection of Door Chimes and Decorator Pushbuttons to builders, con-tractors and homeowners ... more styles, more features plus quality guaranteed!

mpp

Lighting

NuTone Low-Profile Track Lighting offers a choice of over 25 fixtures and three finishes. Choose from energy efficient low voltage or standard fixtures plus micro-size electronic low voltage styles.

Compact Fluorescent Under Cabinet Lights provide energy-saving light even in the tightest spots – under cabinets and shelves, over counters and in work areas. Can be mounted in runs.

Ceiling Fans

NuTone Ceiling Fans help reduce utility costs all year long. Direct air flow down in summer to feel cooler, up in winter to move heated air that collects at ceiling. You stay comfortable while you cut back on air conditioning and heating bills!

Choose from a wide variety of Fan and Light Kit styles.

mpp

NuTone®
BUILT-IN HOME PRODUCTS

Madison and Red Bank Roads, Cincinnati, Ohio 45227-1599
*For your nearest NuTone Sales Outlet, Service Center
or a free Full Line Catalog,
DIAL 1-800-543-8687 in the contiguous U.S.*

Product specifications subject to change without notice

SHOWER DOOR

Crystal Collection

*A*MERICAN SHOWER DOOR presents the *Crystal Collection* for ⅜″ and ½″ glass. The finest in custom engineering and solid brass hardware highlight our elegant "Crystal" designs.

Finished to your specifications, we offer a wide range of extrusions either in architectural brass or polished aluminum. Our polycarbonate strike adds leakproof and steam applications to your options. Feel the difference of these quality engineered AMERICAN SHOWER DOORS.

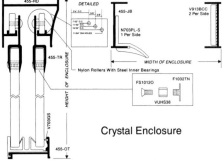

Crystal Enclosure

*A*MERICAN SHOWER DOOR warrants to the purchaser for one year that the product will be free from any defect in material and workmanship. Units are carefully manufactured to strictly adhere to all applicable codes and standards that are in particular delineated by: UBC Code Section 5407; UPC Code Section 909c; California Title 24, part 2-2-1711 and HCD.

American
S H O W E R   D O O R

*A*MERICAN SHOWER DOOR, 6920 E. Slauson Avenue, City of Commerce, CA 90040. (213) 726-2478.

Crystal Specifications:

Glass: ⅜" or ½" tempered. All glazing material shall meet or exceed ANSI Z97.1 - 1984 and CPSC Standard 16 CFR 1201 Category I and II.

Extrusions: Extruded shapes shall be either 385 architectural bronze, specification AS-1567-38D; or aluminum 6463-T5 or 6063-T5 alloy depending on application.

Hardware: Heavy duty solid brass hinges with 20° offset spring load. Leakproof with screw cover plates for a smooth finish; handles solid brass, polished stainless steel or as specified. Heavy-duty ball bearing roller system. All ASD screws are rustproof stainless steel.

Finishes: All solid brass (see page 5) or all aluminum (see page 7).

*W*e will personalize your design with options of artistic or etched glass; curved, beveled, or mitered construction; and custom hardware matched to your decorator plans.

Door Strike Options:

Polycarbonate to Glass

Jamb to Glass

Glass to Glass (non-leakproof)

Panel Inserts:

Into Marble

Inside Jamb

Jamb with Header

Hinges:

Wall to Glass (non-leakproof)

Jamb to Glass

Glass to Glass

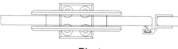

Pivot

SHOWER DOOR

Solid Brass

The Vintage solid brass collection – a trademark of the AMERICAN SHOWER DOOR tradition – incorporates fully framed hinged doors and enclosures with framed or frameless panel systems. Using clear or decorative glass patterns, with an option of heavy glass panels, this program is another opportunity to design installations to your specifications – by AMERICAN SHOWER DOOR.

Fine imported architectural brass is cleaned, polished and buffed. Then it is chrome plated to a mirror quality reflection; baked enameled to highlight the natural beauty of the solid brass; or plated to any finish specified – including brushed and 24 Karat gold.

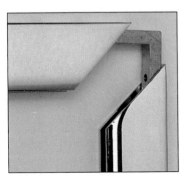

Double corner construction ensures that solid brass frames will last into antiquity.

Pivot Transom

Grill

Hinged Transom

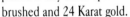

American
SHOWER DOOR

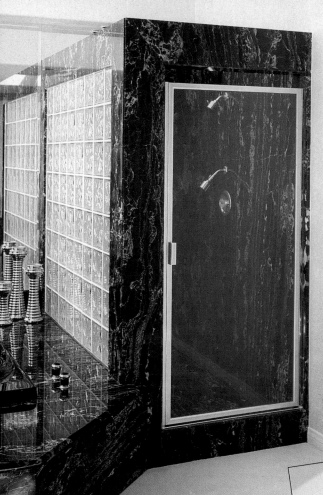

*A*MERICAN SHOWER DOOR, 6920 E. Slauson Avenue, City of Commerce, CA 90040. (213) 726-2478.

Brass Specifications:

Glass: $\frac{3}{16}''$ or $\frac{1}{4}''$ tempered ($\frac{3}{8}''$ or $\frac{1}{2}''$ for frameless applications). All glazing material shall meet or exceed ANSI Z97.1 - 1984 and CPSC Standard 16 CFR 1201 Category I and II. Clear, obscure, etched, patterned or custom option.

Extrusions: Extruded shapes shall be 385 architectural bronze, specification AS-1567-38D.

Hardware: Classic piano hinge; handles are solid brass, polished stainless steel, or as specified. Heavy-duty ball bearing enclosure roller system. All ASD screws are rustproof stainless steel.

Finish: Chrome plated brass – brass shall be polished, buffed, degreased and then plated; nickel plate QQ-N-290, Class 1, Type VI copper flash plus .0003 bright nickel. Chrome plating per QQ-C-320, Class 1, Type 1 decorative plating, bright chrome 0.00001. Baked enameled brass shall be polished, buffed, degreased, hand wiped, and baked enameled at minimum 300°F.

Standard brass finishes include: Polished or brushed chrome/enameled brass; pewter; antique brass enameled; brushed nickel and 24K gold plated.

Architectural Brass Extrusions:

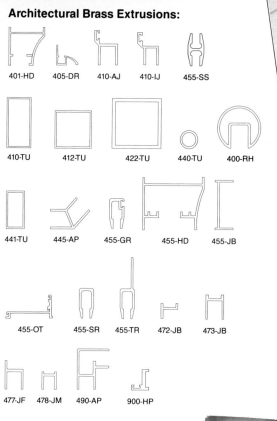

401-HD 405-DR 410-AJ 410-IJ 455-SS

410-TU 412-TU 422-TU 440-TU 400-RH

441-TU 445-AP 455-GR 455-HD 455-JB

455-OT 455-SR 455-TR 472-JB 473-JB

477-JF 478-JM 490-AP 900-HP

American
SHOWER DOOR

Doors & Daylites

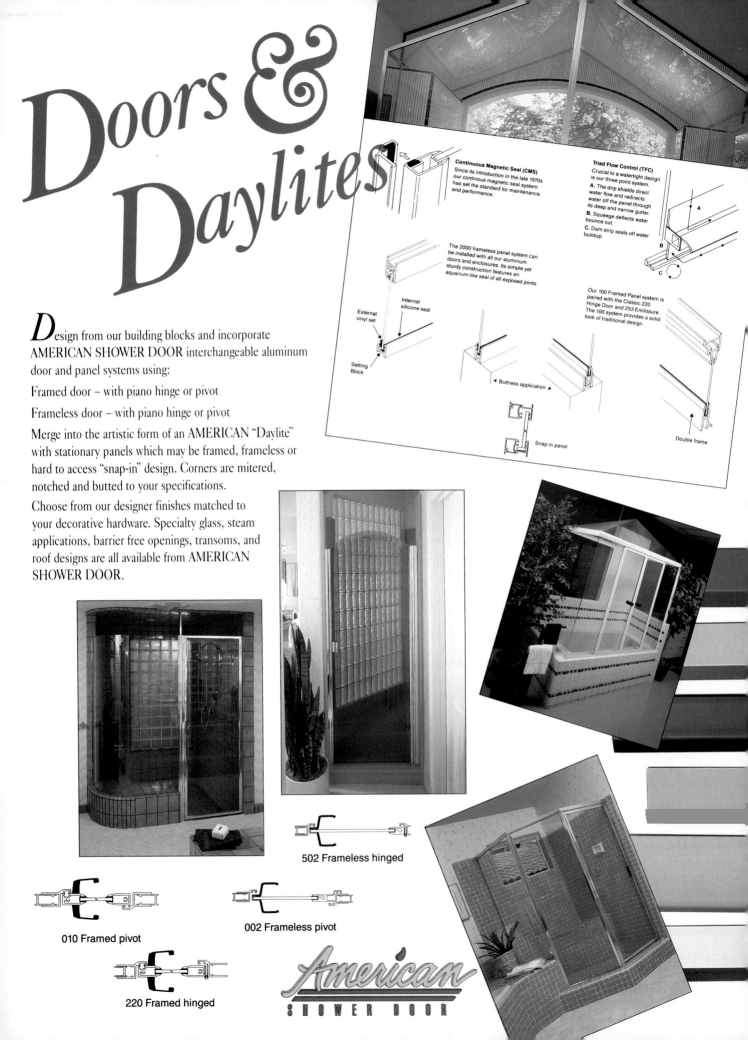

Design from our building blocks and incorporate AMERICAN SHOWER DOOR interchangeable aluminum door and panel systems using:

Framed door – with piano hinge or pivot

Frameless door – with piano hinge or pivot

Merge into the artistic form of an AMERICAN "Daylite" with stationary panels which may be framed, frameless or hard to access "snap-in" design. Corners are mitered, notched and butted to your specifications.

Choose from our designer finishes matched to your decorative hardware. Specialty glass, steam applications, barrier free openings, transoms, and roof designs are all available from AMERICAN SHOWER DOOR.

Continuous Magnetic Seal (CMS)
Since its introduction in the late 1970s our continous magnetic seal system has set the standard for maintenance and performance.

Triad Flow Control (TFC)
Crucial to a watertight design is our three point system.
A. The drip shields direct water flow and redirects water off the panel through its deep and narrow gutter.
B. Squeege deflects water bounce out.
C. Dam strip seals off water buildup.

The 2000 frameless panel system can be installed with all our aluminum doors and enclosures. Its simple yet sturdy construction features an aquarium-like seal of all exposed joints.

Our 100 Framed Panel system is paired with the Classic 220 Hinge Door and 253 Enclosure. The 100 system provides a solid look of traditional design.

External vinyl set

Internal silicone seal

Setting Block

◄ Buttress application ►

Snap in panel

Double frame

502 Frameless hinged

010 Framed pivot

002 Frameless pivot

220 Framed hinged

American
SHOWER DOOR

Enclosures

"805" Reversible contemporary or traditional header for ³⁄₁₆" or ¼" glass

*A*MERICAN SHOWER DOOR, 6920 E. Slauson Avenue, City of Commerce, CA 90040. (213) 726-2478.

Aluminum Specifications:

Glass: ³⁄₁₆" or ¼" tempered. All glazing material shall meet or exceed ANSI Z97.1 - 1984 and CPSC Standard 16 CFR 1201 Category I and II.

Extrusions: Extruded shapes shall be aluminum 6463-T5 or 6063-T5 alloy depending on application.

Hardware: Aluminum, solid brass, polished stainless steel, or as specified. Patented (FRS) fail safe adjustable roller system. Aluminum piano hinge and stainless steel pivot bolts. All ASD screws are rustproof stainless steel.

Finish: Brite dip anodized aluminum – 6463-T5 alloy to be selectively A1 buffed to AA-C31-A21 brite dip silver specification; and AA-C31-A23 brite dip brass, tawny brass specification. Satin anodized aluminum – 6063-T5 alloy to be anodized to a commercial AA-C22-A21 satin silver and AA-C22-A23 satin gold specification. Powder coat – modified polymer to be thermo set and cured at a minimum 400°F as per AAMA-603 specifications.

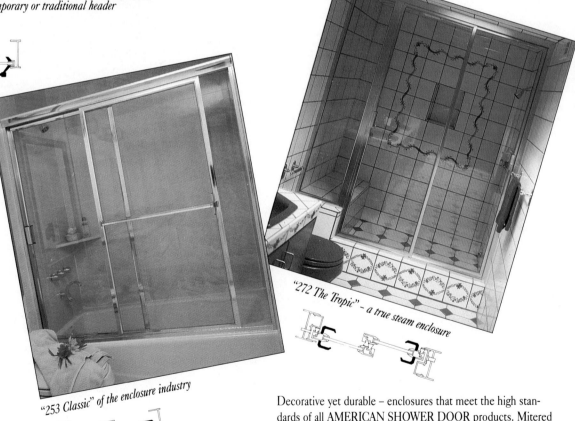

"272 The Tropic" – a true steam enclosure

"253 Classic" of the enclosure industry

Decorative yet durable – enclosures that meet the high standards of all AMERICAN SHOWER DOOR products. Mitered corners, open "L" track for clean maintenance-free operation, and our fail-safe roller system make AMERICAN the quality choice of the tub and shower enclosure market. All designs are interchangeable with our door and panel systems.

American

SHOWER DOOR

Specification Guide

DOORS	#	Model	Standard Dimensions (in Inches)	Maximum Dimensions	Standard Finishes	Suggested Applications
FRAMELESS: Pivot	002	Infinity	20-1/2 - 35-1/2×67-1/2	74 High	SS-BS-BB-TB	Contemporary master shower – frameless sculptured glass design – 1" adjustability
Piano Hinged	502	Infinity	30×67	24×78	SS-BS-BB-TB	Piano hinge gives maximum stability with contemporary frameless appeal
FRAMED: Pivot – 200 Rail	212	Magnum	21 - 37×63-5/16 or 21 - 37×69-5/16	37×72	SS-SG-BS-BB-TB	Strong modular design for large and heavy traffic showers – 2" adjustability
Pivot – 355 Rail	353	Atlas	41-1/2 - 43-1/4×63-5/16	46×72	SS-BS-BB	Commercial modular design meets 36" barrier free requirement
Hinged – 200 Rail (regular or steam)	220	Classic	30×62-5/16 or 30×72	33×84	SS-SG-BS-BB-TB	Symmetrical custom fit for the master bath
Hinged – 355 Rail (regular or steam)	355	Max	30×70	36×96	SS-BS-BB	Large custom floor to ceiling steam shower
Hinged Cafe Doors – 200 Rail (regular or steam)	440	Smithsonian	60×70	60×84	SS-SG-BS-BB-TB	Double swing cafe doors with 60" barrier free opening
*SOLID BRASS AND 3/8" GLASS: Hinged Solid Brass – 455 Rail (regular or steam)	455	Vintage	33×72	33×84	Finishes are plated, brushed or powder coated on solid brass	Classic piano hinged for elite solid brass luxury in the master shower
Pivot – 3/8" Glass	905	Crystal	30×72	30×84		Our brass pivot system has a "minimal" look
Hinged – 3/8" Glass (regular or steam)	902	Crystal	2 hinges/75 lbs.	3 hinges or more 80+ lbs. or steam		All glass shower room with brass "crystal" hinges
Hinged – Aluminum	802	Crystal	2 hinges/75 lbs.		BS-BB with brass hinges	Aluminum extrusions with solid brass hardware for affordability

ENCLOSURES	#	Model	Standard Dimensions (in Inches)	Maximum Dimensions	Standard Finishes	Suggested Applications
FRAMELESS: With Frameless Panels	805	Infinity-E	59-3/8×56-7/8 or 68-7/8	72×76	SS-BS-BB-TB	A new reversible unit with stay clean track. 3/16" or 1/4" glass may be used
	2805	Infinity-E+	59×48×56-7/8 or 68-7/8	76 High	SS-BS-BB-TB	Adds a water tight environment without visual barriers
FRAMED - 200 RAIL:	253	Classic-E	59-3/8×58-1/2 or 70-1/2	72×80	SS-BS-BB-TB	Traditional master tub/shower with sturdy quality extrusions
With Framed Panels	253A	Classic E+	59×48×58-1/2 or 70-1/2	80 High	SS-BS-BB-TB	Framed Panels
With Frameless Panels	2253	Classic E+	Same as above plus angle	80 High	SS-BS-BB-TB	'Quik-stall' panel system for easy and leakproof installation
STANDARD – 703 RAIL:	703	Starlite	58-7/8×57-3/4 or 69-3/4	72×76	SS-SG-BS-BB	Secondary tub/shower for children and multi-unit applications
With Frameless Panels	2703	Starlite+	59×48×57-3/4 or 69-3/4	76 Max.	SS-SG-BS-BB	Maximizes visual space
FRAMED STEAM:	272	Tropic	60×76	96 High with transom	BS-BB	Residential/commercial steam room for tub or shower
BI-FOLD:	814	Aqua Maid	22-1/2 to 68-1/2×57-1/2	69-3/4 High	SS-SG	Obscure vinyl stacking panels designed for mobile or tight space/maximum opening
*SOLID BRASS AND 3/8" GLASS: Framed – 455 Rail	453	Vintage-E	Custom Sizes	Custom Sizes	Finishes are plated, brushed or powder coated on solid brass	Elite solid brass double slide enclosure
With Framed Panels	453A	Vintage-E+	Custom Sizes	Custom Sizes		Solid brass headers and jambs – may add brass towel bars or handles
Framless 3/8" Glass	953	Crystal-E+	Custom Sizes	Custom Sizes		3/8" tempered glass with solid brass headers
With Framless Panels	2953	Crystal-E+	Custom Sizes	Custom Sizes		Contemporary look of invisibility
With Aluminum Extrusions	853	Crystal	Custom Sizes	Custom Sizes	BS-BB	Elegance with less expensive aluminum extrusions and brass hardware

DAYLITES	#	Model	Standard Dimensions (in Inches)	Maximum Dimensions	Standard Finishes	Suggested Applications
FRAMELESS: Pivot Door – Frameless Panels	020	Infinity+	71 High	74 High	SS-BS-BB-TB	Sturdy contemporary 2000 framless panel system with our 002 Infinity door
Hinged Door – Frameless Panels	5020	Infinity+	71 High	24×78 Door	SS-BS-BB-TB	Adds stability of piano hinge to the system
FRAMED Pivot Door – 200 Rail	2100	Magnum+	71 High	74 High	SS-BS-BB-TB	Magnum pivot door with our 2000 frameless panel system
Hinged Door – 200 Rail	100	Classic+	69-5/16 High	84 High	SS-SG-BS-BB	Classic door with 100 framed panel system gives a solid look of traditional design
Hinged Door – 200 Rail With Frameless Panels (regular or steam)	5100	Classic+	71 High	84 High	SS-BS-BB-TB	Classic hinged door with 2000 frameless panel system
Hinged Door – 355 Rail With Frameless Panels (steam)	3100	Max+	To 96 High	To 96 High	SS-BS-BB	Maximum strength door with invisible panels for the steam shower
*SOLID BRASS AND 3/8" GLASS: Hinged – Solid Brass Doors With Framed Panels	421	Vintage+	Custom Sizes	Custom Sizes	Finishes are plated, brushed or powder coated on solid brass	Solid brass piano hinged with sturdy framed panels
Hinged – Solid Brass Doors With 3/8" Frameless Panels	491	Vintage+	Custom Sizes	Custom Sizes		The same sturdy door with invisible 3/8" frameless panels
Hinged 3/8" Crystal (regular or steam)	9000	Crystal+	Custom Sizes	Custom Sizes		Invisible leakproof design for the shower
Pivot 3/8" Crystal	9050	Crystal+	Custom Sizes	Custom Sizes		A unique new concept in invisibility
With Aluminum Extrusions	8000	Crystal+	Custom Sizes	Custom Sizes	BS-BB	Brass hardware with aluminum extrusions

Color codes ALUMINUM: SS = satin silver; SG = satin gold; BS = brite dip silver; BB = brite dip brass (true brass match); TB = tawny brass. A wide range of powder coat options: brushed brite dip silver; brushed brite dip brass; special anodized finishes on request. **SOLID BRASS:** polished chrome, polished brass, brushed pewter, brushed nickel, antique brass, 24k gold, or custom.

Suggested tempered glass styles: Clear, obscure, bronze, grey, reed, rain, glue chip, silk screen, etched, v-grooved, UltraGlas and other custom designs.

Panel systems: In-line, 90 degree, 135 degree, or off angle with or without buttress. Custom engineering and manufacturing for any wall, ceiling or panel design.

*All 3/8" applications also applicable to 1/2" glass.

American

6920 E. Slauson Avenue • City of Commerce, CA 90040

HELO SAUNA & STEAM

For Over 40 Years, More American Architects
Have Specified Helo Than Any Other.

HELO

A World-Class Reputation for Quality and Capabilities!

HELO SAUNAS–A WORLDWIDE QUALITY STANDARD!
Helo has become the world's largest sauna manufacturer through innovation, through product development and an uncompromising commitment to quality. Helo saunas, at first glance, are very impressive; they become even more so upon careful examination.

Helo quality is immediately evident by our use of woods—clear and graded to the lightest of colors. It continues with Helo styling. The sauna itself, of course, but also the sleek, contemporary heaters and user-friendly controls.

Yes, careful thought has gone into every aspect of Helo saunas and this is the basis of Helo quality. It means superior value and years of satisfaction delivered in the name of relaxation and good health.

HELO SAUNA CONTROLS

HELO CONTROLS OFFER TODAY'S BEST TECHNOLOGY.
Offering both mechanical and programmable/digital technology, Helo controls are state-of-the-art, reliable and very friendly to the user. Whether built in to the heater or wall-mounted, Helo controls are compact and attractive.

All Helo heaters and controls manufactured in our factory are UL listed and now carry the ISO 9001 certificate of quality assurance. For years, this certification has been the international symbol of quality assurance in Europe. Now it has come to be similarly recognized in the United States, Canada and Mexico, too.

ME-1T and ME-2T

MB

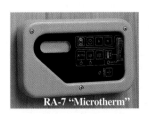

RA-7 "Microtherm"

RA-8 "Saunastat"

Control contains on/off switch for sauna light, 1-hr. timer with 9-hour pre-set and calibrated thermostat. ME-1T for use with BE Series heaters. ME-2T for use with HF Series heaters. Surface mounted, 8⁵/₈"H x 9⁵/₈"W x 3"D.

Control includes 60-minute timer, light switch, and thermostat. Recessed/flush mounted. Rough-in size: 6³/₄"K x 8³/₄"W x 3³/₄"D. Use with BE series heaters.

24-hour programmability, sleek European design, only 1" thick. Surface mounted. 4¹/₂"H x 7¹/₂"W x 1"D. Use with contactor model MA-4. Contractor is recessed/flush mounted. Rough-in size: 10¹/₈"H x 9¹/₂"W x 3³/₄"D. Use with SO and HF series heaters.

7-day programmability, shows set time and actual time, set temp. & actual temp., on/off light switch, Easy to program. Use with contactor model MA-5. Contractor is recessed/flush mounted. Rough-in size: 10¹/₈"H x 9¹/₂"W x 3³/₄"D. Use with SO and HF series heaters. 3¹/₂"H x 6¹/₄"W x 1³/₈"D.

A Sauna can Only be as Good as its Heater!

THE WORLD'S MOST ADVANCED HEATERS ARE FROM HELO!

Among the reasons today's Helo heaters can deliver a better heat with greater efficiency is our larger rock capacity with more of the rocks in direct contact with the heating elements themselves. More rocks means a softer, more gentle heat and the ability to create soft, comfortable steam. Never the less, the styling remains sleek and contemporary! Helo heaters are easy-to-oper-ate, have triple walls for safety and are crafted using a variety of non-corrosive metals and two-toned baked enamel finish. The name Helo means years and years of attractive dependable service.

MODELS: 21T AND 30T: Perfect for personal size saunas or 2 person saunas. Easy to use, side mounted and reversible controls. Timer includes 9-hour time delay feature.

MODELS: SO-45-BE, SO-45-S, SO-60-BE, SO-60-S, SO-80-BE, SO-80-S.

- *Wall mounted or with optional floor stand*
- *Increased rock capacity (70#)*
- *Symmetrical construction for a finished look on all four sides (Ideal for saunas with windows)*
- *Use with separate controls (RA or ME Series) or,*
- *Built-in controls mounted at a higher level on the side for easy access and visibility. Timer includes 9 hour time delay feature.*

MODELS: HF-84, HF-120 : Fantasy Series Heaters: A new idea sets a new standard! The old way: heat some rocks and then have the rocks heat the air. In commercial saunas, left on for hours, the air can get too hot and the rocks aren't hot enough.

Helo's new Fantasy Series uses a patented new idea: heat the rocks and air separately and independently! The results are amazing! Helo's "Turbo System"™ *delivers 45% more heat per kilowatt* and the heat and steam delivered is soft and soothing–a new standard.

Other important features include Octagonal Design (great for mid-sauna placement), a huge rock capacity (over 200 pounds capacity), choice of stainless or baked enamel exterior, and choice of controls built-in or separate. Optional built-in heater guard rail.

21T, 30T
Minnette 17" H x 15" W x 7" D 25 lb. rocks

SO-45-S, SO-60-S, SO-80-S
22" H x 18 3/4" W x 11" D 70 lb. rocks

SO-45-BE, SO-60-BE, SO-80-BE
22" H x 18 3/4" W x 11" D 70 lb. rocks

HF-84, HF-120
Fantasy Series 31½"H x 21¾"W x 21¾"D
200 lbs. to 230 lbs. rocks

Heaters with Built-In Controls

Heater Model No.	Minimum CU. FT. Sauna Room	Maximum CU. FT. Sauna Room	Watts	Amps	Voltage	Phase	Wire Size 90°C Copper	Control Model No.	Shipping Weight
21T	45	100	2100	17.5	120	1	10	Built-In	14
21T	45	100	2100	8.75	240	1	12	Built-In	14
30T	70	150	3000	25.0	120	1	10	Built-In	16
30T	70	150	3000	12.5	240	1	12	Built-In	16
SO-45-S	100	200	4500	18.8	240	1	10	Built-In	35
SO-60-S	175	300	6000	25	240	1	10	Built-In	36
SO-60-S/3	175	300	6000	16.8	208	3	12	Built-In	36
SO-80-S	250	420	8000	33.3	240	1	8	Built-In	37
SO-80-S/3	250	420	8000	22.2	208	3	10	Built-In	37

Heaters with Separate Controls

Heater Model No.	Minimum CU. FT. Sauna Room	Maximum CU. FT. Sauna Room	Watts	Amps	Voltage	Phase	Wire Size 90°C Copper	Control Model No.	Shipping Weight
SO-45-BE	100	200	4500	18.8	240	1	10	RA or ME	35
SO-60-BE	175	300	6000	25	240	1	10	RA or ME	36
SO-60-BE/3	175	300	6000	16.8	208	3	12	RA or ME	36
SO-80-BE	250	420	8000	33.3	240	1	8	RA or ME	37
SO-80-BE/3	250	420	8000	33.3	208	3	10	RA or ME	34
Fantasy 84	300	650	8,400	35	240	1	8	Built-In ME or RA	70
Fantasy 84	300	650	8,400	20.2	240	3	10	Built-In ME or RA	70
Fantasy 84	300	650	8,400	23.3	208	3	10	Built-In ME or RA	70
Fantasy 120	600	950	12,000	50	240	1	6	Built-In ME or RA	70
Fantasy 120	600	950	12,300	29.6	240	3	8	Built-In ME or RA	70
Fantasy 120	600	950	12,300	34.2	208	3	8	Built-In ME or RA	70

UL Listed   CUL Certified

HELO CUSTOM-CUT SAUNAS

From Your Design — Pre-Cut Material Packages

Your Options are Limitless.

CUSTOM-CUT IS A SAUNA BUILT TO FIT ANY SPACE. From your blueprint, floor plan or dimensions, you can have a sauna under a stairway, as part of a corporate fitness center, even outside on the deck.

CUSTOM-CUT SAUNAS are perfect for new construction or remodeling:

- *Residences*
- *Hotels*
- *Corporate Fitness Centers*
- *Health Clubs*
- *Apartment Buildings*

YOU SUPPLY THE IMAGINATION. Go ahead—angles, curves, dramatic use of glass, unusual door designs—if you can design it, we can build it. Once designed, you merely supply the studding, insulation and exterior walls. We do the rest. Each kit contains:

- *interior walls and ceilings. Cut-to-length, tongue and groove, clear western red cedar (or other woods of your choice)*
- *all interior trim*
- *a genuine Helo heater, rocks and heater guard*
- *pre-assembled benches and headrests*
- *pre-hung door with glass window or all-glass door*
- *room light, duckboard flooring, thermometer, all hardware*
- *and, of course, the wooden bucket and ladle.*

In addition to standard sizes shown on pages 4 & 5, Helo offers a limitless variety of custom-made, pre-fabricated rooms.
Call 1-800-882-4352 for free design assistance and alternative layouts.

For Custom-Cut packages, dimensions shown on pages 4 & 5 are I.D. of framed walls. For Panel-Built packages dimensions shown on pages 4 & 5 are approximate O.D. of pre-built panels.

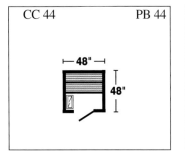
CC 44 / PB 44 — 48" × 48"

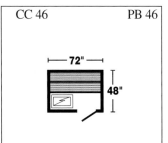
CC 46 / PB 46 — 72" × 48"

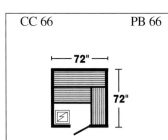
CC 66 / PB 66 — 72" × 72"

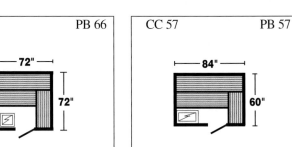
CC 57 / PB 57 — 84" × 60"

4

HELO PANEL-BUILT SAUNAS

Our Pre-Manufactured Designs are Modular and Portable!

One Hour and it's Working - Beautifully!

HELO PANEL-BUILT SAUNAS ARE A PERFECT ADDITION to any home or yard. They are beautiful, of the highest quality, and ready for assembly in as little as 60 minutes.

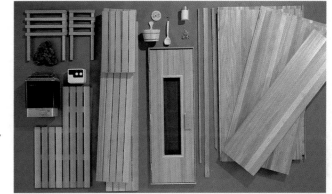

PANEL-BUILT KITS INCLUDE EVERYTHING:

- *all wall and ceiling prefabricated panels*
- *panels are finished inside and out, with clear, tongue and groove, western red cedar, fully insulated, and includes a foil vapor barrier*
- *all interior and exterior trim*
- *Plywood paneling available as option for exterior walls to be hidden, painted, papered or tiled*
- *genuine Helo heater, rocks, and heater guard*
- *pre-hung door with glass window or all-glass door*
- *pre-assembled benches, headrest and duckboard flooring*
- *room light, thermometer, all hardware; yes, even the wooden bucket and ladle!*

HELO PANEL-BUILT MEANS NO CONSTRUCTION NEEDED.

Because they are free-standing and each panel is fully insulated, no studding is necessary and these wonderful saunas can be moved and re-assembled on any hard floor. You should check, but in most cases a building permit won't be necessary.

Helo saunas are ideal for fitness centers.

Shown above: Helo 6-sided pre-fab sauna in a corporate fitness center

For Panel-Built packages dimensions shown on pages 4 & 5 are approximate O.D. of pre-built panels. For Custom-Cut packages, dimensions shown on pages 4 & 5 are I.D. of framed walls.

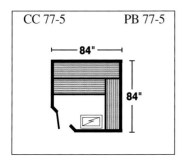

CC 77-5   PB 77-5
84"
84"

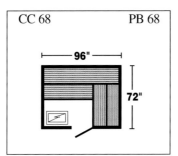

CC 68   PB 68
96"
72"

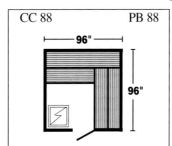

CC 88   PB 88
96"
96"

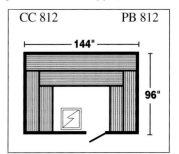

CC 812   PB 812
144"
96"

Unforgettable Steam.

STEAM ROOMS

Helo's beautiful high glaze acrylic steam rooms are pre-fabricated and easy-to-install. And because they are modular, these free-standing complete packages allow you, in no time at all, to enjoy the soothing relaxation of steam. A Helo steam room can provide perfect comfort for two to eleven people, and will fit into almost any residential or commercial space.

Helo means easy cleaning and little maintenance because there is no grout to clean, no tiles to replace. Our modules are of gleaming 8mm acrylic sheeting with ABS reinforcement. Yet another reason why Helo means an optimum steam experience.

Configurations of Helo modular, prefab rooms

Shown above, nine person steam room; sizes available for two to eleven persons.

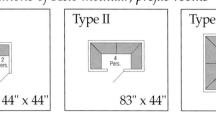

Type I	Type II	Type III 5-Sided	Type IV	Type V	Type VI
2 Pers.	4 Pers.	6 Pers.	7 Pers.	9 Pers.	11 Pers.
44" x 44"	83" x 44"	83" x 83"	83" x 83"	113" x 83"	144" x 83"

Soothing Steam for the Body and Soul.

HELO STEAM GENERATORS, THE NEW INDUSTRY STANDARD.

Helo's steam generator designs are intelligent and feature top quality material and workmanship. You might say, "They've thought of everything!" Each is compact, good looking, and Helo's fitting kit assures very easy installation with all accessories and controls simply plugging into the face of the generator. Helo steam generators have stainless steel tanks with Incalloy 825 elements for high output and long life. Each provides continuous steam, dispersed evenly, and has an electronic low-water cut-out, a 25 minute timer and a safety pressure release valve. Other features include: an on/off air button for use in the steam room, an LED to indicate when in the steam cycle, and an "essence reservoir" for mixing scent with steam. Options include an automatic flush and electrical cord for easy plug-in.

CLUB-STEAM SERIES

Featuring a 1" top-quality polished chrome steamhead with a fragrance reservoir, a continuous water feed system, sight glass, VariTemp control, steam pressure gauge and drain, Helo's Club-Steam Series is reliable, dependable and built to accommodate even the largest steambaths found in health clubs and resorts.

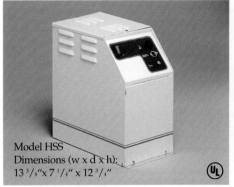

Model HSS
Dimensions (w x d x h):
13 $^3/_8$"x 7 $^1/_4$" x 12 $^3/_4$"

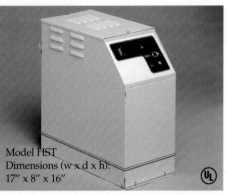

Model HST
Dimensions (w x d x h):
17" x 8" x 16"

Model HCS
Dimensions (w x d x h):
26" x 20" x 20"

Built to ASME Standards

Model	Max. cu. ft.	kW	Amps	Voltage	Phase
HSS-30	50	3	12.5	240	1
HSS-45	100	4.5	18.75	240	1
HSS-65	200	6.5	27.1	240	1

For commercial applications, the HSS Series is available with 208 volt elements.

Model	Max. cu. ft.	kW	Amps	Voltage	Phase
HST-80	300	8	33.3	240	1
HST-80	300	8	19.3	208	3
HST-100	400	10	41.7	240	1
HST-100	400	10	27.8	208	3
HST-120	500	12	50	240	1
HST-120	500	12	33.6	208	3

Model	Max. cu. ft.	kW	3 Phase Voltage	Max. Amps
HCS-135	600	13.5	208/240	240
HCS-195	800	19.5	208/240	208
HCS-255	1200	25.5	208/240	240
HCS-300	1500	30.0	208/240	208

Model HSW
Dimensions (w x d x h):
12 $^1/_4$"x 6" x 17 $^3/_4$"

INTERNAL THERMOSTATIC CONTROL

Install within the steambath. LED temperature display when generarator is turned on. Thermostatically maintains the temperature within the steam bath, to your preset temperature. Shows set temp. and actual temp. Flush mount. Dimensions: 3 $^1/_2$" x 3 $^1/_2$".

EXTERNAL THERMOSTATIC CONTROL

Install outside the steam bath. 24 hr. programmability. LCD clock display shows set time and actucal time, set temperature and actual temperature changes to display the steam bath temperature when generator is turned on. Flush mount. Dimensions: 4" x 5 $^7/_8$".

The HSW steam generator is splash proof (IP34) and designed for wall hanging adjacent to the enclosure. The output power is variable in three steps – 1650 W, 2475 W and 3300 W. The generator is supplied ready for connection with 5 ft. water hose, 5 ft. steam hose with outlet head and 5 ft. power cable. The new model is suitable for steam rooms up to 90 cu. ft.

STEAM SUITE

Helo Acrylic Steam Suites are perfect for new or remodeling bathroom projects. Replace standard tubs and showers with these beautiful self-contained, vapor-proof enclosures. Available in single piece construction or 3-piece "renovator" unit to fit through standard interior doorways. Call 1-800-882-4352 for complete catalog on the six steam suite sizes and designs.

HELO SPECIFICATIONS

GENERAL: Sauna room(s) shall be manufactured by Helo Sauna, Inc., 575 East Cokato St., Cokato, MN 55321. The following specifications include design parameters for Helo prefab/modular saunas, as well as for Helo Custom-Cut material packages.

WORK TO BE DONE BY OTHERS: All work set forth below will be included under other sections for the specifications:

For all Helo sauna types:

1. Finish painting and/or staining of exterior surfaces.

2. Subfloor and/or foundation work.

3. All electrical work from supply, including connections to control, heater and light.

For Helo Custom-Cut saunas:

4. Installation of stud walls (or firrings strips) and ceiling joists.

5. Installation of insulation and vapor barrier between wall studs and ceiling joists.

CODE REQUIREMENTS: All materials, components and work shall conform to all applicable local, state and federal building and safety codes, ordinances and regulations.

TYPE CONSTRUCTION: HELO CUSTOM CUT MATERIAL PACKAGES (for installation on previously framed walls)

Wall framing shall be on 16" centers. Standard framed wall shall have 2" x 4" studs, bottom base plate treated, and ceiling lowered to 7' I.D. from floor to framing. Existing masonry walls shall have firring strips on 16" centers; metal studs shall have firring strips—for nailing of T&G wall boards.

Walls and ceiling shall be insulated with R11 rated fiberglass insulation, with foil vapor barrier.

When ordering: sauna material package, shall be Helo model CC_____ . Provide interior dimensions of the framed space, and indicate direction of ceiling joists.

Walls and ceiling interior materials shall be 1" x 4" V-joint, kiln dried to 11% or less, T&G clear, Western Red Cedar, or clear, vertical grain Redwood, or clear vertical grain Western Hemlock. Boards to be blind nailed using 5p galvanized nails, or comparable galvanized staples.

TYPE CONSTRUCTION: HELO PANEL-BUILT SAUNA PACKAGES (free-standing, modular units).

No framed walls are required for Helo Panel-Built packages. Install on any level, water proof fioor.

Wall and ceiling panels shall be framed of 2" x 2" Douglas Fir or cedar, insulated with fiberglass batts, vapor barrier of type C Reynolds Building foil. Panel interior and exterior shall be lined with 1" x 4", V-joint, kiln dried, clear Western Red Cedar (or optional Redwood or Hemlock). Optional: panel exterior can be 1/4" smooth Plywood on walls to be hidden or walls to be covered with drywall or tile.

TYPE CONSTRUCTION: ALL TYPES—CUSTOM CUT AND PANEL BUILT.

BENCHES: Shall be preassembled. Face and Tops of clear, kiln-dried Western Red Cedar (or Redwood), S4S, 1" x 4" (tops with 1/2" spacing). Internal frames of Western Red Cedar (or Redwood or Douglas Fir) 2" x 4"; internal cross framing of clear 1" x 4" Cedar (or Redwood). Tops fastened from bottom with stainless steel screws. Bench supports of clear, kiln-dried Western Red Cedar (or Redwood or Douglas Fir) 2" x 4".

INTERIOR AND EXTERIOR TRIM: Corner and cove molding of clear, kiln-dried Western Red Cedar (or Redwood). Panel-Built saunas also include facia of same material.

HEATER GUARD RAIL: Shall be constructed of clear cedar or redwood, to surround heater. Dimensions shall match UL requirements for proper spacing between heater and guard rail.

DOOR: Shall be one of three standard Helo types. Helo Model 'DF 24/80': 2' 0" x 6' 8" of vertical grain Douglas Fir rails with sealed, double pane, tempered glass window (15" x 64"), prehung on clear Cedar (or Redwood) jamb; or Helo Model 'CC 24/72': 2' 0" x 6' 0" hand-crafted, triple thick, clear Western Red Cedar or Redwood door, with sealed, double pane, tempered glass window (12" x 60"), prehung on clear Cedar (or Redwood) jamb; or Helo Model 'AG 24/72': a 2' 0" x 6' 0" all-glass door (no wood on the door portion), using 5/16" bronze tinted, tempered glass, mounted on 2" thick Cedar (or Redwood) jamb. All doors include handles, casing, jamb, and threshold. Hardware on wood doors to include two 4" self closing hinges (no catches).

Douglas Fir DF 24/80	Cedar CC 24/72	Glass AG 24/72
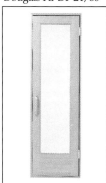	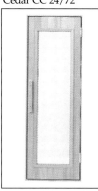	

SAUNA HEATER: Shall be Helo Model_____ , sized according to the size room as shown on page 3. Heater shall be UL listed. Shall include peridotite igneous rocks.

CONTROLS: Shall be Helo Model_____ , UL listed, and matched with heater according to charts on page 2 and 3.

FLOOR: Floor shall be of cement, ceramic tile, vinyl flooring or similar waterproof type (no carpeting). Removable duckboard floor of Cedar or Redwood is provided for walk area in front of benches.

LIGHT: Shall be wall-mounted, UL listed, vapor-proof Progress P5511. Frosted white globe with satin finish, neoprene gasket, brushed aluminum base.

ACCESSORIES: All sauna packages include standard accessories of thermometer, wood bucket, wood ladle, head/back rests, duckboards. A wide range of additional accessories are available. Request Helo's accessory catalog for more information.

WARRANTY: All Helo sauna room components are fully warranted for one year. Helo heaters have a five-year limited warranty (one year for commercial saunas) against defects in material and workmanship. Controls have a one-year limited warranty against defects in material and workmanship. For further information regarding the Helo warranty, please contact Helo or your local authorized Helo dealer.

DESIGN ASSISTANCE: Helo's design staff will gladly offer any assistance you may require when designing or specifying sauna rooms and heaters, steambaths and steam generators.

Helo reserves the right to change specifications and design without notice.
© 1996 Helo Sauna Inc   Printed in U.S.A.

Your Helo Distributor is:

For more information contact:

1-800-882-4352

HELO SAUNA INC.
575 East Cokato Street
Cokato, Minnesota 55321
612-286-6304 ● Fax 612-286-2224

HELO FACTORIES LTD.
Oy Saunatec Ltd.
PB 15
10901 HANKO Finland

Design, quality, elegance. Discover the magic of TradeWind Whirlpools.

Tradewind Whirlpool Baths are available in a variety of marvelous shapes and sizes to compliment any decor—from the traditional to the ultra-modern. Each unit is crafted from the finest color-fast acrylic available. Every Tradewind is built to the same exacting standards that insure countless years of almost maintenance-free enjoyment. In fact every unit we make is completely tested by our design technicians before it receives the Tradewind name plate. Our own stamp of approval. The hydro-therapy massage jets are fully adjustable and are placed low in the tub for maximum massage benefit and optimum water conservation. The tough full one-horse power pump gives you all the power you need. All units are pre-plumbed for easy installation, and are available in a variety of popular decorator colors. Tradewind, discover the luxury for yourself.

TRADEWIND®
ACRYLIC
WHIRLPOOLS

STANDARD SERIES WHIRLPOOLS

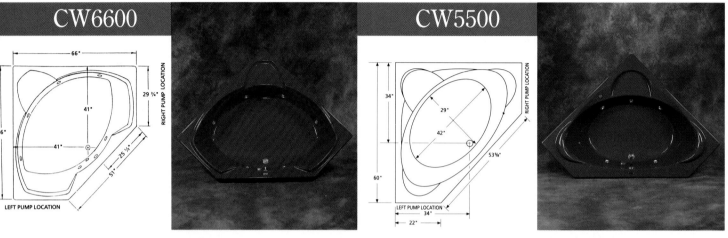

CW6600
Operating capacity-70 GAL.

CW5500
Operating capacity-40 GAL.

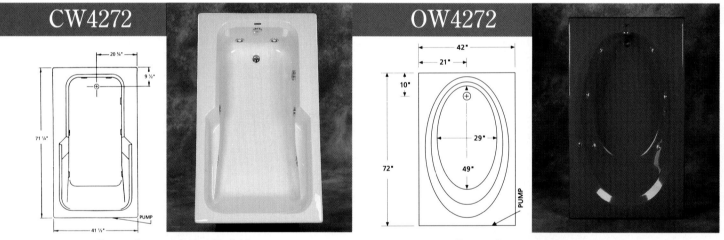

CW4272
Operating capacity-52 GAL.

OW4272
Operating capacity-42 GAL.

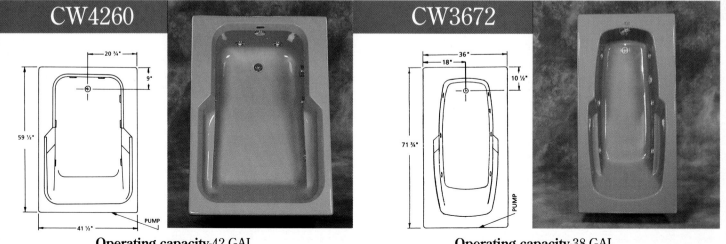

CW4260
Operating capacity-42 GAL.

CW3672
Operating capacity-38 GAL.

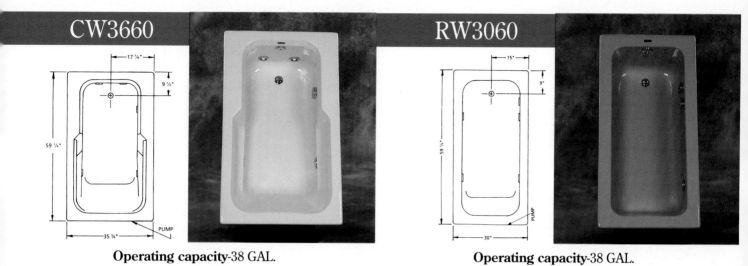

CW3660

17 ⅞"
9 ½"
59 ¼"
35 ¾"
PUMP

Operating capacity-38 GAL.

RW3060

15"
9"
59 ½"
30"
PUMP

Operating capacity-38 GAL.

PUMP LOCATION MAY BE RELOCATED TO
DRAIN END AS REMOTE MOUNT OPTION.

LUXURY SERIES WHIRLPOOLS

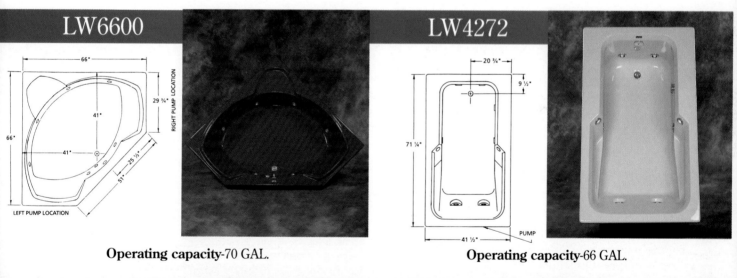

LW6600

66"
41"
66"
41"
29 ¾"
RIGHT PUMP LOCATION
51"
25 ½"
LEFT PUMP LOCATION

Operating capacity-70 GAL.

LW4272

20 ¾"
9 ½"
71 ¼"
41 ½"
PUMP

Operating capacity-66 GAL.

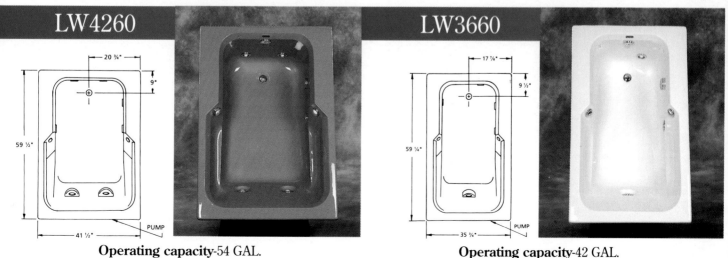

LW4260

20 ¾"
9"
59 ½"
41 ½"
PUMP

Operating capacity-54 GAL.

LW3660

17 ⅞"
9 ½"
59 ¼"
35 ¾"
PUMP

Operating capacity-42 GAL.

MODEL OW4270

Turn back the clock to a quieter time –
a time for you from TradeWind!

Run your hand over the delicate lines. The sensual curves. The graceful form of this beautiful oval whirlpool was inspired by another time. A quieter time when things were a bit slower, more relaxed, more elegant. This Victorian inspired beauty comes with all the TradeWind features that you've come to expect and more. Like the fully adjustable hydro-therapy jets located just right to give you maximum massage benefit. Then there's the automatically balanced air control system to give you the right combination of airflow and water. All our whirlpools are made of beautiful color-fast acrylic and are pre-plumbed and factory tested. Available in most decorator colors. S-o-o-o-o turn back the clock to a quieter time and relax courtesy of TradeWind.

TOP VIEW

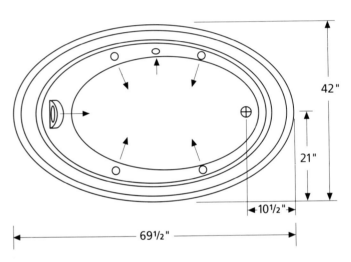

 Listed 93FO
hydromassage bathtub

FEATURES

- Durable acrylic surface always warm to the touch and easy to maintain
- Fully adjustable hydro-therapy massage jets
- Low volume design for water conservation
- 1 horsepower quiet run pump
- Self drain system
- Integral stuctural platform base
- Durable Polyester® backside reinforcement
- UL Listed
- Slip-resistive surface
- Limited 5-year warranty
- Built to last a lifetime
- Inside depth to allow total submersion
- Automatically balanced air control system
- Available in most decorator colors
- Many options available
- Meets ANSI Z124.1 and A119.12.7
- Pneumatic switch standard

Model OW4270
SPECIFICATIONS

PUMP	1 H.P.
ELECTRICAL	115 V.A.C.
LENGTH	70"
WIDTH	40"
INSIDE DEPTH	20"
OUTSIDE DEPTH	22"
OPERATING CAPACITY	45 GAL.

MODEL CW3260
Form following function –
TradeWind –
We've got your whirlpool!

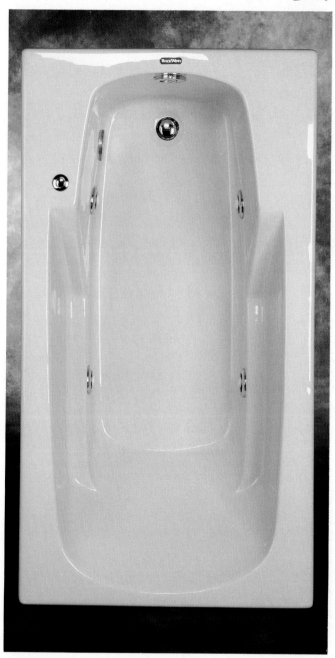

An elegant, functional whirlpool specifically designed to fit the tightest scheme. The essence of comfort as well as beauty. This whirlpool could be precisely what you've been looking for with fully adjustable hydro-therapy jets and an automatically balanced air control system. Each unit is pre-plumbed and factory tested. It's made of beautiful color-fast acrylic for long life and is available in most decorator colors. For a lifetime of carefree enjoyment that you will appreciate, it's got to be a TradeWind. Detachable apron (Model SK6020) available. Soaking tub (Model CT3260) available.

TOP VIEW

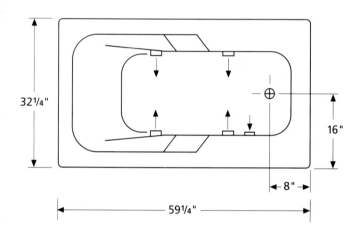

 Listed 93FO
hydromassage bathtub

FEATURES
- Durable acrylic surface always warm to the touch and easy to maintain
- Fully adjustable hydro-therapy massage jets
- Low volume design for water conservation
- 1 horsepower quiet run pump
- Self drain system
- Integral stuctural platform base
- Durable Polyester® backside reinforcement
- UL Listed
- Slip-resistive surface
- Limited 5-year warranty
- Built to last a lifetime
- Inside depth to allow total submersion
- Automatically balanced air control system
- Available in most decorator colors
- Many options available
- Meets ANSI Z124.1 and A119.12.7
- Pneumatic switch standard

Model CW3260
SPECIFICATIONS

PUMP	1 H.P.
ELECTRICAL	115 V.A.C.
LENGTH	59 1/4"
WIDTH	32 1/4"
INSIDE DEPTH	20"
OUTSIDE DEPTH	18"
OPERATING CAPACITY	26 GAL.

OPTIONAL EQUIPMENT

TradeWind®
ACRYLIC WHIRLPOOLS

Tradewind's *Easy Touch* ™ Electronic Control has built-in twenty minute timer and low water safety sensor. Simply fill the tub and touch the Tradewind nameplate and sit back, relax and enjoy.

Tradewind's factory installed safety grab bars provide excellent gripping capabilities especially for the physically impaired bather. Available in Chrome, Polished Brass or Antique Brass.

Tradewind's Thermal Wrap Heat Transfer System provides proper water temperature maintenance. The system extracts waste heat from the pump motor and transfers it to the bathing water. The most economical and efficient whirlpool heater available. Requires no extra electrical hookup or electricity to maintain your bath temperature.

BAR SINKS

Tradewind BAR SINKS are manufactured to the same exacting standards as our entire line of whirlpool baths. The acrylic surface is durable and is available in all the decorator colors. They are designed with a full sink strainer drain and are built to accept a garbage disposer. The 15" x 15" design is perfect for most all bar applications and is deep enough for large glasses and decanters.

OTHER ACRYLIC PRODUCTS

Tradewind offers other items not shown. We have a limited line of shower bases, laundry sinks (self rimming drop-in design much like the bar sink shown above), and bathroom lavatories. Please contact us for further information on these and any other new products that we may offer.

7612 Drag Strip Road • Fairview, TN 37062
Phone 615/799-8300 • FAX 615/799-8477

RainDancer, the wonderful shower/massage system that functions like a whirlpool. It massages! It soothes! It invigorates! You have at your command 13 sprayers that massage and are controlled electronically in 5 independent zones. You may select from constant or pulsating spray modes for any or all of the zones. Made of durable acrylic, available in most decorator colors.

RainDancer — experience it!

Shown with chrome trim — polished brass trim available.

Shower cascade
Relax as the gentle spray of the shower cascade caresses your head, neck and shoulders. You can manually vary the intensity of the spray to your own personal desire and you can choose the pulsating mode for a more invigorating shower.

Shoulder spray
Twin bullet sprayers massage your neck and shoulders to help relieve tension.

Lateral spray
Six body sprayers, three along each side, gently massage your body. Each sprayer is directionally adjustable for your showering pleasure.

Hand held spray
The hand held spray allows the freedom of more direct massage control. Add pulsation and create your own personal hydro-massage. Right hand shown, left hand available

Electronic control panel
RainDancer's electronic control panel gives you an accurate visual display of water temperature and allows you to choose from any of five spray/massage zones. You may select constant or pulsating spray modes all at the touch of your fingertips.

Temperature control
Thermostatically-controlled valve for safety

Lumbar massage
Three bullet sprayers massage your lower back and hips. Choose either the constant spray or the invigorating pulsating mode.

Electrical requirements:
120 volt A.C./15-20 amp G.F.C.I. circuit required.

Plumbing requirements:
3/4" supply lines for hot and cold water inlets. Minimum of 45 p.s.i. actual working pressure required. Unit may work on less flow and pressure, but manufacturer makes no claims as to total performance of unit under these conditions.

Warranty:
Acrylic Unit Warranted for 5 years (limited). All electronic and plumbing warranted for 1 year (limited). See written warranty for specific limitations. Due to variances in water pressures and flow rates at each individual installation location, all functions of RainDancer may not be able to be used simultaneously. RainDancer requests a minimum working pressure of 45 p.s.i. and 3/4" supply lines to work at optimum. RainDancer reserves the right to improve this product, or revise specifications and dimensions without prior notice. Rough-in dimensions W=25" x H=53". Dimensions may vary so take actual measurements from unit prior to installation. Contact your local RainDancer distributor for current information on this product.

RainDancer™

A DIVISION OF **TRADEWIND** INDUSTRIES INC.®

7612 Drag Strip Road • Fairview, TN 37062
Phone 615/799-8300 • FAX 615/799-8477

TW0295RD Printed in USA   © TradeWind Industries, Inc., 1995

For the Look And Feel of A Real Fire.

Turn Your House into A Warm Beautiful Home

SINGLE SIDED Wood Burning Fireplaces

EM48
The Energy Master, Model EM48, offers both style and performance for a BIG IMPACT. Its high output fan system picks up instant heat generated inside your firebox and forces it through a stainless steel concealed tubular heat converter into your home. The high output fan combined with the fireplace's double wall design and seam locked firebox will offer consumers maximum heat potential with the beauty of a traditional fireplace look.

FEATURES
- Brass Trimmed doors
- Front Glass Door 42" x 24"
- Large Basket Grate
- Wire Mesh Fire Screens
- Refractory Lined Firebox
- Optional Blower

EM42
Warm up those cool nights with Heat-N-Glo's high performance Energy Master Series. This highly efficient (up to 50%), insulated fireplace has the heat circulation benefits of internal stainless steel heat tubes and installation advantages of a zero-clearance fireplace. It is certain to warm your heart, and your home.

FEATURES
- Brass Trimmed doors
- Front Glass Door 36" x 20 3/4"
- Refractory Lined Firebox
- Large Basket Grate
- Wire Mesh Fire Screens
- Standard Blower

EM41
The EM41 is sure to make a warm addition to any home. The unique option on this Energy Master fireplace is the blower positioned at the back of the fireplace. This positioning eliminates air flow resistance and more effectively moves the heat accumulated at the back of the fireplace into the room. This upscale heat circulating fireplace is a great alternative for those wanting a large viewing area, true efficiency and a great value for the dollar.

FEATURES
- Brass Trimmed doors
- Front Glass Door 31 1/2" x 20"
- Basket Grate
- Wire Mesh Fire Screens
- Refractory Lined Firebox
- Optional Blower

CBS-41
Heat-N-Glo proudly introduces the first clean burning system with a large glass door area to pass all four phases of EPA Phase II testing. The benefits of this **CLEAN BURN SYSTEM** (CBS) are two-fold: first both wood fuel and secondary gases are burned creating a very clean burn and drastically reducing emissions; and second, the unit is very efficient, using all potential energy available. The EPA approval allows this unit to be installed where wood-burning restrictions apply.

FEATURES
- Front Glass Door 36" x 19"
- Large Basket Grate
- Refractory Lined
- Wire Mesh Fire Screen
- Optional Blower

GRATE HEATER

GRATE HEATER
The GRATE HEATER is an energy efficient woodburning fireplace insert that can be used with almost any set of glass doors, even those already in place. The concealed fan circulates up to 40,000 BTU/hr, is thermostatically controlled and has a variable speed control. Custom heaters are available to fit almost any fireplace.

SEAL TIGHT GLASS DOORS
These doors not only provide a tight seal that can <u>double</u> your fireplace burn time, but can also enhance the looks of any masonry fireplace. They are available in four different finishes and eight standard sizes. When they are combined with a GRATE HEATER, the end result is a very attractive and efficient fireplace insert.

With A Heat-N-Glo Woodburning Fireplace

MULTIPLE SIDED Wood Burning Fireplaces

HST-48
The Twin Glo Model HST-48 is Heat-N-Glo's newest and largest woodburning see-thru fireplace. It offers a large unobstructed opening 42" x 24" and has an unmatched brick to brick opening of 37". Its clean face allows finishing products to be placed right up to the opening, giving the appearance of a masonry see-thru.

FEATURES
- Brass Trimmed doors
- Front Glass Door 42" x 24"
- Large Basket Grate
- Wire Mesh Fire Screens
- Refractory Lined Firebox

HST-42
This see thru offers style as well as the flexibility to develop the look you want. There are many options available, including arched glass doors and various trim kits; one right to suit the decor of your home. Available as a heat circulator or a clean face.

FEATURES
- Brass Trimmed doors
- Front Glass Door 36" x 20 3/4"
- Refractory Lined Firebox
- Large Basket Grate
- Wire Mesh Fire Screens
- Optional Blower

HST-38
For space or budget limitations, the Model HST-38 is the solution. Just as beautiful as our other see-thru models, but in a smaller size. The compact size makes for easy installations and yet will accommodate a 24" log to create a bright, beautiful fire.

FEATURES
- Brass Trimmed doors
- Front Glass Door 31 1/2" x 20"
- Basket Grate
- Wire Mesh Fire Screens
- Refractory Lined Firebox
- Optional Blower

BAY
The BAY provides the traditional qualities and advantages of a fireplace in a unique and modern design. The large front viewing area (36" x 19") with brass trimmed full view glass doors and two large side glass viewing areas (19" x 18") creates a true three dimensional effect. The BAY is available in a heat circulating version called **The BAY SUPREME.**

FEATURES
- Front Glass Door 36" x 19"
- Two Large Glass Sides 19" x 18"
- Large Basket Grate
- Refractory Lined
- Wire Mesh Fire Screen
- Clean Face

PIER
The PIER has two full size openings - a full 36" each - with the third side being the stationary end. This double-opening approach gives the homeowner the option of using a full-view fireplace as a room divider with a view from three sides. As with the BAY, a special heat-circulating unit called **The PIER SUPREME** can be special ordered.

FEATURES
- Side Glass Doors 36" x 19"
- Front Glass Door 23" x 19"
- Wire Mesh Fire Screens
- Large Basket Grate
- Clean Face

OASIS
We've got you covered from every angle! This very unique four-sided fireplace will bring out the planning creativity in architects, builders and homeowners alike. The large viewing area offers an outstanding view from all sides.

FEATURES
- Front and Rear Glass Door 36" x 19"
- Side Glass Doors 19 3/4" x 22"
- Large Basket Grate
- Wire Mesh Fire Screens
- Clean Face

DIRECT VENT Gas Fireplaces

Direct Vent Gas fireplaces were first developed and patented by Heat-N-Glo Fireplace Products in 1987. These (no chimney) gas fireplaces vent out the back of the unit eliminating the need for a chimney, making installations easy and inexpensive. Because these units take no room air for combustion, they are especially efficient (up to 70%+). These elegant gas fireplaces provide the look and feel of a wood burning fireplace, while eliminating the inconvenience and expense of burning wood.

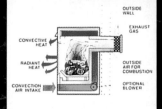

The balanced flue system eliminates the expense of a chimney system.

8000GDVFL

A grand new view. With its large viewing area, this direct vent will add warmth and efficiency to your home for years to come. As with all Heat-N-Glo gas fireplace products, the 8000GDVFL is available with a hand-held remote control for the ultimate in convenience.

FEATURES
- 26,000-38,000 BTU/hr Input
- High Thermal Efficiency (up to 70%+)*
- Six Ceramic Fiber Logs and Burning Embers
- Airtight & Clean Burning
- A.G.A. Design Certified, CGA Certified
- Optional Blower and Remote Control

6000GDVFL

The 6000GDVFL was the first and is still our most popular direct vent model. As with all direct vents, it offers the flexibility to fit almost any application. The high efficiency and heat output will make any room the coziest one in your home. Whether you want the charm of a traditional setting - or something original such as in a corner entertainment center, or under a window - *This unit will set the scene.*

FEATURES
- 19,000 - 27,000 BTU/hr Input
- High Thermal Efficiency (up to 70%+)*
- Six Ceramic Fiber Logs and Burning Embers
- Airtight & Clean Burning
- A.G.A. Design Certified, CGA Certified
- Optional Blower and Remote Control

6000XLS

Heat-N-Glo has created a fire with split fiber logs that duplicates the look and feel of a traditional campfire. In addition to this fireplace's distinct appearance, it offers all the advantages of a direct vent fireplace, including an air tight combustion chamber to keep the warm air in and the cold air out. This will maintain indoor air quality and allow for great energy efficiency. With an A.F.U.E. rating 65+%, the 6000 XLS is tested to the same standards required for todays high efficiency furnaces.

FEATURES
- 24,000-35,000 BTU/hr Input
- 6 Split Ceramic Fiber Logs
- Variable Flame Height and BTU Input
- Burning Embers and Yellow Flame
- Air Tight Combustion Chamber
- A.G.A. Designed Certified, CGA Certified

5000GDV

This mid-sized direct vent provides a great view of the fire without a significant space requirement. The generous heating capacity for this size unit will warm up the average living or family room. This unit has ceramic logs.

FEATURES
- 21,000 BTU/hr Input
- High Thermal Efficiency (up to 70%+)*
- Six Logs and Burning Embers
- Airtight & Clean Burning
- A.G.A. Design Certified, CGA Certified
- Optional Blower and Remote Control

SL-3000

The SL-3000 is a slim (12"), heat circulating, rear vent direct vent fireplace or wall heater that requires minimal space for installation. This model's compact dimensions create unlimited installation opportunities without sacrificing the view of a beautiful fire. With Heat-N-Glo's optional Trim Kits available for this model, the SL-3000 will add a dramatic look to any decor.

FEATURES
- 18,000 BTU/hr Input (NG); 16,000 (LP)
- Thermal Efficiency (75%)
- A.F.U.E. Rating of 65%
- Three Ceramic Fiber Logs Installed for Enhanced Glow and Realism
- Slim Profile (12") for Easy Installation, Compact Dimensions
- Burning Embers
- A.G.A. Design Certified, CGA Certified
- Optional Blower
- Optional Hand Held Remote Thermostat (RC-Stat)
- Optional Almond Finish
- Optional Trim Kits to Match Any Decor

These fireplaces are A.F.U.E. rated (Annual Fuel Utilization Efficiency). They are tested to the same standards required for today's high efficiency furnaces.

*As tested by Gas Technologies, Inc.

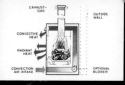

♦ TOP VENT Gas Fireplaces

8000TVFL
Make a BIG impact with this top venting gas fireplace. For the great room, a large family or living room this unit will make a beautiful centerpiece. Six realistic looking oak logs, burning embers and yellow flames make this unit a pleasure to enjoy.

FEATURES
- 24,000-35,000 BTU/hr Input
- Energy Efficiency (up to 50%)*
- Fixed Mesh Screen with Brass Trim
- A.G.A. Design Certified, CGA Certified
- Optional Blower and Remote Control

6000TVFL
The most popular fireplace in our top vent line, the 6000TVFL is the perfect size for most applications. The six realistic looking oak logs and brass trim make these fireplaces beautiful even when they are not burning.

FEATURES
- 20,000-29,000 BTU/hr Input
- Energy Efficiency (up to 50%)*
- Fixed Mesh Screen with Brass Trim
- A.G.A. Design Certified, CGA Certified
- Optional Blower and Remote Control
- Ceramic Fiber Logs

5000TV
If you are looking for a top vent fireplace adaptable to smaller spaces, take a look at the 5000TV. Add charm and warmth to your home without a large expense. This unit has ceramic logs.

FEATURES
- 21,000 BTU/hr Input
- Energy Efficiency (up to 50%)*
- Six Realistic Looking Oak Logs
- Fixed Mesh Screen with Brass Trim
- A.G.A. Design Certified, CGA Certified

FIBER LOG SETS

Create the instant atmosphere of a beautiful woodburning fire with the touch of a button. Heat-N-Glo's new gas log sets are the perfect solution for people who want the radiant look of a woodburning fire with all the convenience of clean burning gas. These ceramic fiber log sets are the first of their kind. The intricate design of the logs makes them the most authentic looking logs on the market today. Designed to fit most fireplaces and yet offer a generous size, these log sets come in three sizes 18'' (FLS-18), 24'' (FLS-24) and 30'' (FLS-30). Additionally, model ST-FLS-24 offers the realistic view of the logs, flames and embers from two sides.

GAS INSERTS *Efficiency, beauty and convenience for your existing fireplace.*

THE BAY-INSERT
offers homeowners a striking view with all the convenience of gas. Its three-sided viewing area offers a spectacular view from anywhere in the room. Additional true heating efficiency is gained due to its airtight combustion chamber.

FEATURES
- 19,000 - 27,000 BTU/hr Input
- Fixed Panel of Ceramic Glass
- Realistic Looking Ceramic Fiber Oak Logs with Bar Grate
- A.G.A. Design Certified, CGA Certified
- Requires 3'' Liners
- Standard Blower

SL-INSERT
features Heat-N-Glo's Slim Line Technology to provide an easy installation anywhere, even where space is limited. Its standard blower and variable valve offer true efficiency and convenience, with an air tight energy combustion chamber to keep the warm air in and the cold air out.

FEATURES
- 16,000 - 23,000 BTU/hr Input
- Fixed Panel of Ceramic Glass
- Realistic Looking Ceramic Fiber Oak Logs with Bar Grate
- A.G.A. Design Certified, CGA Certified
- Requires 4'' Liner
- Standard Blower

DVT-INSERT
The DVT-INSERT offers an airtight combustion chamber, keeping indoor air warm <u>and</u> clean. This unique insert is also tested as a wall furnace - giving you maximum heat output with exceptional heating efficiency. The CrossFyre flame-control design more closely resembles the natural burning of wood, complete with glowing embers. **Also available is the 4000 SUPREME INSERT.**

FEATURES
- 20,000- 28,500 BTU/hr Input
- High Thermal Efficiency (up to 75%+)*
- A.F.U.E. Rating of up to 66.7%*
- Variable Flame Height & BTU Output
- Enhanced Burner and Ember Flames
- Warnock Hersey Approved for Masonry and Zero Clearance Fireplaces
- Standard Blower

TOP VENTING-DIRECT VENT Gas Fireplaces

A Top venting version of our patented direct vent system was designed for installations such as a basement that could not accommodate a back venting direct vent. Although the natural pull of gravity will always make any top venting fireplace less efficient, the patented design of Model 6000DVTFL makes it one of the most energy efficient top venting direct vents on the market today.

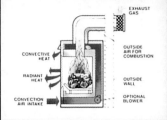

The balanced flue system eliminates the expense of a chimney system.

🔥 **GRAND 50** The largest gas direct-vent fireplace available on the market today, the grand view is sure to make a dramatic impression to any room. With a viewing area of 48"x 30", this fireplace will give you everything you've been looking for in a fireplace and *MORE*!

FEATURES
- 31,000 - 60,000 BTU/hr Input NG
- High Efficiency (up to 60%+)*
- Sealed Combustion Chamber
- CrossFyre Technology: New Pan Burner and Ceramic Fiber Logs
- Polished Brass Hood and Trim
- A.G.A. Design Certified, CGA Certified
- Optional 160 CFM Blower
- Optional Hand-Held Remote Control

🔥 **8000DVTFL** For those wanting the installation advantages of a direct vent, but require a vertical vent off the top (i.e. basement, side wall application) the 8000DVTFL is for you. The 8000DVTFL, along with all the 8000 Series, uses Heat-N-Glo's CrossFyre Technology to add a spectacular glow and duplication of a woodburning fire.

- 24,000 - 35,000 BTU/hr Input
- Airtight Combustion Chamber
- High Thermal Efficiency (60%+)*
- Six Ceramic Fiber Logs
- Variable Valve to Alter Flame Height and Heat Output
- Large Glass Door Area
- Safety: High Temperature Limit Switch
- Burning Embers and Yellow Flames
- Piezo Igniter and Safety Pilot
- Installed Junction Box for Blower and/or Remote Control
- Fixed Mesh Screen (Polished Brass Trim)
- Polished Brass Decorative Hood
- A.G.A. Design Certified, CGA Certified

🔥 **6000ARCH** Until now, having an arch fireplace has always been a compromise between beauty and cost. The 6000ARCH brings you both, without the compromise. You can finish the front of your fireplace right up to the opening giving you the look of a masonry fireplace. The 6000ARCH's realistic logs and golden embers offer the most attractive and realistic fire on the market. This unique direct vent is a beautiful centerpiece for any room.

FEATURES
- 19,000 -27,000 BTU/hr Input
- Variable Flame Height and Heat Output
- Airtight and Clean Burning
- Wall Switch Included
- A.G.A. Design Certified, CGA Certified

🔥 **6000DVTFL** For those wanting the installation advantages of a direct vent but requiring a vertical vent off the top, (i.e. basement, sidewall applications), the 6000DVTFL is the answer. Look is similar to 6000GDVFL.

FEATURES
- 19,000 - 27,000 BTU/hr Input
- Energy Efficient (up to 60%)*
- Airtight Combustion Chamber
- A.G.A. Design Certified, CGA Certified
- Optional Blower and Remote Control

🔥 **DVT-STOVE** This fireplace offers the warmth and look of a traditional stove with the convenience of gas. The CrossFyre Stove has a beautiful flame with realistic looking logs and glowing embers underneath. With its airtight combustion chamber, high efficiency and controllable heat output (AFUE rating of 64%), you can be confident your energy dollars are well utilized.

FEATURES
- 20,000 -28,500 BTU/hr Input
- High Thermal Efficiency (up to 75%+)*
- Variable Flame Height and Heat Output
- Warnock Hersey Listed
- Requires 6"/4" Venting
- Optional Blower and Remote Control
- Optional Legs or Pedestal

🔥 **TOWNSEND STOVE** The Townsend Stove, a cast iron gas stove, will heat up your room conveniently, while you enjoy the traditional look and old fashioned charm of a woodburning cast iron stove, without any hassles. This stove is available in six colors for homeowners to compliment their current decorating scheme and with an AFUE rating of 68%, the units' efficiency will pay for itself.

FEATURES
- 19,000 -28,000 BTU/hr Input
- High Thermal Efficiency 78%*
- A.F.U.E. Rating 68+%
- Variable Flame Height and Heat Output
- Air Tight and Clean Burning
- Sturdy, Cast Iron Construction
- Ceramic Glass
- Burning Embers and Yellow Flames
- Installed Junction Box
- Gas Shut-Off
- Dual-Level Flame
- Warnock Hersey Approved
- Optional 160 CFM Fan with Thermal Sensor
- Optional Hand Held Remote Control (RCH-09A)
- Ceramic Fiber Log Set

Heat-N-Glo has incorporated our CrossFyre Technology in most all Heat-N-Glo products (unless ceramic logs are installed). CrossFyre Technology is the combination of Heat-N-Glo's patented stainless steel burner and ceramic fiber logs for the optimum glow and realism.

*As tested by Gas Technologies, Inc.

MULTISIDED *Gas Fireplaces*

Several years ago Heat-N-Glo was the first fireplace manufacturer to develop and patent a multi-sided woodburning fireplace. Using this fireplace technology we have developed a complete line of direct vent and top vent multi-sided gas fireplaces.

ST-GDV

Our patented direct vent system is also available in a see-thru unit, providing a truly energy efficient see-thru fireplace. The large glass viewing area allows you to enjoy this heart warming fireplace from two rooms.

FEATURES
- 48,000 BTU/hr Input
- High Thermal Efficiency (up to 70%)*
- Fixed Mesh Screens
- Wall Switch Included
- A.G.A. Design Certified, CGA Certified
- Optional Blower

VENTED WALL FURNACE

BAY-GDV

The first fireplace to combine a spectacular view with the efficiency of a wall furnace. The BAY-GDV's three-sided viewing area allows you to warm to the fire's glow from anywhere in the room. For a three-sided viewing area in a more compact size-perfect for bedrooms, sunrooms and starter homes - the BAY-30 was designed with this in mind. Both the BAY-GDV and BAY-30 introduce an HV system that can be turned to accommodate either a horizontal or vertical termination, allowing for multiple installation applications. The BAY-GDV and BAY-30 are the answers for beautiful views, real heat output and easy installations.

FEATURES
- 22,000-32,000 BTU/hr Input
- High Thermal Efficiency (up to 75.6%)*
- A.F.U.E. Rating of 68.5%
- Fixed Panel of Glass on Three Sides
- A.G.A. Design Certified, CGA Certified
- Optional Blower

CORNER-DV

The Left and Right Corner Direct Vent fireplaces offer innovative designs which allow you to place this modern fireplace in a corner or between rooms. This design allows for unique, yet practical installations, while offering the view of a realistic fire from two sides.

FEATURES
- 48,000 BTU/hr Input
- High Thermal Efficiency (up to 70%)*
- Fixed Mesh Screens
- Wall Switch Included
- A.G.A. Design Certified, CGA Certified
- Optional Blower

PIER-GDV

The PIER-GDV is a three-sided direct vent fireplace. The realistic look of this fireplace and the direct venting capabilities make non-conventional installations especially stunning. Some unique installations include within a bar or as a room divider. For the same look as the PIER-GDV but using top venting direct vent, the PIER-DVT is an alternative option for additional convenience on your installations.

FEATURES
- 48,000 BTU/hr Input
- High Thermal Efficiency (up to 70%)*
- Fixed Mesh Screens
- Wall Switch Included
- A.G.A. Design Certified, CGA Certified
- Optional Blower

COFFEE TABLE

This fireplace not only provides the usual social pleasures of beauty and warmth, but also the usefulness of a table. It's grand size, radiant flames, burning embers and oak frame make it a beautiful focal point for any room. Although the COFFEE TABLE fireplace does provide some warmth, it is designed to operate in all seasons and climates.

FEATURES
- 39,000 BTU/hr Input
- Yellow Flames and Burning Embers
- Four Pieces of Ceramic Glass
- Ceramic Fiber Logs
- On/Off Rocker Switch
- Oak Surround with Brass Trim
- Standard Refractory Firebox Base
- A.G.A. Design Certified, CGA Certified
- Optional Remote (RCH-09A)
- Standard Wall Switch

ST-42GTV

This model is the newest and largest of our line of top vent gas see-thru fireplaces. The generous glass door area allows for a spectacular view of the six logs, golden flames and burning embers in not only one, but two rooms. The ST-38GTV is a smaller version of this see-thru fireplace with a 31" opening.

FEATURES
- 38,000 BTU/hr Input
- Fixed Panel of Glass on Each Side
- Requires 6" B-vent
- A.G.A. Design Certified, CGA Certified

PIER-TV and CORNER TV

Create a room with a view. This three sided top venting fireplace has six logs, burning embers and generous flames providing a warm glow on all three sides. Great as a room divider or centerpiece. For a two sided top venting fireplace, the CornerTV creates a unique corner or between rooms installation, while providing a view of a glowing fire from two sides. Available as a left or right corner unit.

FEATURES
- 35,000 BTU/hr Input
- Fixed Panel of Glass on Each Side
- Requires 6" B-vent
- A.G.A. Design Certified, CGA Certified

QUALITY FIREPLACE PRODUCTS SINCE 1975

HEAT-N-GLO Fireplace Products, Inc. 6665 W. Hwy 13, Savage, MN 55378
(612) 890-8367   Fax (612) 890-3525
h&g@winternet.com

GAS LOGS

ACTUAL LOG SET DIMENSIONS

LOG SET	FRONT WIDTH	DEPTH	BACK WIDTH	HEIGHT
FLS-18	25"	10 3/4"	16 3/4"	16"
FLS-24	27 3/4"	14 1/2"	17 1/2"	17"
FLS-30	29 3/4"	14 1/2"	16 3/4"	17"
ST -FLS	22 1/2"	14 "	22 1/2"	18"
HEARTH GLO	22"	15"	17"	12"

MINIMUM FIREBOX DIMENSIONS

LOG SET	FRONT WIDTH	DEPTH	BACK WIDTH	HEIGHT
FLS-18	26 1/2"	11 1/4"	17 1/2"	17
FLS-24	28"	14 3/4"	17 1/2"	17
FLS-30	30"	14 3/4"	17 1/2"	17
ST -FLS	24"	17 "	24"	18
RECTANGULAR SHAPE HEARTH GLO	25"	16"	25"	22"
TRAPEZOID SHAPE HEARTH GLO	31"	16"	21"	22"

* HEARTH GLO is available in Natural Gas only.
ALL MEASUREMENTS ARE IN INCHES.

QUALITY FIREPLACE PRODUCTS SINCE 1975

HEAT-N-GLO Fireplace Products, Inc. has developed and patented several 'firsts' in the fireplace industry. Our reputation as an Industry leader has resulted from our commitment to advanced technology, innovation and quality.

WOOD FIREPLACE PRODUCTS

SPECIFICATIONS

MODEL	HEIGHT		FRONT WIDTH		BACK WIDTH		DEPTH		FRONT GLASS OPENING
	ACTUAL	FRAMING	ACTUAL	FRAMING	ACTUAL	FRAMING	ACTUAL	FRAMING	
EM-48	42	43	48	49	30½	49	25	25½	42 x 24
EM-42	41	41½	42¼	43¾	42¼	43¾	25⅛	25⅝	36 x 19⅛
EM-41	38¼	38¾	41	42	26½	27½	21½	22	35½ x 20¾
CBS-41 RH/41 RS/41	38¼	38¾	41	42	26½	27½	21½	22	35½ x 20¾
ROYAL	37½	37¾	41	42	26 1/32	27 1/32	23	23½	35½ x 20¾
HST-48	45½	46	48	49½	48	49½	25⅛	24⅛*	42 x 24
HST-42	38¼	38¾	42¼	43¾	42¼	43¾	25⅛	24⅛*	36 x 20¾
HST-38	38	38½	37¾	39¼	37¾	39¼	22¼	21¼*	31½ x 20
BAY	39½	40	36½	35½*	36½	35½*	23½	23*	36 x 19
PIER	39½	40	42½	42*	42½	42*	23¼	22¼*	36 x 19
OASIS	39½	40	36½	35½*	36½	35½*	23	22*	36 x 19

HEAT-N-GLO reserves the right to update units periodically.   MINIMUM FRAMING DIMENSIONS

GAS FIREPLACE PRODUCTS

SPECIFICATIONS

MODEL	HEIGHT		FRONT WIDTH		BACK WIDTH		DEPTH		FRONT GLASS OPENING	BTU INPUT
	ACTUAL	FRAMING	ACTUAL	FRAMING	ACTUAL	FRAMING	ACTUAL	FRAMING		
8000GDVFL	42	42½	48	49	30½	31½	24¾	25¼	37¾ x 23	26,000/38,000 ADJ
6000GDV	38¼	38¾	41	42	26½	27½	22	22½	34 x 20	19,000/27,000 ADJ
6000GDVFL	38¼	38¾	41	42	26½	27½	22	22½	34 x 20	19,000/27,000 ADJ
6000DVTFL	38¼	38¾	41	42	26½	27½	22	22½	34 x 20	19,000/27,000 ADJ
6000ARCH	42¼	42¾	47⅝	48⅝	26½	27½	22	22½	34 x 20	19,000/27,000 ADJ
6000CF	42¼	42¾	47⅝	48⅝	26½	27½	22	22½	34 x 20	19,000/27,000 ADJ
5000GDV	29⅝	30⅛	36	37‡	35¼	36¼	17½	18‡	31 x 14½	21,000
SL-3000	32¼	32¼	28¼	28¼	28¼	28¼	12	12	17 x 12	18,000
DVT-STOVE	34	NA	31¼	NA	30	NA	30	NA	25¾ x 15	20,000/28,500 ADJ
8000TVFL	42	42½	48	49	30½	31½	24¾	25¼	37¾ x 23	24,000/35,000 ADJ
6000TVFL	38¼	38¾	41	42	26½	27½	22	22½	34 x 20	20,000/29,000 ADJ
5000TV	31½	32	38	38½‡	26	27½	17½	18‡	31½x14½	21,000
ST-GDV	46¼	46¾	44½	46	44½	46	24½	23½*	34 x 22	48,000
HORIZONTAL BAY-GDV	32⅝	32⅞ RR38	38⅛	38⅛	31¾	32¾	20½	13¼	FR 29 x 19 SIDE 5x19	22,000/32,000 ADJ
VERTICAL	32⅝	FR32⅞	38⅛	38⅛	33⅜	38⅛	20½	17¼		
HORIZONTAL BAY-30	25¼	25½	33	33	20 1/16	33	17 11/16	11½	29½x13½ SIDE 4x12	19,000/27,000 ADJ
VERTICAL	25¼	25½	33	33	20 1/16	33	17 11/16	14⅞		
CORNER-DV	46¼	46¾	41	41‡	41	41	25⅜	24⅞*	34 x 22	48,000
PIER-GDV	46¼	46¾	41	41‡	41	41*	24⅜	23⅜*	34 x 22	48,000
ST-42 GTV	38	38½	42⅛	43⅝	42⅛	43⅝	25	24*	36 x 21	38,000
PIER-TV	39⅛	39⅝	42½	42⅛‡	42½	42½*	23¾	21⅞*	36¼ x 18	35,000

SPECIFICATIONS

MODEL	FRONT HEIGHT	FIREBOX HEIGHT	FRONT WIDTH	FIRE BOX WIDTH		FIREBOX DEPTH	FRONT GLASS DOOR	VENTING	BTU INPUT PER HOUR
				FRONT	REAR				
BAY INSERT	30	21¾	40	26½	16¼	9¾	29½ x 13½	Dual 3''	19,000/27,000 ADJ
DVT INSERT	28¾	20½	41½	29¼	26¼	17¾	26 x 15¼	Dual 3''	20,000/28,500 ADJ
SL-INSERT	26 11/16	19	34 1/16	28⅛	14⅝	14 7/16	22 x 12 1/16	4'' Flex	16,000/23,000 ADJ
4000 INS	28¾	21	41½	26⅛	26⅛	16½	27¼ x 15	4'' Flex	21,000/30,000 ADJ
AT-INSERT	28⅝	21½	41 5/16	28¾	19⅜	15 9/16	31x 15	Dual 3''	15,000/22,000 ADJ

Lumére® Module Selection Guide

CREATE A MOOD.

Task Lighting's Lumére® lighting system is for creative, sensitive people who like to design a total space for beauty, function, and feeling. Lumére® allows you to accentuate your design by allowing one to see the effect, not the source.

Lumére® uses: LISTED

- **under cabinets**
- **in toe spaces**
- **under wall hung vanities**
- **inside cabinets & hutches**
- **tucked into valances**
- **lighting skylights at night**
- **high-lighting architectural features such as beams and vaulted ceilings**
- **radius curves and around corners**
- **lighting stairs**

Photo courtesy of USG Corporation

Lumére® is a UL Listed System with a three year warranty. TASK 12 volt PWT series transformers, Listed by UL, are available from Task Lighting Corporation in 170, 300, and 600 watt capacities.

Each basic Lumére ® module is four inches long, 5/8 inches high, and two and one eighth inches deep with the reflector and has two wedge based bulbs. Bulbs are available in either 3 watt or 5 watt, providing a total of 6 watts or 10 watts per module.

Modules may be plugged into one another or spaced with gap connectors so that cabinet elevations, depth changes, and / or custom spacing may be accomplished.

Lumére® was selected in 1987 by the Illuminating Engineering Society of North America for inclusion in their *IES Progress Report.*

With Task Lighting

Photograph by Robert A. Ikeler

Without Task Lighting

Photograph by Robert A. Ikeler

The Lumére® modular lighting system is a patented, low voltage, incandescent, flexible concept that is truly the quiet light for residential, commercial, recreational, and industrial applications.

Ambiance is easily changed by effective use and installation of one of several UL listed, low voltage rated dimmers.

Lumére® Quick Reference

1. All transformers and switches should be installed by a licensed electrician.
2. All switches should be placed on 120V (household current) side of transformer. (Task's ILS switch may be used on the low voltage side)
3. Twelve gauge (12 ga.) wire must be used after the transformer. (low voltage side)
4. Maximum number of 4LM10 modules is **17** on each Starter Connector and **28** 4LM6 modules on each Starter Connector. *(There may be more than one Starter Connector per transformer as long as you don't exceed the wattage of the transformer).*
5. A 600 watt transformer requires a minimum of (2) Starter Connectors.
6. Location of transformer should be within 20 feet of the light run.
7. All dimming devices must be designated "low voltage".
8. Contact Task Lighting Corporation for further assistance.

Photograph by Joel Armstrong

Lumére® Lighting Module — 4LM10 / 4LM6

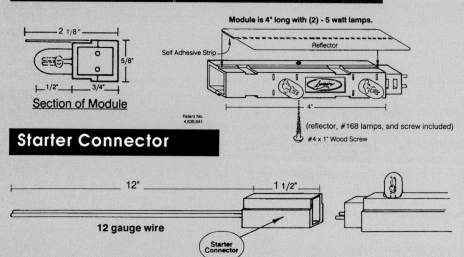

2 1/8″ — 5/8″ — 1/2″ — 3/4″
Section of Module

Module is 4″ long with (2) - 5 watt lamps.
Self Adhesive Strip
Reflector
Patent No. 4,639,841
4″
(reflector, #168 lamps, and screw included)
#4 x 1″ Wood Screw

Photograph by Gene Hinrichs

Starter Connector

12″ — 1 1/2″
12 gauge wire
Starter Connector

Gap Connectors are needed to bridge the gap between units.

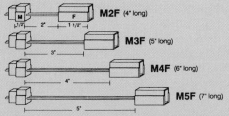

M2F (4″ long)
1/2″ 2″ 1 1/2″
M3F (5″ long)
3″
M4F (6″ long)
4″
M5F (7″ long)
5″

Transformers and Maximum Number of Modules

Transformer	4LM6	4LM10
PWT-170	28	17
PWT-300*	50	30
PWT-600**	100	60

* Two Circuits Provided
** Four Circuits Provided

MAX. LOAD 170 WATTS PER CIRCUIT

Where to locate transformer

- Within 20 feet of the beginning of the light run.
- In a mechanical area below the installation.
- In a sink base cabinet.
- In a pantry or closet adjacent to installation.

 LISTED

Photograph by Robert A. Ikeler

Luche'® Fixtures Guide

The Luche' lighting system offers a variety of fixtures to provide quiet lighting from a concealed source.

The KC and LX series are ideally suited for undercabinet applications in the kitchen, desk and office areas. Work surfaces are evenly illuminated and shadows disappear.

The TS series is the most economical fixture for lighting large areas. Use it for perimeter / cove light, toe space or open soffits, bathroom night lights and stairway handrails.

With Luche' the possibilities are endless.

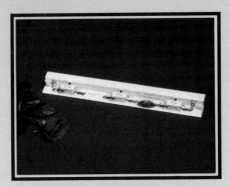

Luche "KC" Series

Length	Series	Total Watts
9"	KC	20
15"	KC	30
21"	KC	40
24"	KC	50
30"	KC	60
36"	KC	70

The KC Series is designed for undercabinet use to light countertop and work areas. The compact size 3/4" H x 2 5/8" D allows the fixture to be installed behind the front rail of most cabinets and not be visible. This series comes in 6 sizes from 9" to 36" and uses 5 watt incandescent lamps. Average lamp life is 7,000 hours.

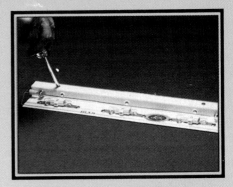

Luche "LX" Series

Length	Series	Total Watts
9"	LX	24
15"	LX	36
21"	LX	48
24"	LX	60
30"	LX	72
36"	LX	84

The LX Series, designed for use undercabinets, comes in 6 sizes from 9" to 36". This fixture, with 6 watt Xenon lamps, produces approximately 35% more light and is brighter and whiter than incandescent. The 7/8" H x 2 5/8" D fixture has a removable lens. Average lamp life is 14,000 hours.

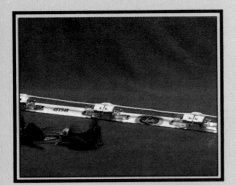

Luche "TS" Series

Length	Series	Total Watts
48"	TS	48
48"	TS	80
48"	TS	64Xenon
48"	TS	96Xenon

The TS Series is available in 4 lamp wattages - 48TS48 (3 watt), 48TS80 (5 watt), 48TS64X (4 watt Xenon), 48TS96X (6 watt Xenon). All fixtures are 48" L x 7/8" W x 3/4" H and can be field cut. The double lamp sockets are 6" on center. Mounting is easy with bonding tape or screws.

PWT 12v Transformers

Power supplies are available in three sizes - PWT170, PWT300 and PWT600. Wattage load is designated by the number 170, 300 or 600. PWT transformers have an electrostatic shield and a fuse and thermal device on the line voltage side. In addition, thermal devices protect each low voltage circuit. Installation is easy with screw-down terminal blocks. The 3' grounded power cord plugs into a switched outlet.

All fixtures & power supplies are UL Listed Misc. Light Fixtures

69X5

Toll Free (800) 445-6404

Lighting Corporation

P.O. Box 1090
Kearney, NE 68848-1090
Fax (308) 234-9401